The SAGE
Handbook *of*

Social Cognition

Advisory Board

The SAGE
Handbook *of*

Social Cognition

Edited by
Susan T. Fiske and
C. Neil Macrae

Los Angeles | London | New Delhi
Singapore | Washington DC

First published 2012

SAGE Publications Ltd
1 Oliver's Yard
55 City Road
London EC1Y 1SP

SAGE Publications Inc.
2455 Teller Road
Thousand Oaks, California 91320

SAGE Publications India Pvt Ltd
B 1/I 1 Mohan Cooperative Industrial Area
Mathura Road, Post Bag 7
New Delhi 110 044

SAGE Publications Asia-Pacific Pte Ltd
3 Church Street
#10-04 Samsung Hub
Singapore 049483

Library of Congress Control Number: 2011932696

British Library Cataloguing in Publication data

A catalogue record for this book is available from the British Library

ISBN 978-0-85702-481-7

Typeset by Cenveo Publisher Services
Printed in India at Replika Press Pvt Ltd.
Printed on paper from sustainable resources

Contents

Notes on Contributors

Henk Aarts (PhD, 1996, Radboud University) is Professor of Psychology at Utrecht University. His research deals with several topics related to the role of goals in social cognition and behavior, with a special interest in the interplay between conscious and unconscious processes in the control and experiences of goal-directed behavior. Dr Aarts has authored over 100 publications in fundamental (e.g., *Science*) and applied journals (e.g., *Health Psychology Review*), edited several books (e.g., *Goal-Directed Behavior*, 2011) and journals (e.g., *Psychological Science*), and has received several awards for his research contributions (e.g., Netherlands Science Foundation VICI Award). For more information: www.goallab.nl.

Joshua M. Ackerman is the Class of 1957 Career Development Professor of Marketing at the MIT Sloan School of Management. He received his BA from Duke University and his PhD in social psychology from Arizona State University. Professor Ackerman's research focuses on the role that adaptive psychological mechanisms play, often outside of conscious awareness, within consumption and decision-making environments. This has included work on topics such as self-control, embodiment, disease and contagion, intergroup processing, and various forms of signaling behavior, and has appeared in journals such as *Science, Journal of Personality and Social Psychology, Personality and Social Psychological Review*, and *Psychological Science*.

Martha W. Alibali is Professor of Psychology and Educational Psychology at the University of Wisconsin – Madison. She received her PhD from the University of Chicago. Her primary areas of research are cognitive development and mathematics learning. She has a special interest in the role of gesture in learning and communication, particularly in educational settings. She is the author of more than 70 peer-reviewed publications, and her research is currently supported by the National Science Foundation and the Institute of Education Sciences.

Daniel R. Ames is a Professor of Management at Columbia University. His work revolves around social judgment and behavior, including how people understand, and sometimes fail to understand, themselves and the people around them and how this comes to life in relationships, influence, cooperation, and conflict. His work has been published in variety of social psychological and organizational outlets, including *Psychological Science, Journal of Experimental Social Psychology, Journal of Personality and Social Psychology, Organizational Behavior and Human Decision Processes,* and *Personality and Social Psychology Bulletin.*

Susan M. Andersen (PhD, Stanford 1981) is Professor of Psychology at New York University. Her research interests span a number of areas in social psychology (social cognition), personality, and clinical; and her central research focus concerns how everyday interpersonal relations are influenced by past relationships with significant others. This primary line of research examines mental representations of significant others, their structure in memory in relation to the self, and what my colleagues and I have termed the social-cognitive model of transference. She also studies private and covert aspects of self, conceptions of future suffering in depression, and identity change. Professor Andersen's work has appeared in *Psychological Review, New Directions in Psychological Science,* and numerous times in the *Journal of Personality and Social Psychology.*

John A. Bargh is Professor of Psychology and Cognitive Science at Yale University. He received his PhD in 1981 from the University of Michigan, under the guidance of Robert B. Zajonc. Professor Bargh's research focuses on automatic and unconscious influences on social cognition, motivation, and behavior; most recently, he has focused on how concrete physical experiences and concepts influence analogous social and psychological experiences and concepts. In recognition of this work, he received the annual Dissertation Award (1982) and more recently, the Scientific Impact Award (2007) from the Society for Experimental Social Psychology, the Early Career Contribution Award from the American Psychological Association, a Guggenheim fellowship, the Donald T. Campbell Lifetime Achievement Award from the Society for Personality and Social Psychology, and an honorary doctorate from Radboud University, the Netherlands. Professor Bargh was elected to the American Academy of Arts and Sciences in 2011.

Avi Ben-Zeev is an Associate Professor of Cognitive Psychology at San Francisco State University (SFSU). He received his PhD degree from Yale University in 1997. Previous to his tenure at SFSU, Dr Ben-Zeev was a faculty member in the Cognitive and Linguistic Sciences Department at Brown University and in the Psychology Department at Williams College. Dr Ben-Zeev's scholarship has centered on explicating cognitive underpinnings of social categorization and stereotyping, especially in regard to identifying contextual factors that cause stigmatized individuals to underperform intellectually (i.e., social identity threat). He has published and edited several books such as *Complex Cognition: The Psychology of Human Thought* (with Robert Sternberg) and a variety of research articles in journals such as *Psychological Science, Journal of Experimental Social Psychology,* and *Cognitive Science.* More recently, Dr Ben-Zeev has been investigating how basic categorization processes associated with essentialist thought are implicated in the perception of social-artifactual categories as "natural."

Mahzarin R. Banaji received her PhD from Ohio State University, taught at Yale for 15 years and since 2002 has been Richard Clarke Cabot Professor of Social Ethics at Harvard University. She studies social cognition with a focus on nonconscious processes in adults and young children. With Susan Gelman she has edited a forthcoming book, *Navigating the Social World: The Early Years.* Professor Mahzarin is a fellow of the Society of Experimental Psychologists, Herbert Simon Fellow of the Association for Political and Social Science and the American Academy of Arts and Sciences and served as President of the Association for Psychological Science in 2011–2012.

Genna M. Bebko is a post-doctoral associate at the Western Psychiatric Institute and Clinic of the University of Pittsburgh Medical Center. She holds a BS in Neuroscience and Psychology from Allegheny College and a PhD in Neuroscience from Northwestern University. Dr Bebko's research interests include emotion regulation, prosocial behavior, and reward processing. Her most recent publication in the journal *Emotion* examined the perceptual strategies underlying emotion regulation. Her current projects focus on identifying biomarkers of bipolar disorder in adults and at-risk children populations.

Jennifer S. Beer is an Associate Professor at the University of Texas at Austin where she directs the Self-Regulation Lab. She received her PhD in Social Personality Psychology from the University of California, Berkeley. Her research focuses on the self, emotion, social cognition, and frontal lobe function. She has published more than 45 articles and chapters and edited *Methods in Social Neuroscience* and a special issue of *Brain Research on Social Cognitive Neuroscience.* Her research has received funding from the National Institutes of Health and the National Science Foundation. Dr Beer serves on the editorial boards for the *Frontiers in Human Neuroscience, Journal of Personality and Social Psychology, Social Cognition, Emotion,* and *Social, Cognitive, and Affective Neuroscience.* She was a recipient of a Harrington Faculty Fellowship and was recognized as the 7th most cited Assistant Professor in Social-Personality Psychology by the Society for Personality and Social Psychology. Dr Beer serves on the Executive Committees of the Society for Experimental Social Psychology and is a co-founder of the Social and Affective Neuroscience Society.

Galen V. Bodenhausen is the Lawyer Taylor Professor of Psychology and a Professor of Marketing at Northwestern University. He studies a variety of issues concerning the structure and function of social attitudes and beliefs, particularly in the domain of intergroup perception. He has served as an Editor or Associate Editor of several journals, including *Personality and Social Psychology Review*, *Journal of Experimental Social Psychology*, *Personality and Social Psychology Bulletin*, and *Social Cognition*. A fellow in several learned societies, Professor Bodenhausen is also a recipient of the Friedrich Wilhelm Bessel Research Prize from the Alexander von Humboldt Foundation in Germany.

Bobby K. Cheon is a doctoral student in the Social Psychology program at Northwestern University. He received his BA in Cognitive Science from the University of Virginia. His research explores the role of culture on the psychological and neurobiological processes that underlie stigma and intergroup bias. He has conducted research in the United States, South Korea, and Singapore, examining how culture may shape cognitions, evaluations, and emotions towards out-groups and stigmatized groups. His most recent contribution to social-cultural neuroscience, published in the journal *NeuroImage*, examines cultural influences on the neural processes that underlie empathic biases for the suffering of in-group relative to out-group members.

Joan Y. Chiao is an Assistant Professor in the Department of Psychology at Northwestern University. She received her PhD in Psychology from Harvard University in 2006, studying social psychology and cognitive neuroscience. Her main research interests include cultural neuroscience of emotion and social interaction, social and affective neuroscience across development, social dominance and affiliation, and integrating psychology and neuroscience research with public policy and population health issues. Dr Chiao currently serves on the board of several journals, including *Journal of Experimental Psychology: General*, *Social Neuroscience*, *Social Cognitive and Affective Neuroscience*, *Frontiers in Cultural Psychology*, *Frontiers in Human Neuroscience* and *Biology of Anxiety and Mood Disorders*. In 2009–10, she served as Editor for an edited volume of *Progress in Brain Research* on cultural neuroscience called "Cultural Neuroscience: Cultural Influences on Brain Function" and a special issue on cultural neuroscience in *Social Cognitive and Affective Neuroscience*. Dr Chiao is a recipient of funding from the National Science Foundation and Japan Society for the Promotion of Science and Technology.

Ellen Delvaux is a doctoral student at the Center of Social and Cultural Psychology, University of Leuven, Belgium. She is interested in intergroup as well as intragroup emotional processes. Her doctoral research focuses on the emotional dynamics in groups. She has published on the time dynamics of emotion and on emotional labor.

David Dunning is Professor of Psychology at Cornell University. He received his BA from Michigan State University and his doctorate from Stanford University, both in psychology. He is best known for his work on misguided self-evaluation, which borrows principles from judgment and decision making and motivated reasoning to explain why people so often misjudge their competence, character, and status in the social world. Much of his approach is reviewed in his book *Self-insight: Roadblocks and Detours on the Path to Knowing Thyself* (Psychology Press, 2005), and has been supported financially by grants from the National Institutes of Health and the National Science Foundation. He is the former executive officer of the Society for Personality and Social Psychology.

Richard P. Eibach (PhD, Cornell University) is an Assistant Professor of Social Psychology at the University of Waterloo (Canada). His research on such topics as perceptions of self and social change, visual perspective in mental imagery, idealization of parenthood, and judgments of progress towards racial and gender equality has been published in *Journal of Personality and Social Psychology*, *Psychological Science*, *Advances in Experimental Social Psychology*, *Journal of Experimental Psychology: General*, *Personality and Social Psychology Bulletin*, and *Journal of Experimental Social Psychology*.

Melissa J. Ferguson is currently an Associate Professor in the Psychology Department at Cornell University. Her main area of interest is implicit social cognition, and she studies the topics of attitudes, goals, ideology, and decision-making. Her work has appeared in journals such as the *Journal of Social and Personality Psychology, Psychological Science, Trends in Cognitive Science,* and *Proceedings of the National Academy of Sciences.* Her research has been funded by the National Institutes of Mental Health, the National Science Foundation, and the Binational Science Foundation.

Susan T. Fiske is Eugene Higgins Professor of Psychology, Princeton University (Ph.D., Harvard University; honorary doctorates, Université Catholique de Louvain-la-Neuve, Belgium; Universiteit Leiden, Netherlands). Author of over 250 publications in outlets such as *Science, Psychological Science, Personality and Social Psychology Science,* and the *Annual Review of Psychology*, she investigates how people make sense of each other, especially cognitive stereotypes and emotional prejudices, at cultural, interpersonal, and neural levels. She recently edited *Beyond Common Sense: Psychological Science in the Courtroom* and the *Handbook of Social Psychology* (5/e). She wrote *Social Beings: Core Motives in Social Psychology* (2/e) and *Social Cognition: From Brains to Culture* (3/e). Her most recent book, supported by a Guggenheim and published by Russell Sage Foundation, is *Envy Up and Scorn Down: How Status Divides Us.* Recently, she won the American Psychological Association's Distinguished Scientific Contribution Award and Association for Psychological Science's William James Award, as well as being elected a Fellow of the American Academy of Arts and Sciences and the American Academy of Political and Social Sciences.

Rebecca S. Frazier received her BS in Psychology and Cognitive Science from the University of Richmond in 2009 and is currently a PhD student in the Department of Psychology at the University of Virginia. In 2010, she received the Jacob K. Javits fellowship from the Department of Education as well as an honorable mention from the National Science Foundation's Graduate Research Fellowship Program. Her research interests include implicit social cognition, morality, ethics, ideology, group dynamics, group-level identification, and leadership.

Jun Fukukura is a fifth-year graduate student in the Psychology Department at Cornell University where she is an advisee of Melissa Ferguson. Her research interests are primarily in decision-making in consumer contexts, materialism, and psychological distance.

Margarida V. Garrido is an Assistant Professor at the Department of Social and Organizational Psychology, ISCTE- University Institute of Lisbon, Portugal and a researcher at CIS/ISCTE-IUL. Her current research interests focus on the influence of informational, environmental, and social contexts on person memory, and the interplay between encoding and retrieval of information in individual and collaborative conditions. She is also interested in exploring the spatial grounding of abstract concepts such as time and politics, as well as in the role of context salience in constraining metaphor use. For more information, see www.cis.com.pt.

Carlee Beth Hawkins graduated summa cum laude with a BS in psychology from Southern Illinois University Edwardsville in 2006. In 2010, she received a MA in social psychology from the University of Virginia, and was awarded the Maury Pathfinder award for best pre-dissertation. She is currently pursuing her PhD at the University of Virginia and is a researcher with Project Implicit, a virtual laboratory for research and education of implicit cognition – thoughts and feelings outside of conscious awareness or control. Carlee's research interests concern identity and ideology, and their influence on judgment and behavior, and strategies for overcoming implicit bias, including intentions for objectivity and resisting group influence.

Julie D. Henry received her doctoral degree from the University of Aberdeen, Scotland (2003). Previously she worked at the University of New South Wales, and is currently an Associate Professor and Australian Research Fellow at the University of Queensland. Her research focuses broadly on the effects of aging and brain disease on cognition, emotion, and social functioning. She is the author of over 80 research articles in journals that include *Psychology and Aging, Neuropsychology, Neuropsychologia, Brain,* and *Journal of Abnormal Psychology.* Dr Henry is Associate Editor for the *British Journal of Clinical Psychology*, a journal of the British Psychological Society (BPS), and an Editorial Board Member for the oldest journal devoted to gerontological research, *Gerontology.* She has received several prestigious grants and awards for her work.

Ying-Yi Hong is a Professor at the Nanyang Business School of Nanyang Technological University, Singapore. She received her PhD from Columbia University in 1994, specializing in experimental social psychology. She taught at the Hong Kong University of Science and Technology from 1994 to 2002 before moving to the University of Illinois at Urbana-Champaign (UIUC), where she taught at the Department of Psychology for six years. Her main research interests include culture and cognition, self, identity, and intergroup relations. Dr Hong has published over 90 journal articles and book chapters mainly on multiculturalism and identity. She co-authored *Social Psychology of Culture* with Chi-yue Chiu and co-edited *Understanding Culture: Theory, Research, and Application* with Robert Wyer and Chi-yue Chiu. She is currently an editor of *Advances in Culture and Psychology*, a book series published by Oxford University Press. Dr Hong is the recipient of the Otto Klineberg Intercultural and International Relations Award in 2001, the Young Investigator Award (conferred by the International Society of Self and Identity) in 2004, and was elected Fellow of the Association for Psychological Science, and Associate of the Center for Advanced Study, UIUC.

Autumn B. Hostetter is Assistant Professor of Psychology at Kalamazoo College. She received her PhD from the University of Wisconsin – Madison. Her research interests include the cognitive underpinnings of speech-accompanying gesture and the role of gesture in communication. Recent publications have appeared in *Psychological Bulletin, Journal of Memory and Language,* and *Psychonomic Bulletin and Review.*

Julie Yun-Ju Huang holds an MS and PhD in social psychology from Yale University. She is currently a Postdoctoral Fellow at Rotman School of Management at the University of Toronto. Her research explores how non-conscious psychological processes drive individual judgments and behaviors, with a particular focus on how incidental physical experiences affect ongoing goal pursuit.

Sonia K. Kang is an Assistant Professor in the Rotman School of Management at the University of Toronto. She received her PhD from the University of Toronto in 2010 and worked as a Postdoctoral Fellow with Galen Bodenhausen at Northwestern University during 2010–2011. Her research examines the development, experience, and consequences of stereotyping, prejudice, and discrimination across the life span. Dr Kang's work has appeared in a variety of outlets, including the *Journal of Personality and Social Psychology*, the *Journal of Experimental Social Psychology*, the *Journal of Social Issues*, and *The Gerontologist.*

Aaron C. Kay (PhD, Stanford University, 2005) is Associate Professor of Management and Associate Professor of Psychology and Neuroscience at Duke University. Dr Kay's research focuses on the relation between motivation, implicit social cognition, and social issues. He has a particular interest in how basic motivations and needs manifest as specific social and societal beliefs. These include (but are not limited to) the causes and consequences of stereotyping and system justification, religious belief, political ideology, and the attitudes people hold towards their organizations and institutions. He also studies processes underlying priming effects. Dr Kay has been awarded the SAGE Young Scholar Award from the Foundation of Personality and Social Psychology (2010), the Early Career Contribution Award from the International Society of Justice Researchers (2010), the Early Researchers Award from the Ontario Ministry of Research and Innovation (2009), and Dissertation Awards from the Society for the Psychological Study of Social Issues (2006) and the Society of Experimental Social Psychology (runner-up; 2006).

Arie W. Kruglanski is a Distinguished University Professor at the University of Maryland, College Park. He has published over 250 works on human judgment and belief formation, motivated cognition, and psychology of goals. His articles have been published in leading journals, including *Journal of Personality and Social Psychology, Psychological Review, Psychological Bulletin,* and *Psychological Science.* Awards include the NIMH Research Scientist Award, the Senior Humboldt Award, the Donald Campbell Award, and the Distinguished Scientific Contribution Award from the Society of Experimental Social Psychology. He is co-director at the National Consortium for the Study of Terrorism and Responses to Terrorism (START).

Nira Liberman is Professor of Psychology at Tel Aviv University. Her doctoral degree is from Tel Aviv University (1997). As one of the authors of Construal Level Theory, much of her research focuses on psychological distance – how it affects and is being affected by mental construal, prediction, decision making, persuasion, performance, interpersonal relations, etc. She has also made contributions to other areas of theory and research, all of which come under the general umbrella of the interface between motivation and cognition: an attributional theory of thought suppression, the question of how goals affect construct accessibility, how regulatory foci affect decision making. Her research has been funded by the Israeli Science Foundation and the US–Israel Binational Science Foundation. She has served as an Associate Editor for *Journal of Personality and Social Psychology.*

Robert W. Livingston is an Assistant Professor at the Kellogg School of Management at Northwestern University. He received his PhD in Social Psychology from the Ohio State University. Dr Livingston's research investigates topics related to stereotyping, prejudice, intergroup discrimination, and social hierarchy. Specifically, his research focuses on the affective and affective processes underlying intergroup attitudes and the role of physical appearance in person perception. Dr Livingston's research has been published in numerous top-tiered journals of social psychology, including the *Journal of Personality and Social Psychology, Personality and Social Psychology Bulletin, Journal of Experimental Social Psychology*, and *Psychological Science.* He has received awards for outstanding research and teaching from Division 9 of the American Psychological Association and the University of Wisconsin – Madison, respectively, and currently serves on the editorial board of the *Personality and Social Psychology Bulletin.*

C. Neil Macrae is Professor of Social Cognition at the School of Psychology, University of Aberdeen, Scotland. His current research focuses on person perception and mental time travel. His work has appeared in journals such as *Science, Nature, Nature Neuroscience, Proceedings of the National Academy of Sciences, Psychological Science* and *Cognition* and he is the recipient of several career awards (APA Early Career Award, BPS Spearman Medal, EASP Jaspars Award, EASP Kurt Lewin Award). He is a Fellow of the British Academy (FBA) and the Royal Society of Edinburgh (FRSE).

Claudia Marinetti is a Research Fellow at the Cultural and Social Psychology Center at the University of Leuven, Belgium. She received her BA and MA at the Università degli Studi di Padova, and her PhD at the University of Oxford. Her main research interest lies in the nature and impact of emotion experience at individual, interpersonal, and intergroup level. She has published on a range of topics such as emotions in social interactions, emotion experience and infrahumanization in intergroup conflict, and the social nature of emotions.

Malia F. Mason is an Associate Professor of Management at Columbia University. Her research documents and analyzes the tactics that people use to understand and explain the behavior of others (e.g., mind reading, perspective taking, stereotyping), and how the brain mediates social interactions. She uses both brain imaging (fMRI) and traditional experimental techniques to investigate these interests. Professor Mason has published in a variety of journals, including *Science, Psychological Science, Journal of Personality and Social Psychology, Social Cognitive Affective Neuroscience,* and *Journal of Experimental Social Psychology.*

Takahiko Masuda is an Associate Professor of Psychology at the University of Alberta, Canada. He received his PhD degree from the University of Michigan in 2003. His current research interests include cultural variations in perceptual and cognitive processes between East Asians, Asian Immigrants in Canada, and North Americans. His work has been published in *Journal of Personality and Social Psychology, Personality and Social Psychology Bulletin, Journal of Experimental Psychology, Cognitive Science, Psychological Science,* and *Proceedings of the National Academy of Sciences of the United States of America.* He serves on the editorial boards of *Personality and Social Psychology Bulletin* and *Journal of Cross-Cultural Psychology.* His awards include a Japanese Psychological Association Award for International Contributions to Psychology (Award for Distinguished Early and Middle Career Contributions).

Batja Mesquita is a Professor of Emotion and Motivation at the Center of Cultural and Social Psychology, University of Leuven, Belgium. Most of her research focuses on the mutual constitution of emotions and sociocultural contexts. Mesquita co-edited *The Mind in Context* (2010), and has served on a large number of peer-reviewed journals in the areas of Emotion and Social Psychology. Currently, she is an Associate Editor of *Psychological Science.* Professor Mesquita is a fellow of the Royal Dutch Academy of Sciences, the American Psychological Society, the American Psychological Association, and the Society for Personality and Social Psychology.

Lynden K. Miles is a Research Fellow in the School of Psychology, University of Aberdeen, Scotland. His research is concerned with the role of perception and action in social contexts.

Beth Morling is an Associate Professor of Psychology at the University of Delaware. After receiving her PhD from the University of Massachusetts Amherst, she conducted postdoctoral work at Kyoto University. With many colleagues, she has investigated how culture shapes motivation in social situations, such as interpersonal adjustment and social support. She recently returned from a year as a Fulbright scholar, teaching and conducting research in Kyoto, Japan. Her work has been published in *Personality and Social Psychology Review* and *Psychological Bulletin.* In addition to writing about cultural psychology, she recently authored an undergraduate research methods book.

Ezequiel Morsella is an Assistant Professor of Neuroscience at San Francisco State University and an Assistant Adjunct Professor in the Department of Neurology at the University of California, San Francisco. His research focuses on the difference between the conscious and unconscious brain processes responsible for human action. He conducted his doctoral research at Columbia University and his post-doctoral training at Yale University. His theoretical and experimental research on the basic mechanisms underlying human action has appeared in journals such as *Psychological Review*, *Neurocase*, and *Journal of Experimental Psychology: Learning, Memory, and Cognition.* Dr Morsella is the editor of the *Oxford Handbook of Human Action* (with John Bargh and Peter Gollwitzer).

Nora A. Murphy is an Assistant Professor of Psychology at Loyola Marymount University in Los Angeles, CA. She earned a PhD in experimental psychology with a specialization in social and personality psychology from Northeastern University in Boston, MA; and she completed a postdoctoral fellowship at Brandeis University in Waltham, MA. Her research centers on nonverbal behavior and nonverbal communication, particularly in the areas of impression formation; emotions and aging; and social identities as portrayed in 3D environments. She has published several book chapters and numerous articles appearing in journals such as *Cyberpsychology, Behavior, and Social Networking; Journal of Nonverbal Behavior; Personality and Social Psychology Bulletin;* and *Psychology and Aging.*

Paula M. Niedenthal received her PhD at the University of Michigan and was on the faculty of the Departments of Psychology at Johns Hopkins University and Indiana University. She is currently Director of Research in the National Centre for Scientific Research and a member of the Laboratory in Social and

Cognitive Psychology at Blaise Pascal University in Clermont-Ferrand, France. Her areas of research include emotion–cognition interaction and representational models of emotion. Author of more than 100 articles and chapters, and several books, Dr Niedenthal is a fellow of the Society for Personality and Social Psychology.

Brian A. Nosek received a PhD in psychology from Yale University in 2002 and is an Associate Professor in the Department of Psychology at the University of Virginia. In 2007, he received early career awards from the International Social Cognition Network (ISCON) and the Society for the Psychological Study of Social Issues (SPSSI). He directs Project Implicit (http://projectimplicit.net/) an Internet-based multi-university collaboration of research and education about implicit cognition – thoughts and feelings that exist outside of awareness or control. Nosek's research interests include implicit cognition, automaticity, social judgment and decision-making, attitudes and beliefs, stereotyping and prejudice, ideology, morality, identity, memory, and the interface between theory, methods, and innovation.

Tomás A. Palma is currently a PhD candidate at ISCTE- University Institute of Lisbon,, Portugal, and at the University of Utrecht, The Netherlands and a researcher at CIS/ISCTE-IUL. His research interests focus on the situated and embodied nature of cognition, in particular the interplay between context and person memory, how they interact, and how one can constrain the other. He is also currently working on how "gender" is grounded. For additional information, see his homepage at www.cratylus.org.

B. Keith Payne is Associate Professor of Psychology at the University of North Carolina at Chapel Hill. His research focuses on the interaction between intentionally controlled and automatic aspects of behavior. He studies these topics in the context of prejudice, stereotyping, and discrimination as well as moral judgment and decision making more generally. He is currently Associate Editor at *Social Cognition*, and his research has been recognized with awards including the Sage Young Scholars Award and the International Social Cognition Network Early Career Award. He recently co-edited the *Handbook of Implicit Social Cognition*.

Destiny Peery is a JD/PhD candidate at Northwestern University; she expects to receive both degrees in 2012. Her primary line of research examines racial categorization processes for multiracial or racially ambiguous targets, including more general investigation of the construction of race as a category from psychological and legal and political perspectives. Her work has appeared in such outlets as *Psychological Science*, *Psychological Inquiry*, and the *Du Bois Review*.

Elizabeth Pellicano, PhD, is Senior Lecturer at the Centre for Research in Autism and Education at the Institute of Education, London. Her research develops subtle theoretical models of the distinctive challenges faced by people with autism and traces the impact of those challenges on daily life, especially in childhood and in a range of learning environments. Dr Pellicano has published widely on this work, including in *Current Biology* and *Proceedings of the National Academy of Sciences (PNAS)*. She has been awarded several national and international prizes for her research, including the Michael Young Prize from UK's Economic and Social Research Council for research likely to have a significant public impact.

Elizabeth Przybylinski is a PhD candidate in the Social Psychology at New York University (degree expected in 2013), having received her undergraduate degree from Barnard College. Her research focuses mainly on the social-cognitive process of transference and the relational self, examining the epistemological functions of the process and goal strategies that may enable the regulation of the process and its effects. She has presented her work at numerous conferences, including among others, the Association for Psychological Science (APS) and the Society for Personality and Social Psychology (SPSP) conventions. Liz is a co-author of a chapter in the forthcoming *Warsaw lectures on personality and social psychology* and of an article in *Social and Personality Psychology Compass*.

SoYon Rim is a Postdoctoral Research Fellow in Public Policy at the Harvard Kennedy School of Government. She received her PhD in Social Psychology from New York University. Dr Rim's research interests are centered on understanding the effect of perceived psychological distance on representation and decision-making, particularly with respect to issues of causality. She has also conducted research that examines implicit impression formation within a functionality framework.

S. Adil Saribay (PhD, New York University, 2008) is Assistant Professor of Psychology at Boğaziçi University in İstanbul, Turkey. His research interests are person perception, social cognition, interpersonal processes, the relational self, social-cognitive transference, and intergroup processes. His work has appeared in the *Annual Review of Psychology* and *Personality and Social Psychology Bulletin*.

Jonathan W. Schooler is a Professor of Psychological and Brain Sciences at the University of California Santa Barbara, where he pursues research on consciousness, meta-cognition, memory, and creativity. A former holder of a Tier 1 Canada Research Chair, he is a fellow of APS, the recipient of grants from both US (e.g. NIMH, Department of Education) and Canadian (e.g. NSERC, CIHR, SSHRC) government agencies, and has served on the editorial boards of *Memory and Cognition, Applied Cognitive Psychology, Consciousness and Cognition, Psychological Science, Social Cognitive and Affective Neuroscience, Encyclopedia of Consciousness,* and *the Journal of Imagination, Cognition and Personality*.

Gün R. Semin is an Academy Professor with The Netherlands Royal Academy of Arts and Sciences at Utrecht University and also Professor of Psychology at Koç University, Istanbul. He has previously served as Professor and Chair of the Department of Social Psychology at the Free University (1990–2004) and as Research Director (2000–2003) of the Faculty of Psychology and Education. Professor Semin was also the founding Scientific Director of the Kurt Lewin Institute (1992–1996), the inter-university graduate school in social psychology, the Netherlands. He has been on the editorial board of journals in his field (e.g., *Journal of Personality and Social Psychology, Personality and Social Psychology Review, Personality and Social Psychology Bulletin, European Journal of Social Psychology*). His main research interest is in embodied social cognition, communication, language, and social neuroscience – aside from specific research projects he is currently running on affect and affective processes and the action–perception link. Further information about his research and publications can be obtained at www.cratylus.org.

Oren Shapira is a researcher of social psychology at the Department of Psychology at Tel Aviv University. His research topics include implicit social cognition, mental construal, and problem solving. He is now examining whether psychological distance and a high level of mental construal can help people reason analogically and solve problems. He has also studied the psychological effects of terrorism and forced evacuation as part of a research group at the National Security Studies Center at the University of Haifa.

Anna Sheveland holds a BA in psychology, a BA in economics and government and politics, and an MS in psychology from the University of Maryland, where she is currently a doctoral candidate in the Psychology Department. Her research interests include motivated cognition, the ascription of epistemic authority, political ideology, and terrorism.

Alexander Todorov received his PhD from New York University in 2002. Currently, he is an Associate Professor of Psychology and Public Affairs at Princeton University with a joint appointment in the Department of Psychology and the Woodrow Wilson School of Public and International Affairs. He is also an affiliated faculty of the Princeton Neuroscience Institute and a visiting professor at Radboud University, the Netherlands. His research focuses on the cognitive and neural basis of social cognition, with a particular emphasis on face perception. In addition to publications on judgments and decision-making, he has over 40 peer-reviewed publications on various topics of face perception published in psychology journals, neuroscience journals, computer science journals, and in general journals such as *Science* and

Proceedings of the National Academy of Sciences. His research has been funded by the National Science Foundation. He is a recipient of the SAGE Young Scholar Award from the Foundation for Personality and Social Psychology, and fellowships from the Guggenheim Foundation and the Russell Sage Foundation.

Yaacov Trope earned a PhD in Psychology from the University of Michigan in 1974 and is a Professor of Psychology at New York University. He is a recipient of several awards, including the Fulbright Fellowship and the American Psychological Society Fellowship. Professor Trope's research has focused on motivation and cognition, dual-mode processing of social information, self-control, and the mental construal processes that afford predicting, emoting, and taking action with respect to psychologically distant objects.

William von Hippel is Professor and Head of the School of Psychology at the University of Queensland. He received his PhD in Social Psychology from the University of Michigan. His research interests are broad, and include the impact of aging on self-control processes and the role of evolution in shaping thought and behavior. He has authored more than 80 articles and chapters with funding from the National Institute of Aging and the Australian Research Council. Professor von Hippel serves on the editorial boards of several social psychology journals and is President-Elect of the Society of Australasian Social Psychologists.

Piotr Winkielman (PhD 1997 Michigan, post-doc OSU) is Professor of Psychology at the University of California, San Diego. His current research focuses on the relation between emotion, cognition, embodiment, and consciousness using psychological and psychophysiological approaches. His research has been supported by NSF, NIMH, and NAAR. He co-edited the books *Emotion and Consciousness* (2005) and *Social Neuroscience* (2008). He has served on the editorial boards of the *Journal of Personality and Social Psychology* and *Personality and Social Psychology Bulletin*. From 2006 to 2008 he was Associate Editor of *Emotion*, and from 2008 to 2010 of *Psychological Review*.

Talee Ziv holds a BA from Tel Aviv University, and is currently a PhD candidate in the Department of Psychology at Harvard University. She has studied infants' visual preference for own-race faces cross-culturally, and her present research focuses on understanding the mechanisms underlying this phenomenon as well as its link to later developing racial attitudes.

Revisiting the Sovereignty of Social Cognition: Finally Some Action

C. Neil Macrae & Lynden K. Miles

> We see persons engaging in actions that have a psychological content.
>
> Asch (1952, p. 151)

For lay psychologists, airport bookstores have traditionally been an uninspiring place to hang out. While perusal of the shelves reliably reveals the secrets of wealth management, dietary restraint and enviable abdominal muscles, it rarely returns much in the way of genuine psychological wisdom. Or at least that was the case until quite recently. Now, outlets are packed with products offering insights into the nature and vagaries of the human condition. For example, if you want to know why winning the lottery makes you feel less happy than you had imagined, what the contents of your bedroom reveal about your inner personality, and how to overcome the perils of procrastination, simply pay a visit to the bookstore next time your flight is delayed (e.g., Ariely, 2008; Gilbert, 2007; Gosling, 2008). Social psychology is everywhere, with much of the available material focusing on the topic of the current chapter (and indeed book) – *social cognition*.

That the general public display a thirst for social-cognitive knowledge is unsurprising. Social cognition, after all, is the medium through which our worlds are construed and actions initiated (Fiske, 1992; James, 1890). As Ostrom famously opined, "The field of social cognition reigns sovereign" (1984, p. 29). Unable to cut the mustard on our own, we thrive and succeed via communal

living (Dunbar, 1993). The demands of such a lifestyle, however, are many. Sometimes our goals and objectives are achieved through mutual cooperation, other times by the manipulation and deception of conspecifics. Sometimes it is advantageous to raise one's head above the parapet and show dissent, on other occasions to sit anonymously and go along with the crowd. Little wonder, therefore, that people are fascinated by the stuff of social cognition, the tactics and strategies that facilitate social interaction and how these are supported in the brain (e.g., Beer & Ochsner, 2006; Fiske, 1992; Mitchell, 2009).

Underpinning current interest in social cognition is around 30 years of research and theorizing on the topic (see Fiske & Taylor, 1984; Hamilton, 1981; Macrae & Bodenhausen, 2000; Wyer & Srull, 1984). Our objective in the present chapter, thankfully, is not to review this enormous body of work, as such an undertaking would be impossible and decidedly soporific. Instead, our goal is to take a broad overview of social cognition and raise some issues and observations that have prompted us to pause for thought and reflection in the course of our own recent research. As a guiding route map, in the course of the current chapter we will touch upon: the nature, basis and function of social cognition; why action serves as the bedrock of social cognition; and how work in social cognition can be integrated with broader themes across the sciences. The views and opinions expressed in this chapter are entirely personal and will likely fall short of universal appeal. Nevertheless, they reflect insights and opinions distilled from numerous conversations with colleagues in coffee shops, wine bars and yes, you guessed it, airport bookstores.

THINKING ABOUT SOCIAL COGNITION

So what exactly is social cognition and why does it (allegedly) reign supreme (Ostrom, 1984)? As it turns out, this delicious question has generated passionate debate for years, most conspicuously at major social-psychological conferences and conventions. Indeed, were it not for the rapid intervention of dinner, visits to the restroom, or unconsciousness, fist-fights may have broken out between social psychologists during these verbal jousts. The problem, we think, can be identified quite easily. Over the years some rather unhelpful definitions of social cognition have been advanced which, in turn, have caused difficulties for individuals working in field, particularly experimental social psychologists. As comparison cases, consider how social cognition has advanced in other branches of psychology, notably developmental psychology and neuropsychology. After much scratching of heads, we cannot think of a single occasion on which researchers in either of these fields has been witnessed arguing by the water cooler about the definition of social cognition. Moreover, it is nothing peculiar about babies or brains that has precipitated this state of affairs. Elsewhere in the discipline, research has been guided by the working assumption that social cognition is an *activity* that enables people to understand and interact successfully with others (Adolphs, 1999; Frith, 2007; Olson & Dweck, 2008). It is regrettable that, on occasion, experimental social psychologists have diverged somewhat from this viewpoint.

In his seminal article on the sovereignty of social cognition, Ostrom (1984) identified a messy definitional landscape that continues to hamper integrative progress in the field. From the clutter of definitions available, one in particular has arguably been problematic. For many researchers, social cognition is not so much an activity or area of inquiry, but rather a methodological approach to the study of human social interaction. Ironically, an influential community of scholars, the International Social Cognition Network, advances just such a position. As stated on their website,

> We view social cognition not as a content area, but rather as an approach to understanding a wide variety of social psychological phenomena pertaining to many content areas ... the major concerns of the approach are the processes underling the perception, memory and judgment of social stimuli; the effects of social, cultural, and affective factors on the processing of information; and the behavioral and interpersonal consequences of cognitive processes.

(International Social Cognition Network, 2011)

This overtly cognitivist (and individualistic) approach is not without virtue. By borrowing terminology (e.g., encoding, representation, retrieval), tasks (e.g., lexical decision tasks, dual-task procedures) and measures (e.g., reaction times, recognition accuracy) from cognitive psychology, researchers have been able to provide a process-oriented account of core aspects of social-cognitive functioning (e.g., impression formation, person categorization, self, attitudes; see Fiske, 1992; Higgins & Bargh, 1987; Macrae & Bodenhausen, 2000). As Ostrom himself remarked, "Principles of interest to cognitive psychologists are directly pertinent to understanding the phenomena of social psychology" (1984, p. 29). In the eyes of many, however, the strengths of this approach fail to conceal some fundamental limitations, a couple of which are worthy of passing mention.

First, immersed in the world of information-processing metaphors and terminology, social cognition can appear to be little more than reheated cognitive psychology – specifically, cognitive psychology with different (albeit more interesting) stimulus materials. Indeed, such an observation has prompted several wise minds to raise the question of what is actually "social" about social cognition at all (e.g., Forgas, 1983). Second, and closely related, a reliance on cognitive methodologies has resulted in the worrisome disappearance of a critical dependent measure from the investigative landscape – meaningful behavior (Fiske, 1992). That is, despite universal acknowledgement that behavioral relevance is critical to the empirical enterprise, the majority of contemporary research continues to measure only social cognitions, in the form of impressions, judgments and memories (see Baumeister, Vohs, & Funder, 2007; Patterson, 2008). The pitfalls of this approach are obvious. By moving away from meaningful behavior, social-cognitive research creates an explanatory gap between the measuring instruments it employs (e.g., questionnaires, reaction times) and the phenomena it strives to explain (e.g., stereotyping). The result is the generation of phenomenon-specific theories that necessarily fragment a unified account of social-cognitive functioning. To be sure there is nothing inherently wrong with participants making "pencil marks" and "computer keystrokes," one must simply exercise caution and restraint when generalizing from these responses to meaningful social action.

In proclaiming the sovereign status of social cognition, Ostrom (1984) identified issues that continue (perhaps unnecessarily) to engender debate and discussion. Two in particular are worthy of consideration as they pertain to the nature of social understanding: (i) differences between social and non-social knowledge; and (ii) action as the foundation of social knowledge. To set the stage for the second section of this chapter, attention now turns to these issues.

Social vs non-social knowledge

Whereas Ostrom (1984) remained agnostic about potential differences in the operations that support social versus non-social perception (see Brewer, 1988), he offered valuable insights into the different properties that social and non-social objects possess. Take, for example, his prototypical object of choice, a rock. The first and perhaps most obvious difference between rocks and persons pertains to the stability of their physical appearance through time. Ordinarily, a rock in the garden will look pretty much the same next year as it did over a decade (or perhaps even a century) ago. The same, however, cannot be said of Aunt Peggy, Bill Clinton, and for that matter either of the current authors. While objects retain their general appearance and composition for years, persons are in a constant state of flux (as evidenced by moment-to-moment changes in their posture, expression and movements, not to mention longer-term shifts in size, shape and appearance). This, of course, has important implications for the acquisition of knowledge. Whereas person knowledge is gleaned from the perception of behavioral events that unfold over time (Heider, 1958), object knowledge is often garnered from a single, discrete sensory-motor experience. Herein resides a critical insight into the conceptualization of social cognition and the primacy of action (Ostrom, 1984). In order to elucidate the acquisition of person knowledge, it is essential to model social cognition in a dynamic manner (Marsh, Richardson, Baron, & Schmidt, 2006).

A second fundamental difference between persons and non-social objects resides in the forces that produce change and the explanations that are offered for these effects. As Ostrom (1984) noted, "A vase may appear different in the sunlight versus the shadows, its color might fade if scrubbed with a strong detergent, it might break if pushed off the table. All these forces are external to the object" (p. 10). Critically, virtually all the changes

that are observed in non-social objects reflect the operation of these forces. As such, transformations in the non-social world are characteristically attributed to the operation of external causal factors (Heider, 1958). For example, a house window cracks because of excessive frost, not because the pane was especially annoyed or frustrated. Whereas persons are similarly subject to the operation of external causal influences (e.g., ever fallen asleep while sunbathing?), change can also be fashioned by (supposedly) unobservable internal factors (Heider, 1958). To paraphrase Ostrom, unlike non-social objects, people act with agency.

This difference between social and non-social objects has well-stated implications for social-cognitive understanding. Compared to inert non-social objects, people are deemed to be purposive, self-initiating agents the behavior of whom is driven by an extensive inventory of psychological forces (e.g., goals, beliefs, intentions). For example, we punch the boss because we believe he flirted with our partner, not because a gust of wind propelled our hand toward his chin. Naturally, therefore, compared to non-social objects, people are viewed through a quite different explanatory lens. Whereas mechanistic explanations are sufficient for rocks, paper and scissors, purposive explanation is the currency of human social cognition. Through possession of a Theory of Mind (ToM) and adoption of what has been termed the *intentional stance* (Dennett, 1987), people ascribe the actions of others to their hidden mental states and unobservable behavioral proclivities (i.e., mental state attribution). Notwithstanding the psychological flavor of these social-cognitive explanations however, they must nevertheless be grounded in the lawful properties of the natural world. A vexatious problem for experimental social psychologists has therefore been to establish how internal psychological causation fits within the natural world order.

Differences between rocks and persons aside, our own particular viewpoint on this matter is quite straightforward – *all cognition is social*. Through natural selection, organisms adapt to the specific environmental challenges they face. For people, these challenges have primarily (though not exclusively) been social. When one's very survival depends on the ability to coexist successfully and harmoniously with other people, precise skills are required. In this respect, just as echolocation provides a fundamental "survival skill" for bats (i.e., locating and identifying objects in the environment), social cognition does so for people, in that it enables them to navigate the complexities of human social interaction. Put simply, social cognition is the medium through which daily exchanges are realized. The pivotal status of social cognition is revealed most directly when this capacity is disrupted or absent. Take, for example, the difficulties encountered by individuals with autism or Asperger's syndrome. Without a fully developed ToM, these persons are unable to intuit the contents of other minds. In particular, they encounter considerable difficulty understanding and predicting people's emotional states and reactions (Baron-Cohen, 1997; Frith, 2003). Stripped of this essential ability, they are unable to comprehend or transmit the subtle signals that underlie successful (or for that matter unsuccessful) social interaction. A similar message emerges following insult to the brain, particularly damage to the orbitofrontal cortex (Damasio, 1996). Without social inhibitions, prefrontal patients exhibit behaviors that would make even the most liberal of individuals cringe. The message that emerges here then is illuminating. When social cognition is impaired, effective interpersonal exchange is near nigh impossible.

Action as the foundation of social knowledge

For Ostrom (1984), action is the critical element of social cognition. As he declared, "A priority concern… for… social cognition is to tackle the theoretical and empirical implications of action as the basis of social knowledge" (p. 19). In so doing, of course, Ostrom was reiterating a well-rehearsed argument in psychology (James, 1890). Developmental psychologists have long maintained that knowledge derives from our actions on the world (e.g., E. J. Gibson, 1969; Piaget, 1954). In social psychology, however, this viewpoint has taken longer to gain a significant foothold (see Fiske, 1993). For many years, despite Ostrom's clarion call, social-cognitive research largely ignored the concept of action (Markus & Zajonc, 1985; Wyer & Srull, 1984). It did so, moreover, even when the importance of action was articulated in some of the field's most influential writings. Asch (1952), for one, was an advocate of this position. As he argued:

> Our problem of relating actions to inward experiences would be solved if we could abandon the assumption that phenomenological facts and the actions that correspond to them are utterly heterogeneous, if we could reverse this assumption and say that the organized properties of experience are structurally similar to those of the corresponding actions (p. 158).

Interestingly, with these words, Asch was clearly arguing for a non-mentalistic account of social knowledge, a viewpoint that was later expanded

on in Gibson's work on the direct perception of affordances (J. J. Gibson, 1979).

Inspired in no small part by J. J. Gibson's (1979) influential writings, the last 25 years have witnessed something of a sea change in the character of social-cognitive research. Building upon early ecological accounts of social perception (e.g., McArthur & Baron, 1983; Valenti & Good, 1991), recent theoretical treatments have emphasized the situated and embodied nature of social knowledge (e.g., Marsh, Richardson, Baron, & Schmidt, 2006; Niedenthal, Barsalou, Winkielman, Krauth-Gruber, & Ric, 2005; Smith & Semin, 2005). Guiding these viewpoints is the assumption of the reciprocity of perception and action, with social cognition characterized as a dynamic transaction between the person and their (social) environment. From this perspective, the critical relationship between knower and known is one of mutuality and interdependence. Thus, it may have taken some time, but finally social-cognitive research has responded to the sage advice of Asch (1952) and Ostrom (1984) and elevated action to a position of theoretical prominence. Reflecting this renewed interest in action as a core component of social cognition, attention now turns to a consideration of how action-oriented theorizing can integrate social-cognitive research with broader themes across the sciences.

THINKING ABOUT ACTION

If Ostrom's (1984) "call for action" is to be given genuine consideration as a guiding principle for researchers exploring social cognition, the nature of action must be taken seriously. Psychological approaches to understanding how people act traditionally postulate a mechanistic view whereby so-called motor programs or commands are issued to relevant body parts by either neural structures or some form of executive controller. However, aside from the missing homunculus and a reliance on a theoretically dubious mind–body dualism, critics of this thesis suggest it is computationally untenable – the degrees of freedom required to capture the complexity and flexibility of action cannot be accommodated by a discrete set of motor programs (e.g., see Berstein, 1967; Kelso, 1995; Kugler & Turvey, 1987; Turvey, 1990, 2007). Instead, there is growing enthusiasm for psychologists to adopt the more general stance of dynamical systems theory (DST) in order to best characterize the organization of motor behavior.

In the following sections we will briefly outline aspects of DST that provide a foundation for viewing patterns of behavior through a more general theoretical lens.[1] Our goal is to point out how human action can be subject to the same lawful principles that guide change across a range of living and non-living systems. Using examples from both our own and other labs, we hope to demonstrate that by viewing action in this manner, core aspects of social cognition do not have to be reduced to hidden mental processes, but can be grounded in the lawful properties of the natural world (Richardson, Marsh, & Schmidt, 2010).

The promise of dynamics

In essence, a dynamical system is one that changes over time as a consequence of the interactions between its elements. To this end, DST attempts to describe the nature of such change. With origins in mathematics, DST provides a foundation for modeling events across all domains of science, from physics and chemistry (e.g., Tel, de Moura, Grebogi, & Karolyi, 2005) to meteorology (e.g., Lorenz, 1963), population ecology (e.g., Hanski, 1998) and epidemiology (e.g., Anderson & May, 1991). Moreover, psychological phenomena have not been entirely overlooked. Neural activity (e.g., Buzsáki & Draguhn, 2004), emotion and development (e.g., Lewis & Granic, 2000), personality (e.g., Shoda, LeeTiernan, & Mischel, 2002), cognition (e.g., Spivey & Dale, 2006), mental illness (e.g., Johnson & Nowak, 2002) and social psychology (e.g., Vallacher & Nowak, 1994) are among a range of topics that been viewed from a dynamical perspective. Of significance, a key concept to emerge from the science of dynamics is that of *self-organization* – namely, the fact that patterns of activity can occur solely through the interactions of the components of a system without the need for external input. Here then is the utility of a dynamical approach to action – ordered behavior can be understood without appealing to commands or motor programs issued by a source external to the behavior itself (e.g., executive controllers, homunculi).

Coordination dynamics

To date, perhaps the most influential application of DST to psychological activity has been with respect to coordination dynamics (for recent overviews, see Kelso, 2009; Schmidt & Richardson, 2008). This field has sought to identify the lawful principles that underlie instances of coordinated activity. Take, for example, a pair of pendulum clocks hung on a common wooden support. Huygens (1665, as cited in Pikovsky, Rosenblum, & Kurths, 2001) observed that regardless of their starting positions, after a period the pendula would synchronize: that is, their respective oscillations would coincide in time, and remain that way. With a little poetic license, Huygens described this phenomenon as the "sympathy of two clocks," and went on to hypothesize that motions of the common support communicated the movement trajectories of the pendula. As it turns out, Huygens' speculations were on the money. Contemporary accounts of synchrony point to the necessity of some form of *coupling* between the elements of a system in order for coordination to emerge. In the case of the clocks, the two swinging pendula were coupled via vibrations transmitted through the wooden support, with each pendulum's motion influencing the other until they fell into a stable, coordinated pattern. In this way, the synchronous motions of the respective pendula were self-organized – no external force or controller was necessary for coordination to emerge. Curiously, precisely the same effects have been observed, and formalized, with respect to human movement.

Kelso (1981, 1984) reported a series of studies in which participants performed rhythmic bimanual movements: for instance, moving their index fingers at a common frequency. Just as Huygens had observed with the clocks, people's finger movements showed spontaneous coordination. Specifically, despite there being an infinite number of possible patterns this coordination could take, only two forms emerged, *in-phase* (where the respective fingers are at equivalent points of the movement cycle at a given time) and *anti-phase* (where the fingers are at opposite points of the movement cycle at a given time). Moreover, as the frequency of movements was increased, individuals who were coordinated in the anti-phase mode spontaneously transitioned to the in-phase mode (but never the opposite).[2] In effect, Kelso had demonstrated self-organized coordination between movements of a finger on each hand, coupled by the nervous system. Soon after, these effects were modeled mathematically, reproducing the precise pattern of coordination observed by Kelso (and for that matter Huygens over 300 years earlier). The outcome of this model, the Haken–Kelso–Bunz (HKB) equation (Haken, Kelso, & Bunz, 1985), has formed a basis for the science of coordination dynamics.

The examples of coordination detailed so far have involved a physical coupling (e.g., a wooden beam, a nervous system) between effectors (e.g., pendula, fingers). But what happens when there is no such mechanism present? Is it possible that, for example, the rhythmic movements of two individuals (in effect two distinct nervous systems) may be subject to the same dynamics that bring about coordination in physically coupled systems?

The answer to this question is a resounding "yes." Early hints of just such an effect came from observations of South-East Asian fireflies, which, when congregated in groups numbering in the thousands, produce a spectacular display of rhythmic and coordinated flashing (Buck & Buck, 1976). Of note, there is no physical coupling between the fireflies, nor is there any "leader" to set a pace or rhythm. Instead the timing of each flash is thought to inform, and be informed by, the others; that is, to be self-organized (Strogatz, 2003). Might then, interpersonal coordination, a mainstay of social interaction, also be organized in this way? Again, the extant research is in support of this view. In the first such demonstration, Schmidt, Carello, and Turvey (1990) reported that pairs of participants, who were instructed to synchronize the swinging of their legs, spontaneously transitioned from anti-phase to in-phase coordination as movement frequency increased. The predictions of the HKB equation were again borne out, but this time in a system with no physical coupling. Instead, the participants were visually coupled, yet the same dynamic applied and synchrony emerged. It is in this way that dynamics provide general, lawful principles that universally describe the emergence of self-organized coordinated activity (Schmidt & Richardson, 2008).

As it turns out, the self-organized nature of interpersonal coordination influences, and is influenced by, social factors. For example, imagine you are taking a stroll with a friend. Often your footsteps will spontaneously become entrained, resulting in the two of you walking in almost perfect step (Zivotofsky & Hausdorff, 2007). Now imagine you are taking the same stroll without your friend, but with others also using the same path. Will you coordinate to the same extent with the movements of strangers? We suspect not. At issue is the functional nature of coordination: specifically, the notion that synchronous actions form a foundation for, and display of, social bonding. It is probably no accident that rhythmic activities such as drumming, singing, and dancing are at the basis of social rituals across all cultures. Indeed, a number of theorists have suggested that engaging in these practices draws people together, uniting them via common experience (e.g., Freeman, 2000; MacNeil, 1995). Several lines of empirical evidence also support this view. Moving in time with others elicits feelings of connectedness, liking, and rapport (e.g., Berneiri, 1988; Hove & Risen, 2009; LaFrance, 1979), blurs self–other boundaries (Paladino, Mazzurega, Pavani, & Schubert, 2010), enhances cooperation (e.g., Wiltermuth & Heath, 2009), cooperative ability (e.g., Valdesolo, Ouyang, & DeSteno, 2010), and altruistic behavior (Valdesolo & DeSteno, 2011), and is accompanied by the release of endorphins (Cohen, Ejsmond-Frey, Knight, & Dunbar, 2010). Behavioral synchrony between parents and infants is indicative of an effective bond, while a lack of such coordination may signal developmental problems (Feldman, 2007). In short, synchronous activity promotes positive social outcomes.

Evidence from our own lab also testifies to this idea. We have shown that the characteristics of a social encounter can influence the emergence of synchrony. Participants who were made to wait for a tardy confederate synchronized less on a movement task than those who endured no such delay (Miles, Griffiths, Richardson, & Macrae, 2010). Similarly, an arbitrary difference between participants and a confederate led to enhanced levels of synchrony as a means to reduce this perceived social distance (Miles, Lumsden, Richardson, & Macrae, 2011). Importantly, in these studies participants were not instructed to coordinate in any way and their actions were incidental to the tasks at hand – yet coordination was manifest in a manner consistent with both a self-organized dynamic (i.e., when coordination was observed it was only in the in-phase mode) as well as social mores and conventions. In other words, social factors appear to be integral to the coordination dynamics that underlie the emergence of interpersonal synchrony.

Perhaps more relevant to the present volume, our own research has also revealed the converse relationship – synchrony can influence social cognition. Macrae, Duffy, Miles, and Lawrence (2008) had participants perform hand movements (i.e., extension/flexion about the wrist) in time with a metronome. Simultaneously, a confederate performed the same movements, intentionally coordinating with the participant in either an in-phase or anti-phase mode and spoke words aloud (allegedly as a distraction). Subsequently, participants were given a surprise recall test, whereby they were asked to recount as many of the words as they could, and to identify the confederate from a series of photographs. Remarkably, following the period of activity, participants who experienced in-phase coordination recalled more words, and were more accurate in recognizing the confederate than those in the anti-phase condition. That is, following the most *stable* mode of coordination (i.e., in-phase) participants demonstrated enhanced memory for central aspects of interaction – what others look like, and what they say. The dynamics of coordination shaped social cognition.

In a follow-up study, we explored further the role of coordination stability during social exchange (Miles, Nind, Henderson, & Macrae, 2010). Again, participants performed a repetitive action (i.e., arm curls) while a confederate coordinated with them in either an in-phase or anti-phase mode. In addition, both the confederate and participant heard words played over head-phones and were required to repeat them out loud, alternating between each other. Next, we meas-ured the participant's incidental recall of self- and other-related information (i.e., words spoken by themselves or the confederate). Consistent with the memory literature (e.g., self-reference effect; Symons & Johnson, 1997), participants demon-strated an advantage for recalling more of the words they spoke compared to words the confed-erate uttered when coordination was anti-phase. However, this effect was eliminated when the confederate coordinated in an in-phase mode. In this condition, participants recalled an equivalent number of words regardless of the source (i.e., self or other). Of note, in other contexts an absence of the self-memory advantage is generally only seen for established interpersonal relationships (e.g., when the "other" is well known to the "self"). Here, however, the confederate was previously unknown to the participant and their interaction was limited to the exchange described above, yet stable coordination led to shifts in social cognition consistent with those seen for more long-standing relationships. Furthermore, measurements of coordination stability (i.e., standard deviation of relative phase) within each dyad were shown to be related to the ratio of self-to-other words recalled by the participant. More stable coordination was associated with a greater attenuation of the self-memory advantage. Once again, properties inher-ent to self-organized coordination seem to be intimately entwined with the very core of social-cognitive functioning.

Perceiving the dynamics

To this point, we have focused primarily on the application of the science of coordination dynam-ics to understanding how interpersonal synchrony can emerge spontaneously and without recourse to any form of external or executive controller. In doing so, we have briefly detailed how action can be self-organized, and how the characteristics of self-organized systems (e.g., phase relationship, stability) have been shown to influence, and be influenced by, social cognition. However, a skep-tical reader might still question the general utility of this approach for psychologists. After all, there is a lot more to social cognition than apparently quirky parallels between fireflies and flapping hands (Macrae et al., 2008). If we are to take "action as the basis of social knowledge" to be a guiding principle for social cognition, what becomes of genuinely psychological constructs – the attitudes, beliefs, biases, emotions, feelings,

goals, intentions, motives, moods, thoughts, and whims that color everyday behavior? Surely, these are "special types" of natural phenomena, beyond the purview of a general dynamical approach to order? Perhaps not. Drawing heavily from the Gibsonian notion of information (e.g., J. J. Gibson, 1979; Michaels & Carello, 1981), Runeson and Frykholm (1983) set out the kinematic specifica-tion of dynamics (KSD) principle, a theoretical framework for incorporating dynamics into our more general understanding of social knowing.

In short, the KSD principle states that move-ments specify their causes (Runeson & Frykholm, 1983): i.e., *kinematics* (i.e., spatio-temporal pat-terns of movement) reveal *dynamics* (i.e., the forces that cause and constrain movement). Take the (relatively) simple example of human gait. By attending to gait patterns (i.e., kinematics) we can glean a host of socially relevant information. We can tell if someone is male or female (Kozlowski & Cutting, 1977), what actions they are perform-ing (Dittrich, 1993), and who they are (Cutting & Kozlowski, 1977). Runeson and Frykholm argue that such information is available for perception, as the form that movements take is structured by the forces that determine (and constrain) them. Differences between, for instance, the anatomical make-up of males and females (e.g., hip and shoulder width) lead to sex-specific differences in the center of movement (i.e., a kinematic property) that in turn is used by perceivers when determining sex from gait (Cutting, Proffitt, & Kozlowski, 1978). From this perspective, social knowledge can be veridically specified as patterns of movement.[3]

Returning to the case of interpersonal syn-chrony, work in our lab has revealed that perceiv-ers utilize kinematic patterns that are consistent with self-organized coordination dynamics when making social judgments (Miles, Nind, & Macrae, 2009). We simulated dyads (i.e., pairs of walkers) using either stick figure animations or audio recordings of footsteps. Importantly, we varied the relative phase relationship between the strides of the walkers in equal increments, ranging from in-phase to anti-phase. This manipulation had the effect of systematically changing the mode of coordination while keeping the amount of coordi-nation constant (i.e., phase relationship did not vary within trials). Participants were asked to view (or listen to) each trial and rate the rapport they associated with the simulated interaction. As it turned out, these ratings followed a curvilinear relationship, whereby perceived rapport was high-est when the kinematics revealed stable modes of coordination (i.e., in-phase and anti-phase), and lowest at the intermediate phase relationships (i.e., the least stable modes). In line with the KSD principle, perceptions of the quality of a social exchange corresponded with the kinematic properties that result from self-organized coordination dynamics.

Importantly, the KSD principle extends beyond biomechanical factors and coordinative structures to include inherently psychological constructs such as emotions, intentions, and expectations. As Koffka (1935) illustrates:

> The slow dragging movements of the depressed, the jerky, discontinuous movements of the irritable, correspond, indeed, to the leaden state of depression or the disrupted state of irritability ... characteristics of overt behavior will map characteristics of the field in which this behavior is started (p. 658).

In this way, Heider's (1958) apparently unobservable internal causes of behavior are the very forces that give rise to overt, perceivable, patterns of movement. Furthermore, consistent with DST, these kinematic patterns are thought to be self-organized (e.g., Lewis, 2000) – no homunculus or executive process is required to register, for example, a depressed mood and issue the motor command to be slow. Instead, the shape of action is thought to unfold by virtue of the interactions between the factors that support and constrain such action. Here again, the utility of understanding the characteristics of action as emergent, self-organized properties of the dynamics that order behavior is evident. Knowing what form actions take can equate to knowing precisely how those actions came about: i.e., in a social context, knowing what those actions mean.

REVISITING THE SOVEREIGN STATE

Over the course of this chapter we have touched, albeit lightly, on several issues that we believe are central to situating social cognition at the forefront of psychological science. First, we see it as critical that researchers abandon the view that social cognition is an approach or set of methodological tools, but rather recognize social cognition as an activity that keeps us in contact with our social worlds. One important implication that arises from this perspective is the need for social-cognitive research to (re)focus on action as the basis of social knowledge (Ostrom, 1984). Although much has been learned from viewing social cognition as a set of internalized processes, less consideration has been given to the extent such mentalizing is borne out in the things people do – their behavior. However, rather than lament this apparently narrow focus, we suggest it is time

to reinvigorate Ostrom's call for action in order to best capitalize on what we now know. To do so, we have advocated casting the theoretical net somewhat wider than social scientists are typically accustomed, in order to locate social-cognitive research within a more general understanding of the natural world.

Second, we have briefly introduced dynamical systems theory as a general framework for understanding the nature of change, or more specific to the current work, how actions are ordered. To this end, we have considered how action can be self-organized, thereby relegating so-called hidden mental processes to be, at best, descriptive constructs rather than causal factors in the patterning of behavior. This approach also helps situate psychological phenomena within the realm of the natural sciences whereby universal, scale-free principles can be employed to guide our understanding of social behavior. Of course, we have only brushed the surface: there is much work to be done here – knowing that coordination dynamics underlie the spontaneous emergence of synchronous activity does not directly inform quite how, for example, emotions guide the self-organization of goal-directed action (but see Lewis, 2000). It does, however, provide researchers with a general set of principles that can, at the very least, guide theorizing and experimentation. To this end, we remain resolute that social cognition can, and should, be viewed from a more general perspective, one that is in keeping with the lawful principles of the natural world.

Finally, we return to Ostrom's (1984) declaration that social cognition stands sovereign. With over a quarter of a century of theory and research under our collective belts, it may now be time to revisit this issue. Has social cognition retained its sovereign status? Our response is twofold. On the one hand, the phenomena continue to reign supreme. Psychologists and lay persons alike spend much of their waking hours trying to figure out the intricacies of social behavior. On the other hand, it may be time to renounce social cognition as an approach, and instead plump for more general explanatory tools. In this way, the intricacies of human social behavior can be firmly embedded within a scientific, principled, and lawful understanding of the natural world.

ACKNOWLEDGMENTS

Portions of this work were supported by a Royal Society Wolfson Fellowship awarded to C.N.M., and a Research Councils of the United Kingdom Academic Fellowship awarded to L.K.M. We are grateful to Michael J. Richardson for helpful discussions and insights regarding several of the main themes of this chapter and to Joanne Lumsden and Louise Nind for their contributions to this work.

NOTES

1   A comprehensive treatment of DST is beyond the scope of this chapter; however, we refer readers to any of several excellent accounts of dynamics as a set of organizing principles for psychological activity (e.g., Kelso, 1995, 2009; Lewis & Granic, 2000; Marsh et al., 2006; Marsh, Richardson, & Schmidt, 2009; Nowak & Vallacher, 1998; Oullier & Kelso, 2009; Richardson et al., 2010; Schmidt & Richardson, 2008; Vallacher & Nowak, 1994; Warren, 2006).

2   Importantly, although in-phase and anti-phase are both stable modes of coordination (i.e., attractor states for coordinated activity), in-phase is relatively more stable than anti-phase and therefore tends to dominate at higher movement frequencies.

3   A good deal of work in this area has employed Johansson's (1973) point-light technique as a means to isolate and display kinematic information. Some contemporary examples of this approach appear, however, to ignore the relationship between dynamics and kinematics, instead employing point-light displays that, in all likelihood, simply caricature aspects of biological motion. For instance, actors in these displays are often asked to move "as if" they were experiencing emotion, performing an action, engaging with others, etc. Given deceptive intent can be revealed in kinematics (e.g., Runeson & Frykholm, 1983, E3) we suggest that dynamical factors be recreated (e.g., via emotion induction procedures, the actual performance of actions, presence of others, etc.) rather than relying on stereotyped approximations of kinematic information when generating displays using this technique.

REFERENCES

Adolphs, R. (1999). Social cognition and the human brain. *Trends in Cognitive Sciences, 3,* 469–479.

Anderson, R. M., & May, R. M. (1991). *Infectious diseases of humans: Dynamics and control.* Oxford, UK: Oxford University Press.

Ariely, D. (2008). *Predictably irrational: The hidden forces that shape our decisions.* New York, NY: Harper Collins.

Asch, S. E. (1952). *Social psychology.* Englewood Cliffs, NJ: Prentice Hall.

Baron-Cohen, S. (Ed.). (1997). *The maladapted mind. Classic readings in evolutionary psychopathology.* Hove, UK: Erlbaum.

Baumeister, R. F., Vohs, K. D., & Funder, D. C. (2007). Psychology as the science of self-reports and finger movements. Whatever happened to actual behavior? *Perspectives on Psychological Science, 2,* 396–403.

Beer, J. S., & Ochsner, K. N. (2006). Social cognition: A multi level analysis. *Brain Research, 1079,* 98–105.

Berneiri, F. J. (1988). Coordinated movement and rapport in teacher–student interactions. *Journal of Nonverbal Behavior, 12,* 120–138.

Bernstein, N. (1967). *The co-ordination and regulation of movements.* Oxford, UK: Pergamon Press.

Brewer, M. B. (1988). A dual process model of impression formation. In R. S. Wyer, Jr. & T. K. Srull (Eds.), *Advances in social cognition* (Vol. 1, pp. 1–36). Hillsdale, NJ: Erlbaum.

Buck, J., & Buck, E. (1976). Synchronous fireflies. *Scientific American, 234,* 74–85.

Buzsáki, G., & Draguhn, A. (2004). Neural oscillations in cortical networks. *Science, 304,* 1926–1929.

Cohen, E. E. A., Ejsmond-Frey, E., Knight, N., & Dunbar, R. I. M. (2010). Rowers' high: Behavioural synchrony is correlated with elevated pain thresholds. *Biology Letters, 6,* 106–108.

Cutting, J. E., & Kozlowski, L. T. (1977). Recognizing friends by their walk: Gait perception without familiarity cues. *Bulletin of the Psychonomic Society, 9,* 353–356.

Cutting, J. E., Proffitt, D. R., & Kozlowski, L. T. (1978). A biomechanical invariant for gait perception. *Journal of Experimental Psychology: Human Perception and Performance, 4,* 356–372.

Damasio, A. R. (1996). The somatic marker hypothesis and the possible functions of the prefrontal cortex. *Philosophical Transactions of the Royal Society B: Biological Sciences, 315,* 1413–1420.

Dennett, D.C. (1987). *The intentional stance.* Cambridge, MA: MIT Press.

Dittrich, W. H. (1993). Action categories and the perception of biological motion. *Perception, 22,* 15–22.

Dunbar, R. (1993). Coevolution of neocortex size, group size and language in humans. *Behavioral and Brain Sciences, 16,* 681–735.

Feldman, R. (2007). Parent–infant synchrony. *Current Directions in Psychological Science, 16,* 340–345.

Fiske, S. T. (1992). Thinking is for doing: Portraits of social cognition from daguerreotype to laserphoto. *Journal of Personality and Social Psychology, 63,* 877–889.

Fiske, S. T. (1993). Social cognition and social perception. In M. R. Rosenzweig & L. W. Porter (Eds.), *Annual review of psychology* (Vol. 44, pp. 155–194). Palo Alto, CA: Annual Reviews.

Fiske, S. T., & Taylor, S. E. (1984). *Social cognition.* New York, NY: Random House.

Forgas, J.P. (1983). What is social about social cognition? *British Journal of Social Psychology, 22,* 129–144.

Freeman, W. (2000). A neurobiological role of music in social bonding. In N. L. Wallin, B. Merker, & S. Brown (Eds.),

The origins of music (pp. 411–424). Cambridge, MA: MIT Press.

Frith, C. D. (2007). The social brain? *Philosophical Transactions of the Royal Society B: Biological Sciences, 362,* 671–678.

Frith, U. (2003). *Autism: Explaining the enigma* (2nd ed.). Oxford, UK: Blackwell.

Gibson, E. J. (1969). *Principles of perceptual learning and development.* New York, NY: Appleton-Century-Crofts.

Gibson, J. J. (1979). *The ecological approach to visual perception.* Hillsdale, NJ: Erlbaum.

Gilbert, D. (2007). *Stumbling on happiness.* New York, NY: Random House.

Gosling, S. D. (2008). *Snoop: What your stuff says about you.* New York, NY: Basic Books.

Haken, H., Kelso, J. A. S., & Bunz, H. (1985). A theoretical model of phase transitions in human hand movements. *Biological Cybernetics, 51,* 347–356.

Hamilton, D. L. (Ed.). (1981). *Cognitive processes in stereotyping and intergroup behavior.* Hillsdale, NJ: Erlbaum.

Hanksi, I. (1998). Metapopulation dynamics. *Nature, 396,* 41–49.

Heider, F. (1958). *The psychology of interpersonal relations.* New York, NY: John Wiley & Sons.

Higgins, E. T., & Bargh, J. A. (1987). Social perception and social cognition. *Annual Review of Psychology, 38,* 369–425.

Hove, M. J., & Risen, J. L. (2009). It's all in the timing: Interpersonal synchrony increases affiliation. *Social Cognition, 27,* 949–960.

International Social Cognition Network (2011). Retrieved July 6, 2011, from www.socialcognition.eu/node/22

James, W. (1890). *The principles of psychology.* New York, NY: Henry Holt.

Johansson, G. (1973). Visual perception of biological motion and a model for its analysis. *Perception and Psychophysics, 14,* 201–211.

Johnson, S. L., & Nowak, A. (2002). Dynamical patterns in bipolar depression. *Personality and Social Psychology Review, 6,* 380–387.

Kelso, J. A. S. (1981). On the oscillatory basis of movement. *Bulletin of the Psychonomic Society, 18,* 63.

Kelso, J. A. S. (1984). Phase transitions and critical behavior in human bimanual coordination. *American Journal of Physiology: Regulatory, Integrative and Comparative, 15,* R1000–R1004.

Kelso, J. A. S. (1995). *Dynamic patterns: The self-organization of brain and behavior.* Cambridge, MA: MIT Press.

Kelso, J. A. S. (2009). Coordination dynamics. In R. A. Myers (Ed.), *Encyclopedia of complexity and systems sciences* (pp. 1537–1564). Berlin: Springer-Verlag.

Koffka, K. (1935). *Principles of gestalt psychology.* New York, NY: Harcourt Brace.

Kozlowski, L. T., & Cutting, J. E. (1977). Recognizing the sex of a walker from a dynamic point-light display. *Perception and Psychophysics, 21,* 575–580.

Kugler, P. N., & Turvey, M. T. (1987). *Information, natural law, and the self-assembly of rhythmic movement.* Hillsdale, NJ: Erlbaum.

LaFrance, M. (1979). Nonverbal synchrony and rapport: Analysis by the cross-lag panel technique. *Social Psychology Quarterly, 42,* 66–70.

Lewis, M. D. (2000). Emotional self-organization at three time scales. In M. D. Lewis, & I. Granic (Eds.), *Emotion, development, and self-organization. Dynamical systems approaches to emotional development.* Cambridge, UK: Cambridge University Press.

Lewis, M. D., & Granic, I. (Eds.). (2000). *Emotion, development, and self-organization. Dynamical systems approaches to emotional development.* Cambridge, UK: Cambridge University Press.

Lorenz, E. (1963). Deterministic nonperiodic flow. *Journal of Atmospheric Science, 20,* 282–293.

Macrae, C. N., & Bodenhausen, G. V. (2000). Social cognition: Thinking categorically about others. *Annual Review of Psychology, 51,* 93–120.

Macrae, C. N., Duffy, O. K., Miles, L. K., & Lawrence, J. (2008). A case of hand waving: Action synchrony and person perception. *Cognition, 109,* 152–156.

Markus, H., & Zajonc, R. B. (1985). The cognitive perspective in social psychology. In G. Lindzey & E. Aronson (Eds.), *Handbook of social psychology* (3rd ed., pp. 137–229). New York: Random House.

Marsh, K. L., Richardson, M. J., Baron, R. M., & Schmidt, R. C. (2006). Contrasting approaches to perceiving and acting with others. *Ecological Psychology, 18,* 1–37.

Marsh, K. L., Richardson, M. J., & Schmidt, R. C. (2009). Social connection through joint action and interpersonal coordination. *Topics in Cognitive Science, 1,* 320–339.

McArthur, L. Z., & Baron, R. M. (1983). Toward an ecological theory of social perception. *Psychological Review, 90,* 215–238.

McNeill, W. H. (1995). *Keeping together in time: Dance and drill in human history.* Cambridge, MA: Harvard University Press.

Michaels, C. F., & Carello, C. (1981). *Direct perception.* Englewood Cliffs, NJ: Prentice-Hall.

Miles, L. K., Griffiths, J. L., Richardson, M. J., & Macrae, C. N. (2010). Too late to coordinate: Contextual influences on behavioral synchrony. *European Journal of Social Psychology, 40,* 52–60.

Miles, L. K., Lumsden, J., Richardson, M. J., & Macrae, C. N. (2011). Do birds of a feather move together? Group membership and behavioral synchrony. *Experimental Brain Research, 211,* 495–503.

Miles, L. K., Nind, L. K., & Macrae, C. N. (2009). The rhythm of rapport: Interpersonal synchrony and social perception. *Journal of Experimental Social Psychology, 45,* 585–589.

Miles, L. K., Nind, L. K., Henderson, Z., & Macrae, C. N. (2010). Moving memories: Behavioral synchrony and memory for self and others. *Journal of Experimental Social Psychology, 46,* 457–460.

Mitchell, J. P. (2009). Social psychology as a natural kind. *Trends in Cognitive Sciences, 13,* 246–251.

Niedenthal, P. M., Barsalou, L. W., Winkielman, P., Krauth-Gruber, S., & Ric, F. (2005). Embodiment in attitudes, social perception, and emotion. *Personality and Social Psychology Bulletin, 9,* 184–211.

Nowak, A., & Vallacher, R. R. (1998). *Dynamical social psychology*. New York, NY: Guilford.

Olson, K. R., & Dweck, C. S. (2008). A blueprint for social cognitive development. *Perspectives on Psychological Science, 3*, 193–202.

Ostrom, T. M. (1984). The sovereignty of social cognition. In R. S. Wyer, & T. K. Srull (Eds.), *Handbook of social cognition* (Vol. 1, pp. 1–38). Hillsdale, NJ: Erlbaum.

Oullier, J. A., & Kelso, J. A. S. (2009). Social coordination from the perspective of coordination dynamics. In R. A. Myers (Ed.), *Encyclopedia of complexity and systems sciences* (pp. 8198–8212). Berlin: Springer-Verlag.

Paladino, M-P., Mazzurega, M., Pavani, F., & Schubert, T. W. (2010). Synchronous multisensory stimulation blurs self-other boundaries. *Psychological Science, 21*, 1202–1207.

Patterson, M. L. (2008). Back to social behavior: Mining the mundane. *Basic and Applied Social Psychology, 30*, 93–101.

Piaget, J. (1954). *The construction of reality in the child*. New York, NY: Basic Books.

Pikovsky, A., Rosenblum, M., & Kurths, J. (2001). *Synchronization. A universal concept in nonlinear sciences*. Cambridge, UK: Cambridge University Press.

Richardson, M. J. Marsh, K. L., & Schmidt, R. C. (2010). Challenging egocentric notions of perceiving, acting, and knowing. In L. F. Barrett, B. Mesquita, & E. Smith. (Eds.), *The Mind in Context* (pp. 307–333). New York, NY: Guilford.

Runeson, S., & Frykholm, G. (1983). Kinematic specification of dynamics as an informational basis of for person-and-action perception: Expectation, gender recognition, and deceptive intent. *Journal of Experimental Psychology: General, 4*, 585–615.

Schmidt, R. C., Carello, C., & Turvey, M. T. (1990). Phase transitions and critical fluctuations in visual coordination of rhythmic movements between people. *Journal of Experimental Psychology: Human Perception and Performance, 16*, 227–247.

Schmidt, R. C., & Richardson, M. J. (2008). Dynamics of interpersonal coordination. In A. Fuchs, & V. K. Jirsa (Eds.), *Coordination: neural, behavioral and social dynamics* (pp. 281–307). Berlin: Springer.

Shoda, Y., LeeTiernan, S., & Mischel, W. (2002). Personality as a dynamical system: Emergence of stability and distinctiveness from intra- and interpersonal interactions. *Personality and Social Psychology Review, 6*, 316–325.

Smith, E. R., & Semin, G. R. (2005). Socially situated cognition: Cognition in its social context. *Advances in Experimental Social Psychology, 36*, 53–117.

Spivey, M. J., & Dale, R. (2006). Continuous dynamics in real-time cognition. *Current Directions in Psychological Science, 15*, 207–211.

Strogatz, S. H. (2003). *Sync: The emerging science of spontaneous order*. New York, NY: Hyperion Press.

Symons, C. S., & Johnson, B. T. (1997). The self-reference effect in memory: A meta-analysis. *Psychological Bulletin, 121*, 371–394.

Tel, T., de Moura, APS., Grebogi, C., & Karolyi, G. (2005). Chemical and biological activity in open flows: A dynamical system approach. *Physics Reports, 413*, 91–196.

Turvey, M. T. (1990). Coordination. *American Psychologist, 45*, 938–953.

Turvey, M. T. (2007). Action and perception at the level of synergies. *Human Movement Science, 26*, 657–697.

Valdesolo, P., & DeSteno, D. (2011). Synchrony and the social tuning of compassion. *Emotion, 11*, 262–266.

Valdesolo, P., Ouyang, J., & DeSteno, D. (2010). The rhythm of joint action: Synchrony promotes cooperative ability. *Journal of Experimental Psychology, 46*, 693–695.

Valenti, S. S., & Good, J. M. M. (1991). Social affordances and interaction I: Introduction. *Ecological Psychology, 3*, 77–98.

Vallacher, R. R., & Nowak, A. (Eds.). (1994). *Dynamical systems in social psychology*. San Diego, CA: Academic Press.

Warren, W. H. (2006). The dynamics of perception and action. *Psychological Review, 113*, 358–389.

Wiltermuth, S. S., & Heath, C. (2009). Synchrony and cooperation. *Psychological Science, 20*, 1–5.

Wyer, R. S., & Srull, T. K. (Eds.) (1984). *Handbook of social cognition* (Vol. 1). Hillsdale, NJ: Erlbaum.

Zivotofsky, A. Z., & Hausdorff, J. M. (2007). The sensory feedback mechanisms enabling couples to walk synchronously: An initial investigation. *Journal of Neuroengineering and Rehabilitation, 4*, 28.

2

Control, Awareness, and Other Things We Might Learn to Live Without

B. Keith Payne

If you ask a person why they did something, they will give you a reason. If you ask a social psychologist why that person did something, they will give you a cause. Aside from the vexation of ordinary people trying to talk to social psychologists at dinner parties, this explanatory gap reveals something about why social psychologists have always been drawn to the automatic and the unconscious. This is in part because social psychology's emphasis on the situational causes of behavior lends itself to explaining in terms of mechanisms rather than reasons. In an influential chapter, Wegner and Bargh (1998) noted that many of the classic experiments in social psychology implied automatic influences of the situation. Milgram's (1963) obedience studies, Festinger and Carlsmith's (1959) dissonance study, Asch's (1952) work on conformity, and Schacter and Singer's (1962) studies of emotion all demonstrated influences of which participants were apparently not aware, and which would disappear if participants became aware of them.

To these observations we can add that the deeply counter-intuitive nature of many social psychology findings (both classic and contemporary) tends to focus our explanations on the automatic and the unconscious. When I tell my undergraduate students for the first time about all of the effects a simple priming stimulus can have on people's perceptions and behavior, they look at me like they are waiting for the punch line.

They simply can't imagine, they say, that these experimental participants would be influenced that way. A reasonable enough response, if we were talking about reasons. When people imagine how participants would behave, they are really imagining how they themselves would behave. And when they imagine how they would behave, they are telling a story about how reasonable people ought to behave (Nisbett & Wilson, 1977).

The fact that the causes of behavior sometimes have little to do with reasons for behaving forces us to look elsewhere for explanations. The more counter-intuitive a finding is, the more likely its explanation is to be found in automatic mental mechanisms whose operation is invisible to introspection. And so, social cognition researchers, even more than social psychologists at large, tend to favor automatic explanations as they seek to identify mental mechanisms. To explain the profound effects of subtle cues in the situation by relying only on reasons alone would be too unbelievable, even for the participants themselves.

This chapter concerns what social cognition has learned about automatic and unconscious processes. It is about what we are learning to live without, in two senses. First, it is about how we have learned to explain behavior in many cases without the introspective, reason-based explanations that are easy to generate based on self-report methods. This is the story of explaining people's explanations, in many cases as justifications or confabulations rather than causal factors in behavior. In a second sense, the chapter is about learning to do without the simple dualistic thinking that characterized early research on automatic thought. Although such broad distinctions as automatic/controlled, implicit/explicit, or System 1/System 2 are convenient shorthand, research over the last three decades has revealed complexities and nuances that cannot be captured by such simple distinctions. Mastering these nuances means accepting a bit more complexity in return for greater precision about how automatic and unconscious processes guide behavior, and how they relate to their opposites, control, and awareness.

The first section reviews what the field means by automatic processing. Automaticity is a hodge-podge of related ideas, rather than a simple definition or a clean dichotomy. This means that a simple duality between automatic and controlled thought is not likely to capture the range and complexity that automatic processing encompasses. This complexity sets the stage for certain confusions that have caused misunderstandings of social cognition research from time to time. The second section takes a look at how we arrived at our current ideas, by considering disparate research traditions that gave rise to distinct criteria for automaticity. Understanding these different traditions helps clarify some of those misunderstandings by placing them in a broader context. The third section draws on contemporary research to summarize six lessons about automaticity in social cognition. These lessons are rooted in the field's traditional understanding of automaticity, but they represent updates or contrasts to views that were widely held 10 or 20 years ago (and in some quarters today).

DEFINING AUTOMATICITY

The roots of automatic social cognition lie mainly in cognitive psychology research of the 1970s and 1980s. These ideas did not have a single inception, but developed in many different laboratories and were applied to many different problems at around the same time. The result is that researchers began invoking a handful of related but distinct ideas for a variety of different purposes, and only later did scholars attempt to organize them into an integrated framework. The most influential framework for thinking about automatic processes in social cognition has been Bargh's (1994) description of four criteria: Awareness, Intentionality, Controllability, and Efficiency. Automatic processes are defined as outside of awareness, lacking intentionality or controllability, and as operating efficiently.

Awareness

In Bargh's (1994) scheme, unconscious processes become a subset of automatic processes because lacking awareness of a process means that it is impossible to control it. People might be unaware of a stimulus itself, as in the case of subliminal perception. In such cases, effects of a subliminal stimulus would necessarily be automatic because if the participant is unaware that any stimulus was presented then the participant cannot be aware of its consequences; or, participants might be perfectly aware of the stimulus but unaware of its impact. Supraliminal primes, such as words embedded in puzzles, are often used to instigate effects of this kind. Participants are aware, for example, that they saw particular words in a word-search puzzle, but they are unaware that the words might have affected their perceptions or behavior (Bargh, 1992). This type of unconscious influence is especially relevant for everyday life because there are few cases outside the laboratory in which people are exposed to truly subliminal stimuli. Instead, unconscious influence in everyday life is most likely to happen because people are simply not attending to a stimulus or because they do not notice how the stimulus is affecting them.

In many cases, participants may be unaware of the effects of a stimulus because of a misattribution. If participants believe they are behaving competitively because they perceive their opponent as being competitive, then they cannot be aware that prime words are the true cause of their behavior. Because people tend to assume that the cause of their reaction is whatever is the salient focus of attention, they are vulnerable to sleights of hand, from magic tricks to priming experiments (Clore & Gasper, 2000; Higgins, 1998).

Intentionality and control

Intentionality and control are so tightly interwoven that they are best considered together. Intentionality refers to how much choice people have over initiating a process, whereas controllability refers to the ability to stop or inhibit it. A lack of intentionality is the focus of most studies in which the automatic *activation* of some idea is key. Automatic evaluation of attitude objects and automatic activation of stereotypes are common examples. Controllability typically concerns whether activated information is actually applied in judgments, decisions, or behaviors. The alternative is to exercise control over activated ideas, by correcting judgments (Martin, Seta, & Crelia, 1990; Wilson & Brekke, 1994), or making a "hard choice" to engage in more elaborate thought processes by seeking out additional information (Fiske, 1989).

Although the four criteria for automaticity are conceptually distinguishable, they often interact, which means that in ordinary life they can be difficult to separate. For example, if a psychology student is unaware that he has been exposed to a prime then he cannot intend to activate the primed thought, nor does he have any basis to attempt to stop it. In more ecologically realistic settings, if a police officer is unaware that racial stereotypes are coloring her impression that a driver looks suspicious, then she will have no reason to suspect that she needs to exert control. The proof is (apparently) evident in the driver's suspicious behavior. And so, exercising intention and control may sometimes depend on awareness. Yet in others cases, as will be discussed in more detail below, awareness may be irrelevant for intent and control, because automatic influences may be so powerful that people are unable to overcome the influence despite being aware of it and overtly attempting to curtail it.

Efficiency

One reason that people may be unable to curtail an automatic influence is because they lack the cognitive capacity to do so. When people "multitask" by trying to hold a conversation on a cell phone while driving, or watching television while studying, they are inevitably reminded of what psychologists have known for years: the human mind can be brilliant, but for only one thing at a time. Such distracting conditions highlight efficiency, the fourth criterion for automaticity. Whereas controlled processes require cognitive resources including effort, attention, and time, automatic processes are relatively impervious to these needs. The efficiency of a process is sometimes demonstrated by measuring or manipulating the speed of responses. If an effect occurs as strongly (or more strongly) at very fast speeds as compared to slow speeds, then this provides evidence that the effect is efficient. A second way to demonstrate efficiency is to impose a cognitive load such as rehearsing numbers to usurp some of the available cognitive resources. If an effect occurs as strongly (or more strongly) under cognitive load as compared to full attention, then this provides evidence of efficiency.

Efficiency may be the most ubiquitous feature of automatic processing in everyday life, simply because the mind's processing capacity is always limited. Some studies suggest that when a person attempts to focus attention on a task, the mind wanders away from the task up to 50% of the time (Smallwood & Schooler, 2006). Even when we are successful at concentrating attention on the task at hand, efficient processing may influence us to a striking extent. This is because whenever we pay attention to, say, a newspaper article, we are under cognitive load with respect to everything else in the world. And if we then shift attention from the newspaper to an itch on our left foot, we are now under cognitive load from the foot, leaving us vulnerable to automatic influences from the newspaper – and everything else. The fact that we can pay close attention only to one, or at most a few events at once, means that at any one moment we are exercising deliberate control over a tiny fraction of all the influences potentially affecting us.

Relations among awareness, intent, control, and efficiency

Awareness, intent, control, and efficiency are thus too closely related to treat them as if they are independent of each other. I once sat down to draw a box and arrows diagram of how these ideas could relate to each other, and ended up with four boxes and a web of bi-directional arrows cementing every possible connection. Needless to say, this was not a very informative diagram. And yet, these four criteria are connected loosely enough to cause trouble. Despite cautions to the contrary (e.g., Bargh, 1994), researchers sometimes assume that if an effect seems to be automatic by one criteria then it is automatic by other criteria. For example, if stereotypes are shown to influence judgments efficiently, then the effects of stereotypes must also be uncontrollable. This kind of reasoning neglects the fact that although the criteria for automaticity sometimes depend on each other, they do not necessarily have to.

To clarify this state of affairs, several authors have proposed taxonomies to organize thinking and terminology (Bargh, 1989, 1994; De Houwer, Teige-Mocigemba, Spruyt, & Moors, 2009). The message common to these taxonomies is that in order to prevent confusion, authors should use terms that are consistent with the methods used to demonstrate automaticity. For example, if an experiment has used a cognitive load manipulation to demonstrate efficiency, then the effects should be discussed in terms of efficiency, rather than unconsciousness or uncontrollability. Nonetheless, these details are often relegated to methods sections and footnotes. The general terms *automatic* and *unconscious* serve as a common shorthand to communicate a simple idea to a broad audience. For this reason the broader, if less precise, terminology is likely to remain common. Just as these taxonomic approaches encourage authors to be specific in writing, readers are well advised to be aware of these nuances in order to avoid misunderstandings.

How did these complexities come about? In large part, they result from the fact that social cognition researchers drew on two different research traditions in cognitive psychology when developing the current understanding. The first tradition is research on selective attention and working memory. The second is research on implicit memory. Although there was certainly some cross-talk between these fields, they used different experimental methods and different terminology, the consequences of which are still evident in today's social cognition research. The next section traces these separate influences and highlights how they foreshadowed important findings in implicit social cognition.

TWO TRADITIONS OF RESEARCH

Legacies of attention research: Intent, control, and efficiency

Many early studies of automatic processes in social cognition are rooted in a tradition of research on selective attention and working memory (e.g., Broadbent, 1971; Treisman, 1969). Especially influential for social cognition were studies of attention (Posner & Snyder, 1975; Shiffrin & Schneider, 1977) and studies of working memory (Baddeley, 1986). The key idea in this research was that information processing could be divided into controlled and automatic modes, whose features are close but not identical to the criteria we have been discussing. Automatic processing did not demand attention, was not limited in capacity, and could not be voluntarily initiated or altered, which is to say that this work was concerned with intentionality, controllability, and efficiency. Conscious awareness was not much emphasized. This tradition was especially influential for the development of (a) priming measures in social cognition, which focused on the lack of intent and control over the activation of mental content, and (b) research on the limited capacity of human cognition, which emphasized the efficiency of automatic processing.

Sequential priming measures

Fazio and colleagues' seminal work showing that attitudes can be automatically activated built on these cognitive theories of automatic and controlled processing (Fazio, Sanbonmatsu, Powell, & Kardes, 1986; see also Dovidio, Evans, & Tyler, 1986; Gaertner & McLaughlin, 1983). Fazio's approach was parallel to semantic priming studies (e.g., Neely, 1977) in which a prime item preceded a target item, and participants made a simple judgment about the target. In Fazio's approach, the primes consisted of pictures or words depicting the object of the attitude. For example, the word "coffee" might be presented as a prime to measure attitudes toward coffee. After a fraction of a second, a second word would appear on the screen. This word had a clear evaluative meaning, such as "wonderful" or "horrible." Participants were instructed to press one of two keys to evaluate the second word as pleasant or unpleasant. Response times to evaluate the second word were used to reveal how participants had spontaneously evaluated the first word. If their evaluation of the prime was positive, then it would facilitate responses to a pleasant target and inhibit responses to an unpleasant target.

Here too, there was little concern with consciousness. For Fazio et al. the key feature of automatic activation was a lack of controllability. In the work of Shiffrin and Schneider (1977) and Posner and Snyder (1975) the degree of learning was critically important for automaticity. Well-learned items were detected or retrieved from memory automatically, whereas poorly learned items required cognitive effort to search for them. Based on these assumptions, Fazio and colleagues distinguished between well-learned (i.e., strong) attitudes that should be activated automatically, and poorly learned (i.e., weak) attitudes that should not.

The connection between the strength of attitudes and their ability to be automatically activated set the stage for the use of sequential priming techniques to measure attitudes without asking participants to report them (Fazio, Jackson, Dunton, & Williams, 1995). This novel approach to indirect measurement would soon become important across many areas of psychology and a central concern in social cognition. Initially, the usefulness of this approach was most obvious for studying racial attitudes. Racial attitudes had always presented challenges for researchers because self-presentation motives meant many participants would not honestly report their attitudes. Priming methods seemed to offer the potential for a *bona fide* pipeline to reach respondents' true attitudes (Fazio et al., 1995).

The challenge of racial attitudes was taken up by both Fazio et al. (1995), who applied his priming technique to measure attitudes toward photos of Black and White people, and Devine (1989). Devine (1989) presented participants subliminally with a list of words that in one condition was mostly related to the stereotype of African Americans, and in the other condition mostly unrelated to that stereotype. Next, participants evaluated the personality of a person whose race was unspecified. Regardless of their level of prejudice on a self-report questionnaire, participants primed with words mostly related to stereotypes of African Americans liked the new person less than the control group.

These studies both found spontaneous negative reactions to African Americans, even among respondents who denied prejudiced attitudes in their self-reports. Both studies were informed by cognitive theories of automatic and controlled processing (Posner & Snyder, 1975; Shiffrin & Schneider, 1977) and priming techniques (Neely, 1977); both had little to say about conscious awareness of attitudes; and both emphasized the idea that well-learned associations should be activated automatically, but weakly learned associations require cognitive effort to be retrieved.

For Fazio, the implication was that individuals with weak or neutral racial attitudes simply would not show any priming effects, whereas those with strongly negative attitudes or strongly positive attitudes should show corresponding priming effects. But for Devine the important distinction was between the *knowledge* of a social stereotype versus the personal *endorsement* of the stereotype. Because everyone in a culture learns stereotypes in the same way they learn about other categories, such as birds or foods, knowledge of stereotypes should be well-learned for virtually everyone. Stereotypes should therefore be automatically activated for everyone. Personally endorsed beliefs, on the other hand, should vary with one's values and motivations. Thus, in Devine's approach, inescapable stereotype activation was universal; it was endorsed beliefs that distinguished prejudiced from unprejudiced individuals. Both approaches offered an answer to the riddle of continued inequality and discrimination amidst changing values and social norms that took a dim view of racial prejudice. Changing social norms may affect how people intentionally act, but automatic forms of prejudice may nonetheless shape perceptions and behaviors in ways that are unintended and difficult to control (Dovidio, Kawakami, & Gaertner, 2002).

Although sequential priming was initially imported to social cognition for the purpose of measuring prejudice, the method has since been used to study a wide range of constructs. These include political attitudes (e.g., Kam, 2007; Payne, Krosnick, Pasek, et al., 2010), stereotypes (Blair & Banaji, 1996), addictive and impulsive behaviors (Austin & Smith, 2008; Friese & Hofmann, 2009), goals (Ferguson, 2008; Ferguson & Bargh, 2004), and more. A recent meta-analysis suggests that sequential priming measures are reliable predictors of behavior, with an average correlation of 0.28 (Cameron, Brown-Ianuzzi, & Payne,

in press). Researchers in recent years have frequently described the results of such studies as reflecting unconscious attitudes, in contrast to earlier applications of these techniques. I discuss whether such interpretations may be warranted later in the section on lessons learned.

Perilously limited capacity

The idea that humans have limited capacity to process information is not new with social cognition, nor with cognitive psychology research. William James' (1890) theorizing on selective attention provided a touchstone for all psychology research that followed on this topic. As James noted, selectivity entails limited capacity, because for some objects to be selected, others must be left out. Therefore the focus of attention must always be a limited subset of the potential information available. The fact of limited capacity had a multitude of consequences for social cognition. These were highlighted by Fiske and Taylor's (1984) portrayal of perceivers as "cognitive misers," stingy with their limited supply of attention and therefore content to take shortcuts with social judgment. Fiske and Taylor's (1991) refinement of that portrait as "motivated tacticians" portrayed people as misers under some conditions but cognitive spendthrifts under others. This view highlighted the importance of goals and motivations in shaping how much effort people put into their thought processes, consistent with attention theories that acknowledged a role for motivation in regulating attentional capacity (Kahneman, 1973).

Reviewing the literature on selective attention a century later, Johnston and Dark (1986) seemed to conclude that James may have understood attention better than the experimentalists who followed. Nonetheless, research on executive control of working memory (Baddeley, 1986; Logan, 1979) made substantial advances by experimentally dissociating modality-specific control systems (visuo-spatial and auditory/phonological) from domain-general central executive resources. These different control systems could be disrupted by different kinds of secondary tasks. The kinds of tasks that disrupted the central executive (active rehearsal and manipulation of information) turned out to have powerful consequences for social judgments.

Some of the foundational research on efficient processing in social cognition focused on the role of social categories, including stereotypes, in guiding social judgment (Allport, 1954; Brewer, 1988; Fiske & Neuberg, 1990; Lippman, 1922). Drawing on tasks or states known to disrupt central executive processing, social cognition researchers highlighted the counter-intuitive role of cognitive resources in social judgment with dramatic effect. For example, circadian rhythms in arousal, known to affect executive processing, also influenced whether social judgments were biased by stereotypes (Bodenhausen, 1990). Morning people stereotyped more in the evening, whereas night owls stereotyped more in the morning. Lay intuition holds that people stereotype because of stable beliefs. This research showed that holding beliefs constant, fluctuations in cognitive resources that have nothing to do with beliefs, intent, or other morally relevant cognitions, dictated whether a target was the victim of stereotypical judgments (see also Bodenhausen & Lichtenstein, 1987; Kruglanski & Freund, 1983; Macrae, Hewstone, & Griffiths, 1993; Pratto & Bargh, 1991).

The idea that people stereotype as a way to save effort suggested another counter-intuitive consequence explored by Macrae, Milne, and Bodenhausen (1994). If people have finite attentional capacity, then when they save effort by using stereotypes they should consequently have more capacity left over for other uses. In a series of elegant experiments, Macrae and colleagues (1994) found that when a stereotype was available to help form an impression of a target person, participants performed better on a cognitively demanding secondary task, as compared to a control condition in which no stereotype was available. Studies of dual-task performance and social categorization suggested two novel reasons for the persistence of stereotyping. First, when people are distracted, tired, or otherwise occupied, they may stereotype because stereotyping is more efficient that considering all of the particulars of an individual (Fiske & Neuberg, 1990). Second, the ease afforded by stereotyping offers functional advantages, creating incentives to stereotype.

At about the same time as the efficiency of social categorization was being established, Gilbert and colleagues conducted a series of influential studies demonstrating the efficiency of dispositional, as opposed to situational judgments. The tendency to attribute other people's behavior to dispositional factors and largely ignore situational factors was established in classic experiments before the contemporary concern with automatic processing (Jones & Harris, 1967). Quattrone (1982) suggested a mechanism for the effect in that people begin by assuming a dispositional explanation but then adjust, albeit insufficiently in most cases, to take account of the situation. Gilbert and colleagues elaborated this account and experimentally manipulated the cognitive resources available as perceivers made social judgments (Gilbert & Osborne, 1989; Gilbert, Pelham, & Krull, 1988). Distracted perceivers were less likely to adjust for the situation than those with full attention, suggesting that

dispositional assumptions were efficient but adjusting for the situation required attention.

This two-step correction model – in which perceivers automatically (i.e., efficiently) make initial assumptions based on scant evidence, and then slowly and effortfully revise those impressions – was subsequently broadened into a more general model of inference. The framework was used to explain why people tend to assume whatever they read or hear is true (Gilbert, 1991; Gilbert, Krull, & Malone, 1990). This credulity bias was exaggerated by cognitive load and speeded responding, suggesting that it is efficient to believe a statement, whereas revising that belief in light of contradictory knowledge requires attentional resources. Similar models have been applied to understand why cognitive load increases stereotyping as reviewed above (Gilbert & Hixon, 1991) and how people adjust judgments to take account of their own biases more broadly (Gilbert & Gill, 2000). Although such models use the language of automatic and controlled processes, experiments testing them have relied mainly on manipulations of attentional resources and therefore the sense of automaticity in question is primarily efficiency. Although this suggests that cognitive resources are necessary to exert control over biases, it does not imply that these biases are necessarily automatic in the sense of intention, control, or awareness.

Thin slice judgments: Efficient accuracy

The research just reviewed highlighted the ways that stereotypes and other biases can automatically bias social judgments. In each case, effortful controlled processing was an antidote to these errors and biases. Yet research on "thin slice" judgments (also called zero acquaintance judgments) suggests that there are many aspects of social judgment that can take place with surprising efficiency and accuracy. An influential study showed that silent video clips of teachers displayed for 30, 10, or even 2 seconds were sufficient evidence to make judgments about teaching effectiveness (Ambady & Rosenthal, 1993). Ratings of effectiveness by naïve judges correlated reliably with teacher evaluations from the teachers' classes.

Studies have since demonstrated thin-slice accuracy in many domains. A quick glimpse at the face or body can reveal information about a person's personality traits (Yeagley, Morling, & Nelson, 2007), sexual orientation (Ambady, Hallahan, & Conner, 1999; Rule & Ambady, 2008a), political ideology (Rule et al., 2010); prejudiced attitudes (Richeson & Shelton, 2005), and intelligence (Murphy, Hall, & Colvin, 2003).

Psychologists know how difficult it is to predict future behavior, but ordinary social perceivers have some skill at doing just that from observing mere thin slices of behavior. Naïve judges successfully predicted patient outcomes from viewing thin slices of physical therapists at work (Ambady, Koo, Rosenthal, & Winograd, 2002). Judgments of political candidates' competence based on photos predicted the candidates' chances of winning congressional elections (Todorov, Mandisodza, Goren, & Hall, 2005). Judgments of Fortune 100 chief executive officers' success based on photos predicted their company's yearly profits (Rule & Ambady, 2008b).

These findings are surprising and impressive when judged against the common intuition that thin slices should provide no valid information for such judgments. To place the findings in context, it is important to note that the levels of accuracy in these studies are reliably above chance, but not close to 100%. The striking aspect of the results is their efficiency. In many studies, the accuracy achieved after a few seconds is not improved by additional viewing time.

There is an apparent inconsistency between research showing that, on the one hand, effortful correction is necessary to counteract the biasing influences of social categories and stereotypes, and yet, on the other hand, people are adept at efficiently extracting accurate information from thin slices. This inconsistency, however, is more apparent than real. One reason is conceptual. Although bias and accuracy are often thought of as opposites, they are actually independent of each other (in the sense of sensitivity and response bias in signal detection theory). A second reason is methodological. In studies of bias, the target stimuli are typically held constant, save for the critical biasing influence (e.g., describing the target as a man in one condition and a woman in the other condition). In contrast, studies of accuracy typically hold biasing factors constant (or let them vary randomly) and the stimuli vary systematically in the factors of interest (e.g., actual sexual orientation, electoral success, etc.). Because of these different experimental approaches, effects that are the "signal" to one researcher are "noise" to another.

A final reason is psychological. Social perception is not a fixed phenomenon that happens the same way regardless of time, place, and context. Instead, it is something people do. That means that people may do it in a variety of ways. The kinds of information that people extract efficiently is likely to depend on their goals and social motives. As an example, participants in one study were primed with photos of men and women, as well as objects, each of which was followed by a letter string (Macrae et al., 1997). The letter strings included non-words, and words that were stereotypical of men and women. Participants were divided into three groups, each of which had a different goal regarding the photos. One group made a meaningful semantic judgment of whether it was animate or inanimate; a second group judged whether or not there was a white spot on the photo; and the third group simply indicated when anything appeared on the screen. Results showed that the photos of men and women facilitated responses to gender-stereotypic words, but only in the condition where the faces were processed semantically. Seeing the same faces apparently did not activate stereotypes when participants were treating them simply as visual features rather than living people.

Wheeler and Fiske (2005) found that processing goals also affected neural activity in response to Black versus White faces. When participants judged Black and White faces using social categories (i.e., sorting by age), amygdala activation was greater in response to Black than White faces. However this difference vanished when making visual feature judgments (i.e., detecting a dot on the photo) and was reversed when judging the photos as individuals (e.g., guessing each individual's preferences). These studies highlight that evidence of efficiency is not evidence of inevitability.

Legacies of implicit memory research: Awareness, awareness, awareness

The studies discussed so far have focused on the distinction between automatic and controlled processing, emphasizing notions of inescapability and efficiency rather than unconsciousness. But in the following years the automatic/controlled distinction often gave way to the dichotomy between conscious and unconscious processes (or the synonymous terms *implicit* and *explicit*). Despite the fact that awareness is only a subset (i.e., one of four criteria) of automaticity, the language of unconscious processing has caught on faster than the language of automaticity. A *Psychinfo* search using the terms *automatic* and *social cognition* returned 413 results. A search using *unconscious or implicit* and *social cognition* returned more than 22,000. This shift was inspired in part by Greenwald and Banaji's (1995) influential review, which built on a different research tradition of cognitive psychology. Rather than building on theories of attention and short-term memory, they drew on research on implicit memory.

Implicit memory has been defined as influences of past experience on later performance, in the absence of conscious memory for the earlier experience (Graf & Schacter, 1985; Jacoby & Dallas, 1981; Schacter, 1987). Whereas explicit memory may be measured by recognition tests (e.g., presenting a word and asking whether it was on a previously studied list) and recall tests (e.g., presenting a word stem such as el_____ and asking participants to complete the stem with a previously studied word), implicit memory is measured without reference to previous experience. For example, researchers might present a word stem (el_____) and ask participants to complete it with the first word that comes to mind. Participants are more likely to complete such items with previously studied words, even if they cannot consciously recall studying the item. Amnesic patients, for example, tend to perform at chance when asked to recognize words they have previously studied. But when asked to guess how to complete word fragments, they perform more accurately for studied than unstudied words (Warrington & Weiskrantz, 1968). The effect of prior study on later performance, despite the inability to consciously remember it, is taken to indicate implicit memory.

This idea strongly shaped Greenwald and Banaji's (1995) definition of implicit attitudes as "introspectively unidentified (or inaccurately identified) traces of past experience that mediate favorable or unfavorable feeling, thought, or action toward social objects" (p.8). Just as implicit memory was defined as consequences of past experience in the absence of conscious awareness for the experience, implicit attitudes were defined as traces of past experience in the absence of conscious awareness for the experience. Implicitness was identified with unconsciousness.

Although the parallel between concepts of implicit memory and implicit attitudes is close, it is not complete. There was a subtle shift between the two concepts that has important consequences for implicit social cognition. In the case of implicit memory, it is the experience of some past event that is not consciously available. In memory studies, the "event" is often the presentation of a particular word or a picture in a learning task. The experimenter has control over whether a particular stimulus was presented, and therefore knows with certainty whether the participant experienced a particular learning episode. Moreover, the definition of implicit memory focuses on performance, which is an operational definition. From this perspective, implicit memory is based on the effects of past experiences, controlled by the experimenter, on later performance, which is directly observable. For implicit attitudes, in contrast, the definition refers to *traces* of past experience which *mediate* later responses. This definition is more mentalistic than for implicit memory.

In fact, implicit social cognition researchers usually do not control conscious awareness of past experiences giving rise to attitudes, stereotypes, and other such traces. Unlike implicit memory tests, the measures employed in implicit social cognition research do not test for awareness of the formative experiences. Moreover, although Greenwald and Banaji (1995) referred to unawareness of the experiences giving rise to attitudes, subsequent writers have sometimes conflated awareness of the source with awareness of the attitude itself. The degree to which the constructs measured with cognitive tests may be unconscious, and how to empirically confirm such claims remains a topic of debate, discussed in greater detail in the section on lessons learned.

Some of the early approaches to measuring implicit social cognition had direct parallels in implicit memory research. For instance, Greenwald and Banaji (1995) adapted Jacoby's false fame paradigm from implicit memory to study gender stereotypes (Jacoby, Kelley, Brown, & Jasechko, 1989). Jacoby and colleagues asked participants to read a list of non-famous names, explicitly labeled as such. After a day's delay participants judged whether previously studied and new names were famous. Because explicit memory for the names faded over the delay but the fluency gained by reading the names persisted, participants misjudged the non-famous names they had previously seen as famous. Greenwald and Banaji (1995) modified the procedure by separately analyzing male and female names. They reasoned that status differences stereotypically associated with men and women would lead male names to be misremembered as famous at higher rates than female names. As predicted, gender stereotypes were reflected in false fame judgments.

The false fame procedure places explicit memory for the names in opposition to implicit memory processes (fluency or familiarity) because explicit memory for reading non-famous names would provide a basis for knowing that the names were not famous. Only if explicit memory fails and the name seems familiar should participants falsely claim that it is famous. In this paradigm, it is clear what conscious awareness refers to: the source of apparent fame. Stereotyping in this procedure is unconscious in the sense that participants are influenced by a prior exposure and by stereotypic knowledge, but they misattribute those influences to the name being famous. Because they are unaware of the true source of apparent fame, they are left with no basis for exerting control over the bias. This procedure therefore establishes a lack of awareness, which in turn determines controllability.

Implicit memory paradigms such as the false fame procedure have the advantage of theoretical clarity. It is clear how performance can be mapped onto notions of awareness and control. However, implicit memory paradigms often have low internal consistency (Buchner & Wippich, 2000) and therefore are problematic for individual difference measures. Perhaps for this reason, Greenwald and Banaji shifted their focus from implicit memory to developing an implicit test based on response compatibility.

Implicit Association Test

With the development of the IAT (Greenwald et al., 1998), implicit social cognition research rapidly accelerated. The IAT maps four response categories onto only two response keys. For example, participants decide whether words are related to *flowers* versus *insects*, and also whether they are *good* versus *bad*. In a compatible block of trials, one response key might be labeled "flowers or good" and the other key labeled "insects or bad." In another block, the pairings would be rearranged to be incompatible ("flowers or bad" and "insects or good"). Associations between flowers versus insects and good versus bad evaluations are measured by comparing response times on compatible versus incompatible blocks. Although sequential priming tasks had been available for several years (e.g., Dovidio et al., 1986; Fazio et al., 1986; Gaertner & McLaughlin, 1983), researchers now had a task that seemed to make implicit social cognition research much easier. Facilitation scores from priming procedures often suffered from low reliability and relatively small effect sizes. But the IAT had good reliability and very large effects.

The IAT has been used in hundreds of studies with millions of participants, making it the most widely used measure of individual differences in implicit social cognition. Reviewing this large body of research is beyond the scope of this chapter, but readers are referred to two meta-analyses that summarize the relationships between the IAT and behaviors (Greenwald, Poehlman, Uhlmann, & Banaji, 2009) and explicit attitude measures (Hofmann, Gawronski, Gschwendner, Le, & Schmitt, 2005).

In what sense are IAT effects automatic? IAT effects are driven by reduced speed in incompatible blocks. Aside from the occasional botanophobic entomologist, most people simply cannot respond as fast when flowers are paired with bad and insects are paired with good, compared to when these pairing are reversed. The involuntary nature of IAT effects suggests that they lack both intention and controllability. And the fact that associated pairs are processed fast can be seen as evidence of efficiency. The only criterion for automaticity that is not readily apparent is awareness.

Ironically, this is the criterion most commonly attached to IAT studies, which are frequently described as demonstrations of unconscious social cognition. Claims of unconsciousness often rest on a lack of correlation between implicit measures such as the IAT and self-report measures. This evidence is evaluated more fully in the section on lessons learned.

Effects of primes on behaviors and goals

Among the most influential work on automatic and unconscious processes has been research demonstrating that passive exposure to primes can influence subsequent behavior and goals. These studies are striking because they suggest that the slightest of stimuli (e.g., prime words) can have the most potent of effects. Implicit memory research, as reviewed above, had demonstrated that primes can influence memory accuracy and performance on a variety of tasks such as judgments of fame, familiarity, or pleasantness. Research on impression formation had shown that priming personality traits or social categories could influence personality impressions (Higgins, Rholes, & Jones, 1977; Srull & Wyer, 1979). But demonstrations that simple primes could increase aggressive behavior (Bargh, Chen, & Burrows, 1996), increase intelligent performance (Dijksterhuis & van Knippenberg, 1998) or alter voting patterns (Berger, Meredith, & Wheeler, 2008) suggested that automatic influences might be more profound than previously thought (see Bargh & Chartrand, 1999).

This research is included under legacies of implicit memory research with some hesitation, because it was influenced by multiple research traditions in addition to implicit memory. It drew upon earlier research in learning theory showing that verbal cues associated with a behavior could activate that behavior (Berkowitz & LePage, 1967; Loew, 1965). It also drew upon cueing paradigms and associative models used in person memory research (Hamilton et al., 1980; Higgins, Rholes, & Jones, 1977; Srull & Wyer, 1986). Nonetheless, one factor that made this new research program so influential was that great care was taken to ensure that participants were not aware that their behaviors were influenced by the priming event. As with implicit memory research, primes influenced behaviors in the absence of conscious awareness of the source of influence.

Automaticity in this research was thus defined in terms of the awareness criterion. In some studies, participants are rendered unaware of the priming stimuli themselves by presenting them subliminally. In other studies, participants are aware of processing the primes, say, as part of a word puzzle, but they are unaware of the connection between the priming manipulation and later tasks. Awareness of the stimulus does not seem to matter so long as the connection to later behavior remains unknown (Bargh, 1992). As with implicit memory studies, it is the influence of prior exposure to a stimulus that is outside of awareness. Lacking awareness of the influence, in turn, means that no intent is required to set the process in motion, and there is little reason for participants to attempt to control such influences. Still, this does not imply that effects of primes on behavior are inescapable. When primed goals are in conflict with consciously adopted goals, the conscious goal may prove to be the dominant force (Macrae & Johnston, 1998).

The logic of opposition

The most direct descendent of implicit memory research in social cognition is an approach based on the process dissociation procedure, which was developed as a means of separating conscious and unconscious influences of memory (Jacoby, 1991). In social cognition studies, the approach has been used not only to study social influences on memory (Hense, Penner, & Nelson, 1995; Payne, Jacoby, & Lambert, 2004) but also stereotypes (Payne, 2001; Payne, Lambert, & Jacoby, 2002), attitudes (Payne, Cheng, Govorun, & Stewart, 2005), and decision making (Ferreira, Garcia-Marques, Sherman, & Sherman, 2006) more generally. The key idea is that performance on any given task is likely to reflect a combination of automatic and controlled processes that jointly contribute to responses. These processes can be separated by arranging experimental conditions that place automatic and intentional influences in opposition in some cases, and in concert in others. This is what Jacoby (1991) has termed *the logic of opposition.*

As an example, Payne (2001) used a priming task to demonstrate effects of race stereotypes in mistaking harmless objects for weapons. A priming task presented Black and White faces as primes, followed on each trial with a briefly presented target object (half were guns, the other half were tools). Participants were more likely to mistake a harmless tool for a gun when it was primed by a Black face. From the perspective of traditional social cognition approaches this would be considered to be an automatic effect because participants attempted to distinguish guns from tools, but they were biased unintentionally by the primes. This, however, assumes that the task reflects only automatic processing and no controlled processing. From the process dissociation perspective, the task is assumed to reflect both automatic and controlled processing, and the aim is to estimate the influence of each using a simple algebraic model.

By this model, if a process is automatic it influences responses regardless of whether it is consistent with intent or inconsistent with intent. In contrast, when a process is controlled it influences responses only when intended, but not otherwise. Thus, automatic and controlled processes are defined in terms of intent and control. When a Black face precedes a gun, stereotypes and intent are in concert. Responding based on either will lead to the correct response. When a Black face precedes a harmless object, stereotypes and intent are in opposition. The relationships between intentional control, automatic stereotyping, and behavioral responses can be formalized using algebraic equations (Jacoby, 1991; Payne, 2001). We can then decompose responses into numeric estimates of two processes: automatic stereotyping and cognitive control.

Applying the model to the studies just reviewed sheds light on the factors driving the weapon bias. For example, the race of the primes influenced only the automatic component, and implicit measures of race attitudes correlated with the automatic but not the controlled component (Payne, 2005). In other cases, differences in intentional control are critical. For example, time pressure (Payne, 2001) and self-regulation depletion (Govorun & Payne, 2006) affected only the controlled component. Notice that the process estimates are defined in terms of intent and controllability, but once they are computed they can be used to test other varieties of automaticity such as efficiency by examining effects of speed, cognitive depletion, and so forth (for reviews of process dissociation in social cognition see Payne, 2008; Payne & Bishara, 2009).

When the task is to distinguish between weapons and harmless objects there is a correct answer, and accuracy can be useful in estimating how much control one has over responses. Yet in many cases in life there is no correct answer. Such ambiguous cases have been captured by a different priming task. In the affect misattribution procedure (AMP) participants are asked to evaluate the pleasantness of an abstract symbol such as a Chinese pictograph, following the presentation of a pleasant or unpleasant prime (Murphy & Zajonc, 1993; Payne, Cheng, Govorun, & Stewart, 2005). Participants are explicitly warned not to let the primes influence their pleasantness ratings of the symbols, but the primes nonetheless influence ratings reliably. Individual differences in performance on this task can be used to predict a wide range of behaviors. For example, presenting a cigarette as a prime tends to elicit unpleasant judgments from non-smokers, but pleasant responses from smokers who are craving a cigarette. The AMP has been used to predict behavior in the domains of cigarette smoking (Payne,

McClernon, & Dobbins, 2007), alcohol consumption (Payne, Govorun, & Arbuckle, 2008), prejudice (Payne, Burkley, & Stokes, 2008), electoral politics (Payne, Krosnick, Pasek, et al., 2010), and moral judgment (Hofmann & Baumert, 2010).

The AMP is similar to sequential priming tasks reviewed earlier, except that the outcome of interest is the respondents' evaluations of ambiguous items rather than response times to unambiguous items. The task generates large effect sizes and high reliability like the IAT, but it also has the simplicity of sequential priming tasks. The AMP is conceptually aligned with the process dissociation approach because the warning pits participants' intentional strategies against the unintended influence of the primes. Still, results of this test cannot be said to purely reflect automatic processing, because some participants may succeed to some degree in ignoring or correcting for influences of the primes. A process dissociation-like model has been developed to mathematically separate three components of task performance (Payne, Hall, Cameron, & Bishara, 2010). This model separates task performance into automatic influences of the primes (A), the likelihood of misattributing affective responses from the primes to the target pictographs (M), and evaluations of the pictographs themselves (P). Thus, by placing intentional response strategies in opposition to automatic effects of primes, the process dissociation approach which began as a means for separating conscious and unconscious forms of memory can be used to separate a range of automatic and controlled contributions to social cognition. Applications of this and similar models in social cognition have expanded in recent years. In addition to the process dissociation model and the AMP model described above, a variety of related multinomial models have been developed to model a range of specific processes and tasks (Conrey et al., 2005; Klauer, Voss, Schmitz, & Teige-Mocigemba, 2007; Stahl & Degner, 2007).

SIX LESSONS

The remarkable growth of research on automatic and unconscious processes has led to rapid advances in social cognitive theory. In the final section of this chapter, I review what I regard as important lessons learned in the past few decades. In some cases, these lessons were surprising correctives to early assumptions that turned out to be wrong. In reviewing these lessons it becomes apparent how far the field has come in our understanding of automatic and unconscious thought.

Lesson 1: Automaticity by some criteria but not others does not constitute a "weak" form of automaticity

Reviewing early research on automatic processing in social psychology, Bargh (1989) observed that cognitive psychology research had defined automaticity as an all-or-none affair, in which effects considered automatic by one criteria were also considered automatic by the others. However, Bargh pointed out that unlike the constrained laboratory paradigms used in studies of basic cognition, most social phenomena of interest to social psychologists were more complex. As a result, we are not likely to find many phenomena that are automatic in every possible way. Instead, the different criteria for automaticity are qualitatively different, and they may or may not co-occur (Bargh, 1994).

I occasionally read reviews or hear comments in talks expressing the belief that if a process is not automatic by all criteria, then it is not automatic in an important way. This way of thinking confuses quantity for quality. To see why, consider the research reviewed earlier suggesting that attitudes measured by implicit tests are automatic in that they are activated without intention or control, but that in many cases participants are well aware of the attitude being measured. If attitude activation is uncontrollable, then awareness does not weaken its consequences for judgments and behaviors. For example, in research on weapon bias, participants are able to accurately express when they have made a mistake after the fact (Payne, Shimizu, & Jacoby, 2005); however, that does not allow them to prevent making racially biased mistakes when responding quickly. If an automatic influence leads a police officer to discriminate, or if it leads consumers to change their purchasing decisions, or if it leads voters to change their votes, then it matters little whether the influence is automatic by many criteria or few. Automaticity by many versus few criteria, therefore, is not "better" or "worse" in any meaningful sense. The four criteria for automaticity are qualitative differences, not a four-point scale.

Lesson 2: Measures of automatic effects are not pure measures of automatic processes

As just reviewed, most phenomena in social psychology are sufficiently complex that they are not automatic in all senses. They are also not likely to be completely automatic or completely controlled. It is common in social psychology to categorize some measure, task, or behavior as either automatic or controlled. Yet doing so overlooks the likelihood that both automatic and controlled processes contribute to any given behavior. One common example is the use of implicit tests to measure implicit attitudes. Although the implicit attitude is assumed to be a purely automatic evaluation, the test that measures it depends not only on an automatic evaluation but also on how the evaluation affects processing in the main task (e.g., categorization of words and pictures). Scores on any given test, then, reflect a combination of intentional processes aimed at completing the main task, as well as unintended influences that interfere with the main task.

Recent efforts using process dissociation and related models, as just noted, have begun to separate the processes underlying tests from the test scores themselves. This is important because the different processes contributing to task performance often relate differentially to other variables of interest. For example, research using process dissociation to study automatic stereotyping has found that intentional control over responses is reduced by speeded responding (Payne et al., 2002), self-regulation depletion (Govorun & Payne, 2006), and ironically by anxiety over being perceived as biased (Lambert et al., 2003). Controlled estimates were associated with individual differences in measures of executive functioning and attention control (Payne, 2005) and event-related potential (ERP) signatures related to conflict detection and executive control (Amodio, 2010; Amodio et al., 2004). None of these factors affected estimates of automatic stereotyping. Instead, automatic bias was affected by the race of primes (Payne, 2001), was ironically increased by warnings against being biased (Payne et al., 2002), and was associated with individual differences in implicit measures of prejudice (Payne, 2005). Similar dissociations were found for other topics. Ferreira and colleagues (2006) used the process dissociation procedure to separate rule-based (controlled) reasoning from heuristic (automatic) reasoning in classic decision-making tasks. They found that controlled estimates were reduced by cognitive load, increased by instructions to response logically, and increased by training in logical reasoning. In contrast, the automatic component was increased by a prime that encouraged participants to respond intuitively.

These findings suggest that when researchers interpret a difference between experimental conditions as "an automatic effect" or "a controlled effect" they will tend to gloss over important differences. Although most research on this topic has been conducted in the context of implicit measures, it is equally relevant to experimental paradigms such as behavioral priming. The effects observed on behaviors likely reflect the joint operation of automatic and controlled influences.

The factors affecting automatic contributions and those affecting controlled contributions are each of interest in their own rights. They can only be studied on their own if they are separated, rather than equating measurement techniques or experimental paradigms with automatic processes.

Lesson 3: Measures of automatic effects do not necessarily measure unconscious constructs (although they have the potential to do so)

The distinction between unconsciousness and other aspects of automaticity is by now quite clear. The lesson described here is about what researchers can – and cannot – conclude from results of measures (such as the IAT or priming tasks) or laboratory paradigms (such as behavior priming). If we take seriously the differences between separate criteria for automaticity, then it becomes clear that simply because a cognition is activated automatically (e.g., without intent) it does not follow that the cognition is unconscious. Yet it is common to administer an implicit measure or experimental procedure and then draw conclusions about unconscious beliefs, thoughts, and feelings.

One way to illustrate this point is with a simple example. Suppose a researcher measured your preference for Coke versus Pepsi using an implicit test. You probably know your own preference very well in this case. Now, just because the researcher has applied an implicit test there would seem to be no reason to conclude that the attitude measured must be unconscious. In fact, when attitudes toward such mundane topics are measured, implicit and explicit tests usually agree (Nosek, 2007). In most cases, claims of unconscious attitudes are based on a lack of correlation between implicit and explicit measures. However, there are many reasons the implicit and explicit tests might not be related. These include measurement reliability (i.e., implicit tests sometimes have low reliability which limits correlations), procedural differences between tests (i.e., implicit and explicit tests often ask participants to do very different things and measure responses of different scales), and social desirability (i.e., implicit tests are often used when participants will not be candid on self-reports). Because all of these factors (and more) are sufficient reason for null correlations between implicit and explicit tests, such null correlations are not strong evidence for unconsciousness (Gawronski, Hofmann, & Wilbur, 2006).

Nevertheless, some research suggests that implicit tests might in some cases measure attitudes of which respondents are unaware. In one study, implicit and explicit measures of attitudes toward a referendum vote were measured among respondents who either had decided or had not decided how they would vote (Galdi, Arcuri, & Gawronski, 2008). Among those who had decided, the explicit measure was more predictive than the implicit measure of later voting. Among the undecided, in contrast, the implicit measure was more predictive. This suggests that implicit tests have the potential to assess attitudes before the respondent has made up his or her mind. This finding does not depend on a null correlation between measures, and so it provides stronger evidence than previous research that implicit tests may reflect attitudes of which the respondent is unaware. It does not follow, of course, that every time an implicit measure is used the construct must be unconscious. This highlights that unconsciousness, like other criteria for automaticity, are not properties of a particular measure or paradigm. They are features that describe momentary states which may depend on a variety of contextual factors, as discussed next.

Lesson 4: Control and awareness are often momentary states

Terms like "implicit attitudes" or "the unconscious mind" suggest stable structures that are hidden from awareness. But such a static view of automaticity is inconsistent with much that is known about the nature of attention and its relationship to control and awareness. Theories of selective attention often invoke the metaphor of a spotlight. This emphasizes that attention is always focused on some things at the expense of others. It also emphasizes the transient nature of focal attention, as the spotlight may zip from one target to another. The transient nature of attention implies that mental representations that are unconscious at one moment may become conscious with a shift of attention. This principle can apply to many mental and physical states, from your breathing rate, to your posture, to your attitude toward gays and lesbians. The same argument applies to intention and control. A process that operates without intention or control when attention is elsewhere may operate with intention and control when one focuses attention on it. At some times when driving we may stop at a light without intention or awareness because we are absorbed in a conversation; but at other times we may stop with conscious intent. These examples highlight that when some experimental effect is described as unconscious or unintentional, these are statements about participants in the specific context of the experiment. At other times and under other conditions, the unconscious may become conscious and the uncontrolled may become controlled.

It is of course possible that some mental content is inaccessible to consciousness and control under all circumstances. However, it is difficult to produce empirical evidence for such a claim. Recent research has made good progress toward acknowledging the transience of awareness and control. One study measured implicit attitudes toward gay people and also asked participants to explicitly rate their attitudes toward gays using scales that distinguished between "gut reactions" and "actual feelings." (Ranganath, Smith, & Nosek, 2008). Whereas "actual feelings" did not correlate with the implicit measure, ratings of "gut feelings" correlated significantly with implicit attitudes. This pattern suggests that participants may have conscious access to implicit attitudes, at least when their attention is properly directed. Depending on how participants interrogate their own reactions, they may appear to be aware or unaware of their implicit attitudes.

Recent theoretical perspectives that emphasize the role of metacognition in the processing of implicit responses seem well equipped to explain such findings. Hofmann and Wilson's (2010) self-inference model argues that although people never have direct access to mental processes themselves, they can make use of subjective feelings or observable behaviors that accompany them to make inferences about their own minds. For example, although people cannot perceive the activation of an idea, they may be aware of the content that is currently in mind, as well as feelings of processing fluency that may have accompanied the idea as it popped easily to mind. If a person has negative thoughts that pop easily to mind when they encounter a gay man, they may infer that they have negative attitudes toward gays. However, the kinds of inferences they draw depend on the focus of selective attention. If the person is not paying attention to his or her mental states at all, then he or she may draw no inferences. As a result, the attitude would remain outside of awareness.

In line with the study by Ranganath and colleagues, drawing attention to key distinctions between "gut reactions" and "actual feelings" may change the kinds of inferences people make. Models such as the self-inference model are valuable because they provide a framework for thinking about the mechanisms by which mental content can become conscious or unconscious as the result of specific metacognitive operations (see also Petty & Briñol, 2006; Gawronski & Bodenhausen, 2006). These models highlight that awareness and control may be present at some moments and absent at others. Thus, awareness and control vary with attention and other cognitive processes, rather than varying as a function of specific representations or specific paradigms.

Lesson 5: Automatic does not mean unchangeable

If awareness and control fluctuate from one context to the next, this challenges the common assumption that automatic influences are unchangeable. This assumption grew from early theorizing based on attention and learning, which argued that well-learned responses are activated automatically (Shiffrin & Schneider, 1977). Given this, it was a reasonable assumption that automatically activated ideas must have been very well learned, and should therefore be very resistant to change. However, many studies have demonstrated that scores obtained with implicit measures often increased, decreased, or even reversed as a function of the context. Spending five minutes imagining a "strong woman" led to weaker implicit gender stereotyping (Blair, Ma, & Lenton, 2001). Pictures of African Americans in the role of prisoners evoked negative implicit evaluations, but presenting the same individuals in the role of lawyers elicited positive implicit evaluations (Barden, Maddux, Petty, & Brewer, 2004; see also Dasgupta & Greenwald, 2001; Wittenbrink, Judd, & Park, 2001). These findings suggested that implicit responses were highly malleable.

Effects of primes on behavior also depend on the context. For example, Loersch and colleagues (2008) found that watching a competitive game of tennis engendered competitive behavior when the tennis players belonged to the participants' in-group but not otherwise. Cesario and colleagues (2010) found that when participants were enclosed in a small space, exposing them to primes related to African Americans increased aggressive behavior, replicating earlier research (Bargh, Chen, & Burrows, 1996). However, when participants were in a wide open space, the same primes led to distancing behavior. These studies suggest that the meaning of the primes within a social context shapes the kinds of behaviors that are activated. Although it is tempting to equate automaticity with rigidity, the evidence suggests that automatic responses are not necessarily difficult to change.

Lesson 6: Automatic responses are not more genuine than controlled responses

There is a tendency in social cognition to treat implicit tests as lie detectors. This grows largely out of the fact that early efforts with implicit measurement were aimed at studying prejudice, a topic in which self-reports are suspect. Indeed, there is a great deal of evidence that social desirability and motivations to conceal prejudice affect explicit measures of attitudes and beliefs much more than they affect implicit tests (e.g., Friese, Hofmann, & Schmitt, 2008). Taken alone, these findings would suggest that the major difference between implicit and explicit measures is susceptibility to dissembling. As discussed earlier, however, there are many reasons that implicit and explicit tests may disagree.

The question of whether automatic or controlled responses are more "genuine" is a bit like the question of whether drunken behavior is more or less reflective of a person's true character than sober behavior. On the one hand, we can argue that spontaneous responses reveal a person's attributes at some deep level because they are unedited for self-presentation. On the other hand, we could argue that everybody has thoughts and impulses that they reject, and what distinguishes genuine responses is whether a person reflectively endorses or rejects them. Both perspectives can be found in scholarship on the idea of the "true self." Some suggest that what counts as a person's "true self" involves only those attitudes that are reflectively endorsed, whereas others suggest that the most revealing attitudes are the ones that occur spontaneously and unintentionally.

At bottom this is a philosophical question, not an empirical one. A more empirically defensible position is to assume that both automatic and controlled responses reflect genuine aspects of the mind, to the extent that they matter for behavior. The empirical questions may then concern the conditions under which each drives behaviors. Some research suggests that implicit attitudes are associated primarily with spontaneous responses such as non-verbal behavior, whereas explicit attitudes are associated with deliberative responses such as overt judgments (e.g., Dovidio, Kawakami, & Gaertner, 2002). Other studies have found that implicit and explicit attitudes are independently associated with the same behaviors (e.g., Payne, Krosnick, Pasek, et al., 2010). This may be because many behaviors include both spontaneous and deliberative aspects. For the purposes of what we have learned about automatic processes, however, the lesson seems clear. Experimental methods that identify automatic processes cannot reveal if the automatic response is genuine or not: therefore, assumptions that automatic responses reveal the true self are suspect.

CONCLUSION

In this chapter I traced the development of two traditions of research on automatic and unconscious processes. Research in the tradition of selective attention studies has tended to emphasize intent, control, and efficiency. Research in the tradition of implicit memory, however, has emphasized awareness. Maintaining clear distinctions among these criteria helps prevent confusions that have sometimes obscured understanding of automatic processes in social cognition. Applying this principle led to six lessons that social cognition research has generated over the past few decades, some of which overturned early assumptions.

Some readers may wonder whether these lesson steal some of the excitement away from studies of automatic social cognition. For example, if automatic responses are not necessarily unconscious; if awareness and control are momentary rather than fixed; if automatic responses do not provide a lie detector to reveal one's true self, then are automatic processes as important as we once assumed?

In my view the answer is absolutely yes. Automatic social cognition is the logical culmination of classic studies on the power of the situation and research showing that we know less about the causes of our own behavior than we think (Nisbett & Wilson, 1977). Automatic social cognition is important, not because it is always unconscious (although it sometimes is). It is important not because automatic cognition is fixed or rigid, or because it reveals the true inner self (although it sometimes does). The study of automatic and unconscious processes is important because it has changed the way scientists see human behavior. It has overturned the intuitive reliance on introspection as an explanation for why we behave as we do. Beliefs that we are always aware of the causes and in control of our behaviors have an intuitive appeal. But these are beliefs that we may be learning to live without.

REFERENCES

Allport, G. W. (1954). *The nature of prejudice*. Oxford, England: Addison-Wesley.

Ambady, N., Hallahan, M., & Conner, B. (1999). Accuracy of judgments of sexual orientation from thin slices of behavior. *Journal of Personality and Social Psychology, 77*, 538–547.

Ambady, N., Koo, J., Rosenthal, R., & Winograd, C. (2002). Physical therapists' nonverbal communication predicts geriatric patients' health outcomes. *Psychology and Aging, 17*, 443–452.

Ambady, N., & Rosenthal, R. (1993). Half a minute: Predicting teacher evaluations from thin slices of nonverbal behavior and physical attractiveness. *Journal of Personality and Social Psychology, 64*, 431–441.

Amodio, D. M. (2010). Coordinated roles of motivation and perception in the regulation of intergroup responses:

Frontal cortical asymmetry effects on the P2 event-related potential and behavior. *Journal of Cognitive Neuroscience, 22*, 2609–2617.

Amodio, D. M., Harmon-Jones, E., Devine, P. G., Curtin, J. J., Hartley, S. L., & Covert, A. E. (2004). Neural signals for the detection of unintentional race bias. *Psychological Science, 15*, 225–232.

Asch, S. E. (1952). Effects of group pressure on the modification and distortion of judgments. In G. E. Swanson, T. M. Newcomb, & E. L. Hartley (Eds.), *Readings in social psychology* (2nd ed., pp. 2–11). New York: Holt.

Austin, J., & Smith, J. (2008). Drinking for negative reinforcement: The semantic priming of alcohol concepts. *Addictive Behaviors, 33*, 1572–1580.

Baddeley, A. D. (1986). *Working memory*. London: Oxford University Press.

Barden, J., Maddux, W. W., Petty, R. E., & Brewer, M. B. (2004). Contextual moderation of racial bias: The impact of social roles on controlled and automatically activated attitudes. *Journal of Personality and Social Psychology, 87*, 5–22.

Bargh, J. A. (1989). Conditional automaticity: Varieties of automatic influence in social perception and cognition. In J. S. Uleman & J. A. Bargh (Eds.), *Unintended thought* (pp. 3–51). New York: Guilford Press.

Bargh, J. A. (1992). Does subliminality matter to social psychology? Awareness of the stimulus versus awareness of its influence. In R. Bornstein & T. Pittman (Eds.), *Perception without awareness* (pp. 236–255). New York: Guilford Press.

Bargh, J. A. (1994). The four horsemen of automaticity: Awareness, intention, efficiency, and control in social cognition. In R. S. Wyer & T. K. Srull (Eds.), *Handbook of social cognition* (2nd ed., Vol. I). Hillsdale, NJ: Erlbaum.

Bargh, J. A., & Chartrand, T. L. (1999). The unbearable automaticity of being. *American Psychologist, 54*, 462–479.

Bargh, J. A., Chen, M., & Burrows, L. (1996). Automaticity of social behavior: Direct effects of trait construct and stereotype activation on action. *Journal of Personality and Social Psychology, 71*, 230–244.

Berger, J., Meredith, M., & Wheeler, S. C. (2008). Contextual priming: Where people vote affects how they vote. *Proceedings of the National Academy of Sciences, 105*, 8846–8849.

Berkowitz, L., & LePage, A. (1967). Weapons as aggression-eliciting stimuli. *Journal of Personality and Social Psychology, 7*, 202–207.

Blair, I. V., & Banaji, M. R. (1996). Automatic and controlled processes in stereotype priming. *Journal of Personality and Social Psychology, 70*, 1142–1163.

Blair, I. V., Ma, J., & Lenton, A. (2001). Imagining stereotypes away: The moderation of implicit stereotypes through mental imagery. *Journal of Personality and Social Psychology, 81*, 828–841.

Bodenhausen, G. V. (1990). Stereotypes as judgmental heuristics: Evidence of circadian variations in discrimination. *Psychological Science, 7*, 319–322.

Bodenhausen, G. V., & Lichtenstein, M. (1987). Social stereotypes and information processing strategies: The impact of task complexity. *Journal of Personality and Social Psychology, 52,* 871–880.

Brewer, M. B. (1988). A dual process model of impression formation. In R. S. Wyer Jr., & T. K. Srull (Eds.), *Advances in social cognition* (Vol. 1, pp. 1–36). Hillsdale, NJ: Erlbaum.

Broadbent, D. E. (1971). *Decision and stress.* Oxford, England: Academic Press.

Buchner, A., & Wippich, W. (2000). On the reliability of implicit and explicit memory measures. *Cognitive Psychology, 40,* 227–259.

Cameron, C. D., Brown-Iannuzzi, J. L., & Payne, B. K. (in press). Sequential priming measures of implicit social cognition: A meta-analysis of associations with behavior and explicit attitudes. *Personality and Social Psychology Review.*

Cesario, J., Plaks, J. E., Hagiwara, N., Navarrete, C., & Higgins, E. (2010). The ecology of automaticity: How situational contingencies shape action semantics and social behavior. *Psychological Science, 21,* 1311–1317.

Clore, G. L., & Gasper, K. (2000). Feeling is believing: Some affective influences on belief. In N. H. Frida & A. Manstead (Eds.), *Emotions and belief: How feelings influence thoughts. Studies in emotion and social interaction* (pp. 10–44). New York: Cambridge University Press.

Conrey, F. R., Sherman, J. W., Gawronski, B., Hugenberg, K., & Groom, C. (2005). Separating multiple processes in implicit social cognition: The Quad-Model of implicit task performance. *Journal of Personality and Social Psychology, 89,* 469–487.

Dasgupta, N., & Greenwald, A. G. (2001). On the malleability of automatic attitudes: Combating automatic prejudice with images of admired and disliked individuals. *Journal of Personality and Social Psychology, 81,* 800–814.

De Houwer, J., Teige-Mocigemba, S., Spruyt, A., & Moors, A. (2009). Implicit measures: A normative analysis and review. *Psychological Bulletin, 135,* 347–368.

Devine, P. G. (1989). Stereotypes and prejudice: Their automatic and controlled components. *Journal of Personality and Social Psychology, 56,* 5–18.

Dijksterhuis, A., & van Knippenberg, A. (1998). The relation between perception and behavior, or how to win a game of Trivial Pursuit. *Journal of Personality and Social Psychology, 74,* 865–877.

Dovidio, J. F., Evans, N., & Tyler, R. B. (1986). Racial stereotypes: The contents of their cognitive representations. *Journal of Experimental Social Psychology, 22,* 22–37.

Dovidio, J. F., Kawakami, K., & Gaertner, S. L. (2002). Implicit and explicit prejudice and interracial interaction. *Journal of Personality and Social Psychology, 82,* 62–68.

Fazio, R. H., Jackson, J. R., Dunton, B. C., & Williams, C. J. (1995). Variability in automatic activation as an unobtrusive measure of racial attitudes: A bona fide pipeline? *Journal of Personality and Social Psychology, 69,* 1013–1027.

Fazio, R. H., Sanbonmatsu, D. M., Powell, M. C., & Kardes, F. R. (1986). On the automatic activation of attitudes. *Journal of Personality and Social Psychology, 50,* 229–238.

Ferguson, M. (2008). On becoming ready to pursue a goal you don't know you have: Effects of nonconscious goals on evaluative readiness. *Journal of Personality and Social Psychology, 95,* 1268–1294.

Ferguson, M., & Bargh, J. (2004). Liking is for doing: The effects of goal pursuit on automatic evaluation. *Journal of Personality and Social Psychology, 87,* 557–572.

Ferreira, M. B., Garcia-Marques, L., Sherman, S. J., & Sherman, J. W. (2006). A dual-process approach to judgment under uncertainty. *Journal of Personality and Social Psychology, 91,* 797–813.

Festinger, L., & Carlsmith, J. M. (1959). Cognitive consequences of forced compliance. *Journal of Abnormal and Social Psychology, 58,* 203–210.

Fiske, S. T. (1989). Examining the role of intent: Toward understanding its role in stereotyping and prejudice. In J. S. Uleman, & J. A. Bargh, (Eds.), *Unintended thought* (pp. 253–283). New York: Guilford Press.

Fiske, S. T., & Neuberg, S. L. (1990). A continuum of impression formation, from category-based to individuating processes: Influences of information and motivation on attention and interpretation. In M. P. Zanna (Ed.), *Advances in experimental social psychology* (Vol. 23, pp. 1–74). New York: Academic Press.

Fiske, S. T., & Taylor, S. E. (1984). *Social cognition.* New York: Random House.

Fiske, S. T., & Taylor, S. E. (1991). *Social cognition* (2nd ed.). New York: McGraw-Hill.

Friese, M., & Hofmann, W. (2009). Control me, or I will control you: Impulses, trait self-control, and the guidance of behavior. *Journal of Research in Personality, 43,* 795–805.

Friese, M., Hofmann, W., & Schmitt, M. (2008). When and why do implicit measures predict behaviour? Empirical evidence for the moderating role of opportunity, motivation, and process reliance. *European Review of Social Psychology, 19,* 285–338.

Gaertner, S. L., & McLaughlin, J. P. (1983). Racial stereotypes: Associations and ascriptions of positive and negative characteristics. *Social Psychology Quarterly, 46,* 23–30.

Galdi, S., Arcuri, L., & Gawronski, B. (2008). Automatic mental associations predict future choices of undecided decision-makers. *Science, 321,* 1100–1102.

Gawronski, B., & Bodenhausen, G. V. (2006). Associative and propositional processes in evaluation: An integrative review of implicit and explicit attitude change. *Psychological Bulletin, 132,* 692–731.

Gawronski, B., Hofmann, W., & Wilbur, C. (2006). Are "implicit" attitudes unconscious? *Consciousness and Cognition, 15,* 485–499.

Gilbert, D. T. (1991). How mental systems believe. *American Psychologist, 46,* 107–119.

Gilbert, D. T., & Gill, M. J. (2000). The momentary realist. *Psychological Science, 11,* 394–398.

Gilbert, D. T., & Hixon, J. (1991). The trouble of thinking: Activation and application of stereotypic beliefs. *Journal of Personality and Social Psychology, 60,* 509–517.

Gilbert, D. T., Krull, D. S., & Malone, P. S. (1990). Unbelieving the unbelievable: Some problems in the rejection of false information. *Journal of Personality and Social Psychology, 59*, 601–613.

Gilbert, D. T., & Osborne, R. E. (1989). Thinking backward: Some curable and incurable consequences of cognitive busyness. *Journal of Personality and Social Psychology, 57*, 940–949.

Gilbert, D. T., Pelham, B. W., & Krull, D. S. (1988). On cognitive busyness: When person perceivers meet persons perceived. *Journal of Personality and Social Psychology, 54*, 733–740.

Govorun, O., & Payne, B. K. (2006). Ego depletion and prejudice: Separating automatic and controlled components. *Social Cognition, 24*, 111–136.

Graf, P., & Schacter, D. L. (1985). Implicit and explicit memory for new associations in normal and amnesic subjects. *Journal of Experimental Psychology: Learning, Memory, and Cognition, 11*, 501–518.

Greenwald, A. G., & Banaji, M. R. (1995). Implicit social cognition: Attitudes, self-esteem, and stereotypes. *Psychological Review, 102*, 4–27.

Greenwald, A. G., McGhee, D. E., & Schwartz, J. K. L. (1998). Measuring individual differences in implicit cognition: The Implicit Association Test. *Journal of Personality and Social Psychology, 74*, 1464–1480.

Greenwald, A. G., Poehlman, T., Uhlmann, E., & Banaji, M. R. (2009). Understanding and using the Implicit Association Test: III. Meta-analysis of predictive validity. *Journal of Personality and Social Psychology, 97*, 17–41.

Hamilton, D. L., Katz, L. B., & Leirer, V. O. (1980). Organizational processes in impression formation. In R. Hastie, T. M. Ostrom, E. B. Ebbesen, R. S. Wyer, Jr., D. L. Hamilton, & D. E. Carlston (Eds.), *Person memory: The cognitive basis of social perception* (pp. 121–153). Hillsdale, NJ: Erlbaum.

Hasher, L., & Zacks, R. T. (1979). Automatic and effortful processes in memory. *Journal of Experimental Psychology: General, 108*, 356–388.

Hense, R. L., Penner, L. A., & Nelson, D. L. (1995). Implicit memory for age stereotypes. *Social Cognition, 13*, 399–415.

Higgins, E. T. (1998). The aboutness principle: A pervasive influence on human inference. *Social Cognition, 16*, 173–198.

Higgins, E., Rholes, W. S., & Jones, C. R. (1977). Category accessibility and impression formation. *Journal of Experimental Social Psychology, 13*, 141–154.

Hofmann, W., & Baumert, A. (2010). Immediate affect as a basis for intuitive moral judgement: An adaptation of the affect misattribution procedure. *Cognition and Emotion, 24*, 522–535.

Hofmann, W., Gawronski, B., Gschwendner, T., Le, H., & Schmitt, M. (2005). A meta- analysis on the correlation between the Implicit Association Test and explicit self-report measure. *Personality and Social Psychology Bulletin, 31*, 1369–1385.

Hofmann, W., & Wilson, T. D. (2010). Consciousness, introspection, and the adaptive unconscious. In B. Gawronski & B. K. Payne (Eds.), *Handbook of implicit social cognition: Measurement, theory, and applications* (pp. 197–215). New York: Guilford Press.

Jacoby, L. L. (1991). A process dissociation framework: Separating automatic from intentional uses of memory. *Journal of Memory and Language, 30*, 513–541.

Jacoby, L., & Dallas, M. (1981). On the relationship between autobiographical memory and perceptual learning. *Journal of Experimental Psychology: General, 110*, 306–340.

Jacoby, L. L., Kelley, C., Brown, J., & Jaschko, J. (1989). Becoming famous overnight: Limits on the ability to avoid unconscious influences of the past. *Journal of Personality and Social Psychology, 56*, 326–338.

James, W. (1890). *Principles of Psychology.* New York: Holt.

Johnston, W. A., & Dark, V. J. (1986). Selective attention. *Annual Review of Psychology*, 37, 43–75.

Jones, E. E., & Harris, V. A. (1967). The attribution of attitudes. *Journal of Experimental Social Psychology, 3*, 1–24.

Kahneman, D. (1973). *Attention and effort.* Englewood Cliffs, NJ: Prentice Hall.

Kam, C. D. (2007). Implicit attitudes, explicit choices: When subliminal priming predicts candidate preference. *Political Behavior, 29*, 343–367.

Klauer, K. C., Voss, A., Schmitz, F., & Teige-Mocigemba, S. (2007). Process-components of the Implicit Association Test: A diffusion model analysis. *Journal of Personality and Social Psychology, 93*, 353–368.

Kruglanski, A. W., & Freund, T. (1983). The freezing and unfreezing of lay inferences: Effects on impression primacy, ethnic stereotyping, and numerical anchoring. *Journal of Experimental Social Psychology, 19*, 448–468.

Lambert, A. J., Payne, B. K., Shaffer, L. M., Jacoby, L. L., Chasteen, A., & Khan, S. (2003). Stereotypes as dominant responses: On the 'social facilitation' of prejudice in anticipated public contexts. *Journal of Personality and Social Psychology, 84*, 277–295.

Lippman, W. (1922). *Public opinion.* New York: Harcourt & Brace.

Loersch, C., Aarts, H., Payne, B. K., & Jefferis, V. E. (2008). The influence of social groups on goal contagion. *Journal of Experimental Social Psychology, 44*, 1555–1558.

Loew, C. A. (1965). *Acquisition of a hostile attitude and its relationship to aggressive behavior.* Doctoral dissertation, State University of Iowa.

Logan, G. D. (1979). On the use of concurrent memory load to measure attention and automaticity. *Journal of Experimental Psychology: Human Perception and Performance, 5*, 189–207.

Macrae, C. N., Bodenhausen, G. V., Milne, A. B., Thorn, M. J. T., & Castelli, L. (1997). On the activation of social stereotypes: The moderating role of processing objectives. *Journal of Experimental Social Psychology, 33*, 471–489.

Macrae, C. N., Hewstone, M., & Griffiths, R. J. (1993). Processing load and memory for stereotype-based information. *European Journal of Social Psychology, 23*, 77–87.

Macrae, C. N., & Johnston, L. (1998). Help, I need somebody: Automatic action and inaction. *Social Cognition, 16*, 400–417.

Macrae, C., Milne, A. B., & Bodenhausen, G. V. (1994). Stereotypes as energy-saving devices: A peek inside the cognitive toolbox. *Journal of Personality and Social Psychology, 66*, 37–47.

Martin, L. L., Seta, J. J., & Crelia, R. A. (1990). Assimilation and contrast as a function of people's willingness and ability to expend effort in forming an impression. *Journal of Personality and Social Psychology, 59*, 27–37.

Milgram, S. (1963). Behavioral study of obedience. *Journal of Abnormal and Social Psychology, 67*, 371–378.

Murphy, N. A., Hall, J. A., & Colvin, C. (2003). Accurate intelligence assessments in social interactions: Mediators and gender effects. *Journal of Personality, 71*, 465–493.

Murphy, S. T., & Zajonc, R. B. (1993). Affect, cognition, and awareness: Affective priming with optimal and suboptimal stimulus exposures. *Journal of Personality and Social Psychology, 64*, 723–739.

Neely, J. H. (1977). Semantic priming and retrieval from lexical memory: Roles of inhibitionless spreading activation and limited-capacity attention. *Journal of Experimental Psychology: General, 106*, 226–254.

Nisbett, R. E., & Wilson, T. D., (1977). Telling more than we can know: Verbal reports on mental processes. *Psychological Review, 84*, 231–259.

Nosek, B. A. (2007). Implicit–explicit relations. *Current Directions in Psychological Science, 16*, 65–69.

Payne, B. K. (2001). Prejudice and perception: The role of automatic and controlled processes in misperceiving a weapon. *Journal of Personality and Social Psychology, 81*, 181–192.

Payne, B. K. (2005). Conceptualizing control in social cognition: How executive control modulates the expression of automatic stereotyping. *Journal of Personality and Social Psychology, 89*, 488–503.

Payne, B. (2008). What mistakes disclose: A process dissociation approach to automatic and controlled processes in social psychology. *Social and Personality Psychology Compass, 2*, 1073–1092.

Payne, B. K., & Bishara, A. J. (2009). An integrative review of process dissociation and related models in social cognition. *European Review of Social Psychology*, 272– 314.

Payne, B. K., Burkley, M., & Stokes, M. B. (2008). Why do implicit and explicit attitude tests diverge? The role of structural fit. *Journal of Personality and Social Psychology, 94*, 16–31.

Payne, B. K., Cheng, C. M., Govorun, O., & Stewart, B. (2005). An inkblot for attitudes: Affect misattribution as implicit measurement. *Journal of Personality and Social Psychology, 89*, 277–293.

Payne, B. K., Govorun, O., & Arbuckle, N. L. (2008). Automatic attitudes and alcohol: Does implicit liking predict drinking? *Cognition and Emotion, 22*, 238–271.

Payne, B. K., Hall, D., Cameron, C. D., & Bishara, A. J. (2010). A process model of affect misattribution. *Personality and Social Psychological Bulletin, 36*, 1397–1408.

Payne, B. K., Jacoby, L. L., & Lambert, A. J. (2004). Memory monitoring and the control of stereotype distortion. *Journal of Experimental Social Psychology, 40*, 52–64.

Payne, B. K., Krosnick, J. A., Pasek, J. Lelkes, Y., Akhtar, O., & Tompson, T. (2010). Implicit and explicit prejudice in the 2008 American presidential election. *Journal of Experimental Social Psychology, 46*, 367–374.

Payne, B. K., Lambert, A. J., & Jacoby, L. L. (2002). Best laid plans: Effects of goals on accessibility bias and cognitive control in race-based misperceptions of weapons. *Journal of Experimental Social Psychology, 38*, 384–396.

Payne, B. K., McClernon, J. F., & Dobbins, I. G. (2007). Automatic affective responses to smoking cues. *Experimental and Clinical Psychopharmacology, 15*, 400–409.

Payne, B. K., Shimizu, Y., & Jacoby, L. L. (2005). Mental control and visual illusions: Toward explaining race-biased weapon identifications. *Journal of Experimental Social Psychology, 41*, 36–47.

Petty, R. E., & Briñol, P. (2006). A metacognitive approach to 'implicit' and 'explicit' evaluations: Comment on Gawronski and Bodenhausen (2006). *Psychological Bulletin, 132*, 740–744.

Posner, M. I., & Snyder, C. R. R. (1975). Attention and cognitive control. In R. L. Solso (Ed.), *Information processing and cognition: The Loyola Symposium*. Hillsdale, NJ: Lawrence Erlbaum Associates.

Pratto, F., & Bargh, J. A. (1991). Stereotyping based upon apparently individuating information: Trait and global components of sex stereotypes under attention overload. *Journal of Experimental Social Psychology, 27*, 26–47.

Quattrone, G. A. (1982). Overattribution and unit formation: When behavior engulfs the person. *Journal of Personality and Social Psychology, 42*, 593–607.

Ranganath, K. A., Smith, C., & Nosek, B. A. (2008). Distinguishing automatic and controlled components of attitudes from direct and indirect measurement methods. *Journal of Experimental Social Psychology, 44*, 386–396.

Richeson, J. A., & Shelton, J. (2005). Brief report: Thin slices of racial bias. *Journal of Nonverbal Behavior, 29*, 75–86.

Rule, N. O., & Ambady, N. (2008a). Brief exposures: Male sexual orientation is accurately perceived at 50 ms. *Journal of Experimental Social Psychology, 44*, 1100–1105.

Rule, N. O., & Ambady, N. (2008b). The face of success: Inferences from chief executive officers' appearance predict company profits. *Psychological Science, 19*, 109–111.

Rule, N. O., Ambady, N., Adams, R. B., Jr., Ozono, H., Nakashima, S., Yoshikawa, S., et al. (2010). Polling the face: Prediction and consensus across cultures. *Journal of Personality and Social Psychology, 98*, 1–15.

Schachter, S., & Singer, J. (1962). Cognitive, social, and physiological determinants of emotional state. *Psychological Review, 6*, 379–399.

Schacter, D. (1987). Implicit memory: History and current status. *Journal of Experimental Psychology: Learning, Memory, and Cognition, 13*, 501–518.

Shiffrin, R. M., & Schneider, W. (1977). Controlled and automatic human information processing: II. Perceptual learning, automatic attending and a general theory. *Psychological Review, 84*, 127–190.

Smallwood, J., & Schooler, J. W. (2006). The restless mind. *Psychological Bulletin, 132*, 946–958.

Srull, T. K., & Wyer, R. S., Jr. (1979). The role of category accessibility in the interpretation of information about persons: Some determinants and implications. *Journal of Personality and Social Psychology, 37*, 1660–1672.

Srull, T. K., & Wyer, R. S., Jr. (1986). The role of chronic and temporary goals in social information processing. In R. M. Sorrentino & E. T. Higgins (Eds.), *Handbook of motivation and cognition: Foundations of social behavior* (Vol. 1, pp. 503–549). New York: Guilford Press.

Stahl, C., & Degner, J. (2007). Assessing automatic activation of valence: A multinomial model of EAST performance. *Experimental Psychology, 54*, 99–112.

Todorov, A., Mandisodza, A. N., Goren, A., & Hall, C. C. (2005). Inferences of competence from faces predict election outcomes. *Science, 308*, 1623–1626.

Treisman, A. M. (1969). Strategies and models of selective attention. *Psychological Review, 76*, 282–299.

Warrington, E. K., & Weiskrantz, L. (1968). A new method of testing long-term retention with special reference to amnesic patients. *Nature, 217*, 972–974.

Wegner, D. M., & Bargh, J. A. (1998). Control and automaticity in social life. In D. T. Gilbert, S. T. Fiske, & G. Lindzey (Eds.), *The handbook of social psychology, Vols. 1 and 2* (4th ed., pp. 446–496). New York: McGraw-Hill.

Wheeler, M. E., & Fiske, S. T. (2005). Controlling racial prejudice: Social-cognitive goals affect amygdala and stereotype activation. *Psychological Science, 16*, 56–63.

Wilson, T. D., & Brekke, N. (1994). Mental contamination and mental correction: Unwanted influences on judgments and evaluations. *Psychological Bulletin, 116*, 117–142.

Wittenbrink, B., Judd, C. M., & Park, B. (2001). Spontaneous prejudice in context: Variability in automatically activated attitudes. *Journal of Personality and Social Psychology, 81*, 815–827.

Yeagley, E., Morling, B., & Nelson, M. (2007). Nonverbal zero-acquaintance accuracy of self- esteem, social dominance orientation, and satisfaction with life. *Journal of Research in Personality, 41*, 1099–1106.

3

Implicit Social Cognition

Brian A. Nosek, Carlee Beth Hawkins,
& Rebecca S. Frazier

Some of the most influential examples of scientific genius start with a powerful idea followed by development of methods to evaluate it. Einstein's theories of relativity were a remarkable insight that inspired decades of methodological innovation to confirm them. Most scientists, however, are no Einstein. Scientific progress can also accelerate rapidly in the reverse direction. Methods may generate evidence that inspires new ideas and theories. This is evident, for example, in Nobel Prize winner citations over a 13-year span for Physics, Chemistry, and Physiology and Medicine. Eighty-four percent of the citations credited a methodological achievement as the primary basis for the prize as opposed to a theoretical advance (Greenwald, 2001). In empirical research, theory and method are interdependent. Theoretical advances may spur methodological innovation by identifying a new possibility that has not yet been investigated. Methodological advances may spur theoretical innovation by producing evidence that existing theories are not prepared to explain, and by providing new avenues for empirical study. The rapid growth of knowledge in implicit social cognition over the last two decades can credit methodological more than theoretical innovation.

The theoretical foundation of implicit social cognition has a long history. Helmholtz (1910/1925) suggested that many mental processes occurred outside conscious awareness. Freud (1900/1972) brought ideas about the unconscious into the public sphere, kindling the imagination and adding trepidation about offering a banana to one's mother. While Freud's methods have gone the way of the Cro-Magnon, the idea that mental processes can escape introspective access and influence behavior is an ancestor of

the modern field of implicit social cognition. This field started to congeal following the emergent understanding that people do not observe their mental processes (Nisbett & Wilson, 1977). People can be mistaken, perhaps quite easily, about why they do the things they do. Following that, measurement innovation in cognitive psychology initiated investigation of memory without requiring that the respondent be able to report the memory (see Roediger, 1990 for a review). These methods and ideas were then applied to social cognition (Greenwald & Banaji, 1995).

The invention of two methods – sequential evaluative priming (EP; Fazio et al., 1986, 1995) and the Implicit Association Test (IAT; Greenwald, McGhee, & Schwartz, 1998) – launched a surge of research. These methods and their kin have stimulated growth in theory and evidence about thoughts and feelings that occur outside of conscious awareness or conscious control and how they impact social perception, judgment, and action. In this chapter, we attempt to synthesize the last 15 years of research in implicit social cognition in 16,000 words or less. More words are available in the marvelous 29-chapter *Handbook of Implicit Social Cognition* (Gawronski & Payne, 2010).

DEFINITION: WHAT IS IMPLICIT? HOW DO WE DECIDE?

A disquieting answer to the question "What is implicit?" is that there is no correct answer. Definitions of concepts are created in the service of theory and interpretation of evidence. Psychological constructs are unobservable – not because we do not know where to look, but because they are not physical objects. As such, the definitions that describe those constructs are arbitrary. Their correctness is a function of how useful they are in connecting theory with evidence. Construct definitions and theory are refined to better reflect observed measurement, and measurement is improved to assess constructs as they are represented in definition and theory. This illustrates the fundamental interdependence of theory and measurement (e.g., Ostrom, 1989).

As a consequence, a question like – Are implicit social cognitions unconscious? – is not an interesting question. The answer could be *definitively yes* or *definitively no* without conducting any research. If the definition is fixed in advance, the only empirical question would be whether a measure can be invented to assess implicit social cognition. If no measure can be found, then either implicit social cognition does not exist, or scientists are not creative enough to measure it. In this scenario, the researcher has two options – invent more measurement methods to assess implicit social cognition, or change the construct definition toward what the available measurement methods measure. The first is theory driven and might be preferred when there is a strong theoretical expectation (e.g., the intensive methodological innovation to find evidence for Einstein's theories of relativity). The second is measurement driven and might be preferred when something interesting has been observed and is not yet understood (e.g., the years of intensive theoretical innovation to explain the insufficient justification effect: Bem, 1967; Festinger, 1957; Greenwald & Ronis, 1978; Harmon-Jones & Mills, 1999). In implicit social cognition research, the invention of implicit measures occurred because self-reported social cognitions were not as successful predicting some behaviors that they theoretically should be predicting (e.g., differential behavior with Black or White targets that is unrelated to self-reported racial attitudes). Following their invention, it became clear that implicit measures revealed effects that went well beyond existing theoretical predictions. As such, implicit social cognition is an example of the interactive feedback between theory and measurement – an initial theoretical insight spurred methodological advances that have, in turn, stimulated theoretical innovation to explain the new findings.

Greenwald and Banaji (1995) introduced the term *implicit social cognition* for describing thoughts and feelings that occur outside of conscious awareness or conscious control in relation to social psychological constructs – attitudes, stereotypes, and self-concepts (the

original focus of the latter had been on self-esteem in particular). Greenwald and Banaji defined implicit constructs this way: "An implicit [construct] is the introspectively unidentified (or inaccurately identified) trace of past experience that mediates [the relevant category of responses]" (1995, p. 5). For example, the relevant category of responses for the construct *attitudes* might be *evaluations of social concepts*.

The definition's phrase, "trace of past experience" suggests that the content need not be believed by possessor as true or false, or used with intention to have it influence social judgment. People may intend a course of action explicitly, but still do something different because of cognitions operating implicitly. Also, the definition uses "unidentified" to refer to the measured content. This is importantly different from "unidentifiable." "Unidentified" does not require that people cannot, across time, place, or situation, *ever* identify the relevant traces of past experience, just that they are not identified in that circumstance. In fact, the additional clause "inaccurately identified" denotes that the person may have some experience of the relevant content, but not report it accurately because they do not want others to know it, they do not believe it themselves, or they do not know how to translate the mental content into a report (Nosek & Greenwald, 2009).

This definition of "implicit" is descriptive. It is agnostic to the particular cognitive processes that might be influential in implicit social cognition. This has important consequences. As a descriptive term, *implicit* is not committed to any particular theoretical interpretation of the mechanisms underlying implicit social cognition. The term is inclusive of a heterogeneous family of processes. Many theoretical positions can (and have) emerged to explain implicit social cognition with distinct mechanisms. A common theme is a dual-process orientation in which the implicit–explicit distinction is understood to reflect different systems or processes such as automatic–controlled, spontaneous–deliberate, associative–rule-based, heuristic–systematic, unconscious–conscious, efficient–effortful, unintentional–intentional, and impulsive–reflexive (Chaiken & Trope, 1999; Smith & DeCoster, 2000). By adopting a descriptive definition, the understanding of "What is implicit?" will change as evidence accumulates.

With a diversity of measurement methods and a growing understanding of how they function, there is an emerging foundation for evaluating and refining the taxonomy of implicit social cognition. "Implicit" may be an umbrella concept for component processes that have unique influences on thinking and behavior, leading to a richer network of constructs and theory that will provide specific predictions about resulting behavior (Moors &

De Houwer, 2006). And, if the taxonomy that emerges leaves out important ideas of what could be influential in implicit processes, it may cycle back and spur a new round of methodological innovation to measure those cognitions.

MEASUREMENT

The signature feature of implicit measures is that their assessment of social cognition is *indirect*.[1] With an explicit measure, the response directly reflects the content. Answering "Yes" or "No" to the question "Do you like Hillary Clinton?" is a direct assessment of liking of Hillary Clinton. Those responses to the same question could also be *indirect* assessments of attitudes toward female leaders, women, or Americans. There is a long history of designing self-report measures for which the content of interest may not be apparent to the respondent. The Modern Racism Scale (McConaughy, 1986), for example, was designed to assess racial attitudes indirectly by asking people about policy positions that have racial implications. The directly measured contents are the policy positions, and the indirect content of interest is racial attitude that may influence these policy positions.

These examples illustrate two challenges for implicit measurement. For one, extraneous variation is more likely with indirect than direct measurement. Individual differences in attitudes toward Hillary Clinton, the individual, could add unwanted variation for measuring attitudes toward female leaders, women, or Americans (not to mention that this measure would provide identical estimates of all three of these attitudes). Likewise, attitudes toward the policy position items of the Modern Racism Scale may be influenced by factors distinct from racial attitudes, such as conservatism (e.g., Fazio et al., 1995; Weigel & Howes, 1985). To the extent that the directly measured content has meaningful variation independent of the indirect construct-of-interest, validity of the measure will be reduced.

The second challenge is that *indirectness* of measurement is not always guaranteed. For example, if respondents understand the Modern Racism Scale to be assessing racial attitudes, then the *direct* response may – in fact – be their racial attitude, not their policy preferences. Recognizing the measure as a direct assessment of racial attitudes gives respondents awareness and control over their responses. Nonetheless, a variety of measures productively use self-reports to make inferences about implicit social cognition (Karpinski, Steinberg, Versek, & Alloy, 2007;

Maass, Salvi, Arcuri, & Semin, 1989; Nuttin, 1985; Sekaquaptewa, Espinoza, Thompson, Vargas, & von Hippel, 2003) by examining responses in ways that respondents are quite unlikely to anticipate and control.

Other methods, such as EP (Fazio et al., 1986) provide more confidence about the indirectness of measurement because of their procedural features. In EP, target words such as "wonderful" or "terrible" appear one-at-a-time on a computer screen and participants rate them as pleasant or unpleasant as quickly as they can. Right before the target word is presented, a prime – such as a face, word, or image – appears briefly. If the prime is negative it may facilitate (speed up) ratings of negative target words and disrupt (slow down) ratings of positive target words. In this case, the direct response is the response latency of rating the target word – the response itself has nothing to do with the prime. The indirect assessment of evaluation is *inferred* by a comparison of behavioral responses: the average response latency of categorizing pleasant words after flashing a positive prime, and the average response latency of categorizing the same positive words after flashing a negative prime.

These methods increase the likelihood that assessment is indirect, but still do not guarantee it. For example, using the Affect Misattribution Procedure (AMP; Payne, Cheng, Govorun, & Stewart, 2005), a similar procedure to EP, Bar-Anan and Nosek (2011) found that, despite instructions to ignore the primes, some participants reported rating primes instead of targets. Without those participants the AMP's internal consistency and relations with criterion measures were much weaker. Likewise, the "personalized" procedural changes to the IAT format (Olson & Fazio, 2004) appear to promote more direct evaluation of target concepts among some participants, and this may account for the former's stronger correlation with self-reported attitudes (Nosek & Hansen, 2008a).

The common theme in these examples is that participants may not perform implicit tasks as instructed because they misunderstand what they are supposed to do, or otherwise fail to do it. With explicit measurement, participant misunderstanding or misbehavior usually damages the possibility for the measure to relate to anything of interest. This is possible with indirect measurement too. Responding randomly in EP, the AMP or the IAT will reduce its correlation with covariates. However, as in the above examples, if the failure to follow instructions turns an *indirect* measure into a *direct* measure, then the resulting effects could appear to be sensible and even increase relations with criterion variables. The problem is that the effects might be misunderstood to indicate implicit social cognition when it is actually explicit.

To summarize, the virtues of implicit measures are that they do not depend on the respondent's willingness and ability to report the content of interest. As long as respondents follow task instructions, indirect content may influence responses without awareness, intention, or control. Implicit measures get, and deserve, more scrutiny than explicit measures because they often lack the face validity of direct measures: the content-of-interest is not clearly indicated by the responses. And, because of their indirectness, implicit measures often have weaker internal consistency and are influenced by more extraneous factors. These have implications for the power and validity of implicit measurement.

Implicit measurement procedures

There are a variety of measurement methods for implicit social cognition. Many are flexible procedures that can be adapted to assess a variety of social constructs (e.g., attitudes, identities, stereotypes, beliefs, self-esteem). Nosek, Hawkins, and Frazier (2011) conducted a citation analysis of 20 articles that introduced an implicit measurement procedure to estimate each measure's impact and use. They found that: (a) the IAT accounted for more than 40% of the total citations and about 50% of citations in the most recent year (2010), (b) EP was the second most cited, with 20% of total citations and about 12% of citations in 2010, (c) a cluster of the AMP, Go/No-go Association Task (GNAT; Nosek & Banaji, 2001), Single-Target Implicit Association Test (STIAT; Karpinski & Steinman, 2006), Lexical Decision Task (LDT; Wittenbrink, Judd, & Park, 1997), and Extrinsic Affective Simon Task (EAST; De Houwer, 2003b) each had between 4 and 6% of the citations, and (d) a recent burst of new methods suggests continuing growth and innovation in implicit measurement.

The IAT and EP have been extensively reviewed elsewhere (Fazio & Olson, 2003; Lane, Banaji, Nosek, & Greenwald, 2007; Nosek, Greenwald, & Banaji, 2007; Teige-Mociemba, Klauer, & Sherman, 2010; Wentura & Degner, 2010). We review them here briefly in the context of a broader view of implicit measures. Several criteria have been put forward for determining what makes a measure implicit (De Houwer & Moors, 2010; De Houwer, Teige-Mocigemba, Spruyt, & Moors, 2009). Here, we organize implicit measures into four categories: indirect self-report tasks, priming tasks, categorization tasks, and approach–avoid tasks.

Indirect self-report tasks

The Linguistic Intergroup Bias (LIB; Maass et al., 1989) uses self-reported explanations of others' behavior to measure implicit cognition. The linguistic category model (Semin & Fiedler, 1991) outlines categories for describing human behavior that range from concrete (e.g., single behaviors such as *to touch*) to abstract (e.g., dispositions such as *aggressive*). In the LIB, participants describe the actions of cartoons showing in-group or out-group members. Positive actions performed by in-group members are described abstractly, whereas the same action performed by out-group members are described more concretely (e.g., Maass et al., 1989). The linguistic descriptions suggests that identical positive behavior is credited as indicating good character for in-group members, but not for out-group members. Other indirect self-report measures draw on similar linguistic principles, such as the Stereotype Explanatory Bias (SEB; Sekaquaptewa et al., 2003) for measuring implicit stereotyping, and the Breadth-based Adjective Rating Task (BART; Karpinski et al., 2007) for measuring implicit self-esteem.

The Name Letter Effect (NLE; Nuttin, 1985) also uses self-report for measuring implicit self-evaluation. Participants evaluate how much they like the letters of the alphabet. People reliably prefer letters in their own name compared to other letters (Nuttin, 1985), and the numbers of their birthday compared to other numbers (Koole, Dijksterhuis, & van Knippenberg, 2001). Variation in the strength of liking letters or numbers associated with the self is related to outcome variables such as parenting style (DeHart, Pelham, & Tennen, 2006) and future depressive symptoms (Franck, De Raedt, & De Houwer, 2007). An obvious concern is that, for some participants, evaluating letters in their name more positively could generate a direct, intentional evaluation of the self, thereby undermining the measure's implicitness ("H is for Haven. That's me!").

Priming tasks

Priming tasks were the first widely-used individual difference measures of implicit cognition (Fazio et al., 1986; Wentura & Degner, 2010). Evaluative priming established that evaluations can be activated automatically upon encountering a social object (Fazio et al., 1986). This automatic evaluation may occur universally (Bargh et al., 1992), even for objects that the person has never experienced previously (Duckworth, Bargh, Garcia, & Chaiken, 2002). Evaluative priming is most commonly used to measure attitudes, but the paradigm has been extended to measure automatic goals (Ferguson, 2007), in-group liking in the minimal group paradigm (Otten & Wentura, 1999), self-concept (Hetts, Sakuma, & Pelham, 1999), and self-esteem (Spalding & Hardin, 1999).

Lexical Decision Task is procedurally similar to EP – a prime is presented (e.g., BLACK or WHITE) quickly followed by a judgment of whether a target stimulus is a word or not. As in EP, the lexical decision is facilitated by the prime. For example, WHITE primes accelerate identifying words that are stereotypically associated with White people and BLACK primes facilitate identifying words that are stereotypically associated with Black people. The AMP is procedurally similar to EP and LDT – a prime is presented followed quickly by a Chinese pictograph. The pictograph is presented only briefly, and participants' task is to evaluate the pictograph as *unpleasant* (less pleasant than the average pictograph) or *pleasant* (more pleasant than the average pictograph). Unlike EP and LDT, AMP scores are calculated based on the proportion of pleasant ratings, not average response times.

These procedures are similar, but their unique features may be important for how they function. Lexical Decision Task and EP are the same except for the response decision – "Is it a word?" versus "Is the word good or bad?" Facilitation of these decisions by the primes may be a function of distinct processes (De Houwer, 2003a). And, because the AMP targets are designed to be evaluatively neutral, the pleasantness decision in the AMP is not a function of the evaluative match or mismatch between prime and target, as it is in EP and LDT; rather, it is a result of misattributing affect elicited by the prime to the neutral target (Payne et al., 2005).

An important feature shared by EP, LDT, and possibly the AMP is that their effects are more influenced by the items than the categories (Olson & Fazio, 2003). Unique features of the individual primes can elicit very different effects, even if they are drawn from the same social category (Livingston & Brewer, 2002). In most applications of these tasks, respondents are told to ignore, remember, or do nothing with the primes, but rarely are they instructed to identify the social categories the primes exemplify. As such, priming effects tend to be more sensitive to characteristics of individual stimulus items unless a category is made accessible. When the category of the primes is made accessible, the reliability of the effect increases as does its relation with category-driven implicit measures (Olson & Fazio, 2003).

Categorization tasks
Whereas priming tasks assess the respondent's spontaneous reactions to primes, categorization tasks define the feature or features for how

stimulus items should be processed. For example, presenting Barack Obama as a prime in EP might activate evaluations of Barack Obama, men, Black people, or US presidents (among other things) and those activations might influence responses to the subsequent target. In a categorization task, Barack Obama might be presented as a stimulus, but the task would define whether he should be categorized as his individual identity, or as an example of men, Black people, or US presidents. As a consequence, categorization tasks tend to be more sensitive to the defined categories compared to priming tasks, unless there are alternative categories that are accessible and can be applied to all stimuli (Govan & Williams, 2004; Mitchell, Nosek, & Banaji, 2003; Nosek, Greenwald, & Banaji, 2005).

The IAT is a categorization task. Participants categorize stimuli into concept categories (e.g., *Democrats* and *Republicans*) and attribute categories (e.g., *self* and *other*). One concept category and one attribute category share a response key (e.g., *Democrat* and *self* are categorized with the 'e' key) and the other concept and attribute category share a separate response key (e.g., *Republican* and *other* are categorized with the 'i' key). Then, the concept categories are switched – *Democrat* and *other* share a response key and *Republican* and *self* share a response key (Greenwald et al., 1998). The difference in average response latency to categorize the items between those response conditions is taken to indicate the relative strength of association between concepts and attributes. Most Democrats are faster at categorizing the items when *Democrat* and *self* share a response key compared to *Republican* and *self*; whereas Republicans are the opposite (Lindner & Nosek, 2009).

The IAT is the most popular implicit measure partly because this procedure is easily adapted to measure a variety of mental contents by changing the categories and stimuli representing them. Also, compared to other implicit measures, its internal consistency and test–retest reliability are strong, which makes it easier to observe relations with other variables (Nosek et al., 2007). Nonetheless, like all measures, its procedural format puts constraints on its applicability, and it is vulnerable to extraneous influences. The IAT reveals relative association strengths among four categories (Nosek et al., 2005). Some alternate measures have been created that measure associations without defining a contrast category – for example, the GNAT, Brief IAT (BIAT; Sriram & Greenwald, 2009), and STIAT. Novel procedural formats have been introduced recently to eliminate potential differences in response strategies between blocks, such as the Single Block Implicit Association Test (SB-IAT; Teige-Mocigemba,

Klauer, & Rothermund, 2008), the Recoding Free Implicit Association Test (IAT-RF; Rothermund, Teige-Mocigemba, Gast, & Wentura, 2009), and the Sorting Paired Features task (SPF; Bar-Anan, Nosek, & Vianello, 2009). Very little is known about their psychometric properties in comparison to established measures.

Several mechanisms have been proposed to explain IAT effects (Teige-Mocigemba et al., 2010). A multinomial model called the QUAD model proposes that four processes contribute to IAT effects: automatic activation of associations, the ability to determine a correct response, success of overcoming the activated associations, and guessing (Conrey, Sherman, Gawronski, Hugenberg, & Groom, 2005). Such models explicitly represent the fact that no measure is process-pure. Identification and parsing of operative processes can improve understanding of the measurements operation itself, and anticipate relations among implicit measures that will each employ a unique constellation of processes.

Approach–avoid tasks

Approach–avoid tasks incorporate movement toward or away from presented stimuli to detect whether concepts automatically elicit approach or avoidance tendencies. For example, the Implicit Association Procedure (IAP; Schnabel, Banse, & Asendorpf, 2006) is the IAT but instead of pressing response keys to categorize stimuli to the left or right, participants pull a joystick toward the self (approach) or push it away from the self (avoid; Schnabel et al., 2006). In a shyness IAP, shy and me would be mapped to the pull response and non-shy and not-me would be mapped to the push response; then the two concepts (shy and non-shy) are reversed. Self-associations with shyness are reflected by faster approach responses when shy is mapped to pulling the joystick toward oneself than when it is mapped to the pushing away response (avoid), suggesting that associations can be measured with physical actions of pushing and pulling in relation to the self. Similarly, in the Stimulus Response Compatibility Task (SRCT; Mogg, Bradley, Field, & De Houwer, 2003) participants use arrow keys to move an image of a person toward or away from a stimulus, such as a cigarette (see also Brendl et al., 2005).

These tasks reveal embodied implicit responses to objects in the environment and have been applied primarily to domains in which approach–avoidance tendencies have implications for social functioning, such as tendencies to approach or avoid (a) drugs and alcohol (e.g., Mogg et al., 2003), (b) crowds among socially anxious individuals (Lange et al., 2008), and

(c) spiders among children with spider fear (Klein, Becker, & Rinck, 2010).

Next steps for implicit measurement

Despite there being a healthy diversity of measures available, current uses of implicit measures suggest that the research is dominated by the IAT and, to a lesser degree, EP (Nosek et al., 2011). Measurement procedures exist in the service of identifying psychological constructs. Only in rare cases is it worthwhile to treat a single procedure as the only means of assessing a construct. As such, attention to the refinement of existing measurement practices and invention of new techniques will facilitate construct validation that is not constrained to the idiosyncratic features of specific measurement tools.

STRUCTURE: CONSTRUCT VALIDITY OF IMPLICIT SOCIAL COGNITIONS

Construct validation is a cumulative process of gathering evidence to form a "nomological network" for conceptual and empirical justification of a construct (Cronbach & Meehl, 1955). Psychological constructs are not physical things; they are abstractions that transform a continuous, distributed, cacophony of mental activity into tractable units. Constructs are the building blocks of theories that explain how those constructs operate and interact to produce human behavior. Despite their arbitrariness, some construct taxonomies are more effective than others by using as few constructs as are needed, accounting for as much variation as possible, and providing means for the resulting theories to be generative, testable, and comprehendible. Research in implicit social cognition suggests that the taxonomy of social cognitions – attitudes, stereotypes, beliefs, self-concepts – is usefully divided into two components, explicit and implicit.

Convergent and divergent validity

Validating distinct implicit and explicit social cognitions requires evidence for divergent validity – that measures of the constructs are not assessing the same thing, and simultaneously requires evidence for convergent validity – that the implicit and explicit measures are reasonably interpreted as assessing the same *type* of thing (Greenwald & Nosek, 2008). Such evidence comes in multiple forms, such as demonstrations that both implicit and explicit measures predict expected group differences, that implicit and explicit effects follow predictions from theories of social cognition, and that implicit and explicit measures have related and distinct components.

Known-group differences

A straightforward approach for construct validation is to identify groups for which there is a strong theoretical or pre-existing empirical basis to expect them to differ on a social cognition and then demonstrate this difference. For example, implicit measures have been used to distinguish omnivores from vegetarians (Swanson, Rudman, & Greenwald, 2001), socially anxious from non-anxious controls (Lange, Keijsers, Becker, & Rinck, 2008), gay people from straight people (Snowden, Wichter, & Gray, 2007), and people with snake fears versus spider fears (Teachman, Gregg, & Woody, 2001). In some cases, these group differences show convergent validity with self-report, and in others, implicit measures were more sensitive to detecting the group difference than was self-report. Demonstrating the latter, convicted pedophiles are very reluctant to self-report attraction to children, but an IAT measuring associations of sex with adults or children distinguished pedophiles from other violent offenders who had not committed sexual crimes against children (Gray, Brown, MacCulloch, Smith, & Snowden, 2005; see also Brown, Gray, & Snowden, 2009).

Theory testing

The prior section advances the evidence for convergent validity that implicit and explicit measures show expected known groups differences, and divergent validity because implicit measures predict group differences that are not effectively predicted by self-report. Divergent validity can also be demonstrated when implicit measures do not show a group difference that is observed explicitly and follows theoretical expectations (i.e., is not just a failure to observe a difference that should have been detected).

One example comes from system justification theory. Preference for one's in-groups compared to out-groups is a pervasive human characteristic (Tajfel & Turner, 1986). In-group preference emerges implicitly as well, with minimal-group inductions in which the mere assignment to a group leads to a preference for it (Ashburn-Nardo, Voils, & Monteith, 2001). However, system justification theory offers a hypothesis about conditions under which in-group favoritism may not be observed, particularly implicitly (Jost, Banaji,

& Nosek, 2004). System justification theory suggests that people are motivated to view the existing system as just, including status and hierarchy differences. As a consequence, members of lower-status groups may show weak or no in-group favoritism to justify their lower status. This pattern is often *not* observed in self-reported attitudes about one's own group. However, implicitly, members of lower-status groups tend to show weaker implicit in-group preference than members of higher-status groups show for theirs, including San Jose State students compared to neighboring Stanford (Jost, Pelham, & Carvallo, 2002), Black people compared to White people (Nosek et al., 2007), and gay people compared to straight people (Jost et al., 2004).

Another example of theory testing demonstrating construct validity comes from balanced identity theory, which anticipates relations among attitudes, stereotypes, and self-concepts following cognitive consistency principles (Greenwald, Banaji, et al., 2002). Among gender identity, academic gender stereotypes, and academic identity, for example, one construct should be predicted by the product of the other two. Women who identify with female and associate female with math should likewise associate self with math to maintain cognitive consistency (Nosek, Banaji, & Greenwald, 2002). Greenwald, Banaji, et al. (2002) found that balanced identity patterns are more consistently observed implicitly than explicitly. Theory testing provides useful support for construct validation, particularly when such evidence is not anticipated or observed with explicit measures.

Implicit–explicit relations

Early construct validity evidence emphasized divergent validity by showing the lack of relationship between implicit and explicit measures of the same concepts (Fazio et al., 1995; Greenwald & Banaji, 1995; Greenwald et al., 1998). As the nomological net for explicit social cognition was already well-developed, this led some to wonder if implicit measures were valid assessments of social cognition at all (Arkes & Tetlock, 2004; Karpinski & Hilton, 2001; see Banaji, 2001, for a counter view). A good deal of evidence for convergent validity has since accumulated showing that implicit and explicit social cognitions are distinct, but related (Cunningham, Preacher, & Banaji, 2001; Hofmann, Gawronski, Gschwendner, Le, & Schmitt, 2005; Hofmann, Gschwendner, Nosek & Schmitt, 2005; Nosek, 2005, 2007; Nosek & Hansen, 2008b; Nosek & Smyth, 2007).

The early evidence tilted strongly toward dissociation of implicit and explicit social cognition for at least two reasons. First, the investigations did not account for the very low internal consistency of some implicit measures. When latent modeling is used to remove random error, relations between implicit and explicit measures are substantially strengthened (Cunningham et al., 2001; Nosek, 2007). Second, evidence of implicit–explicit dissociation was most apparent because the initial applications of implicit measures were those domains in which dissociation with self-report was anticipated. Many people are reluctant to report anything other than equal evaluations of Blacks and Whites, but nonetheless may possess social cognitions about race that predict behavior. Fazio and colleagues (Fazio et al., 1995; see also Dovidio et al., 2002; McConnell & Leibold, 2001) showed that EP detected variability in racial evaluations that was not related to self-report and this variation predicted differential behavior with Black and White targets. As the application of implicit measurement diversified to domains that did not have significant self-presentational demands, stronger implicit–explicit relations were observed. Large studies across 57 (Nosek, 2005) and 98 topics (Nosek & Hansen, 2008b) showed that implicit–explicit correlations range from near zero (e.g., future vs past, $r = 0.14$; forgiveness vs punishment, $r = 0.16$) to strongly positive (e.g., pro-choice vs pro-life, $r = 0.62$; cats vs dogs, $r = 0.59$), with an average correlation across topics of 0.36 for both studies, that increased to 0.48 after accounting for measurement error (Nosek & Smyth, 2007). Notably, there are no known, replicable instances of implicit and explicit measures of the same construct having a reliable *negative* correlation. Implicit and explicit social cognitions are positively related to varying degrees.

Moderators of the relationship between implicit and explicit social cognition

The positive relationship between implicit and explicit social cognition supports convergent validity. What accounts for the variation in implicit–explicit relations? Divergent validity would not be supported if that variability was attributable to extraneous factors, such as individual difference tendencies to select extreme answers on self-report measures or individual differences in average response time for categorizing stimuli in implicit measures that use response latency as a dependent variable. To demonstrate divergent validity, the evidence must show that the explanation of the difference between measures has something to do with the construct, not just extraneous procedural factors.

Extraneous influences

All measurement is imperfect. Some error is random – reducing the reliability, power, and sensitivity to experimental manipulations. Other error is systematic and results from features of the measurement procedure or influences that are immaterial to the construct. For example, in EP, priming effects can be eliminated or reversed when participants are directed to prepare for opposite-valence targets following the primes, suggesting that automatic evaluation isn't the only influence on EP effects (Klauer & Teige-Mocigemba, 2007). In tasks like the IAT and GNAT, participants can deliberately slow down their responding in one condition to alter their score, though this strategy may be partly detectable and correctable (Cvencek et al., 2010). The bulk of evidence on faking suggests that participants need some experience with a measure first, and it may not occur spontaneously very frequently (Fiedler & Bluemke, 2005; Kim, 2003; Steffens, 2004). Nonetheless, the cautious conclusion is to presume that no implicit measure is impervious to manipulation and that detection methods and measurement innovation should be pursued to identify and minimize their impact.

Most research on extraneous influences focuses on implicit measures that contrast performance conditions and use response latency as a dependent variable. With the IAT, for example, the performance condition performed first (e.g., categorize *Democrats* with *self* and *Republicans* with *other*) can increase the difficulty of completing the condition performed second (i.e., *Democrats* with *other*, and *Republicans* with *self*). Ideally, the discovery of extraneous factors leads to measurement innovation to reduce their influence. In this case, a simple procedural change in practice trials can reduce this extraneous influence (Nosek, Greenwald, & Banaji, 2005). Another well-known extraneous factor is average response latency. In any paradigm comparing performance across conditions using speeded response time as a dependent variable, people who perform the task faster on average will tend to show smaller mean latency differences between conditions than people who perform the task slower on average (Blanton et al., 2006; Sriram, Greenwald, & Nosek, & 2010). This is a function of response latency distributions and is an interpretation threat for difference scores. A scoring procedure, called the D-algorithm (Greenwald, Nosek, & Banaji, 2003), reduces this influence by scaling the difference between conditions by the overall variability in response times, creating an individual effect size (Cai, Sriram, Greenwald, & McFarland, 2004; Nosek & Sriram, 2007). A related influence, average differences in task switching ability, are likewise reduced by the D-algorithm (Mierke & Klauer, 2003).

Do extraneous factors like these account for variation in implicit–explicit relations? At a minimum, extraneous influences will reduce implicit–explicit relations overall (unless the same extraneous factor affects implicit and explicit measures). For example, Payne, Burkley, and Stokes (2008) demonstrated that minimizing the structural differences in implicit and explicit measurement methods increased the correlation between the measures. It is likely that the reduction of extraneous differences contributed to this result. Nosek and Smyth (2007) conducted a multitrait-multimethod (Campbell & Stanley, 1966) investigation with seven topics and found that the distinction between IAT and self-reported attitude measures was not accounted for by systematic methodological influences. However, strong validation requires determining what *does* account for differences between implicit and explicit measures, as opposed to just showing that extraneous influences do not account for variation in that relationship.

Person versus culture

Implicit social cognitions are presumed to reflect experience with a social concept whether or not the individual believes the information to be true (Banaji et al., 2004; Gawronski & Bodenhausen, 2006; Nosek & Hansen, 2008b). Explicit social cognitions, on the other hand, are endorsed by the virtue of the individual reporting them as his or her thoughts or feelings. As such, identifying experiences that the individual might have but not endorse could help clarify the divergence between implicit and explicit social cognition.

One manifestation of this potential moderator of implicit–explicit relations is cultural knowledge – what a person perceives to be culturally valued or believed. For example, one could personally have a strong preference for gay people compared to straight people, but simultaneously perceive that the culture has a strong preference in the opposing direction. Explicit assessments would primarily reflect the former, and implicit assessments might be influenced by both. Two perspectives anticipate this, but have different interpretations of its implications. From one perspective, cultural knowledge would be an extraneous influence, getting in the way of measuring "personal" thoughts and feelings (Arkes & Tetlock, 2004; Karpinski & Hilton, 2001; Olson & Fazio, 2004). From another perspective, sensitivity to cultural knowledge is part of what makes implicit social cognition substantively distinct from explicit social cognition (Banaji et al., 2004; Gawronski & Bodenhausen, 2006; Gawronski, Peters, & LeBel, 2008; Nosek & Hansen, 2008b). An investigation measuring personal attitudes

(How much do you like X?) and cultural knowledge (How much does the culture like X?) showed that across about 100 topics only personal attitudes were independently related to the IAT (Nosek & Hansen, 2008b). Even so, this does not rule out the possibility that cultural *experience* that is not reflected in self-reported cultural knowledge is influential on implicit measurement.

Other evidence supports the claim that information that is experienced, but not believed, accounts for part of the distinction between implicit and explicit social cognition. Gregg, Seibt, and Banaji (2006) introduced participants to novel groups – one whose members did mostly positive things, the other whose members did mostly negative things. Prior to measuring attitudes toward the groups, participants in one condition were told that there was an error and the information about the groups was backwards – the behaviors performed by one group were actually performed by the other. Participants were able to reverse their explicit evaluations based on the updated knowledge, but implicit evaluations were consistent with the original training. Likewise, explicitly, people resist using the actions of one person to evaluate another person belonging to the same group. However, implicitly, Ranganath and Nosek (2008) found that participants could not resist transferring attitudes formed toward one person to other same-group members. Moreover, after a multiple-day delay, participants no longer had sufficient memory for the details of who-did-what to separate their explicit evaluations of group members, and both implicit and explicit attitudes formed toward one person transferred to another member of the group. This suggests that what was experienced, but not believed initially, will be believed eventually. This illustrates an interactive process between implicit and explicit social cognition.

Other substantive moderators

A variety of other moderators of the implicit–explicit relationship exist, though most of the evidence comes from research on attitudes (Hofmann et al., 2005). If there are content differences in moderators by constructs – identity, beliefs, stereotypes, motivations – they have not yet been identified.

Implicit measures were developed, in part, because respondents may be unwilling or unable to report all of the relevant contents of their minds. The *unwilling* component of this is self-presentation concerns. People may have thoughts or feelings that they recognize, but do not wish to report either because they don't believe them, or because they have concerns about social consequences of reporting such thoughts. Fazio's MODE model (1990) and subsequent research evidence supported the claim that people may have automatic reactions that are identified by implicit measures, but are adjusted prior to report (Fazio & Olson, 2003; Nosek, 2005).

However, self-presentation appears to account for only a portion of the difference between implicit and explicit measures. Other factors that moderate the relationship include: (1) *elaboration*, importance, or strength of the social cognition (Karpinski, Steinman, & Hilton, 2005) – evaluations that are more important or more elaborated show greater consistency between implicit and explicit assessment; (2) *distinctiveness*, the perception that one's evaluation uniquely identifies the person as different than cultural norms (Nosek, 2005) – more distinct evaluations are associated with stronger implicit–explicit correspondence; and (3) *dimensionality*, the extent to which the attitude has a simple bipolar structure with anchors for positive and negative evaluation (Judd & Kulik, 1980; Nosek, 2005) – simpler structure is associated with stronger implicit–explicit correspondence.

Relations among implicit measures

The prior discussion treats implicit and explicit measures as coherent, unitary assessments of their constructs. They are not. There are a wide variety of implicit measurement procedures, and they may capture distinct components of implicit social cognition. An early study of implicit measures of self-esteem, for example, found that they were weakly related (Bosson et al., 2000). Part of this can be understood as a result of very weak internal consistency of some of the measures (Cunningham et al., 2001). It may also reflect variation in the degree to which the implicit measures are valid assessments of self-esteem. If some measures are less vulnerable to extraneous influences than others, it will be reflected with weaker interrelationships. But, it may also reflect the fact that no single measure assesses all aspects of implicit social cognition, and implicit social cognition may not be a unitary construct. De Houwer (2003a), for example, noted that some implicit measurement procedures can be categorized by whether they rely on stimulus–stimulus compatibility or stimulus–response compatibility in measurement. These different procedural factors may draw on distinct psychological processes (Gawronski & Bodenhausen, 2005).

Despite the lack of consistency among implicit measures being widely recognized, there have been surprisingly few comparative investigations of implicit measures (Bosson et al., 2000;

Cunningham et al., 2001; De Houwer & De Bruycker, 2007; Ranganath, Smith, & Nosek, 2008). A major task for the next generation of implicit social cognition research will be to understand the relations among implicit measures in an effort to both clarify the operative processes of each, and to improve the taxonomic description of implicit social cognition.

Representations and processes

How many representations?

The preceding (and later) sections provide evidence justifying a distinction between two forms of social cognition constructs. Implicit and explicit social cognitions are related, but distinct, meeting the simultaneous criteria of convergent and divergent validity. This construct distinction, however, does not have direct implications for whether there are one or two mental representations (Nosek & Smyth, 2007). Theories differ in terms of describing implicit and explicit social cognitions as comprising distinct mental representations (e.g., Strack & Deutsch, 2004; Wilson et al., 2000), or being a product of distinct processes on a single mental representation (Fazio, 1990; Fazio & Olson, 2003). Because social cognitions are unobservable constructs, there is no definitive answer to which of these is correct (Greenwald & Nosek, 2008). Decisions about whether to parse implicit and explicit constructs on the basis of representation, process, or an admixture of the two is based on the parsimony and power of the resulting theoretical description. As described by Nosek and Smyth (2007), both can be used simultaneously without contradiction. The variations of snow, ice, water, and steam can be considered multiple representations or a single representation (H_2O) interacting with processes such as heating and condensation. Nonetheless, the accumulated evidence suggests that implicit and explicit social cognition are not the same thing, so, whether they use distinct representations, processes, or both, theoretical frameworks are emerging to account for their distinctiveness.

Dual-process theories

The most popular approach for parsing social cognition is to posit at least two modes of cognitive processing – one that is explicit, or deliberate, conscious, effortful, rule-based, reflective, or systematic and another that is implicit, or spontaneous, unconscious, effortless, associative, impulsive, or heuristic (Chaiken & Trope, 1999; Smith & DeCoster, 2000). The varieties of theoretical perspectives share the presumption that behavior is a product of the independent and interactive effects of these processes. The framework has been very useful to motivate and organize investigations for when behavior will be influenced by something other than the actor's deliberate intentions. Eventually, the variety of perspectives that differ in their details may merge into a common model that predicts when and how implicit and explicit processes influence behavior.

FUNCTION: IMPLICIT SOCIAL COGNITION PREDICTING PERCEPTION, JUDGMENT, AND ACTION

The prior section provided evidence for the construct validity of implicit social cognition as related to but distinct from explicit social cognition. Predictive validity also contributes to construct validation – what the construct *does* is informative for understanding what it *is*. Does implicit social cognition predict human behavior? Yes, but how and when is not yet clear.

In a recent meta-analysis of IAT–behavior relations across nine domains (e.g., intergroup behavior, political preferences) with 184 independent samples, both explicit measures ($r = 0.361$) and the IAT ($r = 0.274$) predicted criterion variables (physiological measures, judgments, and actions; Greenwald, Poehlman, Uhlmann, & Banaji, 2009). Implicit and explicit social cognitions were positively correlated ($r = 0.214$), but both demonstrated predictive validity independent of the other. Prediction was strongest for both implicit ($r = 0.483$) and explicit ($r = 0.709$) evaluations for political preferences. Explicit measures were a better predictor than the IAT overall, though the IAT outperformed explicit measures in socially sensitive domains like race and intergroup behavior (IAT r's = 0.236, 0.201; explicit r's = 0.118, 0.120). Also, predictive validity was stronger for both implicit and self-report in domains in which implicit–explicit correlations were strong. This could mean that consistency between the two constructs is mutually reinforcing for influencing behavior (Greenwald, Poehlman, Uhlmann, & Banaji, 2009).

This meta-analysis organized the evidence for predictive validity by the topic of study. Here, we complement that meta-analysis with two alternative organizational schemes. We first review evidence that implicit social cognitions predict within-the-person variables (such as brain activity, physiological responses, or perception), social or interpersonal variables (such as social judgment and action), and group-level variables (such as national estimates of implicit social cognitions

predicting cultural differences). Second, we identify conditions that moderate the extent to which implicit social cognition predicts behavior, such as whether the behavior is spontaneous or subject to social desirability concerns (see also Perugini, Richetin, & Zogmaister, 2010).

Predicting variables within the person to across cultures

Intrapersonal variables
Correlates of neurological activity are predicted by implicit cognition. For example, the amygdala is associated with emotion processing and evaluation. Cunningham et al. (2004) found stronger amygdala activation after a brief presentation (30 ms) of Black faces compared to White faces, and the strength of the activation pattern was predicted by the individual's implicit preferences for Black compared to White people (see also Phelps et al., 2000). Notably, when the presentation time was extended (525 ms), differential amygdala activation for Black and White faces no longer occurred, but differences were observed in the prefrontal cortex and anterior cingulate, areas associated with inhibitory control. These results provide converging evidence that implicit measures reflect automatic responses that may be inhibited or otherwise altered by control processes (Cunningham et al., 2004; see also Quadflieg et al., 2009; Richeson et al., 2003).

Implicit cognition predicts physiological and hormonal responses in social and intergroup contexts. Implicit anxiety (associating self with anxious) predicted increased systolic and diastolic blood pressure and heart rate during and after a stressful speech preparation and delivery (Egloff, Wilhelm, Neubauer, Mauss, & Gross, 2002). Low levels of implicit racial bias predicted increased release of the hormone dehydroepiandrosterone (DHEA) sulfate, which is thought to manage stress levels, during an interracial interaction. The researchers interpreted this finding to suggest that egalitarian attitudes may have adaptive effects for managing stress in interracial interactions (Mendes, Gray, Mendoza-Denton, Major, & Epel, 2007). Similarly, Page-Gould, Mendoza-Denton, and Tropp (2008) simulated friendship-building in the lab over a 3-week period and found that people with high levels of implicit racial bias had higher levels of cortisol – a hormone activated in response to stressors – following the initial interracial interaction, but they showed decreased cortisol levels over the course of developing the interracial friendship.

Implicit cognition also predicts visual perception. Hugenberg and Bodenhausen (2003) showed participants short video clips of Black or White faces that were initially very angry but became neutral and then happy. Participants' pressed a key when they perceived the angry facial expression to be gone. Implicit racial attitudes, but not explicit racial attitudes, predicted the speed of detecting the emotion change, but only for the Black faces, suggesting that the visual perception of anger lingers longer when associated with Black faces than White faces, and this is moderated by implicit attitudes (Hugenberg & Bodenhausen, 2003).

Social judgments and actions

Most evidence for the predictive validity of implicit social cognition assesses social judgments and actions. Early investigations of implicit social cognition primarily concerned intergroup bias, particularly race bias. Interest in predicting these behaviors with implicit measures continues, presumably because of the lack of success in predicting them with explicit measures. For example, stronger implicit preferences for Whites over Latinos predicts stronger support for exclusionary immigration policy proposals (Pérez, 2010), the combination of implicit and explicit race bias of physicians predicted their patients' satisfaction with patient–physician interaction (Penner et al., 2010), implicit bias against intravenous drug users among nurses working with that population predicted their intention to change jobs (von Hippel et al., 2008), and hiring managers' implicit Arab–Swedish (Rooth, 2010) and obese–thin (Agerström & Rooth, 2011) biases predicted likelihood of inviting Arab and obese job applicants for an interview.

As measurement has diversified, so has the application to other areas of social judgment and behavior. For example, implicit positivity toward risk-taking behavior among pilots predicted risky behavior in flight simulation tests (Molesworth & Chang, 2009), implicit associations of self with collaboration predicted employees' collaborative engagement in a firm (Srivastava & Banaji, 2011), implicit romantic attraction to one's partner predicted relationship longevity (Lee, Rogge, & Reis, 2010), implicit moral attitudes predicted decisions during a decision-making exercise about business ethics (Marquardt & Hoeger, 2009), stronger implicit associations of science with male predicted weaker engagement and achievement in science (Nosek & Smyth, 2011), implicit self-positivity predicted self-selected seating distance from someone with the same initials (Kocan & Curtis, 2009), and implicit associations of self with aggressiveness among semi-professional basketball players predicted their playing time and game performance (Teubel, Asendorpf, Banse,

& Schnabel, in press). These illustrate a remarkable diversity in areas of application and predictive validity, and they anticipate the growth of application of implicit measures to business, education, relationships, and human factors.

Health and medicine are well-ahead of these areas in the breadth of application of implicit measures, as well as the accumulated evidence for predictive validity. For example, stronger implicit associations of self with death predicted greater likelihood of a suicide attempt in the following six months among psychiatric ER patients (Nock et al., 2010; see also Glashouwer & de Jong, 2010), implicit associations about panic predicted symptom severity and behavioral distress among a sample of people with panic disorder (Teachman, Smith-Janik, & Saporito, 2007), implicit self-stigma and associations of mental illness with shame or guilt among people with affective disorders or schizophrenia predicted disorder-related beliefs and quality of life (Rüsch et al., 2010), and implicit associations with alcohol, tobacco, and drugs predict addiction-related behavior (Chassin, Presson, Sherman, Seo, & Macy, 2010; Payne, McClernon, & Dobbins, 2007; Wiers, Rinck, et al., 2010a).

Group-level variables

The preceding examples all concern implicit social cognitions predicting individual behavior. Aggregating implicit social cognition in a group, region, or culture may provide insight into variations across groups and cultures that are not manifested in explicit cultural beliefs. For example, Nosek et al. (2009) found that variation across nations' implicit stereotypes associating men with science more than women with science predicted sex differences in science achievement across those nations, even after controlling for national differences in explicit gender stereotypes.

Toward a model: Conditions that moderate predictive validity of implicit social cognition

The evidence for the predictive validity of implicit social cognition is plentiful, but the field has not yet produced a comprehensive or dominant model of when and how implicit cognitions will predict behavior. Here, we identify factors that have some empirical support as moderators of implicit–behavior relations, and fit with a variety of existing theoretical conceptualizations (Chaiken & Trope, 1999; Fazio, 1990; Smith & DeCoster, 2000; Strack & Deutsch, 2004). Explicit social cognitions are expected to direct behavior when the individual has the *motivation* to deliberately direct behavior, the *opportunity* to initiate relevant actions, the *ability* to control the actions, and the *awareness* of the factors that are influencing the actions (Nosek et al., 2011). To the extent that any of these factors are not employed effectively, implicit social cognition may become a better predictor of behavior.

Introspective access and self-presentational concerns

Implicit measures were invented because researchers believed that social cognitions exist that people are unable or unwilling to report. Inability refers primarily to a lack of awareness of the content, and unwillingness refers primarily to a motivation to report content that is accessible but personally or socially inadvisable to report. For example, people are hesitant to report liking or doing illegal or stigmatized behaviors, such as marijuana (Ames et al., 2007) and tobacco use (Sherman et al., 2009), and violent tendencies among at-risk offenders in a treatment program (Polaschek, Bell, Calvert, Takarangi, 2010). In these cases, implicit measurement predicts behavior better than does self-report. Likewise, self-presentation concerns are usually strong for interracial and intergroup behavioral contexts, as evidenced by Greenwald and colleagues' (2009) findings that the IAT predicted outcomes better than self-reported preferences in these domains, and findings such as implicit racial attitudes predicting support for Barack Obama and his policies (Greenwald, Smith, et al., 2009; Knowles, Lowery, Schaumberg, 2010; Payne et al., 2010). In all these cases, it is difficult to distinguish whether the comparative lack of predictive validity for explicit measures is evidence of introspective failure or self-presentation. It could be that people are unaware of their implicit cognitions or are unaware of the link between the implicit cognition and the behavior. It could also be that people have some kind of relevant introspective experience but fail to report it. We suspect that both occur and depend on conditions that are not yet known.

Spontaneous versus deliberate behavior

People may be motivated to behave in a particular way, and even be aware of the mental contents that may influence their behavior, but nonetheless fail to behave as intended because they do not have the opportunity to initiate deliberate actions (Fazio, 1990). For example, non-verbal behavior is understood to be much more difficult to control than the content of one's speech. In interracial interactions, Dovidio, Kawakami, and Gaertner (2002) found

that implicit racial attitudes predicted non-verbal behavior (e.g., blinking rate, amount of eye contact), but explicit racial attitudes did not. Simultaneously, explicit racial attitudes predicted verbal behavior, but implicit racial attitudes did not (see also Fazio et al., 1995; McConnell & Leibold, 2001).

Rudolph, Schröder-Abé, Riketta, and Schütz (2010) found that implicit self-esteem, but not explicit self-esteem, predicted experimenter-rated anxiety and spontaneous self-confident behaviors in anxiety-producing situations. And, explicit self-esteem, but not implicit self-esteem, predicted self-reported anxiety and controlled self-confidence behaviors during the same tasks. Asendorpf, Banse, and Mücke (2002) found a similar pattern of implicit and explicit shyness differentially predicting spontaneous and deliberate behaviors in an interpersonal context.

These examples could be the basis for a very simple model – implicit processes predict spontaneous behavior and explicit processes predict deliberate behavior. This is too simplistic. On the one hand, explicit goal setting in advance can automate behavioral responses when the relevant context occurs (Gollwitzer, 1999). This gives explicit processes some influence over spontaneous behavior "at a distance." But, even more damaging for the simple hypothesis is evidence that implicit social cognition can add incremental predictive validity beyond explicit social cognition even for highly deliberate behaviors. For example, voting may be the prototypical deliberate behavior – people know that it is occurring well in advance, there is ample opportunity for processing the relevant information to decide one's vote, and the person must initiate planned actions in order to carry out the vote. Nonetheless, multiple studies find that voting is predicted by implicit social cognitions beyond what is accounted for by explicit measures (Friese, Bluemke, & Wänke, 2007; Greenwald et al., 2009; Payne et al., 2010), particularly when the person reported being undecided prior to the vote (Galdi et al., 2008; Roccato & Zogmaister, 2010). As such, the present state of evidence suggests that spontaneity contributes to understanding when implicit social cognition will predict behavior, but it is not the exclusive influence.

Cognitive resources and self-regulation

Whereas spontaneity emphasizes the *opportunity* to control one's response, the availability of cognitive resources and self-regulation emphasizes the *ability* to control that response even if it does not occur spontaneously or rapidly. For example, there are individual differences in working memory capacity (WMC), the ability to hold multiple pieces of information in mind for complex thinking and reasoning, suggesting that there may be individual differences in the ability to exert deliberate control over one's behavior. Thush et al. (2008) found that among a group of high-risk youths, implicit alcohol associations predicted alcohol use one month later more strongly for individuals with low WMC than high WMC, whereas the reverse was true for explicit alcohol associations. In other domains, when cognitive processing resources were depleted, implicit attitudes toward potato chips predicted consumption of chips, whereas explicit attitudes predicted eating chips when resources were not depleted (Friese, Hofmann, & Wänke, 2008). Likewise, reducing cognitive processing resources increased the predictive validity of implicit racial attitudes in an interracial interaction (Hofmann, Gschwendner, Castelli, & Schmitt, 2008).

In summary, the predictive validity evidence suggests that implicit and explicit social cognitions each contribute to many aspects of human behavior. The next challenge for the field is to converge on a model that anticipates under what conditions each will show predictive validity, and to explain how implicit and explicit processes work independently or interactively to produce behavior (e.g., Strack & Deutsch, 2004).

FORMATION, MALLEABILITY, AND CHANGE

The preceding sections evaluate implicit social cognitions as they operate during the moment of measurement. Just as it is not possible to understand a film by looking at individual frames, it is not possible to understand implicit social cognition without examining its structure and function over time. The development of implicit social cognition over the life span is virtually uncharted territory (Olson & Dunham, 2010). And, of the research that has been done, very little of it actually investigates *development* – formation and change over time. Rather, most "developmental" studies are cross-sectional investigations using samples of children. These studies highlight the importance of taking development seriously. Across the life span, the understanding of "What is implicit?" and the interaction of implicit and explicit processes may change (Olson & Dunham, 2010). Does infant cognition fit dual-process notions, or – for example – do explicit processes have a developmental trajectory? Likewise, longitudinal investigations of aging suggest that a variety of cognitive functions that should be related to implicit cognition change (Salthouse,

2010). This could lead to distinct operative processes at different points of the life span or, at least, shifts in the interaction and functioning of explicit and implicit processes (e.g., Gonsalkorale, Sherman, & Klauer, 2009; Stewart, von Hippel, & Radvansky, 2009). Failing to take stock of the development of implicit social cognition will retard progress in development of effective theories of its structure and function.

Despite the lack of developmental research, there is a healthy literature on formation, malleability, and change of implicit social cognition (Blair, 2002; Gawronski & Sritharan, 2010). Perhaps the key insight from this research is its contrast to early models that emphasized how mental contents that could be activated automatically were slow to form, relatively insensitive to situational features, and slow to change (e.g., Schneider & Shiffrin, 1977; Smith & DeCoster, 2000). Each of these ideas has been challenged, to some degree, by recent findings in implicit social cognition.

Formation

Implicit social cognitions can form very rapidly. A variety of demonstrations show that in the context of a single experimental session, implicit social cognitions can be created via evaluative conditioning (see Hofmann, De Houwer, Perugini, Baeyens, & Crombez, 2010 for a review), minimal group manipulations (e.g., Ashburn-Nardo et al., 2001; Paladino & Castelli, 2008), and associating the novel object with the self (e.g., Prestwich, Perugini, Hurling, & Richetin, 2010). And, even with a training session of less than five minutes, evaluations formed toward novel groups can persist for at least a week (Ranganath & Nosek, 2008), perhaps much longer.

Given how quickly they form, an interesting follow-up question is how little information is necessary to form an implicit evaluation? Gawronski, Walther, and Blank (2005) used as few as three descriptive statements to create implicit evaluations toward a novel target. Greenwald, Pickrell, and Farnham (2002) found that people formed an implicit preference for a hypothetical group after just reading the names of its members. De Houwer, Beckers, and Moors (2007) found that merely suggesting that one would be learning positive information about one group and negative information about another was sufficient to elicit an implicit preference for the former. They interpreted this to indicate that the observed effects were faked, but other evidence suggests that the instruction actually formed an attitude (Bar-Anan, Ratliff, & Nosek, 2011).

This pushes the boundary to a minimum of experience with a concept to form implicit evaluations of it. But, even that may not be the lower limit. Duckworth, Bargh, Garcia, and Chaiken (2002) found that implicit evaluations could be measured for targets that had never been experienced previously. Van Leeuwen and Macrae (2004; see also Richetin, Croizet, & Huguet, 2004) showed that features of novel items (e.g., attractiveness of faces) affected implicit evaluations. Gregg, Seibt, and Banaji (2006) had to conduct extensive pre-testing of implicit evaluations of novel groups to find two that were evaluated similarly. And, providing some insight on how automatic evaluations might exist for targets for which there is little to no direct experience, Walther (2002) found that conditioning evaluations to one target could transfer to other targets that were associated with the conditioned target. Rapid assessments of similarity with previously experienced social content may drive automatic evaluation of novel social objects.

Malleability

The remarkable simplicity of forming new associations, and evidence that implicit evaluation can occur toward concepts that have never been experienced previously, makes it easy to anticipate that implicit social cognitions are quite malleable. This was not always so easy to imagine. Early conceptualizations of automaticity seemed to consider it akin to fixed action patterns. Once automatized, the same response would occur each time it was activated and be relatively insensitive to the social context. Gawronski and Sritharan (2010) reviewed many factors that elicit shifts in implicit social cognition, including (1) the context of evaluation suggesting that a target was more or less positive (Barden et al., 2004; Wittenbrink et al., 2001), (2) making information about target concepts salient such as positive exemplars, roles or memories of one group and negative exemplars, roles or memories of a comparison group (Dasgupta & Greenwald, 2001; Mitchell, Nosek, & Banaji, 2003; Sassenberg & Wieber, 2005), (3) increasing participants motivation to affiliate with another person whose beliefs are apparent (Sinclair, Lowery, Hardin, & Colangelo, 2005), and (4) altering the participants' state such as eliciting greater positivity toward smoking among deprived than non-deprived smokers (Sherman et al., 2003; Payne et al., 2007) and higher levels of implicit bias among threatened than non-threatened participants (Gonsalkorale, Carlisle, & von Hippel, 2007; Rudman, Dohn, & Fairchild, 2007). A full review of the present literature might lead one to conclude that there is very little stability in implicit social cognition and effects are very sensitive to the social context. That may well be true. However, partly because of the historical emphasis on stability, and partly because of prejudice against the null hypothesis (Greenwald, 1975), the present literature may overestimate malleability. It is less likely that studies of malleability that elicit no difference across situations will be reported (but see Joy-Gaba & Nosek, 2010; Schmidt & Nosek, 2010). With a literature biased toward confirmation of malleability, it will be more difficult to generate an effective theoretical model for when malleability will, and will not, occur.

At present, the model best prepared to account for malleability effects is the Associative–Propositional Evaluation (APE) model (Gawronski & Bodenhausen, 2006). The APE model provides an organizing framework for predicting when implicit social cognitions will be malleable, particularly in comparison to explicit social cognitions. Associative processes are the activation of associations based on past experience. Propositional processes involve the validation of information that is based on these associations – i.e., deciding whether it is true or false. Implicit measures are presumed to reflect the outcome of associative activations and explicit measures reflect the outcome of propositional thinking. This model thus anticipates multiple routes to malleability and change of implicit social cognition. In particular, manipulations that shift association strengths or make accessible different associations should be effective on implicit measures alone if the respondent rejects the new information as false (e.g., Gawronski & LeBel, 2008), but on both implicit and explicit measures if the information is accepted as true (e.g., Whitfield & Jordan, 2009). Furthermore, manipulations that initiate propositional processing and lead to new associations that are consistent with that processing should affect both implicit and explicit measures (e.g., Gawronski & Walther, 2008), but if the propositional processing leads the person to reject an existing association as false, then explicit measures alone should be affected (Gregg et al., 2006). This model should apply both to malleability and change.

Change

One way to conceive of the difference between malleability and change is that the former are shifts that are bounded by the circumstances of measurement, and the latter are shifts that persist beyond the immediate setting. By this definition, there is surprisingly little research on change in implicit social cognition. Almost all research on shifting implicit social cognition occurs within a single laboratory session during which both the manipulation and measurement are completed. However, there is comparatively little evidence for change that persists beyond the immediate experimental context (exceptions include Dasgupta & Greenwald, 2001; Kawakami et al., 2000; Olson & Fazio, 2006).

The exceptions to this trend illustrate that changing implicit social cognition is possible, but do not clarify whether it is the case that minimal manipulations that are sufficient for formation or to elicit malleability effects will be similarly effective for eliciting change. Most of the documented evidence for change involves intensive interventions such as weeks of cognitive behavioral therapy for spider phobia showing change on implicit spider fear two months after therapy (Teachman & Woody, 2003), changing implicit racial biases following a semester-long experience with a diversity education course (Rudman, Ashmore, & Gary, 2001) or a Black roommate (Shook & Fazio, 2008), having female instructors changing implicit gender stereotypes over the course of a semester (Dasgupta & Asgari, 2004; Stout, Dasgupta, Hunsinger, & McManus, 2011), and a social competence training program changing implicit aggressiveness at a follow-up session four months later (Gollwitzer, Banse, Eisenbach, & Naumann, 2007). Some cross-sectional studies also suggest evidence of change from naturally occurring events such as an apparent decline in implicit preferences for White compared to Black people following the candidacy of Barack Obama for US president (Plant et al., 2009; but see Schmidt & Nosek, 2010).

Unlike the other sections of this chapter, the evidence of change summarized here is not a small sampling of a large pool of citations. This subsection cites most of the evidence for "real" change. It may well be the case that many of the factors that have been shown to impact implicit measures within a single session will show lasting effect. But, it could also be that some manipulations are "merely" situational effects and others are long-lasting. Explaining when and how malleability and change effects will differ is virtually uncharted theoretical territory.

CONCLUSION AND WHAT'S NEXT?

As a discipline, implicit social cognition materialized following Greenwald and Banaji's (1995) review and the invention of EP and the IAT. The rapid ascension into a field deserving a chapter in the *Handbook of Social Cognition* is illustrated by citation patterns in the *Journal of Personality and Social Psychology*. Two articles about implicit social cognition were among the top 100 cited articles in that journal during the 1980s. In both the 1990s and 2000s, the first, fourth, and ninth most-cited articles of the decade were about implicit social cognition (retrieved from *Publish or Perish*, February 28, 2011). The present evidence provides a foundation of construct validity for the next generation of research questions, including identification of the mechanisms underlying implicit measures (De Houwer et al., 2009), developing a theoretical model for the independent and interactive effects of implicit and explicit processes in producing social behavior, clarification of when and how implicit social cognitions will be altered by the situation and amenable to change, and understanding how implicit and explicit processes develop across the life span. Likewise, whereas implicit social cognition theory and evidence is established already in social psychology, its application to problems in neighboring disciplines has begun and is accelerating (e.g., Nosek, Graham, & Hawkins, 2010; Perkins & Forehand, 2010; Snowden & Gray, 2010; Teachman, Cody, & Clerkin, 2010; Wiers et al., 2010b). One of the most intriguing issues concerns the potential for implicit social cognition research to impact law, public policy, and organizational practices (Chugh, 2004; Greenwald & Krieger, 2006; Jost et al., 2009; Lane, Kang, & Banaji, 2007; Nosek & Riskind, 2011; Tetlock & Mitchell, 2009). What, for example, are the implications of behavior being shaped by thoughts and feelings that exist outside of conscious awareness and control for legal theory that places such a strong emphasis on intent as a determinant of responsibility and culpability? Such questions confront the basic researcher to consider how all this research matters.

ACKNOWLEDGMENTS

This project was supported by Project Implicit, Inc. Brian Nosek is an officer and Carlee Beth Hawkins is a consultant of Project Implicit, a nonprofit organization that includes in its mission "To develop and deliver methods for investigating and applying phenomena of implicit social cognition, including especially phenomena of implicit bias based on age, race, gender or other factors."

NOTE

1 Implicit measures are indirect, but not all indirect assessments are implicit measures.

REFERENCES

Agerström, J., & Rooth, D. (2011). The role of automatic obesity stereotypes in real hiring discrimination. *Journal of Applied Psychology, 96*, 790–805.

Ames, S.L., Grenard, J.L., Thush, C., Sussman, S., Wiers, R.W., & Stacy, A.W. (2007). Comparison of indirect assessments of association as predictors of marijuana use among at-risk adolescents. *Experimental and Clinical Psychopharmacology, 15*(2), 204–218.

Arkes, H.R., & Tetlock, P.E. (2004). Attributions of implicit prejudice, or "would Jesse Jackson 'fail' the Implicit Association Test?". *Psychological Inquiry, 15*(4), 257–278.

Asendorpf, J.B., Banse, R., & Mücke, D. (2002). Double dissociation between implicit and explicit personality self-concept: The case of shy behavior. *Journal of Personality and Social Psychology, 83*(2), 380–393.

Ashburn-Nardo, L., Voils, C.I., & Monteith, M.J. (2001). Implicit associations as the seeds of intergroup bias: How easily do they take root? *Journal of Personality and Social Psychology, 81*(5), 789–799.

Banaji, M.R. (2001). Implicit attitudes can be measured. In H.L. Roediger, J.S. Nairne, I. Neath, & A.M. Surprenant (Eds.), *The nature of remembering: Essays in honor of Robert G. Crowder* (pp. 117–150). Washington, DC: American Psychological Association.

Banaji, M.R., Nosek, B.A., & Greenwald, A.G. (2004). No place for nostalgia in science: A response to Arkes and Tetlock. *Psychological Inquiry, 15*(4), 279–310.

Bar-Anan, Y., & Nosek, B.A. (2011). Perceptions of intentionally causing unintentional attitude effects: The case of the Affective Misattribution Procedure. Unpublished manuscript.

Bar-Anan, Y., Nosek, B.A., & Vianello, M. (2009). The sorting paired features task: A measure of association strengths. *Experimental Psychology, 56*(5), 329–343.

Bar-Anan, Y., Ratliff, K.A., & Nosek, B.A. (2011). Unpublished data.

Barden, J., Maddux, W.W., Petty, R.E., & Brewer, M.B. (2004). Contextual moderation of racial bias: The impact of social roles on controlled and automatically activated attitudes. *Journal of Personality and Social Psychology, 87*(1), 5–22.

Bargh, J.A., Chaiken, S., Govender, R., & Pratto, F. (1992). The generality of the automatic attitude activation effect. *Journal of Personality and Social Psychology, 62,* 893–912.

Bem, D.J. (1967). Self-perception: An alternative interpretation of cognitive dissonance phenomena. *Psychological Review, 74*(3), 183–200.

Blair, I.V. (2002). The malleability of automatic stereotypes and prejudice. *Personality and Social Psychology Review, 6*(3), 242–261.

Blanton, H., Jaccard, J., Gonzales, P.M., & Christie, C. (2006). Decoding the implicit association test: Implications for criterion prediction. *Journal of Experimental Social Psychology, 42*(2), 192–212.

Bosson, J.K., Swann, W.B., & Pennebaker, J.W. (2000). Stalking the perfect measure of implicit self-esteem: The blind men and the elephant revisited? *Journal of Personality and Social Psychology, 79*(4), 631–643.

Brendl, C.M., Markman, A.B., & Messner, C. (2005). Indirectly measuring evaluations of several attitude objects in relation to a neutral reference point. *Journal of Experimental Social Psychology, 41*(4), 346–368.

Brown, A.S., Gray, N.S., & Snowden, R.J. (2009). Implicit measurement of sexual associations in child sex abusers: Role of victim type and denial. *Sexual Abuse, 21*(2), 166–180.

Cai, H., Sriram, N., Greenwald, A.G., & McFarland, S.G. (2004). The Implicit Association Test's D measure can minimize a cognitive skill confound: Comment on McFarland and Crouch (2002). *Social Cognition, 22,* 673–684.

Campbell, D.T., & Fiske, D.W. (1959). Convergent and discriminant validation by the multitrait-multi method matrix. *Psychological Bulletin, 56,* 81–105.

Campbell, D.T., & Stanley, J.C. (1966). *Experimental and quasi-experimental designs for research.* Chicago, IL: Rand McNally.

Chaiken, S. & Trope, Y. (Eds.) (1999). *Dual-process theories in social psychology.* New York: Guilford.

Chassin, L., Presson, C.C., Sherman, S.J., Seo, D., & Macy, J.T. (2010). Implicit and explicit attitudes predict smoking cessation: Moderating effects of experienced failure to control smoking and plans to quit. *Psychology of Addictive Behaviors, 24*(4), 670–679.

Chugh, D. (2004). Societal and managerial implications of implicit social cognition: Why milliseconds matter. *Social Justice Research, 17*(2), 203–222.

Conrey, F.R., Sherman, J.W., Gawronski, B., Hugenberg, K., & Groom, C.J. (2005). Separating multiple processes in implicit social cognition: The quad model of implicit task performance. *Journal of Personality and Social Psychology, 89*(4), 469–487.

Cronbach, L.J., & Meehl, P.E. (1955). Construct validity in psychological tests. *Psychological Bulletin, 52,* 281–302.

Cunningham, W.A., Preacher, K.J., & Banaji, M.R. (2001). Implicit attitude measures: Consistency, stability, and convergent validity. *Psychological Science, 12*(2), 163–170.

Cunningham, W.A., Johnson, M.K., Raye, C.L., Gatenby, J.C., Gore, J.C., & Banaji, M.R. (2004). Separable neural components in the processing of Black and White faces. *Psychological Science, 15*(12), 806–813.

Cvencek, D., Greenwald, A. G., Brown, A., Snowden, R., Gray, N. (2010). Faking of the Implicit Association Test is statistically detectable and partly correctable. *Basic and Applied Social Psychology, 32,* 302–314.

Dasgupta, N., & Asgari, S. (2004). Seeing is believing: Exposure to counterstereotypic women leaders and its effect on automatic gender stereotyping. *Journal of Experimental Social Psychology, 40,* 642–658.

Dasgupta, N., & Greenwald, A.G. (2001). On the malleability of automatic attitudes: Combating automatic prejudice with images of admired and disliked individuals. *Journal of Personality and Social Psychology, 81*(5), 800–814.

De Houwer, J. (2003a). A structural analysis of indirect measures of attitudes. In J. Musch & K.C. Klauer (Eds.), *The psychology of evaluation: Affective processes in cognition and emotion* (pp. 219–244). Mahwah, NJ: Lawrence Erlbaum Associates.

De Houwer, J. (2003b). The Extrinsic Affective Simon Task. *Experimental Psychology, 50*(2), 77–85.

De Houwer, J., Beckers, T., & Moors, A. (2007). Novel attitudes can be faked on the Implicit Association Test. *Journal of Experimental Social Psychology, 43*(6), 972–978.

De Houwer, J., & De Bruycker, E. (2007). The implicit association test outperforms the extrinsic affective Simon task as an implicit measure of inter-individual differences in attitudes. *British Journal of Social Psychology, 46*(2), 401–421.

De Houwer, J., & Moors, A. (2010). Implicit measures: Similarities and differences. In B. Gawronski and B.K. Payne (Eds.), *Handbook of implicit social cognition* (pp. 176–196). New York: Guilford.

De Houwer, J., Teige-Mocigemba, S., Spruyt, A., & Moors, A. (2009). Implicit measures: A normative analysis and review. *Psychological Bulletin, 135*(3), 347–368.

DeHart, T., Pelham, B.W., & Tennen, H. (2006). What lies beneath: Parenting style and implicit self-esteem. *Journal of Experimental Social Psychology, 42*(1), 1–17.

Dovidio, J.F., Kawakami, K., & Gaertner, S.L. (2002). Implicit and explicit prejudice and interracial interaction. *Journal of Personality and Social Psychology, 82*(1), 62–68.

Duckworth, K.L., Bargh, J.A., Garcia, M., & Chaiken, S. (2002). The automatic evaluation of novel stimuli. *Psychological Science, 13*(6), 513–519.

Egloff, B., Wilhelm, F.H., Neubauer, D.H., Mauss, I.B., & Gross, J.J. (2002). Implicit anxiety measure predicts cardiovascular reactivity to an evaluated speaking task. *Emotion, 2*(1), 3–11.

Fazio, R.H. (1990). Multiple processes by which attitudes guide behavior: The MODE model as an integrative framework. In M.P. Zanna (Ed.), *Advances in experimental social psychology* (Vol. 23, pp. 75–109). New York: Academic Press.

Fazio, R.H., Jackson, J.R., Dunton, B.C., & Williams, C.J. (1995). Variability in automatic activation as an unobtrusive measure of racial attitudes: A bona fide pipeline? *Journal of Personality and Social Psychology, 69*(6), 1013–1027.

Fazio, R.H., & Olson, M.A. (2003). Implicit measures in social cognition research: Their meaning and use. *Annual Review of Psychology, 54*(1), 297–327.

Fazio, R.H., Sanbonmatsu, D.M., Powell, M.C., & Kardes, F.R. (1986). On the automatic activation of attitudes. *Journal of Personality and Social Psychology, 50*(2), 229–238.

Ferguson, M.J. (2007). On the automatic evaluation of end-states. *Journal of Personality and Social Psychology, 92*, 596–611.

Festinger, L. (1957). *A theory of cognitive dissonance.* Stanford, CA: Stanford University Press.

Fiedler, K., & Bluemke, M. (2005). Faking the IAT: Aided and unaided response control on the Implicit Association Tests. *Basic & Applied Social Psychology, 27*(4), 307–316.

Franck, E., Raedt, R.D., & Houwer, J.D. (2007). Implicit but not explicit self-esteem predicts future depressive

symptomatology. *Behaviour Research and Therapy, 45*(10), 2448–2455.

Freud, S. (1900/1972). *Interpretation of dreams.* New York: Basic Books.

Friese, M., Bluemke, M., & Wänke, M. (2007). Predicting voting behavior with implicit attitude measures: The 2002 German parliamentary election. *Experimental Psychology, 54*(4), 247–255.

Friese, M., Hofmann, W., & Wänke, M. (2008). When impulses take over: Moderated predictive validity of explicit and implicit attitude measures in predicting food choice and consumption behaviour. *The British Journal of Social Psychology, 47*(3), 397–419.

Galdi, S., Arcuri, L., & Gawronski, B. (2008). Automatic mental associations predict future choices of undecided decision-makers. *Science, 321*(5892), 1100–1102.

Gawronski, B., & Bodenhausen, G.V. (2005) Accessibility effects on implicit social cognition: The role of knowledge activation versus retrieval experiences. *Journal of Personality and Social Psychology, 89*, 672–685

Gawronski, B., & Bodenhausen, G.V. (2006). Associative and propositional processes in evaluation: An integrative review of implicit and explicit attitude change. *Psychological Bulletin, 132*(5), 692–731.

Gawronski, B., & LeBel, E.P. (2008). Understanding patterns of attitude change: When implicit measures show change, but explicit measures do not. *Journal of Experimental Social Psychology, 44*(5), 1355–1361.

Gawronski, B., & Payne, B.K. (2010). *Handbook of implicit social cognition: Measurement, theory, and applications.* New York: Guilford Press.

Gawronski, B., Peters, K.R., & LeBel, E.P. (2008). What makes mental associations personal or extra-personal? Conceptual issues in the methodological debate about implicit attitude measures. *Social and Personality Psychology Compass, 2*(2), 1002–1023.

Gawronski, B., & Sritharan, R. (2010). Formation, change and contextualization of mental associations: Determinants and principles of variations in implicit measures. In B. Gawronski & B.K. Payne (Eds.), *Handbook of implicit social cognition: Measurement, theory, and applications.* New York: Guilford Press.

Gawronski, B., & Walther, E. (2008). The TAR effect: When the ones who dislike become the ones who are disliked. *Personality & Social Psychology Bulletin, 34*(9), 1276–1289.

Gawronski, B., Walther, E., & Blank, H. (2005). Cognitive consistency and the formation of interpersonal attitudes: Cognitive balance affects the encoding of social information. *Journal of Experimental Social Psychology, 41*(6), 618–626.

Glashouwer, K.A., & de Jong, P.J. (2010). Disorder-specific automatic self-associations in depression and anxiety: Results of the Netherlands study of depression and anxiety. *Psychological Medicine, 40*(07), 1101–1111.

Gollwitzer, M., Banse, R., Eisenbach, K., & Naumann, A. (2007). Effectiveness of the Vienna social competence training on explicit and implicit aggression: Evidence from an aggressiveness-IAT. *European Journal of Psychological Assessment, 23*(3), 150–156.

Gollwitzer, P.M. (1999). Implementation intentions: Strong effects of simple plans. *American Psychologist, 54*(7), 493–503.

Gonsalkorale, K., Carlisle, K., & von Hippel, W. (2007). Intergroup threat increases implicit stereotyping. *International Journal of Psychology and Psychological Therapy, 7,* 189–200.

Gonsalkorale, K., Sherman, J.W., & Klauer, K.C. (2009). Aging and prejudice: Diminished regulation of automatic race bias among older adults. *Journal of Experimental Social Psychology, 45*(2), 410–414.

Govan, C.L., & Williams, K.D. (2004). Changing the affective valence of the stimulus items influences the IAT by re-defining the category labels. *Journal of Experimental Social Psychology, 40*(3), 357–365.

Gray, N.S., Brown, A.S., MacCulloch, M.J., Smith, J., & Snowden, R.J. (2005). An implicit test of the associations between children and sex in pedophiles. *Journal of Abnormal Psychology, 114*(2), 304–308.

Greenwald, A.G. (1975). Consequences of prejudice against the null hypothesis. *Psychological Bulletin, 82,* 1–20.

Greenwald, A.G. (2001). Nothing so practical as a good method. Invited address at meeting of the Person Memory Interest Group, Coeur d'Alene, ID.

Greenwald, A.G., & Banaji, M.R. (1995). Implicit social cognition: Attitudes, self-esteem, and stereotypes. *Psychological Review, 102*(1), 4–27.

Greenwald, A.G., Banaji, M.R., Rudman, L.A., Farnham, S.D., Nosek, B.A., & Mellott, D.S. (2002). A unified theory of implicit attitudes, stereotypes, self-esteem, and self-concept. *Psychological Review, 109*(1), 3–25.

Greenwald, A.G., & Krieger, L.H. (2006). Implicit bias: Scientific foundations. *California Law Review, 94*(4), 945–967.

Greenwald, A.G., McGhee, D.E., & Schwartz, J.L.K. (1998). Measuring individual differences in implicit cognition: The implicit association test. *Journal of Personality and Social Psychology, 74*(6), 1464–1480.

Greenwald, A.G., & Nosek, B.A. (2008). Attitudinal dissociation: What does it mean? In R.E. Petty, R.H. Fazio, & P. Brinol (Eds.), *Attitudes: Insights from the new implicit measures* (pp. 65-82). Hillsdale, NJ: Lawrence Erlbaum Associates.

Greenwald, A.G., Nosek, B.A., & Banaji, M.R. (2003). Understanding and using the Implicit Association Test: I. An improved scoring algorithm. *Journal of Personality and Social Psychology, 85*(2), 197–216.

Greenwald, A.G., Pickrell, J.E., & Farnham, S.D. (2002). Implicit partisanship: Taking sides for no reason. *Journal of Personality and Social Psychology, 83*(2), 367–379.

Greenwald, A.G., Poehlman, T.A., Uhlmann, E.L., & Banaji, M.R. (2009). Understanding and using the Implicit Association Test: III. Meta-analysis of predictive validity. *Journal of Personality and Social Psychology, 97*(1), 17–41.

Greenwald, A.G., & Ronis, D.L. (1978). Twenty years of cognitive dissonance: Case study of the evolution of a theory. *Psychological Review, 85*(1), 53–57.

Greenwald, A.G., Smith, C.T., Sriram, N., Bar-Anan, Y., & Nosek, B.A. (2009). Race attitude measures predicted vote in the 2008 U. S. Presidential Election. *Analysis of Social Issues and Public Policy, 9,* 241–253.

Gregg, A.P., Seibt, B., & Banaji, M.R. (2006). Easier done than undone: Asymmetry in the malleability of implicit preferences. *Journal of Personality and Social Psychology, 90*(1), 1–20.

Harmon-Jones, E., & Mills, J. (Eds.) (1999). *Cognitive dissonance: Progress on a pivotal theory in social psychology.* Washington, DC: American Psychological Association.

Helmholtz, H. (1925). *Treatise on physiological optics* (3rd ed., Vol. 3; J.P.C. Southall, Trans.). Menasha, WI: Banta. (Original 3rd ed. published 1910.)

Hetts, J.J., Sakuma, M., & Pelham, B.W. (1999). Two roads to positive regard: Implicit and explicit self-evaluation and culture. *Journal of Experimental Social Psychology, 35*(6), 512–559.

Hofmann, W., De Houwer, J., Perugini, M., Baeyens, F., & Crombez, G. (2010). Evaluative conditioning in humans: a meta-analysis. *Psychological Bulletin, 136*(3), 390–421.

Hofmann, W., Gawronski, B., Gschwendner, T., Le, H., & Schmitt, M. (2005). A meta-analysis on the correlation between the Implicit Association Test and explicit self-report measures. *Personality and Social Psychology Bulletin, 31*(10), 1369–1385.

Hofmann, W., Gschwendner, T., Castelli, L., & Schmitt, M. (2008). Implicit and explicit attitudes and interracial interaction: The moderating role of situationally available control resources. *Group Processes & Intergroup Relations, 11*(1), 69–87.

Hofmann, W., Gschwendner, T., Nosek, B.A., & Schmitt, M. (2005). What moderates implicit–explicit consistency? *European Review of Social Psychology, 16*(1), 335–390.

Hugenberg, K., & Bodenhausen, G.V. (2003). Facing prejudice: Implicit prejudice and the perception of facial threat. *Psychological Science, 14*(6), 640–643.

Jost, J.T., Banaji, M.R., & Nosek, B.A. (2004). A decade of system justification theory: Accumulated evidence of conscious and unconscious bolstering of the status quo. *Political Psychology, 25*(6), 881–919.

Jost, J.T., Pelham, B.W., & Carvallo, M.R. (2002). Nonconscious forms of system justification: Cognitive, affective, and behavioral preferences for higher status groups. *Journal of Experimental Social Psychology, 38*(6), 586.

Jost, J.T., Rudman, L.A., Blair, I.V., Carney, D.R., Dasgupta, N., Glaser, J., et al. (2009). The existence of implicit bias is beyond reasonable doubt: A refutation of ideological and methodological objections and executive summary of ten studies that no manager should ignore. *Research in Organizational Behavior, 29,* 39–69.

Joy-Gaba, J.A., & Nosek, B.A. (2010). The surprisingly limited malleability of implicit racial evaluations. *Social Psychology, 41*(3), 137–146.

Judd, C.M., & Kulik, J.A. (1980). Schematic effects of social attitudes on information processing and recall. *Journal of Personality and Social Psychology, 38*(4), 569–578.

Karpinski, A., & Hilton, J.L. (2001). Attitudes and the Implicit Association Test. *Journal of Personality and Social Psychology, 81,* 774–788.

Karpinski, A., Steinberg, J.A., Versek, B., & Alloy, L.B. (2007). The Breadth-Based Adjective Rating Task (BART) as an indirect measure of self-esteem. *Social Cognition*, *25*(6), 778–818.

Karpinski, A., & Steinman, R.B. (2006). The Single Category Implicit Association Test as a measure of implicit social cognition. *Journal of Personality and Social Psychology*, *91*(1), 16–32.

Karpinski, A., Steinman, R.B., & Hilton, J.L. (2005). Attitude importance as a moderator of the relationship between implicit and explicit attitude measures. *Personality and Social Psychology Bulletin*, *31*(7), 949 –962.

Kawakami, K., Dovidio, J.F., Moll, J., Hermsen, S., & Russin, A. (2000). Just say no (to stereotyping): Effects of training in the negation of stereotypic associations on stereotype activation. *Journal of Personality and Social Psychology*, *78*(5), 871–888.

Kim, D.Y. (2003). Voluntary controllability of the Implicit Association Test (IAT). *Social Psychology Quarterly*, 83–96.

Klauer, K.C., & Teige-Mocigemba, S. (2007). Controllability and resource dependence in automatic evaluation. *Journal of Experimental Social Psychology*, *43*(4), 648–655.

Klein, A.M., Becker, E.S., & Rinck, M. (2010). Approach and avoidance tendencies in spider fearful children: The Approach–Avoidance Task. *Journal of Child and Family Studies*.

Knowles, E.D., Lowery, B.S., & Schaumberg, R.L. (2010). Racial prejudice predicts opposition to Obama and his health care reform plan. *Journal of Experimental Social Psychology*, *46*(2), 420–423.

Kocan, S.E., & Curtis, G.J. (2009). Close encounters of the initial kind: Implicit self-esteem, name-letter similarity, and social distance. *Basic & Applied Social Psychology*, *31*(1), 17–23.

Koole, S.L., Dijksterhuis, A., & van Knippenberg, A. (2001). What's in a name: Implicit self-esteem and the automatic self. *Journal of Personality and Social Psychology*, *80*(4), 669–685.

Lane, K.A., Banaji, M.R., Nosek, B.A., & Greenwald, A.G. (2007). Understanding and using the Implicit Association Test: IV: What we know (so far) about the method. In B. Wittenbrink & N. Schwarz (Eds.), *Implicit measures of attitudes* (pp. 59–102). New York: Guilford Press.

Lane, K. A., Kang, J., & Banaji, M. R. (2007). Implicit social cognition and law. *Annual Review of Law and Social Science*, *3*, 427–451.

Lange, W., Keijsers, G., Becker, E.S., & Rinck, M. (2008). Social anxiety and evaluation of social crowds: Explicit and implicit measures. *Behaviour Research and Therapy*, *46*(8), 932–943.

Lee, S., Rogge, R.D., & Reis, H.T. (2010). Assessing the seeds of relationship decay. *Psychological Science*, *21*(6), 857–864.

Lindner, N.M., & Nosek, B.A. (2009). Alienable speech: Ideological variations in the application of free-speech principles. *Political Psychology*, *30*(1), 67–92.

Livingston, R.W., & Brewer, M.B. (2002). What are we really priming? Cue-based versus category-based processing of facial stimuli. *Journal of Personality and Social Psychology*, *82*(1), 5–18.

Maass, A., Salvi, D., Arcuri, L., & Semin, G.R. (1989). Language use in intergroup contexts: The Linguistic Intergroup Bias. *Journal of Personality and Social Psychology*, *57*(6), 981–993.

Marquardt, N., & Hoeger, R. (2009). The effect of implicit moral attitudes on managerial decision-making: An implicit social cognition approach. *Journal of Business Ethics*, *85*(2), 157–171.

McConahay, J.B. (1986). Modern racism, ambivalance, and the modern racism scale. In J.F. Dovidio & S.L. Gaertner (Eds.), *Prejudice, discrimination and racism* (pp. 91–126). New York: Academic Press.

McConnell, A.R., & Leibold, J.M. (2001). Relations among the Implicit Association Test, discriminatory behavior, and explicit measures of racial attitudes. *Journal of Experimental Social Psychology*, *37*(5), 435–442.

Mendes, W.B., Gray, H.M., Mendoza-Denton, R., Major, B., & Epel, E.S. (2007). Why egalitarianism might be good for your health. *Psychological Science*, *18*(11), 991–998.

Mierke, J., & Klauer, K.C. (2003). Method-specific variance in the Implicit Association Test. *Journal of Personality and Social Psychology*, *85*(6), 1180–1192.

Mitchell, J.P., Nosek, B.A., & Banaji, M.R. (2003). Contextual variations in implicit evaluation. *Journal of Experimental Psychology: General*, *132*(3), 455–469.

Mogg, K., Bradley, B.P., Field, M., & De Houwer, J. (2003). Eye movements to smoking-related pictures in smokers: relationship between attentional biases and implicit and explicit measures of stimulus valence. *Addiction*, *98*(6), 825–836.

Molesworth, B.R.C., & Chang, B. (2009). Predicting pilots' risk-taking behavior through an Implicit Association Test. *Human Factors*, *51*(6), 845–857.

Moors, A., & De Houwer, J. (2006). Automaticity: A conceptual and theoretical analysis. *Psychological Bulletin*, *132*, 297–326.

Nisbett, R.E., & Wilson, T.D. (1977). The halo effect: Evidence for unconscious alteration of judgments. *Journal of Personality and Social Psychology*, *35*(4), 250–256.

Nock, M.K., Park, J.M., Finn, C.T., Deliberto, T.L., Dour, H.J., & Banaji, M.R. (2010). Measuring the suicidal mind. *Psychological Science*, *21*(4), 511–517.

Nosek, B.A. (2005). Moderators of the relationship between implicit and explicit evaluation. *Journal of Experimental Psychology: General*, *134*(4), 565–584.

Nosek, B.A. (2007). Understanding the individual implicitly and explicitly. *International Journal of Psychology*, *42*(3), 184–188.

Nosek, B.A., & Banaji, M.R. (2001). The go/no-go association task. *Social Cognition*, *19*(6), 625–666.

Nosek, B.A., Banaji, M.R., & Greenwald, A.G. (2002). Math = male, me = female, therefore math ≠ me. *Journal of Personality and Social Psychology*, *83*(1), 44–59.

Nosek, B.A., Graham, J., & Hawkins, C. (2010). Implicit political cognition. In B. Gawronski & B.K. Payne (Eds.), *Handbook of implicit social cognition: Measurement, theory, and applications*. New York: Guilford Press.

Nosek, B.A., & Greenwald, A.G. (2009). (Part of) the case for a pragmatic approach to validity: Comment on De Houwer, Teige-Mocigemba, Spruyt, and Moors (2009). *Psychological Bulletin, 135*(3), 373–376.

Nosek, B.A., Greenwald, A.G., & Banaji, M.R. (2005). Understanding and using the Implicit Association Test: II. Method variables and construct validity. *Personality and Social Psychology Bulletin, 31*(2), 166–180.

Nosek, B.A., Greenwald, A.G., & Banaji, M.R. (2007). The Implicit Association Test at age 7: A methodological and conceptual review. In J.A. Bargh (Ed.), *Social psychology and the unconscious: The automaticity of higher mental processes* (pp. 265–292). New York: Psychology Press.

Nosek, B.A., & Hansen, J.J. (2008a). Personalizing the Implicit Association Test increases explicit evaluation of target concepts. *European Journal of Psychological Assessment, 25*, 226–236.

Nosek, B.A., & Hansen, J.J. (2008b). The associations in our heads belong to us: Searching for attitudes and knowledge in implicit evaluation. *Cognition and Emotion, 22*, 553–594.

Nosek, B.A., Hawkins, C.B., & Frazier, R.S. (2011). Implicit social cognition: From measures to mechanisms. *Trends in Cognitive Sciences, 15*, 152–159.

Nosek, B.A., & Riskind, R.G. (2011). Policy implications of implicit social cognition. *Social Issues and Policy Review.*

Nosek, B.A., & Smyth, F.L. (2007). A multitrait-multimethod validation of the Implicit Association Test: Implicit and explicit attitudes are related but distinct constructs. *Experimental Psychology, 54*(1), 14–29.

Nosek, B.A., & Smyth, F.L. (2011). Implicit social cognitions predict sex differences in math engagement and achievement. *American Educational Research Journal.*

Nosek, B.A., Smyth, F.L., Sriram, N., Lindner, N.M., Devos, T., Ayala, A., et al. (2009). National differences in gender–science stereotypes predict national sex differences in science and math achievement. *Proceedings of the National Academy of Sciences, 106*(26), 10593–10597.

Nosek, B.A., & Sriram, N. (2007). Faulty assumptions: A comment on Blanton, Jaccard, Gonzales, and Christie (2006). *Journal of Experimental Social Psychology, 43*, 393–398.

Nuttin, J.M. (1985). Narcissism beyond Gestalt and awareness: The name letter effect. *European Journal of Social Psychology, 15*, 353–361.

Olson, K.R., & Dunham, Y. (2010). The development of implicit social cognition. In B. Gawronski & B.K. Payne (Eds.), *Handbook of implicit social cognition: Measurement, theory, and applications.* New York: Guilford Press.

Olson, M.A., & Fazio, R.H. (2003). Relations between implicit measures of prejudice. *Psychological Science, 14*(6), 636–639.

Olson, M.A., & Fazio, R.H. (2006). Reducing automatically activated racial prejudice through implicit evaluative conditioning. *Personality and Social Psychology Bulletin, 32*(4), 421–433.

Olson, M.A., & Fazio, R.H. (2004). Reducing the influence of extrapersonal associations on the Implicit Association Test: Personalizing the IAT. *Journal of Personality and Social Psychology, 86*(5), 653–667.

Ostrom, T.M. (1989). Interdependence of attitude and measurement. In A.R. Pratkanis & S.J. Breckler (Eds.), *Attitude structure and function* (pp. 11–36). Hillsdale, NJ: Lawrence Erlbaum Associates.

Otten, S., & Wentura, D. (1999). About the impact of automaticity in the minimal group paradigm: Evidence from affective priming tasks. *European Journal of Social Psychology, 29*(8), 1049–1071.

Page-Gould, E., Mendoza-Denton, R., & Tropp, L.R. (2008). With a little help from my cross-group friend: Reducing anxiety in intergroup contexts through cross-group friendship. *Journal of Personality and Social Psychology, 95*(5), 1080–1094.

Paladino, M., & Castelli, L. (2008). On the immediate consequences of intergroup categorization: Activation of approach and avoidance motor behavior toward ingroup and outgroup members. *Personality and Social Psychology Bulletin, 34*(6), 755–768.

Payne, B.K., Burkley, M.A., & Stokes, M.B. (2008). Why do implicit and explicit attitude tests diverge? The role of structural fit. *Journal of Personality and Social Psychology, 94*(1), 16–31.

Payne, B.K., Cheng, C.M., Govorun, O., & Stewart, B.D. (2005). An inkblot for attitudes: Affect misattribution as implicit measurement. *Journal of Personality and Social Psychology, 89*(3), 277–293.

Payne, B.K., Krosnick, J.A., Pasek, J., Lelkes, Y., Akhtar, O., & Tompson, T. (2010). Implicit and explicit prejudice in the 2008 American presidential election. *Journal of Experimental Social Psychology, 46*(2), 367–374.

Payne, B.K., McClernon, F.J., & Dobbins, I.G. (2007). Automatic affective responses to smoking cues. *Experimental and Clinical Psychopharmacology, 15*(4), 400–409.

Penner, L.A., Dovidio, J.F., West, T.V., Gaertner, S.L., Albrecht, T.L., Dailey, R.K., et al. (2010). Aversive racism and medical interactions with Black patients: A field study. *Journal of Experimental Social Psychology, 46*(2), 436–440.

Pérez, E.O. (2010). Explicit evidence on the import of implicit attitudes: The IAT and immigration policy judgments. *Political Behavior, 32*, 517-545.

Perkins, A., & Forehand, M. (2010). Implicit social cognition and indirect measures in consumer behavior. In B. Gawronski & B.K. Payne (Eds.), *Handbook of implicit social cognition.* New York: Guilford Press.

Perugini, M., Richetin, J., & Zogmaister, C. (2010). Prediction of behavior. In B. Gawronski and B.K. Payne (Eds.), *Handbook of implicit social cognition* (pp. 255–277). New York: Guilford Press.

Phelps, E.A., O'Connor, K.J., Cunningham, W.A., Funayama, E.S., Gatenby, J.C., Gore, J.C., et al. (2000). Performance on indirect measures of race evaluation predicts amygdala activation. *Journal of Cognitive Neuroscience, 12*(5), 729–738.

Plant, E.A., Devine, P.G., Cox, W.T., Columb, C., Miller, S.L., Goplen, J., et al. (2009). The Obama effect: Decreasing implicit prejudice and stereotyping. *Journal of Experimental Social Psychology, 45*(4), 961–964.

Polaschek, D.L.L., Bell, R.K., Calvert, S.W., & Takarangi, M.K.T. (2010). Cognitive-behavioural rehabilitation of high-risk violent offenders: Investigating treatment change with explicit and implicit measures of cognition. *Applied Cognitive Psychology*, *24*(3), 437–449.

Prestwich, A., Perugini, M., Hurling, R., & Richetin, J. (2010). Using the self to change implicit attitudes. *European Journal of Social Psychology*, *40*(1), 61–71.

Quadflieg, S., Turk, D.J., Waiter, G.D., Mitchell, J.P., Jenkins, A.C., & Macrae, C.N. (2009). Exploring the neural correlates of social stereotyping. *Journal of Cognitive Neuroscience*, *21*(8), 1560–1570.

Ranganath, K.A., & Nosek, B.A. (2008). Implicit attitude generalization occurs immediately; explicit attitude generalization takes time. *Psychological Science*, *19*(3), 249–254.

Ranganath, K.A., Smith, C.T., & Nosek, B.A. (2008). Distinguishing automatic and controlled components of attitudes from direct and indirect measurement methods. *Journal of Experimental Social Psychology*, *44*(2), 386–396.

Richeson, J.A., Baird, A.A., Gordon, H.L., Heatherton, T.F., Wyland, C.L., Trawalter, S., et al. (2003). An fMRI investigation of the impact of interracial contact on executive function. *Nature Neuroscience*, *6*(12), 1323–1328.

Richetin, J., Croizet, J.-C., & Huguet, P. (2004). Facial make-up elicits positive attitudes at the implicit level: Evidence from the implicit association test. *Current Research in Social Psychology*, *9*(11), 145–164.

Roccato, M., & Zogmaister, C. (2010). Predicting the vote through implicit and explicit attitudes: A field research. *Political Psychology*, *31*(2), 249–274.

Roediger, H.L. (1990). Implicit memory: Retention without remembering. *American Psychologist*, *45*(9), 1043–1056.

Rooth, D. (2010). Automatic associations and discrimination in hiring: Real world evidence. *Labour Economics*, *17*(3), 523–534.

Rothermund, K., Teige-Mocigemba, S., Gast, A., & Wentura, D. (2009). Minimizing the influence of recoding in the Implicit Association Test: The Recoding-Free Implicit Association Test (IAT-RF). *Quarterly Journal of Experimental Psychology*, *62*(1), 84–98.

Rudman, L.A., Ashmore, R.D., & Gary, M.L. (2001). "Unlearning" automatic biases: The malleability of implicit prejudice and stereotypes. *Journal of Personality and Social Psychology*, *81*(5), 856–868.

Rudman, L.A., Dohn, M.C., & Fairchild, K. (2007). Implicit self-esteem compensation: Automatic threat defense. *Journal of Personality and Social Psychology*, *93*(5), 798–813.

Rudolph, A., Schröder-Abé, M., Riketta, M., & Schütz, A. (2010). Easier when done than said! Implicit self-esteem predicts observed or spontaneous behavior, but not self-reported or controlled behavior. *Zeitschrift für Psychologie,*, *218*(1), 12–19.

Rüsch, N., Corrigan, P.W., Todd, A.R., & Bodenhausen, G.V. (2010). Implicit self-stigma in people with mental illness. *The Journal of Nervous and Mental Disease*, *198*(2), 150–153.

Salthouse, T.A. (2010). *Major issues in cognitive aging.* New York: Oxford University Press.

Sassenberg, K., & Wieber, F. (2005). Don't ignore the other half: The impact of ingroup identification on implicit measures of prejudice. *European Journal of Social Psychology*, *35*(5), 621–632.

Schmidt, K., & Nosek, B.A. (2010). Implicit (and explicit) racial attitudes barely changed during Barack Obama's presidential campaign and early presidency. *Journal of Experimental Social Psychology*, *46*(2), 308–314.

Schnabel, K., Banse, R., & Asendorpf, J. (2006). Employing automatic approach and avoidance tendencies for the assessment of implicit personality self-concept. *Experimental Psychology*, *53*(1), 69–76.

Schneider, W., & Shiffrin, R.M. (1977). Controlled and automatic human information processing: 1. Detection, search, and attention. *Psychological Review*, *84*(1), 1–66.

Sekaquaptewa, D., Espinoza, P., Thompson, M., Vargas, P., & von Hippel, W. (2003). Stereotypic explanatory bias: Implicit stereotyping as a predictor of discrimination.

Semin, G., & Fiedler, K. (1991). The linguistic category model, its bases, applications and range. In W. Stroebe & M. Hewstone (Eds.), *European review of social psychology* (Vol. 2, pp.1–30). Chichester, England: Wiley.

Sherman, S.J., Chassin, L., Presson, C., Seo, D., & Macy, J.T. (2009). The intergenerational transmission of implicit and explicit attitudes toward smoking: Predicting adolescent smoking initiation. *Journal of Experimental Social Psychology*, *45*(2), 313–319.

Sherman, S.J., Rose, J.S., Koch, K., Presson, C.C., & Chassin, L. (2003). Implicit and explicit attitudes toward cigarette smoking: The effects of context and motivation. *Journal of Social and Clinical Psychology*, *22*(1), 13–39.

Shook, N.J., & Fazio, R.H. (2008). Interracial roommate relationships: An experimental field test of the contact hypothesis. *Psychological Science*, *19*(7), 717–723.

Sinclair, S., Lowery, B.S., Hardin, C.D., & Colangelo, A. (2005). Social tuning of automatic racial attitudes: The role of affiliative motivation. *Journal of Personality and Social Psychology*, *89*(4), 583–592.

Smith, E.R., & DeCoster, J. (2000). Dual-process models in social and cognitive psychology: Conceptual integration and links to underlying memory systems. *Personality and Social Psychology Review*, *4*(2), 108–131.

Snowden, R.J., & Gray, N.S. (2010). Implicit social cognition in forensic settings. In B. Gawronski & B. K. Payne (Eds.), *Handbook of implicit social cognition.* New York: Guilford Press.

Snowden, R.J., Wichter, J., & Gray, N.S. (2007). Implicit and explicit measurements of sexual preference in gay and heterosexual men: A comparison of priming techniques and the Implicit Association Task. *Archives of Sexual Behavior*, *37*(4), 558–565.

Spalding, L.R., & Hardin, C.D. (1999). Unconscious unease and self-handicapping: Behavioral consequences of individual differences in implicit and explicit self-esteem. *Psychological Science*, *10*(6), 535–539.

Sriram, N., & Greenwald, A.G. (2009). The brief implicit association test. *Experimental Psychology*, *56*(4), 283–294.

Sriram, N., Greenwald, A.G., & Nosek, B.A. (2010). Correlational biases in mean response latency differences. *Statistical Methodology*, *7*(3), 277–291.

Srivastava, S., & Banaji, M.R. (2011). Behind the front: Collaborative networks and implicit cognition in organizations. *American Sociological Review, 76*, 207–233.

Steffens, M.C. (2004). Is the implicit association test immune to faking? *Experimental Psychology, 51*(3), 165–179.

Stewart, B.D., von Hippel, W., & Radvansky, G.A. (2009). Age, race, and implicit prejudice. *Psychological Science, 20*(2), 164–168.

Stout, J. G., Dasgupta, N., Hunsinger, M., & McManus, M. (2011). STEMing the tide: Using ingroup experts to inoculate women's self-concept and professional goals in science, technology, engineering, and mathematics (STEM). *Journal of Personality and Social Psychology, 100*, 255–270.

Strack, F., & Deutsch, R. (2004). Reflective and impulsive determinants of social behavior. *Personality and Social Psychology Review, 8*(3), 220–247.

Swanson, J.E., Rudman, L.A., & Greenwald, A.G. (2001). Using the Implicit Association Test to investigate attitude-behavior consistency for stigmatized behavior. *Cognition and Emotion, 15(2)*, 207–230.

Tajfel, H., & Turner, J.C. (1986). The social identity theory of intergroup behavior. In S. Worchel & W. G. Austin (Eds.), *Psychology of intergroup relations* (pp. 7–24). Chicago, IL: Nelson-Hall Publishers.

Teachman, B.A., Cody, M., & Clerkin, E. (2010). Clincial applications of implicit measures. In B. Gawronski & B.K. Payne (Eds.), *Handbook of implicit social cognition*. New York: Guilford Press.

Teachman, B.A., Gregg, A.P., & Woody, S.R. (2001). Implicit associations for fear-relevant stimuli among individuals with snake and spider fears. *Journal of Abnormal Psychology, 110*(2), 226–235.

Teachman, B.A., Smith-Janik, S.B., & Saporito, J. (2007). Information processing biases and panic disorder: Relationships among cognitive and symptom measures. *Behaviour Research and Therapy, 45*(8), 1791–1811.

Teachman, B.A., & Woody, S.R. (2003). Automatic processing in spider phobia: Implicit fear associations over the course of treatment. *Journal of Abnormal Psychology, 112*(1), 100–109.

Teige-Mocigemba, S., Klauer, K.C., & Rothermund, K. (2008). Minimizing method-specific variance in the IAT: A single block IAT. *European Journal of Psychological Assessment, 24*(4), 237–245.

Teige-Mocigemba, S., Klauer, K.C., & Sherman, J.W. (2010). A practical guide to Implicit Association Tests and related tasks. In B. Gawronski and B. K. Payne (Eds.), *Handbook of implicit social cognition* (pp. 117–139). New York: Guilford Press.

Tetlock, P., & Mitchell, G. (2009). Implicit bias and accountability systems: What must organizations do to prevent discrimination? In B. Staw & A. Brief (Eds.), *Research in organizational behavior* (Vol. 29, pp. 71–72). New York: Elsevier.

Teubel, T., Asendorpf, J.B., Banse, R., & Schnabel, K. (in press). Implicit but not explicit aggressiveness predicts performance outcome in basketball players. *International Journal of Sport Psychology.*

Thush, C., Wiers, R.W., Ames, S.L., Grenard, J.L., Sussman, S., & Stacy, A.W. (2008). Interactions between implicit and explicit cognition and working memory capacity in the prediction of alcohol use in at-risk adolescents. *Drug and Alcohol Dependence, 94*(1–3), 116–124.

van Leeuwen, M.L., & Macrae, C.N. (2004). Is beautiful always good? Implicit benefits of facial attractiveness. *Social Cognition, 22*(6), 637–649.

von Hippel, W., Brener, L., & von Hippel, C. (2008). Implicit prejudice toward injecting drug users predicts intentions to change jobs among drug and alcohol nurses. *Psychological Science, 19*(1), 7–11.

Walther, E. (2002). Guilty by mere association: Evaluative conditioning and the spreading attitude effect. *Journal of Personality and Social Psychology, 82*(6), 919–934.

Weigel, R.H., & Howes, P.W. (1985). Conceptions of racial prejudice: Symbolic racism reconsidered. *Journal of Social Issues, 41*(3), 117–138.

Wentura, D., & Degner, J. (2010). A practical guide to sequential priming and related tasks. In B. Gawronski and B.K. Payne (Eds.), *Handbook of implicit social cognition* (pp. 95–116). New York: Guilford Press.

Whitfield, M., & Jordan, C.H. (2009). Mutual influence of implicit and explicit attitudes. *Journal of Experimental Social Psychology, 45*(4), 748–759.

Wiers, R.W., Houben, K., Roefs, A., de Jong, P.J., Hofmann, W., & Stacy, A.W. (2010b). Implicit cognition in health psychology: Why common sense goes out the window. In B. Gawronski & B.K. Payne (Eds.), *Handbook of implicit social cognition*. New York: Guilford Press.

Wiers, R.W., Rinck, M., Kordts, R., Houben, K., & Strack, F. (2010a). Retraining automatic action-tendencies to approach alcohol in hazardous drinkers. *Addiction, 105*, 279–287.

Wilson, T.D., Lindsey, S., & Schooler, T.Y. (2000). A model of dual attitudes. *Psychological Review, 107*(1), 101–126.

Wittenbrink, B., Judd, C.M., & Park, B. (1997). Evidence for racial prejudice at the implicit level and its relationship with questionnaire measures. *Journal of Personality and Social Psychology, 72*(2), 262–274.

Wittenbrink, B., Judd, C.M., & Park, B. (2001). Spontaneous prejudice in context: Variability in automatically activated attitudes. *Journal of Personality and Social Psychology, 81*(5), 815–827.

4

Consciousness, Metacognition, and the Unconscious

Piotr Winkielman & Jonathan W. Schooler

What are we aware of? What do we know about our own thoughts and feelings? These questions about consciousness and metacognition lie at the heart of social cognition – a field that relies on concepts and methods of cognitive psychology, cognitive science, and neuroscience to understand how people think about others and themselves. Importantly, these questions need answers not only because they are scientifically fascinating but also because it is practically important to examine how in daily life people manage to (sometimes) answer questions like: "What are you thinking about right now?", "How do you feel right now?", "How much do you want to drink?", "Do you want to smoke?", "Do you dislike this social group?", "Do you find this person attractive?", "Did you enjoy this piece of music?", "Did you notice this object?", "Do you understand this passage of text?", and "Were you influenced by this message?" These standard questions require the ability of the person to access, evaluate, and express the cognitive and affective contents of her own mind. And though these answers may often come to our mind effortlessly, giving the illusion of "self-transparency," the process of reaching them is actually tricky and may be fraught with error. After all, not all mental states are conscious. Furthermore, those states that are conscious can be so in various forms and to different degrees. Finally, translating our consciousness into a report may introduce a variety of distortions.

Our chapter reviews theorizing and empirical research on consciousness and metacognition, using the following organizational structure. We start with a few historical remarks, highlighting

the growing interest in psychology in questions of consciousness and metacognition. We then review selected findings on consciousness and metacognition, using an important distinction between mental states that are simply conscious and mental states that are accompanied by rich metacognitive representations of those states. We then move to a discussion of cognition and emotion in the absence of consciousness. Throughout, we address neural correlates of consciousness and metacognition and touch on questions concerning the relationship between social cognition and self-cognition.

HISTORICAL PERSPECTIVE

Just like the actual phenomena, the history of thinking about consciousness and metacognition undergoes a pattern of waxing and waning. Descartes famously argued that consciousness is the only undeniable reality. Everything else could be created by a malicious demon, but our very own thoughts and feelings are necessarily true. For Descartes, consciousness also comes with metacognitive transparency, making our own mental states self-apparent. It is worth noting this because the Cartesian view still underlies much of everyday intuitions about the mind and, as we describe later, is being challenged by modern social-cognitive research that argues that even one's own thoughts may be subject to misrepresentation, in the form of temporal and translational dissociations, or may even be completely obscured, as in the case of unconscious goals and unconscious affect.

Following some 19th-century philosophers (e.g., Husserl, Brentano), early psychologists had focused on the nature of intentionality and the structure of experience (Boring, 1953). Their method – introspection – assumed that the critical constituents of mental life (thoughts, feelings, volitions) are in principle consciously accessible. They also argued psychology should be fundamentally interested in content-bearing intentional states (thoughts, intentions, goals), but not so much in non-conscious events (e.g., associative chains, reflexes, physiology), which are best left to biologists. As we discuss in detail later, these foundational notions are being challenged by modern researchers in social cognition who argue that states, such as goals, can operate unconsciously.

From the perspective of modern social cognition, another interesting historical aspect was the early interest in social foundations of self-awareness. This was particularly pronounced in the writing of symbolic interactionists (e.g., Mead, 1934) as well as some developmental psychologists (e.g., Vygotsky, 1962). For them, self-consciousness is partly created by the necessity to function in a social community. After all, social coordination requires the individual to be able to adjust to others, see things from their perspective, anticipate their reactions, self-regulate, and, critically, learn to adapt towards oneself the stance of a "generalized other." As we discuss later, these historical themes are reflected in contemporary social-cognitive research on self-monitoring, self-regulation, and self-awareness.

Though consciousness was of central importance for the early psychologists, still they admitted some role for unconscious processes. For example, Helmholtz proposed that vision involves unconscious inferences, whereas James wrote about habits and the subconscious (Kihlstrom, 2007). Behaviorism, and the ambition to make psychology "objective" and equal to other natural sciences, brought disfavor to the methods of introspection and to mentalistic concepts like consciousness. Along with this came the belief that behavior is ultimately under the control of the environment, rather than mysterious "internal forces." This behaviorist credo still guides some modern researchers in social cognition who tend to highlight how much of social behavior is under "environmental control," at least in the sense of "power of the situation" (e.g., Bargh, 2007). Behaviorists also assumed that providing mechanistic explanations of behavior will make concepts like "consciousness" and "volition" disappear from the psychological vocabulary, the way concepts like "phlogiston' or "life force" disappeared from modern scientific physical and

biological vocabulary. Elements of this view are also visible in modern social cognition when researchers argue that as psychological science identifies more and more simple, low-level, and thus unconscious mechanisms it will no longer need complex, high-level concepts, like "consciousness" (e.g., Bargh, 2007). This view is related to a position in philosophy called "eliminative materialism," which proposes replacing high-level mental concepts with references to low-level biological substrates (Churchland, 1981). For example, instead of talking about "seeing," science should talk about specific visual computations in the occipital lobe. However, note that this reductionist argument is logically problematic. For one, it confuses the identification of low-level mechanisms with a satisfying explanation of high-level concepts (Fodor, 1968). But, low-level explanations often offer an uninteresting or even obscuring reduction. For example, providing a complete low-level explanation of physical materials that money is made out of (paper, metal) is not interesting, and does not in any way make the explanations of money in terms of its functions superfluous. In fact, it is counter-productive as it occludes relevant properties (e.g., that a $1 coin functions exactly the same as $1 paper bill). Furthermore, the argument that consciousness can be reduced to smaller, mechanistic, unconscious parts is also problematic because consciousness is an emergent phenomenon that requires an interaction of many (possibly dumb) parts, and thus by definition not reducible to any single one of them. As an analogy, it is impossible to understand the concept of "driving," or how a car works by considering its parts separately.

In the general experimental psychology, the anti-consciousness behaviorist stance started to relax in the mid-1970s when researchers began to tackle issues like controlled and automatic processing (Shiffrin & Schneider, 1977), attentional selection (Kahneman, 1973), and unconscious perception (Marcel, 1983), leading to recognition that consciousness is "respectable, useful, and probably necessary" (Mandler, 1975). Now, the legitimacy of the topic is fully reestablished and "everyone who is conscious, is studying consciousness" (Churchland, 2005).

Social cognition researchers have always been in the game of understanding "consciousness," though, often with the goal of demonstrating its limits. Thus, a pioneering study showed that a stimulus' value can be enhanced via its unconscious mere exposure (Kunst-Wilson & Zajonc, 1980). Another pioneering study showed that people's conscious beliefs about the causes of their own behavior can be at odds with actual causes (Nisbett & Wilson, 1977). These early studies opened the way to a wealth of demonstrations of unconscious influences on social perception, affect, reasoning, decision, and behavior (e.g., Bargh, 1989; Wegner, 2002; Wilson, 2002). Some researchers became so excited about these findings that they began to argue that "most of a person's everyday life is determined not by their conscious intentions and deliberate choices but by mental processes that are put into motion by features of the environment and that operate outside of conscious awareness and guidance" (Bargh & Chartrand, 1999, p. 462). Along with all the excitement about the unconscious in social cognition came fascination with all things "implicit" – perception, learning, attitudes, self-esteem, self-concepts, stereotypes, partisanship, goals, etc. (Greenwald et al., 2002). Perhaps capturing all this, it is telling that the latest *Handbook of Social Psychology* has a chapter on "Automaticity and the unconscious" but no chapter on consciousness (Fiske, Gilbert, & Lindzey, 2010).

However, there have also been attempts to highlight the limits of the unconscious mind. In fact, some cognitive psychologists seem to relish their role as an empirical and theoretical "police" on more spectacular abilities attributed to the unconscious in social cognition (Kihlstrom, 2008; Merikle & Reingold, 1998; Shanks, 2005, 2006). Some critiques of the scientific as well as public misconceptions about the unconscious also came from within social psychology (e.g., Greenwald, 1992). Interestingly, there has been fairly constant interest within social psychology in processes underlying conscious self-control (Metcalfe & Mischel, 1999) and in the questions of self-regulation and, more recently, "free will" (Baumeister, 2008; Schooler, 2010). Recently, social psychologists have also become more interested in the question of the social origins of consciousness – an interesting return to ideas of Mead and Vygotski (e.g., Baumeister & Masicampo, 2010).

A few historic remarks on metacognition

The history of ideas about metacognition is a bit less oscillatory. Some of this is because the basic concept of metacognition carries less philosophical baggage. After all, few doubt that people have some capacity to think about their own mental states, skills, and capacities. Consequently, there is little controversy in the science of metacognition, understood as an effort to uncover the relation between people's mental states and their beliefs about those mental states (Koriat, 2006).

Specifically, since the time of Piaget, psychologists have wanted to know how much children, and adults, know about their own cognitive processes and skills (comprehension, memory,

emotion, intelligence), and how they can improve them to make their cognitive functioning more efficient. Accordingly, research on the developmental and educational aspect of metacognition has a long history (Flavell, 1979). This history continues to have resonance today. For example, there has recently been some enthusiasm about a Vygotsky-inspired curriculum ("tools-of-the mind") which, among other things, teaches children self-knowledge and self-regulation skills in a social setting (Diamond et al., 2007).

Somewhat trickier problems arise when metacognition invokes concepts such as "a sense of uncertainty," "feeling-of-knowing," "tip-of-the-tongue," or "sense of agency" (Koriat, 2006; Nelson, 1996). These require stronger commitment to a view of metacognition as a particular kind of inward-directed, self-reflective, metaconscious capacity. This capacity is a necessarily complex skill, as it involves re-representing one's own current thoughts (i.e., in addition to thoughts, having thoughts about those thoughts). Also, this capacity is necessarily introspective, implying rich subjectivity, with the ability to discern subtle internal states (e.g., a feeling that one knows the answer, without being able to think of the answer right now). These mentalistic and introspective elements of metacognition make some researchers uncomfortable. But explanations of performance on tests of "metacognitive abilities" that do not postulate any kind of access to introspective "private" information have trouble explaining some basic data (e.g., why first-person observers are so much better in making metacognitive judgments than third-party observers; Jameson et al., 1993). Furthermore, as we will elaborate below, it is hard to non-introspectively explain the main metacognitive issues that we will discuss here, which have to do with a person waxing and waning out of "metacognitive" awareness as a function of her attention to the direction of her own thoughts (Schooler, 2002). As a result, the metacognitive perspective is increasingly gaining in popularity, including in social cognition. Since about the mid-1990s there have been many conferences, books, and papers dedicated to social metacognition and several comprehensive reviews are available (Jost, Kruglanski, & Nelson, 1998; Petty, Briñol, Tormala, & Wegener, 2007; Schwarz, 2004).

Definition and distinctions

But what exactly is "consciousness" – with and without the "meta"? Some writers on consciousness devote pages to the elucidation of different meanings (e.g., Zeeman, 2002), but we will highlight only two different senses in which the term appears in psychological literature.

This will also allow us to briefly comment on some current debates in social cognition.

Conscious as "awake and mindful"

The word "conscious" can refer to a global state of an individual. One use of this word is similar to "awake" or "vigilant," as opposed to "asleep" or "comatose." The sleepy–vigilant dimension is typically investigated by neurologists, though some interesting social cognition studies have shown that anesthetized patients form implicit, but not explicit, memory for events during surgery (Kihlstrom et al., 1990). A more relevant meaning of "conscious" as a description of a global state refers to a "mindful," as opposed to a "robot-like," dimension. In that sense, being conscious is the ability to have subjective experiences, wishes, desires, and complex thoughts, and to perform flexible, self-initiated, purposeful behaviors. For example, patients in a persistent vegetative state (PVS) maintain regular sleep–wake cycles, respond to simple stimulation (e.g., withdraw their hand from sharp objects), yet are not considered conscious and possessive of "personhood" by medical experts. This is because PVS patients are unable to make choices, process complex information, show flexible behavior, and initiate purposive actions (Laureys et al., 2002). Interesingly, some recent work that investigated everyday criteria for attribution of a "mind" found that college students basically use two dimensions in their decisions – capacity for agency and capacity for experience – and that these dimension predict how much the "organism" is valued (Gray, Gray, & Wegner, 2007).

It is interesting to contrast the above medical, legal, and everyday view that conscious experience and purposeful action is essential for "personhood" with the dominant view in social cognition that minimizes the role of consciousness in complex thought, choice, and purposive behavior. We actually doubt that, despite some radical "anti-consciousness" declarations in articles and chapters, modern social cognition researchers privately believe there is little distinction between people and complex robots. We also noticed that in informal discussion those researchers readily concede that only *some* thoughts, attitudes, goals or decisions are unconscious, and that only *sometimes* a sense of voluntary control is illusory. We will return to this issue later.

Conscious as "subjectively experienced" and "available for report and intentional use"

A major cluster of meanings for "conscious" centers on the subjective status of a particular mental content (perception, thought, or feeling). First, being conscious of x means having x represented in subjective experience – it "feels like something" to be in a conscious state of, say, seeing red (as opposed to just unconsciously reacting to red). Second, being conscious of x means having x potentially available to report and to use in intentional control of behavior. It is in that second sense that psychologists are interested in whether there are unconscious perceptions, memories, goals, attitudes, or emotions (Bargh, 1989; Greenwald, 1992; Winkielman & Berridge, 2004).

Metaconsciousness

The interest in what makes certain mental content "conscious," and what makes it available for report and control, binds together the research on consciousness with research on metacognition. As mentioned earlier, much of the work under the heading of metacognition simply asks about a person's beliefs about her own comprehension, memory, intelligence, etc. However, other researchers, including one of us in particular (J.W.S.), are interested in metacognition as it reveals the ability (and failures) of human thought to represent itself. Specifically, about a decade ago, Schooler (2001, 2002, Schooler & Schreiber, 2004) proposed a distinction between conscious thoughts that occur without the additional element of explicit self-reflection, and thoughts that are accompanied by the explicit representation of having a thought. That is, mental content could be "experientially conscious," a constituent of ongoing experience, without being explicitly reflected upon. One example of this is the experience of mind-wandering while reading where people can temporarily fail to notice that their eyes are moving across the page but their mind is completely elsewhere. But, mental content can also be "metaconscious" (or "meta-aware") and explicitly represented as a content of one's own consciousness. As for example, when one suddenly realizes that one has been mind-wandering instead of paying attention to what was being read. It is this type of consciousness that is typically assessed when an experimenter asks participants questions like, "What are you thinking about now?", "What goal are you currently pursuing?" or "How happy do you feel right now?" An example of metaconscious affect would be feeling happy and at the same time having an articulated thought: "I am happy now" (Schooler, Ariely, & Loewenstein, 2003; Schooler & Mauss, 2010).

The above distinction between consciousness and metaconsciousness is allied with some terms that have been introduced over the years. For example, it roughly corresponds to the distinction between "first-order" and "second-order" consciousness. For example, Lambie and Marcel (2002) argued that individuals with alexithymia have a first-order experience of emotions but lack a second-order awareness of the fact that they are experiencing the emotions. However, it is also worth noting also that others use the term "second-order consciousness" in a manner that does not directly map on to the notion of metaconsciousness as used by Schooler and colleagues. For example, philosopher Ned Block (1995) introduced a distinction between phenomenal consciousness (first order) and access consciousness (second order), which resembles a distinction between "perceptual vs conceptual" content. This diverges from the present view, in which both perceptual and conceptual content can become metaconscious. Similarly, a popular distinction in social cognition concerns "construal levels" (see Chapter 12), but again we propose that information from any construal level can become "metaconscious." Finally, Rosenthal (1986) has emphasized a philosophical distinction between first-order and higher-order mental states. In his view, consciousness (of any kind) only occurs when a mental representation is accompanied by a higher-order state explicitly articulating the content of a first-order thought. This is different from our view that first-order mental states can be conscious, even when they are not accompanied by explicit knowledge of their occurrence. For further discussion of these issues, see Winkielman and Schooler (2011).

Functions of consciousness and metaconsciousness

A central assumption in social cognition is that mental information is represented on several levels. Accordingly, much research attention focuses on understanding how these different levels relate to each other (Smith & DeCoster, 2000; Strack & Deutsch, 2004). Here, we ask what distinguishes unconscious, conscious, and metaconscious representations. This question touches on a more general problem of the purpose of consciousness – a problem that has received a variety of functional and mechanistic answers in the psychological literature. In general, researchers have emphasized the idea that consciousness is associated with (i) special access to mental content, and (ii) special functions that can be performed on this content.

Conscious access

Several theories posit that consciousness is a representational system characterized by special access to mental content. One useful framework is the Global Workspace Theory, which proposes

that consciousness functions to allow communication and coordination between the many isolated, parallel sub-processors in the human mind (Baars, 1988). Consciousness constitutes a "global workspace" where various local processors can "broadcast" their outputs and talk to each other in a common internal code. As a result, the previously independent and isolated local processes can coordinate, sequence, and structure their actions, thus helping the organism achieving its goals. For example, by representing tactile, visual, and auditory processes in a common matrix, the putative global workspace allows for the identification of novel cross-modal and cross-temporal connections (e.g., "The sequence of musical notes I just heard has the same pattern as the sequence of colored lights I saw before."). Of course, like almost anything else, cross-modal integration can be automatized into unconscious, suggesting that access in the global workspace might be only needed to initially connect novel sensations and responses. More importantly, the global accessibility of conscious representations makes them available for verbal report and for high-level processes such as conscious judgment, reasoning, and the planning and guiding of action.

But what gives representations conscious or "global" access? Cognitive researchers often emphasize the role of representation "strength" (Cleermans, 2005). The notion of "strength" captures the idea that representations require a certain stability and quality before they can enter working memory, where they can be actively maintained, and become accessible for potential report. One determinant of "strength" is activation, which in turn is determined by many factors, such as stimulus energy (longer presented items are more likely to become conscious than briefly presented items) and recency (more recent items are more likely to become conscious than older items), and so forth. Representational strength is also influenced by focused attention – a perceptual amplifier and selector of events (conscious and non-conscious) that fall within its scope. Thus, an objectively very weak stimulus can reach consciousness, if it receives attentional processing and there is little perceptual competition (Breitmeyer & Ogmen, 2006). Interestingly, recent research shows, somewhat paradoxically, that focused conscious attention may be necessary for some unconscious processes (Koch & Tsuchiya, 2007). For example, subliminal priming is enhanced by attentional cuing of location (Sumner et al., 2006) and limbic responses are stronger if brief affective stimuli fall in the scope of focused attention (Pessoa et al., 2002). These observations may explain why so many successful subliminal priming paradigms in social cognition require that the subject is paying attention to a specific area on the screen (even if the prime remains invisible). It may also explain why many social-cognitive studies on unconscious processes use "unobtrusive" rather than subliminal priming. In those studies, participants are exposed to stimuli in a definitely conscious, attended, and prolonged fashion (e.g., as a part of a sentence-unscrambling task or a crossword puzzle), with the "unconscious" element being the relevance of the task to subsequent judgment or the importance of a particular stimulus dimension. In short, focused attention might be a precondition for many unconscious effects.

Another factor that modulates whether or not mental content is conscious has to do with ana-tomical and functional disconnection. Thus, a visual representation in blindsight patients can be strong (e.g., it can drive pointing behavior), but remains unconscious because it is restricted to lower visual pathways (Weiskrantz, 1986). Similarly, habits (e.g., biking) may involve repre-sentations that are very robust, but unconscious, because they are only instantiated in the motor system (Cleermans, 2005). A functional discon-nection may occur when input fails to cohere with currently processed information. For example, a distinct, prolonged, unusual, and dynamic event (e.g., a gorilla slowly walking through a room of people passing balls to each other) can remain unconscious, when participants "look" at the scene and closely attend to its more familiar features (Simons & Chabris, 1999). One explana-tion of this "blindness" is that the event is incom-patible with the current mental model (i.e., generalized schema) of the situation or with par-ticipants' current perceptual goals.

Finally, there is some exciting neuroscientific research on the mechanisms of conscious access. Some evidence suggests that consciousness repre-sents a form of multiregional activation, which is perhaps integrated by oscillatory activity (Tononi, 2004). For example, conscious perception of a stimulus is associated with synchronous activation of higher associative cortices, particularly pari-etal, prefrontal, and anterior cingulate areas, whereas unconscious perception is associated only with a local activation (Dehaene et al., 2006). Synchronized oscillations may serve as a mecha-nism for binding information in the "global work-space" discussed earlier. Consistent with these ideas, clinical work has shown that the previously mentioned patients in a PVS (awake but uncon-scious) show only localized, modality-specific responses to stimuli, whereas patients in a minimally conscious state show coherent responses across multiple sensory and associative systems (Laureys et al., 2002).

Conscious thinking

Some argue that consciousness enables higher-order, meaning-based, logically well-structured processing of information (Block, 1995; Searle, 1997). In contrast, the unconscious is restricted to simpler, associative forms of processing. This distinction resembles, but does not completely overlap with, "dual process" theories in social cognition. For example, Strack and Deutsch (2004) suggest that social cognition is carried out by two systems: a reflective system that relies on knowl-edge about facts and values, and an impulsive system based on associative links and motivational orientations. The differential information base upon which the two systems rely determines the types of responses they engender. The reflective system, drawing on propositions about the world, leads to responses based on rational considera-tions. In contrast, the impulsive system, drawing on associations and impulses, leads to non-reasoned actions.

Does processing of meaning require conscious-ness? This question is a subject of long debate, which touches on tricky issues of the relation between semantic cognition and associationism (McClelland & Rogers, 2003). It is now widely accepted that subliminally presented pictures and words can activate related semantic and affective categories (Greenwald, Draine, & Abrams, 1996; Marcel, 1983). Even subliminally presented single digits can activate magnitude information (Dehaene et al., 2006). Thus, there is no doubt that complex content can be unconsciously activated across meaning dimension. However, the evidence for unconscious semantic processing, rather than automatic activation, is sparse. For example, unconscious priming responds to partial- rather than whole-word information (e.g., fragments of affectively negative words "smut" and "bile" prime the affectively positive word "smile"), is not sensitive to basic operations like negations ("not," "un-," or "dis-"), and cannot process two-digit numbers (Abrahms & Greenwald, 2000). One may wonder whether these limitations arise because subliminal presentations afford very weak stimulus input. However, similar results hold when the input is conscious and only conscious processing capacity is reduced. Thus, processing relational information such as negation ("no dis-ease") or causality ("smoke causes fire") requires conscious capacity, whereas processing informa-tion about association does not (Deutsch, Gawronski, & Strack, 2006; Hummel & Holyoak, 2003). In a straightforward but telling demonstra-tion of this point, DeWall et al. (2008) presented participants with a standard set of graduate record examination (GRE) analytical problems, and asked them to solve these problems under typical conditions or under cognitive load. Not surprisingly, loaded participants did much worse.

Note that even if some complex cognitive skills can ultimately be automatized, it does not follow that the initial acquisition and mastery of these skills is possible without consciousness. For example, most adults can do basic multiplication table automatically, via associative recall (2 × 2 is 4). However, no one believes that the unconscious actually does multiplication. It is generally thought that highly trained operations become automatic over time and can eventually be performed by "dumb" associative retrieval (Logan, 1998; Rickard, 2005; Smith & DeCoster, 2000). As an example, solving a novel mathematical problem, like 78 × 56, is not helped by "thinking about it unconsciously," under cognitive load, or by "sleeping on it."

All this seems to suggest that the unconscious is rather "dumb" (Loftus & Klinger, 1992). Yet, this image has recently been challenged by claims that complex decision are often better made by "unconscious thought" (Dijksterhuis et al., 2006). For example, in one study, participants were presented with 12 attributes for each of four different cars (e.g., "car A has a cup holder," "car B is safe"). That is, participants learned about 48 attributes total. One car had 75% positive attributes, two had 50% positive attributes, and one had 25% positive attributes. Note that the presentation of car–attribute pairs was all mixed, which makes it rather hard to keep track of all the information. Participants were then asked to choose the best car. One group of participants (termed "conscious thinkers") made their decision after 4 minutes of deliberation, and another group (termed "unconscious thinkers") after 4 minutes of engaging in a distracting anagram-solving task. Interestingly, the results showed that 60% of "unconscious thinkers" chose the ostensibly "best" car (i.e., the one with the greatest number of positive attributes), while only 20% of the "conscious thinkers" did so. For the authors, these results show that the unconscious thinking not only facilitates decisions but also is actually better than conscious thinking. To quote: "It should benefit the individual to think consciously about simple matters and to delegate thinking about more complex matters to the unconscious" (Dijksterhuis et al., 2006, p. 1007).

However, other interpretations are possible. First, it is not clear why distraction by anagrams eliminates conscious thought, rather than reducing its amount. If so, perhaps distraction is advantageous because it helps to prevent overthinking (cf. Rey, Goldstein, & Perruchet, 2009). This is not unlike other "verbal overshadowing" effects, to which we return later (Wilson & Schooler, 1991). Also, reduction in capacity may encourage a reliance on simple heuristics that are more effective in that particular case. In fact, when the "best" solution to a problem is to simply count the number of positive (+) vs negative (−) attributes, engaging in deeper processing that focuses on the attribute meaning (cup holder vs safety) might lead to a suboptimal decision making (Gigerenzer & Goldstein, 1996). Accordingly, the benefits of "unconscious thought" may only apply to so-called "linear integration problems," where the attribute content (cup holder vs safety) either does not matter, or can be consciously translated into attribute weights before unconscious "thought." Also, note that it is strange that giving people 4 minutes to think consciously about a simple choice produces such a low response – only 20% correct in the conscious thinking group! After all, it is not that complicated to figure out that a car with 12 (75%) positive attributes is better than a car with 4 (25%) positive attributes. This suggests that the problem encountered by "conscious thinkers" may simply lie in greater confusion about the original attributes and their assignments to cars – perhaps because recall is susceptible to primacy or recency effects and interference by the intermediate task (Shanks, 2006). It may also suggest that conscious thinkers have no problem at all. After all, there are some normative issues with this task, as it is not clear whether a response that simply maximizes + vs − is optimal for most subjects in these types of task (e.g., Why is it best to treat cup holders and safety as equivalent attributes?). In short, while recent evidence does suggest some limitations to extensive deliberation, the degree to which this research implicates truly intelligent unconscious processing remains to be determined. Some doubts about the power of "unconscious thought" are also raised by the fact that the finding of superiority of the decisions in the distraction conditions, over control conditions, is empirically fragile (Acker, 2008). Perhaps reflecting these critiques, more recent writings tone down the radical earlier claims about the general superiority of unconscious processes for decision making (Bongers & Dijksterhuis, 2009).

Conscious control

Consciousness is associated not only with special access to mental content but also with special operations that can be performed on this content. Several of these operations fall under the umbrella name "control," thus linking consciousness to what cognitive scientists call "executive functions" (Norman & Shallice, 1986). One aspect of control is selection. Thus, conscious content can be preferentially attended to and maintained in working memory or discarded if not needed. Another aspect of control is intentionality. Action can be deliberately started and stopped, or can be delayed until appropriate conditions materialize. Scheduling conflicts can be resolved, and new hierarchies can be established. Finally, with control comes flexibility. Thus, extant mental content can be redeployed in adaptive, non-routine ways, and old response chains can be broken up and rearranged. This simple point was recently elegantly demonstrated in a study where participants had to come up with novel titles, musical improvisations, or interesting drawings. Not surprisingly, participants under cognitive load produced repetitive, inflexible, and uninspiring works (Baumeister, Schmeichel, DeWall, & Vohs, 2007).

One interesting aspect of conscious control is its restricted capacity. Thus, only few elements can be consciously manipulated at any one time, operations must be performed in a serial rather than parallel fashion, and processing is subject to severe bottlenecks (Pashler, 1998). In fact, it is hard to be overwhelmed by the power of the unconscious given how many accidents are caused by ill-advised attempts to multitask (e.g., talking on the cell phone while driving; Levy, Pashler, & Boer, 2006).

Of course, not all forms of control are conscious. The world is filled with very complex mechanical devices that automatically monitor the conditions of subordinate processes and adjust their operation (Shinskey, 1979). The human body has many systems of complex control loops (e.g., homeostatic temperature and blood sugar mechanisms). Furthermore, several "mental" processes automatically adjust their operation based on contextual conditions (Carver & Scheier, 1990). Thus, people unconsciously regulate eye movements to facilitate text processing (Reichle, Pollatsek, Fisher, & Rayner, 1998) and unconsciously adjust hand movements to capture the desired object (Triesch et al., 2003). Finally, people are typically unaware of several layers of control required for coherent speaking and writing.

Reflecting the preceding, and other considerations, Bargh (1989) pointed out that it should be possible to dissociate consciousness and control in social cognition. Subsequently, various forms of automatic control have been proposed (Fitzsimons & Bargh, 2004). One case is the pursuit of "unconscious goals" (see also Chapter 5). Evidence comes from studies where individuals who are primed subliminally or unobtrusively with goal-related words (e.g., "cooperate," "achieve," "memorize") show corresponding adjustment in their behavior (e.g., show more helpful behavior, solve more problems, or remember more details). Furthermore, these adjustments appear to be sensitive to conditions under which the goal is appropriate and to track success at goal pursuit. These findings are interesting, but note that the type of "control" explored in these studies is rather

different than in research on executive functions. First, the "unconscious goal" paradigms rely on an unobtrusive activation of preformulated, standard goals, rather than on the formulation of novel goals. Second, those goals do not require participants to overcome stronger alternative behavior (e.g., go against a prepotent tendency), but operate in situations where behavioral choices are already predetermined (participants can either cooperate or compete, with the likelihood of either action relatively equal). Third, the outcomes are fairly unimportant and do not require participants to reflect on the meaning or consequences of their actions. Accordingly, we suspect that many effects attributed to unconscious goals simply reflect the influence of primes on the interpretation of a vague experimental situation, including giving participants an idea of what and how much they are supposed to do (see Förster, Lieberman, & Friedman, 2007 for discussion). Furthermore, in some "unconscious goal" paradigms participants could also be actually conscious of the goal, but just confused about its source. As we discuss later, there are also multiple ways in which goals could be conscious, but not verbally reported because of temporal and translation dissociations.

Finally, while unconscious goal activation clearly operates under some conditions, unconscious goals have yet to be shown to possess anything approaching the potency or flexibility of conscious goals. To illustrate this, imagine a following experiment. Participants are in a room with both food and drink. Participants are first told once, consciously, that their goal is to eat. Next, participants are given an unconscious priming procedure with multiple words related to the goal of drinking. We predict that very few, if any participants, would behave in accordance with the more recent, but unconscious "goal" to drink.

Indeed, in addition to offering a skewed perspective on the role of consciousness in mediating behaviors, the present trend towards attributing the bulk of human action to unconscious mechanisms may have undesirable effects on people's self-regulatory ability. Evidence supporting this concern comes from Vohs and Schooler (2008), who asked some participants to read an excerpt from Francis Crick's *The Astonishing Hypothesis* that articulates the view that conscious control is an epiphenomenon; i.e., that people lack any meaningful sort of free will. Compared to controls, participants exposed to the message that conscious control is illusory behaved more immorally on a passive cheating task. Moreover, their increased cheating was mediated by decreased belief in free will. In a second experiment, exposure to deterministic statements led participants to overpay themselves on a cognitive test, relative to participants who were exposed to statements endorsing free will. Of course, such findings do not speak to the actual efficacy of conscious control. Nevertheless, they do raise concerns about the impact that a scientific dismissal of conscious control might have on the population at large, and thus further highlight the importance of not overstating the degree to which science has shown consciousness to be impotent (Schooler, 2010; Shariff, Vohs, & Schooler, 2008).

META-CONSCIOUS MONITORING

As we have discussed, some forms of control might be automatized and unconscious, but others clearly involve consciousness. In fact, one form of control may require explicitly articulating the content of the conscious state to bring it into metaconsciousness. Thus, periodically, the mind encounters situations which require more resource-dependent conscious monitoring processes. In effect, this occurs anytime one explicitly attempts to answer the question, "What am I thinking or feeling?" Given that the answer requires an explicit representation of one's state, over and above the state itself, it offers individuals the opportunity to step out of the situation, which may be critical for many of the innovative behaviors of which individuals are capable. However, it also raises the possibility that in the re-description process individuals might get it wrong.

There are two kinds of dissociations between levels of mental representation that follow from the claim that metaconsciousness involves the intermittent re-representation of the contents of consciousness (Schooler, 2002). *Temporal dissociations* occur when metaconsciousness temporarily fails to take stock of the current contents of thought (e.g., failing to notice that one is mind-wandering during reading). *Translation dissociations* occur if the meta-representation process misrepresents the original experience. Such dissociations are particularly likely when one verbally reflects on non-verbal experiences or attempts to takes stock of ambiguous experiences. Several interesting social-cognitive phenomena illustrate these metacognitive dissociations.

Temporal dissociations

Mind-wandering

We suspect that all readers have had the experience of suddenly realizing that, despite their best intentions and the fact that their eyes have continued to move across the page, they have no idea what they have been reading. Such examples

suggests that tacit monitoring systems failed to catch the mind's drifting, and that it takes a higher-level explicit monitoring process to take stock of the specific contents of thought and alert one to the fact that they have wandered off task. Over the last several years, Schooler and colleagues have used the mind-wandering phenomenon to examine the function of meta-awareness in a domain where mind-wandering is antithetical to success (see Smallwood & Schooler, 2006 for a review). Specifically, Schooler, Reichle, and Halpern (2005) developed a paradigm to identify temporal lapses of meta-awareness during the attentionally demanding task of reading. In this research, participants read passages of text and indicated every time they caught their minds zoning out. They were then asked whether they had been aware that they had been zoning out prior to reporting it. In a second condition, participants were additionally probed intermittently and asked to indicate whether they had been zoning out at that moment. The results revealed that participants: (1) frequently caught themselves zoning out during reading; (2) were still often caught zoning out by the probes; and (3) frequently reported that they had been unaware that they had been zoning out, particularly when they were caught by the probes. These findings demonstrate that individuals frequently lack meta-awareness of drifting off, even when they are specifically instructed to be vigilant for such lapses.

Additional studies have elucidated the distinct processes associated with the occurrence of mind-wandering (as revealed by probe-caught episodes) and meta-awareness of mind-wandering (as revealed by self-caught episodes). These studies also examined the role that self-awareness may play in the transition from consciousness to meta-consciousness. For example, Sayette, Reichle and Schooler (2009) examined the impact of alcohol on participants' self-caught and probe-caught mind-wandering during reading. Alcohol was an excellent candidate as a variable likely to impact meta-awareness, given its well-established capacity to reduce people's more general self-awareness (e.g. Hull, 1981). In this study, half of the participants received a real alcoholic beverage, whereas the other half of participants received a placebo that they believed contained alcohol. Participants then engaged in a reading task, in which they read *War and Peace* while their mind-wandering was assessed using both the probe-caught and self-caught procedures. Results showed that alcohol had different effects on self-caught vs probe-caught mind-wandering. Despite mind-wandering more than twice as often as participants in the placebo group (as revealed by the probe measure), participants in the alcohol group were no more likely (and, indeed, were slightly less likely) to catch themselves in the act. One can argue that participants in the alcohol group should have had many more opportunities to catch themselves, but they did not catch themselves more often than the sober participants. Apparently, they were impaired in their ability to notice mind-wandering episodes, whereas sober participants were more capable of detecting mind-wandering when it occurred.

A related study by Sayette, Schooler, & Reichle (2010) further illustrates the value of the self-caught/probe-caught methodology for assessing the conditions that impact on meta-awareness. This study also explored the role of motivation in meta-awareness. Specifically, this study focused on the effect of cigarette craving on people's mind-wandering and their meta-awareness thereof. Like alcohol consumption, craving is a factor that might reasonably be expected to impact on meta-awareness. This is because craving may engage working memory and self-regulation resources that otherwise might be directed toward noticing that one has become distracted, thereby simultaneously increasing the occurrence of one's mind-wandering and decreasing the probability of catching it. To explore this issue, Sayette et al. employed the reading task described above with smokers, but in this case half of the participants were induced into a craving state by refraining from smoking for at least 6 hours prior to the experiment. All participants were then given the reading task with both self-caught and probe-caught assessment of mind-wandering. The results revealed that craving significantly impacted on participants' meta-awareness of their mind-wandering. Despite mind-wandering more than three times as often as participants in the no-craving condition, participants in the craving condition were not more likely to spontaneously catch themselves mind-wandering.

These findings suggest that craving, like alcohol, disrupts individuals' meta-awareness of the current contents of thought. In so doing, they also highlight possible reasons why it is so difficult to self-regulate during craving states. While conventional wisdom holds that individuals are fully aware of their cravings, some researchers suggest that cravings can occur unconsciously (Robinson & Berridge, 1993). This debate assumes that cravings must be either conscious or unconscious. The alternative framework suggested here, in which consciousness is divided into experiential consciousness (contents of experience) and meta-consciousness (explicit awareness of the contents of consciousness) suggests that individuals can be conscious of craving but lack metaconsciousness of the fact that they are craving. Such a mental state, in turn, might contribute to relapses. Considerable research suggests that relapse behaviors may occur absent-mindedly, with individuals

failing to explicitly notice that they are relapsing (Tiffany, 1990). Traditionally, the occurrence of absent-minded relapses was taken to suggest that cravings need not trigger relapse. However, the view suggested by the present perspective is that absent-minded relapses may be associated with craving states in which one lacks metaconsciousness of the cravings (see Cheyene, Carriere, & Smilek, 2006). By simultaneously promoting absent-mindedness and decreasing meta-awareness, the unnoticed craving state may induce a unique condition in which individuals are maximally likely to engage in a relapse behavior and minimally likely to notice themselves doing so.

Another approach for investigating the role of meta-awareness in mind-wandering is simply asking participants after probe-caught mind-wandering episodes whether or not they had been previously aware that their minds had drifted. Although it is not self-evident that participants would necessarily be able to accurately reflect on the prior meta-awareness of their mental states, a variety of studies suggest that they can accurately discern whether or not they were meta-aware of their mind-wandering, as evidenced by the consistent differences between mind-wandering episodes characterized as occurring with vs without meta-awareness. For example, in one study participants read text one word at a time and were warned that it would periodically stop making sense – become gibberish (Schooler, McSpadden, Reichle, & Smallwood, 2010). We found that although participants typically noticed the occurrence of gibberish as soon as it began, if they failed to notice it right away, they often continued for several sentences before they did. Moreover, if participants were probed following extended durations of missing gibberish, they were markedly more likely to report mind-wandering without meta-awareness than if they were probed at random intervals. Similarly, Smallwood et al. (2008) found that if individuals reported mind-wandering without meta-awareness prior to encountering clues in a Sherlock Holmes story, they were markedly less likely to solve the whodunnit. Mind-wandering with meta-awareness proved far less disruptive to the construction of a mental model.

When mind-wandering episodes are characterized as having proceeded without meta-awareness, they are not only more disruptive to task performance but also more neurocognitively distinct from on-task performance. In a recent study (Christoff et al., 2009), we scanned participants during a non-demanding vigilance task in which they had to respond to every digit that appeared on the screen with the exception of a specific rarely presented target item for which they had to withhold a response. Because the targets are relatively rare, it is common to mind-wander during this task and then accidently respond when a target is presented. In this study, participants were periodically probed and asked whether they had been mind-wandering, and if so whether or not they had been aware of that fact. Two sets of regions were more active prior to periods in which individuals reported having been mind-wandering relative to having been on-task. One was the default network (including the medial prefrontal cortex (PFC), posterior cingulate cortex/precuneus region and the temporoparietal junction) which is known to become increasingly recruited with decreasing external task demands. This result is interesting, as the default network is often implicated in stimulus-independent thought (Mason et al., 2007). The second set of regions was the executive network, including the dorsal anterior cingulate cortex (ACC) and the dorsolateral PFC (DLPFC), which becomes activated when individuals engage in demanding mental activity. Of particular interest to the present discussion was the further finding that the discrepancy between areas of neural activity associated with on-task vs off-task thought was markedly more pronounced when individuals lacked meta-awareness of the fact that they were mind-wandering.

The fact that participants' awareness of their mind-wandering impacted on the magnitude of discrepancy between on-task vs off-task thinking suggests potentially important implications for conceptualizing metaconsciousness. First, it reveals the robustness of the distinction between those mental states that are accompanied by meta-awareness and those that are not. One might easily have conjectured that participants would have a hard time reliably characterizing their mind-wandering as having been associated with meta-awareness. However, these findings suggest that this distinction was easy for participants to make. After all, mind-wandering episodes accompanied by meta-awareness (vs no meta-awareness) were associated with different patterns of brain activation. Second, one might have thought that when participants were mind-wandering without realizing it, that their brains would show relatively little activity compared to being on-task. To the contrary, it was during periods of mind-wandering without meta-awareness that individuals showed the maximum distinctive regions of brain activation. Apparently, while mind-wandering without meta-awareness may be especially counterproductive to ongoing task performance, the mind is far from being empty and rather is engaging in vigorous brain activity.

Well-being appraisals

We often fail to explicitly notice our own emotional states (e.g., sullenness, cheerfulness) until someone points them out to us. If we commonly lack metaconsciousness of affective states, the induction of continuous metaconsciousness may alter the quality of affective experience. Schooler et al. (2003) explored this issue by asking participants to report on-line happiness while listening to hedonically ambiguous music (Stravinsky's *Rite of Spring*). The results showed that continuous hedonic monitoring reduced individuals' post-music ratings of happiness, relative to a condition in which participants listened to music without monitoring. The fact that hedonic monitoring altered participants' experience suggests that (by default) individuals are, at most, only intermittently metaconscious of their affective state.

Automaticity

Automatic behaviors are often assumed to be unconscious (Bargh, 1997; Wood et al., 2002). However, there is a peculiarity to this designation. Consider a person driving automatically while engaging in some secondary task (e.g., talking). Although such driving is compromised, one still experiences the road at some level. Thus, a more appropriate characterization of the consciousness of automatic behaviors may be that they are experienced but lack metaconsciousness, the latter only taking hold when individuals run into difficulty.

Unwanted thoughts

Wegner (1994) suggested that individuals possess an implicit monitoring system that tracks unwanted thoughts (e.g., of a white bear) in order to veer away from them. But what exactly is this system monitoring? Wegner suggests that it is monitoring the contents of preconsciousness (i.e., thoughts that are near, but below, the threshold of consciousness). However, another, and perhaps more intuitive, possibility is that these systems actually monitor the contents of consciousness itself: that is, perhaps individuals can consciously think about a white bear, without explicitly realizing that they are doing so. In this case, the monitoring system can catch the unwanted thought and raise it to the level of meta-awareness, in effect saying: "There you go again, thinking about that unwanted thought." Recent evidence for this account comes from a study in which participants were asked to try not to think about a previous romantic relationship while reading or while simply sitting quietly (Fishman, Smallwood, & Schooler, 2006). As in standard unwanted-thought paradigms, participants were asked to self-report every time they noticed an unwanted thought coming to mind. In addition, however, they were periodically randomly asked whether at that particular moment they were having the unwanted thought.

The results revealed that participants frequently experienced "unnoticed unwanted thoughts" about their previous relationship, which they experienced but failed to notice until they were probed. Furthermore, these unnoticed unwanted thoughts were detrimental to participants' performance on a test of the reading material, suggesting again that they were conscious. Intriguingly, participants for whom the unwanted thoughts carried emotional weight (i.e., they still wished they were in the relationship) were less likely than participants who no longer wanted to be in the relationship to notice the thoughts themselves, and more likely to be caught having the thought. This suggests that cognitive defenses do not banish disturbing thoughts to the unconscious, but rather prevent us from reflecting on them (Schooler, 2001).

Translation dissociations

The idea that metaconsciousness involves a re-representation of the contents of consciousness suggests that, as with any recoding process, some information may get lost or distorted in translation. The likelihood of noise perturbing the translation process may be particularly great when individuals: (1) verbally reflect on inherently non-verbal experiences; (2) are motivated to misrepresent their experience; or (3) possess a lay theory that is inconsistent with their actual experience.

Verbal reflection

Some experiences are inherently difficult to put into words: the structure of a face, the taste of a wine, the complex tonalities of Stravinsky, and the intuitions leading to insights. If individuals attempt to verbalize these inherently non-verbal and holistic experiences, the resulting re-representations may fail to do justice to the original experience. Schooler and Engstler-Schooler (1990) examined the effects of describing faces, which, because of their holistic nature, are notoriously difficult to capture in words. Participants viewed a face and subsequently either described it in detail or engaged in an unrelated verbal activity. When given a recognition test that included a different photograph of the target face, along with similar distractors, verbalization participants performed substantially worse than controls. This effect of verbalization, termed "verbal overshadowing," has been found in variety of other domains of visual memory (Schooler, Fiore, & Brandimonte, 1997), including colors (Schooler & Engstler-Schooler, 1990), shapes (Brandimonte, Schooler, & Gabbino, 1997), as well as other modalities such as audition (Schooler et al., 1997) and taste (Melcher & Schooler, 1996). Similar disruptions

resulting from verbal reflection have also been observed in various other domains hypothesized to rely on non-verbal cognition. Thinking aloud during problem solving can disrupt the intuitive processes associated with insight problem solving while having no effect on the logical processes associated with analytical problem solving (Schooler, Ohlsson, & Brooks, 1993). Verbally reflecting on the basis of affective judgments can interfere with the quality of affective decision making, as assessed both by the opinions of experts (Wilson & Schooler, 1991) and by post-choice satisfaction (Wilson, Lisle, Schooler, Hodges, Klaaren, & LaFleur, 1993). Verbally articulating the basis of the match between analogical stories can reduce people's sensitivity to meaningful deep-structure relationships, while increasing their emphasis on superficial surface–structure relationships (Sieck, Quinn, & Schooler, 1999). Of course, in many cases verbal analysis can be helpful. This occurs when experiences are readily translated into words, due either to the nature of the task (e.g., logical problem solving, Schooler et al., 1993) or to individuals' unique verbal expertise (e.g., wine experts, Melcher & Schooler, 1996). However, the process of articulating experiences can sometimes result in translation dissociations, where meta-awareness misrepresents conscious content.

Motivation

In some situations, people may be motivated to misrepresent their experiences to themselves. For example, homophobic individuals may not want to recognize when they are aroused by depictions of homosexual acts (Adams, Wright, & Lohr, 1996): that is, individuals may consciously experience the arousal but, because of their motivation, fail to become meta-aware of it (see also Lambie & Marcel, 2002). Our perspective also suggests a different view of repression. Freud argued that repression prevented unwanted feelings from coming to consciousness, but we would say that it primarily prevents such feelings from reaching meta-awareness (Schooler, 2001; Schooler & Schreiber, 2004).

Stereotyping

The distinction between conscious and metaconscious states also provides a way of potentially reconceptualizing existing findings in the domain of stereotyping. For example, several researchers work with the notion of "aversive racists," defined as individuals who reveal evidence of implicit racism but are not conscious of their racist tendencies (e.g., Gaertner & Dovidio, 1986; Son Hing et al., 2008). This idea speaks directly to the disparities that can emerge when discrepant motivations exist at different levels of consciousness. Aversive racists are identified empirically as being those individuals who score high on racism when gauged with implicit measures – i.e., the Implicit Association Test (IAT) – but low when gauged with explicit measures. Evidence for the importance of this distinction comes from the examination of aversive racists' evaluations of stories depicting other-race target individuals, who vary with respect to the degree to which low liking ratings can be attributed to something else besides race. When aversive racists have no excuse for holding negative attitudes towards other-race individuals (e.g., when the target person is characterized as acting politely), then they behave very much like individuals with no racist tendencies. However, when there is an opportunity to justify their discriminatory behavior in a manner that does not necessarily invoke the label of "racist" (e.g., when the target individual behaves in a slightly unfriendly manner), these individuals do act like racists. Son Hing et al. (2008) suggest that aversive racists behave in this fashion because they hold non-conscious racist views that are inconsistent with their conscious views and can only rely on their racist tendencies when they can avoid construing them as such. However, the distinction between consciousness and metaconsciousness raises another possibility: namely, that when individuals experience racist tendencies, they simply do not recognize this experience due to motivation not to take stock of racist reactions. Accordingly, when confronted with the behaviors of an individual towards whom they have racist attitudes, aversive racists experience negative affect. If a justification for this affect exists that is consistent with their views of themselves (i.e., that the individual behaved somewhat rudely), then they embrace this affect. However, when no such outlet is available, they ignore it. Critical to this account, however, is the notion that aversive racists are actually experiencing the affect; it is simply a matter of whether or not they are prepared to allow themselves to take stock of it. Thus, a reasonable alternative way to characterize aversive racists is to suggest that they experience racism but lack explicit awareness of this experience – or, in the terms of metaconsciousness theory, that they exhibit translation dissociations due to a motivation not to acknowledge their racist tendencies.

Implicit attitudes

The distinction between consciousness and metaconsciousness may also have important implications for the study of implicit attitudes more generally (Greenwald et al., 2002). According to the standard view, attitudes are either consciously held (as revealed by standard attitudinal measures) or else inaccessible to consciousness (as revealed by implicit measures such as the IAT). However, the distinction between consciousness and metaconsciousness raises the possibility that some measures that have been characterized as implicit might instead be conscious but lacking in metaconsciousness. According to this view, there may be some situations in which individuals experience negative attitudes but do not acknowledge them as such, as was suggested as an interpretation of the earlier described findings by Song Hing and colleagues. Some implicit measures may in fact tap such experienced but non-reported attitudes. In contrast, other implicit measures may tap attitudes that are truly unconscious and never experienced. This account may explain why various tests of implicit attitudes such as the IAT versus implicit priming can often be uncorrelated (Gawronski & Payne, 2010). Some tests may be measuring truly unconscious attitudes whereas others may be measuring attitudes that are experienced but occur without meta-awareness.

Faulty theories

Finally, translation dissociations can occur if individuals have a faulty theory about what they should be feeling in a particular situation, which then colors their appraisal of their actual experience. Individuals' theories of how they think they should feel may also color their retrospective appraisal of prior experiences.

We have explored this possibility in the fascinating but controversial domain of childhood memory and childhood happiness. It is likely that at least some aspects of one's answer to the question "How happy was your childhood?" are constructed using one's naïve theories of how one "must have felt" (Skurnik, Schwarz, & Winkielman, 2000). One cue to this assessment comes from cognitive outcomes, such as one's memory for the period, with the bridge linking memory and happiness provided by naïve theories. To investigate this process, Winkielman and Schwarz (2001) first asked participants to recall few (easy task) or many (difficult task) examples from their childhood. Participants were then asked to evaluate the quality of their childhood. After completion of the recall task, but prior to rating their childhood happiness, participants were provided with two different theories. Some participants were told that psychologists have found that a poor childhood memory indicates an unhappy childhood, because many unpleasant experiences are purged from memory. Others were told that psychologists have found that a poor childhood memory indicates a happy childhood, because many unpleasant experiences are ruminated upon. For both groups, it was emphasized that these are poorly supported hypotheses and that the relevant evidence is limited to small and unusual clinical samples, making it worthwhile to test these hypotheses with a general college population. As predicted, participants' ratings of their childhood depended on the naïve theory offered to them and the subjective difficulty of retrieving memories. When participants found it difficult to retrieve childhood events, participants who were told that happy events fade from memory evaluated their childhood as happier than did participants who were told that bad events fade from memory. The opposite happened when the retrieval was easy.

Distortions in retrospective meta-awareness may also be one reason why individuals come to characterize childhood abuse experiences as having been previously forgotten (Schooler, 2001). Recent evidence suggests that characterizations of abuse experiences as having been long forgotten and suddenly remembered may at least sometimes be the result of metacognitive failures in which individuals overestimate the degree to which the memory was previously forgotten (Geraerts et al., 2008, Schooler, 2001). Factors that may contribute to such distortions are faulty theories in which individuals assume that they would surely recall having thought about past trauma, unless it was actively repressed. Evidence in partial support of this view comes from a survey study (Joslyn & Schooler, 2006) in which participants' recollections of prior inappropriate sexual experiences were influenced by the manner in which questions about the experience were asked. Participants were asked to define what experiences constitute sexual abuse either before or after they were asked if those experiences had ever happened to them. Individuals who defined sexual abuse before considering whether they had been abused themselves were more likely to identify themselves as having been abused, and reported being more upset at the time that the event occurred. Apparently, thinking about the experience in the context of sexual abuse invoked theories about how upsetting the experience must have been, which in turn colored the way they recalled feeling at the time. If, as adults, individuals believe they were more traumatized by abuse than they actually were as children, then the experience may not have been as significant at the time, and thus no special forgetting mechanisms may have been required for the experience to have been forgotten.

COGNITION AND AFFECT WITHOUT CONSCIOUSNESS

So far we have emphasized that many mental states are actually conscious, though lacking metacognitive representations. However, there are clearly cases when a mental state has a demonstrable influence on behavior, but cannot be directly accessed by consciousness. It is now almost universally accepted that many perceptual and cognitive operations can occur without individuals being conscious (Kihlstrom, 2007). One classic example comes from research on so-called blindsight patients with damaged primary visual cortex (area V1 of striate cortex) but intact subcortical visual pathways. These patients can discriminate simple visual features (e.g., location, or shape), as revealed in pointing and guessing behavior, while denying any awareness of the discriminated features (Weiskranz, 1986). In that case, the mental representation (e.g., "x is a square") is genuinely unconscious – the patients truly do not know that they "know" what shape was presented. Another classic example is patients with visual agnosia who cannot consciously recognize visual features, but have largely intact sensorimotor abilities, and can pursue actions in response to these "unconscious" features (Milner & Goodale, 1995). As discussed earlier, the social cognition literature is rich with demonstrations of unconscious processing in behavioral experiments (Bargh, 1997).

But what about affect? There is certainly research suggesting that briefly presented affective stimuli can work as unconscious triggers of conscious affective states (Kihlstrom, 2007; Öhman, Flykt, & Lundqvist, 2000; Zajonc, 1994). But can affect itself be consciously inaccessible? In recent years, one strand of our work has focused on exploring a dissociation which occurs when a person is in a demonstrable affective state (as evidenced by its impact on behavior, physiology, and cognition) without having conscious access to that state (Winkielman & Berridge, 2004). The idea of "unconscious affect" may s eem initially strange – after all, how can there be feelings that are not felt? Note, though, that evolutionarily speaking, conscious representation of affect in the form of a "feeling" is a late achievement compared with the ability to respond affectively to relevant stimuli, which is present in animals that extend deep into our evolutionary ancestry, such as fish and reptiles. Accordingly, the basic affective neurocircuitry is contained in the subcortical brain, and can operate even in the absence of cortex (Berridge, 2003). A reader interested in a recent review of neuroscientific evidence for "unconscious emotion" may want to consult Winkielman, Berridge, and Sher (2011). However, evolutionary and neuroscientific considerations can only be suggestive of unconscious affect in typical humans. We thus embarked on a program of psychological research to test this possibility using standard experimental paradigms with normal college participants.

Impact of subliminal affective stimuli on behavior, but not on subjective experience

One way of testing unconscious emotion involves separating the impact of affective stimuli on behavior from their impact on conscious feelings. This was done in a series of studies by Winkielman, Berridge, and Wilbarger (2005). In Study 1 participants were first presented with a series of subliminal emotional facial expressions – happy, neutral, or angry. Immediately after this affect induction, participants were given two counterbalanced tasks. One task required participants to self-report on conscious feelings of valence and arousal – a measure of introspective access to the current affective state. The other task was a measure of behavioral impact of the current affective state and asked participants to take a pitcher of lemonade-like beverage and to pour into their cup as much as they wanted and to drink as much as they wanted.

The results of this study illustrate that subliminal emotional expressions can influence people's actual consumption behavior. Subliminal happy facial expressions caused participants to pour more into their own cup, and to drink more than angry facial expressions. Importantly, participants reported no conscious awareness of any intervening change in their subjective state, as measured by their reports of valence and arousal: that is, they did not report feeling more pleasant (or aroused) after happy facial expressions than angry expressions.

This study suggests that consciously inaccessible affective states can drive behavior. However, how does unconscious affect accomplish this result? After all, many steps of the consumption behavior are consciously mediated, in the sense that they require the ability to understand verbal instructions, form an intention, and execute complex movements. To understand this process, we tested the idea that unconscious affect directly modifies the perceived value of presented options, without changing conscious feelings. In Study 2, we presented people with the same series of subliminal happy or angry faces. Then some participants were given just a single sip of the fruit beverage, and were asked to rate its perceived

value. Other participants rated various shades of their current feelings on a 20-item scale. The results showed that the subliminal expressions influenced the perceived value of the drink, with happy faces leading to higher ratings of willingness to pay and the desire to drink. Again, no changes in feelings were found. In sum, this study supported the idea that unconscious affect works via change in the perception of the desirability and value of presented options, without manifesting itself as a change in subjective experience.

It is also worth highlighting that in both studies described above, the effect of prime was amplified by thirst (Winkielman et al., 2005). This is consistent with other work from social psychology suggesting that unconscious cues interact with affective and motivational states in determining goal-oriented behavior (see Chapter 5; see also Custers & Aarts, 2010; Ferguson, 2007). However, our interpretation is that thirst does not represent an "unconscious goal," but rather a low-level motivational amplifier of incoming affective cues (Winkielman et al., 2011).

True dissociation or lack of meta-awareness?

One can ask whether participants in the above studies had no experience of their affective reaction (true unconscious affect) or whether they simply lacked meta-awareness of conscious affective states (experienced but unrealized affect). After all, it is possible that participants were not attending on-line to their feelings, or did not consider their subliminally biased feelings as a potential impairment to their judgments and thus ignored them. Other studies from our lab have addressed this possibility.

In one series of studies, participants were subliminally flashed facial expressions of happiness and anger that were masked by to-be-rated Chinese ideographs (Winkielman, Zajonc, & Schwarz, 1997). In addition, the studies employed various attributional manipulations in which some participants were informed about the possibility of change in their affective experience and offered possible causes of such change (irrelevant "other" pictures, irrelevant background music). If participants' feelings are indeed consciously accessible and form the basis of their judgments, such attributional manipulations should trigger corrective processes, such as discounting and augmenting (Schwarz & Clore, 1983). However, the results of these studies showed no evidence of any discounting or augmenting effects, as predicted by the attributional account (Winkielman et al., 1997). Furthermore, there was also no evidence for feelings in participants' self-reports of experience, again consistent with the idea that the facially triggered affect was unconscious.

Results of a recent study reaffirmed this conclusion with another paradigm (Bornemann, Winkielman, & van der Meer, 2011). The study investigated whether people can somehow "feel" their reactions to briefly presented emotional stimuli by deliberately focusing on their internal subjective state. Specifically, participants were briefly flashed happy, neutral or angry faces and were asked to identify their valence. One group of participants was instructed to do this task while focusing on their feelings. One control group was instructed to use a visual focus strategy, and another group received no strategy instructions. The results showed no beneficial effect of feeling-focus instruction on detection rates, suggesting that the affective responses to faces were unconsciously unavailable, despite participants trying to use them.

Physiological consequences: Unfelt but genuine affect

One issue often raised about these findings is the nature of the unconscious affective states. Are the unconscious states elicited by subtle and brief stimuli (like faces) simply "evaluative," in the sense of changes in activation of value-related, but cold concepts like "goodness" or "badness"? Or are they genuinely "hot" – in the sense of being represented across multiple physiological and psychological systems? This is a difficult question, especially since unconscious affective states are likely to be weaker and less differentiated (Clore, 1994). Still, some recent evidence from our lab suggests that unconscious affect involves genuine physiological changes and is distinguishable from pure evaluative states.

In the just-described study by Bornemann et al. (2011), in addition to behavioral responses, we monitored participants' physiological activity using facial electromyography (EMG). The results revealed distinct physiological responses for different stimulus valences. Angry faces produced the strongest reactions on the frown-generating corrugator supercilii, and happy faces produced the lowest reactions. This suggests that briefly presented and unfelt faces generate at least some muscular reactions.

However, one could argue that the facial EMG responses to faces could simply represent motor mimicry. Thus, in other studies we assessed the reactions to unconsciously presented facial pictures using physiological measures that serve as an index of activation of a low-level positive

affective system, such as post-auricular startle reflex (Starr, Lin, & Winkielman, 2007). Participants showed more post-auricular startle reflex to unconscious happy rather than angry faces, suggesting genuine, albeit weak, activation of the low-level affect system. Recently, we followed up on this finding and presented participants with affective pictures (faces or pictures) designed to induce an affective state, and evaluative words (adjectives and nouns) selected to activate relevant semantic dimensions. As expected, faces and pictures elicited stronger physiological responses than valence-matched words. Critically, changes in behavior were driven more strongly by pictures and faces, consistent with the notion that the behavioral changes reflect genuine "hot" affect, rather than cold evaluation (Starr, Winkielman, Golgolushko, 2008).

In sum, a range of findings from behavioral and physiological experiments suggest that one can obtain genuine dissociation between an underlying affective process and its conscious, experiential awareness. As such, they give credence to the notion of "unconscious affect." Importantly, though, the idea of "unconscious emotion" does not imply that conscious feelings are an unnecessary "icing on the emotional cake" (LeDoux, 1996). Conscious happiness, anxiety, anger, guilt, and sadness are critical in people's life. They may as well be what makes life worth living. As an example, most people probably would not spend money on substances that make them only "unconsciously happy," but result in "happy" behavior. In contrast, they are clearly willing to spend on substances, like alcohol or drugs, which influence conscious states, without doing much good to behavior. Besides recreational reasons, conscious emotions are actually useful in judgments and decisions, giving the decision makers valuable feedback that they might, but are not forced to, explicitly consider in making choices (Winkielman, Knutson, Paulus, & Trujillo, 2007).

Unconscious or not metaconscious?

The preceding discussion argued for some cases where mental states, like affect, can remain genuinely unconscious. However, this discussion also illustrates how hard it is to distinguish empirically between processes that are genuinely unconscious or conscious but not meta-aware. This is tricky, as a failure of verbal report can result from either an absence of experience or an absence of meta-awareness. However, future studies may help to adjudicate between them. For example, if unreported states are indeed represented in consciousness, then in principle they should be influenced by manipulations targeting consciousness, such as cognitive load or explicit monitoring. Experiences in the absence of meta-awareness can also be revealed retrospectively. For example, it is possible to catch conscious, but not meta-aware, states with the external probe procedure, which, as described earlier, was successfully employed in research on zoning out and unnoticed, unwanted thoughts. In principle, similar strategies could be used in other paradigms. For example, perhaps individuals who fail to spontaneously report a goal (e.g., competition) could be caught consciously experiencing such goal states, if probed at the right time. It may also be possible to refine individuals' ability to carefully scrutinize their prior state. For example, if individuals are experiencing something without concurrent meta-awareness, then in principle it may be possible to have them later recall and metacognitively represent their prior state, when some additional source of self-insight (e.g., mindfulness training) is provided or biases due to motivation are removed. Thus, individuals going through the break-up of a romantic relationship may retrospectively recognize past experiences of jealously or anger that had previously escaped meta-awareness. Of course, retrospective analyses have their own pitfalls, as it is possible to infer states that may not have actually been experienced at the time (Joslyn & Schooler, 2006). However, if individuals are capable of retrospectively reporting states for which they lack a basis for inference (e.g., determining whether they were subject to subliminally presented mood manipulations), then the conclusion that the state was experienced seems reasonable. Ultimately, determination of whether or not unreported states are genuinely unconscious, or experienced but not meta-aware, will come down to an assessment of the preponderance of evidence in each case.

SUMMARY AND IMPLICATIONS

This chapter discussed the conscious, metaconscious, and the unconscious, focusing on the domain of social cognition. Our goal here was to offer not only a review of theories and findings from our and related labs but also to problematize some common assumptions and provide a fresh perspective on classic issues. We began by emphasizing the resurgence of consciousness in contemporary science, and contrasted this view with eliminativism of mainstream social cognition. We then discussed what makes mental events conscious, and highlighted the role of consciousness in complex thought and action. Following this, we distinguished between conscious and metaconscious states. We considered various disconnections between conscious and metaconscious representations, highlighting both temporal and translation dissociations. We also highlighted the possibility that some seemingly unconscious states may in fact be conscious states lacking in meta-awareness, and showed how this possibility affects the interpretation of some major social-cognitive phenomena. Finally, we considered some genuinely unconscious mental events, including the curious phenomenon of "unconscious affect."

What are some implications of all this for social cognition? Let's start with some concrete recommendations. First, as we have discussed throughout, researchers need to test more thoroughly if a mental content – a thought, a goal, or a feeling – is possibly experienced but not metacognitively available before declaring it unconscious. Besides psychological tools, there are now plenty of physiological tools available that can facilitate such determination. Second, given that metacognition necessarily involves a process of translation, often into a verbal form, of participants' thoughts and feelings, researchers should use methods which capture the "first-order" nature of these states . This may again involve behavioral techniques as well as psychophysiology. More theoretically, as we have emphasized throughout, many of today's popular frameworks depend (both in the sense of conceptual foundations as well as popularity) on the assumption that the process is unconscious (e.g., unconscious goals, unconscious thought, unconscious emotion, etc.). Challenging this assumption may require major reformulation of these theories.

CONCLUSION

Over the last several years there has been remarkable progress in the psychology and neuroscience of consciousness and metacognition. Clearly, some believe that certain features of consciousness, like subjectivity, qualia, and intentionality, will never submit to scientific scrutiny (Searle, 1997). Others believe that as research progresses, "consciousness" will disappear from the scientific vocabulary (Rey, 1983). In contrast, we believe that future scientific advances will only increase our appreciation of the marvels of consciousness and metacognition. We hope that social cognitive researchers will continue to contribute vigorously to this progress.

ACKNOWLEDGMENT

We thank Shlomi Sher for his generous comments.

REFERENCES

Abrams, R. L., & Greenwald, A. G. (2000). Parts outweigh the whole (word) in unconscious analysis of meaning. *Psychological Science, 11*, 118–124.

Acker, F. (2008). New findings on unconscious versus conscious thought in decision making: additional empirical data and meta-analysis. *Judgment and Decision Making, 3*, 292–303.

Adams, H. E., Wright, L. W., & Lohr, B. A. (1996). Is homophobia associated with homosexual arousal? *Journal of Abnormal Psychology, 105*, 440–445.

Baars, B. J. (1988). *A cognitive theory of consciousness.* New York: Cambridge University Press.

Bargh, J. A. (1989). Conditional automaticity: Varieties of automatic influence in social perception and cognition. In J. S. Uleman & J. A. Bargh (Eds.), *Unintended thought* (pp. 3–51). New York: Guilford Press.

Bargh, J. A. (1997). Advances in social cognition. In R. S. Wyer, Jr. (Ed.), *The automaticity of everyday life* (pp. 1–61). Mahwah, NJ: Erlbaum.

Bargh, J. A. (2007). Social psychological approaches to consciousness. In P. Zelazo, M. Moscovitch, & E. Thompson (Eds.), *The Cambridge handbook of consciousness.* New York: Cambridge University Press.

Bargh, J. A., & Chartrand, T. L. (1999). The unbearable automaticity of being. *American Psychologist, 54*, 462–479.

Baumeister, R. F. (2008). Free will in scientific psychology. *Perspectives on Psychological Science, 3*, 14–19.

Baumeister, R. F., & Masicampo, E. J. (2010). Conscious thought is for facilitating social and cultural interactions: How mental simulations serve the animal–culture interface. *Psychological Review, 117*, 945–971.

Baumeister, R. F., Schmeichel, B. J., DeWall, C. N., & Vohs, K. D. (2007). Is the conscious self a help, a hindrance, or an irrelevance to the creativity process? In A. M. Colombus (Ed.), *Advances in psychology research* (Vol. 53, pp. 137–152). New York: Nova.

Berridge, K. C. (2003). Comparing the emotional brain of humans and other animals. In: R. J. Davidson, H. H. Goldsmith, & K. Scherer (Eds.), *Handbook of affective sciences* (pp. 25–51). New York: Oxford University Press.

Block, N. (1995). On a confusion about a function of consciousness. *Behavioral and Brain Sciences 18*, 27–287.

Bongers, K. C. A., & Dijksterhuis, A. (2009). Consciousness as a trouble-shooting device? The role of consciousness in goal-pursuit. In E. Morsella, J. A. Bargh, & P. Gollwitzer (Eds.), *The Oxford handbook of human action* (pp. 589–604). New York: Oxford University Press.

Boring, E. G. (1953). A history of introspection. *Psychological Bulletin, 50*, 169–189.

Bornemann, B., Winkielman, P., & van der Meer (2011). Can you feel what you don't see? Using bodily feedback to detect briefly presented emotional stimuli. *International Journal of Psychophysiology.* doi:10.1016/j.ijpsycho.2011.04.007

Brandimonte, M. A., Schooler, J. W., & Gabbino, P. (1997). Attenuating verbal overshadowing through visual retrieval cues. *Journal of Experimental Psychology: Learning, Memory, and Cognition, 23*, 915–931.

Breitmeyer, B. G., & Ogmen, H. (2006). *Visual masking: Time slices through conscious and unconscious Vision* (2nd ed.). New York: Oxford University Press.

Carver, C. S., & Scheier, M. S. (1990). Origins and functions of positive and negative affect: A control-process view. *Psychological Review, 197*, 19–35.

Cheyene J. A., Carriere J. S. A., & Smilek D. (2006). Absentmindedness: Lapses of conscious awareness and everyday cognitive failures. *Consciousness & Cognition, 3*, 578–592.

Christoff, K., Gordon, A. M., Smallwood, J., Smith, R., & Schooler, J. W. (2009). Experience sampling during fMRI reveals default network and executive system contributions to mind wandering. *Proceedings of the National Academy of Sciences, 106*, 8719–8724.

Churchland, P. M. (1981). Eliminative materialism and the propositional attitudes. *Journal of Philosophy, 78*(2), 67–90.

Churchland, P. S. (2005). Brain wide shut. *New Scientist*, 30 April, pp. 46–49.

Cleeremans, A. (2005). Computational correlates of consciousness. *Progress in Brain Research, 150*, 81–98.

Clore, G. L. (1994). Why emotions are never unconscious. In P. Ekman & R. J. Davidson (Eds.), *The nature of emotion: Fundamental questions* (pp. 285–290). New York: Oxford University Press.

Crick, F. (1994). *The astonishing hypothesis.* New York: Scribner's.

Custers, R., & Aarts, H. (2010). The unconscious will: How the pursuit of goals operates outside of conscious awareness. *Science, 329*, 47–50.

Dehaene, S., Changeux, J. P., Naccache, L., Sackur, J., & Sergent, C. (2006). Conscious, preconscious, and subliminal processing: A testable taxonomy. *Trends in Cognitive Sciences, 10*, 204–211.

Deutsch, R., Gawronski, B., & Strack, F. (2006). At the boundaries of automaticity: Negation as reflective operation. *Journal of Personality and Social Psychology, 91*, 385–405.

DeWall, C. N., Baumeister, R. F., & Masicampo, E. J. (2008). Evidence that logical reasoning depends on conscious processing, *Consciousness and Cognition, 17*, 628–645.

Diamond, A., Barnett, W. S., Thomas, J., & Munro, S. (2007). Preschool program improves cognitive control. *Science, 318*, 1387–1388.

Dijksterhuis, A., Bos, M. W., Nordgren, L. F., & van Baaren, R. B. (2006). On making the right choice: The deliberation-without-attention effect. *Science, 311*, 1005–1007.

Ferguson, M. J. (2007). On the automatic evaluation of end-states. *Journal of Personality and Social Psychology, 92*, 596–611.

Fishman, D., Smallwood, J., & Schooler, J. W. (2006). Unwanted and meta-unknown. Unpublished manuscript.

Fiske, S. T., Gilbert, D. T., & Lindzey, G. (Eds.) (2010). *Handbook of social psychology* (5th ed.). New York: Wiley.

Fitzsimons, G. M., & Bargh, J. A (2004). Automatic self-regulation. In Baumeister, R. F. & Vohs, K. D. (Eds.),

Handbook of self-regulation: Research, theory and applications (pp. 151–170). New York: Guilford Press.

Flavell, J. H. (1979). Metacognition and cognitive monitoring: A new area of cognitive-developmental inquiry. *American Psychologist, 34*, 906–911.

Fodor, J. (1968). *Psychological explanation.* New York: Random House.

Förster, J., Liberman, N., & Friedman, R. (2007). Seven principles of automatic goal pursuit: A systematic approach to distinguishing goal priming from priming of non-goal constructs. *Personality and Social Psychology Review, 11*, 211–233.

Gaertner, S. L., & J. F. Dovidio. (1986). The aversive form of racism. In: J. F. Dovidio & S. L. Gaertner (Eds.), *Prejudice, discrimination and racism: Theory and research* (pp. 61–89). Orlando, FL: Academic Press,

Gawronski, B., & Payne, B. K. (Eds.) (2010). *Handbook of implicit social cognition: Measurement, theory, and applications.* New York: Guilford Press.

Geraerts, E., Lindsay, D. S., Merckelbach, H., Jelicic, M., Raymaekers, L., Arnold, M. M., et al. (2008). Cognitive mechanisms underlying recovered memory experiences of childhood sexual abuse. *Psychological Science, 20*, 1.

Gigerenzer, G., & Goldstein, D. (1996). Reasoning the fast and frugal way: Models of bounded rationality. *Psychological Review, 103*, 650–669.

Gray, H. M., Gray, K., & Wegner, D. M. (2007). Dimensions of mind perception. *Science, 315*, 619.

Greenwald, A. G. (1992). New Look 3: Reclaiming unconscious cognition. *American Psychologist, 47*, 766–779.

Greenwald, A.G., Banaji, M. R., Rudman, L. A., Farnham, S. D., Nosek, B. A., & Mellott, D. S. (2002). A unified theory of implicit attitudes, stereotypes, self-esteem, and self-concept. *Psychological Review, 109*, 3–25.

Greenwald, A.G., Draine, S. C., & Abrams, R. L. (1996). Three cognitive markers of unconscious semantic activation. *Science, 273*, 1699–1702.

Hull, J. G. (1981). A self-awareness model of the causes and effects of alcohol consumption. *Journal of Abnormal Psychology, 90*, 586–600.

Hummel, J. E., & Holyoak, K. J. (2003). A symbolic-connectionist theory of relational inference and generalization. *Psychological Review, 110*, 220–264.

Jameson, A., Nelson, T. O., Leonesio, R. J., & Narens, L. (1993). The feeling of another person's knowing. *Journal of Memory and Language, 32*, 320–335.

Joslyn, S., & Schooler, J.W. (2006). Influences of the present on the past: The impact of interpretation on memory for abuse. In L.G. Nilsson & N. Ohta (Eds.), *Memory and society: Psychological perspectives.* New York: Psychology Press.

Jost, J. T., Kruglanski, A. W., & Nelson, T. O. (1998). Social metacognition: An expansionist review. *Personality and Social Psychology Review, 2*, 137–154.

Kahneman, D. (1973). *Attention and effort.* Englewood Cliffs, NJ: Prentice Hall.

Kihlstrom, J. F. (2007). The psychological unconscious. O. John, R. Robins, & L. Pervin (Eds.), *Handbook of*

Personality: Theory and Research (3rd ed.). New York: Guilford Press.

Kihlstrom, J. F. (2008). The automaticity juggernaut. In J. Baer, J. C. Kaufman, & R. F. Baumeister (Eds.), *Are we free? Psychology and free will* (pp. 155–180). New York: Oxford University Press.

Kihlstrom, J. F., Schacter, D. L., Cork, R. L., Hurt, C. A., & Behr, S. E. (1990). Implicit and explicit memory following surgical anesthesia. *Psychological Science, 1*, 303–306.

Koch, C., & Tsuchiya, N. (2007). Attention and consciousness: Two distinct brain processes. *Trends in Cognitive Science. 11*, 16–22.

Koriat, A. (2006). Metacognition and consciousness. In: *Cambridge handbook of consciousness.* New York: Cambridge University Press.

Kunst-Wilson, W. R., & Zajonc, R. B. (1980). Affective discrimination of stimuli that cannot be recognized. *Science, 207*, 557–558.

Lambie, J. A., & Marcel, A. J. (2002). Consciousness and the varieties of emotion experience: A theoretical framework. *Psychological Review, 109*, 219–259.

Laureys, S., Antoine, S., Boly, M., Elincx, S., Faymonville, M. E., & J. Berre, J., et al. (2002). Brain function in the vegetative state. *Acta Neurol Belg, 102*, 177–185.

LeDoux, J. (1996). *The emotional brain: The mysterious underpinnings of emotional life.* New York: Simon & Schuster.

Levy, J., Pashler, H., & Boer, E. (2006). Central interference in driving: Is there any stopping the psychological refractory period? *Psychological Science, 17*, 228–235.

Loftus, E. F., & Klinger, M. R. (1992). Is the unconscious smart or dumb? *American Psychologist, 47*, 761–765.

Logan, G. D. (1988). Toward an instance theory of automatization. *Psychological Review, 95*, 492–527.

Mandler, G. (1975). Consciousness: Respectable, useful, and probably necessary. In R. Solso (Ed.), *Information processing and cognition: The Loyola Symposium* (pp. 229–254). Hillsdale, NJ: Lawrence Erlbaum Associates.

Marcel, A. J. (1983). Conscious and unconscious perception: Experiments on visual masking and word recognition. *Cognitive Psychology, 15*, 197–237.

Mason, M. F., Norton, M. I., Van, J. D., Wegner, D. M., Grafton, S. T., & Macrae, C. N. (2007). Wandering minds: The default network and stimulus independent thought. *Science, 315*, 393–395.

McClelland, J. L., & Rogers, T. T. (2003). The parallel distributed processing approach to semantic cognition. *Nature Reviews Neuroscience,*

Mead, G. H. (1934). *Mind, self, & society.* Chicago, IL: University of Chicago Press.

Melcher, J., & Schooler, J. W. (1996). The misremembrance of wines past: Verbal and perceptual expertise differentially mediate verbal overshadowing of taste. *The Journal of Memory and Language, 35*, 231–245.

Merikle, P. M., & Reingold, E. M. (1998). On demonstrating unconscious perception. *Journal of Experimental Psychology: General, 127*, 304–310.

Metcalfe, J., & Mischel, W. (1999). A hot/cool system analysis of delay of gratification: Dynamics of willpower. *Psychological Review, 106*, 3–19.

Milner, D., & Goodale, M. (1995). *The visual brain in action.* Oxford: Oxford University Press.

Nelson, T. O. (1996). Consciousness and metacognition. *American Psychologist, 51*(2), 102–116.

Nisbett, R. E., & Wilson, D. S. (1977). Telling more than we can know: Verbal reports on mental processes. *Psychological Review, 84,* 231–253.

Norman, D. A., & Shallice, T. (1986). Attention to action: Willed and automatic control of behaviour. In R. J. Davidson, G. E. Schwartz, & D. Shapiro (Eds.), *Consciousness and self-regulation: Advances in research and theory.* New York: Plenum Press.

Öhman, A., Flykt, A., & Lundqvist, D. (2000). Unconscious emotion: Evolutionary perspectives, psychophysiological data and neuropsychological mechanisms. In R. D. Lane, L. Nadel & G. Ahern (Eds.), *Cognitive neuroscience of emotion* (pp. 296–327). New York: Oxford University Press.

Pashler, H. E. (1998). *The psychology of attention.* Cambridge, MA: MIT Press.

Petty, R. E., Briñol, P., Tormala, Z. L., & Wegener, D. T. (2007). The role of meta-cognition in social judgment. In E. T. Higgins & A. W. Kruglanski, (Eds.), *Social psychology: A handbook of basic principles* (2nd ed., pp. 254–284). New York: Guilford Press.

Pessoa, L., McKenna M., Gutierrez E., & Ungerleider, L. G. (2002). Neural processing of emotional faces requires attention. *Proc Natl Acad Sci USA, 99,* 11458–11463.

Reichle, E., Pollatsek, A., Fisher, D.L., & Rayner, K. (1998). Toward a model of eye movement control in reading. *Psychological Review, 105,* 125–157.

Rey, A., Goldstein, R. M., & Perruchet, P. (2009). Does unconscious thought improve complex decision making? *Psychological Research, 73,* 372–379. doi:10.1007/s00426-008-0156-4

Rey, G. (1983). A reason for doubting the existence of consciousness. In R. Davidson, G. Schwartz, & D. Shapiro (Eds.), *Consciousness and self-regulation* (Vol. 3, pp. 1–39). New York: Plenum Press.

Rickard, T. C. (2005). A revised identical elements model of arithmetic fact representation. *Journal of Experimental Psychology: Learning, Memory, and Cognition, 31,* 250–257.

Robinson, T. E., & Berridge, K. C. (1993). The neural basis of drug craving: an incentive-sensitization theory of addiction. *Brain Research Reviews, 18,* 247–291.

Rosenthal, D. (1986). Two concepts of consciousness. *Philosophical Studies, 49,* 329–359.

Sayette, M. A., Reichle, E. D., & Schooler, J. W. (2009). Lost in the sauce: The effects of alcohol on mind-wandering. *Psychological Science, 20,* 747–752.

Sayette, M. A., Schooler, J. W., & Reichle, E. D. (2010). Out for a smoke: The impact of cigarette craving on zoning-out during reading. *Psychological Science, 21,* 26–30.

Schooler, J. W. (2001). Discovering memories in the light of meta-awareness. *The Journal of Aggression, Maltreatment and Trauma, 4,* 105–136.

Schooler, J. W. (2002). Re-representing consciousness: Dissociations between consciousness and meta-conscious-ness. *Trends in Cognitive Science, 6,* 339–344.

Schooler, J. W. (2010). What science tells us about free will. In R. F. Baumeister, A. R. Mele, & K. D. Vohs (Eds.), *Free will and consciousness: How might they work?* (pp. 191–218). Oxford: Oxford University Press.

Schooler, J. W., Ariely, D., & Loewenstein, G. (2003). The pursuit and assessment of happiness can be self-defeating. In I. Brocas & J. Carrillo (Eds.), *The psychology of economic decisions.* Oxford: Oxford University Press.

Schooler, J. W., & Engstler-Schooler, T. Y. (1990). Verbal overshadowing of visual memories: Some things are better left unsaid. *Cognitive Psychology, 17,* 36–71.

Schooler, J. W., Fiore, S. M., & Brandimonte, M. A. (1997). At a *loss* from words: Verbal overshadowing of perceptual memories. In D. L. Medin (Ed.), *The psychology of learning and motivation* (pp. 293–334). San Diego, CA: Academic Press.Schooler, J. W. & Mauss, I. B. (2010). To be happy and to know it: The experience and meta-awareness of pleasure. In K. Berridge & M. Kringlebach (Eds.), *Pleasures of the brain.* Oxford: Oxford University Press.

Schooler J. W., McSpadden M., Reichle E. D., Smallwood J. (2010). Unnoticed nonsense: Mind-wandering can prevent people from realizing that they are reading gibberish. Manuscript submitted for publication.

Schooler, J. W., Ohlsson, S., & Brooks, K. (1993). Thoughts beyond words: When language overshadows insight. *Journal of Experimental Psychology: General, 122,* 166–183.

Schooler, J. W., Reichle, E. D., & Halpern, D. V. (2005). Zoning-out during reading: Evidence for dissociations between experience and meta-consciousness. In D. T. Levin (Ed.), *Thinking and seeing: Visual metacognition in adults and children* (pp. 204–226). Cambridge, MA: MIT Press.

Schooler, J., & Schreiber, C.A. (2004). Experience, meta-consciousness, and the paradox of introspection. *Journal of Consciousness Studies, 11* (7–8), 17–39.

Schwarz, N. (2004). Meta-cognitive experiences in consumer judgment and decision making. *Journal of Consumer Psychology, 14,* 332–348.

Schwarz, N., & Clore, G. L. (1983). Mood, misattribution, and judgments of well-being: Informative and directive functions of affective states. *Journal of Personality and Social Psychology, 45,* 513–523.

Searle, J. (1997). *The mystery of consciousness.* New York: New York Review Press.

Shanks, D. R. (2005). Implicit learning. In K. Lamberts & R. Goldstone (Eds.), *Handbook of cognition* (pp. 202–220). London: Sage.

Shanks, D. R. (2006). Are complex choices better made unconsciously? *Science, 313,* 716.

Shariff, A., Schooler, J. W., & Vohs, K. (2008). The hazards of claiming to have solved the hard problem of free will. In J. Baer and R. Baumeister (Eds.), *Psychology and free will* (pp. 181–204). Oxford: Oxford University Press.

Shiffrin, R. M., & Schneider, W. (1977). Controlled and automatic human information processing: II. Perceptual learning, automatic attending and a general theory. *Psychological Review, 84,* 127–190.

Shinskey, F. G. (1979). *Process control systems* (2nd ed.). New York: McGraw-Hill.

Skurnik, I., Schwarz, N., & Winkielman, P. (2000). Drawing inferences from feelings: The role of naive beliefs. In H. Bless & J. P. Forgas (Eds.), *The message within: The role of subjective experience in social cognition and behavior* (pp. 162–175). Philadelphia: Psychology Press.

Sieck, W. R., Quinn, C. N., & Schooler, J. W. (1999). Justification effects on the judgment of analogy. *Memory and Cognition, 27*, 844–855.

Simons, D. J., & Chabris, C. F. (1999). Gorillas in our midst: Sustained inattentional blindness for dynamic events. *Perception, 28*, 1059–1074.

Smallwood, J., McSpadden, M. C., & Schooler, J. W. (2008). When attention matters: The curious incident of the wandering mind. *Memory & Cognition, 36*, 1144–1150.

Smallwood, J., & Schooler, J. W. (2006). The restless mind. *Psychological Bulletin, 132*, 946–958.

Smith, E. R., & DeCoster, J. (2000). Dual process models in social and cognitive psychology: Conceptual integration and links to underlying memory systems. *Personality and Social Psychology Review, 4*, 108–131.

Son Hing, L. S., Chung-Yan, G. A., Hamilton, L. K., & Zanna, M. P. (2008). A two-dimensional model that employs explicit and implicit attitudes to characterize prejudice. *Journal of Personality and Social Psychology, 94*, 971–987.

Starr, M. J., Lin, J., & Winkielman, P. (2007). The impact of unconscious facial expressions on consumption behavior involves changes in positive affect: Evidence from EMG and appetitive reflex-modulation. Poster presented at 47th Annual Meeting of Society for Psychophysiological Research, Savannah, GA.

Starr, M. J., Winkielman, P., & Gogolushko, K. (2008). Influence of affective pictures and words on consumption behavior and facial expressions. Poster presented at Society for Psychophysiological Research, Austin, TX.

Strack, F., & Deutsch, R. (2004). Reflective and impulsive determinants of social behavior. *Personality and Social Psychology Review, 8*, 220–247.

Sumner, P., Tsai, P-C., Yu, K., & Nachev, P. (2006). Attentional modulation of sensorimotor processes in the absence of perceptual awareness. *PNAS, 103*, 10520–10525

Tiffany, S. T. (1990). A cognitive model of drug urges and drug-use behavior: Role of automatic and nonautomatic processes. *Psychological Review, 97*, 147–168.

Tononi, G. (2004). An information integration theory of consciousness. *BMC Neuroscience, 5*, 42.

Triesch J, Ballard D. H., Hayhoe, M. M., Sullivan, B. T. (2003). What you see is what you need. *Journal of Vision, 3*, 86–94.

Vohs, K. D., & Schooler, J. W. (2008). The value of believing in free will: Encouraging a belief in determinism increases cheating. *Psychological Science, 19*, 49–54.

Vygotsky, L. S. (1962). *Thought and language.* Cambridge, MA: MIT Press.

Wegner, D. M. (1994). Ironic processes of mental control. *Psychological Review, 101*, 34–52.

Wegner, D. M. (2002). *The illusion of conscious will.* Cambridge, MA: MIT Press.

Weiskrantz, L. (1986). *Blindsight: A case study and its implications.* Oxford: Oxford University Press.

Wilson, T. D. (2002). *Strangers to Ourselves: Discovering the adaptive unconscious.* Cambridge, MA: Belknap Press of Harvard University Press.

Wilson, T. D., Lisle, D. J., Schooler, J. W., Hodges, S. D., Klaaren, K. J., & LaFleur, S. J. (1993). Introspecting about reasons can reduce post-choice satisfaction. *Personality and Social Psychology Bulletin, 19*, 331–339.

Wilson, T. D., & Schooler, J. W. (1991). Thinking too much: Introspection can reduce the quality of preferences and decisions. *Journal of Personality and Social Psychology, 60*, 181–192.

Winkielman, P. & Berridge, K. C. (2004). Unconscious emotion. *Current Directions in Psychological Science, 13*, 120–123.

Winkielman, P., Berridge, K., & Sher, S. (2011). Emotion, consciousness, and social behavior. In J. Decety & J. T. Cacioppo (Eds.), *Handbook of social neuroscience* (pp 195–211). New York: Oxford University Press.

Winkielman, P., Berridge, K. C., & Wilbarger, J. L. (2005). Unconscious affective reactions to masked happy versus angry faces influence consumption behavior and judgments of value. *Personality and Social Psychology Bulletin, 1*, 121–135.

Winkielman, P., Knutson, B., Paulus, M. P., & Trujillo, J. T. (2007). Affective influence on decisions: Moving towards the core mechanisms. *Review of General Psychology, 11*, 179–192.

Winkielman, P. & Schooler, J. (2011). Splitting consciousness: Unconscious, conscious, and metaconscious processes in social cognition. *European Review of Social Psychology, 22*, 1–35.

Winkielman, P., & Schwarz, N. (2001). How pleasant was your childhood? Beliefs about memory shape inferences from experienced difficulty of recall. *Psychological Science, 12*, 176–179.

Winkielman, P., Zajonc, R. B., & Schwarz, N. (1997). Subliminal affective priming resists attributional interventions. *Cognition and Emotion, 11*, 433–465.

Wood, W., Quinn, J., & Kashy, D. (2002). Habits in everyday life: Thought, emotion, and action. *Journal of Personality and Social Psychology, 83*, 1281–1297.

Zajonc, R. B. (1994). Evidence for nonconscious emotions. In P. Ekman & R. J. Davidson (Eds.), *The nature of emotion: Fundamental questions* (pp. 293–297). New York: Oxford University Press.

Zeeman, A. (2002). *Consciousness: A user's guide.* New Haven, CT: Yale University Press.

5

Goals, Motivated Social Cognition, and Behavior

Henk Aarts

Human behavior is sensitive to learning, is influenced by past experiences, and tends to be organized and structured in the service of future action. Research in the tradition of behaviorism has shown that behavior follows from rigid responses to stimuli that are reinforced by rewards. According to this work, the environment organizes and determines human behavior. However, acting on fixed stimulus–response rules, such as saying "yeah" when someone is knocking on the door, is not the whole story. Our behavior is more flexible to deal with the varying circumstances we encounter in daily social life. Such flexibility relies on our capacity to mentally represent what we want and do, and to control behavior in line with the representations. Accordingly, a substantial component of human behavior is directed at goals that motivate and control the behavioral system in a dynamic environment.

This chapter provides an analysis of the role of goals in social behavior. Fortunately, there are a few recent excellent volumes on goals (Aarts & Elliot, 2012; Moskowitz & Grant, 2009; Shah & Gardner, 2008), so there is no need to review the literature on this topic in all its details here again. Instead, this chapter aims to offer an examination of the general principles that govern goal pursuit. Goal-directed behavior has been mainly conceptualized and studied as the product of our conscious mind. That is, goal setting and control is believed to rely on consciousness, because people are often consciously aware of the goals they pursue. However, the discovery that decisions start in the unconscious (Libet et al., 1983; Soon et al., 2008), and the importance of unconscious processes in social cognition and behavior (Bargh, 2007) has questioned the causal status of consciousness in goal-directed behavior. Here we examine the origin and control of conscious goal-directed behavior and the possibility that goals operate outside awareness. However, we first briefly discuss a few research programs suggesting that the role of goals in social cognition is not taken for granted, and that we should be careful in considering the goal concept as an explanatory tool for social behavior.

THE DEBATE OF GOALS IN SOCIAL COGNITION

The idea that our behavior is goal-directed appears to be well-accepted by most contemporary researchers, but this was (and, in some instances, still is) not always the case in the study of social cognition. This dispute about the role of goals is rooted primarily in the cognitive revolution, in which there was no room for motivation, and cognition was seen as the more parsimonious account for behavior.

In the study on reasoning, the notion that goals affect attitudes (Festinger, 1957), attributions (Heider, 1958), and beliefs (Kruglanski, 1996) has been put forth by some psychologists and challenged by others. For instance, goals have been posited to lead people to make self-serving attributions for success and failure, even though such attributions do not reflect the actual cause of behavior. However, this motivational view of self-serving attributions has been challenged, as effects of goals on attributional reasoning could be interpreted in entirely cognitive, non-motivational terms as the result of prior beliefs and expectancies that people have about success and failure (Miller & Ross, 1975). This dispute between motivation-driven versus cognition-driven accounts for self-serving attributions is still alive, but recently attempts to reconcile have been made by suggesting that cognitive and motivational processes often work in tandem (Shepperd, Malone, & Sweeny, 2008).

In the study on stereotyping and prejudice, it has been argued that stereotypes are automatically activated and applied upon encountering members of stereotyped groups. Thus, exposure to a bagpipe blower automatically leads to the activation and application of stereotypical traits, such as brave and dry sense of humor. This activation of stereotypical traits, however, is facilitated by context and specific processing goals (Kunda & Spencer, 2003). Furthermore, once stereotypes are activated, goals, such as the desire to avoid being prejudiced or to be egalitarian (Devine, 1989; Moskowitz, Gollwitzer, Wasel, & Schaal, 1999), can control the application of stereotypes. Thus, goals guide the activation as well as the control of different aspects of social stereotyping, and seem to impinge on social behavior in the early stage of attention and social information processing.

In a third area of research examining the boundaries of automatic processes in social cognition, psychologists became interested in the question whether stereotypes and other socially meaningful information can unconsciously prime overt behavior. Indeed, stereotypes (e.g., of professors) automatically trigger actions (e.g., being smart in a quiz) consistent with the content of stereotypes (e.g., Dijksterhuis & Bargh, 2001). These effects were initially conceptualized as resulting from a common coding between perception and action (Prinz, 1997; cf. the ideomotor principle, James, 1890). Thus, priming stereotype knowledge directly leads to action. Despite the parsimoniousness of this cognitive account, it should be noted that some direction and control is required to engage in most of the studied behaviors, suggesting that behavioral priming result from goals and are motivational in nature (Custers & Aarts, 2010).

A great deal of past empirical work on the role of goals in social cognition has been open to a cognitive account because it has often neglected to precisely specify what goals are, and how they emerge and execute control over behavior. Fortunately, this has changed over the past two decades. Given this state of affairs about the concept of goals in social cognition research, it therefore seems opportune to devote a chapter to the process by which the mind creates goals and controls social behavior. In doing this, we address three basic questions that organize current research on goal-directed behavior: How do people represent goals? Where do goals come from? And what do goals do in the process of regulation? In examining these questions, we first focus on research suggesting that goals and their pursuit rely on consciousness. Next, we look into research revealing the possibility that the pursuit of goals occurs outside of conscious awareness. Finally, we briefly address a few challenging issues in the study of conscious and unconscious processes in goal pursuit.

HOW DO PEOPLE REPRESENT GOALS?

When asking people to indicate the goal that drives their behavior at a certain point in time, most of them can provide an answer within a few seconds – no matter whether these answers reflect the true goal of their behavior. Some goals may appear trivial, such as scratching one's nose, turning on the light to find the house keys, making coffee, or writing an email, while other goals seem more important, such as going out with friends, earning a lot of money, being a good parent, or treating people equal. Although goals can differ between people and may vary in meaning, there is common agreement that the goals we explicitly articulate refer to some kind of outcome that we desire to attain. Thus, researchers define goals as desired outcomes (Carver & Scheier, 1998; Cooper & Shallice, 2006; Gollwitzer & Moskowitz, 1996).

Defining goals as desired outcomes may be tricky, because this definition can be applied to any entity or system that is capable of action in response to specific conditions in the world, such as the meat-eating plant's goal of opening the flower to invite insects for dinner, or the heating system's goal of keeping the temperature in the house at a constant level. The operation of these biological and mechanical systems corresponds with a cybernetic approach to human behavior in which the actual state of the world is controlled by a reference value or standard (Wiener, 1948). However, most social psychologists treat the concept of goals in a different way by assigning a dedicated role to the mind in controlling behavior. Accordingly, to study the role of goals in human behavior empirically it is important to be a bit more precise.

Although it seems reasonable to assume that the mind plays a vital role in goal-directed behavior, psychology as a science started out quite differently. In the behaviorists' highly influential approach to human behavior (e.g., Skinner, 1953), the term *goal* was used to refer to a particular object or event in the world (water, food, mating partner) that is chosen by the investigator to study a subject's response to the selected object. For example, if water is studied as a goal to a thirsty person, then the goal does simply refer to the notion that water pulls the person to the object. In other words, whether an object is treated as a goal relies on the investigator's mind, and not on the subject's mind. On this view, human behavior is controlled by goals only at the moment the person is exposed to the goal object. It is in this sense that behaviorists consider human behavior to follow from automatic stimulus–response (S–R) associations without the need to propose a mind that controls behavior.

A large part of our behavior relies on the S–R association principle, and this principle does well when behavior occurs under similar circumstances. However, human behavior is suggested to benefit from being more adaptive and flexible in the dynamic world we live in. Such flexibility is thought to originate from the human (or the brain's) capacity to predict and represent the outcomes of actions and the rewards they produce, and to control behavior such that rewarding outcomes are attained (Frith, Blakemore, & Wolpert, 2000; Gilbert & Wilson, 2007; Powers, 1973; Suddendorf & Corballis, 2007; Tolman, 1939). This temporal view on human behavior implies a few key features that are inherent to goals. First, goals are mentally represented in terms of outcomes of actions. Second, goals become active before perceiving the goal object and controlling behavior (e.g., we can think about eating an apple before we actually eat it). Third, the rewarding property of goals motivates the person, such that effort is invested and resources are recruited to attain goals. Thus, while the behaviorists' approach delegates the control of human behavior completely to the environment on the basis of well-learned responses to desired goal objects, the cognitive approach opens the possibility that these goal objects are mentally represented as desired outcomes that motivate and flexibly control behavior before the actual outcome is observed and attained.

One way to understand how such internal representations of goals are acquired and capable of guiding action is to consider human behavior from an instrumental action perspective (Dickinson & Balleine, 1995; Thorndike, 1911), and to propose a bi-directional link between actions and effects that is stored in memory when effects are perceived to result from action performance (Hommel, Muesseler, Aschersleben, & Prinz, 2001). Therefore, thinking about the effect prepares and directs the associated action leading to the effect. In a study testing this idea (Elsner & Hommel, 2001), participants first learned to randomly alternate two actions which were consistently followed by specific outcomes (e.g., pressing a left key produced a low tone and pressing a right key produced a high tone). After practice, participants were exposed to the tones just before a response was required. It turned out that random responding became more difficult, as was revealed by a response bias towards the tones. These results suggest that representations of outcomes (low tone) that previously served as actual effects of actions (pressing a left key) can operate as a goal for people's actions.

From this perspective, human goal-directed behavior can be understood to evolve from simple movement goals to more complex social goals (Maturana & Varela, 1987). We first learn to orchestrate our limbs and motor movements before we pick up a phone and make a date to go out, so to speak. In this way, certain patterns of motor movements become associated with their observable outcomes in terms of sensory/perceptual and semantic/cognitive codes (Aarts & Veling, 2009). Indeed, studies have demonstrated that the acquisition of sensory–motor goal representations involved in goal-directed behavior generalizes to more abstract features of outcomes, such that goal representations become more socially meaningful (e.g., Beckers, De Houwer, & Eelen, 2002; Hommel, Alonso, & Fuentes, 2003; Kray et al., 2006). Furthermore, as suggested by contemporary research on incentive learning (Berridge, 2001), such goals acquire motivational significance when effects of actions are accompanied by rewarding properties (e.g., when meeting friends in a bar evokes pleasure). Whereas people (including researchers) may express this motivation in different ways (e.g., importance, value, utility, commitment, aspiration, wanting, striving), on an operational level goals act as desired action–outcomes that stir up behavior when the actual state of the world is discrepant with the desired outcome.

It is important to note that considering goals as mental representations of desired outcomes indicates that goals are subjective and rely on specific psychological processes in order to become active and manifest. This raises the question where goals as a psychological internal state start.

WHERE DO GOALS COME FROM?

In understanding the nature of goal-directed behavior, most research in experimental psychology (including social cognition) has treated goals as an independent variable: goals are manipulated by explicitly asking subjects to execute one goal versus another (much like behaviorists select the goal object for subjects), such that one can examine the processes and consequences of pursuing a goal. Surely, this is a viable way in which goals are arrived at in a given moment. Yet focusing on instances when goals are provided to people from external sources, usually in the form of task instructions, circumvents an important question. It ignores how people set their own goals, and removes the issue to the external goal setter: i.e. How do external agents set the goal of setting other people's goal?

Accordingly, to understand where goals come from we have to consider the psychological processes that occur before a goal is set and materializes. The common perspective on this matter is to conceptualize goal setting as a conscious and intentional process. Theories differ in the specifics of the information involved in this process, but they all share the basic idea that goals emerge from expected values (see e.g., Bandura, 1997; Fishbein & Ajzen, 1975; Gollwitzer, 1990; Locke & Latham, 2002; Vroom, 1964). Specifically, the person is treated as a decision maker bringing a potential goal or outcome to mind available in her repertoire in response to a challenge or opportunity in the environment, and computing an expected value of the outcome to determine whether the outcome should be set as a goal one wants to attain. In essence, the expected value principle holds that the motivation to produce an outcome is the product of its rewarding value and the expectancy of being able to realize it. In other words, whether a particular outcome is set as a goal one is motivated to attain depends on its perceived desirability and feasibility.

Because the expected value of an outcome is conceived of as an important determinant of the goals that people set, several research programs have examined how expected values can be changed. One major approach concerns the role of persuasion in altering the perceived desirability of outcomes. For instance, much research on dual-process models of attitude formation and change has illustrated that the perceived desirability of an outcome is changed by superficial or elaborate information processing, depending on the person's motivation and ability to process the relevant information (Chaiken, 1987; Petty & Cacioppo, 1986; for a recent review, see Albarracin & Vargas, 2010). Also, research has examined how fluctuations in basic needs (e.g., food, water, social contact) contribute to perceived desirability of outcomes, and how needs interact with other sources of desirability in goal setting (Veltkamp, Aarts, & Custers, 2009). For instance, people who

perceive a soft drink as desirable to quench their thirst are more likely to set the goal to consume a soft drink when thirsty, and this need effect can be simulated by increasing the desirability by means of evaluative conditioning (Veltkamp, Custers, & Aarts, 2011). Thus, both internal needs and externally shaped desirability cause people to set goals for action.

Other research has targeted the perceived feasibility of outcomes. In this approach, people are subjected to a treatment in the hope to augment their belief in being able to perform an action that produces the outcome (Bandura, 1997; Strecher et al., 1986). In other words, people are taught to perceive and experience themselves as strong agents that are capable of controlling their own behavior. Thus, the perceived feasibility (or self-efficacy) increases when people undergo a skill training required to reach the outcome. Perceived feasibility can also be augmented by observing role models executing actions that lead to the outcome (also known as vicarious learning) or exposure to a pep talk. By and large, this research suggests that the perceived feasibility of attaining an outcome relies on actual skills and the subjective confidence of carrying them out.

Changing the perceived desirability and feasibility of outcomes is one major strategy to demonstrate that people compute expected values to set favorable goals. Another, more recent approach is to examine contextual conditions that cause people to consider pre-existing perceptions of desirability or feasibility of given outcomes in setting them as goals. For instance, in testing their temporal construal theory, Liberman and Trope (1998) showed that when people consider an outcome (e.g., eating healthy food) to be attained in the far future, they focus more on outcome desirability. However, when the outcome is seen as something that one aims to attain in the near future, people focus more on feasibility. Thus, the desirability and feasibility of outcomes receive different weights in the process of goal setting, depending on the temporal construal of the outcome that a person has in mind to deal with a challenge or opportunity. Similar modulation effects on the contribution of desirability and feasibility have been suggested for other contextual factors, such as counterfactual thinking (Epstude & Roese, 2008), the anticipation of self-control problems (Mischel, Shoda, & Rodriguez, 1989), the introduction of discrepancies (Moskowitz et al., 1999), attributions of feedback on behavior (Fishbach, Eyal, & Finkelstein, 2010), and probing one's current mood states (Clore et al., 2001).

Expected values of outcomes play a central role in the specific goals that people set and the extent to which they are motivated to attain them. However, people's goals do not only depend on expected values. Goals are also structured by the (learned) context in which people bring potential goals and outcomes to mind. Such context frames the reference value or standard in guiding cognition and behavior of a goal, thus offering an explanation for why two persons with the same goal respond differently. For instance, goals that people set might be framed in terms of approach or avoidance (Elliot, 2008), or gains or losses (Higgins, 1997). For example, a person who is challenged by his teacher to be a good student may set the goal of pleasing his teacher as either approaching good manners or avoiding bad manners. Thus, the reference value of the same goal is toward positive versus negative actions, respectively. The idea that context structures the way people label the goals they set has been explored in other research programs, including the study on action identification in terms of means/ends (Vallacher & Wegner, 1987), and achievement motivation as a function of internal/external (social) standards (Dweck, 1999).

Importantly, once an outcome is set as a goal, the person can act on it. This transition from deliberation to actual goal pursuit is considered to require an act of conscious will that creates an intention to pursue the goal (Bandura, 1997; Fishbein & Ajzen, 1975; Gollwitzer, 1990; Locke & Latham, 2002). These intentions are proposed to form the input for initiating and regulating behavior.

WHAT DO GOALS DO IN THE PROCESS OF REGULATION?

To understand how goals regulate behavior we need to take into consideration that goals often are part of knowledge structures including the context, the goal itself, and actions as well as objects that may aid goal pursuit, that are shaped by direct experience and other types of learning (Aarts & Dijksterhuis, 2003; Bargh & Ferguson, 2000; Kruglanski et al., 2002). For example, the goal of consuming fruit may be related to eating a banana while having lunch in the university cafeteria. Or, a visit to a bar may be connected to interacting with friends and the desire to socialize. Thus, when intending to pursue goals (e.g., eating fruit, socializing), we do not access a single concept, but rather a rich structure containing, among others, cognitive, affective, and behavioral information (Bargh, 2006).

Accordingly, the goals that people set have distinctive effects on information processing in the service of goal achievement. These effects can be classified in two categories: (1) effects that

pertain to the processing of relevant information in order to enhance the probability to act on the goal and (2) effects that deal with the control of goal-directed behavior once goal pursuit is launched. The first category of effects has been mainly studied in the context of biases in perception and evaluation of goal-relevant attributes, and such biases direct behavior by causing stimuli in the environment related to goals to pop out relative to other stimuli (Bruner, 1957; Lewin, 1935). The second category of effects has been examined in the context of top-down attention and cognitive operations that are assumed to facilitate effective goal attainment. These operations are also known under the umbrella of working memory or executive control (Baddeley & Hitch, 1974; Miyake & Shah, 1999), and involve processes that render goal-directed behavior stable and adaptive. Below we will first examine the effects of goals on biases in information processing. Next, we examine goal effects on executive control processes.

Goals and biases in information processing

Goals and biases in visual perception
Research on vision has shown that perceived object size depends on factors like retinal image size, angle, and contextual cues (Rookes & Willson, 2000). Thus, objects that are bigger pop out in the environment and appear to be closer in space. However, apart from such objective factors, size perception is also influenced by subjective factors. Based on this notion, Bruner and Goodman (1947) argued that objects related to goals are perceived as bigger, such that they are more easily identified. The empirical support provided by Bruner and Goodman for this idea was heavily criticized (see e.g., Tajfel, 1957), but research on perceptual biases as a function of goals has recently re-entered the field using novel ways of experimentation.

In a recent study, for example, a group of thirsty and non-thirsty students estimated the size of different objects as they appear on a computer screen (Veltkamp, Aarts, & Custers, 2008b). One of the objects was a glass of water. However, just before they saw the glass, some participants were reminded of the potential goal of drinking, and others were not. Results showed that, compared to non-thirsty participants, thirsty participants perceived the glass of water as bigger, but only when the goal to drink was brought to mind. The fact that non-thirsty participants' size perception was unaffected by the reminder of drinking indicates that the effects were not merely cognitive, based on the mental accessibility of drinking. What was needed for size perception to be accentuated was the motivation to drink. Perceiving goal objects to be bigger when motivated may not be the only way in which goals facilitate their attainment. Objects that are perceptually accentuated also appear to be closer as size is an important cue to distance. In line with this notion, studies have demonstrated that the perceived distance to goal objects is biased as a function of consciously held goals (Balcetis & Dunning, 2010; Witt, Proffitt, & Epstein, 2004).

It is not entirely clear yet how goals biases basic perception of size, but neuro-scientific models on vision suggest that objects or tools that are functional for current behavior are allocated more processing resources (i.e., brain cells) and therefore occupy a larger area of the visual cortex (e.g., Serences & Yantis, 2006). These objects may be perceived as being bigger in relation to other stimuli in the visual field. Perhaps more disturbing, one may wonder whether perceiving objects to be bigger makes it more difficult to actually grasp the objects. Studies on vision and action suggest that it does not. The visual system can be separated in two largely independent operating streams, one dealing with object identification (ventral), the other with the action execution on the objects (dorsal; Goodale & Milner, 1992). As a result, increased size perception facilitates detection of the object, but this perceptual accentuation does not impinge on the information that is used by the system that deals with object prehension and utilization. In short, goals render goal-relevant objects to be perceived as bigger, thus promoting an easier mode of detecting them.

Goals and biases in evaluations

Goals do not only bias perceptual processing of goal-relevant objects to enhance the probability to act on the goal. Goals also bias the evaluation of objects (see also Chapter 9). Such biasing follows from the idea that goals represent desired outcomes that people want to attain, and hence people like objects that promote goal achievement and dislike objects that hamper the goal. Goal instrumental objects thus become more appealing than goal non-instrumental objects.

Ferguson and Bargh (2004; see also, Seibt, Häfner, & Deutsch, 2007), for example, asked participants to refrain from drinking for 3 hours before the experiment. One (non-thirsty) group quenched their thirst, and another (thirsty) group were made even more aware of their goal to drink by asking them to consume salty food. Next, participants took part in an affective priming task (Fazio et al., 1986), assessing their implicit evaluations of goal-related objects. It was found that goal-relevant objects (e.g., water) evoked more positivity in thirsty than in non-thirsty participants. These biases in evaluative processing did not show up for goal-unrelated objects (e.g., shoe). Other studies have shown that consciously held goals can have corollaries for the evaluation of objects that hamper the goal (e.g., Ferguson, 2007; Markman & Brendl, 2000). It is not (yet) clear how these biases in evaluation occur. They may result from a conscious rule-based process (e.g., "If I want to drink, then I like a glass of water") or an implicit associative process (e.g., affective priming in a knowledge network). However, these studies at least show that people feel good or bad towards objects that support or hinder goal pursuit, respectively.

It is interesting to note that goals not only play a role in biased valence processing of goal objects but also in responses to the affect-laden object itself. For instance, Chen and Bargh (1999) have shown that participants are faster to pull a lever toward the body (an approach reaction) after perception of positive stimuli, and to push a lever away from the body (an avoidance reaction) after perception of negative stimuli, than vice versa. These results are often conceptualized in terms of automatic responses, in that positive objects unintentionally evoke an approach and negative objects an avoidance response. However, recent research suggests that these approach and avoidance responses are not fully automatic, but are contingent on the compatibility between valence of response and valence of stimuli (Eder & Rothermund, 2008; Lavender & Hommel, 2007). Specifically, responses are facilitated when valence of response codes (e.g., away = negative and toward = positive) and valence of stimuli codes match independent of specific muscle movements. Whereas this work does not rule out that affect-laden objects can unintentionally prepare approach/avoidance movements (Krieglmeyer, Deutsch, De Houwer, & De Raedt, 2010), it suggests that such movements are responsive to how they are represented in terms of their effect, hence rendering them goal-dependent.

Goals and biases in decision making

The detection of goal-relevant information is an important step in the process of goal pursuit. In this step, internal representations of goals and associated knowledge interact with environmental features, such that top-down and bottom-up processes work together in initiating goal-directed behavior. If a suitable goal response is available in one's repertoire, action is launched and the goal can be attained. For instance, if a person wants to call a friend, action can be directly implemented upon seeing the cell phone on the table. Indeed, research on skills and habits indicates that setting a goal can directly lead to the execution of habitual actions leading to the goal (Aarts & Dijksterhuis, 2000; Sheeran et al., 2005; Wood & Neal, 2007).

However, it is important to stress that direct effects of goals (via perception and evaluation) on behavior do not always occur. People may have different options at their disposal, and be motivated to carefully select one (e.g., induced by the goal to be accurate or to justify one's choices; Neuberg & Fiske, 1987; Tetlock, 1985). In that case, they may compute expected values of each means, and select the one with the highest value. The literature on decision making offers several rational choice models that describe the weighing and decision rules that people should apply to select the best option, as well as models that take into account the bounded rationality of decision makers (Payne, Bettman, & Johnson, 1993; see also Chapter 13).

Interestingly, the notion that goals are mentally represented in knowledge structures implies that the activation of goals leads to enhanced accessibility of goal-related information in memory that guides attention, similar to other social constructs such as stereotypes and scripts (Bargh, 1997). For example, a person who associates the goal to meet friends with going to an Irish pub is likely to bring that pub and related attributes to mind (e.g., Irish music, playing darts, pint, and no foam). This enhanced accessibility of goal-related information can bias the decision-making process, such as the search of information and the weights people place on options and attributes of options (Aarts, Verplanken, & Van Knippenberg, 1998; Beach & Mitchell, 1987; Verplanken & Holland, 2002). In a demonstration of this idea, Verplanken and Holland (2002) asked participants to select a TV out of 20 options that were described on different attributes (e.g., screen quality, environmental friendliness). They showed that the environmental friendliness dimension was given more weight in the decision process, but only for participants who had the goal to protect the environment. These findings indicate that goals motivate biases in decision making, resembling effects of directional goals on confirmation biases (Kunda, 1990).

Goals and executive control of behavior

The biases in processing of goal-relevant information and the selection of means form a vital part of goal pursuit, but a real challenge starts when people have to control their mind and action to attain the goal. Such challenges occur when the situation does not allow for direct execution of means or skills, or contains distractions and temptations that push the current goal out of attention. In that case, we may need to postpone our goals, shield them from interfering (unwanted) responses, check the current status of our goals, and act on feedback and opportunities to attain them. People may experience these challenges as demanding and effortful (Kahneman, 1973), as they involve a set of executive control functions to aid effective goal pursuit. Research on executive control processes has flourished in the last decade. This research has been especially fruitful in understanding how people control attention and action in accord with goals, and in providing a neurocognitive account for how this ability is biologically implemented (Funahashi, 2001; Miller & Cohen, 2001; Miyake & Shah, 1999). A common framework proposed in this research is that the prefrontal cortex (PFC), anterior cingulate cortex (ACC), and posterior parietal cortex (PPC) are the main areas taking care of attentional and control processes.

According to research on executive control, stable and adaptive cognition and behavior depend on: (1) active maintenance of ordered information; (2) attention to task-relevant information and inhibition of task-irrelevant information; and (3) monitoring and feedback processing. These characteristics concur with the following functions underlying goal-directed thought and action: (1) holding goal-relevant information active in mind for a critical period of time; (2) keeping focused and shielding goals from interfering information; and (3) checking up the current state of goal pursuit, and supporting progress of goal attainment by taking advantage of opportunities and adapting to the situation at hand. In studying the regulatory nature of social behavior, research in social cognition employs tasks that rely on these control functions, such as tasks that ask subjects to resist temptations, impulses, and automatic tendencies, and tasks that put them under cognitive load in a dual-task context. Because these functions often operate jointly in the process of executive control, it is difficult to demonstrate their unique contribution to goal pursuit. However, there are a few lines of research that have tried to isolate the operation of these functions to offer clues about the workings of the goal-directed mind.

Active maintenance of goal-relevant information

Effective goal pursuit requires a mechanism that keeps the representation of goals and related information alive for a critical period of time, especially when this information is no longer externally present. Consistent with this idea, research shows that goal representations maintain active in memory – in comparison to semantic knowledge, which shows a rapid decay of activation in memory over short periods of time, usually within a few seconds (Baddeley & Logie, 1999; Joordens & Becker, 1997; McKone, 1995).

One research area in which this process has been tested is that of prospective memory. Goschke and Kuhl (1993) asked participants to study a series of actions (e.g., making coffee) and informed them that they had to perform some of these actions later on (goal condition) or to merely study or observe another person performing them (no-goal condition). Using a recognition paradigm, they established that actions were recognized faster when participants had the goal to execute them in comparison to the no-goal condition, indicating sustained accessibility of the goal in memory (see also, Marsh, Hicks, & Bink, 1998). Other research shows that this active maintenance process of consciously set goals is dependent on the expected value or motivational strength of the goal (Förster, Liberman, & Higgins, 2005).

Another area in which active maintenance processes of goal pursuit are studied concerns the effects of rewards, i.e., the perceived value part of goals. Because working memory has limited capacity, and thus not all information in the environment can be attended to and maintained at the same time, this research suggests that a reward-driven modulation of working memory is highly adaptive (Miller & Cohen, 2001; Pessoa, 2009; Veling & Aarts, 2010). For instance, Heitz, Schrock, Payne, and Engle (2008) tested the effects of monetary rewards on performance on a reading span task and found that participants performed significantly better when they could earn money. Gilbert and Fiez (2004) used functional magnetic resonance imaging (fMRI) to study the effect of money on active maintenance performance, and also found that participants performed better when performance was rewarded. Informatively, during the delay period of rewarded (compared to not rewarded) trials, greater activation was found in the dorsolateral prefrontal cortex (DLPFC), an area that is typically recruited during the active maintenance of information after it is no longer externally present.

Keeping focused and shielding goals from interfering information

Another challenge that people encounter when pursuing goals is distractions. For instance, a person going to the kitchen to do the dishes may suddenly find himself doing something else, such as taking a sausage from the refrigerator. Similarly, a student having the goal to work on a paper may start typing an email and forgets all about the initial goal. More generally, other meaningful or personally relevant information may interfere with keeping focused on the goal. Such information may be triggered by environmental cues associated with habits (e.g., when passing the fridge in the kitchen) and from internally represented information that is accessible but not relevant for the goal at hand (e.g., remembering an unfinished email conversation). In both cases, people are distracted from pursuing the original goal. Accordingly, effective goal pursuit requires a cognitive control mechanism that enhances focus and stability of the goal and shields the goal from interference of competing information by inhibiting it.

The potentials of an inhibition system in promoting effective goal pursuit have been studied in several research programs. In the realm of stereotyping, Moskowitz and colleagues (1999; Moskowitz, 2010) propose that people who have egalitarian goals are motivated to inhibit stereotypical traits upon exposure to stereotyped groups. In a series of studies, they have demonstrated this mechanism in several ways, using goal induction methods such as introducing goal discrepancies, and testing goal effects on reaction time tasks assessing the activation of stereotypes. It is important to note that studies on egalitarian goals and stereotype inhibition use individual differences in motivation, such that goal effects on inhibition are correlational. Although suggestive, these studies are not conclusive, as they may illustrate differences in goal activation, pre-existing knowledge structures, or both.

In a recent study, Danner and colleagues (Danner, Aarts, Papies, & De Vries, 2011) tested effects of goal activation on the inhibition of habitual tendencies while keeping pre-existing knowledge constant. In line with goal system theory (Kruglanski et al., 2002), they proposed that goals are associated with multiple means that enjoy inhibitory links in the service of goal pursuit. Hence, when people have the goal to perform new goal-directed behaviors (e.g., taking the bus to go to work), habitual means (e.g., the car) should be inhibited to protect the goal from habit intrusion. In their study, participants first studied habitual and new behaviors for various goals. Next, following the procedure of Goschke and Kuhl (1993), participants set the goal to perform some of the new behaviors later on (goal condition), while other new goal-directed behaviors only had to be studied (no-goal condition). Employing a recognition task, results showed that the new behaviors were recognized faster when participants had the goal to perform them compared to the no-goal condition, indicating that the new goal-directed behaviors maintained active in memory. Importantly, in the goal condition, habitual behaviors were less accessible than in the no-goal condition, showing that habitual behaviors were inhibited. Thus, participants kept focus on their active new goals by shielding attention from habit intrusion.

Whereas inhibition of interfering information plays a role in staying tuned to current goals, other studies have provided insight in inhibition processes during task switching or when goals are no longer valid. For instance, Mayr (2002) conducted research on the inhibition of action rules in a task-switch paradigm as a function of accessibility (i.e., recent vs non-recent use of action rules), and showed that action rules that are recently used but not relevant are inhibited, while action rules engaged in less recently are not inhibited. Thus, the rationale here is that a previously used task rule as part of a sequential action is inhibited if it causes interference (i.e., is accessible) when switching to another task rule. If the previous task rule does not interfere (i.e., is not accessible), there is no need to inhibit it. In a similar vein, research on prospective memory suggests that goals that are completed or canceled are inhibited, which is assumed to be functional in switching and attending to new goals (Marsh, Hicks, & Bink, 1998; Marsh, Hicks, & Bryan, 1999).

Goals and monitoring and feedback processing

Human goal pursuit often starts with the detection of a discrepancy between the desired outcome or goal and the actual state of the world. That is to say, the person wants something she does not have, or she encounters a situation she does not want to be in. Moreover, once the process of goal pursuit is launched, people have to check up the current state of goal pursuit and to keep an eye out to identify ways to reduce the discrepancies. In other words, they engage in monitoring and feedback processing.

Over the last 20 years, several studies have explored the neural correlates of this internal performance monitoring system. Measuring event-related potentials (ERPs), Gehring and colleagues (1990) discovered a neural response to errors that is now called the error-related negativity (ERN). The ERN consists of a large negative shift in the response-locked ERP occurring within 100 ms after subjects have made an erroneous response. Typically observed at fronto-central recording sites, the ERN has its source in the anterior cingulate cortex (Dehaene et al., 1994). Indeed, the ACC is involved in the processing of outcomes that deviate from conscious task-performance goals (reward prediction-errors; Matsumoto, Matsumoto, Abe, & Tanaka, 2007), and responds with increased activation when subjects commit errors (Ullsperger, Nittono, & Von Cramon, 2007), when feedback indicates that outcomes are below expectations (Nieuwenhuis, Schweizer, Mars, Botvinick, & Hajcak, 2007), or when performance is socially disapproved (Boksem, Ruys, & Aarts, 2011).

Most social psychological models on goal pursuit recognize that discrepancy detection and reduction plays an essential role in attaining and maintaining desired goals (Carver & Scheier, 1998; Hyland, 1988; Lewin, 1935). In research, these discrepancies are at times introduced by external agents (such as negative feedback from a significant other) and are at times introduced by the individual's own monitoring processes. A wide range of studies, relying on a variety of goals (from reducing one's prejudice, to affirming one's worth as a smart person), have illustrated effects on people's tendency to pursue a goal when confronted with such explicit discrepancies (e.g., Elliot & Dweck, 1988; Monteith, 1993; Steele, Spencer, & Lynch, 1993; Wicklund & Gollwitzer, 1982). Other research in the context of failure feedback suggests that discrepancies detection effects on motivation are moderated by reasoning processes, such as attributions (Fishbach et al., 2010; Weiner, 1986).

It is important to note that most studies on goals and discrepancies alluded to above assessed effects on measures indexing people's motivation to pursue or adhere to goals. These motivational responses to discrepancies offer clues that people engage in goal-directed monitoring and feedback processing, but do not directly speak to the operation of an executive control process that induces behavioral adaptation to the situation at hand. As far as behavioral effects have been studied, they mainly concern the goal-setting effect itself. That is, most studies on goal setting can be seen as relying on discrepancy detection, as goal setting usually occurs in a context in which goal discrepancy is inherent because the goal has yet to be achieved (Custers & Aarts, 2005a). However, this confound makes it difficult to determine whether the behavior resulted from "simple" goal setting, or whether it involves a reaction to a detected discrepancy as a function of monitoring. In a recent attempt to solve this issue, Custers and Aarts (2007a) manipulated discrepancies of a goal which typically needs to be maintained over time (the goal of looking well-groomed). They showed that these discrepancies (e.g., the shoes are dirty) trigger actions (e.g., polishing) to restore the discrepancy. However, this effect only occurred in people who are chronic well-groomers (as a result of pursuing the goal frequently), suggesting that adaptive behavior is supported by goal-directed monitoring and feedback processing.

Who sets and controls the goals that we pursue?

We observed that humans bring outcomes to mind in a current situation. Outcomes are set as goals when they are rewarding and attainable on the basis of an expected value analysis. These goals render behavior persistent, effortful, and flexible, directed at attaining desired outcomes. Thus, goals motivate people to process information in the environment and to employ a set of executive functions that promote effective goal pursuit.

As mentioned earlier, research on goal pursuit commonly assumes that goal setting and execution rely on conscious processes. This assumption is central to research on volitional behavior (Haggard, 2008), and the role of the self in controlling behavior (e.g., Baumeister, Schmeichel, & Vohs, 2007). The idea that behavior is controlled by the self is intuitively appealing. After all, the actions we conduct and the outcomes they produce are often accompanied by feelings of self-causation and belonging to oneself. However, there has been some debate about the uniqueness of the self in processing goal-relevant information (Greenwald & Banaji, 1989) and the brain areas involved in such processes (Legrand & Ruby, 2009). Furthermore, research suggests that our sense of self as an agent is likely to result from inferences that we draw from controlling behavior, whether we are the actual cause or not (Aarts, Custers, & Marien, 2009; Ruys & Aarts, in press; Wegner, 2002).

Accordingly, the human pursuit of goals may not (always) result from an agent that consciously sets and controls goals. Perhaps, then, the origin and control of our goal pursuit happens somewhere else. Recent theorizing about human motivation and goal-directed behavior takes an evolutionary perspective on this matter. Specifically, modern goal pursuit is suggested to be primarily based on old brain systems that take care of goal pursuit in an unconscious fashion. The more recent brain systems involved in higher cognitive processes (including consciousness) build on these old systems (Bargh & Morsella, 2008). Thus it is likely that goal-directed processes rely on existing unconscious structures to control behavior in dynamic environments. Others even suggest that consciousness (as we know it) is a relatively young capacity in terms of human evolution, and therefore we should be cautious in assigning a specific function to it (Dennett, 1991; Jaynes, 1976; Pinker, 1997).

These convergent views on the (modest) role of consciousness in behavior underscore the idea that our behavior starts in the unconscious, and is often directed and motivated by goals outside of conscious awareness, even though we share the belief and experience that we consciously set and pursue goals. We now turn to the empirical research that has tested this possibility. We first focus on research that explored whether goals and the subsequent motivation and regulation of behavior can be triggered outside of conscious awareness. We then briefly survey the potential mechanism that enables people to pursue and attain goals unconsciously.

UNCONSCIOUS PROCESSES IN GOAL PURSUIT

In a remarkable experiment conducted about three decades ago (Libet, Gleason, Wright, & Pearl, 1983), participants were instructed to freely choose when to move their index finger while the timing of the action itself, of its preparation in the brain, and of when the subject became aware of the decision to act were measured. Although the decision did indeed precede the action, the preparation of the finger movement in the brain was well on its way by the time people consciously decided to act. Apparently, when people consciously set the goal to engage in behavior, their conscious will to act starts out unconsciously.

The finding that the pursuit of the goals that we consciously set and adopt is prepared unconsciously, at least in the earliest moments before we act on them, is intriguing. Research in social cognition, however, goes even one step further. This research suggests that goals themselves can arise and operate unconsciously. Social situations and stimuli in the surroundings activate goals in people's minds outside of their awareness, thereby motivating and guiding behavior.

Goal priming and unconscious effects on motivated behavior

One of the first empirical demonstrations of this notion comes from Bargh et al.'s (2001) research program on goal priming effects on achievement. In one of their studies, they unobtrusively exposed students to words such as "strive" and "succeed" to prime the goal of achievement in a first task, and then gave them the opportunity to perform well in a second task (solving anagrams). Results indicated that students primed with the achievement goal outperformed those who were not primed with the goal. Further experimentation established that such goal priming effects have motivational qualities, such as persistence in solving puzzles. Extensive debriefing revealed that the students did not experience an influence of the first task on their responses to the second. These findings indicate that the mere activation of a goal representation suffices to motivate and direct goal pursuit without conscious thought and intent (for more evidence of achievement priming effects, see Bongers, Dijksterhuis, & Spears, 2010; Custers, Aarts, Oikawa, & Elliot, 2009; Eitam, Hassin, & Schul, 2008; Engeser, Wendland, & Rheinberg, 2006; Hart & Albarracin, 2009; Hassin, 2008; Oikawa, 2004; Shantz & Latham, 2009).

Recently, researchers have started to identify the specific aspects in the social environment that may cause people to automatically set and pursue goals. Through their associations with particular goals, these aspects *indirectly* prime goal representations. For instances, goal pursuit is automatically triggered when goals are inferred from the behavior of others, an effect dubbed goal contagion (Aarts, Gollwitzer, Hassin, 2004; Dik & Aarts, 2007; Friedman, Deci, Elliot, Moller, & Aarts, 2010; Loersch, Aarts, Payne, Jefferis, 2008). In addition, goals and their pursuit materialize after exposure to important others (Fitzimons & Bargh, 2003; Kraus & Chen, 2009; Shah, 2003), and members of social groups that contain the representation of a goal that is believed to be held by that group (Aarts et al., 2005; Custers, Maas, Wildenbeest, & Aarts, 2008).

It is important to stress that most studies on social triggers of unconscious goal pursuit alluded to above employ a so-called unrelated studies setup: participants are exposed to consciously visible goal primes in a first task and effects on behavior are tested on a second unrelated task. However, these studies have been criticized for allowing participants to be aware of the primes (Custers & Aarts, 2010). Even though participants report being unaware of the influence of the goal priming on their behavior, they could still have formed conscious intentions at the moment they consciously perceived the goal information. Hence, their goal pursuit may still be caused by an act of conscious will.

To offer even more compelling evidence for unconscious goal pursuit, researchers have recently resorted to more stringent methods such as subliminal stimulation, which prevents conscious perception of the primes. Typically, people cannot consciously detect these stimuli, but they are nevertheless influenced by them. Whether subliminal stimulation can convey meaningful information has been debated for quite some time, especially in light of the question of whether the unconscious is dumb (rigid responses) or smart (flexible cognitive processes) when people are exposed to stimuli with an intensity that is too low to reach the threshold of conscious awareness

(Loftus & Klinger, 1992). Nevertheless, recent findings provide strong evidence that subliminal primes affect people's responses (Schlaghecken & Eimer, 2004), activate semantically related knowledge (Naccache & Dehaene, 2001), and even influence cognitive control (Lau & Passingham, 2007).

Research also has demonstrated effects of subliminal stimulation on goal pursuit. Priming of achievement-related words increases task performance (Gendolla & Silvestrini, 2010; Hart & Albarracín, 2009); priming drinking-related words enhances fluid consumption in a taste task (Strahan, Spencer, & Zanna, 2002; Veltkamp, Aarts, & Custers, 2008b), and priming of monetary rewards increases the recruitment of effort on physical and cognitive tasks (Bijleveld, Custers, & Aarts, 2009; Pessiglione et al., 2007). Furthermore, studies have shown an increase in motivated social behaviors (e.g., helping another person) after priming names of significant others (e.g., a good friend) or occupations (e.g., nurse) associated with these goals (Aarts et al., 2005; Fitzsimons & Bargh, 2003). Importantly, in most of these subliminal goal priming studies, subjects are asked in retrospect to report whether they were motivated to pursue the primed goal. The general finding is that, although reported motivation sometimes correlates with behavior (e.g., people who worked harder report to be more motivated), these reports are not influenced by the primes. This suggests that subliminal priming of goals does not affect goal pursuit because people become conscious of their motivation to pursue the goal after it is primed.

Goal priming and unconscious effects on the regulation of behavior

The studies discussed above indicate that goal priming leads to motivated behavior. However, apart from effects on motivated behavior, studies have shown that goal priming also biases information processing. For instance, in a study on drinking behavior (Veltkamp et al., 2008a) participants' level of fluid deprivation was measured in an unobtrusive way, such that they were unaware of being thirsty at the time of testing. Some participants were subliminally exposed to drinking-related words in a stimulus detection task, others were not. It was found that subliminal exposure to drinking words caused thirsty participants to perceive a glass of water as bigger compared to nonthirsty participants and to thirsty participants who were not primed. Thus, only in participants for which drinking was a desired goal, priming caused perceptual accentuation of goal-instrumental objects. In the context of biases in evaluation,

Ferguson (2008) showed that priming goals outside of awareness leads to stronger positive affective responses toward goal-instrument objects.

Furthermore, goal priming shapes executive control processes supporting goal pursuit. For instance, research has demonstrated that goals that are activated unconsciously maintain active over time (Aarts, Custers, & Holland, 2007; Aarts, Custers, & Veltkamp, 2008; Aarts et al., 2009). For instance, Aarts et al. (2007) examined how the mental accessibility of a goal after a short interval changes as a function of subliminally priming the goal. In one of their studies, participants were primed or not with the goal to socialize, and 2.5 minutes later tested for accessibility of the goal in a lexical decision task. Results showed that the representation of the goal remained accessible when participants were primed to attain the goal. Similar persistent activation effects – even after 5 minutes of goal priming – have been obtained for behavioral measures (e.g., Aarts et al., 2004; Bargh et al., 2001), suggesting that some kind of active maintenance process keeps goal-relevant information alive non-consciously.

The role of unconscious goals in active maintenance processes has also been studied in the context of reward priming. For instance, in one study (Zedelius, Veling, & Aarts, 2011) participants could earn money (1 cent or 50 cents) by accurately reporting a set of studied words after a delay. The rewards were presented as coins just before a trial, and the coins were either consciously visible or subliminal. Thus, effects of conscious and unconscious reward cues could be compared within one experiment. Results showed that performance on the maintenance task was higher for 50 cents trials than for 1 cent trials, regardless of whether the coins were presented consciously or unconsciously. Another study showed that both conscious and unconscious presentation of high (vs low) monetary rewards increase the dilation of the pupil during the maintenance task, indicating that participants invested more mental effort (Bijleveld et al., 2009). Interestingly, these effects only showed up when the reward required considerable mental effort to obtain (i.e., when 5 rather than 3 words had to be retained), suggesting that people unconsciously react to reward information by recruiting resources to support the active maintenance process.

Other work has started to explore whether humans can keep their eyes on their ongoing goal pursuit in a non-conscious manner when competing information conflicts with their pursuit (Aarts et al., 2007; Papies, Stroebe, & Aarts, 2008; Shah, Friedman, & Kruglanski, 2002). For instance, Shah and colleagues (2002) demonstrated that non-consciously instigating participants to pursue a given goal (by subliminally exposing them to words representing the goal, e.g., of studying) caused them to inhibit competing accessible goals (e.g., going out); moreover, this inhibition facilitated the achievement of the non-consciously activated goal. These findings provide support for the existence of a non-conscious attention/inhibition mechanism that shields goals from distracting thoughts. Shah et al. speculated that these goal-shielding effects require extensive and effortless practice, thus arguing for a well-learned automated mechanism. Recent studies, however, indicate that the inhibitory effects in goal-directed behavior may kick in rather rapidly – i.e., after a few practice trials (Danner, Aarts, & De Vries, 2007; McCulloch et al., 2008; Veling & Aarts, 2009).

Finally, there are a few studies that show that people engage in unconscious monitoring and feedback processing and that situations that are discrepant with non-consciously activated goals encourage people to adapt their behavior (Custers & Aarts, 2005a, 2007a; Fourneret & Jeannerod, 1998: Slachevsky et al., 2001). For instance, Custers and Aarts (2007a) non-consciously activated the goal of looking well-groomed or not in a parafoveal priming task, just before participants were confronted with a situation that was discrepant with the goal. Their findings showed that the non-consciously activated goal facilitated the identification of actions reducing the discrepancy. However, these goal priming effects did not emerge when the situation was not discrepant with the primed goal (Custers & Aarts, 2005a).

In sum, several lines of research suggest that goals that we pursue are often triggered by the social environment. Apparently, people do not (always) consciously bring potential goals or outcomes to mind and assess the desirability and feasibility of the outcomes in order to consciously set and regulate goals. People are motivated to initiate and control behaviors when goals are primed, even though they are not aware of the primed goal or its effect on their motivation and behavior. In other words, the pursuit of goals seems to be set and flexibly regulated in the unconscious. This unconscious flexibility fits well with research showing that human functioning (information encoding, memory use, evaluation, inferences, social perception, and judgment) is largely rooted in cognitive processes that do not require conscious control (Bargh, 2007).

How does the unconscious pursue goals?

Although the unconscious goal pursuit effects reported in the literature are intriguing and impressive, they may leave (some) readers with the pressing question how this all works: How do people resolve whether to pursue a given goal and to invest effort or recruit resources to attain it without involvement of conscious will?

In an attempt to examine the potential mechanism of unconscious goal pursuit, Custers and Aarts (2005b, 2010) propose that unconscious goal pursuit is likely to occur when the activation of a goal representation available in a person's repertoire is immediately followed by the activation of a positive affective tag. Specifically, goals are suggested to consist of two distinctive features that allow people to pursue goals without conscious intervention: a representation of an outcome and a reward signal attached to the outcome. An outcome is likely to operate as a potential goal when one has learned to represent the outcome in terms of effects resulting from actions. For instance, a person may represent the event of "calling a friend" or "earning money" as outcomes of one's own actions, but not events such as "flying to the moon" or "being Clint Eastwood" (though the last events could be fantasies). The outcome representation thus provides a reference point in directing perception and action: i.e., actions can be initiated by processing information about outcomes, because actions and outcomes are associated on a perceptual, sensory, and motor level. Therefore, bringing to mind the outcome representation prepares and directs perception and action to produce the outcome without much thought. Many of the unconscious behavioral priming studies reported in the literature qualify as such a priming effect (Dijksterhuis, Chartrand, & Aarts, 2007), indicating that outcome representations can be processed and acted upon unconsciously.

However, although priming an outcome representation prepares and directs action, it does not necessarily motivate and control action (Aarts, Custers, & Marien, 2008). For motivation and control to occur a second feature is required: namely, the outcome should be attached to a positive affect or a reward signal that motivates goal-directed behavior. Neuroimaging research has revealed that reward cues are processed by limbic structures such as the nucleus accumbens and the ventral striatum. These subcortical areas play a central role in determining the rewarding value of outcomes and are connected to frontal areas in the cortex that modulate executive control in goal pursuit (e.g., Aston-Jones, & Cohen, 2005). These reward centers in the brain respond to evolutionarily relevant rewards such as food and sexual stimuli, but also to learned rewards (e.g., money, status), or words (e.g., good, nice) that are associated with praise or rewards (Schultz, 2006). Thus, regardless of their shape or form,

positive stimuli can induce a reward signal that is readily picked up by the brain.

The analysis discussed above suggests that the representation of an outcome and an accompanying reward signal provide the building blocks for unconscious goal pursuit. Specifically, when a desired outcome or goal is primed, activation of the mental representation of this outcome is immediately followed by the activation of an associated positive tag, which acts as a reward signal for pursuing the primed goal. The positive reward signal attached to a goal thus unconsciously facilitates the actual selection of the goal and the subsequent mobilization of effort and resources to control goal-directed behavior, unless other (e.g., more strongly activated or rewarding) goals gain priority. This affective-motivational process relies on associations between the representations of outcomes and positive reward signals that are shaped by one's history (e.g., when a person was happy when making money or performing well). In this case, the goal is said to pre-exist as a desired state in mind, and priming the representation of the goal motivates people to pursue the goal because of its association with positive affect (Custers & Aarts, 2007a; Ferguson, 2007).

Unconscious goal pursuit can also be simulated by externally triggering the affective signal just after activation of a potential goal or outcome representation. This ability to respond to the mere co-activation of goal representations and positive affective cues is thought to play a fundamental role in social learning (Miller & Dollard, 1941) and considered as basic in motivational analyses of human behavior (Shizgal, 1997). Thus, when a child observes her mother's smile upon munching homemade cookies, or a student witnesses a hilarious joke upon entering the classroom, this can cause the goal representations that are primed by those situations (eating candy, achieving at school) to acquire an intrinsic reward value, which motivates and regulates goal-directed behavior.

A decent number of studies, testing simple action goals as well as more abstract social goals, have shown that the co-activation of a goal representation and positive affect produces unconscious goal pursuit (Aarts et al., 2008a, 2008b; Capa et al., 2011; Custers & Aarts, 2005b; Holland et al., 2009; Van den Bos & Stapel, 2009; Veltkamp et al., 2008a, 2011). In addition, priming a goal representation in temporal proximity to the activation of positive affect has been demonstrated to bias information processing of goal objects, such as size perception (Aarts et al., 2008b; Veltkamp et al., 2008) and to evoke executive control processes supporting the goal, such as active maintenance (Aarts et al., 2008b, 2009) and overcoming well-learned responses to swiftly switch to alternative courses of action (Marien, Aarts, & Custers, in press).

ISSUES IN THE STUDY OF CONSCIOUS AND UNCONSCIOUS GOAL PURSUIT

So far, the examination of the general principles that govern goal pursuit indicates that people engage in flexible and effortful regulation of goal pursuit. Such regulation results from conscious as well as unconscious processes. The new insight that both conscious and unconscious processes contribute to the pursuit of goals, and its consequence for our understanding of how goals control behavior, lead to a number of interesting issues that require further scrutiny.

First of all, although research suggests that unconscious goal pursuit involves adaptive and flexible processes, understanding exactly how unconscious goals flexibly control behavior remains a challenge. One way to approach this issue is by proposing that goals direct attention and behavior, even without awareness of the goal (Bargh & Ferguson, 2000; Dijksterhuis & Aarts, 2010). In other words, we need attention to flexibly pursue goals, but not necessarily consciousness. Attention is a functional process that selects and biases the flow of incoming information and internal representations in the service of goal attainment. Thus, the content of attention represents the goals that are active at a specific moment in time. Consciousness in the context of goal pursuit usually refers to mental processes that are accompanied by (reported) awareness of certain aspects of the process and/or awareness of relevant contents or perceptual products (Blackmore, 2003; Gray, 2004).

In everyday life, attention and consciousness are correlated, basically because a stimulus that one pays more attention to is more likely to enter conscious awareness. However, this does not mean that attention and consciousness are the same. In fact, recent conceptualizations treat attention and consciousness as orthogonal (Dehaene, Changeux, Naccache, Sackur, & Sergent, 2006; Koch & Tsuchiya, 2006; Lamme, 2003). From this perspective, it would be interesting to offer stricter tests of the possible mediating role of attention in the relation between goals and behavior (independent of consciousness). Such an enterprise may call for new methods and operationalizations that allow us to distinguish attention from consciousness as to the content and workings of the goal-directed mind (Lau, 2009; Seth et al., 2008), and to establish their unique contribution in unconsciously triggered goal pursuit.

Second, we still know surprisingly little about how consciously and unconsciously activated goals differ in their control of behavior. There is quite some research showing that consciously set goals (vs no goal at all) facilitate human functioning in several ways (e.g., Alonso, Fuentes, & Hommel, 2006; Baddeley, 1993; Locke & Latham, 2002), and these data portray the general picture that consciousness plays a causal status in goal-directed behavior. Although tempting, this conclusion may be wrong or at least premature, as most studies lack the proper controls to exclude the possibility that attention actually does the work (Custers & Aarts, 2011; Lau, 2009). The research discussed here indicates that conscious goals (often induced by explicit task instructions) and unconscious goals (induced by priming) have similar effects on tasks that rely on executive control. This suggests that conscious and unconscious goals (partly) rely on the same functional architecture of attention and information processing in which the same cognitive functions or hardware are recruited and shared to pursue goals (Aarts, 2007; Badgaiyan, 2000). How, then, may consciously and unconsciously activated goals differ in directing behavior?

Recent research has started to explore this question. This research looks for instances in which conscious goals would produce different effects on behavior than unconscious goals. In a study on effects of the goal to earn money on performance (Bijleveld, Custers, & Aarts, 2010), participants had to solve an arithmetic problem in a speed–accuracy paradigm to attain a consciously or unconsciously presented high- or low-value coin. Unconscious high (vs low) rewards made participants more eager (i.e., faster, but equally accurate). In contrast, conscious high (vs low) rewards caused participants to become more cautious (i.e., slower, but more accurate). However, the effects of conscious rewards mimicked those of unconscious rewards when the tendency to make speed–accuracy tradeoffs was reduced. These findings suggest that pursuing monetary rewards initially facilitate effort to work on a task regardless of whether or not people are aware of them, but affect speed–accuracy tradeoffs only when the reward information gains access to consciousness.

Another recent study demonstrates that conscious, but not unconscious, pursuit of monetary rewards can deteriorate instead of improve performance (Zedelius et al., 2011). In this study, participants had to retain words in memory. When rewards were presented before participants saw the words, both conscious and unconscious high rewards improved performance. However, when rewards were presented just after the presentation of the words (during the active maintenance process), only unconscious high rewards improved performance, whereas conscious high rewards impaired performance. This pattern is consistent with the idea that unconscious rewards boost task effort, causing people to do well. When rewards are consciously processed, conscious concerns (e.g., "Will I do well?") may interfere with the task, causing people to perform worse. This latter effect concurs with studies on choking under pressure, showing that conscious reflection on behavior or rewards taxes the limited capacity of conscious processes and distracts attention away from the task (Beilock, 2007; Mobbs et al., 2009).

The research alluded to above suggests that consciousness interferes with goal-directed attentional processes that we usually engage in skillfully. However, we should not conclude from this that consciousness is always defective in the pursuit of goals, as we do not yet know whether there are special cases in which consciousness (apart from attention) facilitates goal-directed performance. One such case pertains to situations in which no information or action is available in one's repertoire to deal with challenges or opportunities posed. Often, this implies the preparation of a course of action that is totally new or has never been executed before in the situation at hand. According to Global Workspace Theory (e.g., Baars, 1997), consciousness then helps to mobilize and integrate brain functions and representations/processes that otherwise operate independently in the course of building up a new action. It offers a "facility for accessing, disseminating, and exchanging information, and for exercising global coordination and control" (Baars, 1997, p. 7).

Consistent with this idea, research has shown that conscious planning leads to more successful goal achievement, as such plans integrate and establish links between representations of relevant actions and cues (Gollwitzer & Sheeran, 2006). Moreover, recent research suggests that conscious planning has more stable and reliable effects on goal attainment than merely attending to information of the plan (Papies, Aarts, & de Vries, 2009). Whether these beneficial effects of planning rely on consciousness itself is not clear yet, as there may be other factors that contribute to stronger effects of planning on behavior (e.g., motivation, enhanced attentional processing). However, a large sample of studies in various fields suggest that it may be wise to consciously plan behavior ahead in time when facing new goals and actions.

CONCLUSION

The present chapter indicates that the concept of goals is an important construct in understanding and studying the potential causes, processes, and consequences of people's behavior in their social surroundings. Research on the role of goals in motivated social cognition and behavior thus demonstrates how social and contextual settings cause people to set goals they are motivated to attain, and how such goals shape subsequent information processing and executive control that promote the actual attainment of goals. In so doing, goals play a vital role in rendering human behavior flexible and effortful, suited to meet the dynamics of the environment. This flexible and effortful regulation of goal pursuit can be largely engaged in without conscious intervention. Accordingly, whereas the causal status of consciousness in human behavior is often taken for granted, people seem to navigate their goal-directed behavior quite adequately without a need to postulate an inner agent that sets and controls goal pursuit by an act of conscious will. In the search for the mental faculties that make human behavior goal-directed, then, it is important to further our understanding of how people pursue goals unconsciously, and how conscious processes evolve from, and build on, unconscious processes in promoting effective goal pursuit.

ACKNOWLEDGMENT

The preparation of this chapter was supported by VICI grant 453-06-002 from the Netherlands Organization for Scientific Research.

REFERENCES

Aarts, H. (2007). Health behavior and the implicit motivation and regulation of goals. *Health Psychology Review, 1*, 53–82.

Aarts, H., Chartrand, T. L., Custers, R., Danner, U., Dik, G., Jefferis, V., et al. (2005). Social stereotypes and automatic goal pursuit. *Social Cognition, 23*, 464–489.

Aarts, H., Custers, R., & Holland, R. W. (2007). The nonconscious cessation of goal pursuit: When goals and negative affect are coactivated. *Journal of Personality and Social Psychology, 92*, 165–178.

Aarts, H., Custers, R., & Marien, H. (2008). Preparing and motivating behavior outside of awareness. *Science, 319*, 1639.

Aarts, H., Custers, R., & Marien, H. (2009). Priming and authorship ascription: When nonconscious goals turn into conscious experiences of self-agency. *Journal of Personality and Social Psychology, 96*, 967–979.

Aarts, H., Custers, R., & Veltkamp, M. (2008a). Goal priming and the affective-motivational route to nonconscious goal pursuit. *Social Cognition, 26*, 555–577.

Aarts, H., & Dijksterhuis, A. (2000). Habits as knowledge structures: Automaticity in goal-directed behavior. *Journal of Personality and Social Psychology, 78*, 53–63.

Aarts, H., & Dijksterhuis, A. (2003). The silence of the library: Environment, situational norm and social behavior. *Journal of Personality and Social Psychology, 84*, 18–28.

Aarts, H., & Elliot, A. (2012). *Goal-directed behavior.* New York: Psychology Press.

Aarts, H., Gollwitzer, P. M., & Hassin, R. R. (2004). Goal contagion: Perceiving is for pursuing. *Journal of Personality and Social Psychology, 87*, 23–37.

Aarts, H., & Veling, H. (2009). Do resonance mechanisms in language and action depend on intentional processes? *European Journal of Social Psychology, 39*, 1188–1190.

Aarts, H., Verplanken, B., & Van Knippenberg, A. (1998). Predicting behavior from actions in the past: Repeated decision making or a matter of habit? *Journal of Applied Social Psychology, 28*, 1356–1375.

Albarracín, D., & Vargas, P. (2010). Attitudes and persuasion. In S. T. Fiske, D. T. Gilbert, & G. Lindzey (Eds.), *Handbook of social psychology* (pp. 394–427). New York: Wiley.

Alonso, D., Fuentes, L. J., & Hommel, B. (2006). Unconscious symmetrical inferences: A role of consciousness in event integration. *Consciousness and Cognition, 15*(2), 386–396.

Aston-Jones, G., & Cohen, J. D. (2005). An integrative theory of locus coeruleus-norepinephrine function: Adaptive gain and optimal performance. *Annual Review of Neuroscience, 28*, 403–450.

Baars, B. J. (1997). *In the theatre of consciousness: The workspace of the mind.* New York: Oxford University Press.

Baddeley, A. D. (1993). Working memory and conscious awareness. In A. Collins & S. Gathercole (Eds.), *Theories of memory* (pp. 11–28). Hillsdale, NJ: Lawrence Erlbaum Associates.

Baddeley, A. D., & Hitch, G. (1974). Working memory. In G. Bower (Ed.), *The psychology of learning and motivation: Advances in research and theory* (Vol. 8, pp. 47–89). New York: Academic Press.

Baddeley, A. D., & Logie, R. H. (1999). Working memory: The multiple-component model. In A. Miyake & P. Shah (Eds.), *Models of working memory: Mechanisms of active maintenance and executive control* (pp. 28–61). New York: Cambridge University Press.

Badgaiyan, R. D. (2000). Executive control, willed actions, and nonconscious processing. *Human Brain Mapping, 9*, 38–41.

Balcetis, E., & Dunning, D. (2010). Wishful seeing: More desired objects are seen as closer. *Psychological Science, 21*, 147–152.

Bandura, A. (1997). *Self-efficacy: The exercise of control.* New York: W.H. Freeman.

Bargh, J. A. (1997). The automaticity of everyday life. In R. S. Wyer (Ed.), *The automaticity of everyday life: Advances in social cognition* (Vol. 10, pp. 1–61). Mahwah, NJ: Erlbaum.

Bargh, J. A. (2006). What have we been priming all these years? On the development, mechanisms, and ecology of nonconscious social behavior. *European Journal of Social Psychology, 36*, 147–168.

Bargh, J. A. (2007). *Social psychology and the unconscious: The automaticity of higher mental processes.* New York: Psychology Press.

Bargh, J. A., & Ferguson, M. J. (2000). Beyond behaviorism: On the automaticity of higher mental processes. *Psychological Bulletin, 126*, 925–945.

Bargh, J. A., Gollwitzer, P. M., Lee Chai, A., Barndollar, K., & Trötschel, R. (2001). The automated will: Nonconscious activation and pursuit of behavioral goals. *Journal of Personality and Social Psychology, 81*, 1014–1027.

Bargh, J. A., & Morsella, E. (2008). The unconscious mind. *Perspectives on Psychological Science, 3*, 73–79.

Baumeister, R. F., Schmeichel, B. J., & Vohs, K. D. (2007). Self-regulation and the executive function: The self as controlling agent. In A. W. Kruglanski & E. T. Higgins (Eds.), *Social psychology: Handbook of basic principles* (2nd ed., pp. 516–539). New York: Guilford Press.

Beach, L. R., & Mitchell, T. R. (1987). Image theory: Principles, goals, and plans in decision making. *Acta Psychologica, 66*, 201–220.

Beckers, T., De Houwer, J., & Eelen, P. (2002). Automatic integration of non-perceptual action effect features: The case of the associative affective Simon effect. *Psychological Research, 66*, 166–173.

Beilock, S. L. (2007). Choking under pressure. In R. F. Baumeister & K. D. Vohs (Eds.), *Encyclopedia of social psychology* (pp. 140–141). Thousand Oaks, CA: SAGE.

Berridge, K. C. (2001). Reward learning: Reinforcement, incentives, and expectations. In D. L. Medin (Ed.), *The psychology of learning and motivation: Advances in research and theory* (Vol. 40, pp. 223–278). San Diego, CA: Academic Press.

Bijleveld, E., Custers, R., & Aarts, H. (2009). The unconscious eye opener: Pupil dilation reveals strategic recruitment of mental resources upon subliminal reward cues. *Psychological Science, 20*, 1313–1315.

Bijleveld, E., Custers, R., & Aarts, H. (2010). Unconscious reward cues increase invested effort, but do not change speed–accuracy tradeoffs, *Cognition, 115*, 330–335.

Blackmore, S. (2003). *Consciousness.* New York: Oxford University Press.

Boksem, M. A. S., Ruys, K. I., & Aarts, H. (2011). Facing disapproval: Performance monitoring in a social context. *Social Neuroscience, 6*, 360–368.

Bongers, K. C. A., Dijksterhuis, A., & Spears, R. (2010). On the role of consciousness in goal pursuit. *Social Cognition, 28*, 262–272.

Bruner, J. S. (1957). On perceptual readiness. *Psychological Review, 64*, 123–152.

Bruner, J. S., & Goodman, C. C. (1947). Value and need as organizing factors in perception. *Journal of Abnormal and Social Psychology, 42*, 33–44.

Capa, R. L., Cleeremans, A., Bustin, G. M., Bouquet, C. A., Hansenne, M. (2011). Effects of subliminal priming on nonconscious goal pursuit and effort-related cardiovascular response. *Social Cognition, 29*, 430–444.

Carver, C. S., & Scheier, M. F. (1998). *On the self-regulation of behavior.* New York: Cambridge University Press.

Chaiken, S. (1987). The heuristic model of persuasion. In M. P. Zanna, J. M. Olson, & C. P. Herman (Eds.), *Social influence: The Ontario Symposium* (Vol. 5, pp. 3–39), Hillsdale, NJ: Erlbaum.

Chen, M., & Bargh, J. A. (1999). Consequences of automatic evaluation: Immediate behavioral predispositions to approach or avoid the stimulus. *Personality and Social Psychology Bulletin, 25*, 215–224.

Clore, G. L., Wyer, B., Dienes, K., Gasper, C., Gohm, W., & Isbell, L. (2001). Affective feelings as feedback: Some cognitive consequences. In L. L. Martin & G. L. Clore, (Eds.), *Theories of mood and cognition. A user's handbook* (pp. 27–62). Mahwah, NJ: Erlbaum.

Cooper, R. P., & Shallice, T. (2006). Hierarchical schemas and goals in the control of sequential behavior. *Psychological Review, 113*, 887–916.

Custers, R., & Aarts, H. (2005a). Beyond accessibility: The role of affect and goal-discrepancies in implicit processes of motivation and goal-pursuit. *European Review of Social Psychology, 16*, 257–300.

Custers, R., & Aarts, H. (2005b). Positive affect as implicit motivator: On the nonconscious operation of behavioral goals. *Journal of Personality and Social Psychology, 89*, 129–142.

Custers, R., & Aarts, H. (2007a). Goal-discrepant situations prime goal-directed actions if goals are temporarily or chronically accessible. *Personality and Social Psychology Bulletin, 33*, 623–633.

Custers, R., & Aarts, H. (2007b). In search of the nonconscious sources of goal pursuit: Accessibility and positive affective valence of the goal state. *Journal of Experimental Social Psychology, 43*, 312–318.

Custers, R., & Aarts, H. (2010). The unconscious will: How the pursuit of goals operates outside of conscious awareness. *Science, 329*, 47–50.

Custers, R., & Aarts, H. (2011). Learning of predictive relations between events depends on attention, not on awareness. *Consciousness and Cognition, 20*, 368–378.

Custers, R., Aarts, H., Oikawa, M., & Elliot, A. (2009). The nonconscious road to perceptions of performance: Achievement priming, success expectations and self-agency. *Journal of Experimental Social Psychology, 45*, 1200–1208.

Custers, R., Maas, M., Wildenbeest, M., & Aarts, H. (2008). Nonconscious goal pursuit and the surmounting of physical and social obstacles. *European Journal of Social Psychology, 38*, 1013–1022.

Danner, U. N., Aarts, H., & De Vries, N. K. (2007). Habit formation and multiple options to goal attainment: Repeated selection of targets means causes inhibited access to alternatives. *Personality and Social Psychology Bulletin, 33*, 1367–1379.

Danner, U. N., Aarts, H., Papies, E. K., & De Vries, N. K. (2011). Paving the path for habit change: Cognitive shielding of intentions against habit intrusion. *British Journal of Health Psychology, 16*, 189-200.

Dehaene, S., Changeux, J. P., Naccache, L., Sackur, J., & Sergent, C. (2006). Conscious, preconscious, and subliminal processing: A testable taxonomy. *Trends in Cognitive Sciences, 10*, 204–211.

Dehaene, S., Posner, M. I., & Tucker, D. M. (1994). Localization of a neural system for error-detection and compensation. *Psychological Science, 5*(5), 303–305.

Dennett, D. C. (1991). *Consciousness explained*. Boston, MA: Little, Brown.

Devine, P. G. (1989). Stereotypes and prejudice: Their automatic and controlled components. *Journal of Personality and Social Psychology, 56*, 5–18.

Dickinson, A., & Balleine, B. W. (1995). Motivational control of instrumental action. *Current Directions in Psychological Science, 4*, 162–167.

Dik, G., & Aarts, H. (2007). Behavioral cues to others' motivation and goal-pursuits: The perception of effort facilitates goal inference and contagion. *Journal of Experimental Social Psychology, 43*, 727–737.

Dijksterhuis, A., & Aarts, H. (2010). Goals, attention, and (un)consciousness. *Annual Review of Psychology, 61*, 467–490.

Dijksterhuis, A., & Bargh, J. A. (2001). The perception-behavior expressway: Automatic effects of social perception on social behavior. In M. P. Zanna (Ed.), *Advances in experimental social psychology* (Vol. 33, pp. 1–40). San Diego, CA: Academic Press.

Dijksterhuis, A., Chartrand, T., & Aarts, H. (2007). Effects of priming and perception on social behavior and goal pursuit. In J.A. Bargh (Ed.), *Social psychology and the unconscious: The automaticity of higher mental processes* (pp. 51–131). New York: Psychology Press.

Dweck, C. S. (1999). *Self-theories: Their role in motivation, personality and development*. Philadelphia, PA: Psychology Press.

Eder, A., & Rothermund, K. (2008). When do motor behaviors (mis)match affective stimuli? An evaluative coding view of approach and avoidance reactions. *Journal of Experimental Psychology: General, 137*, 262–281.

Eitam, B., Hassin, R. R., & Schul, Y. (2008). Nonconscious goal pursuit in novel environments: The case of implicit learning. *Psychological Science, 19*, 261–267.

Elliot, A. J. (2008). *Handbook of approach and avoidance motivation*. Mahwah, NJ: Lawrence Erlbaum Associates.

Elliott, E. S., & Dweck, C .S. (1988). Goals: An approach to motivation and achievement. *Journal of Personality and Social Psychology, 54*, 5–12.

Elsner, B., & Hommel, B. (2001). Effect anticipation and action control. *Journal of Experimental Psychology: Human Perception and Performance, 27*, 229–240.

Engeser, S., Wendland, M., & Rheinberg, F. (2006). Nonconscious activation of behavioral goals, a methodologically refined replication. *Psychological Reports, 99*, 963.

Epstude, K., & Roese, N. J. (2008). The functional theory of counterfactual thinking. *Personality and Social Psychology Review, 12*, 168–192.

Fazio, R. H., Sanbonmatsu, D. M., Powell, M. C., & Kardes, F. R. (1986). On the automatic activation of attitudes. *Journal of Personality and Social Psychology, 50*, 229–238.

Ferguson, M. J. (2007). On the automatic evaluation of end-states. *Journal of Personality and Social Psychology, 92*, 596–611.

Ferguson, M. J. (2008). On becoming ready to pursue a goal you don't know you have: Effects of nonconscious goals on evaluative readiness. *Journal of Personality and Social Psychology, 95*, 1268.

Ferguson, M. J., & Bargh, J. A. (2004). Liking is for doing: The effects of goal pursuit on automatic evaluation. *Journal of Personality and Social Psychology, 87*, 557–572.

Festinger, L. (1957). *A theory of cognitive dissonance.* Stanford, CA: Stanford University Press.

Fishbach, A., Eyal, T., & Finkelstein, S. R. (2010). How positive and negative feedback motivate goal pursuit. *Social and Personality Psychology Compass, 4*, 517–530.

Fishbein, M., & Ajzen, I. (1975). *Belief, attitude, intention, and behavior: An introduction to theory and research.* Reading, MA: Addison-Wesley.

Fitzsimons, G. M., & Bargh, J. A. (2003). Thinking of you: Nonconscious pursuit of interpersonal goals associated with relationship partners. *Journal of Personality and Social Psychology, 84*, 148–163.

Förster, J., Liberman, N., & Higgins, E. T. (2005). Accessibility from active and fulfilled goals. *Journal of Experimental Social Psychology, 41*, 220–239.

Fourneret, P., & Jeannerod, M. (1998). Limited conscious monitoring of motor performance in normal subjects. *Neuropsychologia, 36*, 1133–1140.

Friedman, R., Deci, E. L., Elliot, A., Moller, A., & Aarts, H. (2010). Motivation synchronicity: Priming motivational orientations with observations of others' behavior. *Motivation and Emotion*, 34, 34–38.

Frith, C. D., Blakemore, S. J., & Wolpert, D. M. (2000). Abnormalities in the awareness and control of action. *Philosophical Transactions of the Royal Society of London, 355*, 1771–1788.

Funahashi, S. (2001). Neuronal mechanisms of executive control by the prefrontal cortex. *Neuroscience Research, 39*, 147–165.

Gehring, W. J., Coles, M. G. H., Meyer, D. E., & Donchin, E. (1990). The error-related negativity: an event-related brain potential accompanying errors. *Psychophysiology, 27*, s34.

Gendolla, G. H. E., & Silvestrini, N. (2010). The implicit "Go": Masked action cues directly mobilize mental effort. *Psychological Science, 21*, 1389–1393.

Gilbert, A. M., & Fiez, J. A. (2004). Integrating rewards and cognition in the frontal cortex. *Cognitive, Affective & Behavioral Neuroscience, 4*, 540–552.

Gilbert, D. T., & Wilson, T. D. (2007). Prospection: Experiencing the future. *Science, 317*, 1351–1354.

Gollwitzer, P. M. (1990). Action phases and mindsets. In R. M. Sorrentino & E. T. Higgins (Eds.), *Handbook of motivation and cognition.* New York: Guilford Press.

Gollwitzer, P. M., & Moskowitz, G. B. (1996). Goal effects on action and cognition. In E. Higgins & A. W. Kruglanski (Eds.), *Social psychology: Handbook of basic principles* (pp. 361–399). New York: Guilford Press.

Gollwitzer, P. M., & Sheeran, P. (2006). Implementation intentions and goal achievement: A meta-analysis of effects and processes. In M. P. Zanna (Ed.), *Advances in experimental social psychology* (Vol. 38, pp. 69–119). San Diego, CA: Elsevier Academic Press.

Goodale, M. A., & Milner, D. A. (1992). Separate visual pathways for perception and action. *Trends in Neurosciences, 15*, 20–25.

Goschke, T., & Kuhl, J. (1993). Representation of intentions: Persisting activation in memory. *Journal of Experimental Psychology: Learning, Memory, and Cognition, 19*, 1211–1226.

Gray, J. A. (2004). *Consciousness: Creeping up on the hard problem.* New York: Oxford University Press.

Greenwald, A. G., & Banaji, M. R. (1989). The self as a memory system: Powerful, but ordinary. *Journal of Personality and Social Psychology, 57*, 41–54.

Haggard, P. (2008). Human volition: Towards a neuroscience of will. *Nature Reviews: Neuroscience, 9*, 934–946.

Hart, W., & Albarracín, D. (2009). The effects of chronic achievement motivation and achievement primes on the activation of achievement and fun goals. *Journal of Personality and Social Psychology, 97*, 1129–1141.

Hassin, R. R. (2008). Being open minded without knowing why: Evidence from nonconscious goal pursuit. *Social Cognition, 26*, 578–592.

Heider, F. (1958). *The psychology of interpersonal relations.* New York: Wiley.

Heitz, R. P., Schrock, J. C., Payne, T. W., & Engle, R. W. (2008). Effects of incentive on working memory capacity: Behavioral and pupillometric data. *Psychophysiology, 45*, 119–129.

Higgins, E. T. (1997). Beyond pleasure and pain. *American Psychologist, 52*, 1280–1300.

Holland, R. W., Wennekers, A. M., Bijlstra, G., Jongenelen, M. M., & Van Knippenberg, A. (2009). Self-symbols as implicit motivators. *Social Cognition, 27*, 579–600.

Hommel, B., Alonso, D., & Fuentes, L. J. (2003). Acquisition and generalization of action effects. *Visual Cognition, 10*, 965–986.

Hommel, B., Muesseler, J., Aschersleben, G., & Prinz, W. (2001). The theory of event coding (tec): A framework for perception and action planning. *Behavioral and Brain Sciences, 24*, 849–937.

Hyland, M. E. (1988). Motivational control theory: An integrative framework. *Journal of Personality and Social Psychology, 55*, 642–651.

James, W. (1890). *The principles of psychology.* London: Macmillan.

Jaynes, J. (1976). *The origin of consciousness in the breakdown of the bicameral mind.* Boston, MA: Houghton Mifflin.

Joordens, S., & Becker, S. (1997). The long and short of semantic priming effects in lexical decision. *Journal of Experimental Psychology: Learning, memory and cognition, 23*, 1083–1105

Kahneman, D. (1973). *Attention and effort.* Englewoods Cliffs, NJ: Prentice Hall.

Koch, C., & Tsuchiya, N. (2006). Attention and consciousness: Two distinct brain processes. *Trends in Cognitive Sciences, 11*, 16–22.

Kraus, M. W., & Chen, S. (2009). Striving to be known by significant others: Automatic activation of self-verification goals in relationship contexts. *Journal of Personality and Social Psychology, 97*, 58.

Kray, J., Eenshuistra, R., Kerstner, H., Weidema, M., & Hommel, B. (2006). Language and action control: The acquisition of action goals in early childhood. *Psychological Science, 17,* 737–741.

Krieglmeyer, R., Deutsch, R., De Houwer, J., & De Raedt, R. (2010). Being moved: Valence activates approach–avoidance behavior independent of evaluation and approach–avoidance intentions. *Psychological Science, 21,* 607–614.

Kruglanski, A. W. (1996). Motivated social cognition: Principles of the interface. In E. T. Higgins & A. W. Kruglanski (Eds.), *Social psychology: A handbook of basic principles* (pp. 493–522). New York: Guilford Press.

Kruglanski, A. W., Shah, J. Y., Fishbach, A., Friedman, R., Chun, W. Y., & Sleeth-Keppler, D. (2002). A theory of goal-systems. In M. P. Zanna (Ed.), *Advances in Experimental Social Psychology* (Vol. 34). New York: Academic Press.

Kunda, Z. (1990). The case for motivated reasoning. *Psychological Bulletin, 108,* 480–498.

Kunda, Z., & Spencer, S. J. (2003). When do stereotypes come to mind and when do they color judgment? A goal-based theory of stereotype activation and application. *Psychological Bulletin, 129,* 522–544.

Lamme, V. A. F. (2003). Why visual attention and awareness are different. *Trends in Cognitive Sciences, 7,* 12–18.

Lau, H. (2009). Volition and the function of consciousness. In E. M. Gazzaniga (Ed.), *Cognitive neurosciences IV* (pp. 1191–1200). Cambridge, MA: MIT Press.

Lau, H. C., & Passingham, R. E. (2007). Unconscious activation of the cognitive control system in the human prefrontal cortex. *Journal of Neuroscience, 27,* 5805.

Lavender, T., & Hommel, B. (2007). Affect and action: Towards an event-coding account. *Cognition and Emotion, 21,* 1270–1296.

Legrand, D., & Ruby, P. (2009). What is self-specific? Theoretical investigation and critical review of neuroimaging results. *Psychological Review, 116,* 252–282.

Lewin, K. (1935). *A dynamic theory of personality: Selected papers.* New York: McGraw-Hill.

Liberman, N., & Trope, Y. (1998). The role of feasibility and desirability considerations in near and distant future decisions: A test of temporal construal theory. *Journal of Personality and Social Psychology, 75,* 5–18.

Libet, B., Gleason, C. A., Wright, E. W., & Pearl, D. K. (1983). Time of conscious intention to act in relation to onset of cerebral activity (readiness-potential): The unconscious initiation of a freely voluntary act. *Brain, 106,* 623–642.

Locke, E. A., & Latham, G. P. (2002). Building a practically useful theory of goal setting and task motivation: A 35-year odyssey. *American Psychologist, 57,* 705–717.

Loersch, C., Aarts, H., Payne, B. K. & Jefferis, V.E. (2008). The influence of social groups on goal contagion. *Journal of Experimental Social Psychology, 44,* 1555–1558.

Loftus E. F., & Klinger M. R. (1992). Is the unconscious smart or dumb? *American Psychologist, 47,* 761–765.

Marien, H., Aarts, H., & Custers, R. (in press). Being flexible or rigid in goal-directed behavior: When positive affect implicitly motivates the pursuit of goals or means. *Journal of Experimental Social Psychology.*

Markman, A. B., & Brendl, C. M. (2000). The influence of goals on value and choice. In D. L. Medin (Ed.), *The psychology of learning and motivation* (Vol. 39, pp. 97–129). San Diego, CA: Academic Press.

Marsh, R. L., Hicks, J. L., & Bink, M. L. (1998). Activation of completed, uncompleted and partially completed intentions. *Journal of Experimental Psychology: Learning, Memory, and Cognition, 24,* 350–361.

Marsh, R. L., Hicks, J. L., & Bryan, E. S. (1999). The activation of unrelated and canceled intentions. *Memory and Cognition, 27,* 320–327.

Matsumoto, M., Matsumoto, K., Abe, H., & Tanaka, K. (2007). Medial prefrontal cell activity signaling prediction errors of action values. *Nature Neuroscience, 10*(5), 647–656.

Maturana, H. R., & Varela, F. G. (1987). *The tree of knowledge: The biological roots of human understanding.* Boston, MA: Shambhala.

Mayr, U. (2002). Inhibition in action rules. *Psychonomic Bulletin and Review, 9,* 93–99.

McCulloch, K. C., Aarts, H., Fujita, J., & Bargh, J. A. (2008). Inhibition in goal systems: A retrieval-induced forgetting account. *Journal of Experimental Social Psychology, 44,* 857–865.

McKone, E. (1995). Short-term implicit memory for words and nonwords. *Journal of Experimental Psychology: Learning, Memory and Cognition, 21,* 1108–1126.

Miller, D. T., & Ross, M. (1975). Self-serving biases in the attribution of causality: Fact or fiction? *Psychological Bulletin, 82,* 213–225.

Miller, E. K., & Cohen, J. D. (2001). An integrative theory of prefrontal cortex function. *Annual Review of Neuroscience, 24,* 167–202.

Miller, N. E., & Dollard, J. (1941). *Social learning and imitation.* New Haven, CT: Yale University Press.

Mischel, W., Shoda,Y., & Rodriguez, M.I. (1989). Delay of gratification in children. *Science, 244,* 933–938.

Miyake, A., & Shah, P. (1999). *Models of working memory: Mechanisms of active maintenance and executive control.* New York: Cambridge University Press.

Mobbs, D., Hassabis, D., Seymore, B., Marchant, J. L., Weiskopf, N. Dolan, R. J., et al. (2009). Choking on the money. Reward-based performance decrements are associated with midbrain activity. *Psychological Science, 20,* 955–962.

Monteith, M.J. (1993). Self-regulation of prejudiced responses: Implications for progress in prejudice reduction efforts. *Journal of Personality and Social Psychology, 65,* 469–485.

Moskowitz, G. B. (2010). On the control over stereotype activation and stereotype inhibition. *Social and Personality Psychology Compass, 4,* 140–158.

Moskowitz, G. B., Gollwitzer, P. M., Wasel, W., & Schaal, B. (1999). Preconscious control of stereotype activation through chronic egalitarian goals. *Journal of Personality and Social Psychology, 77,* 167–184.

Moskowitz, G. B., & Grant, H. (2009). *The psychology of goals.* New York: Guilford Press.

Naccache, L., & Dehaene, S. (2001). Unconscious semantic priming extends to novel unseen stimuli. *Cognition, 80,* 215–229.

Neuberg, S. L., & Fiske, S. T. (1987). Motivational influences on impression formation: Outcome dependency, accuracy-driven attention, and individuating processes. *Journal of Personality and Social Psychology, 53*, 431–444.

Nieuwenhuis, S., Schweizer, T. S., Mars, R. B., Botvinick, M. M., & Hajcak, G. (2007). Error-likelihood prediction in the medial frontal cortex: A critical evaluation. *Cerebral Cortex, 17*(7), 1570–1581.

Oikawa, M. (2004). Moderation of automatic achievement goals by conscious monitoring. *Psychological Reports, 95*, 975–980.

Papies, E. K., Aarts, H., & de Vries, N. K. (2009). Planning is for doing: Implementation intentions go beyond the mere creation of goal-directed associations. *Journal of Experimental Social Psychology, 45*, 1148–1151.

Papies, E. K., Stroebe, W., & Aarts, H. (2008). Healthy cognition: Processes of self-regulatory success in restrained eating. *Personality and Social Psychology Bulletin, 34*, 1290–1300.

Payne, J. W., Bettman, J. R., & Johnson, E. J. (1993). *The adaptive decision maker*. New York: Cambridge University Press.

Pessiglione, M., Schmidt, L., Draganski, B., Kalisch, R., Lau, H., Dolan, R. J., et al. (2007). How the brain translates money into force: A neuroimaging study of subliminal motivation. *Science, 316*, 904–906.

Pessoa, L. (2009). How do emotion and motivation direct executive control? *Trends in Cognitive Sciences, 13*, 160–166.

Petty, R. E., & Cacioppo, J. T. (1986). *Communication and persuasion: Central and peripheral routes to attitude change*. New York: Springer-Verlag.

Pinker, S. (1997). *How the mind works*. New York: Norton & Company.

Powers, W. T. (1973). *Behavior: The control of perception*. Chicago, IL: Aldine.

Prinz, W. (1997). Perception and action planning. *European Journal of Cognitive Psychology, 9*, 129–154.

Rookes, P., & Willson, J. (2000). *Perception: Theory, development and organization*. London: Routledge.

Ruys, K. I., & Aarts, H. (in press). I didn't mean to hurt you! Unconscious origins of experienced self-agency over other's emotions. *Emotion*.

Schlaghecken, F., & Eimer, M. (2004). Masked prime stimuli can bias "free" choices between response alternatives. *Psychonomic Bulletin and Review, 11*, 463–468.

Schultz, W. (2006). Behavioral theories and the neurophysiology of reward. *Annual Review of Psychology, 57*, 87.

Seibt, B., Häfner, M., & Deutsch, R. (2007). Prepared to eat: How immediate affective and motivational responses to food cues are influenced by food deprivation. *European Journal of Social Psychology, 37*, 359–379.

Serences, J. T., & Yantis, S. (2006). Selective visual attention and perceptual coherence. *Trends in Cognitive Sciences, 10*, 38–45.

Seth, A. K., Dienes, Z., Cleeremans, A., Overgaard, M., & Pessoa, L. (2008). Measuring consciousness: Relating behavioral and neurophysiological approaches. *Trends in Cognitive Sciences, 12*, 314–321.

Shah, J. Y. (2003). Automatic for the people: How representations of significant others implicitly affect goal pursuit. *Journal of Personality and Social Psychology, 84*, 661–681.

Shah, J. Y., Friedman, R., & Kruglanski, A. W. (2002). Forgetting all else: On the antecedents and consequences of goal shielding. *Journal of Personality and Social Psychology, 83*, 1261–1280.

Shah, J. Y., & Gardner, W. (2008), *Handbook of motivation science*. New York: Guilford Press.

Shantz, A., & Latham, G. P. (2009). An exploratory field experiment of the effect of subconscious and conscious goals on employee performance. *Organizational Behavior and Human Decision Processes, 109*, 9–17.

Sheeran, P., Aarts, H., Custers, R., Rivis, A., Webb, T. L., & Cooke, R. (2005). The goal-dependent automaticity of drinking habits. *British Journal of Social Psychology, 44*, 47–63.

Shepperd, J. A., Malone, W., & Sweeny, K. (2008). Exploring causes of the self-serving bias. *Social and Personality Psychology Compass, 2*, 895–908.

Shizgal, P. (1997). Neural basis of utility estimation. *Current Opinion in Neurobiology, 7*, 198–208.

Skinner, B. F. (1953). *Science and human behavior*. Oxford, England: Macmillan.

Slachevsky A., Pillon B., Fourneret P., Pradat-Diehl P., Jeannerod M., & Dubois B. (2001). Preserved adjustment but impaired awareness in a sensory–motor conflict following prefrontal lesions. *Journal of Cognitive Neuroscience, 13*, 332–340.

Soon, C. S., Brass, M., Heinze, H. J., & Haynes, J. D. (2008). Unconscious determinants of free decisions in the human brain. *Nature Neuroscience, 11*, 543–545.

Steele, C. M., Spencer, S. J., & Lynch, M. (1993). Self-image resilience and dissonance: The role of affirmational resource. *Journal of Personality and Social Psychology, 64*, 885–896.

Strahan, E. J., Spencer, S. J., & Zanna, M. P. (2002). Subliminal priming and persuasion: Striking while the iron is hot. *Journal of Experimental Social Psychology, 38*, 556–568.

Strecher V., DeVellis B., Becker M., & Rosenstock I. (1986). The role of self-efficacy in achieving health behavior change. *Health Education Quarterly, 13*, 73–91.

Suddendorf, T., & Corballis, M. C. (2007). The evolution of foresight: What is mental time travel and is it unique to humans? *Behavioral and Brain Sciences, 30*, 299–313.

Tajfel, H. (1957). Value and the perceptual judgment of magnitude. *Psychological Review, 64*, 192–204.

Tetlock, P. E. (1985). Accountability: The neglected social context of judgment and choice. In B. Staw & L. Cummings (Eds.), *Research in organizational behavior* (Vol. 7, pp. 297–332). Greenwich, CT: JAI Press.

Thorndike, E. L. (1911). *Animal intelligence*. New York: Macmillan.

Tolman, E. C. (1939). Prediction of vicarious trial and error by means of the schematic sow bug. *Psychological Review, 46*, 318–336.

Ullsperger, M., Nittono, H., & von Cramon, D. Y. (2007). When goals are missed: Dealing with self-generated and externally induced failure. *Neuroimage, 35*(3), 1356–1364.

Vallacher, R. R., & Wegner, D. M. (1987). What do people think they're doing? Action identification and human behavior. *Psychological Review, 94,* 3–15.

Van Den Bos, A., & Stapel, D. A. (2009). Why people stereotype affects how they stereotype: The differential influence of comprehension goals and self-enhancement goals on stereotyping. *Personality and Social Psychology Bulletin, 35,* 101–113.

Veling, H., & Aarts, H. (2009). Putting behavior on hold decreases reward value of need-instrumental objects outside of awareness. *Journal of Experimental Social Psychology, 45,* 1020–1023.

Veling, H., & Aarts, H. (2010). Cueing task goals and earning money: Relatively high monetary rewards reduce failures to act on goals in a Stroop task. *Motivation and Emotion, 34,* 184–190.

Veltkamp, M., Aarts, H., & Custers, R. (2008a). On the emergence of deprivation-reducing behaviors: Subliminal priming of behavior representations turns deprivation into motivation. *Journal of Experimental Social Psychology, 44,* 866–873.

Veltkamp, M., Aarts, H., & Custers, R. (2008b). Perception in the service of goal pursuit: Motivation to attain goals enhances the perceived size of goal-instrumental object. *Social Cognition, 26,* 720–736.

Veltkamp, M., Aarts, H., & Custers, R. (2009). Unravelling the motivational yarn: A framework for understanding the instigation of implicitly motivated behaviour resulting from deprivation and positive affect. *European Review of Social Psychology, 20,* 345–381.

Veltkamp, M., Custers, R., & Aarts, H. (2011). Subliminal conditioning in the absence of basic needs: Striking even when the iron is cold. *Journal of Consumer Psychology, 21,* 49–56.

Verplanken, B., & Holland, R. (2002). Motivated decision-making: Effects of activation and self-centrality of values on choices and behavior. *Journal of Personality and Social Psychology, 82,* 434–447.

Vroom, V. H. (1964). *Work and motivation.* New York: Wiley.

Wegner, D. M. (2002). *The illusion of conscious will.* Cambridge, MA: MIT Press.

Weiner, B. (1986). *An attributional theory of motivation and emotion.* New York: Springer-Verlag.

Wicklund, R. A., & Gollwitzer, P. M. (1982). *Symbolic self-completion.* Hillsdale, NJ: Lawrence Erlbaum Associates.

Wiener, N. (1948). *Cybernetics: Or control and communication in the animal and the machine.* Cambridge, MA: MIT Press.

Witt, J. K., Proffitt, D. R., & Epstein, W. (2004). Perceiving distance: A role of effort and intent. *Perception, 33,* 570–590.

Wood, W., & Neal, D. T. (2007). A new look at habits and the interface between habits and goals. *Psychological Review, 114,* 843–863.

Zajonc, R. B. (1980). Feeling and thinking: Preferences need no inferences. *American Psychologist, 35,* 151–175.

Zedelius, C. M., Veling, H., & Aarts, H. (2011). Boosting or choking – How conscious and unconscious reward processing modulate the active maintenance of goal-relevant information. *Consciousness and Cognition, 20,* 355–362.

6

The Social Perception of Faces

Alexander Todorov

Faces are one of the most potent social stimuli conveying information about social categories (e.g., sex, age, race), mental states (e.g., puzzled), emotional states (e.g., angry), attractiveness, and identity. People also infer a host of personality characteristics from facial appearance such as trustworthiness and competence (Todorov, Said, & Verosky, 2011), although these inferences are not necessarily accurate (Olivola & Todorov, 2010a). People can rapidly extract information from faces about:

- identity (Grill-Spector & Kanwisher, 2005; Yip & Sinha, 2002)
- race and gender (Cloutier, Mason, & Macrae, 2005; Martin & Macrae, 2007; Ito & Urland, 2003, 2005)
- emotional expressions (Esteves & Öhman, 1993; Whalen et al., 1998)
- attractiveness (Locher, Unger, Sociedade, & Wahl, 1993; Olson & Marshuetz, 2005)
- a variety of social trait inferences (Bar, Neta, & Linz, 2006; Rudoy & Paller, 2009; Rule & Ambady, 2008a; Rule, Ambady, & Adams, 2009; Todorov, Pakrashi, & Oosterhof, 2009; Willis & Todorov, 2006)
- and can recognize familiar faces after more than 50 years (Bahrick, Bahrick, & Wittlinger, 1975).

These are amazing cognitive feats. In fact, decades of computer science research have not been able to produce computer models that match human performance (Bowyer et al., 2006; Sinha et al., 2006).

Not only are social inferences from faces rapidly formed but also they are consequential.

Such inferences predict a range of social outcomes, including economic decisions (Scharlemann, Eckel, Kacelnik, & Wilson, 2001; Van't Wout & Sanfey, 2008), sentencing decisions (Blair, Judd, & Chapleau, 2004; Eberhardt, Davies, Purdie-Vaughns, & Johnson, 2006; Porter, ten Brinke, & Gustaw, 2010; Zebrowitz & McDonald, 1991), occupational success (Hamermesh & Biddle, 1994; Langlois et al., 2000; Mazur, Mazur, & Keating, 1984; Montepare & Zebrowitz, 1998; Mueller & Mazur, 1996; Rule & Ambady, 2008b), and electoral success (Antonakis & Delgas, 2009; Ballew & Todorov, 2007; Little, Burriss, Jones, & Roberts, 2007; Olivola & Todorov, 2010b; Todorov, Mandisodza, Goren, & Hall, 2005).

This chapter is organized in five sections. The first two sections review evidence about the "special" status of faces. Section I reviews the major behavioral findings suggesting that perception of faces is different from perception of objects. Section II reviews the major neuropsychology, neurophysiology, and functional neuroimaging findings suggesting that there are neural circuits dedicated to perceptual analysis of faces. The next three sections review research on social perception of faces. Section III reviews research on social inferences from faces. Section IV describes computational models of social perception of faces. Finally, based on a recent meta-analysis of functional magnetic resonance imaging (fMRI) studies (Mende-Siedlecki, Said, & Todorov, in press), section V describes the potential brain network dedicated to social perception of faces. This network comprises not only regions involved in the perceptual analysis of faces (section II) but also a number of subcortical and prefrontal regions.

SECTION I: THE SPECIAL STATUS OF FACES – PERCEPTUAL AND COGNITIVE PROCESSES

Several early studies have shown that newborns with minimal visual experience preferentially orient to face-like stimuli than to equally complex stimuli (Fantz, 1963; Johnson et al., 1991; Valenza et al., 1996). These findings have been challenged on the grounds that newborns visual preferences are tuned to general geometric configurations (e.g., top-heavy patterns with more elements on the top than on the bottom) rather than to faces (Turati, 2004). However, it is not clear why such general perceptual biases should be present at birth. In contrast, an innate preference for faces (in the form of sensitivity to face-like templates) provides a parsimonious explanation of the findings. In a recent, extensive replication of the earlier studies, newborns with postnatal age from 13 to 168 hours were exposed to a number of different stimulus configurations (Farroni et al., 2005). The key property of stimuli that biased infants' visual preferences was contrast polarity (darker areas around the eyes and the mouth) in an upright face configuration. Moreover, infants preferred faces lit from above (i.e., the natural lighting conditions) than faces lit from below. These findings strongly suggest an innately specified bias to faces in their natural lighting conditions. Importantly, infant monkeys reared without exposure to faces for 6 to 24 months still show preference for faces over other objects (Sugita, 2008). Studies with human newborns also show that they prefer faces with open eyes (Batki et al., 2000) and direct gaze (Farroni et al., 2002), suggesting an early bias to communicative cues in the face. Such early biases can facilitate learning about faces, individuals, and social relations. Undoubtedly, face perception abilities undergo important developmental changes, and experience is critical for tuning these abilities (Pascalis & Kelly, 2009), a topic that is revisited in section III.

In addition to developmental evidence for the special status of faces, there is rich evidence for differences in processing of faces and objects (Farah, Wilson, Drain, & Tanaka, 1998; McKone, Kanwisher, & Duchaine, 2007; Sinha et al., 2006; Yue, Tjan, & Biederman, 2006). Some of the best documented phenomena include the inversion effect, the part-whole effect, and the composite face effect. For example, face recognition is much more dependent on orientation – with dramatic reduction in performance for inverted faces – than object recognition. Similarly, recognition of facial parts (e.g., a mouth) is more accurate when these parts are embedded in the face rather than

presented in isolation and this effect is more pronounced for faces than objects (e.g., a door and a house). Both of these phenomena can be explained by the hypothesis that faces are processed holistically in an upright orientation (Maurer, Le Grand, & Mondloch, 2002): processed as gestalts so that the perception of individual features changes when integrated with other features.

Perhaps, the best paradigm illustrating holistic processing is the composite face paradigm (Young, Hellawell, & Hay, 1987). In the original demonstration of the composite face effect, the alignment of the top half of a familiar face with the bottom half of another face interfered with the recognition of the identity of the original face (e.g., top half). Since this demonstration, similar effects have been demonstrated for perception of gender (Baudouin & Humphreys, 2006), race (Michel, Corneille, & Rossion, 2007), attractiveness (Abbas & Duchaine, 2008), trustworthiness (Todorov, Loehr, & Oosterhof, 2010), and emotional expressions (Calder, Young, Keane, & Dean, 2000). In the case of social judgments, facial halves of "positive" faces (attractive and trustworthy) are judged more negatively when aligned with facial halves of "negative" faces (less attractive and less trustworthy looking), although participants are instructed to ignore the irrelevant halves (Abbas & Duchaine, 2008; Todorov et al., 2010). That is, participants are unable to ignore the "irrelevant" face information. Importantly, this effect is substantially reduced or eliminated when the faces are inverted or the facial halves misaligned, demonstrating the nature of holistic processing. The two facial halves fuse to form a new face.

In addition to holistic processing, another distinctive feature of face processing is the extremely high tolerance for perceptual degradation of familiar faces (Sinha et al., 2006). People can recognize familiar faces under a number of suboptimal conditions: blurring of the face images (leaving primarily low spatial frequency information in the face) and perceptual distortions such as compression of the face and caricatures of the face: i.e., people maintain highly robust representations of familiar faces.

Finally, face perception depends on both shape and reflectance (surface) information (O'Toole, Vetter, & Blanz, 1999; Sinha et al., 2006; Todorov & Oosterhof, 2011). Dependence on surface information accounts for findings that contrast polarity inversion (e.g., as if looking at the negative of a picture) interferes with face recognition and sex identification (Bruce & Langton, 1994; Russell et al., 2006), as well as social judgments from faces (Santos & Young, 2008). Studies that model separately shape and surface information (see section IV) also show that these types of information have relatively equal effects on face recognition (O'Toole et al., 1999) and social judgments from faces (Todorov & Oosterhof, 2011).

SECTION II: THE SPECIAL STATUS OF FACES – NEURAL BASIS

Given the developmental and behavioral data described in the previous section, it should not be surprising that there are brain regions dedicated to face processing. Cases of prosopagnosia – an inability to recognize familiar faces while being able to recognize people by using other cues such as voice, gait, or clothing – have been described as early as the 19th century (Mayer & Rossion, 2005). This perceptual impairment is most frequently caused by bilateral or right lateralized lesions in the inferior part of temporo-occipital regions (fusiform and lingual gyrus). While cases of acquired prosopagnosia are extremely rare, there have been many recent documented cases of developmental prosopagnosia (Duchaine, 2011), and there is evidence that this impairment has a genetic component (Duchaine & Nakayama, 2006).

The data from lesions are largely consistent with neurophysiology and neuroimaging studies. Face-selective neurons were discovered in the inferior temporal (IT) cortex of the macaque brain in the 1970s (Bruce, Desimone, & Gross, 1981; Desimone, 1991; Perrett, Rolls, & Caan, 1982). A number of subsequent studies also recorded from face-selective neurons in the superior temporal sulcus (STS) (Allison, Puce, & McCarthy, 2000; Perrett, Hietanen, Oram, & Benson, 1992).

Consistent with these findings, positron emission tomography (PET) studies of humans in the early 1990s reported face responsive regions in fusiform and inferior temporal regions (Haxby et al., 1993; Sergent, Ohta, & MacDonald, 1992).

Subsequent fMRI studies used a functional localizer approach in which the brain response to faces is contrasted to a number of other categories such as houses, hands, chairs, flowers, etc. Such studies identified several face-selective regions: a region in the fusiform gyrus – labeled the fusiform face area (FFA; see Fig. 6.1A) – (Kanwisher et al., 1997; McCarthy et al., 1997; Tong et al., 2000) a region in the occipital gyrus – labeled the occipital face area (OFA) – (Gauthier et al., 2000; Puce et al., 1996) and a face-selective region in the posterior STS (pSTS, Allison, Puce, & McCarthy, 2000; Puce et al., 1996). These three regions are usually considered the regions comprising the core system for perceptual analysis of faces (Haxby et al., 2000; Said, Haxby, & Todorov, 2011). These regions can be reliably identified in most individual subjects and, at least in the case of FFA, the results are robust with respect to task demands and control categories (Berman et al., 2010).

Two of the most exciting recent developments in the field are the combination of fMRI and single cell recordings in macaques (Tsao et al., 2008) and the use of transcranial magnetic stimulation (TMS) in humans (Pitcher et al., 2007). Tsao and her colleagues used fMRI to identify face-selective patches in the macaque brain and then recorded from these patches. In contrast to previous studies, which have rarely reported more than 20% of face-selective neurons from the sample of recorded neurons, Tsao and her

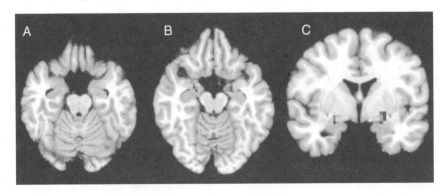

Figure 6.1   An example of fMRI research using a functional localizer. Brain regions respond more strongly to faces than to chairs: bilateral fusiform gyri (A) and bilateral amygdala (B & C). The regions were identified in a group analysis (n = 37), p < 0.001 (uncorrected). Face-selective voxels can also be identified at the level of individual brains.

colleagues reported more than 90% of face-selective neurons in some of the patches. Pitcher and his colleagues used TMS to transiently disrupt the activity of the right OFA (it is not possible to target the FFA) and found that this affected performance on face perception tasks, providing evidence for the causal significance of the OFA in face processing.

In addition to functional neuroimaging and single unit recording studies, electrophysiological studies have also identified face-selective responses. Studies recording directly from the fusiform gyrus in epileptic patients found negative potentials (N200) evoked by faces (Allison et al., 1994; Allison, Puce, Spencer, & McCarthy, 1999). Studies recording from the skull also consistently identify a negative potential selective for faces: the N170 (for an excellent review, see Rossion & Jacques, 2008). This potential emerges between 130 and 200 ms from stimulus onset and peaks at about 170 ms at occipito-temporal sites of recording. A similar response, traceable to the fusiform gyrus, has been observed in magnetoencephalography (MEG) studies (Halgren, Raij, Marinkovic, Jousmaki, & Hari, 2000).

It is likely that faces automatically evoke responses not only in the posterior face-selective network (FFA, OFA, and pSTS) but also in regions in the medial temporal lobe (MTL; see Fig. 6.1B and C) (Todorov, 2011). Recent studies have also shown face selectivity in the lateral orbitofrontal cortex of the macaque's brain (Rolls et al., 2006; Tsao et al., 2008). This is not surprising given the affective and social significance of faces. At about the time of the discovery of face-selective neurons in IT cortex, a number of neurophysiology studies reported face responsive neurons in the macaque's amygdala (Leonard et al., 1985; Perrett et al., 1982; Rolls, 1984; Wilson & Rolls, 1993; for a review see Rolls, 2000). Recent studies have confirmed these findings (Gothard et al., 2007; Kuraoka & Nakamura, 2007; Nakamura et al., 1992). Importantly, the monkey neurophysiology findings have been replicated in human studies (Fried, MacDonald, Wilson, 1997; Kreiman, Koch, & Fried, 2000). Fried and his colleagues recorded from neurons in the MTL of patients undergoing treatment for epilepsy. They found face-selective neurons in the amygdala, hippocampus, and entorhinal cortex. Subsequent studies have shown that the responses of some of these neurons are modulated by face familiarity (Quiroga et al., 2005; Viskontas, Quiroga, & Fried, 2009).

In addition to data from single unit recordings, data from meta-analyses of functional neuroimaging studies also support a general role of the amygdala in face processing. Two large meta-analyses of PET and fMRI studies on emotional processing showed that faces are one class of stimuli that most consistently elicit responses in the amygdala (Costafreda, Brammer, David, & Fu, 2008; Sergerie, Chochol, & Armony, 2008) and that these responses do not depend on the valence of the faces (e.g., positive vs negative expressions). Two recent meta-analysis of studies on social perception of mostly emotionally neutral faces have also shown that the amygdala is consistently activated across these studies (Bzdok et al., 2011; Mende-Siedlecki et al., in press). These findings are revisited in section V.

SECTION III: SOCIAL PERCEPTION OF FACES – EMPIRICAL FINDINGS

Most of the research reviewed in sections I and II has been the exclusive purview of cognitive psychologists and vision scientists. But the study of face perception is at the intersection of cognition, affect, and motivation. As noted in the introduction, people make a variety of social inferences from faces and often act on these inferences: i.e., perceptual information extracted from facial appearance brings to mind relevant social knowledge that can provide a basis for multiple social attributions. For example, attractiveness is associated with a number of social attributions, including social and intellectual competence, concern for others, integrity, and adjustment (Eagly, Makhijani, Ashmore, & Longo, 1991). So is facial maturity (Montepare & Zebrowitz, 1998) and group categorization (Fiske, Cuddy, & Glick, 2007), although they are associated with different sets of social attributions. In a particularly disturbing example, people with more stereotypical African-American appearance are likely to receive harsher legal sentences (Blair et al., 2004; Eberhardt et al., 2006; for a general review of how stereotypical appearance within the same social category affects perception, see Maddox, 2004).

Models of person perception make a fundamental distinction between social category and individuating information and assume that category information is more accessible (Bodenhausen & Macrae, 1998; Brewer, 1988; Fiske & Neuberg, 1990). In fact, there is a lot of evidence that basic categorizations such as age, gender, and race are rapidly extracted from facial appearance (e.g., Cloutier, Mason, & Macrae, 2005; Ito, Thompson, & Cacioppo, 2004; Ito & Urland, 2003; Mason, Cloutier, & Macrae, 2006). However, there is also a lot of evidence that information that could be considered "individuating" is rapidly extracted. This includes information about identity (Jacques & Rossion, 2006; Ramon,

Caharel, & Rossion, 2011; Macrae et al., 2005); attractiveness (Locher et al., 1993; Olson & Marshuetz, 2005; van Leeuwen & Macrae, 2004); facial maturity, masculinity, and threat (Bar et al., 2006; Rule et al., 2009; Willis & Todorov, 2006); general valence of the face often measured with trustworthiness judgments (Todorov et al., 2009); emotional states (Esteves & Öhman, 1993; Whalen et al., 1998); and current focus of attention (e.g., eye gaze, see Frischen, Bayliss, & Tipper, 2007).

For example, people can extract information from subliminal presentation of faces about emotional states (Whalen et al., 2004), attractiveness (Olson & Marshuetz, 2005), and face valence (Todorov et al., 2009). Event-related potential (ERP) studies are particularly informative about the speed of these processes. As noted in section II, the first face-specific ERP responses emerge around 130 ms and peak around 170 ms (Rossion & Jacques, 2008). Within the same time window, people can discriminate between different facial identities (Jacques & Rossion, 2006), and differences between responses to trustworthy- and untrustworthy-looking faces emerge between 200 and 400 ms after the stimulus onset of the faces (Rudoy & Paller, 2009).

In general, these findings suggest that in addition to basic social categories (e.g., age, sex, and race), people extract information from faces relevant to several other basic dimensions. At a minimum, these include familiarity, attractiveness, valence, dominance, and emotional states. Furthermore, inferences about social, personality characteristics are most likely in the service of inferring intentions (Ames, Fiske, & Todorov, 2011) and can be derived from similarity to various cues with adaptive significance (Todorov, Said, Engell, & Oosterhof, 2008; Zebrowitz & Montepare, 2008), including self-resemblance (DeBruine, 2002; Krupp et al., 2008; Verosky & Todorov, 2010a), resemblance to familiar people (Kraus & Chen, 2010; Verosky & Todorov, 2010b) and familiar groups (Zebrowitz, Bronstad, & Lee, 2007; Zebrowitz, Wieneke, & White, 2008), and resemblance to emotional expressions (Montepare & Dobish, 2003; Neth & Martinez, 2009; Oosterhof & Todorov, 2009; Said, Sebe, & Todorov, 2009; Zebrowitz, Kikuchi, & Fellous, 2010). For example, structural similarity of emotionally neutral faces to expressions of anger leads to attributions of aggressiveness and dominance (Said, Sebe, et al., 2009).

As noted in section I, social perception of faces is holistic (Santos & Young, 2008, 2010; Todorov et al., 2010), and one of the important questions is how multiple cues (e.g., sex, race, eye gaze) are integrated. A holistic account would predict that this integration is rapid and that changing a single cue can easily change the resulting categorizations

and downstream consequences. A good example is research by MacLin and Malpass (2001, 2003), who showed that imposing an African or Latino hairstyle on the same racially ambiguous face changes the categorization of the face and leads to memory advantage for faces categorized as own race. Interestingly, the original interpretation of these findings was that a single feature changes face perception and that this featural processing is inconsistent with holistic accounts. However, the holistic account posits that the perception of individual features changes when integrated with other features, whether a single feature or multiple features (Maurer et al., 2002). In fact, face identification is impaired when one creates a composite of a familiar face and a familiar hairstyle of another person (picture Bill Clinton's face with Al Gore's hairstyle; Sinha & Poggio, 1996).

More importantly, people integrate multiple facial cues that include identity, gender, age, race, attractiveness, emotional states, eye gaze, and cues indicating membership in social groups with respect to the self. There have been many research demonstrations of "compound" effects, where one cue changes the effects of another cue (Hess, Adams, Grammer, & Kleck, 2009). These include race cues and emotional expressions (Bijlstra, Holland, & Wigboldus, 2010; Hugenberg & Bodenhausen, 2004; Hutchings & Haddock, 2008), gender cues and emotional expressions (Hess, Adams, Grammer, & Kleck, 2009), trustworthiness cues and emotional expressions (Oosterhof & Todorov, 2009), eye gaze and emotional expressions (Adams & Franklin, 2009; Adams & Kleck, 2003), race cues and eye gaze (Adams et al., 2010), and race cues and personality trait cues (Dotsch, Wigboldus, & van Knippenberg, 2011). These findings await a common account.

A question that has received substantial attention and is of both theoretical and practical significance is how people get attuned to specific category distinctions (Bukach, Gauthier, & Tarr, 2006). For example, one of the well-documented effects in face recognition is the own-race bias effect in memory for faces (Meissner & Brigham, 2001; Sporer, 2001). People are much better at recognizing faces of their own race than faces of other races. This finding has been of tremendous importance for understanding eyewitness errors in cross-race identifications. What leads to such biases in perception and memory? The best-supported hypothesis is that prolonged visual experience with members of a specific social category leads to better perceptual discrimination and memory for members of this category as opposed to members of less familiar categories.

Developmental evidence strongly supports the "expertise" hypothesis. In section I, I mentioned a study that showed that infant monkeys reared without exposure to faces retain their preference for faces (Sugita, 2008). However, their first (1-month) exposure to specific types of faces – human vs monkey – was critical for the development of their perceptual expertise. For example, monkeys only exposed to human faces for a month easily discriminated different human faces but had difficulties discriminating monkey faces afterwards. In a similar vein, human studies show that whereas 6-month-old infants can recognize both human and monkey faces, 9-month-old infants recognize only human faces, showing evidence for perceptual narrowing (Pascalis, de Haan, & Nelson, 2002). Importantly, showing monkey faces to 6-month-old infants on a consistent basis preserves their ability to recognize these faces when they are 9 months old (Pascalis et al., 2005). Finally, whereas newborns do not show a preference for own-race faces, 3-month-old infants do (Kelly et al., 2005). And this preference can be reversed as a result of one's visual experience. Adults who were born in Korea but adopted as children by French parents show better recognition of Caucasian than Asian faces (Sangrigoli et al., 2005).

Adult studies are largely consistent with the expertise hypothesis. This includes evidence for more holistic processing of own- than other-race faces (Michel, Caldara, & Rossion, 2006; Tanaka, Kiefer, & Bukach, 2004), enhanced neural responses in the FFA to own-race faces (Golby et al., 2001), and better recognition of own-race faces (Meissner & Brigham, 2001). Both responses in the FFA and holistic processing have been shown to predict face recognition (Richler, Cheung, & Gauthier, 2011; Golarai et al., 2007). The evidence also includes better recognition of emotional expressions of own-culture faces (Elfenbein & Ambady, 2002, 2003). The expertise hypothesis also fits computational models of face perception that posit that faces are represented in a multi-dimensional face space (see section IV; Caldara & Abdi, 2006).

However, at least in the case of adult studies, the expertise hypothesis is not sufficient to account for a number of recent findings. Specifically, social categorization models posit that the mere categorization of faces as in-group or out-group produces a number of downstream consequences, including those mimicking the impaired recognition of other-race faces (Hugenberg et al., 2010; Hugenberg & Sacco, 2008; but see Rhodes et al., 2010). For example, Bernstein, Young, and Hugenberg (2007) showed that Caucasian subjects had a better memory for Caucasian faces that were categorized as in-group than for Caucasian faces categorized as out-group. Similar effects have been observed for the identification of emotional expressions (Young & Hugenberg, 2010). Other research has shown that categorizing other-race faces as members of an in-group reduces implicit race biases (Van Bavel & Cunningham, 2009) and enhances neural responses in both the amygdala and fusiform gyrus to in-group faces (Van Bavel, Packer, & Cunningham, 2008).

These findings are very interesting because cues exogenous to facial appearance per se (e.g., a color background of the face) signaling in-group/out-group status can dramatically change how faces are processed. In fact, it appears that the mere categorization of faces as out-group reduces holistic processing (Hugenberg & Corneille, 2009; Michel, Corneille, & Rossion, 2007, 2010). One interesting implication of social categorization models is that inducing individuating learning of other-race faces may enhance memory for these faces (Hugenberg, Miller, & Claypool, 2007), as well as reduce negative implicit biases against members of other races (Lebrecht et al., 2009; Van Bavel & Cunningham, 2009).

Often, the expertise and social categorization hypotheses are contrasted, but this need not be the case. First, these hypotheses are not mutually exclusive. Second, some empirical findings are best explained by both hypotheses. When no specific individuation learning is induced, in-group categorizations seem to enhance memory for in-group own-race faces but not for in-group other-race faces. For example, learning White and Black faces in the context of rich and poor environments enhanced memory for White but not Black faces in rich environments (Shriver et al., 2008). Thus, the advantage for White faces was preserved but only when these faces were motivationally significant. Similar considerations apply to studies where the motivational significance of faces is manipulated by eye gaze (Adams, Pauker, & Weisbuch, 2010). More troubling for the expertise hypothesis are findings showing that individuating learning can eliminate memory advantages for own-race faces (Hugenberg et al., 2007; Lebrecht et al., 2009). However, most adults with normal face perception ability have sufficiently rich face representations that can accommodate perception of "other" yet familiar race faces. The interesting practical question is to what extent learning to individuate other-race faces would generalize to settings outside the specific experiments.

One of the important questions for future research is how learning shapes face perception and to what extent different types of perceptual learning can explain different biases (Lebrecht et al., 2009). For example, in a recent paper, Halberstadt, Sherman, and Sherman (2011) provided a simple learning/attentional account of hypodescent, the tendency to classify mixed-race faces as minority faces. Specifically, they argued that because one first learns faces of majority members, learning of minority members requires attention to distinctive features. This specific strategy leads to minority categorization of mixed-race faces. In fact, whereas Caucasian subjects tended to categorize morphs of Chinese and Caucasian faces as Chinese, Chinese subjects tended to categorize the morphs as Caucasian. Experimentally inducing this learning strategy led to similar effects. Assuming that majority faces are perceived as more typical than minority faces, it should be noted that the hypodescent effect is also predicted by the attractor field model (Tanaka & Corneille, 2007; Tanaka, Giles, Kremen, & Simon, 1998) – a computation model within the face space framework (see section IV).

Learning specific person information, especially when this information has affective value, is also inextricably linked to face perception. For example, there are many behavioral studies showing that people spontaneously infer evaluations and traits from behaviors and that such inferences are associated with the faces that accompanied the behaviors (Bliss-Moreau, Barrett, & Wright, 2008; Carlston & Skowronski, 1994; Goren & Todorov, 2009; Todorov & Uleman, 2002, 2003, 2004). Such learning occurs after minimal time exposure to faces and behaviors, is relatively independent of availability of cognitive resources and explicit goals to form impressions, and subsequent effects on perception and judgments are independent of explicit memory for the behaviors (Bliss-Moreau et al., 2008; Todorov & Uleman, 2003). Several studies on patients with brain lesions provide evidence consistent with the idea of robust person learning mechanisms and their effects on face perception (Croft et al., 2010; Johnson et al., 1985; Todorov & Olson, 2008; Tranel & Damasio, 1993). For example, patients with amnesia due to hippocampal lesions are nevertheless able to preserve affective responses to faces that were acquired by learning person information about the faces (Croft et al., 2010; Todorov & Olson, 2008). Finally, intensive learning ("day in the life" stories) about unfamiliar people over a 5-day period can modulate early N170 responses to faces (Heisz & Shedden, 2009). The N170 response is attenuated when unfamiliar faces are repeated, but not when famous faces are repeated. Heisz and Shedden (2009) showed that, as in the case of famous faces, the N170 response was not attenuated after repetition of faces associated with rich behavioral, social information. This was not the case for faces associated with non-social information (e.g., stories about volcanoes).

As people learn over time more and more about their social environment, social face perception and social knowledge begin to mesh together. Beliefs about a person's character influence the expected facial appearance of the person (Hassin & Trope, 2000) and evaluation of novel faces is influenced by their similarity to known faces (Kraus & Chen, 2010; Verosky & Todorov, 2010b). Likewise, beliefs and attitudes about a group influence the expected facial appearance of group members (Dotsch, Wigboldus, Langner, & van Knippenberg, 2008; Dotsch, Wigboldus, & van Knippenberg, 2011) and greater familiarity with in-group (within-race) faces relative to out-group faces can partially explain in-group face preferences (Zebrowitz et al., 2007, 2008). Individual differences in these expectations have been shown to drive face categorization as a function of prejudice (Hugenberg & Bodenhausen, 2004), although this relationship is complex (Dotsch, Wigboldus & van Knippenberg, 2011).

SECTION IV: SOCIAL PERCEPTION OF FACES – COMPUTATIONAL MODELS

Models of representation of faces can be used as tools for modeling social perception (e.g., Oosterhof & Todorov, 2008; Todorov & Oosterhof, 2011; Walker & Vetter, 2009) or as testable hypotheses of how faces are represented in the brain (e.g., Leopold, Bondar, & Giese, 2006; Loffler, Yourganov, Wilkinson, & Wilson, 2005; Rhodes & Jeffery, 2006; Said, Dotsch, & Todorov, 2010). Both uses are invaluable. Models are (a) explicit in specifying the parameters important for face perception, (b) testable because of their explicitness, and (c) an excellent tool for generation of novel faces and for parametric manipulation of faces on parameters of experimental interest. As a general rule, statistical approaches for characterizing the commonalities and differences among individual faces attempt to reduce high-dimensional face representations (e.g., pixel values of photographs or three-dimensional (3D) points that define the skin surface) to a lower-dimensional "face space". The dimensions of the face space define abstract, global properties of faces that are not reducible to single features.[1] Within this space, faces are represented as points, where each dimension is a property of the face.

The conceptual idea of face space was proposed by Valentine (1991), who used this idea to account for a number of face recognition findings, including effects of distinctiveness (recognition advantage for distinctive faces and high false recognition of typical faces) and race (recognition advantage for own-race faces). For example, to explain the first phenomenon, one needs to assume that distinctive faces are located in less dense regions of the face space. Subsequently, statistical face models were defined using a principal components analysis of either the pixel intensities of two-dimensional (2D) facial images (Turk & Pentland, 1991) or points on the face surface extracted from 3D laser scans of faces (Blanz & Vetter, 1999, 2003). These multidimensional models provide a powerful representational framework that can account for variations in face identity and facial expressions (Calder & Young, 2005; Neth & Martinez, 2009), race (Caldara & Abdi, 2006; Furl, Jonathon, & O'Toole, 2002; O'Toole, Abdi, Deffenbacher, & Valentin, 1995), attractiveness (Potter & Corneille, 2008; Potter, Corneille, Ruys, & Rhodes, 2007; Said & Todorov, 2011), and social perceptions of various personality characteristics (Oosterhof & Todorov, 2008; Todorov & Oosterhof, 2011; Walker & Vetter, 2009).

As described in section I, perception of faces is holistic. This poses serious problems for modeling social perception: i.e. deriving the facial features that lead to specific social perceptions such as trustworthiness and dominance. Changes in any facial feature (e.g., the shape of the eyebrows) could lead to changes in social judgments, and the same feature would be perceived differently in the context of other features. Furthermore, it is not even clear what constitutes a proper feature (e.g., mouth vs upper lip vs segment of the face). Finally, the various feature combinations rapidly proliferate even for a relatively small number of features (10 binary features result in 1024 feature combinations, and 20 binary features result in 1,048,576 combinations).

Data-driven approaches based on face space models are particularly well suited for modeling the complexity of social perception (Todorov, Dotsch, Wigboldus, & Said, 2011). These approaches allow for the stimuli to vary across the whole face (and therefore all possible features) without limiting the search to specific features. This makes it possible for solutions to emerge that not only show effects of specific features but also effects of interacting features on social perception. For example, using a statistical face model, it is possible to uncover the variations in the structure of faces that lead to any social judgment whether on personality characteristics (e.g., trustworthiness, extroversion; see Fig. 6.2) or on social categories (e.g., the typical face for a particular group). Generally, the statistical model is used to randomly generate faces that are precisely characterized on the face dimensions. Subsequently, social judgments of these faces are analyzed as a function of the position of the faces in the multidimensional space. This analysis allows for the construction of new dimensions in the face space that account for the maximum variability in the judgments and, importantly, can be used to visualize the differences in facial structure that lead to specific judgments, as well as manipulate faces along these dimensions (Todorov

et al., 2008). Using this approach, a number of social judgments have been successfully modeled (Oosterhof & Todorov, 2008; Todorov & Oosterhof, 2011; Walker & Vetter, 2009).

Whereas the above research uses face space models as tools for modeling social perception, these models were originally proposed as models of how faces are really represented in the brain. In principle, there are two versions of these models, according to which faces are either coded as exemplars or relative to a population norm – the average or prototypical face (Tsao & Freiwald, 2006; Valentine, 1991). The major difference between the exemplar and norm-based models is the importance of the average face. In the norm-based model, all faces are represented with respect to the average face. One way to think of the average face is as the prototype of faces extracted from one's experience and as the face at the origin of the multidimensional face space.[2] In fact, there is evidence that 3-month-old infants are capable of extracting face prototypes (de Haan, Johnson, Maurer, & Perrett, 2001).

Two types of behavioral evidence strongly support the norm-based model. First, people are faster recognized from caricatures of their faces, which have been obtained by exaggerating the difference between the faces and the average face, than from the original faces (Lee, Byatt, & Rhodes, 2000; Rhodes, Brennan, & Carey, 1987). Second, in norm-based models, each face has an anti-face (i.e., the opposite identity of the face) – the face across the origin (the average face) of the space (think of multiplying the face vector by −1). Importantly, the face and its anti-face are very dissimilar (Rhodes & Jeffery, 2006). Yet, adaptation to the anti-face facilitates identification of its corresponding face (Leopold, O'Toole, Vetter, & Blanz, 2001; Leopold, Rhodes, Müller, & Jeffery, 2005; Rhodes & Jeffery, 2006). Norm-based models easily accommodate these findings (Tsao & Freiwald, 2006). Neurophysiological and neuroimaging research also supports these models: both single unit recordings and fMRI studies have shown increased responses in face-selective regions as a function of the distance from the average face (Leopold et al., 2006; Loffler et al., 2005). Moreover, recent work shows that such models could also account for neural responses to the social value of faces (Said et al., 2010), a topic revisited at the end of section V.

SECTION V: THE NEURAL BASIS OF SOCIAL PERCEPTION OF FACES

Section II outlined the regions involved in the perceptual analysis of faces. These include the

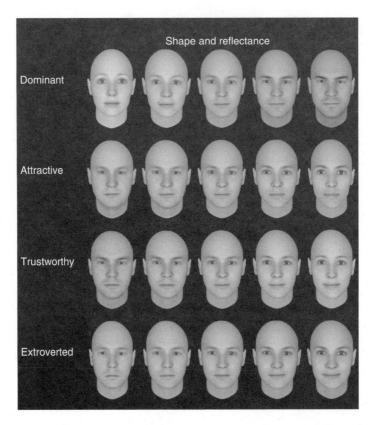

Figure 6.2　Variations of face shape and face reflectance on four social dimensions derived from judgments of dominance, attractiveness, trustworthiness, and extroversion. The perceived value of the faces on the respective dimensions increases from left to right.

FFA, the OFA, and face-selective regions in pSTS. But what are the regions involved in social perception of faces?[3] In the last decade, there has been a flurry of functional neuroimaging studies on social perception of faces (Todorov, Said, & Verosky, 2011). Most of these studies have focused either on perceived attractiveness or perceived trustworthiness. Importantly, about half of these studies used implicit paradigms, in which subjects are not instructed to explicitly evaluate the faces (Mende-Siedlecki et al., in press). Thus, one can draw conclusions that are not generally limited to specific evaluations of trustworthiness and attractiveness.

There have been a number of inconsistencies within attractiveness studies and within trustworthiness studies, as well as inconsistencies between these two types of studies. For example, the guiding assumption of attractiveness studies is that attractive faces should activate reward-related brain regions. Consistent with this assumption, many studies have observed increased activation

to attractive faces in medial orbitofrontal cortex (mOFC; e.g., Cloutier et al., 2008; Kranz & Ishai, 2006; O'Doherty et al., 2003; Winston et al., 2007) and some studies have observed similar responses in the nucleus accumbens (NAcc; e.g., Aharon et al., 2001; Cloutier et al., 2008). However, many other studies have not observed activations in NAcc (e.g., Kampe et al., 2001; O'Doherty et al., 2003; Kranz & Ishai, 2006; Winston et al., 2007).

Most neuroimaging studies on trustworthiness have focused on the role of the amygdala, following research with patients with bilateral amygdala lesions showing that they have a bias to perceive untrustworthy and unapproachable faces – as assessed by judgments of normal controls – as trustworthy and approachable (Adolphs, Tranel, & Damasio, 1998). Although subsequent fMRI studies with normal participants have confirmed the amygdala's involvement in perceptions of trustworthiness, there have been inconsistencies in the nature of the observed responses. Whereas some studies have observed linear responses – the amygdala responded more strongly to untrustworthy-looking faces (Engell, Haxby &, Todorov, 2007; Winston et al., 2002), other studies have observed non-linear responses – the amygdala responded more strongly to both trustworthy- and untrustworthy-looking faces than to faces in the middle of the continuum (Said, Baron, & Todorov, 2009; Said et al., 2010; Todorov, Said, Oosterhof, & Engell, 2011). Similar non-linear amygdala responses have also been observed in studies on attractiveness (Liang et al., 2010; Winston et al., 2007). Finally, it is puzzling that studies on attractiveness and trustworthiness emphasize different sets of regions (Todorov, Said, & Verosky, 2011), given that judgments of attractiveness and trustworthiness are highly correlated with each other (with correlations ranging from 0.60 to 0.80; see Oosterhof & Todorov, 2008; Todorov et al., 2008).

In addressing these issues, meta-analytic methods are especially helpful. These methods can be used to identify regions that are consistently activated across a large number of studies of the same psychological phenomenon. Recently, Mende-Siedlecki and colleagues (Mende-Siedlecki et al., in press) conducted a multi-level kernel density analysis (MKDA) of 28 studies on face evaluation. In contrast to standard approaches, the MKDA approach accounts for the fact that individual activation peaks are nested within contrast maps, making these maps the unit of analysis rather than individual peaks (Wager et al., 2008), and also weights contrasts so that studies with larger sample sizes and more statistically rigorous analyses contribute more to the results of the meta-analysis (Kober et al., 2008).

Across studies, Mende-Siedlecki and colleagues (in press) observed consistently stronger activations to negatively evaluated than to positively evaluated faces in right amygdala. Less consistent areas of activation were observed in left amygdala, right anterior insula, right inferior frontal gyrus, right ventrolateral prefrontal cortex, and right globus pallidus. Consistently stronger activations to positively evaluated than to negatively evaluated faces were observed in left caudate extending into NAcc/mOFC, vmPFC, dACC/pgACC, right thalamus, as well as less consistent activations in right amygdala, bilateral insula, IFG, and vlPFC. Interestingly, these patterns of activations in response to negative and positive faces parallel activations in response to angry and happy faces, respectively. These findings are consistent with the emotion overgeneralization hypothesis (see section III; Montepare & Dobish, 2003; Neth & Martinez, 2009; Oosterhof & Todorov, 2009; Said, Sebe, & Todorov, 2009; Zebrowitz, Kikuchi, & Fellous, 2010) and the

hypothesis that novel faces are automatically evaluated with respect to their approach/avoidance value (Todorov, 2008).

Separate analyses of trustworthiness and attractiveness studies showed that these studies were associated with different loci of activations: right amygdala in trustworthiness studies, and the NAcc/caudate and vmPFC/pgACC in attractiveness studies. However, most of these differences could be attributed to differences in the face stimuli used in the respective studies. Specifically, attractiveness studies that used extremely attractive faces were the ones leading to more consistent activations in the NAcc/caudate and vmPFC/pgACC (see Figure 6.3). These findings show that the type of face stimuli used in a particular study could determine the nature of the observed behavioral and neural responses, a topic that is revisited later.

Importantly, the MKDA analysis revealed several brain regions consistently activated across studies on face evaluation in implicit paradigms not requiring face evaluation. These included bilateral amygdala, vmPFC, bilateral caudate, and NAcc/mOFC. These regions seem to be automatically engaged upon the presentation of faces. Most likely, the region that is central for the face evaluation network is the amygdala (Todorov, 2011). This is consistent with both anatomical studies of the macaque's brain (Amaral et al., 1992) and neurophysiology findings of face-selective responses in the amygdala (Gothard et al., 2007; Nakamura et al., 1992; Rolls, 2000). The amygdala receives input from the inferior temporal (IT) cortex and projects back not only to IT cortex but also to extrastriate and striate visual areas. The amygdala also has strong interconnections with anterior cingulate cortex, orbitofrontal cortex, medial prefrontal cortex, basal ganglia, and anterior insula. This anatomical position of the amygdala allows for it to serve as an affective hub of information.

Future research needs to establish the functions of the regions involved in social perception of faces. Based on the literature, Mende-Siedlecki and colleagues (in press) have argued that highly processed face information in inferior temporal regions can be further processed in the amygdala for determining the affective significance of the faces. Faces that are deemed significant either by virtue of their atypicality (Said et al., 2010) or emotional expressions (Vuilleumier et al., 2004) can be more deeply processed in these regions via feedback projections from the amygdala. Faces that are tagged as affectively significant in the amygdala can be further processed in prefrontal regions. Prefrontal-amygdala connections have been explored in the vmPFC (Quirk et al., 2003, Heinz et al., 2004), as well as the pgACC

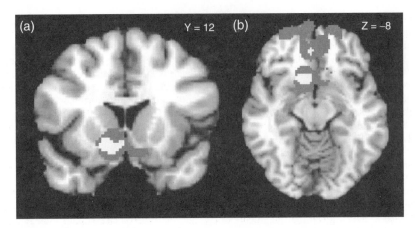

Figure 6.3   More consistently activated areas in studies that used extremely attractive faces than in studies that used more typical faces a) NAcc extending into mOFC, b) pgACC and vmPFC. (The opposite contrast did not produce regions of consistent activation.) Brighter voxels withstood height-based thresholding and darker voxels withstood extent-based thresholding (p < .001). The thresholding was based on Monte Carlo simulations (see Kober et al., 2008 and Mende-Siedlecki, in press, for technical details).

(Stein et al., 2007; Zink et al., 2010), both of which were observed as consistently activated to positively evaluated faces. Finally, the consistent activation in the left caudate nucleus, extending broadly into the NAcc, suggests that the impressions from faces may depend, in part, on the recruitment of structures implicated in reward-processing (Haruno et al., 2004; Knutson et al., 2001a, 2001b). However, as noted above, activations in these regions seem to be driven by extremely attractive faces.

One of the important and unresolved research questions is what properties of faces are coded in the different regions comprising the face evaluation network. The models reviewed in section IV could be particularly useful in guiding this research. In the context of face space models, Said and colleagues recently tested whether the FFA and the amygdala respond to general face properties characterized by the distance to the average face (i.e., face typicality) rather than to more specific "social" properties (Said et al., 2010). Specifically, they compared the responses to faces parametrically manipulated by a statistical model of face valence and faces that were matched on the distance from the average face but varied to a much lesser extent in their perceived valence. Both the amygdala and the FFA responded more strongly to faces distant from the average face irrespective of the valence of the faces.

This finding suggests that these regions are tracking face typicality. Importantly, this finding

accounts for previous inconsistencies in the literature. Studies that found a linear relationship between the amygdala response and face valence (e.g., Todorov & Engell, 2008) used faces for which there was a linear relationship between valence and typicality (with more positive faces perceived as more typical). Studies that found a non-linear relationship between the amygdala response and face valence (e.g., Todorov, Said et al., 2011) used faces for which there was a non-linear relationship between valence and typicality (with more positive and more negative faces perceived as less typical). Finally, although typicality and valence (and many specific social attributions) can be un-confounded in experimental contexts, they are highly correlated in real life. In fact, non-evaluative judgments of typicality correlated with 13 out of 14 evaluative social judgments (Said et al., 2010). In general, these findings suggest that brain regions involved in face evaluation may be coding general properties of faces that are extracted from statistical learning. Yet, these properties would be diagnostic for many social perceptions.

CONCLUSION

Faces are special in many ways. Primates are born with perceptual biases to attend to faces.

Face perception involves processes that are distinct from processes in object perception. For example, perception of faces is holistic and not reducible to single features. There are neural circuits dedicated to face perception. But most importantly, from a social cognition point of view, people extract information from faces that is used for social category and personality judgments. Moreover, people act on these judgments and their effects could be consequential. The challenge for future research would be to provide a common computational account of the various facets of social perception of faces and to characterize the functions of the brain regions involved in this perception.

ACKNOWLEDGMENT

I thank Ron Dotsch for comments on previous versions of this chapter. This work was supported by National Science Foundation grant 0823749 and the Russell Sage Foundation.

NOTES

1   Occasionally, the dimensions of face space can be interpreted as related to specific facial features such as mouth, eyes, etc. – e.g., MacLin and Malpass (2001) – but this is rarely the case in actual statistical models.

2   There is some work suggesting that people may hold different prototypes for distinctive groups of faces (Jaquet, Rhodes, & Hayward, 2008; Little, DeBruine, Jones, & Watt, 2008; Potter & Corneille, 2008).

3   A more detailed treatment of this topic can be found in Todorov and Mende-Siedlecki (in press).

REFERENCES

Abbas, Z.-A., & Duchaine, B. (2008). The role of holistic processing in judgments of facial attractiveness. *Perception, 37*(8), 1187–1196.

Adams R.B., Jr., & Franklin, R.G., Jr. (2009). Influence of emotional expression on the processing of gaze direction. *Motivation & Emotion, 33*, 106–112.

Adams, R.B., Jr., & Kleck, R.E. (2003). Perceived gaze direction and the processing of facial displays of emotion. *Psychological Science, 14*, 644–647.

Adams, R.B., Jr., Pauker, K., & Weisbuch, M. (2010). Looking the other way: The role of gaze direction in the cross-race

memory effect. *Journal of Experimental Social Psychology, 46(2)*, 478–481.

Adolphs, R., Tranel, D., & Damasio, A.R. (1998). The human amygdala in social judgment. *Nature, 393*, 470–474.

Aharon, I., Etcoff, N., Ariely, D., Chabris, C.F., O'Connor, E., & Breiter, H.C. (2001). Beautiful faces have variable reward value: fMRI and behavioral evidence. *Neuron, 32*, 537–551.

Allison, T., McCarthy, G., Nobre, A., Puce, A., & Belger, A. (1994). Human extrastriate visual cortex and the perception of faces, words, numbers, and colors. *Cerebral Cortex, 4*, 544–554.

Allison, T., Puce, A., & McCarthy, G. (2000). Social perception from visual cues: Role of the STS region. *Trends in Cognitive Sciences, 4*, 267–278.

Allison, T., Puce, A., Spencer, D.D., & McCarthy, G. (1999). Electrophysiological studies of human face perception. I. Potentials generated in occipitotemporal cortex by face and non-face stimuli. *Cerebral Cortex* 9, 415–430.

Amaral, D.G., Price, J.L., Pitkänen, A., & Carmichael, S.T. (1992). Anatomical organization of the primate amygdaloid complex. In J. P. Aggleton (Ed.), *The amygdala: Neurobiological aspects of emotion, memory, and mental dysfunction* (pp. 1–66). New York: Wiley-Liss.

Ames, D.L., Fiske, S.T., & Todorov, A. (2011). Impression formation: A focus on others' intents. In J. Decety & J. Cacioppo (Eds.), *The Oxford Handbook of Social Neuroscience* (pp. 419–433). Oxford University Press.

Antonakis, J. & Dalgas, O. (2009). Predicting elections: Child's play! *Science, 323*, 1183.

Bahrick, H.P., Bahrick, P.O., & Wittlinger, R.P. (1975). Fifty years of memory for names and faces: A cross-sectional approach. *Journal of Experimental Psychology: General, 104*(1), 54–75.

Ballew, C.C., & Todorov, A. (2007). Predicting political elections from rapid and unreflective face judgments. *Proceedings of the National Academy of Sciences of the USA, 104*, 17948–17953.

Bar, M., Neta, M., & Linz, H. (2006). Very first impressions. *Emotion, 6*, 269–278.

Batki, A., Baron-Cohen, S., Wheelwright, S., Connellan, J., & Ahluwalia, J. (2000). Is there an innate gaze module? Evidence from human neonates. *Infant Behavior &Development* 23, 223–229.

Baudoin, J-Y., & Humphreys, G.W. (2006). Configural information in gender categorization. *Perception, 35*(4), 531–540.

Berman, M.G., Park, J., Gonzalez, R., Polk, T.A., Gehrke, A., Knaffla, S., et al. (2010). Evaluating functional localizers: The case of the FFA. *NeuroImage, 50*(1), 56–71.

Bernstein, M.J., Young, S.G., & Hugenberg, K. (2007). The cross-category effect: Mere social categorization is sufficient to elicit an own-group bias in face recognition. *Psychological Science, 18*(8), 706–712.

Bijlstra, G., Holland, R.W., & Wigboldus, D.H.J. (2010). The social face of emotion recognition: Evaluations versus stereotypes. *Journal of Experimental Social Psychology, 46* (4), 657–663.

Blair, I.V., Judd, C.M., & Chapleau, K.M. (2004). The influence of Afrocentric facial features in criminal sentencing. *Psychological Science, 15,* 674–699.

Blanz, V., & Vetter, T. (1999). A morphable model for the synthesis of 3D faces. In *Proceedings of the 26th Annual Conference on Computer Graphics and Interactive Techniques,* 187–194.

Blanz, V., & Vetter, T. (2003). Face recognition based on fitting a 3D morphable model. *IEEE Transactions on Pattern Analysis and Machine Intelligence, 25,* 1063–1074.

Bliss-Moreau, E., Barrett, L.F., & Wright, C.I. (2008). Individual differences in learning the affective value of others under minimal conditions. *Emotion, 8*(4), 479–493.

Bodenhausen, G.V., & Macrae, C.N. (1998). Stereotype activation and inhibition. In R.S. Wyer, Jr. (Ed.), *Stereotype activation and inhibition: Advances in social cognition* (Vol. 11, pp. 1–52). Mahwah, NJ: Erlbaum.

Bowyer, K.W., Chang, K., & Flynn P. (2006). A survey of approaches and challenges in 3D and multi-modal 3D & 2D face recognition. *Computer Vision and Image Understanding, 101,* 1–15.

Brewer, M.C. (1988). A dual process model of impression formation. In R. Wyer and T. Scrull (Eds.), *Advances in social cognition* (Vol. 1, pp. 1–36). Hillsdale, NJ: Erlbaum.

Bruce, V., Desimone, R., & Gross, C.G. (1981). Visual properties of neurons in a polysensory area in a superior temporal sulcus of the macaque. *Journal of Neurophysiology, 46,* 369–384.

Bruce, V., & Langton, S. (1994). The use of pigmentation and shading information in recognising the sex and identities of faces. *Perception 23,* 803–822.

Bukach, C.M., Gauthier, I., & Tarr, M.J. (2006). Beyond faces and modularity: The power of an expertise framework. *Trends in Cognitive Sciences, 10*(4), 159–166.

Bzdok, D., Langner, R., Caspers, S., Furth, F., Habel, U., Zilles, K., et al. (2011). ALE meta-analysis on facial judgments of trustworthiness and attractiveness. *Brain Structure and Function, 215,* 209–223.

Caldara, R., & Abdi, H. (2006). Simulating the "other-race" effect with autoassociative neural networks: Further evidence in favor of the face-space model. *Perception, 35,* 659–670.

Calder, A.J., & Young, A.W. (2005). Understanding the recognition of facial identity and facial expression. *Nature Reviews Neuroscience, 6,* 641–651.

Calder, A.J., & Young, A.W., Keane, J., & Dean, M. (2000). Configural information in facial expression perception. *Journal of Experimental Psychology: Human Perception and Performance, 26*(2), 527–551.

Carlston, D.E., & Skowronski, J.J. (1994). Saving in the relearning of trait information as evidence for spontaneous inference generation. *Journal of Personality and Social Psychology, 66,* 840–856.

Cloutier, J., Heatherton, T.F., Whalen, P.J., & Kelley, W.M. (2008). Are attractive people rewarding? Sex differences in the neural substrates of facial attractiveness. *Journal of Cognitive Neuroscience, 20,* 941–951.

Cloutier, J., Mason, M.F., & Macrae, C.N. (2005). The perceptual determinants of person construal: Reopening the

social-cognitive toolbox. *Journal of Personality and Social Psychology, 88,* 885–894.

Costafreda, S.G., Brammer, M.J., David, A.S., & Fu, C.H.Y. (2008). Predictors of amygdala activation during the processing of emotional stimuli: A meta-analysis of 385 PET and fMRI studies. *Brain Research Reviews, 58,* 57–70.

Croft, K.E., Duffa, M.C., Kovacha, C.K., & Anderson, S.W. (2010). Detestable or marvelous? Neuroanatomical correlates of character judgments. *Neuropsychologia, 48,* 1789–1801.

de Haan, M., Johnson, M.H., Maurer, D., & Perrett, D.I. (2001). Recognition of individual faces and average face prototypes by 1- and 3-month old infants. *Cognitive Development, 16,* 659–678.

DeBruine, L. M. (2002). Facial resemblance enhances trust. *Proceedings of the Royal Society B. 269,* 1307–1312.

Desimone, R. (1991). Face-selective cells in the temporal cortex of monkeys. *Journal of Cognitive Neuroscience, 3,* 1–8.

Dotsch, R., Wigboldus, D.H.J., Langner, O., & van Knippenberg, A. (2008). Ethnic out-group faces are biased in the prejudiced mind. *Psychological Science, 19*(10), 978–980.

Dotsch, R., Wigboldus, D.H.J., & van Knippenberg, A. (2011). Biased allocation of faces to social categories. *Journal of Personality and Social Psychology, 100,* 999–1014.

Duchaine, B. (2011). Developmental prosopagnosia. In A. Calder, J.V. Haxby, M. Johnson, & G. Rhodes (Eds.), *Handbook of face perception* (pp. 821–838). Oxford, UK: Oxford University Press.

Duchaine, B. & Nakayama, K. (2006). Developmental prosopagnosia: A window to content-specific face processing. *Current Opinion in Neurobiology, 16,* 166–173.

Eagly, A.H., Makhijani, M.G., Ashmore, R.D., & Longo, L.C. (1991). What is beautiful is good, but – a meta-analytic review of research on the physical attractiveness stereotype. *Psychological Bulletin, 110*(1), 109–128.

Eberhardt, J.L., Davies, P.G., Purdie-Vaughns, V.J., & Johnson, S.L. (2006). Looking deathworthy: Perceived stereotypicality of Black defendants predicts capital-sentencing outcomes. *Psychological Science, 17,* 383–386.

Elfenbein, H.A., & Ambady, N. (2002). On the universality and cultural specificity of emotion recognition: A meta-analysis. *Psychological Bulletin, 128,* 203–235.

Elfenbein, H.A., & Ambady, N. (2003). Universals and cultural differences in recognizing emotions of a different cultural group. *Current Directions in Psychological Science, 12,* 159–164.

Engell, A.D., Haxby, J.V., & Todorov, A. (2007). Implicit trustworthiness decisions: Automatic coding of face properties in human amygdala. *Journal of Cognitive Neuroscience, 19,* 1508–1519.

Esteves, F. & Öhman, A. (1993). Masking the face: Recognition of emotional facial expressions as a function of the parameters of backward masking. *Scandinavian Journal of Psychology, 34,* 1–18.

Fantz, R.L. (1963). Pattern vision in newborn infants. *Science, 140* (3564), 296–297.

Farah, M.J., Wilson, K.D., Drain, M., & Tanaka, J.N. (1998). What is "special" about face perception? *Psychological Review, 105(3)*, 482–498.

Farroni, T., Csibra, G., Simion, F., Johnson, M.H. (2002). Eye contact detection in humans from birth. *Proceedings of the National Academy of Sciences of the USA, 99*, 9602–9605.

Farroni, T., Johnson, M.H., Menon, E., Zulian, L., Faraguna, D., & Csibra, G. (2005). Newborns' preferences for face-relevant stimuli: Effects of contrast polarity. *Proceedings of the National Academy of Sciences of the USA, 102*, 17245–17250.

Fiske, S.T., Cuddy, A.J.C., & Glick, P. (2007). Universal dimensions of social cognition: Warmth and competence. *Trends in Cognitive Sciences, 11*, 77–83.

Fiske, S.T., & Neuberg, S.L. (1990). A continuum of impression formation, from category-based to individuating processes: Influences of information and motivation on attention and interpretation. *Advances in Experimental Social Psychology, 23*, 1–73.

Fried, I., MacDonald, K.A., Wilson, C. (1997). Single neuron activity in human hippocampus and amygdala during recognition of faces and objects. *Neuron 18*, 753–765.

Frischen, A., Bayliss, A.P., & Tipper, S.P. (2007). Gaze cueing of attention: Visual attention, social cognition, and individual differences. *Psychological Bulletin, 133*, 694–724.

Furl, N., Jonathon, P., & O'Toole, A.J. (2002). Face recognition algorithms and the other-race effect: Computational mechanisms for a developmental contact hypothesis. *Cognitive Science, 26*, 797–815.

Gauthier, I., Tarr, M.J., Moylan, J., Skudlarski, P., Gore, J.C., & Anderson, A.W. (2000). The fusiform "face area" is part of a network that processes faces at the individual level. *Journal of Cognitive Neuroscience, 12(3)*, 495–504.

Golarai G., Ghahremani D.G., Whitfield-Gabrieli S, Reiss A, Eberhardt J.L., Gabrieli J.D., Grill-Spector K. (2007). Differential development of high-level visual cortex correlates with category-specific recognition memory. *Nature Neuroscience, 10*, 512–522.

Golby, A.J., Gabrieli, J.D.E., Chiao, J.Y., & Eberhardt, J.L. (2001). Differential responses in the fusiform region to same-race and other-race faces. *Nature Neuroscience, 4*, 845–850.

Goren, A., & Todorov, A. (2009). Two faces are better than one: Eliminating false trait associations with faces. *Social Cognition, 27(2)*, 222–248.

Gothard, K.M., Battaglia, F.P., Erickson, C.A., Spitler, K.M., & Amaral, D.G. (2007). Neural responses to facial expression and face identity in the monkey amygdala. *Journal of Neurophysiology, 97*, 1671–1683.

Grill-Spector, K., & Kanwisher, N. (2005). Visual recognition: As soon as you know it is there, you know what it is. *Psychological Science, 16*, 152–160.

Halberstadt, J., Sherman, S.J., & Sherman, J.W. (2011). Why Barack Obama is Black: A cognitive account of hypodescent. *Psychological Science, 22(1)*, 29–33.

Halgren, E., Raij, T., Marinkovic, K., Jousmaki, V., & Hari, R. (2000). Cognitive response profile of the human fusiform face area as determined by MEG. *Cerebral Cortex, 10*, 69–81.

Hammermesh, D., & Biddle, J. (1994). Beauty and the labor market. *The American Economic Review, 84*, 1174–1194.

Haruno, M., Kuroda, T., Doya, K., Toyama, K., Kimura, M., Samejima, K., et al. (2004). A neural correlate of reward-based behavioral learning in caudate nucleus: A functional magnetic resonance imaging study of a stochastic decision task. *Journal of Neuroscience, 24*, 1660–1665.

Hassin, R., & Trope, Y. (2000). Facing faces: Studies on the cognitive aspects of physiognomy. *Journal of Personality and Social Psychology, 78(5)*, 837–852.

Haxby, J.V., Hoffman, E.A., & Gobbini, M.I. (2000). The distributed human neural system for face perception. *Trends in Cognitive Sciences, 4*, 223–233.

Haxby, J.V., Grady, C.L., Horwitz, B., Salerno, J., Ungerleider, L.G., Mishkln, M., et al. (1993) Dissociation of object and spatial visual processing pathways in human extra-striate cortex. In B. Gulyas, D. Ottoson, & P.E. Roland (Eds.), *Functional organisation of the human visual cortex* (pp. 329–340). Oxford: Pergamon.

Heisz, J.J., & Shedden, J.M. (2009). Semantic learning modifies perceptual face processing. *Journal of Cognitive Neuroscience, 21*, 1127–1134.

Heinz, A., Braus, D.F., Smolka, M.N., Wrase, J., Puls, I., Hermann, D., et al. (2004). Amygdala–prefrontal coupling depends on a genetic variation of the serotonin transporter. *Nature Neuroscience, 8*, 20–21.

Hess, U., Adams, R.B., Jr., Grammer, K., & Kleck, R.E. (2009). Face gender and emotion expression: Are angry women more like men? *Journal of Vision, 9(12)*: 19, 1–8.

Hugenberg, K., & Bodenhausen, G.V. (2004). Ambiguity in social categorization: The role of prejudice and facial affect in race categorization. *Psychological Science, 15*, 342–345.

Hugenberg, K., & Corneille, O. (2009). Holistic processing is tuned for in-group faces. *Cognitive Science, 33*, 1173–1181.

Hugenberg, K., Miller, J., & Claypool, H. M. (2007). Categorization and individuation in the cross-race recognition deficit: Toward a solution to an insidious problem. *Journal of Experimental Social Psychology, 43*, 334–340.

Hugenberg, K., & Sacco, D.F. (2008). Social categorization and stereotyping: How social categorization biases person perception and face memory. *Social and Personality Psychology Compass, 2(2)*, 1052–1072.

Hugenberg, K., Young, S., Bernstein, M., & Sacco, D.F. (2010). The Categorization-Individuation Model: An Integrative Account of the Cross Race Recognition Deficit. *Psychological Review, 117*, 1168–1187.

Hutchings, P.B., & Haddock, G. (2008). Look Black in anger: The role of implicit prejudice in the categorization and perceived emotional intensity of racially ambiguous faces. *Journal of Experimental Social Psychology, 44(5)*, 1418–1420.

Ito, T.A., Thompson, E., & Cacioppo, J.T. (2004). Tracking the timecourse of social perception: The effects of racial cues on event-related brain potentials. *Personality and Social Psychology Bulletin, 30(10)*, 1267–1280.

Ito, T.A., & Urland, G.R. (2003). Race and gender on the brain: Electrocortical measures of attention to the race and gender of multiply categorizable individuals. *Journal of Personality and Social Psychology, 85*(4), 616–626.

Ito, T.A., & Urland, G.R. (2005). The influence of processing objectives on the perception of faces: An ERP study of race and gender perception. *Cognitive Affective & Behavioral Neuroscience, 5*(1), 21–36.

Jacques, C., & Rossion, B. (2006). The speed of individual face categorization. *Psychological Science, 17,* 485–492.

Jaquet, E., Rhodes, G., & Hayward, W.G. (2008). Race-contingent aftereffects suggest distinct perceptual norms for different race faces. *Visual Cognition, 16,* 734–753.

Johnson, M.H., Dziurawiec, S., Ellis, H., & Morton, J. (1991). Newborns' preferential tracking of face-like stimuli and its subsequent decline. *Cognition, 40,* 1–19.

Johnson, M.K., Kim, J.K., & Risse, G. (1985). Do alcoholic Korsakoff's syndrome patients acquire affective reactions? *Journal of Experimental Psychology: Learning, Memory, and Cognition, 11,* 22–36.

Kampe, K K.W., Frith, C.D., Dolan, R.J., & Frith, U. (2001). Reward value of attractiveness and gaze. *Nature, 413,* 589–589.

Kanwisher, N., McDermott, J., Chun, M.M. (1997). The fusiform face area: A module in human extrastriate cortex specialized for face perception. *Journal of Neuroscience, 17*(11), 4302–4311.

Kelly, D.J., Quinn, P.C., Slater, A.M., Lee, K., Gibson, A., Smith, M., et al. (2005). Three-month-olds, but not newborns, prefer own-race faces. *Developmental Science, 8,* F31–F36.

Knutson, B., Adams, C.M., Fong, G.W., & Hommer, D. (2001a). Anticipation of increasing monetary reward selectively recruits nucleus accumbens. *Journal of Neuroscience, 21,* 1–5.

Knutson, B., Fong, G.W., Adams, C.M., Varner, J.L., & Hommer, D. (2001b). Dissociation of reward anticipation and outcome with event-related fMRI. *NeuroReport, 12,* 3683–3687.

Kober, H., Barrett, L.F., Joseph, J., Bliss-Moreau, E., Lindquist, K., & Wager, T.D. (2008). Functional grouping and cortical–subcortical interactions in emotion: A meta-analysis of neuroimaging studies, *NeuroImage, 42,* 998–1031.

Kranz, F., & Ishai, A. (2006). Face perception is modulated by sexual preference. *Current Biology, 16,* 63–68.

Kraus, M.W., & Chen, S. (2010). Facial-feature resemblance elicits the transference effect. *Psychological Science, 21,* 518–522.

Kreiman, G., Koch, C., Fried, I. (2000). Category-specific visual responses of single neurons in the human medial temporal lobe. *Nature Neuroscience, 3,* 946–953.

Krupp, D.B., DeBruine, L.M., & Barclay, P. (2008). A cue of kinship promotes cooperation for the public good. *Evolution and Human Behavior, 29,* 49–55.

Kuraoka, K., & Nakamura, K. (2007). Responses of single neurons in monkey amygdala to facial and vocal emotions. *Journal of Neurophysiology, 97,* 1379–1387.

Langlois, J.H., Kalakanis, L., Rubenstein, A.J., Larson, A., Hallam M., & Smoot, M. (2000). Maxims or myths of beauty? A meta-analytic and theoretical review. *Psychological Bulletin, 126,* 390–423.

Lebrecht, S., Pierce, L.J., Tarr, M.J., & Tanaka, J.W. (2009). Perceptual other-race training reduces implicit racial bias. *PLoS One,* 4(1), e4215. Epub.

Lee, K., Byatt, G., & Rhodes, G. (2000). Caricature effects, distinctiveness and identification: Testing the face-space framework. *Psychological Science, 11,* 379–385.

Leonard, C.M., Rolls, E.T., Wilson, F.A.W., & Baylis, G.C. (1985). Neurons in the amygdala of the monkey with responses selective for faces. *Behavioural Brain Research, 15,* 159–176.

Leopold, D.A., Bondar, I.V., & Giese, M.A. (2006). Norm-based face encoding by single neurons in the monkey inferotemporal cortex. *Nature, 442* (7102), 572–575.

Leopold, D.A., O'Toole, A.J., Vetter, T., & Blanz, V. (2001). Prototype-referenced shape encoding revealed by high-level aftereffects. *Nature Neuroscience, 4,* 89–94.

Leopold, D.A., Rhodes, G., Müller, K.-M., & Jeffery, L. (2005). The dynamics of visual adaptation to faces. *Proceedings of the Royal Society of London, Series B, 272,* 897–904.

Liang, X., Zebrowitz, L.A., & Zhang, Y. (2010). Neural activation in the "reward circuit" shows a nonlinear response to facial attractiveness. *Social Neuroscience, 5,* 320–334.

Little, A.C., Burriss, R.P., Jones, B.C., & Roberts, S.C. (2007). Facial appearance affects voting decisions. *Evolution and Human Behavior, 28,* 18–27.

Little, A.C., DeBruine, L.M., Jones, B.C., & Watt, C. (2008). Category contingent aftereffects for faces of different races, ages and species. *Cognition, 106,* 1537–1547.

Locher, P., Unger, R., Sociedade, P., & Wahl, J. (1993). At first glance: Accessibility of the physical attractiveness stereotype. *Sex Roles, 28,* 729–743.

Loffler, G., Yourganov, G., Wilkinson, F., & Wilson, H.R. (2005). fMRI evidence for the neural representation of faces. *Nature Neuroscience, 8*(10), 1386–1390.

Macrae, C.N., Quinn, K.A., Mason, M.F., & Quadflieg, S. (2005). Understanding others: The face and person construal. *Journal of Personality and Social Psychology, 89,* 686–695.

MacLin, O.H., & Malpass, R.S. (2001). Racial categorization of faces: The ambiguous-race face effect. *Psychology, Public Policy, and Law, 7,* 98–118.

MacLin, O.H., & Malpass, R.S. (2003). The ambiguous-race face illusion. *Perception, 32,* 249–252.

Maddox, K.B. (2004). Perspectives on racial phenotypicality bias. *Personality and Social Psychology Review, 8*(4), 383.

Martin, D. & Macrae, C.N. (2007). A boy primed Sue: Feature based processing and person construal. *European Journal of Social Psychology, 37,* 793–805.

Mason, M.F., Cloutier, J., & Macrae, C.N. (2006). On construing others: Category and stereotype activation from facial cues. *Social Cognition, 24,* 540–562.

Maurer, D., Le Grand, R., & Mondloch, C. J. (2002). The many faces of configural processing. *Trends in Cognitive Sciences, 6,* 255–260.

Mayer, E., & Rossion, B. (2007). Prosopagnosia. In O. Godefroy and J. Bogousslavsky (Eds.), The Behavioral and Cognitive Neurology of Stroke (pp. 315–334). Cambridge University Press.

Mazur, A., Mazur, J., & Keating, C. (1984). Military rank attainment of a West Point class: Effects of cadets' physical features. *American Journal of Sociology, 90,* 125–150.

McCarthy, G., Puce, A., Gore, J.C., & Allison, T. (1997). Face-specific processing in the human fusiform gyrus. *Journal of Cognitive Neurosciences, 9,* 605–610.

McKone, E., Kanwisher, N., & Duchaine, B. (2007). Can generic expertise explain special processing for faces? *Trends in Cognitive Sciences, 11,* 8–15.

Mende-Siedlecki, P., Said, C.P., & Todorov, A. (in press). The social evaluation of faces: A meta-analysis of functional neuroimaging studies. *Social, Cognitive, & Affective Neuroscience.*

Meissner, C.A., & Brigham, J.C. (2001). Thirty years of investigating the own-race bias in memory for faces: A meta-analytic review. *Psychology, Public Policy, and Law, 7*(1), 3–35.

Michel, C., Caldara, R., Rossion, B. (2006). Same-race faces are perceived more holistically than other-race faces. *Visual Cognition,* 14, 55–73.

Michel, C., Corneille, O., & Rossion, B. (2007). Race categorization modulates holistic face encoding. *Cognitive Science, 31,* 911–924.

Michel, C., Corneille, O., & Rossion, B. (2010). Holistic face encoding is modulated by perceived face race: Evidence from perceptual adaptation. *Visual Cognition, 18,* 434–455.

Montepare, J.M., & Dobish, H. (2003). The contribution of emotion perceptions and their overgeneralizations to trait impressions. *Journal of Nonverbal Behavior, 27,* 237–254.

Montepare, J.M., & Zebrowitz, L.A. (1998). Person perception comes of age: The salience and significance of age in social judgments. *Advances in Experimental Social Psychology, 30,* 93–161.

Mueller, U., & Mazur, A. (1996). Facial dominance of West Point cadets as a predictor of later military rank. *Social Forces, 74,* 823–850.

Nakamura, K., Mikami, A., & Kubota, K. (1992). Activity of single neurons in the monkey amygdala during performance of a visual discrimination task. *Journal of Neurophysiology, 67,* 1447–1463.

Neth, D., & Martinez, A.M. (2009). Emotion perception in emotionless face images suggests a norm-based representation. *Journal of Vision, 9*(1), 5, 1–11.

O'Doherty, J., Winston, J., Critchley, H., Perrett, D., Burt, D.M., & Dolan, R.J. (2003). Beauty in a smile: The role of medial orbitofrontal cortex in facial attractiveness. *Neuropsychologia, 41,* 147–155.

Olivola, C.Y., & Todorov, A. (2010a). Fooled by first impressions? Reexamining the diagnostic value of appearance-based inferences. *Journal of Experimental Social Psychology, 46*(2), 315–324.

Olivola, C.Y., & Todorov, A. (2010b). Elected in 100 milliseconds: Appearance-based trait inferences and voting. *Journal of Nonverbal Behavior, 34*(2), 83–110.

Olson, I.R., & Marshuetz, C. (2005). Facial attractiveness is appraised in a glance. *Emotion, 5,* 498–502.

Oosterhof, N.N., & Todorov, A. (2008). The functional basis of face evaluation. *Proceedings of the National Academy of Sciences of the USA, 105,* 11087–11092.

Oosterhof, N.N., & Todorov, A. (2009). Shared perceptual basis of emotional expressions and trustworthiness impressions from faces. *Emotion, 9,* 128–133.

O'Toole, A.J., Abdi, H., Deffenbacher, K.A., Valentin, D. (1995). A perceptual learning theory of the information in faces. In T. Valentine (Ed.), *Cognitive and computational aspects of face processing* (pp. 159–182). London: Routledge.

O'Toole, A.J., Vetter, T., & Blanz, V. (1999). Three-dimensional shape and two-dimensional surface reflectance contributions to face recognition: An application of three-dimensional morphing. *Vision Research, 39,* 3145–3155.

Pascalis, O., de Haan, M., & Nelson, C.A. (2002). Is face processing species-specific during the first year of life? *Science, 296,* 1321–1323.

Pascalis, O., & Kelly, D.J. (2009). The origins of face processing in humans: Phylogeny and ontogeny. *Perspectives on Psychological Science, 2*(2), 200–209.

Pascalis, O., Scott, L.S., Kelly, D.J., Shannon, R.W., Nicholson, E., Coleman, M., et al. (2005). Plasticity of face processing in infancy. *Proceedings of the National Academy of Science, USA, 102,* 5297–5300.

Perrett, D.I., Hietanen, J.K., Oram, M.W., & Benson, P.J. (1992). Organization and functions of cells responsive to faces in the temporal cortex. *Philosophical Transactions of the Royal Society of London. Series B, Biological Sciences, 335,* 23–30.

Perrett, D.I., Rolls, E.T., & Caan, W. (1982) Visual neurons responsive to faces in the monkey temporal cortex. *Experimental Brain Research, 47,* 329–342.

Pitcher, D., Walsh, V., Yovel, G., & Duchaine, B. (2007). TMS evidence for the involvement of the right occipital face area in early face processing. *Current Biology, 17,* 1568–1573.

Porter, S., ten Brinke, L., & Gustaw, C. (2010). Dangerous decisions: The impact of first impressions of trustworthiness on the evaluation of legal evidence and defendant culpability. *Psychology, Crime & Law, 16*(6), 477–491.

Potter, T., & Corneille, O. (2008). Locating attractiveness in the face space: Faces are more attractive when closer to their group prototype. *Psychonomic Bulletin & Review, 15,* 615–622.

Potter, T., Corneille, O., Ruys, K.I. & Rhodes, G. (2007). S/he's just another pretty face: A multidimensional scaling approach to face attractiveness and face variability. *Psychonomic Bulletin and Review, 14,* 368–372.

Puce, A., Allison, T., Asgari, M., Gore, J.C., McCarthy, G. (1996). Differential sensitivity of human visual cortex to faces, letterstrings, and textures: A functional magnetic resonance imaging study. *Journal of Neuroscience 16*(16), 5205–5215.

Quirk, G.J., Likhtik, E., Pelletier, J.G., & Paré, D. (2003). Stimulation of medial prefrontal cortex decreases the responsiveness of central amygdala output neurons. *Journal of Neuroscience, 23,* 8800–8807.

Quiroga, Q.R., Reddy, L., Kreiman, G., Koch, C., & Fried, I. (2005). Invariant visual representation by single neurons in the human brain. *Nature, 435,* 1102–1107.

Ramon, M., Caharel, S., & Rossion, B. (2011). The speed of personally familiar face recognition. *Perception, 40,* 437–449.

Rhodes, G., Brennan, S., & Carey, S. (1987). Identification and ratings of caricatures: Implications for mental representations of faces. *Cognitive Psychology, 19*, 473–497.

Rhodes, G., & Jeffery, L. (2006). Adaptive norm-based coding of facial identity. *Vision Research, 46*, 2977–2987.

Rhodes, G., Lie, H.C., Ewing, L.A., Evangelista, E., & Tanaka, J.W. (2010). Does perceived race affect discrimination and recognition of ambiguous-race faces? A test of the socio-cognitive hypothesis. *Journal of Experimental Psychology: Learning, Memory & Cognition, 36*, 217–223.

Richler, J.J., Cheung, O.S., & Gauthier, I. (2011). Holistic processing predicts face recognition. *Psychological Science, 22*, 464–471.

Rolls, E.T. (1984). Neurons in the cortex of the temporal lobe and in the amygdala of the monkey with responses selective for faces. *Human Neurobiology, 3*, 209–222.

Rolls, E.T. (2000). Neurophysiology and function of the primate amygdala, and neural basis of emotion. In J.P. Aggleton (Ed.), *The amygdala: A functional analysis* (pp. 447–478). New York: Oxford University Press.

Rolls, E.T., Critchley, H.D., Browning, A.S., & Inoue, K. (2006). Face-selective and auditory neurons in the primate orbitofrontal cortex. *Experimental Brain Research, 170*, 74–87.

Rossion, B., & Jacques, C. (2008). Does physical interstimulus variance account for early electrophysiological face sensitive responses in the human brain? Ten lessons on the N170. *NeuroImage, 39*, 1959–1979.

Rudoy, J.D., & Paller, K.A. (2009). Who can you trust? Behavioral and neural differences between perception and memory-based influences. *Frontiers in Human Neuroscience, 3*, 1–6.

Rule, N.O., & Ambady, N. (2008a). Brief exposures: Male sexual orientation is accurately perceived at 50 ms. *Journal of Experimental Social Psychology, 44*, 1100–1105.

Rule, N.O., & Ambady, N. (2008b). The face of success: Inferences from chief executive officers' appearance predict company profits. *Psychological Science, 19*(2), 109–111.

Rule, N.O., Ambady, N. & Adams, R.B., Jr. (2009). Personality in perspective: Judgment consistency across orientations of the face. *Perception, 38*(11), 1688–1699.

Russell, R., Sinha, P., Biederman, I., & Nederhouser, M. (2006). Is pigmentation important for face recognition? Evidence from contrast negation. *Perception, 35*, 749–759.

Said, C.P., Baron, S.G., & Todorov, A. (2009). Nonlinear amygdala response to face trustworthiness: Contributions of high and low spatial frequency information. *Journal of Cognitive Neuroscience, 21*, 519–528.

Said, C.P., Dotsch, R., & Todorov, A. (2010). The amygdala and FFA track both social and non-social face dimensions. *Neuropsychologia, 48*, 3596–3605.

Said, C. P., Haxby, J. V., & Todorov, A. (2011). Brain systems for assessing the affective value of faces. *Philosophical Transactions of the Royal Society, B, 336*, 1660–1670.

Said, C., Sebe, N., & Todorov, A. (2009). Structural resemblance to emotional expressions predicts evaluation of emotionally neutral faces. *Emotion, 9*, 260–264.

Said, C.P., & Todorov, A. (2011). A statistical model of facial attractiveness. *Psychological Science, 22*, 1183–1190.

Sangrigoli, S., Pallier, C., Argenti, A.-M., Ventureyra, V.A.G., & de Schonen, S. (2005). Reversibility of the other-race effect in face recognition during childhood. *Psychological Science, 16*, 440–444.

Santos, I., & Young, A.W. (2008). Effects of inversion and negation on social inferences from faces. *Perception, 37*(7), 1061–1078.

Santos, I., & Young, A.W. (2010). Inferring social attributes from different face regions: Evidence for holistic processing. *The Quarterly Journal of Experimental Psychology*, First published on 17 November 2010 (iFirst), doi: 10.1080/17470218.2010.519779.

Scharlemann, J.P., Eckel, C.C., Kacelnik, A., & Wilson, R.K. (2001). The value of a smile: Game theory with a human face. *Journal of Economic Psychology, 22*(5), 617–640.

Sergent, J., Ohta, S., & MacDonald, B. (1992). Functional neuroanatomy of the face and object processing: A positron emission tomography study. *Brain, 115*, 15–36.

Sergerie, K., Chochol, C., & Armony, J.L. (2008). The role of the amygdala in emotional processing: A quantitative meta-analysis of functional neuroimaging studies. *Neuroscience and Biobehavioral Reviews, 32*(4), 811–830.

Shriver, E.R., Young, S.G., Hugenberg, K., Bernstein, M. J., & Lanter, J. R. (2008). Class, race, and the face: Social context modulates the cross-race effect in face recognition. *Personality and Social Psychology Bulletin, 34*(2), 260–274.

Sinha, P., Balas, B., Ostrovsky, Y., & Russell, R. (2006). Face recognition by humans: Nineteen results all computer vision researchers should know about. *Proceedings of the IEEE, 94*, 1948–1962.

Sinha, P., & Poggio, T. (1996). I think I know that face … *Nature, 384*, 404.

Sporer, S.L. (2001). Recognizing faces of other ethnic groups: An integration of theories. *Psychology, Public Policy, and Law, 7*, 36–97.

Stein, J. L., Wiedholz, L. M., Bassett, D. S., Weinberger, D. R., Zink, C. F., Mattay, V. S., & Meyer-Lindenberg, A. (2007). A validated network of effective amygdala connectivity. *NeuroImage, 36*, 736–745.

Sugita, Y. (2008) Face perception in monkeys reared with no exposure to faces. *Proceedings of the National Academy of Sciences, USA, 105*, 394–398.

Tanaka, J.W., & Corneille, O. (2007). Typicality effects in face and object recognition: Further evidence for the attractor field model. *Perception & Psychophysics, 69*, 619–627.

Tanaka, J.W., Giles, M., Kremen, S., & Simon, V. (1998). Mapping attractor fields in face space: The atypicality bias in face recognition. *Cognition, 68*, 199–220.

Tanaka, J.W., Kiefer, M., & Bukach, C.M. (2004). A holistic account of the own-race effect in face recognition: Evidence from a cross-cultural study, *Cognition, 93*, B1–B9.

Todorov, A. (2008). Evaluating faces on trustworthiness: An extension of systems for recognition of emotions signaling approach/ avoidance behaviors. In A. Kingstone & M. Miller (Eds.), The Year in Cognitive Neuroscience 2008, *Annals of the New York Academy of Sciences, 1124*, 208–224.

Todorov, A. (2011). The role of the amygdala in face perception and evaluation. *Motivation & Emotion.* Published online August 2, 2011, doi: 10.1007/s11031-011-9238-5.

Todorov, A., Dotsch, R., Wigboldus, D., & Said, C P. (2011). Data-driven methods for modeling social perception. *Social and Personality Psychology Compass, 5,* 775–791.

Todorov, A., & Engell, A. (2008). The role of the amygdala in implicit evaluation of emotionally neutral faces. *Social, Cognitive, & Affective Neuroscience, 3,* 303–312.

Todorov, A., Loehr, V., & Oosterhof, N.N. (2010). The obligatory nature of holistic processing of faces in social judgments. *Perception,* 39, 514–532.

Todorov, A., Mandisodza, A.N., Goren, A., & Hall, C.C. (2005). Inferences of competence from faces predict election outcomes. *Science, 308,* 1623–1626.

Todorov, A., & Mende-Siedlecki (in press). The cognitive and neural basis of impression formation. In K. Ochsner & S. Kossyln (Eds.), *The Oxford handbook of cognitive neuroscience.* New York: Oxford University Press.

Todorov, A., & Olson, I.R. (2008). Robust learning of affective trait associations with faces when the hippocampus is damaged, but not when the amygdala and temporal pole are damaged. *Social Cognitive and Affective Neuroscience, 3*(3), 195–203.

Todorov, A., & Oosterhof, N.N. (2011). Modeling social perception of faces. *Signal Processing Magazine, IEEE, 28,* 117–122.

Todorov, A., Pakrashi, M., & Oosterhof, N.N. (2009). Evaluating faces on trustworthiness after minimal time exposure. *Social Cognition, 27,* 813–833.

Todorov, A., Said, C.P., Engell, A.D., & Oosterhof, N.N. (2008). Understanding evaluation of faces on social dimensions. *Trends in Cognitive Sciences, 12,* 455–460.

Todorov, A., Said, C.P., Oosterhof, N.N., & Engell, A.D. (2011). Task-invariant brain responses to the social value of faces. *Journal of Cognitive Neuroscience, 23,* 2766–2781.

Todorov, A., Said, C.P., & Verosky, S.C. (2011) Personality impressions from facial appearance. In A. Calder, J.V. Haxby, M. Johnson, & G. Rhodes (Eds.), *Handbook of face perception* (pp. 631–652). Oxford: UK: Oxford University Press.

Todorov, A., & Uleman, J.S. (2002). Spontaneous trait inferences are bound to actors' faces: Evidence from a false recognition paradigm. *Journal of Personality and Social Psychology, 83*(5), 1051–1065.

Todorov, A., & Uleman, J.S. (2003). The efficiency of binding spontaneous trait inferences to actor's faces. *Journal of Experimental Social Psychology, 39,* 549–562.

Todorov, A., & Uleman, J.S. (2004). The person reference process in spontaneous trait inferences. *Journal of Personality and Social Psychology, 87*(4), 482–493.

Tong, F., Nakayama, K., Moscovitch, M., Weinrib, O., & Kanwisher, N. (2000). Response properties of the human fusiform face area. *Cognitive Neuropsychology, 17,* 257–279.

Tranel, D., & Damasio, A.R. (1993). The covert learning of affective valence does not require structures in hippocampal system or amygdala. *Journal of Cognitive Neuroscience, 5*(1), 79–88.

Tsao, D.Y., & Freiwald, W.A. (2006). What's so special about the average face? *Trends in Cognitive Sciences, 10*(9), 391–393.

Tsao, D.Y., Schweers, N., Moeller, S., & Freiwald, W.A. (2008). Patches of face-selective cortex in the macaque frontal lobe. *Nature Neuroscience, 11,* 877–879.

Turati, C. (2004). Why faces are not special to newborns: An alternative account of the face preference. *Current Directions in Psychological Science, 13*(1), 5–8.

Turk, M., & Pentland, A. (1991). Eigenfaces for recognition. *Journal of Cognitive Neuroscience, 3*(1), 71–86.

Valentine, T. (1991). A unified account of the effects of distinctiveness, inversion, and race in face recognition. *Quarterly Journal of Experimental Psychology, 43*(2), 161–204.

Valenza, E., Simion, F., Macchi Cassia, V., & Umilta, C. (1996). Face preference at birth. *Journal of Experimental Psychology: Human Perception and Performance, 22,* 892–903.

Van Bavel, J.J., & Cunningham, W.A. (2009). Self-categorization with a novel mixed-race group moderates automatic social and racial biases. *Personality and Social Psychology Bulletin, 35,* 321–335.

Van Bavel, J.J., Packer, D.J., & Cunningham, W.A. (2008). The neural substrates of in-group bias: A functional magnetic resonance imaging investigation. *Psychological Science, 19,* 1131–1139.

van Leeuwen, M.L., & Macrae, C.N. (2004). Is beautiful always good? Implicit benefits of facial attractiveness. *Social Cognition, 22,* 637–649.

Van't Wout, M., & Sanfey, A.G. (2008). Friend or foe: The effect of implicit trustworthiness judgments in social decision making. *Cognition, 108,* 796–803.

Verosky, S.C., & Todorov, A. (2010a). Differential neural responses to faces physically similar to the self as a function of their valence. *NeuroImage, 49,* 1690–1698.

Verosky, S.C., & Todorov, A. (2010b). Generalization of affective learning about faces to perceptually similar faces. *Psychological Science, 21,* 779–785.

Viskontas, I.V., Quiroga, R.Q., & Fried, I. (2009). Human medial temporal lobe neurons respond preferentially to personally relevant images. *Proceedings of the National Academy of Sciences of the USA, 106,* 21329–21334.

Vuilleumier, P., Richardson, M., Armony, J.L., Driver, J., & Dolan, R.J. (2004). Distant influences of amygdala lesion on visual cortical activation during emotional face processing. *Nature Neuroscience, 7,* 1271–1278.

Wager, T.D., Barrett, L.F., Bliss-Moreau, E., Lindquist, K., Duncan, S., & Kober, H., (2008). The neuroimaging of emotion, In M. Lewis, J.M. Haviland-Jones, & L.F. Barrett, (Eds.), *Handbook of emotion* (3rd ed., pp. 249–271). New York: Guilford Press.

Walker, M., & Vetter, T. (2009). Portraits made to measure: Manipulating social judgments about individuals with a statistical face model. *Journal of Vision, 9*(11), 12, 1–13.

Whalen, P.J., Bush, G., McNally, R.J., Wilhelm, S., McInerney, S.C., Jenike, M.A., et al. (1998). The emotional counting stroop paradigm: A functional magnetic resonance imaging probe of the anterior cingulate affective division. *Biological Psychiatry, 44,* 1219–1228.

Whalen, P.J., Kagan, J., Cook, R.G., Davis, F.C., Kim, H., Polis, S., et al. (2004). Human amygdala responsivity to masked fearful eye whites. *Science, 306,* 2061.

Whalen, P.J., Rauch, S.L., Etcoff, N.L., McInerney, S.C., Lee, M. B., and Jenike, M. A. (1998). Masked presentations of emotional facial expression modulate amygdala activity without explicit knowledge. *Journal of Neuroscience, 18,* 411–418.

Willis, J., & Todorov, A. (2006). First impressions: Making up your mind after 100 ms. exposure to a face. *Psychological Science, 17,* 592–598.

Wilson, F.A.W., & Rolls, E.T. (1993). The effects of stimulus novelty and familiarity on neuronal activity in the amygdala of monkeys performing recognition memory tasks. *Experimental Brain Research, 93,* 367–382.

Winston, J., O'Doherty, J., & Dolan, R.J. (2003). Common and distinct neural responses during direct and incidental processing of multiple facial emotions. *NeuroImage, 20,* 84–97.

Winston, J., O'Doherty, J., Kilner, J.M., Perrett, D.I., & Dolan, R.J. (2007). Brain systems for assessing facial attractiveness, *Neuropsychologia, 45,* 195–206.

Winston, J.S., Strange, B.A., O'Doherty, J., & Dolan, R.J. (2002). Automatic and intentional brain responses during evaluation of trustworthiness of faces. *Nature Neuroscience, 5*(3), 277–283.

Yip, A.W., & Sinha, P. (2002). Contribution of color to face recognition. *Perception, 31*(8), 995–1003.

Young, A.W., Hellawell, D., & Hay, D.C. (1987). Configurational information in face perception. *Perception, 16*(6), 747–759.

Young, S.G., & Hugenberg, K. (2010). Mere social categorization modulates identification of facial expressions of emotion. *Journal of Personality and Social Psychology, 99*(6), 964–977.

Yue, X., Tjan, B.S., & Biederman, I. (2006). What makes faces special? *Vision Research, 46,* 3802–3811.

Zebrowitz, L.A., Bronstad, P.M., & Lee, H.K. (2007). The contribution of face familiarity to ingroup favoritism and stereotyping. *Social Cognition, 25,* 306–338.

Zebrowitz, L.A, Kikuchi, M., & Fellous, J.M. (2010). Facial resemblance to emotions: group differences, impression effects, and race stereotypes. *Journal of Personality and Social Psychology, 98,* 2, 175–189.

Zebrowitz, L.A., & McDonald, S.M. (1991). The impact of litigants' babyfacedness and attractiveness on adjudication in small claims courts. *Law and Human Behavior, 15,* 603–623.

Zebrowitz, L.A., & Montepare, J.M. (2008). Social psychological face perception: Why appearance matters. *Social and Personality Psychology Compass, 2,* 1497–1517.

Zebrowitz, L.A., Wieneke, K., & White, B. (2008). Mere exposure and racial prejudice: Exposure to other-race faces increases liking for strangers of that race. *Social Cognition, 26,* 259–275.

Zink, C.F., Stein, J.L., Kempf, L., Hakimi, S., & Meyer-Lindenberg, A. (2010). Vasopressin modulates medial prefrontal cortex-amygdala circuitry during emotion processing in humans. *Journal of Neuroscience, 30,* 7017–7022.

7

Mind Perception

Daniel R. Ames & Malia F. Mason

What will they think of next? The contemporary colloquial meaning of this phrase often stems from wonder over some new technological marvel, but we use it here in a wholly literal sense as our starting point. For millions of years, members of our evolving species have gazed at one another and wondered: What are they thinking right now ... and what will they think of next? The interest people take in each other's minds is more than idle curiosity. Two of the defining features of our species are our behavioral flexibility – an enormously wide repertoire of actions with an exquisitely complicated and sometimes non-obvious connection to immediate contexts – and our tendency to live together. As a result, people spend a terrific amount of time in close company with conspecifics doing potentially surprising and bewildering things. Most of us resist giving up on human society and embracing the life of a hermit. Instead, most perceivers proceed quite happily to explain and predict others' actions by invoking invisible qualities such as beliefs, desires, intentions, and feelings and ascribing them without conclusive proof to others. People cannot read one another's minds. And yet somehow, many times each day, most people encounter other individuals and "go mental," as it were, adopting what is sometimes called an *intentional stance*, treating the individuals around them as if they were guided by unseen and unseeable mental states (Dennett, 1987). Many scholars say that mind perception is more than a fortuitous development – this capacity itself may be the essence of human evolution (e.g., Byrne & Whiten, 1988). Nothing could be more necessary and familiar. But perhaps nothing could be more strange.

In this chapter, we move between the strangeness and familiarity of mind perception through the lens of social cognition. We define *mind perception* as the everyday inferential act of a perceiver ascribing mental states such as intentions, beliefs, desires, and feelings to others. For the present chapter, we use the term *mind reading* interchangeably with mind perception. We begin by focusing on *how* perceivers do this, drawing on accounts ranging from protocentrism to social projection as well as models of how perceivers shift between inferential strategies. We then turn to *how well* perceivers read one another's minds. As the social psychological literature is fond of pointing out, perceivers are far from perfect in their judgments of others. We review accounts of various distortions and also describe conditions under which judgments show better and worse validity. Lastly, we describe work showing how mind perception comes to life in a number of important domains, such as intergroup relations and interpersonal conflict, addressing selected contexts *where* perceivers engage in mind reading. We hasten to note that a growing tradition of work examines the ascription of mental states to things other than human minds, such as anthropomorphism of non-living objects or attributions of agency to religious figures or deities (e.g., Epley, Waytz, Cacioppo, 2007; Gilbert, Brown, Pinel, & Wilson, 2000). While this work is fascinating, we restrict our current scope to how human minds attempt to model other human minds.

Mind perception is a vibrant, active topic across academia, drawing in primatologists, developmental psychologists, philosophers, and neuroscientists, among others. Even a partial survey of the field can occupy an entire book or edited volume – and often does (e.g., Apperly, 2010; Decety & Ickes, 2009; Leslie & German, in press;

Malle & Hodges, 2005). We focus in this chapter on work that relates most directly to social cognition. Some of the relevant work in this field has been done through the broader lens of person perception and trait judgment (Gilbert, 1998). We see mind reading and person perception as thoroughly intertwined and so we draw on that tradition of work in our description of what we currently know and what questions remain.

HOW WE DO IT

At first glance, mind perception seems impossible. Indeed, philosophers often speak of the "problem of other minds" as a basic and punishing conundrum: people can never really be sure that other people even *have* minds, not to mention the challenge of figuring out what might be going on in them. Yet somehow most people solve this problem each day, at least to their own satisfaction. How? Over the past few decades, scholars have identified various routes perceivers take to read other minds. Many of these accounts are single-strategy models, focusing on an individual mechanism or source, such as social projection or behavioral evidence. In recent years, several bridging models have emerged, describing ways in which perceivers shift between various inferential tools. In the sections that follow, we review models of mind-reading strategies as well as models of how perceivers shift between strategies.

Reading situations

Sometimes all we need to know to read someone's mind are their circumstances. A delivery person steps onto a porch to find a snarling pit bull, a programmer's painstakingly crafted code finally executes correctly after a dozen revisions, a lecturer realizes mid-talk that the front zipper on his pants is wide open. For these cases and countless others, at least some of the contents of actors' minds seem obvious, a reflection of the situation. Philosopher Daniel Dennett (1987) argued as much in his account of the intentional stance whereby onlookers ascribe beliefs and desires to actors based on "their place in the world." A foundational principle of social psychology is that a good deal of people's cognitions and behaviors are a product of the situations they face (Ross & Nisbett, 1991). While everyday perceivers may be susceptible to overlooking such effects, some models of social judgment attempt to capture folk

situationism. For instance, Trope's (1986) model of disposition inference suggests that perceivers often use situations to disambiguate an actor's behaviors and mental states. Trope presented perceivers with photos featuring ambiguous facial displays (e.g., a look that could suggest either anger or happiness) and manipulated the situation in which the display was described as occurring (e.g., a coach whose team is winning or losing). The situational contexts had a dramatic effect on the emotions perceivers ascribed to the actors (e.g., winning coaches were seen as happy, losing ones as angry).

Karniol (e.g., 1986, 2003) has been a central figure in advancing a situation-based mind-reading account. She identified a series of "transformation rules" that perceivers use to predict an actor's thoughts and feelings. For instance, when asked to read the mind of a target seeing a boat, perceivers might first assume the target's thoughts reflect the characteristics of the stimulus itself (e.g., "He thought about what a big boat it was"). Karniol's (1986) account posits that perceivers work through an ordered series of stimulus-related links in the process of mind reading. For instance, after stimulus characteristics, perceivers might consider stimulus-directed desires (e.g., "He wanted to buy the boat") and cognitions about similar category members (e.g., "He thought it looked like his uncle's boat"). This account turns on the idea that perceivers' reason from prototypes, starting with a "default" view of what human agents think, want, and feel in various circumstances. Perceivers may then adjust from this prototype or default view to reason about themselves and about specific other individuals (Karniol, 2003).

Reading behavior

A substantial amount of social cognition and person perception research in the past half century has roots in attribution theory and research. Tracing back to Heider's "naïve analysis of action" (1958), attribution theory suggests that perceivers often read targets' minds by attempting to read the causes of their behavior. In the wake of Heider, attribution scholars embraced and elaborated this approach, unpacking the ways in which perceivers perform causal analyses of behaviors (e.g., Jones & Davis, 1965; Jones & Harris, 1967; Kelley; 1973; Nisbett & Ross, 1980). A major theme in this work is that perceivers seem especially ready to assume that an actor's intentions faithfully correspond to displayed behavior or achieved outcomes – a *correspondent inference* (Gilbert & Malone, 1995). Recent work has also considered how perceivers read behavioral profiles *across* situations. For instance, Kammrath, Mendoza-Denton, and Mischel (2005) showed that perceivers were sensitive not only to the base rate of behavior (e.g., semi-frequent friendliness) but also to its covariance with situational features (e.g., friendly to superiors but not subordinates).

Several accounts have focused on the ubiquity with which, and processes by which, perceivers posit mental states underlying behaviors. Malle (2004) proposed a framework for describing folk explanations for behavior, an inferential chain flowing backwards from intentional behavior to intentions, reasons, and the causal history of reasons. Malle (2004) found that the vast majority of spontaneous explanations offered for others' intentional behavior feature reasons (e.g., "Why did she hire him? Because he was the best candidate.") and that these reasons typically entailed inferences about the actor's desires (e.g., "She wanted to hire the best candidate") and/or beliefs (e.g., "She believed he was the best candidate"). Elsewhere, Reeder (2009) has argued that perceivers attend to the *soft constraints* in situations, such as instructions from authorities or bribes that shape the motives ascribed to actors. Read and Miller (e.g., 2005) have suggested that perceivers look for a fit between observed behavior and their pre-existing schemas – script-like knowledge structures that can organize episodes around actors' goals. For example, through a process of explanatory coherence, a perceiver might apply a narrative of *vindication* to an observed episode, which would feature an initial harm, an attempted harm in response, and an underlying goal of retribution.

The human impulse to read minds from behavior starts very early: by age two, infants show evidence of interpreting the intentions underlying behaviors and discriminating between intentional and unintentional acts (e.g., Meltzoff, 1995). Other work shows that perceivers naturally parse streams of behavior into meaningful units based in part on an actor's intentions and the fulfillment of goals (e.g., Baird & Baldwin, 2001; Newtson, 1973). Recent research suggests that perceivers read intentions from behavior with great speed, perhaps even automatically (e.g., Fiedler & Schenck, 2001). In short, perceivers often read minds by reading behavior, parsing ongoing and sometimes ambiguous streams of situated action into meaningful *acts* and then instinctively if imperfectly ascribing corresponding beliefs, desires, and feelings to actors. Along with reading arcs of intentional action, perceivers also draw inferences from non-verbal behavior and voice; Murphy (Chapter 10) discusses these dynamics in greater detail.

Reading faces

Reading minds by reading faces has a long history, tracing back at least to Aristotle, who noted that hooked noses suggest ferocity and small foreheads imply fickleness. While there are reasons to think that perceivers may read far too much into faces, or commonly misread them altogether, the readiness of perceivers to do so, and the inferential paths perceivers take, continue to be actively studied (see Todorov, Chapter 6).

One tradition of research has examined the ways in which static facial features affect social judgments. Zebrowitz (1997) has reviewed how various qualities and configurations, such as attractiveness, are taken as cues by onlookers of a person's character and attitudes. Zebrowitz has also documented the ways in which a target's *baby-facedness* – a constellation of child-like facial qualities, including a pronounced forehead, large eyes, and a softened chin – affects perceivers' judgments and behavior (e.g., Friedman & Zebrowitz, 1992). Baby-faced individuals are expected to be comparatively warm, submissive, and naïve. Recently, Todorov, Said, Engell, and Oosterhof (2008) argued that perceivers spontaneously draw judgments – such as trustworthiness and dominance – from faces within a fraction of a second. These judgments endure, shaping other inferences and behavior, such as voting for political candidates.

Other research has focused on the perception of emotional expressions. Darwin (1872) was one of the first scholars to portray emotional displays as having a signaling and coordinating function between people. For such coordination to work, perceivers must be reasonably adept at reading emotional states from displays. Scholars disagree about whether faces are a reliable guide ·to the experience of emotion, with some seeing facial displays as more of an automatic, non-culture-bound readout of experience (e.g., Ekman, 2003; Ekman & Friesen, 1971) and others seeing displays as more of a contrived message produced within cultural frames for social consumption (e.g., Russell & Fernandez-Dols, 1997). Yet most scholars agree that perceivers show facility in recognizing emotional displays and exhibit a readiness to ascribe feelings and intentions on the basis of such displays. Recent work suggests that emotion recognition may even be automatic and effortless on the part of perceivers (Tracy & Robins, 2008).

Perceivers also seem ready to leap beyond inferring current emotional states from displays. Numerous scholars have found overgeneralization effects whereby perceivers draw broader, characterological inferences about a target based on a single emotional display ("That smile means she's a friendly person" vs "That smile means she's happy right now"; Knutson, 1996; Montepare & Dobish, 2003).

Ames and Johar (2009) argued that facial displays are often read in conjunction with the behavior or outcomes they accompany. They suggested that positive affective displays (e.g., expressions of happiness and satisfaction) can *augment* behavior-based inferences, whereas negative displays (e.g., expressions of remorse or dissatisfaction) can *discount* behavior-based inferences. They found that perceivers ascribed less benign intentions to helpers when their acts were accompanied by negative compared to positive displays (i.e., seemingly reluctant helpers are seen less positively), but that perceivers ascribed less sinister intentions to harm-doers when their acts were accompanied by negative compared to positive displays (i.e., seemingly reluctant harm-doers are seen more positively). Identical affective displays can thus have divergent effects on mind reading, depending on which behaviors they accompany. Ames and Johar (2009) also showed that the augmenting and discounting effects of affective displays diminished over the course of accumulating behavioral evidence. As perceivers observe more of an actor's behavior, their mind reading appears to reflect more behavior-based inferences and less affective display-based adjustments.

Faces play another important role in mind reading: they can signal category memberships that are taken as diagnostic. Perceivers appear to spontaneously extract category membership information – such as sex, race, and age – from facial displays, even under taxing conditions (e.g., Macrae, Quinn, Mason, & Quadflieg, 2005). As we discuss in the next section, social category information may have a direct impact on mind reading and can also shape how perceivers interpret facial expressions and behavior.

Reading groups and members

Stereotyping is a pervasive aspect of social judgment (see Bodenhausen et al., Chapter 16). Here, we consider the direct impact of stereotypes on mind perception as well as how stereotypes act as lenses.

Direct effects

Stereotype content is more than just "those people are bad" or "these people are good." In recent years, numerous scholars (e.g., Cuddy, Fiske, & Glick, 2008; Judd, James-Hawkins, Yzerbyt, & Kashima, 2005) have argued that stereotypes revolve around two dimensions: warmth and

competence. Some groups are stereotyped as comparatively high in warmth but low in competence (e.g., the elderly), whereas other groups are stereotyped in the reverse fashion (e.g., the rich). Ascribing competence to a target may not be a matter of mind reading per se, but we believe attributing warmth or its opposite to a group or an individual entails suppositions about goals and intentions (Read & Miller, 2005). Thus, the content of many stereotypes can have direct entailments for the mental states perceivers ascribe to targets.

The axis of warmth and cooperativeness is a recurring theme in the large body of research on gender stereotypes (e.g., Eagly & Mladinic, 1989). In the United States, women are often seen as more communal, cooperative, and emotional, whereas men are often seen as more individualistic, competitive, and rational (e.g., Heilman, 1995). Another large body of work on racial and ethnic stereotypes reveals expectations that can shape mind perception, perhaps even without the perceiver's awareness (e.g., Brigham, 1971; Devine, 1989). For instance, Krueger (1996) found evidence of cultural stereotypes among Whites in the United States, characterizing Blacks as aggressive, unmotivated, arrogant, and violence-prone. Thus, a perceiver's stereotypes can lead directly to inferences about the mental states of targets based on category memberships, including gender and race.

Stereotypes as lenses

A young schoolboy walks down a hallway between class periods and another walks up and bumps into him. Is the act mean and threatening or friendly and playful? The difference depends on what's in the bumping boy's mind – and the answer may turn on his race. Sagar and Schofield (1980) presented this scenario and similar ambiguous behaviors to schoolchildren, varying the race of the actors. Both Black and White participants rated Black actors as more mean and threatening than White actors. Racial and other stereotypes can thus act as a lens, governing how perceivers read the intentions that underlie ambiguous behaviors (Devine, 1989).

Stereotypes can also act as lenses for interpreting facial behavior. Hugenberg (2005) found that European American participants were faster to correctly categorize happy White faces as happy than they were to categorize angry White faces as angry. The reverse was true for Black faces: respondents took longer to identify the happy faces than the angry ones. In other work, Hugenberg and Bodenhausen (e.g., 2003) have linked differences in interpretations of racially-varying faces to different levels of perceivers' implicit prejudice.

Mentalizing

Before closing this section on the role of stereo-types in mind reading, we want to highlight one additional way in which stereotypes can have an impact. Some extreme stereotypes portray certain groups and members as less-than-human, targets for which a perceiver might not even adopt an intentional stance (e.g., Haslam, 2006). In some cases, perceivers may even resist ascribing certain distinctly human emotions (e.g., guilt, hope) to out-groups even though they grant them more basic emotions (e.g., fear, anger; e.g., Leyens et al., 2000). We return to dehumanization in greater detail later in this chapter.

Reading oneself to read others

In many cases, perceivers gauge what others think, want, and feel by consulting what they themselves think, want, and feel. Using one's own mind as a template for understanding others is common – and some accounts go so far as to say that the self provides an irrepressible anchor for reading others. In this section, we'll consider several species of using oneself as a template, starting with a basic mechanism of projection (my attitudes are your attitudes) and moving on to more elaborate processes (I imagine what it would be like to be you in your situation and ascribe that to you).

From me to you: Simple social projection

The most basic form of social projection emerges when a perceiver ascribes or projects his or her own general attitudes and mental states to a target. Hundreds of studies have documented and explored projection, sometimes under the label of *false consensus*, an effect whereby people overestimate the extent to which others share their attitudes and attributes (e.g., Ross, Greene, & House, 1977; see Krueger, 2000 for an overview). Various mechanisms have been proposed, including motivational processes such as wanting to belong or feel normal (e.g., Pyszczynski et al., 1996). Other explanations posit cognitive mechanisms, such as naïve realism, or the sense that one's own attitudes are a natural and sensible reaction to reality, rather than an idiosyncratic or subjective construal (Ross & Ward, 1996). Put another way, I prefer brown bread and I assume others do, too, because it is simply and obviously *better* than white bread (i.e., the difference is in the bread, not in me). In this vein, Krueger (1998) argued that, "Projection is a perceptual rather than a cognitive-motivational phenomenon. The perception of consensus is assumed to be part of the initial encoding of the stimulus rather than the outcome of subsequent higher level processes" (p. 202).

From me to you in your situation: Simulation and perspective taking

Perceivers may assume that others share their general taste in bread or films, but what do perceivers do when they have to judge a person in a particular situation, such as how they might respond when asked to donate to a particular charity or how they might feel when offered payment for a potentially embarrassing lip-synching performance in front of a large audience.

Here, too, many accounts suggest that people will turn to themselves as a template for understanding others, but these inferences involve a more active kind of transformation: putting oneself into another person's shoes in a particular situation, a process variously referred to as *simulation* or *perspective taking*.

Van Boven and Loewenstein (2005) argued that this involves two distinct steps: first, a perceiver imagines himself or herself in a target person's situation ("How would *I* feel if offered payment in exchange for lip synching?"); and, second, the perceiver then translates this into a judgment about how a target person would react ("How would *she* feel if offered payment in exchange for lip synching?"). Multiple streams of research suggest that people do frequently anchor on themselves in simulation and perspective taking. For instance, Epley, Keysar, Van Boven, and Gilovich (2004) showed that perceivers were anchored on their own interpretations of ambiguous messages when guessing others' interpretations – and that this anchoring was exacerbated under time pressure. Elsewhere, Epley, Morewedge, and Keysar (2004) found that children and adults both had initial egocentric interpretations of instructions in a coordination task but that adults more readily adjusted from them to take the perspective of their uninformed counterparts. Together, these accounts converge on the notion that a natural starting point for judging others is to start with the self – and when cognitive development and resources allow, to make adjustments for the situation and the target.

Which tool when? Process moderation and multi-process accounts

Having briefly reviewed a variety of inferential tools for reading minds, the puzzle seems to shift from "How could a person possibly understand what's happening in someone else's mind?" to "When is each of these many tools used?"

Answers to this question are beginning to emerge (e.g., Ames, 2005).

While perspective taking is reflexive for some people, scholars have found that prompting perceivers to actively take another's perspective seems to affect their inferences. These changes hold suggestions about how mind-reading tools may combine with or supplant one another. For instance, Galinsky and Moskowitz (2000) showed that asking people to imagine and write about a day in the life of an elderly person ("looking at the world through his eyes and walking through the world in his shoes") appeared to reduce the accessibility and application of stereotypes. Moreover, active perspective taking appears to increase the overlap between self-representations and judgments about a target (Davis, Conklin, Smith, & Luce, 1996).

These accounts suggest that perceivers may shift between the self and stereotypes as templates for reading minds. What draws perceivers toward one template or the other? Group boundaries appear to matter. Clement and Krueger (2002) found that projection appeared to be diminished for certain out-group targets. Jones (2004) found similar effects, suggesting that perceived social distance accounts for the difference. Other scholars have shown that the type of relationship between groups matters: a cooperating out-group may evoke more projection than a competing out-group (Riketta & Sacramento, 2008; Toma, Yzerbyt, & Corneille, 2010).

These results highlight that differences – group boundaries, social distance, competition – might draw perceivers away from projection. Some evidence suggests that differences might draw perceivers toward stereotyping. Kunda and Spencer (2003) found that a perceiver's accessibility of target stereotypes appears to diminish over the course of an interaction with a target, but that a disagreement with the target – a reminder of differences – can reactivate the stereotype.

Attempting to account for shifts between stereotyping and projection in mind reading, Ames (2004a, 2004b) built on this prior work to offer a *similarity contingency* model (see also Ames, Weber, & Zou, in press). This model argues that when direct evidence, such as behavior, is ambiguous, perceivers may turn to projection and stereotyping, guided in their use of these templates by their subjective sense of similarity to the target. Ames (2004a) showed that mind readers are inclined to overgeneralize from isolated markers of similarity. Presented with a few similarities to a novel target person (e.g., shared appreciation for a particular comedian), perceivers appeared to engage in widespread projection and reduced stereotyping; perceivers learning about dissimilarities seemingly eschewed projection and embraced their stereotypes of the targets' groups.

Other work (Ames, 2004b) found a similar pattern in judgments about groups: Perceivers directed to identify similarities to the group engaged in greater levels of subsequent projection and less stereotyping; perceivers directed to identify differences seemed to shift away from projection and toward stereotyping. Importantly, Ames argued that the subjective sense of similarity was not necessarily closely linked with *actual* similarity. Indeed, his studies found that feelings of similarity and actual similarity between a perceiver and target were at most weakly related, if they were linked at all.

This view of mind readers as shifting between the templates of self and stereotypes presents a more complex account than historical views of the "cognitive miser" (Fiske & Taylor, 1991). A stereotyping view of the cognitive miser suggests that mind readers face the choice between effortful individuation and easy stereotyping. A projection view of the cognitive miser suggests that mind readers face the choice between effortful adjustment and easy anchoring on the self. The similarity contingency account portrays the perceiver as having multiple low-effort mind-reading heuristics – including projection and stereotyping – and shifting between them in predictable ways depending on a (fallible) subjective sense of similarity.

Recent work in social-cognitive neuroscience converges with this view. Mitchell, Macrae, and Banaji (2006) found that different brain regions showed differential activity when making inferences about similar and dissimilar others: mentalizing about similar (vs dissimilar) others appeared to evoke greater activity in the ventral medial prefrontal cortex, a region that has been linked to self-referential thought. In other work, Mitchell, Ames, Jenkins, and Banaji (2009) identified the right frontal cortex as showing heightened activity during stereotyping judgments; this region has been linked with semantic retrieval and categorization. Building on the emerging evidence for multiple tools and tool switching, Mitchell (2009) argued that

> Rather than debating which singular process gives rise to human social abilities, a central aim of social cognition should be identification of the full range of available mentalizing processes and a delineation of the contexts in which one or another is brought to bear on the problem of understanding others (p. 1310).

Initial answers to the "Which tool when?" question have emerged, suggesting when people might shift between routes such as projection and stereotyping en route to reading minds. More refined and elaborate accounts of "Which tool when?" are sure to follow.

Reading via technology

Before concluding our discussion of how perceivers read minds, we want to briefly acknowledge technology-enabled communication as a source of mind reading that has received increased attention in recent years and will likely be a focus of more work in the years ahead. Scholars have begun to explore how people read and misread one another through electronically mediated channels. For instance, Kruger, Epley, Parker, and Ng (2005) found that email recipients have difficulty decoding the tone (e.g., sarcastic or funny) of a message, even though message senders believe their intended signals are exceedingly clear. Other scholars have found that such misunderstandings can compound, with email leading to reduced cooperation and outcomes in negotiation (e.g., Morris, Nadler, Kurtzberg, & Thompson, 2002) and to unproductive escalation of conflicts (e.g., Friedman & Currall, 2003). However, other work shows that electronically mediated communication can yield effective social judgments. For instance, Vazire and Gosling (2004) found that judges reviewing personal websites reached some valid conclusions about the site's creators, including inferences about their openness to experience; the authors argued that these inferences were based on cues in the sites themselves, not simply a product of sex or age stereotypes. While online social networking profiles can be a chance to present an idealized version of oneself, research suggests that perceivers have some ability to separate the wheat from chaff and draw accurate judgments about targets, based on their digital presence (Back et al., 2010).

HOW WELL WE DO IT

In the preceding section, we reviewed a variety of routes everyday mind readers use to get inside others' heads. When it comes to inferential arrows, the folk psychology quiver is hardly empty. But that does not necessarily mean the arrows fly straight or hit their mark. In this section, we address questions of accuracy in mind perception, including how to define it and the extent to which, and the conditions under which, it emerges.

Defining and determining accuracy

Social psychologists have grappled with questions of accuracy in social perception for decades (e.g., Cronbach, 1955; Taft, 1955). We discuss some basic ideas here, drawing in part on more extensive discussions elsewhere that include not only mind perception but also person perception more generally (e.g., Funder, 1995; Gilbert, 1998; Swann, 1984).

As several scholars have noted, accuracy takes variant forms. Both Kruglanski (1989) and Funder and West (1993) suggest that theoretical perspectives of accuracy in social judgment take three basic forms, each with its own unique view of what accurate mind reading entails. The *pragmatic* perspective emphasizes the practical value or utility of a judgment and therefore defines success in terms of the outcome of personal interaction (Jussim, 1991; Swann, 1984). Accurate judgments are those that facilitate performance in the social environment. The *constructivist* perspective often defines accuracy in terms of degree of consensus between observers (Kenny, 1994; Kruglanski, 1989). Many, but certainly not all, researchers who adopt this concept of accuracy consider traits and mental states to be social constructions, not necessarily real characteristics belonging to people (indeed, some philosophers of mind suggest that folk psychological concepts such as "belief" and "desire" are groundless and should be abandoned; e.g., Churchland, 1999). Finally, the *realistic* view of accuracy assumes that, despite their intangibility, mental states and personality more generally are genuine properties of people. Researchers working from this perspective believe one can and should identify criteria against which participants' judgments can legitimately be compared, such as the target's self-rating (Funder, 1995; Kenny & Albright, 1987). Yet another view of accuracy and bias comes from a focus on *inferential processes*, often implying normative views of how judgments ought to be made. From this perspective, perceivers whose social judgments are influenced in ways that they should not be (or are not influenced in ways they should be) are distorted, even if the final judgment cannot readily be compared with a criterion value (Gilbert, 1998).

Even researchers who adopt the same theoretical perspective on accuracy tend to measure mind-reading acuity in their own idiosyncratic ways. Some researchers assess participants' knowledge (e.g., Ickes & Tooke, 1988), some measure their physiological reactivity to a target's experiences (e.g., Levenson & Reuf, 1992), and others are concerned primarily with participants' behavioral responses to a target (e.g., Bernieri, Davis, Rosenthal, & Knee, 1994). Despite the diversity in how accuracy is defined and studied, many – but not all – scholars argue that it emerges less often and less strongly than it should. A significant share of scholarly attention is channeled toward examining biases in mind perception and we review some of the most-studied culprits in the section that follows.

The dark side of mind reading

People are far from flawless when it comes to perceiving other minds. One domain that highlights the challenge is the detection of others' deception and lying. Research suggests that most perceivers fair little better than chance at detecting others' deception (Bond & DePaulo, 2006). To make matters worse, it appears that perceivers generally have little to no idea about how well or badly they fare in deception detection and other forms of mind reading (e.g., Ames & Kammrath, 2004). We cannot survey the entire literature on mind perception biases here, but we discuss several of the most-studied varieties below.

Misreading the self and misprojection

As they age, children generally outgrow their initial extreme egocentrism, coming to recognize that not everyone shares their religious beliefs, food aversions, or fashion tastes (e.g., Flavell, Botkin, Fry, Wright, & Jarvis, 1968). A wealth of social psychology research suggests we never fully outgrow this egocentrism and that this innate inclination to perceive, understand, and interpret the world in terms of the self compromises the effectiveness with which we perform the task. As discussed earlier, perceivers often use their own mind as a template for understanding other people's minds. *False consensus* refers to people's tendency to overestimate the degree to which other individuals share their beliefs, attitudes, and values (e.g., Ross et al., 1977). This "egocentric attribution" (Heider, 1958) or "attributive projection" (Holmes, 1968) habit leads people to overestimate the prevalence of their own mental states. Although some scholars question whether false consensus really represents a bias (e.g., Dawes, 1989), many regard it as a pervasive distortion in mind perception and numerous explanations have been offered for the effect.

Motivational accounts argue that assumed consensus bolsters confidence and reassures people of the soundness and legitimacy of their attitudes (e.g., Sherman, Presson, & Chassin, 1984). Selective exposure explanations emphasize the fact that people generally eat, work, and socialize with like-minded individuals (Ross et al., 1977). People's beliefs may be biased because they tend to sample their immediate social circles and not a more diverse population when making these estimates (Kahneman & Tversky, 1973). Some scholars suggest the effect is a stubborn byproduct of basic perceptual processes, with perceivers anchoring on themselves despite feedback on their performance and warnings about the bias (e.g., Krueger & Clement, 1994). Other scholarship has identified boundaries, such as research suggesting that egocentric projection biases may diminish when perceivers have more cognitive resources, time for judgment, and incentives for accuracy (e.g., Epley et al., 2004). The similarity contingency model (Ames, 2004a) argues that when perceivers sense dissimilarity to a target, even if the sense of dissimilarity is itself exaggerated or baseless, they may shift away from projection and instead embrace stereotypes, although this shift from one heuristic to another is no guarantee of increased accuracy.

Misreading behaviors and situations

Among the attributional distortions perceivers display, the tendency to overweight dispositional factors (e.g., "He's so kind") and underweight situational determinants ("His mother is watching") when assigning causes to others' behaviors – the *correspondence bias* – continues to be widely referenced and fiercely debated (e.g., Gilbert & Malone, 1995; Jones & Harris, 1967; Malle, 2006; McClure, 2002). From a mind perception perspective, the correspondence bias suggests that perceivers have a tendency to assume a target's actions and outcomes are consistent with, and caused primarily by, their underlying intentions and attitudes ("She's grouchy and dismissive today because she dislikes people, not because her back hurts").

Motivational accounts of the correspondence bias suggest that people are prone to reverse engineer mental causes from behavioral outcomes because this assumption fulfills a basic need to believe that the world is predictable and fair (Gilbert & Malone, 1995). An unfortunate consequence of this desire can be assigning blame to victims and ascribing intentionality to failed attempts and chance occurrences. In contrast, proponents of processing accounts of the correspondence bias argue that this impulse is a consequence of the two-step manner in which people explain behavior. Rather than consider the internal and external causal drivers simultaneously, perceivers first automatically and spontaneously intuit an agent's attitudes and dispositions and then engage in an effortful correction process that acknowledges situational, external causal factors (Gilbert & Malone, 1995; Trope, 1986). Under cognitive load, or even everyday conditions, perceivers may perform this correction process incompletely, if at all.

Although the precise nature of the bias and its underlying mechanisms remain topics of study, these accounts generally converge on the conclusion that perceivers are often overzealous about assigning internal, mentalistic explanations for others' actions and outcomes.

Expectations, selective perception, and resistance to updating

A wealth of research suggests that mind reading is compromised by perceivers' discomfort with ambiguity, their pre-existing expectations, and the manner in which they collect information and test their intuitive theories about the causal forces behind others' actions (e.g., Roese & Sherman, 2007).

Evidence suggests that one source of inaccuracy in mind reading is the tendency to embellish a single interpersonal interaction or data point to arrive at a coherent impression of someone. The *halo effect* (e.g., Nisbett & Wilson, 1977) refers to perceivers' habit of generating initial, global evaluations (e.g., "She's a good person") and drawing wide-ranging inferences about the individual that are consistent with the evaluation ("She kind, creative, punctual …"). A principal source of the illusory halo appears to be intuitive theories that perceivers hold about trait/attitude covariance (e.g., Shweder & D'Andrade, 1980). Perceivers' tendency to see other people as either all good or all bad can lead them to overlook the nuances in a target's collection of traits, attitudes, and beliefs.

Social judgment also lends itself to the *confirmation bias,* perceivers' preference for testing hypotheses by looking for confirming instances rather than by seeking both potentially confirming and disconfirming cases (e.g., Ross, Lepper, Strack, & Steinmetz, 1977; Snyder & Swann, 1978). Perceivers tend to overlook highly diagnostic evidence that is disconfirming, are insensitive to negative features, and are often incapable of incorporating data that take the form of nonoccurrences (Nickerson, 1998). A handful of confirmatory "hits" seems sufficient to validate even the most erroneous hunches and people seem resistant to revising or improving their skewed social hypothesis-testing approaches. The notion that people jeopardize their mind reading by tenaciously clinging to their initial beliefs or expectations features prominently in a diverse set of literatures, including research on impression formation (e.g., Carlston, 1980), self-fulfilling prophecies (e.g., Jussim, 1986), stereotyping and prejudice (e.g., Macrae & Bodenhausen, 2000), and implicit personality (e.g., Schneider, 1973).

Taken in their entirety, these findings about biases in mind perception suggest that even the most heroic attempts at mind reading risk being thwarted by perceivers' tendency to put too much faith in initial hunches, to selectively attend to information that is consistent with initially favored hypotheses, to limit themselves to positive hypothesis testing, and to disregard information that challenges the veracity of their expectations and initial beliefs. Put another way, despite the variety of tools perceivers employ, the problem of other minds remains a real problem. In a technical sense, we cannot read minds. And in a practical sense, it appears we often don't.

Not quite so dark

Are everyday mind readers really so faulty? Before we describe work on the conditions that appear to promote or inhibit effective mind perception, we wish to briefly highlight accounts that push back against the characterization of perceivers as largely inept (Krueger & Funder, 2004; Kruglanski & Ajzen, 1983; Swann, 1984). While people and their behavior are sometimes puzzling to one another, perceivers hardly spend their days chronically bewildered by the complicated creatures that share their lives. And while society certainly has troubles and conflicts, somehow billions of people make it through each day unharmed and with their relationships intact, having coordinated their behavior with numerous others.

Critics of the view that people are largely inept at mind reading generally acknowledge that misjudgments have the potential to expose the inference process and that detecting them is therefore key to developing a theoretically rich model for how people interpret and predict their social world. Their concerns center primarily on researchers' willingness to infer fundamental mind-reading inadequacy from misjudgments that are detected in contrived experimental settings. Several researchers (e.g., Funder, 1987; Kruglanski & Ajzen, 1983) have noted a widespread failure to distinguish judgment errors from unequivocal mistakes: whereas the former are deviations from a normative model, the latter refer to something incorrectly done or believed. Funder (1987) contends that narrowly defined misjudgments of artificial stimuli are useful for assessing the validity of the normative model purported to capture the reasoning process. Errors are not in themselves informative about whether people have fundamentally flawed reasoning faculties. And while some errors observed in social inference studies might very well reflect an inherent flaw in a perceiver's mind-reading toolkit, some researchers argue that determining this requires broader criteria than scholars typically employ in their studies. Furthermore, these authors point out that what seems like flawed logic in an experimental setting may be viewed as sound, if not adaptive, when considered in a broader context (Haselton, Nettle & Andrews, 2005; Hogarth, 1981; Kenny & Acitelli, 2001). Indeed, as we note later in the section on conflict, some kinds of misreading can have benefits.

These critiques suggest a more balanced view of mind perception ability. They highlight the need for studies that consider how deviations from a normative model might be adaptive and suggest that mind perception scholarship can fruitfully advance from multiple vantage points, including the question of "Why aren't mind readers perfect?" as well as the question of "How can people ever read minds at all?" (Krueger & Funder, 2004; Mason & Macrae, 2008).

Better or worse

We now move beyond the question of whether people can or cannot read minds and turn to factors that may account for variance in mind-reading accuracy. We adopt a modified version of Funder's (1995) interpersonal accuracy framework, highlighting three factors that predict mind-reading success: the characteristics of the judge (i.e., good judge), the properties of the target (i.e., good target), and the quality of the data on which the inference is based (i.e., good data).

Good judges

The notion that certain people make more effective interpersonal judgments has a long history in social psychology research (Taft, 1955). In this section, we consider the stable personality characteristics, interpersonal styles, and demographic factors that distinguish "good" and "poor" judges. It is worth noting that, with the exception of research on empathic accuracy (e.g., Ickes, 1993), non-verbal communication (e.g., Riggio, 1986), and emotion reading (e.g., Mayer & Salovey, 1997), most researchers have been concerned primarily with determining who excels at judging stable personality characteristics and not mental states per se. However, one might reasonably expect that the individual characteristics that enable effective trait reading would also promote, or perhaps rely on, effective reading of more transient mental features (e.g., Hall, Andrzejewski & Yopchick, 2009; Ickes, Buysse et al., 2000).

Interpersonal orientation and social sensitivity

Two of the more consistent findings in interpersonal accuracy research are the superiority of those who are interpersonally oriented and those who are socially sensitive. Skilled interpersonal judges tend to exhibit greater interest in the social environment (Riggio & Carney, 2003) and are more open to new experiences (Matsumoto et al., 2000); they are more conscientious and tolerant (Hall et al., 2009) and are generally more communal (Vogt & Colvin, 2003) than less-adept mind readers. Consistent with this notion that astute readers are more attuned to the surrounding social environment is evidence that they tend to be more empathic (Funder & Harris, 1986) and that they score higher on measures of self-monitoring (Ames & Kammrath, 2004). Effective readers also tend to score high on measures of extraversion (Hall et al., 2009) and expressiveness (Riggio & Carney, 2003). Finally, it is worth noting the small but reliably negative correlation observed between interpersonal accuracy and neuroticism, shyness, and depression (Hall et al., 2009).

Intelligence and cognitive style
Some evidence suggests that greater reasoning ability and intelligence are associated with an enhanced capacity for mind reading (Davis & Kraus, 1997; Murphy & Hall, 2011). Why this relationship might exist is not yet fully understood. There is also evidence that certain cognitive styles are associated with greater effectiveness on social judgment tasks. Wood (1980) reported that people who score high on measures of interpersonal cognitive and attributional complexity were more effective with an impression-formation task. In their meta-analysis of predictors of success on social-inference tasks, Davis and Kraus (1997) report finding a strong relationship between participants' performance and measures of cognitive/attributional complexity (see also Fletcher, Danilovics, Fernandez, Peterson & Reeder, 1986). This relationship suggests that people who are motivated to develop elaborate and intricate models of others become more attuned to the idiosyncratic collection of characteristics their subjects possess.

Gender
Gender differences appear to exist in social judgment validity; however, the source of this performance discrepancy is the subject of debate. Several of Hall's studies reveal that women are generally more effective than men at drawing interpersonal inferences (1978, 1984). This gender difference has been observed in young children, across cultures, and is present across face, body, and voice judgments (e.g., McClure, 2000; Rosenthal et al., 1979). There is reason to suspect that these differences reflect varying levels of motivation (e.g., Ickes, Gesn, & Graham, 2000) or experience discussing and reflecting on personal interactions (e.g., Cross & Madson, 1997), rather than innate differences (see, however, Hall, Blanch, Horgan, Murphy,

Rosip, & Schmid-Mast, 2009). In recent work, Klein and Hodges (2001) reported that the initial gender differences they detected disappeared when participants were offered monetary incentives for their performance.

Culture

Other work has considered the role of acculturation in mind reading. People commonly communicate their attitudes through facial expressions, gestures, posture, and other body movements (Ekman & Friesen, 1967; Mesquita & Frijda, 1992). While perceivers recognize emotions at better-than-chance levels both within and across cultures, there are cultural variations both in the display of emotions and in the rules perceivers use to decode their significance (e.g., Matsumoto, 1993). Consequently, accuracy is higher when non-verbal manifestations of attitudes are expressed and perceived by members of the same cultural group.

Social habits

For some, effectiveness simply comes down to their natural social interaction habits. Whether intentional or not, some interpersonal styles are more likely to elicit disclosure from others (Miller, Berg, & Archer, 1983). Women tend to elicit more disclosure than men and friends tend to elicit more disclosure than strangers (e.g., Rubin & Shenker, 1978). People who express interpersonal warmth and positivity (Taylor, Altman, & Sorrentino, 1969) or who convey interest by establishing eye contact with their interaction partner also tend to elicit more disclosure from others (Jourard & Friedman, 1970).

While the notion that certain individuals are more effective readers seems beyond dispute, it is worth highlighting that cross-paradigm or cross-domain performance correlations are generally quite low. Mind-reading performance in one domain is usually not highly correlated with mind-reading performance in another domain (e.g., Ames & Kammrath, 2004). Thus, while the question of "Who is a good judge?" continues to attract deserved attention, there may be real limits on the extent to which universally good judges exist.

Good targets

The bulk of the existing work on mental state inference focuses on perceiver characteristics that predict accuracy, yet one would expect that validity would also depend on features of the target. Despite the relative paucity of work on who makes a good mind-reading target, the existing research indicates that both the target's *capacity* to express himself or herself and his or her *willingness* to do this affects mind perception outcomes.

Expressivity

Expressivity is often defined as the accuracy with which an individual indicates her motivations and needs via emotions (Sabatelli & Rubin, 1986), distinct from emotionality (typically characterized as volatility or fluctuation). Buck (e.g., 1985) has argued that expressive displays evolved to provide "an external readout of those motivational-emotional processes that have had social implications during the course of evolution" (1985, p. 396). In other words, expressions, in the broad sense of the term, are a means by which people provide others access to thoughts and experiences that would otherwise be trapped underneath their skin. To the extent that social exchange partners effectively express their emotional and motivational states, they are better understood, laying the groundwork for effective coordination with others (Zaki, Bolger, & Ochsner, 2008).

Expressivity tends to be higher in people who are talkative and sociable, as is evidenced by its correlation with measures of extraversion (e.g., Kring, Smith & Neale, 1994), in individuals high in self-esteem, and in people with fewer social inhibitions (e.g., Buck, 1979). Expressivity is also associated with a predisposition for anxiety, hostility, or depression, as is evidenced by its correlation with measures of neuroticism (Kring et al., 1994). Several researchers report that women are generally more spontaneously expressive than men (Buck, 1979; Riggio & Carney, 2003). Six-month-old females are both more expressive and more effective at regulating negative emotion states (e.g., irritability) than their infant male counterparts (Weinberg, Tronick, Cohn, & Olson, 1999). Other evidence reveals modest trends in expressivity across the human life span. While older adults more effectively regulate their negative emotions, they are also slightly less expressive than their younger counterparts (Gross et al., 1997).

Importantly, people's spontaneous expression of emotion depends on both the nature of the emotion being communicated, the relationship they have with the recipient of the message, and the interaction of the two. Whereas expressivity is inhibited in the presence of unfamiliar others, it is enhanced in the presence of familiar, or even similar others, though this effect may be strongest when positive emotions are involved (e.g., Buck, Losow, Murphy, & Costanzo, 1992; Wagner & Smith, 1991).

Disclosure

A target's capacity to emit expressions with good signal value matters less if he is reticent in revealing his attitudes, intentions, and beliefs: i.e., expressivity is valuable if it accompanies disclosure. One central challenge facing mind readers is eliciting mental states from their interaction partners (Andersen, 1984). Who tends to be effective at encouraging others to share clues about their desires, beliefs, and feelings?

A number of researchers have reported enhanced interpersonal judgment in familiar vs unfamiliar dyads, an effect that is purported to be at least partially mediated by the amount of information disclosed (Funder & Colvin, 1988; Stinson & Ickes, 1992; Thomas & Fletcher, 2003). When people trust their interaction partner, they are more inclined to reveal information that is diagnostic of their underlying attitudes, intentions, and beliefs. In fact, the most consistent and frequently cited finding regarding the interpersonal effects of self-disclosure is disclosure reciprocity. Countless studies have demonstrated that recipients who are disclosed to respond in kind at a comparable level of intimacy (e.g., Cozby, 1973). Several researchers have tracked patterns of sharing over time between partners, friends, and romantic couples. For example, Taylor (1968) demonstrated a rapid increase in non-intimate disclosures, paralleled by a gradual increase in intimate disclosures over time among new male roommates.

Although these findings suggest that disclosure is determined by relational factors, there are also relatively stable individual differences in self-disclosing behavior (e.g., Berg & Derlega, 1987). Individual variations in self-disclosure manifest in the amount that people reveal, the content of their revelations, and its appropriateness (Cozby, 1973).

Good data

We end the section on mind-reading accuracy with a consideration of the role of data quantity and mental-state visibility in social inference. As one might expect, mind perception validity tends to improve when drawn from a large and relevant sample of behavioral data points.

Acquaintanceship and data quantity   Although some scholars suggest that interpersonal accuracy may be nearly as good after brief exposure as after extended experience (e.g., Ambady & Rosenthal, 1992), other evidence indicates that mind reading improves when the target and perceiver have a history of past interactions (e.g., Funder & Colvin, 1988; Thomas, Fletcher & Lange, 1997). Compared to strangers, close acquaintances provide significantly better estimates of both personality traits (Funder & Colvin, 1988; Paunonen, 1989) and transient psychological states (e.g., Stinson & Ickes, 1992). For example, Stinson and Ickes (1992) report that, on average, male friends had empathic accuracy scores that were

50% higher than male strangers, while Thomas and Fletcher (2003) reported improvements in interpersonal accuracy across increasing levels of interpersonal closeness.

What is the source of this acquaintanceship advantage? There is reason to suspect that some of this enhancement reflects a greater willingness among friends to exchange information (Stinson & Ickes, 1992). Others suggest that acquaintances are privy to targets' covert and latent behavioral tendencies and that they utilize this knowledge when drawing inferences about their behavior. From this perspective, extensive experience with a target gives perceivers an opportunity to develop theories about the idiosyncratic beliefs and desires motivating the individual's behavior. Consistent with this latter position is evidence that friends are more effective than strangers at predicting each other's behavior in future and hypothetical scenarios (Colvin & Funder, 1991; Stinson & Ickes, 1992). There is also evidence that the more acquainted a perceiver is with a target, the less their judgment validity depends on the observability of the trait/state in question (Paunonen, 1989).

Visibility   Research on personality inference suggests that trait visibility (i.e., observability) is an important determinant of judgment accuracy (Funder & Colvin, 1988; Hayes & Dunning, 1997; see Vazire, 2010). Traits that are associated with observable behaviors (e.g., extraversion) are more reliably judged than traits characterized by private thought patterns (e.g., neuroticism; Vazire & Gosling, 2004). While limited work has focused on mental-state visibility, the trait inference literature clearly suggests that mental states that manifest in visible behaviors will be more accurately judged.

WHERE WE DO IT

Thus far in this chapter, we have reviewed the various inferential tools perceivers appear to use to read minds. We have also described shortcomings in mind perception and factors that seem to promote or inhibit judgment validity. We turn now to several domains in which mind perception comes to life – in effect, discussions of *where* we do it. In most cases, these domains map on to academic literatures that may not be focused on mind perception per se, but that hold insights for the psychology of mind perception and that also beg to be informed by mind perception scholarship. We begin with culture, and then move on to intergroup relations and conflict.

Culture

Is mind perception the same across cultures? The question is a fundamental and important one because the answer can clarify whether, how, and when mind perception draws on innate modules that are fundamental, universal, hard-wired parts of human psychology as well as culturally informed folk theories, representations, and values. Accounts differ, but most scholars acknowledge layers of similarities and differences (e.g., Ames, Knowles, Rosati, Morris, Kalish, & Gopnik, 2001; Lillard, 1998). It appears that perceivers in virtually all cultures (a) see others as having mental lives and (b) are guided in their everyday interactions by inferences about others' minds. However, differences exist in dimensions such as the extent to which private mental lives are discussed publicly, in the folk ontologies used to describe and distinguish between mental contents, and in the ways in which intentions are ascribed to others (e.g., Lillard, 1998; Mason & Morris, 2010). We discuss some of these differences in the sections that follow (see Chapter 22, for additional discussion of culture).

Situationism

As noted earlier in our discussion of the correspondence bias, considerable work suggests that perceivers tend to explain a target person's acts in terms of the target's underlying attitudes and dispositions, often overlooking or underweighting situational factors. However, the classic evidence for these effects comes from Western studies (e.g., Jones & Harris, 1967); evidence that has emerged from other cultures in the past few decades suggests a somewhat more complicated picture. Consistent with the view that self and other construal differences predispose members of interdependent cultures to consider social-relational causes of action, Miller (1984) demonstrated that East Asians are more inclined to view actions as arising from social contexts than Westerners. The diminished tendency of East Asians to draw on dispositional factors and their enhanced reliance on social contextual factors when constructing explanations for other people's behaviors has subsequently been replicated by a number of researchers (e.g., Knowles, Morris, Chiu, & Hong, 2001; Miyamoto & Kitayama, 2002; Morris and Peng, 1994; see, however, Krull et al., 1999).

This relatively recent research suggests that mind perception is partly rooted in intuitive lay beliefs that people have about the causes of behavior (Heider, 1958). From this perspective, different cultural conceptualizations of self, other, and self–other relationships are thought to promote different intuitive lay beliefs about agency. In turn, such differences lead to discrepancies in how a given behavior is interpreted by members of different cultures. Although cultural belief systems have thus been implicated in behavior interpretation and mind perception, this does not mean the process is necessarily explicit or effortful. In recent years, a number of scholars have argued that these effects can unfold spontaneously (e.g., Maass et al., 2006), with cultural differences emerging most strongly when need for closure is high (e.g., Chiu, Morris, Hong, & Menon, 2000), and perceived cultural consensus around belief systems is substantial (e.g., Zou et al., 2009). A challenge for future researchers is to determine whether attribution differences reflect greater situational correction, more automatized situational correction, or a greater likelihood of anchoring on situational causes by members of interdependent cultures (e.g., Knowles et al., 2001; Mason & Morris, 2010).

Routes to mind reading

Perceivers in different cultures may have different material to work with and may take different routes to drawing inferences about others' minds. Anthropologist Edward Hall (1976) distinguished between low- and high-context cultures: individuals in the former trade messages that are more direct, explicit, and openly confrontational, whereas individuals in the later communicate less directly, variously through allusion, silence, and reliance on contextual cues (see also Ting-Toomey, 1985). Some research shows, for instance, that US negotiators rely more heavily on direct information-sharing strategies, conveying priorities and interests explicitly, whereas Japanese negotiators rely more on indirect strategies (Adair, Okumura, & Brett, 2001). Matsumoto and colleagues (e.g., 2008) have found that members of collectivist cultures show a greater tendency to mask emotional expressions, following more discrete cultural "display rules" for expressivity. Thus, some cultures appear to provide more direct behavioral evidence for mind readers; in other cultures, perceivers may turn to other inferential routes. Evidence of these inferential shifts is beginning to emerge. For instance, Wu and Keysar (2007) recently found that members of interdependent cultures seem more inclined to spontaneously adopt a counterpart's perspective, suggesting a readiness to see things from another's point of view without having to hear or observe more overt or behavioral evidence.

Intergroup relations

Mind perception often occurs, or has the potential to occur, in the context of intergroup relations.

One important dynamic that can emerge in such cases is the denial of fully human mental experiences and capacities, often in the case of outgroup member perception (e.g., Harris & Fiske, 2009; Haslam, 2006). The stakes for how people mentalize groups – or resist mentalizing them – are considerable: Conceiving of others as lacking humanness weakens commitments to moral strictures and norms of fairness; diminishes a sense of responsibility, remorse, and guilt for transgressions; unfetters aggression and discrimination; allows people to justify oppressive and violent acts; and bolsters a sense of personal superiority (e.g., Bar-Tal, 2000; Bar-Tal & Teichman, 2005; Castano & Giner-Sorolla, 2006; Cehajic et al., 2009; Opotow, 1990; Staub, 1989). In recent years, scholars have distinguished various forms of dehumanization and infrahumanization. These different dynamics vary in their implications for mind perception and we briefly discuss each in turn in the sections that follow.

Dehumanization

Haslam's (2006) theoretical framework distinguishes between animalistic and mechanistic dehumanization. Dehumanization takes an *animalistic* form when targets are denied uniquely human characteristics (e.g., intelligence, moral sensibility, sophistication) or the qualities that distinguish them from other animals. Animalistic dehumanization is associated with feelings of disgust and revulsion in the perceiver, and often elicits feelings of shame in the target (e.g., Hodson & Costello, 2007). Targets of animalistic dehumanization tend to be seen as acting from obtuseness or to satisfy some appetitive demand. This form of dehumanization seems particularly prevalent in racial and ethnic conflicts and captures discrimination towards people with cognitive disabilities (O'Brien, 2003).

Dehumanization takes a *mechanistic* form when targets are denied the qualities that define the core of the human concept (e.g., warmth, flexibility, individual agency) or the qualities that distinguish them from robots, tools, or machines (e.g., Montague & Matson, 1983). Targets are perceived as fungible, dependent, lacking agency, cold and emotionally void, and tend to elicit indifference and ambivalence in the perceiver. This form of dehumanization is perhaps best exemplified by the objectification of women (e.g., Cikara, Eberhardt, & Fiske, 2010; Fredrickson & Roberts, 1997).

Infrahumanization

In the last generation, scholars have focused increased attention on *infrahumanization*, a more subtle and prevalent form of dehumanization that involves denying others "secondary emotions" (e.g., pride, contentment) and prosocial sentiments (e.g., empathy, compassion; Demoulin et al., 2004; Leyens et al., 2000). Emotion researchers distinguish between two basic types of emotions. *Primary emotions* are assumed to exist in all cultures, to have both ontogenetic and phylogenetic primacy, to serve a biological function, and to be experienced by other animals (e.g., Izard, 1977). *Secondary emotions*, in contrast, are uniquely human, developed through the socialization process, and are generally less intense and reactive than primary emotions (e.g., Leyens et al., 2000).

People may accept or reject others through the attribution or denial of secondary emotions (e.g., Fiske, Xu, Cuddy, & Glick, 1999; Leyens et al., 2003). Consistent with this notion, a number of recent studies reveal that people attribute more secondary emotional experiences to in-group than out-group members (e.g., Gaunt, Leyens, & Demoulin, 2002). Importantly, this reluctance to ascribe to others secondary emotional experiences appears to have important behavioral consequences and implications for interpersonal exchange (e.g., Vaes, Paladino, Castelli, Leyens, & Giovanazzi, 2003).

Animalistic dehumanization, mechanistic dehumanization, and infrahumanization each hold implications for mind perception, especially in intergroup settings. Perhaps most obvious is the ontology of mental contents and processes denied to group members: animalistically dehumanized groups may be seen as void of moral values and reasoning; mechanistically dehumanized groups may be seen as void of agency and will; and infrahumanized groups may be seen as void of pride. But just as some mental processes are de-emphasized in these intergroup perception dynamics, other processes may be highlighted and govern how groups are expected to act and react and, accordingly, how they are treated. If group members are seen as animals or lesser humans whose behavior is driven by fear, they may be treated in ways designed to intimidate or terrify them. If group members are seen as obedient, non-agentic tokens whose behavior is a relatively mindless product of an ideology, then harming any (interchangeable) member may seem like an option for attacking the ideology.

Re-minding

An open question is to what extent these dynamics can be overridden or counteracted – whether dehumanized groups can be "re-minded." Evidence suggests that, on the one hand, manipulations that encourage people to reflect on a target's mental state or to individuate him/her diminish the effects of dehumanization (e.g., Haslam & Bain, 2007; Lederach, 1997). Preliminary evidence also suggests that these biases attenuate with increased exposure to out-group members (e.g., Harwood, Hewstone, Paolini & Voci, 2005). However, it is worth noting that manipulations that remind people of in-group responsibility or prompt people to experience collective guilt can have the unfortunate consequence of increasing victim infrahumanization (e.g., Cehajic et al., 2009).

Conflict

Conflicts – between nations, groups, and individuals – frequently turn on the perception of intentions and other mental states. Effective conflict resolution often involves parties achieving some accurate, or at least different, understanding of one another's mental states. A growing body of research has revealed the processes by which mind perception unfolds in conflict as well as its fallibility. We survey some of these accounts and results here.

Projection
As noted earlier, people display a seemingly widespread impulse to project their own mental states onto others. Situations of conflict are no exception. In the domain of close relationships, scholars have shown that spouses tend to project their own emotions onto one other during conflict interactions (e.g., Papp, Kouros, & Cummings, 2010). In the domain of social dilemmas and strategic games, researchers have found a tendency to project one's own expectations and intentions onto others (e.g., Acevedo & Krueger, 2005; Ames et al., in press). Negotiation scholars have documented a seemingly widespread "fixed pie" bias, whereby negotiators tend to project their own interests and priorities onto their counterparts, readily assuming situations are zero-sum when opportunities exist to satisfy both parties (e.g., Pinkley, Griffith, & Northcraft, 1995). In research on negotiations, Bottom and Paese (1997) demonstrated that, in the absence of stereotypic or individuating information, negotiators tended to assume that other parties shared their own preferences, an inference leading to fixed pie assumptions and suboptimal settlements.

Assumed malice and bias
Social projection in conflict and elsewhere may flow in part from a perceiver assuming she or he sees things as they "really are" and further assuming that if someone else were facing the same situation, that person would see the same thing. Ross and colleagues (Ross et al., 1977) observed as much in their seminal work on false consensus. More recently, this "naïve realism" account has been applied to conflict situations and extended to capture perceptions of bias (e.g., Pronin, 2007; Robinson, Keltner, Ward, & Ross, 1995; Ross & Ward, 1996). If a perceiver assumes she sees a disputed situation as it really is, she might assume other reasonable onlookers would see the same thing; if another party sees something different, her reasoning would suggest that they are biased. A number of studies have documented such effects, showing that disagreements can lead to ascriptions of self-interested motives and bias (e.g., Reeder, Pryor, Wohl, & Griswell, 2005). Kennedy and Pronin (2008) showed that these perceptions of bias can fuel conflict, leading parties to make conflict-escalating responses that in turn prompt counterparts to perceive bias.

Another tradition of work has examined the role of hostile attribution biases as a factor in conflict and aggression. Growing out of developmental research on aggression in children (e.g., Dodge & Crick, 1990), this work suggests that ascribing hostile intentions to others is a potent precursor to anger, aggression, and retaliation. Research in this vein also suggests that aggressive individuals may be especially prone to attribute hostile intentions to others (Dill, Anderson, Anderson, & Deuser 1997; Epps & Kendall, 1995). This research on interpersonal aggression converges with a stream of work on cognition in social dilemmas. There, Kelley and Stahelski (1970) proposed a triangle hypothesis to account for how cooperative and competitive players ascribed cooperative and competitive intentions to counterparts. The researchers found support for their prediction that cooperative players anticipate greater variance in counterpart intentions, whereas competitive players are more inclined to expect competitive intentions – a notion that has received additional support and attention in recent work (e.g., Van Lange, 1992).

Plous (e.g., 1993) offered a mind-reading take on social dilemmas in his formulation of the "perceptual dilemma." Such a condition arises, he argued, when both sides in a dilemma prefer a mutually cooperative outcome but assume each other prefers unilateral dominance, thereby adopting what seems like an appropriate position of defensive hostility (see also Ames et al., in press). Plous argued that the post-World-War-II nuclear arms race between the United States and the former Soviet Union was essentially a perceptual dilemma, with each side misreading the other's preference. The ascription of malice to a conflict counterpart shapes choices, even though it might be unwarranted – and once embraced, these beliefs about a counterpart's sinister objectives and preferences may be very hard to change.

Perspective taking

In conflict and negotiation, people are often egocentrically biased (e.g., Babcock & Loewenstein, 1997), which can lead to the fixed pie bias, impasses, and foregone opportunities for effective solutions. Does explicit, effortful perspective taking improve matters? Galinsky, Maddux, Gilin, and White (2008) suggest that it does, finding that negotiators instructed to take their counterpart's perspective were better able to discover hidden agreements and to claim value in negotiations. Work by Epley, Caruso, and Bazerman (2006) highlights that perspective taking may carry costs as well. They found that taking the perspective of other parties in a conflict altered perceptions: those who looked at things from others' points of view had less self-serving assessments of what a fair outcome or allocation for themselves would be. However, the authors found that this did *not* improve cooperation in the situations they studied, such as a commons dilemma featuring a scarce resource (Epley et al., 2006). Those who considered others' points of view tended to assume that others would behave in a self-serving fashion, so they themselves raised their defenses, attempting to claim more resources and acting more competitively. As the authors put it, perspective taking led to taking.

The benefits of misreading

Under some circumstances, there may be advantages to misreading counterparts in conflict. Overlooking or discounting a counterpart's negative cognitions can avoid an unproductive spiral of conflict; treating an ambivalent or unsympathetic party in a cooperative fashion could spark a constructive self-fulfilling prophecy. Along these lines, in the domain of relationship research, Srivastava and colleagues (Srivastava, McGonigal, Richards, Butler, & Gross, 2006) found that optimists in romantic relationships perceived greater support from their partners during a conflict and reported higher levels of relationship satisfaction. This converges with earlier work by Simpson, Orina, and Ickes (2003) showing that, in conflict conversations, spouses who fared worse at reading their marriage partner's relationship-threatening cognitions felt closer to their spouses – though the researchers also found that accurate reading of non-threatening cognitions also promoted closeness. In their work on the hostile attribution bias, Epps and Kendall (1995) remarked on a similar

effect, finding that non-hostile perceivers tended to ignore hostile cues, concluding that, "Adjustment, in some cases, may be associated with distorted, albeit healthy, information processing …" (p. 175). In the case of conflict, certain kinds of mind-blindness may foster better outcomes.

CONCLUSION

Most of us deal with dozens of other people each day – at work, in traffic, at home, at the store – and yet most days do not end in catastrophe. Given the incredible range of behavior people are capable of producing, and the complicated interactions we often enter into, this is in many ways remarkable. To pull this off, people often find ways to get inside one another's heads to read their intentions, beliefs, desires, and feelings. Strictly speaking, perceivers cannot do this. And yet they seem to manage well enough to get by. When things do go awry – such as unconstructive conflicts – some form of misreading minds is often involved.

As we close, we want to clarify that mind perception does not itself equal the totality of social experience and interpersonal relations. Perceivers navigate parts of the social world without judging, or needing to judge, what is at work in others' minds. For instance, work on social scripts (e.g., Schank & Abelson, 1977) has revealed how knowledge structures inform interactions. In some cases, we do not need to ascribe an entire internal mental world to a counterpart in an interaction; we just need to know what comes next. We can get through some routinized exchanges – such as buying the morning coffee – without having to bother with the problem of other minds. And yet much of life is off-script and much of what we see from others is, on the face of it, subtly puzzling. We often make sense of what's happening in our social worlds, and what will happen next, by ascribing invisible mental properties to the actors around us. What are they thinking, we wonder? And what will they think of next?

REFERENCES

Acevedo, M., & Krueger, J. I. (2005). Evidential reasoning in the Prisoner's Dilemma. *The American Journal of Psychology, 118*, 431–457.

Adair, W. L., Okumura, T., & Brett, J. M. (2001). Negotiation behaviors when cultures collide: The U.S. and Japan. *Journal of Applied Psychology, 86*, 371–385.

Ambady, N., & Rosenthal, R. (1992). Thin slices of expressive behavior as predictors of interpersonal consequences: A meta-analysis. *Psychological Bulletin, 111*, 256–274.

Ames, D. R. (2004a). Inside the mind reader's tool kit: Projection and stereotyping in mental state inference. *Journal of Personality and Social Psychology, 87*, 340–353.

Ames, D. R. (2004b). Strategies for social inference: A similarity contingency model of projection and stereotyping in attribute prevalence estimates. *Journal of Personality and Social Psychology, 87*, 573–585.

Ames, D. R. (2005). Everyday solutions to the problem of other minds: Which tools are used when? In B. F. Malle & S. D. Hodges (Eds.), *Other minds: How humans bridge the divide between self and others* (pp. 158–173). New York: Guilford Press.

Ames, D. R., & Johar, G. V. (2009). I'll know what you're like when I see how you feel: How and when affective displays influence behavior-based impressions. *Psychological Science, 20*, 586–593.

Ames, D. R., & Kammrath, L. K. (2004). Mind-reading and metacognition: Narcissism, not actual competence, predicts self-estimated ability. *Journal of Nonverbal Behavior, 28*, 187–209.

Ames, D. R., Knowles, E. D., Rosati, A. D., Morris, M. W., Kalish, C. W., & Gopnik, A. (2001). The social folk theorist: Insights from social and cultural psychology on the contents and contexts of folk theorizing. In B. Malle, L. Moses, & D. Baldwin (Eds.), *Intentions and intentionality: Foundations of social cognition* (pp. 307–329). Cambridge, MA: MIT Press.

Ames, D. R., Weber, E. U., & Zou, X. (in press). Mind-reading in strategic interaction: The impact of perceived similarity on projection and stereotyping. In press at *Organizational Behavior and Human Decision Processes.*

Andersen, S. M. (1984). Self-knowledge and social inference: II. The diagnosticity of cognitive/affective and behavioral data. *Journal of Personality and Social Psychology, 46*, 294–307.

Apperly, I. (2010). *Mindreaders: The cognitive basis of "theory of mind."* Hove, East Sussex: Psychology Press.

Babcock, L., & Loewenstein, G. (1997). Explaining bargaining impasse: The role of self-serving biases. *Journal of Economic Perspectives, 11*, 109–126.

Back, M. D., Stopfer, J. M., Vazire, S., Gaddis, S., Schmukle, S. C., Egloff, B., et al. (2010). Facebook profiles reflect actual personality not self-idealization. *Psychological Science, 21*, 372–374.

Baird, J. A., & Baldwin, D. A. (2001). Making sense of human behavior: Action parsing and intentional inference. In B. F. Malle, L. J. Moses, & D. A. Baldwin (Eds.), *Intentions and intentionality: Foundations of social cognition* (pp. 193–206). Cambridge, MA: MIT Press.

Bar-Tal, D. (2000). *Shared beliefs in a society: Social psychological analysis.* Thousand Oaks, CA: Sage.

Bar-Tal, D., & Teichman Y. (2005). *Stereotypes and prejudice in conflict: Representations of Arabs in Israeli Jewish society.* Cambridge, UK: Cambridge University Press.

Berg, J. H., & Derlega, V. J. (1987). Themes in the study of self-disclosure. In V. J. Derlega & J. H. Berg (Eds.), *Self-disclosure: Theory, research, and therapy* (pp. 1–8). New York: Plenum Press.

Bernieri, F. J., Davis, J. M., Rosenthal, R., & Knee, R. (1994). Interactional synchrony and rapport: Measuring synchrony in displays devoid of sound and facial affect. *Personality and Social Psychology Bulletin, 20*, 303–311.

Bond, C. F., Jr., & DePaulo, B. M. (2006). Accuracy of deception judgments. *Personality and Social Psychology Review, 10*, 214–234.

Bottom, W. P., & Paese, P. W. (1997). False consensus, stereotypic cues, and the perception of integrative potential in negotiation. *Journal of Applied Psychology, 27*, 1919–1940.

Brigham, J. C. (1971). Ethnic stereotypes. *Psychological Bulletin, 76*, 15–38.

Buck, R. (1979). Measuring individual differences in the nonverbal communication of affect: The slide-viewing paradigm. *Human Communication Research, 6*, 47–57.

Buck, R. (1985). PRIME theory: An integrated approach to motivation and emotion. *Psychological Review, 92*, 389–413.

Buck, R., Losow, J. I., Murphy, M. M., & Costanzo, P. (1992). Social facilitation and inhibition of emotional expression and communication. *Journal of Personality and Social Psychology, 63*, 962–968.

Byrne, R. W., & Whiten, A. (1988). *Machiavellian intelligence: Social expertise and the evolution of intellect in monkeys, apes, and humans.* New York: Oxford University Press.

Carlston, D. E. (1980). The recall and use of traits and events in social inference processes. *Journal of Experimental Social Psychology, 16*, 303–328.

Castano, E., & Giner-Sorolla, R. (2006). Not quite human: Infra-humanization as a response to collective responsibility for intergroup killing. *Journal of Personality and Social Psychology, 90*, 804–818.

Cehajic, S., Brown, R., & Gonzalez, R. (2009). What do I care? Perceived ingroup responsibility and dehumanization as predictors of empathy felt for the victim group. *Group Processes & Intergroup Relations, 12*, 715–729.

Chiu, C.-Y., Morris, M. W., Hong, Y.-Y., & Menon, T. (2000). Motivated cultural cognition: The impact of implicit cultural theories on dispositional attribution varies as a function of need for closure. *Journal of Personality and Social Psychology, 78*, 247–259.

Churchland, P. M. (1999). Eliminative materialism and the propositional attitudes. In W. G. Lycan (Ed.), *Mind and cognition: An anthology* (2nd ed.). Malden, MA: Blackwell Publishers.

Cikara, M., Eberhardt, J. L., & Fiske, S. T. (2010). From agents to objects: Sexist attitudes and neural responses to sexualized targets. *Journal of Cognitive Neuroscience,* online only.

Clement, R. W., & Krueger, J. (2002). Social categorization moderates social projection. *Journal of Experimental Social Psychology, 38*, 219–231.

Colvin, C. R., & Funder, D. C. (1991). Predicting personality and behavior: A boundary on the acquaintanceship effect. *Journal of Personality and Social Psychology, 60*, 884–894.

Cozby, P. C. (1973). Self-disclosure: A literature review. *Psychological Bulletin, 79,* 73–91.

Cronbach, L. (1955). Processes affecting scores on "understanding of others" and "assumed similarity." *Psychological Bulletin, 52,* 177–193.

Cross, S. E., & Madson, L. (1997). Models of the self: Self-construals and gender. *Psychological Bulletin, 122,* 5–37.

Cuddy, A. J. C., Fiske, S. T., & Glick, P. (2008). Warmth and competence as universal dimensions of social perception: The stereotype content model and the BIAS map. *Advances in Experimental Social Psychology, 40,* 61–149.

Darwin, C. R. (1872). *The expression of the emotions in man and animals.* London: John Murray.

Davis, M. H., Conklin, L., Smith, A., & Luce, C. (1996). Effect of perspective taking on the cognitive representation of persons: A merging of self and other. *Journal of Personality and Social Psychology, 70,* 713–726.

Davis, M. H., & Kraus, L. A. (1997). Personality and empathic accuracy. In W. Ickes (Ed.), *Empathic accuracy* (pp. 144–168). New York: Guilford Press.

Dawes, R. M. (1989). Statistical criteria for establishing a truly false consensus effect. *Journal of Experimental Social Psychology, 25,* 1–17.

Decety, J., & Ickes, W. (2009). *The social neuroscience of empathy.* Cambridge, MA: MIT Press.

Demoulin, S., Leyens, J. P., Paladino, M. P., Rodriguez, R. T., Rodriguez, A. P. & Dovidio, J. F. (2004). Dimensions of "uniquely" and "nonuniquely" human emotions. *Cognition & Emotion, 18,* 71–96.

Dennett, D. C. (1987). *The intentional stance.* Cambridge, MA: MIT Press.

Devine, P. (1989). Stereotypes and prejudice: Their automatic and controlled components. *Journal of Personality and Social Psychology, 56,* 5–18.

Dill, K. E., Anderson, C. A., Anderson, K. B., & Deuser, W. E. (1997). Effects of aggressive personality on social expectations and social perceptions. *Journal of Research in Personality, 31,* 272–292.

Dodge, K. A., & Crick, N. R. (1990). Social information-processing bases of aggressive behavior in children. *Personality and Social Psychology Bulletin, 16,* 8–22.

Eagly, A. H., & Mladinic, A. (1989). Gender stereotypes and attitudes toward women and men. *Personality and Social Psychology Bulletin, 15,* 543–558.

Ekman, P. (2003). *Emotions revealed.* New York: Times Books.

Ekman, P., & Friesen, W. V. (1967). Head and body cues in the judgment of emotion: A reformulation. *Perceptual and Motor Skills, 24,* 711–724.

Ekman, P., & Friesen, W. V. (1971). Constants across cultures in the face and emotion. *Journal of Personality and Social Psychology, 17,* 124–129.

Epley, N., Caruso, E. M., & Bazerman, M. H. (2006). When perspective taking increases taking: Reactive egoism in social interaction. *Journal of Personality and Social Psychology, 91,* 872–889.

Epley, N., Keysar, B., Van Boven, L., & Gilovich, T. (2004). Perspective taking as egocentric anchoring and adjustment. *Journal of Personality and Social Psychology, 87,* 327–339.

Epley, N., Morewedge, C., & Keysar, B. (2004). Perspective taking in children and adults: Equivalent egocentrism but differential correction. *Journal of Experimental Social Psychology, 40,* 760–768.

Epley, N., Waytz, A., & Cacioppo, J. T. (2007). On seeing human: A three-factor theory of anthropomorphism. *Psychological Review, 114,* 864–886.

Epps, J., & Kendall, P. C. (1995). Hostile attribution bias in adults. *Cognitive Therapy and Research, 19,* 159–178.

Fiedler, K., & Schenck, W. (2001). Spontaneous inferences from pictorially presented behaviors. *Personality and Social Psychology Bulletin, 27,* 1533–1546.

Fiske, S. T., & Taylor, S. E. (1991). *Social cognition.* New York: McGraw-Hill.

Fiske, S. T., Xu, J., Cuddy, A. C., & Glick, P. (1999). (Dis) respecting versus (dis)liking: Status and interdependence predict ambivalent stereotypes of competence and warmth. *Journal of Social Issues, 55,* 473–491.

Flavell, J. H., Botkin, P. T., Fry, C. L., Wright, J. W., & Jarvis, P. E. (1968). *The development of role-taking and communication skills in children.* New York: Wiley.

Fletcher, G. J. O., Danilovics, P., Fernandez, G., Peterson, D., & Reeder, G. D. (1986). Attributional complexity: An individual differences measure. *Journal of Personality and Social Psychology, 51,* 875–884.

Fredrickson, B. L. & Roberts, T. (1997). Toward understanding women's lived experiences and mental health risks. *Psychology of Women Quarterly, 21,* 173–206.

Friedman, H., & Zebrowitz, L. A. (1992). The contribution of facial maturity to sex-role stereotypes. *Personality and Social Psychology Bulletin, 18,* 430–438.

Friedman, R. A. & Currall, S. C. (2003). E-mail escalation: Dispute exacerbating elements of e-mail communication. *Human Relations, 56,* 1325–1348.

Funder, D. C. (1987). Errors and mistakes: Evaluating the accuracy of social judgment. *Psychological Bulletin, 101,* 75–90.

Funder, D. C. (1995). On the accuracy of personality judgment: A realistic approach. *Psychological Review, 102,* 652–670.

Funder, D. C., & Colvin, C. R. (1988). Friends and strangers: Acquaintanceship, agreement, and the accuracy of personality judgment. *Journal of Personality and Social Psychology, 55,* 149–158.

Funder, D. C., & Harris, M. J. (1986). On the several facets of personality assessment: The case of social acuity. *Journal of Personality, 54,* 528–550.

Funder, D. C., & West, S. G. (1993). Consensus, self-other agreement, and accuracy in personality judgment: An introduction. *Journal of Personality, 61,* 457–476.

Galinsky, A. D., Maddux, W. W., Gilin, D., & White, J. B. (2008). Why it pays to get inside the head of your opponent: The differential effects of perspective-taking and empathy in negotiations. *Psychological Science, 19,* 378–384.

Galinsky, A. D., & Moskowitz, G. B. (2000). Perspective taking: Decreasing stereotype expression, stereotype accessibility and in-group favoritism. *Journal of Personality and Social Psychology, 78,* 708–724.

Gaunt, R., Leyens, J. P., & Demoulin, S. (2002). Intergroup relations and the attribution of emotions: Control over memory for secondary emotions associated with ingroup or outgroup. *Journal of Experimental Social Psychology, 38*, 508–514.

Gilbert, D. T. (1998). Ordinary personology. In D. T. Gilbert, S. T. Fiske, & G. Lindzey (Eds.), *The handbook of social psychology* (Vol. 2, 4th ed., pp. 89–150). Boston, MA: McGraw-Hill.

Gilbert, D. T., Brown, R. P., Pinel, E. C., & Wilson, T. D. (2000). The illusion of external agency. *Journal of Personality and Social Psychology, 79*, 690–700.

Gilbert, D. T., & Malone, P. S. (1995). The correspondence bias. *Psychological Bulletin, 117*, 21–38.

Gross, J. J., Carstensen, L. L., Pasupathi, M., Tsai, J., Skorpen, C. G., & Hsu, A. Y. C. (1997). Emotion and aging: Experience, expression, and control. *Psychology and Aging, 12*, 590–599.

Hall, E. T. (1976). *Beyond culture*. New York: Anchor Press.

Hall, J. A. (1978). Gender effects in decoding nonverbal cues. *Psychological Bulletin, 85*, 845–857.

Hall, J. A. (1984). *Nonverbal sex differences: Communication accuracy and expressive style*. Baltimore, MD: Johns Hopkins University Press.

Hall, J. A., Andrzejewski, S. A., & Yopchick, J. E. (2009). Psychosocial correlates of interpersonal sensitivity. *Journal of Nonverbal behavior, 33*, 149–180.

Hall, J. A., Blanch, D. C., Horgan, T. G., Murphy, N. A., Rosip, J. C., & Schmid-Mast, M. S. (2009). Motivation and interpersonal sensitivity: Does it matter how hard you try? *Motivation and Emotion, 33*, 291–302.

Harris, L. T., & Fiske, S. T. (2009). Dehumanized perception: The social neuroscience of thinking (or not thinking) about disgusting people. In M. Hewstone & W. Stroebe (Eds.), *European review of social psychology* (Vol. 20, pp. 192–231). London: Wiley.

Harwood, J., Hewstone, M., Paolini, S., & Voci, A. (2005). Grandparent–grandchild contact and attitudes toward older adults: Moderator and mediator effects. *Personality and Social Psychology Bulletin, 31*, 393–406.

Haselton, M. G., Nettle, D., & Andrews, P. W. (2005). The evolution of cognitive bias. In D. M. Buss (Ed.), *Handbook of evolutionary psychology* (pp. 724–746). Hoboken, NJ: Wiley.

Haslam, N. (2006). Dehumanization: An integrative review. *Personality and Social Psychology Review, 10*, 252–264.

Haslam, N., & Bain, P. (2007). Humanizing the self: Moderators of the attribution of lesser humanness to others. *Personality and Social Psychology Bulletin, 33*, 57–68.

Hayes, A. F., & Dunning, D. (1997). Construal processes and trait ambiguity: Implications for self-peer agreement in personality judgment. *Journal of Personality and Social Psychology, 72*, 664–677.

Heider, F. (1958). *The psychology of interpersonal Relations*. New York: John Wiley & Sons.

Hodson, G., & Costello, K. (2007). Interpersonal disgust, ideological orientations, and dehumanization as predictors of intergroup attitudes. *Psychological Science, 18*, 691–698.

Hogarth, R. M. (1981). Beyond discrete biases: Functional and dysfunctional aspects of judgmental heuristics. *Psychological Bulletin, 90*, 197–217.

Holmes, D. S. (1968). Dimensions of projection. *Psychological Bulletin, 69*, 248–268.

Hugenberg, K. (2005). Social categorization and the perception of facial affect: Target race moderates the response latency advantage for happy faces. *Emotion, 5*, 267–276.

Hugenberg, K., & Bodenhausen, G. V. (2003). Facing prejudice: Implicit prejudice and the perception of facial threat. *Psychological Science, 14*, 640–643.

Ickes, W. (1993). Empathic accuracy. *Journal of Personality, 61*, 587–610.

Ickes, W., Buysse, A., Pham, H., Hancock, M., Kelleher, J., & Gesn, P. R. (2000). On the difficulty of distinguishing "good" and "poor" perceivers: A social relations analysis of empathic accuracy data. *Personal Relationships, 7*, 219–234.

Ickes, W., Gesn, P. R., & Graham, T. (2000). Gender differences in empathic accuracy: Differential ability or differential motivation? *Personal Relationships, 7*, 95–109.

Ickes, W., & Tooke, W. (1988). The observational method: Studying the interactions of minds and bodies. In S. W. Duck (Ed.), *Handbook of personal relationships* (pp. 79–98). New York: Wiley.

Izard, C. E. (1977). *Human emotions*. New York: Plenum Press.

Jones, E. E., & Davis, K. E. (1965). From acts to dispositions: The attribution process in person perception. In L. Berkowitz (Ed.), *Advances in experimental social psychology* (Vol. 2, pp. 219–226). New York: Academic Press.

Jones, E. E., & Harris, V. A. (1967). The attribution of attitudes. *Journal of Experimental Social Psychology, 3*, 1–24.

Jones, P. E. (2004). False consensus in social context: Differential projection and perceived social distance. *British Journal of Social Psychology, 43*, 417–429.

Jourard, S. M., & Friedman, R. (1970). Experimenter–subject "distance" and self-disclosure. *Journal of Personality and Social Psychology, 15*, 278–282.

Judd, C. M., James-Hawkins, L., Yzerbyt, V., & Kashima, Y. (2005). Fundamental dimensions of social judgment: Understanding the relations between judgments of competence and warmth. *Journal of Personality and Social Psychology, 89*, 899–913.

Jussim, L. (1986). Self-fulfilling prophecies: A theoretical and integrative review. *Psychological Review, 93*, 429–445.

Jussim, L. (1991). Social perception and social reality: A reflection-construction model. *Psychological Review, 98*, 54–73.

Kahneman, D., & Tversky, A. (1973). On the psychology of prediction. *Psychological Review, 80*, 237–251.

Kammrath, L. K., Mendoza-Denton, R., & Mischel, W. (2005). Incorporating if … then … signatures in person perception: Beyond the person–situation dichotomy. *Journal of Personality and Social Psychology, 88*, 605–618.

Karniol, R. (1986). What will they think of next? Transformation rules used to predict other people's thoughts and feelings. *Journal of Personality and Social Psychology, 51*, 932–944.

Karniol, R. (2003). Egocentrism versus protocentrism: The status of self in social prediction. *Psychological Review, 110,* 564–580.

Kelley, H. H. (1973). The process of causal attribution. *American Psychologist, 28,* 107–128.

Kelley, H. H., & Stahelski, A. J. (1970). The inference of intention from motives in the Prisoner's Dilemma Game. *Journal of Experimental Social Psychology, 6,* 401–419.

Kennedy, K. A., & Pronin, E. (2008). When disagreement gets ugly: Perceptions of bias and the escalation of conflict. *Personality and Social Psychology Bulletin, 34,* 833–848.

Kenny, D. A. (1994). Models of non-independence in dyadic research. *Journal of Social and Personal Relationships, 13,* 279–294.

Kenny, D. A., & Acitelli, L. K. (2001). Accuracy and bias in the perception of the partner in a close relationship. *Journal of Personality and Social Psychology, 80,* 439–448.

Kenny, D. A., & Albright, L. (1987). Accuracy in interpersonal perception: A social relations analysis. *Psychological Bulletin, 102,* 390–402

Klein, K. J. K., & Hodges, S. D. (2001). Gender differences, motivation, and empathic accuracy: When it pays to understand. *Personality and Social Psychology Bulletin, 27,* 720–730.

Knowles, E. D., Morris, M. W., Chiu, C.-Y., & Hong, Y.-Y. (2001). Culture and the process of person perception: Evidence for automaticity among East Asians in correcting for situational influences on behavior. *Personality and Social Psychology Bulletin, 27,* 1344–1356.

Knutson, B. (1996). Facial expressions of emotion influence interpersonal trait inferences. *Journal of Nonverbal Behavior, 20,* 165–181.

Kring, A. M., Smith, D. A., & Neale, J. M. (1994). Individual differences in dispositional expressiveness: Development and validation of the Emotional Expressivity Scale. *Journal of Personality and Social Psychology, 66,* 934–949.

Krueger, J. (1996). Personal beliefs and cultural stereotypes about racial characteristics. *Journal of Personality and Social Psychology, 71,* 536–548.

Krueger, J. (1998). On the perception of social consensus. In M. P. Zanna (Ed.), *Advances in experimental social psychology* (Vol. 30). San Diego, CA: Academic Press.

Krueger, J. (2000). The projective perception of the social world: A building block of social comparison processes. In J. Suls & L. Wheeler (Eds.), *Handbook of social comparison: Theory and research* (pp. 323–351). New York: Plenum/Kluwer.

Krueger, J., & Clement, R. W. (1994). The truly false consensus effect: An ineradicable and egocentric bias in social perception. *Journal of Personality and Social Psychology, 67,* 596–610.

Krueger, J. I., & Funder, D. C. (2004). Towards a balanced social psychology: Causes, consequences, and cures for the problem-seeking approach to social behavior and cognition. *Behavioral and Brain Sciences, 27,* 313–327.

Kruger, J., Epley, N., Parker, J., & Ng, Z. (2005). Egocentrism over email: Can we communicate as well as we think? *Journal of Personality and Social Psychology, 89,* 925–936.

Kruglanski, A. W. (1989). The psychology of being "right": The problem of accuracy in social perception and cognition. *Psychological Bulletin, 106,* 395–409.

Kruglanski, A. W., & Ajzen, I. (1983). Bias and error in human judgment. *European Journal of Social Psychology, 13,* 1–44.

Krull, D. S., Loy, M. H., Lin, J., Wang, C., Chen, S., & Zhao, X. (1999). The fundamental attribution error: Correspondence bias in individualist and collectivist cultures. *Personality and Social Psychology Bulletin, 25,* 1208–1219.

Kunda, Z., & Spencer, S. J. (2003). When do stereotypes come to mind and when do they color judgment? A goal-based theory of stereotype activation and application. *Psychological Bulletin, 129,* 522–544.

Lederach, J. (1997). *Building peace: Sustainable reconciliation in divided societies.* Washington, DC: United States Institute of Peace.

Leslie, A., & German, T. (in press). *Handbook of theory of mind.* New York: Psychology Press.

Leung, A. K.-Y., & Cohen, D. (2007). The soft embodiment of culture: Camera angles and motion through time and space. *Psychological Science, 18,* 824–830.

Levenson, R. W., & Reuf, A. M. (1992). Empathy: A physiological substrate. *Journal of Personality and Social Psychology, 63,* 234–246.

Leyens, J. P., Cortes, B. P., Demoulin, S., Dovidio, J., Fiske, S. T., Gaunt, R., et al. (2003). Emotional prejudice, essentialism, and nationalism. *European Journal of Social Psychology, 33,* 703–717.

Leyens, J. P., Paladino, P. M., Rodriguez-Torres, R., Vaes, J., Demoulin, S., Rodriguez-Perez, A., et al. (2000). The emotional side of prejudice: The attribution of secondary emotions to ingroups and outgroups. *Personality and Social Psychology Review, 4,* 186–197.

Lillard, A. (1998). Ethnopsychologies: Cultural variations in theories of mind. *Psychological Bulletin, 123,* 3–32.

Maass, A., Karasawa, M., Politi, F., & Sayaka, S. (2006). Do verbs and adjectives play different roles in different cultures? A cross-linguistic analysis of person perception. *Journal of Personality and Social Psychology, 90,* 734–750.

Macrae, C. N., & Bodenhausen, G. V. (2000). Social cognition: Thinking categorically about others. *Annual Review of Psychology, 51,* 93–120.

Macrae, C. N., Quinn, K. A., Mason, M. F., & Quadflieg, S. (2005). Understanding others: The face and person construal. *Journal of Personality and Social Psychology, 89,* 686–695.

Malle, B. F. (2004). *How the mind explains behavior: Folk explanations, meaning, and social interaction.* Cambridge, MA: MIT Press.

Malle, B. F. (2006). The actor-observer asymmetry in attribution. *Psychological Bulletin, 132,* 859–919.

Malle, B. F., & Hodges, S. D. (2005). *Other minds: How humans bridge the divide between self and others.* New York: Guilford Press.

Marsh, A. A., Elfenbein, H. A., & Ambady, N. (2003). Nonverbal "accents": Cultural differences in facial expressions of emotion. *Psychological Science, 14,* 373–376.

Mason, M. F., & Macrae, C. N. (2008). Perspective-taking from a social neuroscience standpoint. *Group Processes and Intergroup Relations, 11,* 215–232.

Mason, M. F., & Morris, M. W. (2010). Culture, attribution and automaticity: A social cognitive neuroscience view. *Social Cognitive Affective Neuroscience, 5,* 292–306.

Matsumoto, D. (1993). Ethnic differences in affect intensity, emotion judgments, display rule attitudes, and self-reported emotional expression in an American sample. *Motivation and Emotion, 17,* 107–123.

Matsumoto, D., LeRoux, J., Wilson-Cohn, C., Raroque, J., Kooken, K., Ekman, P., Yrizarry, N., Loewinger, S., Uchida, H., & Yee, A. (2000). A new test to measure emotion recognition ability: Matsumoto and Ekman's Japanese and Caucasian Brief Affect Recognition Test (JACBART). *Journal of Nonverbal Behavior, 24,* 179–209.

Matsumoto, D., Yoo, S. H., Fontaine, J., Anguas-Wong, A. M., Arriola, M., Ataca, B., et al. (2008). Mapping expressive differences around the world: The relationship between emotional display rules and Individualism v. Collectivism. *Journal of Cross-Cultural Psychology, 39,* 55–74.

Mayer, J. D., & Salovey, P. (1997). What is emotional intelligence? In P. Salovey & D. Sluyter (Eds.), *Emotional development and emotional intelligence: Implications for educators* (pp. 3–31). New York: Basic Books.

McClure, E. B. (2000). A meta-analytic review of sex differences in facial expression processing and their development in infants, children, and adolescents. *Psychological Bulletin, 126,* 424–453.

McClure, J. (2002). Goal-based explanations of actions and outcomes. *European Review of Social Psychology, 12,* 201–23.

Meltzoff, A. N. (1995). Understanding the intentions of others: Re-enactment of intended acts by 18-month-old children. *Developmental Psychology, 31,* 838–850.

Mesquita, B., & Frijda, N. H. (1992). Cultural variations in emotions: A review. *Psychological Bulletin, 112,* 179–204.

Miller, J. G. (1984). Culture and the development of everyday social explanation. *Journal of Personality and Social Psychology, 46,* 961–978.

Miller, L. C., Berg, J. H., & Archer, R. L. (1983). Openers: Individuals who elicit intimate self-disclosure. *Journal of Personality and Social Psychology, 44,* 1234–1244.

Mitchell, J. P. (2009). Inferences about other minds. *Philosophical Transactions of the Royal Society B, 364,* 1309–1316.

Mitchell, J. P., Ames, D. L., Jenkins, A. C., & Banaji, M. R. (2009). Neural correlates of stereotype application. *Journal of Cognitive Neuroscience, 21,* 594–604.

Mitchell, J. P., Macrae, C. N., & Banaji, M. R. (2006). Dissociable medial prefrontal contributions to judgments of similar and dissimilar others. *Neuron, 50,* 655–663.

Miyamoto, Y., & Kitayama, S. (2002). Cultural variation in correspondence bias: The critical role of attitude diagnosticity. *Journal of Personality and Social Psychology, 83,* 1239–1248.

Montague, A., & Matson, F. (1983). *The dehumanization of man.* New York: McGraw-Hill.

Montepare, J. M., & Dobish, H. (2003). The contribution of emotion perceptions and their overgeneralizations to trait impressions. *Journal of Nonverbal Behavior, 27,* 237–254.

Morris, M., Nadler, J., Kurtzberg, T., & Thompson, L. (2002). Schmooze or lose: Social friction and lubrication in e-mail negotiations. *Group Dynamics: Theory, Research, and Practice, 6,* 89–100.

Morris, M. W., & Peng, K. (1994). Culture and cause: American and Chinese attributions for social and physical events. *Journal of Personality and Social Psychology, 67,* 949–971.

Murphy, N. A., & Hall, J. A. (2011). Intelligence and interpersonal sensitivity: A meta-analysis. *Intelligence, 39,* 54–63.

Newtson, D. (1973) Attribution and the unit of perception of ongoing behavior. *Journal of Personality and Social Psychology, 28,* 28–38.

Nickerson, R. S. (1998). Confirmation bias: A ubiquitous phenomenon in many guises. *Review of General Psychology, 2,* 175–220.

Nisbett, R. E., & Ross, L. D. (1980). *Human inference: Strategies and shortcomings of social judgment.* Englewood Cliffs, NJ: Prentice Hall.

Nisbett, R. E., & Wilson, T. D. (1977). The halo effect: Evidence for unconscious alteration of judgments. *Journal of Personality and Social Psychology, 35,* 250–256.

O'Brien, G. V. (2003). People with cognitive disabilities: The argument from marginal cases and social work ethics. *Social Work, 48,* 331–337.

Opotow, S. (1990). Moral exclusion and injustice: An introduction. *Journal of Social Issues, 46,* 1–20.

Papp, L. M., Kouros, C. D., & Cummings, E. M. (2010). Spouses' emotions in marital conflict interactions: Empathic accuracy, assumed similarity, and the moderating context of depressive symptoms. *Journal of Social and Personal Relationships, 27,* 327–349.

Paunonen, S. V. (1989). Consensus in personality judgments: Moderating effects of target-rater acquaintanceship and behavior observability. *Journal of Personality and Social Psychology, 56,* 823–833.

Pinkley, R. L., Griffith, T. L., & Northcraft, G. B. (1995). Fixed pie a la mode: Information availability, information processing, and the negotiation of sub-optimal agreements. *Organizational Behavior and Human Decision Processes, 62,* 101–112.

Plous, S. (1993). The nuclear arms race: Prisoner's Dilemma or Perceptual Dilemma? *Journal of Peace Research, 30,* 163–179.

Pronin, E. (2007). Perception and misperception of bias in human judgment. *Trends in Cognitive Sciences, 11,* 37–43.

Pyszczynski, T., Wicklund, R. A., Floresku, S., Koch, H., Gauch, G., Solomon, S., et al. (1996). Whistling in the dark: Exaggerated consensus estimates in response to incidental reminders of mortality. *Psychological Science, 7,* 332–336.

Read, S. J., & Miller, L. C. (2005). Explanatory coherence and goal-based knowledge structures in making dispositional inferences. In B. Malle, & S. Hodges (Eds.), *Other minds* (pp. 124–139). New York: Guilford Press.

Reeder, G. (2009). Mindreading: Judgments about intentionality and motives in dispositional inference. *Psychological Inquiry, 20,* 1–18.

Reeder, G. D., Pryor, J. B., Wohl, M. J. A., & Griswell, M. L. (2005). On attributing negative motives to others who disagree with our opinions. *Personality and Social Psychology Bulletin, 31,* 1498–1510.

Robinson, R. J., Keltner, D., Ward, A., & Ross, L. (1995). Actual versus assumed differences in construal: "Naive realism" in intergroup perception and conflict. *Journal of Personality and Social Psychology, 68,* 404–417.

Riggio, R. E. (1986). Assessment of basic social skills. *Journal of Personality and Social Psychology, 51,* 649–660.

Riggio, R. E., & Carney, D. R. (2003). *Social skills inventory manual* (2nd ed.). Redwood City, CA: MindGarden.

Riketta, M., & Sacramento, C. (2008). 'They cooperate with us, so they are like me': Perceived intergroup relationship moderates projection from self to outgroups. *Group Processes and Intergroup Relations, 11,* 115–131.

Roese, N. J., & Sherman, J. W. (2007). Expectancy. In A. W. Kruglanski & E. T. Higgins (Eds.), *Social psychology: A handbook of basic principles* (Vol. 2, pp. 91–115). New York: Guilford Press.

Rosenthal, R., Hall, J. A., DiMatteo, M. R., Rogers, P. L., & Archer, D. (1979). *Sensitivity to nonverbal communication.* Baltimore, MD: Johns Hopkins University Press.

Ross, L., Greene, D., & House, P. (1977). The "false consensus effect": An egocentric bias and social perception and attribution processes. *Journal of Experimental Social Psychology, 13,* 279–301.

Ross, L., & Nisbett, R. E. (1991). *The person and the situation: Perspectives of social psychology.* Philadelphia, PA: Temple.

Ross, L., & Ward, A. (1996). Naive realism in everyday life: Implications for social conflict and misunderstanding. In E. Reed, E. Turiel, & T. Brown (Eds.), *Values and knowledge* (pp. 103–135). Mahwah, NJ: Lawrence Erlbaum.

Ross, L. D., Lepper, M. R., Strack, F., & Steinmetz, J. (1977). Social explanation and social expectation: Effects of real and hypothetical explanations on subjective likelihood. *Journal of Personality and Social Psychology, 35,* 817–829.

Rubin, Z., & Shenker, S. (1978). Friendship, proximity, and self-disclosure. *Journal of Personality, 46,* 1–22.

Russell, J. A., & Fernandez-Dols, J. (1997). *The psychology of facial expression.* Cambridge, UK: Cambridge University Press.

Sabatelli, R. M., & Rubin, M. (1986). Nonverbal expressiveness and physical attractiveness as mediators of interpersonal perceptions. *Journal of Nonverbal Behavior, 10,* 120–133.

Sagar, H. A., & Schofield, J. W. (1980). Racial and behavioral cues in Black and White children's perceptions of ambiguously aggressive acts. *Journal of Personality and Social Psychology, 39,* 590–598.

Schank, C., & Abelson, R. P. (1977). *Scripts, plans, goals and understanding: An inquiry into human knowledge structures.* Hillsdale, NJ: Lawrence Erlbaum.

Schneider, D. J. (1973). Implicit personality theory: A review. *Psychological Bulletin, 79,* 294–309.

Sherman, S. J., Presson, C. C., & Chassin, L. (1984). Mechanisms underlying the False Consensus Effect: The special role of threats to the self. *Personality and Social Psychology Bulletin, 10,* 127–138.

Shweder, R., & D'Andrade, R. (1980). The systematic distortion hypothesis. In R. Shweder & D. Fiske (Eds.), *New directions for methodology of behavioral science: Fallible judgment in behavioral research* (pp. 37–58). San Francisco, CA: Jossey-Bass.

Simpson, J. A., Orina, M. M., & Ickes, W. (2003). When accuracy hurts, and when it helps: A test of the empathic accuracy model in marital interactions. *Journal of Personality and Social Psychology, 85,* 881–893.

Snyder, M., & Swann, Jr., W. B. (1978). Hypothesis-testing processes in social interaction. *Journal of Personality and Social Psychology, 36,* 1202–1212.

Srivastava, S., McGonigal, K. M., Richards, J. M., Butler, E. A., & Gross, J. J. (2006). Optimism in close relationships: How seeing things in a positive light makes them so. *Journal of Personality and Social Psychology, 91,* 143–153.

Staub, E. (1989). *The roots of evil: The origins of genocide and other group violence.* New York: Cambridge University Press.

Stinson, L., & Ickes, W. (1992). Empathic accuracy in the interactions of male friends versus male strangers. *Journal of Personality and Social Psychology, 62,* 787–797.

Swann, Jr., W. B. (1984). Quest for accuracy in person perception: A matter of pragmatics. *Psychological Review, 91,* 457–477.

Taft, R. (1955). The ability to judge people. *Psychological Bulletin, 52,* 1–23.

Taylor, D. A. (1968). The development of interpersonal relationships: Social penetration processes. *Journal of Social Psychology, 75,* 79–90.

Taylor, D. A., Altman, I., & Sorrentino, R. (1969). Interpersonal exchange as a function of rewards and costs and situational factors: Expectancy confirmation–disconfirmation. *Journal of Experimental Social Psychology, 5,* 324–339.

Thomas, G., Fletcher, G., & Lange, C. (1997). On-line empathic accuracy in marital interaction. *Journal of Personality and Social Psychology, 72,* 839–850.

Thomas, G., & Fletcher, G. J. O. (2003). Mind-reading accuracy in intimate relationships: Assessing the roles of the relationship, the target, and the judge. *Journal of Personality and Social Psychology, 85,* 1079–1094.

Ting-Toomey, S. (1985). Toward a theory of conflict and culture. In W. Gudykunst, L. Stewart, & S. Ting-Toomey (Eds.), *Communication, culture and organizational processes.* Beverly Hills, CA: Sage.

Todorov, A., Said, C. P., Engell, A. D., & Oosterhof, N. N. (2008). Understanding evaluation of faces on social dimensions. *Trends in Cognitive Sciences, 12,* 455–460.

Toma, C., Yzerbyt, V., & Corneille, O. (2010). Anticipated cooperation vs. competition moderates interpersonal projection. *Journal of Experimental Social Psychology, 46,* 375–381.

Tracy, J. L., & Robins, R. W. (2008). The automaticity of emotion recognition. *Emotion, 7,* 789–801.

Trope, Y. (1986). Identification and inferential processes in dispositional attribution. *Psychological Review, 93,* 239–257.

Vaes, J., Paladino, M. P., Castelli, L., Leyens, J. Ph., & Giovanazzi, A. (2003). On the behavioral consequences of infra-humanization: The implicit role of uniquely human emotions in intergroup relations. *Journal of Personality and Social Psychology, 85,* 1016–1034.

Van Boven, L., & Loewenstein, G. (2005). Cross-situational projection. In M. Alicke, J. Krueger, & D. Dunning (Eds.), *Self in social judgment* (pp. 43–64). New York: Psychology Press.

Van Lange, P. A. M. (1992). Confidence in expectations: A test of the triangle hypothesis. *European Journal of Personality, 6,* 371–379.

Vazire, S. (2010). Who knows what about a person? The Self–Other Knowledge Asymmetry (SOKA) model. *Journal of Personality and Social Psychology, 98,* 281–300.

Vazire, S., & Gosling, S. D. (2004). e-Perceptions: Personality impressions based on personal websites. *Journal of Personality and Social Psychology, 87,* 123–132.

Vogt, D. S., & Colvin, C. R. (2003). Interpersonal orientation and the accuracy of personality judgments. *Journal of Personality, 71,* 267–295.

Wagner, H. L., & Smith, J. (1991). Facial expression in the presence of friends and strangers. *Journal of Nonverbal Behavior, 15,* 201–214.

Weinberg, M. K., Tronick, E. Z., Cohn, J. F., & Olson, K. L. (1999). Gender differences in emotional expressivity and self-regulation during early infancy. *Developmental Psychology, 35,* 175–188.

Wu, S., & Keysar, B. (2007). Cultural effects on perspective taking. *Psychological Science, 18,* 600–606.

Zaki, J., Bolger, N., & Ochsner, K. (2008). It takes two: The interpersonal nature of empathic accuracy. *Psychological Science, 19,* 399–404.

Zebrowitz, L. A. (1997). *Reading faces: Window to the soul?* Boulder, CO: Westview.

Zou, X., Tam, K., Morris, W. M., Lee, L., Lau, I., & Chiu, C.Y. (2009). Culture as common sense: Perceived consensus vs. personal beliefs as mechanisms of cultural influence. *Journal of Personality and Social Psychology, 97,* 579–597.

8

Socially Situated Cognition: Recasting Social Cognition as an Emergent Phenomenon

Gün R. Semin, Margarida V. Garrido, & Tomás A. Palma

In this chapter, we present human cognitive processes as situated and dynamic, a perspective identified by the umbrella term 'situated cognition', or 'socially situated cognition' (SSC). We argue that while the SSC approach does not present a theoretically unified framework, it constitutes an approach offering a set of general principles and emphases cutting across many scientific disciplines and with holding the promise of leading to a unified perspective on human functioning.

In the following we present the five pillars upon which SSC rests, namely that cognition is: an *emergent* phenomenon; is constrained by the architecture of our bodies; is for the adaptive co-regulation of action; and is biologically distributed across agents and the social world as well as tools as *scaffolds*. In conclusion, we raise theoretically and empirically unanswered issues and some open questions that are likely to direct future research.

Cognition *emerges* from dynamic and adaptive sensorimotor interactions with the social and physical environment. Human cognitive processes are welded to a changing social world, are inherently interactive, and grounded by the constraints of the human body and the environment. Acknowledging these characteristics of human cognition results in a view of cognitive processes as situated. The perspective that locates cognition in such a dynamic landscape is identified by the umbrella term "situated cognition", or "socially situated cognition" (Semin & Smith, 2002; Smith & Semin, 2004).

Situated cognition is not an overarching theoretical framework, but serves the generic function of covering a broad range of orientations that have emerged over the last two decades across the cognitive sciences, robotics, anthropology, philosophy, inter alia (cf. Robbins & Aydede, 2009). Notably, situated cognition consists of a set of general principles and emphases cutting across many scientific disciplines and with the potential of developing a unified perspective on human functioning.

As with the cycles of fashions and fads, intellectual traditions come and go. Some traces of the ideas on situated cognition can be found already by the mid-19th century psychology and were articulated in intellectual endeavors designed to overcome the then prevailing individual-centered orientation in German psychology. The first half of the 20th century figured prominent names such as William James, Vygotsky, Bartlett, Mead, and Dewey who emphasized the significance of environmental and situational determinants of human cognition and action. The ascendance of the cognitive revolution, heralded amongst other developments by Chomsky's influential critique (1959) of

Skinner's *Verbal Behavior*, introduced the "mind" as the object proper of scientific inquiry and isolated the focus of research across the cognitive sciences to the processing and representation of information. While this shift was very important in drawing attention to "cognitive processes", it also marked the beginning of an extended period which ignored the contextually embedded and embodied nature of human cognition. The metaphor of the mind and human functioning became the computer, which captured scientific as well as popular imagination: namely, an isolated, solitary tool with immense information-processing capacities. The situated cognition perspective developed as a reaction to explanations of human functioning that did not take context into account. This is not to deny the existence of innovative theoretical perspectives that incorporated the interaction between cognition and the environment during this period (e.g., Brunswik, 1955; Gibson, 1979).

In contrast to the metaphor of the human brain as the isolated, solitary information-processing device, advocates of the situated cognition perspective (e.g., A. Clark, 2008; Semin, 2000) maintain that cognitive activities extend to the social and physical environment, which become integral parts of cognitive activity in their own right (e.g., Hutchins, 1995).

Understanding the nature of situated social cognition therefore requires developing an idea of what is its appropriate level of analysis. This is the task of this chapter's five sections, which constitute the five pillars upon which situated cognition rests. In the *first* section, we locate socially situated cognition as an *emergent phenomenon*: namely, a level superseding individual cognition and action. The important implication of such localization is that the level of the phenomenon can be captured only with a macroscopic view because emergent phenomena control the parts that generate and constitute it and not vice versa (cf. Abler, 1989; Gazzaniga, 2010; Semin, 2008). A microscopic view focused on the analysis of the parts (i.e., the individual level) loses contact with the "plot" (i.e., the examination of socially situated cognition as an emergent phenomenon). Thus, an important aspect of situated cognition is the attempt to capture a level of analysis that supersedes the traditional individual- and representation-centered focus in mainstream psychology and its many disciplinary branches – including social psychology.

The *second* section introduces a feature of *social* cognition that is unique. Social cognition is not only socially but also biologically distributed across agents due to the fact that the architecture of the human perceptual-motor system is specifically designed for the reproduction of movements of conspecifics in a privileged way (Semin & Cacioppo, 2008, 2009). Research emerging since the 1990s on the mirror neuron system (cf. Rizzolatti & Craighero, 2004) has not only underlined the unique nature of conspecific cognition – namely, that it is distributed across brains – but is also a further window to how "the epistemic gulf separating single individuals can be overcome" (Gallese, 2006, p. 16).

The *third* section gets to the heart of the issue and to a principle that is central to the socially situated cognition perspective. Cognition is not detached thought but rather *adaptive co-regulation* of action. This emphasis on cognition as adaptive action is a distant cry from the traditional information-processing or representational perspective that loses sight of the function of social cognition. Obviously, adaptive action is not merely mind-play, but also involves successful physical interaction with other agents and the world.

The types of actions we can engage in are constrained by the architecture of our bodies – the cognitive and emotional implications of this constraint are the subject of the *fourth* section on *embodiment*. This section focuses on the neglected role that our physical bodies play in shaping cognition in a variety of different ways. We experience the world through bodily interactions and the architecture of human functioning is constrained and regulated by our bodies and brains. This particular aspect of the situated cognition approach, i.e., embodied cognition, is one of the central converging issues of current interest in philosophy, cognitive science, psychology, robotics, and neuroscience (cf. Schubert & Semin, 2009; Smith & Semin, 2004). However, research in social cognition that preceded these developments (e.g., Cacioppo, Priester, & Berntson, 1993; Strack, Martin, & Stepper, 1988; Valins, 1966; Wells & Petty, 1980) has already illustrated how sensorimotor processes affect mental states.

The *final* section draws attention to the *distributed nature* of social cognition, namely that in implementing action we make use of tools as well as the social world. Tools provide, in A. Clark's (1997) terms, *scaffolds* for cognitive activity. Such scaffolds release cognitive space, and contain knowledge that has been downloaded to different tools (e.g., the multiplication operation of a calculator) or persons with complementary knowledge and expertise.

In the concluding section to this chapter, we raise issues that remain unanswered both theoretically and empirically and pose some of the open questions that are likely to direct future research.

THE FIVE PILLARS OF SITUATED COGNITION

Determining the level of analysis: Emergence

Understanding the nature of social cognition requires developing an idea of what is its appropriate level of analysis. If, as a situated cognition perspective would suggest, social cognition is for adaptive co-regulation (e.g., the regulation of social interaction; Semin & Cacioppo, 2008, 2009), then the phenomenon to be explained and understood is at a macroscopic level: namely, social interaction in specific contexts and the processes driving it. This requires capturing the phenomenon at a level of analysis that surpasses the traditional individual- and representation-centered focus in mainstream psychology and social psychology. In other words, the molecular level impacts the atomic level. Such a higher-level organization has an entirely different quality than the single units that in their composition give rise to an emergent quality with a distinctive composition of the individual parts.

To illustrate, understanding the physical properties of atoms of hydrogen, silicon, sulfur, and oxygen is informative. However, their unique compositions at a higher level of organization – as in the cases of water (H_2O), sand (SiO_2), and sulfur dioxide (SO_2) or sulfuric acid (H_2SO_4) – constitute emergent molecular compounds that do not display any of the characteristics of the individual elements from which they are composed. The larger unit (e.g., H_2O) has an emergent quality. This is a feature that is not only specific to the composition of chemical compounds. The same recursive compositionality can be seen in the genetic makeup of the species that relies on the four nucleotide bases of DNA, abbreviated C (cytosine), G (guanine), A (adenine), and T (thymine) or for that matter in language use (cf. Semin, 2006). Language use displays the same recursive qualities and relies on a discrete set of basic units (*phonemes*) as constituents at the primary level of organization, with *morphemes* at the second, *phrase structure* at the third, and *utterance* at the fourth levels. The fourth level is where "situated meaning" is brought to expression with utterances (cf. Semin, 2006).

The distinctive feature of these examples is that the different syntheses of a set of discrete "elements" give rise to something that is not present in any of the constituents of the syntheses – in fact the range of creative syntheses is unlimited, as Humboldt (1836/1971) observed in the context of language: i.e., that language "makes infinite use of finite media" (p. 70) whose "synthesis creates something that is not present *per se* in any of the associated constituents" (p. 67). This is "emergence". What may at first glance appear to be remote from socially situated cognition is in fact a much more general principle and applies to all self-diversifying systems (cf. Abler, 1989). Moreover, it has a number of interesting implications that are relevant to socially situated phenomena that have gone largely unnoticed (cf. Abler, 1989 for a notable exception).

The permutation and combination of "units" leading to even larger units in a hierarchy of compositionality (e.g., atoms to molecules; words to sentences to utterances) yields an unbounded diversity of form and function. This is the distinctive and creative characteristic of situated social cognition: namely, infinite diversity as the outcome of a recursively generated system.

An important feature of such recursively generated systems is that each level of organization displays a new emergent quality. The variable combinations at different levels of organization display qualities and properties that are absent in their constituent elements. H_2O has properties and qualities that are distinctly different from the elements of H and O of which it is composed. Higher levels of organization have a propensity to act as shells, which enclose or hide their constituents – a consequence of the fact that the compositions are emergent and display unique and novel qualities. This does not mean that the constituents (e.g., phonemes, morphemes or atoms) lose their identity or are not retrievable – on the contrary. However, the fact that the higher-order compound conceals the characteristic properties of its constituents also means that these are not necessarily accessible and in the case of social phenomena are very likely to escape conscious access. When uttering a sentence we do not have access to the constituent elements from which it is composed.

The general implication of these considerations for the analysis of emergent phenomena such as adaptive co-regulation is a point that Gazzaniga recently made (2010). His observation is in the context of neuroscientific inquiries but has more general relevance: namely, emergent phenomena control the parts that generate and constitute it and not vice versa. It is the goals of a dialogue that organize the utterances and their compositionality and not the phonemes and morphemes that organize the utterance! Consequently, it is the higher level of organization that enables an understanding of how the parts are composed and not the reverse, as is the case, when parts are analyzed without the insight of the emergent whole as a guiding perspective. This is precisely what is meant with setting the level of analysis.

Two observations ensue from these considerations about the level of analysis in social cognition cast in the traditional mold. The first is that the prevailing mode of thinking about social cognition is driven by setting an erroneous level of analysis, which is based on the assumption that explaining a phenomenon at a lower level, for instance the individual level, will open the window to grasp something at a more complex level. This can be illustrated in the paradoxical nature of the classic domain of social cognition (e.g., Devine, Hamilton, & Ostrom, 1994; Jones, 1985) that has focused on individual processes and functioning by conveniently replacing the object of individual cognitive processes by mental structures and processes about social objects, such as stereotypes, persons, and social events. In this traditional mode, social cognition is treated as a disembodied structure: i.e., as a set of symbols and "rules" about how to combine them (e.g., Fodor, 1980; Smith, 1998). The second observation is the difficulty of identifying the macroscopic level of analysis that is appropriate for socially situated cognition. The insight of the emergent nature of socially situated cognition needs to be transduced into an operational handle that presents a researchable agenda. The next four sections are designed to deliver the pillars to this agenda. They address the details of the arguments that conspecific cognition is unique, that cognition is for adaptive action, is constrained by our bodies and the environment, and the significance of distributed knowledge as scaffolds for cognition. Together, these sections anchor the level and types of analysis that are introduced by a socially situated perspective.

The unique nature of social cognition

Understanding the social in *social* cognition has presented a number of challenges that have been with us from the very beginnings of "modern" psychology (cf. Semin, 1986). One of these is to come to terms with what the "social" means. As Gallese has noted recently: "The hard problem in "social cognition" is to understand how the epistemic gulf separating single individuals can be overcome" (Gallese, 2006, p. 16). This issue has occupied "modern" psychology in waves from the mid-19th century onwards. The dominant view resulted in an individual-centered view of mainstream social cognition and was underlined with reference to the biological finitude of the individual. Theory and research in psychology ended up regarding cognitive activity as processes that are locked in the cranial vault, and fostered the "epistemic gulf".

The way in which we represent the *social world* is fundamentally connected with the actions that our bodies perform.

An adaptive and dynamic view of social cognition suggests that a model of social cognition should address the constraints and capacities provided by the perceptuomotor apparatus and the complex and continuously changing demands of the social environment in which social cognition evolved. Neural systems evolved that were tuned to particular embodiments and environments. In this view, social cognition is best understood as grounded in (rather than abstracted from) perceptuomotor processes and intertwined with a wealth of interpersonal interaction and specialized for a distinctive class of stimuli. In the course of our lives, we are exposed to a vast range of stimuli, cars, buildings, trees, household objects, books, and, of course, other humans and an array of other life forms. Other human beings and their bodily movements constitute a distinctive class of stimuli, because the movements of other human beings can be mapped onto our own bodies (Semin & Cacioppo, 2008, p. 120).

There is substantial evidence (cf. Iacobini, 2009; Rizzolatti & Craighero, 2004) showing this isomorphism and suggesting it to be a species-specific mapping process (cf. Buccino et al., 2004). The research also underlines the view that such isomorphism in mapping movements is due to "synchronization" processes that result from the formation of a type of sensory neural representation that has an entirely different ontological status than knowledge about the world in general. One can therefore regard this type of neurally emergent isomorphism as a *heritable foundation of communication and the embodied building block of social cognition* (Semin, 2007). In order to communicate efficiently, two or more agents have to be on the same page at multiple levels, from the neural to "content" (i.e., common ground, cf. H. Clark & Brennan, 1991), to subfeatures of a dialogue (cf. Pickering & Garrod, 2011).

The important point is that processes that rely on mutually privileged access drive human knowledge about conspecifics. Thus, the basis for "social cognition" relies on access due to being able to map the movements of another upon our own bodies. This gives a source of information above and beyond interacting. Thus, we can interact with objects and other species. These interactions define our knowledge of object worlds as well as our knowledge of other species (their affordances). However, our knowledge of our conspecifics has the added advantage of being mutually able to reproduce each other's movements. This species-specific advantage furnishes mutual access and the foundations of communication (cf. Semin, 2007).

The adaptive function of cognition

The standard representational or information-processing paradigm of social cognition involves the construction and manipulation of inner representations that have no bearing to real interaction in and with the world. One can characterize this view of cognition as a "glass bead game" (Hesse, 1943) that is for its own sake, and without much contact to the reality of the world in which bodily and verbal interactions define an agent's place and existence in relation to the social and physical environment. The representational view, locked in the cranial vault, has the further burden of explaining how it is possible for two individuals to achieve sociality (intersubjectivity), since the individual-centered conceptualization of cognition does not allow for the active reciprocal and co-regulative nature of social behavior.

Therefore, a minor change has to be introduced to the standard question "What is cognition?" from the socially situated perspective resulting in "What is cognition *for?*", introducing a set of significant implications. The answer to this, from both biological and cognitive scientific perspective, is "for action", for producing the next action. The fundamental evolutionary demands on cognition are the organism's survival and reproduction, which requires adaptive action and (for humans) always takes place in a social context (Caporael, 1997; Fiske, 1992). Thus, from a socially situated perspective, cognition has evolved for the control of adaptive action, not for its own sake. Accordingly, social cognition is for the adaptive regulation and adaptive co-regulation of behavior (Semin & Cacioppo, 2009). Consequently, understanding socially situated cognition entails explicating the processes by which the adaptive regulation of others' behavior and the co-regulation of social interaction is achieved. From this view, cognition is not coterminous with detached thought but with adaptively successful interaction with other agents and with the world. The mind contains "inner structures that act as operators upon the world via their role in determining actions" (Clark, 1997, p. 47).

One of the important implications of viewing cognition as adaptive action is to be found in the way we conceptualize, represent, and think about objects and persons. If cognition is for the control of action, then objects and persons must be represented in terms of their relations to the agent and not some abstract features as "objective" qualities. The type of actions and interactions that are possible between an agent and an object – their *affordances* (cf. Gibson, 1979) – or another person determines one's relation to them (see Glenberg, 1997, 2008).

The significance of actions that define relationships between an agent and the social and physical environment for the construction of meaning and concepts becomes clearer when one contrasts it with standard representational approaches to concepts. They are derived implicitly from a model of textual representations (propositions) or equivalent symbolic structures (schemas, etc.). In representational approaches, concepts were typically considered as abstract and amodal, such as semantic networks or feature lists. Being abstract, these descriptions are without a "subject" and constitute an extra-individual and systematic set of abstract properties with a life of its own. But feature lists present problems. Boroditsky and Prinz (2008) illustrate these problems with the instance of "ducks" as a category. A feature list of a duck is likely to include feet, feathers, a bill, swimming, and so on. Such an abstracted, amodal list has the advantage that we can actually use these features for representations of many different categories aside from ducks. Now, let us consider for the time being that you have no idea what ducks are. You have never seen one, but have access to only these features. How do you know, as Boroditsky and Prinz (2008) put it, the difference between a duck and a Las Vegas showgirl, who shares the same features with a duck: namely, feet, feathers, and swimming? This is the problem that arises when language and cognition are regarded as a closed loop of symbols or an internal model of the world, with the meaning of each symbol defined only by other symbols. This is analogous to learning Chinese from its ideograms in a dictionary. The ideograms provide no connection between anything outside of the dictionary. Any unknown character is defined only by reference to other unknown characters. The result is the so-called "symbol grounding" problem (Harnad, 1990).

We now review research that has a bearing upon the adaptive function of cognition as action. If the evolution of human minds was primarily for the on-line control of action under the demands of survival, then there should be a close connection between cognition and action. This section consists of two parts: the first part addresses the role of context as the arbiter of cognition and action; the second part focuses on what it means to say that cognition is for action and reviews the relevant research.

Context and cognition

Human cognition emerges in the interaction with a constantly changing social and physical environment (e.g., Semin & Smith, 2002). These dynamic contexts require adaptive responses that cannot be found and rely upon static and invariant internal representations. Obviously, off-line cognition (Wilson, 2002) is important in a variety of situations involving, for instance, forward planning. Nevertheless, even so-called "off-line" intrapsychological processes are the result of interpsychological functioning, as Vygotsky (e.g., 1981) has argued. Thus, even "off-line" cognition is situated in that it is a contextually simulated mental activity.

This section reviews research that highlights the situational influences on cognitive processes with adaptive implications. In the following we begin by reviewing work that displays the context sensitivity of mental representations and the research on the effects of context on cognitive processes and behavior. Subsequently, we expand on the notion of context, introducing the physical features of the environment as factors that influence cognition and action.

Context effects on mental representations and action

Modeling cognition in terms of abstract, detached symbolic representations has meant treating mental representations as invariant, timeless, and largely immune to contextual influences. This particular assumption has been the driving force across a number of fields from "classic" views on person and social cognition, to attitudes, and stereotypes, to name a few (e.g., Hamilton & Trolier, 1986). This view was also endorsed because enduring mental structures were assumed to play a key role in attaining cognitive economy. The principle of cognitive economy, it has been argued, is functional to the extent that processing potentially infinitely variable detail would induce a state of informational complexity that the cognitive apparatus would not be able to cope with (e.g., Crocker, Fiske, & Taylor, 1984; Taylor, 1981). Consequently, representations such as stereotypes were assumed to exhibit temporal inertia as well as resistance to fleeting contextual influences (e.g., Hamilton & Trolier, 1986; Snyder, 1981).

This pre-paradigmatic assumption was further bolstered with "evidence" suggesting that across a set of different conditions mental representations such as stereotypes are automatically activated, escaping conscious access (e.g., Bargh, 1999; Bargh, Chen, & Burrows, 1996; Devine, 1989), and therefore making their situational adjustment less likely.

Assuming that mental representations are immune to contextual factors flies in the face of the necessity of cognition to be adaptive to situational requirements and tuned flexibly. Indeed, there is cumulative empirical evidence

documenting, for instance, that attitudes, frequently described as "enduring mental dispositions", are vulnerable to a multitude of contextual effects (e.g., Schwarz & Sudman, 1992). Similarly, stereotypes have been shown to display considerable malleability in the face of changing contexts and their spontaneous activation is neither inevitable nor universal. Rather than representing abstract and stable knowledge structures, stereotypes can be malleable and responsive to the changing contextual demand of situations (e.g., Blair, 2002). For instance, there is an extensive research tradition that has established that the accessibility of specific exemplars or group members affects category and subtype descriptions (e.g., Coats & Smith, 1999; Smith & Zaraté, 1992) as well as central tendency and variability judgments about the group as a whole (Garcia-Marques & Mackie, 1999, 2001). Different members of a group can also apparently make stereotypes differentially accessible (e.g., Macrae, Mitchell, & Pendry, 2002). Stereotypes are sensitive to subtle contextual cues (e.g., Wittenbrink, Judd, & Park, 2001) and to context stability (Garcia-Marques, Santos, & Mackie, 2006).

For example, Schwarz and Bless (1992) have shown that making the membership of a wellregarded politician to a specific political party salient increased the evaluation of his party, whereas its exclusion resulted in lower overall party evaluation. Similarly, recalling politicians that were involved in a scandal decreased evaluations of the trustworthiness of politicians in general. In a similar vein, the incidental exposure to atypical exemplars of a social group (e.g., exposure to well-liked successful African Americans like Oprah Winfrey), in a task-irrelevant context, was shown to be sufficient to produce the expression of more sympathetic beliefs about the group (Bodenhausen, Schwarz, Bless, & Wänke, 1995). The effect of variations in category exemplars on stereotypes was also investigated by Macrae and colleagues (2002), who observed faster judgments about stereotypic attributes when category exemplars had familiar names (John and Sarah) rather than unfamiliar ones (Isaac and Glenda).

Moreover, even subtle changes in the context were shown to significantly affect the stereotype content automatically activated (Macrae, Bodenhausen, & Milne, 1995). Participants who watched a woman with chopsticks in her hand (vs makeup brush) were faster to respond, in a lexical decision task, to personality traits related with "Chinese" than with "Women", and viceversa. Similar subtle context manipulations such as presenting a picture of a Black American person in the context of a street scene produced more automatic negativity toward Black Americans than presenting the same picture framed in a church context, in which significant automatic positivity towards African Americans was observed (Wittenbrink et al., 2001).

Garcia-Marques and colleagues (2006) asked participants to read the description of a group member and to complete a stereotype trait assembling task across two sessions with a two-week interval. Stereotypes were stable when the context remained identical (i.e., the description of the group member was stereotype-consistent or stereotype-inconsistent across both sessions). However, stereotype stability declined considerably when the context differed across the two sessions.

A number of other lines of research support the claim that social context influences and shapes cognitive processes and outcomes which were assumed to be driven automatically and therefore stable. One illustration reveals the context sensitivity of the "fundamental attribution error" (Gilbert, 1991; Ross, 1977), allegedly driven by automatic and invariant cognitive processes, such as the increased salience of an actor in a relatively static situational background (Heider, 1958). However, as Norenzayan and Schwarz (1999) demonstrated, subtle situational cues could easily influence these "fundamental and automatic cognitive processes". When asked to provide causal explanations for a mass murder reported in a newspaper, participants responding to a questionnaire with a letterhead "Institute for Social Research" produced more situational explanations, whereas those responding to a questionnaire for the "Institute of Personality Research" produced more dispositional accounts.

These and other studies constitute compelling evidence of the adaptive and context sensitive nature of knowledge, and that such malleability depends on the incorporation of currently context-activated information into mental structures (e.g., stereotypes) and subsequent action. However as Smith and Semin (2007) noted, the context sensitivity of stereotypes has often been considered as reflecting a deliberate attempt to conceal socially undesirable stereotypic thoughts (cf. Fazio & Olson, 2003). Recent research contradicts this by revealing that stereotypes as assessed with implicit measures (more immune to intentional response bias) are also context sensitive (Blair, 2002). Moreover, non-social concepts, which are not subject to social desirability concerns, also reveal context sensitivity (Yeh & Barsalou, 2006).

It may perhaps appear to be self-evident that mental representations must be responsive to situated demands and thus be context sensitive if they are to guide adaptive responses. Obviously, mental representations would be useless if they were completely malleable, as would a complete lack of responsiveness to changing circumstances be.

The systemic view espoused by a situated approach to human functioning assumes the interdependence between psychological processes, the human body, and the material conditions of the environment, (e.g., Proffitt, 2006; Williams & Bargh, 2008a). Recent research has started to document the effects of the physical features of the environment upon social cognitive processes. Williams and Bargh (2008a) have shown that the actual physical sensation of warmth induced by a warm cup led participants to see a target person as more sociable and to become more generous relative to a physically cold condition induced by a cold cup. Warmer room temperature has also been demonstrated to lead to higher reported social proximity to a target person (Ijzerman & Semin, 2009) relative to colder room temperatures. Zhong and Leonardelli (2008) have taken the opposite implication and revealed that social exclusion leads people to feel colder. Another physical feature that has been shown to affect social judgment is distance. For example, participants primed with spatially proximal coordinates reported stronger bonds to their family members and their hometown than those primed with distant coordinates (Williams & Bargh, 2008b). More recently, Ijzerman and Semin (2010) have shown that inducing experiences of physical and verbal proximity gives rise to perceptions of higher temperature.

Scents have also been shown to affect cognition and behavior across a variety of contexts. For instance, the exposure to a cleaning scent makes the cleaning concept more accessible, accelerates the reaction time to cleaning-related words, guides expectations relative to future cleaning-related activities, and influences actual cleaning behavior (Holland, Hendriks, & Aarts, 2005). Other studies report that pleasant fragrances make it more likely that people help others (Baron, 1997); that human odors affect social interaction, including attraction to others (cf. Stockhorst & Pietrowsky, 2004); that neutral faces are rated as more likable (Li, Moallem, Paller, & Gottfried, 2007); and that male faces are rated by females as more attractive (Demattè, Österbauer, & Spence, 2007).

In a recent integration, Semin and Garrido (2012) have documented the significance of the physical features of the environmental context in person perception and judgment. Specifically, environmental contexts characterized by warm temperature, close distance, and pleasant smells promoted generalized positive evaluations not only of a social target but also of uninvolved others such as the experimenter, in contrast to the cold, distant, and unpleasant smell conditions. These and other findings highlight the interdependence between the material conditions of the environment and psychological processes – which opens new vistas to explore the role of not only physical features of the environment but also the significant role that modalities aside from the traditional ones (visually and linguistically manipulated variables) play in shaping human functioning.

Cognition as action

The "adaptive function of cognition" theme is continued here, first with an overview of the research highlighting the *functions* of mental representations – namely, as guides for action rather than internal states locked in the cranial vault. The action-oriented nature of representations is further underlined with research demonstrating how situated social *motives* and *relationships* with others shape mental representations, and guide psychological, communicative, and behavioral processes. In concluding the third pillar of socially situated cognition, we provide a brief overview of the situationally driven *informative function of feelings* in alerting us to the demands of social events and how we fine-tune our cognitive processes and actions to adapt to such circumstances.

Mental representations as guides for action

Mental representations are tuned and oriented toward adaptive action as a growing body of evidence suggests. Social perceivers seek, process, and retrieve information driven by pragmatic or functional concerns, aiding them to shape their actions flexibly in continuously changing situations. For example, the functional value of attitudes as action-oriented representations can be illustrated by the fact that they not only influence how a person thinks and represents an object but also they shape perceptions, judgments, and actions towards that object (e.g., whether to approach or avoid). Whether a person dislikes pre-Renaissance art, thinks highly of John Stewart, enjoys chocolate soufflé, or supports gay rights will influence the person's judgments and actions in the social and physical world. Automatically activated attitudes have a similar function; however, in this case, without a person's intent and awareness (e.g., Fazio, Sanbonmatsu, Powell, & Kardes, 1986). From the perspective of the social perceiver, the rapidity and flexibility of the automatic evaluation processes represent highly adaptive features of the evaluative system that is pragmatically responsive to dynamic changes in the social and physical environment (e.g., Schwarz, 2007; Smith & Semin, 2007).

Like attitudes, person impressions are also action-oriented representations, and have a functional value in guiding appropriate social action. We protect those we perceive as "vulnerable", recruit those who are "competent", and stay away from those who are "opportunistic". Indeed, research on the *stereotype content model* (SCM, e.g., Cuddy, Fiske, & Glick, 2008; Cuddy et al., 2009; Fiske, Cuddy, Glick, & Xu, 2002) has shown that "warmth" and "competence" constitute core dimensions that underlie perceptions of others and play an important role in the regulation of behavior and emotional reactions. Moreover, Fiske and her colleagues have argued that these dimensions are universal (Cuddy et al., 2008, 2009) because their adaptive function is central in regulating interpersonal relationships. Thus, person impressions contain useful cues about other's abilities, roles, and distinctive behaviors (Cantor & Kihlstrom, 1989; Carlston, 1994; Mischel & Shoda, 1998), as well as the type of relationships one has with different social targets (e.g., Baldwin, 1992; Fiske & Haslam, 1996; Fiske, Haslam, & Fiske, 1991; Holmes, 2000). The reliance on such representations facilitates interaction that underlines the pragmatic nature of social perception and is relevant for social interaction (Semin & Smith, 2002).

Adaptive action requires the rapid adaptation to the situated demands of a dynamically changing environment. Often, we have to orientate ourselves in novel situations without the advantage of much time and information. This means producing "good enough judgments" of other's makeup (e.g., Fiske, 1992) by means of heuristic methods. Such shortcuts facilitate smooth social interaction (Snyder, 1993; Snyder & Cantor, 1998), and suggest that in social interaction we are not necessarily driven by accuracy goals but by pragmatic concerns of processing efficiency that ensure sufficient accuracy to suit everyday demands for rapid adaptive action (Fiske, 1992). What was originally regarded as "biases", namely cognitive shortcuts and heuristics (e.g., Chaiken, Liberman, & Eagly, 1989), or the supposedly lazy and error-prone social perceiver (e.g., Nisbett & Ross, 1980), can be regarded as adaptive and functional processes that serve pragmatic ends.

Social motives as guides for action

Cognition and action are not neutral and detached. Distinct motives and goals that a perceiver pursues mold cognition and action and serve the perceiver's interests. As mentioned earlier, the influence of contextual factors upon knowledge structures such as stereotypes displays their malleability, but context effects do not exhaust the factors contributing to their flexibility. The content of even implicitly measured stereotypes is apparently vulnerable to perceivers' current motives (e.g., Sinclair & Kunda, 1999), processing strategies (e.g., Blair, Ma, & Lenton, 2001), focus of attention (e.g., Macrae, Bodenhausen, Milne, Thorn, & Castelli, 1997), and emotional states in a given situation (Schwarz, 2002). For example, people rated their own abilities as high when the trait domain in question was personally relevant (Kunda, 1987; Kunda & Sanitioso, 1989), or when the outcome was desirable or important (Weinstein, 1980). Other studies revealed that participants' definitions of personality traits were not objective or invariant, but were shaped in self-serving ways by their own perceived standings on those traits (Dunning & Cohen, 1992). In situations of outcome dependency, perceivers attempt to form more accurate impressions in order to predict the other's behavior better and thus have greater control over their own outcomes. Outcome dependency thus facilitates the use of relatively individuating impression formation processes and less reliance on category-based impressions (Neuberg & Fiske, 1987).

Sinclair and Kunda (1999) highlight a different facet of how induced motives affect which of two stereotypes is activated in the case of a target person who is a member of both a negative and positive stereotype (e.g., an African American physician). They show in a lexical decision task that when the target criticizes the participant, then the negative stereotype is activated. In contrast, when the participant is praised, then the positive stereotype is activated. However, these effects were not found when the participants simply observed the target person praising or criticizing someone else, suggesting that the perceiver's current motives to accept praise and discard criticism differentially modulate the activation and use of stereotypes.

Other research reveals that the way social perceivers tune their attention and cognition to process social information in the environment depends on their current social connectedness needs (e.g., scoring high in loneliness or after social exclusion). Individuals high in the need to belong were particularly attentive to and accurate in decoding social cues (e.g., vocal tone, facial emotion; Pickett, Gardner, & Knowles, 2004).

Personal relevance, egocentric judgment, outcome dependency, self-serving motives, social connectedness needs, among others, illustrate that mental representations in the social domain are not invariant processes and depend, among other factors, upon perceivers' goals and motives. Such motivational factors trigger cognitive strategies that are used flexibly to meet the situational demands and to accomplish one's goals.

Feelings as guides for situated action

A further factor giving shape to cognition and action are feeling states that provide us with important information about the processing requirements we face (e.g., Martin & Clore, 2001; Schwarz & Clore, 2007). As Schwarz (2002) points out, different situations provide different affective cues depending on whether they are benign or problematic situations. These feeling or affective states, induced by the characteristics of different situations, regulate our cognitive processes, judgments, and behaviors as a substantial research tradition on mood and cognitive processing styles has uncovered.

The general pattern that has emerged in this literature is that benign situations induce a positive mood, signaling safety. In contrast, a negative mood arises if the nature of a situation is understood as problematic. This affective information leads to cognitive processes being tuned to the respective demands of different situations. According to the feelings-as-information hypothesis (for a review see Schwarz, 2011) and the mood-as-general-knowledge assumption derived from it (for a review see Bless, 2001), people in a positive mood are more likely to rely on past experience, reflecting generalized regularities, and to activate heuristic or global processing. They rely on general knowledge (Bless, Bohner, Schwarz, & Strack, 1990; Isen, 1987; Mackie & Worth, 1989) such as stereotypes or scripts (e.g., Bless, Schwarz, & Wieland, 1996; Bodenhausen, Kramer, & Süsser, 1994; Park & Banaji, 2000), use more inclusive categories when sorting exemplars (Hirt, Levine, McDonald, Melton, & Martin, 1997; Isen & Daubman, 1984), process visual stimuli more globally (Gasper & Clore, 2002), and are more prone to the fundamental attribution error (Forgas, 1998). In contrast, situations that signal danger and induce a negative mood lead to the adoption of a more effortful, analytic, and systematic processing style (for reviews, see Bless, Schwarz, & Kemmelmeier, 1996; Schwarz, Bless, & Bohner, 1991).

Situationally induced affect can also influence cognition in terms of its *content* (Schwarz & Clore, 2007). Thus, content, namely the information retrieved from memory and the current affective state of the person is reportedly congruent (e.g., Bower, 1981; Forgas, 1995; Sedikides, 1995). A range of judgments such as life satisfaction (Schwarz & Clore, 1983), risk (Gasper & Clore, 1998), and political judgments (Forgas & Moylan, 1987) have also been shown to be influenced by affect.

The relevance of this research from a situated cognition perspective lies in the significance of different situations inducing different moods or affective states, which in turn shape the style and content of our cognitive processes and thus also have an impact on our actions.

Cognition as constrained by our bodies

Our experience of the world and our functioning is constrained by a set of relatively invariable conditions (e.g., ecological, existential, material), including our body morphology, which determine the nature of the actions and interactions that we can engage in. Human functioning is therefore embodied.

As was argued earlier, the *meaning of an object or a person* is not determined by some abstract set of features, but by the nature of the actions that one can engage in with an object or the interactions with a person. This is one of the important senses in which cognition is *embodied*, since our experiences of the world (social or otherwise) originate from bodily interactions. This particular account of embodiment takes the "body" in embodiment as the direct reference point. Ideas that have entertained or fed into this perspective are to be found in early motor theories of perception such as William James' account of "ideomotor action" (1890/1950) or Jean Piaget's developmental psychology according to which cognitive abilities grew out from sensorimotor abilities, as well as the aforementioned ecological psychology of J. J. Gibson (1966). The more recent impetus comes from A. Clark (e.g., 2008), and developments in robotics (e.g., Brooks, 1999), but also from W. Prinz's (e.g., 1984) *common coding theory*, which claims a shared representation or common code for perception and action.

The embodiment perspective contrasts with previously described amodal approaches that conceptualize psychological functioning in terms of a closed loop of symbols or an internal model of the world. As a consequence, such amodal views are not perceptually grounded and have difficulties furnishing an informed answer to how adaptively successful interaction with other agents and the world emerges.

This section is organized into four parts. The first part reviews social psychological research that antedates the current surge in this field and its more current follow-ups. The second part describes how motor performance, bodily feedback, or behavior, influence language and evaluative judgments. The third part provides an overview of a substantial research area that has emerged over the last 10 years or so and has demonstrated what is currently referred to as "*motor resonance*". This "phenomenon", which has been demonstrated both by behavioral and neurophysiological research, indicates that words (language) recruit and activate the same neural substrates and motor programs that are active when the person is performing the action represented in the sentence. The reverse has also been shown to hold. Movement, or action, enhances accessibility of language related to the movement. Research findings in neuroscience have demonstrated the link between neural mapping of language and action verbs, in particular (cf. Pulvermüller, 2005). The final part of this section provides a brief overview of how abstract entities such as time, morality, and valence are grounded.

Social psychology and embodiment

Social psychology has had a long-standing tradition of investigating the interface between the body and cognition that precedes the current surge of interest in embodiment (Cacioppo et al., 1993; Strack et al., 1988; Valins, 1966; Wells & Petty, 1980). This research literature has revealed that the human body is more than an output device for the cognitive machinery on which most psychological theories seem to have relied (e.g., Adelmann & Zajonc, 1989; Laird, 1984; Neumann, Förster, & Strack, 2003; Niedenthal, 2007; Zajonc & Markus, 1984).

Surprisingly, and despite this rich research tradition, the role of the body, or, in short, "*embodiment*", has never occupied a central stage for theorizing and research in social psychology.

Nevertheless, one finds a collection of creative studies within this amodal framework which, although not formulated in terms of a "language and motor resonance" framework, highlight the relationship between language – broadly defined – and motor action. A classic illustration of this can be found in research reported by Bargh and colleagues (1996) in which participants who had constructed sentences with words implying the elderly (e.g., *Florida, gray, sentimental, bingo, wise*) were shown to walk significantly slower down the hallway than those in a control condition.

Macrae, and colleagues (1998) report a similar finding. They introduced a reading test, which was either labeled "The Shimuhuru Word Reading Test" or "The Schumacher Word Reading Test" (at the time Schumacher was the most famous Formula 1 driver). Participants' task was to speak each word on a list aloud while they were surreptitiously timed. Participants in the "Schumacher Word Reading Test" condition produced the words more quickly. In another study, Macrae and Johnston (1998) showed that participants primed with the concept of "helpfulness" were more likely to help the experimenter in picking pens than participants in a control group. Indeed, research in social psychology is replete with creative experiments such as these (for reviews, see Niedenthal, Barsalou, Winkielman, Krauth-Gruber, & Ric, 2005; Smeesters, Wheeler, & Kay, 2010).

This research reveals that linguistic stimuli (e.g., in the form of primes) influence or shape motor behavior. However, while creative imagination establishing empirical connections has been in abundance, theory construction has been barren when it comes to explaining the precise nature of the processes mediating the link between language and behavior.

The *motor resonance question* is precisely about *the processes* mediating the relationship between language and motor behavior and would benefit this field considerably by elucidating the processes mediating this link. Notably, this type of inquiry is being conducted outside of what is generally regarded as social cognition and social psychology (see Fischer & Zwann, 2008; Semin & Smith, 2008; Zwann, 2009) as it is illustrated in the third part of this section. However, besides examining how language affects behavior a substantial amount of research also illustrates how motor performance, bodily feedback, or behavior, influence language and evaluative judgments. We review this research in the next part of this section.

Body action, social cognition, and evaluation

This subject has a long tradition, starting with the early days of research on how inferences from one's body influence attitudes. For instance Valins' (1966) classic work showed how manipulated feedback of one's heartbeat rate increases one's liking for an "object" that one is observing. The role that the body (e.g., physical posture) plays in the acquisition and expression of attitudes has early origins (Darwin, 1965; Galton, 1884). Wells and Petty (1980) provided one of the very first demonstrations of this idea by revealing the importance of body movements in shaping attitudinal responses. Specifically, their results showed that for both pro- and counter-attitudinal messages, participants who had nodded their heads agreed more with the message than participants who had shaken their heads (see also Tom, Pettersen, Lau, Burton, & Cook, 1991). Moreover, vertical and horizontal head movements have been shown to impact also the degree of confidence people have in their own thoughts towards those messages (Briñol & Petty, 2003; for a review, see Briñol & Petty, 2008).

In an early seminal study, Solarz (1960) reported that participants were faster in pulling a lever towards themselves for objects they liked and faster in pushing the lever away from themselves for disliked objects. These results conform to the general embodiment argument that motor action congruent with the valence of the words would be facilitated (see also Chen & Bargh, 1999; Neumann & Strack, 2000). Cacioppo and colleagues (1993) also revealed the significance of approach and avoidance movements in the evaluation of neutral stimuli. Their study showed that participants rated more highly a set of novel Chinese ideographs while making approaching movements (press against the palm of their hand upwards from the bottom of a table) than while making avoidance movements (press downwards). This remarkable finding and its arm movement paradigm inspired a range of subsequent studies. In another study reporting the motor congruence effect, the authors showed that when participants were asked to generate names of famous people while performing approach and avoidance movements, the former facilitated the retrieval of liked names while the latter facilitated the retrieval of disliked names (Förster & Strack, 1997, 1998). Kawakami, Phills, Steele, and Dovidio (2007) applied this paradigm to attitudes towards stereotyped groups and showed that positive attitudes towards African Americans improved after participants had performed approach actions compared to avoidance actions (see also Paladino & Castelli, 2008).

In general, social psychology has had a long-standing tradition of showing the contribution of bodily factors on attitudes and persuasion (for a review, see Briñol & Petty, 2008). However, recent research suggests that the connection between specific arm movements and stimulus valence may not be an invariant one, but rather depends, for example, on the self-relevance of the movement (Wentura, Rothermund, & Bak, 2000), the initial stimulus valence (Centerbar & Clore, 2006), the goal-relevant outcomes of actions (Maxwell & Davidson, 2007), the subjective representation of the self (Markman & Brendl, 2005), or on contextual factors (Bamford & Ward, 2008).

Other subtler bodily processes have been shown to influence the way we experience and act towards the world. In a classic experiment, Strack and colleagues (1988) reported that participants judged a set of cartoons to be funnier when holding a pen between their teeth (inductor of a smile expression) than between their lips (inhibiting smiling; see also Ito, Chiao, Devine, Lorig, & Cacioppo, 2006; Stepper & Strack, 1993). In a set of studies addressing the relationship between action and language, Mussweiler (2006) induced participants to move in a portly manner, revealing that they were more likely than participants in a control condition to describe a neutral target person as overweight. If participants were induced to move in a typically elderly manner (i.e., slowly), then they were more likely to describe a neutral target person as old. Moreover, he showed that they responded faster to words associated with features of the stereotypically elderly.

Language and body: The research

The research on how language affects motor performance and recruits neural activity comes from two complementary research orientations: namely, behavioral and neurophysiological. The binding theoretical and empirical frameworks come from neurophysiological (cf. Rizzolatti & Arbib, 1998; Rizollatti & Craighero, 2004,) and action theory (Hommel, Müsseler, Aschersleben, & Prinz, 2001) backgrounds, as well as cognitive psychology (e.g., Barsalou, 1999; Glenberg, 2008) – all of which have converging assumptions, which are outlined briefly along with the distinctive features of their demonstrations.

The embodiment argument suggests that the comprehension of concepts (e.g., a dog) or action language involves the activation of the sensorimotor modalities that are recruited on-line and which can be reactivated off-line. The *perceptual symbol systems* (PSS; Barsalou, 1999) perspective suggests that multimodal stimuli give rise to *on-line* experiences inducing modal states in the somatosensory system, the visual system as well as in affective systems. According to PSS, once established in the brain, knowledge about the categories that are represented by multimodal associative structures can be used across a number of cognitive tasks. In this view, the representations that arise in dedicated input systems during sensation and motor action can be stored and used "off-line" by means of mental simulations that have become functionally autonomous from their experiential sources.

Hearing a sentence such as "She is brushing her teeth" activates the motor system that is related to the semantic content of the description and does so somatotopically. A number of studies, including functional magnetic resonance imaging (fMRI) research, provide support for this argument (see Hauk, Johnsrude, & Pulvermüller, 2004 for a review). A large range of research for the motor grounding of concrete concepts come from the language comprehension research providing evidence that a motor modality is involved in the comprehension of language describing actions (e.g., Fischer & Zwaan, 2008; Glenberg & Kaschak, 2002; Glenberg & Robertson, 1999; Zwaan & Taylor, 2006; however, see Ghazanfor & Schroeder, 2006; Mahon & Caramazza, 2008).

A substantial amount of research shows that the comprehension of language takes place by means of sensorimotor simulations or what Barsalou refers to as "the reenactment of perceptual, motor,

and introspective states acquired during the interaction with the word, body, and mind." (2008, p. 618). A general, but not exclusive, feature of these studies is the use of perceptual and motoric "primes", which are either congruent or incongruent with the perceptual or motoric features in a sentence. What these studies essentially uncover is that congruence between "primes" and "sentence features" provides a comprehension and reading speed advantage, *inter alia*, and incongruence has, relative to the congruence condition, a disadvantage on the same variables. These studies revealed that *perceptual* (e.g., Connell, 2007; Holt & Beilock, 2006; Kaschak, Zwaan, Aveyard, & Yaxley, 2006; Richardson, Spivey, Barsalou, & McRae, 2003; Zwaan, Madden, Yaxley, & Aveyard, 2004) and *motoric* (e.g., Borreggine & Kaschak, 2006; Glenberg & Kaschak, 2002; Zwaan & Taylor, 2006) information is recruited during the processing of sentences.

In the following, we provide a few illustrative examples of this research. For instance, Zwaan and Yaxley (2003) show that spatial iconicity affects semantic-relatedness judgments. For instance, when word pairs were presented in iconic relation (e.g., *attic* presented above *basement*), then semantic-relatedness judgments were significantly faster than when they were presented in reverse iconic relation (e.g., *basement* above *attic*). Borghi, Glenberg, and Kaschak (2004) report a series of studies showing that the speed of part verification (e.g., steering wheel vs. tires) varied with the perspective imposed on the object by the language used to name the object (e.g., "You are driving a car" vs. "You are fueling a car"). Participants were slower when the perspective (e.g., driving) was incongruent with the position of the object (e.g., tires) compared to a congruent match (driving and steering wheel) – (see also Glenberg & Kaschak, 2002; Matlock, 2004; Spivey, Tyler, Richardson, & Young, 2000).

An embodied perspective suggests that language is modality specific – an idea that is alien to an amodal view: i.e., words that have to do with auditory input must be coded differently than words that are coded by visual input. From this, Pecher, Zeelenberg, and Barsalou (2003) have argued that modality specificity would mean that switching from one modality (e.g., auditory) to another (e.g., visual) when processing the features of the same object should have costs. The participant's task was to determine if an object had a particular feature or not (e.g., Is a blender loud?). This was preceded by another judgment that was modality congruent (e.g., Do leaves rustle?). When the modality between two judgments was incongruent (e.g., Are leaves green?), there was an increase in the time required to confirm the feature as belonging to the object.

Most of the behavioral studies that have been done and the small sample that we have reviewed for illustrative purposes have been conducted with either single words or entire sentences. However, two recent reports have investigated how motor resonance unfolds during sentence comprehension, providing some novel insights into the temporal resolution of motor resonance (cf. Taylor & Zwaan, 2008; Zwaan & Taylor, 2006).

Another field of investigation that reveals motor resonance effects is to be found in research on the consequences of facial expressions of emotions and its more recent extension to the link between linguistic expressions of facial expressions and how they affect facial musculature. It is well known that the observation of a smiling or frowning face induces a subtle movement of the smiling muscles (*zygomatic major*) and frowning muscles (*corrugator supercilii* muscle region; e.g., Dimberg & Petterson, 2000; Dimberg, Thunberg, & Elmehed, 2000). This occurs even when such faces are presented subliminally. These experiments suggest what has been referred to as an automatic mimicry effect. Recently, Foroni and Semin (2009) demonstrated an interesting motor resonance effect: namely, that reading or hearing a verb (e.g., to smile, to frown) or an adjective (e.g., happy, angry) has the same sensorimotor consequences as seeing a happy or angry face, providing further evidence for the motor resonance induced by language in the specific domain of emotional expressions and states (see Chapter 11).

Finally, there is evidence of the neural mapping of language and action verbs in particular (Pulvermüller, 2005). In a recent fMRI study, Hauk and colleagues (2004) showed that listening to verbs referring to leg actions activates regions of the motor cortex responsible for control of the leg; in the case of verbs referring to hand actions, motor cortex regions responsible for hand control are activated, and so on. Using fMRI, Tettamanti et al. (2005) demonstrated somatotopic representation of actions described by simple sentences (e.g., "I kick the ball"). Although the fMRI research constitutes a fascinating illustration of the neural grounding of action verbs, the data remain ambiguous: they might reflect simulation of action after hearing action verbs (i.e., an association), or they might instead indicate that activity in motor areas of the brain is important for understanding these verbs.

Grounding abstract concepts

While an embodied approach to action-driven sensorimotor-based grounding of concrete concepts and categories presents some plausibility, the direct sensorimotor-based grounding runs into difficulties when it comes to concepts that we cannot touch, see, taste, or smell (cf. Boroditsky & Prinz, 2008). There is an abundance of abstract concepts such as time, morality, truth, happiness, health, and valence. This question has been at the heart of recent discussions in embodied approaches to cognition (cf. Barsalou, 2008; Dove, 2009; Glenberg et al., 2008; Mahon & Caramazza, 2008).

One solution to this puzzle is furnished by *conceptual metaphor theory* (CMT; Lakoff & Johnson, 1999). In this view, thinking about abstract concepts is structured by perceptual experiences, such as space (Tversky, Kugelmass, & Winter, 1991). According to CMT (Lakoff & Johnson, 1980), only a few concrete concepts are learned through bodily experience such as spatial orientation and containment, while the majority of concepts are more abstract and their understanding is "accomplished" through repeated pairings with the concrete domains (e.g., Landau, Meier, & Kiefer, 2010). Thus, abstract concepts are understood through analogical extensions from concrete, bodily experienced domains. We review some illustrative domains to highlight the grounding of the abstract concepts: namely, morality, time, and valence.

The concept of *morality* is abounding with metaphors of cleanliness (e.g., Kövecses, 2000), including expressions such as a "clean conscience" or a "disgusting act". The interesting question this metaphorical association raises is: Do people "embody" the concept of morality with activities to do with cleaning? The first example comes from Zhong and Liljenquist (2006) who showed that recalling unethical actions or events from memory enhances the accessibility of cleansing-related words (e.g., soap or shower) and influences participants' desire and preference for cleansing products compared to recalling ethical behaviors.

Research by Schnall, Benton, and Harvey (2008) shows a bidirectional relationship between morality and physical cleanliness. They found that when participants were primed with cleanliness they made less severe moral judgments than participants in a neutral condition. In a second study, and after being exposed to a disgusting film clip, participants who washed their hands were milder in their judgments in moral dilemmas compared to those who had not washed their hands (see also Schnall, Haidt, Clore, & Jordan, 2008, and Wheatley & Haidt, 2005, for evidence of the link between disgust and morality). Refining the relevance of the cleanliness metaphor, Lee and Schwarz (2010) demonstrated that the metaphor *morality-cleanliness* is specific to the *type* of action involved in the production of the immoral action. They argue and show that people are more likely to purify those specific body parts involved in the production of the moral transgression.

Thus, participants who lied via voice mail preferred a mouthwash product and those who lied via e-mail preferred a hand sanitizer.

The abundance of metaphors that locate *time* spatially is comparable to those grounding morality with cleanliness (e.g., a *short* while ago, a *long* break, going for a *long* journey, looking *forward* to tomorrow). Moreover, the diverse devices that mark time physically resort to spatial relationships (analog watches, time-lines, clocks, sundials, hourglasses, etc. – see A. Clark, 1997; Traugott, 1978; Tversky et al., 1991). Deriving from CMT (Lakoff & Johnson, 1999), which proposes that thoughts about abstract concepts such as time are structured by perceptual experiences such as space, recent work has revealed the intricate subtleties through which the cognitive representation of time is inherently intertwined with the representation of space (Boroditsky, 2000, 2001; Boroditsky & Ramscar, 2002; Casasanto & Boroditsky, 2008) or the categorization of time-related words (Lakens, Semin, & Garrido, 2011).

For instance, bimanual response tasks have revealed compatibility effects between time-related stimuli and the spatial position of response keys (e.g., Ishihara, Keller, Rossetti, & Prinz, 2008). Similar stimulus–response compatibility effects have also been observed in other studies (e.g., Vallesi, Binns, & Shallice, 2008; Vallesi, McIntosh, & Stuss, 2011; Weger & Pratt, 2008). Lakens and colleagues (2011) showed that when past and future referent words are presented auditorily with equal loudness to both ears, participants disambiguate the auditorily equally balanced future words to the right ear and the past words to the left ear.

While the studies cited above examine spatial grounding that anchors time on an axis that runs from the left (past) to the right (future) that is cultural and probably writing direction specific, this is by no means universal. Research to date has shown time to be represented from not only left to right, but also right to left, front to back, or back to front (e.g., Boroditsky, 2000; Boroditsky & Ramscar, 2002; Fuhrman & Boroditsky, 2010). Notably, the reference point for these instances of grounding is relative to the body. In a recent paper, Boroditsky and Gabi (2010) report that Pormpuraawans (an Australian Aboriginal Community) arranged time according to *cardinal directions: east to west*. This fascinating report reveals both the relativity and generality of how the abstract concept of time is understood. Time is grounded spatially, which appears to be a universal: however, the spatial referents that ground time vary considerably across cultures.

Similar to time, *affect* is represented in space: however, now with the vertical dimension (e.g., "good is up") or alternatively as fluid in a container (She was filled with sadness. He was overflowing with joy) or as natural forces (She was swept off her feet. He was engulfed by anger) – (see Crawford, 2009).

Empirical evidence investigating the relation between affect and verticality has evidenced an explosive growth (cf. Crawford, 2009; Landau, et al., 2010), supporting the argument that metaphors alluding to the vertical spatial orientation like "I'm feeling up" or "I'm feeling down" serve to structure the way people think and represent affect-related concepts. For instance, Meier and Robinson (2004) were able to show that positive words (e.g., ethical and friendly) were classified more rapidly as positive when they were presented at the top rather than at the bottom of a monitor, while the opposite was true for negative words (see Casasanto, 2009). This idea of grounding affect in vertical space was soon extended to other areas beyond categorization, such as to spatial memory. For instance, Crawford, Margolies, Drake, and Murphy (2006), observed that participants' retrieval of presented images revealed an upward position bias for positive images and a downward bias for negative images. Recently, Casasanto and Dijkstra (2010) reported that people were faster in retrieving and generating positive autobiographical memories when performing upward movements and negative memories when performing downward movements (see also Lanciano, Curci, & Semin, 2010; Palma, Garrido, & Semin, 2011).

Another line of research has been showing the link between valence and size. For example, Meier, Robinson, and Caven (2008) have shown that positive words presented in a large font were evaluated more quickly and accurately than those presented in a small font, whereas the reverse pattern was true for negative words.

Other research has explored the metaphorical use of "bright" (e.g., "Bright ideas") or "dark" ("Dark days") to refer to positive or negative aspects, respectively, which seems to be an established association across different cultures (e.g., Adams & Osgood, 1973). Experimentally, this association finds support in the work of Meier, Robinson, and Clore (2004) who observed that participants' responses were facilitated when the word meaning (e.g., gentle) and the font color (white) were congruent with the metaphor. Related research has shown that stimulus valence biases brightness judgments in metaphor-congruent ways. For instance, Meier, Robinson, Crawford, and Ahlvers (2007) report that participants judge squares to be the lighter more often after evaluating positive words than negative words.

These diverse studies reveal that the different metaphors about space, size, or brightness affect the classification of valenced stimuli and have effects on memory and evaluative processes as a function of the congruence or incongruence between the source and target. With these studies on abstract concepts and how they are grounded, we come to the conclusion of the section on the fourth pillar of socially situated cognition.

Scaffolding cognitive activity

When we need money or wish to post a letter we resort to cultural artifacts such as cash dispensers or red postboxes (in some countries). When we want to know which platform the next train to our destination departs from we ask a railway official. Such artifacts and "experts" constitute crucial landmarks that provide reference points with their distinct markers (i.e., red boxes, uniforms) for the organization of complex goal-directed action, and also serve as external memory tools (cf. Caporeal, 1997).

Cognition makes use of tools and other aspects of the individual's environment, aside from people and groups. Moreover, to lean on people and groups one also needs tools (e.g., language) to coordinate and synchronize social interaction.

Tools provide scaffolds for cognitive activity (A. Clark, 1997). Mechanical tools such as hammers, saws, and drills provide scaffolds that aid achieving solutions (e.g., building a chair). Their absence would make such solutions difficult if not impossible. Other types of tools such as language (Semin, 1998) are used to synchronize and coordinate communication between, for instance, different crew members of a ship who are navigating it (cf. Hutchins, 1995). Such coordinated action is achieved by resorting to both physical tools (charts and compasses) as well as utilizing and coordinating the socially distributed knowledge between crew members through communication via language in which knowledge is literally stored. Thus, the physical tools and the coordinated use of socially distributed knowledge become scaffolds for the successful navigation of a large ship. Both internal (e.g., concepts) and external resources (e.g., tools) contribute to the regulation of action. It is self-evident that closer attention has to be paid to such artifacts in order to understand the coordination of social interaction (Hodges & Baron, 1992).

Social and material scaffolds are the result of cognitive efforts to find adaptive solutions to problems and constitute standardized solutions to recurring problems. What is the best solution to drive a nail into hard material? How do I navigate a vessel over open water? In short, scaffolds constitute solutions to problems. Their properties emerge adaptively for the type of task that is confronted. Moreover, they furnish socially situated cognition by delegating processing demands to external aids, and resources such as experts. Once they are shaped over time, they preserve the functional knowledge that has shaped their structure. Therefore, constraints upon human cognition are determined not only by the architecture of our minds and bodies but also by external resources or scaffolds.

Non-social scaffolds: Tools and the architecture of the human body

Tools and their shapes have evolved in order to solve recurrent situated problems. Thus, their design was constrained by the nature of the task they were expected to solve. But that contributes only to part of their design. The other part is they have to be adapted to the human body (cf. Semin, 1998, p. 230–231). The unique quality of such tools is their two-way adaptation. Tools are dually adapted to the constraints of the human body and to the constraints of the object to which they extend human action.

The design of tools is therefore highly informative because they display information about the constraints that have shaped their dual adaptation. They carry information about the type of task they have been constructed for. But equally important, they display information about the constraints that are introduced by our brain–body makeup. This is illustrated with the example of a pair of scissors. The shape of a scissors' handle is an adaptation to the particular grip that is the most efficient way of distributing pressure by the hand. In the case of writing, the particular spacing between letters in a word and between words is informative of the facilitatory link between perceptual processing, reading, and text comprehension. An interesting insight of tool properties can therefore be informative about both psychological and task constraints. Examining tool properties can also be informative about how an agent is coupled to the problem or task.

One of the ways in which the situated cognition approach opens new ways of thinking is by drawing attention to how much we rely on the environment to unload information and thus facilitate and structure cognition. An often-cited example of how such unloading takes place is illustrated by how we solve a difficult arithmetic operation like multiplying two three-digit numbers. The mental operations in this case are distributed by using pencil and paper. As we manipulate symbols, these external resources become part of an overall cognitive system, functioning as memory storage, offering cues for what digits to process next, and so on (A. Clark, 1999). Other classical examples of how we manipulate the physical environment as an aid for memory is leaving an empty milk bottle by the door as a reminder to get milk the next time we go out or placing important material on top of one's desk in order to focus one's attention on the relevant task (Kirsch, 1995; Kirsch & Maglio, 1994).

Another example of how people actively structure their immediate environment to optimize their performance can be observed in how bartenders structure bartending activities (Beach, 1988). Expert bartenders who are confronted with a number of diverse drinks orders line up differently shaped glasses. These glasses correspond to different kinds of drinks in a spatial order that reproduces the temporal sequence of drink orders. This type of exploitation of the physical environment releases memory resources. With the spatial organization of the glasses, the expert bartender does not have to think about either the sequence or the type of drinks that have to be prepared. Bartending is driven by cued action and recall, i.e., by *epistemic* actions (cf. A. Clark, 2008). In contrast to mere *physical* actions, epistemic actions make computation easier, faster, and more reliable. These types of epistemic actions that involve (*inter alia*) the exploitation of space by ordering glasses on the bar in a distinct fashion simplify choice and perception. These types of scaffolds induced by epistemic actions are different from designed tools such as a slide ruler, which reduces demands upon internal memory (cf. A. Clark, 2008). These examples illustrate how the external actions an agent performs on the physical environment can change its own computational state or otherwise cue, prioritize, and structure even the most demanding cognitive tasks.

While cognition can surely be distributed across artifacts and situations that effectively facilitate and structure cognition, extending cognitive processes out beyond the individual, a large amount of evidence emphasizes that cognition is also distributed across other people who participate in the construction of mental representations and the processing of information in a way that extends our cognitive powers.

Social scaffolds: Socially distributed cognition

Socially distributed cognition is best exemplified in tasks that supersede the abilities of an individual. Take navigating a large vessel (e.g., Hutchins, 1995) or performing open-heart surgery. These are tasks that require the finely tuned coordination of activities that brings together teams of "experts" who lean on each other's knowledge to be able to perform a collective task efficiently and successfully. What are the distinctive features of such teams? They consist of diverse experts (e.g., in the case of the heart surgery team, the surgeon, the

anesthetist, etc.). They each have their own specialty and their unshared knowledge base that is highly relevant for the performance of the task at hand. What the team shares is knowledge about the joint activity and the coordination of these activities. Thus, the specialized knowledge that each individual holds is crucial for the performance of the task, and this knowledge is distributed across the individual members of the team. The coordinated product of the individuals constitutes a type of collectively constituted knowledge or cognition that is unique because the entire process of the operation is not a single person's production but a collectively coordinated "cognition as action" that drives the operation from its beginning to its end. Thus, the successful accomplishment of such tasks that supersede an individual's capabilities relies on members "leaning" on each other's competencies and being scaffolded by the others in the team without having to know the details of the other member's expertise.

Hutchins (1995) provides an excellent analysis of this type of socially distributed cognition with a systematic investigation of how a large Navy ship is navigated. The particular activity of navigating is a cyclical one and involves processing complex, socially distributed information. The task is executed by a number of individuals with discrete roles (reading a timepiece, identifying a landmark, communicating a bearing, etc.), who in turn are served by a number of physical and computational tools (charts, protractors, compasses, etc.). The performance of the task is achieved in a series of coordinated activities between a number of different individuals who draw on each other's expertise and thus establish a type of knowledge that supersedes the unique specialisms of the individuals involved. A team member does not need to know the specialized knowledge that is distributed among the other members. However, the execution of the task requires that the members share knowledge, which makes it possible to apply the distributed expertise. Thus, similar to our knowledge of how to use "tools", we utilize each other's specialized knowledge to perform a task, thereby engaging in a process that "extends out beyond the individual" (A. Clark & Chalmers, 1998).

One of the best examples of socially distributed processing in social psychology is the study of *transactive memory* (e.g., Wegner, 1986, 1995; Wegner, Erber, & Raymond, 1991; Wegner, Giuliano, & Hertel, 1985). This research highlights how memory becomes progressively specialized, socially shared, indexed, and complementary among people who know each other well. The research conducted on this subject suggests that individuals in close relationships develop a distributed memory system, such that they divide responsibility for the encoding, storage, and retrieval of information from different domains, according to their implicitly shared knowledge of each other. Through self-disclosure and shared experiences, members of the system become aware not only of what information they themselves know but also what the other members know across knowledge domains. The important aspect of transactive memory in this context is that the coordination of the inter-individual memory expertise gives rise to a *qualitatively different memory system*. By leaning on each other, the individual minds are enhanced by the socially available and accessible scaffolds. This scaffolded memory system is more elaborate than that of any single individual member's memory (Wegner, 1986). Transactive memory is a system that is irreducible, operates at the group level, and depends on a distribution of specializations within this system, as in the case of partners (Wegner, 1995). Note that each person in the system individually lacks critical pieces of information. Nevertheless, such specialization reduces the cognitive load of each individual, while providing the dyad or group access to a larger pool of information across domains and reduces the wasted cognitive effort represented by overlapping individual knowledge.

This is illustrated by the fact that friends and couples jointly remember information better than strangers do (e.g., Andersson & Rönnberg, 1995; Hollingshead, 1998a,1998b; Wegner, 1986, 1995; Wegner et al., 1991). Other findings about collaborative remembering in older couples lend additional support to this idea. Although elderly individuals exhibit memory deficits relative to younger adults, when elderly couples who have been married for 40 year or more are allowed to work together, they remember just as much as young couples (Dixon & Gould, 1996). By this account, individual memory systems can become involved in larger, organized social memory systems that have emergent group mind properties not traceable to the individuals.

The comparison of individual and group performance constitutes a further related line of research, exploring the distributed nature of cognition. A common and not surprising set of findings are that: groups recall more than a single individual (e.g., Lorge & Solomon, 1961); group recognition is more accurate (Clark, Hori, Putnam, & Martin, 2000; Hinsz, 1990); groups are more confident in their answers, but discriminate less well between their accurate and inaccurate answers (e.g., Stephenson, 1984); and groups show more extreme biases in their recall than do individuals. Finally, there is evidence that groups arrive at stable accounts of their experience more rapidly than do individuals, implying that group

recollection may lead to a more rapid consolidation of a long-term account of an event (Clark & Stephenson, 1989; Weldon, 2001; Weldon & Bellinger, 1997). These studies constitute specific instances of socially scaffolded memory.

Notably, distributed cognitive processes do not always result in positive outcomes. An example is the case of groupthink phenomena (Janis, 1972), collaborative memory (e.g., Barnier & Sutton, 2008; Barnier, Sutton, Harris, & Wilson, 2008; Echterhoff & Hirst, 2009; Garcia-Marques, Garrido, Hamilton, & Ferreira, 2012; Garrido, Garcia-Marques, & Hamilton, 2012a, 2012b; see Rajaram & Pereira-Passarin, 2010 for a review) or even socially induced false remembering. Groupthink (e.g., Janis, 1972), constitutes an example of group cognition in which certain conditions lead groups to make risky and poor decisions. Other studies have shown that memory performance is impaired when people collaborate at recall compared to nominal groups (created by pooling the non-redundant responses of individuals working alone), a phenomenon termed *collaborative inhibition* (Basden, Basden, Bryner, & Thomas, 1997; Basden, Basden, & Henry, 2000; Meudell, Hitch, & Boyle, 1995; Meudell, Hitch, & Kirby, 1992). Another illustration is to be found in research on the social contagion of memory, where the incorporation of others' memories may lead to socially induced false remembering (e.g., Meade & Roediger, 2002; Roediger, Meade, & Bergman, 2001).

The "harmful consequences" of collaboration on memory and other distributed cognitive processes have met resistance because they are counterintuitive, given lay and scholarly beliefs in the benefits of collaboration. This is probably the result of the mainstream emphasis on accuracy and efficiency. However, other social, cultural, and political goals such as the development of positive social relationships (Clark & Stephenson, 1989), arriving at a shared representation of the past (Coman, Manier, & Hirst, 2009; Cuc, Ozuru, Manier, & Hirst, 2006), or to establish group identity (Hirst & Manier, 2008; Wertsch, 2008) constitute substantial benefits of distributed cognitive processes in general, and collaborative memory in particular. Shared memories also facilitate communication of events, interpersonal relations, group histories, and government and social policy, as well as the characterization of groups and institutions (Weldon & Bellinger, 1997). Indeed, even the social contagion of memory may have an adaptive function. People with a bad memory can rely on others who can supply detailed accounts of events that have been collectively experienced, and thus update their memoires (Meade & Rodiger, 2002). As Rajaram and Pereira-Pasarin (2010) have pointed out, taken together, the advantages of collaborative memory systems may overcome their ill effects.

Given the pervasiveness of distributed cognition in our daily social lives (e.g., Levine, Resnick, & Higgins, 1993) it is surprising to note that relatively little social psychological research has explored its dynamics. Notably, a purely individual level of explanation fails to account for the often distributed nature of cognition, nor does it address the possible influence of the social contexts and purposes that often determine the processes and contents of our cognitive activity. Nevertheless, many cognitive processes are distributed, and to study and account for them seems crucial for a complete understanding of our social-cognitive processes.

CONCLUSION AND OPEN QUESTIONS

The main goal of the preceding five sections started with a specification of the level of analysis afforded by a socially situated approach to cognition. The dynamic nature of the phenomena under examination – namely, their emergent nature – supersedes individual cognition and action and is best captured with a macroscopic view because emergent phenomena control the parts that generate and constitute it and not vice versa.

The way cognition emerges from the interaction with the social and physical world is driven by unique features of the architecture of the human perceptual-motor system that is specifically designed for the reproduction of movements of conspecifics. This biologically driven advantage furnishes privileged knowledge about conspecifics and constitutes the basis for interaction, namely communication.

Another important assumption that is made throughout this chapter is that "cognition is for adaptive action". The implications of this assumption are unfolded in the subsequent sections. If cognition is for action, then concepts cannot be understood as abstracted, timeless, amodal representations. They have to be understood as the result of the interaction between an agent and the social and physical world. As such cognition can only be addressed by considering the contextual and situational influences that shape cognitive processes and behavior as well as the functional role of our mental representations, goals and feelings as guides for action.

A situated view of cognition holds that objects and persons retain in their representations the sensorimotor features of the actions that bond them with agents. This bonding is retained in the nature of concepts, and fundamental sensorimotor experiences are used to ground even abstract concepts, which do not have any "immediate" bodily experiential elements. The fact that sensorimotor bonding is necessary invites the integration of "body architecture" into how concepts have evolved, i.e., embodiment.

Finally, our interactions with the social and physical environment are not mere "direct" physical exchanges but largely mediated by "tools". Tools are culturally evolved artifacts that are designed for the specific and regular tasks that are faced in everyday realities. They (e.g., pocket calculators, hammers, languages) have very distinctive features in their design – they are adapted to both human propensities (body, brain) and the task at hand (putting a nail into a hard surface or communication). Moreover, a distinctive feature of our social environment is that we contribute to this environment and utilize it at the same time, since we are an integral part of a socially distributed network of knowledge that supersedes individual cognition. Thus, instead of using a single computer with massive processing power as the model for human cognition, the socially situated perspective invites thinking of cognition as a network of interconnected computers that have computational resources superseding the capacities and potential of a single computer. This metaphor captures the essence of socially situated cognition but needs biologically endowed bodies as its operational basis.

The socially situated cognition perspective is no more than a set of pre-paradigmatic assumptions in the Thomas Kuhnian sense. They represent the rumblings of dissatisfaction with the "standard representational" paradigm, but the current situation is no way near to having a fully interwoven, integrated, and mature theoretical framework to guide systematic research. Certain elements of situated cognition's pre-paradigmatic assumptions have captured the imagination and opened visions of research that would not have been possible prior to these developments. Chief amongst these is the work emerging under the broad but diffuse and ill-defined notion of embodiment. The number of demonstrations (Pillar 4) across a whole range of issues – from language and motor resonance to abstract concepts such as time, morality, and valence – is breathtaking. Nevertheless, the theoretical integration is loose and mostly local, with a somewhat global reference to metaphors. Other elements – such as the socially distributed cognition as action – require the introduction of novel research paradigms. For instance, Richardson's work on joint perception is one such innovative approach (e.g., Richardson, Hoover, & Ghane, 2008).

What stands out in the research streams evolving under the situated cognition perspective is the discrepancy between the individual foci that have captured attention (e.g., embodiment, cognition is for action, cognition is socially distributed) and the lack of integration between the different pillars, assumptions. For instance, embodiment research as a burgeoning field does not even pay lip service to the social aspect of concepts. The entire work in the embodiment field refers to individual reasoning, thinking, and representation. Obviously, concepts not only evolve to serve individual reasoning but also social communication. They are fundamental in grounding the basis for socially distributed cognition. Not surprisingly, communication constraints must play an important role in the evolution of concepts – abstract or concrete – since concepts are as much for communication as they are for intra-psychological processes. Thus, the cross-fertilization between the pre-paradigmatic assumptions is not necessarily current, but an integrated vision of human functioning requires an integrated conceptual framework rather than succumbing to the inspiration of one of the pillars at the expense of considering the informative constraints of the other pillars.

Most of the work developed by those who claim a socially situated nature of cognition has not yet been incorporated into mainstream social psychology and social cognition. Nevertheless, the central assumptions of situated cognition are crucial for the development of an informed and informative social cognition that is not merely a subdomain of social psychology, but a centerpiece of any psychology.

REFERENCES

Abler, W. (1989). On the particulate principle of self-diversifying systems. *Journal of Social and Biological Structures, 12,* 1–13.

Adams, F. M., & Osgood, C. E. (1973). Cross-cultural study of affective meanings of color. *Journal of Cross-Cultural Psychology, 4,* 135–156.

Adelman, P. K., & Zajonc, R. (1989). Facial efference and the experience of emotion. *Annual Review of Psychology, 40,* 249–280.

Andersson, J., & Rönnberg, J. (1995). Recall suffers from collaboration: Joint recall effects of friendship and task complexity. *Applied Cognitive Psychology, 9,* 199–211.

Baldwin, M. W. (1992). Relational schemas and the processing of social information. *Psychological Bulletin, 112,* 461–484.

Bamford, S., & Ward, R. (2008). Predispositions to approach and avoid are contextually sensitive and goal dependent. *Emotion, 8,* 174–183.

Barnier, A. J., & Sutton, J. (2008). From individual to collective memory: theoretical and empirical perspectives. *Memory, 16,* 177–182.

Barnier, A. J., Sutton, J., Harris, C. B., & Wilson, R. A. (2008). A conceptual and empirical framework for the social distribution of cognition: the case of memory. *Cognitive Systems Research, 9,* 33–51.

Bargh, J. A. (1999). The cognitive monster: The case against the controllability of automatic stereotype effects. In S. Chaiken and Y. Trope (Eds.), *Dual-process theories in social psychology* (pp. 361–382). New York: Guilford Press.

Bargh, J. A., Chen, M., & Burrows, L. (1996). Automaticity of social behavior: Direct effects of trait construct and stereotype activation on action. *Journal of Personality and Social Psychology, 71,* 230–244.

Baron, R. A. (1997). The sweet smell of helping: Effects of pleasant ambient fragrance on prosocial behavior in shopping malls. *Personality and Social Psychology Bulletin, 23,* 498–503.

Barsalou, L. W. (1999). Perceptual symbol systems. *Behavioral and Brain Sciences, 22,* 577–660.

Barsalou, L. W. (2008). Grounded cognition. *Annual Review of Psychology, 59,* 617–645.

Basden, B. H., Basden, D. R., Bryner, S., & Thomas, R. L. (1997). A comparison of group and individual remembering: Does group participation disrupt retrieval? *Journal of Experimental Psychology: Learning, Memory and Cognition, 23,* 1176–1189.

Basden, B. H., Basden, D. R., & Henry, S. (2000). Cost and benefits of collaborative remembering. *Applied Cognitive Psychology, 14,* 497–507.

Beach, K. (1988). The role of external mnemonic symbols in acquiring an occupation. In M. M. Gruneberg & R. N. Sykes (Eds.), *Practical aspects of memory* (Vol. 1, pp. 342–346). New York: Wiley.

Blair, I. V. (2002). The malleability of automatic stereotypes and prejudice. *Personality and Social Psychology Review, 6,* 242–261.

Blair, I. V., Ma, J. E., & Lenton, A. P. (2001). Imagining stereotypes away: The moderation of implicit stereotypes through mental imagery. *Journal of Personality and Social Psychology, 81,* 828–841.

Bless, H. (2001). Mood and the use of general knowledge structures. In L. L. Martin & G. L. Clore (Eds.), *Theories of mood and cognition: A user's guidebook* (pp. 9–26). Mahwah, NJ: Lawrence Erlbaum Associates.

Bless, H., Bohner, G., Schwarz, N., & Strack, F. (1990). Mood and persuasion: A cognitive response analysis. *Personality and Social Psychology Bulletin, 16,* 331–345.

Bless, H., Schwarz, N., & Kemmelmeier, M. (1996). Mood and stereotyping: The impact of moods on the use of general knowledge structures. In M. Hewstone & W. Stroebe (Eds.), *European Review of Social Psychology, 7,* 63–93.

Bless, H., Schwarz, N., & Wieland, R. (1996). Mood and the impact of category membership and individuating information. *European Journal of Social Psychology, 26,* 935–959.

Bodenhausen, G. V., Kramer, G. P., & Süsser, K. (1994). Happiness and stereotypic thinking in social judgment. *Journal of Personality and Social Psychology, 66,* 621–632.

Bodenhausen, G. V., Schwarz, N., Bless, H., & Wänke, M. (1995). Effects of atypical exemplars on racial beliefs: Enlightened racism or generalized appraisals? *Journal of Experimental Social Psychology, 31,* 48–63.

Borghi, A. M., Glenberg, A. M., & Kaschak, M. P. (2004). Putting words in perspective. *Memory & Cognition, 32,* 863–873.

Boroditsky, L. (2000). Metaphoric structuring: Understanding time through spatial metaphors. *Cognition, 75,* 1–28.

Boroditsky, L. (2001). Does language shape thought?: Mandarin and English speakers' con-ceptions of time. *Cognitive Psychology, 43,* 1–22.

Boroditsky, L., & Gaby, A. (2010). Remembrances of Times East: Absolute spatial representations of time in an Australian Aboriginal community. *Psychological Science, 21,* 1635–1639.

Boroditsky, L., & Prinz, J. (2008). What thoughts are made of. In G. R. Semin & E. R. Smith (Eds.), *Embodied grounding: Social, cognitive, affective, and neuroscientific approaches* (pp. 98–115). New York: Cambridge University Press.

Boroditsky, L., & Ramscar, M. (2002). The roles of body and mind in abstract thought. *Psychological Science, 13,* 185–189.

Borreggine, K. L., & Kaschak, M. P. (2006). The action–sentence compatibility effect: It's all in the timing. *Cognitive Science, 30,* 1097–1112.

Bower, G. H. (1981). Mood and memory. *American Psychologist, 36,* 129–148.

Brinõl, P., & Petty, R. E. (2003). Overt head movements and persuasion: A self-validation analysis. *Journal of Personality and Social Psychology, 84,* 1123–1139.

Briñol, P., & Petty, R. E. (2008). Embodied persuasion: Fundamental processes by which bodily responses can impact attitudes. In G. R. Semin & E. R. Smith (Eds.), *Embodied grounding: Social, cognitive, affective, and neuroscientific approaches* (pp. 184–207). New York: Cambridge University Press.

Brooks, R. A. (1999). *Cambrian intelligence.* Cambridge, MA: MIT Press.

Brunswik, E. (1955). Representative design and probabilistic theory in a functional psychology. *Psychological Review, 62,* 193–217.

Buccino, G., Lui, F., Canessa, N., Patteri, I., Lagravinese, G., Benuzzi, F., et al. (2004). Neural circuits involved in the recognition of actions performed by non-conspecifics: An fMRI study. *Journal of Cognitive Neuroscience, 16,* 114–126.

Cacioppo, J. T., Priester, J. R., & Berntson, G. G. (1993). Rudimentary determinants of attitudes. II. Arm flexion and extension have differential effects on attitudes. *Journal of Personality and Social Psychology, 65,* 5–17.

Cantor, N., & Kihlstrom, J. F. (1989). Social intelligence and cognitive assessments of personality. In R. S. Wyer & T. K. Srull (Eds.), *Advances in social cognition* (Vol. 2, pp. 1–59). Hillsdale, NJ: Lawrence Erlbaum Associates.

Caporael, L. (1997). The evolution of truly social cognition: The core configurations model. *Personality and Social Psychology Review, 1,* 276–298.

Carlston, D. E. (1994). Associated systems theory: A systematic approach to the cognitive representation of persons and events. In R. S. Wyer (Ed.), *Advances in social cognitio* (Vol. 7, *Associated systems theory,* pp. 1–78). Hillsdale, NY: Lawrence Erlbaum Associates.

Casasanto, D. (2009). When is a linguistic metaphor a conceptual metaphor? In V. Evans & S. Pourcel (Eds.), *New directions in cognitive linguistics* (pp. 127–145). Amsterdam: John Benjamins.

Casasanto, D., & Boroditsky, L. (2008). Time in the mind: Using space to think about time. *Cognition, 106,* 579–593.

Casasanto, D. & Dijkstra, K. (2010). Motor action and emotional memory. *Cognition, 115,* 179–185.

Centerbar, D., & Clore, G. L. (2006). Do approach–avoidance actions create attitudes? *Psychological Science, 17,* 22–29.

Chaiken, S., Liberman, A., & Eagly, A. H. (1989). Heuristic and systematic information processing within and beyond the persuasion context. In J. S. Uleman & J. A. (Eds.), *Unintended thought* (pp. 212–252). New York: Guilford Press.

Chen, S., & Bargh, J. A. (1999). Consequences of automatic evaluation: Immediate behavior predispositions to approach or avoid the stimulus. *Personality and Social Psychology Bulletin, 25,* 215–224.

Chomsky, N. (1959). Review of verbal behavior by B. F. Skinner. *Language, 35,* 26–58.

Clark, A. (1997). *Being there: Putting brain, body and world together again.* Cambridge, MA, MIT Press.

Clark, A. (1999). Where brain, body, and world collide. *Cognitive Systems Research, 1,* 5–17.

Clark, A. (2008). *Supersizing the mind. Embodiment, action and cognitive extension.* Oxford: Oxford University Press.

Clark, A., & Chalmers, D. (1998). The extended mind. *Analysis, 58,* 1, 7–19.

Clark, H., & Brennan, S. (1991). Grounding in communication. In L. B. Resnick, J. M. Levine & S. D. Teasley (Eds.), *Perspectives on socially shared cognition* (pp. 127–149). Washington, DC: APA.

Clark, N. K., & Stephenson, G. M. (1989). Group remembering. In P. B. Paulus (Ed.), *Psychology of group influence* (pp. 357–391). Hillsdale, NJ: Lawrence Erlbaum Associates.

Clark, S. E., Hori, A., Putnam, A., & Martin, T. P. (2000). Group collaboration in recognition memory. *Journal of Experimental Psychology: Learning, Memory, and Cognition, 26,* 578–588.

Coats, S., & Smith, E. R. (1999). Perceptions of gender subtypes: Sensitivity to recent exemplar activation and in-group/out-group differences. *Personality and Social Psychology Bulletin, 25,* 515–526.

Coman, A., Manier, D., & Hirst, W. (2009). Forgetting the unforgettable through conversation: Socially shared retrieval-induced forgetting of September 11 memories. *Psychological Science, 20,* 627–633.

Connell, L. (2007). Representing object color in language comprehension. *Cognition, 102,* 476–485.

Crawford, L. E. (2009). Conceptual metaphors of affect. *Emotion Review, 1,* 129–139.

Crawford, L. E., Margolies, S. M., Drake, J. T., & Murphy, M. E. (2006). Affect biases memory of location: Evidence for the spatial representation of affect. *Cognition and Emotion, 20,* 1153–1169.

Crocker, J., Fiske, S. T., & Taylor, S. E. (1984). Schematic bases of belief change. In R. Eiser (Ed.), *Attitudinal judgment* (pp.197–226). New York: Springer.

Cuc, A., Ozuru, Y., Manier, D., & Hirst, W. (2006). On the formation of collective memories: The role of a dominant narrator. *Memory & Cognition, 34,* 752–762.

Cuddy, A. J. C., Fiske, S. T., & Glick, P. (2008). Warmth and competence as universal dimensions of social perception: The Stereotype Content Model and the BIAS Map. *Advances in Experimental Social Psychology, 40,* 61–149.

Cuddy, A. J. C., Fiske, S. T., Kwan, V.S.Y., Glick, P., Demoulin, S., Leyens, J. Ph., et al. (2009). Stereotype content model across cultures: Universal similarities and some differences. *British Journal of Social Psychology, 48,* 1–33.

Darwin, C. (1965). *The expression of emotions in man and animals.* Chicago, IL: University of Chicago Press. (Original work published 1872.)

Demattè, M. L., Österbauer, R., & Spence, C. (2007). Olfactory cues modulate facial attractiveness. *Chemical Senses, 32,* 603–610.

Devine, P. G. (1989). Stereotypes and prejudice: Their automatic and controlled components. *Journal of Personality and Social Psychology, 56,* 5–18.

Devine, P. G., Hamilton, D. L., & Ostrom, T. M. (1994). *Social cognition: Impact on social psychology.* Orlando, FL: Academic Press.

Dimberg, U., & Petterson, M. (2000). Facial reactions to happy and angry facial expressions: Evidence for right hemisphere dominance. *Psychophysiology, 37,* 693–696.

Dimberg, U., Thunberg, M., & Elmehed, K. (2000). Unconscious facial reactions to emotional facial expressions. *Psychological Science, 11,* 86–89.

Dixon, R., & Gould, O. (1996). Adults telling and retelling stories collaboratively. In P. B. Baltes & U. M. Staudinger (Eds.), *Interactive minds: Life-span perspectives on the social foundation of cognition* (pp. 221–241). New York: Cambridge University Press.

Dove, G. (2009). Beyond perceptual symbols: A call for representational pluralism. *Cognition, 110,* 412–431.

Dunning, D., & Cohen, G. L. (1992). Egocentric definitions of traits and abilities in social judgment. *Journal of Personality and Social Psychology, 63,* 341–355.

Echterhoff, G., & Hirst, W. (2009). Social influence on memory. *Social Psychology, 40,* 106–110.

Fazio, R. H., & Olson, M. A. (2003). Implicit measures in social cognition research: Their meaning and use. *Annual Review of Psychology, 54,* 297–327.

Fazio, R. H., Sanbonmatsu, D. M., Powell, M. C., & Kardes, F. R. (1986). On the automatic activation of attitudes. *Journal of Personality and Social Psychology, 50,* 229–238.

Fischer, M. H., & Zwaan, R. A. (2008). Embodied language: A review of the role of the motor system in language comprehension. *Quarterly Journal of Experimental Psychology, 61,* 825–850

Fiske, A. P., & Haslam, N. (1996). Social cognition is thinking about relationships. *Current Directions in Psychological Science, 5,* 137–142.

Fiske, A. P., Haslam, N., & Fiske, S. T. (1991). Confusing one person with another: What errors reveal about the elementary forms of social relations. *Journal of Personality and Social Psychology, 60,* 656–674.

Fiske, S. T. (1992). Thinking is for doing: Portraits of social cognition from daguerreotype to laserphoto. *Journal of Personality and Social Psychology, 63,* 877–889.

Fiske, S. T., Cuddy, A. J. C., Glick, P., & Xu, J. (2002). A model of (often mixed) stereotype content: Competence and warmth respectively follow from status and competition. *Journal of Personality and Social Psychology, 82,* 878–902.

Fodor, J. A. (1980). Methodological solipsism considered as a research strategy in cognitive psychology. *Behavioral and Brain Sciences, 3,* 63–109.

Forgas, J. P. (1995). Mood and judgment: The Affect Infusion Model (AIM). *Psychological Bulletin, 117,* 39–66.

Forgas, J. P. (1998). On being happy but mistaken: Mood effects on the fundamental attribution error. *Journal of Personality and Social Psychology, 75,* 318–331.

Forgas, J. P., & Moylan, S. (1987). After the movies: The effects of transient mood states on social judgments. *Personality and Social Psychology Bulletin, 13,* 478–489.

Foroni, F., & Semin, G. R. (2009).Language that puts you in touch with your bodily feelings. The multimodal responsiveness of affective expressions. *Psychological Science, 20,* 974–980.

Förster, J., & Strack, F. (1997). The influence of motor actions on retrieval of valenced information: A motor congruence effect. *Perceptual and Motor Skills, 85,* 1419–1427.

Förster, J., & Strack, F. (1998). Motor actions in retrieval of valenced information: II. Boundary conditions for motor congruence effects. *Perceptual and Motor Skills, 86,* 1423–1426.

Fuhrman, O., & Boroditsky, L. (2010). Cross-cultural differences in mental representations of time: Evidence from an implicit non-linguistic task. *Cognitive Science, 8,* 1430–1451.

Ghazanfar, A. A., & Schroeder, C. E. (2006). Is neocortex essentially multisensory? *Trends in Cognitive Sciences, 10,* 278–285.

Gallese, V. (2006). Intentional attunement: A neurophysiological perspective on social cognition and its disruption in autism. *Brain Research, 1079,* 15–24.

Galton, F. (1884). Measurement of character. *Fortnightly Review, 42,* 179–185.

Garcia-Marques, L., Garrido, M. V., Hamilton, D. L., & Ferreira, M. (2012). Effects of correspondence between encoding and retrieval organization in social memory. *Journal of Experimental Social Psychology, 48,* 200–206.

Garcia-Marques, L., & Mackie, D. M. (1999). The impact of stereotype-incongruent information on perceived group variability and stereotype change. *Journal of Personality and Social Psychology, 77,* 979–990.

Garcia-Marques, L., & Mackie, D. M. (2001). Not all stereotype-incongruent information is created equal: The impact of sample variability on stereotype change. *Group Processes & Intergroup Relations, 4,* 5–20.

Garcia-Marques, L., Santos, A. S., & Mackie, D. M. (2006). Stereotypes: Static abstractions or dynamic knowledge structures? *Journal of Personality and Social Psychology, 91,* 814–831.

Garrido, M. V., Garcia-Marques, L. & Hamilton, D. L. (2012). Hard to recall but easy to judge: Retrieval strategies in social information processing. *Social Cognition, 30,* 57–71.

Garrido, M. V., Garcia-Marques, L. & Hamilton, D. L. (2012, in press). Enhancing the comparability between part-list cueing and collaborative recall: A gradual part-list cueing paradigm. *Experimental Psychology.*

Gasper, K., & Clore, G. L. (1998). The persistent use of negative affect by anxious individuals to estimate risk. *Journal of Personality and Social Psychology, 74,* 1350–1363.

Gasper, K., & Clore, G. L. (2002). Attending to the big picture: Mood and global versus local processing of visual information. *Psychological Science, 13,* 33–39.

Gazzaniga, M. S. (2010). Neuroscience and the correct level of explanation for understanding mind. *Trends in Cognitive Sciences, 14,* 291–292.

Ghazanfar, A. A., & Schroeder, C. E. (2006). Is neocortex essentially multisensory? *Trends in Cognitive Sciences, 10,* 278–285.

Gibson, J. J. (1966). *The senses considered as perceptual systems.* Boston, MA: Houghton Mifflin.

Gibson, J. J. (1979). *The ecological approach to visual perception.* Hillsdale, NJ: Lawrence Erlbaum Associates.

Gilbert, D. T. (1991). How mental systems believe. *American Psychologist, 46,* 107–119.

Glenberg, A. M. (1997). What memory is for. *Behavioral and Brain Sciences, 20,* 1–55.

Glenberg, A. M. (2008). Radical changes in cognitive process due to technology: A jaundiced view. In I. Dror & S. Harnad (Eds.), *Cognition distributed: How cognitive technology extends our minds* (pp. 71–82). Amsterdam: John Benjamins.

Glenberg, A. M., & Kaschak, M. P. (2002). Grounding language in action. *Psychonomic Bulletin & Review, 9,* 558–565.

Glenberg, A. M., & Robertson, D. A. (1999). Indexical understanding of instructions. *Discourse Processes, 28,* 1–26.

Glenberg, A. M., Sato, M., Cattaneo, L., Riggio, L., Palumbo, D., & Bucino, G. (2008). Processing abstract language modulates motor system activity. *Quarterly Journal of Experimental Psychology, 61,* 905–919.

Hamilton, D. L., & Trolier, T. K. (1986). Stereotypes and stereotyping: An overview of the cognitive approach. In J. Dovidio, & S. L. Gaertner (Eds.), *Prejudice, discrimination, and racism* (pp. 127–163). New York: Academic Press.

Harnad, S. (1990). The symbol grounding problem. *Physica D, 42,* 335–346.

Hauk, O., Johnsrude, I., & Pulvermüller, F. (2004). Somatotopic representation of action words in human motor and premotor cortex. *Neuron, 41,* 301.

Heider, F. (1958). *The psychology of interpersonal relations.* New York: Wiley.

Hesse, H. (1943/1955) (1943). *Das Glasperlenspiel (The glass bead game)* (also published as *Magister ludi*): Frankfurt: Suhrkamp.

Hinsz, V. B. (1990). Cognitive and consensus processes in group recognition: Memory performance. *Journal of Personality and Social Psychology, 59,* 705–718.

Hirst, W., & Manier, D. (2008). Towards a psychology of collective memory. *Memory, 16,* 183–200.

Hirt, E. R., Levine, G. M., McDonald, H. E., Melton, R. J., & Martin, L. L. (1997). The role of mood in quantitative and qualitative aspects of performance: Single or multiple mechanisms? *Journal of Personality and Social Psychology, 33,* 602–629.

Hodges, B. H., & Baron, R. M. (1992). Values as constraints on affordances: Perceiving and acting properly. *Journal for the Theory of Social Behaviour, 22,* 263–294.

Holland, R., Hendriks, M., & Arts, H. (2005). Nonconscious effects of scent on cognition and behavior: Smells like clean spirit. *Psychological Science, 16,* 689–693.

Hollingshead, A. B. (1998a). Communication, learning and retrieval in transactive memory systems. *Journal of Experimental Social Psychology, 34,* 423–442.

Hollingshead, A. B. (1998b). Retrieval processes in Transactive Memory Systems. *Journal of Personality and Social Psychology, 74,* 659–671.

Holmes, J. (2000). Social relationships: The nature and function of relational schemas. *European Journal of Social Psychology, 30,* 447–497.

Holt, L. E., & Beilock, S. L. (2006). Expertise and its embodiment: Examining the impact of sensorimotor skill expertise on the representation of action-related text. *Psychonomic Bulletin & Review, 13,* 694–701.

Hommel, B., Müsseler, J., Aschersleben, G., & Prinz, W. (2001). The theory of event coding (TEC): A framework for perception and action planning. *Behavioral and Brain Sciences, 24,* 849–878.

Humboldt, W. von (1836). *Über die Verschiedenheit Einfuss des menschlichen Sprachaufbaus und ihren Einfluß auf die geistige Entwicklung des Menschengeschlechts.* Berlin: Royal Academy of Sciences. Republished in G. C. Buck & F. Raven (Trans.) (1971). *Linguistic variability and intellectual development.* Baltimore, MD: University of Miami Press.

Hutchins, E. (1995). *Cognition in the wild.* Cambridge, MA: MIT Press.

Iacoboni, M. (2009). Imitation, empathy, and mirror neurons. *Annual Review of Psychology, 60,* 653–670.

Ijzerman, H., & Semin, G. R. (2009). The thermometer of social relations: Mapping social proximity on temperature. *Psychological Science, 20,* 1214–1220.

Ijzerman, H., & Semin, G. R. (2010). Temperature perceptions as a ground for social proximity. *Journal of Experimental Social Psychology, 46,* 867–873.

Isen, A. M. (1987). Positive affect, cognitive processes and social behavior. In L. Berkowitz (Ed.), *Advances in experimental social psychology,* (pp. 203–253). New York: Academic Press.

Isen, A. M., & Daubman, K. A. (1984). The influence of affect on categorization. *Behavior and Human Decision Processes, 37,* 1–13.

Ishihara, M., Keller, P. E., Rossetti, Y., & Prinz, W. (2008). Horizontal spatial representations of time: Evidence for the STEARC effect. *Cortex, 44,* 454–461.

Ito, T. A., Chiao, K. W., Devine, P. G., Lorig, T. S., & Cacioppo, J. T. (2006). The influence of facial feedback on race bias as measured with the Implicit Association Test. *Psychological Science, 17,* 256–261.

James, W. (1890). *The principles of psychology.* (Reprinted 1950. New York: Dover.)

Janis, I. (1972). *Victims of groupthink,* Boston: Houghton-Mifflin

Jones, E. E. (1985). Major developments in social psychology during the last five decades. In G. Lindzey & E. Aronson (Eds.), *Handbook of social psychology* (Vol. 1, pp. 47–107). New York: Random House.

Kaschak, M. P., Zwaan, R. A., Aveyard, M., & Yaxley, R. H. (2006). Perception of auditory motion affects language processing. *Cognitive Science, 30,* 733–744.

Kawakami, K., Phills, C. E., Steele, J. R., & Dovidio, J. F. (2007). (Close) Distance makes the heart grow fonder: Improving implicit racial attitudes and interracial interactions through approach behaviors. *Journal of Personality and Social Psychology, 92,* 957–971.

Kirsh, D. (1995). The intelligent use of space. *Artificial Intelligence, 73,* 31–68.

Kirsh, D., & Maglio, P. (1994). On distinguishing epistemic from pragmatic action. *Cognitive Science, 18,* 513–549.

Kövecses, Z. (2000). *Metaphor and emotion: Language, culture, and body in human feeling.* New York: Cambridge University Press.

Kunda, Z. (1987). Motivated inference: Self-serving generation and evaluation of causal theories. *Journal of Personality and Social Psychology, 53,* 636–647.

Kunda, Z., & Sanitioso, R. (1989). Motivated changes in the self-concept. *Journal of Experimental Social Psychology, 25,* 272–285.

Laird, J. D. (1984). The real role of facial response in the experience of emotion: A reply to Tourangeau and Ellsworth, and others. *Journal of Personality and Social Psychology, 47,* 909–917.

Lakens, D., Semin, G. R., & Garrido, M. V. (2011). The sound of time: Cross-modal convergence in the spatial structuring of time. *Consciouness and Cognition, 20,* 437–443.

Lakoff, G., & Johnson, M. (1980). *Metaphors we live by.* Chicago, IL: University of Chicago Press.

Lakoff, G., & Johnson, M. (1999). *Philosophy in the flesh. The embodied mind and its challenge to western thought.* New York: Basic Books.

Lanciano, T., Curci, A., & Semin, G. R. (2010). The emotional and reconstructive determinants of emotional memories: An experimental approach to flashbulb memory investigation. *Memory, 18,* 473–485.

Landau, M. J., Meier, B. P., & Keefer, L. A. (2010). A metaphor-enriched social cognition. *Psychological Bulletin, 136,* 1045–1067.

Lee, S. W. S., & Schwarz, N. (2010). Dirty hands and dirty mouths: Embodiment of the moral-purity metaphor is specific to the motor modality involved in moral transgression. *Psychological Science, 21,* 1423–1425.

Levine, J., Rensick, L., & Higgins, E. (1993). Social foundations of cognition. *Annual Review of Psychology, 44,* 588–612.

Li, W., Moallem, I., Paller, K. A., & Gottfried, J. A. (2007). Subliminal smells can guide social preferences. *Psychological Science, 18,* 1044–1049.

Lorge, I., & Solomon, H. (1961). Group and individual behavior in free recall. In J. H. Criswell, H. Solomon, & P. Suppes (Eds.), *Mathematical methods in small group processes* (pp. 221–231). Stanford, CA: Stanford University Press.

Mackie, D. M., & Worth, L. T. (1989). Processing deficits and the mediation of positive affect in persuasion. *Journal of Personality and Social Psychology, 57,* 27–40.

Macrae, C. N., Bodenhausen, G. V., & Milne, A. B. (1995). The dissection of selection in person perception: Inhibitory processes in social stereotyping. *Journal of Personality and Social Psychology, 69,* 397–407.

Macrae, C. N., Bodenhausen, G. V., Milne, A. B., Castelli, L., Schloerscheidt, A. M., & Greco, S. (1998). On activating exemplars. *Journal of Experimental Social Psychology, 34,* 330–354.

Macrae, C. N., Bodenhausen, G. V., Milne, A. B., Thorn, T. M., & Castelli, L. (1997). On the activation of social stereotypes: The moderating role of processing objectives. *Journal of Experimental Social Psychology, 67,* 808–817.

Macrae, C. N., & Johnston, L. (1998). Help, I need somebody: Automatic action and inaction. *Social Cognition, 16,* 400–417.

Macrae, C. N., Mitchell, J. P., & Pendry, L. F. (2002). What's in a forename? Cue familiarity and stereotypical thinking. *Journal of Personality and Social Psychology, 38,* 186–193.

Mahon, B. Z., & Caramazza, A. (2008). A critical look at the embodied cognition hypothesis and a new proposal for grounding conceptual content. *Journal of Physiology, 102,* 59–70.

Markman, A. B., & Brendl, C. M. (2005). Constraining theories of embodied cognition. *Psychological Science, 16,* 6–10.

Martin, L. L., & Clore, G. (Eds.) (2001). *Theories of mood and cognition: A user's guidebook.* Mahwah, NJ: Lawrence Erlbaum Associates.

Matlock, T. (2004). Fictive motion as cognitive simulation. *Memory & Cognition, 32,* 1389–1400.

Maxwell, J. S., & Davidson, R. J. (2007). Emotion as motion: Asymmetries in approach and avoidant actions. *Psychological Science, 18,* 1113–1119.

Meade, M. L., & Roediger, H. L. (2002). Explorations in the social contagion of memory. *Memory & Cognition, 30,* 995–1009.

Meier, B. P., & Robinson, M. D. (2004). Why the sunny side is up. *Psychological Science, 15,* 243–247.

Meier, B. P., Robinson, M. D., & Caven, A. J. (2008). Why a Big Mac is a good mac: Associations between affect and size. *Basic and Applied Social Psychology, 30,* 46–55.

Meier, B. P., Robinson, M. D., & Clore, G. L. (2004). Why good guys wear white: Automatic inferences about stimulus valence based on color. *Psychological Science, 15,* 82–87.

Meier, B. P., Robinson, M. D., Crawford, L. E., & Ahlvers, W. J. (2007). When "light" and "dark" thoughts become light and dark responses: Affect biased brightness judgments. *Emotion, 7,* 366–376.

Meudell, P. R., Hitch, G. J., & Boyle, M. (1995). Collaboration in recall: Do pairs of people cross cue each other to produce new memories? *Quarterly Journal of Experimental Psychology, 48,* 141–152.

Meudell, P. R., Hitch, G. J., & Kirby, P. (1992). Are two heads better than one? Experimental investigations of the social facilitation of memory. *Applied Cognitive Psychology, 6,* 525–543.

Mischel, W., & Shoda, Y. (1998). Reconciling processing dynamics and personality dispositions. *Annual Review of Psychology, 49,* 229–258.

Mussweiler, T. (2006). Doing is for thinking! Stereotype activation by stereotypic movements. *Psychological Science, 17,* 17–21.

Neuberg, S. L., & Fiske, S. T. (1987). Motivational influences on impression formation: Outcome dependency, accuracy-driven attention, and individuating processes. *Journal of Personality and Social Psychology, 53,* 431–444.

Neumann, R., Förster, J., & Strack, F. (2003). Motor compatibility: The bidirectional link between behavior and evaluation. In J. Musch & K. C. Klauer (Eds.), *The psychology of evaluation. Affective processes in cognition and emotion.* (pp. 371–391). Mahwah, NJ: Lawrence Erlbaum Associates.

Neumann, R., & Strack, F. (2000). Approach and avoidance: The influence of proprioceptive and exteroceptive cues on encoding of affective information. *Journal of Personality and Social Psychology, 79,* 39–48.

Niedenthal, P. M. (2007). Embodying emotion. *Science, 316,* 1002–1005.

Niedenthal, P. M., Barsalou, L. W., Winkielman, P., Krauth-Gruber, S., & Ric, F. (2005). Embodiment in attitudes, social perception, and emotion. *Personality and Social Psychology Review, 9,* 184–211.

Nisbett, R. E., & Ross, L. (1980). *Human inference: Strategies and shortcomings of social judgment.* Englewood Cliffs, NJ: Prentice Hall.

Norenzayan, A., & Schwarz, N. (1999). Telling what they want to know: Participants tailor causal attributions to researchers' interests. *European Journal of Social Psychology, 29,* 1011–1020.

Paladino, P., & Castelli, L. (2008). On the immediate consequences of intergroup categorization: Activation of approach and avoidance motor behavior toward ingroup and outgroup members. *Personality and Social Psychology Bulletin, 34,* 755–768.

Palma, T., Garrido, M. V., & Semin, G. R. (2011). Grounding person memory in space: Does spatial anchoring of behaviors improve recall? *European Journal of Social Psychology, 41,* 275–280.

Park, J., & Banaji, M. R. (2000). Mood and heuristics: The influence of happy and sad states on sensitivity and bias in stereotyping. *Journal of Personality and Social Psychology, 78,* 1005–1023.

Pecher, D., Zeelenberg, R., & Barsalou, L. W. (2003). Verifying properties from different modalities for concepts produces switching costs. *Psychological Science, 14,* 119–124.

Pickering, M. J. & Garrod, S. (2011). The use of prediction to drive alignment in dialogue. In G. R. Semin & G. Echterhoff (Eds.), *From neurons to shared cognition and culture* (pp. 175–192). New York: Psychology Press.

Pickett, C. L., Gardner, W. L., & Knowles, M. (2004). Getting a cue: The need to belong and enhanced sensitivity to social cues. *Personality and Social Psychology Bulletin, 30,* 1095–1107.

Prinz, W. (1984). Modes of linkage between perception and action. In W. Prinz & A.-F. Sanders (Eds.), *Cognition and motor processes* (pp. 185–193). Berlin: Springer.

Proffitt, D. R. (2006). Embodied perception and the economy of action. *Perspectives on Psychological Science, 1,* 110–122.

Pulvermüller, F. (2005). Brain mechanisms linking language and action. *Nature Reviews Neuroscience, 6,* 576–582.

Rajaran, S., & Pereira-Pasarin, L. P. (2010). Collaborative memory: Cognitive research and theory. *Perspectives on Psychological Science, 5,* 649–663.

Richardson, D. C, Hoover, M. A., & Ghane, A. (2008). Joint perception: Gaze and the presence of others. In B. C. Love, K. McRae & V. M. Sloutsky (Eds.), *Proceedings of the 30th Annual Conference of the Cognitive Science Society* (pp. 309–314). Austin, TX: Cognitive Science Society.

Richardson, D. C., Spivey, M. J., Barsalou, L. W., & McRae, K. (2003). Spatial representations activated during real-time comprehension of verbs. *Cognitive Science, 27,* 767–780.

Rizzolatti, G., & Arbib, M. A. (1998). Language within our grasp. *Trends in Neurosciences, 21,* 188–194.

Rizzolatti, G., & Craighero, L. (2004). The mirror-neuron system. *Annual Review of Neuroscience, 27,* 169–192.

Robbins, P., & Aydede, M. (Eds.) (2009). *The Cambridge handbook of situated cognition.* Cambridge: Cambridge University Press.

Roediger, H. L., III, Meade, M. L., & Bergman, E. T. (2001). Social contagion of memory. *Psychonomic Bulletin & Review, 8,* 365–371.

Ross, L. (1977). The intuitive psychologist and his shortcomings: Distortions in the attribution process. In L. Berkowitz (Ed.), *Advances in experimental social psychology* (Vol. 10, pp. 174–221). New York: Academic Press.

Schnall, S., Benton, J., & Harvey, S. (2008). With a clean conscience: Cleanliness reduces the severity of moral judgments. *Psychological Science, 19,* 1219–1222.

Schnall, S., Haidt, J., Clore, G. L., & Jordan, A.H. (2008). Disgust as embodied moral judgment. *Personality and Social Psychology Bulletin, 34,* 1096–1109.

Schubert, T., & Semin, G. R. (2009). Embodiment as a unifying perspective for psychology. *European Journal of Social Psychology, 39,* 1135–1141.

Schwarz, N. (2002). Feelings as information: Moods influence judgment and processing style. In T. Gilovich, D. Griffin & D. Kahneman (Eds.), *Heuristics and biases: The psychology of intuitive judgment* (pp. 534–547). Cambridge: Cambridge University Press.

Schwarz, N. (2007). Attitude construction: Evaluation in context. *Social Cognition, 25,* 638–656.

Schwarz, N. (2011). Feelings-as-information theory. In P. Van Lange, A. W. Kruglanski, & E. T. Higgins (Eds.), *Handbook of theories of social psychology* (pp. 289–311). Thousand Oaks, CA: Sage.

Schwarz, N., & Bless, H. (1992). Scandals and the public's trust in politicians: Assimilation and contrast effects. *Personality and Social Psychology Bulletin, 18,* 574–579.

Schwarz, N., Bless, H., & Bohner, G. (1991). Mood and persuasion: Affective states influence the processing of persuasive communications. *Advances in Experimental Social Psychology, 24,* 161–199.

Schwarz, N., & Clore, G. L. (1988). How do I feel about it? Informative functions of affective states. In K. Fiedler & J. Forgas (Eds.), *Affect, cognition, and social behavior* (pp. 44–62). Toronto, Canada: Hogrefe International.

Schwarz, N., & Clore, G. L. (2007). Feelings and phenomenal experiences. In E. T. Higgins & A. Kruglanski (Eds.), *Social psychology: Handbook of basic principles* (2nd ed., pp. 385–407). New York: Guilford Press.

Schwarz, N., & Clore, G. L. (1983). Mood, misattribution, and judgments of well-being: Informative and directive functions of affective states. *Journal of Personality and Social Psychology, 45,* 513–523.

Schwarz, N. & Sudman, S. (Eds.) (1992). *Context effects in social and psychological research.* New York: Springer Verlag.

Sedikides, C. (1995). Central and peripheral self-conceptions are differentially influenced by mood: Tests of the differential sensitivity hypothesis. *Journal of Personality and Social Psychology, 69,* 759–777.

Semin, G. R. (1986). The individual, the social and the social individual. *British Journal of Social Psychology, 25,* 177–180.

Semin, G. R. (1998). Cognition, language. and communication. In S. R. Fussell & R. J. Kreuz (Eds.), *Social and cognitive psychological approaches to interpersonal communication* (pp. 229–257). Hillsdale, NJ: Laurence Erlbaum Associates.

Semin, G. R. (2000). Communication: Language as an implementational device for cognition. *European Journal of Social Psychology, 30,* 595–612.

Semin, G. R. (2006). Modeling the architecture of linguistic behavior: Linguistic compositionality, automaticity, and control. *Psychological Inquiry, 17,* 246–255.

Semin, G. R. (2007). Grounding communication: Synchrony. In A. Kruglanski & E. T. Higgins (Eds.), *Social psychology: Handbook of basic principles* (2nd ed., pp. 630–649). New York: Guilford Press.

Semin, G. R. (2008). Language puzzles: A prospective retrospective on the Linguistic Category Model [Special issue], *Journal of Language and Social Psychology, 27,* 197–209.

Semin, G. R. & Cacioppo, J. T. (2008). Grounding social cognition: Synchronization, entrainment, and coordination. In G. R. Semin & E. R. Smith (Eds.), *Embodied grounding: Social, cognitive, affective, and neuroscientific approaches* (pp.119–147*).* New York: Cambridge University Press.

Semin, G. R. & Cacioppo, J. T. (2009). From embodied representation to co-regulation. In J. A. Pineda (Ed.), *Mirror neuron systems: The role of mirroring processes in social cognition* (pp.107–120). Totowa, NJ: Humana Press.

Semin, G. R. & Garrido, M. V. (2012). A systemic approach to impression formation: From verbal to multimodal processes. In J. Forgas, K. Fiedler, & C. Sedikides (Eds.), *Social thinking and interpersonal behavior* (pp. 81–96). New York: Psychology Press.

Semin, G. R., & Smith, E. R. (2002). Interfaces of social psychology with situated and embodied cognition. *Cognitive Systems Research, 3,* 385–396.

Semin, G. R., & Smith, E. R. (2008). *Embodied grounding: Social, cognitive, affective, and neuroscientific approaches.* New York: Cambridge University Press.

Sinclair, L., & Kunda, Z. (1999). Reactions to a black professional: Motivated inhibition and activation of conflicting stereotypes. *Journal of Personality and Social Psychology, 77,* 885–904.

Smeesters, D., Wheeler, S. C., & Kay, A. C. (2010). Indirect prime-to-behavior effects: The role of perceptions of the self, others, and situations in connecting primed constructs to social behavior. *Advances in Experimental Social Psychology, 42,* 259–317.

Smith, E. R. (1998). Mental representation and memory. In D. Gilbert, S. Fiske & G. Lindzey (Eds.), *Handbook of social psychology* (4th ed., Vol. 1, pp. 391–445). New York: McGraw-Hill.

Smith, E. R., & Semin, G. R. (2004). Socially situated cognition: Cognition in its social context. *Advances in Experimental Social Psychology, 36,* 53–117.

Smith, E. R., & Semin, G. R. (2007). Situated social cognition. *Current Directions in Psychological Science, 16,* 132–135.

Smith, E. R., & Zárate, M. A. (1992). Exemplar based model of social judgment. *Psychological Review, 99,* 3–21.

Snyder, M. (1981). On the self-perpetuating nature of social stereotypes. In D. L. Hamilton (Ed.), *Cognitive processes in stereotyping and intergroup behavior* (pp.183–212). Hillsdale, NJ: Lawrence Erlbaum Associates.

Snyder, M. (1993). Basic research and practical problems: The promise of a "functional" personality and social psychology. *Personality and Social Psychology Bulletin, 19,* 251–264.

Snyder, M., & Cantor, N. (1998). Understanding personality and social behavior: A functionalist strategy. In D. Gilbert, S. Fiske, & G. Lindzey (Eds.), *The handbook of social psychology* (Vol. 1, 4th ed., pp. 635–679). New York: McGraw-Hill.

Solarz, A. K. (1960). Latency of instrumental responses as a function of compatibility with the meaning of eliciting verbal signs. *Journal of Experimental Psychology, 59,* 239–245.

Spivey M. J., Tyler M., Richardson D. C., & Young, E. (2000). Eye movements during comprehension of spoken scene descriptions. *Proceedings of the Twenty-Second Annual Meeting of the Cognitive Science Society* (pp. 487–492). Mawhah, NJ: Lawrence Erlbaum Associates.

Stephenson, G. M. (1984). Accuracy and confidence in testimony: A critical review and some fresh evidence. In D. J. Muller, D. E. Blackman & A. J. Chapman (Eds.), *Psychology and law: Topics from an international conference* (pp. 229–250). Chichester, England: Wiley.

Stepper, S., & Strack, F. (1993). Proprioceptive determinants of emotional and nonemotional feelings. *Journal of Personality and Social Psychology, 64*, 211–220.

Stockhorst, U., & Pietrowsky, R. (2004). Olfactory perception, communication, and the nose-to-brain pathway. *Physiology and Behavior, 83*, 3–11.

Strack, F., Martin, L. L., & Stepper, S. (1988). Inhibiting and facilitating conditions of the human smile: A nonobtrusive test of the facial feedback hypothesis. *Journal of Personality and Social Psychology, 54*, 768–777.

Taylor, L. J., & Zwaan, R. A. (2008). Motor resonance and linguistic focus. *Quarterly Journal of Experimental Psychology, 61*, 896–904.

Taylor, S. E. (1981). A categorization approach to stereotyping. In D. L. Hamilton (Ed.), *Cognitive processes in stereotyping and intergroup behavior* (pp. 83–114). Hillsdale, NJ: Lawrence Erlbaum Associates.

Tettamanti, M., Buccino, G., Saccuman, M. C., Gallese, V., Danna, M., Scifo, P., et al. (2005). Listening to action-related sentences activates fronto-parietal motor circuits. *Journal of Cognitive Neuroscience, 17*, 273–281.

Tom, G., Pettersen, P., Lau, T., Burton, T., & Cook, J. (1991). The role of overt head movement in the formation of affect. *Basic and Applied Social Psychology, 12*, 281–289.

Traugott, E. (1978). On the expression of spatiotemporal relations in language. In J. H. Greenberg (Ed.), *Universals of human language* (Vol. 3, *Word structure*, pp. 369–400). Stanford, CA: Stanford University Press.

Tversky, B., Kugelmass, S., & Winter, A. (1991). Cross-cultural and developmental trends in graphic productions. *Cognitive Psychology, 23*, 515–557.

Valins, S. (1966). Cognitive effects of false heart-rate feedback. *Journal of Personality and Social Psychology, 4*, 400–408.

Vallesi, A., Binns, M. A., & Shallice, T. (2008). An effect of spatial-temporal association of response codes: Understanding the cognitive representations of time. *Cognition, 107*, 501–527.

Vallesi, A., McIntosh, A. R., & Stuss, D. T. (2011). How time modulates special responses. *Cortex, 47*, 148–156.

Vygotsky, L. S. (1981). The genesis of higher mental functions. In J. V. Wertsch (Ed.), *The concept of activity in Soviet psychology* (pp. 156–172). Armonk, NY: Sharpe.

Wegner, D. M. (1986). Transactive memory: A contemporary analysis of the group mind. In B. Mullen & G. R. Goethals (Eds.), *Theories of group behavior* (pp. 185–208). New York: Springer-Verlag.

Wegner, D. M. (1995). A computer network model of human transactive memory. *Social Cognition, 13*, 319–339.

Wegner, D. M., Erber, R., & Raymond, P. (1991). Transactive memory in close relationships. *Journal of Personality and Social Psychology, 61*, 923–929.

Wegner, D. M., Giuliano, T., & Hertel, P. (1985). Cognitive interdependence in close relationships. In W. J. Ickes (Ed.), *Compatible and incompatible relationships* (pp. 253–276). New York: Springer-Verlag.

Wegner, U. W., & Pratt, J. (2008). Time flies like an arrow: Space-time compatibility effects suggest the use of a mental time line. *Psychonomic Bulletin & Review, 15*, 426–430.

Weinstein, N. (1980). Unrealistic optimism about future life events. *Journal of Personality and Social Psychology, 39*, 806–820.

Weldon, M. S. (2001). Remembering as a social process. In D. L. Medin (Ed.), *The psychology of learning and motivation* (Vol. 40, pp. 67–120). San Diego, CA: Academic Press.

Weldon, M. S., & Bellinger, K. D. (1997). Collective memory: Collaborative and individual processes in remembering. *Journal of Experimental Psychology: Learning, Memory and Cognition, 23*, 1160–1175.

Wells, G. L., & Petty, R. E. (1980). The effects of head movement on persuasion: Compatibility and incompatibility of responses. *Basic and Applied Social Psychology, 1*, 219–230.

Wentura, D., Rothermund, K., & Bak, P. (2000). Automatic vigilance: The attention grabbing power of approach- and avoidance-related social information. *Journal of Personality and Social Psychology, 78*, 1024–1037.

Wertsch, J. V. (2008). Collective memory. In J. H. Byrne (Series Ed.) & H. L.Roediger III (Vol. Ed.), *Learning and memory: A comprehensive reference* (Vol. 2, *Cognitive psychology of memory*, pp. 927–939). Oxford, England: Elsevier.

Wheatley, T., & Haidt, J. (2005). Hypnotically induced disgust makes moral judgments more severe. *Psychological Science, 16*, 780–784.

Williams, L. E., & Bargh, J. A. (2008a). Experiencing physical warmth promotes interpersonal warmth. *Science, 322*, 606–607.

Williams, L. E., & Bargh, J. A. (2008b). Keeping one's distance: The influence of spatial distance cues on affect and evaluation. *Psychological Science, 19*, 302–308.

Wilson, M. (2002). Six views of embodied cognition. *Psychonomic Bulletin and Review, 9*, 625–636.

Wittenbrink, W., Judd, C. M., & Park, B. (2001). Spontaneous prejudice in context: Variability in automatically activated attitudes. *Journal of Personality and Social Psychology, 81*, 815–827.

Yeh, W., & Barsalou, L. W. (2006). The situated nature of concepts. *American Journal of Psychology, 119*, 349–384.

Zajonc, R. B., & Markus, H. (1984). Affect and cognition: The hard interface. In C. Izard, J. Kagan & R. B. Zajonc (Eds.), *Emotion, cognition, and behavior* (pp. 73–102). Cambridge, UK: Cambridge University Press.

Zwaan, R. A. (2009). Mental simulation in language comprehension and social cognition. *European Journal of Social Psychology, 37*, 1142–1150.

Zwaan, R. A., Madden, C. J., Yaxley, R. H., & Aveyard, M. E. (2004). Moving words: Dynamic mental representations in language comprehension. *Cognitive Science, 28*, 611–619.

Zwaan, R. A., & Taylor, L. J. (2006). Seeing, acting, understanding: Motor resonance in language comprehension. *Journal of Experimental Psychology: General, 135,* 1–11.

Zwaan, R. A., & Yaxley, R. H. (2003). Spatial iconicity affects semantic-relatedness judgments. *Psychonomic Bulletin and Review, 10,* 954–958.

Zhong, C. B., & Leonardelli, G. J. (2008). Cold and lonely: Does social exclusion literally feel cold? *Psychological Science, 19,* 838–842.

Zhong, C. B., & Liljenquist, K. (2006). Washing away your sins: Threatened morality and physical cleansing. *Science, 313,* 1451–1452.

9

Likes and Dislikes: A Social Cognitive Perspective on Attitudes

Melissa J. Ferguson & Jun Fukukura

The vast majority of articles and chapters about attitudes (including this one) introduce the topic by referencing the famous quote by Gordon Allport that attitudes are "the most distinctive and indispensable concept in contemporary social psychology" (Allport, 1935). Although it might seem a little suspicious that such a claim is offered by the very people who study the construct, it also happens to have some merit. Attitudes have occupied a central place in the annals of social psychological scholarship from the beginning of the last century up through today (e.g., for reviews, see Albarracín, Johnson, & Zanna, 2005; Eagly & Chaiken, 1993), and this is evident given, for example, the citation count of attitudes articles in any search through the literature.

A long history of scholarship denotes the persistent importance of, and interest in, the construct, but it also suggests that there is continued disagreement about issues. Indeed, there have been long-standing debates about many aspects of attitudes, including the most basic question of what they are. In the current review chapter, we offer a social cognitive perspective on "what they are" and describe the latest cutting-edge research and pressing theoretical questions. We try to shed light on what we now know to be reliably descriptive of attitudes, and also on the major outstanding questions.

We begin by commenting on the terminology in this area, and then describe some of the standard methods of measurement. With such preliminaries out of the way, we turn then to what we consider to be the big questions about attitudes, including how they are generated, how they influence downstream processing and behavior, their stability and contextual dependence, and how they develop in the first place. Along the way we address some of the most central debates in the literature. A social-cognitive perspective means that we pay special attention to the social-cognitive literature on attitudes, which in turns consists of those articles that pay special attention to the cognitive (broadly defined) processes and mechanisms enabling what we talk about when we talk about attitudes. Describing all of the social-cognitive attitudes literature would be an encyclopedic endeavor and outside the scope of this chapter, however, and so we instead focus on studies that are especially illustrative of a theoretical or methodological question, debate, or issue.

WHAT DO WE TALK ABOUT WHEN WE TALK ABOUT ATTITUDES?

The definition of an attitude has – not surprisingly – fluctuated over the last 100 years (e.g., Allport, 1935; Doob, 1947; Osgood, Suci, & Tannenbaum, 1957; Sarnoff, 1960; M. B. Smith, Bruner, & White, 1956; Thurstone, 1931). In the 1950s and 1960s, researchers argued that attitudes should be understood in terms of the tripartite model, whereby an attitude consists of affect toward the stimuli, beliefs about the object, and behaviors toward the objects (e.g., Rosenberg & Hovland, 1960). This eventually shifted to the current contemporary definition of an attitude as a "psychological tendency that is expressed by evaluating a particular entity with some degree of favor or disfavor" (Eagly & Chaiken, 1993). A great deal of the social-cognitive research on attitudes has assumed the more specific definition put forth by Fazio and colleagues that an attitude is a positive or negative summary evaluation of the corresponding stimulus (Fazio, 1986; Fazio, Chen, McDonel, & Sherman, 1982). This definition differs from the Eagly and Chaiken one by including assumptions about the cognitive architecture underlying an attitude: i.e., an attitude is the summary evaluation that is associatively linked in memory with the object of that evaluation. The association between an attitude and an object can fluctuate in accessibility, which raises numerous testable questions about the precursors to and downstream consequences of attitude accessibility. For example, accessibility of the link between the evaluation and corresponding stimulus relates to characteristics traditionally examined in the attitudes literature, including strength, spontaneous activation, complexity, and certainty (e.g., Fazio & Williams, 1986; see also Fazio, 1990; Fazio et al., 1986).

This social-cognitive definition still leaves room for lots of debate, however, and indeed, researchers have argued over whether an attitude is a hypothetical construct developed by psychologists (e.g., Eagly & Chaiken, 1993; Schwarz, 2007) or corresponds to a specifiable state in the brain (Fazio, 2007). This debate requires more consideration and discussion about how the brain might enable expressions of favor or disfavor, but to cut to the chase we argue that it comes down to whether one wants to equate an attitude as a person's general tendency across time and situations to respond to a stimulus in a favorable or unfavorable manner (so, in this case, averaging over many distinct brain states, and thus, existing as an average, a hypothetical construct, or a latent variable) or as a particular response to a stimulus (which could be identified as a specific brain state). The implications of these views require a little more theoretical heavy lifting and so we return to the nuances of the definition of an attitude during our discussion of how attitudes are generated.

Attitude as a label

One recurring source of confusion surrounding the terminology in this area is the use of the terms evaluation versus attitude. Are they the same? Although many researchers use these terms interchangeably, the term attitude carries with it considerable conceptual baggage, whereas the term evaluation does not. Attitudes have been frequently assumed to be stable, and, as mentioned, to reflect psychological tendencies (real or hypothetical) that could potentially influence behavior. Evaluations, on the other hand, have sometimes been understood as behavioral responses to stimuli (the expression of an attitude; e.g., Cunningham, Zelazo, Packer, & Van Bavel, 2007).

People's likes and dislikes have been studied in various ways across the social sciences, and some terms seem to be confined to particular literatures, making thematic connections across disciplines difficult. The term *preferences* has been used in judgment and decision making and behavioral economics research and is probably more aligned with the common interpretation of the term *evaluation* as a behavioral manifestation of an underlying attitude or set of attitudes. It is also used most commonly to indicate *relative* preferences (or choices). The term *taste* also shows up in the behavioral economics literature and is meant to reflect someone's strong likes and dislikes.

What is an attitude object?

The term attitude object is used throughout the attitudes literature to refer to the target being evaluated (e.g., Allport, 1935; Bargh et al., 1992; Fazio, 2001; Fazio et al., 1986; Sarnoff, 1960; M. B. Smith, et al., 1956; Thurstone, 1931). It is important to note that although the term object might imply a material, physical thing, it can refer to anything that can be discriminated in psychological experience and so can include for instance, abstract concepts, smells, sounds, and the contents of our mental life more generally (Eagly & Chaiken, 1993). This means that we can consider attitudes as our likes and dislikes toward, well, anything. One interesting area for future research might be to take this wide definitional latitude seriously and test how attitudes toward traditional stimuli (e.g., people, issues, material objects) compare with attitudes towards less traditional ones (e.g., behavioral intentions, goals, emotions; see Ferguson, 2007a) in terms of basic issues such as predictive validity.

HOW WE MEASURE ATTITUDES

The bulk of scholarship on attitudes over the past approximately 100 years has mostly employed self-report measures wherein the respondent is asked to report her liking or disliking of a stimulus (see Krosnick, Judd, & Wittenbrink, 2005 for a review). There is commonsense appeal to finding out what someone likes or dislikes simply by asking them, and this kind of measure is still frequently used within social cognition research, and used almost exclusively in other social sciences. Self-report measures tend to consist of a Likert unipolar or bipolar scale (e.g., a scale of 1–11), and respondents are asked to circle the number, for instance, that best represents how they feel about the stimulus.

Because the reporting of how we feel about something or someone is generally under our control (e.g., Schwarz & Bohner, 2001), people can provide answers that depart from their actual feelings about the stimulus of interest, perhaps to please the experimenter, or perhaps to present themselves (to others, or to themselves) in a flattering light (see Orne, 1962; Rosenberg, 1969). This becomes especially likely (and thus problematic) when people are asked about other people, things, or issues that are socially stigmatized and tend to elicit normatively socially desirable responses (Dovidio, Mann, & Gaertner, 1989; Jones & Sigall, 1971; Katz & Hass, 1988; McCauley & Stitt, 1978; McConahay, 1986). Researchers' efforts to circumvent such strategic editing increased considerably in the 1970s and 1980s and have resulted in a major theoretical (as well as methodological) shift in terms of what an attitude is thought to be.

Self-report attitude measures can be considered "direct" measures (Bassili & Brown, 2005; Fazio & Olson, 2003; Ranganath, Smith, & Nosek, 2008) because they consist of asking the respondent directly about her or his attitude. Indirect measures, on the other hand, are those that consist of inferring a person's attitude from other sorts of data, whether behavioral or neural. Direct measures tend to be referred to as explicit measures in reference to explicit memory, which involves cases when one is asked to recall or recognize something. In contrast, indirect measures are frequently referred to as implicit under the assumption that such measures depend on implicit memory.

Although the adjective *explicit* seems to adequately fit self-report measures, the term *implicit* may be a misnomer, as one of us has argued previously (Ferguson, 2007b). *Implicit memory* is a term from cognitive psychology and refers to the influence of a memory on a response wherein the person cannot introspectively identify that memory (Roediger, 1990; Squire & Kandel, 1999; Tulving & Craik, 2000). That is, implicit memory in the cognitive sciences always refers to cases where the person is consciously unaware of the memory.

In social cognition work, however, there has been very little, if any (e.g., see Gawronski, LeBel, & Peters, 2007), evidence that implicitly measured attitudes are beyond the reach of one's awareness. Instead, they are usually called implicit because they are spontaneously evoked by the stimulus without the person intentionally evaluating that stimulus.

Many of the current social-cognitive questions concerning attitudes involve a comparison between directly versus indirectly measured attitudes (for a comprehensive review, see De Houwer, Teige-Mocigemba, Spruyt, & Moors, 2009), and we address this issue wherever appropriate. Throughout this paper, we use the terms *direct attitudes* and *indirect attitudes* as shorthand for directly versus indirectly measured attitudes. The use of these terms does not imply any specific assumptions regarding representational, process, or system differences between the two, beyond the issue of whether the person is asked (or not) about her or his attitudes.

Indirect measures are based on either behavioral responses or on specific regions of neural activation. Below we describe a few of the most commonly used indirect measures. More detailed descriptions of other indirect measures can be found elsewhere (see De Houwer, 2003; De Houwer & Eelen, 1998; Dovidio, Kawakami, Johnson, & Johnson, 1997; Koole, Dijksterhuis, & van Knippenberg, 2001; Niedenthal, 1990; Nosek & Banaji, 2001; Payne, Cheng, Govorun, & Stewart, 2005).

Evaluative priming

Evaluative priming is measured with a paradigm that was first developed by Fazio and colleagues (Fazio et al., 1986). The paradigm was developed to measure the degree to which people's attitudes are activated spontaneously from memory upon perception of the corresponding attitude objects. In this paradigm, which was modeled after priming work in semantic cognition (Logan, 1980; Meyer & Schvaneveldt, 1971; Neely, 1976, 1977; Posner & Snyder, 1975; Shiffrin & Schneider, 1977), participants were presented on a computer with a series of sequentially presented prime–target pairs of stimuli. The prime appears first for a fraction of a second, and the respondent is not asked to respond to it. The target then appears, and the respondent usually is asked to make an evaluative (Is this a good or bad word?) or lexical (Is this a real or nonsense word?) decision about it. Given certain parameters of the paradigm, it produces evaluative priming such that people are faster to respond to targets when the target and prime are similarly (vs dissimilarly) valenced. The phenomenon of priming itself appears to be reliable and robust, and has been interpreted as evidence that people spontaneously evaluate the primes, which then influences the readiness with which people can respond to the positive versus negative targets. There are ongoing debates though about the generality of the effect across different kinds of stimuli (i.e., whether attitude strength moderates automatic attitude activation; Castelli, Zogmaister, Smith, & Arcuri, 2004; Chaiken & Bargh, 1993; Fazio, 1993; Krosnick & Schuman, 1988), the type of response task (e.g., Klauer & Musch, 2003; Wentura, 1999, 2000), and the underlying processes and mechanisms (e.g., Fazio, 2001; Ferguson & Bargh, 2003; Klauer & Musch, 2003; Klauer & Stern, 1992; Klinger, Burton, & Pitts, 2000; Wentura, 1999).

The existence of evaluative priming has enabled researchers to use the paradigm as an indirect measure of the evaluations of the prime stimuli (e.g., Fazio et al., 1995; Ferguson & Bargh, 2004; Wittenbrink, Judd, & Park, 1997, 2001). That is, it is possible to compare the degree to which a certain prime (e.g., a photo of a Black face) facilitates responses to the positive and negative targets as a function of different conditions, or as compared with other prime stimuli (e.g., a photo of a White face).

Implicit Association Test (IAT)

The Implicit Association Test (IAT; Greenwald, McGhee, & Schwarz, 1998) was developed by Greenwald and colleagues and captures the ease with which people can associate a particular category (e.g., women) with pleasant or unpleasant stimuli (for reviews, see Fazio & Olson, 2003; Greenwald, Poehlman, Uhlmann, & Banaji, 2009). The respondent is asked to complete two different sorting tasks simultaneously. For one sorting task, the respondent has to indicate whether each of a series of stimuli is pleasant or unpleasant by pressing one of two keys. For the other, the respondent has to categorize each of a series of stimuli (e.g., female and male names) as belonging to one possible category (female) or another (male). The critical part of this measure is that there are only 2 keys for the 4 possible responses, and so the responses are paired together, such that, for example, pleasant and female names share the same response key and unpleasant and male names share the same response key; thus, it is possible to compare how easily the respondent can perform this version of the sorting tasks compared with the reverse pairing. If the person can respond more easily when female names are paired with

pleasant stimuli (versus the reverse), then the inference is that female names are implicitly preferred over male names.

The IAT has been employed to examine a variety of different topics, including self-esteem (Greenwald & Farnham, 2000), prejudice (e.g., Ashburn-Nardo, Voils, & Monteith, 2001; Blair, Ma, & Lenton, 2001; McConnell & Leibold, 2001), social identity (Greenwald, Banaji, Rudman, Farnham, Nosek, & Mellott, 2002), and personality traits (e.g., Jordan, Spencer, & Zanna, 2003; Marsh, Johnson, & Scott-Sheldon, 2001). There is still ongoing debate about the exact mechanisms underlying the effect, as well as the boundary conditions and predictive validity of the measure (e.g., see Hofmann, Gawronski, Gschwendner, Le, & Schmitt, 2005; Karpinski & Hilton, 2001; Mierke & Klauer, 2003; Nosek, Greenwald, & Banaji, 2005; Olson & Fazio, 2004).

Event-related potentials and functional magnetic resonance imaging

In addition to indirect attitude measures based on behavior, researchers have also inferred people's evaluative processes indirectly by examining what regions of the brain are active while viewing evaluative versus non-evaluative stimuli (e.g., Amodio, Harmon-Jones, & Devine, 2003; Cunningham, Johnson, Raye, Gatenby, Gore, & Banaji, 2004; Ito & Cacioppo, 2000; Phelps, O'Connor, Cunningham, Funayama, Gatenby, Gore, & Banaji, 2000). For instance, Ito and Cacioppo (2000) recorded event-related brain potentials (ERP) and showed that people are sensitive to the evaluative nature of stimuli even when they are not intentionally evaluating those stimuli. Participants were asked to decide whether various kinds of stimuli (e.g., a chocolate bar, a couple hugging) included people or not. The focal task was to report whether people were present or absent, and in this way did not involve any evaluative processing per se. The results showed that whenever a series of stimulus involved evaluative inconsistency (positive and negative stimuli) versus consistency (only positive or only negative stimuli), there was an increase in participants' electroencephalographic activity, suggesting greater cognitive effort.

Researchers have also used functional magnetic resonance imaging (fMRI) to identify the specific regions of the brain that become active during evaluation. For example, the amygdala seems to be particularly active when normatively negative stimuli are processed (e.g., LeDoux, 2000;

Phelps et al., 2000), and this happens even when the stimuli are processed outside of awareness (e.g., Cunningham, Raye, & Johnson, 2004; Morris, Ohman, & Dolan, 1998). Cunningham and colleagues (Cunningham et al., 2003) have also found increased amgydala activity in response to negative versus positive stimuli, both when participants are intentionally evaluating those stimuli and even when they are not. This work also shows that this negativity occurs especially in the very early milliseconds of processing negative stimuli (30 ms), compared with relatively later in the processing stream (525 ms).

Research also shows that irrespective of whether a person is intentionally evaluating stimuli, the perception of normatively negative versus positive stimuli leads to greater activity in the amygdala and right inferior prefrontal cortex (PFC; e.g., see Cunningham et al., 2003). When people are intentionally assessing the valence of stimuli, there is greater activity in the medial and ventrolateral PFC, especially when the stimuli are evaluatively complex (Cunningham et al., 2003; Cunningham, Raye, & Johnson, 2004). These neuroscience methods have provided information that converges with the behavioral measures to suggest that evaluation seems to be a pervasive, easily triggered process. However, it also pinpoints the regions of the brain that are involved in different kinds of evaluation, which can then inform and constrain theorizing about evaluation more generally (Cunningham, 2010).

HOW ARE ATTITUDES GENERATED?

There are numerous assumptions in the current attitudes literature about how attitudes are generated. These assumptions involve the issues of representation, process, and system, and we address each one here. Throughout this discussion, the importance in the literature of indirectly versus directly measured attitudes will be apparent. The two types of measures are commonly assumed to tap different representations, processes, or systems, or all three. Issues about how attitudes are generated in the brain are at the center of a social-cognitive perspective.

Representation

What is a representation? A popular definition in the social psychological literature is that mental representations reflect information stored in memory. But, it is important to note that this construct is the subject of a historically long-standing

and intense debate among cognitive scientists, with many varieties of theoretical stances that are not normally seen in the pages of social psychological journals. The only thing strongly agreed upon in the cognitive science literature about representation is that there is no agreement about representation (e.g., Barsalou, 2009; Dietrich & Markman, 2003; Dretske, 1995; Haugeland, 1991; Palmer, 1978; Markman & Dietrich, 2000). Scholars differ in their opinions about the content, format, and architectural nature of mental representations. So, the most basic nature of a representation is still open for debate, both conceptually and empirically.

Some of the questions from this debate have made their way into the literature on attitudes (as well as on other social psychological topics; see, e.g., Carlston & Smith, 1996; Smith & Conrey, 2007). The most common question is whether (or, when) representations are discrete (symbolic/amodal) versus continuous (distributed/modal). Discrete representations are often defined as non-overlapping representations that are symbolic and are separate from the brain's modal systems for perception, action, and internal states (i.e., interoception, introspection, and emotion; see Barsalou, 2009). They are usually assumed to symbolize meaningful information, such as concepts (see Dietrich & Markman, 2003 for more detailed discussions). On the other hand, distributed representations are considered to be modal in that they are generated using the same mechanisms as in the brain's modal systems. They are commonly defined as patterns of activation among (i.e., distributed across) many units of processing (e.g., neurons), wherein the units are not themselves meaningfully correspondent with information in the same way as are discrete representations. A popular analogy to illustrate distributed representations is the television monitor, consisting of many pixels that individually take on only simplistic variations (e.g., binary) of information such as color, but together interactively provide an astoundingly large (though not infinite, in this case) number of possible images.

The two types of representational formats each have their strengths and weaknesses. Distributed representations possess relatively more biological plausibility in that it is possible to conceive of how they would be implemented by the brain via neurons and populations codes. This strength of distributed representations – biological plausibility – is in turn one of the major weaknesses of discrete representations. There are few ideas about how discrete representations could be implemented in the brain (though, see e.g., Devaney, 2003).

Distributed representations have successfully explained a wealth of lower-order phenomena in, for example, perception, language, and categorization (e.g., Elman et al., 1996; Grossberg et al., 1997; McClelland & Rogers, 2003; Seidenberg & McClelland, 1989; E. Smith, 2009; Spivey, 2007; Thelen & L. Smith, 1994). Network models assuming distributed representations have even been able to explain dissociation data that previously were thought to provide strong evidence for two qualitatively distinct processes (see Spivey, 2007). In the social psychological literature, a number of researchers have argued that distributed representations are implicated in attitude generation (Bassili & Brown, 2005; Ferguson, 2007b; Gawronski & Bodenhausen, 2006; Mitchell et al., 2003; Smith & Conrey, 2007; Smith & DeCoster, 2000; Strack & Deutsch, 2004). In particular, theories on attitudes almost uniformly hold that indirectly measured attitudes are reflective of distributed representations.

The strength of discrete representations, on the other hand, is precisely the weakness of distributed representations. Namely, multiple theorists have argued that basic functions of cognition would just not be possible without discrete representations (see Carey, 1985; Dietrich & Markman, 2003; Markman & Dietrich, 2000; Keil, 1989; Marcus, 2001; Spivey, 2007; cf. Thagard, 1991; Van Overwalle & Van Rooy, 2001). For example, Dietrich and Markman (2003) argue that categorization, reasoning, and decision making all require discrete representations. They argue that although distributed representations might be able to explain or reproduce data from lower-level processing, they would be unable to reproduce/explain data from higher-order cognition. And, in fact, there is very little evidence to dispute that claim. Although some social psychologists have started to apply models assuming distributed representations to higher-order cognition, this research is in its infancy. Critically, it is noteworthy that some of the fiercest advocates of distributed representations acknowledge that such a representational format may never be able to explain some higher-order cognition (Spivey, 2007, pp. 284–285). Attitude theorists have tended to imply (though usually not explicitly) that in addition to distributed representations being involved in attitude generation, discrete representations are involved as well. The assumption is that indirect attitudes draw on distributed representations, while direct attitudes draw on both distributed as well as discrete representations (e.g., see Gawronski & Bodenhausen, 2006; Smith & Conrey, 2007; Strack & Deutsch, 2004).

Some cognitive scientists concede that there are probably both types of these representations, along with other variations in format (Barsalou, 2009; Dietrich & Markman, 2003; Jilk, Lebiere, O'Reilly, & Anderson, 2008) and then the question becomes *where* (in the brain) and *when* these representations play a role in cognition (broadly defined). For the attitudes literature then, these questions about discrete versus distributed representation need to be addressed. Although the current consensus is that indirectly measured attitudes reflect distributed representations, as noted, there is very little evidence for, and powerful philosophical arguments against, the notion that distributed representations could explain conscious, higher-order cognition. And, if indirect attitudes involve this sort of high-order cognition, then this poses a problem for theory concerning this issue. Do indirect attitudes involve high-order cognition? This depends on one's definition of "higher-order" cognition, but, at the least, there is considerable neural connectivity between limbic structures typically involved in immediate affective responding and cortical regions that are traditionally assumed to underlie higher-order cognition-like decision making and goal pursuit. Moreover, some indirect attitude measures are correlated with controlled processes (Klauer & Mierke, 2005; Klauer, Schmitz, Teige-Mocigemba, & Voss, 2010; Payne, 2005), which are traditionally assumed to be integrally involved in higher-order cognition.

For theorists who assume discrete representations, there is little theoretical development about how such representations could be biologically implemented in the brain, as noted. Furthermore, a major challenge to any theorist who assumes both types of representation is how they interact. There is some recent speculation that the mathematics involved in dynamical systems (which assume distributed representations) can handle discrete, or binary, decisions. This sub-field has been dubbed "symbolic dynamics," but its development is occurring outside of the social psychological literature (Devaney, 2003). In sum, any glance at the cognitive science literature on representation reveals some serious questions about representation and these debates challenge current assumptions about the types of representations underlying attitudes, or any social psychological construct or process.

Process

The definition of process depends on one's view of representations. For advocates of distributed representations, the representation is the process (e.g., see Conrey & Smith, 2007). A distributed representation is the pattern of activation across simple processing units that are interconnected by weighted functions. So, the activation of a representation from this perspective is the way in which the representation is processed. In other words, it is not necessary to postulate any external, orthogonal processes to act on the distributed representations. But, for discrete theorists, process is something external to the representation. And, although process is rarely defined, when it is defined in the social psychological literature it usually is meant to imply a transformation of mental representations. Its meaning is more fleshed out when it is used to compare associative or rule-based processing – two modes of thought that have received a lot of attention in both cognitive and social psychology (e.g., see Chaiken & Trope, 1999). Associative processing means processing that is based on the statistical covariance (in space or time) of stimuli. That is, through Hebbian learning (Hebb, 1949), the association in memory between stimuli strengthens as those stimuli are experienced close together in space or time. This kind of computation is used for predicting weather systems and the stock market, for instance, and is invaluable in the generation of responses to stimuli that are likely given past experience. This kind of processing is usually characterized as relatively fast, effortless, non-conscious, uncontrollable, and spontaneous. Associative processing is very similar to automatic processing, and the two terms are often used synonymously in the social psychological literature (see Moors & De Houwer, 2006). This type of processing is largely assumed to recruit (or, be synonymous with) distributed representations. Research over the last two decades shows that attitudes can be activated in memory in response to a wide array of stimuli, and under conditions of limited processing, awareness, intention, and control (e.g., see Ferguson & Zayas, 2009; Wittenbrink & Schwarz, 2007). This sort of evidence supports the notion that indirect attitudes are produced through associative or automatic processing.

Associative processing is often contrasted with rule-based processing. This type of processing is assumed to follow rules, where rules are abstract statements about the logical relations between variables (see Sloman, 1996). Rule-based processing is assumed to actually proceed according to steps or procedures of rules, rather than just being able to be described by rules (associative processing can be described by rules even if it does not operate according to them). For instance, rule-based processing is assumed to characterize thinking about probability and logical reasoning. Rule-based processing is often characterized as slow, effortful, conscious, controllable, and intentional. It is often synonymous with "controlled" processing in the social psychological literature. This type of processing is assumed to recruit both distributed as well as discrete representations. Direct attitudes are assumed to be more flexible,

changeable, and context-dependent due to the controlled nature of the underlying processing (e.g., see Wilson et al., 2000).

Most theories state, tacitly imply, or are consistent with the notion that associative processing underlies indirect attitude measures, while both associative and rule-based processing underlie direct attitude measures (Gawronski & Bodenhausen, 2006; Smith & Conrey, 2007). And yet, the notion that these two types of attitude measures tap into distinct cognitive processes has already been challenged by work showing that multiple processes underlie any measure (Jacoby, 1991; Payne, 2005; Sherman, 2009; Sherman, Gawronski, Gonsalkorale, Hugenberg, Allen, & Groom, 2008). Work on the quad model, in particular, shows evidence for four distinct processes, which demonstrates that that there are at least more than two and probably more than four (Sherman, 2009). There is still the question of what (multiple) processes underlie attitude generation during indirect versus direct measurement, and there are likely interesting differences. After all, the behavior captured by these two types of measurement often differs in terms of intentionality, speed, and effort (see De Houwer et al., 2009). The degree to which the measures differ in awareness is still an open empirical question (see Gawronski et al., 2007). But, these different characteristics suggest differences in the underlying processes and at this point it is unclear how many processes are operating, and when. At the least, the evidence suggests strongly that there are more than two, and that direct versus indirect measures do not map exclusively onto different processes.

System

Although the constructs of process and system are often used interchangeably, they are different conceptually and empirically, and arguably exist at different levels of analysis (Keren & Schul, 2009). A system can be classified according to the information it acts on (input), the processes or rules of operation that transform that information, and the accompanying neural substrates (Schacter & Tulving, 1994; for alternative definitions see e.g., Bechtel, 2008; Sperber, 2005; Tooby & Cosmides, 2005).

The notion that there are two systems of cognition has a long tradition, and is closely related to the proposal of two different kinds of processes. There are numerous dual system models in the social psychological literature, and the characteristics and functions of these systems vary (Chaiken & Trope, 1999), which means that either there are considerably more than two systems, or the characteristics of the systems are not correct (see Gilbert, 1999). There have been some recent critical papers on dual-system models in social psychology (Evans, 2008; Keren & Schul, 2009). Keren and Schul (2009) point out the conceptual and empirical vagueness with which dual systems tend to be defined and operationalized (and tested), and argue that the notion of duality in the mind more generally requires considerably more empirical and conceptual support than exists currently in the literature.

Dual systems have been proposed for reasoning (e.g., Kahneman & Frederic, 2002; Sloman, 1996), self-regulation (Metcalf & Mischel, 1999), persuasion (Chaiken, 1980; Petty & Wegener, 1999), attitudes (Rydell, McConnell, Mackie, & Strain, 2006), and affect and emotion (e.g., Epstein, 1994), among others. The attitudes literature in particular though seems to rely most strongly on the assumption that there are separable systems of *memory*. There is an extensive literature on the assertion that explicit and implicit memory are separate systems, with considerable supporting evidence (McClelland, McNaughton, & O'Reilly, 1995; O'Keefe & Nadel, 1978; Schacter & Tulving, 1994; Sherry & Schacter, 1987; E. Smith & DeCoster, 2000; Tulving, 1983). There are also convincing arguments for the evolutionary development and need for separable memory systems. For example, Sherry and Schacter (1987) discuss how human and non-human animals have memory needs that are functionally incompatible. Birds, for example, need memory to enable frequently revised food cache locations as well as revision-impervious song learning. These two needs would seem to pose distinct, functionally incompatible memory capacities and may have prompted the development of separate memory systems. Sherry and Schacter also discuss how primates and humans likely have needs such as habit forming and episodic memory that would similarly seem incompatible. Although there is recently some work challenging the notion of separable memory systems (e.g., Berry, Shanks, & Henson, 2008), there is generally consensus behind the idea given empirical evidence and functional arguments.

Do attitudes differentially rely on these separable memory systems? The assumption seems to be, as the terms implicit and explicit attitudes suggest, that indirect attitudes tap implicit memory while explicit attitudes tap explicit memory. There are multiple purported differences between explicit and implicit memory in the cognitive literature, but the difference that emerges in the pages of the attitudes literature most commonly is the ease with which implicit versus explicit memories are learned and can be revised. Whereas explicit memory allows for fast learning, implicit memory allows for slow learning. The assumption that

indirect attitudes exhibit slow learning is frequently assumed in the literature. This is despite the fact that there are several notable exceptions to this assumption that show that indirect attitudes can form relatively quickly (Ashburn-Nardo et al., 2001; Castelli et al., 2004; De Houwer et al., 1998; Gregg, Seibt, & Banaji, 2006). For instance, Ashburn-Nardo et al. (2001) used a minimal group paradigm to assign participants to one of two different artists. Participants were told that they showed a preference for either the artist Quan or the artist Xanthie. They then completed an IAT testing their preference for others who prefer Quan or Xanthie with the understanding that names that contained a *q* reflected Quan fans while names with an *x* indicated Xanthie fans. Although participants developed their preference only moments earlier, and on the basis of novel information, they showed a significant preference for fans of the artist to which they had been assigned. This shows relatively fast learning. Even stronger evidence for fast learning comes from Gregg, Seibt, and Banaji (2006). In this paper, participants learned about two novel groups of people, one of which was described as good and the other evil. They learned this information either quickly and abstractly (e.g., read that one group was good and the other bad) or concretely (e.g., read lots of detailed information about the character of the two groups). They then completed an IAT to measure their preference for the two groups, and participants showed a significant preference for the good group, regardless of whether they had learned about the groups in an abstract or concrete manner. This again shows that indirect attitudes can respond to relatively fast learning. These examples strongly contradict the assumption in the current attitudes literature that indirect attitudes operate exclusively on the basis of a slow-learning implicit memory system.

However, Gregg et al. (2006) then tested whether newly formed indirect attitudes would be able to be revised with new (countervailing) information. Participants who had learned about the two novel groups then learned that the two groups actually had the opposite character. They learned this in either an abstract manner ("suppose the two groups were switched in character") or in a concrete manner (they read a long and detailed explanation for how the good group eventually turned bad, and how the bad group eventually turned good). They found that although direct attitudes tracked the instructions and were revised accordingly, indirect attitudes were largely resistant to change. Gregg et al. reasoned that indirect attitudes may be like perceptual defaults in that once an evaluation about a stimulus has been learned (perhaps quickly, or through conscious appraisal), it then becomes largely resistant to change thereafter.

This latter conclusion – that indirect attitudes are "stuck" once they have been formed – is consistent with the general assumption that they are unable to be revised quickly, and in line with assumptions about implicit memory underlying indirect attitudes. Still, these findings concerning the fast formation of indirect attitudes challenge the widely adopted view that indirect attitudes rely exclusively on implicit memory. The findings would seem to pose a challenge either for this claim, or for the claim that implicit memory is slow learning. The more parsimonious implication is that indirect attitudes do not rely exclusively on implicit memory.

In addition to assuming differences between indirect and direct attitudes in terms of the speed of learning, researchers have also argued that they differ in the types of information they are influenced by *during* learning (Rydell et al., 2006). Rydell and colleagues have argued that if indirect attitudes are reliant on implicit memory and associative processes, they should be especially sensitive to subliminally presented information that is activated in close proximity with the novel stimulus. Direct attitudes, on the other hand, should be more sensitive to verbal information that is described as being about the novel stimulus. They tested this by presenting participants with information about a novel target named Bob. They presented many stimuli pairs consisting of a picture of Bob and behavioral information about Bob. The behavioral information was positive or negative in valence, and was described as being characteristic or not characteristic of Bob. Immediately before each presentation of the picture of Bob, however, highly positive or negative words were also subliminally presented. The valence of the subliminal information was always in opposition to the valence of the verbally presented information, and Rydell et al. examined how this learning paradigm would influence participants' indirect and direct attitudes toward Bob. They found that direct attitudes were sensitive to the verbally presented information, while indirect attitudes were sensitive to the subliminally presented information. They concluded that these two different types of attitude measures capture different attitudes in memory, form within different systems, and consist of different representations.

Although the results of the Rydell et al. paper are intriguing, they raise multiple questions. First, if learning evaluative information about novel stimuli is modularized in this way, then other findings from other lines of research are puzzling. For instance, research on mere exposure has found that different frequencies in the exposure to subliminally presented stimuli lead to differences on direct attitude measures. Similarly, research on subliminal evaluative conditioning has also found

effects on direct attitude measures. As for whether indirect attitudes are sensitive to verbally presented information, although there is little work on the formation of indirect attitudes, the previously described studies by Ashburn-Nardo et al. (2001) and Gregg et al. (2006) are two examples against it. Thus, it is not clear how the interpretation of the dissociation in the Rydell et al. paper can be squared with other work. It may be the case that indirect and direct attitudes differ in the kinds of information that will exert an influence under some circumstances, and these circumstances need to be identified. However, if indirect attitudes can be revised or formed by exposure to verbally presented information and conscious reasoning, for instance, it would imply that the two types of attitude measures do not map exclusively or consistently into distinct memory systems as is assumed in the attitudes literatures.

We have already described how indirect attitudes depend on multiple processes that have been characterized as controlled, and they also may be conscious (unlike implicit memory as it has been operationalized in cognitive science), and so there would seem to be multiple reasons to assume that indirect and direct attitudes do not map onto implicit and explicit memory systems. Given the preceding discussion, we now turn to some of the most central debates within the attitudes literature and argue that some of them depend on assumptions about representation, process, system, or some combination of these issues.

DISSOCIATION DATA ACCORDING TO MEASUREMENT

If indirect and direct attitudes each consist of discrete and distributed representations, each rely on an assortment of processes, and each potentially involve implicit as well as explicit memory, what exactly explains the fact that they occasionally diverge? There are multiple reasons why attitudes from these two different types of measure might be dissociated (se De Houwer et al., 2009; Nosek, 2005; Wittenbrink & Schwarz, 2007). First, even though the previous discussion suggested that they might not map exclusively onto different types of representations, processes, or systems, this does not mean that they involve the same proportion or extent of representations, processes, or systems. They may differ in the degree to which they rely on implicit versus explicit memory, or the degree to which they involve multiple automatic processes, for instance. So, the preceding discussion does not preclude the possibility that these measures are tapping different kinds of informational formats (representations), operate according to different kinds of rules (sets of processes), and implicate different neural substrates (systems). This remains a wide-open empirical question. Any of these possibilities could potentially explain dissociation data.

Alternatively, researchers have identified reasons for divergence in data from these two types of measures that do not necessarily point to underlying (substantive) differences in type of representation, process, or system. There are differences in the structural fit of the two tasks, method, task, and instruction differences, response bias, and presentation norms (e.g., Olson, Fazio, & Hermann, 2007; Payne, Burkley, Stokes, 2008; Smith & Nosek, 2011). These would seem to be superficial reasons for dissociation, but it is important to note that some processes, for example, may be triggered by particular task constraints, and so differences in methodology do not necessarily preclude differences in underlying cognitive process (nor do they necessarily point to them).

One obvious difference between the measures is the time that elapses between the perception of the stimulus and the respondent's behavior toward that stimulus. In an indirect measure it is often a matter of a hundred milliseconds or less, whereas in direct measures it can be multiple seconds. This is a considerable difference in cognitive processing time, and it is important to appreciate how cognition can vary over such a time lapse. An object and its associated attitude are not activated in memory and then frozen – they likely undergo repeated iterations in processing that recruit other information, with the influence of some kinds of information waxing or waning, etc. Thus, one important difference is the point in time that the measure captures the dynamic processing stream that is constantly changing (e.g., Cunningham, Zelazo, Packer, & Van Bavel, 2007; Fazio, 1995; Lamme & Roelfsema, 2000; O'Reilly, 1998; Spivey, 2007). This is not to say that we cannot hold a piece of information in mind for a spell, to concentrate on it, or keep it in working memory. We can, but it is not easy (e.g., Smallwood & Schooler, 2006). The mind does not stand still (see Spivey, 2007). And, the processing that likely accompanies attitude measures is constantly dynamically evolving. This is consistent with the view that some of the same representations or processes underlying indirect measures may be exerting an influence also during explicit measurement (e.g., see Cunningham et al., 2007; Fazio, 1995; Wojnowicz, Ferguson, Dale, & Spivey, 2009). A complete disconnect between the representations and processing underlying each type of measure would of course suggest orthogonal constructs, and the data to date do not support this.

STABILITY VERSUS CONTEXTUAL DEPENDENCE

One persistent debate is the extent to which attitudes are trait-like and stable or constructed on the spot, and thus heavily dependent on the context. There are two different levels at which this issue can be analyzed: one level concerns questions of generation in memory, and the other level concerns observed data. In fact, conflating these two levels leads to all kinds of confusion. Let's begin with the level of observed data. Do attitudes seem to persist regardless of time and context? Does someone's liking of pizza, for instance, emerge regardless of whether she is hungry or bored? As we review below, there is a lot of evidence both for stability across time as well as for sensitivity according to the context.

How do researchers tend to interpret this kind of evidence? Their explanations depend on their theory about how attitudes are generated, or what attitudes reflect. One view is that attitudes are relatively stable, trait-like constructs (e.g., Dovidio, Kawakami, & Beach, 2001; Petty et al., 2006; Rudman, 2004; Wilson et al., 2000). Fazio and colleagues (Fazio, 2007), for instance, have argued that many stimuli have summary evaluations associated with them in memory, and that a summary can be formed from many kinds of sources (feelings, beliefs, behaviors). Once this summary evaluation is formed, it can be relatively stable, especially if the summary is well learned, or highly accessible. From this view, a stimulus would be evaluated in roughly the same way regardless of time and context. Any fluctuation in observed attitudes across time and situations would simply mean that the stimulus was categorized in different ways across time and situations. Thus, attitudes – especially strong attitudes that can be activated spontaneously – are generally stable and durable across time. Evidence for fluctuation across time or situation is simply evidence that the object of judgment, rather than the judgment of the object (Asch, 1948, p. 256), is changing. This view would seem to assume that attitudes are discrete representations. Or, in the parlance of social psychological terminology, attitudes would be considered as abstract, generalized prototypes (summaries) of evaluative knowledge concerning stimuli.

The view that attitudes are instead constructed on the spot has been understood as a contrast to the traits/stability view (e.g., Bassili & Brown, 2005; Schwarz, 2007; Schwarz & Bohner, 2001; Tesser, 1978; Wilson & Hodges, 1992; see also Gawronski & Bodenhausen, 2006), and has also gained popularity over the years, for example in the preferences literature (for a review, see

Lichtenstein & Slovic, 2006). What does "constructed on the spot" mean exactly? The only logically possible definition is that for each stimulus, some computation (or integration) is performed across stored sources of evaluative knowledge and information. In this way, there are stored memories about what is good or bad, and these are combined in some way to predict a particular person's particular response to a particular stimulus at a particular time. This view seems most harmonious with the notion of distributed representations (e.g., Ferguson, 2007b), or the notion that any given attitude reflects the online computation across many specific similar instances (i.e., exemplar models of cognition).

One important question for this perspective concerns the nature of the computation or integration (see Betsch, Plessner, Schwieren, & Gütig, 2001). Additionally, some have questioned how such a constructivist process could be economical, given that it would mean that a person would have to "reconstruct" something in order to know whether it is good or bad (see Fazio, 2007; Wilson et al., 2000). However, such "recomputation" does not necessarily need to be effortful, and, in fact, construing an object on the basis of its salient features and the attendant evaluative implications is selectively narrowing down all the available information about the object and presumably making its resulting evaluation more precise, and computationally tractable. Furthermore, there is a great deal of evidence that non-evaluative object knowledge is context-dependent (e.g., see Barsalou, 2008, 2009; Yeh & Barsalou, 2006), so why would evaluative knowledge be computed differently?

After a closer look, however, one might ask how these two views concerning stability and contextual dependence are actually different. There seems to be more agreement between them than might be evident at first glance. First, the two views agree that attitudes reflect stored knowledge. According to the trait/stable view, the observed attitude is the stored summary evaluation. According to the constructivist view, the observed attitude is computed from different sources of stored evaluative information. It is also true that both views assume that the context influences the attitude. The trait/stable view assumes that the context influences the interpretation (or construal, or categorization) of the stimulus, which then (neatly) determines the attitude that is activated. This still means that attitudes are dependent on the context; it is just that the context is influential at the level of object construal, and once the object has been categorized, the attitude presumably follows from that without further interference from the context. In the constructivist view, the attitudes themselves are dependent on the context.

Critically, this of course means that both views are also entirely consistent with stability and variation in observed data across time and situations. If the many elements comprising the context in which a stimulus is encountered are uniform in valence, then the observed attitude could be highly stable, even though it (and/or the stimulus) would still be constructed according to the nature of the context (see Gawronski, Rydell, Vervliet, & De Houwer, 2010). This means that any amount of evidence for contextual dependence cannot really adjudicate between these views.

Instead, the real point of difference is in what the observed attitude reflects. The trait/stable view maintains that the attitude reflects a stored summary evaluation, and the constructivist view argues that it reflects an integration of evaluative information across various sources. These views are suggestive of different types of cognitive architectural commitments. The trait view would seem to assume discrete representations (though see Fazio, 2007), as well as a separation in processing between object recognition or categorization, and attitude activation. And, the constructivist view would seem to be most consistent with distributed representations, although theoretically a computation could operate across discrete representations (see Ferguson, 2007b).

This discussion makes it apparent that the two views are not really that different in terms of the question of whether the context matters, and whether stored knowledge is implicated in attitudes. What is not clear are the assumptions underlying these two views concerning representation, process, and system. We have already identified the many open questions with respect to these issues. These two views therefore require conceptual discussion about representation, process, and system, and cannot be decided simply from evidence of contextual variability in observed attitudes. As Schwarz has noted, deciding whether context variability represents a latent variable of an attitude with noise, or different evaluative responses, is not possible to answer empirically.

Moderators of stability and context dependence of direct attitudes

What is the evidence regarding stability versus context dependence? Demonstrating attitude stability is complicated in that an empirical demonstration would require null results, which are more difficult to interpret than results that reflect a significant difference. Thus, often the most memorable and most cited research on attitudes is when relatively small changes in the context have strong effects on attitude change (e.g., Wittenbrink et al., 2001). Although researchers may not be able to quantify the precise degree to which attitudes are stable versus context dependent, they can identify the moderators that predict when attitudes are more or less likely to be stable versus context dependent (see Petty & Krosnick, 1995).

Although attitude strength would seem to be a likely candidate as a predictor of attitude stability, there is some debate on the relationship between attitude strength and attitude stability. Researchers have identified about a dozen strength attributes of attitudes, including attitude importance, knowledge, elaboration, certainty, ambivalence, accessibility, intensity, extremity, structural consistency, (see Petty & Krosnick, 1995). Across 27 experiments conducted in national surveys, Krosnick and Schuman (1988) showed that none of three strength-related attitude properties (importance, intensity, and certainty) was found to reliably moderate the impact of question variations known to produce response effects, such as question order, wording, or form of questions.

In contrast, in a study done by different researchers, attitude importance, elaboration, certainty, extremity, ambivalence (reverse scored), and intensity, were each shown to each be correlated with resistance to attitude change (Lavine, Huff, Wagner, & Sweeney, 1998). When each attribute was examined individually, Lavine et al. found strong and significant context effects for target issues among participants whose attitudes were highly ambivalent, low in prior elaboration, low in attitude certainty, low in attitude extremity, and low in intensity.

Although it is not entirely clear why seemingly conflicting findings have emerged, there are some key differences in the methodology that may have led to the differing results. Visser, Bizer, and Krosnick (2006) have suggested that Lavine and his colleagues' findings are limited to a specific kind of question order context effect. In contrast, Lavine et al. (1998) have argued that Krosnick and his colleagues' findings may be particular to the attitude issue and that attitude strength measures must be sufficiently broad to demonstrate an effect on attitude stability. Taken together, the research indicates that particular response effects are affected by different attitude attributes and that these effects may also interact differently depending on the attitude object.

There may also be chronic individual differences in attitude stability. Individual differences can also moderate attitude stability. People high in the *need for affect*, the tendency to become involved in emotion-inducing situations (Maio & Esses, 2001), versus people high in the *need for cognition*, the tendency to engage in and enjoy effortful cognitive activity (Cacioppo & Petty, 1982), maintain different degrees of attitude stability in the face of different kinds of persuasive

messages. Huskinson and Haddock (2004) found that people who are high in the need for affect are more persuaded by affect-based appeals than are people high in the need for cognition. In contrast, those high in the need for cognition find cognitive, rather than affective, appeals more persuasive.

Moderators of stability and context dependence of indirect attitudes

One of the central questions guiding research on indirect attitudes over the past 10 or so years has been the extent to which such evaluations are stable across time and contexts. Initially, attitudes measured by implicit methods were thought to be a potentially stable measurements precisely because they were assumed to be independent of the context in which they were measured (e.g., Banaji, 2001; Bargh et al., 1992, 1996; Devine, 1989; Fazio et al., 1995; Greenwald et al., 1998; Wilson & Hodges, 1992) unlike the contextual influences inherent in direct attitude measurement (see Banaji, 2001; Fazio et al., 1995; Schwarz & Bohner, 2001). Because indirect measures were assumed to assess participants' evaluations without their awareness (cf. Gawronski et al., 2007), participants were assumed to be unable to strategically modify their responses (for a review see Ferguson, 2007b).

As data on direct and indirect attitude measures accumulated, evidence began to emerge that indirect attitudes are often weakly correlated or completely unrelated to direct attitudes (e.g., Fazio et al., 1995; Greenwald & Banaji, 1995; Karpinski & Hilton, 2001; though, see Cunningham, Preacher, & Banaji, 2001; McConnell & Leibold, 2001; Wittenbrink, Judd, & Park, 1997). Although some degree of disconnect between the two types of measures is expected, given the differences in the nature of the measures, a complete lack of correspondence worried researchers, and some questioned the construct validity of indirect attitudes and evaluations (see Banaji, 2001 for a discussion). If indirect measures are tapping people's "true" attitudes and preferences (Fazio et al., 1995), then they should at least partially correspond with related measures in some situations, in line with basic conventions regarding convergent and criterion validity. This concern provoked considerable research efforts at examining the stability and contextual independence of indirect attitudes and the relation between indirect and direct measures in general (e.g., for a review see Blair et al., 2001; Dovidio et al., 2001; Fazio & Olson, 2003; Nosek, 2005).

The findings suggest many contextual influences on indirect attitudes, contrary to the initial assumptions of contextual independence. Specifically, findings suggest that the direction and strength of an indirect attitude toward a given object vary, depending on the type of recently activated, or repeatedly learned, object-relevant information (e.g., Dasgupta & Greenwald, 2001; Karpinski & Hilton, 2001; Lowery, Hardin, & Sinclair, 2001; Mitchell et al., 2003; Wittenbrink et al., 2001). For instance, researchers found that participants displayed significantly less negative indirect attitudes toward group members who are commonly targets of prejudice after being exposed to pro-elderly stimuli (Karpinski & Hilton, 2001) and exemplars of well-liked African Americans and disliked White people (Dasgupta & Greenwald, 2001).

Recent work has shown that indirect attitudes are also influenced by the goal that the perceiver is currently pursuing (e.g., Ferguson, 2008; Ferguson & Bargh, 2004; Lowery et al., 2001; Moore, Ferguson, & Chartrand, 2011; Moors & De Houwer, 2001; Sherman et al., 2003) and by the perceiver's chronic motivations (Maddux, Barden, Brewer, & Petty, 2005). For example, Lowery et al. (2001) found that participants who completed an IAT administered by a Black (vs White) experimenter exhibited significantly reduced negative attitudes toward Blacks, demonstrating that indirect attitude measures may be susceptible to social influence pressures. Ferguson and Bargh (2004) investigated how the extent to which a goal is completed affects indirect attitudes. They found that participants who were currently pursuing a goal (or not) completed an evaluative priming paradigm that measured their indirect attitudes toward objects that varied in their relevance to the goal. The results suggest that objects that were relevant to the goal were evaluated as most positive when the perceiver was still pursuing the goal versus had already completed it. For example, participants who were thirsty evaluated the highly thirst-relevant objects (e.g., water, juice) as more positive, than other objects (e.g., chair, table), compared to participants who had just quenched their thirst. These findings demonstrate that indirect evaluations are sometimes prospective with regard to the utility of the objects, as opposed to solely a function of recent experience with the objects.

People's chronic goals can also influence indirect attitudes. Maddux et al. (2005) demonstrated that the impact of contextual cues on participants' indirect attitudes toward Black people depended on participants' chronic motivation to avoid being prejudiced. Participants low in this motivation exhibited negative attitudes toward Blacks in contexts that were threatening (e.g., a prison cell) compared to non-threatening (e.g., a church). In contrast, participants high in the motivation to avoid being prejudiced actually showed less negative evaluations of Blacks in the threatening context, compared with other participants overall and also with high-motivation participants in the non-threatening context. Interestingly, these participants' less negative attitudes resulted from an inhibition of negative information in the threatening condition. This work suggests that people's chronic motivations can determine the way in which they respond to contextual cues regarding the nature of the evaluated stimuli (see also Moskowitz, Gollwitzer, Wasel, & Schaal, 1999).

The research on both indirect and direct methods of attitude measurement have uncovered a variety of moderators that predict when attitudes are likely to be more stable or context dependent. Situational differences, such as recently activated or chronic exemplars and goals, as well as individual differences in people, can influence the extent to which attitudes will be influenced by contextual cues. The question is not whether attitudes are basically stable versus constructed, but rather *when* each is true.

CHANGING OUR LIKES AND DISLIKES

What does attitude "change" mean? Attitude change is typically meant to imply that some manipulation produces changes in the underlying representations. But, how can we infer this? On the one hand, evidence for the contextual dependence of attitudes (reviewed above) would seem to imply that attitudes "change" quite readily. But, this would be misleading because such change could result from the stimulus being categorized differently across contexts, and with resulting differences in evaluations, but without any (significant) accompanying change at the level of representations. So, how might we address this question?

It is important to note that recent research on memory suggests that each time a stimulus is encountered (even in highly familiar situations), there are corresponding changes in the relevant representations (e.g., see Nader, Schafe, & LeDoux, 2000). Every encounter with a stimulus changes (e.g., strengthens) the underlying associations (or, weights) with those representations of accompanying stimuli, and weakens those with absent stimuli. This would be true presumably for both discrete and distributed representations. In this way, every encounter with a given stimulus is a learning/changing instance.

Given this, what is meant by attitude change? Probably what is most often meant by change is when an attitude shifts toward recently over previously learned, and *countervailing*, information. In other words, change is when the intensity or direction of the attitude becomes more aligned with recently learned information. (This is a slightly different version than the case where one learns evaluative information about a novel stimulus.) From this perspective, "slow" change is what happens every time we process a stimulus, and this could be understood in terms of the attitude incrementally aligning with recent over previous information. "Fast" change, on the other hand, would be an instance of an attitude shifting relatively more quickly toward recently acquired, countervailing information.

Most of the work on attitude change has focused on direct attitudes with the assumption that attitudes are relatively stable. Recently Gawronski and Bodenhausen (2006) presented a model for how direct and indirect attitudes can be expected to change. The model is called the associative–propositional evaluation (APE) model, and, as its name implies, it assumes that attitude change can be understood in terms of associative and propositional processes. Whereas attitudes activated by associative processes are independent of whether the person endorses those attitudes (i.e., their subjective "truth value"), attitudes based on propositional processes have undergone an assessment (relying on capacity and motivation) for their truth value and endorsement. Gawronski and Bodenhausen (2006) outline the circumstances in which both direct and indirect attitudes should show change. For example, they note that the two types of measures might show asymmetric change in that indirect attitudes are changed without any change in direct attitudes, as well as the reverse. The former might happen when, for example, people undergo evaluative conditioning of which they are aware (e.g., Karpinski & Hilton, 2001). Although the evaluative conditioning changes the kinds of evaluative information tapped in an indirect measure, during direct measurement people can reject that newly learned information, given their awareness of the potentially biasing nature of that paradigm. Direct attitudes, on the other hand, might show change when people have recently learned propositional information about the stimulus that is not well-learned enough to show up on indirect measures (Gregg et al., 2006). We now briefly comment on social-cognitive work on direct versus indirect attitude change.

Direct attitude change

Changing direct attitudes has long been a traditional topic of interest within the attitudes literature, and generally falls under the umbrella of persuasion research. There is a voluminous literature that addresses the circumstances under which people's self-reported attitudes can be influenced by persuasive appeals. Although reviewing this literature is beyond the purview of the current chapter, we note that much of this work is consistent with a social-cognitive perspective, and the debates in this literature recently have been social cognitive in nature. For example, one debate has been whether persuasion should be understood in terms of a dual-process model versus a uni-process model. The bulk of the research has assumed that people can respond to persuasive appeals in one of two ways (e.g., Chaiken, 1980, 1987; Chaiken & Stangor, 1987; Petty & Cacioppo, 1986). In a systematic or central manner, the person carefully and deliberately analyzes the message-relevant information and is influenced by the strength of the message. The other route is called heuristic or peripheral, and occurs when people are responding with considerably less effort and attention. In this situation, a person might be influenced by cues that are unrelated to the strength of the message, such as the attractiveness or expertise of the spokesperson, the amount of information provided, or even the fluency of the information. This work relies on dual-process assumptions that were described in an earlier section of this current chapter. People are assumed to follow a central or systematic route whenever they are motivated to be accurate and have sufficient cognitive resources. A considerable amount of research shows that people seem to be influenced by superficial cues when they are unmotivated or cognitively taxed, and are influenced by message-relevant information when they are motivated and have the resources.

In contrast with this perspective is the uni-model, by Kruglanski and colleagues (Kruglanski, Erb, Chun, Pierro, & Mannetti, 2003; Kruglanski, Thompson, & Spiegel, 1999). They argue that people actually use syllogistic reasoning in response to any persuasive appeal and so the process is the same regardless of the constraints of the situation and appeal. Differences emerge in terms of what people use for their reasoning process according to the placement and salience of the information in the appeal. Kruglanski and colleagues have argued that previous persuasion research has introduced a confound, wherein cues that have been identified as indicative of the heuristic or peripheral route have been easier to process (e.g., presented early in an appeal), whereas information that would be indicative of the central or systematic route has been more deeply embedded in the appeal.

Indirect attitude change

In terms of changing indirect attitudes, there has been less empirical activity. Much of this work has used the learning paradigm of evaluative conditioning to try to alter (not just change the categorization of) existing indirect attitudes. The phenomenon of evaluative conditioning has received increased empirical attention recently from social psychologists (e.g., Hofmann, De Houwer, Perugini, Baeyens, & Crombez, 2010; Jones et al., 2009; Walther, Nagengast, & Trasselli, 2005). There are still various questions about the precise mechanisms and boundaries of evaluative conditioning (see Hofmann et al., 2010; Jones et al., 2009); however, multiple papers provide evidence for the effect itself. For instance, although there is evidence that evaluative conditioning emerges when the primes are presented subliminally or when participants report no awareness of the prime–target pairings (Aarts, Custers, & Holland, 2007; Aarts, Custers, & Marien, 2008; Baeyens, Eelen, & Van der Bergh, 1990; Custers & Aarts, 2005; Dijksterhuis, 2004; Jones et al., 2009; Jones, Pelham, Carvallo, & Mirenberg, 2004; Olson & Fazio, 2001, 2002, 2006; Ruys & Stapel, 2009; Walther, 2002; Walther & Nagengast, 2006), there is also evidence that it does not emerge when participants do not have at least some awareness (Dawson et al., 2007; Field, 2000; Pleyers et al., 2007; Stahl, Unkelbach, & Corneille, 2009). This is an ongoing debate.

Of most relevance to this topic of attitude change (vs formation), evaluative conditioning has emerged for familiar (vs novel) objects (Aarts et al., 2007; Custers & Aarts, 2005; Dijksterhuis, 2004; Karpinski & Hilton, 2001; Kawakami, Dovidio, Moll, Hermsen, & Russin, 2000; Olson & Fazio, 2006; Ruys & Stapel, 2009; Rudman, Asmore, & Gary, 2001), and can last until at least 2 days (Olson & Fazio, 2006). For example, Olson and Fazio (2006) found that participants who had received positive conditioning of African American faces later showed significantly less prejudice toward the group. This work is also consistent with recent research showing that participants who repeatedly associated approach movements toward a given stimulus later showed more positive indirect attitudes toward it (e.g., Kawakami, Phills, Steele, & Dovidio, 2007). Given the close correspondence between arm movements and evaluation (e.g., Chen & Bargh, 1999), these findings speak to how indirect attitudes can be changed.

THE FORMATION OF LIKES AND DISLIKES

The formation of attitudes has been an understudied topic in the attitudes literature, as noted repeatedly (Albarracín et al., 2005; Eagly & Chaiken, 1993; Fazio & Olson, 2003). Whereas the topic of changing attitudes concerns cases where new (often countervailing) information is provided about familiar stimuli, the formation of attitudes concerns cases where information is provided about novel or unfamiliar stimuli. Most of the work has been conducted with direct attitudes, but some recent work has examined the formation of indirect attitudes. These two areas of research on development are briefly described below.

Direct attitudes

Although some early research focused on unconscious processes underlying the formation of attitudes (e.g., Staats & Staats, 1958), the majority of research until the past few years has focused on the formation of attitudes that people can verbalize. The subjective–expected–utility approach to decision making, first articulated by the statistician Leonard Savage (1954), became popular among social psychologists attempting to explain attitude formation (e.g., Fishbein & Ajzen, 1974; Rosenberg, 1956; Wyer, 1973). This approach assumes that people are basically rational – people form beliefs based on information they receive, form attitudes based on those beliefs, and choose actions based on those attitudes and the expected probabilities of the outcomes. Later approaches to direct attitude formation focused on shortcut strategies (e.g., Chaiken, 1980; Petty & Cacioppo, 1986). These approaches assumed that people, if they are not rational, at least want to be rational in that they are motivated to hold correct beliefs and attitudes and act accordingly. However, it is also assumed that people are motivated to conserve cognitive resources. Thus, people will maintain attitudes based on superficial (peripheral) cues unless they are sufficiently motivated to seek out more in-depth information and have the cognitive resources to process and seek out information more rigorously. For example, the quality of the arguments has a greater impact on persuasion under conditions of high- than low-issue involvement (Petty & Cacioppo, 1979) and for individuals high than low in need for cognition (Cacioppo, Petty, & Morris, 1983). Conversely, peripheral cues such as the attractiveness of the communicator have a greater impact on persuasion under conditions of low than high involvement (Chaiken, 1980; Petty, Cacioppo, & Goldman, 1981).

An especially interesting examination of the formation of direct attitudes was by Betsch et al. (2001). In this paper, the authors tested whether direct attitudes could form during exposure to only superficially processed evaluative information. Participants were asked to watch a series of ads on a computer, and while they were doing so, information about the share value of novel stocks appeared at the top of the screen. Betsch et al. wanted to examine not only whether participants would form evaluations of the stocks based on such subtle exposure but also how the pieces of evaluative information would be combined. Although some research (e.g., Anderson, 1983) suggests that pieces of evaluative information would be averaged, other work from animal learning suggests that it might be summed. Betsch et al. found evidence that participants reported attitudes toward the novel stocks according to the overall summation of the positive information. This research is an especially interesting demonstration of not only how direct attitudes can be formed with minimal processing of the evaluative information but also of how they are formed in terms of process.

Indirect attitudes

What are the circumstances in which people form attitudes that can be measured indirectly? In other words, when and how are people able to form attitudes toward stimuli that can be activated unintentionally, rapidly, and perhaps at times even without awareness? Recent work has taken various different strategies to try to instill indirect attitudes.

Almost all of the work on the formation of indirect attitudes has provided a large number of trials in which the novel object is paired repeatedly with evaluative information. For example, Olson and Fazio (2001) developed an evaluative conditioning paradigm and examined whether it would lead to the formation of indirect attitudes. In this study, participants were presented with various stimuli randomly on a computer screen, and the stimuli consisted of images as well as words. Their task was to press a key whenever they saw a specific target stimulus. The conditioned stimulus (CS) was a Pokemon character (participants were unfamiliar with these stimuli), and the unconditioned stimuli (US) were highly positive (e.g., ice cream sundae) or negative (e.g., cockroach) stimuli. The CS was presented simultaneously with the US, and they were never the target stimulus that participants were monitoring. Participants did not report any awareness of the covariation, and yet still showed a significant preference for the positively conditioned stimulus both on direct as well as indirect measures (see also De Houwer, Baeyens, & Field, 2005; De Houwer, Thomas, & Baeyens, 2001; Martin & Levy, 1978; Walther, Nagengast, & Trasselli, 2005).

As another example of the formation of indirect attitudes through an extensive amount of learning, earlier in this chapter we described research by Rydell and colleagues (Rydell et al., 2006) that showed newly formed indirect attitudes toward a novel target. Participants were presented with many (100) trials in which the novel stimulus (Bob) was paired with positive or negative subliminally presented information as well as positive or negative verbally presented information. Participants' indirect attitudes developed in line with the valence of the subliminally presented information.

The methodological strategy of trying to form indirect attitudes through extensive new pairings or information is consistent with the notion that such attitude rely on implicit memory which only enables slow learning. However, as we have argued already, there are examples of relatively fast formation of indirect attitudes by Ashburn-Nardo et al. (2001) and Gregg et al. (2006). There is also research by De Houwer et al. (1998) and Castelli et al. (2004) showing that novel stimuli that have been only briefly and recently classified as positive or negative can themselves lead to consistent evaluations on indirect measures. For example, De Houwer et al. (1998) found that nonwords that had been briefly paired with highly positive or negative words were themselves indirectly evaluated in line with those positive or negative classifications. And, Castelli and colleagues (2004) showed that recently learned evaluative information about people determined participants' indirect attitudes toward those people. Participants viewed a series of novel people, and these people were described simply as being either child molesters or child counselors. The classification of each person was brief, and yet minutes later, participants indirectly evaluated those novel targets in line with the classification. This work, too, shows that relatively novel stimuli can become evaluatively "stamped" relatively quickly and easily, and in such a way that allows for later unintentional and rapid evaluation.

The idea that stimuli can quickly take on an evaluative connotation is consistent with animal learning literature on single-trial learning. A wide variety of animals and insects, including worms, flies, monkeys, and humans, seem able to develop fear responses after a single experience with a threatening stimulus (see LeDoux, 2000). Rats who are electrically shocked in a specific cage, for instance, later show fear responses to the cage. It is interesting to note that humans as well as non-human animals can retain and express learned preferences even without any accompanying explicit memory about the stimulus or its evaluative meaning (e.g., Squire, 1992; Squire & Kandel, 1999). For instance, if a person with anterograde amnesia has an unpleasant experience with a new acquaintance, the person will show evidence for the implicit memory of that evaluative experience even when he or she of course cannot retain any explicit awareness for the acquaintance.

WHAT ATTITUDES PREDICT

For decades, researchers have puzzled over the weak relationship between attitudes and behavior (e.g., LaPiere, 1934; Thurstone, 1928; Wicker, 1969). The oft-cited paper of Wicker (1969) showed that a meta-analysis of 45 studies yielded a mean correlation of 0.15 between attitudes and behaviors. More recently, researchers have become more optimistic about the consistency between the two variables. In a meta-analysis of 88 studies, Kraus (1995) found that the average attitude–behavior correlation was 0.38, with over half of the studies showing a correlation of above 0.30.

Efforts to explain the attitude–behavior relationship are of two kinds: moderator variable research and methodological research. The consistency (and lack thereof) between attitudes and behaviors can be explained by moderating variables that boost or weaken the relationship. These moderators can be situational, socio-cognitive, or personality variables. Alternatively, other research focuses on showing how methodological flaws yield a certain relationship, while improvements can lead to a stronger relationship. Specifically, indirect attitude researchers have argued that indirect measures of attitudes do not have the demand effects and other weaknesses that explicit measures have, and demonstrate a stronger attitude–behavior relationship (Greenwald, McGhee, & Schwarz, 1998).

In terms of theoretical work, one of the most influential theories concerning predictions about attitudes and behavior is Fazio's MODE model (Motivation and Opportunity as Determinants of the attitude–behavior relation; Fazio, 1986, 1990; Olson & Fazio, 2009). As previously discussed, according to Fazio, an attitude is a learned association in memory between an object and a positive or negative evaluation of that object. Consistent with other dual processing theories (e.g., Chaiken & Trope, 1999), the model claims that attitudes can be activated either in a controlled, deliberative manner or an automatic, spontaneous manner.

Based on the MODE model, indirect attitudes will lead to behaviors consistent with the attitude depending on two moderators: motivation and opportunity. Automatically activated attitudes are the starting point of the attitude-to-behavior process.

When there is a lack of sufficient motivation and/ or cognitive capacity to process information (opportunity), overt judgments and behaviors are hypothesized to reflect the automatically activated attitude. In contrast, sufficient motivational factors and/or opportunity can intercept the automatic attitude, such that the subsequent behavior is less influenced by the automatically activated attitude. Alternatively, in situations when there is no motivation and/or opportunity, nor chronically accessible automatic attitudes, the behavior is more likely to be determined by salient cues associated with the attitude object. According to the MODE model, automatic or spontaneous activation is reflective of strong attitudes. When a strong link has been established in memory, it is more likely to be automatically activated, and thus, is more chronically accessible.

Therefore, the MODE model predicts that attitudes should be good predictors of behaviors when they are readily accessible from memory. In contrast, attitudes should be relatively poor predictors of behaviors when they are not readily accessible. Indeed, research testing this hypothesis has shown that attitude accessibility (as operationalized by response latency), predicts attitude–behavior consistency in domains such as voting (Fazio & Williams, 1986) and prejudiced behavior (Fazio et al., 1995).

Direct attitudes and behavior consistency

Several moderators between direct attitudes and behavior consistency have been identified in the literature, such as attitude accessibility, certainty, and temporal stability. Because there are several excellent recent reviews and meta-analyses on the relationship between direct attitudes and behavior consistency (see Cooke & Sheeran, 2004; Crano & Prislin, 2006; Glasman & Albarracín, 2006), they will not be further discussed in this chapter.

Implicit attitudes and behavior consistency

More recent research has focused on the extent to which attitude–behavior consistency can be predicted by implicit measures of attitudes, such as the Implicit Association Test (IAT, Greenwald et al., 1998). The IAT and other implicit measures of attitudes have received much attention, in part, because they have been shown to be resistant to self-presentational concerns that can mask personally or socially undesirable attitudes (Greenwald et al., 1998).

The IAT has also been demonstrated to predict behaviors, in some cases better than explicit measures of attitudes. In a review of 32 studies on attitudes toward African-American–White interracial behavior, predictive validity of IAT measures significantly exceeded that of self-report measures (Greenwald, Poehlman, Uhlmann, & Banaji, 2009). Although an impressive amount of research has utilized the IAT and other implicit measures of attitudes to predict behaviors, some researchers have questioned the predictive validity of implicit measures (e.g., Blanton, Jaccard, Klick, Mellers, Mitchell, & Tetlock, 2009).

Implicit measures of attitudes appear to be better at predicting behaviors that are uncontrolled and/or not overt compared to more controlled behaviors. For example, Vanman, Saltz, Nathan, and Warren (2004) showed that IAT measures of racial bias did not correspond with discrimination against African Americans, as measured by participants not choosing the African-American candidate among two other equally strong candidates to win a fellowship. However, studies which measured less overt behaviors have demonstrated that the IAT is a significant predictor. McConnell and Leibold (2001) showed that indirect measures of racial bias predicted a greater discrepancy in how the White and the African-American confederates rated their interaction with the participant, such that the White confederate rated the interaction more positively, while the African-American confederate rated the interaction more negatively. Indirect measures of racial bias correlated with negative nonverbal behaviors while direct measures of prejudice did not. Similarly, indirect measures of racial bias, but not direct measures of prejudice, predicted the distance White participants placed their chair from an African-American confederate's belongings (Amodio & Devine, 2006).

Other implicit measures of prejudice have been shown to relate to intergroup behavior. Fazio, Jackson, Dunton, and Williams (1995) developed a supraliminal affective priming measure which was shown to predict the warmth and interest a participant displayed toward an African-American confederate while responses to the Modern Racism Scale did not. Using a subliminal affective priming task, Dovidio, Kawakami, Johnson and Johnson (1997) demonstrated that indirect measures of racial bias predicted negative nonverbal behaviors toward an African-American confederate but did not predict deliberative race-related responses.

The most powerful demonstrations in science tend to be those that show a real-world effect. After demonstrating that roommate relationships of randomly paired interracial freshmen are more likely to dissolve than randomly paired White freshmen (Study 1), Towles-Schwen and Fazio (2006) found that the indirect measure of racial bias of the White roommate (via a superluminal affective priming procedure) predicted roommate longevity between interracial roommates (Study 2). Meanwhile, the White roommate's explicit motivation to control for his or her prejudice did not predict the relationship outcome.

In an international study of impressive scale, Nosek et al. (2009) used the IAT to measure people's indirect attitudes toward women, men, and science from a sample of almost a half a million people in 34 countries. The researchers found that the more strongly people of a certain country associated men with science, the larger the gender gap of math and science achievement among 8th graders of that country. Direct (self-report) measures of attitudes toward men, women, and science did not provide additional predictive validity of the achievement gap. Taken together, these studies suggest that indirect measures of attitudes serve as powerful predictors of important real-world behavioral outcomes, particularly in contexts such as race, gender, or harmful habits, where responses on more direct measures may be intentionally or unintentionally biased.

CONCLUSION

In this chapter, we have provided a social cognitive perspective on the construct of attitudes. We have reviewed some of the most widely agreed upon characteristics about the construct, including that they predict judgment and behavior, can vary across time and situation, and can form relatively easily. We have also discussed some of the more contentious and ongoing conceptual questions in this area such as how to think about attitude generation according to the issues of representation, process, and system. Throughout the chapter we have noted the contemporary emphasis on differences between indirectly and directly measured attitudes, and the possible basis of such differences. It seems safe to say that the current state of social cognitive interest in and work on attitudes speaks well for the continued quoting of Allport's (1935) famous stance on attitudes.

REFERENCES

Aarts, H., Custers, R., & Holland, R. W. (2007). The nonconscious cessation of goal pursuit: When goals and negative affect are coactivated. *Journal of Personality and Social Psychology, 92,* 165–178.

Aarts, H., Custers, R., & Marien, H. (2008). Preparing and motivating behavior outside of awareness. *Science, 319*, 1639.

Albarracín, D., Johnson, B. T., & Zanna, M. P. (2005). *The handbook of attitudes*. Mahwah, NJ: Lawrence Erlbaum Associates.

Allport, G. W. (1935). Attitudes. In C. Murchison (Ed.), *Handbook of social psychology* (pp. 798–844). Worcester, MA: Clark University Press.

Amodio, D. M., & Devine, P. G. (2006). Stereotyping and evaluation in implicit race bias: Evidence for independent constructs and unique effects on behavior. *Journal of Personality and Social Psychology, 91*, 652–661.

Amodio, D. M., Harmon-Jones, E., & Devine, P. G. (2003). Individual differences in the activation and control of affective race bias as assessed by startle eyeblink responses and self-report. *Journal of Personality and Social Psychology, 84*, 738–753.

Anderson, J. R. (1983). *The architecture of cognition*. Cambridge, MA: Harvard University Press.

Arkes, H. R., & Tetlock, P. E. (2004). Attributions of implicit prejudice, or "Would Jesse Jackson 'fail' the Implicit Association Test?". *Psychological Inquiry, 15*, 257–278.

Ashburn-Nardo, L., Voils, C. I., & Monteith, M. J. (2001). Implicit associations as the seeds of intergroup bias: How easily do they take root? *Journal of Personality and Social Psychology, 81*, 789–799.

Asch, S. E. (1948). The doctrine of suggestion, prestige, and imitation in social psychology. *Psychological Review, 55*, 250–276.

Baeyens, F., Eelen, P., & Van den Bergh, O. (1990). Contingency awareness in evaluative conditioning: A case for unaware affective-evaluative learning. *Cognition and Emotion, 4*(1), 3–18.

Banaji, M. R. (2001). Implicit attitudes can be measured. In H. L. Roediger, J. S. Nairne, I. Neither, & A. Surprenant (Eds.), *The nature of remembering: Essays in honor of Robert G. Crowder* (pp. 117–150). Washington, DC: American Psychological Association.

Bargh, J. A. (1994). The Four Horsemen of automaticity: Awareness, efficiency, intention, and control in social cognition. In R. S. Wyer, Jr., & T. K. Srull (Eds.), H*andbook of social cognition* (2nd ed., pp. 1–40). Hillsdale, NJ: Lawrence Erlbaum Associates.

Bargh, J. A., Chaiken, S., Govender, R., & Pratto, F. (1992). The generality of the automatic attitude activation effect. *Journal of Personality and Social Psychology, 62*, 893–912.

Bargh, J. A., & Ferguson, M. J. (2000). Beyond behaviorism: On the automaticity of higher mental processes. *Psychological Bulletin, 126*, 925–945.

Barsalou, L. W. (2008). Grounded cognition. *Annual Review of Psychology, 59*, 617–645.

Barsalou, L. W. (2009). Simulation, situated conceptualization, and prediction. *Philosophical Transactions of the Royal Society of London: Biological Sciences, 364*, 1281–1289.

Bassili, J. N., & Brown, R. D. (2005). Implicit and explicit attitudes: Research, challenges, and theory. In D. Albarracín,

B. T. Johnson & M. P. Zanna (Eds.), *The handbook of attitudes* (pp. 543–574). Mahwah, NJ: Lawrence Erlbaum Associates.

Bechtel, W. (2008). *Mental mechanisms: Philosophical perspectives on cognitive neuroscience*. London: Routledge.

Berry, C. J., Shanks, D. R., & Henson, R. N. A. (2008). A unitary signal-detection model of implicit and explicit memory. *Trends in Cognitive Sciences, 12*, 367–373.

Betsch, T., Plessner, H., Schwieren, C., & Gütig, R. (2001). I like it but I don't know why: A value-account approach to implicit attitude formation. *Personality and Social Psychology Bulletin, 27*, 242–253.

Blair, I. V., Ma, J. E., & Lenton, A. P. (2001). Imagining stereotypes away: The moderation of implicit stereotypes through mental imagery. *Journal of Personality and Social Psychology, 81*, 828–841.

Blanton, H., Jaccard, J., Klick, J., Mellers, B., Mitchell, G., & Tetlock, P. E. (2009). Strong claims and weak evidence: Reassessing the predictive validity of the IAT. *Journal of Applied Psychology, 94*, 567–582.

Cacioppo, J. T., & Petty, R. E. (1982). The need for cognition. *Journal of Personality and Social Psychology, 42*, 116–131

Cacioppo, J. T., Petty, R. E., & Morris, K. (1983). Effects of need for cognition on message evaluation, recall, and persuasion. *Journal of Personality and Social Psychology, 45*, 805–818.

Carlston, D. E., & Smith, E. R. (1996). Principles of mental representation. In E. T. Higgins, & A. W. Kruglanski (Eds.), *Social psychology: Handbook of basic principles* (pp. 184–210). New York: Guilford Press.

Carey, S. (1985). *Conceptual change in childhood*. Cambridge, MA: Bradford Books, MIT Press.

Castelli, L., Zogmaister, C., Smith, E.R., Arcuri, L. (2004). On the automatic evaluation of social exemplars. *Journal of Personality and Social Psychology, 86*, 373–387.

Chaiken, S. (1980). Heuristic versus systematic information processing and the use of source versus message cues in persuasion. *Journal of Personality & Social Psychology, 39*(5), 752–766.

Chaiken, S. (1987). The heuristic model of persuasion. In Zanna, M. P., Olson, J. M., & Herman, C. P. (Eds.), *Social influence: The Ontario Symposium* (Vol. 5, pp. 3–39). Hillsdale, NJ: Lawrence Erlbaum Associates.

Chaiken, S., & Bargh, J. A. (1993). Occurrence versus moderation of the automatic attitude activation effect: Reply to Fazio. *Journal of Personality & Social Psychology, 64*, 759–765.

Chaiken, S., & Stangor, Ch. (1987). Attitudes and attitude change. *Annual Rewiew of Psychology, 38*, 575–630.

Chaiken, S., & Trope, Y. (1999). *Dual-process theories in social psychology*. New York:Guilford Press.

Chen, M., & Bargh, J. A. (1999). Consequences of automatic evaluation: Immediate behavioral predispositions to approach and avoid the stimulus. *Personality and Social Psychology Bulletin, 25*, 215–224.

Conrey, F. R., & Smith, E. R. (2007). Attitude representation: Attitudes as patterns in a distributed, connectionist representational system. *Social Cognition, 25*, 739–758.

Cooke, R., & Sheeran, P. (2004). Moderation of cognition–intention and cognition–behaviour relations: A meta-analysis of properties of variables from the theory of planned behaviour. *British Journal of Social Psychology, 43,* 159–186.

Crano, W. D., & Prislin, R. (2006). Attitudes and persuasion. *Annual Review of Psychology, 57,* 345–374.

Cunningham, W. A. (2010). In defense of brain mapping in social and affective neuroscience. *Social Cognition, 28,* 716–721.

Cunningham, W. A., Johnson, M. K., Gatenby, J. C., Gore, J. C., & Banaji, M. R. (2003). Neural components of social evaluation. *Journal of Personality and Social Psychology, 85,* 639–649.

Cunningham, W. A., Johnson, M. K., Raye, C. L., Gatenby, J. C., Gore, J. C., & Banaji, M. R. (2004). Separable neural components in the processing of Black and White faces. *Psychological Science, 15,* 806–813.

Cunningham, W. A., Preacher, K. J., & Banaji, M. R. (2001). Implicit attitude measures: Consistency, stability, and convergent validity. *Psychological Science, 12,* 163–170.

Cunningham, W. A., Raye, C. L., & Johnson, M. K. (2004). Implicit and explicit evaluation: fMRI correlates of valence, emotional intensity, and control in the processing of attitudes. *Journal of Cognitive Neuroscience, 16,* 1717–1729.

Cunningham, W. A., Zelazo, P. D., Packer, D. J., & Van Bavel, J. J. (2007). The iterative reprocessing model: A multilevel framework for attitudes and evaluation. *Social Cognition, 25,* 736–760.

Custers, R., & Aarts, H. (2005). Positive affect as implicit motivator: On the nonconscious operation of behavioral goals. *Journal of Personality and Social Psychology, 89*(2), 129–142.

Dasgupta, N., & Greenwald, A. G. (2001). On the malleability of automatic attitudes: Combating automatic prejudice with images of admired and disliked individuals. *Journal of Personality and Social Psychology, 81,* 800–814.

Dawson, M. E., Rissling, A. J., Schell, A. M., & Wilcox, R. (2007). Under what conditions can human affective conditioning occur without contingency awareness? Test of the evaluative conditioning paradigm. *Emotion, 7,* 755–766.

De Houwer, J. (2003). The extrinsic affective Simon task. *Experimental Psychology, 50,* 77–85.

De Houwer, J., Baeyens, F., & Field, A. P. (2005). Associative learning of likes and dislikes: Some current controversies and possible ways forward. *Cognition and Emotion, 19,* 161–174.

De Houwer, J., & Eelen, P. (1998). An affective variant of the Simon paradigm. *Cognition and Emotion, 8,* 45–61.

De Houwer, J., Hermans, D., & Eelen, P. (1998). Affective and identity priming with episodically associated stimuli. *Cognition and Emotion, 12,* 145–169.

De Houwer, J., Teige-Mocigemba, S., Spruyt, A., & Moors, A. (2009). Implicit measures: A normative analysis and review. *Psychological Bulletin, 135,* 347–368.

De Houwer, J., Thomas, S., & Baeyens, F. (2001). Associative learning of likes and dislikes: A review of 25 years of research on human evaluative conditioning. *Psychological Bulletin, 127,* 853–869.

Devaney, Robert L. (2003). *An introduction to chaotic dynamical systems* (2nd ed.). Boulder, CO: Westview Press.

Devine, P. G. (1989). Stereotypes and prejudice: Their automatic and controlled components. *Journal of Personality and Social Psychology, 56,* 5–18.

Dietrich, E., & Markman, A. B. (2003). Discrete thoughts: Why cognition must use discrete representations. *Mind & Language, 18,* 95–119.

Dijksterhuis, A. (2004). Think different: The merits of unconscious thought in preference developments and decision making. *Journal of Personality and Social Psychology, 87,* 586–598.

Doob, L.W. (1947). The behavior of attitudes. *Psychological Review, 51,* 135–156.

Dovidio, J. F., Kawakami, K., & Beach, K. R. (2001). Implicit and explicit attitudes: Examination of the relationship between measures of intergroup bias. In R. Brown & S.L. Gaertner (Eds.), *Blackwell handbook of social psychology* (Vol. 4, *Intergroup Relations*, pp. 175–197). Oxford, UK: Blackwell.

Dovidio, J. F., Kawakami, K., Johnson, C., & Johnson, B. (1997). On the nature of prejudice: Automatic and controlled processes. *Journal of Experimental Social Psychology, 33,* 510–540.

Dovidio, J. F., Mann, J., & Gaertner, S. L. (1989). Resistance to affirmative action: The implications of aversive racism. In F. A. Blanchard & F. J. Crosby (Eds.), *Affirmative action in perspective* (pp. 83–102). New York: Springer-Verlag.

Dretske, Fred, F. (1995). *Naturalizing the mind.* Cambridge, MA: MIT Press.

Eagly, A. H., & Chaiken, S. (1993). *The psychology of attitudes.* Fort Worth, TX: Harcourt Brace Jovanovich.

Elman et al., (1996). *Rethinking innateness: A connectionist perspective on development.* Cambridge, MA: MIT Press.

Epstein, S. (1994). Integration of the cognitive and psychodynamic unconscious. *American Psychologist, 49,* 709–724.

Evans, J. St. B. T. (2008). Dual-processing accounts of reasoning, judgement and social cognition. *Annual Review of Psychology, 59,* 255–278.

Fazio, R. H. (1986). How do attitudes guide behavior? In R. M. Sorrentino & E. T. Higgins (Eds.), *Handbook of motivation and cognition: Foundations of social behavior* (pp. 204–243). New York: Guilford Press.

Fazio, R. H. (1990). Multiple processes by which attitudes guide behavior: The MODE model as an integrative framework. In M. P. Zanna (Ed.), *Advances in experimental social psychology* (Vol. 23, pp. 75–109). New York: Academic Press.

Fazio, R. H. (1993). Variability in the likelihood of automatic attitude activation: Data re-analysis and commentary on Bargh, Chaiken, Govender, and Pratto (1992). *Journal of Personality and Social Psychology, 64,* 753–758, 764–765.

Fazio, R. H. (1995). Attitudes as object–evaluation associations: Determinants, consequences, and correlates of attitude accessibility. In R. E. Petty & J. A. Krosnick (Eds.),

Attitude strength: Antecedents and consequences (pp. 247–282). Hillsdale, NJ: Lawrence Erlbaum Associates.

Fazio, R. H. (2001). On the automatic activation of associated evaluations: An overview. *Cognition and Emotion, 14,* 1–27.

Fazio, R. H. (2007). Attitudes as object–evaluation associations of varying strength. *Social Cognition,* 25, 603–637.

Fazio, R. H., Chen, J., McDonel, E. C., & Sherman, S. J. (1982). Attitude accessibility, attitude–behavior consistency and the strength of the object–evaluation association. *Journal of Experimental Social Psychology, 18,* 339–357.

Fazio, R. H., Jackson, J. R., Dunton, B. C., & Williams, C. J. (1995). Variability in automatic activation as an unobtrusive measure of racial attitudes. A bona fide pipeline? *Journal of Personality and Social Psychology, 69,* 1013–1027.

Fazio, R. H., & Olson, M. A. (2003). Implicit measures in social cognition research: Their meaning and use. *Annual Review of Psychology, 54,* 297–327.

Fazio, R. H., Sanbonmatsu, D. M., Powell, M. C., & Kardes, F. R. (1986). On the automatic activation of attitudes. *Journal of Personality and Social Psychology, 50,* 229–238.

Fazio, R. H., & Williams, C. J. (1986). Attitude accessibility as a moderator of the attitude–perception and attitude–behavior relations: An investigation of the 1984 presidential election. *Journal of Personality and Social Psychology, 51,* 505–514.

Fazio, R. H., & Zanna, M. P. (1978). Attitudinal qualities relating to the strength of the attitude–behavior relationship. *Journal of Experimental Social Psychology, 14,* 398–408.

Ferguson, M. J. (2007a). On the automatic evaluation of end-states. *Journal of Personality and Social Psychology, 92,* 596–611.

Ferguson, M. J. (2007b). The automaticity of evaluation. Invited chapter in J. A. Bargh (Ed.), *Social psychology and the unconscious: The automaticity of higher mental processes* (pp. 219–264). New York: Psychology Press.

Ferguson, M. J. (2008). On becoming ready to pursue a goal you don't know you have: Effects of nonconscious goals on evaluative readiness. *Journal of Personality and Social Psychology, 25,* 557–571.

Ferguson, M. J., & Bargh, J. A. (2003). The constructive nature of automatic evaluation. In J. Musch & K. C. Klauer (Eds.), *The psychology of evaluation: Affective processes in cognition and emotion* (pp.169–188). NJ: Erlbaum.

Ferguson, M. J., & Bargh, J. A. (2004). Liking is for doing: Effects of goal pursuit on automatic evaluation. *Journal of Personality and Social Psychology, 88,* 557–572.

Ferguson, M. J. & Zayas, V. (2009). Nonconscious evaluation. *Current Directions in Psychological Science, 18,* 362–366.

Field, A. P. (2000). Evaluative conditioning is Pavlovian conditioning: Issues of definition, measurement, and the theoretical importance of contingency awareness. *Consciousness and Cognition, 9*(1), 41–49.

Fishbein, M., & Ajzen, I. (1975). *Belief, attitude, intention, and behavior: An introduction to theory and research.* Reading, MA: Addison-Wesley.

Gawronski, B., & Bodenhausen, G. V. (2006). Associative and propositional processes in evaluation: An integrative review of implicit and explicit attitude change. *Psychological Bulletin, 132,* 692–731.

Gawronski, B., LeBel, E. P., & Peters, K. R. (2007). What do implicit measures tell us? Scrutinizing the validity of three common assumptions. *Perspectives on Psychological Science, 2,* 181–193.

Gawronski, B., Peters, K. R., Brochu, P. M., & Strack, F. (2008). Understanding the relations between different forms of racial prejudice: A cognitive consistency perspective. *Personality and Social Psychology Bulletin, 34,* 648–665.

Gawronski, B., Rydell, R. J., Vervliet, B., & De Houwer, J. (2010). Generalization versus contextualization in automatic evaluation. *Journal of Experimental Psychology: General, 139,* 683–701.

Gilbert, D. T. (1999). What the mind's not. In S. Chaiken & Y. Trope (Eds.), *Dual process theories in social psychology.* New York: Guilford Press.

Glasman, L. R., & Albarracin, D. (2006). Forming attitudes that predict future behavior: A meta-analysis of the attitude–behavior relation. *Psychological Bulletin, 132,* 778–822.

Greenwald, A. G., & Banaji, M. R. (1995). Implicit social cognition: Attitudes, self-esteem, and stereotypes. *Psychological Review, 102,* 4–27.

Greenwald, A. G., Banaji, M. R., Rudman, L. A., Farnham, S. D., Nosek, B. A., & Mellott, D. S. (2002). A unified theory of implicit attitudes, stereotypes, self-esteem, and self-concept. *Psychological Review, 109,* 3–25.

Greenwald, A. G., & Farnham, S. D. (2000). Using the Implicit Association Test to measure self-esteem and self-concept. *Journal of Personality and Social Psychology, 79,* 1022–1038.

Greenwald, A. G., McGhee, D. E., & Schwarz, J. L. K. (1998). Measuring individual differences in implicit cognition: The Implicit Association Test. *Journal of Personality and Social Psychology, 74,* 1464–1480.

Greenwald, A. G., Poehlman, T. A., Uhlmann, E., & Banaji, M. R. (2009). Understanding and using the Implicit Association Test: III. Meta-analysis of predictive validity. *Journal of Personality and Social Psychology, 97,* 17–41.

Gregg, A. P., Seibt, B., & Banaji, M. R. (2006). Easier done than undone: Asymmetry in the malleability of implicit preferences. *Journal of Personality and Social Psychology, 90,* 1–20.

Grossberg, S., Boardman, I., & Cohen, M.A. (1997). Neural dynamics of variable-rate speech categorization. *Journal of Experimental Psychology: Human Perception and Performance, 23,* 481–503.

Hamann S., & Mao, H. (2002). Positive and negative emotional verbal stimuli elicit activity in the left amygdala. *Neuroreport, 13,* 15–19.

Haugeland, J. (1991). Semantic engines: An introduction to mind design. In J. Haugeland (Ed.), *Mind dDesign: Philosophy, psychology, artificial intelligence* (pp. 1–34). Cambridge, MA: MIT Press.

Hebb, D.O. (1949). *The organization of behavior.* New York: John Wiley & Sons.

Hofmann, W., De Houwer, J., Perugini, M., Baeyens, F., & Crombez, G. (2010). Evaluative conditioning in humans: A meta-analysis. *Psychological Bulletin, 136,* 390–421.

Hofmann, W., Gawronski, B., Gschwendner, T., Le, H., & Schmitt, M. (2005). A meta-analysis on the correlation between the Implicit Association Test and explicit self-report measures. *Personality and Social Psychology Bulletin, 31,* 1369–1385.

Huskinson, T. L. H., & Haddock, G. (2004). Assessing individual differences in attitude structure: Variance in the chronic reliance on affective and cognitive information. *Journal of Experimental Social Psychology, 40,* 82–90.

Ito, T. A., & Cacioppo, J. T. (2000). Electrophysiological evidence of implicit and explicit categorization processes. *Journal of Experimental Social Psychology, 36,* 660–676.

Jacoby, L. L. (1991). A process dissociation framework: Separating automatic from intentional uses of memory. *Journal of Memory and Language, 30,* 513–541.

Jilk, D. J., Lebiere, C., O'Reilly, R. C., & Anderson, J. R. (2008). SAL: An explicitly pluralistic cognitive architecture. *Journal of Experimental and Theoretical Artificial Intelligence, 20,* 197–218.

Jones, E. E., & Sigall, H. (1971). The bogus pipeline: A new paradigm for measuring affect and attitude. *Psychological Bulletin, 76,* 349–364.

Jordan, C. H., Spencer, S. J., & Zanna, M. P. (2003). "I love me ... I love me not": Implicit self-esteem, explicit self-esteem, and defensiveness. In S. J. Spencer, S. Fein, M. P. Zanna, & J. M. Olson (Eds.), *Motivated social perception: The Ontario Symposium* (Vol. 9, pp. 117–145). Mahwah, NJ: Lawrence Erlbaum Associates.

Jones, C. R., Fazio, R. H., & Olson, M. A. (2009). Implicit misattribution as a mechanism underlying evaluative conditioning. *Journal of Personality and Social Psychology, 96,* 933–948.

Jones, J. T., Pelham, B. W., Carvallo, M., & Mirenberg, M. C. (2004). How do I love thee? Let me count the Js: Implicit egotism and interpersonal attraction. *Journal of Personality and Social Psychology, 87*(5), 665–683.

Kahneman, D. (2003). A perspective on judgment and choice: Mapping bounded rationality. *American Psychologist, 58,* 697–720.

Kahneman, D., & Frederick, S. (2002). Representativeness revisited: Attribute substitution in intuitive judgment. In T. Gilovich, D. Griffin & D. Kahneman (Eds.), *Heuristics and biases: The psychology of intuitive judgment* (pp.49–81). New York: Cambridge University Press.

Karpinski, A., & Hilton, J. L. (2001). Attitudes and the implicit association test. *Journal of Personality and Social Psychology, 81,* 774–788.

Katz, I., & Hass, R. G. (1988). Racial ambivalence and American value conflict: Correlational and priming studies of dual cognitive structures. *Journal of Personality and Social Psychology, 55,* 893–905.

Kawakami, K., Dovidio, J. F., Moll, J., Hermsen, S., & Russin, A. (2000). Just say no (to stereotyping): Effects of training in the negation of stereotypic associations on stereotype activation. *Journal of Personality and Social Psychology, 78,* 871–888.

Kawakami, K., Phills, C. E., Steele, J. R. & Dovidio, J. F. (2007). (Close) Distance makes the heart grow fonder: Improving implicit racial attitudes and interracial interactions through approach behaviors. *Journal of Personality and Social Psychology, 92,* 957–971.

Keil, F. (1989). *Concepts, kinds and cognitive development.* Cambridge, MA: MIT Press.

Keren, G., & Schul, Y. (2009) Two is not always better than one: A critical evaluation of two-system theories. *Perspectives on Psychological Science, 4,* 533–550.

Klauer, K. C., & Mierke, J. (2005). Task-set inertia, attitude accessibility, and compatibility-order effects: New evidence for a task-set switching account of the IAT effect. *Personality and Social Psychology Bulletin, 31,* 208–217.

Klauer, K. C., & Musch, J. (2003). Affective priming: Findings and theories. In K. C. Klauer, & J. Musch (Eds.), *The psychology of evaluation: Affective processes in cognition and emotion* (pp. 7–50). Mahwah, NJ: Lawrence Erlbaum Associates.

Klauer, K. C., Schmitz, F., Teige-Mocigemba, S., & Voss, A. (2010). Understanding the role of executive control in the Implicit Association Test: Why flexible people have small IATeffects. *Quarterly Journal of Experimental Psychology, 63,* 595–619.

Klauer, K. C., & Stern, E. (1992). How evaluations guide memory-based judgments: A two-process model. *Journal of Experimental Social Psychology, 28,* 186–206.

Klinger, M. R., Burton, P. C., & Pitts, G. S. (2000). Mechanisms of unconscious priming: I. Response competition, not spreading activation. *Journal of Experimental Psychology: Learning, Memory, and Cognition, 26,* 441–455.

Koole, S.K., Dijksterhuis, A., & van Knippenberg, A. (2001). What's in a name: Implicit self-esteem. *Journal of Personality and Social Psychology, 80,* 614–627.

Kraus, S. J. (1995). Attitudes and the prediction of behavior: A meta-analysis of the empirical literature. *Personality and Social Psychology Bulletin, 21,* pp. 58–75.

Krosnick, J. A., Judd, C. M., & Wittenbrink, B. (2005). The measurement of attitudes. In D. Albarracín, B. T. Johnson, & M. P. Zanna (Eds.), *The handbook of attitudes* (pp. 21–76). Mahwah, NJ: Lawrence Erlbaum Associates.

Krosnick, J. A., & Schuman, H. (1988). Attitude intensity, importance, and certainty and susceptibility to response effects. *Journal of Personality and Social Psychology, 54,* 940–952.

Kruglanski, A.W., Erb, H. P., Chun, W. Y., Pierro, A., & Mannetti, L. (2003). A parametric model of human judgment: Integrating the dual-mode frameworks in social cognition from a singular perspective. In J. Forgas, Von Hippel, W., & K. Williams (Eds.), *Responding to the social world: Explicit and implicit processes in social judgments and decisions.* Cambridge, UK: Cambridge University Press.

Kruglanski, A. W., Thompson, E. P., & Spiegel, S. (1999). Separate or equal? Bimodal notions of persuasion and a single-process "unimodel". In S. Chaiken & Y. Trope (Eds.),

Dual process models in social cognition: A source book. New York: Guilford Press.

Lamme, V. A. F., & Roelfsema, P. R. (2000). The distinct modes of vision offered by feedforward and recurrent processing. *Trends in Neuroscience, 23,* 571–579.

LaPiere, R. T. (1934). Attitudes vs. actions. *Social Forces, 13,* 230–237.

Lavine, H., Huff, J.W.,Wagner, S. H., & Sweeney, D. (1998). The moderating influence of attitude strength on the susceptibility to context effects in attitude surveys. *Journal of Personality and Social Psychology, 75,* 359–373.

LeDoux, J. (1996). *The emotional brain.* New York: Touchstone.

LeDoux, J. E. (2000). Emotion circuits in the brain. *Annual Review Neuroscience, 23,* 155–184.

Levey, A. B., & Martin, I. (1975). Classical conditioning of human "evaluative" responses. *Behaviour Research and Therapy, 13,* 221–226.

Lewin, K. (1935). *A dynamic theory of personality.* New York: McGraw-Hill.

Liberzon I., Phan, K. L., Decker, L. R., & Taylor, S. F. (2003). Extended amygdala and emotional salience: A PET investigation of positive and negative affect. *Neuropsychopharmacology, 28,* 726–733.

Lichtenstein, S., & Slovic, P. (2006). *The construction of preference.* New York: Cambridge University Press.

Logan, G. D. (1980). Attention and automaticity in Stroop and priming tasks: Theory and data. *Cognitive Psychology, 12,* 523–553.

Lowery, B. S., Hardin, C. D., & Sinclair, S. (2001). Social influence on automatic racial prejudice. *Journal of Personality and Social Psychology, 81,* 842–855.

Maddux, W. W., Barden, J., Brewer, M. B., & Petty, R. E. (2005). Saying no to negativity: The effects of context and motivation to control prejudice on automatic evaluative responses. *Journal of Experimental Social Psychology, 41,* 19–35.

Maio, G. R., & Esses, V. M. (2001). The need for affect: Individual differences in the motivation to approach or avoid emotions. *Journal of Personality, 69,* 583–615.

Marcus, G. F. (2001). *The algebraic mind: Integrating connectionism and cognitive science.* Cambridge, MA: MIT Press.

Markman, A. B., & Dietrich, E. (2000). In defense of representation. *Cognitive Psychology, 40,* 138–171.

Marsh, K. L., Johnson, B. T., & Scott-Sheldon, L. A. J. (2001). Heart versus reason in condom use: Implicit versus explicit attitudinal predictors of sexual behavior. *Zeitschrift für Experimentelle Psychologie, 48,* 161–175.

Martin, I., & Levey, A. B. (1978). Evaluative conditioning. *Advances in Behaviour Research and Therapy, 1,* 57–102.

McCauley, C., & Stitt, C. L. (1978). An individual and quantitative measure of stereotypes. *Journal of Personality and Social Psychology, 36,* 929–940.

McClelland, J. L., McNaughton, B. L., & O'Reilly, R. C. (1995). Why there are complementary learning systems in the hippocampus and neocortex: Insights from the successes and failures of connectionist models of learning and memory. *Psychological Review, 102,* 419–457.

McClelland, J. L., & Rogers, T. T. (2003). The parallel distributed processing approach to semantic cognition. *Nature Reviews Neuroscience, 4,* 310–322.

McConahay, J. (1986). Modern racism, ambivalence, and the Modern Racism Scale. In J. Dovidio (Ed.), *Prejudice, discrimination, and racism* (pp. 91–125). San Diego, CA: Academic Press.

McConnell, A. R., & Leibold, J. M. (2001). Relations among the Implicit Association Test, discriminatory behavior, and explicit measures of racial attitudes. *Journal of Experimental Social Psychology, 37,* 435–442.

Metcalfe, J., & Mischel, W. (1999). A hot/cool system analysis of delay of gratification: Dynamics of willpower. *Psychological Review, 106,* 3–19.

Meyer, D. E., & Schvaneveldt, R. W. (1971). Facilitation in recognizing pairs of words: Evidence of a

dependence between retrieval operations. *Journal of Experimental Psychology, 90,* 227–234.

Mierke, J., & Klauer, K. C. (2003). Method-specific variance in the Implicit Association Test. *Journal of Personality and Social Psychology, 85,* 1180–1192.

Mitchell, J. P., Nosek, B. A., & Banaji, M. R. (2003). Contextual variations in implicit evaluation. *Journal of Experimental Psychology: General, 132,* 455–469.

Moore, S. G., Ferguson, M. J., & Chartrand, T. L. (2011). Affect in the aftermath: How goal pursuit influences implicit evaluations. *Cognition and Emotion, 25,* 453–465.

Moors, A., & De Houwer, J. (2001). Automatic appraisal of motivational valence: Motivational affective priming and Simon effects. *Cognition and Emotion, 15,* 749–766.

Moors, A., & De Houwer, J. (2006). Automaticity: A theoretical and conceptual analysis. *Psychological Bulletin, 132,* 297–326.

Morris, J. S., Ohman, A., & Dolan, R. J. (1998). Conscious and unconscious emotional learning in the human amygdala. *Nature, 393,* 467–470.

Moskowitz, G. B., Gollwitzer, P. M., Wasel, W., & Schaal, B. (1999). Preconscious control of stereotype activation through chronic egalitarian goals. *Journal of Personality and Social Psychology, 77,* 167–184.

Musch, J., & Klauer, K. C. (2003). *The psychology of evaluation: Affective processes in cognition and emotion.* Mahwah, NJ: Lawrence Erlbaum Associates.

Nader, K., Schafe. G. E., & LeDoux. J. E. (2000). The labile nature of consolidation theory. *Nature Review Neuroscience, 1*(3), 216–219.

Neely, J. H. (1976). Semantic priming and retrieval from lexical memory: Evidence for faciliatory and inhibitory processes. *Memory and Cognition, 4,* 648–654.

Neely, J. H. (1977). Semantic priming and retrieval from lexical memory: Roles of inhibitionless spreading activation and limited-capacity attention. *Journal of Experimental Psychology: General, 106,* 225–254.

Niedenthal, P. M. (1990). Implicit perception of affective information. *Journal of Experimental Social Psychology, 26,* 505–527.

Nosek, B. A. (2005). Moderators of the relationship between implicit and explicit evaluation. *Journal of Experimental Psychology: General.*

Nosek, B. A., & Banaji, M. R. (2001). The go/no-go association task. *Social Cognition, 19*(6), 625–666.

Nosek, B. A., Banaji, M. R., & Greenwald, A. G. (2002). Math = Me, Me = Female, therefore Math is not equal to me. *Journal of Personality and Social Psychology, 83*, 44–59.

Nosek, B. A., Greenwald, A. G., & Banaji, M. R. (2005). Understanding and using the Implicit Association Test: II. Method variables and construct validity. *Personality and Social Psychology Bulletin, 31*, 166–180.

Nosek, B. A., Smyth, F. L., Sriram, N., Lindner, N. M., Devos, T., Ayala, A., et al. (2009). National differences in gender-science stereotypes predict national sex differences in science and math achievement. *Proceedings of the National Academy of Sciences, 106*, 10593–10597.

O'Keefe, J., & Nadel, L. (1978). *The hippocampus as a cognitive map.* Oxford, UK: Oxford University Press.

Olson, M. A., & Fazio, R. H. (2001). Implicit attitude formation through classical conditioning. *Psychological Science, 12*, 413–417.

Olson, M. A., & Fazio, R. H. (2002). Implicit acquisition and manifestation of classically conditioned attitudes. *Social Cognition, 20*, 89–103.

Olson, M. A., & Fazio, R. H. (2004). Reducing the influence of extra-personal associations on the Implicit Association Test: Personalizing the IAT. *Journal of Personality and Social Psychology, 86*, 653–667.

Olson, M. A., & Fazio, R. H. (2006). Reducing automatically-activated racial prejudice through implicit evaluative conditioning. *Personality and Social Psychology Bulletin, 32*, 421–433.

Olson, M. A., & Fazio, R. H. (2009). Implicit and explicit measures of attitudes: The perspective of the MODE model. In R. E. Petty, R. H. Fazio, & P. Briñol (Eds.), *Attitudes: Insights from the new implicit measures.* New York: Psychology Press.

Olson, M. A., Fazio, R. H., & Hermann, A. D. (2007). Reporting tendencies underlie discrepancies between implicit and explicit measures of self-esteem. *Psychological Science, 18*, 287–291.

Orne, M. T. (1962). On the social psychology of the psychological experiment: With particular reference to demand characteristics and their implications. *American Psychologist, 17*, 776–783.

O'Reilly, R. C. (1998). Six principles for biologically-based computational models of cortical cognition. *Trends in Cognitive Sciences, 2*, 455–462.

Osgood, C. E., Suci, G. J., & Tannenbaum, P. H. (1957). *The measurement of meaning.* Chicago, IL: University of Illinois Press.

Palmer, S. E. (1978). Fundamental aspects of cognitive representation. In E. Rosch & B. L. Lloyd (Eds.), *Cognition and categorization* (pp. 259–302). Hillsdale, NJ: Lawrence Erlbaum Associates.

Payne, B. K. (2005). Conceptualizing control in social cognition: How executive control modulates the expression of automatic stereotyping. *Journal of Personality and Social Psychology, 89*, 488–503.

Payne, B. K., Burkley, M., & Stokes, M. B. (2008). Why do implicit and explicit attitude tests diverge? The role of structural fit. *Journal of Personality and Social Psychology, 94*, 16–31.

Payne, B. K., Cheng, C. M., Govorun, O., & Stewart, B. (2005). An inkblot for attitudes: Attitude misattribution as implicit measurement. *Journal of Personality and Social Psychology, 89*, 277–293.

Payne, B. K., Govorun, O., & Arbuckle, N. L. (2008). Automatic attitudes and alcohol: Does implicit liking predict drinking? *Cognition & Emotion, 22*, 238–271.

Petty, R. E., & Cacioppo, J. T. (1979). Issue involvement can increase or decrease persuasion by enhancing message-relevant cognitive processes. *Journal of Personality and Social Psychology, 37*, 1915–1926.

Petty, R. E., & Cacioppo, J. T. (1986). *Communication and persuasion: Central and peripheral routes to attitude change.* New York: Springer-Verlag

Petty, R. E., Cacioppo, J. T., & Goldman, R. (1981). Personal involvement as a determinant of argument-based persuasion. *Journal of Personality and Social Psychology, 41*, 847–855.

Petty, R. E., & Krosnick, J. A. (1995). *Attitude strength: Antecedents and consequences.* Hillsdale, NJ: Lawrence Erlbaum Associates.

Petty, R. E., Tormala, Z. L., Briñol, P., & Jarvis, W. B. G. (2006). Implicit ambivalence from attitude change: An exploration of the PAST model. *Journal of Personality and Social Psychology, 90*, 21–41.

Petty, R. E., & Wegener, D. T. (1999). The Elaboration Likelihood Model: Current status and controversies. In S. Chaiken & Y. Trope (Eds.), *Dual process theories in social psychology* (pp. 41–72). New York: Guilford Press.

Phelps, E. A., O'Connor, K. J., Cunningham, W. A., Funayama, E. S., Gatenby, J. C., Gore, J. C., et al. (2000). Performance on indirect measures of race evaluation predicts amygdala activation. *Journal of Cognitive Neuroscience, 12*, 729–738.

Phelps, E. A., O'Connor, K. J., Gatenby, J. C., Grillon, C., Gore, J. C., & Davis, M. (2001). Activation of the human amygdala to a cognitive representation of fear. *Nature Neuroscience, 4*, 437–441.

Pleyers, G., Corneille, O., Luminet, O., & Yzerbyt, V. (2007). Aware and (dis)liking: Item-based analyses reveal that valence acquisition via evaluative conditioning emerges only when there is contingency awareness. *Journal of Experimental Psychology: Learning, Memory & Cognition, 33*, 130–144.

Posner, M. I., & Snyder, C. R. R. (1975). Attention and cognitive control. In R. L. Solso (Ed.), *Information processing and cognition: The Loyola Symposium* (pp. 55–85). Hillsdale, NJ: Lawrence Erlbaum Associates.

Ranganath, K. A., Smith, C. T., & Nosek, B. A. (2008). Distinguishing automatic and controlled components of attitudes from direct and indirect measurement methods. *Journal of Experimental Social Psychology, 44*, 386–396.

Roediger, H. L. (1990). Implicit memory: Retention without remembering. *American Psychologist, 45*(9), 1043–1056.

Rosenberg, M. J. (1956). Cognitive structure and attitudinal affect. *Journal of Abnormal and Social Psychology, 53*, 367–372.

Rosenberg, M. J. (1969). The conditions and consequences of evaluation apprehension. In R. Rosenthal & R. L. Rosnow (Eds.), *Artifact in behavioral research* (pp. 279–349). New York: Academic Press.

Rosenberg, M. J., & Hovland, C. I. (1960). Cognitive, affective, and behavioural components of attitudes. In C. I. Hovland & M. J. Rosenberg (Eds.), *Attitude organisation and change: An analysis of consistency among attitude components* (pp. 1–14). New Haven, CT: Yale University Press.

Rudman, L. A. (2004). Sources of implicit attitudes. *Current Directions in Psychological Science, 13*(2), 80–83.

Rudman, L. A., Ashmore, R. D., & Gary, M. L. (2001). "Unlearning" automatic biases: The malleability of implicit stereotypes and prejudice. *Journal of Personality and Social Psychology, 81*, 856–868.

Ruys, K. I., & Stapel, D. A. (2009). Learning to like or dislike by association: No need for contingency awareness. *Journal of Experimental Social Psychology, 45*, 1277–1280.

Rydell, R. J., McConnell, A. R., Mackie, D. M., & Strain, L. M. (2006). Of two minds: Forming and changing valence inconsistent attitudes. *Psychological Science, 17*, 954–958.

Salancik, G. R., & Conway, M. (1975). Attitude inferences from salient and relevant cognitive content about behavior. *Journal of Personality and Social Psychology, 32*, 829–840.

Sarnoff, I. (1960). Psychoanalytic theory and social attitudes. *Public Opinion Quarterly, 24*, 251–279.

Schacter, D. L., & Tulving, E. (Eds.) (1994). *Memory systems 1994.* Cambridge, MA: MIT Press.

Schuman, H., & Johnson, M. P. (1976). Attitudes and behavior. *Annual Review of Sociology, 2*, 161–207.

Schwarz, N. (2007). Attitude construction: Evaluation in context. *Social Cognition, 25*, 638–656.

Schwarz, N., & Bohner, G. (2001). The construction of attitudes. In A. Tesser & N. Schwarz (Eds.), *Blackwell handbook of social psychology: Intraindividual processes* (Vol. 1, pp. 436–457). Oxford, UK: Blackwell.

Seidenberg, M. S., & McClelland, J. L. (1989). A distributed, developmental model of word recognition and naming. *Psychological Review, 96*, 523–568.

Sherman, J. W. (2009). Controlled influences on implicit measures: Confronting the myth of process-purity and taming the cognitive monster. In R. E. Petty, R. H. Fazio, & P. Briñol (Eds.), *Attitudes: Insights from the new wave of implicit measures* (pp. 391–426). Hillsdale, NJ: Lawrence Erlbaum Associates.

Sherman, J. W., Gawronski, B., Gonsalkorale, K., Hugenberg, K., Allen, T. J., & Groom, C. J. (2008). The self-regulation of automatic associations and behavioral impulses. *Psychological Review, 115*, 314–335.

Sherman, J. W., & Payne, B. K. (2009). Separating automatic and controlled components of implicit measures: Process dissociation in social cognition. In R. E. Petty, R. H. Fazio, & P. Briñol (Eds.), *Attitudes: Insights from the new wave of implicit measures.* New York: Psychology Press.

Sherry, D. F., & Schacter, D. L. (1987). The evolution of multiple memory systems. *Psychological Review, 94*, 439–454.

Shiffrin, R. M., & Dumais, S. T. (1981). The development of automatism. In J. R. Anderson (Ed.), *Cognitive skills and their acquisition* (pp.111–140). Hillsdale, NJ: Lawrence Erlbaum Associates.

Shiffrin, R. M., & Schneider, W. (1977). Controlled and automatic human information processing: II. Perceptual learning, automatic attending, and a general theory. *Psychological Review, 84*, 127–190.

Sia, T. L., Lord, C. G., Blessum, K., Ratcliff, C. D., & Lepper, M. R. (1997). Is a rose always a rose? The role of social category exemplar change in attitude stability and attitude–behavior consistency. *Journal of Personality and Social Psychology, 72*, 501–514.

Sloman, S. A. (1996). The empirical case for two systems of reasoning. *Psychological Bulletin, 119*, 3–22.

Smallwood, J., & Schooler, J.W. (2006). The restless mind. *Psychological Bulletin, 132*(6), 946–958.

Smith, C. T., & Nosek, B. A. (2011). Affective focus increases the concordance between implicit and explicit attitudes. *Social Psychology, 42*, 300–313.

Smith, E. R. (1992). The role of exemplars in social judgment. In L. L. Martin and A.Tesser (Eds.), *The construction of social judgment.* Hillsdale, NJ: Lawrence Erlbaum Associates.

Smith, E. R. (1996). What do connectionism and social psychology offer each other? *Journal of Personality and Social Psychology, 70*, 893–912.

Smith, E. R. (1997). Preconscious automaticity in a modular connectionist system. In R. S. Wyer (Ed.), *Advances in social cognition* (Vol. 10, pp. 181–202). Mahway, NJ: Lawrence Erlbaum Associates.

Smith, E. R. (2009). Distributed connectionist models in social psychology. *Social and Personality Psychology Compass, 3*, 64–76.

Smith, E. R., & Conrey, F. R. (2007). Agent-based modeling: A new approach for theory-building in social psychology. *Personality and Social Psychology Review, 11*, 87–104.

Smith, E. R., & DeCoster, J. (1999). Associative and rule-based processing: A connectionist interpretation of dual-process models. In S. Chaiken, & Y. Trope (Eds.), *Dual process theories in social psychology* (pp. 323–336). New York: Guilford Press.

Smith, E. R., & DeCoster, J. (2000). Dual process models in social and cognitive psychology: Conceptual integration and links to underlying memory systems. *Personality and Social Psychology Review, 4*, 108–131.

Smith, E. R., Fazio, R. H., & Cejka, M. A. (1996). Accessible evaluations influence categorization of multiply categorizable objects. *Journal of Personality and Social Psychology, 71*, 888–898.

Smith, E. R., & Lerner, M. (1986). Development of automatism of social judgments. *Journal of Personality and Social Psychology, 50*, 246–259.

Smith, E. R., & Zarate, M. A. (1992). Exemplar-based model of social judgment. *Psychological Review, 99*, 3–21.

Smith, M. B., Bruner, J. S., & White, R. W. (1956). *Opinions and personality.* New York: Wiley.

Sperber, D. (2005). Modularity and relevance: How can a massively modular mind be flexible and context-sensitive? P. Carruthers, S. Laurence, & S. Stich (Eds.), *The innate mind: Structure and content.*

Spivey, M. J. (2007). *The continuity of mind.* New York: Oxford University Press.

Squire, L. R. (1992). Memory and the hippocampus: A synthesis from findings with rats, monkeys, and humans. *Psychological Review, 99*, 195–231.

Squire, L. R., & Kandel, E. R. (1999). *Memory: From mind to molecules.* New York: Scientific American Library.

Stahl, C., Unkelbach, C., & Corneille, O. (2009). On the respective contributions of awareness of US valence and US identity in attitude formation through evaluative conditioning. *Journal of Personality and Social Psychology, 97,* 404–420.

Staats, A. W., & Staats, C. K. (1958). Attitudes established by classical conditioning. *Journal of Abnormal and Social Psychology, 57,* 3740.

Strack, F., & Deutsch, R. (2004). Reflective and impulsive determinants of social behavior. *Personality and Social Psychology Review, 8*(3), 220–247.

Strack, F., & Deutsch, R. (2004). Reflection and impulse as determinants of "conscious" and "unconscious" motivation. In J. P. Forgas, K. Williams, & S. Laham (Eds.), *Social motivation: Conscious and unconscious processes.* Cambridge, UK: Cambridge University Press.

Tesser, A. (1978). Self-generated attitude change. In L. Berkowitz (Ed.), *Advances in experimental social psychology* (Vol. 11, pp. 289–338). New York: Academic Press.

Tesser, A., & Martin, L. (1996). The psychology of evaluation. In E. T. Higgins, & A.W. Kruglanski (Eds.), *Social psychology: Handbook of basic principles* (pp. 400–432). New York: Guilford Press.

Thagard, P. (1991). Philosophical and computational models of explanation. *Philosophical Studies, 64*(October), 87–104.

Thelen, E., & Smith, L. B., (1994). *A dynamical systems approach to development of cognition and action.* Cambridge, MA: Bradford Books/MIT Press.

Thurstone, L. L. (1928). Attitudes can be measured. *American Journal of Sociology, 33*, 529–554.

Thurstone, L. L. (1931). Measurement of social attitudes. *Journal of Abnormal and Social Psychology, 26*, 249–269.

Tooby, J., & Cosmides, L. (2005). Conceptual foundations of evolutionary psychology. In D. M. Buss (Ed.), *The handbook of evolutionary psychology* (pp. 5–67). Hoboken, NJ: Wiley.

Towles-Schwen, T., & Fazio, R. H. (2006). Automatically-activated racial attitudes as predictors of the success of interracial roommate relationships. *Journal of Experimental Social Psychology, 42*, 698–705.

Tulving, E. (1983). *Elements of episodic memory.* Oxford. UK: Oxford University Press.

Tulving, E., & Craik, F. I. M. (2000). *Handbook of memory.* Oxford, UK: Oxford University Press.

Vanman, E. J., Saltz, J. L., Nathan, L. R., & Warren, J. A. (2004). Racial discrimination by low-prejudiced whites: Facial movements as implicit measures of attitudes related to behavior. *Psychological Science, 15*, 711–714.

Van Overwalle, F., & Van Rooy, D. (2001). How one cause discounts or augments another: A connectionist account of causal competition. *Personality and Social Psychology Bulletin, 27*, 1613–1626.

Visser, P. S., Bizer, G. Y., & Krosnick, J. A. (2006). Exploring the latent structure of strength-related attitude attributes. In M. Zanna (Ed.), Advances in experimental social psychology. New York: Academic Press.

Walther, E. (2002). Guilty by mere association: Evaluative conditioning and the spreading evaluation effect. *Journal of Personality and Social Psychology, 82*, 919–924.

Walther, E., & Nagengast, B. (2006). Evaluative conditioning and the awareness issue: Assessing contingency awareness with the four-picture recognition test. *Journal of Experimental Psychology: Animal Behavior Processes, 32*, 454–459.

Walther, E., Nagengast, B., & Trasselli, C. (2005). Evaluative conditioning in social psychology: Facts and speculations. *Cognition and Emotion, 19,* 175–196.

Wentura, D. (1999). Activation and inhibition of affective information: Evidence for negative priming in the evaluation task. *Cognition and Emotion, 13*, 65–91.

Wentura, D. (2000). Dissociative affective and associative priming effects in the lexical decision task: *Yes* versus *no* responses to word targets reveal evaluative judgmental tendencies. *Journal of Experimental Psychology: Learning, Memory, and Cognition, 26*, 456–469.

Wicker, A. W. (1969). Attitude versus actions: The relationship of verbal and overt behavioral responses to attitude objects. *Journal of Social Issues, 25*(4), 41–78.

Wilson, T. D., & Hodges, S. D. (1992). Attitudes as temporary constructions. In A. Tesser & L. Martin (Eds.), *The construction of social judgment* (pp. 37–65). Hillsdale, NJ: Lawrence Erlbaum Associates.

Wilson, T. D., Lindsey, S., & Schooler, T. Y. (2000). A model of dual attitudes. *Psychological Review, 107*, 101–126.

Wittenbrink, B., Judd, C. M., & Park, B. (1997). Evidence for racial prejudice at the implicit level and its relationship with questionnaire measures. *Journal of Personality and Social Psychology, 72*, 262–274.

Wittenbrink, B., Judd, C. M., & Park, B. (2001). Spontaneous prejudice in context: Variability in automatically activated attitudes. *Journal of Personality and Social Psychology, 81*, 815–827.

Wittenbrink, B., & Schwarz, N. (Eds.) (2007). *Implicit measures of attitudes.* New York: Guilford Press.

Wojnowicz, M. T., Ferguson, M. J., Dale, R., & Spivey, M. J. (2009). The self-organization of explicit attitudes. *Psychological Science, 20*, 1428–1435.

Wyer, R. S. (1973). Category ratings as 'subjective expected values': Implications for attitude formation and change. *Psychological Review, 80*(6), 445–467.

Yeh, W., & Barsalou, L.W. (2006). The situated nature of concepts. *American Journal of Psychology, 119*, 349–384.

10

Nonverbal Perception

Nora A. Murphy

INTRODUCTION AND OVERVIEW

Popular lay books promise to reveal the secrets of nonverbal communication. Various books attest that uncovering these "secrets" will provide opportunities to make fabulous first impressions, meet attractive romantic partners, find career success, and even control others. If these claims rang true, we would all have the perfect partner, our dream job, and interpersonal success would abound. Clearly, this is not the case. Those who study nonverbal behavior recognize that such interpersonal communication cannot be defined in a dictionary-type manual. Shifty eyes do not unequivocally indicate that one is lying, just as every brush to one's arms does not indicate sexual attraction. The messages conveyed across nonverbal channels are much more nuanced and complex than these lay volumes imply. Rather than parsing out the influence of nonverbal cues in interpersonal context, nonverbal researchers recognize and acknowledge that verbal and nonverbal signals work in conjunction to convey messages (Friedman, 1979).

While popular lay books may be misleading in terms of uncovering "secrets" of nonverbal communication, the books do highlight the fundamental importance of nonverbal behavior to social encounters and how we perceive others. Another person's behavior influences our impression of that person just as our own behavior influences others' perceptions of us. If you meet a stranger for the first time and he averts his gaze, refuses to shake your hand, and mumbles a greeting, you are likely to come away with the impression that he is unfriendly, shy, or even perhaps hostile. Furthermore, this impression would (and does) develop in a brief amount of time, without much conscious processing (Bargh, 1994).

Nonverbal perception refers to the process by which individuals (i.e., judges or perceivers) perceive the nonverbal behaviors of others (i.e., targets) and how that perception shapes subsequent judgments and impressions of targets (Ambady & Weisbuch, 2010). As most nonverbal perception occurs in the context of a social interaction, the process of nonverbal perception is social-cognitive in nature. There is a particular emphasis in this chapter on the *accuracy* of nonverbal perception; i.e., How well do individuals accurately decode and interpret the nonverbal behavior of others? The reason for an emphasis on accurate nonverbal perception is explained by Funder (1999), who stated that "the psychological process of accurate [person] judgment is as much social as it is cognitive" (p. 117), and thus, accurate person perception represents a true social-cognitive process. Nonverbal perception plays an essential role in accurately determining the states and traits of others.

Chapter outline

This chapter covers several aspects of nonverbal perception. In the first section, we review some major social-cognitive theories of person perception. These person perception models are presented because nonverbal perception is not only about detecting nonverbal behavior but also includes how that nonverbal perception influences impression formation and whether such impressions are accurate. The models I discuss are the Brunswik (1956) lens model, the Realistic Accuracy Model (RAM; Funder, 1995), the ecological theory of social perception (McArthur & Baron, 1983), the parallel process model (Patterson, 1995), the social relations model

(Kenny & La Voie, 1984), and the PERSON model (Kenny, 2004). Whereas these theories do not represent all social cognitive theories involving nonverbal perception, they do provide a representative array of how social psychologists (as well as others) conceptualize the interplay of nonverbal behavior, qualities of targets and perceivers, and social interaction features in the process of person perception. Each of the models presented involves nonverbal perception as part of the larger process of person perception.

In the next section of the chapter, four essential components of nonverbal perception are reviewed: nonverbal cue qualities, target qualities, perceiver qualities, and interaction qualities. These components are discussed because each component has the potential to affect the accuracy of impressions formed of the target by a perceiver during the process of nonverbal perception. Furthermore, the four components of nonverbal perception represent various factors that are included in most social-cognitive models of person perception. In the final section of chapter, some examples of research domains regarding the perception and accurate detection of various states and traits are discussed, including the accurate detection of emotions, sexual orientation, and prejudice. The aim of this section is to highlight how nonverbal perception affects accurate person perception.

As I discuss the importance of nonverbal signals on impression formation and person perception, the research reviewed in this chapter primarily focuses on two classes of nonverbal cues: kinetics, which includes body movements such as gestures, posture, and gait; and vocal cues, which include speech features outside the content of what is being said, such as pauses, interruptions, and pitch (Burgoon & Hoobler, 2002). In terms of perceiving others, researchers often make the distinction between sending nonverbal signals and receiving nonverbal signals. If a message is being communicated through nonverbal channels, successful transmission of that message depends on the sender (encoder or target) as well as the receiver (decoder or perceiver). Given that the purpose of this chapter is nonverbal *perception*, a greater proportion of research reviewed here focuses primarily on nonverbal decoding: i.e., the perception and interpretation of nonverbal signals. This chapter distinctly focuses on nonverbal cues *outside of* the face, facial expression, or eyegaze (for a discussion of face perception, see Chapter 6). The chapter addresses adult social perception: thus, research involving children or animals is not discussed. Additionally, there is an extensive set of research involving nonverbal cues and deception, and summarizing such research is beyond the scope of this chapter. (For reviews, see DePaulo et al., 2003; Vrij, 2000, 2006.) In general, the research summarized reviews person perception, nonverbal behavior, and accuracy between strangers or in zero-acquaintanceship paradigms (Kenny & West, 2008). Now, let me begin with a discussion of some social-cognitive models of person perception that involve nonverbal perception.

SOCIAL-COGNITIVE MODELS OF PERSON PERCEPTION

Most social-cognitive models of person perception incorporate nonverbal perception, and these models of person perception often test not only what impressions are formed but also whether such impressions are accurate assessments of a target's state or trait. There are several universal elements in the models presented here. All of the models address the accuracy of nonverbal perception. Accuracy is often defined as a significant correlation between targets' measured criteria (e.g., scores of extraversion from the Big Five Inventory) and perceivers' ratings of targets on that variable (e.g., perceivers ratings of targets' extraversion levels); thus, accuracy indicates better-than-chance levels of detecting the state or trait. (See Hall, Andrzejewski, Murphy, Schmid Mast, & Feinstein, 2008 for a discussion of various methods of assessing accuracy in judgments of states and states.) Presumably, this process of accurate person perception is dependent upon the appropriate and accurate decoding of nonverbal behavior, as assessed through nonverbal perception. Each model proposes mechanisms for understanding how a social interaction between a target and perceiver involves nonverbal perception and how such perceptions may affect accurate person perception.

Another universal feature of the presented models is the assumption of (or explicit reference to) automaticity in the process of nonverbal perception, as much of nonverbal perception is considered automatic (Choi, Gray, & Ambady, 2005; Lakin, 2006; see also Chapter 2). As Bargh (1994) noted, automatic processes involve four aspects of cognition: awareness, efficiency, intention, and control. For the most part, nonverbal perception occurs outside awareness, is extremely efficient, occurs without intention, and is not necessarily controllable. Studies show that individuals' impression formations and behaviors are influenced by nonconscious cues (e.g., Chartrand & Bargh, 1996). The automaticity associated with nonverbal perception is reflected in research on mimicry and the "chameleon effect" (Chartrand

& Bargh, 1999). Mimicry is generally considered to be the imitation of others during a social interaction, usually without conscious intent (Hess, Blairy, & Philippot, 1999). Several studies demonstrate the automaticity of such processes by documenting that participants do not report awareness that mimicry took place or accurately describe the processes that led to increased liking of interaction partners who unobtrusively mimicked the participant's behavior (Chartrand & Bargh, 1999; Chartrand, Maddux, & Lakin, 2005). In sum, the social-cognitive models of person perception presented in the next section all involve nonverbal perception, and the accuracy and automaticity associated with that perception. The next section briefly reviews these person perception models.

Brunswik's (1956) lens model, as applied to person perception

The lens model approach is based upon a visual perception paradigm as applied to social situations by Brunswik (1956). This approach employs an individual cue as source of information influencing the resulting impression. A Brunswikian approach to a two-person interaction posits that a perceiver takes in information about a target from many cues. Figure 10.1 presents a modified Brunswik lens model as it applies to social perception. On the left, the perceiver views a target individual and forms an impression. Presumably, this impression is shaped by the middle construct, the nonverbal behavior emitted by the target. On the right exists the target's true personality trait or characteristic that is being assessed. The arrows in Figure 10.1 represent the data or analyses available to the researcher employing a

Brunswikian lens model. The researcher can investigate which cues are influential in a perceiver's impression by comparing the emitted behavior to the perceiver rating (cue utility). A researcher can also explore which cues actually indicate the personality construct of interest by comparing emitted behavior with the target's characteristic (cue validity; Brunswik used the term *ecological validity*). Finally, the comparison between the perceiver's impression and the target's true personality reveals how well the perceiver was able to assess the target. In such instances, the match (or mismatch) of the impression to the existence of an attribute is considered accuracy (Brunswik used the term *achievement* or *functional validity*).

Many applications of the Brunswik lens model involve extensive measurement of many specific nonverbal behaviors, as well as manipulating the presentation of those cues to the perceiver (i.e., judgments made from transcripts of social interactions, audiotape or videotapes, or photographs). For example, several studies also demonstrated that perceivers can accurately perceive intelligence from short excerpts (i.e., "thin slices," as described later) of targets' behavior (Borkenau & Liebler, 1993, 1995; Murphy, 2007; Murphy, Hall, & Colvin, 2003; Reynolds & Gifford, 2001). Each of these studies included the measurement of nonverbal cues related to speech and body position to investigate the association between such behaviors and judgments of intelligence. Other personality traits have been examined in this lens model approach, including agreeableness and dominance (Gifford, 1994), assertiveness (Schmid Mast, Hall, Murphy, & Colvin, 2003), and the Big Five personality traits (extraversion, openness, conscientiousness, agreeableness, and neuroticism; McCrae & Costa, 1990) (Borkenau & Liebler, 1993, 1995; Carney, Colvin, & Hall, 2007; Küfner, Back, Nestler, & Egloff, 2010). Ambady, Bernieri, and Richeson (2000) suggested that the lens model's usefulness in understanding the processes associated with person perception cannot be understated:

> The lens model, by integrating the perceiver, the target, and the mediating cues, provides a theoretical framework and methodological structure that allows an investigator to examine [impressions based on brief exposure to targets] with a degree of precision and perspective that reveals the wealth of information contained within a few brief seconds of expressive behavior (p. 238).

In sum, research employing the Brunswikian lens model demonstrates that nonverbal cue qualities play a prominent role in the impression formation and accuracy of target assessment.

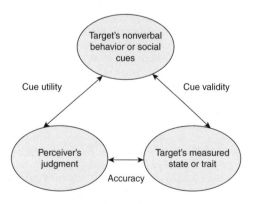

Figure 10.1   Modified Brunswik (1956) lens model as applied to person perception.

McArthur and Baron's (1983) ecological theory of social perception, based on Gibson's (1979) theories of object perception

In response to a number of research studies that employed the Brunswik lensmodel to deconstruct person perception, Zebrowitz and Collins (1997) suggested that the Brunswik lens modelmay be narrow in utility: i.e., researchers may end up with a list of behaviors associated with impressions and personality traits but those lists vary depending on the trait assessed and the behaviors that were measured. Zebrowitz and Collins suggested that such results are far from ideal and provide little theoretical grounding for understanding the construct of person perception accuracy as a whole. Instead, the authors propose that a Gibsonian ecological approach, which is a theoretical application, as opposed to the Brunswikian methodological model, is more appropriate.

Previously, McArthur and Baron (1983) outlined how the Gibson ecological approach could be applied to social perception. The authors distinguished four elements of this model that make it particularly constructive for understanding processes associated with social perception. The four components of the model assert that: (1) the perception of others is an adaptive function where information contained in the environment guides behavior in social interactions; (2) such information is revealed in events such as social interactions; (3) affordances, which are opportunities where the stimulus (e.g., an individual in the social interaction) may be able to act or be acted upon by objects such as another individual in the environment, are revealed in social interactions; and (4) a perceiver in a social interaction must be aware of or be attuned to such affordances in order to complete the impression formation. For example, in order for a perceiver to recognize extraversion in another, the perceiver must notice the hand gestures, vocal qualities, and/or speech patterns related to extraversion. If the perceiver is not paying attention (i.e., he/she is distracted or looking elsewhere), then extraversion cannot be accurately assessed.

According to McArthur and Baron's (1983) ecological perspective, social cues provide affordances that allow the perceiver to detect relevant and important social information. For instance, a heavy-footed walking gait with long strides would indicate anger and inform the perceiver that threatening circumstances may be impending (Montepare, Goldstein, & Clausen, 1987). The ecological perspective emphasizes that focusing on one valid cue may not be sufficient to form an accurate perception. Using extraversion as an example, relying solely on the cue of a loud voice to indicate extraversion may not be sufficient for a perceiver to form an accurate impression, because surely there are individuals who are not extraverted but do possess loud voices. Yet, if we know that the target individual has a loud voice, uses large hand gestures, and is highly talkative, the combination or configured structure of these behaviors could accurately inform the perceiver's impression of extraversion. Zebrowitz and Collins's (1997) ecological theory of social perception has been applied in a variety of research paradigms, including impressions and cues of the Big Five (Church, Katigbak, & del Prado, 2010) and rapport (Tickle-Degnen, 2006).

Funder's (1995) Realistic Accuracy Model

Funder proposed his Realistic Accuracy Model (RAM) as a paradigm for understanding the accurate perception of a target's personality (Funder, 1995, 1999). RAM is based on the premise that personality perception can be accurate and is dependent on several factors, including the detection and availability of behavioral cues. While Funder primarily sets forth a model regarding the accurate perception of personality traits, most of the model's components could also apply to the accurate perception of social states (e.g., emotions, anxiety, etc.). Four elements are essential to RAM. The first element, relevance, is that information or behavior related to the target's trait (or state) must be emitted: for example, an extraverted person emits the behaviors of a loud voice and demonstrative hand gestures. The second element of RAM, availability, is that the behavioral information must be available for the judge to detect it: the target individual must be in a situation by which the nonverbal behavior can be displayed. The third element is detection: the judge must detect the behavior through perception. The fourth and final element of RAM, utilization, occurs when a judge makes use of the behavioral information to make a judgment about the target. According to RAM, when a judge uses each of these elements exactly, achievement of judgment accuracy will occur.

Funder (1999) acknowledges that RAM is influenced by Gordon Allport's perspective on the integration of social psychology and personality psychology, as well as the social perception models of Brunswik's lens model (1956) and Gibson's ecological perspective (1979). Furthermore, the model is interdisciplinary, as elements of the model relate to social psychology (availability), personality psychology (relevance), and social-cognitive psychology (detection, utilization).

Funder argues that investigating person perception accuracy should occur with an interdisciplinary approach and to examine such processes through only one lens (e.g., only social psychology or only personality psychology) would not reveal the complexities of such processes. Studies applying RAM demonstrate its utility in understanding person perception accuracy (Blackman & Funder, 1998; Letzring, Wells, & Funder, 2006; Spain, Eaton, & Funder, 2000).

Patterson's (1995) parallel process model

Patterson (1995) introduced a parallel process model whereby nonverbal communication is not dichotomized into encoding and decoding. Instead, Patterson noted that encoding and decoding are occurring in parallel by any given participant in the interaction. Patterson referred to participants in any given social interaction as actors, and these actors, as well as the outcome of the social interaction, are influenced by a variety of factors. According to the model, person perception is the result of a combination of four related factors: (1) determinants, which are variables such as culture, biology, and personality; (2) social environment, which is (to some extent) the choice of participants in the interaction; (3) cognitive-affective mediators, such as disposition, affect, goals, or cognitive resources of interactants; and (4) person perception and behavioral processes, which include the interactants' attentional focus and cognitive effort, as well as the behavioral intentions and actual behavior. The model encompasses the social-cognitive processing of nonverbal perception by unifying two aspects of social interaction: behavioral processes and social judgments related to nonverbal behavior (Patterson, 2006). Patterson (1996) emphasizes the social-cognitive nature of the parallel by linking the behavioral and cognitive aspects of person perception into one underlying, dynamic system.

Kenny and La Voie's social relations model (1984) and Kenny's (2004) PERSON model

Kenny and La Voie (1984) presented a social relations model (SRM) designed to study the perception of personality within an unstructured social interaction. Various components of the model assess variance attributed to a perceiver, a target, and the interaction ("relationship" effects). One requirement of the model is that multiple interactions occur between targets and perceivers, usually in a round-robin design. Consequently, the SRM can account for independent and non-independent sources of variances within a social interaction (Kenny, 1994; Malloy & Kenny, 1986). Kenny and Albright (1987) then demonstrated how the SRM may be applied to accurate interpersonal judgments by asking whether individuals can accurately perceive the personality of strangers. The SRM has been applied in a variety of research paradigms, from measuring liking between unacquainted pairs (Chapdelaine, Kenny, & LaFontana, 1994) to perceptions of psychopathy (Mahaffey & Marcus, 2006).

Kenny's (2004) PERSON model is a more elaborate design on interpersonal perception. The model was designed to incorporate both categorical information (nonbehavioral information about a target such as physical appearance and demographic features such as age and gender) and behavioral information and how these sources of information combine to influence person perception and accuracy. The model attempts to explain the sources of variance associated with person perception and generally assumes that interpersonal perception contains both accuracy and inaccuracy. The acronym PERSON refers to six possible sources of independent variance in interpersonal judgments: personality, error, residual, stereotypes, opinions, and norms. PERSON is presented as comprehensive model to explain impression formation as it unfolds over time and multiple acts (i.e., target behaviors). The model stresses the importance of understanding interpersonal perception as a complex serious of acts, rather than one single act of perception.

Earlier, Kenny (1991) distinguished between the concepts of consensus and accuracy in interpersonal perception. Consensus refers to how much agreement exists between judges who rate the same set of targets: i.e., Do judges generally agree in their judgments of a target? Accuracy, however, depends upon a criterion or outcome variable that can be used to assess how well judges perceive targets. For example, several judges may give similar ratings of a target's extraversion level but those ratings may not correspond to the target's extraversion level as measured by a self-report questionnaire. In this example, the agreement of the judges amongst themselves reflects consensus, but the judges are not accurate in their perception because their ratings do not match the criterion variable of measured extraversion level. The PERSON model can be used to decipher components of interpersonal perception such as perceiver consensus and acquaintanceship effects and allows for the mathematical computation of different variances involved in interpersonal perception. So far there is little empirical evidence that directly tests PERSON (likely due to its recent formulation), but assumptions and predictions of the model show promise and many studies test various components of the model (e.g., Srivastava, Guglielmo, & Beer, 2010; Vazire & Mehl, 2008).

In sum, the six social-cognitive models of person perception reviewed here all involved the process of nonverbal perception as an essential function in accurately detecting the states and traits of others. Universal features of these models include the role of nonverbal behavior, the automaticity of the processes of person perception, and the accuracy of perceivers in detecting the states and traits of others. Now, let us examine in more detail the process of nonverbal perception. Specifically, we will examine four essential components of nonverbal perception in more detail.

FOUR COMPONENTS OF NONVERBAL PERCEPTION

In terms of a social-cognitive process, nonverbal perception involves four primary components: (1) qualities of the nonverbal behavior being displayed; (2) qualities of the target individual, which may affect the expression of nonverbal behavior; (3) the process of perception by the perceiver, including a perceiver's states and traits, which may affect how that nonverbal behavior is perceived; and (4) qualities of the interaction that may affect the emittence or perception of nonverbal behavior. These four components, and facets of each component, are illustrated in Figure 10.2. Nonverbal cue qualities refers to qualities of the nonverbal behavior being displayed such as speech and voice cues, body cues, and other nonverbal cues such as odor, time, space, and environmental contexts; and whether the cue is presented as static (as in photographs) and/or dynamic (as in video). Target and perceiver qualities refer to aspects of the target or perceiver which may affect how nonverbal behavior is expressed or perceived: these include qualities such as emotional states; personality characteristics (e.g., intelligence, extraversion, etc.); and sociocultural attributes such as age, gender, and culture. Finally, interaction qualities refer to aspects of the interaction between target and perceiver such as the interaction channel (e.g., audio or visual channels), the perceiver's orientation during the interaction (e.g., within the interaction or observing the interaction), interaction length, and the acquaintanceship between perceiver and target. Each component has the potential to affect impressions that are formed based on the

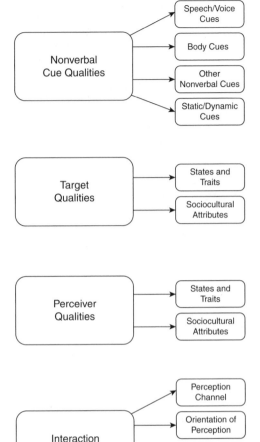

Figure 10.2   Four components of nonverbal perception. Each component contributes to the process of nonverbal perception and consequently has the potential to affect impressions that are formed based on the perception of nonverbal behavior.

perception of nonverbal behavior. Most social-cognitive models of person perception incorporate nonverbal perception, including most, if not all, of these four primary components of nonverbal perception.

Component 1: Nonverbal cue qualities

In this section, various aspects of nonverbal cues and how those features of nonverbal cues may influence or relate to impressions formed during nonverbal perception are discussed.

Nonverbal cues of voice and speech

One nonverbal cue quality that has the potential to shape person perception is paralanguage; paralanguage is the study of the nonverbal components of speech that communicate emotion and meaning. Speech-related qualities such as pauses during speech, the use of fillers (e.g., "um" or "ah") or qualifiers (e.g., "sort of") influence not only how well a speaker communicates but also any subsequent impressions formed by listeners. As Knapp and Hall (2010) noted, listeners are not only influenced by *what* is said by the speaker but also *how* it is spoken. In a classic study, Addington (1968) investigated the effect of voice qualities and speech rate on personality perceptions. Trained male and female speakers were instructed to read a standard passage with seven different voice qualities: breathy, tense, thin, flat, throaty, nasal, and orotund (i.e., richness or fullness). Speakers were also instructed to vary the speech rate (slow, normal, or fast). High reliability was found among judges who rated the speakers for the seven different speech qualities. Raters judged the voices on 40 different personality characteristics such as enthusiastic–apathetic, intelligent–stupid, sensitive–insensitive, kind–cruel, sincere–insincere, and the like. Results showed that voice qualities clearly influenced raters' impressions; for example, breathiness in females was associated with more femininity and being more shallow, while breathiness in males was associated with being younger and more artistic. Other findings showed that a thin voice was associated with being colder and sluggish, a faster speech rate was associated with being more animated and extraverted, and nasality provoked "a wide array of socially undesirable characteristics" (p. 502).

Subsequent research substantiated the influence of various voice qualities on impressions of strangers. Some illustrative findings include research showing individuals with "childlike" voices were perceived as weaker, less capable, and warmer than individuals with more mature-sounding voices (Berry, 1992; Montepare & McArthur, 1987). Childlike voices were described as having higher pitch and greater tightness, as well as less clarity. Jittery voices were perceived as older (Hummert, Mazloff, & Henry, 1999). Submissive voices were rated as more attractive than dominant voices (Raines, Hechtman, & Rosenthal, 1990). Individuals with voices rated as attractive were judged as more warm, honest, and likeable (Berry, 1990, 1992). In sum, voices and vocal qualities influence how individuals are

perceived by others and "whether we like it or not, our voices do elicit stereotyped personality judgments" (Addington, 1968, p. 493).

Nonverbal cues of the body

Nonverbal cues of the body include factors such as body appearance and movement, gait, gestures, posture, and touch. Again, using the example of target attractiveness, one study found that 20% of overall female attractiveness was attributable to body attractiveness (Mueser, Grau, Sussman, & Rosen, 1984). Another study found that female body attractiveness was positively correlated with body femininity, whereas male body attractiveness was associated with body "averageness" and body masculinity (Peters, Rhodes, & Simmons, 2007). Body posture and position can also influence impressions. A listener who leans forward towards a speaker undoubtedly is perceived as a more involved conversation partner than one who leans back or away. Forward-leaning postures are perceived as indicative of rapport, whereas a backward lean can convey the impression of relaxation or boredom. Gender roles suggest that men adopt a "wide" sitting position with legs apart, whereas women sit in a "closed" position; indeed, targets who sat in a wide position were perceived as more masculine and targets who sat in a closed position were perceived as more feminine (Vrugt & Luyerink, 2000). In one detailed study involving computer animation software to pose mannequin figures in a variety of positions and angles, certain target body postures were found to be associated with various emotions (Coulson, 2004). Sadness was perceived when the mannequin was posed with a chest forward bend and arms at sides, whereas surprised was marked with backwards head and chest bends as well as abdominal twisting. Other body cues, such as head positioning, can influence perceptions; a raised head can convey dominance, whereas a bowed head conveys sadness (Mignault & Chaudhuri, 2003).

Gait information can be useful in person perception, and it can be a powerful source of trait impressions (Montepare & Zebrowitz-McArthur, 1988). Some have argued that gait is particularly relevant during person perception because gait information is one of the first cues available of an approaching stranger (Sakaguchi & Hasegawa, 2006). One interesting line of gait perception research has investigated how potential targets of assault are identified by assailants. Research suggests that potential victims are often identified with awkward or inconsistent movements. Targets who walked slowly, with short strides and less arm swinging, were rated as more vulnerable to attacks (Gunns, Johnston, & Hudson, 2002). Targets identified as potential victims (as rated by prison inmates) tended to lack interactional synchrony in their body movements (Grayson & Stein, 1981).

Another body cue related to nonverbal perception is touch. Touches can convey impressions such as dominance and affection. For example, pictures of individuals holding hands or engaged in touching a partner's face were rated highly in perceived affection, whereas pictures of handshaking targets were rated as least affectionate (Burgoon, 1991). Touch also conveys intimacy and emotion (Thayer, 1986). Touch increased rates of compliance (Patterson, Powell, Lenihan, 1986) but touches by strangers were perceived as aversive (Sussman & Rosenfeld, 1978). The form and length of touch, as well as the gender composition of the touch exchange, all affect perceptions of touch; for example, 1-second hugs were perceived more positively than 3-second hugs (Floyd, 1999). Self-touch refers to touching one's own body such as the head, trunk, arms, or legs. Self-touch as a social behavior has been considered a window into psychological functioning but it may also reflect anxiety or depression in the self-toucher (Mehrabian, 1972). Studies of self-touching show that more self-touching in mock interviews increased the likelihood of a hiring recommendation (Goldberg & Rosenthal, 1986). In general, perceptions related to interpersonal touch are complicated by strong cultural norms about appropriate touching, the gender composition of the touch exchange, and the acquaintanceship of the involved individuals.

Other nonverbal cues

A variety of other cues influence nonverbal perception, including signals related to odor, personal space, time, and environmental contexts (see Knapp & Hall, 2010 for a review). For instance, olfactory cues can have powerful influence on how we perceive others. In one study, male target's body odor attractiveness (a composite variable of ratings of pleasant, sexy, and attractive) was rated by women who smelled the T-shirts that the male targets wore to bed two nights in a row (Foster, 2008); the women's fertility affected attractiveness ratings, where body odor attractiveness correlated with overall attractiveness only in the fertile women condition. Additional studies have shown similar results; sexiness ratings of male body odor were correlated with targets' facial attractiveness and dominance, and in turn, these correlations were stronger during female perceivers' peak fertility (Havlicek, Roberts, & Flegr, 2005; Rikowski & Grammer, 1999). Other nonverbal cues include hand gestures and head movements, which are often displayed in conjunction with speech (Hadar, Steiner, & Rose, 1985).

Such movements can help regulate the flow of conversation and signal listening and engagement in a conversation (Birdwhistell, 1983).

Static and dynamic nonverbal cues

Another quality of nonverbal cues to consider is how the cues are displayed to a perceiver; that is, does the perceiver view the nonverbal behavior through static displays (i.e., photographs or drawings), or dynamic displays? Static displays have an extensive history in the study of person perception and impression formation. Though much of this literature emphasized impressions from facial photographs, there is still a substantial portion of research that investigated impression formation from static stimuli of full body or situational contexts. As an example, attractiveness is one area that makes broad use of static stimuli. Research using photographed stimuli showed that lower body mass index (BMI) and hip-to-waist ratio in women's bodies were positively correlated to ratings of attractiveness (e.g., Singh, Dixson, Jessop, Morgan, & Dixson, 2010; Wilson, Tripp, & Boland, 2005). Women with slumped posture (as displayed in photographs) were rated as less attractive than women with standard or upright posture (Osborn, 1996). Other examples of studies involving photos and impression formation include judging emotion in bodily expressions and poses (Coulson, 2004; Ruffman, Sullivan, & Dittrich, 2009), the relative status of individuals in photographs (Hall, Carter, Jimenez, Frost, & Smith LeBeau, 2002), intelligence (Zebrowitz, Hall, Murphy, & Rhodes, 2002), and relationship status (Sternberg & Smith, 1985).

While static stimuli have proffered a wealth of information regarding associations between nonverbal cues and subsequent impressions, judgments based on dynamic displays may be closer to how individuals experience actual interactions than judgments based on static displays. Dynamic displays refer to behavior with active qualities such as movement or auditory information. Dynamic stimuli may also provide temporal information, as well as muscular cues (as in the case of video stimuli), that can only be apparent in dynamic displays as opposed to captured stills of bodies or expressions (Wehrle, Kaiser, Schmidt, & Scherer, 2000). Examples of dynamic displays could be video clips of social interactions or audiotaped discussions. Another example of dynamic stimuli is the use of point-light displays. Point-light displays are typically generated by recording targets in motion (e.g., walking). In a dark background, targets are usually dressed in black clothing and different areas of the body are marked with light points or reflective tape and/or objects (e.g., beads). The perceiver essentially sees small points of light against a black background, with the light points corresponding to the target's movements. Using this technique, researchers have found that perceivers are better-than-chance at detecting characteristics such as gender, age, and emotion (Barclay, Cutting, & Kozlowski, 1978; Montepare & Zebrowitz-McArthur, 1988; Ruffman et al., 2009).

Given that individuals spend a large portion of time in dynamic social interaction, the ecological validity of dynamic displays may present more insight into the influence of behavioral cues on person perception processes. However, as Naumann and colleagues (2009) pointed out, judgments or impressions about others can clearly be shaped by both static (e.g., clothing) and dynamic cues (e.g., voice qualities, body movement). In one study, Naumann et al. found that perceivers were better-than-chance at detecting personality characteristics such as extraversion, emotional stability, and self-esteem from photographs of targets who were instructed to pose in a standardized manner. Another study showed that narcissism could be detected at better-than-chance rates from photographs (Vazire, Naumann, Rentfrow, & Gosling, 2008). Such results suggest that impressions may be formed before any dynamic or expressive cues become available.

The aforementioned Brunswik lens model is one example of a social-cognitive model of person perception that heavily emphasizes the importance of individual nonverbal cues in the process of accurate person perception. And while researchers may often consider cues in isolation, the reality is that we process *patterns* of social behavior and it is these patterns which result in impression formation (Patterson, 1995). Thus, while clearly the discrete signals revealed by the voice, body, or other nonverbal cues can be considered separately, ultimately it is the pattern of these cues that work in conjunction for person perception.

Component II: Qualities of target individuals

Central to nonverbal perception is the expression of nonverbal behavior by a target individual. There are a variety of factors that would affect how, when, and what type of nonverbal behavior is displayed by a target. A target state refers to the target's feelings, emotions, motives, and any situationally specific condition that the target is in, mainly while engaged in a social situation that a perceiver is observing or participating in. A target trait refers to personality characteristics, which are generally more stable across situations than

a target state. Other target qualities include variables such as age, gender, and culture. Such qualities in the target obviously play a role in how that target is perceived. Imagine a female target in a social interaction who is seated and smiling (nonverbal behaviors), attractive (physical appearance), young and Asian (sociocultural attributes), who is relaxed (state) and bright (trait). All of those qualities would interact to potentially affect how that female target is perceived by an interaction partner.

Target states and traits

A target's mood clearly plays a role in the expression of nonverbal behavior. A person who is happy is more likely to smile and walk with a bounce in his/her step; a person who is sad is more likely to move in a slow and sluggish manner. Montepare et al. (1987) found that different emotions were marked with different gait cues: happy gaits tended to be quicker; angry gaits tended to be more heavy-footed; and sad gaits were marked by less arm swinging. Another study showed that sadness was related to slower walking speed and vertical head movements (Michalak, Troje, Fischer, Vollmar, Heidenreich, & Schulte, 2009). Dancers expressing anger displayed strong (in force) and high-speech (in velocity) movements (Sawada, Suda, & Ishii, 2003). Such findings illustrate how a target's mood state would influence the expression of nonverbal behavior.

Another example of a target state that may affect the expression of nonverbal behavior is the target's self-presentation or impression management motives. Impression management theory has demonstrated that individuals can often manipulate their behavior to successfully portray desired impressions (Schlenker, 1980). Research shows the intricate interplay between nonverbal behavior and self-presentation goals where various nonverbal cues may (or may not) be displayed depending on self-presentation motives; in one study, those attempting to appear likeable were less inclined to show negative emotions than those attempting to appear competent (Levine & Feldman, 1997). Similar research showed that individuals attempting to appear likeable tend to nod, smile, and gesture more than individuals without that self-presentation motive (Rosenfeld, 1966). An extensive review of the relationship between self-presentation motives and nonverbal behavior has been published elsewhere (DePaulo, 1992). The review highlighted several reasons why nonverbal behavior is relevant to self-presentation motives; DePaulo emphasized that success at self-presentation depends not only on the actor's ability but also on the perceiver's ability to form impressions from social interactions.

Target traits such as extraversion and dominance are reflected in nonverbal displays. A meta-analysis showed that extraverted people are more emotionally expressive (i.e., expressively animated), whereas neurotic individuals tend to be less emotionally expressive (Riggio & Riggio, 2002). Extraverts also were more likely to display a relaxed stance and less likely to fold their arms, whereas high neuroticism was associated with a tense stance (Naumann et al., 2009). Those with higher intelligence (as measured with IQ scores) tended to use more pauses in their speech (Murphy, 2007). These examples from the literature illustrate how a target's personality would influence nonverbal displays.

Sociocultural attributes

Sociocultural attributes of a target influence nonverbal displays. In terms of nonverbal behavior and age, studies show that older adults tend to use less hand gestures and have more variation in vocal pitch than young adults (Cohen & Borsoi, 1996; Hummert et al., 1999). Gender is another target quality that affects nonverbal displays. The study of gender differences in nonverbal behavior has a long history and is well-documented (e.g., Hall, 1984, 2006; Hall, Carter, & Horgan, 2000). In a meta-analysis, Hall (1978) found that women engage in more expressive movements during a social interaction than men, whereas men display more restless leg and foot movement; men's voices are also louder and lower pitched. Other nonverbal behaviors that show gender differences (with women displaying more than men) include nodding, gazing, forward leaning, and gesturing (Hall, 1984).

Another social factor to consider in nonverbal displays is culture; cultures vary in their nonverbal expressiveness. For example, one study of game-show contestants in the United States and Canada showed that US citizens were more expressive, and US women gestured with their hands more than Canadian women (Waxer, 1985). Other findings show cultural differences in gesturing (e.g., Friesen, Ekman, & Wallbott, 1979), body postures (e.g., Kudoh & Matsumoto, 1985), and emotional expression willingness (Matsumoto, Takeuchi, Andayani, Kouznetsova, & Krupp, 1998). It is not necessary to review widespread stereotypes about various ethnic groups to understand that nonverbal cues (including physical appearance) influence how individuals who belong to a specific ethnic group may be (mis)perceived and affected by those stereotypes.

Weisbuch and Ambady (2008) argue that nonverbal behavior is essential to the communication of culture. The authors reason that a large part of cultural norms are expressed and communicated through social influence and social conformity. From their perspective, much of social influence and conformity is the result of nonverbal gestures and cues (in addition to verbal exchanges of cultural norms and ideals). Social circumstances also teach us cultural display rules, which are rules about how and when to display various nonverbal expressions (Ekman & Friesen, 1969). Studies show that individuals are aware of display rules and these rules vary among ethnicities and cultures (Matsumoto, 1990, 1993). Thus, the culture of a target individual would affect what type of nonverbal cues were displayed. All told, the findings reviewed here demonstrate how target qualities would affect the process of nonverbal perception. Several of the aforesaid models of person perception, including the Brunswik lens model, RAM, and PERSON, highlight the importance of target qualities in nonverbal perception and accurate person perception.

Component III: Perceiver qualities

A third component in our discussion of nonverbal perception involves qualities of the perceiver, including how he/she detects a target's nonverbal behavior, as well as the perceiver's states and traits. Just as qualities about a target may affect the target's nonverbal behavior, qualities of the perceiver affect what impressions are formed. Along these lines, one can imagine how such perceiver qualities could shape the impressions formed of a target. The perception formed by a young, Hispanic, happy, gregarious male perceiver may be very different than the perception formed by an older, Caucasian, anxious female, even if both of those perceivers are judging the same target. Thus, a perceiver's personality traits and emotional states, as well as his/her age, gender, and culture, may affect the process of perceiving nonverbal behavior.

States and traits of the perceiver

There are a variety of states and traits that affect how a perceiver processes nonverbal behavior; much of this research examines how moods and personality traits affect how well (i.e., accurately) perceivers detect the states and traits of targets. Presumably, the perceiver's accuracy in assessing a target hinges on the perception of nonverbal behavior and correct interpretation of that nonverbal behavior. In terms of mood, those in sad moods tend to perform worse on nonverbal decoding tasks than those in neutral or happy moods. For example, those who were experimentally induced into a sad mood were worse at detecting targets' teaching effectiveness (Ambady & Gray, 2002). Another perceiver state to consider is whether the perceiver is under cognitive load. In one study of cognitive load and nonverbal perception, Patterson and Stockbridge (1998) manipulated the cognitive load of participants who were tested on the Interpersonal Perception Task (IPT), a standard measure of interpersonal sensitivity that involves nonverbal perception (Costanzo & Archer, 1989). The authors hypothesized that increased cognitive load would result in higher interpersonal accuracy scores than participants under lower cognitive load condition. Results showed that participants under cognitive load had significantly higher IPT scores than participants with no load. Because nonverbal decoding is primarily automatic, the high cognitive load presumably limited attentional resources such that participants made automatic accurate judgments. On the other hand, participants in the low load condition were distracted by irrelevant cues, because attentional resources were available, leading to inaccurate perceptions. Essentially, the more automatic the judgment, the better decoding accuracy. The pattern of cognitive load leading to more accurate person judgments has been replicated by others (Ambady & Gray, 2002). Overall, such results illustrate how the state of the perceiver (e.g., being under cognitive load) may affect nonverbal perception.

A host of perceiver traits are associated with the decoding of nonverbal behavior. For example, individuals who are high in the need to belong tended to be better at detecting social cues in others (Pickett, Gardner, & Knowles, 2004). Aube and Whiffen (1996) found that those high in self-criticism were more likely to score lower on the IPT, and another study showed that those higher in shyness performed worse on the IPT (Schroeder, 1995). A meta-analysis showed that individuals high in the trait of dominance are better at decoding nonverbal cues (Hall, Halberstadt, & O'Brien, 1997). In another meta-analysis, which investigated personality characteristics associated with decoding accuracy, including 215 independent studies, numerous traits were associated with better decoding, including empathy, conscientiousness, openness, tolerance, and having a high internal locus of control (Hall, Andrzejewski, & Yopchick, 2009). This is only a brief sampling of perceiver states and traits that may affect nonverbal perception, but the overall conclusion is that a variety of a perceiver's states and traits could affect the process of nonverbal perception.

Sociocultural attributes of the perceiver

As mentioned, a perceiver's age, gender, and culture may all affect the process of perceiving nonverbal behavior. In terms of perceiver qualities and gender, not only are women expected to be better at nonverbal perception compared with men (Briton & Hall, 1995) but also they are generally superior in decoding nonverbal behaviors compared with men (Hall, 1978, 1984, 2006). Reviews about gender and nonverbal communication provide further explication on gender similarities and differences in nonverbal perception (Eagly, 1987; Hall, 1984, 2006). With regards to culture, cultural display rules affect expectations and interpretations of nonverbal behavior. For example, Japanese participants reported that positive emotions should be displayed less often compared with Canadian participants (Safdar et al., 2009); such expectations undoubtedly affect how nonverbal behavior is perceived in a social interaction. With regard to age, one meta-analysis showed that older adults (mean age > 65) performed significantly worse at recognizing many emotions from bodies or voices compared with younger adults (Ruffman, Henry, Livingstone, & Sullivan, 2008; see also Chapter 20). Thus, just as target qualities affect how nonverbal behavior is expressed, perceiver qualities affect how that nonverbal behavior is perceived. Social-cognitive models of person perception, such as McArthur and Baron's (1983) ecological approach to person perception, accentuate the significance of perceiver qualities in accurate person perception.

Component IV: Interaction qualities

The fourth component to consider in nonverbal perception relates to the qualities of the interaction: i.e., What is the context in which the nonverbal perception is taking place? When a perceiver is forming an impression of a target, the impression may be shaped by the interaction channel: i.e., how the perceiver is receiving the target information and the perceiver's orientation to the social interaction. The perceiver could be taking in information about a target through various channels, such as photographs or videos of a target, or even through audio channels (e.g., audiotaping of a target's voice). Furthermore, the perceiver could be a participant within the social interaction or could merely be an observer of a target engaged in a social interaction. Interaction length and acquaintanceship between the target and perceiver are other factors to consider. Each of these qualities is considered in more detail below.

Perception channel and perceiver orientation

A perceiver's observation of a target's nonverbal behavior could take place through a variety of channels, such as visual (photographs or video) and/or audio channels, or even interaction through touch. In a study of nonverbal cue channels, judges listened to actors' portrayals of four emotions (happy, sad, anger, and surprise), and judges' accuracy was measured according to how well they decoded the emotions from audiotapes or videos of the actors (Wallbott & Scherer, 1986). Decoding accuracy was significantly higher in the video conditions than in the audio conditions. Perceivers who receive nonverbal cues from visual + auditory stimuli (i.e., video with sound) generally outperform perceiver's who receive cues in visual-only conditions (e.g., Most & Aviner, 2009; Murphy et al., 2003). Another quality of the interaction that could affect person perception is the perceiver's orientation (whether the perceiver is directly interacting with a target or is perceiving the target as an observer).[1] Research suggests that when perceivers are engaged within the social interaction, their accuracy in decoding nonverbal cues is lower than when they observe nonverbal cues from outside the interaction (e.g., watching targets interact in a video). For example, perceivers who interacted with targets were worse at judging targets' intelligence levels than perceivers who judged targets' intelligence from outside the interaction, by viewing targets in videotaped social interaction (Murphy, 2007, Study 1). Similar results were found in a round-robin design where strangers were less accurate in judging intelligence of others with whom they engaged in a 10-minute social interaction, as compared to acquaintances' judgments of intelligence (Vazire, 2010).

Interaction length

Regarding the length of an interaction, research shows that short excerpts (no more than 5 minutes) of target behaviors are sufficient to obtain accuracy in the detection of certain behaviors or traits, such as trustworthiness, extraversion, and anxiety (Ambady & Rosenthal, 1992). These short excerpts of target behavior are known as "thin slices." A thin slice is as "a brief excerpt of expressive behavior sampled from the behavioral stream . . . any excerpt with dynamic information less than 5 min long" (Ambady et al., 2000, p. 203). The Ambady and Rosenthal study also showed that longer excerpt lengths (>30 seconds) did not increase accuracy in comparison to shorter excerpts (<30 seconds). Though another study showed that accurate decoding of nonverbal cues was affected by both the slice length and the type of judgment being made; i.e., accuracy rates increased when perceivers' judged characteristics such as neuroticism and openness at longer excerpts (20 seconds to 5 minutes) compared to

judgments made at shorter excerpt lengths (5 seconds) (Carney et al., 2007). However, that same study showed that individuals are better-than-chance at decoding intelligence, extraversion, openness, agreeableness, conscientiousness, and neuroticism, regardless of slice length (5, 20, 45, or 60 seconds, or 5 minutes). In a review of dozens of studies, Hall and colleagues (2008) found that accurate decoding was only very weakly associated with target exposure length, confirming the Ambady and Rosenthal findings.

Acquaintanceship

Another interaction quality to consider is the relationship between the target and the perceiver. Are the interactants strangers, acquaintances, friends, or family members? This relationship is referred to as the acquaintanceship between target and perceiver and much of the research regarding nonverbal perception involves a zero-acquaintanceship paradigm; i.e., the target and the perceiver are strangers (Kenny & West, 2008). Yet, research investigating whether acquaintanceship affects how well a perceiver detects nonverbal cues suggests that, perhaps not surprisingly, acquainted others are better at predicting personality traits than strangers (Colvin & Funder, 1991). In that study, participants were videotaped interacting with a stranger, and videoclips of these interactions were shown to zero-acquaintance judges, who rated the participants on personality dimensions. Furthermore, participants recruited friends (i.e., acquaintances), who also rated the participants on personality traits. Acquaintances were better at predicting personality traits than strangers; presumably, "judgments by acquaintances . . . yield better predictions of targets' personalities [than strangers' judgments] because of the acquaintances' greater number of experiences" with the target (p. 887). Interestingly, however, both strangers and acquaintances had equal predictive validity in predicting the target's behavior in a specific situation. Colvin and Funder suggest that there is a boundary on the acquaintanceship effect such that acquaintances may be better at detecting personality, but both strangers and acquaintances share equal skill in predicting behavior. Other results support the acquaintanceship effect whereby longer interactions with a target led to higher accuracy predictions of personality (Letzring et al., 2006). However, there is research demonstrating that increased acquaintanceship increases accuracy in perceiving "low observability" traits, such as intelligence and neuroticism, perhaps because these traits are less easily observed through nonverbal behavior than more expressive traits such as extraversion (Vazire, 2010).

In sum, the four components of nonverbal perception presented here illustrate how various aspects of the nonverbal behavior itself, the states and traits of targets and perceivers, and qualities of the interaction could all interact to affect the decoding of nonverbal cues. Each of these components is featured heavily in many social-cognitive models of person perception. In the following section, several examples of research regarding the accurate detection of states and traits are presented as illustrations of the role of nonverbal perception in accurate person perception.

EXAMPLES OF ACCURACY IN PERCEIVING STATES AND TRAITS

In the last section of this chapter, some examples of how nonverbal perception relates to the accurate detection of states and traits are presented. Most of the reviewed research below employs the thin-slice paradigm where perceivers are only exposed to target behavior in short intervals (as described below). Furthermore, in these accuracy paradigms, the detection of states and traits occurs between unacquainted strangers. The aim of this section is to highlight how nonverbal perception affects accurate person perception. Only a few content areas are reviewed below but there exists additional research illustrating the accurate detection of various interpersonal variables such as status (Schmid Mast & Hall, 2004), rapport (Grahe & Bernieri, 1999), and masculinity and femininity (Lippa, 1998), among others.

Detection of emotion from the body and voice

A vast literature exist documents the accurate detection of emotions in others, and much of this research involves the accurate detection of emotion from facial expressions (e.g., Carroll & Russell, 1996; Ekman et al., 1987; Elfenbein & Ambady, 2003; Matsomoto, 1992). The literature investigating the accurate detection of emotions from the voice and body also reveals substantial recognition accuracy. What is clear from such research is that nonverbal cues are heavily influential in the detection of emotion in others. In one informative study, Planalp and colleagues (1996) asked college students and working adults to make observations about how close others (usually roommates or significant others) displayed emotions. Participants reported events where others displayed emotion cues, and listed specific cues they used to assess that the other was experiencing an emotion. Over 95% of respondents reported using more than one cue to detect emotion and respondents reported using an average of 6–7 cues to detect emotion. The most common type of cue was vocal, such as voice pitch, loudness, and rate. Other important cues were facial, indirect verbal (e.g., expletives), and movements or body position. In fact, very few respondents reported using direct verbal cues (e.g., the target explicitly stated the emotion they were feeling). The use of nonverbal cues to decode emotion was probably even greater than what participants reported, given that much of nonverbal perception is automatic and occurred outside the participants' awareness. In general, the study underscored the importance of nonverbal cues in understanding how individuals detect emotions in others.

The literature investigating the accurate detection of emotions from the voice and body reveals substantial recognition accuracy. In one extensive study, Banse and Scherer (1996) audio-recorded actors reading standard sentences with varying emotional intentions. Participants were then asked to listen to the vocal expressions and make judgments as to which emotion was being expressed. Accurate recognition of emotions from the vocal expressions was highest for "hot" anger, boredom, and interest, and lowest accuracy rates were found for shame and disgust. Results suggested that emotions may be recognized from acoustic and vocal qualities and such expressions are marked by distinct acoustic profiles. Emotion recognition from vocal cues is documented in many studies (e.g., Ryan, Murray, & Ruffman, 2010; Scherer, Banse, & Wallbott, 2001; Wickline, Bailey, & Nowicki, 2009).

Other examples of accurate emotion recognition from nonverbal cues outside of facial expressions include accurate emotion recognition from body position, movement, posture, and touch (e.g., Atkinson, Heberlein, & Adolphs, 2007; Montepare, Koff, Zaitchik, & Albert, 1999; Sauter, 2010; Sogon & Masutani, 1989; Wallbott & Scherer, 1986). For instance, there was high agreement and accuracy of perceivers in judging happiness, anger, and sadness from body postures, at rates close to those found with facial stimuli (Coulson, 2004). Perceivers were better than chance at detecting emotions such as happiness and anger from videos of actors instructed to walk in emotional situations (e.g., learning that a roommate ruined a new blouse) (Montepare et al., 1987). One fascinating study of recognizing emotion from touch had participants instructed to touch an unacquainted partner (only on appropriate areas of the body) in any fashion to convey one of eight possible emotions (Hertenstein, Holmes, McCullough, & Keltner, 2009). Participants used various types of touches, including hugs, pats, taps, and strokes, to communicate various emotions; remarkably, previously unacquainted partners were better-than-chance at detecting emotions such as anger, fear, gratitude, and love. These findings confirmed an earlier, similar study that only allowed participants to touch the arm of their unacquainted partner (Hertenstein, Keltner, App, Bulleit, & Jaskolka, 2006). Again, such research accentuates the power of nonverbal cues in the detection and recognition of emotion.

Detection of sexual orientation

Thin-slice research shows that sexual orientation can be detected from nonverbal cues. Ambady, Hallahan, and Conner (1999) investigated whether perceivers could detect sexual orientation from thin slices. Graduate students, who served as targets, were videotaped discussing the balance between extracurricular activities and school work. Perceivers (undergraduate students) were shown silent 10-second clips (extracted from the 25th–35th -second interval in the longer videotaped discussion), a silent 1-second clip (extracted from the 4th–6th-second interval), or eight still photographs of the targets. Perceivers were better-than-chance at detecting sexual orientation and were significantly better at judging sexual orientation from the dynamic, thin-slice conditions (1-second and 10-second silent videos) than the still photos. In a second study, the importance of body movement, posture, and gestures was illustrated when target faces were blocked out and animated figural displays were presented to participants; again, participants were better-than-chance at detecting sexual orientation. Additional studies have confirmed these original findings; perceivers can accurately detect sexual orientation from thin slices of behavior (Johnson, Gill, Reichman, & Tassinary, 2007; Rieger, Linsenmeier, Gygax, Garcia, & Bailey, 2010). Clearly, this detection relies on the perception and recognition of nonverbal cues.

Detection and display of prejudice

Research demonstrates that nonverbal cues may subtly reveal prejudicial attitudes and racial biases. One study investigated whether participants could detect prejudicial attitudes from viewing thin slices of targets' social interactions (Richeson & Shelton, 2005). Black and White targets were video recorded in either same-race or interracial dyadic interactions. The targets also completed measures of racial bias. Twenty-second slices of these interactions were then shown to Black and White participant judges, who were asked to rate the positive affect and appearance of prejudice in the targets. Results showed that Black judges' ratings of targets' positive affect were significantly correlated with White targets' implicit bias scores, but only for the White targets in interracial interactions. Notably, judges only viewed thin slices of single targets; they did not know the race of targets' interaction partners. Thus, Black judges detected racial biases from White targets, but those racial biases are only apparent in interracial interactions (as opposed to same-race interactions). Such results suggest that implicit racial biases can be perceived in context-relevant situations via nonverbal cues.

Other research has found similar results indicating that racial bias is revealed during social interactions via nonverbal behavior. For example, participants with higher measured implicit racial bias engaged in more positive interaction behaviors (assessed with ratings of friendliness, comfort level, and abruptness) during interactions with a White experimenter than a Black experimenter (McConnell & Leibold, 2001). In the same study, higher racial bias scores were correlated with more smiling, greater speaking time, and fewer speech errors and hesitations in interactions with a White experimenter compared to interactions with a Black experimenter. High-prejudiced participants showed more behavioral inhibition (less body and hand movements) during discussions about fraternities on college campuses with a Black experimenter than with a White experimenter, suggesting that high-prejudiced participants inhibited their nonverbal behavior as not to risk appearing prejudiced (Richeson & Shelton, 2003). Once again, such findings illustrate the importance of nonverbal perception in the process of person perception.

CONCLUSION

Nonverbal perception involves the recognition and interpretation of nonverbal cues. The influence of nonverbal cues such as vocal qualities and body movement on the impressions we form of others cannot be understated. As the research reviewed in this chapter illustrates, the processes involved in nonverbal perception consist of four basic components: (1) nonverbal cue qualities; (2) target qualities; (3) perceiver qualities; and (4) the social context, namely interaction qualities. Accurate person perception is a complex process intertwined with the perception of nonverbal cues, and these interpersonal judgments represent a true social-cognitive mechanism. And while we may never achieve a dictionary-style manual that defines which nonverbal signal corresponds to which interpersonal state or trait, nonverbal perception research establishes that nonverbal cues are influential and essential in our everyday interactions with others.

ACKNOWLEDGMENTS

The author wishes to acknowledge the helpful feedback provided by Drs. Adam Fingerhut and Máire Ford on earlier versions of this chapter.

NOTE

1   While perceiver orientation could be considered a perceiver quality, I have categorized it under interaction qualities because perceiver orientation refers to the perceiver's position within the interaction.

REFERENCES

Addington, D. W. (1968). The relationship of selected vocal characteristics to personality perception. *Speech Monographs, 35*, 492–503. doi: 10.1080/03637756809375599

Ambady, N., Bernieri, F. J., & Richeson, J. A. (2000). Toward a histology of social behavior: Judgmental accuracy from thin slices of the behavioral stream. In M. P. Zanna (Ed.), *Advances in Experimental Social Psychology: Vol. 32* (pp. 201–271). San Diego, CA: Academic Press.

Ambady, N., & Gray, H. M. (2002). On being sad and mistaken: Mood effects on the accuracy of thin-slice judgments. *Journal of Personality and Social Psychology, 83*, 947–961. doi: 10.1037/0022-3514.83.4.947

Ambady, N., Hallahan, M., & Conner, B. (1999). Accuracy of judgments of sexual orientation from thin slices of behavior. *Journal of Personality and Social Psychology, 77*, 538–547. doi: 10.1037/0022-3514.77.3.538

Ambady, N., & Rosenthal, R. (1992). Thin slices of expressive behavior as predictors of interpersonal consequences: A meta-analysis. *Psychological Bulletin, 111*, 256–274. doi: 10.1037/0033-2909.111.2.256

Ambady, N., & Weisbuch, M. (2010). Nonverbal behavior. In S. T. Fiske, D. T. Gilbert & G. Lindzey (Eds.*), Handbook of social psychology: Vol. 1.* (5th ed.). Hoboken, NJ: John Wiley and Sons.

Atkinson, A. P., Heberlein, A. S., & Adolphs, R. (2007). Spared ability to recognize fear from static and moving whole-body cues following bilateral amygdala damage. *Neuropsychologia, 45*, 2772–2782. doi: 10.1016/j.neuropsychologia.2007.04.019

Aube, J., & Whiffen, V. (1996). Depressive styles and social acuity: Further evidence for distinct interpersonal correlates of dependency and self-criticism. *Communication Research, 23*, 407–424. doi: 10.1177/009365096023004004

Banse, R., & Scherer, K. R. (1996). Acoustic profiles in vocal emotion expression. *Journal of Personality and Social Psychology, 70*, 614–636. doi: 10.1007/BF00995674

Barclay, C. D., Cutting, J. E., & Kozlowski, L. T. (1978). Temporal and spatial factors in gait perception. *Perception and Psychophysics, 23*, 145–152.

Bargh, J. A. (1994). The Four Horsemen of automaticity: Awareness, efficiency, intention, and control in social cognition. In R. S. Wyer, Jr., & T. K. Srull (Eds.), *Handbook of social cognition* (2nd ed., pp. 1–40). Hillsdale, NJ: Erlbaum.

Berry, D. S. (1990). Vocal attractiveness and vocal babyishness: Effects on stranger, self, and friend impressions. *Journal of Nonverbal Behavior, 14*, 141–153. doi:10.1007/BF00996223

Berry, D. S. (1992). Vocal types and stereotypes: Joint effects of vocal attractiveness and vocal maturity on person perception. *Journal of Nonverbal Behavior, 16*, 41–54. doi: 10.1007/BF00986878

Birdwhistell, R. L. (1983). Background to kinesics. *Etc., 40*, 352–361.

Blackman, M. C., & Funder, D. C. (1998). The effect of information on consensus and accuracy in personality judgment. *Journal of Experimental Social Psychology, 34*, 164–181. doi: 10.1006/jesp.1997.1347

Borkenau, P., & Liebler, A. (1993). Convergence of stranger ratings of personality and intelligence with self-ratings, partner ratings, and measured intelligence. *Journal of Personality and Social Psychology, 65*, 546–553. doi: 10.1037/0022-3514.65.3.546

Borkenau, P., & Liebler, A. (1995). Observable attributes as manifestations and cues of personality and intelligence. *Journal of Personality, 63*, 1–25. doi: 10.1111/j.1467-6494.1995.tb00799.x

Briton, N. J., & Hall, J. A. (1995). Gender-based expectancies and observer judgments of smiling. *Journal of Nonverbal Behavior, 19*, 49–65. doi: 10.1007/BF02173412

Brunswik, E. (1956). *Perception and the representative design of psychological experiments*. Los Angeles, CA: University of California Press.

Burgoon, J. K. (1991). Relational message interpretations of touch, conversational distance, and posture. *Journal of Nonverbal Behavior, 15*, 233–259. doi: 10.1007/BF00986924

Burgoon, J. K., & Hoobler, G. (2002). Nonverbal signals. In M. L. Knapp & J. Daly (Eds.), *Handbook of interpersonal communication* (pp. 240–299). Thousand Oaks, CA: Sage Publications.

Carney, D. R., Colvin, C. R., & Hall, J. A. (2007). A thin slice perspective on the accuracy of first impressions. *Journal of Research in Personality, 41*, 1054–1072. doi: 10.1016/j.jrp.2007.01.004

Carroll, J. M., & Russell, J. A. (1996). Do facial expressions signal specific emotions? Judging emotion from the face in context. *Journal of Personality and Social Psychology, 70*, 205–218. doi: 10.1037/0022-3514.70.2.205

Chapdelaine, A., Kenny, D. A., & LaFontana, K. M. (1994). Matchmaker, matchmaker, can you make me a match? Predicting liking between two unacquainted persons. *Journal of Personality and Social Psychology, 67*, 83–91. doi: 10.1037/0022-3514.67.1.83

Chartrand, T. L., & Bargh J. A. (1996). Automatic activation of impression formation and memorization goals: Nonconscious goal priming reproduces effects of explicit task instructions. *Journal of Personality and Social Psychology, 71,* 464–478. doi: 10.1037/0022-3514.71.3.464

Chartrand, T. L., & Bargh, J. A. (1999). The chameleon effect: The perception–behavior link and social interaction. *Journal of Personality and Social Psychology, 76*, 893–910. doi: 10.1037/0022-3514.76.6.893

Chartrand, T. L., Maddux, W., & Lakin, J. (2005). Beyond the perception–behavior link: The ubiquitous utility and motivational moderators of nonconscious mimicry. In R. Hassin, J. Uleman, & J. A. Bargh (Eds.), *The new unconscious* (pp. 334–361). New York: Oxford University Press.

Choi, V. S., Gray, H. M., & Ambady, N. (2005). The glimpsed world: Unintended communication and unintended perception. In R. R. Hassin, J. S. Uleman, & J. A. Bargh (Eds.), *The new unconscious* (pp. 309–333). New York: Oxford University Press.

Church, A. T., Katigbak, M. S., & del Prado, A. M. (2010). Cultural similarities and differences in perceived affordances of situations for Big Five behaviors. *Journal of Research Personality, 44*, 78–90. doi: 10.1016/j.jrp.2009.11.003

Cohen, R. L., & Borsoi, D. (1996). The role of gestures in description-communication: A cross-sectional study of aging. *Journal of Nonverbal Behavior, 20*, 45–63. doi: 10.1007/BF02248714

Colvin, C. R., & Funder, D. C. (1991). Predicting personality and behavior: A boundary on the acquaintanceship effect. *Journal of Personality and Social Psychology, 60*, 884–894. doi: 10.1037/0022-3514.60.6.884

Costanzo, M., & Archer, D. (1989). Interpreting the expressive behavior of others: The Interpersonal Perception Task. *Journal of Nonverbal Behavior, 13*, 225–245. doi:10.1007/BF00990295.

Coulson, M. (2004). Attributing emotion to static body postures: Recognition, accuracy, confusions and viewpoint dependence. *Journal of Nonverbal Behavior, 28*, 117–139. doi: 10.1023/B:JONB.0000023655.25550.be

DePaulo, B. M. (1992). Nonverbal behavior and self-presentation. *Psychological Bulletin, 111*, 203–243. doi: 10.1037/0033-2909.111.2.203

DePaulo, B. M., Lindsay, J. J., Malone, B. E., Muhlenbruck, L., Charlton, K., & Cooper, H. (2003). Cues to deception. *Psychological Bulletin, 129*, 74–118. doi: 10.1037/0033-2909.129.1.74

Eagly, A. (1987). *Sex differences in social behavior: A social-role interpretation.* Hillsdale, NJ: Erlbaum.

Ekman, P. & Friesen, W. V. (1969). The repertoire of nonverbal behavior categories, origins, usage, and coding. *Semiotica, 1*, 49–98.

Ekman, P., Friesen, W. V., O'Sullivan, M., Chan, A., Diacoyanni-Tarlatzis, I., Heider, K., et al. (1987). Universals and cultural differences in the judgments of facial expressions of emotion. *Journal of Personality and Social Psychology, 53*, 712–717. doi: 10.1037/0022-3514.53.4.712

Elfenbein, H. A., & Ambady, N. (2003). When familiarity breeds accuracy: Cultural exposure and facial emotion recognition. *Journal of Personality and Social Psychology, 85*, 276–290. doi: 10.1037/0022-3514.85.2.276

Floyd, K. (1999). All touches are not created equal: Effects of form and duration on observers' interpretations of an embrace. *Journal of Nonverbal Behavior, 23*, 283–299. doi: 10.1023/A:1021602926270

Foster, J. (2008). Beauty is mostly in the eye of the beholder: Olfactory versus visual cues of attractiveness. *The Journal of Social Psychology, 148*, 765–774. doi: 10.3200/SOCP.148.6.765–774

Friedman, H. S. (1979). The interactive effects of facial expressions of emotion and verbal messages on perceptions of affective meaning. *Journal of Experimental Social Psychology, 15*, 453–469. doi: 10.1016/0022-1031(79)90008-8

Friesen, W. V., Ekman, P., & Wallbott, H. (1979). Measuring hand movements. *Journal of Nonverbal Behavior, 4*, 97–112. doi: 10.1007/BF01006354

Funder, D. C. (1995). On the accuracy of personality judgment: A realistic approach. *Psychological Review, 102*, 652–670. doi: 10.1037/0033-295X.102.4.652

Funder, D. C. (1999). *Personality judgment: A realistic approach to person perception.* San Diego, CA: Academic Press.

Gibson, J. J. (1979). *The ecological approach to visual perception.* Boston, MA: Houghton Mifflin.

Gifford, R. (1994). A lens-mapping framework for understanding the encoding and decoding of interpersonal dispositions in nonverbal behavior. *Journal of Personality and Social Psychology, 66*, 398–412. doi: 10.1037/0022-3514.66.2.398

Goldberg, S., & Rosenthal, R. (1986). Self-touching in the job interview: Antecedents and consequences. *Journal of Nonverbal Behavior, 10*, 65–80. doi: 10.1007/BF00987206

Grahe, J. E., & Bernieri, F. J. (1999). The importance of nonverbal cues in judging rapport. *Journal of Nonverbal Behavior, 23*, 253–269. doi: 10.1023/A:1021698725361

Grayson, B., & Stein, M. I. (1981). Attracting assault: Victims' nonverbal cues. *Journal of Communication, 31*, 68–75. doi: 10.1111/j.1460-2466.1981.tb01206.x

Gunns, R. E., Johnston, L., & Hudson, S. M. (2002). Victim selection and kinematics: A point-light investigation of vulnerability to attack. *Journal of Nonverbal Behavior, 26*, 129–158. doi: 10.1023/A:1020744915533

Hadar, U., Steiner, T. J., & Rose, F. C. (1985). Head movements during listening turns in conversation. *Journal of Nonverbal Behavior, 9*, 214–228. doi: 10.1007/BF00986881

Hall, J. A. (1978). Gender effects in decoding nonverbal cues. *Psychological Bulletin, 85*, 845–857. doi:10.1037/0033-2909.85.4.845.

Hall, J. A. (1984). *Nonverbal sex differences: Communication accuracy and expressive style.* Baltimore, MD: Johns Hopkins University Press.

Hall, J. A. (2006). Nonverbal behavior, status, and gender: How do we understand their relations? *Psychology of Women Quarterly, 30*, 384–391. doi: 10.1111/j.1471-6402.2006.00313.x

Hall, J. A., Andrzejewski, S. A., Murphy, N. A., Schmid Mast, M., & Feinstein, B. A. (2008). Accuracy of judging others' traits and states: Comparing mean levels across tests. *Journal of Research in Personality, 42*, 1476–1489. doi: 10.1016/j.jrp.2008.06.013

Hall, J. A., Andrzejewski, S. A., & Yopchick, J. E. (2009). Psychosocial correlates of interpersonal sensitivity: A meta-analysis. *Journal of Nonverbal Behavior, 33*, 149–180. doi: 10.1007/s10919-009-0070-5

Hall, J. A., Carter, J. D., & Horgan, T. G. (2000). Gender differences in nonverbal communication of emotion. In A. H. Fischer (Ed.), *Gender and emotion: Social psychology perspectives* (pp. 97–117). New York: Cambridge University Press.

Hall, J. A., Carter, J. D., Jimenez, M. C., Frost, N. A., & Smith LeBeau, L. (2002). Smiling and relative status in news photographs. *Journal of Social Psychology, 142*, 500–510. doi: 10.1080/00224540209603914

Hall, J. A., Halberstadt, A. G., & O'Brien, C. E. (1997). 'Subordination' and nonverbal sensitivity: A study and synthesis of findings based on trait measures. *Sex Roles, 37*, 295–317. doi: 10.1023/A:1025608105284

Havlicek J., Roberts, S. C., & Flegr, J. (2005). Women's preference for dominant male odour: Effects of menstrual cycle and relationship status. *Biology Letters, 1*, 256–259. doi: 10.1098/rsbl.2005.0332

Hertenstein, M. J., Holmes, R., McCullough, M., & Keltner, D. (2009). The communication of emotion via touch. *Emotion, 9*, 566–573. doi: 10.1037/a0016108

Herstenstein, M. J., Keltner, D., App, B., Bulleit, B. A, & Jaskolka, A. R. (2006). Touch communicates distinct emotions. *Emotion, 6*, 528–533. doi: 10.1037/1528-3542.6.3.528

Hess, U., Blairy, S., & Philippot, P. (1999). Facial mimicry. In P. Philippot, R. Feldman, & E. Coats (Eds.), *The social context of nonverbal behavior* (pp. 213–241). New York: Cambridge University Press.

Hummert, M. L., Mazloff, D., & Henry, C. (1999). Vocal characteristics of older adults and stereotyping. *Journal of Nonverbal Behavior, 23*, 111–132. doi: 10.1023/A:1021483409296

Johnson, K. L., Gill, S., Reichman, V., & Tassinary, L. G. (2007). Swagger, sway, and sexuality: Judging sexual orientation from body motion and morphology. *Journal of Personality and Social Psychology, 93*, 321–334. doi: 10.1037/0022-3514.93.3.321

Kenny, D. A. (1991). A general model of consensus and accuracy in interpersonal perception. *Psychological Review, 98*, 155–163. doi: 10.1037/0033-295X.98.2.155

Kenny, D. A. (1994). *Interpersonal perception: A social relations analysis.* New York: Guilford Press.

Kenny, D. A. (2004). PERSON: A general model of interpersonal perception. *Personality and Social Psychology Review, 8*, 265–280. doi:10.1207/s15327957pspr0803_3

Kenny, D. A., & Albright, L. (1987). Accuracy in interpersonal perception: A social relations analysis. *Psychological Bulletin, 102*, 390–402. doi: 10.1037/0033-2909.102.3.390

Kenny, D. A., & La Voie, L. (1984). The social relations model. In L. Berkowitz (Ed.), *Advances in experimental social psychology* (pp. 142–182). Orlando, FL: Academic Press.

Kenny, D. A., & West, T. V. (2008). Zero acquaintance: Definitions, statistical model, findings, and process. In J. Skowronski, & N. Ambady (Eds.), *First impressions* (pp. 129–146). New York: Guilford Press.

Knapp, M. L., & Hall, J. A. (2010). *Nonverbal communication in human interaction* (7th ed.). Belmont, CA: Wadsworth.

Kudoh, T., & Matsumoto, D. (1985). Cross-cultural examination of the semantic dimensions of body postures. *Journal of Personality and Social Psychology, 48*, 1440–1446.

Küfner, A. C. P., Back, M. D., Nestler, S., & Egloff, B. (2010). Tell me a story and I will tell you who you are! Lens model analyses of personality and creative writing. *Journal of Research in Personality, 44*, 427–435. doi: 10.1016/j.jrp.2010.05.003

Lakin, J. L. (2006). Automatic cognitive processes and nonverbal communication. In V. Manusov & M. L. Patterson (Eds.), *The SAGE Handbook of Nonverbal Communication* (pp. 59–77). Thousand Oaks, CA: Sage Publications.

Letzring, T. D., Wells, S. M., & Funder, D. C. (2006). Quantity and quality of available information affect the realistic accuracy of personality judgment. *Journal of Personality and Social Psychology, 91*, 111–123. doi: 10.1037/0022-3514.91.1.111

Levine, S. P., & Feldman, R. S. (1997). Self-presentational goals, self-monitoring, and nonverbal behavior. *Basic and Applied Social Psychology, 19*, 505–518. doi: 10.1207/s15324834basp1904_7

Lippa, R. (1998). The nonverbal display and judgment of extraversion, masculinity, femininity, and gender diagnosticity: A Lens Model analysis. *Journal of Research in Personality, 32*, 80–107. doi: 10.1006/jrpe.1997.2189

Mahaffey, K. J., & Marcus, D. M. (2006). Interpersonal perception of psychopathy: A social relations analysis. *Journal of Social and Clinical Psychology, 25*, 53–74. doi: 10.1521/jscp.2006.25.1.53

Malloy, T. E., & Kenny, D. A. (1986). The Social Relations Model: An integrative method for personality research. *Journal of Personality, 54*, 199–225. doi: 10.1111/j.1467-6494.1986.tb00393.x

Matsumoto, D. (1990). Cultural similarities and differences in display rules. *Motivation and Emotion, 14*, 195–214. doi: 10.1007/BF00995569

Matsumoto, D. (1992). American–Japanese cultural differences in the recognition of universal facial expressions. *Journal of Cross-Cultural Psychology, 23*, 72–84. doi: 10.1177/0022022192231005

Matsumoto, D. (1993). Ethnic differences in affect intensity, emotion judgments, display rules, and self-reported emotional expression. *Motivation and Emotion, 17*, 107–123. doi: 10.1007/BF00995188

Matsumoto, D., Takeuchi, S., Andayani, S., Kouznetsova, N., & Krupp, D. (1998). The contribution of individualism vs. collectivism to cross-national differences in display rules. *Asian Journal of Social Psychology, 1*, 147–165. doi: 10.1111/1467-839X.00010

McArthur, L. Z., & Baron, R. M. (1983). Toward an ecological theory of social perception. *Psychological Review, 90*, 215–238. doi: 10.1037/0033-295X.90.3.215

McConnell, A. R., & Leibold, J. M. (2001). Relations among the Implicit Association Test, discriminatory behavior, and explicit measures of racial attitudes. *Journal of Experimental Social Psychology, 37*, 435–442. doi: 10.1006/jesp.2000.1470

McCrae, R. R., & Costa, P. T., Jr. (1990). *Personality in adulthood.* New York: Guilford Press.

Mehrabian, A. (1972). *Nonverbal communication.* Chicago, IL: Aldine-Atherton.

Michalak, J., Troje, N. F., Fischer, J., Vollmar, P., Heidenreich, T., & Schulte, D. (2009). Embodiment of sadness and depression: Gait patterns associated with dysphoric mood. *Psychosomatic Medicine, 71*, 580–587. doi: 10.1097/PSY.0b013e3181a2515c

Mignault, A., & Chaudhuri, A. (2003). The many faces of a neutral face: Head tilt and perception of dominance and emotion. *Journal of Nonverbal Behavior, 27*, 111–132. doi: 10.1023/A:1023914509763

Montepare, J. M., Goldstein, S. B., & Clausen, A. (1987). The identification of emotions from gait information. *Journal of Nonverbal Behavior, 11*, 33–42. doi: 10.1007/BF00999605

Montepare, J. M., Koff, E., Zaitchik D., & Albert, M. (1999). The use of body movements and gestures as cues to emotions in younger and older adults. *Journal of Nonverbal Behavior, 23*, 133–152. doi: 10.1023/A:1021435526134

Montepare, J. M., & McArthur, L. Z. (1987). Perceptions of adults with childlike voices in two cultures. *Journal of Experimental Social Psychology, 23*, 331–349. doi: 10.1016/0022-1031(87)90045-X

Montepare, J. M., & Zebrowitz-McArthur, L. (1988). Impressions of people created by age-related qualities of their gaits. *Journal of Personality and Social Psychology, 55*, 547–556. doi: 10.1037/0022-3514.55.4.547

Most, T., & Aviner, C. (2009). Auditory, visual, and auditory-visual perception of emotions by individuals with cochlear implants, hearing aids, and normal hearing. *Journal of Deaf Studies and Deaf Education, 14*, 449–464. doi: 10.1093/deafed/enp007

Mueser, K. T., Grau, B. W., Sussman, M. S., & Rosen, A. J. (1984). You're only as pretty as you feel: Facial expression as a determinant of physical attractiveness. *Journal of Personality and Social Psychology, 46*, 469–478. doi:10.1037/0022-3514.46.2.469

Murphy, N. A. (2007). Appearing smart: The impression management of intelligence, person perception accuracy, and behavior in social interaction. *Personality and Social Psychology Bulletin, 33*, 325–339. doi: 10.1177/0146167206294871

Murphy, N. A., Hall, J. A., & Colvin, C. R. (2003). Accurate intelligence assessments in social interactions: Mediators and gender effects. *Journal of Personality, 71*, 465–493.

Naumann, L. P., Vazire, S., Renfrew, P. J., & Gosling, S. D. (2009). Personality judgments based on physical appearance. *Personality and Social Psychology Bulletin, 35*, 1661–1671. doi: 10.1177/0146167209346309

Osborn, D. R. (1996). Beauty is as beauty does? Makeup and posture effects on physical attractiveness judgments. *Journal of Applied Social Psychology, 26*, 31–51. doi:10.1111/j.1559-1816.1996.tb01837.x

Patterson, M. L. (1995). A parallel process model of nonverbal communication. *Journal of Nonverbal Behavior, 19*, 3–29. doi: 10.1007/BF02173410

Patterson, M. L. (1996). Social behavior and social cognition: A parallel process approach. In J. L. Nye & A. M. Brower (Eds.), *What's social about social cognition?* (pp. 87–105). Thousand Oaks, CA: Sage Publications.

Patterson, M. L. (2006). The evolution of theories of interactive behavior. In V. Manusov & M. L. Patterson (Eds.), *The SAGE handbook of nonverbal communication* (pp. 21–39). Thousand Oaks, CA: Sage Publications.

Patterson, M. L., Powell, J. L., & Lenihan, M. G. (1986). Touch, compliance, and interpersonal affect. *Journal of Nonverbal Behavior, 10*, 41–50. doi: 10.1007/BF00987204

Patterson, M. L., & Stockbridge, E. (1998). Effects of cognitive demand and judgment strategy on person perception accuracy. *Journal of Nonverbal Behavior, 22*, 253–263. doi:10.1023/A:1022996522793

Peters, M., Rhodes, G., & Simmons, L. W. (2007). Contributions of the face and body to overall attractiveness. *Animal Behaviour, 73*, 937–942. doi: 10.1016/j.anbehav.2006.07.012

Pickett, C. L., Gardner, W. L., & Knowles, M. (2004). Getting a cue: The need to belong and enhanced sensitivity to social cues. *Personality and Social Psychology Bulletin, 30*, 1095–1107. doi: 10.1177/0146167203262085

Planalp, S., DeFrancisco, V., & Rutherford, D. (1996). Varieties of cues to emotion in naturally occurring situations. *Cognition and Emotion, 10*, 137–153. doi: 10.1080/026999396380303

Raines R. S., Hechtman S. B., & Rosenthal R. (1990). Physical attractiveness of face and voice: Effects of positivity, dominance, and sex. *Journal of Applied Social Psychology, 20*, 1558–1578. doi: 10.1111/j.1559-1816.1990.tb01493.x

Reynolds, D. J., & Gifford, R. (2001). The sounds and sights of intelligence: A lens model channel analysis. *Personality and Social Psychology Bulletin, 27*, 187–200. doi: 10.1177/0146167201272005

Richeson, J. A., & Shelton, J. N. (2003). When prejudice does not pay: Effects of interracial contact on executive function. *Psychological Science, 14*, 287–290. doi:10.1111/1467-9280.03437

Richeson, J. A., & Shelton, J. N. (2005). Brief report: Thin slices of racial bias. *Journal of Nonverbal Behavior, 29*, 75–86. doi: 10.1007/s10919-004-0890-2

Rieger, G., Linsenmeier, J. A. W., Gygaz, L., Garcia, S., & Bailey, M. J. (2010). Dissecting "gayday": Accuracy and the role of masculinity–femininity. *Archives of Sexual Behavior, 39*, 124–140. doi: 10.1007/s10508-008-9405-2

Riggio, H. R., & Riggio, R. E. (2002). Emotional expressiveness, extraversion, and neuroticism: A meta-analysis. *Journal of Nonverbal Behavior, 26*, 195–218. doi: 10.1023/A:1022117500440

Rikowski, A., & Grammar, K. (1999). Human body odour, symmetry and attractiveness. *Proceedings of the Royal Society of London, 266B*, 869–887. doi: 10.1098/rspb.1999.0717

Rosenfeld, H. M. (1966). Approval-seeking and approval-inducing functions of verbal and nonverbal responses in the dyad. *Journal of Personality and Social Psychology, 4*, 597–605. doi: 10.1037/h0023996

Ruffman, T., Henry, J. D., Livingstone, V., & Phillips, L. H. (2008). A meta-analytic review of emotion recognition and aging: Implications for neuropsychological models of aging. *Neuroscience and Biobehavioral Reviews, 32*, 863–881. doi: 10.1016/j.neubiorev.2008.01.001

Ruffman, T., Sullivan, S., & Dittrich, W. (2009). Older adults' recognition of bodily and auditory expressions of emotion. *Psychology and Aging, 24*, 614–622. doi: 10.1037/a0016356

Ryan, M., Murray, J., & Ruffman, T. (2010). Aging and the perception of emotion: Processing vocal expressions alone and with faces. *Experimental Aging Research, 36*, 1–22. doi: 10.1080/03610730903418372

Safdar, S., Friedlmeier, W., Matsumoto, D., Yoo, S. H., Kwantes, C., Kakai, H., et al. (2009). Variations of emotional display rules within and across cultures: A comparison between Canada, USA, and Japan. *Canadian Journal of Behavioural Science, 41*, 1–10. doi: 10.1037/a0014387

Sakaguchi, K., & Hasegawa, T. (2006). Person perception through gait information and target choice for sexual advances: Comparison of likely targets in experiments and real life. *Journal of Nonverbal Behavior, 30,* 63–85. doi: 10.1007/s10919-006-0006-2

Sauter, D. (2010). More than happy: The need for disentangling positive emotions. *Current Directions in Psychological Science, 19*, 36–40. doi:10.1177/0963721409359290.

Sawada, M., Suda, K., & Ishii, M. (2003). Expression of emotions in dance: Relation between arm movement characteristics and emotion. *Perceptual and Motor Skills, 97*, 697–708. doi: 10.2466/PMS.97.7.697–708

Scherer, K. R., Banse, R., & Wallbott, H. G. (2001). Emotion inferences from vocal expression correlate across languages and cultures. *Journal of Cross-Cultural Psychology, 32*, 76–92. doi:10.1177/0022022101032001009

Schlenker, B. R. (1980). *Impression management: The self-concept, social identity, and interpersonal relations.* Monterey, CA: Brook/Cole.

Schmid Mast, M., & Hall, J. A. (2004). Who is the boss and who is not? Accuracy of judging status. *Journal of Nonverbal Behavior, 28*, 145–165. doi: 10.1023/B: JONB.0000039647.94190.21

Schmid Mast, M., Hall, J. A., Murphy, N. A., & Colvin, C. R. (2003). Judging assertiveness. *Facta Universitatis, 2*, 731–744.

Schroeder, J. E. (1995). Self-concept, social anxiety, and interpersonal perception skills. *Personality and Individual Differences, 19*, 955–958.

Singh, D., Dixson, B. J., Jessop, T. S., Morgan, B., & Dixson, A. F. (2010). Cross-cultural consensus for waist–hip ratio and women's attractiveness. *Evolution and Human Behavior, 31*, 176–181. doi:10.1016/j.evolhumbehav.2009.09.001

Sogon, S., & Masutani, M. (1989). Identification of emotion from body movements: A cross-cultural study of Americans and Japanese. *Psychological Reports, 65*, 35–46.

Spain, J. S., Eaton, L. G., & Funder, D. C. (2000). Perspectives on personality: The relative accuracy of self versus others for the prediction of emotion and behavior. *Journal of Personality, 68*, 837–867. doi: 10.1111/1467-6494.00118

Srivastava, S., Guglielmo, S., & Beer, J. S. (2010). Perceiving others' personalities: Examining the dimensionality, assumed similarity to the self and stability of perceiver effects. *Journal of Personality and Social Psychology, 98*, 520–534. doi: 10.1037/a0017057

Sternberg, R. J., & Smith, C. (1985). Social intelligence and decoding skills in nonverbal communication. *Journal of Social Cognition, 3*, 16–31.

Sussman, N. M., & Rosenfeld, H. M. (1978). Touch, justification, and sex: Influences on the aversiveness of spatial violations. *Journal of Social Psychology, 106*, 215–225.

Thayer, S. (1986). Touch: Frontier of intimacy. *Journal of Nonverbal Behavior, 10*, 7–11.

Tickle-Degnen, L. (2006). Nonverbal behavior and its functions in the ecosystem of rapport. In V. Manusov & M. L. Patterson (Eds.), *The SAGE handbook of nonverbal communication* (pp. 381–399). Thousand Oaks, CA: Sage Publications.

Vazire, S. (2010). Who knows what about a person? The self-other knowledge asymmetry (SOKA) model. *Journal of Personality and Social Psychology, 98*, 281–300. doi: 10.1037/a0017908

Vazire, S., & Mehl, M. R. (2008). Knowing me, knowing you: The accuracy and unique predictive validity of self-ratings and other-ratings of daily behavior. *Journal of Personality and Social Psychology, 95*, 1202–1216. doi: 10.1037/a0013314

Vazire, S., Naumann, L. P., Rendfrow, P. J., & Gosling, S. D. (2008). Portrait of a narcissist: Manifestations of narcissism in physical appearance. *Journal of Research in Personality, 42*, 1439–1447. doi: 10.1016/j.jrp.2008.06.007

Vrij, A. (2000). *Detecting lies and deceit: The psychology of lying and its implications for professional practice.* Chichester, UK: John Wiley and Sons.

Vrij, A. (2006). Nonverbal communication and deception. In V. Manusov & M. L. Patterson (Eds.), *The SAGE handbook of nonverbal communication* (pp. 341–359). Thousand Oaks, CA: Sage Publications.

Vrugt, A., & Luyerink, M. (2000). The contribution of bodily posture to gender stereotypical impressions. *Social Behavior and Personality, 28*, 91–103. doi: 10.2224/sbp.2000.28.1.91

Wallbott, H. G., & Scherer, K. R. (1986). Cues and channels in emotion recognition. *Journal of Personality and*

Social Psychology, 51, 690–699. doi: 10.1037/0022-3514.51.4.690

Waxer, P. H. (1985). Video ethology: Television as a database for cross-cultural studies in nonverbal displays. *Journal of Nonverbal Behavior, 9*, 111–120. doi: 10.1007/BF00987142

Wehrle, T., Kaiser, S., Schmidt, S., & Scherer, K. R. (2000). Studying the dynamics of emotional expression using synthesized facial muscle movements. *Journal of Personality and Social Psychology, 78*, 105–119. doi: 10.1037/0022-3514.78.1.105

Weisbuch, M., & Ambady, N. (2008). Non-conscious routes to building culture: Nonverbal components of socialization. *Journal of Consciousness Studies, 15*, 159–183.

Wickline, V. B., Bailey, W., & Nowicki, S. (2009). Cultural in-group advantage: Emotion recognition in African American and European American faces and voices. *The Journal of Genetic Psychology: Research and Theory on Human Development, 170*, 5–29. doi: 10.3200/GNTP.170.1.5-30

Wilson, J. M. B., Tripp, D. B., & Boland, F. J. (2005). The relative contributions of waist-to-hip ratio and body mass index to judgements of attractiveness. *Sexualities, Evolution and Gender, 7*, 245–267. doi:10.1080/14616660500238769

Zebrowitz, L. A., & Collins, M. A. (1997). Accurate social perception at zero acquaintance: The affordances of a Gibsonian approach. *Personality and Social Psychology Review, 1*, 204–223. doi: 10.1207/s15327957pspr0103_2

Zebrowitz, L. A., Hall, J. A., Murphy, N. A., & Rhodes, G. (2002). Looking smart and looking good: Facial cues to intelligence and their origins. *Personality and Social Psychology Bulletin, 28*, 238–249. doi: 10.1177/0146167202282009

11

Embodied Social Thought: Linking Social Concepts, Emotion, and Gesture

Autumn B. Hostetter, Martha W. Alibali,
& Paula M. Niedenthal

Social concepts, from relatively simple ones such as "handshake" to more complex ones such as "international relations," are fundamental for successfully anticipating and negotiating the interactions and situations that take place in daily social life. The set of social concepts includes emotion concepts, bases of knowledge that are critical for understanding one's own feeling states and for anticipating and perceiving the feelings of others (e.g., Niedenthal, 2008). Such concepts guide an individual's social behavior because they support acts of categorization, interpretation, and prediction about the attitudes, behaviors, and intentions of other individuals. For example, upon accepting an invitation to a jazz concert, we rely on our concept of this type of social situation in order to choose what to wear, what time to arrive, and how and when to applaud once we are there. We further rely on the concept when we decide to encourage our friend André to come along, but not our friend George. Recent theories of embodied social cognition hold that using a social concept involves reactivating motor, perceptual, and emotional experiences in the brain and in the body's periphery. The neural and peripheral activation of these experiences serve to represent the concept for use in negotiating the social world.

An embodied view therefore has profound implications for how we understand our social world. In this chapter, we will begin by reviewing the evidence that speakers understand others'

intentions, emotions, and language through simulated action and emotion. We then show how such simulations are embedded in the social environment so that they are functionally linked to the situations in which they are used. Finally, we explore how an embodied account of social cognition can be extended to apply to abstract concepts.

SIMULATING CONCEPTS IN SOCIAL THOUGHT AND LANGUAGE

Access to and use of the concept of *jazz concert* in our opening example is relatively easy to understand. Here, the concept is primed directly through the act of linguistic communication about it (i.e., "Do you want to come to a *jazz concert*?"). However, we also understand concepts that are not articulated in the speech of those around us; often, we must form an appropriate conceptualization of a situation based only on the non-linguistic behavior of those around us. Our ability to do so is complicated by the fact that observable behaviors and events are not always straightforward instances of any particular concept. When we see a woman holding five grocery bags and struggling outside a door to find something in her purse, how do we know – as we do with great accuracy much of the time – that she is searching for her keys? She could be looking for any number of things. We seem to "know" that she is looking for her keys because we have the ability to put ourselves "in her shoes," as the old saying goes, and imagine what we would likely be looking for if we were in a similar situation. We perform the same act of perspective taking in the domain of emotion. Although his overt behavior may be quite disorganized or ambiguous, we know what our son is feeling when he receives an award at a ceremony or trips during a soccer game. So, what is the relationship between using a concept and imagining ourselves in a similar situation? According to some recent theories of the conceptual system, there is not much difference at all.

The ability to imagine that we are in someone else's shoes is more than just a charming expression. Recent discoveries in neurophysiology have demonstrated that there are cells in the motor system of primate brains that are activated both when an action is observed and when the action is produced. These *mirror neurons* were first observed in the brains of monkeys (Gallese, Fadiga, Fogassi, & Rizzolatti, 1996; Rizzolatti & Craighero, 2004; Rizzolatti, Fadiga, Gallese, & Fogassi, 1996). Mirror neurons in the monkey's motor cortex, and in particular in area F5, which is responsible for controlling the production of hand and mouth movements, are now considered part of the neural system for comprehending action and intentional movement (Gallese et al., 1996; Rizolatti et al., 1996). Mirror systems that could support both the perception and performance of action have also been described in humans (Fadiga et al., 1995; Gallese et al., 1996; Iacoboni, et al., 1999; Rizolatti et al., 1996). The proposed cellular link between action and perception is groundbreaking because it suggests that understanding the actions of others is fundamentally linked to the experience of our own actions.

But possible accounts go beyond the mirror neuron. Indeed, in recent years, there have been an increasing number of proposals for how our ability to *simulate*, or engage our neural systems in a meaningful way, forms the basis for our ability to understand the actions, intentions, emotions, and language of others (e.g., Barsalou, 1999; Hurley, 2008; Kaschak & Maner, 2009; Sommerville & Decety, 2006; Wilson & Knoblich, 2005). Sometimes referred to as "embodied cognition," the thesis of such views is that cognition is based in our perceptual and motor abilities. Rather than processing the world in abstract, amodal terms that are distinct from motor and perceptual experiences, embodied views propose that cognition occurs because we can recreate motor and perceptual experiences even in the absence of environmental input (see Wilson, 2002). This recreation,

or simulation, relies on the same areas of the brain that are involved in actually experiencing the event.

To return to the jazz concert example, then, when we use this concept, we are not simply accessing a definition of jazz (i.e., *a style of music, native to America, characterized by a strong but flexible rhythmic understructure with solo and ensemble improvisations on basic tunes and chord patterns and, more recently, a highly sophisticated harmonic idiom*) and combining it with a definition of concert (i.e., *a performance given by one or more singers or instrumentalists or both*). Instead, according to these accounts, when we think about the concept *jazz concert*, we simulate the experiences we have had at these events, including how they look, sound, and smell, and of course how they make us feel. This simulation relies on the activation of neural states that are also activated when we are actually attending a jazz concert.

Thus, according to embodied views of social cognition, we understand social concepts by simulating the actions and emotions involved in experiencing the concept. These simulations occur both when we directly perceive the actions or emotions of another person and when we process language about actions and emotions.

Simulation in social information processing

What indicates that someone is simulating a social situation or entity? Perhaps the most obvious manifestation of simulation in social comprehension is overt mimicry. Individuals mimic the nonverbal behavior of those with whom they interact (e.g., Kimbara, 2008), particularly when they perceive a similarity between themselves and their interaction partner (Yabar, Johnston, Miles, & Peace, 2006). Furthermore, engaging in mimicry seems to have advantageous social consequences; we like people better when they have mimicked us (Lakin & Chartrand, 2003) and we are more successful in negotiations when we have mimicked others (Maddux, Mullen, & Galinsky, 2008). Chartrand and Bargh (1999) describe mimicry as facilitating a behavior → perception link; by mimicking the behaviors of those around us, our social perceptions are enhanced.

However, simulation need not be overtly expressed as mimicry in order to influence our social understanding and behavior. Evidence suggests that our behavior is influenced even when we simply think about a particular social concept. For example, Bargh, Chen, and Burrows (1996) found that participants walked significantly more slowly down a hallway when they had just been primed with the stereotype of the elderly than when they had not been primed. In this case, thinking about the elderly appears to have activated the motor system in a way that corresponds to how the elderly often move; the motor system activation then influenced the participants' own subsequent motor activity. In another compelling example, Dijksterhuis and van Knippenberg (1998) found that participants who were primed with the concept of college professors performed significantly better on a subsequent trivia test than did participants who were primed with the concept of soccer hooligans. Such evidence suggests that thinking about social categories unconsciously determines subsequent behavior.

The relation between embodied concepts and behavior holds in the opposite direction, as well. Engaging in a particular motor activity primes corresponding concepts of social situations. For example, Schubert (2004) found that males were more likely to interpret ambiguous situations as relating to the concept of power when they simultaneously made a fist gesture than when they were in a neutral posture. Similarly, in another study, participants were more likely to interpret an ambiguously hostile behavior as aggressive when they simultaneously extended their middle finger than when they did not (Chandler & Schwarz, 2009). These findings suggest that producing a particular action automatically activates knowledge of the situations that are associated with the action. This knowledge then influences the perception of an unrelated situation.

In addition to influencing the categorization of social situations, motor activity appears to guide the categorization of persons as well. In a recent study, Nussinson, Seibt, Häfner, and Strack (2010) had participants view photographs of target individuals while engaging in either an approach motion (flexing the arm in) or an avoidance motion (extending the arm out). Participants were then asked to evaluate how similar the targets were to themselves. Nussinson et al. found that participants believed that the targets were more similar to themselves when they had viewed them while engaged in an approach motion than when they had viewed them while engaged in an avoidance motion. Such findings suggest that when we first encounter someone, engaging in actions that we associate with approach makes us more prone to think that the person is worthy of approaching.

Simulations can also affect the level of specificity with which we think about the actions of others. Libby, Shaeffer, and Eibach (2009) compared participants' tendencies to describe the actions of others (e.g., a person mailing a letter) as concrete (e.g., mailing a letter) or abstract (e.g., communicating). Participants were more likely to interpret the actions of someone else in a concrete way when they imagined the actions from a first-person perspective. In contrast, when they imagined the actions from a third-person perspective, they were more likely to describe the actions in an abstract way. Thus, the specific nature of a particular simulation and whether it relies more on first-person motor simulation or third-person visual simulation influences how abstractly the action is thought about.

Taken together, the evidence outlined above suggests that current motor states, even if irrelevant to the task at hand, can influence and disambiguate social perceptions of situations and entities. Several recent proposals have built on this evidence to articulate how motor simulation might form the basis of all social understanding and interaction (e.g., Decety & Stevens, 2008).

For example, the Shared Circuits Model (SCM) (Hurley, 2008) proposes five layers of progressively more complex abilities that are necessary for human social interaction. First, the SCM proposes that the basis of social interaction is dynamic online motor control, or the ability to adjust motor output given various sensory input. Second, the SCM proposes that online motor control is extended to predict what sensory effects various motor actions will have on the system. Third, the ability to predict sensory effects from motor actions is reversed, so that it is also possible to predict motor actions that will cause various sensory effects. This reversal occurs through mirroring, or activating a motor signal in response to an input sensory signal. Fourth, inhibition is possible, in that it is possible to prevent the motor signals that are automatically generated in response to sensory input from being overtly produced as behavior. Fifth, counterfactual input is possible, such that it is possible to generate motor signals from imagined sensory inputs. Thus, according to the SCM, we understand the actions of others because our cognitive systems are highly adept at generating motor signals from sensory signals and vice versa. We understand one another's actions by engaging our own capacity for similar action, and this happens both when we see another individual's actions as well as when we imagine another individual's actions. Further, it happens regardless of whether we overtly mimic the behavior or inhibit the activated motor signal from being produced.

The Shared Circuits Model (Hurley, 2008) is only one model for how our ability to understand the actions of others might be rooted in the simulation of their actions in our own cognitive system, and to date, there have been no direct empirical tests of the model's claims. However, as the evidence reviewed above suggests, it appears that understanding of others' intentions and actions is connected to, and perhaps caused by, corresponding motor activity. We next consider whether similar motor activity is connected to our understanding of emotions.

Simulation in emotional understanding

Just as we understand the actions of others by simulating their movement in our own motor systems, we may understand the emotions of others by simulating their affective states in our own emotional systems. The idea that producing affective states in the brain and in the body's periphery is critical in representing emotional meaning, and therefore for understanding incoming emotional information, is gaining in popularity (e.g., Atkinson, 2007; Decety & Chaminade, 2003; Gallese, 2003, 2005; Goldman & Sripada, 2005; Keysers & Gazzola, 2007; Niedenthal, 2007; Winkielman, McIntosh, & Oberman, 2009). In this section we review empirical evidence for the claim that people simulate the emotional behaviors of others and that these simulations ground emotional information processing tasks. These behaviors may include, but are not limited to, facial expressions, postures, and vocal parameters that convey emotion. A full review of such effects can be found in Niedenthal, Barsalou, Winkielman, Krauth-Gruber, & Ric (2005). We focus in particular on facial expression here.

In a now classic study, Adolphs and colleagues (2000) instructed 108 patients with a variety of focal brain lesions and 30 normal control participants to perform three visual emotion recognition tasks. In the first task, participants evaluated the intensity of basic emotional facial expressions. In the second task, participants matched a facial expression to its name. In the third task, participants sorted facial expressions into emotional categories. Though each task identified a slightly different group of critical brain regions, damage to primary and secondary somatosensory cortices impaired performance in all three tasks. The finding is now seen as the empirical generator of the notion that emotional information processing involves simulating the relevant state in the perceiver using somatosensory resources (Niedenthal, 2007).

More recently, Pitcher, Garrido, Walsh, and Duchaine (2008) further explored the idea that facial expression recognition is supported by somatovisceral responses linked with the perceived expression. In that experiment, repetitive transcranial magnetic stimulation (rTMS) was used to temporarily inhibit the right occipital face area (rOFA) and the face area of the right somatosensory cortex (rSC) during a facial

expression or facial identity discrimination task. Over trials, participants saw pairs of faces (sample and target pictures) separated by a brief interval. The faces expressed one of six emotions – happiness, sadness, surprise, fear, disgust, and anger – and participants had to recognize the emotion expressed in each face. Results showed that accuracy on the recognition task was reduced for stimulation of both rOFA and the face regions of the rSC. Other findings indicated that stimulation at these sites did not have similar disruptive effects on a face identity task.

There is also evidence for the selectivity of central mechanisms in embodied simulation of specific emotions. Wicker, Keysers, Plailly, Royet, Gallese, and Rizzolatti (2003) had participants inhale odors that generated feelings of disgust. The same participants were later exposed to videos of other individuals expressing disgust. Areas of the anterior insula and, to some extent, the anterior cingulate cortex were activated both when individuals experienced disgust themselves and when individuals observed disgust in others, presumably reflecting simulation. This interpretation is further supported by evidence that damage to the insula results in a corresponding impairment in the experience and recognition of disgust (Calder, Keane, Manes, Antoun, & Young, 2000).

Embodied simulations may be particularly important in decoding emotional signals that are nuanced and complex. Take, for example, the smile. Some smiles express happiness or enjoyment. Other smiles express friendliness or desire for affiliation. Still others express dominance or power (Niedenthal, Mermillod, Marginer, & Hess, 2010). Although the meaning of smiles can sometimes be inferred from the social situation in which they occur, there are few simple physiological markers that definitively distinguish between types of smiles. Yet, most people are able to interpret smiles correctly. For example, when our boss presents a dominance smile, we typically do not mistake it for an affiliative smile and invite him or her out to lunch.

The problem of interpreting nuances in facial expressions can be solved through the use of facial mimicry: i.e., by engagement of the body's peripheral systems as well as central ones. It seems that by mimicking the smiles and other facial expressions of those we encounter, we can gain a better understanding of the nuanced meaning of the expression. People do occasionally mimic the facial expressions of those around them; from the time they are only a few hours old, infants mimic the facial expressions of adults (Meltzoff & Moore, 1977). Adults also mimic facial expressions. For example, Dimberg, Thunberg, and Elmehed (2000) found that adults mimicked positive and negative facial expressions seen in photographs, even when the photographs were displayed for only 30 ms and were thus not consciously perceived. Taken together, this evidence suggests that humans have a tendency to mimic facial expressions that is both innate and unconscious. There is evidence that mimicking facial expressions can improve speed of recognition of the emotion displayed (e.g., Stel & van Knippenberg, 2008) as well as accuracy for fine-grained distinctions in facial expressions (e.g., Niedenthal, Brauer, Halberstadt, & Innes-Ker, 2001). Furthermore, facial mimicry is positively related to empathy (e.g., Sonnby-Borgström, 2002; Zajonc, Adelmann, Murphy, & Niedenthal, 1989).

The importance of facial mimicry in the processing of facial expression of emotion is supported empirically in a pair of studies by Maringer, Krumhuber, Fischer, and Niedenthal (2011). In their first study, they exposed participants to animated smiles that were empirically derived and validated as possessing the characteristics of "true" and "false" smiles (in Krumhuber, Manstead, & Kappas, 2007). The participants saw 20 smiles in all and judged the extent to which each seemed to be a "genuine" (i.e., true) smile. Half of the participants saw only true smiles and the other half saw only false smiles. Furthermore, type of smile was fully crossed with ability to mimic the smiles as they were presented. Thus, half of the participants could freely mimic these expressions, while the remaining participants held a pencil in their mouths so that facial mimicry was effectively inhibited. The results showed that, as expected, free mimicry participants perceived the "true" smiles as being significantly more genuine expressions than the "false" smiles, consistent with the validation studies. However, the mimicry-blocked participants did not perceive a distinction between the two types of smiles; they judged true and false smiles as being equally genuine. Thus, in this case, the perceptual differences did not do the work that feedback from mimicry could provide.

The second study by Maringer et al. (2011) demonstrated that when mimicry is blocked, other situational information is used rather than motor feedback. In that study, participants were exposed to only true smiles. However, they were told either that the smiles occurred in a social situation in which a true smile is expected (according to cultural beliefs and stereotypes) or that the smiles occurred in a social situation in which a false smile is expected. Free mimicry was again blocked in half of the participants, and all participants rated the genuineness of the smiles. The results of this second study demonstrated that free mimicry participants did not use their expectations of the likelihood of a true versus false smile in the given

social situation to rate the genuineness of the smiles. On the other hand, when mimicry was inhibited, smiles that occurred in situations typically associated with true smiles were evaluated as more genuine than those that occurred in situations typically associated with false smiles.

The mimicry findings just reviewed are consistent with the Simulation of Smiles (SIMS) model (Niedenthal et al., in press). The SIMS model proposes that embodied simulations of smiles are triggered in the perceiver by eye contact with the person who is smiling. These simulations involve neural activation in the brain's reward centers of the basal ganglia and motor regions that support motor mimicry. Activation in the motor cortex then activates other relevant brain areas, depending on the type of smile. For example, enjoyment smiles activate the somatosensory cortex, while affiliative smiles also activate the orbitofrontal cortex, which is associated with attachment-related positive affect. This differential neural activity results in very different subjective feelings associated with each type of smile. For example, when the orbitofrontal cortex is activated during the simulation of an affiliative smile, the perceiver experiences positive emotions of attachment and intimacy.

An embodiment model such as the SIMS can be extended to define the neural and bodily "feeling" or meaning of different facial expressions, those other than smiles as well (e.g., Adolphs, 2002; Atkinson, 2007). In addition, all such models need to combine social behavior with the central and peripheral responses of the body in order to be productive.

The SIMS model and the evidence reviewed above suggest that individuals simulate or overtly mimic the facial expressions of those they see. There is also evidence, however, that individuals simulate facial expressions when they are merely thinking about a particular emotion concept. Niedenthal, Winkielman, Mondillon, and Vermeulen (2009) showed that the conceptual processing of emotions involves the production of a corresponding facial expression. For instance, in one study, some participants made emotion judgments about the meaning of emotional concepts such as *CUDDLE, SMILE, POCKET, VOMIT* or *MURDER*. Other participants saw the same concepts but had to indicate whether they were written in capital letters or not. During the emotion or typeface judgment task, the activation of muscles that support facial expressions of anger, disgust, and joy were measured with electromyographic (EMG) recording. Results showed that participants judging the emotional meanings of concepts produced corresponding facial expressions during this task. However, the participants who only had to judge the typeface made no such facial expressions. A follow-up study provided evidence that the simulation of the concept was functional and specific to the requirement of representing the emotional meaning of the word (see also Foroni & Semin, 2009).

Thus, the ability to simulate or mimic facial expressions is important, not only to the ability to process the emotional expressions of those around us but also to the ability to conceptually understand emotional concepts more generally. We next turn to the role of embodied simulation in understanding language about actions and emotions, with an emphasis on how simulations might be expressed in gesture.

Simulation in processing language and gesture

Over the past decade, it has become increasingly evident that the same embodied simulations that support processing of social actions and emotions are also involved in processing language about actions and emotions. Rather than manipulating amodal symbols, language comprehenders appear to run motor and emotion simulations that engage their brains in ways that mimic the behaviors they are reading or hearing about (see Spivey, Richardson, & Gonzales-Marquez, 2005 for a review). The evidence to support this claim comes from a variety of sources, which we review here.

First, studies demonstrate facilitation in sentence comprehension when speakers are engaged in a secondary task that involves their motor, perceptual, or emotional system in a manner complementary to the action, perception, or emotion implied in the sentence they are reading or hearing. In a classic demonstration of this phenomenon, Glenberg and Kaschak (2002) showed that readers are faster to comprehend a sentence like "Open the drawer," which implies motion toward the body, when they respond by moving their hand toward their body than when they respond by moving their hand away from their body. The effect also occurs for actions that are even more specific to particular objects. Masson, Bub, and Warren (2008) trained participants to engage in particular hand grasps following cues. They then cued participants to engage in particular grasps while simultaneously reading them sentences about different objects. They found facilitation for hand grasps that matched the grasp that would be used to manually interact with the object in the sentence. For example, hearing a sentence "The lawyer saw the calculator" primed participants to produce a motion in which their index finger pushed downward.

Similar findings have been reported for sentences about emotion. Havas, Glenberg, and Rinck (2007) had participants produce facial expressions of positive and negative emotions while reading sentences that described either positive or negative valence. They found that participants were faster to judge sentence valence and sensibility when there was a match between their facial posture and the sentence valence (e.g., smiling and reading a happy sentence) than when there was a mismatch (e.g., frowning and reading a happy sentence).

Second, participants experience modality-specific interference in comprehension and semantic judgment tasks. For example, Pecher, Zeelenberg, and Barsalou (2003) showed that people take longer to recognize *TART* as a characteristic of *CRANBERRIES* if they have just judged *RED* as a characteristic of *APPLES* than if they have just recognized *SWEET* as a characteristic of *APPLES*. This suggests that there is a cost involved in switching perceptual modalities, even when the particular perceptual modalities are not relevant to the task. More recently, Bergen, Lau, Narayan, Stojanovic, and Wheeler (2010) found that people have a harder time rejecting an image as corresponding to a particular verb if the action in the image is performed with the same effector as the verb. For example, a picture of a person kicking is harder to reject as being inconsistent with the verb *WALK* than is a picture of a person punching. This evidence suggests that language comprehension is not only facilitated by the engagement of motor and perceptual systems but also that the engagement is actually both modality and effector specific.

Finally, temporarily disabling the ability to simulate an action or emotion temporarily interferes with the ability to process words describing those actions or emotions. Neuroimaging studies have consistently demonstrated that the same cortical areas that are involved in producing an action are also involved in reading words that describe those actions (Pulvermüller, 2005). Delivering TMS to areas of motor cortex impairs the processing of words that describe actions that would be performed with that area (Pulvermüller, Hauk, Nikulin, & Ilmoniemi, 2005). For example, disabling the arm area of motor cortex inhibits recognition of the word *PICK* but not *KICK*. In contrast, disabling the leg area of motor cortex inhibits recognition of *KICK* but not *PICK*. Furthermore, Havas, Glenberg, Gutowski, Lucarelli, and Davidson (2010) examined the effects of BOTOX injections, which temporarily paralyze the facial muscles used in frowning, on sentence processing. They found that patients who had just received BOTOX were slower to read sentences that described negative affect than they were 2 weeks later when the paralyzing effect of BOTOX had worn off. This evidence suggests that simulation is not only involved in language processing, but that without it, language processing is actually impaired.

If the motor system is involved in comprehending sentences, why don't comprehenders routinely act out the sentences they read about? One possibility is that motor simulation may be enough to facilitate understanding; overt motor activity may not be necessary and thus would be a waste of resources in the majority of situations. For example, Willems, Hagoort, and Casasanto (2010) found that reading action verbs (e.g., *PICK*) activated premotor cortex areas that are associated with the hand, but forming an explicit motor image of performing the action activated hand-related areas of both premotor and motor cortex. Thus, it is possible that language comprehension does not necessarily rely on effortful imagery that involves the motor cortex, but instead relies on simulation that occurs less effortfully in the premotor cortex.

Although people do not generally act out the actions they read about, people do quite frequently act out the actions they talk about. Speakers often produce representational gestures that depict the information they are describing (McNeill, 1992). Hostetter and Alibali (2008) have argued that these hand gestures are actually visible reflections of the involvement of motor simulation during language production. According to their Gesture as Simulated Action (GSA) framework, thinking in the interest of producing language naturally relies on simulations of perception and action. These simulations activate the motor system, and when the activation reaches a certain threshold, the activation is produced as a co-speech manual gesture.

As evidence for this claim, Hostetter and Alibali (2010) had participants describe patterns of dots that were connected by lines to form shapes. In half of the trials, participants constructed the patterns by placing small wooden pieces on the table in the position of the dots in the pattern. In the remaining trials, participants only viewed the pattern on a computer screen before describing them. Hostetter and Alibali found that speakers gestured at a higher rate when describing the pattern they had physical experience making than when describing the pattern they had only viewed. This finding is in line with the GSA framework and suggests that speakers gesture when they are thinking about the information they are describing in terms of actions.

The GSA framework predicts that speakers should gesture more with speech about ideas that are highly activated, because motor activation from highly activated simulations should be more likely to exceed the threshold for overt production of gestures. This contrasts with other theories of gesture production, which predict that speakers should gesture more when speech is more difficult to produce (e.g., Krauss, Chen, & Gottesman, 2000). Sassenberg and Van der Meer (2010) addressed this issue in a study of the gestures that speakers produced as they described routes to a listener. Importantly, they compared the gestures that speakers produced the first time that a particular turn was described to those produced when the turn was re-described as the first part of another route. Speakers produced more gestures when re-describing a turn than when describing the turn initially, suggesting that gestures are more likely to accompany representations that are particularly active (because they have been imagined before) than to accompany representations that are particularly hard to describe (because they have never been described before).

If gestures are reflections of simulated action, as the GSA framework claims, why do speakers so frequently produce simulated actions as overt movements when they are speaking but not when they are reading or listening? There are a couple of possibilities. First, the GSA framework contends that it may be difficult to prevent the premotor activity involved in simulation from spreading to motor cortex when the motor system is engaged in the simultaneous task of speaking (Hostetter & Alibali, 2008). Second, it is possible that simulation during language production involves more effortful formation of imagery than does simulation during language comprehension. If this is the case, the simulations needed for successful production may require stronger activation than those required for successful comprehension, and this stronger activation may be more likely to result in gestures. Further research is needed to explore these two possibilities.

Although the GSA framework was conceptualized as a way of explaining how gestures come to be produced, its embodied cognition stance also has implications for how gestures are comprehended. There is much evidence that listeners have better comprehension for messages that are accompanied by gesture than for messages that are not accompanied by gesture (e.g., Church, Ayman-Nolley, & Mahootian, 2004; Hostetter, in press; Valenzeno, Alibali, & Klatzky, 2003). One possibility for why comprehension is facilitated when speech is accompanied by gestures is that listeners simulate a speaker's gestures the same way they simulate the actions of others more generally. This simulation may then result in understanding of the gesture's meaning, which facilitates comprehension of the message as a whole (see Alibali & Hostetter, in press).

In sum, there is much evidence to suggest that understanding the social world involves activation of motor and emotional simulations. Furthermore, these same simulations are involved when we produce and comprehend language about the social world. Next we review theory and research that suggests that simulations are embedded in the social environment, so that they are functionally linked to the situations in which they are used.

EMBEDDEDNESS OF SOCIAL THOUGHT AND LANGUAGE

One of the central tenets of embodied theories is that cognition is not isolated in the mind of the cognizer; instead, it is *situated*, or embedded in the context in which it occurs. Social cognition is intimately intertwined with the environment in that it depends on features of the physical and social environment, it is employed in service of adaptive action in the world, and it sometimes utilizes external objects and representational systems in the service of achieving goals (e.g., Anderson, 2003; Nathan, 2008; Wilson, 2002).

Many lines of research have shown that cognitive processes depend on the specifics of the current situation. Even basic perceptual processes show effects of context. For example, Goldstone (1995) showed that participants' perceptions of the colors of objects were influenced by their category membership as determined by their shape. Objects that belonged to categories that contained redder objects were judged as being more red than objects of the same hue that belonged to other categories. Context also influences higher-level processes, such as categorization, strategy choice, and logical reasoning (e.g., Barsalou, 1983; Carraher, Carraher, & Schliemann, 1985; Griggs & Cox, 1982; Kotovsky, Hayes, & Simon, 1985; McNeil & Alibali, 2005; Yeh & Barsalou, 2006). Many aspects of the context can be relevant, including the task, features of the physical environment, and features of the social context, such as the setting, the participants, their roles and goals, the nature of the social interaction, and the broader cultural norms for the activity and interaction. Another set of potentially relevant features includes the material tools, notational systems, and technological resources that are available in the context.

The notion of simulated action, discussed in the preceding section, is compatible with the view that cognition is embedded in situations. Thus, Barsalou (2008) argues that, "If a conceptual representation simulates a perceptual experience, it should simulate a situation, because situations provide the background of perceptual experience." (p. 241). From this perspective, concepts are never fully removed from the situations in which they are experienced and learned.

An embodied perspective also highlights the *functional* relevance of cognitive processes in enabling adaptive activity. One widely shared perspective is that cognition is "for" action – that is, we perceive, remember, categorize, and reason in order to act in the world in ways that promote our survival and well-being (e.g., Gibson, 1979). Glenberg (1997) argues that the function of memory is to encode and store information relevant to possible patterns of interaction in the physical and social world. Along similar lines, Barsalou (1983) holds that people construct categories online, as needed to achieve their goals. When important for intended action, people readily create "ad hoc categories," such as *items to sell at a garage sale* or *items to take out of a burning house*. Thus, cognitive processes such as perception, memory, and categorization are employed for practical ends that involve actions in the world.

Cognitive processes also sometimes utilize physical objects and external representational systems in strategic ways. People use the environment, either consciously or unconsciously, to store, represent, and manipulate information. For example, I might count on my fingers when determining the number of people who will be attending a party, or I might make a shopping list to help me remember items I wish to purchase at the grocery store. I might use pencil and paper – or perhaps a calculator or spreadsheet – to plan my monthly budget or to figure out how much money I should transfer between my savings and checking accounts. In each of these examples, some aspects of the cognitive work required for a task are *off-loaded* onto the environment (Kirsh & Maglio, 1994; Wilson, 2002). In this sense, the environment is part of the cognitive system.

This same sort of off-loading can also occur with the social environment, as illustrated by the phenomenon of *transactive memory*, which is memory that is shared across individuals (Wegner, Erber, & Raymond, 1991; Wegner, Giuliano, & Hertel, 1985). People in social structures such as dyads or groups need not encode or store all of the information that the structure needs to function. Instead, people store some information themselves, and they remember who in their social group has stored other important information. When that other information is needed, people rely on others' memories. For example, a husband may take the wheel of the car knowing that he does not know how to get to the current destination, but confident that his wife does know the way.

In the following sections, we review research on the ways in which social cognition is shaped, constrained, and even augmented by the physical and social situations in which it occurs. We also consider how language and gesture manifest the embedding of social cognition in situations.

Embeddedness of social and emotional information processing

Like all cognitive processes, social cognition is embedded in situations (Smith & Semin, 2004). As one illustration, a large body of work, reviewed by Blair (2002), suggests that "automatic" stereotypes and prejudice depend both on contextual factors and on the perceiver's goals and intentions. For example, in one study, Wittenbrink, Judd, and Park (2001) found that the same Black faces elicited different racial attitudes depending on the context in which they were presented (e.g., when shown on a street corner vs in a church). In another study, Richeson and Ambady (2003) provided White participants with different goals for an upcoming interaction with a Black partner: either to evaluate the partner's performance, to get along with the partner, or to manage the impression they would make on the partner, who would later evaluate them. Later, participants' implicit prejudice was assessed. Participants who expected to evaluate the partner showed a higher level of prejudice, and those who expected to be evaluated by the partner showed a lower level of prejudice. These studies demonstrate that activation of social stereotypes depends crucially on aspects of the current situation.

In turn, there is evidence that social aspects of situations affect other aspects of cognitive processing. For example, activating social stereotypes can affect basic perceptual processes. Chambon (2009) asked young participants to complete a task that covertly primed the stereotype of the elderly, and then asked them to estimate either the steepness of an incline, or the distance across a grassy field to a target cone. Compared to controls who were not primed, participants for whom the stereotype was primed estimated the inclines to be more steep, and the distance to be farther. Thus, activation of the stereotype affected perceptual judgments.

The processing of emotional information is also affected by context. In addition to (external) social context, researchers have been interested in the (internal) ambient emotional state of the individual as well as the emotional state of the group in which the individual is a member. Emotional state is itself a cognitive context and, as such, it guides the way in which incoming emotional information is encoded and represented.

That emotional information processing is embedded in the social context is well known. An old example is that of canned laughter. Canned laughter is intended to provoke an audience's mirth, positive affective state, and ultimately a positive attitude toward a television series or a product for sale. An experiment by Bush, Barr, McHugo, and Lanzetta (1989) is particularly relevant in demonstrating the information processing effects of canned laughter. Bush and colleagues had participants watch video excerpts of comedy routines. For half of the participants, the video excerpts included close-up images of the faces of various people laughing, and for half of the participants the excerpts contained no such images. The activity of participants' facial muscles involved in producing smiles and participants' evaluations of amusement were measured. Results showed that muscle activity associated with happiness as well as self-reported amusement were higher in the condition in which the videos contained close-up inserts of people laughing than when the images of laughing faces were not presented. Thus, the social context determines a perceiver's responses to incoming emotional information.

Emotional information processing is embedded in the social context in other ways as well. We noted previously that some early research suggested that facial mimicry is fast and often automatic (e.g., Dimberg et al., 2000): however, recent research has demonstrated that there are contextual constraints on facial mimicry. In a study by Likowski and colleagues (Likowski, Muhlberger, Seibt, Pauli, & Weyers, 2008), for instance, single word descriptors were paired with target faces to induce positive or negative attitudes towards the faces. Attitudes modulated facial mimicry of the targets' expressions, such that negative attitudes suppressed mimicry. Further studies have shown that mimicry can be moderated by meaning of the social context for the perceiver (Bourgeois & Hess, 2008), task relevance (Cannon, Hayes, & Tipper, 2009), the perceiver's emotional state (Moody, McIntosh, Mann, & Weisser, 2007), the subliminal priming of competition (Weyers, Muhlberger, Kund, Hess, & Pauli, 2009), empathy (Sonnby-Borgström, Jonsson, & Svensson, 2003), and by levels of circulating testosterone (Hermans, Putman, & van Honk, 2006). Thus, how emotional expressive information is processed depends also on the social context in which it is encountered and the goals and motives that the context engenders.

The internal emotional state of the individual has also long been considered a contextual determinant of emotional information processing. Halberstadt, Niedenthal, and Kushner (1995) showed, for instance, that participants who were in a sad emotional state were more likely to access the sad meanings of homophones (i.e., pairs of words that sound the same but have different meanings) than were participants in a happy emotional state. For instance, the sad individuals were more likely to write down the word *mourning* instead of *morning* when they heard the word/môrnng/. The finding was recently replicated and extended using emotional prosody by Nygaard and Queen (2008), in a study involving words that had either a happy, sad, or neutral meaning. Emotional meanings were fully crossed with prosody of the utterance, such that each word was said in three tones of voice (happy, sad, and neutral). Latency to word naming (i.e., repeating the word that was heard) was the variable of interest. Emotional tone of voice facilitated linguistic processing of emotional words in an emotion-congruent way, suggesting that emotional vocal context determines the processing of linguistic content.

More recently, Halberstadt, Winkielman, Niedenthal, and Dalle (2009) recorded EMG of facial muscles to show how emotional language constrains the processing of facial expressions of emotion. In the study, participants first encoded emotionally ambiguous faces in terms of specific emotion concepts ("angry" or "happy"). They then later viewed the faces passively, without the concepts. Memory for the faces and facial muscle activity were measured. At initial encoding, participants displayed more smiling-related EMG activity when looking at faces paired with "happy" than when looking at faces paired with "angry." Later, in the absence of associated conceptual context, participants were perceptually biased to remember happiness-encoded faces as happier than anger-encoded faces. More importantly, during the passive re-exposure to the ambiguous faces, EMG measures indicated spontaneous emotion-specific mimicry, which in turn predicted perceptual memory bias. That is, when seeing a happiness-encoded expression, individuals spontaneously mimicked happiness, while those who had encoded the same face in terms of anger did not spontaneously mimic happiness. No specific EMG activity was observed when participants encoded or viewed faces with valenced concepts not related to emotion, or when participants encoded or viewed Chinese ideographs. The findings constitute evidence of context-driven changes in emotion perception; participants simulated (and perceived) facial expressions differently depending on the context in which they initially encountered the face.

Taken together, the studies summarized in this section suggest that the processing of emotional information is influenced and constrained by the external social and emotional context as well as the current internal, ambient state of the individual. In what follows, we argue that language and gesture are influenced and constrained in similar ways, as communication is also deeply embedded in context. Speakers' choices of particular ways of communicating depend crucially on aspects of the physical and social environment, and these choices profoundly influence the effectiveness of their communication.

Embeddedness of language and gesture

Communication always occurs in context. For communication to be successful, addressees must be able to reference the speaker's message to objects, events, or concepts that are currently present or that can be imagined or remembered. This is the central tenet of the Indexical Hypothesis (Glenberg & Robertson, 1999, 2000). For example, when a listener comprehends the statement, "Blue cheese is delicious", the listener may index the noun "blue cheese" to a wedge of cheese that is physically present, or to a mental representation of cheese that includes perceptual information, such as information about how blue cheese looks, tastes or smells. In order for the utterance "blue cheese is delicious" to be properly understood, the listener must know what cheese the speaker is referring to. One option, of course, would be for the speaker to clearly articulate precisely which cheese he or she is referring to (e.g., "The blue cheese on the cracker I am eating is delicious"). But such preciseness takes cognitive effort, and speakers are rarely this precise in their utterances.

Instead, research on *audience design* in language production (e.g., Clark & Murphy, 1982; Horton & Gerrig, 2005) suggests that speakers tailor their utterances to the knowledge and needs of their addressees. In the blue cheese example, the speaker may know that the listener has just seen him or her eat a particular blue cheese, and thus assumes that the listener will index "blue cheese" to the blue cheese that was just eaten.

Alternatively, rather than relying solely on the knowledge of the addressee, speakers may index their speech to the environment though gesture, for example, by pointing to the relevant cheese on the table. Speakers' spontaneous gestures are a concrete, physical manifestation of the indexing of speech to the physical environment. Pointing gestures are a prime example of what Goodwin (2007) has called "environmentally coupled gestures," because pointing gestures are generally uninterpretable without the environmental ground that gives them meaning. Speakers commonly use pointing gestures to directly index objects, people, or locations that are physically present, and as such, pointing gestures are deeply dependent on context.

Perhaps surprisingly, speakers can also use pointing gestures to index objects, events, and situations that are not present, in at least three distinct ways (Butcher, Mylander, & Goldin-Meadow, 1991; Morford & Goldin-Meadow, 1997). First, speakers point to perceptually similar objects to index non-present objects. For example, a speaker might point to the bleu cheese that is physically present, to refer to another variety of bleu cheese that she tasted on another occasion. Second, speakers sometimes point to physical locations to index objects or people that are associated with those locations. For example, a child may point to her father's place at the dinner table when referring to her father, even when he is not at home. Third, speakers sometimes metaphorically locate people or objects in their gesture space, and then point to these locations to index those objects or people. For example, McNeill (1992) described a speaker – talking about a movie plot – who used different spaces to represent the "bad guys" and the "good guys", and pointed to those spaces to index those characters over the course of his narrative (p. 155). As these examples illustrate, gestures "anchor" the information expressed in the verbal channel in the physical and material world, either literally or metaphorically (Williams, 2008). In so doing, such gestures manifest the grounding of speech in the physical environment.

Speakers produce other types of gestures besides pointing, and there is evidence that the meaning and production of other gestures is also embedded in the physical and social environment. Iconic gestures are movements that depict the semantic meaning of speech in some way (McNeill, 1992). For example, imagine a speaker who says, "That cheese was delicious" while making a circle of her thumbs and index fingers. The speaker is likely indicating that the particular cheese being referenced was in a circular wheel. Furthermore, the speaker may use this gesture with the referring expression "that cheese" because she knows that only one of the cheeses at the party that she and her listener just attended was presented in a wheel. Thus, the knowledge shared by speaker and listener shapes the gesture and linguistic expression the speaker uses to make reference.

The effects of shared knowledge on the production and interpretation of iconic gestures have been documented in several studies. For example, Gerwing and Bavelas (2004) found that the preciseness of a particular gesture is related to whether or not the gesture conveys information that is already known to the listener. As common ground between speaker and listener increases, gestures become less precise and informative, and also less frequent (see Holler & Stevens, 2007).

In addition to considering common knowledge, speakers are influenced by other characteristics of the social situation as well. Bavelas, Kenwood, Johnson, and Phillips (2002) asked speakers to describe a picture to a recipient who would either see a videotape of their description or hear an audiotape. Speakers gestured at a higher rate and used more non-redundant gestures when they expected that their listeners would see the videotape. Speakers also alter the size and orientation of their gestures as a function of characteristics of the audience. Hostetter, Alibali and Schrager (2011) found that speakers produced more "large" gestures (defined as gestures that crossed outside of neutral space) when they expected their listeners to cooperate with them than when they expected their listeners to compete with them in a game that involved navigating a complex spatial layout. Along similar lines, Özyürek (2002) found that speakers altered the orientation of their gestures depending how their gesture space intersected with the gesture space of their addressees. Taken together, these findings suggest that speakers tailor their gestures to the physical position, expectations, and information needs of their listeners. At a more general level, these findings support the view that cognitive processes such as language and gesture production depend on the particulars of the situation in which they occur.

More broadly, research on communication in language and gestures highlights the fact that cognition is deeply social (see Smith & Semin, 2007). In this regard, it is worth emphasizing that the social nature of cognition goes far beyond the constraining or augmenting effects of social context. Many tasks – for example, raising a barn, performing surgery, performing a military maneuver, navigating a large ship, perhaps even conducting a psychological experiment – extend beyond the capabilities of any single individual, and instead require collaborative action that is mediated by social communication with language and gesture (see Hutchins, 1995). In such cases, it is difficult to say where the cognitive system begins and ends. Cognition is located in the collaborative, communicative process, and in the technical tools that are utilized in the activity, rather than in the mind of any single individual. Communication is an integral aspect of cognition, and the situatedness of communication underscores the situatedness of cognition more generally.

EMBODIMENT AND ABSTRACTIONS

It seems straightforward for an embodied account of cognition to explain understanding of concepts that are concrete and directly based on perception or action. For example, it is easy to imagine how a person's concept of "jazz concert" could be based on perceptions of associated objects (e.g., saxophone, microphone), actions (e.g., dancing, playing music), and bodily experiences (e.g., the sound of the music, the smell of the night). However, it is more challenging for embodied theories to account for abstract concepts, which do not share diagnostic perceptual features, such as "mentor" or "fair-weather friend." Indeed, one of the most commonly raised objections to embodied theories is that they are not able to handle abstractions.

One response to this objection is that we understand abstract domains metaphorically, by analogy to experience-based domains (e.g., Boroditsky & Prinz, 2008). This view builds on the work of Lakoff and Johnson (1980), who argue that the human conceptual system is largely metaphorical. Importantly, many fundamental metaphors are based on image schemas for space, action, forces, and other aspects of bodily experience. For example, we conceive of ideas as objects, the mind as a container, the passage of time as movement in space, numbers as locations in space, mathematical operations as actions on objects, love as a journey, society as a person, and so forth (Boroditsky, 2000; Lakoff & Johnson, 1980; Lakoff & Núñez, 2001).

What is the evidence for the existence of such conceptual metaphors? Lakoff and Johnson (1980) present hundreds of example of such metaphors in everyday language. For example, the metaphor HEALTH IS UP, SICKNESS IS DOWN is manifested in expressions such as "she's in *top* shape" and "his health is *declining*"; the metaphor HAPPINESS IS UP, SADNESS IS DOWN is manifested in expressions such as "that *boosted* my spirits" and "she is feeling *low*." For such metaphors, ties to bodily experiences are quite obvious – when ill, people usually lie down; when sad, people's posture droops. Thus, these metaphors serve to ground abstract concepts in physical actions and perceptions.

Experimental evidence supports the claim that people understand abstract concepts in terms of spatial images. When asked to draw or to choose image schemas to represent abstract verbs, participants show highly consistent performance; for example, almost all participants draw or choose a vertical relationship to represent "respect" (Richardson, Spivey, Edelman, & Naples, 2001). Furthermore, comprehending abstract verbs that activate particular spatial axes (e.g., the vertical axis for *respect*) affects other cognitive processes that rely on those spatial axes, such as visual discrimination or picture memory (Richardson, Spivey, Barsalou, & McRae, 2003). These data support the claim that spatial image schemas underlie abstract verbs.

One abstract concept that has been extensively studied with regard to metaphoric structuring is *time* (e.g., Alverson, 1994; Casasanto & Boroditsky, 2008; Clark, 1973; Núñez & Sweetser, 2006). Experimental evidence indicates that people's conceptions of time are structured by metaphorical mappings to space. In one experiment, priming different spatial representations led participants to make different inferences regarding the following sentence, which is ambiguous about time: "Next Wednesday's meeting has been moved forward two days". Depending on the particular schema that was primed, participants tended to infer that the meeting was either Monday or Friday (Boroditsky, 2000).

Cross-linguistic studies also support the view that time is understood in terms of space. Different languages construe time in terms of space differently – for example, Mandarin Chinese construes time as vertical, whereas English construes it as horizontal. Consistent with these spatial metaphors, native speakers of Mandarin were faster to confirm that March comes before April if they had just seen a vertical array of objects rather than a horizontal array, and the reverse pattern held for native speakers of English (Boroditsky, 2001).

Abstract social and emotion concepts

Are abstract social concepts also understood by analogy to experience-based domains, such as space and action? Indeed, available evidence supports this view. Consider the concept of *social power*. A number of studies indicate that power is understood by metaphorical mappings to space, via the metaphor POWER (CONTROL) IS UP, WEAKNESS (LACK OF CONTROL) IS DOWN. Lakoff and Johnson (1980) highlighted the experiential basis of this metaphor, noting that "physical size typically correlates with physical strength, and the victor in a fight is typically on top" (p. 15). This suggests that people conceptualize power relationships between social groups with the more powerful individual (e.g., boss) above and the less powerful individual (e.g., secretary) below.

Experimental evidence supports the view that people's representations of social power are structured spatially. Schubert (2005) showed that participants' judgments about social power relationships were influenced by the relative vertical positions of the groups to be judged. When the task was to find the powerful group, participants were faster to respond when that group's name was at the top of the computer screen, and when the task was to find the powerless group, participants were faster to respond when that group's name was at the bottom. Similarly, participants were faster to make judgments of powerful groups (presented alone) when they responded with the "cursor up" key, and faster to make judgments of powerless groups (presented alone) when they responded with the "cursor down" key.

There is also evidence that participants' judgments about power are also affected by spatial cues. Schubert (2005) showed that participants rated powerful animals (e.g., lion, grizzly bear) as even more powerful when they were presented at the top of the screen than when they were presented at the bottom. Giessner and Schubert (2007) extended these findings to judgments of human leaders. They asked participants to evaluate a manager of a company, and provided participants with a short text and an organization chart. In the organization chart, boxes at the lower level, which represented employees, were connected by a horizontal line, and the middle box was connected by a vertical line to a box above it, which represented the manager. The length of the vertical line (short or long) was manipulated between participants, yielding either a small or a large vertical difference between the manager and employee in the organizational chart. Participants in the large vertical difference condition evaluated the leader as more powerful than participants in the small vertical difference condition. Moreover, these effects were not found for evaluations of charisma, which is not represented in terms of a vertical spatial schema.

It is not only the case that spatial representations influence evaluations of power; the opposite also holds. That is, judgments of power can influence the spatial representations that people construct. Giessner and Schubert (2007) manipulated whether a leader was described as powerful or non-powerful, and investigated how participants represented the leader's relationships to others spatially. In one study, participants were asked to place a box representing the leader in an organizational chart that included empty boxes to represent other employees the bottom. In another study, participants were asked to place a picture of the leader relative to a circle of six pictures representing the leader's team members, to represent the relation of the leader to the followers. In both studies, participants placed the more powerful leader higher along the vertical dimension than the less powerful leader.

Taken together, this evidence suggests that the abstract social concept of power is grounded by a metaphorical mapping to vertical space, via the metaphor POWER (CONTROL) IS UP, WEAKNESS (LACK OF CONTROL) IS DOWN. Thus, abstract social concepts can be grounded in embodied experience.

Metaphoric structuring has also been investigated in terms of abstract emotion concepts; in particular, concepts regarding emotional valence. These concepts appear to be structured by metaphorical mappings to space, in terms of the broad-based metaphor GOOD IS UP, BAD IS DOWN.

Riskind (1983) showed that people retrieve emotional memories with positive valence more efficiently when sitting erect, and they retrieve emotional memories with negative valence more efficiently when sitting in a slumped position. Along similar lines, Casasanto and Dijkstra (2010) showed that, when participants were given neutral-valence prompts, they retrieved more memories with positive valence when they were instructed to move a set of marbles upward (from one box to another), and they retrieved more memories with negative valence when they were instructed to move marbles downward. Likewise, latency to recall memories with positive valence was shorter when participants were instructed to move marbles upward, and latency to recall memories with negative valence was shorter when participants were instructed to move marbles downward (Casasanto & Dijkstra, 2010).

Embodiment of abstractions in language and gesture

The studies described above are primarily experimental manipulations that have yielded evidence about the conceptual metaphors that underlie abstract social and emotional concepts. However, one need not conduct experiments in order to "see" the metaphorical structuring of abstract concepts. Conceptual metaphors that involve action, space, and other bodily experiences are commonly expressed in everyday language. Indeed, Lakoff and Johnson (1980) based their arguments on evidence from everyday linguistic expressions. For example, the POWER IS UP, WEAKNESS IS DOWN metaphor (described above) is manifested in expressions such as "your *highness*," "*high* and mighty," and "he's *moving up* in the ranks." As another example, consider the metaphor FRIENDSHIP IS PHYSICAL CLOSENESS. This metaphor is manifested in everyday expressions that describe physical closeness, such as "we are really *tight*" or "he's being *distant*."

Conceptual metaphors that involve action, space, and bodily experiences are also commonly expressed in spontaneous gestures. McNeill (1992) was among the first to observe that representational gestures sometimes depict abstract concepts metaphorically; this insight has spawned a large body of research on metaphor in gesture (Cienki & Müller, 2008). One metaphor that McNeill discusses at length is the "conduit" metaphor (see Lakoff & Johnson, 1980; Reddy, 1979), which holds that IDEAS, CONCEPTS, MEANINGS (and so forth) ARE OBJECTS; WORDS, SENTENCES AND OTHER LINGUISTIC EXPRESSIONS ARE CONTAINERS; and COMMUNICATION IS SENDING AND RECEIVING. This metaphor is commonly expressed in gestures that represent holding or transferring objects. For example, a speaker might extend her hand as if holding something, while saying, "I have an idea" or "How shall I say this?"

Metaphors that involve spatial image schemas are also readily expressed in gestures. Consider spatial metaphors for time, as considered at the outset of this section. Núñez and Sweetser (2006) studied conceptual metaphors for time in Aymara, a language spoken in the Andean highlands of western Bolivia, southeastern Peru, and northern Chile. In Aymara, the word for front is also used to mean "past" and the word for back is also used to mena "future." Núñez and Sweetser examined the gestures that Aymara speakers produced to accompany verbal expressions about time, and found that Aymara speakers used the space behind them to represent the future, and the space in front of them to represent the past. Furthermore, Aymara speakers used locations in front of and closer to their bodies to represent more recent past times, and locations in front of and farther from their bodies to represent less recent past times. These gestures complement data from Aymara linguistic expressions to show that metaphoric construals of time in Aymara are quite different from those in other languages, including English.

Many other studies have documented gestures that reflect the metaphoric structuring of abstract concepts in terms of space and action. A few have investigated metaphoric gestures for abstract mathematical concepts. Núñez (2005) presents examples drawn from mathematics professors teaching at the university level. In one example, a professor describes an unbounded monotonic sequence that "goes in one direction," and he represents this sequence using a circular motion of his hand, which he produces while walking forward across the front of the classroom. This case illustrates the NUMBERS ARE LOCATIONS IN SPACE metaphor (Lakoff & Núñez, 2001). In another study, Alibali and Nathan (in press) present examples drawn from middle-school mathematics lessons. In one case, a teacher presents a figure of a (balanced) pan balance with two spheres on one side, and two cylinders and a sphere on the other side, and below it, the associated equation, $s + s = c + c + s$. The teacher first describes removing identical objects from both sides of the balance,

saying, "I am going to take away a sphere from each side," while making a grasping motion over the spheres on each side. She then says, "Instead of taking it off the pans, I am going to take it away from this equation." With this utterance, she first mimes removing a sphere from each side of the pan balance figure, and then makes the same grasping handshapes over the s symbols on the two sides of the equation. With this last gesture, she expresses the metaphor of taking objects away – reflecting the ARITHMETIC IS COLLECTING OBJECTS metaphor described by Lakoff and Núñez (2001) – to give meaning to the abstract principle of subtracting equal quantities from both sides of an equation, by grounding it in the action of removing objects. As these examples show, metaphoric gestures can reflect the grounding of abstract mathematical concepts in space and action.

To our knowledge, there has been little research on gestural expression of metaphors for abstract social concepts, but it seems likely that such concepts would also be readily expressed in gestures. Consider the POWER IS UP, WEAKNESS IS DOWN metaphor, discussed extensively above. It is easy to imagine a speaker producing a gesture of upward movement while saying "she acts so *high* and mighty" or "he's *moving up* in the ranks." Or consider the metaphor FRIENDSHIP IS PHYSICAL CLOSENESS. It is easy to imagine a speaker producing a gesture that represents friendship in terms physical closeness – for example, pressing the palms together while saying "we are best buddies."

Metaphoric gestures may be most informative in situations where speakers do not express the corresponding metaphors overtly in their speech. In the "best buddies" example just described, the metaphor of FRIENDSHIP IS PHYSICAL CLOSENESS is not overtly expressed in speech; however, this metaphor might be manifested in the gestures that accompany that speech. Along similar lines, it would be interesting to ask scientists to describe the composition of their research groups, and to investigate the vertical positioning of their gestures in space, as a possible index of power within the group.

CONCLUSION

Current evidence suggests that we understand social concepts – both concrete and abstract – by simulating relevant motor, perceptual, and emotional experiences, and that our understanding and use of these concepts is embedded in the social and physical environment. The same reliance on simulation, and the same embedding of knowledge and performance, also characterize language comprehension and production. In this chapter we have highlighted gestures as a unique source of data, not only about the role of simulation in cognition but also about the embeddedness of cognition and about the metaphoric embodiment of abstract concepts.

To return once again to the example of the jazz concert, we understand a jazz concert because we can simulate what it is like to be at a jazz concert. Our simulations hearken back to particular situations in which we have experienced jazz concerts (or other sorts of concerts) in the past. We understand how the saxophonist plays by imagining ourselves pressing the keys. We understand the drummer's relaxed state because we can simulate his laid-back smile. And when we invite our friend Andre to join us at the concert, we just might convey the action of the saxophonist and the smile of the drummer in our own gesture and facial expression.

REFERENCES

Adolphs, R. (2002). Recognizing emotion from facial expressions: Psychological and neurological mechanisms. *Behavioral and Cognitive Neuroscience Reviews, 1,* 21–62.

Adolphs, R., Damasio, H., Tranel, D., Cooper, G., & Damasio, A. R. (2000). A role for somatosensory cortices in the visual recognition of emotion as revealed by 3-D lesion mapping. *Journal of Neuroscience, 20,* 2683–2690.

Alibali, M. W., & Hostetter, A. B. (in press). Mimicry and simulation in gesture comprehension. (Commentary on Niedenthal, Mermillod, Maringer, & Hess, The Simulation of Smiles Model.) *Behavioral and Brain Sciences.*

Alibali, M. W., & Nathan, M. J. (in press). Embodiment in mathematics teaching and learning: Evidence from students' and teachers' gestures. *Journal of the Learning Sciences.*

Alverson, H. (1994). *Semantics and experience: Universal metaphors of time in English, Mandarin, Hindi, and Sesotho.* Baltimore, MD: Johns Hopkins University Press.

Anderson, M. L. (2003). Embodied cognition: A field guide. *Artificial Intelligence, 149,* 91–130.

Atkinson, A. (2007). Face processing and empathy. *Empathy in mental illness* (pp. 360– 385). New York: Cambridge University Press.

Bargh, J. A., Chen, M., & Burrows, L. (1996). The automaticity of social behavior: Direct effects of trait concept and stereotype activation on action. *Journal of Personality and Social Psychology, 81,* 1014–1027.

Barsalou, L. W. (1983). Ad hoc categories. *Memory & Cognition, 11,* 211–227.

Barsalou, L. W. (1999). Perceptual symbol systems. *Behavioral and Brain Sciences, 22,* 577–660.

Barsalou, L. W. (2008). Grounded cognition. *Annual Review of Psychology, 59,* 617–645.

Bavelas, J. B., Kenwood, C., Johnson, T., & Phillips, B. (2002). An experimental study of when and how speakers use gestures to communicate. *Gesture, 2,* 1–17.

Bergen, B. K., Lau, A., Narayan, S., Stojanovic, D., & Wheeler, K. (2010). Body part representations in verbal semantics. *Memory & Cognition, 38,* 969–981.

Blair, I. V. (2002). The malleability of automatic stereotypes and prejudice. *Personality and Social Psychology Review, 6*(3), 242–261.

Boroditsky, L. (2000). Metaphoric structuring: Understanding time through spatial metaphors. *Cognition, 75,* 1–28.

Boroditsky, L. (2001). Does language shape thought? English and Mandarin speakers' conceptions of time. *Cognitive Psychology, 43*(1), 1–22.

Boroditsky, L., & Prinz, J. (2008). What thoughts are made of. In G. Semin & E. Smith (Eds.), *Embodied grounding: Social, cognitive, affective, and neuroscientific approaches.* New York: Cambridge University Press.

Bourgeois, P., & Hess, U. (2008). The impact of social context on mimicry. *Biological Psychology, 77*(3), 343–352.

Bush, L. K., Barr, C. L., McHugo, G. J., & Lanzetta, J. T. (1989). The effects of facial control and facial mimicry on subjective reactions to comedy routines. *Motivation and Emotion, 13,* 31–52.

Butcher, C., Mylander, C., & Goldin-Meadow, S. (1991). Displaced communication in a self-styled gesture system: Pointing at the nonpresent. *Cognitive Development, 6,* 315–342.

Calder, A. J., Keane, J., Manes, F., Antoun, N., & Young, A. W. (2000). Impaired recognition and experience of disgust following brain injury, *Nature Neuroscience, 3*(11), 1077–1078.

Cannon, P. R., Hayes, A. E., & Tipper, S. P. (2009). An electromyographic investigation of the impact of task relevance on facial mimicry. *Cognition and Emotion, 5,* 918–929.

Carraher, T. N., Carraher, D. W., & Schliemann, A. D. (1985). Mathematics in the streets and in the schools. *British Journal of Developmental Psychology, 3,* 21–29.

Casasanto, D., & Boroditsky, L. (2008). Time in the mind: Using space to think about time. *Cognition, 106,* 579–593.

Casasanto, D., & Dijkstra, K. (2010). Motor action and emotional memory. *Cognition, 115*(1), 179–185.

Chambon, M. (2009). Embodied perception with others' bodies in mind: Stereotype priming influence on the perception of spatial environment. *Journal of Experimental Social Psychology, 45,* 283–287.

Chandler, J., & Schwarz, N. (2009). How extending your middle finger affects your perception of others: Learned movements influence concept accessibility. *Journal of Experimental Social Psychology, 45*(1), 123–128.

Chartrand, T. L., & Bargh, J. A. (1999). The chameleon effect: The perception– behavior link and social interaction. *Journal of Personality and Social Psychology, 76,* 893–910.

Church, R. B., Ayman-Nolley, S., & Mahootian, S. (2004). The role of gesture in bilingual education: Does gesture enhance learning? *Bilingual Education and Bilingualism, 7*, 303–318.

Cienki, A., & Müller, C. (Eds.). (2008). *Metaphor and gesture.* Amsterdam: John Benjamins.

Clark, H. H. (1973). Space, time, semantics, and the child. In T. Moore (Ed.), *Cognitive development and the acquisition of language* (pp. 27–63). New York: Academic Press.

Clark, H. H., & Murphy, G. L. (1982). Audience design in meaning and reference. In J.-F. L. Ny & W. Kintsch (Eds.), *Language and comprehension.* Amsterdam: North-Holland.

Decety, J., & Chaminade, T. (2003). Neural correlates of feeling sympathy. *Neuropsychologia, 41*, 127–138.

Decety, J., & Stevens, J. A. (2008). Action representation and its role in social interaction. In K. D. Markman, W. M. P. Klein, & J. A. Suhr (Eds.), *The handbook of imagination and mental simulation.* New York: Psychology Press.

Dijksterhuis, A., & van Knippenberg, A. (1998). The relation between perception and behavior or how to win a game of trivial pursuit. *Journal of Personality and Social Psychology, 74*, 865–877.

Dimberg, U., Thunberg, M., & Elmehed, K. (2000). Unconscious facial reactions to emotional facial expressions. *Psychological Science, 11*, 86–89.

Fadiga, L., Fogassi, L., Pavesi, G., & Rizzolatti, G. (1995). Motor facilitation during action observation: A magnetic stimulation study. *Journal of Neurophysiology, 73*, 2608–2611.

Foroni, F., & Semin, G. R. (2009). Language that puts you in touch with your bodily feelings. The multimodal responsiveness of affective expressions. *Psychological Science, 20*, 974–980.

Gallese, V. (2003). The roots of empathy: The shared manifold hypothesis and the neural basis of intersubjectivity. *Psychopathology, 36*, 171–180.

Gallese, V. (2005). "Being like me": Self-other identity, mirror neurons, and empathy. Perspectives on imitation: From neuroscience to social science. Vol. 1: *Mechanisms of imitation and imitation in animals* (pp. 101–118). Cambridge, MA: MIT Press.

Gallese, V., Fadiga, L., Fogassi, L., & Rizzolatti, G. (1996). Action recognition in the premotor cortex. *Brain, 119*, 593–609.

Gerwing, J., & Bavelas, J. B. (2004). Linguistic influences on gesture's form. *Gesture, 4*, 157–195.

Gibson, J. J. (1979). *The ecological approach to visual perception.* Hillsdale, NJ: Erlbaum.

Giessner, S. R., & Schubert, T. W. (2007). High in the hierarchy: How vertical location and judgments of leaders' power are interrelated. *Organizational Behavior and Human Decision Processes, 104*(1), 30–44.

Glenberg, A. M. (1997). What memory is for. *Behavioral and Brain Sciences, 20*, 1–55.

Glenberg, A. M., & Kaschak, M. P. (2002). Grounding language in action. *Psychonomic Bulletin & Review, 9*, 558–565.

Glenberg, A. M., & Robertson, D. A. (1999). Indexical understanding of instructions. *Discourse Processes, 28*, 1–26.

Glenberg, A. M., & Robertson, D. (2000). Symbol grounding and meaning: A comparison of high-dimensional and embodied theories of meaning. *Journal of Memory and Language, 43*, 379–401.

Goldman, A., & Sripada, C. (2005). Simulationist models of face-based emotion recognition. *Cognition, 94*, 193–213.

Goldstone, R. L. (1995). Effects of categorization on color perception. *Psychological Science, 6*, 298–230.

Goodwin, C. (2007). Environmentally coupled gestures. In S. Duncan, J. Cassell & E. Levy (Eds.), *Gesture and the dynamic dimensions of language* (pp. 195–212). Amsterdam/Philadelphia: John Benjamins.

Griggs, R. A., & Cox, J. R. (1982). The elusive thematic-materials effect in Wason's selection task. *British Journal of Psychology, 16*, 94– 143.

Halberstadt, J. B., Niedenthal, P. M., & Kushner, J. (1995). Resolution of lexical ambiguity by emotional state. *Psychological Science, 6*, 278–282.

Halberstadt, J., Winkielman, P., Niedenthal, P. M., & Dalle, N. (2009). Emotional conception: How embodied emotion concepts guide perception and facial action. Psychological Science, 20, 1254–1261.

Havas, D. A., Glenberg, A. M., Gutowski, K. A., Lucarelli, M. J., & Davidson, R. J. (2010). Cosmetic use of botulinum toxin-A affects processing of emotional language. *Psychological Science, 21*, 895–900.

Havas, D. A., Glenberg, A. M., & Rinck, M. (2007). Emotion simulation during language comprehension. *Psychonomic Bulletin & Review, 14*, 436–441.

Hermans, E. J., Putman, P., & van Honk, J. (2006). Testosterone administration reduces empathetic behavior: A facial mimicry study. *Psychoneuroendocrinology, 31*(7), 859–866.

Holler, J., & Stevens, R. (2007). The effect of common ground on how speakers use gesture and speech to represent size information. *Journal of Language and Social Psychology, 26*, 4–27.

Horton, W. S., & Gerrig, R. J. (2005). The impact of memory demands on audience design during language production. *Cognition, 96*, 127–142.

Hostetter, A. B. (in press). When do gestures communicate? A meta-analysis. *Psychological Bulletin.*

Hostetter, A. B., & Alibali, M. W. (2008). Visible embodiment: Gestures as simulated action. *Psychonomic Bulletin & Review, 15*, 495–514.

Hostetter, A. B., & Alibali, M. W. (2010). Language, gesture, action! A test of the gesture as simulated action framework. *Journal of Memory and Language, 63*, 245–257.

Hostetter, A. B., Alibali, M. W., & Schrager, S. M. (2011). If you don't already know, I'm certainly not going to show you! Motivation to communicate affects gesture production. In G. Stam & M. Ishino (Eds.), *Integrating gestures: The interdisciplinary nature of gesture* (pp. 61–74). Amsterdam: John Benjamins.

Hurley, S. (2008). The shared circuits model (SCM): How control, mirroring, and simulation can enable imitation, deliberation, and mindreading. *Behavioral and Brain Sciences, 31*, 1–58.

Hutchins, E. (1995). *Cognition in the wild.* Cambridge, MA: MIT Press.

Iacoboni, M., Woods, R., Brass, M., Bekkering, H., Mazziotta, J., & Rizzolatti, G. (1999). Cortical mechanisms of human imitation. *Science, 286,* 2526–2528.

Kaschak, M. P., & Maner, J. K. (2009). Embodiment, evolution, and social cognition: An integrative framework. *European Journal of Social Psychology, 39*(7), 1236–1244.

Keysers, C., & Gazzola, V. (2007). Integrating simulation and theory of mind: From self to social cognition. *Trends in Cognitive Science, 11,* 194–196.

Kimbara, I. (2008). Gesture form convergence in joint description. *Journal of Nonverbal Behavior, 32*(2), 123–131.

Kirsh, D., & Maglio, P. (1994). On distinguishing epistemic from pragmatic actions. *Cognitive Science, 18*(4), 513–549.

Kotovsky, K., Hayes, J. R., & Simon, H. A. (1985). Why are some problems hard? Evidence from Tower of Hanoi. *Cognitive Psychology, 17,* 248–294.

Krauss, R. M., Chen, Y., & Gottesman, R. F. (2000). Lexical gestures and lexical access: A process model. In D. McNeill (Ed.), *Language and gesture* (pp. 261–283). Cambridge, UK: Cambridge University Press.

Krumhuber, E., Manstead, A. S. R., & Kappas, A. (2007). Temporal aspects of facial displays in person and expression perception. The effects of smile dynamics, head-tilt and gender. *Journal of Nonverbal Behavior, 31,* 39–56.

Lakin, J. L., & Chartrand, T. L. (2003). Using nonconscious behavioral mimicry to create affiliation and rapport. *Psychological Science, 19,* 816–822.

Lakoff, G., & Johnson, M. (1980). *Metaphors we live by.* Chicago, IL: University of Chicago Press.

Lakoff, G., & Núñez, R. (2001). *Where mathematics comes from: How the embodied mind brings mathematics into being.* New York: Basic Books.

Libby, L. K., Shaeffer, E. M., & Eibach, R. P. (2009). Seeing meaning in action: A bidirectional link between visual perspective and action identification level. *Journal of Experimental Psychology: General, 138*(4), 503–516.

Likowski, K. U., Muhlberger, A., Seibt, B., Pauli, P., & Weyers, P. (2008). Modulation of facial mimicry by attitudes. *Journal of Experimental Social Psychology, 44*(4), 1065–1072.

Maddux, W. W., Mullen, E., & Galinsky, A. (2008). Chameleons bake bigger pies: Strategic behavioral mimicry facilitates integrative negotiations outcomes. *Journal of Experimental Social Psychology, 44,* 461–468.

Maringer, M., Krumhuber, E., Fischer, A., & Niedenthal, P. M. (2011). Beyond smile dynamics: Mimicry and beliefs in judgments of smiles. *Emotion, 11,* 181–187.

Masson, M. E. J., Bub, D. N., & Warren, C. M. (2008). Kicking calculators: Contribution of embodied representations to sentence comprehension. *Journal of Memory and Language, 59*(3), 256–265.

McNeill, D. (1992). *Hand and mind: What gestures reveal about thought.* Chicago, IL: University of Chicago Press.

McNeil, N. M., & Alibali, M. W. (2005). Knowledge change as a function of mathematics experience: All contexts are not created equal. *Journal of Cognition and Development, 6,* 285–306.

Meltzoff, A., & Moore, M. (1977). Imitation of facial and manual gestures by human neonates. *Science, 198,* 75–78.

Moody, E. J., McIntosh, D. N., Mann, L. J., & Weisser, K. R. (2007). More than mere mimicry? The influence of emotion on rapid facial reactions to faces. *Emotion, 7*(2), 447–457.

Morford, J., & Goldin-Meadow, S. (1997). From here and now to there and then: The development of displaced reference in homesign and English. *Child Development, 68,* 420–435.

Nathan, M. J. (2008). An embodied cognition perspective on symbols, grounding, and instructional gesture. In M. DeVega, A. M. Glenberg & A. C. Graesser (Eds.), *Symbols and embodiment: Debates on meaning and cognition* (pp. 375–396). Oxford, UK: Oxford University Press.

Niedenthal, P. M. (2007). Embodying emotion. *Science, 316,* 1002–1005.

Niedenthal, P. M. (2008). Emotion concepts. In M. Lewis, J.M. Haviland-Jones, and L. F. Barrett (Eds.), *Handbook of emotion, 3rd Edition.* (pp. 597–600). New York: Guilford.

Niedenthal, P. M., Barsalou, L. W., Winkielman, P., Krauth-Gruber, S., & Ric, F. (2005). Embodiment in attitudes, social perception, and emotion. *Personality and Social Psychology Review, 9,* 184–211.

Niedenthal, P. M., Brauer, M., Halberstadt, J. B., & Innes-Ker, A. H. (2001). When did her smile drop? Contrast effects in the influence of emotional state on the detection of change in emotional expression. *Cognition and Emotion, 15,* 853–864.

Niedenthal, P. M., Mermillod, M., Maringer, M., & Hess, U. (2010). The Simulation of Smiles (SIMS) model: Embodied simulation and the meaning of facial expression. Target article for *Behavioral and Brain Sciences, 33,* 417–480.

Niedenthal, P. M., Winkielman, P., Mondillon, L., & Vermeulen, N. (in press). Embodied emotion concepts. *Journal of Personality and Social Psychology.*

Núñez, R. (2005). Do real numbers really move? Language, thought, and gesture: The embodied cognitive foundations of mathematics. In F. Iida, R. Pfeifer, L. Steels & Y. Kuniyoshi (Eds.), *Embodied artificial intelligence* (pp. 54–73). Berlin: Springer-Verlag.

Núñez, R., & Sweetser, E. (2006). With the future behind them: Convergent evidence from Aymara language and gesture in the crosslinguistic comparison of spatial construals of time. *Cognitive Science, 30,* 401–450.

Nussinson, R., Seibt, B., Häfner, M., & Strack, F. (2010). Come a bit closer: Approach motor actions lead to feeling similar and behavioral assimilation. *Social Cognition, 28,* 40–58.

Nygaard, L. C., & Queen, J.S. (2008). Communicating emotion: Linking affective prosody and word meaning. *Journal of Experimental Psychology: Human Perception and Performance, 34,* 1017–1030

Özyürek, A. (2002). Do speakers design their co-speech gestures for their addressees? The effects of addressee location on representational gestures. *Journal of Memory and Language, 46*(4), 688–704.

Pecher, D., Zeelenberg, R., & Barsalou, L. W. (2003). Verifying different-modality properties for concepts produces switching costs. *Psychological Science, 14*, 119–124.

Pitcher, D., Garrido, L., Walsh, V., & Duchaine, B. (2008). TMS disrupts the perception and embodiment of facial expressions. *Journal of Neuroscience, 28*(36), 8929–8933.

Pulvermüller, F. (2005). Brain mechanisms linking language and action. *Nature Reviews, 6*, 1–6.

Pulvermüller, F., Hauk, O., Nikulin, V. V., & Ilmoniemi, R. J. (2005). Functional links between motor and language systems. *European Journal of Neuroscience, 21*, 793–797.

Reddy, M. J. (1979). The conduit metaphor: A case of frame conflict in our language about language. In A. Ortony (Ed.), *Metaphor and thought* (pp. 164–201). Cambridge, UK: Cambridge University Press.

Richardson, D. C., Spivey, M. J., Barsalou, L. W., & McRae, K., (2003). Spatial representations activated during real-time comprehension of verbs. *Cognitive Science, 27*, 767–780.

Richardson, D. C., Spivey, M. J., Edelman, S., & Naples, A. (2001). "Language is spatial": Experimental evidence for image schemas of concrete and abstract verbs. *Proceedings of the Twenty-third Annual Meeting of the Cognitive Science Society* (pp. 873–878). Mahwah, NJ: Erlbaum.

Richeson, J. A., & Ambady, N. (2003). Effects of situational power on automatic racial prejudice. *Journal of Experimental Social Psychology, 39*, 177–183.

Riskind, J. (1983). Nonverbal expressions and the accessibility of life experience memories: A congruence hypothesis. *Social Cognition, 2*(1), 62–86.

Rizzolatti, G., & Craighero, L. (2004). The mirror-neuron system. *Annual Review of Neuroscience, 27*, 169–192.

Rizzolatti, G., Fadiga, L., Gallese, V., & Fogassi, L. (1996). Premotor cortex and the recognition of motor actions. *Cognitive Brain Research, 3*, 131–141.

Sassenberg, U., & van der Meer, E. (2010). Do we really gesture more when it is more difficult? *Cognitive Science, 34*, 643–664.

Schubert, T. W. (2004). The power in your hand: Gender differences in bodily feedback from making a fist. *Personality and Social Psychology Bulletin, 30*, 757–769.

Schubert, T. W. (2005). Your Highness: Vertical positions as perceptual symbols of power. *Journal of Personality and Social Psychology, 89*(1), 1–21

Smith, E., & Semin, G. (2007). Situated social cognition. *Current Directions in Psychological Science, 16*(3), 132–135.

Sommerville, J. A., & Decety, J. (2006). Weaving the fabric of social interaction: Articulating developmental psychology and cognitive neuroscience in the domain of motor cognition. *Psychonomic Bulletin & Review, 13*, 179–200.

Sonnby-Borgström, M. (2002). Automatic mimicry reactions as related to differences in emotional empathy. *Scandinavian Journal of Psychology, 43*, 433–443.

Sonnby-Borgström, M., Jonsson, P., & Svensson, O. (2003). Emotional empathy as related to mimicry reactions at different levels of information processing. *Journal of Nonverbal Behavior, 27*(1), 3–23.

Spivey, M. J., Richardson, D. C., & Gonzales-Marquez, M. (2005). On the perceptual-motor and image-schematic infrastructure of language. In D. Pecher & R. A. Zwaan (Eds.), *Grounding cognition: The role of perception and action in memory, language, and thinking* (pp. 246–281). Cambridge, UK: Cambridge University Press.

Stel M., & van Knippenberg, A. (2008). The role of facial mimicry in the recognition of affect. *Psychological Science, 19*, 984–985.

Valenzeno, L., Alibali, M. W., & Klatzky, R. (2003). Teachers' gestures facilitate students' learning: A lesson in symmetry. *Contemporary Educational Psychology, 28*, 187–204.

Wegner, D. M., Erber, R., & Raymond, P. (1991). Transactive memory in close relationships. *Journal of Personality and Social Psychology, 61*, 923–929.

Wegner, D. M., Giuliano, T., & Hertel, P. (1985). Cognitive interdependence in close relationships. In W. J. Ickes (Ed.), *Compatible and incompatible relationships* (pp. 253–276). New York: Springer-Verlag.

Weyers, P., Muhlberger, A., Kund, A., Hess, U., & Pauli, P. (2009). Modulation of facial reactions to avatar emotional faces by nonconscious competition priming. *Psychophysiology, 46*, 328–335.

Wicker, B., Keysers, C., Plailly, J., Royet, J. P., Gallese, V., & Rizzolatti, G. (2003). Both of us disgusted in my insula: The common neural basis of seeing and feeling disgust. *Neuron, 40*, 655–664.

Willems, R. M., Hagoort, P., & Casasanto, D. (2010). Body-specific representations of action verbs: Neural evidence from right- and left-handers. *Psychological Science, 21*, 67–74.

Williams, R. F. (2008). Gesture as a conceptual mapping tool. In A. Cienki & C. Müller (Eds.), *Metaphor and gesture* (pp. 55–92). Amsterdam: John Benjamins.

Wilson, M. (2002). Six views of embodied cognition. *Psychonomic Bulletin & Review, 9*, 625–636.

Wilson, M., & Knoblich, G. (2005). The case for motor involvement in perceiving conspecifics. *Psychological Bulletin, 131*, 460–473.

Winkielman, P., McIntosh, D. N., & Oberman, L. (2009). Embodied and disembodied emotion processing: Learning from and about typical and autistic individuals. *Emotion Review, 2*, 178–190.

Wittenbrink, B., Judd, C. M., & Park, B. (2001). Spontaneous prejudice in context: Variability in automatically activated attitudes. *Journal of Personality and Social Psychology, 81*, 815–827.

Yabar, Y., Johnston, L., Miles, L., & Peace, V. (2006). Implicit behavioral mimicry. *Journal of Nonverbal Behavior, 30*, 97–113.

Yeh, W., & Barsalou, L. W. (2006). The situated nature of concepts. *American Journal of Psychology, 119*, 349–384.

Zajonc, R., Adelmann, P., Murphy, S., & Niedenthal, P. (1987). Convergence in the physical appearance of spouses. *Motivation and Emotion, 11*, 335–346.

12

Levels of Mental Construal

Oren Shapira, Nira Liberman,
Yaacov Trope, & SoYon Rim

Philosophical realism is the view that there is a realm of objects and facts that exists independent of the mind (Frege, 1980). Although debated among philosophers, both psychologists and lay people largely subscribe to this view, and the present chapter is no exception. At the same time, it is clear that our construals[1] of objects are far from being mere reflections of objective reality. For one thing, there are multiple ways to construe the same object. For example, the same object could be represented as "a generation 4 iPhone," as "a cellular phone," or as "a communication device." The same action could be seen as aggressive or as desperate.

Because people rely on their senses and do not have direct access to reality, they in fact regulate themselves with respect to construals of objects rather than the objects themselves. For example, people choose between mental representations of different cars, not between cars. People love a mental representation of a partner rather than the partner. It is for this reason that understanding how people form construals is of central importance to psychologists.

Indeed, many subdisciplines in psychology investigate regularities of construal. The psychology of perception studies, among other questions, how we construe input into perception of movement, color, size, and direction. The psychology of cognition studies questions such as how people learn concepts and how they categorize objects. Social psychology studies how people imbue objects with valence and other socially shared, cultural meaning. These subdisciplines of psychology address very different types of construals. Yet, we would like to argue that two issues are universally relevant to construals, and thus run

across these subdisciplines of psychology. The first is the question of accuracy: i.e., the extent of correspondence between construals and objective reality. This question has received much attention in each of the subdisciplines, and we will only refer to it briefly. The second fundamental aspect of construal is its level: i.e., the extent of reduction to what the perceiver designates as the primary elements. This relatively less emphasized dimension of mental construal is the main focus of the present chapter.

ACCURACY: CORRESPONDENCE OF CONSTRUAL TO REALITY

A primary function of construals is to enable self-regulation in reality. For example, we may want to estimate the size of represented objects in order to be able to grasp them or walk through them. As another example, we infer traits of individuals in order to predict their behavior. A primary question of concern is therefore the construals' veridicality: namely, the extent of correspondence between people's construals and objective characteristics of the construed object. Indeed, the question of veridicality runs through many fields in psychology. For example, in perception, the classic psychophysical questions of sensitivity to change in stimulus characteristics and minimal threshold of detection concern the correspondence between mental representations and physical characteristics of objects (e.g., level of energy), or, in our terms, the accuracy of representation. In cognition and social cognition, examples of accuracy-related issues are the questions of accuracy of memory, stereotypes, and trait inferences. Judgment and decision-making research concerns the correspondence between mental representations and objectively verifiable attributes of decision alternatives.

The conclusion in all these disciplines is that construals depart from objective reality in a predictable way. There are many reasons and mechanisms that may explain such departure; many of these mechanisms apply to a wide range of construals, from simple percepts to complex social evaluations. For example, effects of the context of the stimulus and the context of the perceiver – the constructs that happen to be accessible in his or her mind, his/her expectancies, and motivation – have been found in every subdiscipline in psychology. Thus, range frequency theory (Parducci, 1965, 1974) suggests that the context of the evaluated stimulus affects its estimation (e.g., after lifting many heavy objects, a medium-weight object would seem lighter than in another context; after reading a few bad essays, a mediocre essay would seem better than in another context). This theory has been applied successfully to a variety of domains, from perceptual judgments of sizes of squares and darkness of dot patterns (Mellers & Birnbaum, 1982; Parducci & Wedell, 1986) to social judgments of physical attractiveness, equity, and psychopathology (Mellers, 1982, 1986; Wedell, Parducci, & Geiselman, 1987; Wedell, Parducci, & Lane, 1990). As another example, the principle of priming suggests that a perceiver's mind may have varying degrees of readiness to process stimuli (e.g., due to recent encountering, due to active goals, etc.), resulting in faster and more efficient recognition of that stimulus. This principle, too, applies to both processing simple perceptual stimuli (Balcetis & Dunning, 2006; Liberman & Förster, 2009b) and processing of complex, social concepts (e.g., DeCoster & Claypool, 2004; for a review on priming effects, see Förster, Liberman, & Friedman, 2007).

Although construals depart, sometimes markedly from objective reality, people often hold to naïve realism, believing that their construals reflect "what is there." Some important consequences of naïve realism have been described by Griffin and Ross (1991). For example, people are often surprised to find out that other people's construals of the same object differ from their own. People treat construals that deviate from their own with suspicion, and attribute the discrepancy first to the other perceiver's misperception or incompetence and then, if this attribution does not suffice (e.g., if the other perceiver sticks to his/her belief despite being exposed to all of the needed information), they resort to inferring an intentional bias (e.g., Vallone, Ross, & Lepper, 1985).

For example, opponents in a conflict often think that if a third party sympathizes with the other side, it is because they are misled by propaganda. They first attempt to present the third party with what they think is the objectively correct information. When that does not help sway the third party, the conflict partisan may conclude that the third party is biased towards the other side.

To summarize, the question of veridicality has been central to the study of mental construals and has received much attention in psychology. Psychologists have studied both the laws that transform objective properties of stimuli into mental representations and the consequences of imperfect transformation. In this chapter, however, we would like to concentrate on another dimension, besides veridicality, on which construals vary: namely, their level of abstraction.

LEVEL OF CONSTRUAL

As mentioned above, we believe that construals serve self-regulatory needs. Critically, although we directly experience only ourselves, here, and now, we self-regulate towards objects that lie outside of this restricted circle: we plan for the future, draw conclusions from the past, evaluate alternatives to reality, consider the perspectives of other people and of other spatial locations. Effective self-regulation, then, concerns not only objects in the immediate environment of the actor but also objects that are distal in time or space, objects that are part of other people's reality, and objects that are hypothetical rather than real. Distal objects cannot be directly perceived but can be only construed. Construal, then, is necessitated by the need to regulate towards distal objects.

Construal level theory (CLT; Liberman & Trope, 2008; Trope & Liberman, 2010) conceptualizes temporal distance, spatial distance, social distance, and hypotheticality as psychological distances. Obviously, distance changes objects and changes what we might need from them. The need to regulate towards distal objects calls for construing those objects using aspects that are invariant across distances with respect to one's self-regulatory needs. For example, when buying clothes, one may have to consider usefulness in situations that are increasingly different from the current one – situations in which one will have different needs, and in which yet unfamiliar people, perhaps in unfamiliar situations, would look at the clothes.

When regulating towards distal objects, people ask themselves: "What is it about this object that really matters? What are the things that are important to preserve across time, different perspectives, and alternative scenarios?" Such questions form the core of the process of forming higher-level construals. *Whenever we move to a higher-level construct we make a distinction between primary, defining features, which are relatively stable and invariant, and secondary features, which may change with changes in context and hence are omitted from the higher-level representation.* For example, construing a person as "an old woman" renders age- and gender-defining and other attributes such as skill, intellect, or likability, irrelevant. *A higher-level construal is a statement that alternative worlds with different low-level features are similar to each other. In that sense, higher-level constructs form bridges across hypothetical worlds, thereby allowing people to traverse hypotheticality.*

Many acts of reasoning involve forming higher-level construals, and in fact create constructs that remain unchanged across hypothetical variations. For example, when we categorize an object (e.g., "this is a chair"), we suggest that some of its features but not others may vary without causing important change (e.g., changing its color would not change its category, but removing its legs would). As another example, when we reduce a problem to a mathematical formula, we strip it of its content (e.g., calculating velocity or population growth), allowing this content to vary without changing what we see as the underlying structure of the problem. Similarly, when we infer a personality trait (e.g., "smart") from a behavior (e.g., "got an A on an exam"), we allow the specific behavior to vary without changing its meaning. And when we note that a group of elements form a gestalt, we imply that the elements may vary in nature but as long as the relations between them remain, the gestalt will be the same.

CLT contends that regulating towards distal objects requires forming high-level construals: namely, removing from mental construals incidental, mutable aspects and retaining central, invariant aspects. For this reason, according to CLT, distancing and abstraction are cognitively associated, with distancing facilitating abstraction, and abstraction facilitating distancing. Many conceptual distinctions that have been studied within cognitive and social psychology may be related to the dimension of level of construal: namely, may be viewed as distinctions between primary aspects and mutable, secondary aspects. Without denying the uniqueness of each distinction, we propose that it is useful to consider their relations to level of construal. For example, labeling a person "an African American" means "For the present purposes, what I find important about that person is that he is African American; I find other details, such as his personal qualities,

his personal history, or his goals relatively less important." It is also useful to map different conceptual distinctions onto level of construal because, according to CLT, higher-level construals would be used more frequently for more distal objects, and higher-level construals would bring to mind objects that span across a wider range of times, spaces, societies, and hypothetical situations. This prediction has potentially rich implications, as we will see in the review that follows.

In the following sections, we describe how the notion of level of construal can be applied to the distinctions between categories and exemplars, primary and secondary features, gestalt and details, figure and context, superordinate and subordinate elements, theories and noise, as well as symbolic and analog representation. We discuss how each of these may be viewed as a different way of distinguishing between primary and incidental aspects, review extant findings that connect these distinctions to psychological distance, and make new predictions that derive from conceptualizing these distinctions in terms of level of construal. Some constructs we discuss may be classified into more than one category. For example, inferring traits from behavior could be viewed as an instance of applying a causal theory as well as an instance of categorizing an exemplar. This is because causal theories oftentimes (but not always) underlie categories. Despite this partial overlap, we believe that theories, categories, and the other constructs we review are distinct ways of forming high-level construals.

Categories versus exemplars

Exemplars make up categories. For instance, the objects chair, table, sofa, desk, and closet are exemplars of the category "furniture." The many chairs I have seen in the course of my life make up the category "chair." Inanimate objects, events, and people can be represented using different levels of categorization, ranging from low-level, narrow categories, to wider, more inclusive ones.

Moving to a more inclusive category involves a decision about what is primary and what is secondary, and thus more inclusive categories are, in terms of CLT, higher-level construals. For example, representing a dog more abstractly as "a mammal" involves a decision that the feature "gives birth to live offsprings" is more important than the feature "domesticated." Obviously, having a different goal in mind could have afforded a different categorization of the same exemplar. For example, if one wishes to buy a dog, then "a pet" would be a more relevant superordinate category for a dog, because it would suggest a pet shop as a good place to visit. That abstraction, too, involves rendering some features (e.g., size) primary and other features (e.g., reproduction ways) less important.

Because categorization involves a statement about what is primary and what is secondary, it might be offensive when applied to people. For example, categorizing a person as "Latino" implies that race is central, whereas other qualities are less important. This is just fine in some contexts (e.g., when filling out different pieces of information on a form) but perhaps not in others (e.g., when saying "a Latino applied to the job we advertised").

Although categorization is goal-dependent, there are also "default" common abstractions that may seem independent of goals, but actually presume "default goals." For example, "fruit" might seem as a default category for "an apple." Yet, this category would not be applied if instead of eating the apple or serving it (which are the commonly assumed, default goals) the apple is used for an unusual purpose, such as throwing it at someone. In such a case, "hard" and "easy to grasp" would be more pertinent superordinate categories.

Higher-level categories afford psychological distancing more than lower-level categories because they are more likely to apply to distal times, places, individuals, and possibilities. For example, in the more distant future and in more remote counterfactual situations, I can more safely assume that I will need furniture rather than chairs, and hence it is more useful to construe distant future needs in terms of "furniture" rather than "chairs." Also, people from other cultures are more likely to use furniture than chairs, and hence, when communicating to a person from another culture, it is more useful to use the broader category. Similarly, high-level categories bring to mind exemplars that span across a wider range of times, places, social targets, and hypothetical situations, and thus expand one's mental horizons. For example, using the term "food," compared to "macaroni and cheese," connects one to more distal historical periods, to more remote places and social groups, and to less likely hypothetical situations.

Breadth of categories

Consistent with CLT, research has shown that people group objects (e.g., things that one would take to a trip) into fewer, broader categories when they imagine using them in the more distant future (Liberman, Sagristano, & Trope, 2002, Study 1) or in a less likely situation (Wakslak, Trope, Liberman, & Alony, 2006). Likewise, participants primed with high power (an instance of social

distance; Smith & Trope, 2006) were more inclusive in categorizing atypical exemplars (e.g., *sled* for the category *vehicle*) than those primed with low power (Smith & Trope, 2006, Study 1).

It has also been found that broad, general categories promote a sense of psychological distance. A recent series of studies by Wakslak and Trope (2009) manipulated level of categorization and found the predicted effect on event likelihoods. In one study, participants generated either superordinate categories or subordinate exemplars for 40 objects (e.g., *table, sport, book*; Study 2). Next, participants completed a supposedly unrelated questionnaire where they made a series of probability judgments. As expected, participants who had been primed with categories (a high-level construal mindset) indicated that the events were less likely to occur compared to those who had been primed with exemplars (a low-level construal mindset).

Another study (Stephan, 2006, Study 12) supported the same prediction with social distance. Participants read about an actor interacting with either a general category or specific exemplars of the same category (e.g., "Diana is ordering *dessert* vs *cake and ice cream*"). Participants rated the actor as more familiar (i.e., less socially distant) when the sentence included exemplars rather than a category.

Assimilation versus contrast

When perceiving two stimuli in relation to each other (as compared to perceiving the same stimuli separately), a perceiver may assimilate the two stimuli to each other, thereby perceiving them as more similar to each other, or contrast them away from each other, thereby perceiving each of the stimuli as more distinct from the other stimulus (Parducci, Perrett, & Marsh, 1969; Schwarz & Bless, 1992, 2007). For example, when considering a paper of a student in relation to the best paper in class (vs considering it in isolation), the focal paper may be assimilated to the excellent paper and thus seem better, or it may be contrasted away, and thus seem worse. In view of the opposite effects of assimilation versus contrast, the question of what makes each of them more likely becomes crucial (Mussweiler, 2001; Schwarz & Bless, 1992, 2007).

Most germane to the present framework are Schwartz and Bless' inclusion/exclusion model (Schwarz & Bless, 1992, 2007) and Förster, Liberman, and Kuschel's (2008) global/local model (GLOMO) of social judgment. According to these models, because global, high-level construals are more inclusive, using those construals is likely to result in including two stimuli in the same category and produce an assimilation effect.

Using low-level construals, however, is likely to result in applying narrower categories, and hence categorizing the two stimuli as exemplars of separate categories and a contrast effect. Consistent with this view, it has been found that priming of high-level construal and greater temporal distance enhances assimilation and reduces contrast. For example, in one of the studies (Förster et al., 2008, Study 3), participants compared their athletic skills to either a moderately high standard or a moderately low standard and then rated their expected athletic performance in an athletic competition that would take place the next day (a proximal temporal perspective) or a year later (a distal temporal perspective). In the control condition, time was not specified. The results showed that a distant time perspective enhanced assimilation (i.e., produced a high self-rating after comparison to a high standard and a low self-rating after comparison to a low standard), whereas a proximal time perspective enhanced contrast (i.e., produced a low self-rating after comparison to a high standard and a high self-rating after comparison to a low standard).

Group-based stereotypes

Another way in which people may categorize others is based on the social groups they belong to, such as age, gender, or race. In the social cognitive literature, group-based categorization is often contrasted with individuating information, such as the person's actions, intentions, and traits. Using group-based categories implies that information on group belongingness is central, whereas individuating information is secondary and mutable. It is an implicit statement that the target of such categorization is equivalent to other members of that category, and that those of his or her characteristics that are not inferable from category membership are secondary.

To the extent that group-based categorization is a relevant abstraction, CLT predicts that it would be more likely with increasing psychological distance. Indeed, research has shown that individuals are more likely to stereotype out-group members who, in CLT terms, are socially distal, as compared to in-group members, who are socially proximal (for reviews, see Hewstone, Rubin, & Willis, 2002; Hilton & von Hippel, 1996). However, this effect could be attributed to a difference in amount of information, as people generally have more information and more concrete information about in-group vs out-group members. Future studies could examine the influence of social distance on stereotyping when amount of information is held constant. Extensions to other dimensions of psychological distance would be interesting as well.

Inferring traits from behaviors

People in Western cultures tend to interpret others' behavior as exemplifying dispositional traits (Asch, 1946; Heider, 1958; Jones & Davis, 1965). For example, many different behaviors, such as donating money, sharing information, or offering a ride home, could exemplify the trait of helpfulness. It is possible to think of behaviors as exemplars of traits. As with other categories, inferring traits involves a distinction between essential aspects and mutable aspects: namely, using a trait term to describe a behavior typically implies that specific aspects of the behavior (e.g., the identity of the recipient of the action, the objects used in the action) are secondary and mutable, whereas a characteristic of the actor is central. Traits are by their very definition enduring and applicable across many situations, and in that sense, "travel well" across psychological distances.

Research on spontaneous trait inference (STI; Winter & Uleman, 1984) demonstrates that people infer traits from behavior even without explicitly having the intention to form impressions (i.e., through task instructions) and without being aware of having made any inferences. For example, upon reading the sentence "*The secretary solved the mystery halfway through the book*," they spontaneously encode the trait "clever," even under conditions of time pressure or cognitive load (Todorov & Uleman, 2003; Winter, Uleman, & Cunniff, 1985). A CLT analysis of STIs suggests that STI formation will be enhanced for psychologically distal vs proximal actors. Indeed, Rim, Uleman, and Trope (2009) demonstrated more STIs from behaviors of others who were described as being in a spatially remote (vs proximal) location (Study 1), or from the distant (vs recent) past (Study 2).

Converging evidence comes from research that used Semin and Fiedler's (1988) linguistic categorization model (LCM), which classifies linguistic representations of actions into four levels of abstractness. At the most concrete level are descriptive action verbs (*lift, take*), which are typically directly observable. Interpretative action verbs (*pretend, help*) are more abstract, as they involve interpretation and require some knowledge of a context larger than the immediately perceived. Most relevant to the current discussion, it is possible to think of descriptive action verbs as exemplars and of interpretive action verbs as categories. For example, "hand a dollar bill to a homeless person" is an exemplar of "helping." This abstraction rests on a decision that the dollar and the fact that the recipient is homeless are incidental, whereas the presence of a helper and a recipient, as well as an act by the former that is beneficial to the latter, are central. State verbs (*prefer, understand*) are still more abstract, and adjectives (*helpful, aggressive*) are the most abstract category. Using an adjective to describe a behavior is akin to inferring a trait from that behavior.

The LCM is a useful tool for examining the relationships between psychological distance and abstractness (or construal level) of actions. Indeed, various kinds of distance have been found to affect abstractness of language. For example, people used more abstract language when describing another person's actions than their own actions (Semin & Fiedler, 1989; see also Fiedler, Semin, Finkenauer, & Berkel, 1995), when describing spatially distant interactions than spatially near interactions (Fujita, Henderson, Eng, Trope, & Liberman, 2006), and when instructed to address another person politely (i.e., in a socially distant manner) rather than colloquially (Stephan, Liberman, & Trope, 2010a).

Would the reverse direction of influence hold? That is, would linguistic abstractness affect perceived psychological distance? Semin and Smith (1999, Studies 2, 3) provided participants with retrieval cues of varying abstractness and examined the temporal distance of the events they recalled. For example, participants were asked to recall either an occasion in which they helped somebody (i.e., a concrete, behavioral retrieval cue) or an occasion in which they displayed helpfulness (i.e., an abstract, trait retrieval cue). As predicted, trait retrieval cues prompted older memories than memories that were prompted by behavioral retrieval cues.

Relational categorization and analogical mapping

Analogy is a special kind of similarity, in which two situations share a common structure of relationships between their constituent elements, even though the elements themselves may differ (Gentner, 1983; Holyoak, 2005). For example, in a picture-mapping task commonly used to measure analogical thinking (Markman & Gentner, 1993, Experiment 1), participants are shown pairs of pictures. The pictures in each pair share a relational structure (e.g., both exemplify a relation of *giving*), while the elements differ between pictures (e.g., the upper picture shows a man giving food to a woman, whereas the bottom picture shows a woman giving food to a squirrel; Figure 12.1). Analogical mapping involves matching the elements in both scenes based on their similar roles in the relational structure, while ignoring perceptual similarities that might interfere with such mapping (e.g., Gentner & Toupin, 1986; Markman & Gentner, 1993). For example, in order to match the woman in the upper picture with the squirrel in the bottom picture (both in the role of the receiver in the relation), participants have to ignore the perceptual similarities between the woman in the upper picture and that in the bottom picture.

Representing a situation in terms of its relational structure reflects categorization, whereas representing it in terms of its perceptual features reflects attention to concrete, individuating information (which is incidental from the perspective of the relational structure). Categorizing a situation in terms of the relations it exemplifies (e.g., "This scene exemplifies relations of giving and receiving") is based on identifying the relations as primary, and the identity of the actors (a woman, a man, a squirrel) as well as the context of the act (e.g., the type of house where the woman lives) and its content (e.g., what is being given) as incidental.

Psychological distance (vs proximity) should thus promote relational categorization and also analogical mapping, as well as other downstream processes of analogical thinking. In a preliminary study that tested this prediction (Elias & Shapiro-Pavlovsky, 2009), participants were primed with high or low power using a scrambled sentences task. They then performed the picture-mapping task described above (Markman & Gentner, 1993, Experiment 1), where elements in one picture in a pair can be matched with elements in the other picture either based on relational role or perceptual similarity (Figure 12.1). As predicted, participants primed with high power made more relational mappings as compared to participants primed with low power. We are currently exploring effects of other manipulations of psychological distance on analogical mapping and other processes of analogical thinking. For example, we plan to study whether psychological distancing helps people transfer a solution from one insight problem to a problem from a different domain but with the same structure. As processes of analogical thinking are central in learning and problem solving (e.g., Gentner & Colhoun, 2010; Holyoak, 2005), this seems like a promising avenue for research.

It is noteworthy that we think of both trait inferences and analogy by relational structure as instances of high-level construal. For example, when we see one person giving food to another, we may attribute a trait to the actor (e.g., *generosity*), abstract a relation between the figures (e.g., *giving–receiving*), or do both. It would be interesting to examine how distance interacts with factors that sway our mind towards one kind of high-level construal or another. For example, it has been found that people from collectivist cultures or in a collectivist mindset are *less* likely to make trait inferences than people from

Figure 12.1   A pair of pictures exemplifying analogy. Both pictures show a relation of giving, but the role fillers differ between pictures. Adapted from Markman and Gentner (1993).

individualistic cultures or in an individualist mindset (e.g., Choi, Nisbett, & Norenzayan, 1999; Oishi, Wyer, & Colcombe, 2000; Oyserman, Coon, & Kemmelmeier, 2002). It would be interesting to examine also whether people from collectivistic cultures would be also *more* likely to make relational inferences (and analogies), and whether distance would have a different effect on people with individualistic versus collectivistic tendencies.

Primary versus secondary aspects of objects

We mentioned earlier that abstraction rests on a distinction between primary and secondary aspects

of objects. Yet, not all such distinctions amount to forming categories. Regardless of whether or not categories are formed, central, goal-related features of objects constitute high-level construals, whereas peripheral, relatively goal-irrelevant features constitute low-level construal of those objects. Distancing an object should therefore promote construals that focus on primary features and de-emphasize secondary features. Trope and Liberman (2000) found support for this prediction in studies on evaluations of objects and events containing both a primary and a secondary aspect. For instance, participants imagined buying a radio set either the next day or 1 year later, in order to listen to morning programs. In one version, participants read that the sound quality of the radio set (i.e., a goal-relevant, primary aspect) was good, but that the clock that was incidentally included (i.e., a goal-irrelevant secondary aspect) was relatively useless. In another version, participants read that the sound quality of the radio set was poor, but that the clock aspect was quite useful. As expected, thinking about the radio set in the more distant future increased satisfaction when the sound quality was good and the clock poor, but decreased satisfaction when the sound quality was poor and the clock good, indicating that time delay increased the weight of central features and decreased the weight of peripheral features (for related findings in persuasion contexts, see Fujita, Eyal, Chaiken, Trope, & Liberman, 2008). Conceptually similar findings were obtained with social distance, operationalized as interpersonal similarity (Liviatan, Trope, & Liberman, 2008) and social power (Smith & Trope, 2006).

Interestingly, research that compared the decisions people make for themselves to the advice they give to others obtained similar findings. Kray and Gonzalez (1999) and Kray (2000) compared participants' own choices to the advice they gave to socially close and distant others. They found that in advising others, especially socially remote others, participants tended to give more weight to a single attribute which they designated as the most important and less weight to other, more peripheral attributes. For example, when advising another person about choosing between two jobs, participants gave more weight to personal satisfaction (which they viewed as the most important dimension) and less weight to salary and location (the less important dimensions) than when choosing for themselves (Kray, 2000, Study 2). In two other studies, Kray found that this preferential weighting of important attributes was stronger in advising a distant social target (a student in another department) than a closer target (a student in one's own class). Moreover, as advisers, participants rated central attributes as highly important and peripheral ones as unimportant, whereas as deciders they rated the various attributes as relatively similar in importance. In our terms, these findings demonstrate choosing according to more central, high-level aspects for socially distant than social close others.

Goal-dependent importance

As we noted earlier in the discussion of categorization, importance is goal-dependent. When on a diet, caloric value of food becomes primary and its color secondary, but when decorating a plate for a fancy reception, the relative importance of these aspects might reverse. If goal change reverses the relative importance of aspects, then the effect of distance would likewise depend on goals. Support for this prediction comes from a study

that independently manipulated affective and cognitive value, temporal distance, and goals (Trope & Liberman, 2000, Study 5). The study assessed desirability ratings of four films, varying in affective value (funniness) and cognitive value (informativeness). The films were, thus, funny and informative, funny but uninformative, not funny but informative, or neither funny nor informative. Some of the participants expected to watch the films in the same experimental session (i.e., near future), whereas other participants expected to watch them in the second session of the study, 2 months later (i.e., distant future). The goal of watching the films was also manipulated: it was either affective (getting oneself into a good mood) or cognitive (learning about a topic). We assumed that the features of the film that are related to the goal would be more central than the goal-irrelevant aspects, and thus would constitute a high-level construal of the film. Thus, depending on the goal, either affective aspects or cognitive aspects of the films were more central (constituted the high-level construal of the films), whereas the other type of features was rendered goal-irrelevant, and thus part of the low-level construal of the films. Consistent with the predictions of CLT, we found that temporal distance increased the influence of the informativeness versus the funniness of the films when the goal was cognitive, but decreased the influence of informativeness versus the funniness of the films when the goal was affective: i.e., psychological distance increased the importance of the goal-relevant aspect of the film over the goal-irrelevant aspect.

Alternatives versus attributes in choice matrices

Prior to making a decision, people often search for information on the available alternatives. Decision theoretic work has distinguished between searching within attributes – across alternatives and searching within alternatives – across attributes (Tversky, 1972). In a typical study, participants are presented with a matrix of information in which rows represent alternatives (e.g., different apartments), columns represent attributes (e.g., price, location, noise), and cells include the standing of each alternative on the corresponding attribute. Participants search this matrix by exposing the information in each cell, one at a time (see Payne, Bettman, & Johnson, 1988, for a review of this paradigm).

Borovoi, Liberman, and Trope (2010) found that when presented with a choice matrix, participants think of attributes as being more central than alternatives. For example, they tend to think that deleting an entire column (i.e., deleting information on the standing of all the alternatives on a certain attribute) would change the choice situation more than deleting an entire row (i.e., deleting all information on one of the alternatives). Notably, it is probably the case that distance typically changes the alternatives in a choice set more than it changes the attributes. For example, when looking for an apartment in a different place or a long time in advance, the alternatives might be unknown, but the dimensions (e.g., price, location, and size) most likely remain similar to those that apply to proximal sets.

Based on CLT, Borovoi et al. (2010) predicted that within-attribute search would characterize processing of distal decision situations, whereas within-alternative search would characterize processing of proximal decision situations. They tested this prediction with both temporal and social distances. In a study on temporal distance, participants considered a choice for either the near future (e.g., choosing an apartment to rent in the following two weeks) or the distant future (e.g., choosing an apartment to rent a year later). In a study on social distance, participants considered a choice either for themselves or for another student. As expected, there were more within-attribute steps and less within-alternative steps when making decisions for psychologically distal situations than for psychologically proximal situations. Importantly, in both studies participants opened an equal number of cells and invested a similar amount of time in both distance conditions, indicating that they were not less motivated in the distal condition than in the near condition.

Gestalt versus details

We tend to perceive Figure 12.2 as alternating lines of black and white. This perception is a classical demonstration of gestalt. More generally, according to the principle of gestalt, people tend to order their experience in a manner that is regular and simple. Two of the laws of gestalt – similarity and proximity – are of relevance in the example in Figure 12.2: they state, respectively, that similar elements are grouped together into collective entities, and elements that are spatially or temporally proximal to each other are grouped together (Koffka, 1935).

Perceiving a gestalt involves a decision that the elements that make it up are less important than their organization relative to each other. In Figure 12.2, perceiving black and white lines renders the circles that make up these lines unimportant – they could have been replaced by other shapes without affecting the gestalt. In that sense, a perception of a gestalt renders its elements secondary, low-level constructs.

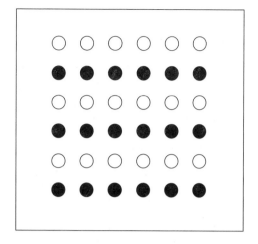

Figure 12.2   Gestalt principles of proximity and similarity.

As noted earlier, abstract categorization is achieved by making *some features of the exemplars which make up the category* primary and some secondary. A gestalt, on the other hand, is achieved by making *the relations between the elements* primary and their particular identities secondary. In that sense, the relation between a gestalt and its elements is not the same as that between a category and its exemplars. Nevertheless, in both cases a higher level of construal is achieved by assigning more importance to some elements of a stimulus than to others.

The laws of gestalt, which specify the conditions that promote organization of elements into gestalts, include, in addition to the laws of similarity and proximity, symmetry, continuity, and common fate. To the extent that all these promote perceptions of a gestalt, they also promote a perception of its elements as secondary, mutable, and relatively unimportant. In other words, the basic notion of gestalt – that the whole is more than the sum of its parts – also means that the parts are unimportant relative to the whole, a notion that might have a troubling flavor when applied to gestalts that are made of people, such as in human pyramids or in military parades.

Distance and composite letters (the Navon task)

Liberman and Förster (2009b) conducted a series of studies in which participants were primed with psychological distance or proximity and then completed the Navon (1977) task. In this well-known task, participants see a series of large letters (the gestalt) made up of smaller letters (the elements), and are asked to indicate as quickly as possible whether a target letter (e.g., *H*) appeared on the screen. As predicted, when primed to think about the distant future (Study 1), a distant spatial location (Study 2), and distant social relations (Study 3), participants were faster to indicate that a target letter (*H*) had appeared on the screen when it was the global (*H* made up of *L*s) vs the local (*L* made up of *H*s) letter. When primed with proximity in time, space, and social relations, participants were faster when the target letter was the local (vs global) letter.

To examine the reverse direction of influence – namely, that of global perception on estimated psychological distance – Liberman and Förster (2009a) procedurally primed participants with either global or local perceptual processing, using a variation of Navon's (1977) task. In the global priming condition, the target letters were always global, and in the local priming condition the target letters were always local, whereas in the control condition the targets were global in half of the trials and local in the other half. Relative to the control condition, global processing led to greater estimates of temporal distance, spatial distance, social distance, and hypotheticality. Local processing had the opposite effect. For example, participants who were primed with global processing estimated temporal distance to a dental visit as longer and spatial distance between themselves and a designated point in the room as larger than participants primed with local processing. In a related vein, Wakslak and Trope (2009) found that priming global processing (vs local processing) through the Navon task led participants to assign lower probability to a variety of everyday-life occurrences.

Distance and gestalt completion

In the Gestalt Completion Test (GCT; Street, 1931; see also Ekstrom, French, Harman, & Derman, 1976) participants are presented with fragmented images, and have to identify them. In this task, performance depends on detecting the global pattern, and attending to details interferes with performance. In a series of studies, participants completed what they believed to be sample items of the GCT, supposedly as a practice version before they performed the actual task. Participants' performance improved when they anticipated working on the actual task in the more distant future (Förster, Friedman, & Liberman, 2004), when they thought the actual task was less likely to take place (Wakslak et al., 2006), and when social distance was enhanced by priming of high social status (Smith & Trope, 2006). Thus, a psychologically distant perspective seems to enable people to better see the gestalt.

While distance improves the ability to perceive the gestalt in a visual array, it should have the opposite effect when the task requires attention to details. Distance should therefore have a detrimental effect on the ability to identify a missing local element within a coherent whole (e.g., a missing hand on a watch, a missing handle on a drawer chest). Wakslak et al. (2006) used the picture completion subtest of the Wechsler Intelligence Scale for Children (WISC; Wechsler, 1991) to test this prediction. As expected, participants did worse on sample items of this task when they believed they were less likely to later complete it.

Segmentation

Segments of continuous events (e.g., events in a movie; stages of a disease) may be regarded as elements of a gestalt that are grouped together due to proximity and continuity. Distance should, therefore, interfere with isolating segments of continuous events. Consistent with this idea, two studies have found that when ongoing events were described as psychologically distal, they were chunked into broader and fewer segments than when they were described as psychologically proximal. In the first study participants watched an animated film clip depicting two triangles and a circle (Heider & Simmel, 1944) and segmented the clip into as many meaningful sections as they thought appropriate. Participants (New York University [NYU] undergraduates) were either told that the film portrayed the actions of three teenagers at a summer camp on the East Coast (spatial proximity condition) or the West Coast (spatial distance condition). As predicted based on the association between distance and level of construal, participants segmented the video into fewer, broader sections when they believed it portrayed a spatially distal (vs proximal) event (Henderson, Fujita, Trope, & Liberman, 2006). Converging evidence was found using subjective probability as a manipulation of psychological distance; unlikely (i.e., more distal) events were chunked into broader units than likely events (Wakslak et al., 2006).

Focal object versus context

The distinction between object and context assigns importance to one element of an array of information and renders the elements surrounding it less important. For example, when observing one's kid in a school yard, one would typically think of the child as the focal element and of the yard (and possibly of other kids) as the surrounding context. It is quite possible that the architect who designed the yard would have the opposite perception, viewing the yard as the focal object and the kids as context. In perception, the conceptually similar distinction between figure and ground assigns more importance to the figure and less importance to the ground: changing the ground or the context would be thought of as less substantial than changing the figure. As with other distinctions between more important and less important aspects of stimuli, the distinction between object and context maps onto level of construal: we consider a decontextualized construal of an object as being of a higher level than a construal rich in contextual detail.

Figure versus ground distinctions in visual input

In complex visual arrays, people tend to identify as the figure elements that are salient – by being bigger, brighter, and/or more mobile than others. For example, Masuda and Nisbett (2001) studied the context sensitivity of American and Japanese participants with animated vignettes of underwater scenes. The vignettes featured "focal fish," which were large, had lively colors and clear shapes, and moved actively. In contrast, the background included smaller water animals, which had pallid colors and unclear shapes, and moved more slowly, along with inert objects, such as vegetation and rocks.

Goal relevance is of course another determinant of figure/ground decisions. For example, if one is looking for the letter *B* among other letters, then *B* is the figure and the rest of the letters form the ground (or the context). CLT predicts that psychological distance would reduce attention to contextual elements and increase focus on the figure. For example, memory for the context (e.g., the nonfocal elements in a visual array) should be poorer if the visual array presents a place that is more geographically distal, a place to be visited in the more distant future, a place to be visited by a more distal person, or a place to be visited with less likelihood. To the best of our knowledge, this prediction still awaits empirical examination.

Dispositional versus situational attributions

In social psychology, the object vs context distinction has been applied to individuals behaving in a situation. A prominent example is Heider's (1958) classic notion that the behavior "engulfs the field" and the common finding that situational forces receive little attention from most observers of the behavior (at least in Western cultures), who identify the actor and his or her dispositions as the object and the situational forces as the (relatively less important) context (e.g., Jones, 1979).

Consistent with this analysis is the correspondence bias, whereby people tend to attribute the behaviors of others to internal, dispositional causes even when they are aware of situational constrains (Gilbert & Malone, 1995; Jones, 1979).

According to this analysis, dispositional factors constitute high-level construals, which should receive more weight with increased psychological distance, whereas situational factors constitute low-level construals, which should receive less weight with increased psychological distance. In other words, according to CLT, the correspondence bias should intensify with psychological distance. In line with this prediction is the actor–observer effect in attribution, which describes the tendency for people to attribute others' behaviors (e.g., failing an exam) to dispositional causes ("because he is stupid") while attributing one's own behaviors to situational causes ("because the exam was unfair"; e.g., Heider, 1958; Jones & Nisbett, 1987). This classic finding lends some support to construal-level theory's prediction, because others are, by definition, more distant than the self. However, differences in amount of information and/or differences in informational salience could account for these effects as well. Thus, an important question is whether psychological distance affects the tendency to give a dispositional attribution for an actor's situationally constrained behavior, controlling for the nature and amount of information given.

Nussbaum, Trope, and Liberman (2003) found an answer in the affirmative. Participants were students at an Israeli university, and they read an essay purportedly written by another student arguing in favor of Israel's withdrawal from Southern Lebanon (which was then occupied by Israel). In the constrained condition, participants were told that the writer was instructed to write the pro-withdrawal essay, and in the unconstrained condition, they were told that the writer was free to express his/her own opinion. Correspondent attitude inferences in the constrained condition were greater after participants had made judgments regarding the writers' distant (vs near) future behaviors. Henderson et al. (2006) replicated this effect manipulating spatial distance: that is, perceivers were more likely to ignore situational information and draw correspondent inferences when the actor was believed to be spatially remote vs proximal. Thus, increasing temporal or spatial distance of the actor's behavior increases the tendency for perceivers to draw correspondent inferences even when amount and type of information given is held constant.

Could the reverse direction of influence hold? That is, would making dispositional rather than situational attributions for actors' behaviors facilitate thinking about those actors as being temporally, spatially, or socially remote? Stephan, Liberman, and Trope (2010b) found support for this prediction with social distance. They found that participants who first provided a dispositional (vs situational) explanation for a person's action thought that the actor was less similar to them, and allocated him or her less of their resources. In another study (Stephan et al., 2010a), a similar manipulation made people address the actor in a more polite manner, signifying a greater sense of social distance.

It is worth noting that people from different cultures do not make as sharp a distinction between figure and ground (for reviews, see Nisbett, Peng, Choi, & Norenzayan, 2001; Norenzayan, Choi, & Peng, 2007). Thus, whereas individuals from West European and North American (independent) cultures process stimuli as isolated from the immediate context, individuals from Asian and South American (interdependent) cultures process stimuli in a more contextual manner, attending more to the relationships between the focal object and the field. Accordingly, people from interdependent cultures seem to be less prone to perform the correspondence bias (e.g., Miller, 1984; for reviews, see Choi et al., 1999; Norenzayan & Nisbett, 2000). It would be interesting to examine whether the effects of psychological distance on correspondent attribution would be attenuated or even reversed among individuals from interdependent cultures (as compared to independent cultures).

Contextual primes

Semantic primes influence the impressions and evaluations people form of other people (for reviews, see DeCoster & Claypool, 2004; Förster et al., 2007; Higgins, 1996). Those primes are oftentimes presented in the context of the target of evaluation. For example, in the classic study by Higgins, Rholes, and Jones (1977), participants' judgments of a person who engaged in risky behaviors were influenced by prior exposure to semantic primes: those who were first presented with words related to adventurousness (a positive construct) rated the target more positively than those primed with recklessness (a negative construct).

If, as CLT contends, distance focuses attention on an object and attenuates attention to its context, then it should also attenuate the effects of contextual primes. Henderson and Wakslak (2010) found support for this prediction. Building on Higgins et al.'s (1977) paradigm, they primed participants with words related to adventurousness or recklessness. They then presented them with pictures of individuals performing behaviors (skydiving,

motor biking) that are ambiguous with respect to being either adventurous or reckless. As predicted, judgments of the targets were influenced by the prime when the target was described as spatially close (Study 1) or as likely to repeat the behavior (Study 2), but not when the target was described as spatially distant or unlikely to repeat the behavior.

Subordination

Feature A is subordinate to feature B when A depends on B more than B depends on A. Consider, for example, arguments in favor of an action (pros) and against an action (cons). In deciding whether to undertake an action, cons are subordinate to pros because the subjective importance of cons depends on whether or not pros are present more than the subjective importance of pros depends on whether or not cons are present. For instance, if we know that a medical treatment has some health benefits (i.e., pros), we would inquire about its potential side effects (i.e., cons) before making a decision. But if the treatment has no benefits, we would decide against taking it without further inquiry about its side effects. In contrast, we would inquire whether a medical treatment has health benefits whether or not it has side effects. Thus, the importance of side effects depends on whether the treatment is known to have benefits, but the importance of benefits is independent of whether the treatment is known to have side effects. Subordinate features, more than superordinate features, may vary without changing the meaning of the object. Relations of subordination exist not only between arguments in favor and against an action, as just explained, but also between ends and means, desirability and feasibility, and value and probability in positive bets, as well as causes and effects.

Because subordination is a property that defines features as high level versus low level, we expect that superordinate features would be more salient relative to subordinate features as the psychological distance from the object increases. We now turn to examine how this prediction bears out with different manifestations of subordination. Because we believe that goals are especially important cognitive structures, we discuss subordination of goals in a separate section.

Arguments in favor versus against an action

As explained above, in deciding whether to undertake an action, cons are subordinate to pros, making pros higher-level construals than cons. Therefore, pros should become more salient as temporal distance from the action increases, whereas cons should become less salient as temporal distance from the action increases. Eyal, Liberman, Trope, and Walther (2004) asked participants to generate arguments in favor and against new (i.e., non-routine) near-future or distant-future actions, such as introducing a new exam procedure (e.g., switching to open-ended questions instead of multiple-choice questions, Study 2), social policies (e.g., restricting private cars in the city center, Study 3), and a variety of personal and interpersonal behaviors (e.g., approaching a fellow student and offering to write an assignment together, Studies 4–6). As predicted, in all the studies, participants generated more pros and less cons as temporal distance from the actions increased.

In an extension of these findings, Herzog, Hansen, and Wänke (2007) suggested that, if pros are more salient as temporal distance increases and cons are more salient as temporal distance decreases, then an increase in temporal distance should make it easier to generate pros and more difficult to generate cons. Furthermore, because attitudes tend to be more in line with content when the retrieval is experienced as easy (Wänke & Bless, 2000), the ease of retrieval associated with generating pros and cons of near- and distant-future activities should influence attitudes toward those activities, even when the number of arguments is held constant. In a test of these ideas, participants read about a proposed action that was to happen in the near or distant future, and were instructed to write down either four pros or four cons regarding the activity. As expected, participants (a) found it easier to generate pros and more difficult to generate cons when the issue concerned the distant rather than near future and (b) had more favorable attitudes toward the action when it was to occur in the distant future.

Value versus probability in positive bets

In the normative expected utility model, probability and payoffs combine multiplicatively and therefore have symmetric weight in determining the attractiveness of gambles. Our studies, however, have demonstrated that people tend to view the probability of winning as subordinate to the payoff: i.e., people tend to think that probability is important only if the payoff is high, but that payoff is important regardless of whether the probability of winning is high or low (Sagristano, Trope, & Liberman, 2002, Study 1). This establishes payoffs as pertaining to a higher construal level than probabilities, and entails a prediction by CLT that people would assign more weight to payoffs and less weight to probabilities in deciding for the more distant future.

A series of studies on preference for near- and distant-future gambles tested this prediction (Sagristano et al., 2002). For example, one of the studies assessed monetary bids for gambles to be played on the same day or 2 months later. Participants were presented with a set of 20 bets that varied in probability of winning (0.1, 0.3, 0.5, 0.7, and 0.9) within each of four levels of expected value ($4, $6, $8, and $10), and were asked to state the amount of money they were willing to bid to play each gamble. The prediction was that near-future participants would prefer to sacrifice payoff for better odds, whereas distant-future participants would be willing to risk poorer odds for higher payoffs. As expected, for near-future gambles, bids were higher for high-probability and low-payoff bets than for low-probability and high-payoff bets, whereas for distant-future gambles, bids were higher for low-probability and high-payoff bets than for high-probability and low-payoff bets.

It would be interesting to test whether other dimensions of psychological distance would have a similar effect. For example, would betting for another person rather than for oneself, buying tickets for a gamble that is unlikely to take place, or about outcomes taking place in other countries (e.g., the Football World Cup) rather than in one's own country make one prefer more risky bets?

Causes versus effects

Effects are subordinate to causes because, by definition, effects depend on causes but causes do not depend on effects. In the cognitive literature on concept representation and categorization, a concept's causal features are considered to be more central than its effect features, because causes are less mutable and afford greater inductive power (Ahn, 1998; Ahn, Kim, Lassaline, & Dennis, 2000; Kim & Ahn, 2002).

Would a psychologically distal perspective facilitate representation of events in terms of their underlying causes rather than effects? Rim, Hansen, and Trope (2010) found a relationship between temporal distance and the frequency of generating causes and effects. Participants were initially induced to be in a temporally distal or proximal mindset by imagining their lives 1 year later or the next day, respectively. Subsequently, they were asked to generate causes or effects for a series of events (e.g., getting a tooth cavity). Those in the temporally distal condition imagined the events as occurring on the day 1 year later, which they described before; those in the temporally proximal condition imagined the same events as occurring the next day. As predicted, participants generated more causes when they had been initially placed in a temporally distal mindset and imagined events as occurring at that distant-future time. They generated more effects when they had been placed in a temporally proximal mindset and imagined events as occurring at that near-future time. There is also evidence for the reverse direction of causality. One study showed that when participants generated causes (vs effects) for various events, they believed that the events were likely to take place in the more distant future. Additional studies extend these ideas using less obtrusive measures to examine spontaneity of inference generation and look into other instances of distance (e.g., spatial distance, social distance, power, and hypotheticality).

Subordination of goals

Actions can be represented in terms of the reasons *why* one performs an action, the ends, or in terms of *how* the action is performed, the means (Vallacher & Wegner, 1989). Means are subordinate to ends because means derive their value from ends rather than vice versa. For example, if I need to get a cab in order to get to the airport, then how important it is for me to get the cab derives from the importance of getting to the airport, but the importance of getting to the airport does not derive from the importance of getting the cab.

Research has found that, when given a choice, people tend to represent psychologically more distal actions in terms of high-level ends rather than low-level means. For example, participants tended to describe more distant future activities (e.g., *studying*) in high-level terms (e.g., *doing well in school*) rather than in low-level terms (e.g., *reading a textbook*; Liberman & Trope, 1998). Similar effects emerged when actions were to take place in a more spatially distant location (Fujita et al., 2006), when the actions were framed as less likely to actually take place (Wakslak et al., 2006), and when the actor was less similar to the perceiver (Liviatan et al., 2008).

It seems also that activating higher-level goals leads people to think of more psychologically distal events. For example, thinking about an activity in high-level, *why* terms rather than low-level, *how* terms led people to think of the activity as taking place in more distant points in time (Liberman, Trope, McCrea, & Sherman, 2007) and led to more delayed enactment (i.e., procrastination; McCrea, Liberman, Trope, & Sherman, 2008). Similarly, participants who described a target's actions in high-level, why terms (vs low-level, how terms) allocated to him or her less of their resources, which indicates greater social distance (Stephan et al., 2010b).

Desirability versus feasibility

When thinking about an action (e.g., attending a guest lecture), desirability refers to the value of the action's end state (e.g., how interesting the lecture is), whereas feasibility refers to the ease or difficulty of reaching the end state (e.g., how convenient the timing of the lecture is). The feasibility of an action is subordinate to its desirability, in that desirability is subjectively important whether the end state is feasible or not, but feasibility is important mainly when the end state is desirable. For example, if a guest lecture is interesting, we will consider attending it regardless of whether the timing is convenient or inconvenient. However, we will not consider attending a boring guest lecture just because its timing is convenient.

Desirability should therefore receive greater weight over feasibility concerns as psychological distance increases. Liberman and Trope (1998) examined this prediction as it pertains to temporal distance. Participants in one study (Study 2), for example, made decisions about three situations (e.g., deciding whether to attend a guest lecture) that they imagined occurring to them in either the near or distant future. For each situation, the desirability of the outcome (e.g., how interesting the lecture was) and its feasibility (e.g., how convenient the timing of the lecture was) were varied between participants. Consistent with CLT, results revealed that the effect of desirability increased over time, whereas the effect of feasibility decreased. Namely, the attractiveness of the options increased or decreased as a function of the source of the attractiveness: when outcomes were desirable but hard to obtain, they were more attractive when imagined to occur in the distant (vs near) future; when outcomes were less desirable but easy to obtain, they were more attractive when imagined to occur in the near (vs distant) future. Similar results have been found for other distance dimensions, including hypotheticality and social distance (e.g., Liviatan et al., 2008; Todorov, Goren, & Trope, 2007; see review by Liberman, Trope, & Stephan, 2007).

Values as guides of behavior

Values are commonly viewed as abstract, trans-situational guides for action (Schwartz & Bilsky, 1987). In our terms, values may be conceptualized as superordinate goals and thus should be more readily applied to and guide intentions for psychologically more distant situations. Eyal, Sagristano, Trope, Liberman, and Chaiken (2009) empirically examined this prediction. One study used Schwartz's (1992) value questionnaire to assess the importance participants assigned to a wide range of values (e.g., power, benevolence, hedonism), and then asked participants to imagine 30 behaviors (e.g., *rest as much as I can*) and to indicate the likelihood of performing each behavior either in the near future or in the distant future. Eyal et al. correlated the rated importance of each value and the mean likelihood of performing the behaviors corresponding to that value. As expected, these correlations were higher when the behaviors were planned for the distant rather than the near future, suggesting that people's values are better reflected in their intentions for the distant future than in their intentions for the immediate future or their actual behavior. For example, being high (vs low) in hedonism might mean planning hedonic activities for the distant future, but not necessarily for the upcoming week.

Extending this line of thought, Eyal, Liberman, and Trope (2008) argued that people judge immoral acts as more offensive and moral acts as more virtuous when the acts are psychologically distant than near. They showed that transgressions against core values that are deemed harmless due to extenuating circumstances (e.g., eating one's dead dog) were judged more severely when imagined from a more distant temporal or social perspective. Conversely, moral acts which might have had ulterior motives (e.g., adopting a disabled child when a government pays high adoption pensions) were judged more positively from temporal distance. The findings suggest that moral criteria are more likely to guide people's judgments of distant rather than proximal behaviors.

Ideology versus social influence
Ideologies, like values, can be conceptualized as superordinate goals, and, as such, constitute high-level constructs. The effect of ideology on people's actions and attitudes can be contrasted with social influence, which, from the perspective of the actor, can be considered as a contextual, low-level factor. CLT therefore predicts that social influence would be stronger when an attitude object is psychologically near, whereas the effect of one's ideology would be stronger with increasing psychological distance.

A series of studies by Ledgerwood, Trope, and Chaiken (2010) tested the hypothesis that attitudes would align with those of another person in the local social context more when psychological distance is low (vs high). For example, one of the studies (Study 3) used an anticipated interaction paradigm, in which participants read about a policy that would increase the deportation of illegal immigrants starting either the week after (near future) or the following year (distant future), and learned that their discussion partner was either in favor of or against deporting illegal immigrants. They then privately reported how likely they

would be to vote in favor of the policy. Participants' voting intentions shifted toward the interaction partner's attitude when the policy was set to be implemented in the near future, but not when it was to be implemented in the distant future. However, voting intentions more strongly reflected participants' previously assessed ideological values when the policy was to be implemented in the distant (vs near) future. Specifically, the more participants valued preserving the societal status quo, the more they supported a distant-future policy that would enforce the deportation of illegal immigrants.

Theories versus noise

Theories make predictions. From the perspective of the theory, non-predicted events are incidental and unimportant. For example, trait theories of human behavior hold that extraverted people would tend to behave in an extraverted way. From these theories' point of view, non-trait-related variations in extraversion are considered incidental and unimportant – they are noise. Of course, one theory's prediction is another theory's noise. For example, situation theories of human behaviors would hold that behavior is determined by situations, and that individual differences in behavior are incidental. In terms of CLT, events that are predicted by theories form higher-level construals, whereas noise, or theory-unpredicted events belong to the low level of construal.

Theories are meant to uncover regularities, and their usefulness for traversing distances is apparent – theories may help to predict the future, to understand the perspective of others, and to simulate hypothetical situations. According to CLT, psychological distance should increase the salience of theory-driven prediction and diminish the weight of noise. This should hold for both scientific prediction and lay theories, as we now turn to discuss.

Theory versus noise is scientific prediction
A study by Nussbaum, Liberman, and Trope (2006, Study 1) examined the confidence of advanced psychology students in replicating classic findings in psychology in either the near future or the distant future. For example, participants imagined entering a class at the university, either the next day or a year later (depending on experimental condition), handing the students a list of words to memorize, and then testing how well they remember it after moving some of the students to a different room. Participants estimated how likely it is that those tested in the same room

would outperform, on average, those that were moved to a different room, thus replicating the encoding specificity effect (Tulving & Thomson, 1973). Participants were more confident that they would replicate this effect when they imagined conducting the experiment in the distant future than in the near future, especially when reminded of the theory underlying prediction. The same pattern of results was obtained with other classic findings in social, cognitive, and developmental psychology (Nussbaum et al., 2006).

We predict similar effects for other distances – people would tend to feel that theories work better for other people, in distal times and places, and in hypothetical situations rather than in practice. From a closer perspective, noise would become more salient and would undermine confidence in prediction.

Global trends versus local deviations

Continuous processes sometimes show a clear global trend despite local deviations from that trend. For example, some experts contend that the globe is steadily warming over the last 100 years, although on a more local scale, some season in some places could be exceptionally cold. It is possible to see the global trend as a theory and the local deviation as noise and predict, based on CLT, that psychological distance would increase the salience of global trends and decrease the salience of local deviations.

In a study on spatial distance (Henderson et al., 2006), NYU participants viewed a series of graphs depicting information from the years 1999–2004 (e.g., average number of photocopies per student). The information was said to pertain to the NYU campus in Manhattan (spatially near condition) or to the NYU campus in Florence, Italy (spatially distant condition). Each graph showed either an upward or downward trend, with the final year (2004) always deviating from that global trend. Participants estimated the likelihood that the year 2005 would follow the global trend and the likelihood that it would follow the more recent local deviation. As expected, spatial distance enhanced the tendency to predict that the global trend would persist rather than the local deviation.

Extending the logic of these findings, we could expect that people would more readily predict from global trends when they think of the more distant future, when they think of hypothetical situations, and when they think of other people and strangers rather than themselves or close others. Global warming, for example, would be more readily detected in noisy data that pertains to spatially, temporally, and socially more distal situations, and in hypothetical data more than in real data. Recession, likewise, would be more clearly

detected from noisy signals in historical data than in current economic indicators.

Primacy versus recency effects

The primacy effect refers to the tendency to form impressions that are more sensitive to the information that is presented earlier in a sequence. In classic studies by Asch and others (Asch, 1946; Hamilton & Zanna, 1974), when positive traits (e.g., intelligent) were presented first and were followed by less positive traits (e.g., envious), participants formed a more favorable impression of the target than when the order was reversed. Different accounts of the primacy effect (Anderson, 1981; Anderson & Jacobson, 1965; Asch, 1946; Dreben, Fiske, & Hastie, 1979; Hamilton & Zanna, 1974) all suggest that traits encountered initially create expectations about the target, which further organize remaining traits into a coherent impression, imbuing meaning to these traits and shifting attention towards traits consistent with the schema and away from other traits. In some sense, the initial traits form a schema, or a mini-theory about the target of impression.

Based on a CLT, Eyal, Hoover, Fujita, and Nussbaum (2011) have proposed that psychological distance should enhance the primacy effect. In their study, participants read a description of an applicant for a job to begin the week after (near future) or 6 months later (distant future). The description included six traits, presented from positive (e.g., *intelligent*) to negative (e.g., *envious*), or vice versa. Participants in the distant-future condition formed more favorable impressions of the target when positive traits appeared first, displaying a primacy effect. Consistent with the predictions and contrary to the primacy effect, participants in the near-future condition formed more favorable impressions of the target when positive traits appeared last.

Self-construal

People have theories not only about the external world but also about themselves. They seek to maintain a sense of themselves as a single entity that has consistent and enduring qualities (Bem & Allen, 1974). As with other theories, CLT predicts that people would apply this view to a greater extent when they think about themselves from a psychologically more distant perspective (Wakslak, Nussbaum, Liberman, & Trope, 2008). Support for this prediction comes from several studies on temporal distance. Using Linville's (1985, 1987) and Donahue and colleagues' (1993) measures of self-complexity, Wakslak et al. found that self-descriptions were more structured and less complex (i.e., less "noisy") when they referred to a distant-future self than to a near-future self. Also related to this point is research by Pronin and Ross (2006), which shows that people more likely view their future and past selves than their present selves in terms of general personality traits. In a related study, Wakslak et al. (2008) asked participants to imagine themselves in different situations either in the near future or in the distant future, and indicate the extent to which their behavior in those situations would reflect each of the Big Five personality traits. It was found that in the distant future, compared to the near future, participants expected to exhibit their traits more consistently across situations. These findings suggest that the distant-future self is represented more in terms of theoretically coherent structures than the near-future self.

It would be interesting to examine in future research the effects of other distances on the self-concept. For example, would thinking of oneself in an unlikely situation or in a remote spatial location make one see oneself in a more coherent way? Does thinking about ourselves from another person's perspective make us see ourselves as more coherent and predictable?

Symbolic versus analog representations

The same object can be represented in a symbolic, digital way, or in an analogical way. Consider a simple example. "A $2 \times 3 \times 4 \ cm^3$ box" is a symbolic, digital representation of an object. To make an analog representation of this object, we could, for example, build a model of the box. Building the model inevitably imbues the symbolic representation of the box with incidental details, such as material, color, strength, and the means that hold the surfaces together. Any model or, for that matter, any simulation is bound to do the same: namely, add incidental details. Conversely, moving from an analog representation to a digital one strips the analog representation of irrelevant details (or rather, omits details that by the very act of moving to the digital representation are rendered irrelevant). In terms of CLT then, symbolic representations are of a higher construal level than analog representations, such as models and simulations. We examine the implications of this theorizing for the distinction between symbolic and embodied representations and between words and pictures.

Symbolic versus embodied representations
Theories of embodied cognition (Barsalou, 1999; Niedenthal, Barsalou, Winkielman, Krauth-Gruber,

& Ric, 2005; Winkielman, Niedenthal, & Oberman, 2008) suggest that mental representations are embodied: namely, involve motor and perceptual simulations (Barsalou, 2008). For example, when representing the concept "water," people simulate in their minds activities that involve interaction with water and include both motor and sensual information (e.g., drinking, swimming, walking in the rain, wiping a flooded floor). In support of this notion, research has shown, for instance, that when participants had to verify the plausibility of sentences including action–object pairs (e.g., "close the drawer"), they responded faster when the response was compatible with the action (e.g., when responding by pressing a button away from themselves, thereby requiring an extension of the arm) rather than incompatible with it (i.e., when responding by pressing a button located closer to themselves, requiring arm flexion; Glenberg & Kaschak, 2002). Thus, it seems that processing the sentences involved simulating the described action, a simulation which either facilitated or inhibited the required response. It was also found that, when processing sentences that describe motor actions, brain areas in the motor and premotor cortex are activated in a way corresponding to when performing those same actions (Hauk, Johnsrude, & Pulvermuller, 2004; Tettamanti et al., 2005).

Is it possible that as psychological distance increases, representation would be less embodied: i.e., would contain less perceptual and motor detail, and would be increasingly more symbolic? For example, in the experiment describe above, would the effect of action compatibility be attenuated if the sentences described actions performed by socially distal people as compared to socially close people?

Words versus pictures
Pictures are icons, analog representations of objects, whereas words are symbolic representations of objects (Amit, Algom, & Trope, 2009a; Amit, Algom, Trope, & Liberman, 2009b). An object's picture bears concrete resemblance to it and contains incidental details, whereas a word to describe the same object is abstract and captures its essence. Even a line drawing of an object is more concrete than a word representing the same object.

Consistent with CLT, participants were faster to identify spatially, temporally, and socially proximal (vs distal) pictures and faster to identify spatially, temporally, and socially distal (vs proximal) words on a speeded identification task (Amit et al., 2009a). Furthermore, distance affected memory for pictures vs words. Using various dimensions of psychological distance (spatial, temporal, and social), Amit, Trope, Rim, and Algom (2010) found that proximal pictures were remembered better than distal pictures, and distal words were remembered better than proximal words. Thus, words and pictures behave like other dimensions of high- and low-level construal and are associated with distance and proximity, respectively.

CONCLUSION

Understanding the nature of mental construal is a central goal of many fields in psychology. One dimension on which construals vary is veridicality – the extent of correspondence between construals and the objective attributes of the objects they represent. Understanding what makes construal more or less veridical has been central to the study of perception, cognition, social psychology, and decision making. Another dimension on which construals vary is level, which we defined as the extent of reduction to primary elements that are central to a representation and omission of incidental elements. We reviewed various manifestations of level of construal that differ in the mapping of their features onto importance: categorization, primary and secondary aspects, gestalt, distinguishing a figure from its context, subordination, theories versus noise, and digitization of construals. Across these different manifestations of level of construal, we suggest that the perspective of construal level enriches our understanding of the constructs.

NOTE

1   Unlike "representation," "construal" conveys an active process rather than a passive reflection of reality. This is the standard view in psychology – even perceptual processes are subject to "top down" influences by prior knowledge, conditioning, and expectations.

REFERENCES

Ahn, W. (1998). Why are different features central for natural kinds and artifacts? The role of causal status in determining feature centrality. *Cognition, 69*(2), 135–178. doi:S0010027798000638

Ahn, W. K., Kim, N. S., Lassaline, M. E., & Dennis, M. J. (2000). Causal status as a determinant of feature

centrality. *Cognitive Psychology, 41*(4), 361–416. doi:10.1006/cogp.2000.0741

Amit, E., Algom, D., & Trope, Y. (2009a). Distance-dependent processing of pictures and words. *Journal of Experimental Psychology: General, 138*(3), 400–415. doi:10.1037/a0015835

Amit, E., Algom, D., Trope, Y., & Liberman, N. (2009b). "Thou shalt not make unto thee any graven image": The distance dependence of representation. In K. D. Markman, W. M. P. Klein, & J. A. Suhr (Eds.), *Handbook of imagination and mental simulation* (pp. 53–68). New York: Psychology Press.

Amit, E., Trope, Y., Rim, S., & Algom, D. (2010). *Do you remember seeing it or reading about it? The distance dependence of memory for pictures and words.* Manuscript submitted for publication.

Anderson, N. H. (1981). *Foundation of information integration theory.* New York: Academic Press.

Anderson, N. H., & Jacobson, A. (1965). Effect of stimulus inconsistency and discounting instructions in personality impression formation. *Journal of Personality and Social Psychology, 2*(4), 531–539. doi:10.1037/h0022484

Asch, S. E. (1946). Forming impressions of personality. *The Journal of Abnormal and Social Psychology, 41*(3), 258–290. doi:10.1037/h0055756

Balcetis, E., & Dunning, D. (2006). See what you want to see: Motivational influences on visual perception. *Journal of Personality and Social Psychology, 91*(4), 612–625. doi:10.1037/0022-3514.91.4.612

Barsalou, L. W. (1999). Perceptual symbol systems. *Behavioral and Brain Sciences, 22*(4), 577–660.

Barsalou, L. W. (2008). Grounded cognition. *Annual Review of Psychology, 59*, 617–645. doi:10.1146/annurev.psych.59.103006.093639

Bem, D. J., & Allen, A. (1974). On predicting some of the people some of the time: The search for cross-situational consistencies in behavior. *Psychological Review, 81*(6), 506–520. doi:10.1037/h0037130

Borovoi, L., Liberman, N., & Trope, Y. (2010). *The effect of psychological distance on information search in decision making.* Unpublished manuscript, Tel Aviv University, Israel.

Choi, I., Nisbett, R. E., & Norenzayan, A. (1999). Causal attribution across cultures: Variation and universality. *Psychological Bulletin, 125*(1), 47–63.

DeCoster, J., & Claypool, H. M. (2004). A meta-analysis of priming effects on impression formation supporting a general model of informational biases. *Personality and Social Psychology Review, 8*(1), 2–27.

Donahue, E. M., Robins, R. W., Roberts, B. W., & John, O. P. (1993). The divided self: Concurrent and longitudinal effects of psychological adjustment and social roles on self-concept differentiation. *Journal of Personality and Social Psychology, 64*(5), 834–846. doi:10.1037/0022-3514.64.5.834

Dreben, E. K., Fiske, S. T., & Hastie, R. (1979). The independence of evaluative and item information: Impression and recall order effects in behavior-based impression formation.

Journal of Personality and Social Psychology, 37(10), 1758–1768. doi:10.1037/0022-3514.37.10.1758

Ekstrom, R. B., French, J. W., Harman, H. H., & Derman, D. (1976). *Manual for kit of factor-referenced cognitive tests.* Princeton, NJ: Educational Testing Service.

Elias, S., & Shapiro-Pavlovsky, A. (2009). *The sense of power as psychological distance: Implications for analogical thinking.* Unpublished manuscript, The Open University of Israel.

Eyal, T., Hoover, G. M., Fujita, K., & Nussbaum, S. (2011). The effect of distance-dependent construals on schema-driven impression formation. *Journal of Experimental Social Psychology, 47*(1), 278–281. doi:10.1016/j.jesp.2010.10.007

Eyal, T., Liberman, N., & Trope, Y. (2008). Judging near and distant virtue and vice. *Journal of Experimental Social Psychology, 44*(4), 1204–1209. doi:10.1016/j.jesp.2008.03.012

Eyal, T., Liberman, N., Trope, Y., & Walther, E. (2004). The pros and cons of temporally near and distant action. *Journal of Personality and Social Psychology, 86*(6), 781–795. doi:10.1037/0022-3514.86.6.781

Eyal, T., Sagristano, M. D., Trope, Y., Liberman, N., & Chaiken, S. (2009). When values matter: Expressing values in behavioral intentions for the near vs. distant future. *Journal of Experimental Social Psychology, 45*(1), 35–43. doi:10.1016/j.jesp.2008.07.023

Fiedler, K., Semin, G. R., Finkenauer, C., & Berkel, I. (1995). Actor–observer bias in close relationships: The role of self-knowledge and self-related language. *Personality and Social Psychology Bulletin, 21*(5), 525–538.

Förster, J., Friedman, R. S., & Liberman, N. (2004). Temporal construal effects on abstract and concrete thinking: Consequences for insight and creative cognition. *Journal of Personality and Social Psychology, 87*(2), 177–189. doi:10.1037/0022-3514.87.2.177

Förster, J., Liberman, N., & Friedman, R. S. (2007). Seven principles of goal activation: A systematic approach to distinguishing goal priming from priming of non-goal constructs. *Personality and Social Psychology Review, 11*(3), 211–233. doi:10.1177/1088868307303029

Förster, J., Liberman, N., & Kuschel, S. (2008). The effect of global versus local processing styles on assimilation versus contrast in social judgment. *Journal of Personality and Social Psychology, 94*(4), 579–599. doi:10.1037/0022-3514.94.4.579

Frege, G. (1980). On sense and meaning. In P. Geach & M. Black (Eds.), *Translations from the philosophical writings of Gottlob Frege* (3rd ed., pp. 578–6). Oxford: Blackwell (Original work published 1892).

Fujita, K., Eyal, T., Chaiken, S., Trope, Y., & Liberman, N. (2008). Influencing attitudes toward near and distant objects. *Journal of Experimental Social Psychology, 227*(21), 9044–9062. doi:10.1016/j.jesp.2007.10.005

Fujita, K., Henderson, M. D., Eng, J., Trope, Y., & Liberman, N. (2006). Spatial distance and mental construal of social events. *Psychological Science, 17*(4), 278–282.

Gentner, D. (1983). Structure-mapping: A theoretical framework for analogy. *Cognitive Science: A Multidisciplinary Journal, 7*(2), 155–170.

Gentner, D., & Colhoun, J. (2010). Analogical processes in human thinking and learning. In B. Glatzeder, V. Goel, & A. Müller (Eds.), *On thinking: Vol. 2. Towards a theory of thinking* (pp. 35–48). Berlin: Springer.

Gentner, D., & Toupin, C. (1986). Systematicity and surface similarity in the development of analogy. *Cognitive Science, 10*(3), 277–300.

Gilbert, D. T., & Malone, P. S. (1995). The correspondence bias. *Psychological Bulletin, 117*(1), 21–38.

Glenberg, A. M., & Kaschak, M. P. (2002). Grounding language in action. *Psychonomic Bulletin & Review, 9*(3), 558–565.

Griffin, D. W., & Ross, L. (1991). Subjective construal, social inference, and human misunderstanding. *Advances in Experimental Social Psychology, 24,* 319–359.

Hamilton, D. L., & Zanna, M. P. (1974). Context effects in impression formation: Changes in connotative meaning. *Journal of Personality and Social Psychology, 29*(5), 649–654. doi:10.1037/h0036633

Hauk, O., Johnsrude, I., & Pulvermuller, F. (2004). Somatotopic representation of action words in human motor and premotor cortex. *Neuron, 41*(2), 301–307.

Heider, F. (1958). *The psychology of interpersonal relations.* Mahwah, NJ: Lawrence Erlbaum Associates. doi:10.1037/10628-000.

Heider, F., & Simmel, M. (1944). An experimental study of apparent behavior. *The American Journal of Psychology, 57,* 243–259 . doi:10.2307/1416950

Henderson, M. D., Fujita, K., Trope, Y., & Liberman, N. (2006). Transcending the "here": The effect of spatial distance on social judgment. *Journal of Personality and Social Psychology, 91*(5), 845–856. doi:10.1037/0022-3514.91.5.845

Henderson, M. D., & Wakslak, C. J. (2010). Psychological distance and priming: When do semantic primes impact social evaluations? *Personality and Social Psychology Bulletin, 36*(7), 975–985. doi:10.1177/0146167210367490

Herzog, S. M., Hansen, J., & Wänke, M. (2007). Temporal distance and ease of retrieval. *Journal of Experimental Social Psychology, 43*(3), 483–488. doi:10.1016/j.jesp.2006.05.008

Hewstone, M., Rubin, M., & Willis, H. (2002). Intergroup bias. *Annual Review of Psychology, 53,* 575–604.

Higgins, E. T. (1996). The "self digest": Self-knowledge serving self-regulatory functions. *Journal of Personality and Social Psychology, 71*(6), 1062–1083. doi:10.1037/0022-3514.71.6.1062

Higgins, E. T., Rholes, W. S., & Jones, C. R. (1977). Category accessibility and impression-formation. *Journal of Experimental Social Psychology, 13*(2), 141–154.

Hilton, J. L., & von Hippel, W. (1996). Stereotypes. *Annual Review of Psychology, 47,* 237–271.

Holyoak, K. J. (2005). Analogy. In K. J. Holyoak & R. G. Morrison (Eds.), *The Cambridge handbook of thinking and reasoning* (pp. 117–142). New York: Cambridge University Press .

Jones, E. E. (1979). Rocky road from acts to dispositions. *American Psychologist, 34*(2), 107–117.

Jones, E. E., & Davis, K. E. (1965). From acts to dispositions: The attribution process in person perception. *Advances in Experimental Social Psychology, 2*(4), 219–266.

Jones, E. E., & Nisbett, R. E. (1987). The actor and the observer: Divergent perceptions of the causes of behavior. In E. E. Jones, D. E. Kanouse, H. H. Kelley, R. E. Nisbett, S. Valins, & B. Weiner (Eds.), *Attribution: Perceiving the causes of behavior* (pp. 79–94). Hillsdale, NJ: Lawrence Erlbaum Associates .

Kim, N. S., & Ahn, W. K. (2002). Clinical psychologists' theory-based representations of mental disorders predict their diagnostic reasoning and memory. *Journal of Experimental Psychology: General, 131*(4), 451–476. doi:10.1037/0096-3445.131.4.451

Koffka, K. (1935). *Principles of Gestalt psychology.* Oxford, England: Harcourt, Brace.

Kray, L., & Gonzalez, R. (1999). Differential weighting in choice versus advice: I'll do this, you do that. *Journal of Behavioral Decision Making, 12*(3), 207–217.

Kray, L. J. (2000). Contingent weighting in self-other decision making. *Organizational Behavior and Human Decision Processes, 83*(1), 82–106. doi:10.1006/obhd.2000.2903

Ledgerwood, A., Trope, Y., & Chaiken, S. (2010). Flexibility now, consistency later: Psychological distance and con-strual shape evaluative responding. *Journal of Personality and Social Psychology, 99*(1), 32–51. doi:10.1037/a0019843

Liberman, N., & Förster, J. (2009a). Distancing from experi-enced self: How global-versus-local perception affects estimation of psychological distance. *Journal of Personality and Social Psychology, 97*(2), 203–216. doi:10.1037/a0015671

Liberman, N., & Förster, J. (2009b). The effect of psycho-logical distance on perceptual level of construal. *Cognitive Science: A Multidisciplinary Journal, 33*(7), 1330–1341.

Liberman, N., Sagristano, M. C., & Trope, Y. (2002). The effect of temporal distance on level of construal. *Journal of Experimental Social Psychology, 38,* 523–534.

Liberman, N., & Trope, Y. (1998). The role of feasibility and desirability considerations in near and distant future deci-sions: A test of temporal construal theory. *Journal of Personality and Social Psychology, 75*(1), 5–18.

Liberman, N., & Trope, Y. (2008). The psychology of tran-scending the here and now. *Science, 322*(5905), 1201–1205. doi:10.1126/science.1161958

Liberman, N., Trope, Y., McCrea, S. M., & Sherman, S. J. (2007). The effect of level of construal on the temporal distance of activity enactment. *Journal of Experimental Social Psychology, 43*(1), 143–149. doi:10.1016/j.jesp.2005.12.009

Liberman, N., Trope, Y., & Stephan, E. (2007). Psychological distance. In E. T. Higgins & A. Kruglanski (Eds.), *Social psychology: Handbook of basic principles* (Vol. 2, pp. 353–381). New York: Guilford Press .

Linville, P. W. (1985). Self-complexity and affective extremity: Don't put all of your eggs in one cognitive basket. *Social Cognition, 3*(1), 94–120.

Linville, P. W. (1987). Self-complexity as a cognitive buffer against stress-related illness and depression. *Journal of Personality and Social Psychology, 52*(4), 663–676.

Liviatan, I., Trope, Y., & Liberman, N. (2008). Interpersonal similarity as a social distance dimension: Implications for perception of others' actions. *Journal of Experimental Social Psychology, 44*(5), 1256–1269. doi:10.1016/j.jesp.2008.04.007

Markman, A. B., & Gentner, D. (1993). Structural alignment during similarity comparisons. *Cognitive Psychology, 25*(4), 431–467. doi:10.1006/cogp.1993.1011

Masuda, T., & Nisbett, R. E. (2001). Attending holistically versus analytically: Comparing the context sensitivity of Japanese and Americans. *Journal of Personality and Social Psychology, 81*(5), 922–934. doi:10.1037//0022-3514.81.5.922

McCrea, S. M., Liberman, N., Trope, Y., & Sherman, S. J. (2008). Construal level and procrastination. *Psychological Science, 19*(12), 1308–1314. doi:10.1111/j.1467-9280.2008.02240.x

Mellers, B. A. (1982). Equity judgment: A revision of Aristotelian views. *Journal of Experimental Psychology: General, 111*(2), 242–270. doi:10.1037/0096-3445.111.2.242

Mellers, B. A. (1986). Fair allocations of salaries and taxes. *Journal of Experimental Psychology: Human Perception and Performance, 12*(1), 80–91.

Mellers, B. A., & Birnbaum, M. H. (1982). Loci of contextual effects in judgment. *Journal of Experimental Psychology: Human Perception and Performance, 8*(4), 582–601.

Miller, J. G. (1984). Culture and the development of everyday social explanation. *Journal of Personality and Social Psychology, 46*(5), 961–978.

Mussweiler, T. (2001). 'Seek and ye shall find': Antecedents of assimilation and contrast in social comparison. *European Journal of Social Psychology, 31*(5), 499–509.

Navon, D. (1977). Forest before trees: Precedence of global features in visual perception. *Cognitive Psychology, 9*(3), 353–383.

Niedenthal, P. M., Barsalou, L. W., Winkielman, P., Krauth-Gruber, S., & Ric, F. (2005). Embodiment in attitudes, social perception, and emotion. *Personality and Social Psychology Review, 9*(3), 184–211. doi:10.1207/s15327957pspr0903_1

Nisbett, R. E., Peng, K. P., Choi, I., & Norenzayan, A. (2001). Culture and systems of thought: Holistic versus analytic cognition. *Psychological Review, 108*(2), 291–310. doi:10.1037//0033-295X.108.2.291

Norenzayan, A., Choi, I., & Peng, K. (2007). Perception and cognition. In S. Kitayama & D. Cohen (Eds.), *Handbook of cultural psychology* (pp. 569–594). New York: Guilford Press .

Norenzayan, A., & Nisbett, R. E. (2000). Culture and causal cognition. *Current Directions in Psychological Science, 9*(4), 132–135.

Nussbaum, S., Liberman, N., & Trope, Y. (2006). Predicting the near and distant future. *Journal of Experimental Psychology: General, 135*(2), 152–161. doi:10.1037/0096-3445.135.2.152

Nussbaum, S., Trope, Y., & Liberman, N. (2003). Creeping dispositionism: The temporal dynamics of behavior prediction. *Journal of Personality and Social Psychology, 84*(3), 485–497. doi:10.1037/0022-3514.84.3.485

Oishi, S., Wyer, R. S., & Colcombe, S. J. (2000). Cultural variation in the use of current life satisfaction to predict the future. *Journal of Personality and Social Psychology, 78*(3), 434–445. doi:10.1037//0022-3514.78.3.434

Oyserman, D., Coon, H. M., & Kemmelmeier, M. (2002). Rethinking individualism and collectivism: Evaluation of theoretical assumptions and meta-analyses. *Psychological Bulletin, 128*(1), 3–72. doi:10.1037/0033-2909.128.1.3

Parducci, A. (1965). Category judgment: A range-frequency model. *Psychological Review, 72*(6), 407–418.

Parducci, A. (1974). Contextual effects: A range-frequency analysis. In E. Carterette & M. Friedman (Eds.), *Handbook of perception* (pp. 127–141). New York: Academic Press .

Parducci, A., Perrett, D. S., & Marsh, H. W. (1969). Assimilation and contrast as range-frequency effects of anchors. *Journal of Experimental Psychology, 81*(2), 281–288.

Parducci, A., & Wedell, D. H. (1986). The category effect with rating scales: Number of categories, number of stimuli, and method of presentation. *Journal of Experimental Psychology: Human Perception and Performance, 12*(4), 496–516.

Payne, J. W., Bettman, J. R., & Johnson, E. J. (1988). Adaptive strategy selection in decision making. *Journal of Experimental Psychology: Learning Memory and Cognition, 14*(3), 534–552.

Pronin, E., & Ross, L. (2006). Temporal differences in trait self-ascription: When the self is seen as an other. *Journal of Personality and Social Psychology, 90*(2), 197–209.

Rim, S., Hansen, J., & Trope, Y. (2010). *Causes and effects of psychologically distant and near events.* Unpublished manuscript, New York University.

Rim, S., Uleman, J. S., & Trope, Y. (2009). Spontaneous trait inference and construal level theory: Psychological distance increases nonconscious trait thinking. *Journal of Experimental Social Psychology, 45*(5), 1088–1097. doi:10.1016/j.jesp.2009.06.015

Sagristano, M. D., Trope, Y., & Liberman, N. (2002). Time-dependent gambling: Odds now, money later. *Journal of Experimental Psychology: General, 131*(3), 364–376.

Schwartz, S. H. (1992). Universals in the content and structure of values: Theoretical advances and empirical tests in 20 countries. In M. P. Zanna (Ed.), *Advances in experimental social psychology* (Vol. 25, pp. 1–65). San Diego, CA: Academic Press .

Schwartz, S. H., & Bilsky, W. (1987). Toward a universal psychological structure of human values. *Journal of Personality and Social Psychology, 53*(3), 550–562.

Schwarz, N., & Bless, H. (1992). Scandals and the public's trust in politicians: Assimilation and contrast effects. *Personality and Social Psychology Bulletin, 18*(5), 574–579.

Schwarz, N., & Bless, H. (2007). Mental construal processes: The inclusion/exclusion model. In D. A. Stapel & J. Suls (Eds.), *Assimilation and contrast in social psychology* (pp. 119–141). New York: Psychology Press .

Semin, G. R., & Fiedler, K. (1988). The cognitive functions of linguistic categories in describing persons: Social cognition and language. *Journal of Personality and Social Psychology, 54*(4), 558–568.

Semin, G. R., & Fiedler, K. (1989). Relocating attributional phenomena within a language–cognition interface: The case of actors and observers perspectives. *European Journal of Social Psychology, 19*(6), 491–508.

Semin, G. R., & Smith, E. R. (1999). Revisiting the past and back to the future: Memory systems and the linguistic representation of social events. *Journal of Personality and Social Psychology, 76*(6), 877–892.

Smith, P. K., & Trope, Y. (2006). You focus on the forest when you're in charge of the trees: Power priming and abstract information processing. *Journal of Personality and Social Psychology, 90*(4), 578–596. doi:10.1037/0022-3514.90.4.578

Stephan, E. (2006). *Social distance and its relations to level of construal, temporal distance, and spatial distance.* Unpublished doctoral dissertation, Tel Aviv University, Israel.

Stephan, E., Liberman, N., & Trope, Y. (2010a). Politeness and psychological distance: A construal level perspective. *Journal of Personality and Social Psychology, 98*(2), 268–280. doi:10.1037/a0016960

Stephan, E., Liberman, N., & Trope, Y. (2010b). The effects of time perspective and level of construal on social distance. *Journal of Experimental Social Psychology.* doi:10.1016/j.jesp.2010.11.001

Street, R. F. (1931). A Gestalt completion test. *Teachers College Contributions to Education, 481*, vii.

Tettamanti, M., Buccino, G., Saccuman, M. C., Gallese, V., Danna, M., Scifo, P., et al. (2005). Listening to action-related sentences activates fronto-parietal motor circuits. *Journal of Cognitive Neuroscience, 17*(2), 273–281.

Todorov, A., Goren, A., & Trope, Y. (2007). Probability as a psychological distance: Construal and preferences. *Journal of Experimental Social Psychology, 43*(3), 473–482. doi:10.1016/j.jesp.2006.04.002

Todorov, A., & Uleman, J. S. (2003). The efficiency of binding spontaneous trait inferences to actors' faces. *Journal of Experimental Social Psychology, 39*(6), 549–562. doi:10.1016/S0022-1031(03)00059-3

Trope, Y., & Liberman, N. (2000). Temporal construal and time-dependent changes in preference. *Journal of Personality and Social Psychology, 79*(6), 876–889.

Trope, Y., & Liberman, N. (2010). Construal-level theory of psychological distance. *Psychological Review, 117*(2), 440–463. doi:10.1037/a0018963

Tulving, E., & Thomson, D. M. (1973). Encoding specificity and retrieval processes in episodic memory. *Psychological Review, 80*(5), 352–373.

Tversky, A. (1972). Elimination by aspects: A theory of choice. *Psychological Review, 79*(4), 281–299.

Vallacher, R. R., & Wegner, D. M. (1989). Levels of personal agency: Individual variation in action identification. *Journal of Personality and Social Psychology, 57*(4), 660–671.

Vallone, R. P., Ross, L., & Lepper, M. R. (1985). The hostile media phenomenon: Biased perception and perceptions of media bias in coverage of the Beirut massacre. *Journal of*

Personality and Social Psychology, 49(3), 577–585. doi:10.1037/0022-3514.49.3.577

Wakslak, C., & Trope, Y. (2009). The effect of construal level on subjective probability estimates. *Psychological Science, 20*(1), 52–58. doi:10.1111/j.1467-9280.2008.02250.x

Wakslak, C. J., Nussbaum, S., Liberman, N., & Trope, Y. (2008). Representations of the self in the near and distant future. *Journal of Personality and Social Psychology, 95*(4), 757–773. doi:10.1037/a0012939

Wakslak, C. J., Trope, Y., Liberman, N., & Alony, R. (2006). Seeing the forest when entry is unlikely: Probability and the mental representation of events. *Journal of Experimental Psychology: General, 135*(4), 641–653. doi:10.1037/0096-3445.135.4.641

Wänke, M., & Bless, H. (2000). The effects of subjective ease of retrieval on attitudinal judgments: The moderating role of processing motivation. In H. Bless & J. P. Forgas (Eds.), *The message within: The role of subjective experience in social cognition and behavior* (pp. 143–161). New York: Psychology Press .

Wechsler, D. (1991). *Wechsler Intelligence Scale for Children* (3rd ed.). San Antonio, TX: Psychological Corporation.

Wedell, D. H., Parducci, A., & Geiselman, R. E. (1987). A formal analysis of ratings of physical attractiveness: Successive contrast and simultaneous assimilation. *Journal of Experimental Social Psychology, 23*(3), 230–249.

Wedell, D. H., Parducci, A., & Lane, M. (1990). Reducing the dependence of clinical judgment on the immediate context: Effects of number of categories and type of anchors. *Journal of Personality and Social Psychology, 58*(2), 319–329.

Winkielman, P., Niedenthal, P. M., & Oberman, L. (2008). The embodied emotional mind. In G. R. Semin & E. R. Smith (Eds.), *Embodied grounding: Social, cognitive, affective, and neuroscientific approaches* (pp. 263–288). New York: Cambridge University Press .

Winter, L., & Uleman, J. S. (1984). When are social judgments made? Evidence for the spontaneousness of trait inferences. *Journal of Personality and Social Psychology, 47*(2), 237–252.

Winter, L., Uleman, J. S., & Cunniff, C. (1985). How automatic are social judgments. *Journal of Personality and Social Psychology, 49*(4), 904–917.

13

Judgment and Decision Making

David Dunning

People often find themselves in situations in which they must judge what is likely to be true versus false, probable versus improbable, and desirable versus undesirable. Then, based on these assessments, they must decide on a course of action to take. They must calculate whether to go on a diet, invest in that trendy new stock, or to sell their car to this particular customer. In a sense, this type of thinking sounds much like social cognition itself, in that people weigh the information in front of them and then come to some sort of conclusion that ultimately leads to action – and scholars have argued, forcefully, that the type of thinking associated with social cognition is ultimately for doing (Fiske, 1992).

If scholars are to build a model of a human being as a decision maker, what should that model look like? What information is the decision maker most interested in? What calculations does that decision maker make? Is the process of decision making the same for all decisions, or does the decision maker approach different types of decisions in unique ways? Scholarly disciplines other than psychology have certainly committed to specific models of the human decision maker in their own theorizing. For example, at the core of economics and related fields stands the *rational actor model*. This model assumes that people are impartial and unflawed thinkers who have an unlimited capacity for analysis and calculation. This actor has firm preferences about what he or she wants and complete information about the surrounding world. First and foremost, this actor is concerned with his or her material self-interest; the interests of other actors do not matter and are given little if any weight. This rational actor, further, is a cold calculator, unmoved by incidental passions, who takes the evidence given and deliberates his or

her way toward a decision. Thus, rational actors make accurate and beneficial judgments about the world, and always choose the most optimal behavior possible. To be sure, under this type of model, errors are allowed, but only random errors that occasionally distract the rational actor from the right judgment and the correct choice. Beyond that, the thinking of the rational actor is flawless (e.g., Becker, 1976; Hicks & Allen, 1934; Pareto, 1971).

Economists, building theories based on the rational actor model, have met with over a century of success in the analysis of human behavior (e.g., Becker, 1976). To the reader, this might seem something of a surprise, in that this model of the human decision maker sounds not much like any flesh-and-blood human being that he or she has met in everyday life. Instead, this completely rational actor sounds a little more like it comes from the realm of science fiction, like Spock for older *Star Trek* fans or Data for newer ones, or like the Cybermen from *Doctor Who*. Thus, might there be revisions or even wholesale changes to this model that might make it more realistic – that better approximate how people approach judgments and decisions in their everyday world?

THE PROJECT OF JUDGMENT AND DECISION-MAKING RESEARCH

Within psychology, research on judgment and decision making (JDM) can be construed as a reaction against the rational actor model, taking as its central goal an attempt to build a description of the human decision maker that better approximates how people go about the business of their daily lives. JDM starts with a different premise from the rational actor model. It assumes that people show systematic flaws and biases about how they weigh evidence and reach decisions. These flaws can be quite fundamental and far-reaching in their consequences.

This alternative model of the human decision maker begins to appear in the psychological literature roughly in the mid-20th century (see Edwards, 1954, 1961). It can found in the thinking of Simon (1957), who noted that people often do not have the cognitive capacity or sufficient time to do all the calculation that the rational actor model often demanded. Instead, he proposed that people frequently fail to conduct an exhaustive analysis of any decision, but instead often stop well before they had completely considered all the evidence before them, a tendency he described as *satisficing*. In roughly the same era, Edwards (1968) discovered that people differed, systematically, in the ways they revised their beliefs in the face of new evidence. He found that people revised their beliefs too little relative to what basic statistical principles said they should, a pattern that became known as *judgmental conservatism*.

But it was with the "heuristics and biases" work of Daniel Kahneman and Amos Tversky (for reviews of early work, see Kahneman, Slovic, & Tverksy, 1982; Nisbett & Ross, 1980) that JDM research took off, and in the 1970s a project began, one which continues to this day, in which the rational actor was placed under close scrutiny to explore the ways in which people differed from that idealized portrait. Commonly, it is from this work on heuristics and biases that JDM traces its lineage. This work has had an impact not only on cognitive, social, personality, developmental, and organizational psychology but also on such diverse fields as medicine, artificial intelligence, sociology, political science, law, accounting, and marketing – and, of course – has a growing impact on economics.

In this chapter, I review research that has flowed from this JDM tradition, and focus on five central insights that this research has thematically revealed. I discuss the implications of these fundamental insights for both basic theory and, where appropriate, applied policy. I also discuss more current and emerging work in JDM, discussing six specific areas in which the discipline seems poised to make central discoveries about human decision making.

Relation to behavioral economics

Two notes should be made about the area of psychology known as JDM. The first note is that it is natural for such an active and increasingly diverse field to have many names – and JDM does, such as decision theory, or behavioral decision theory. When affixed to a specific applied area, it is likely to have the pre-fix "behavioral" attached to it, such as in behavioral law or behavioral accounting.

One name that should not be taken as a synonym, however, is *behavioral economics*, which refers to a related but distinct area of scholarship within economics itself. Behavioral economics is quite active – each year even more so – and shares many of the same concerns as JDM. It asks, for example, how people make risky decisions, or when people will act altruistically rather than in their own selfish interest. Behavioral economics has been informed by many of the insights gained in JDM work. JDM, in return, has gained many insights and inspirations from research in behavioral economics.

But the two fields differ in many fundamental ways. JDM is a psychological field, and as such is interested in *experimentation*: i.e., in empirically identifying the circumstances and dynamics that influence the judgments and decisions that people ultimately reach. Do people, for example, react to potential gains differently from the way they react to potential losses? The scholarship of behavioral economics follows from a fundamentally different method of exploration. Typically, it will take the insights of JDM, as well as insights from elsewhere, and use them to construct *models*. In these models, economists create a hypothetical world in which they identify a set of variables, specify some logical or quantitative relationships between those variables, and then allow the variables to interact to see what outcomes arise (Holcombe, 1989). Economists may explore how their models behave over time, or when many people, not just one individual, are allowed to interact with one another. To be sure, economists at times collect empirical data (there is, after all, a field named *experimental economics*), and psychologists sometimes construct models, but the two fields differ greatly in the central method they use to make their discoveries: psychologists use data to examine how one or a few causal agents influence some outcome, whereas economists construct hypothetical worlds in which a system of variables interact with one another.

The importance of normative benchmarks

The second note is that work in JDM distinguishes itself from other research in social cognition in another central emphasis. Instead of just examining how people reach their decisions, JDM research compares how people do so with how they *should* do so. That is, people's judgments or decisions are compared against some *normative* benchmark from economics, statistical science, or logic describing how a flawless and impartial agent – that rational actor – would have reached a decision.

There is no single normative standard that covers all of JDM work. At times, researchers may just compare judgments and decisions to the truth, to see if people's conclusions comport with reality. People may be asked, for example, how many libraries there are in the United States, and then be asked to place an upper and lower bound on that estimate such that there is a 90% likelihood that the true answer lays within those bounds. Then, people's estimates are compared to the truth: Do their bounds actually contain the true answer 90% of the time? (Usually not: in such exercises their bounds typically contain the true answer less than 50% of the time; see Alpert & Raiffa, 1982; Klayman, Soll, Gonzalez-Vallejo, & Barlas, 1999.)

Alternatively, researchers may examine how well participants' estimates replicate the conclusions reached via some normative technique. One common technique is Bayesian inference, which suggests how people should revise their judgments when combining new evidence with previous suspicions. For example, suppose one is a detective investigating a murder and has a suspect in mind, but rates the chance of this suspect being guilty as only 10%. However, the detective runs a very accurate blood test, and finds that the suspect's blood matches a sample left by the culprit – and, once more, that the blood type matched is very rare, being shared by only 1% of the population. How sure should the detective be of the suspect's guilt now? According to Bayes' theorem, and assuming an accurate test, the detective should move to being 92% sure that the suspect is guilty.[1] Usually, however, people do not revise their suspicions in legal cases as much as they should (Smith, Penrod, Otto, & Park, 1996).

Finally, if truth is difficult to determine, or no precise normative technique exists to guide judgment, researchers can examine whether people's judgments at least follow constraints suggested by mathematics or logic. For example, the logic of transitivity suggests that if someone would prefer object A over B, and object B over C, then he or she must prefer object A over C. There are times, however, when this logic is violated. Tversky (1969) found that most people, most of the time, preferred a 7 out of 24 chance to win $5 over a 9 out of 24 chance to win $4.50, and that this second gamble was preferred a majority of the time over a 11 out of 24 chance to win $4. However, ask people to choose between the first gamble (7/24 chance to win $5) and the third (11/24 to win $4), most people most of the time opted for the latter.

FIVE CENTRAL INSIGHTS OF JDM RESEARCH

If one traces JDM work back to the early research of Simon and Edwards, then psychological researchers have been closely scrutinizing the rational actor model for over a half-century. Thus, it is not a surprise that researchers have discovered many ways in which flesh-and-blood decision makers differ from the ideal embodied in the rational actor model. Although any review of JDM word may differ in its details, there are at least five central ways in which human decision makers appear to differ from the rational ideal. That is, surveying the theorizing and empirical evidence that JDM researchers have developed, one finds five major insights about human decision making. Let us consider each in turn.

Insight #1: Judgments and decisions are often the product of quick and crude heuristics

The primary insight identified with research on judgment and decision making is that judgments of truth, likelihood, and benefit are often not the product of intense, exhaustive, and analytical calculation, but rather the product of quick and crude *heuristics*, or rules of thumb, that potentially get people close to the right answer but which can sometimes lead to dramatic and systematic error. Two specific heuristics, *availability* and *representativeness*, are the ones most featured in JDM work.

Availability

Suppose one were asked whether there are more 7-letter words in the English language that have the form - - - - - n – or - - - - i n g? Most people "know" the answer within seconds, and know it without a comprehensive review of the closest *Webster's Dictionary*. They merely sit back and see if they can generate words with an "- n –" ending or an "-ing" one. For most people, it's the latter that are more easily generated (the author can't help but think of *Dunning* if proper names count) than the former – and so they conclude that "-ing" words are more numerous (Tversky & Kahneman, 1973). But they are necessarily wrong.

Stare at the "- n –" form a little more, and one would realize that all "ing" words fit the "- n –" form. Also, there are many words (*present, benzene*) that fit –n-, and so –n- words must be more common than -ing ones.

The quick-and-crude rule of thumb that produces this error was termed by Kahneman and Tversky (1973) as the *availability heuristic*, which suggests that people think of something as more likely or true to the extent that it (or examples of it) can be easily brought to mind. The heuristic might be a good rule of thumb, but it can lead to systematic mistakes in belief. For example, people believe that homicides are more frequent than suicides, which stands to reason given how often the former is in the news relative to the latter, but the truth is actually the opposite is true. People also overestimate the prevalence of lethal risks such as car accidents, fire, and drowning, in part because these risks are made available in the news, but not more invisible risks such as hepatitis, diabetes, and breast cancer (Lichtenstein, Slovic, Fischhoff, Layman, & Combs, 1978).

The availability heuristic is such a powerful determinant of judgment that it can even defeat the quality and quantity of information people have at their disposal. Schwarz and colleagues asked college students to generate lists of behaviors suggesting that they were emotional people. Some were asked to generate only four examples – a task that was easily completed and, thus, scored high on a feeling of availability. Others were asked to generate 12 examples, an arduous task that left students with a feeling that their emotional behaviors were not that available at all. Thus, it was not surprising that students asked to list a mere four behaviors rated themselves as more emotional than those asked to provide 12, even though the latter group had generated more information indicating they were emotional people (Schwarz, Bless, Strack, Klumpp, Rittenauer-Schatka, & Simons, 1991). What mattered was the feeling of availability associated with the task, not the actual content of information generated.

Representativeness

People tend to believe that an outcome is likely to occur to the extent that it resembles its inputs, a heuristic that Kahneman and Tversky (1972, 1973; see also Tversky & Kahneman, 1983) termed the *representativeness* heuristic. For example, they gave participants the following profile of a college student:

Tom W. is of high intelligence, although lacking in true creativity. He has a need for order and clarity, and for neat and tidy systems in which every detail

finds its appropriate place. His writing is rather dull and mechanical, occasionally enlivened by somewhat corny puns and by flashes of imagination of the sci-fi type. He has a strong drive for competence. He seems to feel little sympathy for other people and does not enjoy interacting with others. Self-centered, he nonetheless has a deep moral sense.

Participants were then asked to rank nine college majors (business administration, law, engineering) in terms of how likely Tom was to be pursuing them. Not surprisingly, most participants thought it much more likely that Tom was an engineer rather than in social science/social work. Consistent with the representativeness heuristic, Tom's personality matched the type of personality participants associated with engineers than it did the character associated with social work – a quite reasonable conclusion.

But, Kahneman and Tversky (1973) cogently argued that this conclusion was much more likely to be an error that participants had not anticipated. Consider the following proposition, which I hope is not too controversial: the probability that an outcome will occur depends on its sheer frequency. Common events happen commonly; rare events only seldomly. Thus, when predicting whether an event will occur, we should consult simply how frequent or probable it is. If this is the case, then one should bend one's prediction in the direction toward Tom being a social science or a social worker major rather than an engineer. The first type of major is quite common among college students; engineering students are much rarer. That is, when making judgments of an uncertain event, one should consult an outcome's *base rate*: namely, the raw likelihood or frequency with which it occurs. Statistical tools such as Bayes' theorem can even be exploited to formally incorporate base rate information into predictive judgments (Howson & Urbach, 2005).

Kahneman and Tversky (1973) discovered that in relying on the representativeness heuristic, people gave short shrift to base rate information, even though it is a prime indicator of whether an event will occur. Convincing people to set aside this *base rate neglect* is often a central tenet of training in many professions. For example, medical students are often exhorted to consider the base rates of the diseases they are considering for a diagnosis, and instructed to pay attention to the obvious – but important – point that a diagnosis of a disease that tends to be frequent is much more likely to be right than a diagnosis of a disease that appears only rarely (Sotos, 2006). To be sure, mistakes will be made, but not as many as there would have been if students had neglected base rates in their diagnostic conclusions.

Reliance on the representativeness heuristic also leads people to disregard other types of valuable information. For example, let me show you two coins, one of which I claim is biased towards heads and away from tails when I flip it. I flip Coin A 4 times, and get heads 3 of those times. I then flip Coin B 13 times, and get heads 8 times. Which coin, A or B, is most likely to be the biased one? Most people, because of the representativeness heuristic, choose A because a 75% "heads" rate looks more like a biased coin than the 61.5% figure produced by B. This conclusion, however, is wrong. Statistically, an unbiased coin will produce 3 heads out of 4 flips 31% of the time, but it will produce 8 heads out of 13 times only 29% of the time. It is close, but my money is on Coin B being the biased one.

Griffin and Tversky (1992) discovered, however, that people, relying so heavily on the representativeness heuristic, failed to consider the quality of the information they had in hand. Using their terminology, they claimed that people were too influenced by the *strength* of the information they were given (e.g., but it's a 75% heads rate!) much more than the *weight* they should give the information (e.g., but its only 4 flips): i.e., people looked at what the information suggested, but failed to consider the credibility they should assign that information.

Insight #2: Reference points matter

According to the traditional treatments of expected utility theory in economics, we can make two assumptions about the preferences of rational actors: first, their preferences are well-formed before they ever encounter a situation in which they must make a choice; second, those preferences are based on the totality of what a person owns – that is, his or her total wealth (e.g., Friedman & Savage, 1948). For example, a poor student with total net worth of near zero should jump at a chance to win $100,000 in a lottery, but a rich business executive whose financial portfolio is already stuffed with assets would be less enthusiastic. A rise in total of wealth of $100,000 would not appear to be as great to the executive, and thus the gamble not worth the time to reach for a wallet.

Work in JDM, in many different ways, has shown that these two assumptions are false. First, people's preferences are often not well-formed prior to making an economic decision. Instead, people often "bootstrap" their preferences on the spot, based on features of the choice presented to them (Hsee & Zhang, 2004). For example, when presented with a sure gain of $2 versus a gamble in which they have a 7 out of 36 (19%) chance of winning $9, only a third of respondents choose the gamble over the sure $2. The reason for this is obvious – $9 is certainly more than $2, but a mere 19% chance of winning is disappointingly low. However, if the bet is revised a little, such that participants now have a 7 out of 36 chance of winning $9 but a 29/36 chance of losing 5¢, the proportion taking the bet for $9 rises to nearly 61% (Slovic, Finucane, Peters, & MacGregor, 2002). But this enhanced enthusiasm for the revised bet is somewhat paradoxical. The revised bet presents worse terms – after all, the original bet presented no chance for a loss – so how can it be that people find it more attractive?

It is more attractive because the meaning that participants assign the $9 is not crystallized before they hear about the bet. Instead, it is constructed once the other features of the gamble are described. In this case, the attractiveness of the $9 depends importantly on how it compares to the other features of the gamble. It compares favorably, for example, to a gain of $2, but not enough to prompt people to take the gamble. However, in the revised gamble, the possible gain of $9 is certainly much more impressive looking when compared to a possible loss of a mere 5¢. Gaining this added attractiveness in the comparison, bootstrapped from a comparison to a small possible loss, participants are moved to take the gamble to try to gain that appealing $9.

Framing

Kahneman and Tversky (1984; see also Tversky & Kahneman, 1981, 1986) provided further demonstrations that local reference points mattered by introducing the notion of *framing* to the JDM literature. Framing meant that choice options could often be presented in different formats that implicitly changed the reference points involved. For example, in a classic example of framing, participants were told that an Asian disease was about to break out which was expected to kill 600 people. There were two possible medical responses that policymakers could adopt: one that would save 200 for sure and one that presented a one-third chance of saving all 600 and a two-thirds chance of saving no one. Given this "frame," close to 75% of participants chose the sure thing of saving 200. However, if the response options were described differently, with one policy meaning that 400 people would die for sure and the other policy meaning there was a 1/3 chance that no one would die but a 2/3 chance that all 600 would, only 20% of people choose the sure thing of 400. Note, however, that the 200 saved under the first frame, a choice most people favored, was exactly the same as the 400 dying under the second. Shifting the reference point, however, had shifted how people evaluated the two options – sure thing versus taking a risk – that they evaluated.

Attraction and compromise effects

Other reference point effects can be introduced by adding irrelevant options among the choices people are deliberating over. In the *attraction effect*, people's choices between two objects are swayed by a third option that no one would choose but which makes one of the original two objects more attractive by comparison. For example, suppose one were deciding between two different apartments to rent. Apartment A is only 10 minutes by car to one's office, and so it presents a short commute, but the rent is $800 per month. Apartment B presents a 30-minute commute, but also a cheaper rent of $550 per month. Which one a person will choose depends on other inferior choices that might also be in the choice set. For example, suppose one also considered Apartment C, which is 12 minutes by car away from the office and which costs $900 to rent. By comparison, Apartment A now looks very good, and so is more likely to be chosen. However, if Apartment C instead presents a 35-minute commute and costs $600 per month, Apartment B now looks attractive by comparison and is more likely to be chosen. Note here that Apartment C is irrelevant in that it is never chosen, but it has its impact by how it shapes people's evaluations of the choices worth considering (Huber, Payne, & Puto, 1982; Simonson, 1989).

Inferior choice options also sway decisions via *compromise effects*, in which a third option makes a particular choice appear to be an appropriate compromise between competing needs. For example, suppose one was thirsty after eating a large bucket of popcorn at a movie, and so go back to the concession counter to buy some soda pop. But what size to buy? A larger-size drink will definitely quench any thirst, but can also be quite expensive and contain too many indulgent calories. A smaller-size soda is more virtuous, but may not be enough to quench one's thirst. Movie theaters often assist customers in solving this dilemma – in the theater's favor, of course – by offering a super-size set of drinks that are so big that very few people buy them. The worth of those drinks for the movie theater, however, is that they make moderately large drinks look like a defensible compromise between the small and super-large sizes, causing people to buy the medium drink over the small (Benartzi & Thaler, 2002; Dhar & Simonson, 2003; Simonson, 1989).

Anchoring

Other work has shown that considering a reference point, even an arbitrary one, influences judgments in systematic and significant ways. Once people consider a reference point, they appear to *anchor* their judgments on it, adjusting their response away from the reference point but still being biased by it. In an initial demonstration, Tversky and Kahneman (1974) asked participants to estimate the percentage of countries in the United Nations that came from Africa. But, before they gave their estimates, the researchers spun a lottery wheel in order to present participants with an initial anchor. For some participants, the lottery wheel stopped at the number 10, and they were asked if the percentage of countries from Africa was more or less than 10%. For the others, the lottery wheel stopped at 65, and participants were asked if the percentage was greater or lesser than 65%. These initial anchors biased participants' subsequent estimates. Those exposed to the 10 ultimately claimed, on average, that 25% of UN countries were from Africa; those exposed to the 65 thought, on average, that the actual percentage was 45%.

Hundreds of studies have demonstrated the power of anchors to distort people's judgments – and even how they behave in situations (for a review, see Chapman & Johnson, 2002). College students estimating how many word puzzles they can complete in a laboratory session provide higher estimates if they have first been exposed to high anchors rather than low anchors – and then persist longer as the puzzles become unsolvable (Cervone & Peake, 1986). How much people are willing to pay for such items as wine and chocolates can also be shaped by patently arbitrary anchors. In one demonstration, students were asked to write down the last two digits of their Social Security number – and then asked if they would pay that amount for a bottle of wine and Belgian chocolates, among other items. They then reported how much they were willing to pay for each item. Even though students knew they might have to buy any product at the price they wrote down, those whose Social Security numbers fell in the highest 20% were willing to pay more than three times for the wine and twice for the chocolates than those whose numbers fell in the lowest 20% (Ariely, Loewenstein, & Prelec, 2003).

Insight #3: People take into account the information handed to them, but not all information that is relevant

People often reach judgments easily by constructing a mental model in their head of the question being posed, based on the information they have been handed. What people fail to appreciate is that building an adequate mental model often means considering information well beyond that which is being supplied. This leads to several problems in judgments and decisions.

Failures to unpack

For example, suppose that I asked someone the probability that an individual died of "natural causes" in the past year. The likelihood this someone will respond with is likely to be much smaller than the estimate of another person who is asked to consider the likelihood that an individual will die of some specific causes such as cancer, heart disease, infectious disease, and so on. A similar pattern holds, for example, if people are asked the chance someone died of homicide in the past year. People provide a lower estimate than they do if the experimenter instead lists all the possible perpetrators one could be a victim of, such as an acquaintance, a lover, or a stranger (Rottenstreich & Tversky, 1997; Tversky and Koehler, 1994). Similarly, doctors discount the likelihood of diagnoses that have not been explicitly specified (Redelmeier, Koehler, Liberman, & Tversky, 1995): i.e., when asked about some class of event, people tend to respond without first "unpacking" that event into its more concrete instantiations. However, if the experimenter does the unpacking for them, people are quite willing to concede that there is a larger possibility that the overall event will occur. They will not do it on their own accord – sticking to only the information given by the experimenter – but if the experimenter provides more guidance, they will easily follow it to a different answer.

Other biases in judgment arise because people fail to "unpack" events into their constituent components. People, for example, commonly underestimate the time they need to complete many projects, like their holiday shopping, their tax returns, or a school assignment (Buehler, Griffin, & MacDonald, 1997; Buehler, Griffin, & Ross, 1994, 2002). Indeed, college seniors, on average, tend to complete their senior theses a week after the date they swore previously would be their "worst case" scenario (Buehler et al., 1994). This overoptimism about getting things done is referred to as the *planning fallacy*, and arises even though people concede quite readily that they have rarely completed projects before some deadline in their past (Buehler et al., 1994).

The planning fallacy, in part, arises because people fail to "unpack" all the concrete steps they have to take in order to get some task done. Led explicitly to consider those steps, however, makes them much more accurate. As a demonstration of this, Kruger and Evans (2004) across many experiments, asked participants to estimate how long it would take them to complete their holiday shopping, prepare for a date, and cook a meal. Relative to a control condition, those asked first to list out all the concrete steps they would have to take to complete the task before providing an estimate were more pessimistic – and less biased – in their predictions. In a more real-world context, Jorgenson (2004) has found that software developers gave more accurate estimates of when they will complete projects if they use a "bottom up" strategy of listing all the concrete sub-tasks they must tackle for the project to be finished, relative to developers, who focus only on the project as a whole.

Partitioning

People also use the form of questions they are posed to suggest the number of possible outcomes they should consider for their answer – not realizing there are often many different ways to partition possibilities into distinct events. For example, if people are asked whether "Sunday will be hotter than any other day next week," people partition possible outcomes into *Sunday is the hottest* or *Some other day will be the hottest*. They then start from their reasoning from a 50% chance – one out of two – that Sunday will be the hottest. However, if asked instead whether "The hottest day of the week will be Sunday," people partition all possible events into seven, one for each day of the week. They will then start their reasoning from 14% – a one in seven chance. Not surprisingly, respondents presented the first frame of the question end up believing the chance that Sunday will be the hottest day to be greater than those presented the second frame – 30% versus 15%, respectively (Fox & Rottenstreich, 2003).

Such partitioning also influences not only judgments but also actual decisions. Respondents asked to distribute their charitable contributions among an international charity and four local ones tend to give 21% to the international one. However, if asked first to split their money between international and local charities first, and then are shown the collection of charities they can contribute to, they choose to donate 55% to the international choice (Fox, Ratner, & Lieb, 2005).

Focalism

If asked about some focal event, people base their answer on some consideration of that event without taking into account that other events matter, as well. *Focalism*, as it is termed, arises in two different guises.

One guise of focalism is that people fail to consider alternative comparison points. If students are asked, for example, if studying for three hours (relative to no studying) will have an impact on their exam grade, they state that studying will have a substantial impact. However, if asked whether not studying those three hours (relative to studying) would have an impact, they state that it will not have much impact (Dunning & Parpal, 1989). Coming to two different assessments depending on which act (studying vs not studying) is highlighted is nonsensical. Both questions are mirror images of one another, and thus the answer under one frame should be the same as it is under the other.

However, people give different answers because of focalism. They focus on the state of the world that is featured (studying vs not studying), and base their answer mostly on what will occur in that state of world, neglecting the other state. Thus, if asked about studying, they will generate reasons why studying will help, and see a large impact. However, if asked about not studying, they think of many compensatory reasons why they would achieve a good grade anyway, thus seeing less impact (Dunning & Madey, 1995).

A similar focalism effect is seen if poker players are asked whether introducing wild cards into a game would help their chances at winning. They typically think it does (Windshitl, Kruger, & Simms, 2003). At some level, this is true. With wild cards, a poker player has more ways to construct a highly imposing hand. But here is the rub: so does every other poker player, and to roughly an equal degree. In reality, each poker player's better chance of constructing an impressive hand is countered by the better chance his or her opponents also have of drawing a better hand – but, via focalism, people tend to neglect this insight. Thus, a poker player is in error in thinking he or she has a better chance of winning when wild cards are introduced.

Another guise of focalism involves disregarding the humdrum of background events that occur in everyday life – but which have an impact on some focal outcome. College students, for example, over-believe how their university's football team winning or losing will impact their mood and well-being (Gilbert, Pinel, Wilson, Blumberg, & Wheatley, 1998; Wilson, Wheatley, Meyers, Gilbert, & Axsom, 2000). Part of this overestimation arises because people focus almost exclusively on the central event they are being asked about (i.e., the football team winning or losing) and fail to take into account that life will provide many other events that will also influence mood. For the college students, papers will be due, this week's episode of *Big Bang Theory* might be especially funny, or an old friend might call out of

the blue. However, if the presence of all this background "noise" is explicitly pointed out to them, people recognize that the impact of any focal event will be diminished, and thus they avoid the overestimation they are prone toward otherwise.

Insight #4: Confirmatory information is privileged over disconfirmatory information

When striving to determine whether some conclusion is true, people are biased in their search for information. They tend to favor information that confirms that conclusion over information that would disconfirm or contradict it. For example, if someone asks me if people are likely to get taller over the next few centuries, I am likely to grope around for facts and theories that suggest that, yes, people will get taller. However, if someone asks me if people are likely to get shorter, my search for information and argument shifts in the opposite direction.

Confirmation bias

One way to describe this *confirmation bias* is that people look for positive matches between the conclusion they are considering and the information they search for (Wason, 1960). The conclusion can come from many different sources. People seem biased to consider, and then confirm, conclusions that they favor over those they dislike (Hoch, 1985; Pyszczynski & Greenberg, 1987; Tabor & Lodge, 2006). People tend to confirm conclusions that fit their expectations (e.g., the sun will rise in the east tomorrow) than those they consider less plausible (Nickerson, 1998). Even the way a question is posed will suggest a conclusion, and thus the direction in which people will seek out information (Snyder & Swann, 1978). For example, participants who were asked to judge whether they were happy with their social life tended to bring to mind positive social experiences, and ended up being much more bullish on their social life than those asked whether they were *un*happy with their social life (Kunda, Fong, Sanitioso, & Reber, 1993).

Confirmation bias can lead to perverse conclusions, with people coming to different decisions based on the way they frame the question in front of them. Suppose that the decision being considered is to which parent a child should be granted custody, with Parent A unremarkable in a remarkable number of ways, but Parent B being an individual with some real strengths and obvious weaknesses as a parent. When participants were asked in one study which parent should be given custody of the child, they tended to go with Parent B. But when asked, instead, which parent should be denied custody, they chose to deny Parent B custody. Apparently, the strengths that suggested good parenting skills under the first frame of the question were ignored under the second frame in favor of those shortcomings and weakened Parent B's case (Shafir, 1983).

The timing when people encounter information can also influence what gets chosen. Across several studies, Russo and colleagues have discovered that people form tentative conclusions about the options they favor when making a choice. And once one option nudges ahead in favoritism, confirmatory bias seals its ultimate selection (Russo, Medvec, & Meloy, 1996; Russo, Meloy, & Medvec, 1998) – a tendency observed among professional auditors, for example, deciding which firm should receive an on-site review (Russo, Meloy, & Wilks, 2000). This tendency for one option to nose ahead in the horse race can also lead to perverse decisions. People will choose an inferior option over a superior one if the first piece of information they receive about the two options just happens to favor the inferior choice. Now ahead in the horse race, confirmation bias speeds its selection, even though it is not the optimal selection to make (Russo, Carlson, & Meloy, 2006).

"Cell A" bias

People show favoritism toward confirmatory information – as a positive match between evidence and outcome – in other ways. Suppose one were a scientist–doctor in the Middle Ages, and wanted to test the idea that bleeding sick people with leeches (in order to remove excess ill-humored blood) tended to improve their health. There is a simple way to test this idea – bleed ill people with leeches and see whether their health improves. Let us say that one does this and finds 10 instances in which patients improve after bloodletting. Is that positive or negative evidence about this treatment?

Readers might be tempted to say "yes" or "no," and others may instead have a sense that more information is needed. That all said, in everyday life, people often take these instances of positive–positive matches between evidence and outcome to decide that some notion is true. They have a flickering thought of a long-lost relative on one day, and the next day that relative calls – perhaps evidence of ESP? Or, they privately wish a curse on an annoying co-worker, only to have that co-worker suffer a severe car accident – tentative evidence of the power of our own thoughts?

Perhaps, but researchers in JDM would not suggest that counting up positive–positive matches

provides enough evidence for any conclusions in the above cases (Beyth-Marom, 1982; Ward & Jenkins, 1965). Essentially, if one considers the presence and absence of an outcome (e.g., the patient improving or not), as well as the presence or absence of an intervention (e.g., bloodletting using leeches), one sees that there are four possible states of the world, depicted in Table 13.1. Our medieval doctor has looked at only those instances in which one of those states attained – those 10 times in which bloodletting was followed by patient improvement, the positive–positive cell, marked as "Cell A" in Table 13.1.

But determining whether bloodletting works clearly means examining the number of times two other states of the world arise – those states which produce a positive–negative instance. Let us imagine that the doctor has noticed the 5 times that he bloodlet the patient and the patient's health did not improve (Cell B), and also that there were 10 times in which the patient refused the bloodletting, but still improved anyway (Cell C). What does this mean for the medical technique? The comparison to Cell B causes bloodletting to look effective, but the comparison to Cell C makes it look less so. Which comparison provides the most accurate answer?

The answer, of course, is that neither does. To determine whether bloodletting actually improves the chances of patients regaining their health, one must look not only at Cells A, B, and C – but Cell D as well. This cell represents the instances in which negative–negative intervention to outcome matches occur, and it is a crucial cell in determining whether the data in Cell A is cause for hope or evidence of folly. Suppose that the doctor observes 20 Cell D instances in which he withholds bloodletting and the patient fails to improve. That would mean that of all 25 times bloodletting was withheld, the patient improved only 5 of those times – but improved 50% of the time when bloodletting was tried. That would be cause for hope. But if the doctor observed no Cell D instances, that means that patients always improve without bloodletting (5 out of 5 times), and that chance is reduced to 50% with bloodletting. That would be cause to seek new forms of treatment.

Table 13.1 Hypothetical counts of experiences with bloodletting and patient cures

Bloodletting	Patient cured		
		Yes	No
Yes	Cell A	10	Cell B 5
No	Cell C	10	Cell D ??

Insight #5: Events matter more when happening with certainty, now, or involve loss

Beyond certain types of information, specific types of events are also given more weight in decisions and actions. People are especially concerned with prospects that will happen with certainty than they are those that occur only at some level of probability. They are more concerned with events that will happen now or in the near future rather than in the more distant future. When weighing risky options, the losses associated with those options loom larger than potential gains.

The certainty effect

Consider two types of car insurance the gentle reader could buy. Insurance Policy A is expensive, but it pays for all expenses – car repair, medical, legal – if the policyholder gets into an accident. Insurance Policy B is only half the price, but it pays for all costs after an accident only 50% of the time on randomly selected days (however, in case it fails to pay, the cost of the insurance is refunded). Which one would the gentle reader prefer? If the reader is like participants in many JDM studies, he or she will likely be one of the 80% who prefer Policy A that pays with certainty (Kahneman & Tversky, 1979).

In effect, people give greater weight to outcomes that will take place with certainty. They favor certain gains over larger ones that are more uncertain. They strive to avoid certain losses, and often opt for gambles that present possibly larger losses (Kahneman & Tversky, 1979). We have already seen the impact of this preference in the earlier discussion about framing effects. Recall that when the choice of a medical plan was described in terms of saving lives, participants preferred the plan that would save 200 with certainty over one that presented only a one-third chance of saving 600. And when the plans were described in terms of lives lost, participants preferred the plan that presented a gruesome gamble – a two-third chance of losing all 600 lives – over the one that presented an inevitable loss of 200 lives (Kahneman & Tversky, 1984).

Future discounting

Like events that happen with certainty, events that happen in the here and now matter more to people than those that take place farther in the future. Given a choice between receiving $50 now versus $100 a year in the future, most people go for the $50. However, given a choice between receiving $50 five years from now versus $100 six years from now, most opt for the delayed $100. In a sense, these two decisions contradict each other. In the first case, people want the smaller award that is given a year earlier; in the second case, they reject that smaller award (Frederick, Loewenstein, & O'Donoghue, 2002; Green, Fry, & Meyerson, 1994).

However, such behavior is made explicable if one assumes that people discount future rewards and punishments, doing at first swiftly as events recede from the present to the near future, and then more slowly as events recede from the nearer future to a more distant time. In essence, people's discounting of future events follows a hyperbolic curve, as depicted in Figure 13.1 (Ainslie, 1992; Loewenstein & Prelec, 1992) – as well as in pigeons, who have been shown to peck a button that produces less food as long as that button produces the food right now (Ainslie & Herrnstein, 1981). In a word, both humans and pigeons are *present-biased*, in that events that occur close to the present weigh much more heavily on decision making than more temporally distant events.

Losses

Finally, losses loom larger than gains in people's decisions about risk. Ask a number of people if they want to bet $20 on a coin flip to win $40, and most will decline the offer. Many will decline the offer even if the amount to be won is $50 or $60 (Kahneman & Tversky, 1979). Essentially, the prospect of losing $20 is given greater weight than the potential prospect of gaining someone else's $20, and so the bet is not attractive enough for most people to take – even after inflating somewhat the amount that can be won. This tendency to weigh potential losses more than potential gains in decision making is referred to as *loss aversion*.

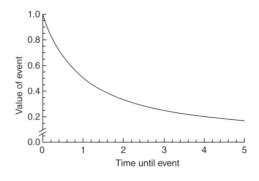

Figure 13.1 Hyperbolic discounting curve of the value of events taking place in the future.

Loss aversion is echoed in the quite similar phenomenon known as the endowment effect. People appear to value objects much more as soon as they own (i.e., are endowed with) them. For example, in one experiment, participants were handed at random either a mug or a pen and then asked if they wanted to exchange the object they had been given for the alternative. Economically, it should not matter which object, mug or pen, participants had been given – but psychologically it did. Most given a pen kept the pen; most given a mug refused to exchange it, indicating that ownership did cause people to inflate the value of what they owned (Kahneman, Knetsch, & Thaler, 1990).

CURRENT DEVELOPMENTS AND FUTURE TRENDS

Research on judgment and decision making is a robust enterprise, and the field seems poised to burst in a number of new directions with potentially important insights as it fleshes out a fuller model of decision making than the one contained in the rational actor model. If one scans the current JDM literature, one finds the following developments already in full bloom.

Experience sampling

Traditionally, JDM work has assigned the blame for judgmental errors on factors that are internal to the people who make them. The research has emphasized people's tendencies to adhere to mistaken heuristics or to neglect valuable information, such as base rate data. Newer work, however, suggests that many errors may instead be produced not by mistaken heuristics but by problems in the information that people tend to encounter. That is, people deal with information they receive just fine; the problem is that their experience with the world just furnishes them with incomplete and biased information.

Why people tend to disappoint

Consider the possibility that other people, over time, tend to disappoint. We meet a person who has exciting characteristics, but over time we find out that he or she really is just ordinary like the rest of us. Why do such initially exciting people tend to disappoint? More importantly, why do people tend not to do the reverse – look ordinary at the beginning and then amaze us as time goes on?

This tendency toward disappointment may come directly from the types of social interactions

people tend to pursue versus the types they tend to avoid – and thus asymmetries in the experiences they have with other people. Meet an amazing person, and people pursue interactions with that person. Over time, they find that that first amazing experience they had with that person was a fluke. Or, they spend enough time to discover that they first encountered the very best of the person, and that the rest is simply more lackluster. However, if the person they encounter is initially lackluster, people do not pursue further social interaction, and thus never discover just how wonderful that other person might be in some other circumstances. Thus, the bias people have is ultimately to spend time and gather experience with people who will initially thrill but then disappoint. People less commonly put themselves in situations in which they could have the opposite experience (Norton, Frost, & Ariely, 2007).

Why people distrust others

The notion that our actions lead us to gain biased or incomplete feedback about the world (i.e., staying in social relationships that will ultimately disappoint) is referred to as an *experience sampling analysis* (Denrell, 2005; Smith & Collins, 2009). It suggests that there might be nothing wrong with how people think about social information once collected. Instead, the major problem is in the information they collect. As another example, consider the fact that people dramatically underestimate the likelihood that strangers will prove to be trustworthy. In studies involving an economic game in which people can choose to invest $5 in a stranger who might – but is not forced to – give $10 in return, people think that only roughly 45% of their peers will give money back when in fact 80% do (Fetchenhauer & Dunning, 2009). Why do people get their peers so wrong? Why are they so unduly cynical?

Fetchenhauer and Dunning (2010) explored an experience sampling explanation of this cynicism that pointed out that people receive biased feedback about the trustworthiness of others. Through their lives, people at times choose to trust another person. Sometimes that trust is honored, but sometimes it is violated – leading people to become more cynical. But what about those times in which people consider trusting but decide not to do it? Here, people receive no feedback. Because they withhold their trust, they never find out if the other person would have reciprocated that trust, pointing out a mistake that might lead them to become more optimistic about their peers.

In a test of this idea, Fetchenhauer and Dunning (2010) showed participants short videotapes of 56 other people. For each, participants were asked to decide whether they would trust the other person in the $5/$10 economic game. Participants all started out overly cynical about their peers, underestimating the chance that each person would honor their trust. Some participants, however, were given feedback about the trustworthiness of others much like Fetchenhauer and Dunning (2010) presumed people received in real life: i.e., participants received feedback only after they made a decision to trust the other person. If they decided to withhold trust, no feedback was given. This type of feedback had no impact on the cynicism that participants expressed about their peers, and did not change the rate at which they trusted the other people they saw in the videotapes. Other participants, however, were given feedback, regardless of whether they decided to trust the other person. Now given complete information about the behavior of others, participants quickly learned how generous and kind their peers were. As a consequence, they were more likely to trust others, and ended up earning more money in the experiment.

A general negativity bias towards others

As can be seen in the two examples above, biases in experience sampling suggest a general negativity bias in impressions about human nature. People who initially leave a favorable impression get lots of chances to disprove that impression; those who initially leave an unfavorable impression never get a chance to correct that impression. An experience sampling account of human error, however, suggests clues about when these negativity biases are more likely to last versus dissolve away. What matters is whether people must continue interactions with people who left negative impressions. In those situations in which people must continue, those others are given ample opportunity to disprove negative impressions. And what types of people are given these opportunities? Family members and co-workers are two such types. In addition, people who fall in the same social circle – i.e., who are socially similar to the person forming the impression – are given the same chance. People with whom we interact with only infrequently, or people who fall into out-groups we rarely deal with or can avoid, are given less of a chance to disprove initial unfavorable impressions (Denrell, 2005). As such, experience sampling may stand as an important explanation for in-group/out-group biases in social cognition. People continue to interact with in-group members in ways that leave them over time with accurate impressions of those individuals, whereas out-group members never get the same opportunity to correct a negative impression that they may make.

Social norms

Beyond the payoffs and probabilities that economists focus on, social norms also have an impact on the decisions that people make (Cialdini, Kallgren, & Reno, 1991; Lindenberg, 2008). People are certainly attuned to whether others are following common social norms. Researchers in the Netherlands took a pristine alleyway and covered it in graffiti, despite the presence of a "no graffiti" sign. Doing so caused people leaving their bicycles in the alley to more frequently leave litter, as shown by what people did with flyers the authors had attached to their bicycle handlebars. Rates of littering the flyers went from 33% when there was no graffiti to 69% when there was. In a follow-up study, setting off firecrackers (known to be illegal) while people picked up their bicycles from a storage shed prompted littering rates to go from 52% to 80% (Keizer, Lindenberg, & Steg, 2008).

Social norms come in two varieties. First are *injunctive* social norms, which refer to dictums about how people should behave – the behaviors people can do that are either socially acceptable or unacceptable. Practically everyone knows that one should hold the door open for an elderly person, but should not steal from his or her wallet or purse. Some social norms are more diffuse and obscure, yet no less impactful on social behavior. For example, if an employee making $9 an hour leaves a business, it is perfectly acceptable for the business owner to offer $7 to any new employee who is hired to do the same work, if that is what other businesses are paying. However, if the business owner merely finds out that other businesses are paying the lower wage, it is not acceptable to unilaterally lower an employee's wage from $9 to $7 (Kahneman, Knetsch, & Thaler, 1986). That is, people respond to rules of fairness – but what is fair depends on many nuances of a social situation, such as whether a person is establishing new ground rules for a relationship or dealing with a relationship with ground rules already established.

Many injunctive norms influence judgments and decisions. Perhaps one of the strongest is reciprocation: If someone does something beneficial for you, you should return the favor. Cialdini and colleagues have demonstrated the power of this norm in an experiment involving inducing hotel guests to reuse their towels and linens, a decision that saves the hotel money but also saves the environment a little bit of wear and tear. What would induce guests to request that their towels not be washed and replaced every day? Reminding hotel guests of their social responsibility to the environment, or even promising to donate to environmental causes does not have much of an impact of the choices hotel guests make. However, having the hotel announce that it had already donated to environmental causes prompted the "re-use" rate among hotel guests to rise from 31% to 45% (Goldstein, Griskevicius, & Cialdini, 2007). Presumably, hotel guests feel impelled to reciprocate the actions that the hotel has already taken on their behalf.

But beyond injunctive norms lay *descriptive* norms, norms not about what people should do but rather what they actually do. Descriptive norms influence behavior to a degree that is surprising. For example, in a follow-up study on hotel guests and their towel usage, telling guests (truthfully) that 75% of their fellow guests opted to re-use their towels caused the re-use rate to leap significantly – and leap even more if guests were informed about the re-use rate of past guests who had stayed in their specific hotel room (Goldstein et al., 2007).

Curiously, although people concede that injunctive norms powerfully shape their behavior, they seem to under-appreciate just how impactful descriptive norms are. In a study of energy conservation, the biggest predictor of Californian residents' behavior was their beliefs about what most people did, but residents thought this was the least impactful consideration in their behavior. Telling residents about other people's conversation efforts had the largest impact on their own efforts, among several other interventions, but residents reported they thought this would be the least impactful intervention (Nolan, Schultz, Cialdini, Goldstein, & Griskevicius, 2008).

Emotional dimensions of decision making

With its central focus on decision making that is economic in nature, JDM research has tended to stick closely to the types of variables that economists presume drive people's decisions, such as the benefit of possible outcomes and the likelihood that those outcomes can be attained. The process of decision making has been thought of as "cool" in nature. The individual sits back, analyzes all the possibilities in a dispassionate manner, and then calmly calculates what decision is in his or her best interest. To be sure, the calculation might be sloppy, and it might be wrong, but it is a cold calculation nonetheless.

That said, economics has often let "hotter" processes such as emotion or visceral states such as hunger or thirst enter the picture. After all, people tend to choose those options they believe will bring them *pleasure* while allowing them to avoid *pain*. However, newer work is increasingly showing that emotions may play an even greater role in judgment and decision making, influencing people's calculations – if there are calculations at all – in a wide variety of ways.

In all, emerging theories of emotion in decision making make four different claims:

1   People, in part, base their decisions on the emotions they anticipate they will feel in the future.
2   Emotions color the interpretation of the elements people consider in their decisions, even if those elements, on the face of it, have nothing to do with the emotion.
3   Emotion can "hijack" the decision-making process away from the typically cold and deliberate analysis that economists envision.
4   People may not perfectly understand how emotions influence their preferences and decisions, leading them to make decision-making errors not anticipated by a model of the decision maker as a cold calculator.

Emotions as inputs in the decision-making calculus

Imagine someone gave you a choice between two gambles. In the first, you have a 50% chance of winning $8; otherwise, you would lose $8. In the second gamble, you have a 20% chance of winning $32, and an 80% chance of losing $8. Assume that you chose the first gamble, but both gambles were played. You win the $8, but you find out that you would have won $32 if you had chosen the second gamble. What would you feel? If you are like most people, you would feel many things, but regret is likely to be in the picture (Mellers, Schwartz, Ho, & Ritov, 1997; Mellers, Schwartz, & Ritov, 1999).

Suppose instead you were given another choice between these two gambles. This time, you choose the second gamble, but you lose. Suppose you would have lost the first gamble, too. Do you feel worse about losing the second gamble than you would about losing the first, or better? People differ, but most people look at that $32 they could have won in the second gamble (vs the mere $8 in the first gamble) and feel worse. Specifically, they feel disappointment in missing out on such a large prize (Mellers, Schwartz, Ho, & Ritov, 1997; Mellers, Schwartz, & Ritov, 1999).

Mainstream work in economics has long suggested that such emotional calculations of regret and disappointment matter (Bell, 1982, 1985; Loomes & Sugden, 1982, 1986). People project themselves into all the possible end states of their decisions, anticipate how they would feel in each end state, and then base their decisions, in part, on what those emotions will be (for a review, see Loewenstein, Weber, Hsee, & Welch, 2001). Empirical work in psychology confirms these economic suspicions (Mellers et al., 1997, 1999), in that the attractiveness of a risky bet depends, in part, on the potential disappointment or regret that it might produce. Once more, this empirical work suggests that level of surprise matters as well. To the extent that a positive event is unexpected, it is even more pleasurable. To the extent that a negative event is a shock, the more displeasurable it is. Such surprise effects have been observed, for example, in both laboratory choices between gambles and in real-world settings such as women taking pregnancy tests (Mellers & McGraw, 2001).

Emotions color the interpretation of decision inputs

Beyond being direct inputs into decisions, emotions have an impact via the way they alter people's interpretation of other decision inputs. Work on the *affect heuristic*, for example, has shown that good moods alter how people perceive potential benefits, with people perceiving possible benefits of their actions to be greater when they are in an overall positive mood, or attach a positive mood to a stimulus they are considering (Slovic, Finucane, Peters, & MacGregor, 2002). For example, participants in one study were asked to examine Chinese ideographs that, for a time, were associated with positive (e.g., beauty) or negative (e.g., disease) meanings. The true, and rather neutral, meanings for all the ideographs (e.g., desks) were then revealed to participants, and they were asked which ideographs they preferred. Participants showed a preference for those ideographs that had been originally colored by positive meaning over those that had been tainted with negative connotations (Sherman, Kim, & Zajonc, 1998).

On the flip side, feelings like sadness or disgust make people see the status quo as worse than they would otherwise, making them more likely to exchange it for an alternative. In a demonstration of the impact of such emotions, Lerner, Small, and Loewenstein (2004) exposed participants to one of three different film clips: one clip, designed to elicit sadness, focused on the tragic death of a boy's mentor; another clip, designed to elicit disgust, depicted a man using an unsanitary toilet; the last clip was neutral in nature, and showed a few minutes of swimming fish. Half of the participants in each film clip condition were given a set of highlighters and asked the price at which they would sell them back to the experimenter. The remaining participants were asked about the price they would pay to purchase the highlighters.

Participants who had viewed the neutral clip displayed the usual endowment effect: those owning highlighters thought their value was higher than those merely considering buying the highlighters. Indeed, potential sellers asked for a dollar more to sell the highlighters back to the experimenters than what potential buyers were willing to pay to acquire them. However, no such endowment effect arose in the disgust condition. Owners asked for a price that was roughly what buyers were willing to pay. Those in the sadness condition actually showed a *reverse* endowment effect. Those given an opportunity to sell named, on average, a price (roughly $3) that was far lower than buyers on average were willing to pay (roughly $4.50).

Fear and anger each also have a unique impact on decision making. Fear makes people see potential risks as more likely to occur, thus prompting them to be more cautious in their decision making. Anger has an opposite effect, making people more certain that any action they take will have an impact on the world (Lerner, Gonzalez, Small, & Fischhoff, 2003; Lerner & Keltner, 2001; Slovic et al., 2002). These impacts toward pessimism with fear and optimism with anger have been shown with national surveys. Those, for example, who expressed more anxiety about the terrorist attacks of September 11, 2001, also believed there was a higher likelihood of a future attack. Those who expressed more desire for vengeance foresaw a lower likelihood of attack. Once more, asking people to review the events of September 11, 2001, also had an impact on risk judgments. Those asked specifically to review what about those events made them fearful were more likely to think that future attacks were likely and to take precautionary steps to protect themselves. Those directed to think about what made them angry about the attacks did the opposite (Lerner et al., 2003).

Emotion as an alternative route to decisions

But emotion can influence economic decision making in an entirely different way, by causing people to abandon the cold and deliberative mental apparatus that economists assume in favor of one that is more intuitive, rapid, and emotional. That is, among psychologists, it is customary to talk about a "two systems" or "dual process" approach to decision making (Chaiken & Trope, 1999; Sloman, 1996). One such system or approach is the economist's system – a decision-making device that consciously, effortfully, and consciously analyzes and calculates its way to a decision based on rules and algorithms. This system is oft-times labeled "System 2" (Kahneman, 2003). The other system or approach is one that quickly conjures a decision out of automatic associations, rapid assessments of similarity, quick rules of thumb, and intuitive leaps. Most of its operation can occur outside of consciousness, and its conduct can be infused with emotion. This more crude and primitive, but fast, system is often referred to as "System 1" (Kahneman, 2003).

Introducing emotion into a decision can enhance the influence of System 1 and negate the influence of System 2. Consider, for example, the following scenario. You are at the control station managing several trolley cars out on the tracks, and one specific trolley car is rapidly approaching five workmen standing on the tracks, unaware of the speeding danger bearing down on them. There is only one chance to save their lives. You can pull a lever at the station that will switch the trolley to a different track. There is, however, a single workman on this other track, and so he would be killed as the other lives are sparred.

Given this scenario, a good number of people reluctantly and regretfully decide to pull the lever and save the five lives at the expense of this other person's life. It is, as best one can tell, the right calculus, as given to us by System 2. However, let's change the scenario in one important detail. In this detail, to save the five lives of the workmen, your only chance is to push a stocky guy onto the tracks – killing him but blocking the trolley from the other five men. Here, very few people decide to push the guy, even though the calculus of losing one life to save five is the same. Why? It appears that people consider this decision to be more rife with emotion, and with that emotion is a discarding of any deliberative calculation of lives saved versus lost (Greene, Sommerville, Nystrom, Darley, & Cohen, 2001).

Other experiments show that calculation flies out the window when vivid emotion or visceral states are introduced into a situation. Consider students who were asked whether they wanted to take a gamble to win some cookies – which they were not shown but which were described to them. In this situation, students paid a good deal of attention to the likelihood that they could win before they decided to gamble. However, when, instead, the experimenter brought freshly baked cookies into the lab room, surrounding participants with the sight and smell of the delectable treats, participants gambled to win them regardless of the risk (Ditto, Pizarro, Epstein, Jacobson, & MacDonald, 2006). Similarly, when weighing how much to gamble to win a $500 discount on their college tuition, participants give much more weight to the chances of winning than when the $500 discount applied to a more emotional event, such as a trip to Paris. On the negative side, when considering how much to pay to avoid a negative outcome, people pay close attention to odds of losing when considering an outcome that carried little emotion with it, such as losing $20, but much less to those odds when the event induces emotion, such as receiving an electric shock (Rottenstreich & Hsee, 2001).

That all said, a few interpretational caveats might be put in place. It is true that active emotion can change how people reach the decisions they reach, but even though it is customary to talk about those changes as moving from a System 2 approach to a System 1 approach, one should not assume that there are actually two physical systems in the brain. There may be, but to what extent there are separate "systems" is something for future research to determine. People may have within them different ways they can approach problems, but whether or not that reflects something about the physiological set-up of the human organism is unknown. One aspect of System 1 versus System 2 suggests that separating these approaches into different physical structures may be difficult, in that asking a handful of researchers to describe the two systems, and one will hear many varying descriptions of what the two systems supposedly are. Does System 1 always operate under awareness? Can it be controlled? Is System 2 devoid of all emotion? Different researchers come to different conclusions, suggesting also that the core difference between the two systems is easy to grasp, but the nuances of how they differ and how they interact with one another is entirely a different matter – leading one to be cautious about whether they should be considered different "systems" at all.

People misunderstand the role played by emotions

Finally, the introduction of emotion into the decision-making mix provides many more opportunities for people to make mistakes in their decisions, and recent work suggests that some of those mistakes arise because people do not anticipate the impact that emotions will have on their preferences and actions. For example, Van Boven and colleagues asked college students in a large lecture class whether they were willing for $5 to go up to the front of the class and dance to the funk classic *Super Freak* by Rick James. When the question was merely hypothetical, over a third of respondents stated that they were willing to volunteer. However, when the request was a real one, only 8% of respondents actually volunteered. When asked how much money would induce them to dance, respondents considering the request hypothetically thought that they would have to be paid, on average, $20. For those considering a real request, the average payment required was over $50 (Van Boven, Loewenstein, & Dunning, 2005;

for similar data, see Van Boven, Loewenstein, Welch, & Dunning, in press).

Van Boven, Loewenstein, and colleagues termed these different preferences to be the result of *empathy gaps*, proposing that people in an emotionally cold state had little insight into how much being placed in a hot state would change how they viewed the situation and what their preferences would be. The reverse was also true: people in hot states would have little access to how they would construe the situation if they were in a more emotionally cold state. In support of this analysis, Van Boven and colleagues found that inducing negative emotions in respondents, such as anxiety or anger, prompted respondents considering hypothetical requests to respond more like respondents considering real requests in the *Super Freak* scenario. They, too, were reluctant to perform potentially embarrassing behaviors in front of their peers. Reducing anxiety did the opposite, leading respondents to considering hypothetical choices to reach conclusions that differed significantly from those considering actual requests (Van Boven et al., in press).

These empathy gaps between people in their cold and hot emotional states may prompt other mistakes in behavior. To the extent that people fail to anticipate the irresistible pull of temptation, they may place themselves in tempting situations that lead to unwanted behavior. Nordgren and colleagues, in their studies of *restraint bias*, found that former smokers who believed they were the able to control their impulses were the ones most likely to place themselves in tempting situations, such as spending time with other smokers. In a follow-up, he found that it was exactly those who placed themselves in those situations who were the ones most likely to have resumed smoking (Nordgren, van Harreveld, & van der Pligt, 2009). That is, a vaulted sense in "cold" situations that one could control one's appetite for cigarettes ultimately led people to approach circumstances in which that appetite would "hot up," leading to a failure to control. Those with the biggest empathy gaps with themselves when it came to smoking were the one's least likely to succeed at quitting.

The presence of empathy gaps may also have implications for social policy. Middle-school teachers were less supportive of policies aimed at curbing bullying unless they were first asked to experience a bout of social pain themselves: namely, a "Cyberball" computer game in which two other players refused to throw a ball to the respondent. After experiencing such social exclusion, teachers were more willing to endorse treatment for bullied students and greater sanctions against those who did the bullying (Nordgren, Banas, & MacDonald, 2011).

Embodiment

Newer work also suggests that a person's physical body may play a direct role in influencing his or her judgments and decisions: i.e., the physical experience people have of the environment shapes how they make decisions, a stance known as *embodied cognition* (Barsalou, 2008; Lakoff & Johnson, 1999; Niedenthal, Barsalou, Winkielman, Krauth-Gruber, & Ric, 2005). Central to the notion of embodied cognition is the assertion that physical experiences influence judgments that would seem, at first blush, to be entirely abstract and conceptual. This impact of the physical body on more conceptual judgments occurs, it is argued, because people's representations of real-world problems are distributed across a number of sensorimotor systems in the brain – some that involve more representations of the body and of the physical world as well as more conceptual knowledge (Barsalou, 2008).

A growing set of examples argues for this physical–conceptual link. For example, when people are surveyed about the importance of various social issues, they rate those issues are more important if the clipboard that holds the questionnaire is heavier rather than lighter (Jostmann, Lakens, & Schubert, 2009). People think global warming is more likely if they are in a hot room, and that drought is more likely to occur if they are thirsty (Risen & Critcher, 2011). When weighing up to take a trip between two cities, participants see the trip as more effortful and costly if the trip involves going north (i.e., up) than the reverse trip going south (i.e., down) (Nelson & Simmons, 2009).

Neuroscientific underpinnings

But, finally, there is the body itself. Clearly, a person's decisions are supported by brain activity, and many scholars are collecting neuroscientific data to see how exactly the brain operates as people strive toward their judgments and decisions. Such data can take on many forms. Through fMRI (functional magnetic resonance imaging) techniques, researchers can examine which areas of the brain are active as people reach decisions. Via single neuron measurement, researchers can examine how active a single neuron is during decision making, although this technique is so invasive it usually is constrained to non-human animals. By measuring ERPs (event-related brain potentials), researchers can record the presence and time-course of neural events associated with decisions. By examining brain-damaged patients, scientists can assess the functions of decision making that are corrupted or disappear due to specific brain injuries (Camerer, Loewenstein, & Prelec, 2005).

Although in their infancy, neuroscientific studies of decision making have already provided key insights. Damasio and colleagues have shown, for example, how a learning history within a certain context can leave *somatic markers*, emotional reactions to potential decisions that guide people's future decisions. In one study, non-patients and patients with damage to their ventromedial prefrontal cortex (VMPFC) played a gambling game in which they could take turns betting on one of two decks of cards. One deck provided for small wins but occasional small losses. The second deck was more risk/reward, and provided for big wins but occasionally massive losses. Immediately after such a loss with this second deck, all participants avoided it, but those with VMPFC damage more quickly returned to bet on that deck than did non-patients. Presumably, VMPFC damage inhibited patients' ability to encode emotional events, such as those massive losses, that feed into a more permanent feature of a somatic marker. Without it, participants were not steered away from the high-risk deck (Bechara, Damasio, Damasio, & Anderson, 1994; Bechara, Damasio, Tranel, & Damasio, 1997).

Neuroscientific data have also been found to validate the distinction, made above, between those decisions made under cold rational analysis (e.g., System 2) versus those that involve more quick emotional reactions (e.g., System 1). Consider the two versions of the trolley problem described above. In the colder version, in which one could save five lives by sacrificing one through the flip of a railroad switch, brain imaging studies have shown that areas associated with conscious and deliberate thinking, such as the parietal lobes and middle frontal gyrus, are more active. In the hotter version, in which one had to push someone onto the tracks to save the five workers, areas more associated with emotion were more active, such as the left and right angular gyrus, bilateral posterior cingulate gyrus, and medial frontal gyrus (Greene et al., 2001).

Neuroscientific data also help to explain why people give much more weight to present events than those events taking place further out in the future. According to McClure, Laibson, Loewenstein, and Cohen (2004), immediate events are processed by the limbic system, which is sensitive to emotional stimuli and which responds to rewards that are immediately available. Events in the future, however, are processed more by frontoparietal regions that tend to be engaged more in higher-order cognitive functioning. As such, when people make a choice between an immediate versus a delayed reward, the comparison is quite different (between a choice eliciting more vivid

emotions than the other) than when people compare two delayed options (which involve a decision residing more in a cool cognitive environment).

Thus, in early extant examples, neuroscientific data has provided a level of explanation for a few economic phenomena, but it also provides a great promise for theoretical development that has yet to be realized. As mentioned earlier, it is the custom of economic theorists to take some variables, postulate some relationships among those variables, construct a model in which those variables are allowed to interact, and then see what results fall out from the model they have thus created. Usually, an implicit assumption of economic models is that there is only one "person" or "system" in the model. For example, in deciding whether to buy a car, there is only one person, one "decider," who is weighing the pros and cons of making a purchase.

Neuroscientific evidence suggests, however, that this may not be the best way to model decision making in many contexts. Instead of being unitary, the decision maker may instead be many decision makers that work in concert or in conflict. For intertemporal choice, for example, there may be one "decider" in the limbic system, and another decider contained in the frontoparietal region. For other choices, there may be emotional systems pulling for one decision and a more rational decider pulling for another. That is, economic modelers in the future may more accurately base their models more on the many distinct processes going on in the brain as people make decisions, and thus may find themselves modeling multiple brain processes (multiple deciders, if you will) more than some ideal picture of an individual lost in contemplation (Loewenstein, Rick, & Cohen, 2008).

Nudging

Finally, efforts are increasing to apply judgment and decision-making principles to real-world problems. One more visible variant of this has been the book *Nudge* by Richard Thaler and Cass Sunstein (2008; see also Thaler & Sunstein, 2003), which suggests that health and well-being can be enhanced by how the *choice architecture* of an individual is constructed – without taking away any of that individual's freedom to make the choice they want.

One simple way to craft the architecture of a choice is by selecting which decision option is a default. It is well-known, via the endowment effect, that people tend to stick with the default option, and so rates of choosing any particular action can be increased by making it a default. Worried that people fail to save enough for retirement? Then, make saving for retirement at a certain rate a default decision that people have the freedom to opt out of (Benartzi & Thaler, 2004). Concerned that too few people donate their organs after their death? Then, make donating one's organs a default decision that they, of course, can reverse (Johnson & Goldstein, 2003).

Other judgment and decision-making principles, trivial to introduce into the decision-making process, can have profound implications for the decision maker. Poorer individuals, for example, have been shown to deposit their money in banks less often than those more affluent, even though the benefits for doing so can be as great, if not greater, for those less well-off. Poorer individuals will sign up for bank accounts if they attend workshops that explain the mechanics of doing so, but individuals will sign up at a greater rate if there is a bank representative on-site to immediately complete the paperwork – thus removing some of the incidental hurdles that prevent people from following through on decisions they favor (Bertrand, Mullainathan, & Shafir, 2006). In addition, making salient important parts of an individual's identity – such as reminding women how much they have invested in their family – causes people to sign up for bank accounts or financial literacy courses (Bertrand et al., 2006).

CONCLUSION

The key to any intellectual enterprise in psychology is to construct a theoretical model of the human being that mimics what real human beings do in their everyday lives. Work in JDM has followed that project in a specific way – by taking the model of the rational actor ascendant in economics and asking how that model could be altered or improved to better mimic decision making in everyday life.

In so doing, JDM work has provided at least five central insights about human decision making and how it is not necessarily rational:

- People follow crude and quick heuristics rather than exhaustive analysis to reach their decisions.
- References points in the environment sway judgments in decisive ways.
- People use the information given to them to make a decision, but often fail to recognize that there is other information they should consult as well.
- They lean heavily on confirmatory evidence and neglect disconfirming information.

- When thinking about possible outcomes, they give disproportionate weight to outcomes that happen with certainty, in the near future, or which feature loss.

In this chapter, I have discussed how these five insights arise again and again across many different life settings and across diverse types of tasks and decisions.

But, in discussing these insights, I hasten to acknowledge that this list is not sacred, and it is likely to be added to in the next few decades of JDM research. Many types of topics, such as the role of emotion in decision making, promise to reveal further ways in which the rational actor model should be revised to create a model that better resembles what humans look like, and how they act, throughout the course of their lives.

Therein lies a pleasant irony. As Herb Simon was fit to say, anything that gives us new knowledge gives us an opportunity to be more rational. Thus, in discovering and delineating the ways in which each of us individually fails to be that perfect rational actor, we give ourselves the best shot to achieve more rational outcomes in the future.

ACKNOWLEDGMENT

The writing of this review was supported by National Science Foundation Grant 0745806. The views expressed in this review do not necessarily reflect those of the Foundation.

NOTE

1 The specifics of Bayes' theorem and how the final answer of 92% is calculated goes beyond the scope of this chapter. However, there are many books that describe the basics of Bayes' theorem and its uses, such as Howsom and Urbach (2005).

REFERENCES

Ainslie, G. (1992). *Picoeconomics*. Cambridge, UK: Cambridge University Press.

Ainslie, G., & Herrnstein, R. J. (1981). Preference reversal and delayed reinforcement. *Animal Learning Behavior, 9,* 476–482.

Alpert, M., & Raiffa, H. (1982). A progress report on the training of probability assessors. In D. Kahneman, P. Slovic, & A. Tversky (Eds.), *Judgment under uncertainty: Heuristics and biases* (pp. 294–305). New York: Cambridge University Press.

Ariely, D., Loewenstein, G., & Prelec, D. (2003). "Coherent arbitrariness": Stable demand curves without stable preferences. *Quarterly Journal of Economics, 118*, 73–105.

Barsalou, L. W. (2008). Grounding symbolic operations in the brain's modal systems. In G. R. Semin & E. R. Smith (Eds.), *Embodied grounding: Social, cognitive, affective, and neuroscientific approaches* (pp. 9–42). New York: Cambridge University Press.

Bechara, A., Damasio, A. R., Damasio, H., & Anderson, S. W. (1994). Insensitivity to future consequences following damage to human prefrontal cortex. *Cognition, 50*, 7–15.

Bechara, A., Damasio, H., Tranel, D., & Damasio, A. R. (1997). Deciding advantageously before knowing the advantageous strategy. *Science, 275*, 1293–1295.

Becker, G. S. (1976). *The economic approach to human behavior.* Chicago: University of Chicago Press.

Bell, D. E. (1982). Regret in decision making under uncertainty. *Operations Research, 30*, 961–981.

Bell, D. E. (1985). Disappointment in decision making under uncertainty. *Operations Research, 33*, 1–27

Benartzi, S., & Thaler, R. H. (2002). How much is investor autonomy worth? *Journal of Finance, 57*, 1593–1616.

Benartzi, S., & Thaler, R.H. (2004). Save more tomorrow: Using behavioral economics to increase employee saving. *Journal of Political Economy, 112,* 164–187.

Bertrand, M., Mullainathan, S., & Shafir, E. (2006). Behavioral economics and marketing in aid of decision making among the poor. *Journal of Public Policy & Marketing, 25*, 8–23.

Beyth-Marom, R. (1982). Perception of correlation reexamined. *Memory & Cognition, 10*, 511–519.

Buehler, R., Griffin, D., & MacDonald, H. (1997). The role of motivated reasoning in optimistic time predictions. *Personality and Social Psychology Bulletin, 23*, 238–247.

Buehler, R., Griffin, D., & Ross, M. (1994). Exploring the "planning fallacy": Why people underestimate their task completion times. *Journal of Personality and Social Psychology, 67*, 366–381.

Buehler, R., Griffin, D., & Ross, M. (2002). Inside the planning fallacy: The causes and consequences of optimistic time predictions. In T. Gilovich, D. Griffin, & D. Kahneman (Eds.), *Heuristics and biases: The psychology of intuitive judgment* (pp. 250–270). Cambridge, UK: Cambridge University Press.

Camerer, C., Loewenstein, G., & Prelec, D. (2005). Neuroeconomics: How neuroscience can inform economics. *Journal of Economic Literature, 43*, 9–64.

Cervone, D., & Peake, P. (1986). Anchoring, efficacy, and action: The influence of judgmental heuristics on self-efficacy judgments and behavior. *Journal of Personality and Social Psychology, 50*, 492–501.

Chaiken, S., & Trope, Y. (Eds.) (1999). *Dual-process theories in social psychology.* New York: Guilford Press.

Chapman, G. B., & Johnson, E. J. (2002). Incorporating the irrelevant: Anchors in judgments of belief and value. In T. Gilovich, D. Griffin, & D. Kahneman (Eds.), *Heuristics and biases: The psychology of intuitive judgment* (pp. 120–138). Cambridge, UK: Cambridge University Press.

Cialdini, R. B., Kallgren, C. A., & Reno, R. R. (1991). A focus theory of normative conduct: A theoretical refinement and reevaluation of the role of norms in human behavior. In M. P. Zanna (Ed.), *Advances in experimental social psychology* (Vol. 24, pp. 202–234). San Diego, CA: Academic Press.

Denrell, J. (2005). Why most people disapprove of me: Experience sampling in impression formation. *Psychological Review, 112*, 951–978.

Dhar, R., & Simonson, I. (2003). The effect of forced choice on choice. *Journal of Marketing Research, 40*, 146–160.

Ditto, P. H., Pizarro, D. A., Epstein, E. B., Jacobson, J. A., & MacDonald, T. K. (2006). Visceral influences on risk taking behavior. *Journal of Behavioral Decision Making, 19*, 99–113.

Dunning , D., & Madey, S. F. (1995). Comparison processes in counterfactual reasoning. In N. Roese & J. Olson (Eds.), *What might have been: The social psychology of counterfactual thinking* (pp. 103–132). Hillsdale, NJ: Erlbaum

Dunning , D., & Parpal , M. (1989). Mental addition versus subtraction in counterfactual reasoning: On assessing the impact of personal actions and life events. *Journal of Personality and Social Psychology, 57*, 5–15.

Edwards, W. (1954). The theory of decision making. *Psychological Bulletin, 41*, 380–417.

Edwards, W. (1961). Behavioral decision theory. *Annual Review of Psychology, 12*, 473–498.

Edwards, W. (1968). Conservatism in human information processing. In B. Kleinmuntz (Eds.), *Formal representation of human judgment* (pp. 17–52). New York: Wiley.

Fetchenhauer, D., & Dunning, D. (2009). Do people trust too much or too little? *Journal of Economic Psychology, 30*, 263–276.

Fetchenhauer, D., & Dunning, D. (2010). Why so cynical? Asymmetric feedback underlies misguided skepticism in the trustworthiness of others. *Psychological Science, 21*, 189–193.

Fiske, S. T. (1992). Thinking is for doing: Portraits of social cognition from daguerreotype to laserphoto. *Journal of Personality and Social Psychology, 63*, 877–889.

Fox, C. R., Ratner, R. K., & Lieb, D. (2005). How subjective grouping of options influences choices and allocation: Diversification bias and the phenomenon of partition dependence. *Journal of Experimental Psychology: General, 134*, 538–551.

Fox, C. R., & Rottenstreich, Y. (2003). Partition priming in judgment under uncertainty. *Psychological Science, 14*, 195–200.

Frederick, S., Loewenstein, G., & O'Donoghue, T. (2002). Time discounting and time preference: A critical review. *Journal of Economic Literature, 40*, 350–401.

Friedman, M., & Savage, L. J. (1948). The utility analysis of choices involving risks. *Journal of Political Economy, 56*, 279–304.

Gilbert, D. T., Pinel, E. C., Wilson, T. D., Blumberg, S. J., & Wheatley, T. P. (1998). Immune neglect: A source of durability bias in affective forecasting. *Journal of Personality and Social Psychology, 75*, 617–638.

Goldstein, N. J., Griskevicius, V., & Cialdini, R. B. (2007). Invoking social norms: A social psychology perspective on improving hotels' linen-reuse programs. *Cornell Hotel and Restaurant Administration Quarterly, 48,* 145–150.

Green, L., Fry, A. F., & Myerson, J. (1994). Discounting of delayed rewards: A life-span comparison. *Psychological Science, 5,* 33–36.

Greene, J. D., Sommerville, R. B., Nystrom, L. E., Darley, J. M., & Cohen, J. D. (2001). An fMRI investigation of emotional engagement in moral judgment. *Science, 293,* 2105–2108.

Griffin, D., & Tversky, A. (1992). The weighing of evidence and the determinants of confidence. *Cognitive Psychology, 24,* 411–435.

Hicks, J., & Allen, R. (1934). A reconsideration of the theory of value. *Economica, N.S. 1,* 52–76 and 196–221.

Hoch, S. J. (1985). Counterfactual reasoning and accuracy in predicting personal events. *Journal of Experimental Psychology: Learning, Memory, and Cognition, 11,* 719–731.

Holcombe, R. (1989). *Economic models and methodology.* New York: Greenwood Press.

Howson, C., & Urbach, P. (2005). *Scientific reasoning: The Bayesian approach* (3rd ed.). Chicago, IL: Open Court.

Hsee, C. K., & Zhang, J. (2004). Distinction bias: Misprediction and mischoice due to joint evaluation. *Journal of Personality and Social Psychology, 86,* 680–695.

Huber, J., Payne, J. W., & Puto, C. (1982). Adding asymmetrically dominated alternatives: Violations of regularity and the similarity hypothesis. *Journal of Consumer Research, 9,* 90–98.

Johnson, E. J., & Goldstein, D. G. (2003). Do defaults save lives? *Science, 302,* 1338–1339.

Jorgensen, M. (2004). Top-down and bottom-up expert estimation of software development effort. *Information and Software Technology, 46,* 3–16.

Jostmann, N. B., Lakens, D., & Schubert, T. W. (2009). Weight as an embodiment of importance. *Psychological Science, 20,* 1169–1174.

Kahneman, D. (2003). Maps of bounded rationality: Psychology for behavioral economics. *American Economic Review, 93,* 1449–1475.

Kahneman, D., Knetsch, J. L., & Thaler, R. H. (1986). Fairness as a constraint on profit seeking: Entitlements and the market. *American Economic Review, 76,* 728–741.

Kahneman, D., Knetsch, J. L., & Thaler, R. H. (1990). Experimental tests of the endowment effect and the Coase theorem. *Journal of Political Economy, 98,* 1325–1348.

Kahneman, D., Slovic, P., & Tversky, A. (1982). *Judgment under uncertainty: Heuristics and biases.* New York: Cambridge University Press.

Kahneman, D., & Tversky, A. (1972). Subjective probability: A judgment of representativeness. *Cognitive Psychology, 3,* 430–454.

Kahneman, D., & Tversky, A. (1973). On the psychology of prediction. *Psychological Review, 80,* 237–251.

Kahneman, D., & Tversky, A. (1979). Prospect theory: An analysis of decision under risk. *Econometrica, 47,* 263–291.

Kahneman, D., & Tversky, A. (1984). Choices, values, and frames. *American Psychologist, 39,* 341–350.

Keizer, K., Lindenberg, S., & Steg, L. (2008). The spreading of disorder. *Science, 322,* 1681–1685.

Klayman, J., Soll, J. B., Gonzalez-Vallejo, C., & Barlas, S. (1999). Overconfidence: It depends on how, what, and whom you ask. *Organizational Behavior and Human Decision Processes, 79,* 216–247.

Kruger, J., & Evans, M. (2004). If you don't want to be late, enumerate: Unpacking reduces the planning fallacy. *Journal of Experimental Social Psychology, 40,* 586–594.

Kunda, Z., Fong, G. T., Sanitioso, R., & Reber, E. (1993). Directional questions direct self-conceptions. *Journal of Experimental Social Psychology, 29,* 63–86.

Lakoff, G., & Johnson, M. (1999). *Philosophy in the flesh: The embodied mind and its challenge to Western thought.* New York: Basic Books.

Lerner, J. S., Gonzalez, R. M., Small, D. A., & Fischhoff, B. (2003). Effects of fear and anger on perceived risks of terrorism: A national field experiment. *Psychological Science, 14,* 144–150.

Lerner, J. S., & Keltner, D. (2001). Fear, anger, and risk. *Journal of Personality and Social Psychology, 81,* 146–159.

Lerner, J. S., Small, D. A., & Loewenstein, G. (2004). Heart strings and purse strings – carryover effects of emotions on economic decisions. *Psychological Science, 15,* 337–341.

Lichtenstein, S., Slovic, P. Fischhoff, B., Layman, M., & Combs, B. (1978). Judged frequency of lethal events. *Journal of Experimental Psychology: Human Learning and Memory, 4,* 751–778.

Lindenberg, S. (2008). Social norms: What happens when they become more abstract? In A. Diekmann, K. Eichner, P. Schmidt, & T. Voss (Eds.), *Rational choice: Theoretische Analysen und empirische Resultate* (pp.63–82). Wiesbaden, Germany: VS Verlag.

Loewenstein, G., & Prelec, D. (1992). Anomalies in intertemporal choice: Evidence and an interpretation. *Quarterly Journal of Economics, 57,* 573–598.

Loewenstein, G., Rick, S., & Cohen, J. D. (2008). Neuroeconomics. *Annual Review of Psychology, 59,* 647–672.

Loewenstein, G. F., Weber, E. U., Hsee, C. K., & Welch, N. (2001). Risk as feelings. *Psychological Bulletin, 127,* 267–286.

Loomes, G., & Sugden, R. (1982). Regret theory: An alternative theory of rational choice under uncertainty. *Economic Journal, 92,* 805–824.

Loomes, G., & Sugden, R. (1986). Disappointment and dynamic consistency in choice under uncertainty. *Review of Economic Studies, 53,* 271–282.

McClure, S. M., Laibson, D. I., Loewenstein, G., & Cohen, J. D. (2004). Separate neural systems value immediate and delayed monetary rewards. *Science, 306,* 503–507.

Mellers, B. A., & McGraw, A. P. (2001). Anticipated emotions as guides to choice. *Current Directions in Psychological Science, 10,* 210–214.

Mellers, B. A., Schwartz, A., Ho, K., & Ritov, I. (1997). Decision affect theory: How we feel about risky options. *Psychological Science, 8,* 423–429.

Mellers, B. A., Schwartz, A., & Ritov, I. (1999). Emotion-based choice. *Journal of Experimental Psychology: General*, 128, 1–14.

Nelson, L. D., & Simmons, J. P. (2009). On southbound ease and northbound fees: Literal consequences of the metaphoric link between vertical position and cardinal direction. *Journal of Marketing Research*, 46, 715–724.

Nickerson, R. S. (1998). Confirmation bias: A ubiquitous phenomenon in many guises. *Review of General Psychology*, 2, 175–220.

Niedenthal, P. M., Barsalou, L. W., Winkielman, P., Krauth-Gruber, S., & Ric, F. (2005). Embodiment in attitudes, social perception, and emotion. *Personality and Social Psychology Review*, 9, 184–211.

Nisbett, R., & Ross, L. (1980). *Human inference: Strategies and shortcomings of social judgment*. Englewood Cliffs, NJ: Prentice Hall.

Nolan, J. M., Schultz, P. W., Cialdini, R. B., Goldstein, N. J., & Griskevicius, V. (2008). Normative social influence is underdetected. *Personality and Social Psychology Bulletin*, 34, 913–923.

Nordgren, L. F., Banas, K., &MacDonald, G. (2011). Empathy gaps for social pain: Why people underestimate the pain of social suffering. *Journal of Personality and Social Psychology*, 100, 120–128.

Nordgren, L. F., van Harreveld, F., & van der Pligt, J. (2009). The restraint bias: How the illusion of self-restraint promotes impulsive behavior. *Psychological Science*, 20, 1523–1528.

Norton, M. I., Frost, J. H., & Ariely, D. (2007). Less is more: The lure of ambiguity, or why familiarity breeds contempt. *Journal of Personality and Social Psychology*, 92, 97–105.

Novemsky, N., Dhar, R., Schwarz, N., & Simonson, I. (2007). Preference fluency in choice. *Journal of Marketing Research*, 44, 347–356.

Pareto, V. (1971). *Manual of political economy* (A. Schwier, Trans.). New York: A. M. Kelley. (Original work published 1909)

Pyszczynski, T., & Greenberg, J. (1987). Toward an integration of cognitive and motivational perspectives on social inference: A biased hypothesis-testing model. In L. Berkowitz (Ed.), *Advances in experimental social psychology* (Vol. 20, pp. 297–340). New York: Academic Press.

Redelmeier, D., Koehler, D. J., Liberman, V., & Tversky, A. (1995). Probability judgment in medicine: Discounting unspecified alternatives. *Medical Decision Making*, 15, 227–230.

Risen, J. L., & Critcher, C. R. (2011). Visceral fit: While in a visceral state, associated states of the world seem more likely. *Journal of Personality and Social Psychology*, 100, 777–793.

Rottenstreich, Y., & Hsee, C.K. (2001). Money, kisses, and electric shocks: On the affective psychology of risk. *Psychological Science*, 12(3), 185–90.

Rottenstreich, Y., & Tversky, A. (1997). Unpacking, repacking, and anchoring: Advances in support theory. *Psychological Review*, 104, 406–415.

Russo, J. E., Carlson, K. A., & Meloy, M. G. (2006). Choosing an inferior alternative. *Psychological Science*, 17, 899–904.

Russo, J. E., Medvec, V. H., & Meloy, M. G. (1996). The distortion of information during decisions. *Organizational Behavior and Human Decision Processes*, 66, 102–110.

Russo, J. E., Meloy, M. G., & Medvec, V. H. (1998). Predecisional distortion of product information. *Journal of Marketing Research*, 35, 438–452.

Russo, J. E., Meloy, M. G., & Wilks, T. J. (2000). Predecisional distortion of information by auditors and salespersons. *Management Science*, 46, 13–27.

Schwarz, N., Bless, H., Strack, F., Klumpp, G., Rittenauer-Schatka, & Simons, A. (1991). Ease of retrieval as information: Another look at the availability heuristic. *Journal of Personality and Social Psychology*, 61, 195–202.

Shafir, E. (1983), Choosing versus rejecting: Why some options are both better and worse than others. *Memory and Cognition*, 21, 546–556.

Sherman, D. A., Kim, H., & Zajonc, R. B. (1998). Affective perseverance: Cognitions change but preferences stay the same. Paper presented at the annual meeting of the American Psychological Society.

Simon, H.A. (1957). *Models of man: Social and rational*. New York: Wiley.

Simonson, I. (1989). Choice Based on Reasons: The Case of Attraction and Compromise Effects. *Journal of Consumer Research*, 16, 158–174.

Sloman, S. A., (1996). The empirical case for two systems of reasoning. *Psychological Bulletin*, 119, 3–22.

Slovic, P., Finucane, M. L., Peters, E., & MacGregor, D. G. (2002). The affect heuristic. In T. Gilovich, D. Griffin, & D. Kahneman (Eds.), *Heuristics and biases: The psychology of intuitive judgment* (pp. 397–420). New York: Cambridge University Press.

Smith, B. C., Penrod, S. D., Otto, A. L., & Park, R. C. (1996). Jurors' use of probabilistic evidence. *Law and Human Behavior*, 20, 49–82.

Smith, E. R., & Collins, E. C. (2009). Contextualizing person perception: Distributed social cognition. *Psychological Review*, 116, 343–364.

Snyder, M., & Swann, W. B. (1978). Hypothesis-testing in social interaction. *Journal of Personality and Social Psychology*, 36, 1202–1212.

Sotos, J. G. (2006). *Zebra cards: An aid to obscure diagnoses*. Mt. Vernon, VA: Mt. Vernon Book Systems.

Tabor, C. S., & Lodge, M. (2006). Motivated skepticism in the evaluation of political beliefs. *American Journal of Political Science*, 50, 755–769.

Thaler, R. H., & Sunstein, C. R. (2003). Libertarian paternalism. *American Economic Review*, 93, 175–179.

Thaler, R. H., & Sunstein, C. R. (2008), *Nudge: Improving decisions about health, wealth, and happiness*. New Haven, CT: Yale University Press.

Tversky, A. (1969). Intransitivity of preferences. *Psychological Review*, 76, 31–48.

Tversky, A., & Kahneman, K. (1971). Belief in the law of small numbers. *Psychological Bulletin*, 76, 105–110.

Tversky, A., & Kahneman, D. (1973). Availability: A heuristic for judging frequency and probability. *Cognitive Psychology, 5,* 207–232.

Tversky, A., & Kahneman, D. (1974). Judgment under uncertainty: Heuristics and biases. *Science, 185,* 1124–1130.

Tversky, A., & Khaneman, D. (1981). The framing of decisions and the psychology of choice. *Science, 211,* 453–458.

Tversky, A., & Kahneman, D. (1983). Extensional versus intuitive reasoning: The conjunction fallacy in probability judgment. *Psychological Review, 90,* 293–315.

Tversky, A., & Kahneman, D. (1986). Rational choice and the framing of decisions. *Journal of Business, 59,* 5251–5278.

Tversky, A., & Koehler, D. J. (1994). Support theory: A nonextensional representation of subjective probability. *Psychological Review, 101,* 547–567.

Van Boven, L., Loewenstein, G., & Dunning, D. (2005). The illusion of courage in social prediction: Underestimating the impact of fear of embarrassment on other people. *Organizational Behavior and Human Decision Processes, 96,* 130–141.

Van Boven, L., Loewenstein, G., Welch, E., & Dunning, D. (in press). The illusion of courage: Underestimating the impact of fear of embarrassment on the self. *Journal of Behavioral Decision Making.*

Ward, W. C., & Jenkins, H. M. (1965). The display of information and the judgment of contingency. *Canadian Journal of Psychology, 19,* 231–241.

Wason, P. (1960). On the failure to eliminate hypotheses in a conceptual task. *Quarterly Journal of Experimental Psychology, 12,* 129–140.

Wilson, T. D., Wheatley, T., Meyers, J., Gilbert, D. T., & Axsom, D. (2000). Focalism: A source of durability bias in affective forecasting. *Journal of Personality and Social Psychology, 78,* 821–836.

Windshitl, P. D., Kruger, J., & Simms, E. (2003). The influence of egocentism and focalism on people's optimism in competitions. *Journal of Personality and Social Psychology, 85,* 389–408.

14

Cognition and Action in the Social World

Ezequiel Morsella & Avi Ben-Zeev

In 2005, Dr Lawrence Summers, then president of Harvard University, was invited to speak to the question of why women were underrepresented in math, science, and engineering domains. Part of his response was that women were intrinsically inferior to men in quantitative domains, as corroborated by women's lower achievement at the high end of aptitude test curves. The same data that allegedly reflected "differential availability at the high end" (Summers, 1/14/2005) have been theorized and shown empirically to stem from social contextual factors, such as stereotype threat (Ben-Zeev, Fein, & Inzlicht, 2005; Schmader, Johns, & Forbes, 2008; Steele, 1997).

If one had to "reverse engineer" the social act performed by Summers, what would be the component (a) knowledge structures, (b) modes of thinking, and (c) action-related mechanisms responsible for it? ("Reverse engineering" is a term used to describe how one could figure out how a machine or some biological product works by taking it apart and looking at how the component parts interact with each other.) Regarding knowledge structures, there must be some difference between those of Dr Summers and those of the audience members who vehemently disagreed with his statement. Did he interpret the statistical data through the lens of a *biological* versus a *social* account of behavior (e.g., Dar-Nimrod & Heine, 2006)? Regarding the *mode* of thinking, were his conclusions based primarily on "intuitive" versus "deliberative" forms of reasoning (Darlow & Sloman, 2010)? Regarding action-related mechanisms, was Dr Summer's consequential act simply a failure of self-control,

spurred by the stimuli comprising that particular environment?

We address these questions from an action-based standpoint, a standpoint which has been neglected in mainstream psychology in America, where psychology has focused on perception and the nature of knowledge representation (e.g., concepts) in the mind/brain (Rosenbaum, 2005). As discussed in the Conclusion section, social psychological research has, unlike mainstream research in psychology, historically always looked to, and benefited from, research on the nuts-and-bolts of behavior, because social psychology always cared about what makes people act the way they do, not only in laboratory settings but also in the natural world (Lewin, 1946). In this spirit, we attempt to answer these kinds of questions by reviewing what is known about the component knowledge structures, modes of thinking, and actional mechanisms responsible for human social action. We focus on those aspects of the component phenomena that are most predictive of the variability found in actions of the social world—why some social acts are non-consequential while others are aired on the evening news.

In accord with previous work on other forms of action (Morsella & Bargh, 2010; Sperry, 1952), we approach the topic of social action from an untraditional perspective – by working backwards from overt action to the underlying (conscious and unconscious) central processes (i.e., processes occurring within the central nervous system). Hence, in Figure 14.1, we work backwards from Stage 4 to Stage 1; the contents of Figure 14.1 will become clearer as the chapter unfolds.

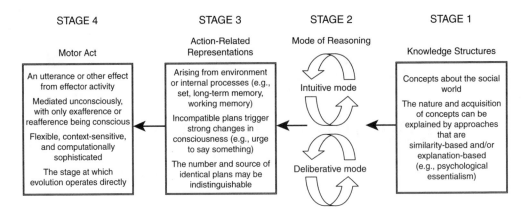

Figure 14.1   The critical components of social action production.

THE REVERSE ENGINEERING OF SOCIAL ACTION

As mentioned above, the history of psychology has been dominated by the study of epistemology (perception and knowledge representation), and the study of action has been neglected, for several reasons (cf., Rosenbaum, 2005). One of the reasons is logistical: In experiments it is much easier to control the nature of the stimuli that are presented to subjects than to control the behavior of subjects (Rosenbaum, 2005), which is far more multi-determined (i.e., influenced by many more factors). Only recently has the study of human action begun to receive the attention it deserves (e.g., Johnson-Frey, 2003; Morsella, Bargh, & Gollwitzer, 2009; Rosenbaum, 2005). In this section, we focus on what has been learned about the study of action that informs social behavior. (The reader interested in the nature of human action more generally should consult Morsella et al., 2009.)

Overt behavior and motor control (Stage 4)

It is important to appreciate that, regarding social phenomena, evolution can operate directly only on overt behavior (Roe & Simpson, 1958): "The main way in which brains actually contribute to the success of survival machines is by controlling and coordinating the contraction of muscles" (Dawkins, 1976, p. 49), or, as stated by T. H. Huxley, "The great end of life is not knowledge, but action." Similarly, Thorndike (1905) asserts, "The function of thoughts and feelings is to influence actions.... Thought aims

at knowledge, but with the final aim of using the knowledge to guide action" (p. 111).

Thus, the nature of one's thoughts, inclinations, desires, subvocalizations (e.g., when one speaks "in one's head"), and social tendencies cannot be the direct targets of evolutionary processes (Morsella, 2009). And there is no such thing as an actionless state (Skinner, 1953); even what one would consider "doing nothing" is actually a form of action. Hence, that which one actually does, and not what one intended or preferred to have done, is what is critical in the social world. It is for this reason that the ability to counteract impulsive action (e.g., when suppressing the urge to say something rude) is essential for a functional social existence (Rankin, 2007). Thus, because overt action is the undisputable "output" of the nervous system (Morsella & Bargh, 2010) and can be construed as the cognitive "unit of analysis" in natural selection, we begin by looking at action and working backwards toward central processing. When one works in this untraditional manner, much can be learned about central processing that cannot be learned otherwise (cf., Morsella & Bargh, 2010; Sperry, 1952).[1]

When observing a social action, one can perceive (directly) only the motor act. It is well established that, as sophisticated as these acts may be (Rosenbaum, Vaughan, Meulenbroek, Jax, & Cohen, 2009), motor control is unconsciously mediated (Gray, 1995, 2004; Grossberg, 1999; Jeannerod, 2006; Rosenbaum, 2002; Rossetti, 2001). Whether in limb control, finger control, or speech production (e.g., during social interaction), one is unconscious of the efferences contracting some muscle fibers but not others. One is often conscious of the perceptual consequences of motor control, through sensory information from the world (*exafference*) or body (*proprioception* from body and *reafference* from nervous processing; Sherrington, 1906). As James (1950) noted, "In perfectly simple voluntary acts there is nothing else in the mind but the kinesthetic idea ... of what the act is to be" (p. 771). From this standpoint, conscious contents regarding ongoing action are primarily of the perceptual (exafferent or reafferent) consequences of action (Jeannerod, 2006). (For a computational explanation of why motor programs must be unconscious, and consciously experienced memories must not be formed for them, see Grossberg, 1999.)

During motor acts such as shaking hands or catching a baseball, highly flexible "online" adjustments are made unconsciously (Goodale & Milner, 2004; Rosenbaum, 2002). (Motor control has historically been associated with the unconscious, dorsal processing stream in the brain; Goodale & Milner, 2004.) Each time an action is performed, new motor programs are generated online in order to deal with peculiarities of each setting. These programs are "scrapped," because the physical spatial relationship between the objects of the world and one's body is seldom unchanging (Grossberg, 1999). Importantly, for the social psychologist interested in the difference between conscious and unconscious processes, motor control serves as one of many examples revealing the degree of sophistication and flexibility found in unconscious processing (see review in Bargh and Morsella, 2008). To appreciate the sophistication of these processes (something which obviously cannot be noted through introspection alone) the reader is referred to Rosenbaum et al. (2009).

Working backwards from overt action to central processing leads us to our next question: What determines the initiation of one motor act versus another? To answer this question, one must move from Stage 4 into Stage 3 in Figure 14.1.

Environmental determinants of action in the social world (Stage 3)

One of the main predictors of the nature of "social action" is the local environment, which is the main predictor of habitual behaviors (Wood, Quinn, & Kashy, 2002) and engenders what is known as *environmentally driven automaticity.* This form of automaticity has been explained in terms of *incidental behavioral priming,* in which supraliminal stimuli (i.e., stimuli that one *is* aware of) influence one systematically, but in ways that one is unaware of (see review in Morsella & Bargh, 2011). Contemporary incidental priming research demonstrates that ambient stimuli can unconsciously influence the degree to which

behavioral dispositions are expressed (Carver, Ganellen, Froming, & Chambers, 1983; Kay, Wheeler, Bargh, & Ross, 2004). For example, business suits prime competitiveness; candy bars prime tempting hedonic goals (Fishbach, Friedman, & Kruglanski, 2003); dollar bills prime greed (Vohs, Mead, & Goode, 2006); scents such as cleaning fluids prime cleanliness goals (Holland, Hendriks, & Aarts, 2005); sitting in a professor's chair primes social behaviors associated with power (Chen, Lee-Chai, & Bargh, 2001; Custers, Maas, Wildenbeest, & Aarts, 2008); control-related words prime the reduction of prejudice (Araya, Akrami, Ekehammar, & Hedlund, 2002); and backpacks and briefcases prime cooperation and competitiveness, respectively (Kay et al., 2004). In addition, when primed with (typically word) stimuli associated with the stereotypes of "elderly" or "library," people walk slower and speak more quietly, respectively (Aarts & Dijksterhuis, 2003; Bargh, Chen, & Burrows, 1996); and when they are primed with the concept "hostility," they become more aggressive (Carver, Ganellen, Froming, & Chambers, 1983). Last, the names of close relationship partners (e.g., mother, friend) prime the goals that those partners have for the individual as well as those goals the individual characteristically pursues when with the significant other (Fitzsimons & Bargh, 2003; Shah, 2003).

These findings have led to the view that there is an automatic *perception–behavior link* from perceptual processing to action planning (Dijksterhuis & Bargh, 2001). With respect to cognitive processing, these effects have been explained at a more nuts-and-bolts level by models in which activation in the nervous system cannot help but flow from perceptuo–semantic stages of processing to action–planning stages (Ganz, 1975), models with names denoting that there is the spillage of activation from one stage of processing to another (e.g., "continuous flow" models [Eriksen & Schultz, 1979] or "cascade models" [McClelland, 1979]). (The nature of such processing is beyond the purview of the present approach; see review in Levine et al., 2007. See psychophysiological evidence for these models in Coles, Gratton, Bashore, Eriksen, & Donchin, 1985.) Learning to associate a response (e.g., a button press) when confronted with a stimulus (e.g., a visual cue) is known as *efference binding* (Haggard, Aschersleben, Gehrke, & Prinz, 2002). Efference binding often occurs consciously, but substantial research has revealed that simple *stimulus→response* ($S{\rightarrow}R$) forms of it can be triggered unconsciously, as through the presentation of subliminal stimuli[2] (Hallett, 2007; Taylor & McCloskey, 1990, 1996). Even though efference binding is a quite complicated process that involves, for example, unconscious context-sensitive motor adjustments, it is useful to conceptualize it as a structure resembling the reflex arc (the most basic form of reflex, in which a stimulus triggers a response), though the common characterization of the reflex is more a convenient fiction than a probable truth, as noted by Sherrington (1906). Regarding unconscious efference binding (which can also occur consciously, of course), subjects can select the correct motor response (e.g., pressing one of two buttons) when confronted with a subliminal cue, suggesting that "appropriate programs for two separate movements can be simultaneously held ready for use, and that either one can be executed when triggered by specific stimuli without subjective awareness" (Taylor & McCloskey, 1996, p. 62).

This datum, that actions can be elicited by stimuli that are consciously imperceptible, has been used as evidence that action in the social world can occur unconsciously. Although this can certainly be taken as evidence that actions can be spurred into being by unconscious processes, it is important to note that many forms of unconsciously triggered or unconsciously motivated actions are actually triggered by stimuli of which one is aware but have effects on motivation or action that one is unaware of (Bargh & Morsella, 2008). Indeed, the findings above from paradigms using *incidental behavioral priming* all involve the presentation of supraliminal stimuli (e.g., library books) that then unconsciously cause people to act in certain ways (e.g., speak more quietly; Aarts & Dijksterhuis, 2003). It was this kind of unconscious that Freud and Helmholtz were concerned about: unconscious processes in motivation (Freud) or perception (Helmholtz) that occurred over consciously perceptible stimuli, stimuli which are often called "supraliminal." Freud, for example, believed that "psychic determinism" could unconsciously influence motivational processes. There is the famous anecdote of a young man telling him that, for some unknown reason, the thought about *X* kept recurring in his mind. Freud explained to the young man that his undesired thoughts about *X* were triggered by having seen *Y*, which was a supraliminal stimulus that had unconscious consequences (Fancher, 1973). Helmholtz (1856) referred to these unconscious machinations as *unconscious inferences*, a term that has historically been used to describe those sophisticated, "consciously impenetrable," mechanisms constituting low-level perceptual analyses (e.g., depth perception, motion detection, color and auditory analyses; Zeki & Bartels, 1999). Helmholtz used the term in a more inclusive manner than it is used today (Morsella & Bargh, 2010). One of his examples of unconscious inference was not about basic visual perception but about the automaticity of word reading – one

is faced with a word (*SOCIAL*) and one cannot help but read it. Above we mentioned that efference binding, a kind of S→R mapping, can occur unconsciously. It should also be mentioned that, à la Helmholtz, the integrating (or "binding") of perceptual processes can also occur unconsciously. This has been called "afference binding" (Morsella & Bargh, 2011). This occurs in intrasensory, feature binding (e.g., the binding of shape to color; Zeki & Bartels, 1999) and in intersensory conflicts, as in the McGurk effect. In the McGurk effect (McGurk & MacDonald, 1976), there are unconscious interactions between visual and auditory processes: an observer views a speaker mouthing "ga" while presented with the sound "ba." Surprisingly, the observer is unaware of any intersensory interaction, perceiving only "da." Knowledge of these different forms of bindings is important for appreciating the various models of action control, the topic of the next section.

Apart from the kinds of unconsciously influenced actions observed in everyday social life, unconscious action of various forms can also be observed in neurological conditions in which consciousness is decoupled from action, as in *blindsight* (a disorder in which visually guided action occurs without visual awareness), *blind-smell* (when olfactory stimuli are imperceptible but influence behavior), *anarchic hand syndrome* (a disorder in which patients' hands perform actions involuntarily), *utilization behavior syndrome* (a disorder in which patients cannot suppress their actions), and in *automatisms* observed during an epileptic seizure (see review of all forms in Morsella & Bargh, 2011).

Action control

One has to reconcile theoretical notions such as stimulus–response automaticity, and the many findings in support of it, with the everyday observation that it is not the case that an environmental stimulus always elicits the behavior to which it is associated. How does one explain this?

During the era of Behaviorism (c.1912–1948), the control of behavior was seen as a function of external stimuli, whether they be in the external world (Sherrington's "exafference") or in the physical body ("proprioception"). Laboratory experiments like those of Tolman (1948) help to falsify this overarching hypothesis. These experiments showed that laboratory rats could solve mazes without the need of any such external stimulus. Tolman proposed that the behavior of the rat was determined by a knowledge structure in its head, the "cognitive map," which the animal acquired passively (without reward) through the exploration of its environment. Once a cognitive map was invoked to explain one kind of behavior (maze solving), then a flurry of other kinds of "mental representation" were invoked to explain other behaviors, including social actions (e.g., Schank & Abelson, 1977). Unlike Tolman's account, many of these subsequent models of action control were influenced by the von Neumann computer, in which processing was dictated by a central processor, a "supervisor" of sorts (Morsella, 2009). In response to these developments, "decentralized" models of action control emerged. In these models, there is no central supervisor in charge of control; control is distributed among multiple, quasi-independent systems. These models are beyond the purview of the present chapter. (The interested reader should consult Arkin, 1998.)

For both social phenomena (e.g., Chaiken & Trope, 1999; Lieberman, 2007) and non-social phenomena, most current models of the control of behavior include a mix of what was proposed by centralized and decentralized frameworks (Morsella, 2009). One species of model mixes "top-down," centralized (and effortful) control with automatic, "bottom-up" (effortless) processing, with the latter being responsible for the unconscious efference binding underlying automatic $S \rightarrow R$ links. In this species of model, a supervisory system (or "central executive," as in the case of control during "working memory"; Baddeley, 2007) would come into play only when processing errors, or conflict involving automatic processes, arise (e.g., Norman & Shallice, 1980; Shallice, 1972; Shallice & Burgess, 1998), as when word-reading plans and color-naming plans conflict in the classic Stroop task (Stroop, 1935). In this task, participants are instructed to name the color in which stimulus words are written. When the color and word mismatch (e.g., BLUE presented in red), response interference leads to increased response times, error rates, and reported urges to make a mistake (MacLeod & McDonald, 2000; Morsella et al., 2009). The effect is due in part to the automatic tendency to "word read" (instead of "color name") when presented with a word, àla Helmholtz (Cohen, Dunbar, & McClelland, 1990; MacLeod & McDonald, 2000). These hybrid approaches have spurred attempts to "reverse engineer" the supervisory system itself so that it, too, could be understood mechanistically. These developments (e.g., Curtis & D'Esposito, 2009; Kimberg, D'Esposito, & Farah, 1997; Roepstorff & Frith, 2004) have been motivated in part by the fear that a "supervisor" or "central executive" account of control does nothing but place all the explanatory power within a "homunculus." In one account (Morsella, 2005), control is not attributed to a single supervisor but to a senate-like arrangement, in which afference binding and efference binding can occur

unconsciously (as mentioned above) but the co-activation of conflicting $S \rightarrow R$ links (known as *efference–efference* binding; Morsella & Bargh, 2011) requires a "crosstalk" mechanism (the physical state we identify as consciousness) that can lead to *integrated action* (e.g., holding one's breath or suppressing the urge to say something to a friend; Morsella & Bargh, 2011). Without consciousness, behavior can be influenced by only one efference-binding stream, leading to *un-integrated actions* such as unconsciously inhaling while underwater or responding to a subliminal stimulus (Morsella & Bargh, 2011). (See meta-analysis of evidence for this approach in Morsella, Berger, & Krieger, 2011).

Thus, competition occurs among action-related representations (action plans) vying for behavioral expression. Although all suppressed actions must be voluntary actions (Passingham, 1995), suppression is only one case of inter-representational dynamics. Dynamics can also lead to modulations such as "voluntarily" increasing one's rate of inhalation in exchange for some reward. It is likely that competing plans come from diverse sources (e.g., brain systems; Morsella, 2005) and modes of thinking. Again, it is important to appreciate that, for various a priori and empirical reasons (Curtis & D'Esposito, 2009; Kimberg, D'Esposito, & Farah, 1997; Roepstorff & Frith, 2004), it is best to think about this dynamic, multi-determined form of action control as *action-related representations competing with each other* (as when there are multiple $S \rightarrow R$ links competing for behavioral expression) rather than as a homunculus reining in one action in order to express another. Action control is best conceptualized as representations vying for behavioral control, with no supervisor or homunculus observing the conflict and with no single brain region in charge of suppressing all unwanted actions (Curtis & D'Esposito, 2009). Two action plans may compete for control in the morning, and two other plans may compete for control in the evening, with no common neural component shared by both conflicts (Curtis & D'Esposito, 2009; Morsella, Berger, & Krieger, 2011). In sum, the activation of action-related mental representations through external stimuli must compete with the activation of action-related representations triggered by other external stimuli or by internal processes, such as top-down activations from "set," long-term memory, or working memory (Figure 14.1, Stage 3).

Within such an arrangement, how does "voluntary" action control emerge? The best "non-homuncular" account of how voluntary processing emerges is *ideomotor theory* (Hommel, 2009), an approach that has informed theories of social mimicry (Chartrand & Dalton, 2009). (For a non-homuncular definition of "voluntary," see Morsella, Lynn, & Riddle, in press; for present purposes, it is adequate to use the loaded and problematic term "voluntary.") Originating in the times of Lotze (1852), Harleß (1861), and Carpenter (1874), James's (1890/1950) popularization of ideomotor processing is that action guidance, and action knowledge, are limited to perceptual-like representations (or, *event codes*; cf., Hommel, 2009; Hommel, Müsseler, Aschersleben, & Prinz, 2001) of action outcomes (e.g., the "image" of one's finger flexing), with the motor programs/events actually responsible for enacting the actions being unconscious, as mentioned above. James (1890/1950) proposed that the conscious mind later uses these conscious perceptual-like representations to voluntarily guide the generation of motor efference, which itself is an unconscious process. In today's renaissance of action research (Agnew, Carlston, Graziano, & Kelly, 2010; Hommel et al., 2001; Morsella, 2009; Nattkemper & Ziessler, 2004), ideomotor processing is one prevalent hypothesis regarding how cognition influences action (Hommel et al., 2001).

It is important to note that Lotze and James's "agents of behavioral suppression" did not refer to a homunculus reining action in, but rather to the actions of an incompatible idea (i.e., a competing action plan). From the ideomotor standpoint, if one imagines one's finger flexing, the finger should flex automatically, unless, of course, one simultaneously holds an incompatible idea (e.g., of the finger not flexing). Because unconscious efference binding is a faster process than consciously mediated action, control from top-down, conscious processing must begin as early as possible, in order to successfully influence overt action (Morsella, Zarolia, & Gazzaley, 2011). Historically, competition amongst representations for *action selection* has been associated with the ventral processing stream[3] (Goodale & Milner, 2004). The co-activation of incompatible action plans (e.g., to look left *and* right) leads to the strongest changes in conscious awareness (Morsella, Berger, & Krieger, 2011; Morsella, Gray, Krieger, & Bargh, 2009). (For the role of consciousness in such conflict, see Morsella, 2005; Morsella, Berger, & Krieger, 2011.)

So far, we have discussed the important nuts-and-bolts of action. However, our story has been limited to unconscious motor control or action-related representations, representations that can be activated by environmental stimuli and that may or may not involve higher-level thought. It is clear that social behavior, and the action-related representations responsible for it, may also arise from different ways of thinking. Thus, when further reverse engineering a social action, one should take into account the *mode of reasoning* giving rise to the action-related representation(s) underlying it. Just as voluntary actions such as blinking, breathing, and saccades differ in various important ways from their reflexive counterparts (cf., Morsella & Bargh, 2011), so too can social actions that are topographically similar eventuate from different types of reasoning and knowledge processing (Stage 2).

MODES OF KNOWLEDGE PROCESSING (STAGE 2)

Sloman (1996; see also Darlow & Sloman, 2010, and Chaiken & Trope, 1999) provides an eloquent argument for a duality of mind composed of *intuitive* (aka "associative") and *deliberative* (aka "rule-based") modes of reasoning. (For a recent "dual-process" model of social phenomena, see Sherman et al., 2008.) The intuitive mode, in accordance with James' (1890/1950) conception of *empirical thinking*, operates effortlessly and automatically. The products of this phylogenetically old mode are conscious, but its processing is unconscious (see discussion of "outputs" in Morsella & Bargh, 2010). In a fast, parallel, and "quick and dirty" fashion, this mode operates independently of working-memory capacity, and thus does not take up resources from "central processing." Hence, it is unrelated to working-memory capacity or general intelligence. The modus operandi of the system rests upon detecting similarities or associations. More specifically, it captures statistical regularities, such as correlations and conditional probability data, resulting in an abstract level of description that captures the central tendency of an empirical domain. The intuitive mode of processing is responsible for the "out of the blue" gut feelings (e.g., "somatic markers"; Damasio, 1996), automatic evaluations (Duckworth, Bargh, Garcia, & Chaiken, 2002; Todorov, Mandisodza, Goren, & Hall, 2005), and inclinations that are a key determinant of social outcomes (Uleman, Newman, & Moskowitz, 1996). It may be this kind of intuitive processing that allows speakers to infer the physical attributes of the voices of unknown speakers (Krauss, Freyberg, & Morsella, 2002).

On the other hand, the deliberative (rule-based) mode is associated with directed reasoning and symbol manipulation, what most people consider to be true "thinking." The mode features *direct cognitive control*, in which one can voluntarily manipulate mental contents. (Intentionally thinking of something scary to make oneself scared would be a case of *indirect cognitive control*;

Morsella, Lanska, Berger, & Gazzaley, 2009.) The mode is symbolic and rests on computational principles (e.g., see Anderson, 1993). To make a formal case for this mode, Sloman highlights the principles of *productivity* and *systematicity* as specified by Fodor and Pylyshyn (1988). Productivity refers to the generative nature of its rules – there are no theoretical limits on the number of new representations its rules could produce, just as there is an infinite number of sentences that one's syntactic system could produce. Systematicity refers to the generalizability of rules from one context to another. Rules contain variables that represent an entire class of objects and therefore are not constrained to specific and concrete instances. The same rules could be instantiated in different situations. In sum, the rule-based mode is a "language of thought" (Sloman, 1996, p. 5) composed of a combinatorial syntax and semantics. The logical, hierarchical, and causal nature of this mode leads to *explanations* (versus *predictions* only as per the associative system) of what people perceive as *natural* versus *social artifactual* categories (also see Rothbart & Taylor, 1992).

It has been proposed that, in social behavior, these two kinds of reasoning stem from distinct brain systems (Darlow & Sloman, 2010; Lieberman, 2007; Sloman, 1996; Strack & Deutsch, 2004). Whether these modes stem from one system (Osman, 2004), two systems, or multiple systems remains controversial (cf., Darlow & Sloman, 2010; Morsella, 2005; Osman, 2004). For present purposes, what matters is that the two modes of thinking – stemming from one or many systems – can eventuate in what Sloman termed *Criterion S*: a situation in which people believe concurrently in two contradictory ideas. Criterion S has ramifications for basic categorization (an avocado might be perceived as a fruit formally and a vegetable informally) as well as social categorization (experiencing disgust when seeing two men kissing while holding a strong explicit belief in the acceptance of homosexuality). Regarding action, one challenge faced by the nervous system is that some of its component systems may have different skeletomotor inclinations (i.e., "action goals") toward the same stimulus situation. (An "action goal" is best defined by Skinner's conception of an operant; Skinner, 1953.) As in the classic theorizing by Lewin (1935), under conditions of conflict, one system may want to approach a stimulus while another system may want to avoid it. For example, one system may be inclined to utter something inappropriate to one's boss, but another system may desire to not do so. These systems often have different agendas, operating principles, phylogenetic origins, and bases of knowledge (Morsella, 2005).

Again, it is well-established that, as predicted by theory (Morsella, 2005), conflict between incompatible plans leads to the strongest changes in consciousness (Morsella, Berger, & Krieger, 2011). It is for this reason that Criterion S may induce subjective effects. For example, in a social psychology priming paradigm, participants were primed with the idea of "competition" and then were asked to work together cooperatively. The participants reported inexplicable changes in their subjective experience, perhaps because of the activation of the incompatible inclinations (Oettingen, Grant, Smith, Skinner, & Gollwitzer, 2006). Research suggests that the activation of action plans countering the will of the self are perceived as foreign from the self (Morsella, Berger, & Krieger, 2011).

Of course there are also situations in which the two kinds of reasoning function cooperatively. In such a case, one may not know which mode of reasoning gave rise to the cognition (Darlow & Sloman, 2010; Sloman, 1996):

> Because the systems cannot be distinguished by the problem domains to which they apply, deciding which system is responsible for a given response is not always easy. It may not even be possible because both systems may contribute to a particular response (Sloman, 1996, p. 6).

Evidence for this is found in the Stroop task, where urges to err are low for the congruent Stroop condition, even though it is known that participants often read the stimulus word inadvertently in the congruent condition of the Stroop task: "The experimenter (perhaps the participant as well) cannot discriminate which dimension gave rise to the response on a given congruent trial" (MacLeod & MacDonald, 2000, p. 386). Urges to err for the congruent condition are comparable to those of the "neutral" condition of the Stroop task, in which the color is presented on an illegible letter string (Morsella et al., 2009). In addition, in a within-subjects Stroop manipulation, "urges to read" are greater when words are presented in standard black font than when the same words are presented in a congruent color (Molapour, Berger, & Morsella, 2011), suggesting that the act of color naming masks introspection of the reading process which may occur automatically (Morsella et al., 2009). This finding has been explained as an instance of *synchrony blindness*, in which one is unaware that two distinct cognitive operations are activated when the operations lead to the same action plan (Morsella et al., 2009). The notion is consistent with the view that one is conscious only of the "outputs" of processes, not of the processes themselves (Lashley, 1951; Morsella & Bargh, 2010).

Inter-representational dynamics as more informative than "system identification"

Is it useful at this stage of understanding to posit that, in the Stroop task, the color-naming and word-reading plans arise from different (or the same) systems? We believe that, at this stage of understanding and with respect to social behavior, whether the two distinct modes of reasoning (intuitive versus deliberate) arise from one or many systems (or whether two action-related representations at Stage 3 stem from one or two systems) is not as critical as understanding the dynamics (e.g., subjective effects) and behavioral consequences from the modes of processing. As Sloman (1996) posits, "Associative thought *feels* like it arises from a different cognitive mechanism than does deliberate, analytical reasoning" (p. 3). Knowing whether two action-related representations (e.g., the color-naming and word-reading plans in the Stroop task) come from one versus more than one "system" is not as critical as understanding the inter-representational dynamics and behavioral consequences of such a pattern of activity. Regarding subjective effects of multiply activated action-related representation, reliable and informative effects include conscious conflict, synchrony blindness, negative affect (e.g., "subjective cost"; Morsella, 2005) and the sense that some plans are countering the will of the self (Morsella, Berger, & Krieger, 2011). The behavioral consequences include phenomena such as slowed response times, post-error corrections, and the ability to fail to execute a desired plan (e.g., a failure in self-control). As Skinner (1953) noted, conflicted behavior resembles other behaviors of weak strength and is thus easily perturbed by external stimuli. Like the classic research on instincts and the nature of their interactions (cf., Campbell & Misanin, 1969; Dempsey, 1951), it is likely that the "one versus many systems" debate will continue for some time, until more is known about the neural correlates and degrees of "encapsulation" of each of the proposed systems, things which are difficult to ascertain in the human brain. Much of this depends on a consensus regarding the meaning of what constitutes a "system" in a highly interactive apparatus like the brain. Regarding social behavior, it seems that there is no shortage of sources for action plans. Action plans vying for behavioral control at Stage 3 may be "evolved" (cf., Bargh & Morsella, 2010) or "acquired" (e.g., from operant conditioning or cultural learning; cf., Morsella, Zarolia, & Gazzaley, 2011), and they may be ramped up or decreased in activation by emotional and motivational processing. In the human animal, culture introduces a major source of action plans

(Baumeister & Masicampo, 2010). We believe that, at this stage of understanding, it is more important to examine how the action plans from different sources or modes of thinking influence behavior and subjective experience.

So far we have considered interactions between different kinds of action-related representations and different modes of reasoning, but what is the nature of the tokens (the representations and knowledge structures) on which these operations take place? We now turn to the tokens of knowledge upon which different modes of reasoning operate. Again, we focus on conceptual structures (Stage 1) that predict most of the variability of action in the social world.

KNOWLEDGE STRUCTURES (STAGE 1)

As explained below, when accounting for behavior in the social world, one cannot simply use the models of knowledge representation that have been useful in accounting for knowledge representation/categorization in the non-social world; it seems that one must invoke more nuanced models, such as those involving "psychological essentialism," a major topic of this section. In order for one to appreciate these models, one must first understand the evolution of theories of categorization and knowledge representation, which we review in brief.

Conceptual knowledge is the product of categorization. In the classical, Aristotelian view of categorization, membership in a category is judged by defining features – a set of features that are individually necessary and jointly sufficient for category membership (e.g., Bruner, Goodnow, & Austin, 1956; Katz, 1972; Katz & Fodor, 1963). For various reasons, this view fails to capture the nature of human categorization, as aptly illustrated by Wittgenstein's (1953) question: What defines whether something is a "game"? In response to the shortcomings of the classical approach, Rosch, Mervis (Mervis & Rosch, 1981; Rosch, 1973, 1975, 1978; Rosch & Mervis, 1975) and colleagues (Rosch, Mervis, Gray, Johnson, & Boyes-Braem, 1976) have proposed an associative view of human categories, based on Wittgenstein's notions of *family resemblance* (Wittgenstein, 1953). This work has led to a variety of "prototype-based" models of categorization (Homa, Sterling, & Trepel, 1981; Posner & Keele, 1968, 1970; Reed, 1972; Rosch, 1973, 1975; J. D. Smith & Minda, 1998, 2002). A "family resemblance" structure contains a set of instances (e.g., robin, penguin, blue jay, crow, among others), where each instance shares at least one attribute with one or more of the other instances in the set (e.g., has wings, flies, sings). Certain members of the set (e.g., robin) are seen as more central than others (e.g., flamingo). According to Rosch and colleagues, an instance is perceived as prototypical of the whole set as a function of the extent to which it shares overlapping attributes with other instances in that set. The prototype serves as the central tendency of the set because it shares the most characteristic attributes with other instances. Categorization judgments are said to result from a comparison between the similarity of a new instance and the prototype, where similarity is operationalized as a function of the number, salience, and perceived importance of features that the object and prototype have in common (e.g., Tversky, 1977). A main advantage of prototype models is that they can explain *typicality effects*: the intuition and perception of graded category membership. For example, instances that have been shown to be prototypical, such as "robin," tend to elicit faster response times than other less prototypical instances, such as "chicken" (e.g., Rips, Shoben, & E. E. Smith, 1973). (See neural evidence for typicality effects in Lei et al., 2010.)

Prototypes in the social world

Cantor and Mischel (1977) were among the first to show that recognition memory was more accurate for prototypical (versus non-prototypical) instances of social categories, specifically those of *extravert* and *introvert*, regardless of whether the manipulation was implicit or explicit (see also, Cantor & Mischel, 1979; Cohen, 1981; Ellis & Nelson, 1999). Cohen (1981) showed a similar prototype-consistency effect in recognition memory in response to other social categories. Participants were asked to watch a videotape of a woman that was labeled as either a waitress or a librarian and were later given a surprise recognition memory test. Accuracy was a function of features that were consistent with participants' prototype of the original (waitress/librarian) label. This effect held regardless of whether participants were given the occupational label before or after watching the videotape. Silvera, Krull, and Sassler (2002) extended this finding by showing that prototypical instances tended to be recalled faster than non-prototypical instances in a free recall paradigm. Recently, Sesko and Biernat (2010) examined prototype effects on memory, in a complex category with intersecting social identities: namely, that of a Black woman. They argued that the comparative non-prototypicality of Black women's race and gender was complicit in Black women's experience of "social invisibility."

Specifically, compared to Black men, White women, and White men, photographs of Black women were recognized less accurately, and Black women's statements were more incorrectly attributed to others (for social invisibility, see also Fryberg & Townsend, 2008; Purdie-Vaughns & Eibach, 2008). The impact of these and of similar findings, as a whole, is that the degree of instance prototypicality affects more than memory recognition and recall and has ramifications for discrimination outside the laboratory.

Explanation-based views of categorization

Despite the utility of prototype models for understanding social cognition, categorization cannot rest on similarity or associative reasoning alone because it fails to provide a comprehensive account of what makes instances in a category cluster together or cohere, especially when instances are dissimilar from each other. For example, penguins, eagles, and robins, are often perceived to be in the same category (birds), but perceptually similar sea animals such as sharks and whales are often grouped in separate categories (Ross & Spalding, 1994). How does this come to be? Goodman (1972) has argued that every object bears some similarity to every other object in the world (e.g., animate and inanimate objects are made of matter). Similarity therefore cannot always explain why exemplars are partitioned into different categories from an infinite set of possibilities. An alternative view is that people use theories that constrain concept acquisition and structure. Instances of a concept are oftentimes related by an explanatory structure, which may or may not correspond to external reality. The "explanation-based" view has been supported empirically by demonstrating dissociations between classification and similarity judgments (Rips, 1989). To stay within the scope of the current chapter's goals, we will focus on a particular theory-based account – *psychological essentialism* – that has received much attention for its basic explanatory power as well as its implications for cognition and action in the social world.

Psychological essentialism

Medin and Ortony (1989), the fathers of psychological essentialism, argued that conceptual features range on a continuum of accessibility from being deeply hidden/abstract (e.g., biological matter) to being easily perceived (e.g., color or shape). The main tenet is that people attend more to surface-structural features, which are believed to be constrained by a central/causal hidden property. For example, two entities that are surface-structurally different (a whale and a bear) become ontologically grouped together as members of the same category (mammals) because of a shared belief in their internal genetic makeup.[4] A large body of cognitive developmental work has shown evidence that essentialism occurs even in young children, which might indicate a natural human predilection for using explanation-based accounts in categorization. For example, Gelman and colleagues (see Gelman, 2009, for a review) have extended previous work on essentialism by arguing that a specific type of essence, namely, a *causal essence* (Gelman & Hirschfeld, 1999), is perceived to account for the more surface or secondary properties in natural kinds versus artifacts (Diesendruck & Gelman, 1999). For instance, the essence of water is typically conceived of as being H_2O (but see Malt, 1994). The main idea (Gelman, 2003, 2009) underlying this important body of work is that causal essentialism is a type of early "cognitive bias" (Gelman, 2009, p. 7) that guides children's language learning, inferences, and decision making. It involves an active search for hidden features that is spontaneous rather than learned.

One corollary from the above theorizing, and consistent with Dweck (1975), is that essentialist beliefs imply immutability among other characteristics (see also Haslam, Rothschild, & Ernst, 2000; Rips, 1989). In support of this and to examine immutability beliefs, Taylor, Rhodes, and Gelman (2009) used a "switched-at-birth" paradigm, such as depicting a baby mouse raised entirely by dogs (Gelman & Wellman, 1991) or a human male baby raised by women only (Taylor, 1996). The aim was to assess whether the target would be judged to develop origin- versus adoptive-category-typical traits. Data indicated a developmental shift from relying on origin essentialism for social and biological categories to considering environmental effects on social categories (i.e., gender). Altogether, these findings point to the important role of naïve biological theory on development of categories and its ramifications for inference making about the biological and social worlds (see also Bloom, 1996; Keil, 1989; Kelemen & Bloom, 1994; Markman, 1989, 1999; Nelson, 1995; Rhodes & Gelman, 2008, Spelke, Von Hofsten, & Kestenbaum, 1989; Waxman, 2010).[5]

Psychological essentialism in the social world

In an evocative thought piece, Prentice and Miller (2007) argued that "all categories are not created equal in the minds' eye" (p. 202) based on work by Haslam and colleagues (e.g., Haslam, Rothschild, & Ernst, 2000), which showed that gender, ethnicity, race, and disability emerged as the most highly essentialized human categories (but also see essentialism of social class [Mahalingam, 2003] and mental disorders [Ahn, Flanagan, Marsh, & Sanislow, 2006]). Importantly, Prentice and Miller argued that the extent to which a category is essentialized is intimately tied to social consequences such as stereotyping and motivation that affect behavior. Prentice and Miller (2006) asked participants to complete a task that allegedly measured participants' perceptual style and that was piloted and found to be perceived as gender neutral. Specifically, participants were asked to estimate the number of dots from several slides presented sequentially. Participants were then told that they were either overestimators or underestimators (without regard to participants' actual performance). In Experiment 1, participants were asked to complete the task alone or with a person of the same or a different gender. In the latter two conditions, both participants were either told that they had the same or a different perceptual style. All participants were then asked to estimate what percentage of each gender would have a given perceptual style. Data indicated that participants endorsed an essentialist view of gender when they were either alone or with a person of a different gender. Specifically, participants predicted that a higher percentage of same-gender individuals would exhibit their assigned perceptual style versus when they were paired with a person of the same gender. In subsequent experiments, participants were asked to complete the same task and with the same (randomly assigned) feedback, but were then given an opportunity "to correct" performance by retaking the task. When participants were alone, they showed a motivation to correct performance by increasing or decreasing their estimates compared to baseline. The same motivation to correct occurred in female-female pairs. However, participants in the male-female pairs failed to correct. Prentice and Miller argued that participants' behavior in the mixed-gender condition indicated a lack of motivation, which resulted from the mere priming of a gender difference. Presumably this priming evoked the belief that performance was gender specific and therefore natural or fixed.

Prentice and Miller's data beg a pragmatic question that brings our discussion full circle to Dr Summer's public comments: Is it possible that a mere suggestion of a biological versus a social cause of gender differences affects women's performance in quantitative domains? Dar-Nimrod and Heine (2006) presented elegant data that provide an affirmative answer. They asked women to read an article about either genetic or social-contextual causes of gender differences before taking a math test. Women who were exposed to the genetics theory performed worse than their counterparts who were introduced to an experiential one. These dramatic findings on the power of priming a scientific theory of human categorization on intellectual performance have social justice implications. We therefore choose to conclude this section with a compelling exhortation from Prentice and Miller (2007):

> In light of this evidence, we maintain that human characteristics become the basis for essentialized categories only to the extent that they are used to explain differences. The process of establishing a causal link between the category essence and its observable manifestations is critical for producing and maintaining an essentialist category structure. Thus, every time people invoke biology to explain gender differences, they further strengthen the view that women and men are different human kinds. The processes through which essentialist explanations for individual and group differences become category representations with divisive social consequences are an important topic for future research (p. 205).

CONCLUSION

Although the eras of Behaviorism (c.1912–1948) and the Cognitive Revolution (c.1948–1990) could be construed as being founded on opposing principles (cf., Morsella, 2009), mainstream research in both eras systematically evaded the study of nebulous action-related constructs such as "subjective urges," "goals," and "motivations." Instead, cognitive researchers focused on epistemology (Rosenbaum, 2005), and Behaviorists avoided discussion of both central processing and the actual mechanics (e.g., motor control) involved in the generation of behavior, focusing instead on the causal role of external stimuli (Skinner, 1953). It is important to note that, historically, it has been the social psychologist who has intrepidly opened the "black box" to examine how things like conflicting urges, plans, and goals can influence action (e.g., Festinger, 1957; Heider, 1958; Lewin, 1935). In short, there has always been a rich cross-fertilization of social psychological research and work on behavior (e.g., from field studies or ethological research; Thorpe, 1964; Zajonc, 1969). This cross-fertilization continues today, when there is an even greater appreciation of the various kinds of actions that humans are capable of expressing in the social world (e.g., Agnew et al., 2010).

In this spirit, we attempted to deconstruct a social act by working backwards from overt action to central processing, referring to the literatures associated with each of the four stages illustrated in Figure 14.1. In the process, we focused on aspects of processing/phenomena that explain a large portion of observed variability in social behavior. When reviewing such disparate literatures, it is important to underscore the ideas for which there is some consensus.

There is a consensus that motor control, and the sophisticated programs underlying it, are unconsciously mediated. The social psychologist interested in the sophistication of unconscious processing can look to these intelligent and highly flexible processes. In addition, there is ample evidence that action plans can be activated, selected, modulated, and, in some cases, expressed without conscious control (cf., Morsella & Bargh, 2011), as in the case of unconscious efference binding (e.g., when responding to a subliminal stimulus), neurological phenomena, and incidental behavioral priming. (This, of course, does not imply that efference binding occurs only unconsciously.)

There is also a growing consensus that, at this stage of understanding, the kinds of conflicts occurring at Stage 3 are best construed as occurring between representations, independent of a homunculus-like supervisor (Curtis & D'Esposito, 2009; Kimberg, D'Esposito, & Farah, 1997; Morsella, Berger, & Krieger, 2011; Roepstorff & Frith, 2004). In addition, though there is controversy regarding whether intuitive and deliberate reasoning stem from one system or whether each stems from a different system (cf., Osman, 2004), there is some agreement about the inter-representational dynamics and behavioral consequences resulting from the co-activation of different kinds of action-related representations (e.g., identical versus incompatible). Few would argue that the voluntary suppression of an action plan can be mediated unconsciously or occur without evoking changes in consciousness. Thus, "system identification" is more difficult than identifying inter-representational dynamics and the behavioral consequences of such dynamics. Similarly, more is certain about the phenomenology of deliberative versus intuitive reasoning than about the systems from which they are proposed to arise (Morsella & Bargh, 2010; Sloman, 1996).

It is important to note that, in the two-systems framework of Sloman (1996), the attribute of something being conscious or unconscious cannot be used to distinguish which system is at play with regard to reasoning. Deliberative-like reasoning can occur unconsciously (Dijksterhuis & Nordgren, 2006; Nisbett & Wilson, 1977; Sloman, 1996). The role of consciousness in action production is far from straightforward and beyond the purview of this chapter (cf., Morsella & Bargh, 2011). That some aspects of action production are conscious while others are unconscious corroborate Miller's (1962) assertion that, "In some sense not yet defined we are both conscious and unconscious at the same time" (p. 37). Future research may increase consensus building regarding conscious versus unconscious processing by examining the social actions of the dream world, where conscious action selection, action conflict, and ideomotor processing seem to occur, but where it is readily evident that processes such as motor programming do not ever occupy the mind (Morsella & Bargh, 2010).

Last, there is a consensus that the knowledge structures biasing social behavior cannot be explained by similarity-based models of categorization alone. It seems that explanation-based models (e.g., those focusing on essentialism) are required.

Figure 14.1 reveals that a social act such as that by Dr Summers is a complicated affair, multi-determined by sources of knowledge, modes of processing, and forms of cognitive control (e.g., inter-representational dynamics) that are far from being fully understood. The sources vying for the control of action – that which is most important in evolution – can at times be at loggerheads with each other. Perhaps what is most elusive about social action pertains to what Lewin (1935) noted – that the organism not only responds to the social world but that, in doing so, it *prefers* certain states over others. This is consistent with the view that, unlike anything else we know of in the physical world, the brain is an "affinity-based" system that prefers certain states (e.g., conflict-free states) over others (e.g., conflict-laden states). It seems that such *intra-psychic* conflict is fundamentally different from what occurs inter-personally in the social world, perhaps because evolution works at the level of the overt behavior of the individual and not at the level of "group behavior" (Mayr, 2001). Inter-personally, understanding does not always imply agreement (Krauss & Morsella, 2000), as in the case of adversaries who understand the views of each other perfectly, but refuse to reach a resolution. It seems that, within the organism, such a conflict is a luxury that is highly taxed – one versus another action plan must always be expressed, for good or for bad.

ACKNOWLEDGMENT

Each author contributed equally to the creation of this chapter.

NOTES

1 The Nobel Laureate Roger Sperry (1952) proposed that examining the outputs of a machine (e.g., a smoothie from a blender) tells one more about the inner workings of the machine (e.g., the blending actions of the blender) than does examining the machine inputs (e.g., fruit and milk). For this reason, Sperry (1952) claimed that overt behavior can reveal more about the workings of the brain than can sensory inputs.

2 For example, participants can select the correct motor response (one of two button presses) when confronted with subliminal stimuli, suggesting that "appropriate programs for two separate movements can be simultaneously held ready for use, and that either one can be executed when triggered by specific stimuli without subjective awareness" (Taylor & McCloskey, 1996, p. 62).

3 Information for action selection has been proposed to reside in the neural circuits of the ventral thalamocortical processing stream (Goodale & Milner, 2004; Sherman & Guillery, 2006), where information about the world is represented in a unique manner (e.g., representing the invariant aspects of the world, involving allocentric coordinates), one unlike that of the dorsal stream (e.g., representing the variant aspects of the world, using egocentric coordinates).

4 Psychological essentialism is different from metaphysical essentialism – the philosophical view that an instance has an essence by virtue of being that instance – because it centers on perceptions of essences, rather than on an external reality. Psychological essentialism is a descriptive versus a normative theory of categorization, which captures people's tendency to invoke an "essence" in categorization, even just as a place holder, and can give rise to conceiving of particular categories, such as race, as natural rather than as artifactual or socially constructed (e.g., Gil-White, 2001; Rothbart & Taylor, 1992). (For arguments that race is in actuality socially constructed, see Tate & Audette, 2001.)

5 The large body on naïve biological theories implies that categorization via essentialist beliefs should be sensitive to causal structure. The approach of Rehder and colleagues (e.g., Rehder & Kim, 2010) to explaining and modeling basic human categorization has attempted to integrate people's existing beliefs about causal mechanisms in conjunction with people's implicit computation of statistical regularities, using computational modeling. The common theme underlying this work is that an instance's category membership is perceived to be a function of whether or not it appears to obey causal laws, which are part of people's implicit theories. The presupposition of an underlying and oftentimes invisible cause results from people's attempt to understand the world by forming explanations and making predictions from observable or surface characteristics

of instances. This theorizing is intimately related to Gelman's (2003, 2009) idea of causal essentialism and includes causal and principled models of categorization (see, for example, Ahn, Kim, Lassaline, & Dennis, 2000; Hampton, 2001; Murphy & Medin, 1985; Opfer & Bulloch, 2006; Prasada, 2000; Prasada & Dillingham, 2006; Rehder, 2003; Rehder & Hastie, 2001; Sloman & Lagnado, 2004; Sloman, Love, & Ahn, 1998).

REFERENCES

Aarts, H., & Dijksterhuis, A. (2003). The silence of the library: Environment, situational norm, and social behavior. *Journal of Personality and Social Psychology, 84,* 18–28.

Agnew, C. R., Carlston, D. E., Graziano, W. G., & Kelly, J. R. (2010). *Then a miracle occurs: Focusing on behavior in social psychological theory and research.* New York: Oxford University Press.

Ahn, W.-k., Flanagan, E. H., Marsh, J. K., & Sanislow, C. A. (2006). Beliefs about essences and the reality of mental disorders. *Psychological Science, 17,* 759–766.

Ahn, W.-k., Kim, N. S., Lassaline, M. E., & Dennis, M. (2000). Causal status as a determinant of feature centrality. *Cognitive Psychology, 41,* 361–416.

Anderson, J. R. (1993). *Rules of the mind.* Hillsdale, NJ: Lawrence Erlbaum Associates.

Araya, T., Akrami, N., Ekehammar, B., & Hedlund, L-E. (2002). Reducing prejudice through priming of control-related words. *Experimental Psychology, 49,* 222–227.

Arkin, R. C. (1998). *Behavior-based robotics.* Cambridge, MA: The MIT Press.

Baddeley, A. D. (2007). *Working memory, thought and action.* Oxford, England: Oxford University Press.

Bargh, J. A., Chen, M., & Burrows, L. (1996). Automaticity of social behavior: Direct effects of trait construct and stereotype activation on action. *Journal of Personality and Social Psychology, 71,* 230–244.

Bargh, J. A., & Morsella, E. (2008). The unconscious mind. *Perspectives on Psychological Science, 3,* 73–79.

Bargh, J. A., & Morsella, E. (2010). Unconscious behavioral guidance systems. In C. R. Agnew, D. E. Carlston, W. G. Graziano, & J. R. Kelly (Eds.), *Then a miracle occurs: Focusing on behavior in social psychological theory and research* (pp. 89–118). New York: Oxford University Press.

Baumeister, R. F., & Masicampo, E. J. (2010). Conscious thought is for facilitating social and cultural interactions: How simulations serve the animal–culture interface. *Psychological Review, 117,* 945–971.

Ben-Zeev, T., Fein, S., & Inzlicht, M. (2005). Arousal and stereotype threat. *Journal of Experimental Social Psychology, 41,* 174–181.

Bloom, P. (1996). Intention, history, and artifact concepts. *Cognition, 60,* 1–29.

Bruner, J. S., Goodnow, J. J., & Austin, G. A. (1956). *A study of thinking.* New York: John Wiley.

Campbell, B. A., & Misanin, J. R. (1969). Basic drives. *Annual Review of Psychology, 20,* 57–84.

Cantor, N., & Mischel, W. (1977). Traits as prototypes: Effects on recognition memory. *Journal of Personality and Social Psychology, 31,* 38–48.

Cantor, N., & Mischel, W. (1979). Prototypicality and personality: Effects on free recall and personality impressions. *Journal of Research in Personality, 13,* 187–205.

Carpenter, W. B. (1874). *Principles of mental physiology.* New York: Appleton.

Carver, C. S., Ganellen, R. J., Froming, W. J., & Chambers, W. (1983). Modeling: An analysis in terms of category accessibility. *Journal of Experimental Social Psychology, 19,* 403–421.

Chaiken, S., & Trope, Y. (1999). *Dual-process theories in social psychology.* New York: Guilford Press.

Chartrand, T. L., & Dalton, A. N. (2009). Mimicry: Its ubiquity, importance, and functionality. In E. Morsella, J. A. Bargh, & P. M. Gollwitzer, *Oxford handbook of human action* (pp. 458–483). New York: Oxford University Press.

Chen, S., Lee-Chai A. Y., & Bargh J. A. (2001). Relationship orientation as a moderator of the effects of social power. *Journal of Personality and Social Psychology, 80,* 173–187.

Cohen, C. E. (1981). Person categories and social perception: Testing some boundary conditions of the processing effects of prior knowledge. *Journal of Personality and Social Psychology, 40,* 441–452.

Cohen, J. D., Dunbar, K., & McClelland, J. L. (1990). On the control of automatic processes: A parallel distributed processing account of the Stroop effect. *Psychological Review, 97,* 332–361.

Coles, M. G. H., Gratton, G., Bashore, T. R., Eriksen, C. W., & Donchin, E. (1985). A psychophysiological investigation of the continuous flow model of human information processing. *Journal of Experimental Psychology: Human Perception and Performance, 11,* 529–553.

Curtis, C. E., & D'Esposito, M. (2009). The inhibition of unwanted actions. In E. Morsella, J. A. Bargh, & P. M. Gollwitzer (Eds.), *Oxford handbook of human action* (pp. 72–97). New York: Oxford University Press.

Custers, R., Maas, M., Wildenbeest, M., & Aarts, H. (2008). Nonconscious goal pursuit and the surmounting of physical and social obstacles. *European Journal of Social Psychology, 38,* 1013–1022.

Damasio, A. R. (1996). The somatic marker hypothesis and the possible functions of the prefrontal cortex. *Philosophical Transactions of the Royal Society of London B, 351,* 1413–1420.

Dar-Nimrod, I., & Heine, S. J. (2006). Exposure to scientific theories affects women's math performance. *Science, 314,* 435.

Darlow, A. L., & Sloman, S. A. (2010). Two systems of reasoning: Architecture and relation to emotion. *Cognitive Science, 1,* 1–11.

Dawkins, R. (1976). *The selfish gene.* New York: Oxford University Press.

Dempsey, E. W. (1951). Homeostasis. In S. S. Stevens (Ed.), *Handbook of experimental psychology* (pp. 209–235). New York: Wiley.

Diesendruck, G., & Gelman, S. A. (1999). Domain differences in absolute judgments of category membership: Evidence for an essentialist account of categorization. *Psychonomic Bulletin & Review, 6,* 338–346.

Dijksterhuis, A., & Bargh, J. A. (2001). The perception–behavior expressway: Automatic effects of social perception on social behavior. In M. Zanna (Ed.), *Advances in Experimental Social Psychology, 33,* 1–40.

Dijksterhuis, A., & Nordgren, L. F. (2006). A theory of unconscious thought. *Perspectives on Psychological Science, 1,* 95–109.

Duckworth, K. L., Bargh, J. A., Garcia, M., & Chaiken, S. (2002). The automatic evaluation of novel stimuli. *Psychological Science, 13,* 513–519.

Dweck, C. S. (1975). The role of expectations and attributions in the alleviation of learned helplessness. *Journal of Personality and Social Psychology, 31,* 674–685.

Ellis, A. E., & Nelson, C. A. (1999). Category prototypicality judgments in adults and children: Behavioral and electrophysiological correlates. *Developmental Neuropsychology, 15,* 193–211.

Eriksen, C. W., & Schultz, D. W. (1979). Information processing in visual search: A continuous flow conception and experimental results. *Perception and Psychophysics, 25,* 249–263.

Fancher, R. E. (1973). *Psychoanalytic psychology: The development of Freud's thought.* New York: W. W. Norton.

Festinger, L. (1957). *A theory of cognitive dissonance.* Evanston, IL: Row, Peterson.

Fishbach, A., Friedman, R. S., & Kruglanski, A. W. (2003). Leading us not unto temptation: Momentary allurements elicit overriding goal activation. *Journal of Personality and Social Psychology, 84,* 296–309.

Fitzsimons, G. M., & Bargh, J. A. (2003). Thinking of you: Nonconscious pursuit of interpersonal goals associated with relationship partners. *Journal of Personality and Social Psychology, 84,* 148–163.

Fodor, J. A., & Pylyshyn, Z. W. (1988). Connectionism and cognitive architecture: A critical analysis. *Cognition, 28,* 3–71.

Fryberg, S. A., & Townsend, S. S. M. (2008). The psychology of invisibility. In G. Adams, M. Biernat, N. R. Branscombe, C. S. Crandall & L. S. Wrightsman (Eds.), *Commemorating brown: The social psychology of racism and discrimination* (pp. 173–193). Washington, DC: American Psychological Association.

Ganz, L. (1975). Temporal factors in visual perception. In E. C. Carterette & M. P. Friedman (Eds.), *Handbook of perception* (Vol. 5, pp. 169–231). New York: Academic Press.

Gelman, S. A. (2003). *The essential child: Origins of essentialism in everyday thought.* New York: Oxford University Press.

Gelman, S. A. (2009). Essentialist reasoning about the biological world. In A. Berthoz & Y. Christen (Eds.), *Neurobiology of "Umwelt": How living beings perceive the world* (pp. 7–16). Berlin: Springer-Verlag.

Gelman, S. A., & Hirschfeld, L. A. (1999). How biological is essentialism? In D. L. Medin & S. Atran (Eds.), *Folkbiology* (pp. 403–446). Cambridge, MA: MIT Press.

Gelman, S. A., & Wellman, H. M. (1991). Insides and essences: Early understandings of the non-obvious. *Cognition, 38,* 213–244.

Gil-White, F. J. (2001). Are ethnic groups biological "species" to the human brain? *Current Anthropology, 42,* 515–554.

Goodale, M., & Milner, D. (2004). *Sight unseen: An exploration of conscious and unconscious vision.* New York: Oxford University Press.

Goodman, N. (1972). Seven strictures on similarity. In N. Goodman (Ed.), *Problems and projects.* New York: Bobbs-Merrill.

Gray, J. A. (1995). The contents of consciousness: A neuropsychological conjecture. *Behavioral and Brain Sciences, 18,* 659–676.

Gray, J. A. (2004). *Consciousness: Creeping up on the hard problem.* New York: Oxford University Press.

Grossberg, S. (1999). The link between brain learning, attention, and consciousness. *Consciousness and Cognition, 8,* 1–44.

Haggard, P., Aschersleben, G., Gehrke, J., & Prinz, W. (2002). Action, binding and awareness. In W. Prinz & B. Hommel (Eds.), *Common mechanisms in perception and action: Attention and performance* (Vol. XIX, pp. 266–285). Oxford, UK: Oxford University Press.

Hallett, M. (2007). Volitional control of movement: The physiology of free will. *Clinical Neurophysiology, 117,* 1179–1192.

Hampton, J. A. (2001). *The roles of similarity in natural categorization.* New York: Oxford University Press.

Harleß, E. (1861). Der Apparat des Willens. *Zeitshrift für Philosophie und philosophische Kritik, 38,* 499–507.

Haslam, N., Rothschild, L., & Ernst, D. (2000). Essentialist beliefs about social categories. *British Journal of Social Psychology, 39,* 113–127.

Heider, F. (1958). *The psychology of interpersonal relations.* New York: John Wiley & Sons.

Helmholtz, H. V. (1856/1925). Treatise of physiological optics: Concerning the perceptions in general. In T. Shipley (Ed.), *Classics in psychology* (pp. 79–127). New York: Philosophy Library.

Holland, R. W., Hendriks, M., & Aarts, H. A. G. (2005). Smells like clean spirit: Nonconscious effects of scent on cognition and behavior. *Psychological Science, 16,* 689–693.

Homa, D., Sterling, S., & Trepel, L. (1981). Limitations of exemplar-based generalization and the abstraction of categorical information. *Journal of Experimental Psychology: Human Learning and Memory, 7,* 418–439.

Hommel, B. (2009). Action control according to TEC (theory of event coding). *Psychological Research, 73,* 512–526.

Hommel, B., Müsseler, J., Aschersleben, G., & Prinz, W. (2001). The theory of event coding: A framework for perception and action planning. *Behavioral and Brain Sciences, 24,* 849–937.

James, W. (1950). *The principles of psychology.* New York: Dover. (Original published 1890)

Jeannerod, M. (2006). *Motor cognition: What action tells the self.* New York: Oxford University Press.

Johnson-Frey, S. (2003). *Taking action: Cognitive neuroscience perspectives on intentional acts.* Cambridge, MA: The MIT Press.

Katz, J. J. (1972). *Semantic theory.* New York: Harper & Row.

Katz, J. J., & Fodor, J. A. (1963). The structure of a semantic theory. *Language, 39,* 170–210.

Kay, A. C., Wheeler, S. C., Bargh, J. A., & Ross, L. (2004). Material priming: The influence of mundane physical objects on situational construal and competitive behavioral choice. *Organizational Behavior and Human Decision Processes, 95,* 83–96.

Keil, F. C. (1989). *Concepts, kinds, and cognitive development.* Cambridge, MA: MIT Press.

Kelemen, D., & Bloom, P. (1994). Domain-specific knowledge in simple categorization tasks. *Psychonomic Bulletin and Review, 1,* 390–395.

Kimberg, D. Y., D'Esposito, M., & Farah, M. J. (1997). Cognitive functions in the prefrontal cortex – Working memory and executive control. *Current Directions in Psychological Science, 6,* 185–192.

Krauss, R. M., Freyberg, R., & Morsella, E. (2002). Inferring speaker's physical attributes from their voices. *Journal of Experimental Social Psychology, 38,* 618–625.

Krauss, R. M., & Morsella, E. (2000/2007). Communication and conflict. In M. Deutsch & P. T. Coleman (Eds.), *The handbook of conflict resolution: Theory and practice* (pp. 131–143). San Francisco, CA: Jossey-Bass.

Lashley, K. S. (1951). The problem of serial order in behavior. In L. A. Jeffress (Ed.), *Cerebral mechanisms in behavior. The Hixon Symposium* (pp. 112–146). New York: Wiley.

Lei, Y., Li, F., Long, C., Li, P., Chen, Q., Ni, Y., & Li, H. (2010). How does typicality of category members affect the deductive reasoning? An ERP study. *Experimental Brain Research, 204,* 47–56.

Levine, L. R., Morsella, E., & Bargh, J. A. (2007). The perversity of inanimate objects: Stimulus control by incidental musical notation. *Social Cognition, 25,* 265–280.

Lewin, K. (1935). *A dynamic theory of personality.* New York: McGraw-Hill.

Lewin, K. (1946). Action research and minority problems. *Journal of Social Issues, 2,* 34–46.

Lieberman, M. D. (2007). The X- and C-systems: The neural basis of automatic and controlled social cognition. In E. Harmon-Jones & P. Winkielman (Eds.), *Fundamentals of social neuroscience* (pp. 290–315). New York: Guilford Press.

Lotze, R. H. (1852). *Medizinische Psychologie oder Physiologie der Seele.* Leipzig: Weidmann'sche Buchhandlung.

MacLeod, C. M., & McDonald, P. A. (2000). Interdimensional interference in the Stroop effect: Uncovering the cognitive and neural anatomy of attention. *Trends in Cognitive Sciences, 4,* 383–391.

Mahalingam, R. (2003). Essentialism, culture, and power: Representations of social class. *Journal of Social Issues, 59,* 733–749.

Malt, B. C. (1994). Water is Not H_2O. *Cognitive Psychology, 27,* 41–70.

Markman, A. B. (1989). LMS rules and the inverse base-rate effect: Comment on Gluck and Bower (1988). *Journal of Experimental Psychology: General, 118,* 417–421.

Markman, A. B. (1999). *Knowledge representation.* Hillsdale, NJ: Lawrence Erlbaum Associates.

Mayr, E. (2001). *What evolution is.* London: Weidenfeld & Nicolson.

McClelland, J. L. (1979). On the time-relations of mental processes: An examination of systems of processes in cascade. *Psychological Review, 86,* 287–330.

McGurk, H., & MacDonald, J. (1976). Hearing lips and seeing voices. *Nature, 264,* 746–748.

Medin, D. L., & Ortony, A. (1989). Psychological essentialism. In S. Vosniadou and A. Ortony (Eds.), *Similarity and analogical reasoning* (pp. 179–195). Cambridge, UK: Cambridge University Press.

Mervis, C. B., & Rosch, E. (1981). Categorization of natural objects. *Annual Review of Psychology, 32,* 89–115.

Miller, G. A. (1962). *Psychology: The science of mental life.* New York: Adams, Bannister, & Cox.

Molapour, T., Berger, C. C., & Morsella, E. (2011). Did I read or did I name? Diminished awareness of processes yielding identical 'outputs.' *Consciousness and Cognition, 20,* 1776–1780.

Morsella, E. (2009). The mechanisms of human action: Introduction and background. In E. Morsella, J. A. Bargh, & P. M. Gollwitzer (Eds.), *Oxford handbook of human action* (pp. 1–32). New York: Oxford University Press.

Morsella, E., & Bargh, J. A. (2010). What is an output? *Psychological Inquiry, 21,* 354–370.

Morsella, E., & Bargh, J. A. (2011). Unconscious action tendencies: Sources of "un-integrated" action. In J. T. Cacioppo & J. Decety (Eds.), *Handbook of social neuroscience* (pp. 335–347). New York: Oxford University Press.

Morsella, E., Bargh, J. A., & Gollwitzer, P. M. (2009). *Oxford handbook of human action.* New York: Oxford University Press.

Morsella, E., Berger, C. C., & Krieger, S. C. (2011). Cognitive and neural components of the phenomenology of agency. *Neurocase, 17,* 209–230.

Morsella, E., Gray, J. R., Krieger, S. C., & Bargh, J. A. (2009). The essence of conscious conflict: Subjective effects of sustaining incompatible intentions. *Emotion, 9,* 717–728.

Morsella, E., Lanska, M., Berger, C. C., & Gazzaley, A. (2009). Indirect cognitive control through top-down activation of perceptual symbols. *European Journal of Social Psychology, 39,* 1173–1177.

Morsella, E., Lynn, M. T., Riddle, T. A. (in press). Voluntary action, Illusion of. In H. Pashler (Ed.), *The encyclopedia of the mind.* New York: Sage.

Morsella, E., Wilson, L. E., Berger, C. C., Honhongva, M., Gazzaley, A., & Bargh, J. A. (2009). Subjective aspects of cognitive control at different stages of processing. *Attention, Perception, and Psychophysics, 71,* 1807–1824.

Morsella, E., Zarolia, P., & Gazzaley, A. (2011). Cognitive conflict and consciousness. In B. Gawronski & F. Strack (Eds.), *Cognitive consistency: A unifying concept in social psychology* (pp. 19–46). New York: Guilford Press.

Murphy, G. L., & Medin, D. L. (1985). The role of theories in conceptual coherence. *Psychological Review, 92,* 289–316.

Nattkemper, D., & Ziessler, M. (2004): Editorial: Cognitive control of action: The role of action effects. *Psychological Research, 68,* 71–73.

Nelson, D. (1995). Principle-based inferences in young children's categorization: Revisiting the impact of function on the naming of artifacts. *Cognitive Development, 10,* 347–380.

Nisbett, R. E., & Wilson, T. D. (1977). Telling more than we can know: Verbal reports on mental processes. *Psychological Review, 84,* 231–259.

Norman, D. A., & Shallice, T. (1980). Attention to action: Willed and automatic control of behavior. In R. J. Davidson, G. E. Schwartz, & D. Shapiro (Eds.), *Consciousness and self-regulation* (pp. 1–18). New York: Plenum Press.

Oettingen, G., Grant, H., Smith, P. K., Skinner, M., & Gollwitzer, P. M. (2006). Nonconscious goal pursuit: Acting in an explanatory vacuum. *Journal of Experimental Social Psychology, 42,* 668–675.

Opfer, J. E., & Bulloch, M. J. (2006). Causal relations drive young children's induction, naming, and categorization. *Cognition, 105,* 206–217.

Osman, M. (2004). An evaluation of dual process theories of reasoning. *Psychonomic Bulletin and Review, 11,* 998–1010.

Passingham, R. (1995). *The frontal lobes and voluntary action.* New York: Oxford University Press.

Posner, M. I., & Keele, S. W. (1968). On the genesis of abstract ideas. *Journal of Experimental Psychology, 77,* 353–363.

Posner, M. I., & Keele, S. W. (1970). Retention of abstract ideas. *Journal of Experimental Psychology, 83,* 304–308.

Prasada, S. (2000). Acquiring generic knowledge. *Trends in Cognitive Science, 4,* 66–72.

Prasada, S., & Dillingham, E. M. (2006). Principled and statistical connections in common sense conception. *Cognition, 99,* 73–112.

Prentice, D. A., & Miller, D. T. (2006). Essentializing differences between women and men. *Psychological Science, 17,* 129–135.

Prentice, D. A., & Miller, D. T. (2007). Psychological essentialism of human categories. *Current Directions in Psychological Science, 16,* 202–206.

Purdie-Vaughns, V. & Eibach, R. P. (2008). Intersectional invisibility: The distinctive advantages and disadvantages of multiple subordinate-group identities. *Sex Roles, 59,* 377–391.

Rankin, K. (2007). Social cognition in frontal injury. In B. L. Miller & J. L. Cummings (Eds.), *The human frontal lobes: Functions and disorders, second edition* (pp. 345–360). New York: Guilford Press.

Reed, S. K. (1972). Pattern recognition and categorization. *Cognitive Psychology, 3*(3), 382–407.

Rehder, B. (2003). Categorization as a causal reasoning. Cognitive Science: A *Multidisciplinary Journal, 27,* 709–748).

Rehder, B., & Hastie, R. (2001). Casual knowledge and categories: The effects of casual beliefs on categorization, induction, and similarity. *Journal of Experimental Psychology: General, 130,* 232–260.

Rehder, B., & Kim, S. W. (2010). Casual status and coherence in casual-based categorization. *Journal of Experimental Psychology: Learning, Memory, and Cognition, 36,* 1171–1206.

Rhodes, M., & Gelman, S. A. (2008). Categories influence predictions about individual consistency. *Child Development, 79,* 1270–1287.

Rips, L. J. (1989). Similarity, typicality, and categorization. In S. Vosniadou & A. Ortony (Eds.), *Similarity and Analogical Reasoning* (pp. 21–59). New York, NY: Cambridge University Press.

Rips, L. J., Shoben, E. J., & Smith, E. E. (1973). Semantic distance and the verification of semantic relations. *Journal of Verbal Learning and Verbal Behavior, 12,* 1–20.

Roe, A., & Simpson, G. G. (1958). *Behavior and evolution.* New Haven, CT: Yale University Press.

Roepstorff, A., & Frith, C. D. (2004). What's at the top in the top-down control of action? Script-sharing and "top-top" control of action in cognitive experiments. *Psychological Research, 68,* 189–198.

Rosch, E. (1975). Cognitive representations of semantic categories. *Journal of Experimental Psychology: General, 104,* 192–233.

Rosch, E. (1978). Principles of categorization. In E. Rosch & B. B. Lloyd (Eds.), *Cognition and categorization* (pp. 27–48). Hillsdale, N J: Erlbaum.

Rosch, E., & Mervis, C. B. (1975). Family resemblances: Studies in the internal structure of categories. *Cognitive Psychology, 7,* 573–605.

Rosch, E. H. (1973). Natural categories.*Cognitive Psychology, 4,* 328–350.

Rosch, E. H., Mervis, C. B., Gray, W. D., Johnson, D. M., & Boyes-Braem, P. (1976). Basic objects in natural categories. *Cognitive Psychology, 8,* 382–439.

Rosenbaum, D. A. (2002). Motor control. In H. Pashler (Series Ed.) & S. Yantis (Vol. Ed.), *Stevens' handbook of experimental psychology: Vol. 1. Sensation and perception* (3rd ed., pp. 315–339). New York: Wiley.

Rosenbaum, D. A. (2005). The Cinderella of psychology: The neglect of motor control in the science of mental life and behavior. *American Psychologist, 60,* 308–317.

Rosenbaum, D. A., Vaughan, J., Meulenbroek, R. G. J., Jax, S., & Cohen, R. G. (2009). Smart moves: The psychology of everyday perceptual–motor acts. In E. Morsella, J. A. Bargh, & P. M. Gollwitzer (Eds.), *Oxford handbook of human action* (pp. 121–135). New York: Oxford University Press.

Ross, B. H., & Spalding, T. L. (1994). Concepts and categories. In R. J. Sternberg (Ed.), *Handbook of perception and cognition* (pp. 119–148). San Diego, CA: Academic Press.

Rossetti, Y. (2001). Implicit perception in action: Short-lived motor representation of space. In P. G. Grossenbacher (Ed.), *Finding consciousness in the brain: A neurocognitive approach* (pp. 133–181). Netherlands: John Benjamins Publishing.

Rothbart, M., & Taylor, M. (1992). Category labels and social reality: Do we view social categories as natural kinds? In G. R. Semin & F. Fiedler (Eds.), *Language, interaction, and social cognition* (pp. 11–36). Newbury Park, CA: SAGE.

Schank, R. C., & Abelson, R. P. (1977). *Scripts, plans, goals, and understanding: An inquiry into human knowledge structures.* Hillsdale, NJ: Erlbaum.

Schmader, T., Johns, M., & Forbes, C. (2008). An integrated process model of stereotype threat effects on performance. *Psychological Review, 115,* 336–356.

Sesko, A. K., & Biernat, M. (2010). Prototypes of race and gender: The invisibility of Black women. *Journal of Experimental Social Psychology, 46,* 356–360.

Shah, J. Y. (2003). The motivational looking glass: How significant others implicitly affect goal appraisals. *Journal of Personality and Social Psychology, 85,* 424–439.

Shallice, T. (1972). Dual functions of consciousness. *Psychological Review, 79,* 383–393.

Shallice, T., & Burgess, P. (1998). The domain of supervisory processes and the temporal organisation of behaviour. In Roberts, A., Robbins, T., Weiskrantz, L. (Eds.), *The prefrontal cortex: Executive and cognitive functions* (pp. 22–35). Oxford, UK: Oxford University Press.

Sherrington, C. S. (1906). *The integrative action of the nervous system.* New Haven, CT: Yale University Press.

Sherman, J. W., Gawronski, B., Gonsalkorale, K., Hugenberg, K., Allen, T. J., & Groom, C. J. (2008). The self-regulation of automatic associations and behavioral impulses. *Psychological Review, 115,* 314–335.

Sherman S. M., & Guillery R. W. (2006). *Exploring the thalamus and its role in cortical function.* Cambridge, MA: MIT Press.

Silvera, D.H., Krull, D.S., & Sassler, M.A. (2002). Typhoid Pollyanna: The effect of category valence on the processing speeds of positive and negative category members. *European Journal of Cognitive Psychology, 14,* 227–236.

Skinner, B. F. (1953). *Science and human behavior.* New York: Macmillan.

Sloman, S.A. (1996). The empirical case for two systems of reasoning. *Psychological Bulletin, 119,* 3–22.

Sloman, S. A., & Lagnado, D. (2004). Causal invariance in reasoning and learning. In B. Ross (Ed.), *The psychology of learning and motivation* (Vol. 44, pp. 287–325). San Diego: Elsevier Science.

Sloman, S. A., Love, B. C., & Ahn, W. (1998). Feature centrality and conceptual coherence. *Cognitive Science, 22,* 189–228.

Smith, J. D., & Minda, J. P. (1998). Prototypes in the mist: the early epochs of category learning. *Journal of Experimental Psychology: Learning, Memory, and Cognition, 24,* 1411–1436.

Smith, J. D., & Minda, J. P. (2002). Distinguishing prototype-based and exemplar-based processes in category learning. *Journal of Experimental Psychology: Learning, Memory, and Cognition, 28,* 800–811.

Spelke, E. S., Von Hofsten, C., & Kestenbaum, R. (1989). Object perception and object-directed reaching in infancy: Interaction of spatial and kinetic information for object boundaries. *Developmental Psychology, 25,* 185–196.

Sperry, R. W. (1952). Neurology and the mind–brain problem. *American Scientist, 40,* 291–312.

Steele, C. M. (1997). A threat in the air: How stereotypes shape intellectual identity and performance. *American Psychologist, 52,* 613–629.

Strack, F., & Deutsch, R. (2004). Reflective and impulsive determinants of social behavior. *Personality and Social Psychology Bulletin, 8,* 220–247.

Stroop, J. R. (1935). Studies of interference in serial verbal reactions. Journal of *Experimental Psychology, 18,* 643–662.

Tate, C., & Audette, D. (2001). Theory and research on "race" as a natural kind variable in psychology. *Theory & Psychology, 11,* 495–520.

Taylor, J. L., & McCloskey, D. I. (1990). Triggering of preprogrammed movements as reactions to masked stimuli. *Journal of Neurophysiology, 63,* 439–446.

Taylor, J. L., & McCloskey, D. I. (1996). Selection of motor responses on the basis of unperceived stimuli. *Experimental Brain Research, 110,* 62–66.

Taylor, M. G. (1996). The development of children's beliefs about social and biological aspects of gender differences. *Child Development, 67,* 1555–1571.

Taylor, M. G., Rhodes, M., & Gelman, S.A. (2009). Boys will be boys; Cows will be cows: Childrens essentialist reasoning about gender categories and animal species. *Child Development, 80,* 461–481.

Thorndike, E. L. (1905). The functions of mental states. In E. L. Thorndike (Ed.), *The elements of psychology* (pp. 111–119). New York: A. G. Seiler.

Thorpe, W. H. (1964). *Learning and instinct in animals.* Cambridge, MA: Harvard University Press.

Tolman, E. C. (1948). Cognitive maps in rats and men. *Psychological Review, 55,* 189–208.

Todorov, A., Mandisodza, A. N., Goren, A., & Hall, C. C. (2005). Inferences of competence from faces predict election outcomes. *Science, 308,* 1623–1626.

Tversky, A. (1977). Features of similarity. *Psychological Review, 84,* 327–352.

Uleman, J. S., Newman, L. S., & Moskowitz, G. B. (1996). People as flexible interpreters: Evidence and issues from spontaneous trait inference. In M. P. Zanna (Ed.), *Advances in experimental social psychology* (Vol. 28, pp. 211–279). San Diego, CA: Academic Press.

Vohs, K. D., Mead, N. L., & Goode, M. R. (2006). The psychological consequences of money. *Science, 314,* 1154–1156.

Waxman, S. (2010). Names will never hurt me? Naming and the development of racial and gender categories in pre-school-aged children. *European Journal of Social Psychology. 40,* 593–610.

Wittgenstein, L. (1953). *Philosophical investigations.* New York, NY: Macmillan.

Wood, W., Quinn, J., & Kashy, D. (2002). Habits in everyday life: Thought, emotion, and action. *Journal of Personality and Social Psychology, 83,* 1281–1297.

Zajonc, R. B. (1969). *Animal social psychology: A reader of experimental studies.* New York: Wiley.

Zeki, S., & Bartels, A. (1999). Toward a theory of visual consciousness. *Consciousness and Cognition, 8,* 225–259.

15

The Social Psychology of Emotion

Batja Mesquita, Claudia Marinetti, & Ellen Delvaux

Emotional phenomena enter into almost every aspect of our social life, and in themselves, emotions are distinctly social processes
(Zajonc, 1998, p. 591).

Emotions are at the heart of social psychology: They are not just, and not even in the first place, subjective feelings, but rather connections to the social world. Emotions constitute who we are, they give direction to our interactions and relationships, they are central to group membership, and they tie us to our culture. What makes emotions social is not just that they occur in social situations, or are elicited by social events. Rather, their very nature is social and cultural.

To fully understand the social nature of emotions, it is important to consider them first, and foremost, as intentions to act (Frijda, 2007; Lazarus, 1991; Zajonc, 1998). Having an emotion means that one has a stance, a relationship with the environment or, put more sharply, a strategy or a goal in the (social) situation (Griffiths & Scarantino, 2009, p. 2; Lutz & Abu-Lughod, 1990). To take anger as an example: the experience of anger implies an attitude of non-acceptance, an assessment that one has a relatively high level of control over (others in) the situation (Frijda, Kuipers, & Terschure, 1989), and an assumption that others will, or at the very least should, accommodate to your wishes, goals, and values (Stein, Trabasso, & Liwag, 1993). A given emotion may thus be seen as a commitment to a certain way of

acting. As such, emotions are highly relevant in the relationships with others (Mesquita, 2010; Parkinson, Fischer, & Manstead, 2005).

In this chapter, we will conceive emotions as motivation to act. Though particular kinds of emotions have been associated with certain classes of behavior, emotional behavior is not fixed. Rather, emotions involve behavioral intentions; the actual behaviors will depend on, and flexibly adjust to, the context (Frijda, 2004). In this chapter, we suggest that emotions do not *happen to* lead to behavior, but rather are *for doing*. This suggestion takes emotions out of the subjective realm of feeling and consciousness, and places it squarely in the domain of social relationships (Mesquita, 2010; Parkinson et al., 2005); that is, in the domain of social psychology.

After a short introduction about the nature and development of emotions, we will discuss the various ways in which emotions figure in our social lives. First, we will review evidence about the role of emotions in dyadic relationships. We will then synthesize research suggesting that we often experience and express the emotions that fit the social context, followed by research on emotions that are at odds with the social context in which they occur. Finally, we will discuss research suggesting that emotions are not isolated events but that, rather, they occur in the context of extended interactions, relationships, and even social network, and are influenced by them. In the last section of this chapter, we will discuss the function of inter-group emotions. Throughout the chapter, we will argue that emotions are an indispensable, but hitherto often ignored, aspect of social psychological processes.

COGNITIVE APPROACHES TO EMOTIONS

There is some debate about the processes that lead up to the emotional action. For purposes of this chapter, it suffices to say that emotional responses are more than knee-jerk reactions, and thus require some representation of the environment that allows for their strategic or appropriate use but that, at the same time, not every instance of emotion requires a conceptual representation of what goes on. There are different views on how exactly the emotional context gets represented.

Appraisal theories of emotions have proposed that emotions start with an assessment of the personal meaning of the situation according to a fixed number of dimensions, such as novelty, valence, goal consistency, coping potential, and norms or values (Ellsworth & Scherer, 2003; Frijda, 1986; Lazarus, 1991). "The idea [is] that appraisals occur sequentially and that the nature of the emotional experience changes with each time a new appraisal is added" (Ellsworth & Scherer, 2003, p. 574). Anger would emerge when the situation is appraised as novel, unpleasant, goal inconsistent, someone else's responsibility, controllable, and against the norms. Appraisal can be, and often is, automatic and non-conscious (Ellsworth & Scherer, 2003; Scherer, Schorr, & Johnston, 2001).

Somewhat orthogonal to the concept of appraisal dimensions, and much less elaborated, is the idea that emotions emerge from the assessment that (and how) a situation is relevant to a person's specific concerns (Frijda, 1986, 2007), including the coping potential (Lazarus, 1991), values, goals, norms (Mesquita & Ellsworth, 2001), and to the self (Arnold, 1960). Anger emerges from a situation that infringes on one's autonomy, if autonomy is valued (Rozin, Lowery, Imada, & Haidt, 1999). The idea is as old as appraisal theory itself (Arnold, 1960), and connects the person with the situation. It recognizes that appraisals are always made from a certain perspective (Solomon, 2004): that they reflect a person's active construction of meaning, referencing his or her expectations, social position, and moral understandings.

More recently, it has been proposed that "emotional content has a fundamentally pragmatic dimension, in the sense that the environment is represented in terms of what it affords the emoter in the way of skillful engagement with it" (Griffiths

& Scarantino, 2009, p. 2). Some authors conceive of these pragmatic representations as a form of embodied appraisal (Frijda, 2007). Others highlight the temporal dynamics of the representations, emphasizing that these representations develop in response to unfolding transactions in the practical and social world (Griffiths & Scarantino, 2009). In the latter view, representations of the environment unfold in an online fashion, and are scaffolded by events in the environment. Thus, during a marital conflict the anger of each partner develops according to the exchanges of the fight. Emotions, according to this view, are "situated" (see also Mesquita, 2010).

Social cognition figures prominently in all cognitive approaches of emotions –regardless of its representation as evaluative, goal-driven, or situated – but not all social cognition is considered emotion. *What then is emotion-specific?* While the term emotion does not relate to a natural category (Barrett, 2006), both lay people and psychologists usually speak of emotion to refer to special cases of social cognition. First, we conceive of emotions as judgments that something is sufficiently positive or negative to be *relevant to the self*. This means that emotions go beyond a positive or negative attitude towards something, but are motivated states: They affect the self and need to be dealt with. For example, an emotion is not merely an assessment that some procedure is unfair, but rather the determination that this procedure needs to be challenged or changed, because it puts you at a disadvantage personally, or because it is unfair to the point of being incompatible with an acceptable state of the world. We speak of emotion when the social cognition is inherently motivating of action. Second, emotions are those motivated states, or "modes of action readiness," that have "control precedence" (Frijda, 2007; Oatley, 1992): They take priority over other types of behavior. Thus, when the appraisal of unfair treatment motivates a person to do anything in her power to stop the unfair treatment, this is called an emotion. Third, and perhaps best thought of as part of the same control precedence, emotions involve physiological changes that prepare the behavior intended or sought after; the physiological signature of challenge, for instance, to prepare for antagonistic behavior (Blascovich & Mendes, 2000).

Emotions are social engagements

Most emotions take place in the context of relationships (Scherer, Matsumoto, Wallbott, & Kudoh, 1988). This is not coincidental: emotions serve important functions in relationships. According to some, the adaptive advantage of emotions is precisely that they help to coordinate and regulate relationships (Jankowiak & Fischer, 1992; Oatley, 2004; Oatley, Keltner, & Jenkins, 2006). From the evidence to be discussed next, it is clear that emotions fulfill an important role in our relationships.

Evidence for the social significance of emotions comes from two research traditions. One starts from the idea that emotions are affect programs, and consist of invariant packages of responses that have some adaptive advantage for establishing or maintaining important relationships with others. For instance, passionate sexual love is "experienced as joyful and energizing, it is enacted in courtship, and it includes a biological core, including increased levels of phenylalanine in the brain" (Oatley, et al., 2006, p. 73). It provides a strong motivation to engage in a particular sexual relationship, to the point of causing pain and longing in absence of the other. Embarrassment is characterized by a temporary loss of self-esteem and/or perceived social exposure, and serves to appease the more powerful (Keltner & Buswell, 1997; Tangney, Miller, Flicker, & Barlow, 1996); and jealousy, an emotion marked by a drop in self-esteem, and aggressive action tendencies, serves to defend our valuable close relationships against rivals (DeSteno, Valdesolo, & Bartlett, 2006).

Based on their most frequent social consequences, emotions have been classified into *affiliative* or *socially engaging* emotions that strengthen the bond between people, and *socially distancing* or *disengaging* emotions that draw clear individual boundaries, emphasize autonomy, and increase interpersonal distance, at least initially (Fischer & Manstead, 2008; Kitayama, Markus, & Kurokawa, 2000; Kitayama, Mesquita, & Karasawa, 2006). For instance, shame and gratitude tend to be seen as prototypes of affiliative or socially engaging emotions, because they commonly involve a motivation to be closer to (or, more accepted by) others, whereas anger and pride are exemplars of socially distancing emotions, since their most common consequence is to distinguish or defend the individual from his or her social environment.

Other evidence stems from a more situationist view, and focuses on emotional episodes as they emerge from the interaction between individuals and their environments (Boiger & Mesquita, 2011; Griffiths & Scarantino, 2009; Mesquita, 2010; Parkinson et al., 2005; Saarni, 2008). Children's unfolding emotions as a response to caregiver's attempts to discipline the child, the escalation of marital conflict, and the establishment of a relationship based on acts of kindness are cases in point (see below). According to this view, emotions are on-line constructions that unfold in ways that are responsive both to cultural concepts, norms, and practices, and to the particular affordances and constraints of the direct (social) environment. This means that emotions may vary across social relationships and cultures, an implication that is at odds with the idea of invariant, universal affect programs.

Our goal for the present chapter is not to weigh the evidence for any particular theoretical model, but rather to show that the joint evidence from all these perspectives suggests a central role of emotions in interpersonal relationships. To this end, we will synthesize the evidence that emotions, however conceived, are relationship engagements.

DEVELOPMENT OF EMOTIONS

Nowhere is it clearer that emotions are social engagements than in the first year of life (cf. Parkinson et al., 2005). The relationship between infants and caregivers revolves around the exchange of emotions. Infants give their caregivers affective messages from the very early beginnings of life. Behaviors like fussing, crying, and smiling communicate to the caregiver that adjustments to the environment need to be made, or conversely, that the interaction is going well (Oatley & Jenkins, 1992; Oatley et al., 2006). This is not to say that infant emotional displays are associated with adult-like emotions: they are not (e.g., Camras, Meng, & Ujie, 2002; Hiatt, Campos, & Emde, 1979). However, caregivers imbue infant displays with emotional meaning by the way they respond. Thus, from a very early age on, expressive emotional behaviors on the part of the infant are at the center of the relationship with the caregiver.

Caregivers' behavior, on the other hand, can be seen as a way to regulate the babies' emotions (Holodynski & Friedlmeier, 2006). For example, mothers were found to maintain a baby's positive state by engaging in mirroring the baby's positive emotions and ignoring or responding with surprise to a baby's negative expressions. Caregivers thus either reduce or increase stimulation, such that good-feeling states of the baby are recognized and sustained, and bad-feeling states are taken into account and discontinued (Oatley et al., 2006). At the infant stage, it is easy to see that emotions are distributed processes that belong to the interaction between caregiver and infant, rather than to each of the interactants separately.

The relationship with the caregiver can also provide emotional meaning to objects outside the infant–caregiver relationship, as is the case in social referencing (Hertenstein & Campos, 2004;

Mumme & Fernald, 2003). Children as young as 11–12 months will appraise a novel object by referencing the emotions of a nearby adult, usually the caregiver, and infer from these emotions the significance of the object. Social referencing has been shown to influence both the infants' expressions and their emotional responses to the novel object. For instance, a caregiver's disgust expressions increase the chances of infants' crying, as well as make the infant less likely to touch or approach the new toy. There is also some evidence that social referencing in the case of negative emotion changes the infant's behavior vis-à-vis the caregiver. Infants tend to stay closer to the mother (Carver & Vaccaro, 2007). Yet again, the infant emotion is inferred in the context of the relationship with the caregiver, and in turn influences the course of this relationship itself.

The relationships with caregivers (and peers) are an important context of emotional development in the years of childhood. During those years emotions are often the object of communication between caregivers and children (Dunn, 2004). Caregivers label, interpret, and evaluate emotions. They do so in two ways. First, caregivers explicitly talk about emotions, communicating rules and beliefs. Furthermore, caregivers' own emotional responses may lend meaning to their children's emotions too (Saarni, 2008). One way of looking at caregiver's (verbal as well as emotional) communications about emotions is that they teach children about the propriety of certain ways of emoting – i.e., certain ways of relational engagement – in particular contexts. Consistent with this interpretation is the finding that parental talk about emotions is an important predictor of a child's social adroitness (Dunn, Brown, & Beardsall, 1991; Harris, 2008). For example, the frequency with which preschool children discuss emotions with caregivers predicts their later ability to understand other people's feelings.

Parental talk about emotions varies across cultural contexts (Cole, Tamang, & Shrestha, 2006; Miller, Fung, & Mintz, 1996), and reflects cultural ideas and practices about valued and devalued types of relational engagements. Thus, one study compared conversations of American and Taiwanese moms with their 2.5 year olds. Consistent with the American cultural model that emphasizes the importance of high self-esteem and independence, American moms emphasized the child's independent achievements, and thus invoked happiness and pride. On the other hand, Taiwanese moms drew attention to the child's transgressions, and how these transgressions had burdened and saddened the mom, thus shaming the child (Cole et al., 2006; Miller et al., 1996). The latter is consistent with the East Asian model of being, in which the individual's accommodation to the needs of the relationship and the avoidance of norm violations are central. Parents thus draw attention to those types of relational engagement – i,e., those types of emotion – that are most likely to render the child into a well-socialized individual in their culture.

Similarly, Cole and colleagues found different socialization practices in two Nepalese groups, the Tamang and the Brahman (Cole, Bruschi, & Tamang, 2002; Cole et al., 2006). The Tamang – Tibetan Buddhists – value self-effacement and compassionate tolerance. In this group, anger is viewed as destructive to social harmony, whereas shame is seen as a valuable emotion by which individuals subject themselves to the larger group. On the other hand, the Brahman – high caste of Hindus – conceive of anger as a way to establish dominance and competence, assuming it gets properly regulated, whereas shame is seen as a sign of weakness. Consistently, adult responses to anger and shame episodes in 3–5 year olds were very different in these two groups. Tamang caregivers responded to children's shame with teaching and nurturing, whereas anger was received with teasing and rebuking. Conversely, Brahman adults ignored signs of shame in their children, but gave their angry children attention, teaching them proper ways of expressing anger. Caregivers' responses to given emotions thus function to enhance and moderate culturally valued emotions, and suppress culturally devalued emotions. In other words, caregivers assist their children in selecting rewarding relational engagements, and suppressing unrewarding ones.

Parents also create the opportunities for their children's emotions, and they do so in ways that are consistent with the prevalent and valued types of relationship engagements. Research comparing German and Japanese mother's disciplining of their disobedient children makes this point (Trommsdorff & Kornadt, 2003). German mothers' way of disciplining tended to incite anger and hurt feelings in their children; both are considered disengaging emotions, in that they reinforce individual boundaries and independence, which are consistent with relationship values in a German context. Japanese mothers' style of disciplining, on the other hand, induced empathy in their children, thus increasing the harmony and oneness that are valued aspects of the Japanese mother–child relationship.

In sum, emotions in the developing child can be seen as engagements with the relationship with their caregiver. At the infant stage, the caregiver acts on the emotional signals of the baby. Emotions at this stage can thus be readily conceived as distributed processes. At later stages, there is a shift in distribution: babies themselves act in limited ways on their emotional representations of the situation, and caregivers help to regulate the babies' emotions. The caregiver does so by modeling, encouraging, and affording the emotions of the child in ways that may be thought to enhance functionality of the emotions to the particular social context (Saarni, 2008). In other words, caregivers regulate their baby's emotion with the aim of enhancing the baby's social fit. Cross-cultural differences in caregiver regulation are consistent with differences in the valued types of relationship.

EMOTIONS IN SOCIAL RELATIONSHIPS

In the adulthood literature, there is also ample evidence for emotions as social engagements. This literature is dominated by a more discrete view of emotions. Particular emotions are seen as commitments to certain kinds of action, which tend to elicit well-described effects in others, and thus to have some predictable social or relational consequences.

Affiliative emotions

Recent work has drawn attention to the affiliative function of gratitude (Algoe, Haidt, & Gable, 2008). It has been proposed that gratitude serves to generate intrinsically motivated kind acts towards the benefactor, and thus would be instrumental towards a communal relationship. Algoe and colleagues (2008) studied gratitude as it helped develop the relationship between little and big sisters of a sorority: little sisters had just joined the sorority, while big sisters had been members of the sorority since the year prior. During little sister week, when big sisters anonymously surprised their little sisters, the gratitude of little sisters was measured. This gratitude was associated with the little sister's appreciation for the relationship with their anonymous big sister. In support of the hypothesis, it was found that, one month later, the little sister's gratitude predicted the quality of the relationship and the amount of time spent together, as reported by the big sister. Gratitude seemed to stand for a relationship commitment on the part of the little sister that was reciprocated by the big sister.

There is also ample evidence for the affiliative or socially engaging nature of several negative emotions. Embarrassment is a good example. Signs of embarrassment, such as blushing, gaze aversion, and smile controls, have been described as "nonverbal apologies" that "inform others of one's genuine contrition and desire to avoid rejection" (Miller, 1996, p. 145). This interpretation is supported by studies that show that the level of felt embarrassment diminishes only after others

have been informed about it. For instance, the embarrassment of respondents who sang out of tune in the presence of an experimenter diminished to the level of a non-embarrassed control group when they thought the experimenter had either seen their ratings of embarrassment or had seen them blushing, but not when they thought their embarrassment had remained hidden from the experimenter (Leary, Landel, & Patton, 1996). "Knowing that their audience was aware of their embarrassment seemed to reduce the severity of their predicament, diminishing the embarrassment they felt. Meanwhile those who had never made their embarrassment plain, seemed to remain motivated to express it" (Miller, 1996, p. 153).

That embarrassment is a social regulator can also be inferred from the finding that anti-social behavior is related to low levels of embarrassment. Specifically, boys judged by their teachers to be "externalizers," and thus to display anti-social behavior, were found to have fewer facial expressions of embarrassment and fear than a well-adjusted comparison group during a standardized test situation (Keltner, Kring, & Bonnano, 1999). The researchers suggest that the relative absence of embarrassment means that the externalizing boys were less concerned about rejection.

Embarrassment tends to be interpreted as intended: namely, as a sign of appeasement (Keltner & Buswell, 1997). Several studies suggest that a person is *liked* better when he or she shows embarrassment than not. Participants who watched videotapes of a person dislodging a large stack of toilet paper liked this person better when he had responded with embarrassment, regardless of whether he restacked the toilet paper or walked away from the mess (Semin & Manstead, 1982). Similarly, people responding with embarrassment to negative feedback about their task performance are better liked than people who respond defiantly (Edelmann, 1982). Moreover, participants judged individuals to be more trustworthy, friendlier, and more likeable when they were described to blush after breaking a valuable in a shop than when they were not (de Jong, 1999). Finally, in studies about teasing, displays of embarrassment on the part of the victims evoked positive emotions in their teasing partners, whether fraternity members or romantic partners, as well as in observers (Keltner, Young, Heerey, Oemig, & Monarch, 1998). The effects of embarrassment on others, however, may go beyond increased liking. Participants bought more condoms after a presentation aimed to increase condom use when the presenter acted embarrassed than when he/she was confident and unembarrassed; perhaps because they liked the embarrassed presenter better, though this was not reported by the authors (Keltner & Stoey, 1996, as cited in Keltner & Busswell, 1997). Together, the evidence suggests that embarrassment serves the purpose of correcting a breach in social norms that could otherwise have led to social rejection.

While embarrassment is important in restoring and maintaining even not so close relationships, guilt appears to be significant in the restoring and maintenance of close and communal relationships (Baumeister, Stillwell, & Heatherton, 1994). It has been hypothesized that guilt emerges when there is a threat of social exclusion or rejection by a significant other. One circumstance for guilt is the individuals' own perception that they have behaved badly towards their partner: for example, by hurting them or causing loss or distress. Indeed, in a self-report study (Baumeister, Stillwell, & Heatherton, 1995), respondents who reported feeling guilty about harming another person held the other in greater esteem than respondents who did not feel guilty. Moreover, fewer guilty than non-guilty respondents reported that they had anticipated the outcome, that their actions were justified, and that the victim helped to provoke their behavior. In other words, guilt feelings were associated with a greater appreciation of the relationship as well as with more self-blame for what happened. Guilt appears to motivate corrective behavior: it increases communal behaviors such as mutual concern and positive treatment, while at the same time reducing the chance of transgressions (Baumeister et al., 1994). Indeed, in the same self-report study quoted above (Baumeister et al., 1995), respondents with guilt feelings reported more often that they had learned a lesson, changed their behavior, and gave apologies after they had harmed another person than respondents who did not feel guilty.

Consistently, experimental research has shown that guilt inductions increase cooperative behavior, especially in those who are uncooperative to begin with. Thus, those respondents who are more liable to self-blame show corrective behavior after guilt induction. In one study, participants cooperated more in a bargaining game after they had been primed with guilt (by having to write about an episode in which they had felt really guilty) than before. Moreover, respondents primed with guilt cooperated more than those who had described a typical day (Ketelaar & Au, 2003). Finally, the guilt prime had the greatest effects on participants who had behaved uncooperatively in the first part of the game. Similarly, respondents primed with guilt (by remembering a time they cheated on their romantic partner), were more likely to cooperate in a ten-coin give-some dilemma game with another participant than respondents in the control condition (De Hooge, Zeelenberg, & Breugelmans, 2007). Again, guilt had the largest effects on those who were least cooperative to begin with: pro-selves, distinguished on the basis

of their low default levels of cooperation, were more likely to show their commitment to the relationship after they were primed with guilt than in the control condition. Differences in level of cooperation between the guilt and the control conditions did not reach significance for the pro-social type participants, due to a ceiling effect.

Guilt also predicted cooperation in an ultimatum game, when feelings of guilt were measured instead of manipulated (Keetelaar & Au, 2003). Participants who had made selfish offers in the first negotiation game, and subsequently reported to feel guilty, made more generous offers in a second round of the game. Participants who had made selfish offers, but had not felt guilty, did not change their negotiation strategy during the second game session.

A final example of an affiliative emotion that we discuss is jealousy. As an affiliative emotion, jealousy has its appearance working against it: it is linked with aggression. Jealousy may be a last-resort emotion under conditions where social exclusion threatens to become, or even has become, a reality and when self-esteem is seriously threatened (DeSteno, Valdesolo, & Bartlett, 2006). After a jealousy induction, when a rival's appearance put an abrupt end to a flattering and successful working relationship with a partner, participants' self-esteem, as measured both on explicit and implicit self-esteem measures, dropped considerably. In a control scenario, where the initial partner excused himself because he needed to make another appointment, the self-esteem of the respondents remained unaffected. Moreover, in a second study with the same jealousy manipulation, the participants tended to add more hot sauce to the taste samples of both the partner and the rival, even though they knew that neither one of them liked their food spicy (DeSteno et al., 2006). The amount of hot sauce added, considered a measure of interpersonal aggression, was mediated by the reduction in participants' self-esteem. Path analysis confirmed that the participants' self-esteem was lowered after their partner chose to work with the rival, which then increased the intensity of their jealousy, which, in turn, led to higher aggression towards both partner and rival.

To our knowledge, there are no studies of the effects of jealous behavior on either the rivals or the partners. We would assume that, at least some of the time, rivals are scared away and partners reminded that the jealous person needs to be taken into consideration. And if this is not the case, then at least the prospect of making one's partner jealous, with the entailing consequences of this person's behavior, may sometimes be instrumental in keeping an existing relationship together. It should be noted that the dichotomy between affiliative and assertive emotions is of limited use in the case of jealousy emotions.

Assertive emotions

Anger is a prime example of an assertive or socially disengaging emotion. In emotional prototype studies, anger, both in self and in others, is associated with verbally attacking the cause of anger, and yelling and screaming (Shaver, Schwartz, Kinson, & O'Connor, 1987). In a study on emotion scripts, married couples reported worrying and brooding as part of their anger episodes (Chow, Tiedens, & Govan, 2008; Fitness, 1996); within romantic relationships these behaviors may be considered disengaging as well. Finally, participants who were made angry in a Cyberball game were more likely to aggress towards their supposed teammates (by giving them the least attractive snack), and this aggression was mediated by the level of anger reported by the respondents (Chow et al., 2008).

That anger has an assertive function in relationships – making claims for status, power, or other means –has been largely inferred from its effects on other people's behavior. People subjected to anger yield, apologize or submit to the angry person (Fischer & Manstead, 2008). In a series of studies, Tiedens (2001) showed that targets expressing anger were conferred with higher status than those expressing sadness, fear, or guilt. In a first study, students watched a video clip of former American President Bill Clinton discussing a sex scandal in which he was purportedly involved. In one condition the clip showed an angry Clinton. In the other condition the President appeared fearful and guilty. Participants who had watched the angry clip were more convinced that Clinton should stay in power than those who saw the fearful, guilty clip. Similar results were obtained showing respondents a fictitious politician who talked about terrorism in either an angry or a sad way. Participants who saw the politician in anger were more likely to vote for him and considered the politician a better leader than participants who saw the same fictitious politician displaying sadness. Moreover, the link between emotion expression and status conferral was mediated by the perceived competence of the politician: the angry politician was rated as more competent than the sad one and, in turn, increased competence led to higher status attribution.

In a final study (Tiedens, 2001, Study 4), the effects of anger and sadness on status attribution were assessed in the context of a job interview. Students of business administration viewed a clip of an applicant reporting a situation in which things had not gone well at his previous job. In one condition the clip ended with the applicant reporting that he felt angry about it; in the other with the applicant saying he felt sad and guilty. Participants offered the job applicant both a high-status position and a better salary when he had expressed anger than when he seemed sad and guilty. Once again, competence ratings fully mediated the emotion-status conferral relationship.

That anger induces yielding on the part of the other person has also been shown by negotiation studies (Van Kleef, De Dreu, & Manstead, 2004). In these studies, participants take part in a computer-simulated negotiation. The computer was programmed to send to the participant messages that expressed anger in one condition, and that were happy and neutral in the other two. Participants whose opponent expressed anger lowered their demands and made larger concessions over time, compared to participants in the other two conditions. Participants in this study thus honored the greater entitlement expressed by the angry negotiators.

When the claim of anger is considered both justified and inescapable, anger brings about an improvement of position. But what happens when the angry person's claim is neither justifiable nor inescapable? In a series of studies by Van Dijk, van Kleef, Steinel, and van Beest (2008), respondents played a computer-mediated ultimatum game with another negotiator (in reality, the computer) who either expressed anger or happiness. Respondents were the allocator in the game, deciding about the distribution of the available chips between themselves and the other person. In the default condition, respondents offered the angry negotiating partner more chips than the happy person, but the anger advantage faded or disappeared when either (a) the game was set up in a way that gave the negotiating partner less power (the results did not change that much whether the offer was accepted or declined), or (b) the participants got the power to misinform the negotiating partner such that the offer seemed more generous than it really was. Thus, anger seems to be effective only if the claims of the angry person are not negotiable. Respondents will use room for negotiating the anger claim, if there is any. In fact, anger backfired in some cases. When the respondents knew that the chips had twice the value to them than to the bargainer, but they thought the bargainer to be unaware of this fact, participants offered fewer chips to the angry bargainer than to the happy one. This can only be explained as either punishment of the angry bargainer or reward to the happy one. Anger effects are thus dependent on the context in which anger is expressed. Anger of people with power is met with the conferral of status and goods. However, anger that can be challenged, will be, if the circumstances allow it.

In sum, emotions may be considered relationship engagements to which others respond. They are strategic bids for certain positions in the social world: affiliative emotions make intimacy bids and socially distancing emotions make status bids. Emotions may make an appeal on others to conform to the strategic bid, to accept the relationship alignment, or to welcome or reject the changed (or alternatively, sustained) relationship engagement. In many cases these bids are accepted, but there are exceptions.

EMOTIONS IN CONTEXT

Emotions that fit the context

If emotions are moves in interactions or strategic bids, one may expect that the prevalence of a given emotion is contingent on its fit with the prevalent relationship goals in that context. In other words, if emoting is largely strategic, then it should be functional to the sociocultural environment in which it occurs. There is much evidence that this is in fact the case. Examples of this principle can be found at the level of social roles as well as the level of culture.

For example, low- and high-status contexts are associated with different rates of emotions. In one study (Tiedens, Ellsworth, & Mesquita, 2000), business students from a mid Western university read a vignette in which a boss and an employee formed a sales team that failed in their mission, and did not reach the customer on time with the product. Responsibility for this bad outcome could not be inferred from the description. Respondents inferred that the level of anger was higher for the boss and the levels of sadness and guilt were higher for the employee. Thus, the emotion that expressed rightfulness and power was associated with the boss; the emotions of powerlessness and regret with the employee. Status roles render certain emotions more appropriate, and therefore more likely. Interestingly, when emotions rather than status roles were given in the same vignettes, respondents recognized the boss in the angry person, and the employee in the sad or guilty person. Emoting is thus engaging in status roles, and from the status roles we can predict which emotions are likely to be experienced. Emotions are functional to these status roles.

The most prevalent emotions in given cultural contexts also appear to be the ones that are consistent with the culturally preferred relationship arrangements (Kitayama et al., 2006a; Mesquita & Leu, 2007). For example, Kitayama and his colleagues found that socially engaging emotions, such as friendly feelings or shame, were more prevalent in the Japanese interdependent than the American independent cultural context; the reverse was true for socially disengaging emotions, such as pride and anger. Engaging emotions underline and reinforce the relatedness between people, and thus fit the interdependent model. This is obviously the case with friendly feeling, but also an emotion of shame signals the acknowledgement of social rules as well as the preparedness to submit to those rules. Socially disengaging emotions tend to signal and contribute to the boundedness and independence of an individual, and thus fit the goals in independent contexts. Data from several studies converged. In one experience sampling study, both positive and negative engaged emotions were more frequent than disengaged emotions in Japanese contexts, whereas the reverse was true in independent European American contexts (Kitayama et al., 2006). In these studies, Japanese and European-American students rated engaged as well as disengaged emotions subsequently in a daily experience sampling study, and in response to 22 very diverse emotional events. In these studies, the largest differences appeared for the disengaged emotions. Whereas Japanese and European American students similarly appraised situations with regard to their implications for relational engagement, European American students reported significantly higher levels of disengaged emotions for both the positive and the negative situations. Thus, the combined work on power and cultural contexts suggests that emotions that have the greatest strategic benefits in the context are those most likely to occur: in other words, the reinforcement structure of the context predicts the likelihood of an emotion occurring. A finding in the same study by Kitayama and colleagues corroborates this idea. Not only were disengaged emotions relatively more frequent in the US samples, and engaged emotions more frequent in the Japanese samples, but also self-reported well-being was best predicted by the culturally valued emotions disengaged in the US and engaged in Japan. Thus, the most frequent emotions may have been the most rewarding, if rewards can be assumed to translate into well-being.

In sum, the studies discussed here suggest that contextualized relationship arrangements may account for the types of emotions that occur. The contextualized norms, habits, or reward structures affect which emotions occur most frequently. Note that these features of the context help us understand the regularities of an individual's emotional life. Thus, what emotions a person is likely to experience can be inferred from the contexts in which his/her emotional life is embedded.

Emotions that do not fit with the context

If emotions can be right within a context, they can be at odds with it too. Context may be defined by culture, power differential, or gender roles. Whether emotions represent successful and legitimate bids, or rather will be challenged or rejected, depends on whether they are judged acceptable given the context.

Gender contexts affect the legitimacy of a number of different emotions. For instance, Brescoll and Uhlmann (2008) found that anger did not elicit the same status conferral when expressed by women as by men. They replicated an earlier study by Tiedens (2001; discussed above), in which respondents viewed a recording of a job applicant who was either angry or sad telling about a mishap that happened at his previous job. Whereas the job applicant in the initial study by Tiedens had been a man, Brescoll and Uhlman replicated the study using both male and female job applicants. For the male job applicants, they replicated the Tiedens' results: respondents conferred more status to angry than to sad male applicants, by offering them better jobs. However, the picture was reversed when the job applicant was a woman: respondents conferred less power on angry than on sad women. (Brescoll & Uhlmann, 2008). Furthermore, participants explained anger in a woman by making negative, internal attributions ("She is not in control"), but they justified anger in men by referring to external circumstances. Thus, women do not gain from being angry, while angry men make successful claims to status. Hence, gender is a constituting context for the interactive meaning of anger. It seems that women in this case did better assuming an emotion that is more consistent with their less agentic stereotype (Best & Williams, 1997).

Stereotypical emotions may not always be the best strategy for women, however. A study by Lewis (2000) suggested that women in astereotypical roles may be judged more positively when their emotions are inconsistent with the female stereotype: i.e., when they do not show emotions. Participants watched videotaped scenarios with a person expressing anger, sadness (by crying), or no emotion at all, and rated this person's leadership effectiveness. Emotions affected perceived leadership efficiency differently in men than in women. Men who were either angry or neutral were perceived as more effective than men who were sad. Women, on the other hand, were considered most effective when they showed no emotion at all. The default judgment of men as effective leaders is only challenged when they show an emotion that is typically associated with low status and low assertiveness. On the other hand, women,

who tend to be stereotyped as emotional, are considered less effective as leaders (cf. Eagly & Karau, 2002) unless they behave in a non-stereotypical way and do not express emotions. In that case, they are exempt from the bad stereotype about their leadership qualities. Thus, what emotions mean for the perception by others is not only dependent on the type of engagement they represent but also on the meaning of this engagement for a person with this specific identity.

Not only the effect of assertive emotions but also that of affiliative emotions may depend on gender. Crying is more prevalent in women than in men, consistent with gender schemas that prescribe strength and independence for men, and emotional expressiveness and connectedness for women (Vingerhoets & Scheirs, 2000). Furthermore, there is some evidence that crying is judged to be more legitimate for women than for men: crying men are helped and comforted less often than crying women (Hendriks, Nelson, Cornelius, & Vingerhoets, 2008).

The status of the relationship may also serve as the context by which the legitimacy of emotions is judged. The impact of guilt, for instance, was suggested to be contingent on the mutual dependence of the dyadic partners. When both partners are committed to the relationship, guilt may operate as an influencing technique for the less powerful person (Baumeister et al., 1994) who invokes it when the outcomes of the relationship are unequally distributed. Guilt induction motivates corrective behavior, such as apologizing or making reparations or amends, but this seems only the case to the extent that the relationship in question is indispensable for the person made to feel guilty. Guilt is more likely to have a negative effect on the relationship in case the guilty partner does not reciprocate the relationship. For example, recipients of unwanted love who feel guilty about it tended to avoid the would-be lover (Baumeister & Wotman, 1992).

Similarly, sadness can be seen as a bid for sympathy and help in others (Bonnano, Goorin, & Coifman, 2008; Keltner & Kring, 1998). However, without mutual commitment to the relationship, sadness does not make an effective appeal. When randomly created same-sex dyads were made to listen to each others' reports of pain and suffering, those low on power (as measured by the Sense of Power scale) reciprocated with distress and compassion, while distress levels of high-power listeners (measured on the same scale) were unrelated to their partners' sadness levels (Van Kleef, Oveis, van der Löwe, LuoKogan, Goetz, & Keltner, 2008). This may be a specific case of the finding that people in high-status positions generally fail to appreciate the mental life of those lower in status (Fiske, 2010).

The meaning of emotional engagements may also vary according to cultural differences in the meanings of certain relationship arrangements. This is clear for shame, an emotion that may be seen as aligning oneself with the social rules and expectations. Whether this act is condoned by others seems to depend on the specific cultural models (Mesquita & Karasawa, 2004). Shame in East Asian cultures tends to be a desirable emotion, as it is consistent with interdependent goals of accommodating to others. It fits the values and practices of modesty and self-criticism that are prevalent in East Asian cultures. On the other hand, shame in Western contexts is an uneasy, painful, and often *invisible* (Scheff, 1988) emotion. It signals that one has failed to achieve the central tasks of an independent self: namely, self-esteem and positive independence.

In some cultures, emotions are more literally taken as bids that can be negotiated if unreasonable. Shame and anger were described as the currency for power negotiations among the Kaluli in Papua New Guinea (Schieffelin, 1983). In the Kaluli cultural model, nearly every reason to be angered, "any loss, wrong, injury, insult, or disappointment, is interpreted in the scheme of reciprocity.... A person who is angry is in some sense owed something: He has a legitimate expectation that he is due redress..." (pp. 186–187). Legitimacy can be challenged by shaming the angry person, implying he is over-asking. Shaming is basically undermining the legitimacy of the appeal that anger makes. Shame is "a situation, or a state of powerlessness and rejection. The legitimacy of one's basic posture of assertion or appeal has been removed." But shaming requires an assessment of power: "A person does not try to shame another if he does not think he can dominate the situation. If one tries to shame a stronger opponent without proper social support, his opponent may become provoked, override shame, and dominate him by intimidation" (p. 190). Thus, the legitimacy of anger in a Kaluli context also seems dependent on social power of the person who is angry.

Lest we give the impression that only the strategic bids or relational engagements associated with negative emotions are negotiated, we will give an example of a positive emotion negotiating in the context of intimate relationships. Gratitude, for instance, can be seen as the currency of many intimate relationships, and thus plays an important role in the negotiation of what is valued in a relationship (Fields, Copp, & Kleinman, 2006). Hochshild (1989, in Fields et al., 2006) found that, as gender culture shifted, with more women participating in the labor market, the marital baseline against which women measured, received, and appreciated gifts, shifted as well, but often men did not follow suit. Women tended to consider their pay checks as gifts, but men would find their wives' financial success shaming. Consequently, women were expecting that men would do their fair share in the household (their spouses folding the laundry was not considered a gift), whereas men would see washing the dishes as a gift. Gratitude or the abstinence from it can thus be considered moves in the relationship that are subject to evaluation and negotiation. Emotions may thus be seen as bids in the negotiation for certain social positions (closeness, dominance); bids that may be acceptable to others in some but not in all contexts.

EMOTIONAL EPISODES: ONGOING INTERACTIONS, SOCIAL SHARING, AND CONVERGENCE OF EMOTIONS

Much of the adult literature is based on experimental research in which a one-time occurrence elicits an emotion, which is measured by a one-time subjective self-report. Moreover, the behavioral response is often channeled to fit a one-time, quantifiable response, such as choosing an unattractive snack, cooperating in a dilemma game, or adding hot sauce. While this type of research has greatly helped our understanding of the social nature of emotions, moving it away from conceptions of emotions as flight-or-fight responses to bears in the woods, it has also skewed the view of emotions towards discrete occurrences. The picture of emotions that emerges from the body of experimental research is of a bounded phenomenon with a clear beginning and end.

In real interactions, emotions appear to be more fluid, ongoing, and "attuned to unfolding transactions with the practical and social world" (Parkinson, 2008, p. 24). This conceptualization of emotions as based in social interaction draws attention to the dynamics of emotions in context and, more importantly, it renders the connection between different instances of emoting more transparent.

In the following, we highlight the importance of studying larger emotional episodes by briefly discussing research that focuses on ongoing interactions, on the social sharing of emotions, and on emotional convergence.

Ongoing emotional interactions

There are not many studies that are attuned to the question of emotions in context, but research on marital dispute provides an interesting exception. Several of these studies have established meaningful couple patterns of emoting (Gottman, Swanson,

& Murray, 1999). One study found, for instance, that some couples' emotional patterns consist of reciprocal negative emotions (contempt, anger), with one spouse's negative emotions predicting the other's on the next interaction turn (even when controlling for the first spouse's own emotions on previous turns). Other couples' dynamics did not show the same reciprocity, because one of the spouses would have a "negativity threshold," meaning that the hostility of the other partner had to be much more pronounced in order for the first partner to respond in kind on the next turn (Gottman et al., 1999). The negativity threshold was predicted not only by the partner's hostility on the previous turn but also by hostility earlier in the interaction. One partner's negative emotions during the first half of the discussion predicted a higher negativity threshold in the other partner during the latter half. One possible interpretation is that those who received too many messages of disapproval from their spouses stopped engaging in the relationship. This interpretation fits with the finding that a negativity threshold predicted failure of the marriage 1 year later.

The important point here is that emotions of the spouses mutually afford or constrain each other, as it may be, even in the course of *one* single interaction. One can only imagine how emotional patterns of partners afford each other in the course of a long-term relationship. In fact, the power of emotions in a relationship is impressively illustrated by another finding from the marital conflict literature (Gottman & Levenson, 2000). The emotions of couples who were invited to the lab to discuss an issue of conflict predicted the chances of divorce reliably 14 years later. Comparing couples headed for divorce and stable couples, those headed for divorce had a much lower positive to negative emotions ratio. Both volatile couples who have lots of positive and lots of negative emotions and harmonious couples who are neither positive nor express very many negative emotions can be successful, as long as the positive emotions outweigh the negative emotions by far. Other good predictors of divorce are "the four horsemen of the apocalypse": emotions that deny the validity of the other person's perspective – being critical of the person, not wanting to really listen to what the other has to say, contempt, and stonewalling (= listener withdrawal) during a discussion in the lab all predicted divorce 7 years later. The in-between processes mediating expression of these emotions and dissolution of the relationship are unknown, but these findings suggest an important, erosive role for these emotions in the relationship that merits further study.

On the positive end of the spectrum, Algoe and colleagues did an experience sampling study that followed the effects of gratitude in romantic relationships (Algoe, Gable, & Maisel, 2010). Gratitude was found to function as a "booster shot." In the study, both partners of heterosexual couples were asked to keep a daily diary on (a) their own and received thoughtful actions, (b) their emotional reactions (e.g., gratitude) towards their partner's actions, and (c) their relationship satisfaction. Thoughtful actions of the partner predicted the experience of gratitude, which in turn led to higher relationship satisfaction for *both* partners the following day. This means that one partner's experience of gratitude not only led the grateful partner to feel more relationally connected, but that it did the same for the partner who had initially acted thoughtfully. Gratitude for "the little things" appears to play an important role in affording relationship growth, and it does so not only for newly formed dyads but also in established relationships on a day-to-day basis.

The mutual constitution of emotions in interactions can also be studied between people who are unfamiliar at the start of the interaction. An example comes from research with undergraduates who were selected to be either very high or very low on social anxiety (Heerey & Kring, 2007). Non-anxious respondents were either paired with non-anxious peers, or alternatively, with socially anxious counterparts. Each pair was instructed to "get to know" each other. Highly anxious participants engaged in more self-talk, asked fewer questions, reciprocated genuine smiles more often with polite smiles and less often with pleasant genuine smiles, and sought more reassurance than the non-anxious participants in either type of dyad. Central to the current argument is that this emotional behavior constituted the emotions of the non-anxious participants who were paired with anxious conversation partners. These non-anxious participants were the only group who did *not* report an increase in positive affect as a result of the interaction. Moreover, they offered more empathy and support to their conversation partners than any other group in the study. Finally, both interaction partners in the socially anxious/non-anxious pair perceived lower quality of interaction, and fidgeted more than the partners of non-anxious pairs. Fidgeting tended to be started by the socially anxious partner, and seemed to be transmitted across interaction partners. Again, the study illustrates how emotions are meaningfully described as an interactive pattern. Moreover, describing emotions this way renders it much more transparent how the emotions of one (i.e. non-anxious) partner in the interaction are constituted by the emotions of the other (i.e. the anxious person) – and perhaps vice versa as well.

In sum, mapping the dynamics of emotions in interaction yields insights not provided by the description of individual emotions only. It shows effectively how emotions are in fact relational processes that are distributed across different partners (cf. Griffiths & Scarantino, 2009). In the above examples, the emotions of one partner could be seen as moves in the interaction to which the other person responded. Moreover, the study of emotions in interaction shows "dynamic coupling" of emotions "to an environment which both influences and is influenced by the unfolding of the emotion" (p. 2). Adopting a contextualized perspective on emotion thus enhances our insight into why and when emoting occurs. It renders transparent the connections between the emotions of different interactants, as well as the connections between those emotions and the interaction or relationship in which they occur.

Social sharing

Most emotional episodes, whether positive or negative, are shared with others who were not part of the emotional situation themselves. This phenomenon has been repeatedly demonstrated, tends to happen soon after the emotion event has taken place, and holds across age and gender. Moreover, the more intense the emotional episode, the more likely it is that it will be shared (see Rimé, Mesquita, Philippot, & Boca, 1991; Rimé, Philippot, Boca, & Mesquita, 1992). This systematic tendency to emotion sharing should imply that individuals gain from it. Indeed, some authors have found that discussing emotion events facilitates cognitive-emotional processes of adjustment to stressors by reducing intrusive thoughts (Lepore, Ragan, & Jones, 2000). However, others have found that sharing may not lead to an immediate emotional recovery or a decrease in the intensity of the emotion (cf. Wetzer, Zeelenberg, & Pieters, 2007).

If self-disclosure of emotion does not persistently lead to immediate benefits in terms of emotion regulation, then, why do people systematically engage in this behavior? The most important reason for sharing seems to be a social one: to gain acceptance for one's emotional stance, to reintegrate after important emotional events. Rimé, Páez, Basabe, and Martínez (2010) propose that "sharing an emotional experience often leads to the completion of a variety of social needs such as need for relatedness, for enhancement of interpersonal relationships and for social integration" (p. 1031). In a longitudinal study on people who had been exposed to the terrorist attacks carried out on March 11, 2004 in Madrid, Spain, these authors measured, among other variables, frequency of social sharing, intensity of the emotions experienced, perceived social support, loneliness,

and post-traumatic growth. Data on these measures were collected from 644 respondents during two or three measurement times (1, 3, and 8 weeks after the event). The impact of the event on respondents' emotions appeared to be severe, and social sharing a week after the event was extremely high (98.9% of the respondents reported self-disclosure). Moreover, the authors' prediction about obtaining important psychosocial benefits from sharing was fully supported. Social sharing was positively related to and predicted perceived social support and post-traumatic growth, while it was negatively linked to loneliness.

Emotion sharing is first of all a social behavior and, as such, this phenomenon cannot be fully grasped by approaching it as happening within the individual. Social sharing happens between people, and has effects not only on the sharer but also on the people with whom the emotion is shared. Participants who had been induced to feel anger in a bogus cooperation game evaluated the other person differently, depending on the reactions of a third party (the experimenter) with whom they shared their experience (Wetzer, Zeelenberg, & Pieters, 2007). Moreover, the experimenter himself was evaluated more positively when confirming the participant's feelings than when de-dramatizing. The authors stress the social nature of self-disclosure of emotions by pointing at the consequences of this behavior on evaluation of the self and of the interaction partner.

Social sharing of emotion also has a more direct impact on the receiver of the emotion information. Christophe and Rimé (1997) tested in two studies the propositions that being exposed to disclosure of emotion is emotion-inducing and that the listener subsequently shares with other persons the emotional episode heard. One hundred and thirty-four participants were asked to retrieve from memory a recent episode of someone sharing with them a personal emotion experience. They were then asked to rate their emotional reaction to the sharing situation, and to what extent, if any, they later shared the emotional episode they heard with others. Participants were then divided into three groups on the basis of their ratings of emotion intensity elicited of the shared episode (low, medium, high). Sixty-six percent of the respondents reported to have shared the episode with third parties, and people whose emotional reaction had been high, talked about it later more recurrently and with more different people than participants with low or medium emotion reactions. In a second study, participants were handed a list comprising 20 emotional life events. Three different types of lists were available, containing low-, moderate-, or high-intensity events. Participants received only one of these lists and were asked to recall a situation in which someone had socially shared with them an emotional episode resembling one of those included in the list. Participants were then asked to report how upset they had been when listening to the shared episode, how they reacted non-verbally and verbally, and to what extent, if any, they had subsequently shared the episode with other people. Subjects in the low-intensity condition had been significantly less emotionally aroused than those in higher-intensity conditions. Also, they engaged less in vocalizing and more in non-verbal comforting when in the high-intensity condition than in the lower ones. Finally, 78.5% of the respondents reported to have shared the emotion episode heard with a third party, and participants in the high-intensity condition reported to have shared more often and with more people than those in lower-intensity conditions.

Curci and Bellelli (2004) replicated these results both with a similar recall procedure and with a diary study in which people were asked to report a socially shared episode as soon as it had taken place and, three weeks later, they answered questions about secondary social sharing. Christophe and Rimé (1997) propose that this secondary social sharing might have both personal and interpersonal advantages. For instance, people would need to verbalize the emotional episode heard in order to free attentional channels from the mental images representing it. On the other hand, interpersonal motives may play a substantial role in secondary emotion sharing by enhancing the person's social visibility and social integration. Also, secondary social sharing can add to collective interests by spreading emotional knowledge within a community and constantly updating and redefining emotion scripts and prototypes.

Hence, social sharing of emotion represents one of the most evident ways in which emotions function as a link between individuals and their environment.

Emotional convergence

Emotions of the members of dyads and groups converge over time. This is another illustration that the emotional processes of interest exceed the boundaries of the individual person.

A first demonstration of emotional convergence came from a study by Zajonc and his colleagues showing that married couples looked more alike after 25 years of marriage than they did at their first anniversary (Zajonc, Adelmann, Murphy, & Niedenthal, 1987). Relationship closeness and marriage satisfaction predicted how much better the couples were recognized after 25 years than after just one by students who were asked to match the faces. The authors postulated imitation

as the underlying process. Relationship closeness might lead to empathy, and to the mimicking of emotions. Twenty-five years of mimicking one's partner, and thus using similar facial muscles, would account for the resemblance between partners' faces.

Not only partners start looking alike emotionally, so do roommates in college, dating couples, group members, and individuals within cultures (Anderson & Keltner, 2004; Anderson, Keltner, & John, 2003; Kim, Mesquita, & Gomez, 2008; Smith, Seger, & Mackie, 2007). In all cases, people who belong together become more emotionally similar over time, or are so at the time of measurement.

Anderson and colleagues (Anderson et al., 2003) reported two experimental studies in which the emotions of roommates and romantic couples were measured at the beginning of the academic year, and then 6 or 9 months later in the year. Emotions were measured both by self-reports and facial coding, and were elicited in a number of different ways (conversations about topics with different valence, watching emotion-eliciting movies). In all cases, convergence of emotions was higher at the second measurement point than at the first. Emotional convergence was related to relationship satisfaction and liking of the partner/roommate, and this was true even when controlling for personality similarities. A third study showed that after 7 months of sharing a room the emotions of roommates were more similar to each other than to randomly chosen other students, even when roommates separately watched emotion-eliciting movies so as to prevent contagion. Thus, living together may lead to similarity in emotional reactivity and, whatever the mechanism, it develops in a relatively short time.

In two different studies, Smith and colleagues (Smith, Seger, & Mackie, 2007) showed that members of in-groups converge on group-level emotions. In these studies, respondents were asked to rate their own emotions, as well as their emotions as a group member (e.g., American, Democrat, or Republican) on 12 emotion scales (e.g., anger, happiness). The scores on those 12 scales constituted their emotion profile. Group emotions had significantly different profiles than individual emotions. Furthermore, an individual's group emotion (e.g., happiness as an American) was predicted by the average group member's group emotion (e.g., the level of happiness averaged across all Americans), when controlling for the individual emotion (e.g., happiness reported by the individual). Thus, emotions of group members converged.

Consistently, there is some evidence for emotional convergence in immigrants as well. In two studies, De Leersnyder and colleagues measured the fit between immigrants' emotions with the emotional patterns of the host country (De Leersnyder, Mesquita, & Kim, 2011). In the first study, the emotional fit of Korean immigrants in the United States was examined, and in the second study, the emotional fit of first- and second-generation Turkish immigrants with Belgian mainstream emotional responses was considered. Respondents in both studies reported emotional events from their own life that varied along the dimensions of valence and social engagement. They subsequently reported how they had felt by rating 30 different emotion scales. Individual emotion profiles were calculated for each type of situation. Individual profiles were then compared with the average host country profile (inferred from the European American responses in the first, and the Belgian responses in the second study). The results were consistent with the findings on in-group convergence. In the first study, Americans' emotion profiles were more similar to the American average emotion profile than were Koreans' emotion profiles. In the second study, Belgian emotion profiles were more similar to the Belgian emotion profile than were both first- and second-generation Turkish emotion profiles. Moreover, immigrants who had spent more years in the host country, as well as those with the highest number of interactions with people from the host culture, were more similar to the average host culture emotion profile than those who had had less contact with the host culture. Presumably, interactions with people from another culture affect one's own emotions.

Convergence of emotions has been established, therefore, for roommates, couples, in-groups, and cultural groups in contact. Convergence is particularly pronounced for those whose connection is a close, happy, or identified one. The mechanism by which convergence emerges is not clear (see Anderson, et al., 2003; Smith, et al., 2007), but we may suggest several reasons (cf. Smith et al., 2007 for similar explanations). First, to the extent that dyads, in-group members, and members of different cultural groups are in each others' presence, they may mimic each others' emotions; those most identified, are expected to mimic most (Lakin & Chartrand, 2003; Lakin, Chartrand, & Arkin, 2008; Niedenthal, Barsalou, Winkielman, Krauth-Gruber, & Ric, 2005; Semin, 2007). Second, groups may facilitate certain appraisals by sharing social norms. For example, individuals who valued social order reported more anger towards those who valued freedom *when* they felt supported by others valuing social order as well: perceived shared norms in this case afforded the expression of anger towards out-group members (Mackie, Devos, & Smith, 2000). Third, emotions may be shared within a group to the extent that

similar events become relevant. This explanation has largely remained untested. Regardless of the precise mechanisms underlying convergence, its occurrence makes a case for conceiving of emotions as a process that exceeds the individual mind.

INTERGROUP EMOTIONS

On the eve of the 2008 presidential elections in the United States, when the Democrat Barak Obama was about to win, the *New York Times* published a graphic display of the emotions of Democrats and Republicans. Excited, proud, victorious, euphoric, and jubilant, as well as anxious, giddy, worried and amazed populated the Democratic landscape of emotions. Clearly, the Democrats felt positive, mostly in control, and not yet legitimately powerful. On the other hand, apprehensive, disappointed, cautious, scared, hijacked, and terrified were important Republican feelings. The Republican emotions were not only negative but also implied that the legitimate power was still with the Republicans. The emotions on each side thus represented the positions and world views. They were not only descriptive of the state of affairs, but also evaluated the world from the perspective of either a Democrat or a Republican. These group emotions were identity enactments: they reflected the identification with that particular group, and in so doing, they adopted that group's perspective on what is important, what is good, and what is moral.

This is the idea of group emotions: people experience emotions as group members. These so-called group emotions arise when people identify with a social group and respond emotionally to events or objects that impinge on this group (Smith & Mackie, 2008). As described before, intergroup emotions theory (Mackie, Silver, & Smith, 2004; Smith, 1993) posits that group emotions emerge when individuals appraise situations as relevant to their group concerns. Guilt feelings result from the acknowledgment of having wronged another party. Dutch people reported feeling guilty about their colonial past, even if they had had no personal involvement in the oppression or discrimination. In two studies – one real-life study where people found out about the involvement of their ancestors in Dutch colonization and one experimental study in which the involvement of people's ancestors was manipulated – it was found that when reading about the negative aspects of the Dutch colonial history, those with high-involvement ancestors reported more guilt feelings than those with low-involvement ancestors

(Zebel et al., 2007). Similarly, the perception of a collective disadvantage may lead to group-based emotions: in one study, faculty members' perception of a pay disadvantage compared to the faculty of other universities gave rise to group-based anger, sadness, and fear (Smith, Cronin, & Kessler, 2008).

Just like individual emotions, the emotions people experience as group members may be seen as intentions to act (Fiske, Cuddy, & Glick, 2007; Parkinson, et al., 2005). Group emotions are for doing: they prepare for (collective) action. Intergroup anger prepares for approaching the out-group, whereas intergroup fear prepares for avoiding the out-group (Crisp, Heuston, Farr, & Turner, 2007; Mackie, et al., 2000). In support of this, Americans who reported anger several months after the attacks on the World Trade Center were found to be more in support of military retaliation against those responsible for the attack than those Americans who reported to be afraid; the latter were more in support of restrictions on civil liberties (Skitka, Bauman, & Mullen, 2004). Likewise, intergroup guilt motivates group members to repair the damage caused to the out-group. In a longitudinal test of the association between collective guilt and reparation attitudes, Brown and colleagues (Brown, Gonzalez, Zagefka, Manzi, & Cehajic, 2008) found that collective guilt at Time 1 predicted reparation motivations at Time 2 (8 weeks later). Also, in support of this, Dutch people who reported collective guilt over their imperial past were both more likely to apologize and more in favor of making reparations for their collective past (Branscombe & Doosje, 2004).

Not only are group emotions associated with action readiness but also successful implementation of the action readiness puts an end to the emotion or makes it fade, whereas failing to act, or acting unsuccessfully, leaves the intensity of the emotion unchanged, presumably because it fails to change the environmental signal that started the emotion (Maitner, Mackie, & Smith, 2006). Students who were angered by professors writing an insulting editorial in their university's newspaper became less angry when other students protested *and* the professors retracted their comments. When the student protest was not met with apologies from the professors, the students became even angrier. In another study by the same authors, intergroup guilt that followed learning about American aggression on another country was diminished after respondents learned that the United States had sent help following the aggression, and increased after respondents had learned that their country carried out renewed attacks. The importance of these findings is that they suggest that intergroup emotions have social

consequences: they regulate behavior towards out-groups.

Even if the relationship between group identification and group emotions is not completely straightforward, group emotions are most likely to happen when group identity is particularly salient; i.e., in the case of social comparison, competition, and conflict with other groups. Group feelings often occur in contrast to other groups, and can be seen to contrast with the feelings for other groups. According to one influential framework, coined the Behaviors from Intergroup Affect and Stereotypes (or BIAS) framework, the emotions towards in- and out-groups correspond to the relative positioning of these groups on the dimensions of warmth and competence and prepare for action towards these groups (e.g., Cuddy, Fiske, & Glick, 2007). The dimensions of warmth and competence stem from an evolutionary perspective: in encountering others, one has to decide whether the other has good or bad intentions, and whether the other is able to act upon these intentions. A proper assessment of others' intentions and abilities leads to a higher chance of survival. Based on social comparison and attributional models of emotions, Cuddy, Fiske and Glick (2007) predict that the relative positioning of groups on these dimensions is associated with specific emotions. With student samples and random US population samples, the authors found that groups high on warmth and competence (e.g., the in-group and reference groups, such as middle class) elicited admiration, groups high on warmth but low on competence (e.g., the elderly) elicited pity, groups low on warmth but high on competence (e.g., the rich) elicited envy, and groups low on warmth and competence (e.g., the poor) elicited contempt. These associations were replicated in an experimental design, in which competence and warmth of the out-group members was manipulated, except for the association between low warmth/low competence and contempt (Caprariello, Cuddy, & Fiske, 2009). Emotions as reported were associated to different types of behavioral dimensions. Cuddy and colleagues (2007) found that admiration was associated with active facilitation (e.g., help) or passive facilitation (e.g., cooperation); pity was associated with active facilitation or passive harm (e.g., neglect); envy was associated with active harm (e.g., attack) or passive facilitation; and contempt was associated with active harm or passive harm. In sum, intergroup behaviors can be predicted from group emotions felt towards the own group and different out-groups.

Group emotions are not shared equally among different group members. Generally, high identifiers are likely to experience more intense – positive and negative – emotions based on their group membership than low identifiers. For instance, high-group identifiers reported higher levels of anger towards an out-group than low-group identifiers (e.g., Smith et al., 2007; Yzerbyt, Dumont, Wigboldus, & Gordijn, 2003). The evidence for a positive link between level of group identification and intensity of group-based emotions is, nevertheless, not unequivocal: some studies find no relationship or a negative one. This is especially true for self-critical emotions such as guilt (Iyer & Leach, 2008). Doosje and colleagues (1998) found a negative association between Dutch national identification and guilt related to the nation's colonization history, especially in the case of ambiguous information about this history. Low identifiers felt guiltier about the nation's colonization history than high identifiers. For high identifiers, denial and legitimization may have been easier than acknowledging that they had inflicted harm on others, because this acknowledgment would have threatened their positive self-image. Similarly, several studies found support that low identifiers considered an aggressive act by their group as more unfair and less justified than high identifiers (Gordijn, Yzerbyt, Wigboldus, & Dumont, 2006; Maitner et al., 2006). In some cases, high- and low-group identifiers have been even shown to experience different emotions with regard to the same event: after their soccer team had lost, high identifiers felt angry and wanted to oppose soccer fans of the other team, whereas low identifiers rather felt sad and wanted to move away from the other team's soccer fans (Crisp et al., 2007).

Furthermore, group emotions may themselves affect identification, as is illustrated by the fact that supporters of a losing football team wear fewer college shirts the Monday after the match than those whose teams won over the weekend (Cialdini et al., 1976). Also, experimental evidence suggests that remembering either a happy in-group event or an event that elicited angry feelings towards an out-group increases group identification, whereas remembering an instance of anger towards the in-group or out-group happiness decreases group identification (Kessler & Hollbach, 2005). Consistently, experimental induction of anger increased in-group favoritism: angry respondents showed more preference for their in-group relative to the out-group on an Implicit Association Test than either fearful or non-emotional respondents (DeSteno, Dasgupta, Bartlett, & Cajdric, 2004). Thus, there seems to be a dynamic interplay between emotion and identification, such that identification affects emotions, and emotions identification.

Lest this picture suggests that people's group emotions are "chronic" (Smith et al., 2007), we should add some caveats. First, group emotions

can change depending on the out-group. For instance, when respondents' student identity was made salient, they felt anger towards the police and respect towards Muslims (Ray, Mackie, Rydell, & Smith, 2008). Moreover, people have multiple identities, and dependent on the identity primed, different emotions will emerge. When respondents identified as a student, they felt anger at the police, but when they identified as an American, they felt respect towards the police (Ray et al., 2008). Furthermore, if respondents thought they shared a common identity with victims of negative behaviors, they felt more anger and fear than when they perceived the victims as an out-group. In two studies, participants were told that the goal of the study was to either compare the opinions of students of one university vs students of another university or those of students vs professors. When sharing a common identity with students of another university, students reported more anger when they found out that the study load would be increased for students at the other university (Gordijn, Wigboldus, & Yzerbyt, 2001) or when they found out that English would become the language of instruction in the master years of another university (Yzerbyt et al., 2003). In another study, Dumont and colleagues (2003) compared the emotional reactions of Westerners vs Arabs or Europeans vs Americans to the 9/11 terrorist attacks. When sharing a common identity with Americans (i.e., when categorized as Westerners), Dutch and Belgian respondents reported more fear than when not sharing this social identity with Americans (i.e., when categorized as Europeans).

CONCLUSION

Psychological insights about emotions have changed: the central research question is shifting from what emotions *are* in the abstract, to what they *do* in concrete social contexts.

While the dominant research focus was once on the properties of individual experiences and responses, much current research is centered on the effects of emotions in interactions. Social context, once considered noise in emotion research, has now become the substance of many studies. Emotions are no longer considered merely individual-level, subjective feelings, but rather are viewed as thoroughly social psychological.

Many emotional phenomena can simply not be studied without putting them in the social context in which they occur. It is impossible to understand the sequences of emotions in interactions unless we consider both partners' emotional responses and the ways they influence each other and follow each other up. Likewise, it is impossible to understand the dynamics of group emotions, emotional convergence, or social sharing of emotions, without exceeding the level of the individual. Social context is an essential part of the study of emotion, and the study of emotion an indispensable part of social psychology.

REFERENCES

Algoe, S. B., Gable, S. L., & Maisel, N. C. (2010). It's the little things: Everyday gratitude as a booster shot for romantic relationships. *Personal Relationships, 17,* 217–233.

Algoe, S. B., Haidt, J., & Gable, S. L. (2008). Beyond reciprocity: Gratitude and relationships in everyday life. *Emotion, 8,* 425–429.

Anderson, C., & Keltner, D. (2004). The emotional convergence hypothesis: Implications for individuals, relationships, and cultures. In L. Z. Tiedens, & C. W. Leach (Eds.), *The social life of emotions* (pp. 144–163). Cambridge, UK: Cambridge University Press.

Anderson, C., Keltner, D., & John, O. P. (2003). Emotional convergence between people over time. *Journal of Personality and Social Psychology, 84,* 1054–1068.

Arnold, M. B. (1960). *Emotion and personality* (Vol. 1). New York: Columbia University Press.

Barrett, L. F. (2006). Are emotions natural kinds? *Perspectives on Psychological Science, 1,* 28–58.

Baumeister, R. F., Stillwell, A. M., & Heatherton, T. F. (1994). Guilt: An interpersonal approach. *Psychological Bulletin, 115,* 243–267.

Baumeister, R. F., Stillwell, A. M., & Heatherton, T. F. (1995). Personal narratives about guilt: Role in action control and interpersonal relationships. *Basic and Applied Social Psychology, 17,* 173–198.

Baumeister, R. F., & Wotman, S. R. (Eds.). (1992). *Breaking hearts: The two sides of unrequited love.* New York: Guilford Press.

Best, D. L., & Williams, J. E. (1997). Sex, gender, and culture. In J. W. Berry, M. H. Segall, & C. Kagitcibasi (Eds.), *Handbook of cross-cultural psychology: Vol.3. Social behavior and applications.* Boston: Allyn & Bacon.

Blascovich, J., & Mendes, W. B. (2000). *Challenge and threat appraisals: The role of affective cues.* New York: Cambridge University Press.

Boiger, M., & Mesquita, B. (2011). The construction of emotion in interactions, relationships, and cultures. *Emotion Review.*

Bonanno, G. A., Goorin, L., & Coifman, K. G. (2008). Sadness and Grief. In M. Lewis, J. M. Haviland-Jones, & L. F. Barett (Eds.), *Handbook of emotions* (3rd ed., pp. 797–810). New York: Guilford Press.

Branscombe, N. R., & Doosje, B. (Eds.) (2004). *Collective guilt: International perspectives.* New York: Cambridge University Press.

Brescoll, V. L., & Uhlmann, E. L. (2008). Can an angry woman get ahead? Status conferral, gender, and expression of emotion in the workplace. *Psychological Science, 9,* 268–275.

Brown, R., Gonzalez, R., Zagefka, H., Manzi, J., & Cehajic, S. (2008). Nuestra culpa: Collective guilt and shame as predictors of reparation for historical wrongdoing. *Journal of Personality and Social Psychology, 94,* 75–90.

Camras, L., Meng, Z., & Ujie, T. (2002). Observing emotion in infants: Facial expression, body behavior, and rater judgments of responses to an expectancy-violating event. *Emotion, 2,* 179–193.

Caprariello, P. A., Cuddy, A. J. C., & Fiske, S. T. (2009). Social structure shapes cultural stereotypes and emotions: A causal test of the stereotype content model. *Group Processes & Intergroup Relations, 12*(2), 147–155.

Carver, L. J., & Vaccaro, B. G. (2007). 12-month-old infants allocate increased neural resources to stimuli associated with negative adult emotion. *Developmental Psychology, 43,* 54–69.

Chow, R. M., Tiedens, L. Z., & Govan, C. L. (2008). Excluded emotions: The role of anger in antisocial responses to ostracism. *Journal of Experimental Social Psychology, 44,* 896–903.

Christophe, V., & Rimé, B. (1997). Exposure to the social sharing of emotion: Emotional impact, listener responses and secondary social sharing. *European Journal of Social Psychology, 27,* 37–54.

Cialdini, R. B., Borden, R. J., Thorne, A., Walker, M. R., Freeman, S., & Sloan, L. R. (1976). Basking in reflected glory: Three (football) field studies. *Journal of Personality and Social Psychology, 34,* 366–375.

Cole, P. M., Bruschi, C. J., & Tamang, B. L. (2002). Cultural differences in children's emotional reactions to difficult situations. *Child Development, 73,* 983–996.

Cole, P. M., Tamang, B. L., & Shrestha, S. (2006). Cultural variations in the socialization of young children's anger and shame. *Child Development, 77,* 1237–1251.

Crisp, R. J., Heuston, S., Farr, M. J., & Turner, R. N. (2007). Seeing red or feeling blue: Differentiated intergroup emotions and ingroup identification in soccer fans. *Group Processes & Intergroup Relations, 10,* 9–26.

Cuddy, A. J. C., Fiske, S. T, & Glick, P. (2007) The BIAS map: Behaviors from intergroup affect and stereotypes. *Journal of Personality and Social Psychology, 92*(4), 631–648.

Curci, A., & Bellelli, G. (2004). Cognitive and social consequences of exposure to emotional narratives: Two studies on secondary social sharing of emotions. *Cognition & Emotion, 18,* 881–900.

De Hooge, I. E., Zeelenberg, M., & Breugelmans, S. M. (2007). Moral sentiments and cooperation: Differential influences of shame and guilt. *Cognition & Emotion, 21,* 1025–1042.

de Jong, P. J. (1999). Communicative and remedial effects of social blushing. *Journal of Nonverbal Behavior, 23,* 197–217.

De Leersnyder, J., Mesquita, B., & Kim, H. (2011). Where do my emotions belong? A study on immigrants' emotional acculturation. *Personality & Social Psychology Bulletin, 37*(4), 451–463. DeSteno, D., Dasgupta, N., Bartlett, M. Y., & Cajdric, A. (2004). Prejudice from thin air: The effect of emotion on automatic intergroup attitudes. *Psychological Science, 15*, 319–324.

DeSteno, D., Valdesolo, P., & Bartlett, M. Y. (2006). Jealousy and the threatened self: Getting to the heart of the green-eyed monster. *Journal of Personality and Social Psychology, 91*, 626–641.

Doosje, B., Branscombe, N., Spears, R., Manstead, A. S. R. (1998). Guilty by association: When one's group has a negative history. *Journal of Personality and Social Psychology, 75*(4), 872–886.

Dumont, M., Yzerbyt, V., Wigboldus, D., & Gordijn, E. H. (2003). Social categorization and fear reactions to the September 11th terrorist attacks. *Personality and Social Psychology Bulletin, 29*, 1509–1520.

Dunn, J. (2004). Individual differences in understanding emotion and mind. In A. S. R. Manstead, N. H. Frijda, & A. H. Fischer (Eds.), *Feelings and emotions. The Amsterdam Symposium* (pp. 303–320). New York: Cambridge University Press.

Dunn, J., Brown, J., & Beardsall, L. (1991). Family talk about feeling states and children's later understanding of others' emotions. *Developmental Psychology, 27*, 448–455.

Eagly, A. H., & Karau, S. J. (2002). Role congruity theory of prejudice toward female leaders. *Psychological Review, 109*, 573–598.

Edelmann, R. J. (1982). The effect of embarrassed reactions upon others. *Australian Journal of Psychology, 34*, 359–367.

Ellsworth, P. C., & Scherer, K. R. (2003). Appraisal processes in emotion. In H. Goldsmith & K. R. Scherer (Eds.), *Handbook of affective sciences* (pp. 572–595). New York: Oxford University Press.

Fields, J., Copp, M., & Kleinman, S. (2006). Symbolic interactionism, inequality, and emotions. In J. E. Stets & J. H. Turner (Eds.), *Handbook of the sociology of emotions* (pp. 155–178). New York: Springer.

Fischer, A. H., & Manstead, A. S. R. (2008). Social functions of emotion. In M. Lewis, J. M. Haviland-Jones, & L. F. Barrett (Eds.), *Handbook of emotions* (3rd ed., pp. 456–468). New York: Guilford Press.

Fiske, S. T. (2010). Interpersonal stratification: Status, power, and subordination. In S. T. Fiske, D. T. Gilbert & G. Lindzey (Eds.), *Handbook of social psychology* (5th ed., pp. 941–982). Hoboken, NJ: John Wiley & Sons.

Fiske, S. T., Cuddy, A. J. C., & Glick, P. (2007). Universal dimensions of social cognition: Warmth and competence. *Trends in Cognitive Sciences, 11*, 77–83.

Fitness, J. (1996). Emotion knowledge structures in close relationships. In G. J. O. Fletcher & J. Fitness (Eds.), *Knowledge structures in close relationships: A social psychological approach* (pp. 195–217). Hillsdale, NJ: Lawrence Erlbaum Associates.

Frijda, N. H. (1986). *The emotions*. Cambridge, UK: Cambridge University Press.

Frijda, N. H. (2004). *Emotions and action*. In A. S. R. Manstead, N. H. Frijda, & A. Fischer (Eds.), *Feelings and emotions:*

The Amsterdam Symposium (pp. 158–173). New York: Cambridge University Press.

Frijda, N. H. (2007). *The laws of emotion*. Mahwah, NJ: Lawrence Erlbaum Associates.

Frijda, N. H., Kuipers, P., & Terschure, E. (1989). Relations betweeen emotion, appraisal and emotional action readiness. *Journal of Personality and Social Psychology, 57*, 212–228.

Gordijn, E. H., Wigboldus, D., & Yzerbyt, V. (2001). Emotional consequences of categorizing victims of negative outgroup behavior as ingroup or outgroup. *Group Processes & Intergroup Relations, 4*, 317–326.

Gordijn, E. H., Yzerbyt, V., Wigboldus, D., & Dumont, M. (2006). Emotional reactions to harmful intergroup behavior. *European Journal of Social Psychology, 36*, 15–30.

Gottman, J. M., & Levenson, R. W. (2000). The timing of divorce: Predicting when a couple will divorce over a 14-year period. *Journal of Marriage and the Family, 62*, 737–745.

Gottman, J., Swanson, C., & Murray, J. (1999). The mathematics of marital conflict: Dynamic mathematical nonlinear modeling of newlywed marital interaction. *Journal of Family Psychology, 13*, 3–19.

Griffiths, P., & Scarantino, A. (2009). Emotions in the wild: The situated perspective on emotion. In P. Robbins & M. Aydede (Eds.), *The Cambridge handbook of situated cognition* (pp. 437–453). New York: Cambridge University Press.

Harris, P. L. (2008). Children's understanding of emotion. In M. Lewis, J. M. Haviland-Jones, & L. F. Barrett (Eds.), *The handbook of emotions* (3rd ed., pp. 320–331). New York: Guilford Press.

Heerey, E. A., & Kring, A. M. (2007). Interpersonal consequences of social anxiety. *Journal of Abnormal Psychology, 116*, 125–134.

Hendriks, M. C. P., Nelson, J. K., Cornelius, R. R., & Vingerhoets, A. J. J. M. (2008). Why crying improves our well-being: An attachment-theory perspective on the functions of adult crying. In A. Vingerhoets, I. Nyklicek, & J. Denollet (Eds.), *Emotion regulation: Conceptual and clinical issues* (pp. 87–96). New York: Springer Science + Business Media.

Hertenstein, M. J., & Campos, J. J. (2004). The retention effects of an adult's emotional display on infant behavior. *Child Development, 75*, 595–613.

Hiatt, S., Campos, J. J., & Emde, R. N. (1979). Facial patterning and infant facial expression: Happiness, surprise, and fear. *Child Development, 50*, 1020–1035.

Holodynski, M., & Friedlmeier, W. (2006). *Development of emotions and emotion regulation*. Boston, MA: Springer (Kluwer International Series in Outreach Scholarship).

Iyer, A., & Leach, C. W. (2008). Emotion in inter-group relations. *European Review of Social Psychology, 19*, 86–125.

Jankowiak, W. R., & Fischer, E. F. (1992). A cross-cultural perspective on romantic love. *Ethnology: An International Journal of Cultural and Social Anthropology, 31*, 149.

Keltner, D., & Buswell, B. N. (1997). Embarrassment: Its distinct form and appeasement functions. *Psychological Bulletin, 122*, 250–270.

Keltner, D., & Kring, A. M. (1998). Emotion, social function, and psychopathology. *Review of General Psychology, 2*(3), 320–342.

Keltner, D., Kring, A., & Bonanno, G. A. (1999). Fleeting signs of the course of life: Facial expression and personal adjustment. *Current Directions in Psychological Science, 8,* 18–22.

Keltner, D., Young, R. C., Heerey, E. A., Oemig, C., & Monarch, N. D. (1998). Teasing in hierarchical and intimate relations. *Journal of Personality and Social Psychology, 75,* 1231–1247.

Kessler, T., & Hollbach, S. (2005). Group-based emotions as determinants of ingroup identification. *Journal of Experimental Social Psychology, 41,* 677–685.

Ketelaar, T., & Au, W. T. (2003). The effects of feelings of guilt on the behaviour of uncooperative individuals in repeated social bargaining games: An affect-as-information interpretation of the role of emotion in social interaction. *Cognition & Emotion, 17,* 429–453.

Kim, H., Mesquita, B., & Gomez, G. (2008). *Emotional concordance: A cultural psychology perspective on acculturation.* Unpublished manuscript, UCSB, Santa Barbara, CA.

Kitayama, S., Markus, H. R., & Kurokawa, M. (2000). Culture, emotion, and well-being: Good feelings in Japan and the United States. *Cognition & Emotion, 14,* 93–124.

Kitayama, S., Mesquita, B., & Karasawa, M. (2006). Cultural affordances and emotional experience: Socially engaging and disengaging emotions in Japan and the United States. *Journal of Personality and Social Psychology, 91,* 890–903.

Lakin, J. L., & Chartrand, T. L. (2003). Using nonconscious behavioral mimicry to create affiliation and rapport. *Psychological Science, 14,* 334–339.

Lakin, J. L., Chartrand, T. L., & Arkin, R. M. (2008). I am too just like you: Nonconscious mimicry as an automatic behavioral response to social exclusion. *Psychological Science, 19,* 816–822.

Lazarus, R. S. (1991). *Emotion and adaptation.* New York: Oxford University Press.

Leary, M. R., Landel, J. L., & Patton, K. M. (1996). The motivated expression of embarrassment following a self-presentational predicament. *Journal of Social Psychology, 64,* 619–636.

Lepore, S. J., Ragan, J. D., & Jones, S. (2000). Talking facilitates cognitive-emotional processes of adaptation to an acute stressor. *Journal of Personality and Social Psychology, 78,* 499–507.

Lewis, K. M. (2000). When leaders display emotion: How followers respond to negative emotional expression of male and female leaders. *Journal of Organizational Behavior, 21,* 221–234.

Lutz, C. A., & Abu-Lughod, L. (Eds.) (1990). *Language and the politics of emotion.* New York: Cambridge University Press.

Mackie, D. M., Devos, T., & Smith, E. R. (2000). Intergroup emotions: Explaining offensive action tendencies in an intergroup context. *Journal of Personality and Social Psychology, 79,* 602–616.

Mackie, D. M., Silver, L. A., & Smith, E. R. (2004). Intergroup emotions: Emotion as an intergroup phenomenon. In L. Z. Tiedens & C. W. Leach (Eds.), *The social life of emotions* (pp. 227–245). Cambridge, UK: Cambridge University Press.

Maitner, A. T., Mackie, D. M., & Smith, E. R. (2006). Evidence for the regulatory function of intergroup emotion: Emotional consequences of implemented or impeded intergroup action tendencies. *Journal of Experimental Social Psychology, 42,* 720–728.

Mesquita, B. (2010). Emoting: A contextualized process. In B. Mesquita, L. F. Barrett, & E. R. Smith (Eds.), *The mind in context* (pp. 83–104). New York: Guilford Press.

Mesquita, B., & Ellsworth, P. C. (2001). The role of culture in appraisal. In K. R. Scherer & A. Schorr (Eds.), *Appraisal processes in emotion: Theory, methods, research* (pp. 233–248). New York: Oxford University Press.

Mesquita, B., & Karasawa, M. (2004). Self-conscious emotions as dynamic cultural processes. *Psychological Inquiry, 15,* 161–166.

Mesquita, B., & Leu, J. (2007) The cultural psychology of emotions. In S. Kitayama & D. Cohen (Eds.), *Handbook for cultural psycholog* (pp.734–759). New York: Guilford Press.

Miller, P. J., Fung, H., & Mintz, J. (1996). Self-construction through narrative practices: A Chinese and American comparison of early socialization. *Ethos, 24,* 237–280.

Miller, R. S. (1996). *Embarrassment: Poise and peril in everyday life.* New York: Guilford Press.

Mumme, D. L., & Fernald, A. (2003). The infant as onlooker: Learning from emotional reactions observed in a television scenario. *Child Development, 74,* 221–237.

Niedenthal, P. M., Barsalou, L. W., Winkielman, P., Krauth-Gruber, S., & Ric, F. (2005). Embodiment in attitudes, social perception, and emotion. *Personality and Social Psychology Review, 9,* 184–211.

Oatley, K. (1992). *Best laid schemes. The psychology of emotions.* New York: Cambridge University Press.

Oatley, K. (2004). *Emotions. A brief history.* Malden, MA: Blackwell Publishing.

Oatley, K., & Jenkins, J. H. (1992). Human emotions: Function and dysfunction. *Annual Review of Psychology, 43,* 55–85.

Oatley, K., Keltner, D., & Jenkins, J. M. (2006). *Understanding emotions* (2nd ed.). Malden, MD: Blackwell Publishing.

Parkinson, B. (2008). Emotions in direct and remote social interaction: Getting through the spaces between us. *Computers in Human Behavior, 24,* 1510–1529.

Parkinson, B., Fischer, A. H., & Manstead, A. S. R. (2005). *Emotion in social relations: Cultural, group, and interpersonal processes.* New York: Psychology Press.

Ray, D. G., Mackie, D. M., Rydell, R. J., & Smith, E. R. (2008). Changing categorization of self can change emotions about outgroups. *Journal of Experimental Social Psychology, 44,* 1210–1213.

Rimé, B., Mesquita, B., Philippot, P., & Boca, S. (1991). Beyond the emotional event: Six studies on the social sharing of emotion. *Cognition and Emotion, 5,* 435–465.

Rimé, B., Páez, D., Basabe, N., & Martínez, F. (2010). Social sharing of emotion, post-traumatic growth, and emotional climate: Follow-up of Spanish citizen's response to the collective trauma of March 11th terrorist attacks in Madrid. *European Journal of Social Psychology, 40*, 1029–1045.

Rimé, B., Philippot, P., Boca, S., & Mesquita, B. (1992). Long-lasting cognitive and social consequences of emotion: Social sharing and rumination. In W. S. M. Hewstone (Ed.), *European review of social psychology* (Vol. 3, pp. 225–258). Chichester, UK: Wiley.

Rozin, P., Lowery, L., Imada, S., & Haidt, J. (1999). The CAD triad hypothesis: A mapping between three moral emotions (contempt, anger, disgust) and three moral codes (community, autonomy, divinity). *Journal of Personality and Social Psychology, 76*, 574–586.

Saarni, C. (2008). The interface of emotional development with social context. In M. Lewis, J. M. Haviland-Jones & L. F. Barrett (Eds.), *Handbook of emotions* (3rd ed., pp. 332–347). New York: Guilford Press.

Scheff, T. J. (1988). Shame and conformity: The deference-emotion system. *American Sociological Review, 53*, 395–406.

Scherer, K. R., Matsumoto, D., Wallbott, H. G., & Kudoh, T. (1988). Emotional experience in cultural context: A comparison between Europe, Japan, and the US. In K. R. Scherer (Ed.), *Facets of emotions* (pp. 5–30). Hillsdale, NJ: Lawrence Erlbaum Associates.

Scherer, K. R., Schorr, A., & Johnston, T. (2001). *Appraisal processes in emotion: Theory, methods, research.* New York: Oxford University Press.

Schieffelin, E. L. (1983). Anger and shame in the tropical rainforest: On affect as a cultural system in Papua New Guinea. *Ethos, 11*, 181–209.

Semin, G. R. (2007). Grounding communication: Synchrony. In A. Kruglanski & E. T. Higgins (Eds.), *Social psychology: Handbook of basic principles* (2nd ed., pp. 630–649). New York: Guilford Press.

Semin, G. R., & Manstead, A. S. R. (1982). The social implications of embarrassment displays and restitution behaviour. *European Journal of Social Psychology, 12*, 367–377.

Shaver, P. R., Schwartz, J. C., Kirson, D., & O'Connor, C. (1987). Emotion knowledge: Further exploration of a prototype approach. *Journal of Personality and Social Psychology, 52*, 1061–1086.

Skitka, L. J., Bauman, C. W., & Mullen, E. (2004). Political tolerance and coming to psychological closure following the September 11, 2001 terrorist attacks. *Personality and Social Psychology Bulletin, 30*, 743–756.

Smith, E. R. (1993). Social identity and social emotions: Toward new conceptualizations of prejudice. In D. M. Mackie & D. L. Hamilton (Eds.), *Affect, cognition and stereotyping: Interactive processes in group perception.* San Diego, CA: Academic Press.

Smith, E. R., & Mackie, D. M. (2008). Intergroup emotions. In M. Lewis, J. M. Haviland-Jones, & L. F. Barrett (Eds.), *Handbook of emotions* (3rd ed., pp. 428–439). New York: Guilford Press.

Smith, E. R., Seger, C. R., & Mackie, D. A. (2007). Can emotions be truly group level? Evidence regarding four conceptual criteria. *Journal of Personality and Social Psychology, 93*, 431–446.

Smith, H. J., Cronin, T., & Kessler, T. (2008). Anger, fear, or sadness: Faculty members' emotional reactions to collective pay disadvantage. *Political Psychology, 29*, 221–246.

Solomon, R. C. (2004). *Thinking About Feeling: Contemporary Philosophers on Emotions.* Oxford University Press.

Stein, N. L., Trabasso, T., & Liwag, M. (1993). The representation and organization of emotional experience: Unfolding the emotion episode. In M. Lewis & J. M. Haviland (Eds.), *Handbook of emotions* (pp. 279–300). New York: Guilford Press.

Tangney, J. P., Miller, R. S., Flicker, L., & Barlow, D. H. (1996). Are shame, guilt and embarrassment distinct emotions? *Journal of Personality and Social Psychology, 70*, 1256–1269.

Tiedens, L., Ellsworth, P. C., & Mesquita, B. (2000). Sentimental stereotypes: Emotional expectations for high- and low-status group members. *Personality and Social Psychology Bulletin, 26*, 560–574.

Tiedens, L. Z. (2001). Anger and advancement versus sadness and subjugation: The effect of negative emotion expressions on social status conferral. *Journal of Personality and Social Psychology, 80*, 86–94.

Trommsdorff, G., & Kornadt, H.-J. (2003). Parent–child relations in cross-cultural perspective. In L. Kuczynski (Ed.), *Handbook of dynamics in parent–child relations* (pp. 271–306). London: Sage.

Van Dijk, E., van Kleef, G. A., Steinel, W., & van Beest, I. (2008). A social functional approach to emotions in bargaining: When communicating anger pays and when it backfires. *Journal of Personality and Social Psychology, 94*, 600–614.

Van Kleef, G. A., De Dreu, C. K. W., & Manstead, A. S. R. (2004). The interpersonal effects of anger and happiness in negotiations. *Journal of Personality and Social Psychology, 86*, 57–76.

Van Kleef, G. A., Oveis, C., van der Löwe, I., LuoKogan, A., Goetz, J., & Keltner, D. (2008). Power, distress, and compassion: Turning a blind eye to the suffering of others. *Psychological Science, 19*, 1315–1322.

Vingerhoets, A., & Scheirs, J. (2000). Sex differences in crying: Empirical findings and possible explanations. In A. H. Fischer (Ed.), *Gender and emotion: Social psychological perspectives* (pp. 143–165). New York: Cambridge University Press.

Wetzer, I. M., Zeelenberg, M., & Pieters, R. (2007). Consequences of socially sharing emotions: Testing the emotion–response congruency hypothesis. *European Journal of Social Psychology, 37*, 1310–1324.

Yzerbyt, V., Dumont, M., Wigboldus, D., & Gordijn, E. H. (2003). I feel for us: The impact of categorization and identification on emotions and action tendencies. *British Journal of Social Psychology, 42*, 533–549.

Zajonc, R. B. (1998). Emotions. In D. T. Gilbert & S. T. Fiske (Eds.), *The handbook of social psychology* (pp. 591–632). New York: McGraw-Hill.

Zajonc, R. B., Adelmann, P.-K., Murphy, S.-T., & Niedenthal, P.-M. (1987). Convergence in the physical appearance of spouses. *Motivation and Emotion, 11*, 335–346.

Zebel, S., Pennekamp, S. F., van Zomeren, M., Doosje, B., van Kleef, G. A, Vliek, M L. W., & van der Schalk, J. (2007). Vessels with gold or guilt: Emotional reactions to family involvement associated with glorious or gloomy aspects of the colonial past. *Group Processes & Intergroup Relations, 10*(1), 71–86.

16

Social Categorization and the Perception of Social Groups

Galen V. Bodenhausen, Sonia K. Kang,
& Destiny Peery

The importance of social categories in everyday life is made woefully evident in daily world news. Consider the case of Sabbar Kashur, a Palestinian living in Jerusalem who by habit adopted a Jewish nickname, Dudu. People just assumed Dudu was Jewish; his life was easier that way. However, after his (consensual) Jewish lover discovered that he was an Arab rather than a Jew, Mr Kashur was accused, arrested, tried, and convicted of rape (Levy, 2010). In an instant, a loving act became a crime, based entirely on a change of social categories. Such is the power of social categories to shape our perceptions of others.

Over the last few decades, social psychologists have been extensively exploring the dynamics of social categorization, the process by which individuals are sorted into various social categories (e.g., women, men, Asian, student, musician, etc.). In the pages that follow, we will attempt to summarize the major conclusions that have been reached regarding the nature of social categories and their impact on the perception of social groups. We begin by considering the diverse psychological functions that social categories serve for perceivers, and then we examine how social categories are mentally represented in ways that facilitate these basic functions. In particular, we review research showing how the stereotypes about particular social groups are acquired and how stereotypic beliefs are organized. Next, we turn to the processes involved in using stereotypes. We summarize the factors that determine whether or not people end up thinking in primarily

categorical ways about particular individuals as well as the factors that determine which specific categories are most likely to be used in a given context. We then discuss how perception, judgment, and behavior can be shaped by activated social categories, and we conclude by considering whether and how social perceivers can avoid relying on categorical stereotypes when they are motivated to do so. The overall picture of social categorization that emerges is of a process that is generally adaptive but also sometimes problematic.

STARTING POINTS: STRUCTURE AND FUNCTION OF SOCIAL CATEGORIES

Psychological functions of social categorization

Categorization is fundamental to human cognition because it serves a basic epistemic function: organizing and structuring our knowledge about the world. By identifying classes of stimuli that share important properties, categorization allows perceivers to bring order and coherence to the vast array of people, objects, and events that are encountered in daily life (e.g., Smith & Medin, 1981). Once a categorical structure is superimposed upon them, the immense diversity of individual entities that we encounter in daily life becomes manageable. General, portable concepts become possible; for example, categorical representations allow us to speak of "horses," rather than having to separately name each equine individual and treat each one as a wholly unprecedented and hence unpredictable entity. Once perceptual rules for establishing category membership are acquired, generic knowledge derived from prior interactions with category members can provide a rich source of inferences about the properties of newly encountered individuals. With the help of categories, the mind transforms the world from chaotic complexity into predictable order.

Social categories are no different from other types of concepts in their capacity to serve these basic knowledge functions. Whether on the basis of demographic features, social roles, kinship networks, shared tasks, or other social cues, identifying an individual as belonging to a particular social category enables inferences about a range of relevant and important issues. We can infer, for example, what the person's goals and intentions might be, what skills and knowledge she might possess, and what general personality traits are likely to characterize her. These sorts of inferences can be exceptionally useful in determining whether and how to interact with other people, just as categorizing physical objects can direct our interactions with them (e.g., we know that "sitting on" is an appropriate interaction with a "chair"). However, categorizing people differs from categorizing objects in one critical respect. When we place an individual into a social category, we are likely to consider our own status with respect to that category (i.e., as a member or non-member). In this way, social categorization allows us to connect with those who share our group memberships (i.e., in-groups); however, it also has the potential to establish psychologically significant dividing lines between the perceiver and the target (i.e., out-groups), as was evident in the case of Sabbar Kashur described above. Thus, in addition to epistemic functions, social categories also serve an important identity function, shaping the perceiver's sense of belonging and connection to – or alienation from – others. Tajfel (1969, 1982) established a rich theoretical tradition exploring the implications of the epistemic and identity functions served by social categories (for a recent review, see Hornsey, 2008).

As the foregoing discussion makes clear, relying on categories when perceiving the social world is in principle functional and adaptive – even essential – although it sometimes can lead to unsavory consequences. Far from being the "rotten generalizations that smelled up the mental household" (Schneider, 2004, p. 562) that were assumed in early research, stereotypes about the general characteristics of social groups are often useful tools for constructing meaningful representations of others. However, to serve the epistemic functions that are ascribed to them in a truly adaptive way, these generalizations would need to possess a reasonable degree of accuracy. Are social stereotypes accurate? This turns out to be a rather complicated question to answer definitively. The best answer seems to be: yes and no. On the one hand, it certainly seems likely that, if groups differ systematically from one another in detectable ways, such differences would be noted by perceivers and reflected in their beliefs. Surely many stereotypes do reflect actual group differences (Lee, Jussim, & McCauley, 1995). The forces producing these differences, however, are not necessarily obvious to perceivers. A variety of social forces can work to produce and reinforce stereotypically expected differences between groups, whether or not they would have emerged spontaneously. For example, when individuals disconfirm stereotypes about their social group, they often face a backlash from others that operates to discourage this counter-stereotypic behavior in the future (e.g., Phelan & Rudman, 2010). Actual differences between social groups reflect not only the intrinsic characteristics of the groups' members but also the social situations they typically face (Eagly, Wood, & Diekman, 2000). For instance, if a group has limited access to high-quality education, it would not be surprising if group members scored lower on standardized tests of learning. In such cases, stereotypes may indeed reflect the social reality, if not the intrinsic character and potential, of the group. An accurate representation of group differences does not necessarily imply an accurate understanding of the reasons for their existence.

On the other hand, research indicates that the accuracy of particular stereotypic beliefs can be constrained by a variety of factors. Forming accurate stereotypes depends on exposure to relevant, unbiased samples of group members. From this standpoint, it is perhaps not surprising that some common gender stereotypes have been shown to be relatively accurate (Swim, 1994), given the extensive direct experience most people have with members of both sexes. However, when one has limited direct exposure to members of a particular group, then beliefs about the group must be mediated by how others communicate about the group; such communications are subject to systematic distortions (e.g., Allport & Postman, 1947). Systematic cognitive distortions can also be an issue when strong a priori expectations about a social group lead to biased perceptions of newly encountered group members (Cameron & Trope, 2004; Hamilton & Sherman, 1994). As we will show when we discuss how stereotypes operate in guiding social perception, the implicit operation of stereotypic expectancies can transform non-stereotypic information into stereotype-congruent representations, creating an illusory sense that one's prior beliefs have been confirmed. Moreover, stereotypic expectancies can result in behavior that unwittingly elicits the expected characteristic, as in the case of self-fulfilling prophecies (Darley & Fazio, 1980; Jussim & Harber, 2005). More generally, pressing psychological needs can sometimes trump epistemic accuracy concerns, leading perceivers to seek motivationally satisfying conclusions, even if this requires parting company with a realistic view of the world (Kunda, 1990). For example, the desire to disparage groups that are perceived to be competing with one's own group (Esses, Jackson, Dovidio, & Hodson, 2005) could lead to unrealistically negative stereotypes of them. Additionally, the strong desire we hold for feeling that the world is fair and just may lead us to form negative stereotypes that can provide a seeming justification for a group's low social status (Jost, Banaji, & Nosek, 2004). Thus, generalizations about social groups can serve ego-gratifying and system-justifying functions as well as epistemic ones, and accurate beliefs are not at all necessary for the satisfaction of these motivational needs.

Cognitive representations of social categories

Cognitive representations of social groups play a key role in (a) determining which individuals belong in a given category, and then (b) generating inferences about these identified category members. The classical view of categories held that category membership is established by a set of features that are individually necessary and jointly sufficient to define the category (e.g., Katz, 1972). This perspective was largely abandoned in light of a variety of conceptual critiques and incompatible empirical findings and replaced with two rival alternatives. The first of these, the probabilistic view (e.g., Rosch, 1978), argued that categories are defined by a set of prototypic features, and perceptions of category membership are governed by the degree of similarity (or "family resemblance") between a particular instance and the category prototype. The second alternative, the exemplar view (e.g., Medin & Schaffer, 1978), rejected the notion of a stable, unitary category prototype and instead argued that a category is represented by the features that characterize its salient individual exemplars. From the exemplar perspective, there is little or no abstraction involved in representing the category; it is instead defined by the characteristics of specific instances.

Most of the research testing the relative merits of these competing perspectives involved the study of non-social categories. What is known about the representation of social groups? Sherman (1996) made a case that both views are correct, but they apply at different points in the development of group representations. When initially encountering members of a novel group, an exemplar-based representation governs category judgments, but once enough experience with group members has occurred, a probabilistic, prototype-based representation appears to emerge.

Regardless of which representational format one presupposes, people clearly do hold consequential beliefs about the features and characteristics that are associated with social groups. Categories are fundamentally represented in terms of descriptive features, but the representations consist of more than just a "laundry list" of characteristics that are individually correlated with category membership. Instead, these features are embedded within causal theories that do more than merely describe the category – they provide explanations for why the category is the way it is (McGarty, Yzerbyt, & Spears, 2002; Murphy & Medin, 1985). Certain features have "causal status" (Ahn, Kim, Lassaline, & Dennis, 2000) in that they are involved in creating other category characteristics, known as effect features. For example, if a group is stereotypically viewed as hard-working, well-educated, and affluent, then "hard-working" might be a feature having causal status in the perceiver's mental model of the group, providing an explanation for the group's educational and financial success. Features having causal status assume greater importance in judgments about category membership and inductive inferences made about category members, compared to effect features (Rehder & Hastie, 2001).

Of course, one can also ask about a causal feature's cause. In the previous example, we could ask, "Why is the group hard-working?" Like a child who asks "Why?" in response to each successive level of a parental explanation, perceivers face a potentially infinite explanatory regress in formulating their category representations. Is there an *ultimate* causal feature that can produce the observed causal chains of features comprising a category representation? In the case of social categories (as well as other categories considered to be "natural kinds"), the ultimate cause of a category's features is typically assumed (whether implicitly or explicitly) to be a defining inner essence (Rothbart & Taylor, 1992; Yzerbyt & Rocher, 2002). This "psychological essentialism" (Medin & Ortony, 1989) emerges early in childhood (Gelman, 2003) and consists of the assumption that there is a deep, inner essence that defines a category and produces its expressed characteristics. From this perspective, surface-feature similarity ("effect" similarity) is not the critical factor in category judgments; rather, the presence or absence of the category essence is determinative. Psychological essentialism provides an intuitive ontological framework for understanding the natural world that need not be taught or supported by explicit beliefs about exactly what the inner essence consists of, but advances in genetics research have provided a seemingly sophisticated basis for speculating about the ultimate inner cause (or essence) defining category membership: DNA. In the case of many kinds of social groups, psychological essentialism is now linked to genetic determinism, with genes providing the ultimate explanation for a group's characteristics (Dar-Nimrod & Heine, 2011; Keller, 2005). Such a view is scientifically questionable, given the abundant evidence that gene expression is commonly environmentally regulated (Gilbert, 2005; Jaenisch & Bird, 2003) and the more general fact that phenotypes represent the interaction of nature and nurture (e.g., Bronfenbrenner & Ceci, 1994). Recognition of these forms of biological plasticity is absent in essentialist thinking, and as a result, representations of many social groups (e.g., gender and ethnic groups) consist of implicitly essentialist theories asserting the immutability of group characteristics (Haslam, Rothschild, & Ernst, 2000).

A different aspect of social category representation is reflected in the nested, hierarchical arrangement of categories. A category such as "African Americans" is nested within more encompassing, superordinate categories (such as "Americans," "human beings," "carbon-based life forms," etc.). In turn, it can also be specified in terms of more and more constrained subcategories (such as "African American politicians" or "conservative African American politicians"). Categories in the middle range of this hierarchy are often considered to be "basic" (Rosch, Mervis, Gray, Johnson, & Boyes-Braem, 1976), in that they are the first categories that are learned, named, and used in infancy, and they constitute the level at which most world knowledge is organized. Between-category differentiation is maximized at the basic level, making it the most generally useful place for making conceptual distinctions (Markman & Wisniewski, 1997), although people with extensive domain expertise may make greater use of more subordinate levels of a category (Tanaka & Taylor, 1991).

In the stereotyping literature, a great deal of work has investigated the hypothesis that representations of basic-level social categories, which seem so useful for everyday distinction-making, are protected from modification by a process of subtyping (e.g., Richards & Hewstone, 2001). When perceivers encounter group members who do not display group-typical qualities, they are likely to construct a specific subcategory that is regarded as a special case, an "exception that proves the rule" (see Kunda & Oleson, 1997). In this way, the original stereotype needs not be modified.

Moving in the other direction within the conceptual hierarchy, researchers have also investigated how broader, more inclusive social categories can provide a mechanism for remedying antagonistic intergroup relations that exist at a more basic level (e.g., Dovidio, Gaertner, & Saguy, 2009). Given the previously noted identity function served by social categories, it can be anticipated that recategorizing at a more inclusive level is likely to shift the dividing lines that determine feelings of connection vs alienation. Thus, for example, different ethnic subgroups within a given country might enjoy better interethnic relations under conditions in which their shared national identity is salient – although this identity would likely also highlight differences from other national groups, shifting the focus of intergroup boundaries. Research on the in-group projection model (Wenzel, Mummendey, & Waldzus, 2007) offers an important caveat to this rosy view of better inter(sub)group relations when a shared, superordinate identity is salient. Specifically, this research indicates that subgroups often represent a shared, superordinate category in ways that render members of their own subgroup more prototypic (and hence superior) exemplars of the superordinate than other subgroups. For example, Italians may represent the superordinate category "Europeans" in ways that privilege the positive characteristics of their own national subgroup. If members of each subgroup engage in this form of in-group projection, the meaning of the superordinate category can become a ground for contestation, rather than for the harmonious alignment of goals and interests. Research in this tradition holds that the way to achieve more agreeable intergroup relations is to develop a richer, more complex representation of the superordinate category, in which multiple prototypes coexist (e.g., a representation in which there are multiple valid ways to be a European).

When researchers speak of category representations being stored or retrieved, it implies a relatively enduring and fixed view of the social world. And indeed, if there were no stability to our representations of social categories, their value in serving our epistemic purposes would be completely undermined. At the same time, a major theme emerging from a variety of different research traditions, including research on the in-group projection model, is the idea that category representations are likely to be tuned to the imme-diate context (Smith & Conrey, 2007), particularly the salient comparative context (e.g., Brown & Turner, 2002). Theoretical notions of category representation have become increasingly dynamic in recent thinking. As Smith and Conrey argue, it may be preferable to think of mental representa-tions as being more like transitory states than enduring entities – although there is most assur-edly a non-trivial degree of continuity in these representational states.

The contextualization of category representa-tions has been documented in a number of studies showing that the automatic associations that are triggered by category members can change across different circumstances. For example, Wittenbrink, Judd, and Park (2001) showed that automatic evaluative associations triggered by African American targets varied as a function of the set-ting in which a target was encountered. The very same individuals elicited more positive evalua-tions when seen in church as compared to on an urban street corner. Along similar lines, Barden, Maddux, Petty, and Brewer (2004) showed that the social role occupied by an African American target moderated the degree of automatic preju-dice that was elicited by exposure to the target; for example, a Black person elicited more favora-ble automatic evaluations when depicted as a lawyer than when depicted as a prisoner. As a final example, Correll, Park, Judd, and Wittenbrink (2007) showed that reading a newspaper story about a Black criminal made participants more likely to commit racially biased errors in a simu-lated police decision-making task requiring them to "shoot" individuals holding weapons (includ-ing being more likely to shoot a Black target holding an innocuous object such as a cell phone). These kinds of effects are typically understood to reflect the fact that some social categories, like "African Americans," are actually quite mul-tifaceted and are likely to be represented in an evaluatively heterogeneous way; only a subset of the potential associations will be activated in any given circumstance, and the particular subset that does become activated is influenced by the salient context (see Gawronski & Bodenhausen, 2006, 2011).

A great deal remains to be learned about what is general and what is context-specific in repre-sentations of social groups. Gawronski, Rydell, Vervliet, and De Houwer (2010) have provided some very promising new insights about this issue in the domain of implicit attitudes. They focus on the role of attention to context cues in determining the generality of automatic evaluation. When indi-viduals form a new evaluative representation of a given category, the surrounding context may or may not be salient. For example, if you meet some friendly Bosnians at a party, you may form a positive impression of Bosnians without particu-larly noting the context in which the positivity was experienced. This experience will thus lead to a relatively decontextualized positive automatic evaluation of the group. However, if you subse-quently have a bad experience with a Bosnian, you are quite likely to be attentive to the context (because the unexpectedness of the event triggers greater analysis). By the logic of Gawronski et al.'s reasoning, this pattern of experiences would tend to produce automatic negative evalua-tions of Bosnians whenever they are encountered within the same context as the negative experience ("occasion setting" in their terminology), but automatic evaluations should be positive in all other situations, activating the decontextualized automatic evaluation that was initially formed (a "renewal effect"). The time is certainly ripe for more research on stable (default) vs context-driven perceptions of social groups.

Lay demography

Thus far, we have written about social categories in a very general manner, focusing on general functional and representational processes. We turn now to some particulars, in an attempt to address the following questions:

1. Which respects for social differentiation are chronically salient to social perceivers?
2. What specific stereotypic content is associated with these salient groups?
3. How is this content acquired?

As much as any object can be, people are infi-nitely categorizable. Imagine encountering an unknown individual at a cocktail party. As your interaction progresses, this same person might be categorized as a woman, a teacher, a brunette, a Liberal, an oenophile, and a person with detached earlobes. Of course, some of these categories are more useful and have more salient cues associated with them than others. As previously noted, research on category representation has estab-lished that some categories are more "basic" than others. In the case of people, researchers have noted that basic demographic distinctions – age, race, gender, and social class – seem to serve as the most chronically salient categories (Brewer, 1988; Fiske & Neuberg, 1990). The relative pre-eminence of these categories no doubt relates to the fact they are typically easily and immediately perceived.

Evidence that individuals spontaneously use sex and race to categorize others was provided by Stangor, Lynch, Duan, and Glass (1992), who showed that memory for statements that had been made by a variety of individuals who differed on race and gender tended to be organized around the race and gender categories. Specifically, when memory errors occurred, it was more likely that a statement would be misattributed to a person having the same race or gender as the actual source, compared to cross-race or cross-sex memory errors. This tendency to group information by sex and race was generally evident, but it was more pronounced among individuals who were higher in prejudice. Using neuroscience methods, Ito and Urland (2003) showed that perceivers are attentive to the race and sex of a face within a fraction of a second of its presentation (within 100 ms for race and 150 ms for gender). Studies of this sort clearly show that certain basic demographic categories are immediately encoded in an automatic manner, although the focus of categorization can subsequently shift across longer time periods (e.g., Kunda & Spencer, 2003).

Stereotype content

The process of categorization initiates the activation of a variety of stereotypes associated with the category in question. Though the content of these stereotypes can be extremely varied (e.g., elderly people are slow; women are bad at math; homeless people are dangerous), over a decade of work on the stereotype content model (SCM; Fiske, Cuddy, Glick, & Xu, 2002) has shown that the content of stereotypes can be understood in terms of two fundamental dimensions: warmth and competence. The dimension of warmth (which encompasses traits like tolerant, warm, good-natured, and sincere) is concerned with a group's goals in relation to the self or in-group. As perceivers, we want to know whether an individual or out-group is a friend or foe – whether the "other" intends to cooperate or compete (Fiske et al., 2002). In addition to knowledge about a target's intention to compete or cooperate, perceivers are also concerned with the target's ability to pursue that intent. This capability to pursue one's relatively positive or negative intentions is described by the second dimension: competence. Competence (which encompasses traits like competent, confident, independent, and intelligent) describes the degree to which a target individual or group will be effective at bringing about desired outcomes. In essence, the SCM asserts that perceivers differentiate individuals and groups according to their predicted impact on the self or in-group using judgments of their perceived intent (warmth) and their ability (competence) to pursue that intent (Cuddy, Fiske, & Glick, 2008). These same dimensions appear to organize social impression

in general (e.g., Judd, James-Hawkins, Yzerbyt, & Kashima, 2005; Wiggins, 1991).

The SCM contends that social groups are often characterized by ambivalent stereotypes, specifically reflected in positive evaluation on one dimension but negative evaluation on the other. For example, in relation to one's in-group, a group could be characterized as warm but not competent (e.g., the elderly). Alternatively, a group could be characterized as competent but not warm (e.g., Asians). Unfortunately, positive evaluation along one dimension is not enough to overcome an overall negative evaluation. Members of ambivalently stereotyped groups are usually devalued and experience prejudice and discrimination relative to groups that are perceived as both warm and competent (e.g., Cuddy, Norton, & Fiske, 2005; Glick, 2005).

The SCM also outlines the emotional responses that are likely to be elicited by groups positioned at different points along the warmth and competence continua. Groups judged as high in both warmth and competence – usually only one's in-group and "societal prototype groups" like Whites, heterosexuals, and middle-class individuals (Cuddy et al., 2008) – elicit admiration. In contrast, groups judged as neither warm nor competent (e.g., poor people, welfare recipients) elicit feelings of contempt. These feelings of contempt are often associated with a host of related negative emotions like disgust, anger, and resentment. The two mixed quadrants also elicit relatively negative emotions. Groups stereotyped as warm but not competent (e.g., elderly people, disabled people) elicit feelings of pity, while groups stereotyped as competent but not warm (e.g., Asians, Jews, rich people) elicit feelings of envy.

A recent extension of the SCM, the "behaviors from intergroup affect and stereotypes (BIAS) map" framework (Cuddy, Fiske, & Glick, 2007), links the contents of stereotypes and associated emotions as identified by the SCM to actual discriminatory behaviors. The BIAS map proposes four distinct classes of out-group-related behaviors that fall along two dimensions: active vs passive and facilitative vs harmful. Active behaviors are those involving directed effort toward the target group (e.g., a targeted attack on a synagogue), while passive behaviors are defined as those having repercussions for an out-group but that involve less directed effort (e.g., failing to hire Jewish job applicants). In addition to the effort with which they are engaged, behaviors can also be differentiated according to their intended effect. This distinction is encompassed by the facilitative vs harmful dimension: facilitation refers to behaviors intended to bring about favorable outcomes or gains (e.g., donating money to an after-school program for inner-city youth), whereas harm refers to behaviors intended to bring about detrimental outcomes or losses (e.g., discrimination in hiring). Linking these dimensions to the SCM, judgments of warmth predict active behaviors, while judgments of competence predict passive behaviors. Groups judged as warm elicit active facilitation (help; e.g., antidiscrimination policy); groups judged as lacking warmth elicit active harm (attack; e.g., legalized segregation). Groups judged as competent elicit passive facilitation (obligatory association, convenient cooperation; e.g., choosing to work with an Asian classmate on a math project); groups judged as lacking competence elicit passive harm (neglect, ignoring; e.g., avoiding eye contact with a homeless person). Much of the research on prejudice and stereotyping has been conducted on a "group-by-group" basis, with some researchers studying sexism, some racism, some ageism, etc. While there are undoubtedly important aspects of prejudice and stereotyping that are unique to these particular groups, it is also important to understand the more general principles that drive these phenomena. The SCM and the BIAS map represent theoretical approaches that can provide an integrative framework for understanding the different manifestations of bias that can emerge toward different social groups.

Acquiring stereotypes

The ability to categorize is a skill displayed very early in development. In the case of gender, for instance, babies are basically experts at distinguishing between males and females' and categorizing individuals accordingly, by 12 months of age (e.g., Leinbach & Fagot, 1993;Quinn, Yahr, Kuhn, Slater, & Pascalis, 2002). Almost as quickly as these categories are learned, they also become attached to stereotypes. Between the ages of 3 and 6 years, and often much earlier, children acquire knowledge of and begin to apply stereotypes in a number of domains, including race (e.g., Bigler & Liben, 1993), gender (e.g., Eichstedt, Serbin, Poulin-Dubois, & Sen, 2002), and age (Seefeldt, Jantz, Galper, & Serock, 1977).

Much of what is known about the development of the ability to categorize and the formation of stereotyping and prejudice has been synthesized into the framework of Developmental Intergroup Theory (DIT; Bigler & Liben, 2006, 2007). DIT is concerned with how children establish the importance of some person attributes (and the relative unimportance of others), how they then categorize individuals based on these salient dimensions, and, finally, how children develop stereotypes and prejudices about these salient groups. We will focus on the first process. Importantly, DIT posits

what children will only categorize based on dimensions that have been made psychologically salient.

Four factors are hypothesized to affect the establishment of the psychological salience of person attributes: perceptual discriminability; proportional group size; explicit labeling and use of social groups; and implicit use of social groups. Perceptual discriminability refers to the ease with which differences between groups can be seen. Children tend to note only perceptually salient attributes of people, so groups that can be readily distinguished by visible qualities (e.g., skin color, eye shape, hair style, clothing) are most likely to become bases for categorization (Bigler, 1995; Patterson & Bigler, 2006). Categories that are not readily distinguished (e.g., religion, nationality) are less likely to be noticed by children, and therefore children are unlikely to categorize individuals according to these groups (Rutland, 1999). Attributes like race, gender, age, and attractiveness all include perceptually salient features, and thus quickly become important for categorization among children. A second important factor in categorization is perceptual group size. Children are sensitive to numerical differences between groups, recognizing relative differences in proportions of various social groups. Smaller (minority) groups tend to be more salient than larger (majority) groups, and can thus more easily become targets of stereotypes and prejudice (Brown & Bigler, 2002).

A major tenet of DIT is that children's categorization closely follows the explicit and implicit use of categories evident in the adult world. Children pay close attention to characteristics that adults mark as important via various verbal and nonverbal (and often very subtle) cues. In contrast, children tend to ignore aspects of human variation which are not attended to by adults. It is important to note that DIT does not posit that children simply imitate adults; rather, DIT proposes that children construct their beliefs about various categories based on cues from adults. When authority figures use labels or some functional organization to distinguish individuals (e.g., boys in this line, girls in this line), children infer that the grouping criterion (e.g., gender, height, etc.) is an important category distinction (Patterson & Bigler, 2006). Category labeling has this effect even when the categories are used in a neutral manner (e.g., "Good morning boys and girls"). In addition, children make inferences about psychological salience based on the presence of social distinctions in the social world, in the absence of any explicit explanation (e.g., gender or racial segregation). Children are sensitive to perceptual similarities of those who are grouped together and, further, infer that these individuals are segregated because they differ in important ways. For example, children tend to think that some jobs are "for Black people" and other jobs are "for White people" even in the absence of any external adult instruction (Bigler, Averhart, & Liben, 2003). According to DIT, this knowledge would be gained simply by observing differences in perceptually salient features that characterize individuals in various professions. In sum, DIT provides a useful framework for understanding how categories are first developed and conceptualized by children.

CATEGORIZATION IN ACTION

Having addressed basic questions about the representational structure, psychological function, and specific content of social categories, we now turn our attention to the processes whereby these categories influence our perceptions, judgments, and behaviors. Here, we address questions about when and how social categories become influential in perceptions of social groups and their individual members.

Categorization versus individuation

Influential models of impression formation portray our perceptions of others as emerging within a tension between viewing others categorically – as group members who are functionally interchangeable with other individuals in the group – vs perceiving them as individuals who are characterized by a unique constellation of personal qualities (Brewer, 1988; Fiske & Neuberg, 1990). One approach to analyzing the differences between categorization and individuation has been to focus on the type of content that is emphasized in impression formation: category cues vs trait cues (see Bodenhausen, Macrae, & Sherman, 1999). On this view, individuation relies on more extensive processing of trait (or behavior) cues, whereas such cues are de-emphasized in categorization in favor of cues indicating membership in some noteworthy social group. A key problem with this approach lies in the fact that the distinction between traits and categories is ultimately hard to defend on the basis of content. A "trait" like neurotic can easily define a category of (from the perceiver's perspective) functionally interchangeable people – i.e., neurotic people – while a "category" membership like Muslim can serve merely as one of many personal descriptors (and not as a basis for viewing the individual as interchangeable with other category members). There are, to be sure, noteworthy differences between

demographically defined social categories vs trait-based ones (see Bodenhausen et al., 1999), but the key difference between categorization and individuation does not appear to be reducible to the type of content (e.g., traits vs demographic cues) emphasized in impression formation. A more promising approach is to build the distinction between categorization and individuation on processing differences (e.g., Fiske & Neuberg, 1990).

When social impressions are categorical, a particular group membership, trait, or other personal feature provides the overarching organizing theme for perception and judgment, and a priori, generic knowledge is used schematically to produce an impression in which the target is, for all intents and purposes, interchangeable with other members of the category defined by this feature. The particulars of the individual are not important; rather, the ways in which the individual typifies that general sort of person is of paramount concern. Individuation, in contrast, refers to a process in which no particular aspect of a person dominates impression formation. Instead, multiple characteristics are considered and their implications are integrated in a more piecemeal process. Its end result is an impression focused on how the target person differs from other persons, rather than on class equivalencies within a given group of persons.

A great deal of research has examined the moderators of categorization vs individuation. Social, motivational, attentional, and dispositional moderating variables have been identified. The importance of the social context is emphasized in self-categorization theory (Turner, Hogg, Oakes, Reicher, & Wetherell, 1987), which holds that in *interpersonal* contexts, it is the differences between *individuals* that are salient; the personal self is predominant and individuated identities are important. However, in *intergroup* contexts, differences between *groups* are salient; the interchangeable social self is predominant and social identities are important. This argument of course begs the question of what constitutes an interpersonal vs an intergroup context. Research has identified several relevant factors. First, when individuals' behavior maps onto distinct category norms (*normative fit*; e.g., Oakes, 1987), the situation is likely to become an intergroup context. For example, consider a conference where social psychologists are asserting the importance of situational factors in shaping behavior, while personality psychologists are arguing for the importance of dispositions. These patterns of behavior align with expected category characteristics, so the situation will seem to be an intergroup context, rather than one in which interpersonal distinctions are pre-eminent. Second, the degree to which patterns of similarities and differences between individuals are aligned with category membership (*comparative fit*; e.g., Wegener & Klauer, 2004) also can trigger intergroup thinking. Consider a mixed-gender group of individuals serving on a jury in a criminal trial. If opinions about the case aligned in such a way that the men on the jury favored the defense while the women on the jury favored the prosecution, this high degree of "meta-contrast" would immediately draw attention to the gender distinction (even if there was nothing particularly gender-stereotypic about the trial content), creating an intergroup situation rather than an interpersonal one. Also important are variables that influence the general salience of categorical identities. For example, distinctiveness based on situational rarity (e.g., solo status; Biernat & Vescio, 1993) or low overall base-rate population frequency (Nelson & Miller, 1995) can make certain categories influential, as can the frequent or recent use of a potentially applicable category (e.g., Rutland & Cinnirella, 2000).

Eitam and Higgins (2010) developed the "relevance of a representation" (ROAR) framework for understanding when an accessible concept or category will be applied to a given target. From this perspective, a category may be available for use in orienting one's impression of another person, but whether or not this happens depends on whether the category has motivational relevance. Motivational relevance can consist of *value relevance* (strong positive or negative value is associated with a given category), *control relevance* (a categorical identity has relevance to the achievement or blockage of goal attainment or task completion), or *truth relevance* (a category is perceived to be meaningful and informative, rather than insignificant or obsolete). When one or more of these forms of motivational relevance is high with respect to a potentially applicable social category, the likelihood that the category will be used to organize a social impression is increased.

Given its schematic quality, categorical impression formation is typically more automatic than individuation, particularly in the senses of being more rapid and efficient (i.e., less dependent on attentional resources; for a review, see Amodio & Mendoza, 2010). Going beyond a stereotypic, categorical impression (i.e., individuation), in contrast, is commonly viewed as a more effortful and resource-dependent phenomenon (see Payne, 2005). Thus, the likelihood of categorical (vs individuated) social impressions also increases to the extent that any variable constrains the perceiver's attentional capacity, motivation for effortful processing, or opportunity to deliberate (for a review, see Macrae & Bodenhausen, 2000). A variety of dispositional variables have relevance here. For example, individuals who are high in the need for structure or closure (i.e., people who want to obtain a rapid, firm sense of the meaning of their experiences) are likely to rely on categorical thinking, which tends to provide rapid, clear, and well-structured impressions (e.g., Kruglanski & Fishman, 2009). Dogmatism (e.g., Rokeach, 1954; see Duckitt, 2009, for a recent review) is a closely related individual difference that has similar implications. On the other hand, openness to experience (one of the "Big 5" personality trait dimensions) is associated with less rigidly categorical social impressions (Flynn, 2005). Numerous situational factors also influence the motivation or opportunity to engage in individuation. Distraction (e.g., Pendry & Macrae, 1994) and time pressure (Kruglanski & Freund, 1983) can result in more category-based impressions by precluding effortful deliberation, while having one's own outcomes depend on the actions of a social target – and other factors triggering strong accuracy concerns – can trigger motivation for carefully individuated impressions (e.g., Neuberg & Fiske, 1987). Finally, situationally generated, incidental affective states (especially anger, anxiety, and happiness) can promote greater categorical thinking (for a review, see Bodenhausen, Mussweiler, Gabriel, & Moreno, 2001).

In sum, categorical thinking is often the most immediate response to social targets, but with ample motivation and opportunity, more deliberated, individuated impressions can arise. Although it is theoretically convenient to think of categorical and individuated impressions as distinct and mutually exclusive ways of thinking about others (and ourselves), researchers have recognized the shades of gray that exist between these two extremes (e.g., Fiske & Neuberg, 1990). Indeed, an important direction in recent research has been the examination of the ways personal/individuated and social/categorical identities can be interlinked (see, e.g., Amiot, de la Sablonnière, Terry, & Smith, 2007; Postmes & Jetten, 2006).

Category selection

Much of the early research on social categorization involved the manipulation of a single focal category (while holding all else constant), in order to determine how the presence or absence of that categorical cue might influence perceptions, evaluations, and behavior. However, in real life, perceivers typically encounter whole persons in their multifarious diversity. Thus, it becomes important to know how a particular category is selected as the focus for social perception, given that many possible bases for categorization are available (for recent reviews, see Bodenhausen, 2010; Bodenhausen & Peery, 2009), and the relevant evaluative and descriptive implications can differ strikingly, depending on which category is salient. For example, Mitchell, Nosek, and Banaji (2003) showed that automatic evaluations of Black athletes were significantly more positive when their occupational category was in contextual focus, compared to when their racial category was salient.

As noted in the prior section, the relevance of particular categories can vary as a function of the comparative context, the behavior and other characteristics of the target, and the motivational states of the perceiver. Moreover, the recency and frequency of a category's prior use can determine its likelihood of being invoked again. But by what process does category selection unfold? Bodenhausen and Macrae (1998) provided a theoretical account of the selection process, based on studies in which perceivers were confronted with targets who could be stereotyped in terms of more than one commonly used social category (ethnicity vs sex; Macrae, Bodenhausen, & Milne, 1995). The central idea of their perspective is that social categorization is dynamic and involves simultaneous activation and inhibition processes that work to highlight or downplay the activation of potentially applicable categories. They propose that in circumstances that favor categorical responses (i.e., situations characterized by low motivation or opportunity for thoughtful individuation, which may characterize a great number of everyday life contexts), a single category will often come to dominate social impressions, depending on the unfolding of the relevant activation/inhibition processes. Initially, multiple categories are activated (e.g., Freeman, Ambady, Rule, & Johnson, 2008), but one or more of these categories is likely to have an activation advantage, accruing more rapid activation because of its contextual or motivational relevance. Once a particular category achieves a sufficient amount of activation, it effectively "wins" the dominance contest, and its rivals are actively inhibited, allowing a coherent focus on the dominant category (see, e.g., Dagenbach & Carr, 1994). As a result, social perceivers are able to cope effectively with this diversity by simplifying the identity-relevant information used in social categorization processes.

It is certainly also possible for perceivers to pay attention to more than one categorical identity at a time and, indeed, research on cross-categorization effects has examined exactly this sort of situation, in which the social perceiver's attention is directed simultaneously to more than one social category (Crisp & Hewstone, 2007; Kang & Chasteen, 2009). Research in this area has focused primarily on the evaluative consequences of cross-categorizations. Broadly speaking, when multiple categories are made salient, social evaluations tend to be affected by the number of category memberships shared by the perceiver and the target (Migdal, Hewstone, & Mullen, 1998); more shared category memberships translate into more positive evaluations. Other, less intuitive effects of cross-categorizations have also been documented. For example, one might expect that a person who belongs to two socially subordinated groups (e.g., "Black" and "gay") would simply be evaluated in a doubly negative way by majority (White, heterosexual) perceivers. However, work by Purdie-Vaughns and Eibach (2008) paints a more complicated picture: they argue that individuals whose identities involve intersection of more than one socially devalued group may experience social invisibility. For example, gay African Americans, because they are non-prototypical of both the respective social groups (i.e., the prototypical gay person is not Black, and the prototypical Black person is not gay), are not considered for true inclusion in either group. Non-prototypical group members are less likely to be noticed, heard, or to have influence over other group members (e.g., Hogg, 2001), thus making these individuals subject to multiple cultural, political, and legal disadvantages that are linked more to their relative invisibility rather than to double-strength animus.

Another way in which perceivers may accommodate multiple categories when perceiving others is to form specific subtypes. When encountered with sufficient frequency, particular category combinations (e.g., Black Republicans) may come to be represented in terms of a specific category of their own. Once established, such subtypes can function much the same as any other category does (e.g., Brewer, Dull, & Lui, 1981), competing with other bases for construal in the category selection process (see Bodenhausen & Macrae, 1998). The constellation of characteristics associated with the subgroup need not necessarily reflect typical features of either of the more inclusive "parent" categories; indeed, a novel set of typical features can emerge for the subtype (Hutter, Crisp, Humphreys, Waters, & Moffitt, 2009; Kunda, Miller, & Claire, 1990). Social perceivers thus seem adept at both highlighting singular, dominant social categories in the face of multiply categorizable individuals, as well as dealing with situations where multiple categories remain salient for a given individual. While these strategies are not necessarily all positive, particularly for the social targets who may find themselves subject to social invisibility, they are effective means for navigating a complex social world where perceivers regularly encounter individuals for whom multiple categories are visible and accessible to perceivers.

A different problem that can sometimes plague the process of category selection is ambiguous category membership. It is clear that category members' prototypicality enhances the likelihood of the category being applied to them (e.g., Eberhardt, Davies, Purdie-Vaughns, & Johnson, 2006; Maddox, 2004). However, what happens when a target does not appear to be a clear match to any established category? How do perceivers deal with ambiguous social targets? As noted above, people often automatically categorize others based on their race and gender. When a person's race or gender cannot be readily ascertained, perceivers may try to assimilate the target into one of the conventional existing categories, but it is also possible that in certain circumstances, the typical demographic categories are not adequate and new categories are needed to represent these individuals (e.g., "multiracials" or "androgynous people"). It may be relatively uncommon to encounter individuals for whom determining gender is difficult. Research suggests that when these individuals are encountered, they are sometimes miscategorized by perceivers on the basis of gender-atypical features (e.g., long hair on a man, leading to his categorization as a woman; see Macrae & Martin, 2007). Research by Freeman, Rule, Adams, and Ambady (2010) indicates that, when judging the sex of faces, perceivers rely on gender-(a)typical traits to make concrete, categorical, and dichotomous gender determinations (although brain activity shows a more graded response to variations in gender-typical facial attributes on a full spectrum from extremely masculine to extremely feminine).

Very recently, there has been an explosion of interest in the question of how perceivers deal with racial/ethnic ambiguity. In one of the earliest studies on the categorization of racially ambiguous faces, South African participants categorized African, European, and mixed-race faces as European or African. White participants were more likely to categorize mixed-race (presumably racially ambiguous) faces as African than European (Pettigrew, Allport, & Barnett, 1958). Nearly half a century later, Castano et al. (2002) showed similar effects, demonstrating that northern Italians were generally likely to categorize ambiguous faces as southern rather than northern Italian. In addition, Pauker, Weisbuch, Ambady, Sommers, Adams, and Ivcevic (2009) demonstrated that both racially ambiguous and other-race faces are remembered less well than same-race faces, suggesting that the ambiguous faces were treated as if they belonged in the out-group, in accordance with the well-established own-race bias (e.g., Malpass & Kravitz, 1969; Meissner & Brigham, 2001; see Hugenberg, Young, Bernstein, & Sacco, 2010, for a review). All of these results comport with the in-group overexclusion effect, which is the tendency to be highly selective about

who qualifies for inclusion in one's in-group (Leyens & Yzerbyt, 1992). These results highlight the fact that not only obvious out-group members but also ambiguous cases are likely to experience exclusion. Thus, for cases where it is not clear whether a target person belongs in one's own group, a primary strategy for resolving the ambiguity question is to assign the target to the out-group.

Just as category-based impressions of individuals holding clear category memberships can be dependent on characteristics of the perceiver, target, or context, so, too, is the categorization process for ambiguous targets affected by these different aspects of the social categorization situation. For example, research indicates that in-group overexclusion is particularly likely among perceivers who are highly identified with their in-group (Castano et al., 2002), among persons who feel psychologically vulnerable (Miller, Maner, & Becker, 2010), as well as among those who are prejudiced against the potential out-group in question (e.g., Blascovich, Wyer, Swart, & Kibler, 1997). Characteristics of ambiguous targets themselves may also play a role in how they are categorized. For example, MacLin and Malpass (2001) demonstrated that hair style and clothing choice can serve to disambiguate otherwise ambiguous targets, leading not only to categorization patterns reflecting conventional, disambiguated categories but also to subsequent, congruent perceptual consequences, such as perceptions of darker skin (on the same target) with a Black vs Hispanic hair style. Eberhardt, Dasgupta, and Banaszynski (2003) also demonstrated that racial labels, once applied, affect subsequent perception of previously ambiguous faces along clear racial lines. This research suggests that when ambiguous targets provide some information, via application of a racial label or choice of cues to category membership such as hair style or clothing style, social perceivers readily receive and use this information in their social judgments of the target.

What happens when ambiguous individuals do not disambiguate themselves and perceivers are not necessarily motivated to pigeonhole them into the out-group? For individuals who identify as multiracial, for example, the racial label they apply to themselves may not serve to disambiguate them to social perceivers. The research described above always relied on the use of conventional racial or ethnic labels provided by the researchers. In research by Peery and Bodenhausen (2008), perceivers were given an opportunity to (a) apply their own label(s) to racially ambiguous targets, and (b) use, if desired, a multiracial label (that either identified an ambiguous individual as a member of both possible categories or as a separate category). In this study, mostly White (and always non-Black) participants were more likely to categorize a racially ambiguous person (resulting from a mixture of Black and White 'parent' faces) as Black and *not* White, but only when information was provided suggesting that this individual had one Black and one White parent. When no information was known about the ambiguous target, participants' category assignments were more variable, although monoracial forms of categorization were the most common (either Black and *not* White, or White and *not* Black). This pattern reflects a historical tradition of in-group overexclusion by Whites in the United States (specifically, the principle of hypodescent, which asserts that mixed-race individuals should be assigned to the racial category corresponding to that of the parent having the lowest social status), highlighting the role that cultural traditions may play in perceivers' categorizations of ambiguous targets (Peery & Bodenhausen, 2008). Thus, just as social perceivers are quite adept at negotiating the complexity of multiple potentially applicable social categories, they also seem to be relatively adept at handling target ambiguity as well. While the categorization patterns they exhibit may not always have desirable consequences for the social targets, they nonetheless demonstrate that social perceivers are effective at making social categorizations in complicated social situations with complex social targets.

Using – and avoiding the use of – selected categories

As just noted, when perceivers engage in a primarily categorical strategy for impression formation, the first problem is to identify which category to use. After a particular category is selected, its mental representation provides a schematic structure for organizing the impression. In particular, features associated with category membership are automatically activated (e.g., Devine, 1989; Dovidio, Kawakami, Johnson, Johnson, & Howard, 1997). Once these representational features are activated in working memory, they can influence a host of fundamental information-processing operations. For example, they can bias the perceiver's attention to stereotype-confirming aspects of the situation (e.g., Bodenhausen, 1988), particularly when perceivers have unconstrained attentional capacity (Allen, Sherman, Conrey, & Stroessner, 2009). They also produce assimilative interpretive biases, such that ambiguous information is given a stereotype-consistent meaning (e.g., Hill, Lewicki, Czyzewska, & Boss, 1989; Kunda & Sherman-Williams, 1993); a well-known example was provided by the news coverage of

the aftermath of Hurricane Katrina, in which African Americans were said to be "looting" convenience stores while European Americans were "finding food." In addition, activated stereotypes can lead to the selective retrieval of stereotype-consistent information from long-term memory (Rothbart, Evans, & Fulero, 1979). Thus, when stereotypic associates of a social category are activated, they can unleash a number of mechanisms that produce a confirmation bias in social impressions. Because perceivers are unlikely to appreciate the constructive aspects of their impressions (i.e., naïve realism; Robinson, Keltner, Ward, & Ross, 1995), they are likely to view their initial stereotypes as having been "objectively" validated after the operation of these confirmatory biases.

The extent of assimilative stereotypic biases is moderated by a range of variables. For example, they are more evident among perceivers who possess stronger category-stereotype associations, as measured with indirect assessments such as the Implicit Association Test (e.g., Allen et al., 2009; Gawronski, Geschke, & Banse, 2003; Hugenberg & Bodenhausen, 2003). It is also important that perceivers feel entitled to make a judgment (Yzerbyt & Corneille, 2005); for example, if the evidence provided to perceivers for forming an impression seems too scant, they may withhold judgment. This kind of finding points to the fact that stereotypes often exert their influence on judgments primarily indirectly, through their impact on evidence processing, rather than in a more direct manner (see also Bodenhausen, 1988; Darley & Gross, 1983). Reality constraints are important too; when a target's behavior or characteristics unambiguously do *not* fit stereotypic expectations, perceptual contrast effects can lead to judgments that are more extreme in a counter-stereotypic direction, at least when the response scale is subjective (e.g., a woman being rated as more assertive than a man, given the identical assertive behavior; see Biernat, 2003).

The amount of deliberation that goes into forming an impression is also of great significance in shaping the degree of bias expressed in social judgments and behavior. Stereotype-based assimilation happens in a largely implicit, automatic manner and is likely to be evident in perceivers' initial reactions (Bodenhausen & Todd, 2010). With more thought, however, it becomes increasingly likely that perceivers will go beyond their most impulsive, stereotypic impressions, possibly considering less stereotypic factors before finalizing their impressions and judgments (Florack, Scarabis, & Bless, 2001). Following the seminal research of Devine (1989), a great deal of research has examined the possibility that, among individuals who are motivated to avoid prejudice, the detection of categorical biases is likely to trigger effortful strategies that are specifically designed to counteract these biases (e.g., Devine, Plant, Amodio, Harmon-Jones, & Vance, 2002; Monteith, 1993; for a review, see Bodenhausen, Todd, & Richeson, 2009). When such concerns are triggered, the additional, effortful processing that occurs is likely to "put the brakes on prejudice" (Monteith, Ashburn-Nardo, Voils, & Czopp, 2002). In addition to the desire to control prejudice per se, deliberative reasoning in the face of racial biases can also be triggered by a desire to restore cognitive consistency when the judgmental implications of automatic reactions clash with explicit beliefs about the group in question or about oneself (Gawronski, Peters, Brochu, & Strack, 2008). Thus, whether or not perceivers are motivated to go beyond their initial, stereotypic reactions to a target can be an important variable moderating the extent of categorical bias. Additionally, factors that impede the *ability* to deliberate, such as distraction and ego depletion, can also heighten the degree of bias in judgments and behavior (Govorun & Payne, 2006; Hofmann, Gschwendner, Castelli, & Schmitt, 2008), because these factors compromise more effortful forms of deliberation but spare the automatic processes responsible for bias.

However, as Gawronski and Bodenhausen (2006, 2011) point out, it is certainly also possible that additional deliberation can simply serve to reinforce initial association-based impressions; this is particularly likely to happen in circumstances where there are motivational forces leading the perceiver to prefer stereotypic interpretations (and thus to generate motivated reasoning strategies; Kunda, 1990). Thus, thoughtful analysis can attenuate or exacerbate categorical thinking, depending on the circumstances (see also Wegener, Clark, & Petty, 2006).

The fact that effortful processes for combating unwanted bias can be compromised by any factor that undermines the motivation or opportunity for deliberative thinking suggests that bias-reduction strategies focusing on attenuating or eliminating automatic biases online (rather than trying to correct for them after they have occurred) may be a more promising strategy. Interestingly, some recent research suggests that the subset of people who are *not* racially prejudiced consists largely of individuals who are not very susceptible to affective conditioning and are thus unlikely to have formed automatic prejudiced associations in the first place (Livingston & Drwecki, 2007). Fortunately, evidence is now accumulating that control of automatic bias is indeed possible (e.g., Sherman, Gawronski, Gonsalkorale, Hugenberg, Allen, & Groom, 2008). For example, fairly straightforward cognitive strategies, such as imagining or thinking about counter-stereotypic group members (Blair, Ma, & Lenton, 2001; Dasgupta & Greenwald, 2001) or taking the perspective of group members (Todd, Bodenhausen, Richeson, & Galinsky, 2011), can effectively reduce implicit and automatic forms of racial bias. Moreover, there is evidence that effortful control of unwanted categorical biases can itself become relatively automatized (see Moskowitz, Li, & Kirk, 2004), increasing the perceiver's prospects of avoiding the pitfalls of distraction, depletion, and other factors that typically make thoughtful self-regulation less successful. Of course, the automatic pursuit of the goal to be more egalitarian is only likely to emerge among individuals who actually have a commitment to this goal.

CONCLUSION

The importance of social categories in shaping social perception has long been recognized by social psychologists, but our understanding of when and how social categories matter continues to evolve as researchers uncover a wealth of new findings in this domain. New insights are emerging from neuroscientific investigations of social categorization (e.g., Kang, Inzlicht, & Derks, 2010). Behavioral techniques for uncovering the cognitive processes underlying group perceptions are being continually refined, and new ones are being created (e.g., De Houwer & Moors, 2010). New connections between emotions and social categories are being discovered (e.g., Yzerbyt & Kuppens, 2009). In this necessarily brief survey, we have tried to provide a representative sample of what social psychological research has revealed about social categorization. However, it is abundantly clear that, despite decades of research, exciting new directions are still emerging in research on social categorization. We look forward to these developments eagerly.

REFERENCES

Ahn, W.-k., Kim, N. S., Lassaline, M. E., & Dennis, M. J. (2000). Causal status as a determinant of feature centrality. *Cognitive Psychology, 41*, 361–416.

Allen, T. J., Sherman, J. W., Conrey, F. R., & Stroessner, S. J. (2009). Stereotype strength and attentional bias: Preference for confirming versus disconfirming information depends on processing capacity. *Journal of Experimental Social Psychology, 45*, 1081–1087.

Allport, G. W., & Postman, L. J. (1947). *The psychology of rumor.* New York: Holt, Rinehart & Winston.

Amiot, C. E., de la Sablonnière, R., Terry, D. J., & Smith, J. R. (2007). Integration of social identities in the self: Toward a cognitive-developmental model. *Personality and Social Psychology Review, 11,* 364–388.

Amodio, D. M., & Mendoza, S. A. (2010). Implicit intergroup bias: Cognitive, affective, and motivational underpinnings. In B. Gawronski & B. K. Payne (Eds.), *Handbook of implicit social cognition: Measurement, theory, and applications* (pp. 353–374). New York: Guilford Press.

Barden, J., Maddux, W. W., Petty, R. E., & Brewer, M. B. (2004). Contextual moderation of racial bias: The impact of social roles on controlled and automatically activated attitudes. *Journal of Personality and Social Psychology, 87,* 5–22.

Biernat, M. (2003). Toward a broader view of social stereotyping. *American Psychologist, 58,* 1019–1027.

Biernat, M., & Vescio, T. K. (1993). Categorization and stereotyping: Effects of group context on memory and social judgment. *Journal of Experimental Social Psychology, 29,* 166–202.

Bigler, R. S. (1995). The role of classification skill in moderating environmental influences on children's gender stereotyping: A study of the functional use of gender in the classroom. *Child Development, 66,* 1072–1087.

Bigler, R. S., Averhart, C. J., & Liben, L. S. (2003). Race and the workforce: Occupational status, aspirations, and stereotyping among African American children. *Developmental Psychology, 39,* 572–580.

Bigler, R. S., & Liben, L. S. (1993). A cognitive-developmental approach to racial stereotyping and reconstructive memory in Euro-American children. *Child Development, 64,* 1507–1518.

Bigler, R. S., & Liben, L. S. (2006). A developmental intergroup theory of social stereotypes and prejudice. In R. V. Kail (Ed.), *Advances in child development and behavior* (Vol. 34, pp. 39–89). San Diego, CA: Elsevier.

Bigler, R. S., & Liben, L. S. (2007). Developmental intergroup theory: Explaining and reducing children's social stereotyping and prejudice. *Current Directions in Psychological Science, 16,* 162–166.

Blair, I. V., Ma, J. E., & Lenton, A. P. (2001). Imagining stereotypes away: The moderation of implicit stereotypes though mental imagery. *Journal of Personality and Social Psychology, 81,* 828–841.

Blascovich, J., Wyer, N. A., Swart, L. A., & Kibler, J. L. (1997). Racism and social categorization. *Journal of Personality and Social Psychology, 72,* 1364–1372.

Bodenhausen, G. V. (1988). Stereotypic biases in decision making and memory: Testing process models of stereotype use. *Journal of Personality and Social Psychology, 55,* 726–737.

Bodenhausen, G. V. (2010). Diversity in the person, diversity in the group: Challenges of identity complexity for social perception and social interaction. *European Journal of Social Psychology, 40,* 1–16.

Bodenhausen, G. V., & Macrae, C. N. (1998). Stereotype activation and inhibition. In R. S. Wyer Jr. (Ed.), *Stereotype activation and inhibition: Advances in social cognition* (Vol. 11, pp. 1–52). Mahwah, NJ: Erlbaum.

Bodenhausen, G. V., Macrae, C. N., & Sherman, J. W. (1999). On the dialectics of discrimination: Dual processes in social stereotyping. In S. Chaiken & Y. Trope (Eds.), *Dual process theories in social psychology* (pp. 271–290). New York: Guilford Press.

Bodenhausen, G. V., Mussweiler, T., Gabriel, S., & Moreno, K. N. (2001). Affective influences on stereotyping and intergroup relations. In J. P. Forgas (Ed.), *Handbook of affect and social cognition* (pp. 319–343). Mahwah, NJ: Erlbaum.

Bodenhausen, G. V., & Peery, D. (2009). Social categorization and stereotyping in vivo: The VUCA challenge. *Social and Personality Psychology Compass, 3,* 133–151.

Bodenhausen, G. V., & Todd, A. R. (2010). Automatic aspects of judgment and decision making. In B. Gawronski & B. K. Payne (Eds.), *Handbook of implicit social cognition: Measurement, theory, and applications* (pp. 278–294). New York: Guilford Press.

Bodenhausen, G. V., Todd, A. R., & Richeson, J. A. (2009). Controlling prejudice and stereotyping: Antecedents, mechanisms, and contexts. In T. Nelson (Ed.), *Handbook of prejudice, stereotyping, and discrimination* (pp. 111–135). New York: Psychology Press.

Brewer, M. B. (1988). A dual process model of impression formation. In T. K. Srull & R. S. Wyer, Jr. (Eds.), *A dual process model of impression formation: Advances in social cognition* (Vol. 1, pp. 1–36). Hillsdale, NJ: Erlbaum.

Brewer, M. B., Dull, V., & Lui, L. (1981). Perceptions of the elderly: Stereotypes as prototypes. *Journal of Personality and Social Psychology, 41,* 656–670.

Bronfenbrenner, U., & Ceci, S. J. (1994). Nature–nurture reconceptualized in developmental perspective: A bioecological model. *Psychological Review, 101,* 568–586.

Brown, C. S., & Bigler, R. S. (2002). Effects of minority status in the classroom on children's intergroup attitudes. *Journal of Experimental Child Psychology, 83,* 77–110.

Brown, P. M., & Turner, J. C. (2002). The role of theories in the formation of stereotype content. In C. McGarty, V. Y. Yzerbyt, & R. Spears (Eds.), *Stereotypes as explanations: The formation of meaningful beliefs about social groups* (pp. 67–89). Cambridge, UK: Cambridge University Press.

Cameron, J. A., & Trope, Y. (2004). Stereotype-biased search and processing of information about group members. *Social Cognition, 22,* 650–672.

Castano, E., Yzerbyt, V., Bourguignon, D., & Seron, E. (2002). Who may enter? The impact of in-group identification on in-group/out-group categorization. *Journal of Experimental Social Psychology, 38,* 315–322.

Correll, J., Park, B., Judd, C. M., & Wittenbrink, B. (2007). The influence of stereotypes on decisions to shoot. *European Journal of Social Psychology, 37,* 1102–1117.

Crisp, R. J., & Hewstone, M. (2007). Multiple social categorization. In M. P. Zanna (Ed.), *Advances in experimental social psychology* (Vol. 39, pp. 163–254). Amsterdam: Elsevier.

Cuddy, A. J. C., Fiske, S. T., & Glick, P. (2007). The BIAS map: Behaviors from intergroup affect and stereotypes. *Journal of Personality and Social Psychology, 92*, 631–648.

Cuddy, A. J. C., Fiske, S. T., & Glick, P. (2008). Warmth and competence as universal dimensions of social perception: The stereotype content model and the BIAS map. *Advances in Experimental Social Psychology, 40*, 61–149.

Cuddy, A. J. C., Norton, M. I., & Fiske, S. T. (2005). This old stereotype: The pervasiveness and persistence of the elderly stereotype. *Journal of Social Issues, 61*, 267–285.

Dagenbach, D., & Carr, T. H. (Eds.) (1994). *Inhibitory processes in attention, memory, and language*. San Diego, CA: Academic Press.

Dar-Nimrod, I., & Heine, S. J. (2011). Genetic essentialism: On the deceptive determinism of DNA. *Psychological Bulletin, 137*, 800–818.

Darley, J., & Fazio, R. H. (1980). Expectancy confirmation processes arising in the social interaction sequence. *American Psychologist, 35*, 867–881.

Darley, J. M., & Gross, P. H. (1983). A hypothesis-confirming bias in labeling effects. *Journal of Personality and Social Psychology, 44*, 20–33.

Dasgupta, N., & Greenwald, A. G. (2001). On the malleability of automatic attitudes: Combating automatic prejudice with images of admired and disliked individuals. *Journal of Personality and Social Psychology, 81*, 800–814.

De Houwer, J., & Moors, A. (2010). Implicit measures: Similarities and differences. In B. Gawronski & B. K. Payne (Eds.), *Handbook of implicit social cognition: Measurement, theory, and applications* (pp. 176–193). New York: Guilford Press.

Devine, P. G. (1989). Stereotypes and prejudice: Their automatic and controlled components. *Journal of Personality and Social Psychology, 56*, 5–18.

Devine, P. G., Plant, E. A., Amodio, D. M., Harmon-Jones, E., & Vance, S. L. (2002). The regulation of explicit and implicit race bias: The role of motivations to respond without prejudice. *Journal of Personality and Social Psychology, 82*, 835–848.

Dovidio, J. F., Gaertner, S. L., & Saguy, T. (2009). Commonality and the complexity of "we": Social attitudes and social change. *Personality and Social Psychology Review, 13*, 3–20.

Dovidio, J. F., Kawakami, K., Johnson, C., Johnson, B., & Howard, A. (1997). The nature of prejudice: Automatic and controlled processes. *Journal of Experimental Social Psychology, 33*, 510–540.

Duckitt, J. (2009). Authoritarianism and dogmatism. In M. R. Leary & R. H. Hoyle (Eds.), *Handbook of individual differences in social behavior* (pp. 298–317). New York: Guilford Press.

Eagly, A. H., Wood, W., & Diekman, A. B. (2000). Social role theory of sex differences and similarities: A current appraisal. In T. Eckes & A. M. Trautner (Eds.), *The developmental psychology of gender* (pp. 123–174). Mahwah, NJ: Erlbaum.

Eberhardt, J. L., Dasgupta, N., & Banaszynski, T. L. (2003). Believing is seeing: The effects of racial labels and implicit beliefs on face perception. *Personality and Social Psychology Bulletin, 39*, 360–370.

Eberhardt, J. L., Davies, P. G., Purdie-Vaughns, V. J., & Johnson, S. L. (2006). Looking deathworthy: Perceived stereotypicality of Black defendants predicts capital-sentencing outcomes. *Psychological Science, 17*, 383–386.

Eichstedt, J. A., Serbin, L. A., Poulin-Dubois, D., & Sen, M. G. (2002). Of bears and men: Infants' knowledge of conventional and metaphorical gender stereotypes. *Infant Behavior and Development, 25*, 296–310.

Eitam, B., & Higgins, E. T. (2010). Motivation in mental accessibility: Relevance of a representation (ROAR) as a new framework. *Social and Personality Psychology Compass, 4*, 951–967.

Esses, V. M., Jackson, L. M., Dovidio, J. F., & Hodson, G. (2005). Instrumental relations among groups: Group competition, conflict, and prejudice. In J. F. Dovidio, P. Glick, & L. A. Rudman (Eds.), *On the nature of prejudice: Fifty years after Allport* (pp. 227–243). Malden, MA: Blackwell Press.

Fiske, S. T., Cuddy, A. J. C., Glick, P., & Xu, J. (2002). A model of (often mixed) stereotype content: Competence and warmth respectively follow from perceived status and competition. *Journal of Personality and Social Psychology, 82*, 878–902.

Fiske, S. T., & Neuberg, S. L. (1990). A continuum model of impression formation from category-based to individuation processes: Influences of information and motivation on attention and interpretation. In M. P. Zanna (Ed.), *Advances in experimental social psychology* (Vol. 23, pp. 1–74). New York: Academic Press.

Florack, A., Scarabis, M., & Bless, H. (2001). When do associations matter? The use of automatic associations toward ethnic groups in person judgments. *Journal of Experimental Social Psychology, 37*, 518–524.

Flynn, F. J. (2005). Having an open mind: The impact of openness to experience on interracial attitudes and impression formation. *Journal of Personality and Social Psychology, 88*, 816–826.

Freeman, J. B., Ambady, N., Rule, N. O., & Johnson, K. L. (2008). Will a category cue attract you? Motor output reveals dynamic competition across person construal. *Journal of Experimental Psychology: General, 137*, 673–690.

Freeman, J. B., Rule, N. O., Adams, R. B. Jr., & Ambady, N. (2010). The neural basis of categorical face perception: Graded representations of face gender in fusiform and orbitofrontal cortices. *Cerebral Cortex, 20*, 1314–1322.

Gawronski, B., & Bodenhausen, G. V. (2006). Associative and propositional processes in evaluation: An integrative review of implicit and explicit attitude change. *Psychological Bulletin, 132*, 692–731.

Gawronski, B., & Bodenhausen, G. V. (2011). The associative–propositional evaluation model: Theory, evidence, and open questions. *Advances in Experimental Social Psychology, 100*, 1027–1042.

Gawronski, B., Geschke, D., & Banse, R. (2003). Implicit bias in impression formation: Associations influence the construal of individuating information. *European Journal of Social Psychology*, *33*, 573–589.

Gawronski, B., Peters, K. R., Brochu, P. M., & Strack, F. (2008). Understanding the relations between different forms of racial prejudice: A cognitive consistency perspective. *Personality and Social Psychology Bulletin*, *34*, 648–665.

Gawronski, B., Rydell, R. J., Vervliet, B., & De Houwer, J. (2010). Generalization versus contextualization in automatic evaluation. *Journal of Experimental Psychology: General*, *139*, 683–701.

Gelman, S. A. (2003). *The essential child: Origins of essentialism in everyday thought*. New York: Oxford University Press.

Gilbert, S. F. (2005). Mechanisms for the environmental regulation of gene expression: Ecological aspects of animal development. *Journal of Biosciences*, *30*, 65–74.

Glick, P. (2005). Choice of scapegoats. In J. F. Dovidio, P. Glick, & L. Rudman (Eds.), *Reflecting on the nature of prejudice* (pp. 244–261). Malden, MA: Blackwell Press.

Govorun, O., & Payne, B. K. (2006). Ego-depletion and prejudice: Separating automatic and controlled components. *Social Cognition*, *24*, 111–136.

Hamilton, D. L., & Sherman, J. W. (1994). Stereotypes. In R. S. Wyer, Jr., & T. K. Srull (Eds.), *Handbook of social cognition* (2nd ed., Vol. 2, pp. 1–68). Hillsdale, NJ: Erlbaum.

Haslam, N., Rothschild, L., & Ernst, D. (2000). Essentialist beliefs about social categories. *British Journal of Social Psychology*, *39*, 113–127.

Hill, T., Lewicki, P., Czyzewska, M., & Boss, A. (1989). Self-perpetuating development of encoding biases in person perception. *Journal of Personality and Social Psychology*, *57*, 373–387.

Hofmann, W., Gschwendner, T., Castelli, L., & Schmitt, M. (2008). Implicit and explicit attitudes and interracial interaction: The moderating role of situationally available control resources. *Group Processes & Intergroup Relations*, *11*, 69–87.

Hogg, M. A. (2001). A social identity theory of leadership. *Personality and Social Psychology Review*, *5*, 184–200.

Hornsey, M. J. (2008). Social identity theory and self-categorization theory: A historical review. *Social and Personality Psychology Compass*, *2*, 204–222.

Hugenberg, K. & Bodenhausen, G. V. (2003). Facing prejudice: Implicit prejudice and the perception of facial threat. *Psychological Science*, *14*, 640–643.

Hugenberg, K., Young, S. G., Bernstein, M. J., & Sacco, D. F. (2010). The categorization–individuation model: An integrative account of the other-race recognition deficit. *Psychological Review*, *117*, 1168–1187.

Hutter, R. R. C., Crisp, R. J., Humphreys, G. W., Waters, G. M., & Moffitt, G. (2009). The dynamics of category conjunctions. *Group Processes & Intergroup Relations*, *12*, 673–686.

Ito, T. A., & Urland, G. R. (2003). Race and gender on the brain: Electrocortical measures of attention to the race and gender of multiply categorizable individuals. *Journal of Personality and Social Psychology*, *85*, 616–626.

Jaenisch, R., & Bird, A. (2003). Epigenetic regulation of gene expression: How the genome integrates intrinsic and environmental signals. *Nature Genetics*, *33*, 245–254.

Jost, J. T., Banaji, M. R., & Nosek, B. A. (2004). A decade of system justification theory: Accumulated evidence of conscious and unconscious bolstering of the status quo. *Political Psychology*, *25*, 881–919.

Judd, C. M., James-Hawkins, L., Yzerbyt, V. Y., & Kashima, Y. (2005). Fundamental dimensions of social judgment: Understanding the relations between judgments of competence and warmth. *Journal of Personality and Social Psychology*, *89*, 899–913.

Jussim, L., & Harber, K. D. (2005). Teacher expectations and self-fulfilling prophecies: Knowns and unknowns, resolved and unresolved controversies. *Personality and Social Psychology Review*, *9*, 131–155.

Kang, S. K., & Chasteen, A. L. (2009). Beyond the double-jeopardy hypothesis: Assessing emotion on the faces of multiply categorizable targets of prejudice. *Journal of Experimental Social Psychology*, *45*, 1281–1285.

Kang, S. K., Inzlicht, M., & Derks, B. (2010). Social neuroscience and public policy on intergroup relations: A Hegelian analysis. *Journal of Social Issues*, *66*, 585–601.

Katz, J. J. (1972). *Semantic theory*. New York: Harper & Row.

Keller, J. (2005). In genes we trust: The biological component of psychological essentialism and its relationship to mechanisms of motivated cognition. *Journal of Personality and Social Psychology*, *88*, 686–702.

Kruglanski, A. W., & Fishman, S. (2009). The need for cognitive closure. In M. R. Leary & R. H. Hoyle (Eds.), *Handbook of individual differences in social behavior* (pp. 343–353). New York: Guilford Press.

Kruglanski, A. W., & Freund, T. (1983). The freezing and unfreezing of lay-inferences: Effects on impressional primacy, ethnic stereotyping, and numerical anchoring. *Journal of Experimental Social Psychology*, *19*, 448–468.

Kunda, Z. (1990). The case for motivated reasoning. *Psychological Bulletin*, *108*, 480–498.

Kunda, Z., Miller, D. T., & Claire, T. (1990). Combining social concepts: The role of causal reasoning. *Cognitive Science*, *4*, 551–577.

Kunda, Z., & Oleson, K. C. (1997). When exceptions prove the rule: How extremity of deviance determines the impact of deviant examples on stereotypes. *Journal of Personality and Social Psychology*, *72*, 965–979.

Kunda, Z., & Sherman-Williams, B. (1993). Stereotypes and the construal of individuating information. *Personality and Social Psychology Bulletin*, *19*, 90–99.

Kunda, Z., & Spencer, S. J. (2003). When do stereotypes come to mind and when do they color judgment? A goal-based theoretical framework for stereotype activation and application. *Psychological Bulletin*, *129*, 522–544.

Lee, Y.-T., Jussim, L. J., & McCauley, C. R. (Eds.) (1995). *Stereotype accuracy: Toward appreciating group differences*. Washington, DC: American Psychological Association.

Leinbach, M. D., & Fagot, B. I. (1993). Categorical habituation to male and female faces: Gender schematic processing in infancy. *Infant Behavior and Development, 16*, 317–332.

Levy, G. (2010, July 22). He impersonated a human. *Haaretz*. Retrieved from http://www.haaretz.com/print-edition/opinion/he-impersonated-a-human-1.303359

Leyens, J. P., & Yzerbyt, V. Y. (1992). The ingroup overexclusion effect: Impact of valence and confirmation of stereotype information search. *European Journal of Social Psychology, 22*, 549–569.

Livingston, R. W., & Drwecki, B. B. (2007). Why are some individuals not racially biased? Susceptibility to affective conditioning predicts nonprejudice toward Blacks. *Psychological Science, 18*, 816–823.

MacLin, O. H., & Malpass, R. S. (2001). Racial categorization of faces: The ambiguous race face effect. *Psychology, Public Policy, and Law, 7*, 98–118.

Macrae, C. N., & Bodenhausen, G. V. (2000). Social cognition: Thinking categorically about others. *Annual Review of Psychology, 51*, 93–120.

Macrae, C. N., Bodenhausen, G. V., & Milne, A. B. (1995). The dissection of selection in social perception: Inhibitory processes in social stereotyping. *Journal of Personality and Social Psychology, 69*, 397–407.

Macrae, C. N., & Martin, D. (2007). A boy primed Sue: Feature-based processing and person construal. *European Journal of Social Psychology, 37*, 793–805.

Maddox, K. B. (2004). Perspectives on racial phenotypicality bias. *Personality and Social Psychology Review, 8*, 383–401.

Malpass, R. S., & Kravitz, J. (1969). Recognition for faces of own and other "race." *Journal of Personality and Social Psychology, 13*, 330–334.

Markman, A. B., & Wisniewski, E. J. (1997). Similar and different: The differentiation of the basic level. *Journal of Experimental Psychology: Learning, Memory, & Cognition, 23*, 54–70.

McGarty, C., Yzerbyt, V. Y., & Spears, R. (Eds.) (2002). *Stereotypes as explanations: The formation of meaningful beliefs about social groups*. Cambridge, UK: Cambridge University Press.

Medin, D. L., & Ortony, A. (1989). Psychological essentialism. In S. Vosniadou & A. Ortony (Eds.), *Similarity and analogical reasoning* (pp. 179–195). New York: Cambridge University Press.

Medin, D. L., & Schaffer, M. M. (1978). A context theory of classification learning. *Psychological Review, 85*, 207–238.

Meissner, C. A., & Brigham, J. C. (2001). Thirty years of investigating the own-race bias in memory for faces: A meta-analytic review. *Psychology, Public Policy, and Law, 7*, 3–35.

Migdal, M., Hewstone, M., & Mullen, B. (1998). The effects of crossed categorization in intergroup evaluations: A meta-analysis. *British Journal of Social Psychology, 37*, 303–324.

Miller, S. L., Maner, J. K., & Becker, D. V. (2010). Self-protective biases in group categorization: Threat cues shape the psychological boundary between "us" and "them." *Journal of Personality and Social Psychology, 99*, 62–77.

Mitchell, J. P., Nosek, B. A., & Banaji, M. R. (2003). Contextual variations in implicit evaluation. *Journal of Experimental Psychology: General, 132*, 455–469.

Monteith, M. J. (1993). Self-regulation of prejudiced responses: Implications for progress in prejudice-reduction efforts. *Journal of Personality and Social Psychology, 65*, 469–485.

Monteith, M. J., Ashburn-Nardo, L., Voils, C. I., & Czopp, A. M. (2002). Putting the breaks on prejudice: On the development and operation of cues for control. *Journal of Personality and Social Psychology, 83*, 1029–1050.

Moskowitz, G. B., Li, P., & Kirk, E. R. (2004). The implicit volition model: On the preconscious regulation of temporarily adopted goals. In M. P. Zanna (Ed.), *Advances in experimental social psychology* (Vol. 36, pp. 317–413). Amsterdam: Elsevier.

Murphy, G. L., & Medin, D. L. (1985). The role of theories in conceptual coherence. *Psychological Review, 92*, 289–316.

Nelson, L. J., & Miller, D. T. (1995). The distinctiveness effect in social categorization: You are what makes you unusual. *Psychological Science, 6*, 246–249.

Neuberg, S. L., & Fiske, S. T. (1987). Motivational influences on impression formation: Outcome dependency, accuracy-driven attention, and individuating processes. *Journal of Personality and Social Psychology, 53*, 431–444.

Oakes, P. J. (1987). The salience of social categories. In J. C. Turner, M. A. Hogg, P. J. Oakes, S. D. Reicher, & M. S. Wetherell (Eds.), *Rediscovering the social group* (pp. 117–141). Oxford, UK: Blackwell Press.

Patterson, M. M., & Bigler, R. S. (2006). Preschool children's attention to environmental messages about groups: Social categorization and the origins of intergroup bias. *Child Development, 77*, 847–860.

Pauker, K., Weisbuch, M., Ambady, N., Sommers, S. R., Adams, R. B. Jr., & Ivcevic, Z. (2009). Not so black and white: Memory for ambiguous group members. *Journal of Personality and Social Psychology, 96*, 795–810.

Payne, B. K. (2005). Conceptualizing control in social cognition: How executive functioning modulates the expression of automatic stereotyping. *Journal of Personality and Social Psychology, 89*, 488–503.

Peery, D., & Bodenhausen, G. V. (2008). Black + White = Black: Hypodescent in reflexive categorization of racially ambiguous faces. *Psychological Science, 19*, 973–977.

Pendry, L. F., & Macrae, C. N. (1994). Stereotypes and mental life: The case of the motivated but thwarted tactician. *Journal of Experimental Social Psychology, 30*, 303–325.

Pettigrew, T. F., Allport, G. W., & Barnett, E. O. (1958). Binocular resolution and perception of race in South Africa. *British Journal of Psychology, 49*, 265–278.

Phelan, J. E., & Rudman, L. A. (2010). Reactions to ethnic deviance: The role of backlash in racial stereotype maintenance. *Journal of Personality and Social Psychology*, *99*, 265–281.

Postmes, T., & Jetten, J. (Eds.) (2006). *Individuality and the group: Advances in social identity*. London: SAGE Publications.

Purdie-Vaughns, V., & Eibach, R. P. (2008). Intersectional invisibility: The distinct advantages and disadvantages of multiple subordinate-group identities. *Sex Roles, 59*, 377–391.

Quinn, P. C., Yahr, J., Kuhn, A., Slater, A. M., & Pascalis, O. (2002). Representation of the gender of human faces by infants: A preference for female. *Perception, 31*, 1109–1121.

Rehder, B., & Hastie, R. (2001). Causal knowledge and categories: The effects of causal beliefs on categorization, induction, and similarity. *Journal of Experimental Psychology: General, 130*, 323–360.

Richards, Z., & Hewstone, M. (2001). Subtyping and subgrouping: Processes for the prevention and promotion of stereotype change. *Personality and Social Psychology Review, 5*, 52–73.

Robinson, R. J., Keltner, D., Ward, A., & Ross, L. (1995). Actual versus assumed differences in construal: "Naïve realism" in intergroup perception and conflict. *Journal of Personality and Social Psychology, 68*, 404–417.

Rokeach, M. (1954). The nature and meaning of dogmatism. *Psychological Review, 61*, 194–204.

Rosch, E. (1978). Principles of categorization. In E. Rosch & B. B. Lloyd (Eds.), *Cognition and categorization* (pp. 27–48). Hillsdale, NJ: Erlbaum.

Rosch, E. H., Mervis, C. B., Gray, W. D., Johnson, D. M., & Boyes-Braem, P. (1976). Basic objects in natural categories. *Cognitive Psychology, 8*, 382–439.

Rothbart, M., Evans, M., & Fulero, S. (1979). Recall for confirming events: Memory processes and the maintenance of social stereotypes. *Journal of Experimental Social Psychology, 15*, 343–335.

Rothbart, M. & Taylor, M. (1992). Category labels and social reality: Do we view social categories as natural kinds? In G. R. Semin & K. Fiedler (Eds.), *Language, interaction, and social cognition* (pp. 11–36). London: Sage Publications.

Rutland, A. (1999). The development of national prejudice, in-group favouritism and self-stereotypes in British children. *British Journal of Social Psychology, 38*, 55–70.

Rutland, A. & Cinnirella, M. (2000). Context effects on Scottish national and European self-categorization: The importance of category accessibility, fragility, and relations. *British Journal of Social Psychology, 39*, 495–519.

Schneider, D. J. (2004). *The psychology of stereotyping*. New York: Guilford Press.

Seefeldt, C., Jantz, R. K., Galper, A., & Serock, K. (1977). Using pictures to explore children's attitudes toward the elderly. *The Gerontologist, 17*, 506–512.

Sherman, J. W. (1996). Development and mental representation of stereotypes. *Journal of Personality and Social Psychology, 70*, 1126–1141.

Sherman, J. W., Gawronski, B., Gonsalkorale, K., Hugenberg, K., Allen, T. J., & Groom, C. J. (2008). The self-regulation of automatic associations and behavioral impulses. *Psychological Review, 115*, 314–335.

Smith, E. E., & Medin, D. L. (1981). *Categories and concepts*. Cambridge, MA: Harvard University Press.

Smith, E. R., & Conrey, F. R. (2007). Mental representations are states, not things: Implications for implicit and explicit measurement. In B. Wittenbrink & N. Schwarz (Eds.), *Implicit measures of attitudes* (pp. 247–264). New York: Guilford Press.

Stangor, C., Lynch, L., Duan, C., & Glass, B. (1992). Categorization of individuals on the basis of multiple social features. *Journal of Personality and Social Psychology, 62*, 207–218.

Swim, J. K. (1994). Perceived versus meta-analytic effect sizes: An assessment of the accuracy of gender stereotypes. *Journal of Personality and Social Psychology, 70*, 1126–1141.

Tajfel, H. (1969). Cognitive aspects of prejudice. *Journal of Social Issues, 25*, 79–97.

Tajfel, H. (1982). Social psychology of intergroup relations. *Annual Review of Psychology, 33*, 1–39.

Tanaka, J. W., & Taylor, M. (1991). Object categories and expertise: Is the basic level in the eye of the beholder? *Cognitive Psychology, 23*, 457–482.

Todd, A. R., Bodenhausen, G. V., Richeson, J. A., & Galinsky, A. D. (in press). Perspective taking combats automatic expressions of racial bias. *Journal of Personality and Social Psychology*.

Turner, J. C., Hogg, M. A., Oakes, P. J., Reicher, S. D., & Wetherell, M. S. (1987). *Rediscovering the social group*. Oxford, UK: Blackwell Press.

Wegener, D. T., Clark, J. K., & Petty, R. E. (2006). Not all stereotyping is created equal: Differential consequences of thoughtful versus nonthoughtful stereotyping. *Journal of Personality and Social Psychology, 90*, 42–59.

Wegener, I., & Klauer, K. C. (2004). Inter-category versus intra-category fit: When social categories match social context. *European Journal of Social Psychology, 34*, 567–593.

Wenzel, M., Mummendey, A., & Waldzus, S. (2007). Superordinate identities and intergroup conflict: The ingroup projection model. *European Review of Social Psychology, 18*, 331–372.

Wiggins, J. S. (1991). Agency and communion as conceptual coordinates for the understanding and measurement of interpersonal behavior. In D. Cicchetti & W. Grove (Eds.), *Thinking clearly about psychology: Essays in honor of Paul Everett Meehl* (pp. 89–113). Minneapolis, MN: University of Minnesota Press.

Wittenbrink, B., Judd, C. M., & Park, B. (2001). Spontaneous prejudice in context: Variability in automatically activated attitudes. *Journal of Personality and Social Psychology, 81*, 815–827.

Yzerbyt, V., & Corneille, O. (2005). Cognitive process: Reality constraints and integrity concerns in social perception. In J. F. Dovidio, P. Glick, & L. A. Rudman (Eds.), *On the nature* of prejudice: Fifty years after Allport (pp. 175–191). Malden, MA: Blackwell Press.

Yzerbyt, V., & Kuppens, T. (2009). Group-based emotions: The social heart in the individual head. In S. Otten, K. Sassenberg, & T. Kessler (Eds.), *Intergroup relations: The role of motivation and emotion* (pp. 143–161). New York: Psychology Press.

Yzerbyt, V. Y., & Rocher, S. (2002). Subjective essentialism and the emergence of stereotypes. In C. McGarty, V. Y. Yzerbyt, & R. Spears (Eds.), *Stereotypes as explanations: The formation of meaningful beliefs about social groups* (pp. 38–66). Cambridge, UK: Cambridge University Press.

17

Self-Evaluation and Self-Knowledge

Jennifer S. Beer

Just as someone might reference Julia Child for a classic French recipe, most researchers reference William James when it comes to classic definitions of the self. In fact, the "Consciousness of the Self" is the longest chapter in the two volumes of *The Principles of Psychology* (James, 1890/1983). James talked about a number of themes that are still present in modern discussions of the self. But perhaps his most unique contribution can be illustrated with a simple example. Grasp your left wrist with your right hand. Simultaneously, you are the perceiver of the wrist – the way the skin and bones feel to touch – and you are the wrist that is perceived. The subjective (i.e., perceiver) and objective (i.e., perceived) nature of the self was central to James' definition. Therefore, in order to understand the self, we need to characterize the processes that contribute to the self as perceiver and perceived. For example, how does the perceiver self learn about the perceived self? Is there something special about the way we represent knowledge about ourselves? Do we dispassionately gather and represent self-knowledge or are these processes influenced by motivational states? And before James was a psychologist, he was a physiologist. So we might ask – What have we learned by examining more physiological aspects of the self? Decades of research have shed light on answers to these questions and, in the process, raised new questions. We learn about ourselves by drawing on both internal and external sources and take extra pains when representing this information. Research has identified a number of motivations that influence how we gather and represent self-knowledge; we are just beginning to understand how we

balance the relative influence of these various motivations. Neurobiological investigations of self-processes have also just begun and promise to be an informative complement to extant behavioral studies.

SELF: A DEFINITION

What is the self? The self consists of internal, external, and socially perceived attributes that are shaped by a number of factors, including culture, time, and motivation. According to William James (1890/1983), the self is defined by the material, social, and spiritual constituents of the perceived self as well as the perception of these constituents. Perhaps the most tangible aspect of the self is the material self. James argues that external attributes such as possessions and family are just as much material aspects of one's self as one's body (James, 1890/1983). In other words, the "material" of your self includes your physical presence but also the clothes you select, the material goods you buy, and the people you call family. The self is also constituted by how you represent yourself in your own mind as well as the less tangible representations in the minds of other people. In other words, the self is partially represented socially through the identity or reputation that you have in other people's eyes. The self is also represented by what James called "spiritual" aspects of the self, which includes internal attributes that researchers more recently might call personality, attitudes, and consciousness. In other words, the self is reflected by your physical presence as much as your reputation for lighting up a party or hiding by the wall, your preference for chocolate over vanilla, and your innermost thoughts and strivings. Since this classic definition, research has helped us understand how these aspects of self sometimes correspond to each other and sometimes do not. Furthermore, research has shown that the centrality of these aspects to the definition of selfhood is affected by culture, temporal construal, and motivation (e.g., Markus & Kitayama, 1991; Markus & Nurius, 1986; Sedikides & Gregg, 2008; Swann, Pelham, & Krull, 1989).

Correspondence between external, internal, and social representations of self

The external, internal, and social representations of self are related but not wholly redundant. People's personalities are related to the types of possessions they own, the clothes they wear, and even the material on their websites (Gosling, Ko, Mannarelli, & Morris, 2002). For example, there is a high correlation between the possessions and characteristics of someone's bedroom (i.e., external attributes), what someone says about their own personality (i.e., internal attributes), and what their friends say about that person's personality (i.e., the social self). A team of observers viewed the bedrooms of target individuals and then formed impressions of the target's personality based on these viewings. The impressions formed solely on the basis of the contents of the bedroom were then compared to self-reports provided by the target individual as well as reports provided by friends who knew the target well. The study found that observer report, self-reports, and friend reports agreed significantly on how much a target was extraverted, agreeable, open to new experiences, conscientious, and neurotic. Furthermore, it was shown that observers used bedroom contents to make their judgments of *conscientiousness* and *openness to new experience*. For example, observers rated targets as highly conscientious to the extent that their bedrooms were well lit, organized, and not cluttered with books or CDs. These same external attributes related to self-reported conscientiousness. Similarly, observers rated targets as highly open to new experiences to the extent that their bedrooms were distinctive among the bedrooms viewed and had a variety of diverse books and magazines. Again, these same external attributes correlated with self-reported openness to new experiences.

Another example of the relation between the self's internal attributes, external attributes, and social representations comes from research on the "beautiful is good" stereotype (e.g., Dion,

Berscheid, & Walster, 1972; Meier, Robinson, Carter, & Hinsz, 2010). People who are physically attractive are more likely to report desirable personality characteristics and observers use physical attractiveness to judge whether a person is likely to have a desirable personality. In the classic study, participants formed impressions of three target people based on their photographs (Dion, Berscheid, & Walster, 1972). They were then presented with a photograph of an unattractive target, an attractive target, and a target of average attractiveness. Compared to the other two targets, participants judged the attractive target to be more outgoing and sociable.

A recent study complements this research by showing that observers' tendency to use physical attractiveness to judge sociability is consistent with internal perceptions of sociability (Meier et al., 2010). Participants were asked to pose in impromptu photographs and provide self-reported personality ratings. Participants who rated themselves as more sociable (e.g., extraverted or agreeable) were perceived as most attractive by observers. These studies illustrate how external attributes such as possessions or physical appearance relate to internal attributes and affect how the self is represented in the minds of other people.

Differences between external, internal, and social representations of self

However, it is not the case that there is always high correlation between the self's external attributes, internal attributes, and social representations. This principle is illustrated by research examining the ways in which people erroneously make inferences about a target's internal attributes on the basis of the objects in their rooms or the objects they hold in their hand. In the bedroom study described above, observers sometimes used external attributes to judge the target's personality, yet these attributes were not related to what the target or their friends had to say about the target's personality (Gosling et al., 2002). For example, observers tended to associate colorful bedrooms with high levels of *agreeableness* and *conscientiousness*, yet targets who reported high levels of those traits were neither more nor less likely to have colorful bedrooms. Furthermore, stereotyping illustrates how social representations of the self may be driven by external attributes of the self that are not necessarily predictive of the internal attributes. For example, participants are more likely to assume an out-group member is holding a gun or is a threat when holding a gun compared to in-group members in the same context (e.g.,

Correll, Park, Judd, & Wittenbrink, 2002; Greenwald, Oakes, & Hoffman, 2003). These studies are just a few examples that illustrate how the self's external attributes (e.g., possessions, skin color) do not always relate to one's own representations or other's representations of the self (e.g., one's personality or aggression).

Culture and self-definition

External attributes, internal attributes, and social representations may also vary in their centrality or importance for defining the self. For example, culture may impact the extent to which people construe their family members or other social groups to be a part of the self. Cultures vary in their emphasis on the relatively independent or interdependent nature of self-construal (Markus & Kitayama, 1991). Independent self-construals emphasize definitions of self based on the external and internal attributes that distinguish an individual from other people. A person is "acting like themselves" as long as they are allowing their unique configuration of internal attributes to shape their appearance and actions. In contrast, interdependent self-construals emphasize defining the self as part of a larger social entity. In this way, interdependent self-construals emphasize the importance of family and other social groups (considered to be material aspects of the self by James, 1890/1983) as well as how the self is represented in other people's minds (considered to be the social self by James, 1890/1983). From this perspective, the self is largely driven by affiliation with social groups and taking into consideration how other people feel about the self. Self-expression may be less focused on emphasizing unique qualities and more about one's role within the group.

Research has shown that participants from cultures emphasizing independence or interdependence will complete repetitions of the sentence "I am…" in different ways (e.g., Bochner, 1994; Bond & Cheung, 1983). Participants from interdependent cultures are more likely to complete these sentences using social roles or social relationships. For example, they may complete the sentences by noting that they are a father, a son, and a brother. In contrast, participants from independent cultures are more likely to complete these sentences by emphasizing their idiosyncratic personality characteristics. For example, they may complete the sentences by noting that they are intelligent, strong, and talented. This research illustrates how culture can influence how much the material, social, and internal aspects are considered to be central or important in self-definition.

Temporal construal and the self

Recent research additionally suggests that we represent our innermost thoughts and strivings not only as they currently are but also as they have been and how they might be in the future (e.g., Bartels & Rips, 2010; Markus & Nurius, 1986; Trope & Liberman, 2010; Wilson & Gilbert, 2005). And temporal construals affect how we perceive our preferences. If given a choice between earning a smaller amount of money today compared to a larger amount in a year, people need the delayed payoff to be considerably larger to justify having to wait. Similarly, people estimate that they will choose to drink significantly less of an unpleasant liquid to advance scientific knowledge if the drinking will occur today compared to 3 months from now (Pronin, Olivola, & Kennedy, 2008). Why do we make different choices for ourselves depending on whether it has consequences for now or the future? One theory is that we identify more closely with our selves in the present and, therefore, we prefer to acquire benefits and avoid costs for our current selves in comparison to our future selves (Parfit, 1984). In support of this theory, a series of studies found that the more people expected their personality to change in the future, the more they wanted to receive $100 before that change occurred (Bartels & Rips, 2010). These studies illustrate that we believe the perceived self has the potential to change over time.

Summary

James argued that the self is equally defined by its constituents (i.e., the perceived) and by the perception of those constituents (i.e., the perceiver). The self consists not only of our external attributes but also how those external attributes and less tangible internal attributes are represented in our minds and the minds of other people (i.e., our social reputation). Sometimes these aspects of self are predictably related to one another, but sometimes they are not. Culture affects how much we favor different aspects when defining the self and temporal construal affects our perception of the contents of the perceived self.

COSTS AND BENEFITS OF HAVING A SELF

As this chapter will illustrate, a number of cognitive, affective, and physiological resources are devoted to maintaining a sense of self. Is this resource expenditure worth it? What do we gain by having a sense of self and do we lose anything? A historical account of the evolution of self-definition highlights that there are both costs and benefits to possessing a sense of self (Baumeister, 1987). A sense of self can be advantageous because it gives us a reference point for organizing the large amount of incoming information from our daily lives (Turk et al., 2003), gives us a sense of agency (Haggard & Tskairis, 2009; Wegner, 2003), and allows for higher-order cognitive processing such as planning, goal setting, and perspective taking (Leary, Estrada, & Allen, 2009). We feel that we are the agents of our behavior and our accountability may motivate us to plan our behavior to make sure it fits with our goals. The dialogue we have with our "selves" allows us to consider what we will do and what it will help us accomplish (Leary, Estrada, & Allen, 2009). Additionally, our internal dialogue may help us understand the perspective of other people (Leary, Estrada, & Allen, 2009). We do not have access to other people's internal experiences and we may use our own experience to try to simulate what someone might be feeling or thinking. The ability to take the perspective of other people is beneficial for a number of social outcomes, including self-regulation and moral judgment (Eisenberg, 2010).

On the other hand, as this chapter will illustrate, our sense of self may lead to costly outcomes. For example, we may underestimate or overestimate ourselves and set ourselves up to fail. People underestimate their ability to cope with negative emotional events and may choose to avoid situations or relationships on the basis of that incorrect sense of the self's capabilities (Eastwick, Finkel, Krishnamurti, & Loewenstein, 2008; Wilson & Gilbert, 2005). Overestimation can lead to trouble as well; overconfidently predicting academic success can lead to disengagement from college (Robins & Beer, 2001). In summary, having a sense of self opens up opportunities for sophisticated cognitive processing and self-regulation but may paradoxically undermine these efforts when self-evaluation diverges too much from reality.

PROCESSES OF SELF-EVALUATION

What are the ways in which we evaluate our external attributes, internal attributes, and social representations? Many different theories have been proposed and they are not mutually exclusive because it is likely that we use several different avenues for gaining self-knowledge. Take the example of picking out a melon at the grocery store. Nothing is better than a ripe melon, but with that thick rind making it difficult to see the insides, it can sometimes feel like it is anyone's guess as to which melon is a good choice. So how do you evaluate a melon? Do you pick one up and observe its features to assess whether it appears fresh (smells like a melon, free from blemishes, heavy for its weight)? You could also refer to the people around you. You could ask someone their opinion or look to see how your melon compares to the melons selected by nearby shoppers. A glance at the research shows that all of these strategies are also useful for gaining self-knowledge and some are more useful for particular situations than others.

Self-perception theory

From the perspective of *self-perception theory* (Bem, 1967, 1972), we get to know ourselves in much the same way we get to know others. Just as we might observe someone's action to make inferences about their desires, we may try to understand our attitudes by observing our own behavior. In Jamesian terms, self-perception theory posits that the perceiver self learns about internal attributes by observing external aspects of the perceived self. Research supports the hypothesis that self-knowledge can be derived from behavior (Festinger, 1957; Festinger & Carlsmith, 1959; Nisbett & Wilson, 1977), but people perceive their internal thoughts and feelings to be more diagnostic of themselves than long-term observation of their overt behavior (Andersen & Ross, 1984). For example, one study required participants to rate how much someone else could learn about them from a sample of their thoughts and feelings compared to a sample of their overt behaviors. Participants rated both sources of information to be at least somewhat informative, but the sample of thoughts and feelings was rated as significantly more informative than a sample of overt behavior (Andersen & Ross, 1984).

More recently, research along these lines has moved away from investigating the relative importance of behavioral observation or introspection for gaining self-knowledge. Instead, research has investigated the differences and similarities between the a priori theories and deductive reasoning used to explain one's own behavior and other's people's behavior. Some research has found evidence of differences (e.g., Jones & Nisbett, 1971; Pronin, Lin, & Ross, 2002). In the study mentioned above, participants felt that long-term observation of overt behavior would likely be more informative about another person than it would about themselves (Andersen & Ross, 1984). On the other hand, the way we explain our own behavior is often similar to the way we make sense of other people's behavior (e.g., Knee,

Patrick, & Lonsbary, 2003; Malle, 2006; Nisbett & Wilson, 1977; Plaks, Levy, & Dweck, 2009; Taylor & Koivumaki, 1976). For example, it was originally hypothesized that people considered situational factors much more when explaining their own behavior compared to another person's behavior (Jones & Nisbett, 1971). In other words, if I asked you why you did not hold the door open for a stranger, you would likely look for something special about that particular instance to explain your behavior (e.g., you did not want to be late to meet someone waiting on you). However, if I asked you why someone else failed to hold the door open, you would be more likely to attribute their behavior to something about their disposition (e.g., they are an inconsiderate person). A recent meta-analysis has shown that these differences are not as robust as previously thought (Malle, 2006); people are only likely to make dramatically different attributions in circumstances where information suggests real differences between the self and other people.

The looking-glass self

Self-perception theory explains one way we can evaluate the self in the absence of other people. Yet most of our lives are spent in social settings; so it is reasonable to wonder whether other people play a role in how we come to know ourselves. From the perspective of the "*looking-glass self*," one way that people help us learn about ourselves is by communicating what they see in us. Other people act as looking glasses: i.e., mirrors in which we can observe ourselves. Rather than observing ourselves directly as in self-perception theory, we observe what other people see in us. From this perspective, people are theorized to imagine how they must appear to other people (i.e., reflected appraisals) and internalize those imagined judgments (e.g., Cooley, 1902; Mead, 1934).

Research has shown that people are more likely to incorporate behaviors into their self-view if they believe the behaviors are observed by another person. In one study, participants were told that they would serve as test cases for graduate students training in clinical observation (Tice, 1992). Participants were told to present themselves as emotionally stable, emotionally unstable, or as possessing a task-irrelevant attribute (i.e., athletic). Participants were then randomly assigned to a condition in which they believed that they were either interacting with a graduate student who could see them through a one-way mirror or being recorded so a graduate student could listen to the responses at another time. A telecom was provided and participants responded to a series

of questions which gave them the opportunity to present themselves as instructed. Afterwards, participants were asked if they could do the experimenter a favor and fill out some questionnaires that were presumably unrelated to the first task. The questionnaires included a self-assessment of emotional stability. The study found that participants were most likely to rate themselves in line with the behavior they had portrayed when they believed they had done so while being watched. In other words, participants rated themselves as more emotionally stable when they had portrayed emotional stability in the condition where they believed they were observed than when they thought someone would listen to their responses at a later time. Similarly, ratings of emotional instability were higher when participants believed they had been observed while portraying emotional instability. A follow-up study found that these effects generalize to public compared to private portrayals of other personality characteristics such as *extraversion* (Tice, 1992). This study illustrates that strong cues to imagine how you are being perceived by another person can affect your perception of your personality.

The looking-glass self also implies that your self-evaluations should be consistent with how other people perceive you and that you should be aware of how you are perceived by others. Although the research is correlational in nature, a large body of work has shown a high level of agreement between how someone perceives themselves and how they are perceived by others, at least on certain dimensions (e.g., Albright, Kenny, & Malloy, 1988; Ambady & Rosenthal, 1992; Gosling et al., 2002; Marcus & Miller, 2003; Norman & Goldberg, 1966). For example, students on the first day of class were assigned to groups and physical attractiveness ratings were collected using a round-robin design (Marcus & Miller, 2003). Not only did each group member rate themselves and all other group members on attractiveness but also they reported how their attractiveness was perceived by each group member. The findings show that people's attractiveness ratings are correlated with how other people see them and that people are aware of how they are seen by others in terms of physical attractiveness. Perhaps this is not that surprising. After all, physical attractiveness is somewhat defined by whether other people agree that you are desirable. However, similar results are found for other dimensions of the self. Another study asked students on the first day of class to rate their own personality and the personalities of the other students in the class. When students agreed that someone appeared friendly, that person tended to rate themselves as friendly (Norman &

Goldberg, 1966). Finally, similar neural systems support making self-judgments and imagining how one is perceived by other people (Ochsner et al., 2005; Pfeifer et al., 2009). The neural commonality between these processes suggests that they share at least some of the same psychological mechanisms. Taken together, this research illustrates a close relationship between self-perceptions and how the self is perceived by other people.

More recently, researchers have taken the looking-glass self perspective a step further and suggested that a fundamental function of self-worth is to signal one's social acceptance by other people (e.g., the sociometer hypothesis: Leary, Tambor, Terdal, & Downs, 1995). In other words, rather than having to imagine how other people see the self, self-esteem functions to quickly signal the degree to which the self is positively (or negatively) viewed by others.

Research has shown that self-esteem is multiply determined, both by how others actually feel about the self and perceptions of other people's regard. For example, one study examined how the relation between self-perceptions, other people's perceptions of the self, and perceived social acceptance unfolded over time (Srivastava & Beer, 2005). Participants were randomly assigned to groups and met once a week for 4 weeks to perform various group tasks. Participants rated themselves, their group members, and how they believed they were perceived by their group members on various attributes. The more participants were rated as likeable by their group members in the first group meeting, the more their self-perceptions rose in subsequent weeks. However, this effect was independent of the effect of perceived regard on self-perceptions. In other words, self-perceptions of likeability appear to increase when the self is well-received by other people, but this effect is not wholly accounted for by awareness of how the self is received by others. It is important to note that this study also examined the opposite possibility: i.e., whether people broadcast aspects of themselves that then influence how they are perceived by other people. However, no significant effects were found for initial self-perceptions predicting other-perceptions in later meetings. When considered in relation to the correlational nature of the research demonstrating agreement between the self and others, this study suggests that those correlations may indeed reflect self-perceptions that are influenced by reflected appraisals. In Jamesian terms, the looking-glass self perspective suggests that the perceiver self uses the observations of other people to learn about the perceived self.

Social comparison theory

So far, we have considered our ability to draw on our own observations and other people's observations to learn about the self. A third perspective, *social comparison theory*, states that people learn about themselves by using other people as a referent point for self-evaluation (Festinger, 1954; Goethals & Darley, 1977; Kruglanski & Mayseless, 1990; Mussweiler & Rueter, 2003). From a Jamesian perspective, social comparison theory suggests that the perceiver self learns about the perceived self by comparing it to other people. For example, if you want to get a sense of your athleticism, you might compare your athletic ability to the athletic ability you see in your peers.

We are particularly likely to draw on social-comparative information when we are uncertain about how to evaluate ourselves (see Kruglanski & Mayseless, 1990). However, there is evidence that, regardless of intent, we make social-comparative judgments (Gilbert, Giesler, & Morris, 1995; Stapel & Blanton, 2004) and, in fact, identify people who are a part of our everyday lives that can serve as relatively chronic reference points (Mussweiler & Rueter, 2003). Research has shown that it takes effort to discount social-comparative information even when you are aware that it is not relevant for self-evaluation. For example, one study found that participants under mental load were unable to prevent themselves from referencing the performance of another person even when it was clearly not relevant for self-evaluation (Gilbert, Giesler, & Morris, 1995). Participants viewed a videotape of a confederate performing a personality impression task. Participants were told that the confederate's task performance was due to external factors. Specifically, if they had viewed a confederate who had done well, they were told that the confederate was doing the task for a second time. If the confederate had done poorly, they were told that the confederate had been given misleading information about how to perform the task. Afterwards, each participant then performed the same personality impression task they had just viewed. Then participants had to rate their competence at the task while maintaining an 8-digit number in their minds (or not). For participants who were not under mental load, their own competence was not affected by whether the confederate had done well or poorly on the task. However, participants in the mental load condition tended to rate themselves as though the confederate were an appropriate benchmark for average performance on the task. Even though they were told that the confederate had advantages they did not have, self-competence was lower when the confederate had done well rather than poorly.

These results suggest that we automatically want to use salient social targets as referents for self-evaluation and that it takes extra cognitive resources to discount them.

Furthermore, recent research suggests that for the sake of efficiency, social comparisons may involve a referent that has been repeatedly useful in the past even if it is not optimal for a particular comparison. We may repeatedly compare ourselves to our friends such that we eventually tend to use them as a routine referent in our social-comparative judgments. In a series of studies, researchers found that self-evaluation and information about a friend tend to facilitate one another (Mussweiler & Rueter, 2003). Participants were faster at recognizing the name of their best friend after making a self-evaluation judgment of a personality trait (when compared to making a personality trait judgment for a celebrity). Furthermore, participants were also faster at judging the personality of their friend after making a self-evaluation judgment of personality trait (when compared to making a personality trait judgment for a celebrity). Importantly, these results held even when the self and best friend did not share the personality characteristic. Taken together, these studies illustrate people's inclination to make social comparisons, and that certain people become such routine referents that probing for self-evaluation increases accessibility of information about those other people.

In summary, people gain knowledge about themselves in myriad ways. They may observe their own behavior much in the way they would observe someone else's behavior to make inferences about their internal states. Additionally, other people play a role in our self-evaluation processes. We may learn about ourselves or be particularly likely to internalize our behavior when we consider the perspective of an external observer. We also learn about ourselves by comparing ourselves to other people. In particular, social comparisons appear to be a particular automatic way in which people gain knowledge about themselves.

COGNITIVE REPRESENTATIONS OF THE SELF

The self is multifaceted, and people use different strategies to gain knowledge about these facets. Once we have acquired information about the self, how do we represent it? Could we answer this question with a survey of the basic principles of knowledge representation? Or does the perceiver self operate on the perceived self in unique ways (see Keenan & Baillet, 1980; Kihlstrom & Cantor, 1984)? While self-knowledge does not draw on

dramatically different principles, it does showcase the effect of intimacy and frequency on knowledge representation. Research on the representations of self-knowledge suggests that they are particularly elaborate and well-organized. Two examples illustrate the unique ways in which we create and access representations of self-information: the self-reference effect and the relation of episodic memory to person judgment.

The self-referent effect

Are you talented, personable, and happy? Is the president jovial, agreeable, and tidy? Which of these words has more than two syllables: conscientious, intellectual, friendly? Say that you answered all of these questions and 10 minutes later, you had to recall the words you judged. Research has shown that there will be a self-reference effect on your memory. That is, you are much more likely to remember the words you judged in relation to yourself than to other social targets such as political figures or low-level characteristics such as syllabic structure (e.g., Kelley et al., 2002; Markus, 1977; Ochsner et al., 2005; Rogers, Kuiper, & Kirker, 1977). Why is information encoded in relation to the self remembered so much better? Does the self engage a unique cognitive process or is it better understood as an extreme of the factors known to promote memory?

A basic principle of cognition is that people organize and guide knowledge using schemas (e.g., Bartlett, 1932; Neisser, 1967; Taylor & Crocker, 1981) and self-knowledge is no exception (Markus, 1977). From this perspective, the knowledge gained by observing the self, imagining other people's perspectives, and social comparison is organized into a schema devoted to information about the self. Self-schemas tend to include information about the self that we deem important or centrally descriptive of the self (Markus, 1977). Schemas organize the information we currently hold and, furthermore, they influence how we process schema-relevant information that we subsequently encounter (e.g., Baldwin, 1992; Markus, Hamill, & Sentis, 1987; Taylor & Crocker, 1981). The self-referent effect is considered to be one more example of schematic influences on information-processing.

Both the elaborative and organizational properties of self-schemas have been implicated in promoting memory for self-referent information (e.g., Ingram, Smith, & Brehm, 1983; Klein & Kihlstrom, 1986; Rogers, Kuiper & Kircher, 1977; Symons & Johnson, 1997). Self-schemata affect how much information is elaborated during encoding. Information that is more extensively elaborated tends to be better remembered (Craik & Tulving, 1975). Given that information judged in relation to the self is better remembered, researchers theorize that the self-schema is especially well-developed compared to other schemas (e.g., Markus, 1977; Rogers, Kuiper, & Kircher, 1977). The rich nature of the self-schema creates myriad opportunities to elaborate on the information being encoded. For example, if I ask you to judge whether you are talented, any number of self-associations may be triggered. Encoding the word "talented" becomes more elaborate to the extent that the meaning of "talent" is analyzed in relation to diverse pre-existing self-information. However, if I ask you if the word "talented" has two syllables, then it is not likely to be processed in terms of its meaning, let alone in a diverse manner. Instead, its pronunciation may be briefly analyzed to assess its syllabic content.

In addition to their promotion of elaboration, self-schemas may be used to organize information (Klein & Kihstrom, 1986; Symons & Johnson, 1997) and organization of information promotes memory (Bower, Clark, Lesgold, & Winzenz, 1969). For example, say I ask you to remember the list: ball, carrot, wrench, glove, pea, and hammer. You will find it easier to remember the words if you organize them into three categories: sports equipment; vegetables; and tools (Bower et al., 1969). Researchers suggest that judging information in relation to self organizes the information into categories (e.g., "me" and "not me"). For example, one study asked people to judge one list of words describing body parts in relation to the self ("Can you think of an incident in which you had an injury or illness associated with your neck?") and to categorize another list of words describing body parts on their internal or external nature (Klein & Kihlstrom, 1986). In contrast to the typical superiority of memory for information in a self-reference condition, memory for the words was not significantly different across the two conditions. In other words, the memory advantage for words encoded in relation to the self is similar to words encoded in relation to organizational cues (e.g., categories of internal and external body parts). These studies suggest that we take extra pains when representing the information we gather about ourselves. Of all of the schematic representations created by the perceiver self (the perceiver), the perceived self (i.e., the perceived) is represented through especially elaborate and well-organized schemas.

The role of abstract and episodic information in self-judgment

Beyond representation, is there anything unique about the relation between the perceiver self and the perceived self? Research suggests that we often make judgments about the self using different aspects of knowledge than we use for making judgments about other people (e.g., Klein, Babey, & Sherman, 1997; Klein, Loftus, & Burton, 1989). For example, if I ask you to decide whether the president is artistic, you are likely to form your judgment by searching through your memory for instances that confirm or dispute the president's artistic talent. But if I ask you to decide whether you are artistic, your answer is not likely to involve a search through autobiographical memories.

Why the difference? Over time, we may create summaries or abstractions of episodic information about ourselves but are less likely to do that for others (Klein, Loftus, Trafton, & Fuhrman, 1992). When judging ourselves, we do not rely on autobiographical memories, so it is likely that we access summaries to draw conclusions about ourselves (e.g., Klein, Babey, & Sherman, 1997; Klein, Loftus, & Burton, 1989). For example, self-description judgments are not facilitated by recalling episodic information about the self: i.e., autobiographical memories. In one study, participants were asked to judge personality trait words for their self-descriptiveness (Klein, Loftus, & Burton, 1989). However, before they made each judgment, the participants performed one of three tasks. They generated a definition of the personality trait word, remembered a time they exhibited the personality trait, or made a self-descriptive judgment. If we make self-descriptive judgments by computing our answers from autobiographical memories, then participants should have been faster when making a self-descriptive judgment after recalling an autobiographical memory than after generating a definition of the trait word. However, that is not what the study found. Instead, participants were equally quick to make self-descriptive judgments when generating a trait definition or when recalling an autobiographical memory. Furthermore, when participants performed one of the above tasks before being asking to recall an autobiographical memory, they were no quicker to do so after recalling an autobiographical memory than generating a semantic definition (Klein, Loftus, & Burton, 1989). These studies show that the processes involved in self-description judgments and retrieving autobiographical memories are not redundant.

It is likely that the lack of reliance on autobiographical memory reflects our chronic experience of ourselves across time and situations. In fact, personality judgments of the self in new contexts do rely on autobiographical memories. For example, one study asked participants to perform the tasks above in relation to contexts in which they had either long-term or short-term experiences (Klein et al., 1992). Specifically, participants were asked to recall memories and make self-description judgments in relation to the way they acted at home with their families or in relation to the way they acted in college. All participants had only about 3 months of experience with their college environments (compared to 18 years of experience in the family environment). The results for judgments made in relation to home matched the results described above: autobiographical recall did not significantly facilitate self-description judgment. However, recalling autobiographical instances from time spent at college did facilitate self-description judgments in the college context. In some sense, these findings are consistent with self-perception theory which emphasizes that we learn about ourselves by observing our behavior. The research on autobiographical memory's facilitative effect on self-description suggests that this theory is particularly relevant for forming impressions of the self in new contexts. Finally, making personality judgments without relying on episodic memory may be mostly unique to the self. For the most part, retrieving episodic memories about one's mother will facilitate personality judgments of her (Klein et al., 1992).

Taken together, the research on the self-referent effect and the role of memory retrieval in self-judgment illustrates unique ways in which the perceiver self operates on the perceived self. In comparison to other kinds of knowledge, we represent knowledge about ourselves in particularly elaborate and well-organized ways. The rich nature of self-knowledge also has implications for how we make self-description judgments. Our experience with ourselves may create abstract representations culled from repeated experiences and, therefore, self-description judgments often do not necessitate the retrieval of autobiographical memories.

MOTIVATION AND SELF-KNOWLEDGE

Are the social-cognitive aspects of the self fully captured by an understanding of how we learn about ourselves and how we represent that knowledge? Not quite. A central theme in diverse disciplines such as psychology, philosophy, and economics is that we are rarely dispassionate when it comes to self-processes. When we evaluate ourselves by observing our behavior, comparing ourselves to other people, or imagining what they think of us, do we passively take in all self-information regardless of whether it is good or bad? If not, what kinds of motivations influence the way we conduct self-evaluation processes and use self-knowledge? Is one motivation more predominant than others? How pervasive are motivational influences: Are there any circumstances in which we tend to remain dispassionate

when evaluating ourselves? These are the kinds of questions that organize a large body of literature on self-perception motives. To date, this research has consistently found evidence for at least three broad motivations that influence self-perception processes and the predominance of their relative influence depends on a number of factors (e.g., Anderson et al., 2006; Kwang & Swann, 2010; Sedikides & Gregg, 2008; Swann, Pelham, & Krull, 1989; Taylor & Brown, 1988; Trope, 1980).

Self-enhancement

Self-enhancement is one motivation that influences self-evaluation processes and cognitive representations of the self (e.g., Alicke et al., 1995; Paulhus, Graf, & van Selst, 1989; Sedikides & Gregg, 2008; Taylor & Brown, 1988). Self-enhancement is the motivation to view the self in a positive manner presumably as a means of protecting self-esteem. A large body of research has shown that people often evaluate themselves in a positively skewed manner: they claim to have more positive traits than negative traits, believe they have done better on a task than indicated by their actual performance, rate themselves as having more desirable personalities than their peers, and attribute their failures to circumstance rather than essential qualities of the self (e.g., Alicke et al., 1995; Beer & Hughes, 2010; Jones & Nisbett, 1971; Klayman et al., 1999; Robins & Beer, 2001; Sedikides & Gregg, 2008; Taylor & Brown, 1988; Taylor & Koivumaki, 1976).

Researchers theorize that such unrealistically positive perceptions of the self are perhaps best explained by the motivation to maintain or inflate self-worth (Sedikides & Gregg, 2008; Taylor & Brown, 1988; but see Chambers & Windschitl, 2004). We want to see ourselves in a positive light and we can accomplish this by influencing what we observe about ourselves, how we compute social comparisons, and imagine how others see us. For example, we can prioritize attention to flattering information about the self or choose to compare the self to people who are worse off. Research has shown that people's positive qualities tend to spring to mind before their negative qualities. They automatically assume they have significantly more positive qualities and fewer negative qualities than other people (e.g., Beer & Hughes, 2010; Paulhus, Graf, & Van Selst, 1989) and select interaction partners who provide positive feedback (Swann, Hixon, Stein-Seroussi, & Gilbert, 1990). Furthermore, people engage in a number of cognitive operations to ensure that they come out favorably when comparing themselves to others. For example, people may idiosyncratically define a personality trait so that they seem exceptional when compared to others (Alicke et al., 1995; Dunning, Meyerowitz, & Holzberg, 1989). If you want to see yourself as a good cook compared to your friends, you can define a good cook as someone who excels at things you can do (e.g., never burn the food) but downplay the importance of things that you do not do (e.g., developing unique recipes). Additionally, people can enhance their self-worth by comparing themselves to people who are worse off (e.g., Kruglankski & Mayseless, 1990). For example, students in a medical training program chose more often to compare themselves to peers with poorer performance when they wanted to ensure positive self-appraisals of their own performance (Buunk, Cohen-Schotanus, & van Nek, 2007). These studies suggest that positive information in self-schemas is more easily accessible than negative information.

In summary, self-enhancement motivation may create lopsided representation or greater elaboration of positive information about the self (compared to negative information about the self). We may evaluate ourselves by observing our behavior or imagining what others think of us, but we do not do this dispassionately. Instead, there is evidence that we ensure positive self-views by focusing on the positive aspects of our behavior and the good things that people have to say about us. Additionally, we ensure positive self-views by comparing ourselves on dimensions or to people that emphasize our positive qualities.

Self-verification

We do not always want to enhance our self-view; evidence indicates that we also strive for self-verification (e.g., Kwang & Swann, 2010; Swann, Pelham, & Krull, 1989). Self-verification theory posits that people want to confirm their current conceptions of themselves. From this perspective, people use their self-view to make sense of the world. To the extent that self-views are consistent and predictable, people are able to feel that the world is predictable and coherent, which gives them a sense of control.

At first blush, it may seem like it would be difficult to disentangle the effects of self-enhancement and self-verification motivations on self-evaluations. Most people have moderate to high levels of self-esteem (e.g., Gray-Little, Williams, & Hancock, 1997), so verification of these views would result in evaluations that are positive in nature. The difference between the two theories is most evident for individuals with low self-esteem. If people are striving to verify their self-view, then people with low self-esteem should not exhibit the positively

slanted self-evaluations mentioned above. Indeed, a large body of literature has shown that people with low self-esteem perpetuate their negative self-views by seeking information and environments that reinforce currently held self-views (see Kwang & Swann, 2010). For example, people find it easier to remember information that is consistent with their self-view. In one study, participants who varied in self-esteem were given false feedback about the desirability of their personality (Story, 1998). Participants were much better at recalling the content of the feedback if it matched their own self-views. In other words, participants with low self-esteem found it easier to remember details of their feedback if it indicated they had undesirable personalities.

Furthermore, even people with high self-esteem admit to having flaws, and they will choose interaction partners that confirm these flaws (Swann, Pelham, & Krull, 1989). Participants were pre-screened to have extremely positive self-views of certain personality attributes and negative self-views of other personality attributes. Participants were then told that their personalities had been ostensibly evaluated by three confederates and asked to rate their preference for interacting further with each of the confederates. The evaluation feedback was bogus and varied in how much it verified either positive or negative aspects of self-ratings of personality. Regardless of whether participants had high or low self-esteem, they preferred to interact with people they believed to share their perceptions of both their positive and negative attributes. These studies illustrate our ability to seek and recall information that reinforces current self-views, even when they are negative. We sometimes focus our self-observations on information that reinforces our current self-views and ensure that our imagined evaluations by others come from people who will confirm our current self-views.

Self-assessment

We wondered earlier whether we could be dispassionate when gathering information about ourselves. In addition to striving toward enhancement or verification, there is also evidence that there are times that people do gather information about themselves in order to gain accurate self-knowledge (e.g., Trope, 1986). The benefit of realistic self-assessment is that it helps people understand their capabilities and how to improve on them (this latter benefit is sometimes referred to as self-improvement motivation and treated independently from the motivation to understand the current self: e.g., Taylor, Neter, & Wayment, 1995). Research on self-assessment motivation has shown that, when given a choice, we prefer feedback compared to no feedback about ourselves (e.g., Dunning, 1995). Our interest in the feedback increases in relation to its objective diagnostic value (Trope, 1975), even when we are aware it may hurt our self-esteem (Trope, 1980). For example, in one study, participants' achievement motivations were measured and several weeks later they completed a battery of six tests that varied in difficulty (Trope, 1975). Participants were then told how much each test had the potential to accurately assess their abilities. When rating their preferences for feedback, participants were most interested in feedback from tests that were presented as highly diagnostic and this was especially true for participants with high achievement motivation. Furthermore, test difficulty did not impact interest in feedback. Research on self-assessment demonstrates our interest in gathering feedback, even when it may not enhance or verify current self-views. From this perspective, a relatively non-defensive curiosity about the self governs at least some of the data gathering and cognitive representation associated with self-evaluation.

Relative influence of each motivation

Self-evaluation processes appear to be pushed around by several different motivations. How should we conceptualize the relative influence of different motivations? Is one predominant over the others or is their influence determined by domain? In a broad sense, research suggests that self-enhancement may be more automatic and affect-driven, whereas self-verification and self-assessment may require more controlled and cognitive processing (e.g., Swann et al., 1990; Trope & Neter, 1994). As mentioned above, people's automatic tendency is to seek self-enhancing information. People's self-description judgments and social comparisons become even more positively skewed when under mental load (e.g., Beer & Hughes, 2010; Paulhus, Graf, & Van Selst, 1989). People under mental load select social interaction partners who enhance their self-view rather than verify them (Swann et al., 1990). However, the automatic tendency towards self-enhancement should not be taken as evidence that it somehow dominates self-evaluation. In fact, there are even certain domains in which self-evaluations are not typically enhanced. For example, people do not inflate their self-perceptions of status on average. One series of studies examined self-perceptions of status in experimentally assigned groups and in naturalistic groups (Anderson et al., 2006). Self-perceptions of status

correlated significantly with group members' judgments. Furthermore, the correlation between self and group-member ratings of status holds for minimally acquainted groups and across time. This illustrates at least one domain in which self-enhancement is not expressed on average. It is unclear whether self-enhancement is simply not automatically engaged in the domain of status or whether cognitive effort is used to attenuate its expression. In other domains, there is evidence that people use additional cognitive effort to accomplish self-verification and self-assessment over self-enhancement. Without the distraction of mental load, people seek interaction partners who verify their negative self-view (Swann et al., 1990). Self-assessment is likely to influence self-evaluations if a cost–benefit analysis reveals that learning something negative about the self will ultimately be useful despite adverse effects on self-esteem (Trope & Neter, 1994).

Beyond differences in automaticity, research continues to investigate factors that influence the activation and expression of self-perception motives. It is tempting to posit that a particular motivation will be pronounced in a domain that is likely to fulfill the goal of the motivation. For example, if people are motivated to assess themselves accurately as a way to promote achievement, then we might except that self-assessment will show a dominant influence on perceptions of achievement-related qualities such as academic ability. However, research has found that people, on average, tend to self-enhance their academic ability (e.g., Robins & Beer, 2001). Furthermore, some research suggests that we are just as likely to respond to the bruise of past and future self-esteem threats with self-enhancement, self-verification, or self-assessment. Participants were presented with descriptions of each motivation and asked to describe the situations in which they had been motivated to enhance, verify, assess, or improve themselves through their self-evaluations (Taylor, Neter, & Wayment, 1995). A narrative analysis of the answers showed that situations of threat, either in the past or future, were equally likely to elicit the different motivations. However, there is evidence that people self-enhance less when recalling a past self-esteem threat when compared to current self-esteem threats (Gramzow & Willard, 2006). Another possibility is that the social nature of self-evaluation might mean that certain relationships tend to elicit particular motivations. A recent meta-analytic review suggests that self-verification motivations may be particularly strong when seeking information in long-term relationships compared to newly forming relationships (Kwang & Swann, 2010). Future research will be beneficial for refining our understanding of how and when self-evaluation processes and representation of self-knowledge are influenced by various motivations.

NEURAL REPRESENTATIONS OF THE SELF

One of the most recent developments in self-research is a wave of studies investigating the neurobiological basis of self-processes. Classically, neuropsychologists noted that frontal lobe damage was often associated with a disruption in self-processes. Frontal lobe injuries are related to clinical observations of impaired self-insight (Blumer & Benson, 1975). Within the last few years, a wave of recent studies has added complementary empirical data to these clinical observations. In particular, recent lesion studies and neuroimaging in healthy populations suggest that different aspects of self-evaluation draw on different frontal lobe sub-regions.

Self-referent encoding

The earliest neuroimaging work investigated the neural basis of the self-referent effect. A large body of literature has found robust, convergent evidence that the medial prefrontal cortex (MPFC) plays a role in encoding and remembering self-referent information. Participants in neuroimaging studies perform the self-referent paradigms typically used in behavioral research. For example, they might rate personality words for their self-descriptiveness, descriptiveness of a political figure, general social desirability, and number of syllables. These experiments find that rating personality trait words in relation to the self (compared to the conditions mentioned above) tends to increase activation in the medial prefrontal cortex (BA 9/10) (Craik et al., 1999; Fossati et al., 2003; Gillihan & Farah, 2005; Kelley et al., 2002; Kircher et al., 2002; Ochsner et al., 2005). Furthermore, the MPFC activation increases as a function of self-descriptiveness. MPFC activation is highest on average when judging information in relation to the self, and the magnitude of its activation for a particular trial correlates with the extent to which the personality trait is considered to be self-descriptive (e.g., Kircher et al., 2002; Macrae et al., 2004; Moran et al., 2006). The association between self-reference and MPFC activation is not specific to personality words. Research has found a similar association between MPFC activation and self-referent faces (Keenan et al., 2000; Kircher et al., 2000) and objects (Kim &

Johnson, 2010). Some studies have asked participants to observe their own face and the faces of a novel person or a close other. When participants observed their own face compared to the face of another person, they show increased activation in the right frontal lobe (e.g., BA 9/10) (e.g., Keenan et al., 2000; Kircher et al., 2000). Another study required participants to perform a transient ownership paradigm in which objects were either associated with self or another person (Kim & Johnson, 2010). Participants were presented with objects and given rules about which objects to place in a basket assigned to the participant or another person. They were further instructed to imagine that they owned the objects that they placed in their basket. MPFC activation was highest when participants placed objects in their own basket.

Furthermore, MPFC activation is implicated in the memory advantage for self-referent information because its activation predicts which self-referent is subsequently remembered (e.g., Kim & Johnson, 2010; Macrae et al., 2004). For example, one study asked participants to rate personality trait words for their self-descriptiveness (Macrae et al., 2004). Afterwards, participants were given a surprise memory test for the words they had seen during the experiment. Activation in the MPFC increased in relation to words that were later remembered compared to those words that were not remembered. Additionally, the relation between MPFC and self-reference extends to objects. In the transient ownership study mentioned above, participants were given a surprise memory test for objects they had placed in their own basket or the basket of another person. MPFC activation derived from the placement task predicted which of the objects assigned to the participant's basket would be later remembered (Kim & Johnson, 2010)

Motivated self-perception

In contrast to the large body of literature on the neurobiology of self-referent encoding, less attention has been paid to the neurobiology of motivated self-perception (Beer, 2007). In fact, of all of the motivations noted above, only self-enhancement has received any sort of consistent attention in the neural literature. When self-enhancement is operationalized by self-evaluations that diverge from objective indicators (e.g., actual performance, base rates), neuroimaging and lesion studies find a robust association between unrealistically positive self-evaluations and reduced orbitofrontal cortex (OFC) function. However, most of these studies do not include threats to the self, making it difficult to know whether these studies truly indicate self-evaluations that are enhanced to maintain positive self-worth. The one functional magnetic resonance imaging (fMRI) study that did include a threat manipulation found that unrealistically positive self-evaluations are predicted by increased OFC and MPFC activation.

The earliest hints of neural regions that might support self-enhancement came from analyses of the neural regions that tracked the social desirability of information judged in relation to the self. For example, studies asked participants to rate the self-descriptiveness of desirable and undesirable personality traits (Beer & Hughes, 2010; Moran et al., 2006) or to evaluate the likelihood that good and bad events would happen to them in the future (Sharot et al., 2007). These studies found convergent evidence that ventral anterior cingulate cortex (vACC) differentiates judgments of desirable attributes from judgments of undesirable attributes. The vACC activation increases when people rate desirable compared to undesirable personality traits and when they evaluate the likelihood that they will experience good events in the future compared to bad events. However, claiming that a desirable attribute is self-descriptive does not necessarily indicate the influence of an active self-enhancement motivation (see Beer & Hughes, 2010; Chambers & Windschitl, 2004). People may genuinely be characterized by a desirable quality, and self-enhancement has been shown to involve both the inflation of desirable attributes and the dismissal of undesirable attributes (Beer & Hughes, 2010; Dunning et al., 1989; Taylor & Brown, 1988). Therefore, it was important to further investigate whether vACC played a role when more direct measures of self-evaluations influenced by a self-enhancement motive were implemented.

An emerging body of research has now shown that unrealistically positive self-evaluations tend to be associated with reduced OFC function rather than changes in vACC activation. The relation to reduced OFC function holds when unrealistically positive self-evaluations are operationalized as discrepancies between self-confidence and actual task performance (Beer, Lombardo, & Bhanji, 2010), base rates compared to self-rankings in social comparisons (Beer & Hughes, 2010), attributions for task success compared to task failure (Blackwood et al., 2003), and self-perceptions compared to other perceptions (Beer et al., 2006).

For example, self-evaluations are considered to be unrealistically positive when they are discrepant from objective indicators such as task performance. Overestimation of success on a trivia task is associated with reduced OFC activation (Beer, Lombardo, & Bhanji, 2010). Participants estimated how confident they were that their answers to trivia about average July temperatures in US cities were correct. When participants had answered the actual trivia question incorrectly, a region of medial OFC was negatively modulated by confidence level. In other words, for those incorrect trials where confidence was unwarranted, people tended to recruit OFC activation less often. It is important to note that the relation could not be explained by confidence level alone; OFC did not predict confidence for trials that were answered correctly. Additionally, participants who tended to be more overconfident about their performance on the task were the least likely to activate OFC.

Another way in which people inflate their self-view is by comparing themselves in an unrealistically positive manner to their peer group. Research shows that people tend to believe they have significantly more desirable personality traits and significantly fewer undesirable personality traits than their peers (e.g., Dunning, Meyerowitz, & Holzberg, 1989). Although each person is likely to be unique on some traits, so is the average peer. Therefore, ranking the self as having significantly more desirable traits and fewer negative traits is theorized to reflect a motive to self-enhance (Taylor & Brown, 1988; but see Chambers & Windschitl, 2004). OFC activation is reduced when people make unrealistically positive social comparisons compared to social comparisons that are more realistically calibrated (Beer & Hughes, 2010). Participants were asked to compare themselves to their average peer on 200 personality traits (100 desirable traits, 100 undesirable traits). The more participants rated themselves as having more desirable traits and fewer negative traits than their average peer, the less likely they were to activate OFC during the social-comparative judgments (Beer & Hughes, 2010).

People also make unrealistically positive attributions for their behavior. They tend to take credit for their successes but then dismiss responsibility for failure (Taylor & Brown, 1988). OFC activation is reduced when people choose to account for their behavior in this self-serving manner (Blackwood et al., 2003). Participants were asked to imagine that they had experienced social success (i.e., a friend gives you a gift) or social failure (i.e., a friend refuses to talk to you). Then participants were asked to rate whether they had imagined the situation arising because of something they had done, something their friend had done, or something about the situation. The researchers compared the trials in which participants attributed their imaginary success or failure to self-serving factors (i.e., self for success, friend or situation for failure) compared to non-self-serving factors (i.e., self for failure, friend or situation for success). Taking credit for success and dismissing self-responsibility for failure was associated with less lateral OFC activation.

Finally, unrealistically positive evaluations of one's task performance are associated with OFC damage. In particular, OFC damage is associated with self-ratings that are more favorable than ratings from judges. Patients with OFC damage overestimate their social skills on a social interaction task when compared to patients with lateral prefrontal cortex damage or healthy control participants (Beer et al., 2006). Participants had to engage in a semi-structured conversation with a stranger. Although all participants reported that social norms dictate that certain kinds of personal information should be held back when speaking with strangers, patients with OFC damage were likely to introduce personal information into the conversation. Patients with orbitofrontal damage were much less likely to note the inappropriateness of their conversation when compared to blind judges' perceptions.

HAVE WE LEARNED ANYTHING PSYCHOLOGICAL FROM THE NEURAL RESEARCH?

The studies above demonstrate a consistent relation between self-enhanced responses and reduced OFC function, but what do they mean in a psychological sense? The nascent nature of social neuroscience investigations of the self have laid important groundwork on understanding how different frontal lobe regions are involved in different aspects of self-processes. However, there is much research left to be done in order to understand the psychological significance of the neurobiology underlying self-evaluation and its motivations. For example, two intriguing possibilities are emerging from the current research.

First, although vACC activation is not related to direct measures of positively skewed self-evaluations, there is reason to believe that vACC may be sensitive to the influence of motivational states on self-evaluation. In these studies reviewed above, vACC differentiated desirable traits from undesirable traits even though participants were not asked to evaluate the traits for their desirability, just their self-descriptiveness. Furthermore, the extent to which vACC differentiates desirable judgment stimuli from undesirable judgment stimuli is modulated by how much we care about viewing the target of the judgment in a positive light. The vACC is especially likely to differentiate desirable from undesirable attributes when we are judging attributes we consider to be highly descriptive of ourselves (Moran et al., 2006)

and people we care about (Hughes & Beer, 2011a). Research on gambling has found that the vACC detects the potential for reward (e.g., Rogers et al., 2004). One possibility is that, in the case of social cognition, vACC plays a role in detecting which attributes are likely to be rewarding and this function is especially engaged when judging the self or people we want to cast in a positive light.

Second, it may be that positively skewed self-evaluations are shaped by at least two distinct mechanisms (Chambers & Windschitl, 2004). The neural profile of unrealistically positive self-evaluations is different depending on whether the self-evaluations are a response to an immediate threat or not. For example, when a threat manipulation is integrated into social comparison judgments (Beer & Hughes, 2010), a different neural profile predicts inflation of desirable traits and dismissal of negative traits (Hughes & Beer, 2011b). Specifically, participants made social-comparative judgments either after they had received feedback that their peers did not find them attractive (i.e., a threat condition) or did find them attractive (Hughes & Beer, 2011b). When participants received threatening social feedback, they were significantly more likely to rate themselves as desirable compared to an average peer. Individual differences in unrealistically positive social comparisons were *positively* associated with OFC activation and positively associated with activation in an additional neural region, the MPFC (Hughes & Beer, 2011b). If unrealistically positive social comparisons are related to different patterns of neural activation depending on whether they are a response for coping with an immediate threat, then it is possible that different mechanisms achieve social comparisons that cast the self in a flattering light when self-esteem concerns are engaged or especially heightened. These are just two examples of the psychological advances that can be achieved through neural investigations of self-processes. Future research is needed to build on these findings and raise new insights.

THE SELF OR JUST PEOPLE IN GENERAL?

Finally, research on the self begs the question of whether the processes discussed thus far characterize the self or extend more broadly in social cognition. In other words, how special is the self? In a broad sense, it is surprising that researchers often study either the self or other people, because an examination of the literature suggests that there are many parallels in the underlying social-cognitive processes. As discussed previously, there is evidence that many of the a apriori theories and heuristics that we use to evaluate ourselves are also in operation when we evaluate others (e.g., Knee, Patrick, & Lonsbury, 2003; Malle, 2006; Nisbett & Wilson, 1977; Plaks, Levy, & Dweck, 2009). The progress of research has permitted meta-analyses that show that classically held differences between self-evaluation and other evaluation are not as robust or extensive as previously thought (Malle, 2006). In addition to these similarities, research suggests that we should expect that the processes that influence self-evaluation and evaluation of others to be particularly similar when the other person is someone we know intimately or someone we perceive to be similar to the self (e.g., Klein et al., 1992; Mitchell, Banaji, & Macrae, 2005; Mitchell, Macrae, & Banaji, 2006; Murray, Holmes, & Griffin, 1996; Neff & Karney, 2005; Symons & Johnson, 1997).

Highly elaborated and well-organized schema for self and close others

For example, the rich elaboration and organization that characterizes self-schemas likely extends to our schemas for people close to us. The memory advantage we gain by encoding information in relation to the self is almost as strong as when we encode information in relation to a close other (e.g, Maki & McCaul, 1985; Ochsner et al., 2005; and see Symons & Johnson, 1997 for a meta-analysis). In other words, if I ask you to judge whether a series of personality traits describes someone close to you such as your spouse, friend, daughter, son, sibling, or parent, then you are likely to remember these personality trait words almost as well as you would remember traits you rated in relation to yourself. And this memory would be even greater than if you judged the relevance of the trait words to a familiar, but not intimate, other person such as a politician (e.g., Maki & McCaul, 1985).

Judgments about self and close others driven by abstract representation

Similarly, the rich development of schemas for close others may also be indicated by similarities in the way we judge ourselves and the highly descriptive personality traits of close others. We do not rely on the retrieval of episodic information to judge whether a personality trait describes us; research shows that the retrieval of episodic information is also not needed when we judge personality traits we deem to be highly descriptive of people we know well. As mentioned previously, autobiographical memory retrieval tends to facilitate personality judgments of one's mother but not the self. The one exception to this finding is that retrieving these memories does not facilitate judgments of the personality traits that are most characteristic of one's mother (Klein et al., 1992). These results suggests that we form abstract representations of the most central aspects of our close other's personalities.

Neural similarities underlie representations of self and close others

Finally, the similarity in the richness of cognitive representation of the self and close others is mirrored at the neural level. There is evidence that a common neural system supports self-evaluation and evaluation of close others (for reviews, see Gilihan & Farah, 2005; Ochsner et al., 2005) and similar others (Mitchell, Banaji, & Macrae, 2005; Mitchell, Macrae, & Banaji, 2006). For example, the significantly higher activation in MPFC associated with trait judgments about the self (Kelley et al., 2002) disappears when self-judgments are compared to judgments of close others such as a romantic partner (e.g., Ochsner et al., 2005). Additionally, the neural systems involved in evaluating a relatively unknown person may overlap with the neural systems involved in self-evaluation to the extent that the person is perceived as similar to the self (Mitchell, Banaji, & Macrae, 2005; Mitchell, Macrae, & Banaji, 2006). For example, one study required participants to evaluate the intangible mental states or overt physical aspects of unknown social targets. Participants were presented with a series of faces and asked to judge whether the face looked pleased (mental state) or symmetric (physical aspect). Afterwards, participants rated the extent to which they estimated the faces from the task to reflect people who were similar or dissimilar to themselves. The ventral MPFC activity associated with making judgments about strangers' mental states tended to increase to the extent that participants believed the stranger to be similar to themselves (Mitchell, Banaji, & Macrae, 2005). The researchers suggest that, in the absence of other information, we may engage the self-system to evaluate novel others, but only to the extent that the self seems like a reasonable proxy for understanding a novel person. Together, these studies illustrate the commonality between cognitive representations of self and close others or other people we perceive to be similar to the self.

Motivated perceptions of both the self and close others

The similarity between self and close others also extends to the type of motivations that may shape the content of cognitive representations and judgments. Just as people exhibit a number of behaviors that indicate their motivation to see themselves in a positive light, they exhibit similar behaviors in relation to their close others (e.g., Murray & Holmes, 1997; Neff & Karney, 2005; Suls, Lemos, & Stewart, 2002; Taylor & Brown, 1988; Taylor & Koivumaki, 1976). For example, we can perceive the social desirability of our romantic partner or friend's personality in a fashion that is as lopsided as our perceptions of the social desirability of our own personalities. The positive skew is specific to close others; we tend to have more even-handed perceptions of the desirability of an unknown, typical person's personality (Suls, Lemos, & Stewart, 2002). Similarly, we are much more likely to excuse away the poor social behavior of ourselves, our friends, and our spouses to situational factors than we are for strangers or people we dislike. For example, a series of studies asked participants to consider poor social behavior such as showing up late to an appointment, having an argument, and ignoring others at a party (Taylor & Koivumaki, 1976). Participants then rated the likelihood that dispositional and situational factors would motivate themselves, their spouses, and acquaintances to act in these ways. The poor social behavior was significantly more likely to be attributed to situational factors for the self and spouses.

Furthermore, similar neural regions support the mechanisms used to accomplish the flattering views of ourselves and the people we care about. People's unrealistically positive social-comparative judgments are associated with reduced OFC activation, regardless of whether the judgments are for the self (Beer & Hughes, 2010) or for a romantic partner and roommate (Hughes & Beer, 2011a). For example, participants compared their romantic partners and assigned roommates to their average peer on a series of 200 personality traits (100 desirable, 100 undesirable). OFC activation was reduced to the extent to which participants considered their romantic partners or roommates to have significantly more desirable personality traits and significantly fewer undesirable personality traits than the average peer.

Finally, self-evaluation and other evaluation share more than enhancement motivations. There is also evidence that just as we influence social environments to confirm our self-view (e.g., choosing to interact with people who confirm our self-view: Swann, Pelham, & Krull, 1989), we also structure environments to confirm our views of other people (e.g., Darley & Gross, 1983; Word, Zanna, & Cooper, 1974) even when we have not consciously accessed those views (Chen & Bargh, 1997). For example, when participants interviewed out-group members (compared to in-group members) for an ostensible job, they tended to cut the interview short, invested less in the interaction, and committed more speech errors (Word, Zanna, & Cooper, 1974). A second set of participants were then trained to use the poorer interview style when interacting with in-group applicants. Under those conditions, the in-group applicants came across as less competent and more nervous. These studies illustrate the ways in which motivational influences known to operate in self-evaluation can extend to evaluations of other people.

CONCLUSION

From a social-cognitive standpoint, William James long ago pointed out that the self is an interesting case that includes both the perceiver and perceived. In the Jamesian recipe for the self, we are as much our physical presence as we are our innermost strivings and social reputations. Recent research has built on this notion and discovered that our perceiver self gathers information about the perceived self in myriad ways, including observing the self through one's own eyes and the eyes of others as well as comparing the self to others. The information we acquire through these processes form self-schemas that tend to be particularly elaborate and well-organized. Although we sometimes gather and represent self-information in an even-handed manner, we are also motivated to enhance or verify our self-view. Recent research has helped us move away from considering the frontal lobes to be a catch-all for any self-processes. Instead, we are beginning to learn about how frontal lobe sub-regions vary in their involvement in different self-processes and the motivations that influence them. Finally, the processes and motivations that shape self-evaluation often extend to evaluations of people close to us or people we perceive to be similar to the self. Future research is needed to further deepen our understanding of the self and two important areas are to understand how we balance competing motivational influences and the psychological significance of the neural architecture of self-processing.

REFERENCES

Albright, L., Kenny, D. A., & Malloy, T. E. (1988). Consensus in personality judgments at zero acquaintance. *Journal of Personality and Social Psychology, 55,* 387–395.

Alicke, M.D., Klotz, M.L., Breitenbecher, D. L., Yurak, T. J., & Vrendenburg, D. S. (1995). Personal contact, individuation, and the above-average effect. *Journal of Personality and Social Psychology, 68,* 804–825.

Ambady, N., & Rosenthal, R. (1992). Thin slices of expressive behavior as predictors of interpersonal consequences: A meta-analysis. *Psychological Bulletin, 111,* 431–441.

Andersen, S. M., & Ross, L. (1984). Self-knowledge and social inference: I. The impact of cognitive/affective and behavioral data. *Journal of Personality and Social Psychology, 46,* 280–293.

Anderson, C. P., Srivastava, S., Beer, J. S., Spataro, S. E., & Chatman, J. A. (2006). Knowing your place: Self-perceptions of status in social groups. *Journal of Personality and Social Psychology, 91,* 1094–1110.

Baldwin, M. W. (1992). Relational schemas and the processing of social information. *Psychological Bulletin, 112,* 461–484.

Bartels, D., & Rips, L. (2010). Psychological connectedness and intertemporal choice. *Journal of Experimental Psychology: General, 139,* 49–69.

Bartlett, F.A. (1932). *A study in experimental and social psychology.* New York: Cambridge University Press.

Baumeister, R. F. (1987). How the self became a problem: A psychological review of historical research. *Journal of Personality and Social Psychology, 52,* 163–176.

Beer, J. S. (2007). The default self: Feeling good or being right? *Trends in Cognitive Sciences, 11,* 187–189.

Beer, J. S., & Hughes, B. L. (2010). Neural systems of social comparison and the "above-average" effect. *NeuroImage, 49,* 2671–2679.

Beer, J. S., John, O. P., Scabini, D., & Knight, R. T. (2006). Orbitofrontal cortex and social behavior: Integrating self-monitoring and emotion–cognition interactions. *Journal of Cognitive Neuroscience, 18,* 871–879.

Beer, J. S., Lombardo, M. V., & Bhanji, J. P. (2010). Roles of medial prefrontal cortex and orbitofrontal cortex in self-evaluation. *Journal of Cognitive Neuroscience. 22,* 2108–2119.

Bem, D. J. (1967). Self-perception: An alternative interpretation of cognitive dissonance phenomena. *Psychological Review, 74,* 183–200.

Bem, D. J. (1972). Self-perception theory. In L. Berkowitz (Ed.), *Advances in experimental social psychology* (Vol. 6, pp. 1–62). New York: Academic Press.

Blackwood, N.J., Bentall, R.P., Simmons, A., Murray, R. M., & Howard, R.J. (2003). Self-responsibility and the self-serving bias: an fMRI investigation of causal attributions. *NeuroImage, 20,* 1076–1085.

Blumer, D., & Benson, D. F. (1975). Personality changes with frontal and temporal lobe lesions. In D. F. Benson & D. Blumer (Eds.). *Psychiatric aspects of neurologic disease* (pp. 151–169). New York: Grune & Stratton.

Bochner, S. (1994). Cross-cultural differences in the self concept: A test of Hofstede's individualism/collectivism distinction. *Journal of Cross-Cultural Psychology, 25,* 273–283.

Bond, M., & Cheung, T. (1983). College students' spontaneous self-concept: The effect of culture among respondents in Hong Kong, Japan, and the United States. *Journal of Cross-Cultural Psychology, 14,* 153–171.

Bower, G.H., Clark, M. C., Lesgold, A. M., & Winzenz, D. (1969). Hierarchical retrieval schemes in recall of categorized word lists. *Journal of Verbal Learning and Verbal Behavior, 8,* 323–343.

Buunk, A., Cohen-Schotanus, J., & van Nek, R. (2007). Why and how people engage in social comparison while learning social skills in groups. *Group Dynamics: Theory, Research, and Practice, 11*(3), 140–152.

Chambers, J. R., & Windschitl, P. D. (2004). Biases in social comparative judgments: The role of nonmotivated factors in above-average and comparative-optimism effects. *Psychological Bulletin, 130,* 813–838.

Chen, M., & Bargh, J. A. (1997). Nonconscious behavioral confirmation processes: The self – fulfilling nature of automatically-activated stereotypes. *Journal of Experimental Social Psychology. 33,* 541–560.

Cooley, C. H. (1902). *Human nature and the social order.* New York: Scribners.

Correll, J., Park, B., Judd, C. M., & Wittenbrink, B. (2002). The police officer's dilemma: Using ethnicity to disambiguate potentially threatening individuals. *Journal of Personality and Social Psychology, 83,* 1314–1329.

Craik, F. I. M., Moroz, T. M., Moscovitch, M., Stuss, D. T., Wincour, G., Tulving, E., et al. (1999). In search of the self: A positron emission tomography study. *Psychological Science, 10,* 26–34.

Craik, F .I. M., & Tulving, E. (1975). Depth of processing and the retention of words in episodic memory. *Journal of Experimental Psychology: General, 11,* 268–294.

Darley, J. M., & Gross, P. H. (1983). A hypothesis-confirming bias in labeling effects. *Journal of Personality and Social Psychology, 44,* 20–33.

Dion, K., Berscheid, E., & Walster, E. (1972). What is beautiful is good. *Journal of Personality and Social Psychology, 24,* 285–290.

Dunning, D. (1995). Trait importance and modifiability as factors influencing self-assessment and self-enhancement motives. *Personality and Social Psychology Bulletin, 21,* 1297–1306.

Dunning, D., Meyerowitz, J. A., & Holzberg, A. D. (1989). Ambiguity and self-evaluation: The role of idiosyncratic trait definitions in self-serving assessments of ability. *Journal of Personality and Social Psychology, 57,* 1082–1090.

Eastwick, P. W., Finkel, E. J., Krishnamurti, T., & Loewenstein, G. (2008). Mispredicting distress following romantic breakup: Revealing the time course of affective forecasting error. *Journal of Experimental Social Psychology, 44,* 800–807.

Eisenberg, N. (2010). Empathy-related responding: Links with self-regulation, moral judgment, and moral behavior. In Mikulincer, M. & Shaver, P. R. (Eds), *Prosocial motives, emotions, and behavior: The better angels of our nature.* Washington DC: American Psychological Association.

Festinger, L. (1954). A theory of social comparison processes. *Human Relations, 7,* 117–140.

Festinger, L. (1957). *A theory of cognitive dissonance.* Stanford, CT: Stanford University Press.

Festinger, L., & Carlsmith, J. M. (1959). Cognitive consequences of forced compliance. *Journal of Abnormal and Social Psychology, 58,* 203–210.

Fossati, P., Hevenor, S. J., Graham, S. J., Grady, C., Keightley, M. L., Craik, F., et al. (2003). In search of the emotional self: an FMRI study using positive and negative emotional words. *American Journal of Psychiatry, 160,* 1938–1945.

Gilbert, D. T., Giesler, R. B., & Morris, K. A. (1995). When comparisons arise. *Journal of Personality and Social Psychology, 69,* 227–236.

Gilihan, S. J., & Farah, M. J. (2005). Is self special? A critical review of evidence from experimental psychology and cognitive neuroscience. *Psychological Bulletin, 131,* 76–97.

Goethals, G. R., & Darley, J. (1977). Social comparison theory: An attributional approach. In J. M. Suls & R. L. Miller (Eds.), *Social comparison processes: Theoretical and empirical perspectives* (pp. 86–109). Washington, DC: Hemisphere.

Gosling, S. D., Ko, S. J., Mannarelli, T., & Morris, M. E. (2002). A room with a cue: Judgments of personality based on offices and bedrooms. *Journal of Personality and Social Psychology, 82,* 379–398.

Gramzow, R. H, & Willard, G. (2006). Exaggerating current and past performance: Motivated self-enhancement versus reconstructive memory. *Personality and Social Psychology Bulletin, 32,* 1114–1125.

Gray-Little, B., Williams, V.S.L., & Hancock, T. D. (199). An item response theory analysis of the Rosenberg Self-esteem scale. *Personality and Social Psychology Bulletin, 23,* 443–451.

Greenwald, A. G., Oakes, M. A., & Hoffman, H. G. (2003). Targets of discrimination: Effects of race on responses to weapons holders. *Journal of Experimental and Social Psychology, 39,* 399–405.

Haggard P. & Tsakiris M. (2009). The experience of agency: feeling, judgment and responsibility. *Current Directions in Psychological Science, 18,* 242–246

Hughes, B. L. & Beer, J. S. (2011a). *Motivated social cognition modulates orbitofrontal cortex and anterior cingulate cortex. Cerebral Cortex.*

Hughes, B. L., & Beer, J. S. (2011b). *Neural systems underlying positivity bias elicited by threat.* Manuscript under review.

Ingram, R. E., Smith, T. W., & Brehm, S. S. (1983). Depression and information-processing: Self-schemata and the encoding of self-referent information. *Journal of Personality and Social Psychology, 45,* 412–420.

James, W. (1983). *The principles of psychology.* Cambridge, MA: Harvard University Press. (Original work published 1890)

Jones, E. E., & Nisbett, R. E. (1971). *The actor and the observer: Divergent perceptions of the causes of behavior.* Morristown, NJ: General Learning Press.

Keenan, J. M., & Baillet, S. D. (1980). Memory for personally and socially significant events. In R. S. Nickerson (Ed.), *Attention and performance* (Vol. 8, pp. 651–669). Hillsdale, NJ: Erlbaum.

Keenan, J. P., Wheeler, M. A., Gallup, G. G., & Pasucal-Leone, A. (2000). Self-recognition and the right prefrontal cortex. *Trends in Cognitive Sciences, 4,* 338–344.

Kelley, W. M., Macrae, C. N., Wyland, C. L., Caglar, S., Inati, S., & Heatherton, T. F. (2002). Finding the self? An event-related fMRI study. *Journal of Cognitive Neuroscience, 14,* 785–794.

Kihlstrom, J.F., & Cantor, N. (1984). Mental representations of the self. In L. Berkowitz (Ed.), *Advances in experimental social psychology.* Vol. 17. New York: Academic Press.

Kim, K., & Johnson, M. K. (2010). Extended self: Medial prefrontal activity during transient association of self and objects. *Social Cognitive and Affective Neuroscience,* Advance online publication.

Kircher, T. T., Brammer, M., Bullmore, E., Simmons, A., Bartels, M., & David, A. S. (2002). The neural correlates of intentional and incidental self processing. *Neuropsychologia, 40,* 683–692.

Kircher, T. T., Senior, C., Phillips, M. L., Benson, P. J., Bullmore, E. T., Brammer, M., et al. (2000). Towards a functional neuroanatomy of self processing: effects of faces and words. *Cognitive Brain Research, 10,* 133–144.

Klayman, J., Soll, J. B., Gonzalez-Vallejo, C., & Barlas, S. (1999). Overconfidence: It depends on how, what, and whom you ask. *Organizational Behavior and Human Decision Processes, 79,* 216–247.

Klein, S. B., Babey, S. H., & Sherman, J. W., (1997). The functional independence of trait and behavioral self-knowledge: Methodological considerations and new empirical findings. *Social Cognition, 15,* 183–203.

Klein, S.B., & Kihlstrom, J.F. (1986). Elaboration, organization, and the self-reference effect in memory. *Journal of Experimental Psychology: General, 115,* 26–39.

Klein, S. B., Loftus, J., & Burton, H. A., (1989). Two self-reference effects: The importance of distinguishing between self-descriptiveness judgments and autobiographical retrieval in self-referent encoding. *Journal of Personality and Social Psychology, 56,* 853–865.

Klein, S. B., Loftus, J., Trafton, J. G., & Fuhrman, R. W. (1992). Use of exemplars and abstractions in trait judgments: A model of trait knowledge about the self and others. *Journal of Personality and Social Psychology, 63,* 739–753.

Knee, C., Patrick, H., & Lonsbary, C. (2003). Implicit theories of relationships: Orientations toward evaluation and cultivation. *Personality and Social Psychology Review, 7*(1), 41–55.

Kruglanski, A. W., & Mayseless, O. (1990). Classic and current social comparison research: Expanding the perspective. *Psychological Bulletin, 108,* 195–208.

Kwang, T., & Swann, W. B., (2010). Do people embrace praise even when they feel unworthy? A review of critical tests of self-enhancement versus self-verification. *Personality and Social Psychology Review, 4,* 263–280.

Leary, M. R., Estrada, M. J., & Allen, A. (2009). The analogue-I and the analogue-Me: The avatars of the self. *Self and Identity.* 8, 147–161.

Leary, M. R., Tambor, E. S., Terdal, S. K., & Downs, D. L. (1995). Self-esteem as an interpersonal monitor: The sociometer hypothesis. *Journal of Personality and Social Psychology, 68,* 518–530.

Macrae, C. N., Moran, J. M., Heatherton, T. F., Banfield, J. F., & Kelley, W. M. (2004). Medial prefrontal activity predicts memory for self-knowledge. *Cerebral Cortex, 14,* 647–654.

Maki, R. H., & McCaul, K. D. (1985). The effects of self-reference versus other reference on the recall of traits and nouns. *Bulletin of the Psychonomic Society, 23,* 169–172.

Malle, B. F. (2006). The actor–observer asymmetry in attribution: A (surprising) meta-analysis. *Psychological Bulletin, 132,* 895–919.

Marcus, D. K. & Miller, R. S. (2003). Sex differences in judgments of physical attractiveness: A social relations analysis. *Personality and Social Psychology Bulletin, 29,* 325–335.

Markus, H., (1977). Self-schemata and processing information about the self. *Journal of Personality and Social Psychology, 35,* 63–78.

Markus, H., Hamill, R., & Sentis, K. P. (1987). Thinking fat: Self-schemas for body weight and the processing of weight relevant information. *Journal of Applied Social Psychology, 17,* 50–71.

Markus, H. R., & Kitayama, S. (1991). Culture and the self: Implications for cognition, emotion, and motivation. *Psychological Review, 98,* 224–253.

Markus, H., & Nurius, P. (1986). Possible selves. *American Psychologist, 41,* 954–969.

Mead, G. H. (1934). *Mind, self and society.* Chicago, IL: University of Chicago Press.

Meier, B., Robinson, M., Carter, M., & Hinsz, V. (2010). Are sociable people more beautiful? A zero-acquaintance analysis of agreeableness, extraversion, and attractiveness. *Journal of Research in Personality, 44,* 293–296.

Mitchell, J., Banaji, M., & Macrae, C. (2005). The link between social cognition and self-referential thought in the medial prefrontal cortex. *Journal of Cognitive Neuroscience, 17*(8), 1306–1315.

Mitchell, J. P., Macrae, C. N., & Banaji, M.R. (2006). Dissociable medial prefrontal contributions to judgments of similar and dissimilar others. *Neuron, 50,* 655–663.

Moran, J. M., Macrae, C. N., Heatherton, T. F., Wyland, C. L., & Kelley, W.M. (2006). Neuroanatomical evidence for distinct cognitive and affective components of self. *Journal of Cognitive Neuroscience, 18,* 1586–1594.

Murray S. L., & Holmes, J. G. (1997). A leap of faith? Positive illusions in romantic relationships. *Personality and Social Psychological Bulletin, 23,* 586–597.

Murray, S. L., Holmes, J. G., & Griffin, D. W. (1996). The benefits of positive illusions: Idealization and the construction of satisfaction in close relationships. *Journal of Personality and Social Psychology, 70,* 79–98.

Mussweiler, T., & Rueter, K. (2003). What friends are for! The use of routine standards in social comparison. *Journal of Personality and Social Psychology, 85*(3), 467–481.

Neff, L., & Karney, B. (2005). To know you is to love you: The implications of global adoration and specific accuracy for marital relationships. *Journal of Personality and Social Psychology, 88*(3), 480–497.

Neisser, U. (1967). *Cognitive psychology.* Englewood Cliffs, NJ: Prentice Hall.

Nisbett, R., & Wilson, T. (1977). Telling more than we can know: Verbal reports on mental processes. *Psychological Review, 84,* 231–259.

Norman, W. T., & Goldberg, L. R. (1966). Raters, ratees, and randomness in personality structure. *Journal of Personality and Social Psychology, 4,* 681–691.

Ochsner, K. N., Beer, J. S., Robertson, E. A., Cooper, J., Gabrieli, J. D. E., Kihlstrom, J. F., et al. (2005). The neural correlates of direct and reflected self-knowledge. *NeuroImage, 28,* 797–814.

Parfit, D. (1984). *Reasons and persons.* Oxford, UK: Oxford University Press.

Paulhus, D. L., Graf, P., & Van Selst, M. (1989). Attentional load increases the positivity of self-presentation. *Social Cognition, 7,* 389–400.

Pfeifer, J. H., Masten, C. L., Borofsky, L. A., Dapretto, M., Fuligni, A.J., & Lieberman, M. D. (2009). Neural correlates of direct and reflected self-appraisals in adolescents and adults: When social perspective-taking informs self-perception. *Child Development, 80,* 1016–1038.

Plaks, J., Levy, S., & Dweck, C. (2009). Lay theories of personality: Cornerstones of meaning in social cognition. *Social and Personality Psychology Compass, 3,* 1069–1081.

Pronin, E., Lin, D., & Ross, L. (2002). The bias blind spot: Perceptions of bias in self versus others. *Personality and Social Psychology Bulletin, 28*(3), 369–381.

Pronin, E., Olivola, C. Y., & Kennedy, K. A. (2008). Doing unto future selves as you would do unto others: Psychological distance and decision making. *Personality and Social Psychology Bulletin, 34,* 224–236.

Robins, R. W., & Beer, J. S. (2001). Positive illusions about the self: Short-term benefits and long-term costs. *Journal of Personality and Social Psychology, 80,* 340–352.

Rogers, T. B., Kuiper, N. A., & Kirker, W. S. (1977). Self-reference and the encoding of personal information. *Journal of Personality and Social Psychology, 35,* 677–688.

Rogers, R. D., Ramnani, N., Mackay, C., Wilson, J. L., Jezzard, P., Carter, C. S., et al. (2004). Distinct portions of anterior cingulate cortex and medial prefrontal cortex are activated by reward processing in separable phases of decision-making cognition. *Biological Psychiatry, 55,* 594–602.

Sedikides, C., & Gregg, A. P. (2008). Self-enhancement: Food for thought. *Perspectives on Psychological Science, 3,* 102–116.

Sharot, T., Riccardi, A.M., Raio, C. M., & Phelps, E. A. (2007). Neural mechanisms mediating optimism bias. *Nature. 450,*102–105.

Srivastava, S., & Beer, J. S. (2005). How self-evaluations relate to being liked by others: Integrating sociometer and attachment perspectives. *Journal of Personality and Social Psychology, 89,* 966–977.

Stapel, D. A., & Blanton, H. (2004). From seeing to being: Subliminal social comparisons affect implicit and explicit self-evaluations. *Journal of Personality and Social Psychology, 87*, 468–481.

Story, A. (1998). Self-esteem and memory for favorable and unfavorable personality feedback. *Personality and Social Psychology Bulletin, 24*, 51–64.

Suls, J., Lemos, K., & Stewart, H. L. (2002). Self-esteem, construal, and comparisons with the self, friends, and peers. *Journal of Personality and Social Psychology, 87*, 252–261.

Swann, W. B., Pelham, B. W., & Krull, D. S. (1989) Agreeable fancy or disagreeable truth? Reconciling self-enhancement and self-verification. *Journal of Personality and Social Psychology, 57*, 782–791.

Swann, W. B., Hixon, J. G., Stein-Seroussi, A., & Gilbert, D. T. (1990). The fleeting gleam of praise: Cognitive processes underlying behavioral reactions to self-relevant feedback. *Journal of Personality and Social Psychology, 59*, 17–26.

Symons, C. S., & Johnson, B. T. (1997). The self-reference effect in memory: A meta-analysis. *Psychological Bulletin, 12*, 371–394.

Taylor, S. E., & Brown, J. D. (1988). Illusion and well-being: A social psychological perspective on mental health, *Psychological Bulletin, 103*, 193–210.

Taylor, S. E., & Crocker, J. (1981). Schematic bases of social information processing. In E. T. Higgins, C. P. Herman, & M.P. Zanna (Eds.), *Social cognition: The Ontario Symposium* (Vol. 1, pp. 89–134). Hillsdale, NJ: Erlbaum.

Taylor, S. E., & Koivumaki, J. H. (1976). The perception of self and others: Acquaintanceship, affect, and actor–observer differences. *Journal of Personality and Social Psychology, 33*, 403–408.

Taylor, S. E., Neter, E., & Wayment, H. A. (1995). Self-evaluation process. *Personality and Social Psychology Bulletin, 21*, 1278–1287.

Tice, D. M. (1992). Self-presentation and self-concept change: The looking-glass self is also a magnifying glass. *Journal of Personality and Social Psychology*, 63, 435–451.

Trope, Y. (1975). Seeking information about one's ability as a determinant of choice among tasks. *Journal of Personality and Social Psychology, 16*, 116–123.

Trope, Y. (1980). Self-assessment, self-enhancement, and task preference. *Journal of Experimental Social Psychology, 16*, 116–129.

Trope, Y. (1986). Self-enhancement and self-assessment in achievement behavior. In R. M. Sorrentino & E. T. Higgins (Eds.), *Handbook of motivation and cognition: Foundations of social behavior* (pp. 350–378). New York: Guilford Press.

Trope, Y., & Liberman, N. (2010). Construal-level theory of psychological distance. *Psychological Review, 117*, 440–463.

Trope, Y., & Neter, E. (1994). Reconciling competing motives in self-evaluation: The role of self-control in feedback seeking. *Journal of Personality and Social Psychology, 66*, 646–657.

Turk, D. J., Heatherton, T. F., Macrae, C. N., Kelley, W. M., & Gazzaniga, M. S. (2003). Out of contact, out of mind: The distributed nature of self. *Annals of the New York Academy of Sciences, 1001*, 65–78.

Wegner, D. M. (2003). The mind's best trick: How we experience conscious will. *Trends in Cognitive Sciences, 7*, 65–69.

Wilson, T., & Gilbert, D. (2005). Affective forecasting: Knowing what to want. *Current Directions in Psychological Science, 14*, 131–134.

Word, C. O., Zanna, M. P., & Cooper, J. (1974). The nonverbal mediation of self-fulfilling prophecies in interracial interaction. *Journal of Experimental Social Psychology, 10*, 109–120.

18

Social Cognition in Close Relationships

Susan M. Andersen, S. Adil Saribay,
& Elizabeth Przybylinski

Close relationships are a source of much joy and of perceived meaning in life, and likewise can also be fraught with painful emotions. Given that people accord so much time and energy to relationships and their maintenance, it is surprising in some respects that the processes and phenomena defining close relationships often occur not with deliberate forethought and intent, but rather, quite automatically based on whatever interpersonal knowledge happens to be active at the moment. Social-cognitive research in this area has thus focused quite centrally on such relational knowledge, how and when it is evoked, and with what consequences.

In this chapter, we present the main theories and the documented phenomena in the social cognition of close relationships. Beginning with the extant theoretical approaches in the literature that take a distinctly social-cognitive approach to close relationships, we proceed to a review of the evidence in the area that speaks to the basic social-cognitive processes and phenomena arising in close relationships. We then conclude by highlighting common themes in the literature – reflecting how cognitive processes involving relational knowledge influence social life, for example, as relationships from the past are perpetuated in the present.

DEFINITIONS

Social cognition in close relationships

For the present purposes, we define social-cognitive research relatively narrowly, focusing on research that tests cognitive assumptions and makes use of social-cognitive paradigms to experimentally manipulate relational representations (by cueing or otherwise activating these structures). The latter work tracks cognitive processes in relationships in fairly fine-grained terms and relatively directly, for example, often by moving beyond simple self-reports and tapping what is automatic or implicit (Baldwin, Lydon, McClure, & Etchison, 2010).

There is of course a far wider literature on close relationships that is important and influential in the field, but not especially focused on cognition or relational representations. For the sake of space, this literature falls largely outside the present scope, even though we do hope to contribute to whatever extent possible to this wider literature. We also do not address many fruitful areas of investigation on the outskirts of close relationships research, such as that on dyadic interaction, unless it explicitly examines close relationships. Likewise, we do not review work in clinical psychology on close relationships, even when cognitively focused, and give little attention to research on cross-cultural differences or to still more relevant work on social neuroscience pertaining to close relationships, even though both hold much promise for future research.

As has been noted, "investigation of automatic processes operating in close relationships is just beginning" (Reis & Downey, 1999, p. 109). Over a decade later, there have been many conceptual and empirical advances and yet the potential of social cognition to contribute to close relationships is as yet not fully realized. In this chapter we aim to underline this potential.

Significant others and close relationships

We form close relationships with individuals who become significant others, whom we care deeply about and in whom we are emotionally invested. We form knowledge representations in memory that designate these especially significant individuals, and these can take the form of n-of-1 exemplars (Smith & Zarate, 1992; e.g., Hinkley & Andersen, 1996) or of more generalized knowledge encompassing more than one relationship (e.g., Klohnen, Weller, Luo, & Choe, 2005).

Significant others are represented richly in memory both because they are repeatedly encountered and provoke inferences about the other's thoughts and intentions in order to effectively navigate these relations (e.g., Chen, 2003). They also have motivational and emotional relevance for satisfying fundamental human needs (or failing to do so). Thus, fundamental needs, such as for human connection or belonging (Baumeister & Leary, 1995; see also Andersen, Reznik, & Chen, 1997; Deci, 1995), autonomy or freedom, competence or control, comprehension or meaning, and a sense of felt security (Andersen & Chen, 2002; Baumeister, 1991; Fiske, 2003) circumscribe how people interact with and conceive close others.

Some significant others who are present early in life may have a particularly profound role (e.g., Ogilvie & Ashmore, 1991). For instance, rudimentary significant-other and self representations are grounded in early experiences with caregivers (e.g., Bowlby, 1969), which then serve as working models for later relationships (Thompson, 1998). Nevertheless, additional representations continue to form throughout life, as people form new relationships in adulthood.

Whether they arise in childhood or adulthood, significant-other representations do not stand alone in memory, but are connected with the self through *linkages* that embody the experiences and the typical relational dynamics with the other. Although exact models of these elements vary (see, e.g., Andersen & Chen, 2002; Aron, Aron, Tudor, & Nelson, 1991; Baldwin, 1992), the relevance of significant others to the self is well understood. Hence, significant-other representations are infused with emotion and motivation, as noted, and the social-cognitive mechanisms that propel forward a variety of interpersonal effects when activated – even if the significant other is

not present – often evoke affect and motivation as well.

Construct activation and automaticity

Representations of significant others are called to the fore or activated (e.g., Bargh, Bond, Lombardi, & Tota, 1986) when a cue is encountered that is sufficiently similar (often minimally so) to the representation, including simply thinking about the close other. When activated, such representations typically exert an assimilative influence on how we think about (attend to, evaluate, remember) and act toward others. Research in the area tends to adopt, implicitly or explicitly, a spreading activation model in which activation of a significant-other or relationship representation facilitates activation of associated aspects of the self, and also provokes relevant inferences, evaluations, and expectancies concerning the other. Both chronic and transient accessibility play a role in whether or not a representation is used (see Bargh et al., 1986; Förster & Liberman, 2007; Higgins, 1996), and accounts for activation of significant-other representations.

Transient activation can occur, for example, based on a match between cues encountered about a new person (e.g., how the new person acts, thinks, speaks, or listens, and his/her preferences, attitudes, and indeed facial features) and a significant-other representation (Chen, Andersen, & Hinkley, 1999). In addition, significant-other representations are accessible even without priming before encountering an applicable person (i.e., they are chronically accessible; Andersen, Glassman, Chen, & Cole, 1995, Study 1) and when triggering cues in a new person are extremely minimal (Chen et al., 1999) or even absent (Andersen et al., 1995, Study 2). Transient cues have been shown to combine additively with chronicity in activating significant-other representations (Andersen et al., 1995; Baldwin, 1997), as with trait concepts (Bargh et al., 1986). Regardless of the temporary or chronic nature of this activation, the use of relational structures often occurs automatically (e.g., Andersen & Glassman, 1996; Andersen, Moskowitz, Blair, & Nosek, 2007).

A process can be considered automatic if it takes place efficiently (i.e., uses minimal cognitive resources), with little or no awareness, intention, or control (Bargh, 1989, 1994). Rather than an all-or-none definition, any one of these indicators is considered sufficient, and moreover, no task or response is likely to be process-pure (entirely automatic or entirely controlled/deliberative) (Jacoby, 1991). Therefore, even when automaticity can be said to occur, it is more matter of degree than of kind. Automatic processes are often triggered by minimal cueing conditions (Bargh, 1989). Hence, conditional automaticity (Bargh, 1994) can either be preconscious (based on subliminal cueing or chronic accessibility with no cueing), postconscious (when cueing stimuli are consciously perceived), or goal-dependent (based on intent, such as to form an impression).

Finally, although these varieties of automaticity are implicated in processes observed in close relationships, the criteria themselves are not commonly delineated or even necessarily measured. Still, our focus where possible is on evidence that taps or implicates automatic relational processes of one variety or another, or potentially contrasts such evidence with that which suggests more deliberative and strategic processes.

SOCIAL-COGNITIVE APPROACHES TO CLOSE RELATIONSHIPS

In the pages that follow, we present some of the most influential social-cognitive models of close relationships, the processes these propose, and the phenomena they predict. In so doing, we describe the methods typically used in each, highlighting automaticity where relevant. Because each model has been presented at length elsewhere, along with evidence supporting it, we aim simply to provide an overview.

Transference and the relational self

The social-cognitive model of transference (Andersen & Glassman, 1996) assumes that cues relevant to a significant other, such as those in a new person that remind one in some way of this other, will activate the representation of the significant other, which is then applied to the new person. In the process, the perceiver infers that the new person has more in common with the significant other than is actually the case, and remembers him or her accordingly (Andersen & Cole, 1990; Chen et al., 1999). Additionally, the relational self model (Andersen & Chen, 2002; Chen, Boucher, & Tapias, 2006) maintains that each significant-other representation is linked in memory to the self by means of linkages to the relationship with this significant other. Activation of the significant other then spreads across the linkage to the relationship and then to the relevant relational self, causing the individual to view the self in these terms.

Research shows that the transference process often arises automatically. The process is evoked relatively implicitly when features presented about a new person happen to be similar to a significant other (a small set embedded among several) and activate the significant-other representation. This occurs even when these features are presented subliminally rather than supraliminally (Glassman & Andersen, 1999a). Because such representations are so chronically accessible, it also can arise preconsciously, based on extremely minimal transient cueing (Andersen et al., 1995; Chen et al., 1999). Furthermore, although participants in the supraliminal cueing paradigm usually have the conscious goal of remembering what they learn about the new person and are sometimes anticipating an upcoming interaction as well (Andersen, Reznik, & Manzella, 1996), they rarely report awareness of the significant-other resemblance, and are thus unlikely to be aware of the activation and use of the significant-other representation and its relevance to their responses. Effects are assessed by means ranging from self-reports to facial affect and overt behavior.

Relational schemas

The relational-schema approach maintains that the cognitive representation of close relationships is schematic, such that self and significant-other knowledge is linked in memory by an interpersonal script consisting of generalizations about how others have tended to respond to the self (Baldwin, 1992, 1997). The temporary or chronic activation of any one of the three components of the schema is thought to elicit the relational schema as a whole (Baldwin, 1992) and thus to elicit generalizations about the self, relationships, and others. Relational schemas typically cut across specific relationships, and are conceived as IF–THEN contingencies (e.g., "If I seek support, then my spouse will provide it"). A contingency, such as "If I make a mistake, then others will reject me," may give rise to pertinent self-generalizations based on repeated experience, as in "If I make a mistake, then I am unworthy" (Baldwin, 1997, p. 329).

Relational schemas are often activated by asking participants to consciously visualize interacting with a significant other (e.g., Baldwin & Holmes, 1987), with effects assessed by ostensibly unrelated tasks – e.g., lexical decision response latencies (e.g., Baldwin & Sinclair, 1996, Study 3). Thus, activation is assumed to be automatic. Subliminal priming (Baldwin, Carrell, & Lopez, 1990) has also been used to show preconscious automatic activation of relational schemas, and effects arising from this, in combination with chronically accessible relational schemas, such as those held by low self-esteem persons (Baldwin & Sinclair, 1996, Study 1).

Inclusion of other in the self

In contrast to the models above, the inclusion-of-other-in-the-self model views close relationships as entailing the incorporation of relationship partners (e.g., their characteristics and perspectives) into the self-concept (Aron et al., 1991) in a merging of self and other representations. The extent to which another person is included in the self is assessed by means of the endorsement of highly overlapping circles designating the self and other, versus more minimally overlapping circles, to reflect the phenomenological experience of as a sense of "we-ness" with the other (Aron et al., 1991; see also Agnew, Van Lange, Rusbult, & Langston, 1998).

Evidence for the model has focused on differential response latencies to endorse self descriptors that are and are not also descriptive of the close other (e.g., Aron et al., 1991). Shorter response latencies to judge the descriptiveness of traits previously endorsed as descriptive of both the self and the other (and vice versa) than to judge traits of self or other that are not shared are taken as evidence that the other is included in the self and thus difficult to distinguish. Because participants are unaware that their response times are being recorded or that they have responded differentially quickly to these traits, such judgments are arguably made relatively automatically.

Relational-interdependent self-construal

The relational-interdependent self-construal model (Cross, Bacon, & Morris, 2000) is based on individual differences in the degree to which the self is defined and evaluated in terms of close relationships. Individuals who see themselves in this way chronically attend to relationally relevant information and process and organize information in terms of relationships (e.g., Cross, Morris, & Gore, 2002), which then serves to maintain a relational self-construal. Although this individual difference is assessed by means of self-report (Cross et al., 2000), research using unobtrusive, implicit measures has documented automatic information processing tendencies predicted by the model. For example, individuals scoring high on relational self-construal are better able to recall relationship-related information about others in a surprise recall task (Cross et al., 2002), presumably because, unknowingly, they selectively attend to

such information. Hence, such effects appear to occur without awareness or intention.

Attachment working models

According to attachment theory, individuals form internal, complementary working models of the self and other (Collins & Read, 1994; Griffin & Bartholomew, 1994; Pietromonaco & Barrett, 2000) based on individual experiences in early interactions with attachment figures. Having responsive and loving attachment figures leads to a sense of the self as competent and worthy of love, and a view of others as available and responsive – i.e., to a *secure* attachment model. Lack of responsiveness in attachment figures often leads to a sense that the self is incompetent and unworthy and/or to a sense that others are unavailable or unresponsive – an *insecure* model – varying along dimensions of attachment anxiety and attachment avoidance. A basic assumption of the theory is that these early working models are stored in memory and can be re-experienced as general templates for later relationships, guiding expectations and behavior (e.g., Bowlby, 1969). Attachment models are considered to be chronically accessible, and thus preconsciously activated as individual differences.

Such models are usually assessed through self-report measures, although usually in a pre-test session separated in time from any experiment activating such models, thus distinguishing temporary activation based simply on completing explicit self-report measures of attachment style. Unobtrusive or implicit measures have also been used, such as response latency measures that tap self-evaluative responses associated with attachment working models (Mikulincer, 1995). Temporary activation of working models has also been shown, and there is growing evidence suggesting that individuals maintain more than one working model in memory (e.g., Baldwin, Keelan, Fehr, Enns, & Koh-Rangarajoo, 1996; see also Overall, Fletcher, & Friesen, 2003). Subliminal priming with attachment-relevant stimuli can also lead to preconscious automatic influences (e.g., Mikulincer, Hirschberger, Nachmias, & Gillath, 2001), just as explicitly visualizing a secure (vs insecure) attachment figure can transiently but postconsciously activate working models and their effects (e.g., Mikulincer, 1995).

Rejection sensitivity

Rejection sensitivity is considered to be a cognitive-affective processing disposition to "anxiously

expect, readily perceive, and overreact" to rejection (Downey & Feldman, 1996) that is learned
from exposure to rejection early in life. While
making no claims about how prior rejection or
rejection expectancies are represented in memory,
the theory has motivated considerable research
showing the ready activation of such response
tendencies in situations in which rejection is possible among individuals scoring higher (vs lower)
on an individual difference measure assessing
such tendencies.

These tendencies are assumed to be chronically
activated, reflecting a form of preconscious automaticity. As with attachment style and relational
self-construal, however, rejection sensitivity is an
individual difference variable assessed using self-
report, typically in a prior setting in advance of
any experiment. In one longitudinal study, for
example, rejection sensitivity assessed before the
study predicted a greater inclination to report several months later that a romantic partner's insensitive behavior was grounded in hurtful intentions
(Downey & Feldman, 1996). Response latencies
have also been used, for example, in a sequential-
priming pronunciation task in which rejection-
sensitive individuals pronounced hostility-related
words more quickly when preceded by rejection
primes, demonstrating their automatic linking of
rejection with hostility (Ayduk, Downey, Testa,
Yen, & Shoda, 1999).

Other approaches

Other social-cognitive approaches delineate
unique relationship categories associated with
distinct relational norms. For example, close relationships are often categorized as communal (vs
exchange) relations, with partners providing for
each other's needs without expecting specific or
immediate remuneration (Clark & Mills, 1979).
Likewise, in the relational models theory, close
relationships are deemed communal sharing relations in which partners treat each other as equivalent and emphasize what is shared rather than
distinct (Fiske, 1992). These models have done
much to illuminate the nature of relationships,
though they do not focus exclusively on close
relationships or particularly on social-cognitive
processes (with some exceptions; Fiske, Haslam,
& Fiske, 1991); they are thus addressed only when
especially relevant.

PROCESSES AND PHENOMENA

What follows is a brief review of the relatively
automatic relationship processes and phenomena

that stem from one or more of the theoretical
perspectives presented above. Instead of presenting existing research findings primarily by model,
we focus on broad classes of processes or phenomena, and, within each class, highlight the
most illuminating evidence stemming from each
theoretical approach, as feasible.

Information processing, inference, and memory

Relational knowledge often influences the manner
in which we attend to, interpret, organize, and
store information as a function of both chronic
and transient activation. Transference, relational
schema, and attachment approaches all presume
that close relationships involve mental representations stored in memory that, once activated, make
it more likely that stimuli encountered will be
encoded, quite automatically, in accordance with
the content of the representation. When a significant-other representation is activated based on
learning about a new person bearing even a minimal descriptive resemblance to this significant
other, individuals will come to use the representation to infer that this new person possesses a
still wider array of features comparable to the
significant other's (Andersen & Cole, 1990;
Andersen et al., 1995; Chen et al., 1999; Glassman
& Andersen, 1999b; for reviews, see Andersen,
Reznik, & Glassman, 2005; Andersen & Saribay,
2005). Such inferences are evoked even based
on mere facial resemblance to the significant
other (Kraus & Chen, 2010), and can arise when
triggering cues are presented subliminally
(Glassman & Andersen, 1999a). Moreover, individuals also falsely remember having learned
significant-other-consistent information that they
did not in fact learn about a new person who
minimally resembles a significant other (e.g.,
Andersen & Cole, 1990; Andersen et al., 1995,
Baum & Andersen, 1999; Berenson & Andersen,
2006; Hinkley & Andersen, 1996). Indeed, such
memory effects are more likely under cognitive
load, such as when participants are experiencing a
circadian rhythm mismatch (Kruglanski & Pierro,
2008). They are also more likely among individuals who score high on need for closure (Pierro &
Kruglanski, 2008) or low on assessment orientation (Pierro, Orehek, & Kruglanski, 2009).

Both relational-interdependent self-construal
and rejection sensitivity reflect forms of selective
encoding. For instance, individuals high in relational interdependence, are, by definition, likely to
attend to and interpret stimuli in terms of relationships (Cross et al., 2002), while rejection-sensitive
individuals are more likely to attend to rejection-
relevant stimuli and to encode ambiguous situations

as instances of rejection (Downey & Feldman, 1996). Indeed, rejection-sensitive individuals show marked attentional disruption in an emotional Stroop task when social threat words (e.g., unwanted, shunned) are encountered, but not unrelated words (Study 1), and attentional avoidance of threatening faces once they are detected (Study 2) (Berenson, Gyurak, Ayduk, Downey, Garner, Mogg, Bradley, & Pine, 2009). Such effects also hold when adjusting for attachment style and self-esteem.

As might be anticipated, avoidant individuals reveal the opposite pattern in an emotional Stroop task, in that they show less interference based on attachment-related (but not unrelated) words (e.g., intimate, loss) (Edelstein & Gillath, 2008). This effect is strongest among those in a romantic relationship when avoidance strategies are particularly engaged. When under cognitive load, however, attachment-related interference returns, suggesting that these avoidance strategies require cognitive effort. Avoidant individuals appear to be especially skillful in rapidly switching attention from one type of decision to another and in resisting distracters (Gillath, Giesbrecht, & Shaver, 2009), even with stimuli and tasks that are not attachment-related. This ability to resist distractors is, however, eliminated when they are led to think in detail about a past experience of insecurity. Thus, when they can exert the effort, avoidant individuals are skilled at intentionally regulating attention to prevent the encoding of distressing cues.

In terms of attachment, the way in which relational inferences are processed also varies, based on secure relative to insecure attachment: i.e., secure (vs insecure) individuals have less need for cognitive closure, are inclined to engage in a wider information search process about others, and are less susceptible to the primacy effect (Mikulincer, 1997). Moreover, both chronic and transiently activated secure models predict greater responsiveness to expectancy-incongruent information about a relationship partner, as shown in greater change in partner perceptions after exposure to such information, especially when the information is positively valenced. Avoidant individuals show the opposite pattern of alerting to potential threats (Mikulincer & Arad, 1999). Likewise, both chronic and experimentally manipulated social avoidance motivation are associated with greater memory for negative information and negatively biased interpretations of ambiguous social cues (Strachman & Gable, 2006).

Attachment orientation can also influence memory for one's own behavior in a dyadic interaction with a partner, with avoidant individuals remembering themselves 1 week after a distressing discussion as having been less supportive than they initially indicated (to avoid dependency), whereas less avoidant persons remember themselves as having been more supportive (fostering a sense of closeness) (Simpson, Rholes, & Winterheld, 2010). Anxiously attached individuals, by contrast, later remember having been less emotionally distant than they initially indicated (in line with their desire to be close). Interestingly, attachment orientation may also interact with communal- and exchange-oriented behaviors (Clark & Mills, 1979), producing benefits in encoding. That is, securely attached participants who experience a novel interaction partner behaving communally toward them not only demonstrate increased accessibility of proximity-seeking (in a lexical decision task) but also better performance on a mental concentration task associated with this accessibility. Anxiously attached participants in the same condition also show increased accessibility of proximity-seeking, although with poorer performance (Bartz & Lydon, 2006, Study 4).

Finally, well-known findings indicate that people are more likely to unintentionally confuse one social actor with another when their own relationship to each actor is characterized by the same relational role (Fiske et al., 1991), as indicated by clustering in recall by relationship type (e.g., in communal-sharing relationships). Indeed, among people who define themselves in terms of their own relationships, memory about others particularly depends on what the individual knows about the relationships these others are in (Cross et al., 2002).

Evaluation and facial affect

Activation of relational knowledge can also elicit a positive or negative evaluation in accord with relational knowledge and can do so quite automatically. Evidence addressing this issue is reviewed here along with that on the elicitation of emotion (e.g., in facial affect). Central to the transference approach, for example, is the notion that the overall positive or negative response one has to the significant other is stored in memory with the representation and is thus evoked when the representation is activated in relation to a new person that resembles the significant other. People report liking a new person more who implicitly resembled a liked vs disliked significant other, an effect not observed in a control condition in which the new person resembled another participant's liked or disliked significant other (e.g., Andersen et al., 1996; Andersen & Baum, 1994; Baum & Andersen, 1999; Berk & Andersen, 2000). Positive evaluation arises even when the loved other is a parent whose standards the individual falls short of and who thus evokes a negative mood in the individual (Reznik & Andersen, 2007).

Automatic affective reactions in transference have been captured more directly in participants' facial affect during exposure to descriptors about an upcoming interaction partner (Andersen et al., 1996). That is, when the partner was made to resemble and thus activate the representation of a positive compared to negative significant other, participants expressed more pleasant affect in their facial expressions – an effect not seen when the partner resembled a yoked participant's significant other. Positive facial affect even occurred when the loved other was a parent who had physically abused the individual while he or she was growing up (Berenson & Andersen, 2006).

Conversely, positive affect does not necessarily always arise from a positive transference (as indicated by positive evaluation of the new person). Emergence of this overall tone in more diffuse mood states at the moment can be disrupted (see Andersen & Saribay, 2005). For example, when a new person resembles a loved significant other but contextual factors suggest that this person cannot fulfill the interpersonal role typically occupied by the significant other (e.g., being an authority figure), this anticipated role violation, even if only implicit, disrupts the positive mood otherwise emerging when the role is not violated. Hostile mood is instead evoked (Baum & Andersen, 1999).

Overall evaluation also arises quite automatically based on significant-other priming. For example, when a significant other's (vs one's own) face/name is subliminally presented prior to encountering a neutral stimulus, the stimulus is then evaluated more favorably (Banse, 1999). Moreover, automatic positive evaluations of a relationship partner with whom one is securely attached are particularly strong and arise automatically, as indexed by the Implicit Association Test (IAT; Zayas & Shoda, 2005). Likewise, activating a secure-base schema through subliminal priming (vs priming a neutral cue or no prime) also leads participants to evaluate neutral stimuli more positively, and this effect occurred both under stressful and under neutral conditions (Mikulincer et al., 2001).

Differences in the actual structure of a significant-other representation are also related to differences in how experiences with a partner are encoded (Graham & Clark, 2006; Showers & Kevlyn, 1999), and thus evaluated. Indeed, using attributes of only one valence to describe a partner, or "compartmentalizing," is associated with more polarized partner perceptions (Showers & Kevlyn, 1999). Such compartmentalization may also underlie the variability over time in spousal evaluations shown by anxiously attached individuals (Graham & Clark, 2006; Study 5). Moreover, individuals with low self-esteem are more likely to functionally segregate positive and negative partner information in memory, such that valenced thoughts about the partner activate thoughts of the same valence, whereas those with high self-esteem are more integrative (Graham & Clark, 2006; Studies 1–4). Indeed, when judging whether positive and negative traits, presented in alternating or non-alternating order, apply to a relationship partner or an inanimate object (Studies 1 and 2), people with low (vs high) self-esteem judge their relationship partners more slowly in the alternating-valence order (but not the inanimate objects). Together, these lines of research suggest that structural differences in how partner information is represented in memory can systematically bias partner evaluations.

Acceptance or rejection expectancies

Expectations that one will be accepted or rejected are central to how people regard others, particularly those who are most significant. Such expectancies can be elicited automatically, and even when the significant other is not present. In the transference and relational self models, these expectations are part of the linkages binding significant others to the self in memory (Andersen & Chen, 2002; Chen et al., 2006) and should thus be activated when the representation of a significant other is activated. Hence, when a newly encountered person is minimally similar to a loved (vs disliked) significant other, and implicitly activates the representation of this other, the individual should expect to be accepted (or rejected) by this new person – as he or she is by the significant other. And people do indeed report expectations of acceptance (rather than rejection) under such conditions, while no such effect occurs in pertinent control conditions (e.g., Andersen et al., 1996). Individuals even expect acceptance when the triggered significant other is a loved parent whom the individual believes holds exacting standards that he or she has failed to meet (Reznik & Andersen, 2007). The positive regard for the relationship is thus what is predictive. That said, such expectancies can be reversed, such as when the individual's sense of trust has been severely violated through physical abuse by a loved parent in childhood. Reported love aside, activation of the parental representation by minimal cues about a new person leads the individual to expect to be rejected by the new person (as compared with a control condition; Berenson & Andersen, 2006).

As noted, interpersonal expectations play a crucial role in the interpersonal scripts examined within relational schemas (Baldwin, 1992), and these should be automatically activated when a relational schema is activated. In a classic study, Roman Catholic women who were subliminally primed with the frowning face of the Pope (vs a frowning stranger), and then read a sexually explicit passage, reported higher levels of tension and anxiety, presumably because they expected to be judged less favorably by this personally significant figure (Baldwin et al., 1990). Research has also examined the degree to which people expect contingent (vs non-contingent) acceptance by significant others. Individuals with chronically low (vs high) self-esteem tend to expect contingent acceptance based on success or failure, and moreover, in spite of these chronic differences, being prompted to visualize a relationship partner who expresses acceptance only contingently (vs without contingency) can activate these same associations (e.g., failure–rejection) across the board (Baldwin & Sinclair, 1996; see also Baldwin & Meunier, 1999). Likewise, work on attachment styles has shown that when securely attached individuals are primed with sentence stems like, "If I depend on my partner, then my partner will…," followed by lexical decision trials involving interpersonal outcomes (e.g., support, reject), they show faster response latencies to positive-outcome words, whereas insecurely attached individuals show faster latencies to negative outcome words (Baldwin, Fehr, Keedian, Seidel, & Thomson, 1993).

Rejection sensitivity, as indicated, is also characterized by automatic expectancies for rejection, hypervigilance to threat cues, and a tendency to perceive rejection in ambiguous responses (Downey & Feldman, 1996; Downey, Mougios, Ayduk, London, & Shoda, 2004). Rejection-sensitive individuals overestimate a relationship partner's dissatisfaction and lack of commitment to the relationship and also interpret ambiguous situations involving strangers in terms of personal rejection (Downey & Feldman, 1996). Likewise, as noted, they tend to be so vigilant to detecting potential rejection that this can interfere with other goals they have, draining attention away from other processing goals when social threat cues are present (Berenson et al., 2009). Equally important, their rejection expectations can lead to negative behaviors that actually elicit rejecting responses (Downey, Freitas, Michaelis, & Khouri, 1998). That is, when discussing unresolved relationship issues with their partner (in a videotaped encounter), they make more demeaning comments about their partner, and accordingly, elicit more anger from him or her (relative to pre-test anger) – with the latter partially accounted for by their own negative behavior. In a related vein, correlational research suggests that people who are insecure about a relationship partner's acceptance, and express their insecurities, ultimately come to doubt the authenticity of the partner's attempts to reassure them. Moreover, when reflected appraisals of vulnerability are experimentally manipulated with an acquaintance, this also leads to increased doubts about the other's authenticity in expressing positive regard (Lemay & Clark, 2008). Expectancies of rejection and unresponsiveness are thus perpetuated quite readily in dyadic encounters.

Self-definition and self-evaluation

As noted, nearly all social-cognitive approaches reviewed here address the ways in which the self is implicated in close relationships. Both the relational-self (transference) and relational-schema frameworks assume linkages between the self and significant others and memory via relationship knowledge. Hence, activating any of these components can evoke the other components. In the transference literature, the focus has been on the ways in which cueing a significant-other representation while learning about a new person activates the relational self with this other, leading these aspects of the self to infuse into the working self-concept (e.g., Hinkley & Andersen, 1996; see also Andersen & Chen, 2002). When a stranger who is a potential interaction partner is presented so as to subtly resemble (or not) a loved or disliked significant other, participants come to freely describe themselves in a manner consistent with how they tend to view themselves when with the significant other (Hinkley & Andersen, 1996). And not only does the content of the self-concept shift in this way, but the valence of that content also shifts as well (with implications for self-worth), with no such effects in control conditions. Furthermore, this process can evoke self-verification processes in that it leads people to seek to verify the relevant relational self with this significant other (Kraus & Chen, 2009). Indeed, whether the significant other was cued in a transference paradigm (Study 2), or simply primed (Studies 1 and 3), participants desired to be viewed in more self-verifying ways (vis-à-vis the relational self) rather than self-enhancing ways.

The relational self has also been examined in terms of standards by which the self may be judged. That is, activating the representation of a parent in such a context will evoke the standards that the parent holds for the individual; hence, if the individual falls short of those standards, the relevant self-discrepancy (see Higgins, 1987) will be activated as well (Reznik & Andersen, 2007). This sense of self, when called to the fore in this relational context, then evokes the specific emotional responses predicted by self-discrepancy theory, depending on the nature of the self-discrepancy: depressed mood from an ideal discrepancy and resentful/hostile mood and lack of calmness from an ought discrepancy. Similarly, in research in which an individual's father is simply primed (vs not), the standards held from the father's standpoint (ideal or ought) are activated, such that actual performance on an anagram task – which pertains to achievement standards – predicts dejection-related affect (from ideal standards) or agitation-related affect (from ought standards) (Shah, 2003b, Study 3).

In terms of self-evaluation, even the earliest work on relational schemas focused on the ways in which relational schemas may influence self-evaluation. For example, when a contingently (vs non-contingently) accepting significant other was primed using a visualization task, individuals evaluated themselves more negatively after they were led to believe they had failed at a task (Baldwin & Holmes, 1987, Study 2). Moreover, graduate-student participants also offered self-evaluations of their own research ideas that were more negative after they were subliminally primed (vs not) with the disapproving face of their department chair (Baldwin et al., 1990, Study 1). While the latter does not address evaluation of the self writ large (but of one's own ideas), it is suggestive of broader effects on self-evaluation.

More recently, research has focused on domain-specific contingencies of self-worth (see Crocker & Wolfe, 2001) in particular relationships, which can then be activated when the mental representation of this significant other is activated (Horberg & Chen, 2010). That is, when a significant other with whom the individual seeks closeness is primed, people report being more invested in the domains that the other values (Study 1), show increases in self-worth if they learn that they have succeeded in such a domain (Study 2), and show decreases in self-worth if they learn they have failed (Study 3), with the latter leading them to feel less close to this other (and to expect less acceptance). Related evidence also suggests that individuals with domain-contingent self-worth linked to experiences with significant others (vanDellen, Hoy, & Hoyle, 2009) automatically assume that these domains are important to various others, as well, and associate outcomes in these domains with thoughts about their relationships. For example, individuals with appearance-contingent self-worth associate negative appearance words with social exclusion, a tendency that does not occur for domains in which self-worth is not contingent.

By definition, attachment working models of the self are composed of positive or negative conceptions of the self that develop in relation to primary attachment figures. Research tapping self-representations implicitly provides compelling evidence for the automatic association between self-evaluation and activated attachment models. In a Stroop task, for example, securely attached individuals show slower color-naming latencies (greater interference) for both positive and negative trait terms that are self-descriptive (vs not), reflecting a "balanced" self-view, whereas those who are anxious-ambivalent are slowest for negative, self-relevant traits, and avoidants are slowest for positive, self-relevant traits (Mikulincer, 1995). Furthermore, the securely attached engage in negative self-synchronization – they modify internal aspects of the self to make them congruent with others, even when this may have negative consequences for the self (Gabriel, Kawakami, Bartak, Kang, & Mann, 2010). This pattern is diminished by priming insecure attachment. Automatic shifts in self-perceptions have also been shown with relational-interdependent self-concepts, in that individuals who see themselves in terms of their relationships are especially likely to define themselves (in unobtrusive measures) in terms of similarities with others to whom they are close (but not with a generalized other) (Cross et al., 2002).

As noted, research on inclusion of the other in the self has long shown the relative automaticity with which people judge the self-concept relevance of features that their significant other happens to share (relative to those he/she does not), as tapped by shorter response latencies (Aron et al., 1991). Consistent with this, forming a new relationship by falling in love predicts greater changes and more diversity in open-ended self-descriptions (Aron, Paris, & Aron, 1995; see also Wright, Aron, McLaughlin-Volpe, & Ropp, 1997). While such changes are expansive and potentially facilitate growth, they also leave individuals particularly vulnerable if the relationship ends (Slotter, Gardner, & Finkel, 2010). Because close relationship dissolution implicates the self as it has come to be defined by this relationship, the content of the post break-up self-concept is vulnerable to reduced clarity. This reduced clarity predicts emotional distress following the break-up.

Beyond self-definition and self-evaluation, one may ask whether or not individuals can regulate their own self-views, for example, to protect themselves from problematic relational experiences. The risk of rejection, in particular, may elicit different motivations and strategies in individuals with low (vs high) self-esteem. Individuals low in self-esteem are especially motivated to avoid rejection, and thus self-protectively underestimate acceptance from potential romantic partners, whereas high self-esteem individuals are motivated to promote new relationships and overestimate acceptance (Cameron, Stinson,

Gaetz, & Balchen, 2010), a difference not present when social risk is not salient. Indeed, social risk activates avoidance and approach goals for low and high self-esteem individuals, respectively, as tapped by a word-recall task and by approach behaviors.

Furthermore, relational selves can be used as a self-affirmation resource. Individuals who view relationships as core to their identity spontaneously refer to relational self-aspects following threat (i.e., a below-average score on a social aptitude test), and this has the impact of repairing self-esteem (Chen & Boucher, 2008). Likewise, high self-esteem people may repair esteem after encountering threat by increasing reported confidence in a romantic partner's love and affection (Murray, Holmes, MacDonald, & Ellsworth, 1998; see also DeHart, Pelham, & Murray, 2004) or by viewing relationship qualities more positively (Lockwood, Dolderman, Sadler, & Gerchak, 2004). Visualizing a positive significant other (vs not) after receiving negative feedback can also enable people to be more receptive to that threatening feedback (Kumashiro & Sedikides, 2005).

Although these studies indicate that self-esteem threats in one domain can be compensated for by indirect self-affirmation in unrelated domains, threats to the need for belonging may not be so flexibly repaired. Based on self-esteem threats involving social rejection (rather than, e.g., intelligence), self-affirmation in other domains may not be as restorative. Belonging regulation may thus be distinct from self-esteem regulation (Knowles, Lucas, Molden, Gardner, & Dean, 2010). We consider other related findings below in addressing self-protective and other-protective processes.

Goal activation and self-regulation

Goals have considerable influence on interpersonal life. The degree to which goals held by or in relation to specific significant others can be automatically activated and pursued is reviewed below along with self-regulatory processes pertaining to the activation and pursuit of such goals, including efforts to protect the self or one's relationships in the face of threat.

Goal activation and pursuit

It is well known that goals can be activated automatically by situational cues. Individuals pursue goals to which they are committed when such goals are activated and they regulate their behavior accordingly (e.g., Bargh, Gollwitzer, Lee-Chai, Barndollar, & Trötschel, 2001). Both the goals that people hold in a given relationship and the goals that the significant other holds for them are stored in memory and can be activated when the significant other is activated (Andersen & Chen, 2002; Fitzsimons & Bargh, 2003; Shah, 2003a, 2003b).

People are particularly likely to pursue fundamental needs for connection and belonging with significant others, and pursuit of such goals can thus be evoked in transference. Specifically, when a loved (vs disliked) significant other is activated in transference, this indirectly activates the goal to be close (e.g., to be open and disclosing rather than emotionally distant) with the new person, as reflected in self-reports (Andersen et al., 1996; Berk & Andersen, 2000), and this effect is distinct from simple evaluation effects reviewed earlier.

Indeed, although people who report loving a parent who in fact physically abused them while growing up may express relatively immediate positive facial affect upon learning about a parent-resembling new person (just as non-abused individuals do), as noted, they report a wish to avoid closeness with this new person, i.e., an unwillingness to evince any vulnerability (Berenson & Andersen, 2006). In a similar vein, individuals whose goals for affection with a loved significant other have chronically gone unsatisfied may report more hostility when the representation of this other is activated in transference (vs not), and yet as this hostility increases, so does their paradoxical pursuit of the frustrated goal behaviorally (Berk & Andersen, 2008). That is, this increases their affection-soliciting behavior toward the new person, which is presumably a counterproductive paring of hostility and affection-seeking.

Indeed, such motivations, when activated by a new person's minimal resemblance to a loved (vs disliked) significant other, can also influence behavior (Berk & Andersen, 2000), eliciting behavioral confirmation from a naïve stranger. The new person's actual conversational behavior in an unstructured telephone encounter ultimately comes to express more positive affect and responsiveness in return, as assessed by blind judges exposed only to the new person's side of the conversation. Additionally, construing the self in terms of one's relationship may itself make confirmation effects more likely, in that these individuals not only evaluate new relationship partners more positively (Cross et al., 2000) but also believe new relationship partners view the relationship more positively (Cross & Gore, 2003) and they are in fact perceived as more responsive and self-disclosing (Cross et al., 2000).

Relatedly, subliminally priming a secure attachment figure increases self-reported willingness to self-disclose (Study 1) and to seek emotional support (Study 2), and priming an insecurity-inducing figure implicitly activates insecure goal words, as assessed by a lexical decision task (Study 3; Gillath, Mikulincer, Fitzsimons, Shaver, Schachner, & Bargh, 2006). Moreover, avoidant individuals are unwilling to seek support even when primed with a security-inducing figure (Study 2), and both attachment anxiety and avoidance moderate goal accessibility following such a prime, interfering with fast responding to secure goals and instead activating anxious or avoidance goals, respectively (Study 3).

More broadly, merely thinking about a significant other or being subliminally exposed to this person's name can activate goals with this other as well as behavioral goal pursuit. That is, individuals perform better and persist longer on an anagram task after having been primed with their mother when they have the goal to make her proud (rather than not) (Fitzsimons & Bargh, 2003, Study 4a), even though they showed no conscious awareness of this or of intending it. Simply thinking about a friend (vs a coworker) appears also to activate the goal of being helpful, as it makes people more likely to subsequently volunteer to help another person when asked to do so by the experimenter (Study 1).

Likewise, the automatic influence of goals that significant others have for the self also occurs based on priming a specific significant other. For example, subliminally priming a significant other increases commitment to one's significant other's goals (Study 1), and increases the accessibility of these goals (assessed in a lexical decision task) and behavioral goal pursuit (in anagram-task performance and persistence), and this is mediated by goal accessibility (Studies 2–5; Shah, 2003a). Moreover, this tendency increases as closeness to the significant other increases, but is less strong if the significant other holds multiple (potentially diverse) goals. Likewise, subliminally priming a significant other who has high expectations for the individual, and regards a task as difficult, leads to believing one can do well on the task and to performing better and persisting longer (again on an anagram task) (Shah, 2003b, Study 1). When the primed significant other highly values attaining a particular goal, this also influences the individual's own goal valuation as well as task performance and persistence (Study 2). Priming a significant other, however, does not always increase the likelihood that a specific goal will be activated and pursued. When a primed significant other is controlling, people may resist by engaging in behavior that directly opposes that person's wishes, without awareness or apparent intent, even when this results in a suboptimal outcome (Chartrand, Dalton, & Fitzsimons, 2007).

Finally, spontaneous, dyadic behaviors among relationship partners may also reflect automatic goal activation and pursuit. Women who are securely attached, for example, spontaneously seek more help from their romantic partner in a stressful situation, as a function of their own anxiety, whereas women with avoidant working models do the opposite (Simpson, Rholes, & Nelligan, 1992). Moreover, secure men in these relationships offer more support as a function of their partners' exhibited anxiety, whereas avoidant men offer less. Subliminal priming of attachment security has also been linked to compassion and altruism (Mikulincer, Shaver, Gillath, & Nitzberg, 2005) – with primed participants reported higher levels of compassion and agreeing to do aversive tasks for the sake of another alleged participant.

Self- and relationship-protective regulation

Two particularly important motives that are pursued within close relationships are self-protection and relationship-protection, especially in response to respective threats. Evidence suggests that such motives may arise automatically and serve self-regulatory functions when significant others are activated and a threat is encountered.

The relational self model, for example, argues that both of these motives can readily be evoked when a significant-other representation is activated (Andersen & Chen, 2002; Chen et al., 2006). In the transference paradigm, for example, implicit activation of a negative significant-other representation leads individuals to experience, as part of the working self-concept, negative self-qualities typically experienced in the relationship, while also simultaneously calling to mind *self-enhancing* personal qualities that are unrelated to the relationship (Hinkley & Andersen, 1996), presumably as a self-protective regulatory response. Although assessed using free-form self-descriptions (self-reports), the relatively implicit activation of the significant other in this paradigm implies an automatic effect (Andersen et al., 2005).

In terms of other-protective motives in transference, evidence shows that upon learning about a new person who minimally resembles (via positive and negative features) a loved significant other, people respond with far more positive facial affect to the *negative* features of this loved other than to the positive features. This did not occur when the features were drawn from another participant's significant other. The effect can presumably compensate for encountering in a new person what one dislikes about a loved significant other, thus serving to protect the loved one and the relationship. Similarly, when a loved parent is activated in transference, people also respond with far more positive facial affect, this time to learning that the person in transference is becoming increasingly irritable and annoyed while awaiting a forthcoming interaction, an effect that occurs even among individuals who were physically abused by this parent in childhood (Berenson & Andersen, 2006). The relative immediacy of these facial expressions suggests that the negative information may have been transformed into a positive response relatively automatically, in a process comparable to that observed in spousal relationships (e.g., Murray & Holmes, 1993).

Self-protective motives are also thought to regulate the behavior of people high in rejection sensitivity in response to interpersonal threat, and to do so automatically. Rejection cues automatically activate the defensive motivational system in rejection-sensitive individuals, while acceptance cues, by contrast, do not activate an appetitive motivational system (Downey et al., 2004; for a review, see Romero-Canyas, Downey, Berenson, Ayduk, & Kang, 2010). Based on exposure to paintings depicting rejection or acceptance, as well as to non-representational paintings of either negative or positive valence, people high in rejection sensitivity showed greater magnitude in startle eye-blinks upon viewing scenes of rejection, relative to negative non-representational paintings; furthermore, their startle magnitude is not attenuated upon viewing acceptance themes relative to positive non-representational paintings.

Indeed, individuals high in rejection sensitivity are particularly susceptible to using self-protective mechanisms even when they lead to negative interpersonal outcomes. For example, heightened rejection sensitivity can lead to less satisfying relationship experiences (Downey & Feldman, 1996). How this defensive motivation plays out can vary depending on context: anxious expectations of rejection predict dating violence among men who are highly invested in their romantic relationship. However, among men reporting relatively low investment in romantic relationships, anxious expectations of rejection predicted reduced involvement in relationships and increased distress in (and avoidance of) social situations (Downey, Feldman, & Ayduk, 2000).

The negative effects of rejection sensitivity on interpersonal outcomes are also moderated by general self-regulation abilities (Ayduk, Mendoza-Denton, Mischel, Downey, Peake, & Rodriguez, 2000). To the extent that they happen to be "good self-regulators" (indexed by ability to delay gratification), highly rejection-sensitive people tend to have fewer negative interpersonal experiences, and function more effectively than those low in rejection sensitivity. Indeed, experimentally inducing the ability to delay gratification leads to a decreased accessibility of hostile thoughts and feelings relevant to rejection (in a lexical decision task, Ayduk et al., 2000; Ayduk, Mischel, & Downey, 2002). Such a process may begin effortfully (see Yovetich & Rusbult, 1994), but can presumably become automatic with practice.

Other direct evidence for automatic self-protection in response to interpersonal threat, and for the way this may interact with relationship-protective motivations, comes from research on dependency regulation processes (Murray, Holmes, & Collins, 2006). In the dependency regulation model, people are assumed to pursue relationship-protective responses by default. When not facing threat, people tend to be motivated to view their partners positively and to seek increased closeness with their partners (Murray, Holmes, & Griffin, 2000; Murray, Holmes, Griffin, Bellavia, & Rose, 2001). When people feel rejected, however, self-protective strategies take over, and as a result, attachment to partners decreases while self-reliance increases. Similar processes have also been shown among low versus high self-esteem individuals – with high self-esteem persons seeking closeness when risk is activated and those low in self-esteem seeking to self-protect (Murray, Derrick, Jaye, Leder, & Holmes, 2008).

Research also shows that such self-regulatory processes can occur outside of awareness in the service of contextually activated higher-order self- and relationship-protecting needs (DeHart et al., 2004). People with chronically low self-esteem, for example, tended to implicitly evaluate their relationship partners in ways contingent on current relationship quality. People with high self-esteem, on the other hand, maintain positive implicit evaluations of their partner, even when things are not going well in the relationship.

Related processes evoked by threat are observed in parent–child relationships in which the parent feels powerless. Such parents engage in physically coercive behavior, and find perceived non-compliance in the child threatening. They also tend to activate dominance and power cognitions in such contexts – particularly when under cognitive load (Bugental, Lyon, Krantz, & Cortez, 1997). With sufficient cognitive capacity, however, even low-power parents can effortfully regulate their responses to perceived threats and respond adaptively.

In attachment processes, people also respond to threat by automatically (without awareness) activating attachment figures in compensatory fashion (Mikulincer, Gillath, & Shaver, 2002). When threat cues are presented subliminally to both secure and anxious individuals, attachment figures are activated, perhaps because they are comforting. Additionally, when threatened, securely attached individuals show heightened

accessibility of self-attributes developed in secu-
rity-enhancing interactions with attachment figures (Mikulincer, 1998). However, those high in
attachment avoidance actually show diminished
accessibility of their attachment figures
(Mikulincer et al., 2002). Indeed, individuals who
are anxiously attached respond to threat cues by
pursuing closeness, derogating the self, and accen-
tuating agreement with the other, while those who
are avoidantly attached accentuate self-reliance,
emotional distance, and self-enhancement
(Mikulincer, 1998; Mikulincer, Orbach, & Iavnieli,
1998). Avoidant individuals suppress distressing
feelings about potentially threatening interpersonal outcomes, such as when they are prompted
to imagine abandonment (Fraley & Shaver, 1997)
and encode less about attachment-relevant experiences in the moment (Fraley, Garner, & Shaver,
2000).

Self-regulatory strategies also influence perceptions of the self and others in adult attachment
relationships. For example, anxiously attached
individuals tend to overestimate their similarity
to attachment figures (Mikulincer et al., 1998),
and also hold a negative view of themselves
(Mikulincer, 1998), a tendency that increases
when these individuals are experiencing negative
affect and are particularly motivated to win others'
approval. By contrast, avoidant individuals underestimate their similarity to attachment figures and
hold an unusually positive view of themselves.
This effect is also exasperated under conditions of
distress, and is related to a desire to validate a
sense of self-reliance. Furthermore, in a diary
study, avoidant individuals reported the benefits
received in their relationship to be less voluntarily
given, which arguably perpetuates independence
and justifies not depending upon the partner (Beck
& Clark, 2010). Avoidance priming also leads
to similar perceptions. Given that these effects
stem from chronically accessible constructs, they
are likely to function at a preconscious level.
Ultimately, chronically activated self-protection
goals can override ideal patterns of mutual non-
contingent responsiveness in relationships, even
in the absence of threat. This can lead to a neglect
of the partner's needs or even attending to a partner's needs to the neglect of the self to ensure he
or she will not leave (Clark, Graham, Williams,
& Lemay, 2008).

In a related vein, communal and exchange
relationship orientations (Clark & Mills, 1979)
differentially influence the perception of self and
others based on motives. Specifically, communal
orientation encourages relationship-promotion
behaviors and the perception that partners
are equally caring and supportive (Lemay &
Clark, 2008). These projected perceptions elicit
more communal behavior from the partner, lead-

ing to increased relationship satisfaction as well as
willingness to invest in the relationship and depend
on the partner: activating communal responsiveness positively affects perceptions of the partner's
responsiveness, evaluations of the partner, and
attraction, warmth, and disclosure in romantic
relationships and close friendships.

Lastly, in order to monitor their goal progress,
individuals can look to their social relationships
for information about their own relative success
or failure. Contrary to the typical upward comparison effect, comparisons with successful
romantic partners can lead to greater motivation,
even in self-relevant domains (Pinkus, Lockwood,
Schimmack, & Fournier, 2008). Individuals with
romantic partners who support their goal pursuit
(Brunstein, Dangelmayer, & Schultheiss, 1996),
or who are willing to be dependent upon a romantic partner (Feeney, 2007), tend to be more
successful in their goal pursuit, across various
domains.

Some evidence shows as well that goal activation based on significant others can be used
strategically. Thinking of a significant other with
good self-control leads to increases in state self-
control, whereas thinking of others with poor
self-control leads to the opposite (vanDellen &
Hoyle, 2010). Additionally, activated goals can
automatically bring to mind significant others
who are instrumental for those goals, heightening
their accessibility relative to non-instrumental
others (Fitzsimons & Shah, 2009). Categorizing
others as such may enable people to approach goal-
instrumental others and avoid goal-obstructing
others, promoting successful goal pursuit
(Fitzsimons & Shah, 2008). For example, when college students primed with academic-achievement
goal draw closer to instrumental others, they end
up studying longer and performing better on a
midterm weeks later. Once the goal is attained,
however, they draw away from these others,
making way for others instrumental for new goals
(Fitzsimons & Fishbach, 2010).

Group and intergroup processes

A particularly exciting area of research has aimed
to examine links between relational and group or
intergroup processes. On the one hand, researchers have commonly applied social-cognitive concepts in close relationships to the study of group/
intergroup issues. For example, research has
examined attachment to groups (Smith, Murphy,
& Coats, 1999), has conceived of rejection sensitivity in terms of race-based rejection sensitivity
(Mendoza-Denton, Downey, Purdie, Davis, &
Pietrzak, 2002), and has considered social identity
as inclusion of the in-group in the self (Smith &

Henry, 1996). The latter research has established the *extended contact effect* by showing that intergroup bias is reduced as a function of observing a member of one's in-group (who, by definition, one includes in the self) engaging in friendly interactions with an out-group member (Wright et al., 1997). This presumably leads the out-group member to be included in the self, as well. Recent evidence suggests that forming cross-group friendships can buffer the negative consequences of race-based rejection sensitivity, e.g., by lessening intergroup anxiety (Page-Gould, Mendoza-Denton, & Tropp, 2008).

On the other hand, processes in close relationships have also been examined in the context of group (social category membership) differences. Recent research, for example, has demonstrated that transference occurs across group boundaries, i.e., when the new person does not share the significant other's political or ethnic group membership, though resembling him or her in other ways (Kraus, Chen, Lee, & Straus, 2010). If the activated significant other is liked or loved, participants in transference may transfer this positive evaluation to the new person despite his or her ethnic out-group status (Kraus et al., 2010, Study 2).

Meanwhile, research has examined how intergroup processes may arise from activation of relationship knowledge. Building on research suggesting that categorical knowledge (and related norms) are activated based on significant-other activation in transference (e.g., social roles, Baum & Andersen, 1999; standards, Reznik & Andersen, 2007), evidence has shown that activating a significant other can also lead this other's ethnic category to be activated and used to categorize the new person (Saribay & Andersen, 2007). Indeed, when the self is also of this same ethnicity, such indirect activation of this ethnic category can also activate the participant's own ethnic identity, and as theory would suggest, can increase intergroup bias in judging unrelated others. That is, if the broader social network of the significant other is ethnically homogenous, this outcome occurs. When, by contrast, the significant other's social network is more expansive and ethnically heterogeneous, the effect is dampened.

Returning to the contact hypothesis, both theory and research have highlighted the role of intergroup friendships (e.g., Brown & Hewstone, 2005; Page-Gould et al., 2008) in the reduction of prejudice. The research just noted addressing social networks of significant others (Saribay & Andersen, 2007) has much in common with this theme and with the extended contact effect in particular (Wright et al., 1997). In that case, the social network of the significant other serves as a record of cross-group affiliations, which can then attenuate or exacerbate bias when the perceivers' ethnic identity is evoked based on activation of a significant other. Of course, actually forming cross-group friendships oneself or directly observing them can also be influential in important ways (Page-Gould, Mendoza-Denton, Alegre, & Siy, 2010), in part by enabling the individual to revise expectations about and response tendencies toward both in-group and out-group others.

Similarly, attachment researchers (Mikulincer & Shaver, 2001) also assume that priming attachment security (i.e., a secure base) should lead to less derogation of out-group members, stemming from personal or collective self-esteem protection. Unsurprisingly, perhaps, dispositional attachment security clearly is negatively correlated with hostility toward out-groups. More importantly, however, priming attachment security (vs positive affect or a neutral prime) does lead to less negative responses toward out-group members, both when it is an attachment figure (a significant other) that is primed and when it is generic attachment knowledge (and whether via subliminal priming or visualization). Indeed, a lower threat appraisal of intergroup encounters appears to mediate the effect of security priming on reduced intergroup bias.

Meaning systems

Close relationships are also crucial in establishing and maintaining a sense of meaning in life, as relationship partners validate people's views of the world in which they live (Baumeister, 1991) and bestow a sense of security. Research on the role of close others in meaning-making and the joint construction of social reality has also begun to address the underlying processes involved.

Shared reality

Shared reality theory suggests that people are motivated to achieve shared perceptions of reality with others to establish, maintain, and regulate social bonds. In so doing, people can come to view their environments (and the self) as predictable and stable. A central assumption of the model is that mutual understanding is critical for establishing and maintaining relationships (Hardin & Conley, 2001; Hardin & Higgins, 1996), and that people cannot interpret stimuli in meaningful ways in the absence of a socially shared basis for interpretation, as such mutual understanding imbues experience with perceived validity (see also Heine, Proulx, & Vohs, 2006; Swann, 1990).

Although little research has directly examined these processes in close relationships, some have examined factors of considerable relevance to such. For example, people are more likely to "socially tune" (Hardin & Higgins, 1996) toward individuals they like and are motivated to approach (Sinclair, Huntsinger, Skorinko, & Hardin, 2005b; Sinclair, Lowery, Hardin, & Colangelo, 2005c) and to tune away from those they dislike and wish to avoid. They also shift their attitudes toward those of close-relationship partners (Davis & Rusbult, 2001), align their self-concepts and self-evaluations with the views of significant persons and even strangers under some circumstances (Sinclair, Dunn, & Lowery, 2005a; Sinclair et al., 2005c), and mimic the characteristics and behaviors of salient individuals (Chartrand & Bargh, 1999). Moreover, evidence has shown that implicit activation of a loved significant other in transference indirectly activates the shared belief system held in common with a significant other – over and above one's own distinct or other's distinct belief systems (Przybylinski & Andersen, 2011). In this case, the individual also socially tunes toward such shared meanings.

Attempts to establish shared reality with others may begin early in life, as infants seek to convert their sensations into meaningful experience. Accordingly, shared reality is most beneficial when trust and dependability are givens, and openness and exploration possible (e.g., Mikulincer & Shaver, 2004). People who report high levels of attachment security and shared reality with family members also report finding their lives as more meaningful (Sakellaropoulo & Baldwin, 2007). Similarly, evidence suggests that religiosity and also prejudice against atheists may be rooted in shared reality within close relationships (Magee & Hardin, 2010), in that securely attached people who believe that their fathers share their religious beliefs (rather than not) are less threatened by exposure to ideas on evolution. The functions of shared meaning in close relationships may thus depend to some extent on the quality of the relationship and the content of the shared beliefs.

Terror management

The meaning-making functions of personal relationships have also been much emphasized in terror management theory (see Greenberg, Solomon, & Pyszczynski, 1997), which assumes that humans are uniquely cognizant of the inevitability of their own death and that this often induces feelings of helplessness or terror. Such feelings can then be reduced by processes that buffer or remove death awareness.

A central focus of the theory is on validating cultural worldviews and on self-esteem enhancement (Greenberg et al., 1997) for reducing existential anxiety. Recently, however, the relevance of close relationships has been increasingly examined (Mikulincer, Florian, & Hirschberger, 2003). For example, among securely attached individuals, imagining separation from or an argument with a romantic partner increases the accessibility of death-related thoughts and instigates worldview defense (Mikulincer, Florian, Birnbaum, & Malishkevich, 2002). Conversely, when these individuals think about one of their parents, it helps buffer the negative effects of reminders of death (Cox, Arndt, Pyszczynski, Greenberg, Abdollahi, & Solomon, 2008, Studies 1–3). Indeed, when these individual are reminded of death, it increases the accessibility of attachment constructs (Mikulincer et al., 2002), heightens their motivation to form and maintain close relationships and to increase intimacy (Florian, Mikulincer, & Hirschberger, 2002; Taubman-Ben-Ari, Findler, & Mikulincer, 2002), and reduces fear of rejection (Taubman-Ben-Ari et al., 2002). More generally, reminders of death may ease the recall of positive maternal interactions (vs negative ones), and increase attraction to a stranger who is similar to one's parent (Cox et al., 2008, Studies 4–5).

OVERARCHING THEMES AND OUTSTANDING ISSUES

An overarching theme arising from this review is that prior and current significant-other knowledge is often perpetuated in present-day encounters. Thus, tendencies learned in prior relationships continue to exert influences beyond the initial relationships themselves, even when the relationship partners are not physically present, or after a given relationship ends. This notion is an essential consequence of many of the social-cognitive mechanisms reviewed here. The social-cognitive model of transference, in particular, documents the ways in which activation of a specific significant-other representation causes prior relational knowledge to resurface with new others. While the transference model focuses both theoretically and empirically on representations of specific significant others and on cues that activate such representations, most other models focus on more generalized knowledge representations. The relational schemas model, for example, tends to emphasize generalized, schematic knowledge and evokes such schemas using generic cues or primes of a specific significant other. Likewise, attachment theory maintains that secure or insecure attachment styles are generic, having been generalized based on early experiences with attachment figures. The attachment system is typically activated generically, or by priming a significant other, who, for example, serves as a secure base.

The representation of specific significant others in memory and their activation can thus be the starting point for research across a wider variety of theoretical perspectives on close relationships, perhaps more so than the theories themselves imply. Indeed, the automatic tendency to expect, perceive, and overreact to potential rejection, as in rejection sensitivity, is thought to develop from prior relational experiences and thus to confirm expectations learned from prior relationships. Similarly, the fact that individuals with a relational self-construal attend so intently to relationships might make them all the more likely to maintain the very relationships that define them. Moreover, even a merging of close others with the self, as in the inclusion-of-other-in-the-self model, provides a means through which a significant other remains present even when not.

It is clear that much of what happens in close relationships may to some extent happen automatically: automatic tendencies guide how people think and feel about close others and themselves, whether in expecting to be accepted or rejected, in self-regulating to attain goals, in group/intergroup perceptions or in epistemic responses. Thus, despite major differences in the exact assumptions and methods underlying research across the models we address, an assumption common to all is that relationship knowledge is readily perpetuated precisely because of the influence it can exert even without awareness, intent, effort, or control. In short, it is automaticity that may lie at the heart of such perpetuation and re-emergence of close relationship patterns.

Nonetheless, relationship processes and phenomena are not *always* automatic. People spend a good deal of conscious, intentional energy deliberating about their interactions with close others (even as they are automatically or unconsciously influenced by relational knowledge). Individuals also care about how their responses to others may be "contaminated" by biases, even if their lay theories about such biases are inaccurate (Wilson & Brekke, 1994) and may experience only the end product of automatic processes, which may at times be undesired. Hence, diverting the automatic processes that give rise to problematic responding is often the focus of clinical work, and further integration of the approaches reviewed here with systematic research in the clinical domain may thus be fruitful. Indeed, the transference concept first arose as a clinical one.

Recent work in fact speaks to the possibility of regulating the influence of relational knowledge, such as that indicating instances when transference is more likely to occur (when experiencing circadian mismatch, Kruglanski & Pierro, 2008; or based on individual differences in motivation, Pierro & Kruglanski, 2008; Pierro et al., 2009). While such work suggests that deficits in attention may be what give rise to the process, this implies that attention or awareness per se should enable the transference process to be overturned. Recent evidence has suggested that this may not be the case, even when motivation to prevent the effect is also high (Liviatan & Andersen, 2010). Of course, to override the automatic influences, one may need an appropriate regulation strategy and sufficient cognitive resources to execute it, if it requires effort. Nonetheless, preliminary evidence suggesting that awareness and motivation may not be sufficient remains of interest. Given the limited cognitive resources, time, and motivation available in daily social life, and how relatively uncommon effective strategies for short-circuiting automatic relational responses may be, gaining further understanding when and why such responses can be regulated and by whom is warranted.

Indeed, even when relationships are maladaptive and/or particularly painful, it may be that the predictability and meaning the relationship affords can make anything other than the maintenance and continual use of relational representations unappealing. Thus, some individuals may tend toward engaging in suboptimal or harmful relationship patterns, perpetuating them over time rather than facing the unknown, uncharted territory of doing otherwise, just as people often seek self-verification even of negative self-views (Swann, 1990). At the same time, people often do know they are suffering from repeating old patterns in new contexts and want to change, and the task that remains is to clearly specify the conditions under which they can be enabled to do so.

Furthermore, the evidence reviewed here suggests that, despite the automatic nature of relational processes, they are by no means simplistic. Indeed, the fact that effective goal pursuit is promoted by the activation of those significant others who are instrumental to the goal (Fitzsimons & Shah, 2008, 2009; vanDellen & Hoyle, 2010), and that once the goal is attained the individual moves away from these others to draw closer to those who are instrumental for new goals (Fitzsimons & Fishbach, 2010), suggests a far more dynamic regulatory process in close relationships than previously understood. This evidence also implies that relatively communal relationships are guided not only by social motives and communal goals but also by instrumental motives and personal goals, and that dual motives can operate in tandem or trade-off rather than showing exclusivity as a function of relationship type. Evidently, individuals adopt different strategic orientations at different times, and perhaps it is the case that some people are more flexible in doing so than others. If properly understood and harnessed, perhaps such strategic flexibility may offer new avenues for the regulation of particularly maladaptive relational processes.

Accordingly, evidence has also demonstrated the complex interplay and tension between self-protective and other-protective regulatory processes in the context of close relationships (Murray et al., 2000, 2001; see also, e.g., Andersen et al., 1996; Andersen & Chen, 2002; Berenson & Andersen, 2006). By default, individuals appear to exhibit relationship-protective responses, and yet the perception of threat can lead to a shift into more self-protective responses, with the perception of threat itself varying across individuals, contexts, and experiences. Given that these processes may function relatively automatically and, thus in some cases, outside of conscious awareness or intention, understanding when and why individuals may choose to protect the other over protecting the self, even at great cost, is important.

New evidence on the self-concept reviewed here also highlights the potential reach of relational knowledge in influencing people's responses, suggesting that much remains to be discovered about both variability and consistency in the relational self. For example, the fact that people seek to validate their relational selves when significant-other representations have been activated (Kraus & Chen, 2009) makes it clear that the spread of activation along self–other linkages not only activates those aspects of the self typically experienced with this other but also consistency motives that underlying self-verification processes. Finally, the broader influence of relational knowledge on social identity and intergroup perception, as well as on epistemic concerns, suggests that these literatures, too, are likely to continue to grow in the coming years.

CONCLUSION

We began by noting the tremendous importance of close others in people's lives, even while the processes known to guide interpersonal life are frequently quite automatic. To fully understand relationship processes, it is of value to ask how and when these processes are relatively automatic and when they are relatively more mindful and deliberative. To facilitate healthy relationship dynamics, it is also important to understand when automatic processes can interfere with conscious intentions. As of now, many questions remain about exactly how people are best able to consciously shape their own relationships and interpersonal lives. Perhaps answers are just around the corner and will reveal themselves as methods and theory advance.

REFERENCES

Agnew, C. R., Van Lange, P. A. M., Rusbult, C. E., & Langston, C. A. (1998). Cognitive interdependence: Commitment and the mental representation of close relationships. *Journal of Personality and Social Psychology, 74,* 939–954.

Andersen, S. M., & Baum, A. B. (1994). Transference in interpersonal relations: Inferences and affect based on significant-other representations. *Journal of Personality, 62,* 460–497.

Andersen, S. M., & Chen, S. (2002). The relational self: An interpersonal social-cognitive theory. *Psychological Review, 109,* 619–645.

Andersen, S. M., & Cole, S. W. (1990). "Do I know you?": The role of significant others in general social perception. *Journal of Personality and Social Psychology, 59,* 384–399.

Andersen, S. M., & Glassman, N. S. (1996). Responding to significant others when they are not there: Effects on interpersonal inference, motivation, and affect. In R. M. Sorrentino & E. T. Higgins (Eds.), *Handbook of motivation and cognition* (Vol. 3, pp. 262–321). New York: Guilford Press.

Andersen, S. M., Glassman, N. S., Chen, S., & Cole, S. W. (1995). Transference in social perception: The role of chronic accessibility in significant-other representations. *Journal of Personality and Social Psychology, 69,* 41–57.

Andersen, S. M., Moskowitz, D. B., Blair, I. V., & Nosek, B. A. (2007). Automatic thought. In E. T. Higgins & A. W. Kruglanski (Eds.), *Social psychology: Handbook of basic principles* (2nd ed., pp. 138–175). New York: Guilford Press.

Andersen, S. M., Reznik, I., & Chen, S. (1997). Self in relation to others: Cognitive and motivational underpinnings. In J. G. Snodgrass & R. L. Thompson (Eds.), *The self across psychology: Self-recognition, self-awareness, and the self-concept* (pp. 233–275). New York: New York Academy of Science.

Andersen, S. M., Reznik, I., & Glassman, N. S. (2005). The unconscious relational self. In R. Hassin, J. S. Uleman, & J. A. Bargh (Eds.), *The new unconscious* (pp. 421–481). New York: Oxford University Press.

Andersen, S. M., Reznik, I., & Manzella, L. M. (1996). Eliciting transient affect, motivation, and expectancies in transference: Significant-other representations and the self in social relations. *Journal of Personality and Social Psychology, 71,* 1108–1129.

Andersen, S. M., & Saribay, S. A. (2005). The relational self and transference: Evoking motives, self-regulation, and emotions through activation of mental representations of significant others. In M. W. Baldwin (Ed.), *Interpersonal cognition* (pp. 1–32). New York: Guilford Press.

Aron, A., Aron, E. N., Tudor, M., & Nelson, G. (1991). Close relationships as including other in the self. *Journal of Personality and Social Psychology, 60*, 241–253.

Aron, A, Paris, M., & Aron, E. N. (1995). Falling in love: Prospective studies of self-concept change. *Journal of Personality and Social Psychology, 69*, 1102–1112.

Ayduk, O., Downey, G., Testa, A., Yen, Y., & Shoda, Y. (1999). Does rejection elicit hostility in rejection sensitive women? *Social Cognition, 17*, 245–271.

Ayduk, O., Mendoza-Denton, R., Mischel, W., Downey, G., Peake, P. K., & Rodriguez, M. (2000). Regulating the interpersonal self: Strategic self-regulation for coping with rejection sensitivity. *Journal of Personality and Social Psychology, 79*, 776–792.

Ayduk, O., Mischel, W., & Downey, G. (2002). Attentional mechanisms linking rejection to hostile reactivity: The role of "hot" versus "cool" focus. *Psychological Science, 13*, 443–448.

Baldwin, M. W. (1992). Relational schemas and the processing of information. *Psychological Bulletin, 112*, 461–484.

Baldwin, M. W. (1997). Relational schemas as a source of if–then self-inference procedures. *Review of General Psychology, 1*, 326–335.

Baldwin, M. W., Carrell, S. E., & Lopez, D. F. (1990). Priming relationship schemas: My advisor and the Pope are watching me from the back of my mind. *Journal of Experimental Social Psychology, 26*, 435–454.

Baldwin, M. W., Fehr, B., Keedian, E., Seidel, M., & Thomson, D. W. (1993). An exploration of the relational schemata underlying attachment styles: Self-report and lexical decision approaches. *Personality and Social Psychology Bulletin, 19*, 746–754.

Baldwin, M. W., & Holmes, J. G. (1987). Salient private audiences and awareness of self. *Journal of Personality and Social Psychology, 52*, 1087–1098.

Baldwin, M. W., Keelan, J. P. R., Fehr, B., Enns, V., & Koh-Rangarajoo, E. (1996). Social-cognitive conceptualization of attachment working models: Availability and accessibility effects. *Journal of Personality and Social Psychology, 71*, 94–109.

Baldwin, M. W., Lydon, J. E., McClure, M. J., & Etchison, S. (2010). Measuring implicit processes in close relationships. In B. Gawronski, & B. K. Payne (Eds.), *Handbook of implicit social cognition* (pp. 426–444). New York: Guilford Press.

Baldwin, M. W., & Meunier, J. (1999). The cued activation of attachment relational schemas. *Social Cognition, 17*, 209–227.

Baldwin, M. W., & Sinclair, L. (1996). Self-esteem and "if...then" contingencies of interpersonal acceptance. *Journal of Personality and Social Psychology, 71*, 1130–1141.

Banse, R. (1999). Automatic evaluation of self and significant others: Affective priming in close relationships. *Journal of Social and Personal Relationships, 16*, 803–821.

Bargh, J. A. (1989). Conditional automaticity: Varieties of automatic influence in social perception and cognition. In J. S. Uleman & J. A. Bargh (Eds.), *Unintended thought* (pp. 3–51). New York: Guilford Press.

Bargh, J. A. (1994). The four horsemen of automaticity: Awareness, intention, efficiency, and control in social cognition. In R. S. Wyer & T. K. Srull (Eds.), *Handbook of social cognition* (2nd ed.). Hillsdale, NJ: Erlbaum.

Bargh, J. A., Bond, R. N., Lombardi, W. J., & Tota, M. E. (1986). The additive nature of chronic and temporary sources of construct accessibility. *Journal of Personality and Social Psychology, 50*, 869–878.

Bargh, J. A., Gollwitzer, P. M., Lee-Chai, A., Barndollar, K., & Trötschel, R. (2001). The automated will: Nonconscious activation and pursuit of behavioral goals. *Journal of Personality and Social Psychology, 81*, 1014–1027.

Bartz, J. A., & Lydon, J. E. (2006). Navigating the interdependence dilemma: Attachment goals and the use of communal norms with potential close others. *Journal of Personality and Social Psychology, 91*, 77–96.

Baum, A. & Andersen, S. M. (1999). Interpersonal roles in transference: Transient mood states under the condition of significant-other activation. *Social Cognition, 17*, 161–185.

Baumeister, R. F. (1991). *Meanings of life.* New York: Guilford Press.

Baumeister, R. F., & Leary, M. R. (1995). The need to belong: Desire for interpersonal attachments as a fundamental human motivation. *Psychological Bulletin, 117*, 497–529.

Beck, L. A., & Clark, M. S. (2010). Looking a gift horse in the mouth as a defense against increasing intimacy. *Journal of Experimental Social Psychology, 46*, 676–679.

Berenson, K. R., & Andersen, S. M. (2006). Childhood physical and emotional abuse by a parent: Transference effects in adult interpersonal relationships. *Personality and Social Psychology Bulletin, 33*, 1509–1522.

Berenson, K. R., Gyurak A., Ayduk, O., Downey G., Garner, M. J., Mogg, K., et al. (2009). Rejection sensitivity and disruption of attention by social threat cues. *Journal of Research in Personality, 43*, 1064–1072.

Berk, M. S., & Andersen, S. M. (2000). The impact of past relationships on interpersonal behavior: Behavioral confirmation in the social-cognitive process of transference. *Journal of Personality and Social Psychology, 79*, 546–562.

Berk, M. S., & Andersen, S. M. (2008). The sting of lack of affection: Chronic dissatisfaction of goals in transference. *Self and Identity, 7*, 393–412.

Bowlby, J. (1969). *Attachment and loss* (Vol. 1, *Attachment*). New York: Basic Books.

Brown, R., & Hewstone, M. (2005). An integrative theory of intergroup contact. In M. P. Zanna (Ed.), *Advances in experimental social psychology* (Vol. 23, pp. 305–331). San Diego, CA: Academic Press.

Brunstein, J. C., Dangelmayer, G., & Schultheiss, O. (1996). Personal goals and social support in close relationships: Effects on relationship mood and marital satisfaction. *Journal of Social and Personal Psychology, 71*, 1006–1019.

Bugental, D. B., Lyon, J. E., Krantz, J., & Cortez, V. (1997). Who's the boss? Differential accessibility of dominance ideation in parent–child relationships. *Journal of Personality and Social Psychology, 79*, 1297–1309.

Cameron, J. J., Stinson, D. A., Gaetz, R., & Balchen, S. (2010). Acceptance is in the eye of the beholder: Self-esteem and motivated perceptions of acceptance from the opposite sex. *Journal of Personality and Social Psychology, 99*, 513–529.

Chartrand, T. L., & Bargh, J. A. (1999). The chameleon effect: The perception–behavior link and social interaction. *Journal of Personality and Social Psychology, 76*, 893–891.

Chartrand, T. L., Dalton, A., & Fitzsimons, G. J. (2007). Nonconscious relationship reactance: When significant others prime opposing goals. *Journal of Experimental Social Psychology, 43*, 719–726.

Chen, S. (2003). Psychological-state theories about significant others: Implications for the content and structure of significant-other representations. *Personality and Social Psychology Bulletin, 29*, 1285–1302.

Chen, S., Andersen, S. M., & Hinkley, K. (1999). Triggering transference: Examining the role of applicability and use of significant-other representations in social perception. *Social Cognition, 17*, 332–365.

Chen, S., & Boucher, H. C. (2008). Relational selves as self-affirmational resources. *Journal of Research in Personality, 42*, 716–73.

Chen, S., Boucher, H. C., & Tapias, M. P. (2006). The relational self revealed: Integrative conceptualization and implications for interpersonal life. *Psychological Bulletin, 132*, 151–179.

Clark, M. S., Graham, S. M., Williams, E., & Lemay, E. P., Jr. (2008). Understanding relational focus of attention may help us understand relational phenomena. In J. Forgas & J. Fitness (Eds.), *Social relationships: Cognitive, affective and motivational processes* (pp. 131–146). New York: Psychology Press.

Clark, M. S., & Mills, J. (1979). Interpersonal attraction in exchange and communal relationships. *Journal of Personality and Social Psychology, 37*, 12–24.

Crocker, J., & Wolfe, C. T. (2001). Contingencies of self-worth. *Psychological Review, 108*, 593–623.

Collins, N. L., & Read, S. J. (1994). Cognitive representations of attachment: The structure and function of working models. In K. Bartholomew & D. Perlman (Eds.), *Attachment processes in adulthood* (Vol. 5, pp. 53–90). London, UK: Jessica Kingsley Publishers.

Cox, C. R., Arndt, J., Pyszczynski, T., Greenberg, J., Abdollahi, A., & Solomon, S. (2008). Terror management and adults' attachment to their parents: The safe haven remains. *Journal of Personality and Social Psychology, 94*, 696–717.

Cross, S. E., Bacon, P. L., & Morris, M. L. (2000). The relational-interdependent self-construal and relationships. *Journal of Personality and Social Psychology, 78*, 791–808.

Cross, S. E., & Gore, J. S. (2003). Cultural models of the self. In M. R. Leary & J. P. Tangney (Eds.), *Handbook of self and identity* (pp. 536–564): New York: Guilford Press.

Cross, S. E., Morris, M. L., & Gore, J. S. (2002). Thinking about oneself and others: The relational-interdependent self-construal and social cognition. *Journal of Personality and Social Psychology, 82*, 399–418.

Davis, J. L., & Rusbult, C. E. (2001). Attitude alignment in close relationships. *Journal of Personality and Social Psychology, 81*, 65–84.

Deci, E. L. (1995). *Why we do what we do*. New York: Putnam.

DeHart, T., Pelham, B. W., & Murray, S. L. (2004). Implicit dependency regulation: Self-esteem, relationship closeness, and implicit evaluation of close others. *Social Cognition, 22*, 126–146.

Downey, G., & Feldman, S. (1996). Implications of rejection sensitivity for intimate relationships. *Journal of Personality and Social Psychology, 70*, 1327–1343.

Downey, G., Feldman, S., & Ayduk, O. (2000). Rejection sensitivity and male violence in romantic relationships. *Personal Relationships, 7*, 45–61.

Downey, G., Freitas, A. L., Michaelis, B., & Khouri, H. (1998). The self-fulfilling prophecy in close relationships: Rejection sensitivity and rejection by romantic partners. *Journal of Personality and Social Psychology, 75*, 545–560.

Downey, G., Mougios, V., Ayduk, O., London, B., & Shoda, Y. (2004). Rejection sensitivity and the defensive motivational system: Insights from the startle response to rejection cues. *Psychological Science, 15*, 668–673.

Edelstein, R. S., & Gillath, O. (2008). Avoiding interference: Adult attachment and emotional processing biases. *Personality and Social Psychology Bulletin, 34*, 171–181.

Feeney, B. C. (2007). The dependency paradox in close relationships: Accepting dependence promotes independence. *Journal of Personality and Social Psychology, 92*, 268–285.

Fiske, A. P. (1992). The four elementary forms of sociality: Framework for a unified theory of social relations. *Psychological Review, 99*, 689–723.

Fiske, S. T. (2003). Five core social motives, plus or minus five. In S. J Spencer, S. Fein, M. P. Zanna, & J. M. Olson (Eds.), *Motivated social perception: The Ontario Symposium* (Vol. 9, pp. 233–246). Mahwah, NJ: Erlbaum.

Fiske, A. P., Haslam, N., & Fiske, S. T. (1991). Confusing one person with another: What errors reveal about the elementary forms of social relations. *Journal of Personality and Social Psychology, 60*, 656–674.

Fitzsimons, G. M., & Bargh, J. A. (2003). Thinking of you: Nonconscious pursuit of interpersonal goals associated with relationship partners. *Journal of Personality and Social Psychology, 84*, 148–164.

Fitzsimons, G. M., & Fishbach, A. (2010). Shifting closeness: Interpersonal effects of personal goal progress. *Journal of Personality and Social Psychology, 98*, 535–549.

Fitzsimons, G. M., & Shah, J. (2008). How goal instrumentality shapes relationship evaluations. *Journal of Personality and Social Psychology, 95*, 319–337.

Fitzsimons, G. M., & Shah, J. Y. (2009). Confusing one instrumental other for another: Goal effects on social categorization. *Psychological Science, 20*, 1468–1472.

Florian, V., Mikulincer, M., & Hirschberger, G. (2002). The anxiety buffering function of close relationships: Evidence that relationship commitment acts as a terror management mechanism. *Journal of Personality and Social Psychology, 82*, 527–542.

Förster, J., & Liberman, N. (2007). Knowledge activation. In A. W. Kruglanski & E. T. Higgins (Eds.), *Social psychology: Handbook of basic principles* (2nd ed., pp. 201–231). New York: Guilford Press.

Fraley, R. C., Garner, J. P., & Shaver, P. R. (2000). Adult attachment and the defensive regulation of attention and memory: Examining the role of preemptive and postemptive defensive processes. *Journal of Personality and Social Psychology, 79*, 816–826.

Fraley, R. C., & Shaver, P. R. (1997). Adult attachment and the suppression of unwanted thoughts. *Journal of Personality and Social Psychology, 73*, 1080–1091.

Gabriel, S., Kawakami, K., Bartak, C., Kang, S., & Mann, N. (2010). Negative self-synchronization: Will I change to be like you when it is bad for me? *Journal of Personality and Social Psychology, 98*, 857–871.

Gillath, O., Giesbrecht, B., & Shaver, P. R. (2009). Attachment, attention, and cognitive control: Attachment style and performance on general attention tasks. *Journal of Experimental Social Psychology, 45*, 647–654.

Gillath, O., Mikulincer, M., Fitzsimons, G. M., Shaver, P. R., Schachner, D. A., & Bargh, J. A. (2006).Automatic activation of attachment-related goals. *Personality and Social Psychology Bulletin, 32*, 1375–1388.

Glassman, N. S., & Andersen, S. M. (1999a). Activating transference without consciousness: Using significant-other representations to go beyond what is subliminally given. *Journal of Personality and Social Psychology, 77*, 1146–1162.

Glassman, N. S., & Andersen, S. M. (1999b). Transference in social cognition: Persistence and exacerbation of significant-other-based inferences over time. *Cognitive Therapy and Research, 23*, 75–91.

Graham, S. M., & Clark, M. S. (2006). The Jekyll and Hyde-ing of relationship partners. *Journal of Personality and Social Psychology, 90*, 652–665.

Greenberg, J., Solomon, S., & Pyszczynski, T. (1997). Terror management theory of self-esteem and cultural worldviews: Empirical assessments and conceptual refinements. In M. P. Zanna (Ed.), *Advances in experimental social psychology* (Vol. 29, pp. 61–139). San Diego, CA: Academic Press.

Griffin, D. W., & Bartholomew, K. (1994). Models of the self and other: Fundamental dimensions underlying measures of adult attachment. *Journal of Personality and Social Psychology, 67*, 430–445.

Hardin, C. D., & Conley, T. D. (2001). A relational approach to cognition: Shared experience and relationship affirmation in social cognition. In G. B. Moskowitz (Ed.), *Cognitive social psychology: The Princeton symposium on the legacy and future of social cognition* (pp. 3–17). Mahwah, NJ: Erlbaum.

Hardin, C. D., & Higgins, E. T. (1996). Shared reality: How social verification makes the subjective objective. In E. T. Higgins & R. M. Sorrentino (Eds.), *Handbook of motivation and cognition: The interpersonal context* (Vol. 3, pp. 28–84). New York: Guilford Press.

Heine, S. J., Proulx, T., & Vohs, K. D. (2006). The meaning maintenance model: On the coherence of human motivations. *Personality and Social Psychology Review, 10*, 88–110.

Higgins, E. T. (1987). Self-discrepancy: A theory relating self and affect. *Psychological Review, 94*, 319–340.

Higgins, E. T. (1996). Knowledge activation: Accessibility, applicability, and salience. In E. T. Higgins & A. W. Kruglanski (Eds.), *Social psychology: Handbook of basic principles* (pp. 133–168). New York: Guilford Press.

Hinkley, K., & Andersen, S.M. (1996). The working self-concept in transference: Significant-other activation and self-change. *Journal of Personality and Social Psychology, 71*, 1279–1295.

Horberg, E. J., & Chen, S. (2010). Significant others and contingencies of self-worth: Activation and consequences of relationship-specific contingencies of self-worth. *Journal of Personality and Social Psychology, 98*, 77–91.

Jacoby, L. L. (1991). A process-dissociation framework: Separating automatic from intentional uses of memory. *Journal of Memory and Language, 30*, 513–541.

Klohnen, E. C., Weller, J. A., Luo, S., & Choe, M. (2005). Organization and predictive power of general and relationships-specific attachment models: One for all, all for one? *Personality and Social Psychology Bulletin, 31*, 1665–1682.

Knowles, M. L., Lucas, G. M., Molden, D. C., Gardner, W. L., & Dean, K. K. (2010). There's no substitute for belonging: Self-affirmation following social and non-social threats. *Personality and Social Psychology Bulletin, 36*, 173–186.

Kraus, M. W., & Chen, S. (2009). Striving to be known by significant others: Automatic activation of self-verification goals in relationship contexts. *Journal of Personality and Social Psychology, 97*, 58–73.

Kraus, M. W., & Chen, S. (2010). Facial-feature resemblance elicits the transference effect. *Psychological Science, 21*, 518–522.

Kraus, M. W., Chen, S., Lee, V. A., & Straus, L. D. (2010). Transference occurs across group boundaries. *Journal of Experimental Social Psychology, 46*, 1067–1073.

Kruglanski, A. W., & Pierro, A. (2008). Night and day, you are the one: On circadian mismatches and the transference effect in social perception. *Psychological Science, 19*, 296–301.

Kumashiro, M., & Sedikides, C. (2005). Taking on board liability-focused feedback: Close positive relationships as a self-bolstering resource. *Psychological Science, 16*, 732–739.

Lemay, E. P., Jr., & Clark, M. S. (2008). "Walking on eggshells": How expressing relationship insecurities perpetuates them. *Journal of Personality and Social Psychology, 95*, 420–441.

Liviatan, I., & Andersen, S. M. (2010). *Just try to stop yourself: Can awareness, prompting, or exhortation short-circuit transference?* Unpublished manuscript.

Lockwood, P., Dolderman, D., Sadler, P., & Gerchak, E. (2004). Feeling better about doing worse: Social comparisons within romantic relationships. *Journal of Personality and Social Psychology, 87*, 80–95.

Magee, M. W., & Hardin, C. (2010). In defense of religion: Shared reality moderates the unconscious threat of evolution. *Social Cognition, 28*, 379–400.

Mendoza-Denton, R., Downey, G., Purdie, V., Davis, A., & Pietrzak, J. (2002). Sensitivity to status-based rejection: Implications for African-American students' college experience. *Journal of Personality and Social Psychology, 83*, 896–918.

Mikulincer, M. (1995). Attachment style and the mental representation of the self. *Journal of Personality and Social Psychology, 69*, 1203–1215.

Mikulincer, M. (1997). Adult attachment style and information processing: Individual differences in curiosity and cognitive closure. *Journal of Personality and Social Psychology, 72*, 1217–1230.

Mikulincer, M. (1998). Adult attachment style and affect regulation: Strategic variations in self-appraisals. *Journal of Personality and Social Psychology, 75*, 420–435.

Mikulincer, M., & Arad, D. (1999). Attachment working models and cognitive openness in close relationships: A test of chronic and temporary accessibility effects. *Journal of Personality and Social Psychology, 77*, 710–725.

Mikulincer, M., Florian, V., Birnbaum, G., & Malishkevich, S. (2002). The death–anxiety buffering function of close relationships: Exploring the effects of separation reminders on death–thought accessibility. *Personality and Social Psychology Bulletin, 28*, 287–299.

Mikulincer, M., Florian, V., & Hirschberger, G. (2003). The existential functions of close relationships: Introducing death in to the science of love. *Personality and Social Psychology Review, 7*, 20–40.

Mikulincer, M., Gillath, O., & Shaver, P. R. (2002). Activation of the attachment system in adulthood: Threat-related primes increase the accessibility of mental representations of attachment figures. *Journal of Personality and Social Psychology, 83*, 881–895.

Mikulincer, M., Hirschberger, G., Nachmias, O., & Gillath, O. (2001). The affective component of the secure base schema: Affective priming with representations of attachment security. *Journal of Personality and Social Psychology, 81*, 305–321.

Mikulincer, M., Orbach, I., Iavnieli, D. (1998). Adult attachment style and affect regulation: Strategic variations in subjective self-other similarity. *Journal of Personality and Social Psychology, 75*, 436–448.

Mikulincer, M., & Shaver, P. R. (2001). Attachment theory and intergroup bias: Evidence that priming the secure base schema attenuates negative reactions to outgroups. *Journal of Personality and Social Psychology, 81*, 97–115.

Mikuliner, M., & Shaver, P. R. (2004). Security-based self-representations in adulthood: Contents and processes. In W. S. Rholes & J. A. Simpson (Eds.), *Adult attachment: Theory, research, and clinical implications* (pp. 159–195). New York: Guilford Press.

Mikulincer, M., Shaver, P. R., Gillath, O., & Nitzberg, R. A. (2005). Attachment, caregiving, and altruism: Boosting attachment security increases compassion and helping.

Journal of Personality and Social Psychology, 89, 817–839.

Murray, S. L., Derrick, S., Jaye, L., Leder, S., & Holmes, J. G. (2008). Balancing connectedness and self-protection goals in close relationships: A levels-of-processing perspective on risk regulation. *Journal of Personality and Social Psychology, 94*, 429–459.

Murray, S. L., & Holmes, J. G. (1993). Seeing virtues in faults: Negativity and the transformation of interpersonal narratives in close relationships. *Journal of Personality and Social Psychology, 65*, 707–722.

Murray, S. L., Holmes, J. G., & Collins, N. L. (2006). Optimizing assurance: The risk regulation system in relationships. *Psychological Bulletin, 132*, 641–666.

Murray, S. L., Holmes, J. G., & Griffin, D. W. (2000). Self-esteem and the quest for felt security: How perceived regard regulates attachment processes. *Journal of Personality and Social Psychology, 78*, 478–498.

Murray, S. L., Holmes, J. G., Griffin, D. W., Bellavia, G., & Rose, P. (2001). The mismeasure of love: How self-doubt contaminates relationship beliefs. *Personality and Social Psychology Bulletin, 27*, 423–436.

Murray, S. L., Holmes, J. G., MacDonald, G., & Ellsworth, P. C. (1998). Through the looking glass darkly? When self-doubt turns into relationship insecurities. *Journal of Personality and Social Psychology, 75*, 1459–1480.

Ogilvie, D. M., & Ashmore, R. D. (1991). Self-with-other representation as a unit of analysis in self-concept research. In R. C. Curtis (Ed.), *The relational self: Theoretical convergences in psychoanalysis and social psychology* (pp. 282–314). New York: Guilford Press.

Overall, N. C., Fletcher, G. J. O., & Friesen, M. D. (2003). Mapping the intimate relationship mind: Comparisons between three models of attachment representations. *Personality and Social Psychology Bulletin, 29*, 1479–1493.

Page-Gould, E., Mendoza-Denton, R., Alegre, J. M., & Siy, J. O. (2010). Understanding the impact of cross-group friendship on interactions with novel outgroup members. *Journal of Personality and Social Psychology, 98*, 775–793.

Page-Gould, E., Mendoza-Denton, R., & Tropp, L. R. (2008). With a little help from my cross-group friend: Reducing anxiety in intergroup contexts through cross-group friendship. *Journal of Personality and Social Psychology, 95*, 1080–1094.

Pierro, A., & Kruglanski, A. W. (2008). "Seizing and freezing" on a significant-person schema: Need for closure and the transference effect in social judgment. *Personality and Social Psychology Bulletin, 34*, 1492–1503.

Pierro, A., Orehek, E., & Kruglanski, A. W. (2009). Let there be no mistake! On assessment mode and the transference effect. *Journal of Experimental Social Psychology, 45*, 879–888.

Pietromonaco, P. R., & Barrett, L. F. (2000). The internal working models concept: What do we really know about the self in relation to others? *Review of General Psychology, 4*, 155–175.

Pinkus, R. T., Lockwood, P., Schimmack, U., & Fournier, M. A. (2008). For better and for worse: Everyday social comparisons between romantic partners. *Journal of Personality and Social Psychology, 95,* 1180–1201.

Przybylinski, E., & Andersen, S. M. (2011). *Systems of meaning and transference: Evoking shared reality through activation of a significant other.* Unpublished manuscript.

Reis, H. T., & Downey, G. (1999). Social cognition in relationships: Building essential bridges between two literatures. *Social Cognition, 17,* 97–117.

Reznik, I., & Andersen, S. M. (2007). Agitation and despair in relation to parents: Activating emotional suffering in transference. *European Journal of Personality, 21,* 281–301.

Romero-Canyas, R., Downey, G., Berenson, K., Ayduk, O., & Kang, N. J. (2010). Rejection sensitivity and the rejection–hostility link in romantic relationships. *Journal of Personality, 78,* 119–148.

Sakellaropoulo, M., & Baldwin, M. W. (2007). The hidden sides of self-esteem: Two dimensions of implicit self-esteem and their relation to narcissistic reactions. *Journal of Experimental Social Psychology, 43,* 995–1001.

Saribay, S. A., & Andersen, S. M. (2007). Relational to collective: Significant-other representations, ethnic categories, and intergroup perceptions. *Personality and Social Psychology Bulletin, 33,* 1714–1726.

Shah, J. (2003a). Automatic for the people: How representations of significant others implicitly affect goal pursuit. *Journal of Personality and Social Psychology, 84,* 661–681.

Shah, J. (2003b). The motivational looking glass: How significant others implicitly affect goal appraisals. *Journal of Personality and Social Psychology, 85,* 424–439.

Showers, C. J., & Kevlyn, S. B. (1999). Organization of knowledge about a relationship partner: Implications for liking and loving. *Journal of Personality and Social Psychology, 76,* 958–971.

Simpson, J. A., Rholes, W. S., & Nelligan, J. S. (1992). Support seeking and support giving within couples in an anxiety-provoking situation: The role of attachment styles. *Journal of Personality and Social Psychology, 62,* 434–446.

Simpson, J. A., Rholes, W. S., & Winterheld, H. A. (2010). Attachment working models twist memories of relationship events. *Psychological Science, 21,* 252–259.

Sinclair, S., Dunn, L., & Lowery, B. (2005a). The influence of parental racial attitudes on children's automatic racial prejudice. *Journal of Experimental Social Psychology, 41,* 283–289.

Sinclair, S., Huntsinger, J. H., Skorinko, J. L., & Hardin, C. (2005b). Social tuning of the self: Consequences for the self-evaluations of stereotype targets. *Journal of Personality and Social Psychology, 89,* 160–175.

Sinclair, S., Lowery, B. S., Hardin, C. D., & Colangelo, A. (2005c). The social tuning of automatic ethnic attitudes: The role of affiliative motivation. *Journal of Personality and Social Psychology, 89,* 583–592.

Slotter, E. B., Gardner, W. L., & Finkel, E. J. (2010). Who am I without you? The influence of romantic breakup on the self-concept. *Personality and Social Psychology Bulletin, 36,* 147–160.

Smith, E. R., & Henry, S. (1996). An in-group becomes part of the self: Response time evidence. *Personality and Social Psychology Bulletin, 22,* 635–642.

Smith, E. R., Murphy, J., & Coats, S. (1999). Attachment to groups: Theory and measurement. *Journal of Personality and Social Psychology, 77,* 94–110.

Smith, E. R., & Zarate, M. A. (1992). Exemplar-based model of social judgment. *Psychological Review, 99,* 3–21.

Strachman, A., & Gable, S. L. (2006). What you want (and don't want) affects what you see (and don't see): Avoidance social goals and social events. *Personality and Social Psychology Bulletin, 32,* 1446–1458.

Swann, W. B., Jr. (1990). To be adored or to be known: The interplay of self-enhancement and self-verification. In R. M. Sorrentino & E. T. Higgins (Eds.), *Foundations of social behavior* (Vol. 2, pp. 408–448). New York: Guilford Press.

Taubman-Ben-Ari, O., Findler, L., & Mikulincer, M. (2002). The effects of mortality salience on relationship strivings and beliefs: The moderating role of attachment style. *British Journal of Social Psychology, 41,* 419–441.

Thompson, R. A. (1998). Early sociopersonality development. In W. Damon (Series Ed.) & N. Eisenberg (Vol. Ed.), *Handbook of child psychology: Vol. 3. Social, emotional, and personality development* (5th ed., pp. 25–104). New York: Wiley.

vanDellen, M. R., Hoy, M. B., & Hoyle, R. H. (2009). Contingent self-worth and social information processing: Cognitive associations between domain performance and social relations. *Social Cognition, 27,* 847–866.

vanDellen, M. R., & Hoyle, R. H. (2010) Regulatory accessibility and social influences on state self-control. *Personality and Social Psychology Bulletin, 36,* 251–263.

Wilson, T. W., & Brekke, N. (1994). Mental contamination and mental correction: Unwanted influences on judgments and evaluations. *Psychological Bulletin, 116,* 117–142.

Wright, S. C., Aron, A., McLaughlin-Volpe, T., & Ropp, S. A. (1997). The extended contact effect: Knowledge of cross-group friendships and prejudice. *Journal of Personality and Social Psychology, 73,* 73–90.

Yovetich, N. A., & Rusbult, C. E. (1994). Accommodative behavior in close relationships: Exploring transformation of motivation. *Journal of Experimental Social Psychology, 30,* 138–164.

Zayas, V., & Shoda, Y. (2005). Do automatic reactions elicited by thoughts of romantic partner, mother, and self relate to adult romantic attachment? *Personality and Social Psychology Bulletin, 31,* 1011–1025.

19

Representations of Social Groups in the Early Years of Life

Talee Ziv & Mahzarin R. Banaji

At some stage in social development, we achieve recognition of ourselves as unique individuals, separate from others. Among the fundamental accompaniments of that process of forming a sense of self is the joint recognition that one is a social being, with membership in some groups and not others. Indeed, young children come to recognize and know that there are clusters of beings out there who are not only individually named but who have group labels associated with them for example, "male" or "female," "dark" or "light," "young" or "elderly." Without even consciously recognizing this to be so, they come to know that these social categories have psychological and social meaning, and that membership creates a clear sense of "us" and "them." What are the roots of full-blown and explicit knowledge about social groups and their properties that typifies the adult state? How early are they in place? What do they reveal about the social nature of our evolutionary history and about the significance of social groups in our learning and development?

In this chapter, we carve out a modest portion of the research on the development of social cognition that has scarcely been presented in compendiums of social psychology before. We select the earliest moments in human development that reveal when and how we perceive others as members of groups and even show preferences for them. By focusing on infants and young children, we not only stand to learn some surprising facts of

early social group perception but also to pose new questions about the structure of our minds, the social nature of early mental life, and how to regard the basic acts of social perception and cognition alongside other domains of core knowledge (see Spelke, Bernier, & Skerry, in press).

Let us start with the adult human state. Members of our kind appear to code and categorize people naturally and easily. The accuracy of such ability aside, there is high consensus as to who is what: male or female, dark or light, old or young, among many other groupings. But our species does far more with such knowledge. Based on a smidgen of information about another's social origins, such as whether they are urban or rural dwellers, we feel confident making predictions about them. Will she like hip-hop or not? Eat sushi or not? Have traveled abroad or not? Be religiously observant or not? Again, the accuracy of predictions is another matter; what is astonishing is that we feel comfortable and even confident making such assessments at all. To us, the ease with which we think about other people through the lens of their groups suggests that we must regard social groups to be decent predictors of individual behavior: enough that we use them profligately, unconsciously, and with ease – whether they are useful and accurate or not.

If social groups are viewed as "good" categories to rely on and thus useful guides to social cognition, the developmental course of the ability to perceive, categorize, and evaluate social groups, and individuals as members of them, is important to understand. In fact, the very question of whether or not this aspect of social cognition is fundamental can, to some extent, be answered by examining its presence in the youngest members of our species. Do they perceive social groups as distinct? Can they tell individual members of a group apart? Do they need experience with a group to do this? How much and how early?

A second set of questions concern whether even in the earliest years of life we prefer some individuals over others because of their inclusion in particular groups over others. What rules do these group-based preferences follow? Is similarity-to-self a sufficient rule to account for the evidence or is there a preference for that which is novel and different from self? And what if the group one belongs to has high or low social status? What wins? Ingroup-ness or group status? We do not have all the answers equally convincingly at hand, but we know a lot more than we did only a few years ago about the development of social cognition and our purpose in this chapter is to lay out the evidence on social group perception and preferences in the early years and in the interim, what it means.

In engaging with these questions, one approach posits that a limited set of innate conceptual systems serve as the basis for later emerging knowledge. Each of these "core knowledge" systems allows us to process different elements of the world around us (for example, numbers, agents, or spatial layouts) that are identified by a unique set of principles. The systems produce abstract but useful representations of these entities and guide the inferences we make about them. Thus it is, for example, that young children and monkeys may have no concrete understanding of "3" and "2," but can nevertheless recognize that a group of 3 is larger than a group of 2. These systems have signatures that allow them to be regarded as core knowledge: they appear evolutionarily ancient, they are shared with non-human animals, they continue to unfold throughout development with minimal refinement, and are culturally universal, observable in Amazonians and New Yorkers alike (Spelke, 2000).

Even by the earliest years of life, we have clocked thousands of hours "on the job" of social cognition. Broadly speaking, social cognition refers to many dimensions of social representations, relationships, and behavior that cannot all be reviewed here. For example, a full understanding of the development of social cognition must engage, among other questions, the role of imitation and learning from others (Gergely, Bekkering, & Király, 2002), the understanding of intention and agency (Johnson, Slaughter, & Carey, 1998; Woodward,

1999), the basis of social trust and creditability (Koenig & Harris, 2005), knowing the minds of others (Baillargeon, Scott, & He, 2010; Wimmer & Perner, 1983), and the development of morality and understanding help versus harm (Hamlin, Wynn, & Bloom, 2007). In fact, an attempt at a more comprehensive review of what we know about the early years of social navigation in its broadest sense has been undertaken to cover these very questions (Banaji & Gelman, in press).

To provide an in-depth look at one central question concerning social cognition we focus our lens on how infants and young children seem to know or learn about social groups. We do so in part because of a growing sense that the capacity to reason about social partners, and in particular the us–them distinction, might constitute a separate domain of core knowledge (Banaji & Gelman, in press; Spelke & Kinzler, 2007). We parcel the evidence into two main sections concerning infants and young children because the differences in their capacities have required the invention and reliance on different forms of measures that can be used with each. Looking-time measures for instance dominate in work with infants but are not amenable for use with older children. Likewise, measures of preference that rely on choosing one of two objects can only be used with older infants who are capable of reaching. Finally, access to language provides a host of measures that can be included in research with 3-year-olds and older children.

SOCIAL GROUP CATEGORIZATION AND PREFERENCES IN INFANCY

Humans come into the world with an innate face template (Meltzoff & Moore, 1977) and a preference for face-like configurations over non-face stimuli (Johnson, Dziurawiec, Ellis, & Morton, 1991; Macchi Cassia, Turati, & Simion, 2004). While the exact mechanism driving the preference for faces is debated (see Turati, 2004, compared to Farroni, Johnson, Menon, Zulian, Faraguna, & Csibra, 2005), this innate capacity no doubt prepares us for identifying potential social partners. Newborns display a number of more nuanced face-processing capabilities as well. They are able to differentiate female faces never before seen (Pascalis & de Schonen, 1994), and are sensitive to facial attractiveness as evidenced by their preference for attractive faces over less attractive ones (Slater et al., 1998). These well-established preferences and perceptual capacities for individual faces set the stage for examining the questions raised in the introduction regarding individuals as representatives of larger social groups. In the remainder of this section we will focus on four of the most studied social groups and what we know about how infants approach them: gender, language, age, and race.

We will be upfront about the most surprising aspect of the data from infants' perception, categorization, and preferences based on these groups. Intergroup cognition and conflict is often assumed to result from years of immersion in culture-specific attitudes. This work, however, has accumulated evidence that long before anything resembling substantial experience or practice with unfamiliar groups or out-groups is achieved, infants display interpersonal preferences that reflect group membership. In most cases, they appear to do so based on the simple rule of familiarity and on the relatively small amounts of information available to them in the first months after birth. These findings have raised questions regarding the underlying mechanisms driving early preferences, and have motivated the examination of their stability over development.

Measures of preference, categorization, and discrimination

There are three standard measures used in the research with infants, each of which seeks to tap a unique aspect of cognition. In the social domain, we can distinguish them as measures of *preference* (where preference need not reflect an evaluation but simply longer engagement with one stimulus over another), measures of *categorization* (the ability to tell two sets apart from each other, e.g., male and female), and *discrimination* (the ability to distinguish individual members of a set from each other).

Looking time serves as the main measure for inferring all three of these underlying processes in infancy. To understand the parameters of looking-time measures – i.e., what it can and cannot tell us – we preface our discussion of the work by tackling some of the basic questions typically raised when encountering data in which the dependent measure of interest is the time spent looking at *x* over *y*, typically measured in seconds.

The procedure for testing categorical representations involves familiarizing infants with multiple stimuli from a single category (for example, different photographs of White females) and then showing them a previously unseen White female and Asian female face. If during the familiarization phase infants extracted the commonality between the presented stimuli and formed a category, they should now look at the item that "breaks" the category (i.e., the Asian face) rather than the face that "continues" the familiarized

category. If no category distinctions are in place the infant should randomly look at the White or Asian face.

Most of the discrimination studies we are about to describe use a similar procedure to categorization studies with the exception that two items within the same category serve as stimuli. For example, if we would like to find out whether infants are capable of telling two Asian faces apart we would begin by presenting a single female Asian face repeatedly during familiarization. Across these trials, infants' looking time typically decreases, a pattern indicating they have fully processed the face and are essentially getting "bored." Once a significant reduction in looking time has been achieved, discrimination is assessed via infants' response to a pair of faces consisting of a novel Asian female alongside the familiarized stimulus. Equal looking at both is taken as evidence that infants cannot distinguish the old face from the new, while increased interest in the new face leads to the inference that the difference between the faces has been detected.

In a standard preference study, each trial involves two stimuli presented side by side, simultaneously competing for the infants' attention. In the social domain, one of these stimuli could be a member of the infant's in-group (for example, a face of the same race as the infant, or a person speaking the infant's native language), while the other stimulus is an out-group member (an other-race face, or a person speaking a foreign language). Looking-time measures of this sort do not always allow for a priori interpretation, thus hypothesizing which face would receive more attention may be elusive. For instance, longer looking time at a person from one's own group may emerge from a preference for that which is familiar, whereas longer looking times for an out-group face may emerge because of a preference for the novel.

In the examples we mentioned using race and language as social categories, babies show a familiarity preference in early infancy, making this result the standard expectation for new research. However, once a consistent looking pattern has been established, the next step requires determining what drives the infant to look in one direction or another. Here multiple factors could come into play, including differences in low-level processing demands, a preference to interact with the familiar other, or an avoidance of the unfamiliar stimulus. Disentangling these possibilities becomes a much more intricate task, and often benefits from evidence using other kinds of methodologies. While keeping these interpretive limitations in mind, we turn to describing the current state of affairs in infants' social group perception and preferences as it relates to the four types of social groupings most studied: race, gender, age, and language. Later in this chapter we examine the expression of social preferences in childhood where measures other than looking time will help to zero in with more confidence on whether the apparent preference in the early months of life indeed carries over to approach or liking in later months and years. To the extent that the later data with new measures are consistent with the earlier data with looking time, the more faith we can have that we are observing the roots of the same preferences in early infancy.

We have chosen these four groups because the bulk of the research evidence is situated in studies of gender, language, age, and race. But each of these categories also presents unique features that allow the jigsaw of early social cognition to be fitted. Some social groups present discrete and even dichotomous social groups to infants. Gender typically is dichotomous, with infants seeing both male and female exemplars. Age is a continuum, but infants mainly interact with adults. Race and language both often present one of many possible categories, although in multilingual and multiracial cultures that is less the case. Most of the extant studies though use unilingual and monoracial cultures, with a minority focusing on the effects of degrees of exposure to varying cultural input. Another dimension along which groups vary is whether group membership is fixed (such as the case with gender or race) versus a multiplicity of options that are open as the child grows (such as with language) or the continuum along which the baby itself moves, as with age. These features of various social groups allow questions of similarity to self, familiarity in early life, and the evolutionary roots of preferences and their acquisition after birth to be examined in interesting ways.

Gender

Gender poses an interesting opportunity to understand social group perception and preference because although most babies are cared for by a female caregiver, males are not completely absent from the environment as is often the case with race, where members of other race groups are typically completely absent. If a preference for female over male is not present at birth, but emerges rapidly after that, we would have evidence that babies can form preferences for the more familiar of two known groups. Moreover, studies that look at preferences based on gender of caregiver can test whether early experience with a single caregiver (male or female) generalizes to preferences for others from that group.

Babies typically show a looking-time preference for female faces when paired alongside a male face; however, this preference is reversed if the baby is brought up by a male primary caregiver (Quinn, Yahr, Kuhn, Slater, & Pascalis, 2002). This result is both indicative of infants' ability to differentiate male and female faces (without which preferential looking could not be obtained), and demonstrates the importance of early experience in preference formation. It also rules out to some extent the possibility of an innate female preference that is not rooted in experience.

Other work has provided evidence for gender category formation, in some cases by 23 weeks of age (e.g. Cornell, 1974; Leinbach & Fagot, 1993; Levy & Haaf, 1994). Recently, however, researchers have pointed to an asymmetry in infant's gender categories such that female faces are categorized earlier and processed more efficiently than male faces (Ramsey, Langlois, & Marti, 2005). For example, Quinn et al. (2002, experiment 6) report that infants display poorer recognition of male faces at 3–4 months of age compared to female faces. After familiarization with 8 different female faces, infants looked longer at a novel female face when paired with one of the faces they previously saw during familiarization. The same procedure with male faces did not elicit a novelty preference.

Infants' poorer task performance with male faces has been attributed to the greater processing effort they must exert when encountering male faces (Ramsey et al., 2005). For example, a meta-analysis of 15 face perception studies revealed that infants spend more time looking during studies that use male face stimuli compared to female faces and this difference increases as the complexity of the experimental task rises. Furthermore, Ramsey et al. (2005) show that 6-month-olds have considerable difficulty in forming a male face prototype compared to the ease with which they abstract a prototype from a series of female faces, even at earlier ages (de Haan, Johnson, Maurer, & Perret, 2001; Rubenstein, Kalakanis, & Langlois, 1999). The observed disadvantage with male faces, according to Ramsey et al. (2005), implies a weaker representation of the male category, at least in babies whose primary caregiver is female.

Such differences in infants' processing and categorization of gender have been attributed to different levels of experience with men and women (Ramsey et al., 2005; Ramsey-Rennels & Langlois, 2006), and indeed tracking infants' facial experience during a 1-week observation period has shown substantially higher exposure to females during the first year of life (Rennels & Davis, 2008). This exposure pattern makes the gender case particularly interesting in comparison to race. Whereas infants' ability to differentiate other-race faces deteriorates over time (Kelly et al., 2007b, Kelly et al., 2009), male face processing improves over the first year of life and into the second. Since a female preference *and* an own-race preference both appear by the age of 3 months, the question of the connection between face processing and face preference at this early age arises. Interestingly, for gender, the initially narrow processing advantage for female faces broadens over the first year of life to include male faces as well. For race, on the other hand, it would appear that the system starts out broad, with openness to the whole spectrum, and narrows down with experience to the most familiar physiognomy.

Newborn infants brought up by a female caregiver do not show a preference for female over male faces, further supporting an experience-based account (Quinn et al., 2008). This is an important discovery because it would seem that gender could be a good candidate for innate social preference (favoring females) but that does not seem to be the case. In addition, based on previous work we reviewed on the malleability of gender preferences (depending on caregiver), we conclude that this preference is shaped after birth and based on experience, yet its precise developmental course is yet to be fully mapped because preferences based on gender have not been tested in later infancy.

Language

Language is unique in that babies are exposed to their parents' speech prenatally, and they indeed display a preference for the sound of their native language over a foreign language from birth (Mehler, Jusczyk, Lambertz, Halsted, Bertoncini, & Amiel-Tison, 1988; Moon, Cooper, & Fifer, 1993). Much in parallel to the race case, newborns exposed to two languages equally prior to birth, do not exhibit a preference for either one of those languages, despite being perfectly capable of telling them apart (Byers-Heinlein, Burns, & Werker, 2010).

Infants can consistently discriminate their own language from other languages at least by 2 months of age (Bahrick & Pickens, 1988; Mehler et al., 1988) and they do so even if the two languages are phonologically very similar by 4 months of age (e.g. Spanish and Catalan; Bosch & Sebastián-Gallés, 1997).

We now know that at least by 6 months of age the native-language preference extends to a preference for the individuals speaking that language, as measured by infants' looking times

(Kinzler, Dupoux, & Spelke, 2007). Specifically, subjects were first introduced to two females, one at a time, each speaking either the infant's native language or a foreign language. When later both women reappeared on screen silently, side by side, infants spent significantly more time looking at the native-language speaker. Remarkably, even when both actresses speak in the infant's native language, but one has a foreign accent, infants will prefer the non-accented speaker.

Early manifestations of social responding based on language have been documented soon after the visual preference is observed. Using a more interactive method, infants 10 months of age were again introduced to two speakers, but this time during the silent test phase each of them appeared to be simultaneously offering the infant identical toys (while actual toys were placed within the infant's reach). The dependent measure was which of the two toys the infant will select, and results indicated a preference to take a toy offered by the native-language speaker (Kinzler et al., 2007).

A similar method has demonstrated 12-month-olds' use of language as a cue to food selection. During introductory trials, actors appeared individually on screen either speaking in a native or foreign language, each eating a different kind of food from a colored container. In the critical silent test trials both actors appeared on screen simultaneously, while the same food-filled containers were presented to the year-old infants. Findings again showed reliably more selection of the food associated with the native-language speaker (Shutts, Kinzler, McKee, & Spelke, 2009).

Such social reactions have not been tested prior to 10 months of age, but they may suggest that the earlier looking preference is a precursor of infants' affiliative predilections. More broadly, the findings on language have started to raise important questions regarding the relative status of different social categories (see Kinzler, Shutts, & Correll, 2010 for a discussion). For example, presenting 10-month-old babies with individuals who differ on race using the toy choice method does not elicit preferential selection of the toy offered by the own-race person, suggesting that language may be a more prominent social group marker at this age (Kinzler & Spelke, 2011). It has been suggested that this results from the fact that, unlike race, languages (and even more so accents) served as important markers of coalitional alliances over evolutionary times (Kinzler & Spelke, 2011). It is important to keep in mind, however, that exposure to language also occurs earlier than visually marked group distinctions like race. In this regard, it would be interesting to find out whether newborns exhibit preferences for native-language speakers. We will return to discussing interactions of language and race when examining social preferences in the preschool years.

Language-based preferences are relatively newly studied in research on infant social cognition. Questions that have been targeted by some of the social groups described in this chapter will surely be relevant for language too. For example, how early will infants show evidence of categorization of multiple individuals based on their language (especially when those individuals differ on other dimensions such as race or gender), and what is the role of exposure in attenuating the observed social preferences in infancy?

Age

Age throws off the simple "liking for familiar" effect and forces us to consider the role of self in early social cognition. Infants are sensitive to the age of the person they interact with, at least by the time they are 4 months old, as evidenced by increased looking time at same-age (i.e. infant) faces in comparison to older children and adult faces (McCall & Kennedy, 1980). Unlike the preference for female faces, this own-age preference cannot be driven by exposure, since infants rarely spend significant amounts of time with other infants their own age and certainly not more so than they do with adults. It is also the case that the own-age preference is quite nuanced and not simply a generalized response to baby-like features of the stimuli: 6-month-olds and 9-month-olds show greater behavioral positivity (as measured by arm movements) toward static images of same-age infants (Sanefuji, Ohgami, & Hashiya, 2006).

Infants also display an elevated-looking pattern toward children compared to adults and produce differing behavioral reactions by age; they respond more positively (e.g., smile) to children, and react negatively (e.g., by averting their gaze or by avoidance) when presented with unfamiliar adults (Bigelow, MacLean, Wood, & Smith, 1990; Greenberg, Hillman, & Grice, 1973), leading some to propose that babies are reacting to a combination of size and facial configuration in these experiments (Brooks & Lewis, 1976).

Whereas the above studies point to early categorization of strangers by age, further evidence has been provided using the intermodal matching technique. In this particular version of the task, dynamic videos of an adult and child (matched for gender) speaking in synchrony were simultaneously presented while either an adult's voice or a child's voice was played in the background. Visual matching of the face–voice pairing was present at 4 months of age (Bahrick, Netto, & Hernandez-Reif, 1998), suggesting that the infant versus adult categories are indeed in place and, remarkably, that voice associations to visual images are present.

Whether infants are better able to differentiate own-age or child faces relative to older faces, or whether they do so with a greater degree of accuracy compared to adults, has not been examined. The existing literature on children's face processing is in fact divided on whether an advantage for similar others (i.e. own age) or for the faces children most often encounter in their environment (i.e. young adults) should be expected. One study, for instance, tested the ability of 3-year-olds to differentiate adult faces and infant faces. The task involved presentation of a target face, followed by a pair of faces – the target and a distracter of the same age. Participants received one block of trials with adult faces and another with infant faces, and discrimination was assessed by children's ability to point to the target. The study showed that while participants with younger siblings were equally able to detect the target in both blocks, participants of the same age without younger siblings (and thus with limited experience with infant faces) showed a recognition advantage for the adult faces, providing yet another example of the effect of exposure on face-processing capabilities (Macchi Cassia, Kuefner, Picozzi, & Vescovo, 2009a). Interestingly, these effects are not limited to experience acquired during childhood, as it has been shown that maternity ward nurses display an enhanced ability to differentiate newborn faces compared to adults without regular contact with newborns (Macchi Cassia, Picozzi, Kuefner, & Casati, 2009b).

In contrast, others have argued for an own-age processing advantage in children. Using a delayed recognition task, one study showed that 5–8-year-olds were better able to remember previously seen photographs of children, compared to young, middle-aged, and older adults (Anastasi & Rhodes, 2005). Furthermore, recording event-related potentials, another study reported a larger amplitude of the face-selective N170 component when 5-year-olds passively viewed own-age faces compared to young and elderly adults, indicating an own-age advantage already present for face encoding (Melinder, Gredebäck, Westerlund, & Nelson, 2010).

While infants' contact with own-age peers is limited, children gradually accumulate more exposure to other children of their own age, beginning in the preschool years. Therefore, it is not unreasonable to suggest that a transition occurs from superior processing of young adults (in infancy) to an own-age processing advantage. This hypothesis is consistent with the studies reported above, as Macchi Cassia et al. (2009a) tested 3-year-olds, whereas Anastasi and Rhodes (2005) and Melinder et al. (2010) tested children from 5 years of age onwards. New research is needed, however, to establish this claim, first of all by testing infants, and later by systematically measuring the correlation between exposure levels to different age groups, and performance on face recognition tasks.

Race

Race is an arbitrary category (Werker & Tees, 1984) and there ought to be no evolutionarily rooted mechanism to distinguish and form preferences along this dimension. However, using standard looking-time measures for one of two visually presented faces, as early as 3 months of age infants from different backgrounds (African, Asian, and European infants) prefer to look at faces with origins on their own continents compared to those of another race (Bar-Haim, Ziv, Lamy, & Hodes, 2006; Kelly et al., 2007a). This early in-group preference observed in monocultural infants does not arise in a biracial environment (Bar-Haim et al., 2006) and is not displayed by newborns (aged 16–120 hours; Kelly et al., 2005).

Collectively, these findings suggest that the infant face-processing system depends on environmental input for forming an own-race preference, and that such preferences may be formed (or not at all) quite quickly. These findings also tell us that by 3 months of age infants are able to visually distinguish the two groups of faces from one another, raising the question of whether they are already forming discrete categories by race. The remainder of the research we summarize concerns this question of categorization as well as infants' ability to discriminate among instances within a group. The latter tests are particularly important because they exemplify the effect of group membership on subsequent representation of the individuals within a category.

In a direct test of categorization, Anzures and her colleagues (Anzures, Quinn, Pascalis, Slater, & Lee, 2009) showed that 9-month-old White infants treat faces from different racial backgrounds as belonging to separate categories. Anzures et al. (2009) showed that after familiarization with a group of White female faces, for example, infants showed increased looking toward an unfamiliar Asian female, but not to an unfamiliar White female. Furthermore, they demonstrated that while babies were able to differentiate individual White faces, they could not tell Asian faces apart, suggesting that infants' own-race category is finer grained compared to the other-race category, perhaps due to enhanced experience with individual exemplars of own-race faces on a daily basis. Further support for qualitative differences between racial categories in infancy comes from a study assessing face processing by 8-month-old White infants (Ferguson, Kulkofsky, Cashon, & Casasola, 2009), which in addition to extending the own-race discrimination advantage to White relative to African faces, also showed that own-race faces are processed holistically (i.e. the relation between the external and internal features of the face are encoded) while other-race faces are processed featurally (see also Liu, Quinn, Wheeler, Xiao, Ge & Lee, 2011 showing a decline between 4 and 9 months of age in Asian infants' fixation on internal features of other-race faces).

Poor discriminability of other-race faces is a well-documented phenomenon in the adult literature, named the *other-race effect* (ORE; for a review, see Meissner & Brigham, 2001). Whether the ORE results from greater experience with own-race faces (Chiroro & Valentine, 1995; Elliott, Wills, & Goldstein, 1973; Stahl, Wiese, & Schweinberger, 2008) or from mere social categorization (Bernstein, Young, & Hugenberg, 2007; Levin, 2000; MacLin & Malpass, 2001) is currently under debate. Does this effect also have its origins early in development? Indeed there is evidence for the ORE in childhood (Pezdek, Blandon-Gitlin, & Moore, 2003; Sangrigoli & de Schonen, 2004a) and it has recently been tracked down to infancy (Kelly et al., 2007b, 2009; but see Hayden, Bhatt, Joseph, & Tanaka, 2007 and Sangrigoli & de Schonen, 2004b for slightly different results), suggesting that the homogeneity of out-groups requires very little experience to be expressed and may be a fundamental principle of social learning.

Specifically, the ORE seems to develop gradually during the first year of life, with 3-month-olds being able to differentiate faces from every racial group presented to them. That is, they can tell two faces of African descent apart with the same ease they can differentiate two Asian or two European faces. By 9 months of age, however, only differentiation of own-race faces is preserved, again presumably due to the tuning of the face-processing system in accord with infants' exposure. Likewise, Korean adults who were adopted as children into White families show enhanced processing of White faces relative to Asian faces (Sangrigoli, Pallier, Argenti, Ventureyra, & de Schonen, 2005), indicating that reversing the ORE is possible even when the onset of intense other-race exposure occurred relatively late in development. Finally, testing short-term exposure effects on face discrimination has revealed that familiarization to only three exemplars of other-race (Asian) faces for a total duration of 120 seconds is enough for infants to regain their ability to tell these faces apart (Sangrigoli & de Schonen 2004b), an impressive result of the malleability of the learning system to input.

Such data raise two issues of interest. First, much like the ability to perceive non-native phonemes, which is lost during the first year of life due to lack of exposure, the ability to discriminate individual members of a group may initially be broad enough to effectively handle a wide range of stimuli, even ones that never appear in the environment. Over time, however, selective tuning of the system will occur at the expense of less frequently encountered groups (Scott, Pascalis, & Nelson, 2007); Second, the system has sufficient plasticity, even after some narrowing has taken place, such that later exposure to unfamiliar input can gradually reorient the system in the relevant direction. For example, we know that Asian adoptees tested earlier in development (6–14 years of age) show equivalent recognition performance for Asian and White faces (de Heering, de Liedekerke, Deboni, & Rossion, 2010), perhaps an intermediate step before the full-blown advantage for White faces is in place, as observed in adult Korean adoptees (Sangrigoli et al., 2005).

Parallels to these exposure effects on face processing have been shown in what has been known as the *other-species effect* – babies 6 months of age can easily tell monkey faces apart, an ability that disappears by the age of 9 months (Pascalis, de Haan, & Nelson, 2002). In other words, the younger the infant, the better the ability to discriminate among the individuals of another species. But by routinely exposing 6-month-olds to individually labeled monkey faces during this critical period, discrimination performance is maintained when infants are again tested at 9 months of age (Pascalis et al., 2005).

Among the most important results from such studies provides evidence for the crucial role of verbal labels in solidifying categorization. One group of infants was shown monkey faces that were paired with individualized names, another received the category label "monkey" when seeing each face repeatedly, and a third control condition passively viewed faces without labels. After 3 months of exposure, infants' discrimination ability was maintained only when the monkeys were given individual labels (Scott & Monesson, 2009). Labels, therefore, seem to be a powerful mechanism enhancing categorization and learning and may explain the inferential richness of categories in humans. We will return to discussing the role of verbal labels in highlighting social groups when we look at findings with older children

with whom more research has been done on this question.

From the data on infant perception of cross-species and cross-race faces, we know that a surprising sensitivity to race of the face is in place within the first months after birth. Not only do infants prefer faces of their own race but also they quickly form distinct categories centering on race. We also observed that cross-race exposure is a key factor both in terms of shaping the emerging own-race preference, and in terms of enhancing the perceptual discriminability of faces that do not belong to one's own racial group. The role of experience is clear from work showing that early cross-race exposure can mute a simple familiarity-based preference. Furthermore, the role of verbal labels in enhancing category distinctions and discriminability points to a unique human mechanism by which social cognition is stamped in.

A remaining open question concerns the underlying nature of the initial own-race preference. Interestingly, it has been proposed that, in contrast to language, race-based visual preferences in infancy might be perceptually driven rather than indicative of a desire for social interaction (Kinzler & Spelke, 2011). Indeed, thus far, no evidence for race-based social preferences in later infancy has been obtained. As mentioned earlier, the toy choice method elicits equal selection of toys from own- and other-race individuals at 10 months of age, and in a similar paradigm even 2.5-year-olds do not show sensitivity to race when given the option to offer a toy to one of two novel individuals (Kinzler & Spelke, 2011). If this pattern of discontinuity is substantiated, a challenge for future research would be to account for how race eventually becomes a socially meaningful category for older children and adults.

NAVIGATING SOCIAL CATEGORIES IN EARLY CHILDHOOD

We have outlined group-based preferences along a number of social categories that appear surprisingly early in infancy. A dominant method used to draw these conclusions was looking time. A question of great interest is whether these preferences are precursors of later-developing group-based preferences. While it is difficult to establish direct links between the behavior of infants and the behavior of children and adults, we will carefully review research on social categories as observed in later childhood and what it says about the continuity of social cognition.

To organize the growing research on this topic we focus on several sets of experiments. First, we look at those that show the use of social categories in service of self, including studies that test whom children decide to learn from to derive their own preferences or to learn culturally relevant information. We continue to draw out the evidence on which social categories might be more salient compared to others, and note that race still appears to be less relevant to children at the earlier ages. We also point to the potential role of environmental input and children's own experiences in guiding behavior.

Next we look at research on how children use their own preferences to make inferences about others; we will see that gender and ethnicity play a role, but these may be specific instantiations of a more general influence of the self on social perception because the results also obtain for minimal groups. We further examine experiments utilizing novel properties, thus allowing us to look at how category-based inductions occur when children's own personal preferences are immaterial to the task. These studies concern the role of social categories relative to personality characteristics in drawing inferences, as well as the effect of physical appearance with and without verbal labeling on drawing category-based induction.

Third, we examine preferences based on group membership, with many studies involving tasks similar to those used with adults (e.g., Implicit Association Test [IAT], memory tasks) and focusing on language, race, gender, and status. In studies using minimal groups, we show that just as in research with adults, even arbitrarily created groups shape in-group favoritism. Some of the factors influencing group bias in this context are physical markers, verbal labels, and status.

Finally, we report on a social preference that is not based on the usual demographic properties, which have been the mainstay of this research, but rather studies how children treat others who they learn are fortunate or not. These studies demonstrate how simple a model of social preference exists in young children – those who are lucky are good.

Imitation and modeling

In the previous section we learned that language serves as an important social cue to infants as they accept objects more from those who sound familiar. Tracking the developmental course of this preference, preschooler's sensitivity to accent as a social group marker was investigated by presenting participants with two distinct ways of manipulating novel objects, each demonstrated either by a person who previously spoke English with a native accent or with a foreign (Spanish)

accent. Monolingual English-speaking children endorsed the object function shown by the native English-speaking model, thus providing further evidence for continuous sensitivity to accent across different ages and context (Kinzler, Corriveau, & Harris, 2011).

Three-year-old children have been shown to spontaneously use social category information to infer their *own* preferences for novel objects and activities (Shutts, Banaji, & Spelke, 2010). Participants were introduced to still images of people differing in gender, race, or age and each member of the pair endorsed a different object or activity unfamiliar to the child. Despite never verbally labeling or highlighting the social distinctions, children went along with the preferences indicated by same-gender and same-age characters, but did not show a consistent pattern of responding based on race cues. These findings fit with other research on social categories' relative perceptual salience, which suggests that gender might be most prominent, followed by race and age (McGraw, Durm, & Durnam, 1989).

A strong demonstration of the influence of early gender identification on the maintenance of gender-based cultural stereotypes has recently been provided by Cvencek and colleagues (Cvencek, Meltzoff, & Greenwald, 2011b). Using both explicit and implicit measures they show that already by school age, boys and girls perceive math as being "for boys." Furthermore, boys (compared to girls) showed greater self-identification with a character that liked math, and showed a stronger association between "self" and math on an IAT.

Further evidence of preschool children's use of gender as a guide to one's own behavior was observed in their selective same-sex modeling of distinct physical movements produced by male and female actors. A follow-up experiment using the same paradigm further revealed preferential same-age imitation when children and adults demonstrated distinct actions. Finally, the authors were able to show that priming one or the other social category (age or gender) led to the primed category having priority on who children chose to imitate, suggesting that the hierarchy of social categories is malleable and dictated to some extent by environmental input (Grace, David, & Ryan, 2008).

While superior imitation of peers relative to adults has been shown as early as 14 months of age (Ryalls, Gul, & Ryalls, 2000), it has also been established that the *type* of knowledge preschoolers are seeking determines who they turn to for information. For example, when pondering why a certain food item is nutritional versus how to play with an unfamiliar toy, children as young as 3 will direct food questions to adults and toy questions to peers (VanderBorght & Jaswal, 2009). These studies do not only show the ability of the preschooler's social apparatus to absorb contextual information: the self serves as an anchor for what is appropriate behavior, but if the environment privileges another type of model or if experience suggests that expertise lies elsewhere, 3-year-olds mold their behavior accordingly.

Perceiving others

Thus far we have described the use of social category information in the service of learning or acquiring information relevant to the self; however, children are also remarkably good at drawing inferences about unfamiliar others based on their social group membership. In some cases, the self is the basis for predictions about others. For example, in a theoretically complementary study to Shutts et al. (2010), a positive correlation between children's own preferences for novel, gender-neutral toys and their predictions for how much same-gender peers would like those same toys was observed (Martin, Eisenbud, & Rose, 1995). In a similar manner, Lam and Leman (2009) found a positive correlation between children's preferences for unfamiliar food items and their predictions of whether other children from their own ethnic group would like those same foods. No relationship was found when asked to predict the preferences of peers belonging to an ethnic out-group.

We see evidence of children projecting the self even upon minimally created groups. When children (aged 5–11) were randomly assigned to "blue" or "red" teams, perceptions of their own academic and athletic competence were highly correlated with their predictions of in-group success in these domains, only 24 hours after group assignment (Patterson, Bigler, & Swann, 2010).

When subjects' personal preferences or abilities are entirely removed from the test setting, category-based inductions still arise. Diesendruck and haLevi (2006) tested which of many social group dimensions (gender, social class, religiosity, and ethnicity) or individual information (i.e., the person's personality) would rise to the top when kindergartners needed to attribute novel preferences and behaviors to different characters. While, generally, children used social category information much more than personality traits to make their inferences, ethnicity (Jewish/Arabic) and social status (rich/poor) emerged as particularly strong inductive bases. The authors ascribe this finding to the current cultural discourse in Israel, where the study was conducted. An important follow-up study established that verbal labels were the crucial factor in guiding children's decisions, much more than physical similarity. When social category and personality information were conveyed only verbally (without any physical markers), children still relied on social categories, and particularly on ethnicity, more than the character's personality when drawing inferences (Diesendruck & haLevi, 2006).

Furthermore, in a recent study, Waxman (2010) gauged children's inductive inferences *only* when physical appearance cues were present, and tested the effect of adding verbal labels. She hypothesized that much like naming in the object domain (e.g. Waxman & Markow, 1995), labeling people would enable children to identify commonalities among them, and to form distinct categories (Waxman, 2010). Specifically, 4-year-olds were shown a target picture (e.g. a White woman), which was either described using a novel social group marker (e.g. "This one is a *Wayshan*"), or a general statement (e.g. "This one *eats big lunches*"). A novel property was then attributed to the target (e.g. likes to go *glaving*), and participants were asked to judge which of a series of test photographs shared this novel property. In one version of the task the test items were pictures of people who matched the gender of the target but differed on race (e.g. Black and White females) and in a second version test items matched the target on race but differed on gender (e.g. White males and females). In both versions test items also included pictures of non-human animals. Results showed that labels enhanced group-based inductions. In the race condition, when no social category marker was given, generalization of the novel property was very broad and encompassed all people (irrespective of race), but excluded non-human animals. However, once group membership was highlighted via labeling, children extended the novel property exclusively to other exemplars of the same race as the target. Interestingly, in the gender condition, even when no label was provided, gender-matching inductions still arose, but this effect became significantly stronger after labeling. Waxman (2010) explains the baseline gender finding as indicative of preschooler's already-developing sensitivity to gender categories, perhaps due to the ample labeling of gender that is already occurring in children's daily life.

Taken together, the evidence thus far suggests that preschool children will readily make inferences based on gender, ethnicity, and age; they will privilege social category information over personality traits as the basis for predictions about novel individuals, and their inductions are strongly influenced by labels for social groups. More generally, this pattern of results has been treated as evidence for "psychological essentialism" (Gelman, 2003; Medin & Ortony, 1989), suggesting that children even at this young age see members of certain social categories as sharing unobservable intrinsic properties, assuming that they are likely innate and stable over time, and denoting "distinct kinds of people" (Waxman, 2010). (For further discussion of this issue and how it relates to the categories of race and gender, see Gil-White, 2001; Hirschfeld, 1995; Taylor, 1996; Taylor, Rhodes, & Gelman, 2009.)

Us and them

So far we have considered how social group categories guide children's behaviors, preferences, and inductions, and have left the question of group evaluation untouched. However, there is ample evidence of own-group preference, especially in the domains of race and gender (e.g. Black-Gutman & Hickson, 1996; McGlothlin & Killen, 2010; Powlishta, Serbin, Doyle, & White, 1994; Yee & Brown, 1994) Children's playmate selections have often provided evidence for own-group affiliations (e.g. Aboud, Mendelson, & Purdy, 2003; Fishbein & Imai, 1993; Graham & Cohen, 1997; Martin & Fabes, 2001; Martin, Fabes, Evans, & Wyman, 1999).

Recently, testing friendship preferences in White English-speaking 5-year-olds, Kinzler and colleagues (Kinzler, Shutts, DeJesus, & Spelke, 2009) found preferential selection of native-language speakers over foreign-language (French) speakers and foreign-accented speakers (French-accented English). Furthermore, when no language information was given, children chose White as opposed to Black targets as their friends; however, when race and language were put in conflict such that the own-race target spoke with a foreign accent, while the other-race target spoke in familiar English, children showed language-based preference, indicating that, in parallel to the findings with 10-month-old infants, language similarity seems to be more important than race similarity.

In another example, Asian children 3–11 years of age were asked: "Who would you like to play with?" in reference to three photographs of an Asian, a White, and a Black child matched for subjects' gender (Kowalski & Lo, 2001). While, as expected, significantly more Asian selections were evident, a couple of additional findings are worth noting. First, the authors ran two trials in which the target photographs were presented and children were instructed to select the one that looks most like them. Across all ages the Asian photograph was selected significantly more often than chance, and an increase in correct responses with age was also observed. Importantly, whether this self-identification task was administered

before or after children made their playmate choices had an influence on the results. Specifically, children who were asked to self-identify at the beginning of the study produced Asian playmate choices more often (when the target photographs were not labeled) than children who received the self-identification task last, presumably due to the increased salience of group membership. In a related manner, Bigler (1995) has shown that the functional use of gender categories in the classroom increases gender stereotyping in elementary school children, particularly those who have low classification skills (see also Hilliard & Liben, 2010 for equivalent findings with even younger children).

Kowalski and Lo (2001) additionally observed that the *least* own-race playmate selections were made in the oldest age group tested, 10–11-year-olds (for similar findings on reduction of bias across age, see Aboud, 1988; Powlishta et al., 1994). This may be due to increased awareness of social norms requiring suppression of biased responses (Apfelbaum, Pauker, Ambady, Sommers, & Norton, 2008; Rutland, Cameron, Milne, & McGeorge, 2005) or perhaps increased attention to individual characteristics (Kowalski & Lo, 2001).

The automaticity of us and them

Measures of implicit attitudes allow us to overcome the demand characteristics described above and, in fact, reveal no reduction in intergroup bias with age. For example, using a child version of the Implicit Association Test (Ch-IAT), Baron and Banaji (2006) showed that implicit pro-White/anti-Black attitudes were identical in magnitude in their White 6-year-old and adult participants. Moreover, a gradual dissociation between the implicit task and an explicit preference task was observed; when asked which of two targets (differing on race) they preferred, 6-year-olds selected the White target 84% of the time, a preference that was attenuated at age 8 (with 68% own-race selection), and completely non-existent in adulthood.

In contrast, the same Ch-IAT comparing own-race to a *high-status* out-group in two different populations (American and Japanese) revealed a lack of implicit racial bias in adults. At age 6, children's in-group preference was equally strong, irrespective of out-group status, but by the age of 10, sensitivity to status seems to be visible as the magnitude of children's implicit own-race bias was greater for low- compared to high-status groups (Dunham, Baron, & Banaji, 2006). In line with this result, Hispanic children (tested in the United States where they are a relatively disadvantaged minority) exhibited implicit pro-Hispanic attitudes only when the comparison group was another disadvantaged out-group (African Americans), and not when compared to the White majority. Responses on the explicit preference measure again diverged from the implicit findings as children exhibited an in-group bias irrespective of the comparison out-group (Dunham, Baron, & Banaji, 2007).

Until recently, the IAT was limited to data collection on adults and on children approximately 6 years of age. To assess the preferences of younger children, Dunham and Banaji (2008) adapted a task established in previous research with adults by Hugenberg and Bodenhausen (2004) that even a 3-year-old could perform. Participants were shown ambiguous race faces (intermediate between Black and White) displaying happy and angry facial expressions, and their task was to answer the question: Is this face like this one (pointing to an unambiguously Black face) or like this one (pointing to an unambiguously White face)? Racially ambiguous angry faces were more often categorized as Black than White if the child was able to categorize unambiguous faces by race. These results show how prepared the mind is to make "us and them" distinctions, and that in-group preference is visible just as soon as intergroup categorization is possible. Such studies also potentially explain recently discussed findings (e.g. Kowalski & Lo, 2001; Waxman, 2010), as presumably the processes of labeling and self-categorization in those studies enhanced children's attention to the relevant category distinctions, which then automatically enabled them do make inductions and preference choices based on those categories.

Implicit racial stereotypes have also been revealed using tasks requiring recall of information, with young children generally remembering stereotypical descriptions better than counter-stereotypical descriptions of targets differing in race (e.g., Bigler & Liben, 1993). In one particularly strong example of top-down effects pertaining to *face* memory, young White children were shown ambiguous race target faces that were constructed by morphing a Black face with a White face. During the task, the ambiguous race target face was named and introduced as the sibling of either the Black or the White face that was used in its construction. Immediately after, children were presented with a test slide displaying the target paired with a distractor (a different Black/White morphed face) and were asked to point to the target. Results revealed that faces paired with their White "sibling" were remembered significantly more often (Shutts & Kinzler, 2007).

Encoding of gender follows the same pattern, with children remembering stereotypical information more accurately (Koblinsky, Cruse, & Sugawara, 1978; Martin & Halverson, 1983; Signorella &

Liben, 1984: for a review, see Signorella, Bigler, & Liben, 1997), and recently it has been shown using the Preschool IAT that by the age of 4, children already display implicit gender attitudes which mimic the adult data, with girls showing a stronger implicit own-gender bias compared to boys (Cvencek, Greenwald, & Meltzoff, 2011a).

Minimal groups

In addition to race, gender, and language, children consistently exhibit in-group preferences even when groups are arbitrarily created. For example, one study (Bigler, Jones, & Lobliner, 1997) manipulated the functional use of social grouping in summer school classrooms of 6–9-year-olds by assigning children to either a "yellow" or "blue" group marked by T-shirt color. In the experimental conditions, teachers regularly referred to the two color groups when organizing the class (e.g. lining up by T-shirt color). In the control condition, children wore colored T-shirts but these were ignored by the teacher. After 4 weeks intergroup attitudes were evaluated, and findings showed that children in the experimental conditions (but not in the control condition) attributed more positive traits to members of the in-group and negative traits to the out-group, perceived the two color groups as more dissimilar from each other, and members of each group as more similar to each other. Despite the visual salience of T-shirt color in the control condition, group bias did not arise, presumably because group membership was irrelevant for classroom functioning (for comparison, see Patterson & Bigler, 2006 with 3–5-year-old subjects showing some in-group bias in the control condition).

Dunham and colleagues (Dunham, Baron, & Carey, 2011) replicated these findings using a much more stringent minimal group paradigm. In their experimental session, 5-year-old subjects were individually tested, randomly assigned to an explicitly labeled color group, given a matching colored T-shirt, and asked to make judgments about target own- and out-group members presented on a computer screen. Adopting these stringent criteria revealed greater explicit liking of own-group members over out-group targets, an own-group preference in resource allocation, as well as a strong implicit own-group bias as measured by the Ch-IAT (which in turn correlated with attribution of positive behavior to the in-group). Significantly weaker effects were found when the colored shirts were described but not referred to as markers of group membership. A final experiment revealed biased memorization even using this minimal manipulation, such that positive information was better recalled when it was attributed to the in-group compared to the out-group.

Similarly, Bigler and her colleagues (Bigler, Brown, & Markell, 2001) randomly assigned group status based on T-shirt color (blue or yellow). In both experimental conditions group status was implicitly conveyed via posters depicting novel group members and their various achievements (e.g., pictures of the winners of an athletic contest, the majority of whom were wearing yellow shirts). Reference to these posters was only made once on the first day of school. The teachers then either avoided emphasizing group membership throughout the study, or made functional use of group labels in addition to displaying the posters. Evaluation of group bias after 4 weeks indicated that only children assigned to a *high-status* group in this latter experimental condition displayed in-group favoritism, while children in the low-status group did not (an effect which was significantly stronger in the younger participants). No preference was observed in either status group when only posters were displayed, again indicating that visual information alone is not sufficient for intergroup attitudes to arise.

Children will also judge others based on criteria that might not mark group boundaries so explicitly in adults. An example of this comes from studies on luck preference (Olson, Banaji, Dwek, & Spelke, 2006; Olson, Dunham, Dwek, Spelke, & Banaji, 2008). Specifically, 5–7-year-old children liked others who experienced an uncontrollable positive event (e.g., finding $5 on the sidewalk) significantly more than those who experienced an uncontrollable negative event (e.g., being rained on while walking to school).

Moreover, mere group membership will produce these effects, such that a novel individual who belongs to a group (marked by T-shirt color) whose members mostly experienced lucky events will be preferred to a novel member of a group that mostly experienced unlucky events, despite never hearing any specific information about the target (Olson et al., 2006). Further testing has produced evidence for the luck preference cross-culturally (in Japanese children), and in children as young as 3 years of age. Also, children not only believe that an unlucky person is more likely to later perform an *intentional* bad action but also predict that the sibling of someone who experienced an uncontrollable negative event is more likely to perform an intentional bad action (Olson et al., 2008).

CONCLUSION

Returning to the questions presented at the outset, we have learned from studies on the social cognition capacities of infants that group-based

preferences develop early – gender and race preference by 3 months of age, age preference by 4 months, and language preference by 6 months. These social group preferences are, in most cases, shaped by the predominant environmental input (with the possible exception of age), and do not appear to need extensive intergroup interaction in order to emerge. Now that these preferences have been uncovered, research has turned to determining what drives the looking-time findings, and whether some group distinctions are more significant to infants than others. Future research will better characterize the natural developmental trajectories of these preferences later on in infancy, and study their malleability, for example, by exposing infants to unfamiliar group members even after a preference has been established.

Studies of categorization – the ability of an infant to recognize that all instances of group X belong to a single set which is distinct from set Y– have been conducted with older infants, showing the ability to categorize age by 4 months, race by 9 months, and an asymmetry in the emergence in infants' gender categories. As in the case with preferences, it is yet unclear whether these categories are solely perceptually driven or whether they are conceptual and could promote further inferences about the individual exemplars within a set, and as such these questions will benefit from future research. Furthermore, there remains a theoretically important question of the relationship between categorization and preference formation: Is this a two-step process, or do preferences co-occur with the formation of categories? The early years provide a natural place to test this question about the intertwining of perceptual and affective learning and development.

As infants turn into toddlers and young children, their social interactions multiply, and begin to involve a greater number of social groups. Groups that had no relevance early in life such as class, ethnicity, and religion now become markers of one's own group membership within the hierarchy of groups in the larger social world. In addition, the greater cognitive and social abilities present in young children allow a variety of measures to be used that rely on language using both self-report as well as implicit measures of cognition. From the early years of childhood we know that some of the preferences observed on more basic measures like looking time in infancy continue on the same path in early childhood (e.g., age preference). In addition, childhood also provides information that us–them divides that are so much an explicit part of adult life, are present early in life. Unlike measures of looking time, we know, for instance, from measures of actual interpersonal approach and choice behavior that these are true forms of preference. On the other hand, looking-time preferences on some dimensions like race in infancy do not seem to show continuity in childhood, supporting evolutionary accounts of race as an arbitrary category. Among the most striking effects seen in early childhood is the role that language plays in taking otherwise irrelevant social categories and turning them into meaningful ones that seem to be rich in inference. When labels are used to categorize groups, young children show implicit preferences that are similar to those of adults, a surprising result given assumptions that sustained experience over development is necessary input to the development of implicit intergroup attitudes.

Although the question of how much social cognition represents a domain of core knowledge remains open, the research reviewed here makes it clear that social cognition as it pertains to discriminating, recognizing, and forming attitudes toward individuals as members of social groups is visible in the earliest days and months after birth and unfolds along the dimensions of familiarity and similarity to self in the early years. As the globe shrinks socially, so much of adult social life requires being able to cut across group boundaries both for work and for assuring personal happiness. It is clear that people who differ from us in nationality, language, race, and age are ones we interact with, learn from, grow to love, and work with. Yet shaking off group distinctions, even when adult humans wish to do so, and even when such shaking off is in our individual and group interest, is difficult perhaps because it is such an entrenched aspect of social development. To do so, as the growing new context of modern social life demands, seems to be a task for conscious, adult minds.

ACKNOWLEDGMENT

We thank Steve Lehr and Susan Fiske for valuable feedback on an early draft. The writing of this chapter was supported by the E. J. Safra Center for the Study of Ethics at Harvard University.

REFERENCES

Aboud, F.E. (1988). *Children and prejudice*. New York: Blackwell.

Aboud, F.E., Mendelson, M.J., & Purdy, K.T. (2003). Cross-race peer relations and friendship quality. *International Journal of Behavioral Development, 27*(2), 165–173.

Anastasi, J.S., & Rhodes, M.G. (2005). An own-age bias in face recognition for children and older adults. *Psychonomic Bulletin and Review, 12*(6), 1043–1047.

Anzures, G., Quinn, P.C., Pascalis, O., Slater, A.M., & Lee, K. (2009). Categorization, categorical perception, and asymmetry in infants' representation of face race. *Developmental Science, 13*(4), 553–564.

Apfelbaum, E.P., Pauker, K., Ambady, N., Sommers, S.R., & Norton, M.I. (2008). Learning (not) to talk about race: When older children underperform in social categorization. *Developmental Psychology, 44*(5), 1513–1518.

Bahrick, L.E., Netto, D., & Hernandez-Reif, M. (1998). Intermodal perception of adult and child faces and voices by infants. *Child Development, 69*(5), 1263–1275.

Bahrick, L.E., & Pickens, J.N. (1988). Classification of bimodal English and Spanish language passages by infants. *Infant Behavior and Development, 11*, 277–296.

Baillargeon, R., Scott, R.M., & He, Z. (2010). False-belief understanding in infants. *Trends in Cognitive Sciences, 14*(3), 110–118.

Banaji, M.R., & Gelman, S.A. (in press). *Navigating the social world: The early years*. Oxford, UK: Oxford University Press.

Bar-Haim, Y., Ziv, T., Lamy, D. & Hodes, R.M. (2006). Nature and nurture in own-race face processing. *Psychological Science, 17*(2), 159–163.

Baron, A.S., & Banaji, M.R. (2006). The development of implicit attitudes: Evidence of race evaluations from ages 6 and 10 and adulthood. *Psychological Science, 17*(1), 53–58.

Bernstein, M.J., Young, S.G., & Hugenberg, K. (2007). The cross-category effect: Mere social categorization is sufficient to elicit an own-group bias in face recognition. *Psychological Science, 18*(8), 706–712.

Bigelow, A., MacLean, J., Wood, C., & Smith, J. (1990). Infants' responses to child and adult strangers: An investigation of height and facial configuration variables. *Infant Behavior and Development, 13*, 21–32.

Bigler, R.S. (1995). The role of classification skill in moderating environmental influences on children's gender stereotyping: A study of the functional use of gender in the classroom. *Child Development, 66*, 1072–1087.

Bigler, R.S., Brown, C.S., & Markell, M. (2001). When groups are not created equal: Effects of group status on the formation of intergroup attitudes in children. *Child Development, 72*(4), 1151–1162.

Bigler, R.S., Jones, L.C., & Lobliner, D.B. (1997). Social categorization and the formation of intergroup attitudes in children. *Child Development, 68*(3), 530–543.

Bigler, R.S., & Liben, L.S. (1993). A cognitive-developmental approach to racial stereotyping and reconstructive memory in Euro-American children. *Child Development, 64*, 1507–1518.

Black-Gutman, D., & Hickson, F. (1996). The relationship between racial attitudes and social-cognitive development in children: An Australian study. *Developmental Psychology, 32*(3), 448–456.

Bosch, L., & Sebastián-Gallés, N. (1997). Native language recognition abilities in 4-month-old infants from monolingual and bilingual environments. *Cognition, 65*, 33–69.

Brooks, J., & Lewis, M. (1976). Infants' responses to strangers: Midget, adult, and child. *Child Development, 47*, 323–332.

Byers-Heinlein, K., Burns, T.C., & Werker, J.F. (2010). The roots of bilingualism in newborns. *Psychological Science, 21*(3), 343–348.

Chiroro, P., & Valentine, T. (1995). An investigation of the contact hypothesis of the own-race bias in face recognition. *The Quarterly Journal of Experimental Psychology, 48A*(4), 879–894.

Cornell, E.H. (1974). Infants' discrimination of photographs of faces following redundant presentations. *Journal of Experimental Child Psychology, 18*, 98–106.

Cvencek, D., Greenwald, A.G., & Meltzoff, A.N. (2011a). Measuring implicit attitudes of 4-year-olds: The Preschool Implicit Association Test. *Journal of Experimental Child Psychology, 109*, 187–200.

Cvencek, D., Meltzoff, A.N., & Greenwald, A.G. (2011b). Math-gender stereotypes in elementary school children. *Child Development, 82*(3), 766–779.

Diesendruck, G., & haLevi, H. (2006). The role of language, appearance, and culture in children's social category-based inductions. *Child Development, 77*(3), 539–553.

Dunham Y., & Banaji, M.R. (2008). *Invariance of intergroup attitudes across the lifespan*. Unpublished manuscript, Harvard University.

Dunham, Y., Baron, A.S., & Banaji, M.R. (2006). From American city to Japanese village: A cross-cultural investigation of implicit race attitudes. *Child Development, 77*(5), 1268–1281.

Dunham, Y., Baron, A.S., & Banaji, M.R. (2007). Children and social groups: A developmental analysis of implicit consistency in Hispanic Americans. *Self and Identity, 6*, 238–255.

Dunham, Y., Baron, A.S., & Carey, S. (2011). Consequences of "minimal" group affiliations in children. *Child Development, 82*(3), 793–811.

de Haan, M., Johnson, M.H., Maurer, D., & Perrett, D.I. (2001). Recognition of individual faces and average face prototypes by 1- and 3-month-old infants. *Cognitive Development, 16*, 659–678.

de Heering, A., de Liedekerke, C., Deboni, M., & Rossion, B. (2010). The role of experience during childhood in shaping the other-race effect. *Developmental Science, 13*(1), 181–187.

Elliott, E.S., Wills, E.J., & Goldstein, A.G. (1973). The effects of discrimination training on the recognition of white and oriental faces. *Bulletin of the Psychonomic Society, 2*(2), 71–73.

Farroni, T., Johnson, M.H., Menon, E., Zulian, L., Faraguna, D., & Csibra, G. (2005). Newborns' preference for face-relevant stimuli: Effects of contrast polarity. *Proceedings of the National Academy of Sciences, 102*(47), 17245–17250.

Ferguson, K.T., Kulkofsky, S., Cashon, C.H., & Casasola, M. (2009). The development of specialized processing of own-race faces in infancy. *Infancy, 14*(3), 263–284.

Fishbein, H.D., & Imai, S. (1993). Preschoolers select playmates on the basis of gender and race. *Journal of Applied Developmental Psychology, 14*, 303–316.

Gelman, S. A. (2003). *The essential child: Origins of essentialism in everyday thought*. New York : Oxford University Press.

Gergely, G., Bekkering, H., & Király, I. (2002). Rational imitation in preverbal infants. *Nature, 415*(6873), 755.

Gil-White, F.J. (2001). Are ethnic groups biological "species" to the human brain? Essentialism in our cognition of some social categories. *Current Anthropology, 42*(4), 515–554.

Grace, D.M., David, B.J., & Ryan, M.K. (2008). Investigating preschoolers' categorical thinking about gender through imitation, attention, and the use of self-categories. *Child Development, 79*(6), 1928–1941.

Graham, J.A., & Cohen, R. (1997). Race and sex as factors in children's sociometric ratings and friendship choices. *Social Development, 6*(3), 355–372.

Greenberg, D.J., Hillman, D., & Grice, D. (1973). Infant and stranger variables related to stranger anxiety in the first year of life. *Developmental Psychology, 9*(2), 207–212.

Hamlin, J.K., Wynn, K., & Bloom, P. (2007). Social evaluation by preverbal infants. *Nature, 450*, 557–559.

Hayden, A., Bhatt, R.S., Joseph, J.E., & Tanaka, J.W. (2007). The other-race effect in infancy: Evidence using a morphing technique. *Infancy, 12*(1), 95–104.

Hilliard, L.J., & Liben, L.S. (2010). Differing levels of gender salience in preschool classrooms: Effects on children's gender attitudes and intergroup bias. *Child Development, 81*(6), 1787–1798.

Hirschfeld, L.A. (1995). Do children have a theory of race? *Cognition, 54*, 209–252.

Hugenberg, K., & Bodenhausen, G.V. (2004). Ambiguity in social categorization: The role of prejudice and facial affect in race categorization. *Psychological Science, 15*(5), 342–345.

Johnson, M.H., Dziurawiec, S., Ellis, H., & Morton, J. (1991). Newborns' preferential tracking of face-like stimuli and its subsequent decline. *Cognition, 40*, 1–19.

Johnson, S., Slaughter, V., & Carey, S. (1998). Whose gaze will infants follow? The elicitation of gaze following in 12-month-olds. *Development Science, 1*(2), 233–238.

Kelly, D.J., Liu, S., Ge, L., Quinn, P.C., Slater, A.M., Lee K., et al. (2007a). Cross-race preferences for same-race faces extend beyond the African versus Caucasian contrast in 3-month-old infants. *Infancy, 11*(1), 87–95.

Kelly, D.J., Liu, S., Lee, K., Quinn, P.C., Pascalis, O., Slater, A.M., et al. (2009). Development of the other-race effect during infancy: Evidence toward universality? *Journal of Experimental Child Psychology, 104*, 105–114.

Kelly, D.J., Quinn, P.C., Slater, A.M., Lee, K., Ge, L., & Pascalis, O. (2007b). The other-race effect develops during infancy: Evidence of perceptual narrowing. *Psychological Science, 18*(12), 1084–1089.

Kelly, D.J., Quinn, P.C., Slater, A.M., Lee, K., Gibson, A., Smith, M., et al. (2005). Three-month-olds, but not newborns, prefer own-race faces. *Developmental Science, 8*(6), F31–F36.

Kinzler, K.D., Corriveau, K.H., & Harris, P.L. (2011). Children's selective trust in native-accented speakers. *Developmental Science, 14*(1), 106–111.

Kinzler, K.D., Dupoux E., & Spelke, E.S. (2007). The native language of social cognition. *Proceedings of the National Academy of Sciences, 104*(30), 12577–12580.

Kinzler, K.D., Shutts, K., & Correll, J. (2010). Priorities in social categories. *European Journal of Social Psychology, 40,* 581–592.

Kinzler, K.D., Shutts, K., DeJesus, J., & Spelke, E.S. (2009). Accent trumps race in guiding children's social preferences. *Social Cognition, 27*(4), 623–634.

Kinzler, K.D., & Spelke, E.S. (2011). Do infants show social preferences for people differing in race? *Cognition, 119,* 1–9.

Koblinsky, S.G., Cruse, D.F., & Sugawara, A.I. (1978). Sex role stereotypes and children's memory for story content. *Child Development, 49,* 452–458.

Koenig, M.A., & Harris, P.L. (2005). The role of social cognition in early trust. *Trends in Cognitive Sciences, 9*(10), 457–459.

Kowalski, K., & Lo, Y.-F. (2001). The influence of perceptual features, ethnic labels, and sociocultural information on the development of ethnic/racial bias in young children. *Journal of Cross-Cultural Psychology, 32*(4), 444–455.

Lam, V., & Leman, P. (2009). Children's gender- and ethnicity-based reasoning about foods. *Social Development, 18*(2), 478–496.

Leinbach, M.D., & Fagot, B.I. (1993). Categorical habituation to male and female faces: Gender schematic processing in infancy. *Infant Behavior and Development, 16,* 317–332.

Levin, D.T. (2000). Race as a visual feature: Using visual search and perceptual discrimination tasks to understand face categories and the cross-race recognition deficit. *Journal of Experimental Psychology, 129*(4), 559–574.

Levy, G.D., & Haaf, R.A. (1994). Detection of gender-related categories by 10-month-old infants. *Infant Behavior and Development, 17,* 457–459.

Liu, S., Quinn, P.C., Wheeler, A., Xiao, N., Ge, L., & Lee, K. (2011). Similarity and difference in the processing of same- and other-race faces as revealed by eye tracking in 4- to 9-month-olds. *Journal of Experimental Child Psychology, 108,* 180–189.

Macchi Cassia, V., Kuefner, D., Picozzi, M., & Vescovo, E. (2009a). Early experience predicts later plasticity for face processing: Evidence for the reactivation of dormant effects. *Psychological Science, 20*(7), 853–859.

Macchi Cassia, V., Picozzi, M., Kuefner, D., & Casati, M. (2009b). Why mix-ups don't happen in the nursery: Evidence for an experience-based interpretation of the other-age effect. *The Quarterly Journal of Experimental Psychology, 62*(6), 1099–1107.

Macchi Cassia, V., Turati, C., & Simion, F. (2004). Can a nonspecific bias toward top-heavy patterns explain newborns' face preference? *Psychological Science, 15*(6), 379–383.

MacLin, O.H., & Malpass, R.S. (2001). Racial categorization of faces: The ambiguous race face effect. *Psychology, Public Policy, and Law, 7*(1), 98–118.

Martin, C.L., Eisenbud, L., & Rose, H. (1995). Children's gender-based reasoning about toys. *Child Development, 66,* 1453–1471.

Martin, C.L., & Fabes, R.A. (2001). The stability and consequences of young children's same-sex peer interactions. *Developmental Psychology, 37*(3), 431–446.

Martin, C.L., Fabes, R.A., Evans, S.M., & Wyman, H. (1999). Social cognition on the playground: Children's beliefs about playing with girls versus boys and their relations to sex segregated play. *Journal of Social and Personal Relationship, 16*(6), 751–771.

Martin, C.L., & Halverson, C.F. (1983). The effects of sex-typing schemas on young children's memory. *Child Development, 54,* 563–574.

McCall, R.B., & Kennedy, C.B. (1980). Attention of 4-month infants to discrepancy and babyishness. *Journal of Experimental Child Psychology, 29,* 189–201.

McGlothlin, H., & Killen, M. (2010). How social experience is related to children's intergroup attitudes. *European Journal of Social Psychology, 40,* 625–634.

McGraw, K.O., Durm, M.W., & Durnam, M.R. (1989). The relative salience of sex, race, age, and glasses in children's social perception. *Journal of Genetic Psychology, 150*(3), 251–267.

Medin, D., & Ortony, A. (1989). Psychological essentialism. In S. Vosniadou & A. Ortony (Eds.), *Similarity and analogical reasoning* (pp. 179–195). New York: Cambridge University Press.

Mehler, J., Jusczyk, P., Lambertz, G., Halsted, N., Bertoncini, J., & Amiel-Tison, C. (1988). A precursor of language acquisition in young infants. *Cognition, 29,* 143–178.

Meissner, C.A., & Brigham, J.C. (2001). Thirty years of investigating the own-race bias in memory for faces: A meta-analytic review. *Psychology, Public Policy, and Law, 7*(1), 3–35.

Melinder, A., Gredebäck, G., Westerlund, A., & Nelson, C.A. (2010). Brain activation during upright and inverted encoding of own- and other-age faces: ERP evidence for an own-age bias. *Developmental Science, 13*(4), 588–598.

Meltzoff, A.N., & Moore, M.K. (1977). Imitation of facial and manual gestures by human neonates. *Science, 198*(4312), 75–78.

Moon, C., Cooper, R.P., & Fifer W.P. (1993). Two-day-olds prefer their native language. *Infant Behavior and Development, 16,* 495–500.

Olson, K.R., Banaji M.R., Dweck, C.S., & Spelke E.S. (2006). Children's biased evaluations of lucky versus unlucky people and their social groups. *Psychological Science, 17*(10), 845–846.

Olson, K.R., Dunham, Y., Dweck, C.S., Spelke, E.S., & Banaji M.R. (2008). Judgments of the lucky across development and culture. *Journal of Personality and Social Psychology, 94*(5), 757–776.

Pascalis, O., de Haan, M. & Nelson, C.A. (2002). Is face processing species-specific during the first year of life? *Science, 296,* 1321–1323.

Pascalis, O., & de Schonen, S. (1994). Recognition memory in 3- to 4-day-old human neonates. *NeuroReport, 5,* 1721–1724.

Pascalis, O., Scott, L.S., Kelly, D.J., Shannon, R.W., Nicholson, E., Coleman, M., et al. (2005). Plasticity of face processing in infancy. *Proceedings of the National Academy of Sciences, 102*(14), 5297–5300.

Patterson, M.M., & Bigler R.S. (2006). Preschool children's attention to environmental messages about groups: Social categorization and the origins of intergroup bias. *Child Development, 77*(4), 847–860.

Patterson, M.M., Bigler, R.S., & Swann, W.B. (2010). When personal identities confirm versus conflict with group identities: Evidence from an intergroup paradigm. *European Journal of Social Psychology, 40*, 652–670.

Pezdek, K., Blandon-Gitlin, I., & Moore, C. (2003). Children's face recognition memory: More evidence for the cross-race effect. *Journal of Applied Psychology, 88*(4), 760–763.

Powlishta, K.K., Serbin, L.A., Doyle, A.-B., & White, D.R. (1994). Gender, ethnic, and body type biases: The generality of prejudice in childhood. *Developmental Psychology, 30*(4), 526–536.

Quinn, P.C., Uttley, L., Lee, K., Gibson, A., Smith, M., Slater, A.M., et al. (2008). Infant preference for female faces occurs for same- but not other-race faces. *Journal of Neuropsychology, 2*, 15–26.

Quinn, P.C., Yahr, J., Kuhn, A., Slater, A.M., & Pascalis O. (2002). Representation of the gender of human faces by infants: A preference for female. *Perception, 31*, 1109–1121.

Ramsey, J.L., Langlois, J.H., & Marti, N.C. (2005). Infant categorization of faces: Ladies first. *Developmental Review, 25*, 212–246.

Ramsey-Rennels, J.L., & Langlois, J.H. (2006). Infants' differential processing of female and male faces. *Current Directions in Psychological Science, 15*(2), 59–62.

Rennels, J.L., & Davis, R.E. (2008). Facial experience during the first year. *Infant Behavior and Development, 31*, 665–678.

Rubenstein, A.J., Kalakanis, L., & Langlois, J.H. (1999). Infant preferences for attractive faces: A cognitive explanation. *Developmental Psychology, 35*(3), 848–855.

Rutland, A., Cameron, L., Milne, A., & McGeorge, P. (2005). Social norms and self-presentation: Children's implicit and explicit intergroup attitudes. *Child Development, 76*(2), 451–466.

Ryalls, B.O., Gul, R.E., & Ryalls, K.R. (2000). Infant imitation of peer and adult models: Evidence for a peer model advantage. *Merrill-Palmer Quarterly, 46*(1), 188–202.

Sanefuji, W., Ohgami, H., & Hashiya, K. (2006). Preference for peers in infancy. *Infant Behavior and Development, 29*, 584–593.

Sangrigoli, S., & de Schonen, S. (2004a). Effect of visual experience on face processing: A developmental study of inversion and non-native, effects. *Developmental Science, 7*(1), 74–87.

Sangrigoli, S., & de Schonen, S. (2004b). Recognition of own-race and other-race faces by three-month-old infants. *Journal of Child Psychology and Psychiatry, 45*(7). 1219–1227.

Sangrigoli, S., Pallier, C., Argenti, A.-M., Ventureyra, V.A.G., & de Schonen, S. (2005). Reversibility of the other-race effect in face recognition during childhood. *Psychological Science, 16*(6), 440–444.

Scott, L.S., & Monesson, A. (2009). The origin of biases in face perception. *Psychological Science, 20*(6), 676–680.

Scott, L.S., Pascalis, O., & Nelson, C.A. (2007). A domain-general theory of the development of perceptual discrimination. *Current Directions in Psychological Science, 16*(4), 197–201.

Shutts, K., Banaji, M.R., & Spelke, E.S. (2010). Social categories guide young children's preferences for novel objects. *Developmental Science, 13*(4), 599–610.

Shutts, K., & Kinzler, K.D. (2007). An ambiguous-race illusion in children's face memory. *Psychological Science, 18*(9), 763–767.

Shutts, K., Kinzler, K.D. McKee, C.B., & Spelke E.S. (2009). Social information guides infants' selection of foods. *Journal of Cognition and Development, 10*(1–2), 1–17.

Sidanius, J., & Pratto, F. (1999). *Social dominance: An intergroup theory of social hierarchy and oppression.* Cambridge, UK: Cambridge University Press.

Signorella, M.L., Bigler, R.S., & Liben, L.S. (1997). A meta-analysis of children's memories for own-sex and other-sex information. *Journal of Applied Developmental Psychology, 18*, 429–445.

Signorella, M.L., & Liben, L.S. (1984). Recall and reconstruction of gender-related pictures: Effects of attitude, task difficulty, and age. *Child Development, 55*, 393–405.

Slater, A., Von der Schulenburg, C., Brown, E., Badenoch, M., Butterworth, G., Parsons, S., et al. (1998). Newborn infants prefer attractive faces. *Infant Behavior and Development, 21*, 345–354.

Spelke, E.S. (2000). Core knowledge. *American Psychologist, 55*(11), 1233–1243.

Spelke, E.S., Bernier, E., & Skerry, A. (in press). Core social cognition. In M. R. Banaji & S. A. Gelman (Eds.), *Navigating the social world: The early years.* New York: Oxford University Press.

Spelke E.S., & Kinzler, K.D. (2007). Core knowledge. *Developmental Science, 10*(1), 89–96.

Stahl, J., Wiese, H., & Schweinberger, S.R. (2008). Expertise and own-race bias in face processing: An event-related potential study. *NeuroReport, 19*(5), 583–587.

Taylor, M.G. (1996). The development of children's beliefs about social and biological aspects of gender differences. *Child* Development, 67, 1555–1571.

Taylor, M.G., Rhodes M., & Gelman, S.A. (2009). Boys will be boys; cows will be cows: Children's essentialist reasoning about gender categories and animal species. *Child Development, 80*(2), 461–481.

Turati, C. (2004). Why faces are not special to newborns: An alternative account of the face preference. *Current Directions in Psychological Science, 13*(1), 5–8.

VanderBorght, M., & Jaswal, V.K. (2009). Who knows best? Preschoolers sometimes prefer child informants over adult informants. *Infant and Child Development, 18*, 61–71.

Waxman, S.R. (2010). Names will never hurt me? Naming and the development of racial and gender categories in preschool-aged children. *European Journal of Social Psychology, 40*, 593–610.

Waxman, S.R., & Markow, D.B. (1995). Words as invitations to form categories: Evidence from 12- to 13-month-old infants. *Cognitive Psychology, 29*, 257–302.

Werker, J.F., & Tees, R.C. (1984). Cross-language speech perception: Evidence for perceptual reorganization during the first year of life. *Infant Behavior and Development, 7,* 49–63.

Wimmer, H., & Perner, J. (1983). Beliefs about beliefs: Representation and constraining function of wrong beliefs in young children's understanding of deception. *Cognition, 13,* 103–128.

Woodward, A.L. (1999). Infants' ability to distinguish between purposeful and non-purposeful behaviors. *Infant Behavior and Development, 22*(2), 145–160.

Yee, M., & Brown, R. (1994). The development of gender differentiation in young children. *British Journal of Social Psychology, 33,* 183–196.

20

Social Cognitive Aging

William von Hippel & Julie D. Henry

Brains and bodies age together. But an old brain has an important advantage over an old back or knee in that the accumulated experience that resides in the mind can help the brain compensate for neurobiological losses brought about by senescence. As a consequence, the cognitive changes that emerge with age paint a complex picture of loss, gain, and stasis, as diminished functioning in some domains offsets or interacts with enhanced knowledge and abilities in others. Social cognitive changes with age are more complex still, as motivational changes brought about by differences in time perspective and changing life goals interact with cognitive changes. Although many of these age-related changes are influenced by personality and circumstance, the overall signature of social cognitive aging is determined primarily by the varying strength of these competing motivational, neurobiological, and cognitive forces.

On the cognitive processing side, loss is the norm with aging, with older adults typically showing declines in the "mechanics of the mind," such as processing speed, memory, executive functioning, reasoning, etc. (Hasher, Zacks, & May, 1999; Park & Gutchess, 2006; Salthouse & Ferrer-Caja, 2003). These cognitive losses often co-occur with other age-related losses, such as reduced strength and visual and auditory functioning, suggesting an underlying general physical decline (Anstey & Smith, 1999; Christensen et al., 2001). Despite the generality of such losses, however, there are also areas of preserved or even enhanced functioning in late life. In domains that tap the "experience of the mind" such as vocabulary (Park, 2000; Salthouse, 1991) and general knowledge (Park & Gutchess, 2006; Salthouse, 1982) smaller age differences emerge, with older adults often out-performing younger adults.

Thus, one determinant of social cognitive change with age is whether the task at hand relies more on mechanics or experience.

Experience does not just accumulate over a lifetime, however, it also differs systematically across historical time periods. Thus, the importance of experience is also evident in the differences between cohorts that are inevitably confounded with age. From a social cognitive perspective it can be important to consider whether age differences are associated with changes in the mechanics of the mind, the accumulated experience of the mind, or the types of experience to which the mind has been exposed. For example, are older adults more prejudiced than younger adults because they came of age in more prejudiced times or because of age-related changes in cognitive or emotional processes? In the absence of longitudinal studies – which are not the norm in social cognition research – questions such as these can be difficult if not impossible to answer.

This picture is then made more complex by the fact that social cognition often involves dual processes, with automatic and controlled processes each contributing to – and sometimes competing for – judgmental and behavioral outcomes (Chaiken & Trope, 1999). Although aging disrupts processing speed and other factors that play a role in automatic processes, the primary impact of age is on controlled processes, with automatic ones relatively spared in late life (Fleischman et al., 2004). Because controlled processes are sometimes recruited to inhibit automatic ones (e.g., Devine, 1989), the influence of automatic processes can become more apparent with age as the influence of controlled processes wanes. Thus, a further determinant of social cognitive change with age is whether the task at hand relies more on automatic or controlled processing and whether automatic and controlled processes tend to work together or at cross-purposes. This interaction between controlled and automatic processes is also influenced by the fact that automatic and controlled processes appear to wax and wane in a compensatory fashion, such that some automatic processes peak when controlled processes are at their weakest (May, Hasher, & Foong, 2005). Older adults might thus be particularly likely to rely on automatic processes when they are tired and show the largest deficits in controlled processing.

In addition to these interacting cognitive forces, there are also motivational shifts that appear to be due to changed time perspective as well as other changes in the brain. Older adults tend to prioritize emotional goals more highly (Blanchard-Fields, 2007) and focus more on positive information (Carstensen & Mikels, 2005) than younger adults, and they are more oriented toward prevention than promotion (Freund, 2006). These motivational changes influence social cognitive processes just as assuredly as the cognitive changes, and can sometimes completely counteract them (von Hippel, Henry, & Matovic, 2008).

In the pages that follow we review research on social cognitive aging in an effort to examine the combined effects of cognitive and motivational changes with age. We first discuss emotional and motivational changes with age and then consider how deficits in executive functions lead to social cognitive changes. We then examine age differences in processes involved in understanding others, in decision making, and in attitude change. We close this review with a consideration of factors that can delay or compensate for age-related cognitive losses. As the research covered in this review makes apparent, the study of social cognitive aging not only provides wide-open vistas for theory testing but it is also a highly generative field in its own right.

EMOTIONAL AND MOTIVATIONAL CHANGES

Positivity

Emotionally salient information is more likely to be recalled and attended to than neutral information, and this emotional enhancement effect is robust across the adult life span (Murphy & Isaacowitz, 2008). Nevertheless, many studies have found that age interacts with the valence of emotional material such that older adults show increased attention to positive and decreased attention to negative information compared to younger adults (Carstensen & Mikels, 2005; Charles et al., 2003; Kwon et al., 2009; Mather & Carstensen, 2005). This finding is in contrast to the cognitive priority given to negative information in young adults, a phenomenon that may be associated with survival mechanisms (Grühn et al., 2005). Some of the clearest evidence for enhanced processing of positive information comes from eye gaze experiments. For example, whereas young adults exhibit mood congruent gaze, older adults in a bad mood look away from negative stimuli and towards positive stimuli (Isaacowitz, Toner, Goren, & Wilson, 2008). These data suggest that older adults use gaze to regulate and improve mood. They also suggest that older adults are sacrificing information integrity in an effort to maintain positivity, a strategy that makes more sense in late life when world knowledge is greater and when threats to immune functioning place a premium on a positive outlook (as positive emotions enhance immune functioning; Marsland, Pressman, & Cohen, 2007).

One possibility is that positivity preferences reflect cognitively demanding "top-down" processes intended to achieve mood-regulatory goals (Kennedy et al., 2004; Mather & Knight, 2005). Alternatively, it may be that these attentional biases reflect "bottom-up" processes, whereby information processing is automatically simplified by defaulting to a positive orientation (Labouvie-Vief, Diehl, Jain & Zhang, 2007). To address this issue, Isaacowitz, Allard, Murphy, and Schlangel (2009) assessed the temporal characteristics of older adults' preferential fixation toward positive stimuli and away from negative stimuli. Their results indicated that in the early stages of stimulus onset (500 ms), no positivity preferences emerged for young or old. Rather, preferences only emerged later on, implying a role for top-down processes. Furthermore, only for older adults did the strength of these preferences increase linearly over time. These data suggest that the preferential fixations seen in late adulthood rely on cognitive control, and are not simply an automatic means of simplifying information processing (see also Leclerc & Kensinger, 2008).

Positivity effects in late adulthood have also been attributed to age-related impairments in adrenergic and amygdala functioning (Cacioppo et al., 2011). Neuroimaging data show that the amygdala is activated less when viewing negative than positive emotional stimuli in older compared to younger adults (Mather et al., 2004). This finding could be evidence of reduced amygdala functioning – a similar pattern of greater response to positive than negative information is shown by individuals with focal amygdala damage but not other types of brain damage (Berntson, Bechara, Damasio, Tranel, & Cacioppo, 2007). Consistent with this interpretation of the positivity effect, St Jacques, Dolcos, and Cabeza (2010) found that older adults experienced negatively valenced stimuli as less negative compared to their younger counterparts, and that these behavioral differences coincided with age-related reductions in functional connectivity with the right amygdala. Older adults in their research had good functional connectivity with ventral anterior regions, but reduced connectivity with posterior brain regions. These functional differences might reflect decreased perceptual processing of negative stimuli, in addition to controlled processes that attenuate responses to negative emotion (see also St Jacques, Dolcos & Cabeza, 2009). Indeed, proponents of the motivational model of positivity argue that these age-related neural changes are the consequence of motivational shifts, not the cause. Whichever perspective is correct, both models predict that in late adulthood emotional arousal to positive information will be preserved, but there will be a diminution in arousal to negative information (see Mather et al., 2004). Consistent with this view, event-related potential measures indicate that neural activity to negative images declines linearly with age, but there is stasis in responses to positive images across most of the adult life span (Kisley, Wood, & Burrows, 2007).

These changes in positivity are considered to be among the most important factors contributing to changes in life satisfaction across the adult life span. Older adults typically report that during everyday life they experience lower intensity of negative emotions and higher frequency of positive emotions than their younger counterparts (Gross et al., 1997; Mroczek & Kolarz, 1998). Consistent with these day-to-day reports, most longitudinal evidence indicates that life satisfaction rises in a non-linear fashion, generally increasing up to the age of 65–70, but then starting to decline. This decline may represent a psychological harbinger of death. Using longitudinal data of deceased participants from Germany, the United Kingdom, and the United States, Gerstorf et al. (2010) found that, "something is seriously wrong at the end of life." In all three nations, well-being was relatively stable across the adult age range until 3–5 years prior to death, when a rapid decline was seen. These findings suggest that mortality-related mechanisms may be responsible for changes in well-being at the end of life. These data also align with other longitudinal evidence showing that higher life satisfaction predicts lower risk of mortality, even after controlling for variables such as age, gender, education, marital status, and health status (Collins, Glei, & Goldman, 2009; Gerstorf et al., 2008). Thus, except for the

end of life, it appears that life satisfaction increases throughout the adult years, and enhanced positivity in late life seems to be the primary cause.

Emotion regulation

Although emotional responses have evolved to be consistent with the consequences of an event for an individual's well-being, emotional responses are not always appropriate for the social setting. We may be delighted at the demise of an archenemy, but laughter at a funeral is still inappropriate. In situations such as these, people have various strategies that they can use to modulate their emotions. Although emotions can feel overwhelming and often arise spontaneously, they are not obligatory and can be regulated (Feldman Barrett, Mesquita, Ochsner, & Gross, 2007). Emotion regulation can involve the experience or expression of emotion, and may result in increasing, decreasing, or sustaining an emotion, either positive or negative, consciously or unconsciously.

Two broad strategies for regulating emotions can be delineated (Gross, 1998). *Antecedent-focused* strategies are applied early in the emotion generation process and influence not only what is expressed behaviorally but also what is experienced subjectively. In contrast, *response-focused* strategies occur after the emotion response tendencies have been triggered, and require management of the ongoing emotional expression and physiological responses. A typical example of the former strategy is reappraisal of the emotion-eliciting situation, while an example of the latter is suppression of emotional impulses that have already arisen. Antecedent-focused strategies are associated with increased positive affect, improved interpersonal functioning, and greater well-being, and response-focused strategies are associated with negative affect, impaired interpersonal functions, and poorer well-being (Gross & John, 2003). These differential outcomes have been attributed to the fact that response-focused strategies produce an incongruence between the emotion experienced and the emotion expressed, leading to a sense of "inauthenticity" and to less effective mood repair. With antecedent-focused strategies no such discrepancy is experienced (Gross & John, 2003).

Gross et al. (1997) argue that life experience typically leads to greater reliance on reappraisal processes, with the end result that older adults should experience less frequent negative affect than younger adults. Although this may be the case, the data suggest that compared to younger adults, older adults are just as effective (if not more so) at both antecedent-focused and response-focused emotion regulation strategies. Despite the fact that behavioral suppression is generally regarded as a poor strategy, one possibility is that its effective use may depend on practice, as it may become automatic by the time people reach late adulthood. Evidence consistent with this possibility can be found in the dissociation between older adults' abilities to engage in cognitive and emotional inhibitory processes. In contrast to the increasing difficulties in deliberate thought and behavioral suppression that emerge among older adults (Kramer, Humphrey, Larish, Logan, & Strayer, 1994; Rabbitt, Lowe, & Shilling, 2001), suppression of emotional expression either improves or remains stable across the life span (Emery & Hess, 2008; Kunzmann et al., 2005; Phillips et al., 2008; Shiota & Levenson, 2009). It appears that emotional suppression incurs fewer cognitive costs for older compared to younger adults, apparently due to a lifetime's accumulated experience of controlling affect (Scheibe & Blanchard-Fields, 2008).

There is less evidence on how age impacts the ability to apply antecedent-focused regulatory strategies, but again, improvement (or at least stasis) in this capacity appears likely. In one study, footage from an undercover documentary that investigated animal abuse was viewed by older and younger adults under conditions of positive refocusing or expressive suppression (Phillips et al., 2008). When instructed to suppress their emotional display, both older and younger adults showed reduced external display of negative affect. When given instructions to regulate emotions by positive refocusing, older adults showed lower levels of experienced and expressed emotions but younger adults did not. This finding suggests that older adults were more effective in implementing at least this particular antecedent-focused regulation strategy than younger adults.

Similar effects have also been suggested by studies of real-life experiences. For example, older adults in an experience-sampling study conducted over 1 week reported as much positive affect as their younger counterparts but less negative affect. Furthermore, when negative affect was experienced, older adults returned to a neutral or positive state more quickly than the younger adults (Carstensen, Pasupathi, Mayr, & Nesselroade, 2000). These results may reflect age differences in positivity, but the latter finding also hints at age-related gains in the proficiency of emotion regulation. Findings such as these are typically attributed to older adults' extensive life experience with interpersonal communication (Dougherty, Abe, & Izard, 1996). Older adults are believed to take advantage of knowledge accumulated throughout their lives to better understand, anticipate, and react to emotional situations (Magai, 2001). Consistent with these behavioral

outcomes, compared to younger adults, older adults also rate themselves as relying on more effective emotion regulation strategies (Gross et al., 1997; Phillips, Henry, Hosie, & Milne, 2006).

Goals

Late life is typically accompanied by physical decline and an awareness of impending mortality. These two uncomfortable facts have a major impact on the goals held by older adults. Decline brings with it a focus on loss prevention, and thus older adults typically move from a promotion frame to a prevention frame (Ebner, Freund, & Baltes, 2006; Freund, 2006). We expand on this change in self-regulatory focus in the section on risk and loss aversion below. Awareness of impending mortality leads to the other major change in goals, as older adults begin to focus on emotion-related goals due to a sense that time is running out (Carstensen, Fung, & Charles, 2003). According to Socioemotional Selectivity Theory, "the approach of endings – the penultimate of which is old age – activates a reorganization of goal hierarchies such that emotionally meaningful goals are prioritized." (Mather & Carstensen, 2003, p. 409). This increased focus on emotionally salient goals is thought to be a major factor leading to improved emotion regulation skills and the increased positivity in late adulthood.

According to Socioemotional Selectivity Theory, as people age and have a sense that time is running out, there is an increased focus on the present rather than the future. This motivational shift leads to a greater investment in important social relationships and less interest in pursuing new or peripheral social contacts. As noted, however, the mechanism underlying this effect is considered not to be age per se, but rather time perspective (Carstensen et al., 2003). In the first study to demonstrate this effect, Fredrickson and Carstensen (1990) asked participants aged 11–94 to choose among three different social partners: a member of the participants' family; the author of a book that the participant had read; or an acquaintance with whom the participant seemed to have much in common. Some participants were asked to make this selection as they would if they were shortly moving across country alone. Results indicated that older adults' preference was always to spend time with the familiar social partner, but only when time was perceived as limited did younger adults also show this preference. The reverse effect has also been shown. When older adults in the United States and Hong Kong were asked to imagine an expansive future in which medical advances ensure 20 more healthy years beyond when they expect to live, their preference for familiar social partners disappeared (Fung, Carstensen, & Lutz, 1999). Findings such as these suggest that the perception of time is an important determinant of social goals.

Because Socioemotional Selectivity Theory predicts an increased focus on positive emotions, older adults should be more effective than younger adults at planning their lives to ensure positive experiences. One strategy for achieving this goal is maintaining contact with people who are already known and loved rather than pursuing interactions with people who are not known well. Consistent with this possibility, older adults typically maintain a similar number of close friends to younger people but a smaller number of peripheral social partners (Fung et al., 2001; Lang, 2001; Lee & Markides, 1990). Proponents of Socioemotional Selectivity Theory contend that such findings are attributable to a selective "pruning" of peripheral social networks towards the end of the life span that prioritizes emotionally close social partners (Carstensen et al., 2003). Of course, cognitive, health, and mobility constraints might also result in such a pattern of selective friendship maintenance.

Risk and loss aversion

Consistent with increased positivity and prioritization of emotional goals, there is evidence for increased hedonic and decreased contra-hedonic motivations in late adulthood. Although people generally strive to attain positivity and reduce negativity, in certain circumstances reduction of positive affect may confer benefits (e.g., by enhancing concentration) as might sustaining negative affective states (e.g., anger may enhance determination). Such contra-hedonic motivations can therefore lead to the attainment of utilitarian goals. In a recent experience sampling study, Riediger, Schmiedek, Wagner, and Lindenberger (2009) found that goals to maintain positive affect and reduce negative affect were strongest in late adulthood, whereas contra-hedonic motivations were most prevalent in adolescence. Notably, Riediger et al. (2009) found that older adults sought to maintain but not enhance positive affect, and suggested that perhaps this regulation strategy is less resource intensive. An alternative possibility is that age leads to change in regulatory focus, with older adults shifting from promotion to a prevention orientation (Ebner et al., 2006; Freund, 2006), and thus older adults may be more focused on preventing losses in positive affect than in promoting gains.

This interpretation is also consistent with predictions from the life span developmental theory of *selection, optimization, and compensation*

(Baltes & Baltes, 1990). According to this model, the increasing salience of resource limitations in late adulthood precipitates a shift in personal goal orientation as the ratio of gains to losses decreases in the second half of life (Baltes, 1987, 1997). These age-related changes in developmental opportunities and constraints are reflected in a shift from an orientation toward growth and gains to an orientation toward maintenance and loss prevention (Ebner et al., 2006). Such shifts in goal orientation are considered necessary and beneficial, in light of the resource limitations in older age. Indeed, Ebner et al. (2006) found that for younger adults well-being was negatively correlated with degree of prevention orientation, whereas for older adults well-being was positively correlated with degree of prevention orientation. Furthermore, younger and older adults alike seem aware of this change, as they associate young adults with promotion goals and older adults with prevention goals (Ebner, Riediger, & Lindenberger, 2009).

These changes in regulatory focus should lead to age-related differences in decision making in various domains. For example, Mikels and Reed (2009) showed that there are age differences in the framing effect, whereby individuals are risk averse when decisions are framed as gains but risk seeking when decisions are framed as losses (Tversky & Kahneman, 1981). Mikels and Reed (2009) presented older and younger adults with a gambling task in which expected outcomes were equal, but framed in terms of keeping a proportion of an initial endowment (e.g., keep $20 of $100) vs losing a proportion of the initial endowment (e.g., lose $80 of $100). Although both younger and older adults were risk averse in the gain frame, only younger adults showed risk seeking in the loss frame.

Changes in regulatory focus provide another perspective for interpreting older adults' tendency to put their energies into a smaller circle of closer friends, with less interest in seeking novel social partners. In the context of Socioemotional Selectivity Theory, such findings are thought to reflect motivational shifts whereby emotion-related goals are prioritized. In the context of regulatory focus theory, these friendship changes can be interpreted in terms of a prevention framework, according to which older adults are focused less on promoting new social opportunities than on preventing the loss of current friendships.

Regret

The experience of regret is common across the life span. Regret is typically accompanied by counterfactual thoughts, such as, "What would have happened if…," and is usually associated with negative emotions such as anger, sadness, or desperation. Regrets can take on greater importance in late life, perhaps because regretted episodes are less easily fixed later in the life (Heckhausen & Schulz, 1995), and thus regrets predict life satisfaction more strongly in older than younger adults (Lecci, Okun, & Karoly, 1994). Indeed, regret intensity predicts increased diurnal cortisol secretion and physical health problems experienced in late adulthood (Wrosch et al., 2007).

Regrets can be divided into many types, but a simple division is into regrets of action vs inaction, or sins of commission vs omission. In the short run, people tend to regret their actions more than their inactions (Kahneman & Tversky, 1982). It seems that the counterfactual is simply more available in the case of actions than inactions, as actions are more easily undone. Nevertheless, this difference in regret is soon reversed, as people overwhelmingly nominate sins of omission as their greatest regrets, and they do so across the life span (Erskine, 1973; Kinnier & Metha, 1989). There are several reasons for this reversal, but perhaps the most important is that regretted actions can typically be undone, but regretted inactions often cannot (Gilovich & Medvec, 1995). Too often, missed opportunities are simply no longer available with the passage of time.

Although regrets of inaction loom larger than regrets of action across adulthood, there is reason to believe that this effect should be exacerbated late in life. As Gilovich and Medvec (1995) explain, "there is an important asymmetry in the perceived negative consequences of regrettable actions and inactions: Regrets of action center around bad things that actually happened; regrets of inaction involve good things that one believes *would have* happened." (p. 386). Because older adults emphasize the positive over the negative, it seems possible that the bad things that happened fade in late life, whereas the good things that did not happen may retain their importance. Weak support for this possibility can be found in Gilovich and Medvec (1994), who reported a nonsignificant trend for older adults to have a higher ratio of inaction to action regrets compared to younger adults. To our knowledge this hint of an age effect has not been pursued in subsequent research, but it would seem to be an issue worthy of further study.

Regrets can be resolved through primary control processes, whereby behavioral changes are made that overcome regrets, such as reconciling with estranged family members. Regrets can also be resolved through secondary control processes, whereby cognitive strategies are engaged, such as reappraising past actions or forgiving oneself.

Life-span control theory suggests that younger adults are more likely to benefit from primary control processes, as early in life there is generally greater opportunity to actively undo the consequences of regrets (Heckhausen & Schulz, 1995). Thus, regret in early adulthood may confer benefits by motivating adaptive actions, and indeed in younger adults self-regulatory efforts such as taking responsibility for a regretted event are associated with lower regret intensity and fewer intrusive thoughts (Wrosch & Heckhausen, 2002).

In contrast, opportunities to overcome regret are likely to be more limited in late adulthood, and thus older adults should benefit from secondary control processes. This perspective implies that effective management of regret in late adulthood will depend on regulation processes related to self-protective attributions and disengagement. Consistent with this possibility, older adults who do not blame themselves for a regretted event or who are disengaged from undoing the consequences of regret report lower levels of regret intensity and higher subjective well-being compared to their peers who do not engage in these regulatory processes (Wrosch & Heckhausen, 2002; Wrosch et al., 2005). Of course, the causal order of these effects is ambiguous, as older adults with milder regrets might be less likely to blame themselves and more likely to be disengaged from the consequences of the regrets.

COGNITIVE CHANGES I: EFFECTS OF EXECUTIVE DECLINE

The mental processes known as executive functions are responsible for initiating, planning, and coordinating the basic cognitive processes with which we navigate our everyday lives. Executive functions include planning, task switching, and inhibition of thought and behavior. Thus, rather than being considered a unitary ability, executive functions refer to the ensemble of higher-order processes that permit contextually sensitive flexible behavior as well as sustained goal pursuit. Because executive functions impose particular demands on frontal neural substrates, and because these structures are subject to age-related deterioration, aging has been linked to diminished executive control (Dempster, 1992; Hasher, Zacks, & May, 1999; West, 1996).

Failures at thought control lead to contamination of ongoing mental activities with unwanted information, and thus age-related deficits in inhibitory ability have been implicated in a variety of cognitive deficits (Hasher et al., 1999). But executive functions are not only important for regulating cognition, they also play a central role in social functioning (Finkel et al., 2009; Macrae, Bodenhausen, Schloerscheidt, & Milne, 1999; Payne, 2005; Richeson & Shelton, 2003). Indeed, many theorists believe that it was the demands of social living that led to the development of such large frontal lobes in humans (Dunbar & Schultz, 2007), and there is considerable evidence for social abnormalities in populations with executive impairment (Stuss & Levine, 2002). Thus, despite the fact that aging is associated with improvement in some aspects of socioemotional functioning (Blanchard-Fields, 2007; Carstensen, Gottman, & Levenson, 1995), age-related executive deficits have the potential to disrupt social judgment and behavior in a variety of domains. In this section we discuss research in two such domains.

Behavioral restraint

Age-related inhibitory losses have been implicated in several types of socially disinhibited behavior. First, older adults are more likely than younger adults to talk excessively and about topics that are irrelevant to the stream of conversation (Pushkar et al., 2000). This "off-target verbosity" is associated with diminished inhibitory ability, which leaves older adults less capable of stopping their conversation and remaining on topic (Pushkar et al., 2000). Verbosity also appears to be related to different conversational goals of younger and older adults, as younger adults are more likely than older adults to be focused on transmitting information (Trunk & Abrams, 2009).

Inhibition also appears to be necessary to restrain oneself from verbalizing thoughts that are better left unsaid (von Hippel & Gonsalkorale, 2005), and thus inhibitory deficits might lead older adults to make socially inappropriate remarks. Consistent with this possibility, von Hippel and Dunlop (2005) found that older adults were more likely than younger adults (according to their peers) to inquire about private issues in public settings, and this age difference in peer-reported social inappropriateness was mediated by inhibitory deficits. Furthermore, these age differences emerged despite the fact that older and younger adults agreed that it is inappropriate to inquire about such issues in public settings. Indeed, older adults in particular felt less close to those who inquired about private issues in public.

This evidence of social disinhibition in older adults was conceptually replicated by Henry, von Hippel, and Baynes (2009), who found that older adults were more likely to engage in a variety of socially inappropriate behaviors than younger adults (again, according to their peers). Furthermore, this peer-reported increase in social inappropriateness was again mediated by participants' own performance on measures of executive functioning. Importantly, this effect of executive decline was found to be independent of the effect of general cognitive decline, suggesting that increased social inappropriateness in late life is specific to executive deficits. Further evidence for this possibility comes from research with younger adults, which also indicates that socially inappropriate behavior is associated with individual differences in executive functioning (von Hippel & Gonsalkorale, 2005).

Findings such as these suggest that disinhibition is socially costly because it often manifests in socially inappropriate behavior. Nevertheless, it seems plausible that there are also benefits to a more disinhibited style of social functioning. Particularly if mixed with warmth and sympathy, an honest but socially difficult appraisal of the situation may sometimes be more valuable than polite disingenuousness. In a test of this possibility, Apfelbaum, Krendl, and Ambady (2010) presented older and younger adults with a photograph of an obese adolescent who reported having a variety of difficulties that are typically associated with obesity (lack of energy, poor social engagement). Participants were then videotaped as they offered advice to the obese adolescent. In this socially awkward situation, it was primarily older adults with poor executive functioning who offered direct advice about the adolescent's obesity – advice that was rated by obesity doctors as most likely to lead to lifestyle changes. Older adults with good executive control and younger adults both chose to dance around the issue, and instead offered briefer and more placebic advice. These data suggest that, in combination with the positivity that is common in older adults, a little disinhibition can be a socially valuable commodity.

Stereotyping and prejudice

In an influential model of prejudice, Devine (1989) proposed that because everyday culture is often suffused with stereotypes, these stereotypes become over-learned and automatically activated upon encounters with individual members of the stereotyped groups. What differentiates non-prejudiced from prejudiced people is not whether prejudiced thoughts are activated, but whether people inhibit those thoughts and replace them with more egalitarian beliefs. Prejudiced people endorse the stereotypic thoughts that are automatically activated, and non-prejudiced people reject and subsequently inhibit the stereotypic thoughts. This model suggests that older adults might be more prejudiced than younger adults because they are less capable of inhibiting their unintentionally activated stereotypes. There are now several lines of research that support this possibility.

In a study of explicit stereotyping and prejudice, von Hippel, Silver, and Lynch (2000) found that older White adults show greater stereotyping and prejudice toward African Americans than younger White adults. This age difference emerged despite the fact that the older adults were more concerned about impression management and more motivated to control their prejudice than the younger adults. Older adults also performed more poorly than younger adults on a measure of inhibitory ability, and this age difference in inhibition mediated the age differences in stereotyping and prejudice. Additionally, individual differences in inhibition were associated with individual differences in prejudice among both older and younger adults. This finding suggests that the link between inhibition and prejudice in older adults is not simply a byproduct of their shared relationship with general cognitive decline. Rather, because younger adults also show a correlation between inhibitory ability and prejudice, there appears to be something unique about inhibition that plays a critical role in the prevention of prejudice.

There are, of course, interpretive problems associated with the findings of von Hippel et al. (2000), and subsequent research has addressed these issues in a variety of ways. First, it is possible that older adults are no more prejudiced than younger adults, but are simply more willing to express their prejudices in the politically correct confines of the university laboratory. To address this possibility, Henry, von Hippel, and Baynes (2009) asked a close friend or family member of the participants to report on the participants' prejudice level. Participants then completed measures of executive functioning. Henry et al. (2009) found that older adults were more prejudiced than younger adults (according to their peers), and that this age difference in peer-reported prejudice was mediated by the participants' own performance on measures of executive functioning.

This finding addresses problems associated with political correctness and social desirability, but it does not circumvent the fact that prejudice is still measured as public expression. To address this issue, Radvansky, Copeland, and von Hippel (2010) conducted an experiment in which older and younger adults were presented with stories that contained stereotype-suggestive sentences that were not explicitly stereotypic. After these suggestive sentences, participants were occasionally interrupted to complete a lexical decision task assessing activation of a word highly related to the stereotypic inference (e.g., after the sentence, "Susan saw that Jamal didn't help," participants were tested with the word *lazy*). Participants were also presented with lexical decisions after inference-inviting sentences that were stereotype neutral (e.g., the sentence, "Jamal watched with anticipation," followed by the word *hungry*) and after sentences in which no inference was likely (which were used as control sentences). Results revealed that, compared to the lexical decisions in the control sentences, younger adults were faster to identify the inference-relevant neutral words but slower to identify the inference-relevant stereotypic words. Older adults were also faster to identify the neutral words, but non-significantly faster rather than slower to identify the stereotypic words.

These findings suggest that younger adults inhibit their stereotypic inferences as they encode new information, but older adults fail to do so. Two different types of modeling data reveal results that are consistent with this possibility. First, Gonsalkorale, Sherman, and Klauer (2009) used the Quadruple Process model (Conrey et al., 2005) to examine the source of age differences in implicit prejudice that emerged in a large national data set with the Implicit Association Test (IAT; Greenwald, McGhee, & Schwarz, 1998). Their modeling results indicate that older adults are less successful than younger adults in regulating automatic bias toward African Americans, but show no differences in degree of bias itself. Second, Stewart, von Hippel, and Radvansky (2009) conceptually replicated this result using the process dissociation procedure (Jacoby, 1991). Stewart et al. (2009) found that age differences in implicit prejudice toward African Americans emerged only in the control component of implicit prejudice, with older adults showing decreased control over their automatic biases. Furthermore, this age difference in prejudice control was mediated by age differences in inhibitory ability. Finally, Stewart et al. also found that self-reported motivation to be non-prejudiced only translated into low-prejudice responses on the IAT when participants also had good control over their automatic biases. The results of Gonsalkorale et al. (2009) and Stewart et al. (2009) suggest that age differences in prejudice are the result of poor inhibitory control of prejudicial associations and are not just evidence of a greater willingness among older adults to express their prejudices.

These experiments provide evidence for unintended stereotyping and prejudice among older adults, but the question remains whether older adults can compensate for these executive losses. In support of such a possibility, recent evidence suggests that older adults can be just as effective as younger adults at inhibiting stereotypes when they know the stereotype is irrelevant at encoding (Radvansky, Lynchard, & von Hippel, 2009). In their research, Radvansky et al. (2009) presented younger and older adults with stories about a person who held a stereotypically male or female occupation (e.g., a plumber vs a babysitter). Half of the time participants were explicitly given a gender label when first learning about the protagonist (e.g., "the babysitter was a young boy who…") and half the time they were not (e.g., "the babysitter was a young teenager who…"). Additionally, half of the time the gender of the protagonist was occupation-stereotypic and half the time it was counter-stereotypic. Later in the story, participants encountered a pronoun that communicated the gender of the protagonist, and the critical measure was whether they read the sentence containing the counter-stereotypic pronoun more slowly than the sentence containing the stereotypic pronoun. Results indicated that both younger and older adults read the sentence containing the counter-stereotypic pronoun more slowly when they had not initially been provided an explicit gender label, but both younger and older adults read the counter-stereotypic pronoun just as quickly as the stereotypic pronoun when they had already been provided a gender label.

This finding suggests that older adults are just as capable as young adults of putting aside their stereotypes when they know at the moment they encounter the person that their stereotypes are irrelevant to the situation at hand. These findings are also consistent with informal observations from our laboratory that older adults are often just as capable as younger adults of suppressing a socially inappropriate response when they know in advance that the need to suppress a response is likely to be imminent. Older adults seem to get into trouble primarily when they do not anticipate the self-regulatory demand in advance and prepare themselves for it.

COGNITIVE CHANGES II: UNDERSTANDING OTHERS

With motivational shifts leading to increased prioritization of emotion-related and relationship maintenance goals in late adulthood, it might be anticipated that older adults would show enhanced social understanding relative to their younger counterparts. In fact, the dominant picture depicts one of loss – with deficits seen in emotion recognition, mental state attributions, and the ability to infer deceit or potential harmful intent in others. Thus, in terms of emotion *recognition*, the predominant pattern across all emotions and modalities is of age-related decline. Most aspects of explicit empathic processing also appear to be disrupted, although the implicit processing of empathic information may be preserved. Analogously, explicit (but perhaps not implicit) detection of deceit and social threat is disrupted. Despite the evidence of deficits in each of these social domains, in at least some contexts older adults appear to use more sophisticated heuristics than their younger counterparts in forming social judgments. These latter findings align with domains in which the accumulation of social experience across the adult life span leads to more sophisticated and accessible knowledge structures.

Emotion recognition and empathy

Age-related difficulties in understanding emotional signals have implications for social interactions in older adults. Indeed, emotion misrecognition in late life is associated with reduced social competence and interest, poor interpersonal functioning and communication, reduced quality of life, and inappropriate social behavior (Carton et al., 1999; Phillips et al., 2010; Shimokawa et al., 2001). A recent meta-analytic review indicates that the predominant pattern across emotions (with the exception of disgust) is of age-related decline – with recognition of anger and sadness particularly impaired (Ruffman, Henry, Livingston, & Phillips, 2008). This particular decline in detection of negative emotions might be a function of the increased positivity/decreased negativity that is associated with late adulthood, as inattention to negative expressions might make them more difficult to identify. Furthermore, significant impairment was seen across all modalities assessed (recognition of emotions from faces, voices, bodies, and matching voices to faces), indicating that this is unlikely to be a face-specific processing deficit. Indeed, tasks that required matching a facial expression to an auditory expression were associated with particularly large age deficits, perhaps because problems in either domain will create problems on a matching task. Evidence also indicates that age-related deficits with emotion recognition extend to video stimuli (Henry et al., 2008), and may reflect difficulty integrating incongruent semantic content (what is said) with affective prosody (how something is said; Dupuis & Pichora-Fuller, 2010).

Older adults' difficulties evaluating social stimuli are not restricted to emotion recognition. Relative to young adults, they also appear to have a poorer understanding of others' complex emotions and mental states (cognitive empathy). In the first study of age-related differences in cognitive empathy, Pratt et al. (1996) asked participants to solve moral dilemmas such as deciding upon the appropriate punishment for a doctor involved in an illegal euthanasia case. Pratt et al. found that young adults showed better perspective-taking skills than their older counterparts. More recent studies have corroborated these age-related deficits in cognitive empathy (German & Hehman, 2006; McKinnon & Moscovitch, 2007; Phillips, MacLean, & Allen, 2002).

These deficits in cognitive empathy appear to emerge from age-related executive decline, with older adults disproportionately impaired on measures that impose greater demands on control operations (Bailey & Henry, 2008; German & Hehman, 2006; McKinnon & Moscovitch, 2007). One possibility is that executive selection processes are relied upon to choose the most appropriate mental state attribution from a number of potential candidates (German & Hehman, 2006). In addition, the self-perspective is regarded as the cognitive default, driven in part by the automatic link between perception and action (Decety et al., 1997). Therefore, to evaluate another's perspective, some form of active inhibitory mechanism is necessary to regulate the prepotent self-perspective. Thus, it appears that as we age it becomes more difficult to see the world from someone else's point of view, with these deficits particularly pronounced when executive demands are high. These deficits in cognitive empathy may then be compounded by older adults' difficulty following eye-gaze cues, which disrupts their ability to engage in joint attention (Slessor, Phillips, & Bull, 2008).

Relatively less research has been conducted on the affective component of empathy, which refers to emotional responses to the cognitive or affective state of another. The few attempts to index affective empathy in late adulthood have been guided by the notion of *motor* empathy (Blair, 2005; Chartrand & van Baaren, 2009; Decety & Jackson, 2004). This form of empathy is the tendency for individuals to automatically mimic the facial expressions and behavior of another (Chartrand & van Baaren, 2009). Two studies to date have assessed facial expression mimicry in late adulthood, and imply that although subconscious facial mimicry is spared in late adulthood (Bailey & Henry, 2009), later stages of the mimicry process may be disrupted by conscious difficulties at emotion recognition (Bailey, Henry, & Nangle, 2009). These data provide preliminary support for the possibility that at least some aspects of affective empathy may decline in late adulthood.

Detecting deception

Detection of deception or nefarious intent in the facial expressions of others is an important aspect of understanding others – and one that seems likely to have significant social and material outcomes, particularly in older adulthood when time to recoup losses is more limited. Given older adults' increased difficulties recognizing emotions and seeing things from other's perspectives, it follows that they may also have difficulties detecting deceitful or harmful intentions, and available evidence indicates that this is the case. For example, relative to their younger counterparts, older adults are at greater risk of becoming victims of fraud (Cohen, 2006), and are up to 10 times more likely to be misled by deceptive information (Jacoby, 1999). Executive and general cognitive decline probably play a role in their susceptibility, but several studies connect emotion recognition problems with difficulties detecting deception and hurtful intent. For example, Stanley and Blanchard-Fields (2008) found an association between older adults' difficulty detecting deceit and reduced recognition of facial expressions of fear (an emotion that might be briefly displayed by a deceptive person who fears being caught in the lie). Older adults also have greater difficulty differentiating between genuine and posed smiles, and are more likely to approach an individual displaying a posed smile (Slessor et al., 2010). Additionally, and similar to adults with amygdala damage (Adolphs, Tranel, & Damasio, 1998), older adults have greater difficulty distinguishing between faces normatively judged as being high or low in threat (Ruffman, Sullivan, & Edge, 2006). These findings suggest that the greater positivity/diminished negativity of older adults might also play a role in their enhanced susceptibility to deception.

Despite these losses in explicit judgments of deception and threat, older adults show some evidence of maintained implicit threat detection mechanisms. Specifically, older adults are faster to detect an emotionally discrepant face in an array if that face displays anger rather than happiness or sadness (Mather & Knight, 2006; Ruffman, Ng, & Jenkin, 2009). This pop-out effect suggests that at least some aspects of implicit threat detection are preserved in older adulthood, although older adults' apparently greater willingness to approach posed smilers (Slessor et al., 2010) suggests that other aspects of implicit threat detection may be compromised.

Attribution and social inference

The preceding sections present a rather grim picture of how age relates to social understanding, with older adults showing deficits in emotion recognition, some aspects of empathy, and the detection of deceit. Such processes rely primarily on the mechanics of the mind, and thus they are diminished by atrophy of the brain. However, some aspects of social inference rely more clearly on the experience of the mind, and here age has the potential to enhance social judgment. A case in point is that age is associated with increased use of trait-diagnostic behavioral information in making social judgments. In one study demonstrating this effect, Hess and Auman (2001) presented individuals aged 20–84 with a series of brief behavioral descriptions. Each description included two positive and two negative behaviors executed by the same target individual, half of which related to honesty, and half of which related to intellect. Participants were asked to form impressions of the target individual. Consistent with the differential diagnosticity of positive and negative information in the domains of competence vs morality (Skowronski & Carlston, 1989), greater weight was given to negative information when character judgments related to honesty but to positive information when judgments related to intelligence. Of particular interest was the finding that this use of trait-diagnostic behavioral information was greatest in late adulthood – as evident in both attentional focus and in the impressions that were formed. With increasing age, greater attention was focused on high diagnostic (dishonest, intelligent) relative to low diagnostic (honest, unintelligent) behavioral information, with corresponding judgments more negative in the honesty domain and more positive in the intelligence domain.

If older adults are more sensitive than younger adults to trait-diagnostic information, then increasing the salience of the trait diagnosticity should attenuate or eliminate this age difference. In a test of this possibility, Leclerc and Hess (2004) presented younger and older adults with behavioral descriptions that varied in the number of diagnostic clues (one vs three), and the extremity of the behavioral information (moderate vs extreme). Increasing either the amount or the extremity of behavioral information affected both age groups, but disproportionately influenced younger adults, thereby eliminating age differences in impressions. These data imply that older adults require fewer cues than younger adults to form clear impressions of others, perhaps because they rely on their greater social experience when forming social judgments.

COGNITIVE CHANGES III: ATTITUDES AND DECISION MAKING

Attitudes and persuasion

Changes in attitudes and persuasibility across the life span implicate a variety of cognitive and motivational processes. Early research on aging and attitudes suggested that older adults might be more rigid in their attitudes, and thus relatively difficult to persuade (Glenn 1974, 1980). Consistent with this possibility, Krosnick and Alwin (1989) found with nationally representative data in the United States that people are most susceptible to attitude change in late adolescence and early adulthood (the "impressionable years" hypothesis: Sears, 1981), and then susceptibility drops precipitously and stays low throughout middle and late adulthood.

As Visser and Krosnick (1998) pointed out, however, there is interpretive ambiguity with these data in that older adults may be less likely to be exposed to counter-attitudinal information. For example, older adults tend to have smaller circles of closer friends, and thus their attitudes may be less likely to be challenged. For this reason, it is important to subject the attitudes of younger and older adults to persuasive attempts to assess whether older adults really are more rigid than younger adults. Visser and Krosnick (1998) went on to hypothesize that older adults might be more rather than less susceptible to attitude change due to (a) cognitive losses with aging (which limit counter-arguing effectiveness), (b) reduced social support for their attitudes, or (c) role changes that bring about attitude changes as well. Consistent with this possibility, when they challenged the attitudes of people of various ages, they found a U-shaped curve, whereby younger and older adults showed the greatest susceptibility to attitude change. They also found the opposite U-shaped curve when they measured attitude certainty, importance, and perceived attitude-relevant knowledge, such that younger and older adults reported the least certainty, importance, and knowledge. These results suggest possible mechanisms for increased susceptibility to persuasion in late life – via reduced certainty, importance, and knowledge – but they do not indicate what the source of these changes might be, as decreased social support, role changes, and cognitive losses could all decrease attitude certainty, importance, and knowledge.

At this point, there is no basis for excluding any of these factors as sources of attitude change late in life. With regard to social roles, two findings appear relevant. First, middle-aged adults are the most likely to be in positions of power, and powerful roles often call for a resolute approach in the face of persuasive attempts (Eaton, Visser, Krosnick, & Anand, 2009). Consistent with this possibility, age changes in the power of social roles partially mediated the effect of aging on persuasibility (Eaton et al., 2009). Second, the changing temporal perspective that underlies Socioemotional Selectivity Theory might also increase susceptibility to attitude change late in life, as people who see time as limited are more likely to modify their attitudes to match their social partners and to achieve peer consensus (DeWall, Visser, & Levitan, 2006). With regard to cognitive loss, evidence suggests that diminished working memory also plays a role in increased susceptibility to persuasion among older adults, as working memory losses mediated age differences in attitude change when people's attitudes were challenged (Wang & Chen, 2006).

Decision making

In the case of decision making we again see evidence for competing consequences of aging. Older adults often make poorer decisions due to general cognitive decline, but they make excellent use of cognitive short cuts, they benefit from their greater life experience, and they often end up happier with their decisions due to their greater positivity. In this sense, the literature on aging and decision making is reminiscent of research with satisficers and maximizers, in which maximizers made more thorough decisions with objectively better outcomes, but satisficers were nonetheless happier with their choices (Iyengar, Wells, & Schwartz, 2006).

Perhaps the most important consequence of the decline in mental mechanics is that older adults show deficits in most aspects of the types of decisions that support everyday life (Thornton & Dumke, 2005). For example, when older adults are presented with vignettes such as, "What should an elderly woman who has no other source of income do if her social security check does not come one month?", they generate fewer effective solutions than younger adults (Heidrich & Denney, 1994). Meta-analysis reveals that this effect is robust across different types of measures, with the exception that older adults' self-ratings often suggest preserved or even better everyday decision making than young adults (Thornton & Dumke, 2005). This latter finding is sometimes interpreted as evidence of effective decision making in late life, but it is also possible that older adults believe they are making better decisions when in fact they are making worse ones, which can be a recipe for disaster. Alternatively, by virtue of their tendency to focus on the positive,

older adults may simply be happier than younger adults with their decisions (Kim et al., 2008).

Despite this overall decline in everyday decision making, there are domains of preserved ability, and this can be seen most clearly with interpersonal decisions. As has been noted elsewhere, older adults sometimes outperform younger adults in interpersonal domains due to their greater experience (Grossman et al., 2010). Older adults have an additional advantage, in that they tend to take a long-term perspective and focus more on preserving relationships than on solving particular problems (Blanchard-Fields, 2007). Older adults also benefit in some tasks by the fact that they do not over-weight negative information, and thus are more capable of balancing positive and negative outcomes (Wood et al., 2005). Lastly, older adults are also strategic about when they engage in controlled processing (Peters, Hess, Västfjäll, & Auman, 2007) – rightly perceiving it as a limited resource – and thus deficits in their decision-making prowess can be more or less apparent depending on situational demands and their willingness to devote limited processing resources (Hess, Leclerc, Swaim, & Weatherbee, 2009; Mata, Schooler, & Rieskamp, 2007).

The age-related pattern of deficits in controlled processes but preservation of automatic processes also has clear implications for a variety of different types of decision processes. On the controlled side of the equation, correction for possible sources of bias is regarded as an effortful process, and thus it follows that older adults should often fail to correct, or under-correct, compared to younger adults. Consistent with this possibility, Chen and Blanchard-Fields (2000) found that older adults were more likely than younger adults to rely on information that had earlier been identified as false. These data suggest failure to correct, but they do not indicate if older adults are incapable of correcting when the situational cues are strong enough. To examine this possibility, Wang and Chen (2004) presented younger and older adults with five Midwestern cities or five exotic vacation spots, and asked them to rate how much they would like to take a vacation to these locations. Participants were then given five additional Midwestern cities to evaluate either with no differentiation from the prior set, with a note that they would now be considering a different group of locations (subtle cue), or with a note that the next group has very different characteristics from the prior group (strong cue). Wang and Chen found the typical contrast effect among young and old participants when there had been no demarcation between groupings, such that those who had previously rated exotic locales subsequently rated Midwestern cities as less appealing than those who had previously rated other Midwestern locales (see Wegener & Petty, 1995). Furthermore, when given the strong cue both young and old participants corrected for this contrast bias, and showed no effect of prior ratings. When given a subtle cue, however, younger adults corrected for their inherent contrast bias but older adults continued to rate the Midwestern cities more negatively if they had previously evaluated exotic locales. These findings suggest that older adults are capable of correcting for contextual biases, but need greater environmental support to engage in such correction processes.

Controlled processes also have the potential to play an important role whenever decision making is enhanced by counterfactual simulations of possible outcomes. Poorer autobiographical memory among older than younger adults (Craik & Salthouse, 2000; Schlagman, Kliegel, Schultz, & Kvavilashvili, 2009) is likely to translate into lower quality simulations, as theory and evidence suggest that episodic memory is one of the foundations for imagining and predicting future events (Schacter & Addis, 2007; Suddendorf & Corballis, 1997, 2008). Consistent with this possibility, recent evidence suggests that older adults have fewer details in their simulations of the future, and this impoverishment in foresight is associated with less detailed recall of the past (Addis, Wong, & Schacter, 2008). Because people often engage in counterfactual reasoning prior to making important decisions, these losses in memory have the potential to result in poorer decisions among older adults.

On the automatic side of the equation, Gigerenzer and colleagues have argued that there are a number of heuristics that enable people to make fast and frugal judgments that are sufficiently accurate for most everyday purposes (Gigerenzer et al., 1999). If fast and frugal heuristics enable people to make reasonably accurate decisions with less cognitive effort, then it follows that older adults should be particularly likely to rely on such strategies. Consistent with this reasoning, Pachur, Mata, and Schooler (2009) found that older adults rely on the recognition heuristic (the notion that if one recognizes an item it is more likely to be important than if one does not) just as younger adults do, and in fact were less capable than younger adults of suspending their reliance on this heuristic when it was identifiably less appropriate.

Automatic processes have the potential to play a further role once the decision has been made, as they can facilitate engagement in the appropriate behavior at the appropriate time. Because implementation intentions automatize planned behaviors by linking behavioral intentions to environmental contingencies (Gollwitzer & Sheeran, 2006), older adults might benefit by forming implementation intentions and thereby automatizing their planned behavior. Consistent with this possibility, older adults were more successful at performing planned medical tests when they made implementation intentions to do so rather than simply rehearsing or deliberating about their plans to do so (Liu & Park, 2004). Thus, data from different domains suggests that older adults can take advantage of their preserved automatic functioning to make good decisions and then execute them.

COGNITIVE CHANGES IV: INDIVIDUAL DIFFERENCES IN LOSS

We end this review by considering the first question that is typically asked about cognitive loss with age: Can it be prevented? It turns out that the answers to this question are intertwined with social cognitive functioning, both long term and acute.

Age stereotypes

Stereotypes create their own reality, but reality also creates stereotypes (Lee, Jussim, & McCauley, 1995). Thus, an important question in aging research is the degree to which stereotypes about cognitive losses in late life – which are widely endorsed by older adults themselves (Ryan, 1992) – can create those very losses. To address this question we turn to the literature on self-stereotyping and stereotype threat among older adults, and the role played by these factors in cognitive maintenance and loss.

The first clear evidence that self-stereotyping might contribute to cognitive loss with aging was provided by Levy and Langer (1994), who demonstrated that older deaf Americans and older Chinese showed smaller memory deficits than older hearing Americans. Importantly, deaf Americans and Chinese have more positive views of aging than are prevalent among hearing Americans, and Levy and Langer (1994) found that these more positive views were associated with smaller cognitive losses. Levy (1996) then reasoned that if these results were a function of positive views of aging in these cultures, it might be possible to prime such positive views to create a similar effect on cognitive performance of older adults. Consistent with this reasoning, Levy (1996) found that priming wisdom among older adults led to better memory performance and priming senility led to worse memory performance. Subsequent research demonstrated that these effects are also domain specific, as frailty primes have a larger effect on physical performance and senility primes have a larger effect on mental performance of older adults (Levy & Leifheit-Limson, 2009).

One interpretation of these behavioral effects is that they are simply evidence of priming, and have little or nothing to do with self-stereotyping. Such priming effects can be seen, for example, in the work of Bargh, Chen, and Burrows (1996), who found that younger adults walked more slowly after being primed with concepts stereotypic of older adults. In contrast to this interpretation, the consequences of these acute manipulations of positive and negative images of older adults appear to be induced primarily by stereotype threat. Three results support this view. First, these cognitive consequences emerged when positive and negative images of older adults (e.g., *wise* vs *senile*) were presented to older but not younger adults (Hess, Hinson, & Statham, 2004; Levy, 1996). Second, these cognitive consequences emerged not only from priming positive and negative images but also from the standard stereotype threat instructions (e.g., *younger adults tend to do better than older adults on these memory tests*; Hess, Emery, & Queen, 2009). Finally, these cognitive consequences emerged primarily when the tests were made particularly challenging (e.g., by limiting time for reflection; Hess et al., 2009).

These data suggest that negative stereotypes of aging can create their own cognitive reality via both chronic and acute effects. The acute effects appear to be a function of stereotype threat, but the chronic effects are likely to be a combination of stereotype threat (e.g., disengagement; Steele, 2010) and self-stereotyping. That is, to the degree that older adults expect to show losses, they are likely to do so. For example, a lack of self-efficacy in cognitive domains can lead older adults not to engage in mental effort even when it is required (Stine-Morrow, Shake, Miles, & Noh, 2006). Self-stereotyping can also change people's view of reality by realigning their past; older adults tend to recollect being worse in their youth on attributes thought to improve with aging and better on attributes thought to decline with aging (McFarland, Ross, & Giltrow, 1992). Perhaps the most dramatic effects of self-stereotyping can be seen in research on health and mortality, in which negative stereotypes about aging measured earlier in life predict a greater likelihood of cardiovascular problems (Levy, Zonderman, Slade, & Ferrucci, 2009) and mortality at a younger age (Levy, Slade, Kunkel, & Kasl, 2002). Of course, such effects are likely to be multiply mediated, as negative stereotypes about aging could emerge from observations of one's parents or from individual experiences with how the body and

brain respond to aging well before people enter late adulthood. Thus, despite the fact that disentangling the effects of stereotyping on reality and reality on stereotyping is no easy task, the data suggest that expectations of cognitive loss in late life are likely to exacerbate those losses.

Mental activity

Intertwined with people's stereotypes about age changes in cognitive functioning are the actual mental activities in which they engage. Although genetic factors play an important role in cognitive losses with age (Reynolds et al., 2005), environmental influences that result in different mental activity levels may play an important role as well. Complexity in leisure and at work has long been thought to provide a protective function against cognitive loss (Kohn & Schooler, 1978, 1983), under the assumption that the facilitating effect of mental activity is analogous to that of physical exercise. Evidence in support of this possibility can be found in meta-analyses that show that complexity in education, at work, and in everyday life all delay the onset of cognitive decline (Valenzuela & Sachdev, 2006). Such evidence is also available from retirement studies, which show that complexity at work is associated with enhanced cognitive functioning primarily while people are still working, as the rate of decline tends to accelerate with retirement (Finkel, Andel, Gatz, & Pederson, 2009). Interestingly, in the Finkel et al. (2009) research, it was only social complexity that appeared to protect older adults from loss; complexity with data and objects appeared to have no effect. Although further research is clearly necessary to validate the importance of social complexity, this finding is consistent with evidence that even brief social interaction enhances processing speed and working memory (Ybarra et al., 2008), and that social engagement preserves processing speed in older adults (Lövdén, Ghisletta, & Lindenberger, 2005). Moderate extraversion is also associated with less cognitive impairment in late life (Crowe et al., 2006), perhaps due to the enhanced social activities of extraverts.

If mental practice preserves functioning in late life, then bilingualism might enhance attentional control processes, as bilinguals must continually inhibit one language to use the other (Green, 1998). Consistent with this possibility, bilingual adults show enhanced executive functioning compared to monolinguals, and this effect is even more evident in late adulthood (Bialystock, Craik, Klein, & Viswanathan, 2004; see Park and Gutchess, 2006, for related cross-cultural effects). These results, and those of job and leisure complexity, reveal practice effects that are undoubtedly based on thousands of hours of mental activity. Nevertheless, effects of very short-term mental activity are also evident, at least with younger adults (Ybarra et al., 2008), and thus it remains possible that older adults would also benefit from acute cognitive training. Consistent with this possibility, 24 hours of training with strategy video games has been shown to enhance performance on a variety of measures of executive functioning (e.g., task switching and working memory; Basak, Boot, Voss, & Kramer, 2008).

Mental activity does not just delay the onset of cognitive aging, it can also compensate for it. One important variety of compensation shown by older adults is neural "over-activation," in which additional neural regions are recruited by older adults to solve the same problems as younger adults (see Reuter-Lorenz & Cappell, 2008). Although there is no single explanation for over-activation, at least some of the time it appears to be compensatory. For example, older adults who recruit both hemispheres to solve problems that are solved unilaterally by younger adults have been shown to suffer performance deficits if activation in either hemisphere is disrupted by transcranial magnetic stimulation (Rossi et al., 2004). Data such as these suggest that older adults compensate for reduced functioning in some areas of the brain by recruiting additional brain regions to solve the same problems. Nevertheless, over-activation can also be evidence of age-related failure to inhibit unwanted or irrelevant cognitive processes (Gazzaley, Cooney, Rissman, & D'Esposito, 2005; Persson, Lustig, Nelson, & Reuter-Lorenz, 2007).

CONCLUSION

As the research reviewed in this chapter indicates, social cognitive aging is a complex process that is subjected to a variety of forces. Age-related deficits in controlled processes are sometimes offset by preserved automatic processes, but sometimes further undermined by them. These processes represent the *mechanics* of the mind, and they underlie changes in a wide variety of mental functions. In contrast, age-related increases in knowledge accumulated through a lifetime of experience enhance social cognitive functioning, particularly with regard to interpersonal processes. These processes represent the *experiences* of the mind, and they too underlie changes in a wide variety of mental functions. Finally, motivational changes with age also play an important role, as advancing age changes people's goals and values, and even their self-perceptions. These various cognitive and motivational changes

interact in numerous ways, some of which are reasonably well understood but most of which remain to be explored. With aging populations worldwide, such explorations are becoming more valuable and more feasible.

REFERENCES

Addis, D. R., Wong, A. T., & Schacter, D. L. (2008). Age-related changes in the episodic simulation of future events. *Psychological Science, 19,* 33–41.

Adolphs, R., Tranel, D., & Damasio, A. R. (1998). The human amygdala in social judgment. *Nature, 393,* 470–474.

Anstey, K. J., & Smith, G. A. (1999). Interrelationships among biological markers of aging, health, activity, acculturation, and cognitive performance in late adulthood. *Psychology and Aging, 14,* 605–618.

Apfelbaum, E. P., Krendl, A. C., & Ambady, N. (2010). Age-related decline in executive function predicts better advice-giving in uncomfortable social contexts. *Journal of Experimental Social Psychology, 46,* 1074–1077.

Bailey, P. E., & Henry, J. D. (2008). Growing less empathic with age: Disinhibition of the self-perspective. *Journal of Gerontology: Psychological Sciences, 63,* 219–226.

Bailey, P. E., & Henry, J. D. (2009). Subconscious facial expression mimicry is preserved in older adulthood. *Psychology and Aging, 24,* 995–1000.

Bailey, P. E., Henry, J. D., & Nangle, M. R. (2009). Electromyographic evidence for age-related differences in the mimicry of anger. *Psychology and Aging, 24,* 224–229.

Baltes, P. B. (1987). Theoretical propositions of life-span developmental psychology: On the dynamics between growth and decline. *Developmental Psychology, 23,* 611–626.

Baltes, P. B. (1997). On the incomplete architecture of human ontogeny: Selection, optimization, and compensation as foundation of developmental theory. *American Psychologist, 52,* 366–380.

Baltes, P. B., & Baltes, M. M. (1990). Psychological perspectives on successful aging: The model of selective optimization with compensation. In P. B. Baltes & M. M. Baltes (Eds.), *Successful aging: Perspectives from the behavioral sciences* (pp. 1–34). New York: Cambridge University Press.

Bargh, J. A., Chen, M., & Burrows, L. (1996). Automaticity of social behavior: Direct effects of trait construct and stereotype activation on action. *Journal of Personality and Social Psychology, 71,* 230–244.

Basak, C., Boot, W. R., Voss, M. W., & Kramer, A. F. (2008). Can training in a real-time strategy video game attenuate cognitive decline in older adults? *Psychology and Aging, 23,* 765–777.

Berntson, G. G., Bechara, A., Damasio, H., Tranel, D., & Cacioppo, J. T. (2007). Amygdala contributions to selective dimensions of emotion. *Cognitive and Affective Neuroscience, 2,* 123–129.

Bialystok, E., Craik, F. I. M., Klein, R., & Viswanathan, M. (2004). Bilingualism, aging, and cognitive control: Evidence from the Simon ask. *Psychology and Aging, 19*, 290–303.

Blair, R. J. (2005). Responding to the emotions of others: Dissociating forms of empathy through the study of typical and psychiatric populations. *Consciousness and Cognition, 14*, 698–718.

Blanchard-Fields, F. (2007). Everyday problem solving and emotion: An adult developmental perspective. *Current Directions in Psychological Science, 16*, 26–31.

Cacioppo, J. T., Berntson, G. G., Bechara, A., Tranel, D., & Hawkley, L. C. (2011). Could an aging brain contribute to subjective wellbeing? The value added by a social neuroscience perspective. In A. Todarov, S. T. Fiske & D. Prentice (Eds.), *Social neuroscience: Toward understanding the underpinnings of the social mind* (pp. 249–262). New York: Oxford University Press.

Carstensen, L. L., Fung, H., & Charles, S. (2003). Socioemotional selectivity theory and the regulation of emotion in the second half of life. *Motivation and Emotion, 27*, 103–123.

Carstensen, L.L., Gottman, J.M., & Levenson, R.W. (1995). Emotional behavior in long-term marriage. *Psychology and Aging, 10*, 140–149.

Carstensen, L.L., & Mikels, J.A. (2005). At the intersection of emotion and cognition: Aging and the positivity effect. *Current Directions in Psychological Science, 14*, 117–121.

Carstensen, L. L., Pasupathi, M., Mayr, U., & Nesselroade, J. R. (2000). Emotional experience in everyday life across the adult life span. *Journal of Personality and Social Psychology, 79*, 644–655.

Carton, J. S., Kessler, E. A., & Pape, C. L. (1999). Nonverbal decoding skills and relationship well-being in adults. *Journal of Nonverbal Behavior, 23*, 91–100.

Chaiken, S., & Trope, Y. (1999) *Dual-process theories in social psychology*. New York: Guilford Press.

Charles, S. T., Mather, M., & Carstensen, L. L. (2003). Aging and emotional memory: The forgettable nature of negative images for older adults. *Journal of Experimental Psychology: General, 132*, 310–324.

Chartrand, T. L., & van Baaren, R. (2009). Human mimicry. *Advances in Experimental Social Psychology, 41*, 219–274.

Chen, Y., & Blanchard-Fields, F. (2000). Unwanted thought: Age difference in the correction of social judgments. *Psychology and Aging, 15*, 475–482.

Christensen, H., Mackinnon, A. J., Korten, A., & Jorm, A. F. (2001). The "common cause hypothesis" of cognitive aging: Evidence for not only a common factor but also specific associations of age with vision and grip strength in a cross-sectional analysis. *Psychology and Aging, 16*, 588–599.

Cohen, C. A. (2006). Consumer fraud and the elderly: A review of Canadian challenges and initiatives. *Journal of Gerontology and Social Work, 46*, 137–144.

Collins, A. L., Glei, D. A., & Goldman, N. (2009). The role of life satisfaction and depressive symptoms in all-cause mortality. *Psychology and Aging, 24*, 696–702.

Conrey, F. R., Sherman, J. W., Gawronski, B., Hugenberg, K., & Groom, C. J. (2005). Separating multiple processes in implicit social cognition: The Quad Model of implicit task performance. *Journal of Personality and Social Psychology, 89*, 469–487.

Craik, F. I. M., & Salthouse, T. A. (Eds.) (2000). *Handbook of aging and cognition* (2nd ed.). Hillsdale, NJ: Erlbaum.

Crowe, M., Andel, R., Pedersen, N. L., Fratiglioni, L., & Gatz, M. (2006). Personality and risk of cognitive impairment 25 years later. *Psychology and Aging, 21*, 573–580.

Decety, J., Grèzes, J., Costes, N., Perani, D., Jeannerod, M., Procyk, E., Grassi, F., & Fazio, F. (1997). Brain activity during observation of actions. Influence of action content and subject's strategy. *Brain, 120*, 1763–1777.

Decety, J., & Jackson, P. L. (2004). The functional architecture of human empathy. *Behavioral and Cognitive Neuroscience Reviews, 3*, 71–100.

Dempster, F. N. (1992). The rise and fall of the inhibitory mechanism: Toward a unified theory of cognitive development and aging. *Developmental Review, 12*, 45–75.

Devine, P. G. (1989). Stereotypes and prejudice: Their automatic and controlled components. *Journal of Personality and Social Psychology, 56*, 5–18.

DeWall, C. N., Visser, P. S., & Levitan, L. C. (2006). Openness to attitude change as a function of temporal perspective. *Personality and Social Psychology Bulletin, 32*, 1010–1023.

Dougherty, L. M., Abe, J. A., & Izard, C. E. (1996). Differential emotions theory and emotional development in adulthood and later life. In C. Magai & S. H. McFadden (Eds.), *Handbook of emotion, adult development and aging* (pp. 27–41). New York: Academic Press.

Dunbar, R., & Shultz, S. (2007). Evolution in the social brain. *Science*, 317, 1344–1347.

Dupuis, K., & Pichora-Fuller, M. K. (2010). Use of affective prosody by young and older adults. *Psychology and Aging, 25*, 16–29.

Eaton, A. A., Visser, P. S., Krosnick, J. A., & Anand, S. (2009). Social power and attitude strength over the life course. *Personality and Social Psychology Bulletin, 35*, 1646–1660.

Ebner, N. C., Freund, A.M., & Baltes, P. B. (2006). Developmental changes in personal goal orientation from young to late adulthood: From striving for gains to maintenance and prevention of losses. *Psychology and Aging, 21*, 664–678.

Ebner, N. C., Riediger, M., & Lindenberger, U. (2009). Schema reliance for developmental goals increases from early to late adulthood: Improvement for the young, loss prevention for the old. *Psychology and Aging, 24*, 310–323.

Emery, L., & Hess, T. M. (2008). Viewing instructions impact emotional memory differently in older and young adults. *Psychology and Aging, 23*, 2–12.

Erskine, H. (1973). The polls: Hopes, fears, and regrets. *Public Opinion Quarterly, 37*, 132–145.

Feldman Barrett, L., Mesquita, B., Ochsner, K. N., & Gross, J. J. (2007). The experience of emotion. *Annual Review of Psychology, 58*, 373–403.

Finkel, D., Andel, R., Gatz, M., & Pedersen, N. L. (2009). The role of occupational complexity in trajectories of cognitive aging before and after retirement. *Psychology and Aging, 24*, 563–573.

Finkel, E. J., DeWall, C. N., Slotter, E. B., Oaten, M., & Foshee, V. A. (2009). Self-regulatory failure and intimate partner violence perpetration. *Journal of Personality and Social Psychology, 97*, 483–499.

Fleischman, D. A., Wilson, R. S., Gabrieli, J. D. E., Bienias, J. L., & Bennett, D. A. (2004). A longitudinal study of implicit and explicit memory in old persons. *Psychology and Aging, 19*, 617–625.

Fredrickson, B. L., & Carstensen, L. L. (1990). Choosing social partners: How old age and anticipated endings make people more selective. *Psychology and Aging, 5*, 335–347.

Freund, A. M. (2006). Age-differential motivational consequences of optimization versus compensation focus in younger and older adults. *Psychology and Aging, 21*, 240–252.

Fung, H. H., Carstensen, L. L., & Lang, F. R. (2001). Age-related patterns in social networks among European Americans and African Americans: Implications for socioemotional selectivity across the life span. *International Journal of Aging and Human Development, 52*, 185–206.

Fung, H. H., Carstensen, L. L., & Lutz, A. M. (1999). Influence of time on social preferences: Implications for life-span development. *Psychology and Aging, 14*, 595–604.

Gazzaley, A., Cooney, J.W., Rissman, J., & D'Esposito, M. (2005). Topdown suppression deficit underlies working memory impairment in normal aging. *Nature Neuroscience, 8*, 1298–1300.

German, T. P., & Hehman, J. A. (2006). Representational and executive selection resources in "theory of mind": Evidence from compromised belief-desire reasoning in old age. *Cognition, 101*, 129–152.

Gerstorf, D., Ram, N., Mayraz, G., Hidajat, M., Lindenberger, U., & Wagner, G. G., (2010). Late-life decline in well-being across adulthood in Germany, the United Kingdom, and the United States: Something is seriously wrong at the end of life. *Psychology and Aging, 25*, 477–485.

Gerstorf, D., Ram, N., Rocke, C., Lindenberger, U., & Smith, J. (2008). Decline in life satisfaction in old age: Longitudinal evidence for links to distance-to-death. *Psychology and Aging, 23*, 154–168.

Gigerenzer, G., Todd, P. M., & the ABC Research Group. (1999). *Simple heuristics that make us smart.* New York: Oxford University Press.

Gilovich, T., & Medvec, V. H. (1994). The temporal pattern to the experience of regret. *Journal of Personality and Social Psychology, 67*, 357–365.

Gilovich T., & Medvec, V. H. (1995). The experience of regret: What, when, and why. *Psychological Review, 102*, 379–395.

Glenn, N. D. (1974). Aging and conservatism. *Annals of the Academy of Political and Social Science, 415*, 176–186.

Glenn, N. D. (1980). Values, attitudes, and beliefs. In O. G. Brim & J. Kagan (Eds.), *Constancy and change in human development* (pp. 596–640). Cambridge, MA: Harvard University Press.

Gollwitzer, P. M., & Sheeran, P. (2006). Implementation intentions and goal achievement: A meta-analysis of effects and processes. *Advances in Experimental Social Psychology, 38*, 69–119.

Gonsalkorale, K., Sherman, J. W., & Klauer, K. C. (2009). Aging and prejudice: Diminished regulation of automatic race bias among older adults. *Journal of Experimental Social Psychology, 45*, 410–414.

Green, D. W. (1998). Mental control of the bilingual lexico-semantic system. *Bilingualism: Language and Cognition, 1*, 67–81.

Greenwald, A. G., McGhee, D. E., & Schwartz, J. K. L. (1998). Measuring individual differences in implicit cognition: The implicit association test. *Journal of Personality and Social Psychology, 74*, 1464–1480.

Gross, J. J. (1998). Antecedent- and response-focused emotion regulation: Divergent consequences for experience, expression, and physiology. *Journal of Personality and Social Psychology, 74*, 224–237.

Gross, J. J., Carstensen, L. L., Pasupathi, M., Tsai, J., Skorpen, C. G., & Hsu, A. Y. (1997). Emotion and aging: Experience, expression, and control. *Psychology and Aging, 12*, 590–599.

Gross, J. J., & John, O. P. (2003). Individual differences in two emotion regulation processes: Implications for affect, relationships, and well-being. *Journal of Personality and Social Psychology, 85*, 348–362.

Grossmann, I., Na, J., Varnum, E. W., Park, D. C., Kitayama, S., & Nisbett, R. E. (2010). Reasoning about social conflicts improves into old age. *Proceedings of the National Academy of Science, 76*, 200–213.

Grühn, D., Smith, J., & Baltes, P. B. (2005). No aging bias favoring memory for positive material: Evidence from a heterogeneity–homogeneity list paradigm using emotionally toned words. *Psychology and Aging, 20*, 579–588.

Hasher, L., Zacks, R. T., & May, C. P. (1999). Inhibitory control, circadian arousal, and age. In D. Gopher & A. Koriat, (Eds.), *Attention and performance XVII: Cognitive regulation of performance: Interaction of theory and application* (pp. 653–675). Cambridge, MA: MIT Press.

Heckhausen, J., & Schulz, R. (1995). A life-span theory of control. *Psychological Review, 102*, 284–304.

Heidrich, S. M., & Denney, N. W. (1994). Does social problem-solving differ from other types of problem-solving during the adult years? *Experimental Aging Research, 20*, 105–126.

Henry, J. D., von Hippel, W., & Baynes, K. (2009). Social inappropriateness, executive control, and aging. *Psychology and Aging, 24*, 239–244.

Henry, J. D., Ruffman, T., McDonald, S., O'Leary, M. A., Phillips, L. H., Brodaty, H., et al. (2008). Recognition of disgust is selectively preserved in Alzheimer's disease. *Neuropsychologia, 46*, 1363–1370.

Hess, T. M., & Auman, C. (2001). Aging and social expertise: The impact of trait-diagnostic information on impressions of others. *Psychology and Aging, 16*, 497–510.

Hess, T. M., Emery, L., & Queen, T. L. (2009). Task demands moderate stereotype threat effects on memory performance. *Journal of Gerontology: Psychological Sciences, 64B*, 482–486.

Hess, T. M., Hinson, J. T., & Statham, J. A. (2004). Explicit and implicit stereotype activation effects on memory: Do age and awareness moderate the impact of priming? *Psychology and Aging, 19*, 495–505.

Hess, T. M., Leclerc, C. M., Swaim, E., & Weatherbee, S. R. (2009). Aging and everyday judgments: The impact of motivational and processing resource factors. *Psychology and Aging, 24,* 735–740.

Isaacowitz, D. M., Allard, E. S., Murphy, N. A., & Schlangel, M. (2009). The time course of age-related preferences toward positive and negative stimuli. *Journal of Gerontology: Psychological Sciences, 64,* 188–192.

Isaacowitz, D. M., Toner, K., Goren, D., & Wilson, H. R. (2008). Looking while unhappy: Mood-congruent gaze in young adults, positive gaze in older adults. *Psychological Science, 19,* 848–853.

Iyengar, S.S., Wells, R.E., & Schwartz, B. (2006). Doing better but feeling worse: Looking for the "best" job undermines satisfaction. *Psychological Science, 17,* 143–150.

Jacoby, L. L. (1991). A process dissociation framework: Separating automatic from intentional uses of memory. *Journal of Memory and Language, 30,* 513–541.

Jacoby, L. L. (1999). Deceiving the elderly: Effects of accessibility bias in cued-recall performance. *Cognitive Neuropsychology, 16,* 417–436.

Kahneman, D., & Tversky, A. (1982). The psychology of preferences. *Scientific American, 246,* 160–173.

Kennedy, Q., Mather, M., & Carstensen, L. L. (2004). The role of motivation in the age-related positivity effect in autobiographical memory. *Psychological Science, 15,* 208–214.

Kim, S., Healey, M. K., Hasher, L., & Wiprzycka, U. J. (2008). Age differences in choice satisfaction: A positivity effect in decision making. *Psychology and Aging, 23,* 33–38.

Kinnier, R. T, & Metha, A. T. (1989). Regrets and priorities at three stages of life. *Counseling and Values, 33,* 182–193.

Kisley, M. A., Wood, S., & Burrows, C. L. (2007). Looking at the sunny side of life: Age-related change in an event-related potential measure of the negativity bias. *Psychological Science, 18,* 838–843.

Kohn, M. L., & Schooler, C. (1978). The reciprocal effects of the substantive complexity of work and intellectual flexibility: A longitudinal assessment. *American Journal of Sociology, 84,* 24–52.

Kohn, M. L., & Schooler, C. (1983). *Work and personality: An inquiry into the impact of social stratification.* Norwood, NJ: Ablex.

Kramer, A. F., Humphrey, D. G., Larish, J. F., Logan, G. D., & Strayer, D. L. (1994). Aging and inhibition: Beyond a unitary view of inhibitory processing in attention. *Psychology and Aging, 9,* 491–512.

Krosnick, J. A., & Alwin, D. F. (1989). Aging and susceptibility to attitude change. *Journal of Personality and Social Psychology, 57,* 416–425.

Kunzmann, U., Kupperbusch, C. S., & Levenson, R. W. (2005). Behavioral inhibition and amplification during emotional arousal: A comparison of two age groups. *Psychology and Aging, 20,* 144–158.

Kwon, Y., Scheibe, S., Samanez-Larkin, G. R., Tsai, J. L., & Carstensen, L. L. (2009). Replicating the positivity effect in picture memory in Koreans: Evidence for cross-cultural generalizability. *Psychology and Aging, 24,* 748–754.

Labouvie-Vief, G., Diehl, M., Jain, E., & Zhang, F. (2007). Six-year change in affect optimization and affect complexity across the adult life span: A further examination. *Psychology and Aging, 22,* 738–751.

Lang, F. R. (2001). Regulation of social relationships in later adulthood. *Journals of Gerontology Series B: Psychological Science and Social Science, 56,* 321–326.

Lee, D. J., & Markides, K. S. (1990). Activity and mortality among aged persons over an eight-year period. *Journal of Gerontology: Social Sciences, 45,* S39-S42.

Lee, Y. T., Jussim, L., & McCauley, C. R. (Eds.) (1995). *Stereotype accuracy: Toward appreciating group differences.* Washington, DC: APA.

Lecci, L., Okun, M. A., & Karoly, P. (1994). Life regrets and current goals as predictors of psychological adjustment. *Journal of Personality and Social Psychology, 66,* 731–741.

Leclerc, C. M., & Hess, T. M. (2007). Age differences in the bases for social judgments: Tests of a social expertise perspective. *Experimental Aging Research, 33,* 95–120.

Leclerc, C. M., & Kensinger, E. A. (2008). Effects of age on detection of emotional information. *Psychology and Aging, 23,* 209–215.

Levy, B. (1996). Improving memory in old age through implicit self stereotyping. *Journal of Personality & Social Psychology, 71,* 1092–1107.

Levy, B., & Langer, E. (1994). Aging free from negative stereotypes: Successful memory in China and among the American deaf. *Journal of Personality and Social Psychology, 66,* 989–997.

Levy, B. R., & Leifheit-Limson, E. (2009). The stereotype-matching effect: Greater influence on functioning when age stereotypes correspond to outcomes. *Psychology and Aging, 24,* 230–233.

Levy, B. R., Slade, M., Kunkel, S., & Kasl, S. (2002). Longitudinal benefit of positive self-perceptions of aging on functioning health. *Journal of Personality and Social Psychology, 83,* 261–270.

Levy, B. R., Zonderman, A., Slade, M. D., & Ferrucci, L. (2009). Age stereotypes held earlier in life predict cardiovascular events in later life. *Psychological Science, 20,* 296–298.

Liu, L. L., & Park, D. C. (2004). Aging and medical adherence: The use of automatic processes to achieve effortful things. *Psychology and Aging, 19,* 318–325.

Lövdén, M., Ghisletta, P., & Lindenberger, U. (2005). Social participation attenuates decline in perceptual speed in old and very old age. *Psychology and Aging, 20,* 423–434.

Macrae, C. N., Bodenhausen, G. V., Schloerscheidt, A. M., & Milne, A. B. (1999). Tales of the unexpected: Executive function and person perception. *Journal of Personality and Social Psychology, 76,* 200–213.

Magai, C. (2001). Emotions over the life span. In J. E. Birren & K. W. Schaie (Eds.), *Handbook of the psychology of aging* (5th ed., pp. 310–344). San Diego, CA: Academic Press.

Marsland, A. L., Pressman, S., & Cohen, S. (2007) Positive affect and immune function. In R. Ader (Ed.), *Psychoneuroimmunology* (4th ed., pp. 261–79). San Diego, CA: Elsevier.

Mata, R., Schooler, L. J., & Rieskamp, J. (2007). The aging decision maker: Cognitive aging and the adaptive selection of decision strategies. *Psychology and Aging, 22,* 796–810.

Mather, M., Canli, T., English, T., Whitfield, S., Wais, P., Ochsner, K., et al. (2004). Amygdala responses to emotionally valenced stimuli in older and younger adults. *Psychological Science, 15,* 259–263.

Mather, M., & Carstensen, L. L. (2003). Aging and attentional biases for emotional faces. *Psychological Science, 14,* 409–415.

Mather, M., & Carstensen, L. L. (2005). Aging and motivated cognition: The positivity effect in attention and memory. *Trends in Cognitive Sciences, 9,* 496–502.

Mather, M., & Knight, M. (2005). Goal-directed memory: The role of cognitive control in older adults' emotional memory. *Psychology and Aging, 20,* 554–570.

Mather, M., & Knight, M. (2006). Angry faces get noticed quickly: Threat detection is not impaired among older adults. *Journal of Gerontology: Psychological Sciences, 61,* 54–57.

May, C. P., Hasher, L., & Foong, N. (2005). Implicit memory, age, and time of day: Paradoxical priming effects. *Psychological Science, 16,* 96–100.

McFarland, C., Ross, M., & Giltrow, M. (1992). Biased recollections in older adults: The role of implicit theories of aging. *Journal of Personality and Social Psychology, 62,* 837–850.

McKinnon, M. C., & Moscovitch, M. (2007). Domain-general contributions to social reasoning: Theory of mind and deontic reasoning re-explored. *Cognition, 102,* 179–218.

Mikels, J. A., & Reed, A. E. (2009). Monetary losses do not loom large in later life: Age differences in the framing effect. *Journal of Gerontology: Psychological Sciences, 64,* 457–460.

Mroczek, D. K., & Kolarz, C. M. (1998). The effect of age on positive and negative affect: A developmental perspective on happiness. *Journal of Personality and Social Psychology, 75,* 1333–1349.

Murphy, N. A., & Isaacowitz, D. M. (2008). Preferences for emotional information in older and younger adults: A meta-analysis of memory and attention tasks. *Psychology and Aging, 23,* 263–286.

Pachur, T., Mata, R., & Schooler, L. J. (2009). Cognitive aging and the adaptive use of recognition in decision making. *Psychology and Aging, 24,* 901–915.

Park, D., & Gutchess, A. (2006). The cognitive neuroscience of aging and culture. *Current Directions in Psychological Science, 15,* 105–108.

Park, D. C. (2000). The basic mechanisms accounting for age-related decline in cognitive function. In D. C. Park & N. Schwarz (Eds.), *Cognitive aging: A primer* (pp. 3–21). Philadelphia, PA: Psychology Press.

Payne, B. K. (2005). Conceptualizing control in social cognition: How executive control modulates the expression of automatic stereotyping. *Journal of Personality and Social Psychology, 89,* 488–503.

Persson, J., Lustig, C.A., Nelson, J.K., & Reuter-Lorenz, P.A. (2007). Age differences in deactivation: A link to cognitive control? *Journal of Cognitive Neuroscience, 19,* 1021–1032.

Peters, E., Hess, T. M., Västfjäll, D., & Auman, C. (2007). Adult age differences in dual information processes: Implications for the role of affective and deliberative processes in older adults' decision making. *Perspectives on Psychological Science, 2,* 1–24.

Phillips, L. H., Henry, J. D., Hosie, J. A., & Milne, A. B. (2006). Age, anger regulation and well-being. *Aging and Mental Health, 10,* 250–256.

Phillips, L. H., Henry, J. D., Hosie, J. A., & Milne, A. B. (2008). Effective regulation of the experience and expression of negative affect in old age. *Journal of Gerontology: Psychological Sciences, 63,* 138–145.

Phillips, L. H., MacLean, R. D., & Allen, R. (2002). Age and the understanding of emotions: Neuropsychological and sociocognitive perspectives. *Journal of Gerontology: Psychological Sciences, 57,* 526–530.

Phillips, L. H., Scott, C., Henry, J. D., Mowat, D., & Bell, S. (2010). Emotion perception in Alzheimer's disease and mood disorders in old age. *Psychology and Aging, 25,* 38–47.

Pratt, M. W., Diessner, R., Pratt, A., Hunsberger, B., & Pancer, S. M. (1996). Moral and social reasoning and perspective taking in later life: A longitudinal study. *Psychology and Aging, 11,* 66–73.

Pushkar, D., Basevitz, P., Arbuckle, T., Nohara-LeClair, M., Lapidus, S., & Peled, M. (2000). Social behavior and off-target verbosity in elderly people. *Psychology and Aging, 15,* 361–374.

Rabbitt, P., Lowe, C., & Shilling, V. (2001). Frontal tests and models for cognitive ageing. *European Journal of Cognitive Psychology, 13,* 5–28.

Radvansky, G. A., Copeland, D. E., & von Hippel, W. (2010). Stereotype activation, inhibition, and aging. *Journal of Experimental Social Psychology, 46,* 51–60.

Radvansky, G. A., Lynchard, N., A., & von Hippel, W. (2009). Aging and stereotype suppression. *Aging, Neuropsychology, and Cognition, 16,* 22–32.

Reuter-Lorenz, P. A., & Cappell, K. A. (2008). Neurocognitive aging and the compensation hypothesis. *Current Directions in Psychological Science, 17,* 177–182.

Reynolds, C. A., Finkel, D., McArdle, J. J., Gatz, M., Berg, S., & Pedersen, N. L. (2005). Quantitative genetic analysis of latent growth curve models of cognitive abilities in adulthood. *Developmental Psychology, 41,* 3–16.

Richeson, J. A., & Shelton, J. N. (2003). When prejudice does not pay: Effects of interracial contact on executive function. *Psychological Science, 14,* 287–290.

Riediger, M., Schmiedek, F., Wagner, G. G., & Lindenberger, U. (2009). Seeking pleasure and seeking pain: Differences in pro-hedonic and contra-hedonic motivation from adolescence to old age. *Psychological Science, 20,* 1529–1535.

Rossi, S., Miniussi, C., Pasqualetti, P., Babiloni, C., Rossini, P. M., & Cappa, S. F. (2004). Age-related functional changes of prefrontal cortex in long-term memory: A repetitive transcranial magnetic stimulation study. *Journal of Neuroscience, 24,* 7939–7944.

Ruffman, T., Henry, J. D., Livingstone, V., & Phillips, L. H. (2008). A meta-analytic review of emotion recognition and aging: Implications for neuropsychological models of aging. *Neuroscience and Biobehavioural Reviews, 32*, 863–881.

Ruffman, T., Ng, M., & Jenkin, T. (2009). Older adults respond quickly to angry faces despite labeling difficulty. *Journal of Gerontology: Psychological Sciences, 64B*, 171–179.

Ruffman, T., Sullivan, S., & Edge, N. (2006). Differences in the way older and younger adults rate threat in faces but not situations. *Journal of Gerontology: Psychological Sciences, 61*, 187–194.

Ryan, E. B. (1992). Beliefs about memory across the life span. *Journal of Gerontology: Psychological Sciences, 47*, 41–47.

Salthouse, T. A. (1982). Duration estimates of 2 information-processing components. *Acta Psychologica, 52*, 213–226.

Salthouse, T. A. (1991). *Theoretical perspectives on cognitive aging.* Hillsdale, NJ: Erlbaum.

Salthouse, T. A., & Ferrer-Caja, E. (2003). What needs to be explained to account for age-related effects on multiple cognitive variables? *Psychology and Aging, 18*, 91–110.

Schacter, D. L., & Addis, D. R. (2007). The cognitive neuroscience of constructive memory: Remembering the past and imagining the future. *Philosophical Transactions of the Royal Society B: Biological Sciences, 362*, 773–786.

Scheibe, S., & Blanchard-Fields, F. (2009). Effects of regulating emotions on cognitive performance: What is costly for young adults is not so costly for older adults. *Psychology and Aging, 24*, 217–223.

Schlagman, S., Kliegel, M., Schulz, J., & Kvavilashvili, L. (2009). Differential effects of age on involuntary and voluntary autobiographical memory. *Psychology and Aging, 24*, 397–411.

Schooler, C., & Mulatu, M. S. (2001). The reciprocal effects of leisure time activities and intellectual functioning in older people: A longitudinal analysis. *Psychology and Aging, 16*, 466–482.

Sears, D. O. (1981). Life stage effects on attitude change, especially among the elderly. In S. B. Kiesler, J. N. Morgan, & V. K. Oppenheimer (Eds.), *Aging: Social change* (pp. 183–204). New York: Academic Press.

Shimokawa, A., Yatomi, N., Anamizu, S., Torii, S., Isono, H., Sugai, Y., et al. (2001). Influence of deteriorating ability of emotional comprehension on interpersonal behaviour in Alzheimer-type dementia. *Brain and Cognition, 47*, 423–433.

Shiota, M. N., & Levenson, R. W. (2009). Effects of aging on experimentally instructed detached reappraisal, positive reappraisal, and emotional behavior suppression. *Psychology and Aging, 24*, 890–900.

Skowronski, J. J., & Carlston, D. E. (1989). Negativity and extremity biases in impression formation: A review of explanations. *Psychological Bulletin, 105*, 131–142.

Slessor, G., Miles, L. K., Bull, R., & Phillips, L. H. (2010). Age-related changes in detecting happiness: Discriminating between enjoyment and nonenjoyment smiles. *Psychology and Aging, 25*, 246–250.

Slessor, G., Phillips, L. H., & Bull, R. (2008). Age-related declines in basic social perception: Evidence from tasks assessing eye-gaze processing. *Psychology and Aging, 23*, 812–822.

Stanley, J. T., & Blanchard-Fields, F. (2008). Challenges older adults face in detecting deceit: The role of emotion recognition. *Psychology and Aging, 23*, 24–32.

Steele, C. M. (2010). *Whistling Vivaldi and other clues to how stereotypes affect us.* New York: Norton.

Stewart, B. D., von Hippel, W., & Radvansky, G. A. (2009). Age, race, and implicit prejudice: Using process dissociation to separate the underlying components. *Psychological Science, 20*, 164–168.

Stine-Morrow, E. A. L., Shake, M. C., Miles, J. R., & Noh, S. R. (2006). Adult age differences in the effects of goals on self-regulated sentence processing. *Psychology and Aging, 21*, 790–803.

St Jacques, P. L., Dolcos, F., & Cabeza, R. (2009). Effects of aging on functional connectivity of the amygdala for subsequent memory of negative pictures: A network analysis of functional magnetic resonance imaging data. *Psychological Science, 20*, 74–84.

St Jacques, P., Dolcos, F., & Cabeza, R. (2010). Effects of aging on functional connectivity of the amygdala during negative evaluation: A network analysis of fMRI data. *Neurobiology of Aging, 31*, 315–327.

Stuss, D. T., & Levine, B. (2002). Adult clinical neuropsychology: Lessons from studies of the frontal lobes. *Annual Review of Psychology, 53*, 401–433.

Suddendorf, T., & Corballis, M. C. (1997). Mental time travel and the evolution of the human mind. *Genetic, Social, and General Psychology Monographs, 123*, 133–167.

Suddendorf, T., & Corballis, M. C. (2007). The evolution of foresight: What is mental time travel, and is it unique to humans? *Behavioral and Brain Sciences, 30*, 299–351.

Thornton, W. J. L., & Dumke, H. A. (2005). Age differences in everyday problem-solving and decision-making effectiveness: A meta-analytic review. *Psychology and Aging, 20*, 85–89.

Trunk, D. L., & Abrams, L. (2009). Do younger and older adults' communicative goals influence off-topic speech in autobiographical narratives? *Psychology and Aging, 24*, 324–337.

Tversky, A., & Kahneman, D. (1981). The framing of decisions and the psychology of choice. *Science, 211*, 453–458.

Valenzuela M. J., & Sachdev P. (2006). Brain reserve and cognitive decline: A non-parametric systematic review. *Psychological Medicine, 36*, 1065–1073.

Visser, P. S., & Krosnick, J. A. (1998). The development of attitude strength over the life cycle: Surge and decline. *Journal of Personality and Social Psychology, 75*, 1389–1410.

von Hippel, W., & Dunlop, S. M. (2005). Aging, inhibition, and social inappropriateness. *Psychology and Aging, 20*, 519–523.

von Hippel, W., & Gonsalkorale, K. (2005). "That is bloody revolting!" Inhibitory control of thoughts better left unsaid. *Psychological Science, 16*, 497–500.

von Hippel, W., Henry, J. D., & Matovic, D. (2008). Aging and social satisfaction: Offsetting positive and negative effects. *Psychology and Aging, 23*, 435–439.

von Hippel, W., Silver, L. A., & Lynch, M. E. (2000). Stereotyping against your will: The role of inhibitory ability in stereotyping and prejudice among the elderly. *Personality and Social Psychology Bulletin, 26,* 523–532.

Wang, M., & Chen, Y. (2004). Age differences in the correction processes of context-induced biases when correction succeeds. *Psychology and Aging, 19,* 536–540.

Wang, M., & Chen, Y. (2006). Age differences in attitude change: Influences of cognitive resources and motivation on responses to argument quality. *Psychology and Aging, 21,* 581–589.

Wegener, D. T., & Petty, R. E. (1995). Flexible correction processes in social judgment: The role of naive theories in corrections for perceived bias. *Journal of Personality and Social Psychology, 68,* 36–51.

West, R. L. (1996). An application of prefrontal cortex function theory to cognitive ageing. *Psychological Bulletin, 120,* 272–292.

Wood, S., Busemeyer, J. B., Koling, A., Cox, C. R., & Davis, H. (2005). Older Adults as Adaptive Decision Makers: Evidence From the Iowa Gambling Task. *Psychology and Aging, 20,* 220–225.

Wrosch, C., Bauer, I., Miller, G. E., & Lupien, S. (2007). Regret intensity, diurnal cortisol secretion, and physical health in older individuals: Evidence for directional effects and protective factors. *Psychology and Aging, 22,* 319–330.

Wrosch, C., Bauer, I., & Scheier, M. F. (2005). Regret and quality of life across the adult life span: The influence of disengagement and available future goals. *Psychology and Aging, 20,* 657–670.

Wrosch, C., & Heckhausen, J. (2002). Perceived control of life regrets: Good for young and bad for old adults. *Psychology and Aging, 17,* 340–350.

Ybarra, O., Burnstein, E., Winkielman, P., Keller, M.C., Manis, M., Chan, E., et al. (2008). Mental exercising through simple socializing: Social interaction promotes general cognitive functioning. *Personality and Social Psychology Bulletin, 34,* 248–259.

21

Atypical Social Cognition

Elizabeth Pellicano

In developmental psychology, arguably one of the most important findings of the last century was that children become able to represent explicitly the mental states of others at around 3–4 years of age (Wimmer & Perner, 1983). In a now seminal study, young children were introduced to a character, Maxi, who was enjoying a bar of chocolate. Having eaten half of his chocolate bar, Maxi put the remainder in the cupboard and went outside to play. While Maxi was outside, his mother found the chocolate and moved it from the cupboard to a drawer. Maxi returns to the kitchen, and the child was asked the crucial test question, "Where will Maxi look for his chocolate?" Typical 4-year-olds answered the question correctly (i.e., "in the cupboard"), suggesting that preschoolers could attribute mental states (in this case, a false belief) to others, and could use these to predict their behavior: that is, they had a "theory of mind" (cf. Premack & Woodruff, 1978). This capacity for understanding *false* beliefs was taken as the hallmark of a theory of mind because beliefs involve representations of reality, and as such, can either be true or false (Dennett, 1978). Younger children, however, performed *worse* than chance, consistently reporting that Maxi would look in the drawer, where the chocolate really is. Their failure on this task could not be due to difficulties remembering the story sequence or the current or previous location of the chocolate. Instead, their difficulties were attributed to a fundamental difficulty understanding that others will act on the basis of their beliefs, rather than on the actual state of affairs.

These findings inspired a new research area focusing on the development of social cognition – one which sought to understand the fundamental ways in which children come to adopt an "intentional stance" (Dennett, 1996), to understand one's own and others' mental states. They also spawned a huge body of work on the *atypical* development of social cognition. This latter work was driven partly by the prospect that a primary cognitive "deficit" in social cognition might explain some – or all – of the defining features of autism spectrum conditions. It was also motivated in part by the possibility that the case of autism could serve as fertile testing ground for theories of how typical children come to know about and act upon the social world. In this chapter, I begin by describing autism and then provide a comprehensive survey and analysis of work on the theory of mind hypothesis, particularly false-belief understanding, in autism, detailing the reasons why researchers have become dissatisfied with the false-belief task as the gold standard for assessing theory of mind. Finally, I turn to more recent work in autism, which goes beyond false-belief attribution and investigates the potential preconditions or "building blocks" for later social cognition, outlining the additional challenges faced by such investigations.

AUTISM: DEFINING FEATURES AND CASE EXAMPLES

Autism is a common neurodevelopmental condition or spectrum of related conditions, which currently include autistic disorder, Asperger syndrome, and pervasive developmental disorder – not otherwise specified (PDD-NOS) (APA, 2000). Although autism is now considered a highly heritable disorder of neural development (Levy, Mandell, & Schultz, 2009), specific genes and biological markers have yet to be identified. The diagnosis of autism therefore relies on a constellation of behavioral symptoms in early childhood, including often severe difficulties in social interaction and verbal and nonverbal communication, and limitations in behavioral flexibility (APA, 2000). There is, however, striking variability in the extent to which individuals manifest these behaviors, and show problems in terms of intellectual functioning and language ability.

Take Jonathan, for example. He is an 8-year-old boy who was diagnosed with autism at the age of 3 years, although many symptoms (especially, limited eye contact) were noticed by his parents much earlier. His speech was severely delayed; he could say single words by the age of 4 and began putting words together at age 6. Although much improved, his speech still contains recurring grammatical errors. He is extremely rigid – he needs his world to operate in a highly predictable way, and becomes very distressed when things are changed or don't follow his normal routine (taking exactly the same route to school, for example). His current obsession is with the "Tellie Tubbies," a popular television show for toddlers, and he will spend hours alone in his room talking gibberish to toy versions of the characters. Despite these difficulties, Jonathan enjoys going to school, where he is in a mainstream classroom receiving 1:1 support for half of the week. He is extremely sensitive to sounds, which makes it difficult for him to concentrate in an often noisy class. But he is interested in his peers – in fact, he'd desperately like to have a friend, and indeed makes many attempts to relate to other children. Sadly, these interactions, which lack the fluidity and natural ease of typically developing children's social exchanges, are often unsuccessful.

Now consider Adam, also aged 8, and also diagnosed with autism at the age of 3. Unlike Jonathan, Adam's scores on standardized tests of intellectual functioning place him in the mild learning disability range. This is probably an underestimate of his true intellectual capacity, however, as his very poor language skills undoubtedly hinder his performance on such tests. Much of what Adam says is repetitive or "echolalic" – he will repeat verbatim what has just been said to him or TV jingles or film scripts he has heard previously. He does use language to communicate about the things he is interested in, which currently include carwashes, bus washes, and washing machines (his family has the cleanest car in town!). But, again, these conversations are almost exclusively one-sided and have a scripted quality to them. In addition, and most unusually, Adam also has echopraxia, meaning that he will copy facial expressions, and emphatic or descriptive gestures. He attends a special unit – which is attached to a mainstream school – specifically for

children with autism, where he shows little interest in his peers and seldom interacts with them, instead appearing content to play on his own.

It is easy to see how Jonathan and Adam, the two case examples, broadly share the core diagnostic features of autism. Yet they are also strikingly different in terms of degree of symptoms (especially interest in other people) and communicative difficulties. This variability in autism is the norm rather than the exception. A large proportion of children with autism (around 50%) have an additional learning disability, and difficulties with receptive and expressive language vary enormously. For some children, language is limited or absent altogether, while for others, speech can be fluent, but even so, their use of language to communicate in social contexts (e.g., conversations) can be odd, awkward, and often one-sided. Furthermore, "stereotyped" and inflexible behaviors range from hand-flapping and finger-twisting to idiosyncratic special interests (e.g., prime numbers, train timetables, drain pipes) and an "insistence on sameness."

EXPLAINING CORE AUTISTIC BEHAVIORS: THE "THEORY OF MIND HYPOTHESIS"

There have been numerous attempts to try to pinpoint the underlying cause(s) of these symptoms. In his first descriptions of autism, Kanner (1943) suggested that we must "assume that these children have come into the world with innate inability to form the usual biologically provided affective contact with people" (p. 50). Although there was a time when practitioners of psychoanalysis – the prevailing dogma of the day – mistakenly believed that autism was an emotional illness caused by "faulty mothering" (Bettelheim, 1967), psychologists in the 1970s and 1980s became increasingly aware that a causal explanation could not lie at the level of behavior: the overt behavioral symptoms of people with autism change with age and ability and, moreover, the same behavior can be shown by different individuals for different reasons.

Research on autism took a turn following Premack and Woodruff's (1978) seminal article, "Does the Chimpanzee Have a Theory of Mind," which had resonated with researchers in London, who questioned whether atypicalities at the level of cognition, specifically difficulties in understanding other minds, might explain the core problems in sociability in autism. In a landmark study, Baron-Cohen, Leslie, and Frith (1985) put this possibility to the test. They administered a simplified version of the Maxi task (known as the "Sally-Ann task") to typically developing preschool children, older children with Down syndrome, and children with autism. Four- and 5-year-old typical children and children with Down syndrome responded correctly to the false-belief question, that Sally would look in the box where she mistakenly believes the marble to be. Yet 80% of their sample of children with autism answered incorrectly – that Sally would look in the basket, where the marble really is, despite the fact that the verbal mental age of these children was well beyond the 4- to 5-year-old level, when success on this task typically occurs.

This striking finding was taken as evidence that false-belief understanding – considered the hallmark of theory of mind at the time – is impaired in autism, which led the authors to propose that the core features of autism could be explained by a single primary cognitive deficit in the ability to understand other minds, thus placing individuals with autism "at a grave disadvantage when having to predict the behavior of other people" (p. 43) (see also Baron-Cohen, 1993, 1995; Baron-Cohen et al., 1985; Frith et al., 1991; Leslie, 1987, 1991). Indeed, Leslie (1987, 1991) and Leslie and Thaiss (1992) argued strongly that individuals with autism specifically lack the modular Theory of Mind Mechanism (ToMM), which in the typically developing child enables the formation of propositional attitudes [e.g., of the form, "X believes that (…)"], and provides insight into others' behavior.

These findings have since generated a huge body of work investigating the possibility that difficulties in theory of mind might play a causal role in the development of autism. In support of this position, a multitude of studies have demonstrated that many persons with autism perform poorly on tasks that require a representational understanding of other minds relative to appropriately matched comparison individuals (see Baron-Cohen et al., 2000, and Tager-Flusberg, 2001, 2007, for reviews), including those tapping the understanding of deception (Baron-Cohen, 1992; Russell, Mauthner, Sharpe, & Tidwell, 1991; Sodian & Frith, 1992), knowledge (Baron-Cohen & Goodhart, 1994; Leslie & Frith, 1988), complex emotions, such as surprise (Baron-Cohen, Spitz, & Cross, 1993), intention (Phillips, Baron-Cohen, & Rutter, 1998; Williams & Happé, 2010), in addition to recognition, comprehension, and expression of mental-state terms (Baron-Cohen et al., 1994; Tager-Flusberg, 1992; Ziatas, Durkin, & Pratt, 1998).

Importantly, according to the hypothesis, not *all* social behaviors should be equally affected by difficulties in theory of mind. Uta Frith and her colleagues sought to elucidate precisely those behaviors that on the surface appeared the same but in fact were functionally different. For example,

Attwood, Frith, and Hermelin (1988) demonstrated that children with autism showed specific problems using expressive gestures (those that communicate an emotional/mental state: e.g., putting the hand to the mouth in embarrassment) but had no problems understanding and using gestures for instrumental purposes (those which influence the behavior of another person: e.g., finger on lips signals "be quiet").

Similarly, Sodian and Frith (1992) showed that the cognitive processes underpinning the ability to perform sabotage and the ability to deceive were fundamentally distinct. In the sabotage condition, children were shown a box with some sweets in it, and were introduced to two characters – a "nice" boy and a "not-so-nice" boy. If the nice boy saw a sweet in the box, then he would put another sweet in the box, and the child could take them home. If, however, the not-so-nice boy saw a sweet in the box, he would try to take it. The child therefore had to devise a way of preventing the not-so-nice boy from stealing the sweet. Sodian and Frith (1988) showed that typical children *and* children with autism were able to sabotage (using a padlock and key) the not-so-nice boy's attempts to take the sweet. In the deception condition, the padlock and key were removed, leaving the children with no physical means of preventing the boy from taking the sweet. Instead, children were required to use their mentalizing skills to trick the not-so-nice boy into thinking that the box was locked. Typical children were overwhelmingly able to "lie" to ensure that the thief did not take their sweet but autistic children of similar mental age could not. Despite broad similarities in the structure of the task, this "fine cuts" method was able to pinpoint those skills with which children with autism had the most difficulty: those that relied most heavily on representing other minds.

Taken together, these findings were exciting. The so-called theory of mind hypothesis seemed to capture what Kanner (1943) first described as "autistic aloneness." Certainly, a limited ability to realize fully what it means to have a mind and to think, know, believe, and feel differently from others should affect one's capacity to predict others' behavior and therefore relate to others socially. It should also influence one's ability to communicate effectively (see Happé, 1993). Indeed, links were made between successful theory of mind task performance and autistic individuals' use of language in a social context (or "pragmatic" skills) (Eisenmajer & Prior, 1991), in addition to "real-life" social difficulties, including the ability to make or keep secrets, offer important information, and recognize surprise and embarrassment (Frith, Happé, & Siddons, 1994; Hughes, Soares-Boucaud, Hochmann, & Frith,

1997; Tager-Flusberg, 2000). Leslie (1987, 1991) argued that a core impairment in "metarepresentation" in autism could also account for the limited imaginative or pretend play in autism during early childhood (see also Baron-Cohen, 1987).

CHALLENGES TO THE THEORY OF MIND HYPOTHESIS

It soon became evident, however, that the theory of mind hypothesis fell short of explaining the full range of autistic behaviors, or even the social features specifically, in all individuals with autism. To begin, the percentage of individuals with autism passing the false-belief task varied considerably among studies. In Baron-Cohen et al.'s (1985) original study, 20% of children with autism passed the critical false belief question.[1] In subsequent studies, this percentage varied from 15% (Reed & Peterson, 1990) to 90% (Dahlgren & Trillingsgaard, 1996). Later studies showed, however, that while some individuals with autism could pass first-order false-belief tasks, they failed more difficult, second-order false-belief attributions (i.e., of the form "Mary thinks that John thinks the ice-cream van is in the park"; Perner & Wimmer, 1985) despite being significantly older than the age at which such tasks are typically passed (6–7 years) (Baron-Cohen, 1989; Perner, Leekam, & Wimmer, 1987; but see Bowler, 1992), and also scored lower than verbal mental age-matched typical individuals on other advanced theory of mind tasks, such as Francesca Happé's (1994) Strange Stories (see also White et al., 2009). On this basis, Baron-Cohen (1989a) proposed that the development of theory of mind is initially delayed in autism rather than completely absent.

One major criticism of these initial studies was that the veracity of the theory of mind hypothesis in many respects hinged on the validity of the false-belief task as the gold standard for assessing theory of mind. Having a theory of mind was portrayed as an "all or nothing" skill, manifested by success or failure on first-order false-belief tasks. Bloom and German (2000) cautioned researchers regarding the ubiquity of the false-belief task as the "litmus test" for theory of mind for two reasons.

First, they suggested that passing the false-belief task required more than simply the capacity for theory of mind. Indeed, in the typical literature, studies had begun to reveal that 3-year-olds could fail standard false-belief tasks not solely due to limitations in representing others' mental states but to difficulties in a set of domain-general processes known collectively as "executive function." On the false-belief task, correctly predicting the protagonist's action relies on the child suppressing his or her own prepotent (albeit mistaken) knowledge of current reality while at the same time keeping track of the protagonist's actions and the location of the object in question. Experimental manipulations of the false-belief task in which the executive demands were reduced (e.g., by making current reality less salient) were shown to enhance typical 3-year-olds' performance (Carlson, Moses, & Hix, 1998; Cassidy, 1998; Hala & Russell, 2001; Leslie & Polizzi, 1998). The possibility that false-belief task performance might be constrained by additional limitations in executive function was a real possibility for children with autism, who showed difficulties in core components of executive function, including the abilities to plan ahead, to switch flexibly between tasks, and to generate novel, flexible behavior (e.g., Ozonoff, Pennington, & Rogers, 1991) – an issue that we shall return to in the sections below.

Second, Bloom and German (2000) further suggested that the emphasis on the false-belief task was misguided because theory of mind encompassed much more than simply understanding false belief. Most critically, they stressed that typically developing 3-year-olds and individuals with autism – both of whom had been characterized as showing "a deficit in theory of mind" – were in reality very different to one another. Typical 3-year-olds showed other early-emerging putative "precursory" mentalizing behaviors, like initiating and responding to bids for joint attention (i.e., looking where someone is looking), engaging in imaginary play, and social referencing (i.e., the ability to use social signals to guide action in novel situations) – behaviors that, by diagnostic definition, are limited in autism. Indeed, this objection posed a real challenge for the theory of mind hypothesis: how could an impairment in theory of mind – as indexed by performance on false-belief tasks *typically passed at the age of 4 years* – explain the earliest symptoms of autism including atypicalities in social responsiveness and reciprocity, gaze behavior, joint attention, and imitation often detected during infancy (e.g., Dawson & Adams, 1984; Klin et al., 1992; Mundy & Sigman, 1989; Volkmar et al., 1987).

In response to these challenges, subsequent theoretical accounts have broadened the definition of theory of mind in order to provide a causal explanation of the *development* of autism. Baron-Cohen (1995) proposed a more extensive "mind-reading" system, which included not only a module for understanding mental states, such as think, believe, know, but also other early-emerging "precursor" modules, including innate mechanisms for eye-gaze detection and shared attention. Like other theorists (e.g., Bretherton, 1991; Tomasello, 1995; but see Moore & Corkum, 1994), Baron-Cohen (1994, 1995) suggested that the early appearance of joint visual gaze, and of shared attentiveness, may mark the beginning of an implicit understanding of mind, and may be a precursor for the ability to represent the full range of mental states. On his view, one of these modules – the Shared Attention Mechanism – is specifically "damaged" in autism, which, as a result, fails to trigger the subsequent development of the modular ToMM.

Tager-Flusberg (2001) proposed an alternative model. She interpreted the earliest symptoms of autism within a componential account of theory of mind, which encompasses a sociocognitive system that allows for mental-state reasoning, in addition to a socioperceptual system that includes eye-gaze perception, face recognition, emotion recognition, and imitation. Both systems are held to be fundamentally impaired in autism, and dissociations among systems may be present in other neurodevelopmental conditions (e.g. Williams syndrome; Tager-Flusberg & Sullivan, 2000). Similarly, others have postulated further that the social difficulties in autism extend beyond the processing of mental-state stimuli to include the on-line processing of social stimuli, including faces, voices, and gestures (e.g. Klin et al., 2002; Klin, Jones, Schultz, & Volkmar, 2003).

The need to explain some of the earliest manifestations of autism combined with the need to move away from the false-belief test as the pinnacle of theory of mind produced a flurry of research on the origins and developmental unfolding of this understanding, including the putative component skills – or "building blocks" – essential for a fully-fledged theory of mind. In the next section, I provide a brief overview of recent contributions to understanding those processes that might be necessary for the typical emergence of theory of mind, and relate these to what we know so far about autism.

BEYOND FALSE BELIEF: EARLY-EMERGING SIGNS OF UNDERSTANDING OTHER MINDS

Typically developing human infants appear to come into the world interested in, and attuned to, other people. Within the first few hours of life, infants can distinguish between a moving schematic face and a scrambled face (Goren, Sarty, & Wu, 1975; Johnson, Dziurawiec, Ellis, & Morton, 1991), and are also able to recognize their mother's face within a few days of birth (Bushnell, Saï, & Mullin, 1989). Newborns are also exquisitely sensitive to others' gaze, preferring to look at faces with direct than averted eye gaze (Farroni, Csibra, Simion, & Johnson, 2002) or eyes closed (Bakti, Baron-Cohen, Wheelwright, Connellan, & Ahluwalia, 2000). And they also appear to have an inbuilt "life detector" (cf. Troje & Westhoff, 2006): 2-day-old infants can discriminate between biological vs non-biological (random) movement, and they look longer at an upright point-light walker compared with the same walker turned upside down (Simion et al., 2008). Indeed, researchers have suggested that biological motion detection is an adaptive mechanism designed to facilitate interaction with conspecifics, directing attention towards another agent and sets up the processing of other important cues (like eye-gaze direction and facial expressions). Some (Klin & Jones, 2008, 2009) have suggested further that the later development of a theory of mind is predicated on an early-emerging "theory of body."

These early-emerging skills are impressive. But typical infants are not only able to detect another agent; they are able to extract causality from the spatiotemporal cues of schematic events (e.g., Leslie & Keeble, 1987; Schlottmann & Surian, 1999), and can further perceive an agent's actions as directed at or about an agent, object, or situation. Woodward (1998) showed that 6-month-old infants can interpret an action (in this case, a grasping hand) as directed to the goal of acquiring a specific object. By 12 months, infants expect agents to achieve their goals in a rational (i.e., the most efficient) way (Gergely, Nádasdy, Csibra, & Bíró, 1995), and are more likely to attribute goals to computer-generated animations that appear to move by themselves than to non-self-propelled agents (Gergely & Csibra, 2003).

Self-propelled motion has been proposed by some authors to be the critical cue for goal-directed agency (Baron-Cohen, 1995; Leslie, 1994; Premack, 1990), although evidence that infants can interpret computer-generated animations as goal-directed even when the cause of the object's movement is not apparent (Csibra et al., 1999) suggests that infants' early understanding of goals might not be mentalistic. Indeed, Csibra and Gergely (1998) have proposed that the infant adopts a "teleological stance" – a non-mentalistic bias to construe an event in terms of goals. This bias extends to non-human phenomena, including simple animated shapes (such as interacting triangles; Heider & Simmel, 1944; Scholl & Treboulet, 2000), which are not only self-propelled but also react to each others' movement, thus showing non-mechanical contingency or "causation-at-a-distance." Interpreting such actions as goal-directed further warrants the attribution of mental states such as agency, intentions, desires, and emotions to such shapes. Indeed, viewing the contingent silent movements of geometric shapes evokes rich anthropomorphic descriptions about their goals, thoughts, and feelings (Heider & Simmel, 1944), and activates regions of the brain (like the posterior superior temporal sulcus) that are normally recruited for theory of mind (Abell et al., 2000; Castelli et al., 2000, 2002).

Infants are also highly attuned very early on to attend to ostensive, communicative signals. Three-month-old infants show an early sensitivity for eye-gaze direction, particularly mutual gaze; they smile less when an adult looks away, and resume smiling when the adult re-initiates eye contact (Hains & Muir, 1996). Also, 4-month-olds rapidly shift their own gaze towards a target only when such shifts are preceded by a period of mutual eye gaze (Farroni et al., 2003). Such sensitivity appears to hold special significance during infant–adult interactions. In one study, Senju and Csibra (2008) examined 6-month-old infants' gaze following as they observed a person looking toward a toy located on either the left or the right. Infants followed the adult's eye movement only when it was preceded by direct eye contact, suggesting an early awareness of the ostensive nature of gaze cues. In another study, 9-month-olds observed a face either always looking towards an object or always looking away from it. Infants preferred to look at an adult making object-directed shifts in eye gaze but, again, only when such shifts were preceded by direct gaze (Senju, Csibra, & Johnson, 2008). These findings suggest that the perception of someone "looking at me" influences subsequent processing of another's socio-communicative intentions.

From the age of 9 months, children begin to *use* eye-gaze direction as an indicator of another's interest or attention: they track spontaneously another's eye gaze to determine precisely what s/he is looking at ("joint attention"). Some theorists (e.g., Corkum & Moore, 1998) are cautious in their interpretation of this phenomenon, suggesting that it might result from a learned association between the direction of an adult's gaze and interesting (and therefore rewarding) events in the world. Yet others afford a rich interpretation to joint attention behavior, suggesting instead that such behavior plays a formative role in children's linguistic (Baldwin, 1995; Tomasello, 2003) and sociocognitive (Baron-Cohen, 1995) development. Indeed, 4-year-olds use eye-gaze direction as a cue to understand the intentions and desires of others (Baron-Cohen, Campbell, Karmiloff-Smith, Grant, & Walker, 1995), and even 15-month-olds can detect a disparity between eye gaze and subsequent action (Onishi & Baillargeon, 2005). This ability not only developmentally precedes an understanding of complex mental states, such as false belief (Pellicano & Rhodes, 2003), but also

is held to afford a "window into the mind" of others (Baron-Cohen, 1995).

Whatever their explanation individually, these foundational abilities to detect another agent, to ascribe intentions and goals to that agent, and also to detect and respond to that agent's ostensive signals (cf. Frith & Frith, 2010) together provide the basis for the development of successful social interactions, and therefore of theory of mind.

ATYPICALITIES IN EARLY-EMERGING THEORY OF MIND IN AUTISM

Consequently, much research in the past decade has focused on whether these early-emerging components of theory of mind follow an atypical trajectory in autism. The detection and analysis of biological motion, which might be critical in how we distinguish living creatures from other objects, does appear to be different in autism. School-age children and adolescents (e.g., Blake et al., 2003; Koldewyn et al., 2010; Jones et al., 2011 for review see Kaiser & Shiffrar, 2009) show a selective atypicality in the perception of biological motion, despite showing typical sensitivity to perceiving non-biological movement and form. And this reduced sensitivity to point-light displays of human movement is evident from an early age. Klin and colleagues showed typically developing toddlers, toddlers with developmental delay but not autism, and toddlers with autism, a point-light animation of biological motion of a children's game (e.g., "pat-a-cake" or "peek-a-boo") on one side of the screen combined with the soundtrack of the actor's vocalizations. On the other side of the screen, children viewed an upside-down version of the same animation. Unlike both comparison groups, the group of toddlers with autism failed to show a looking preference for the upright biological motion, instead looking equally at both sides of the screen. The instance in which toddlers with autism did preferentially attend to biological motion was during one specific animation, pat-a-cake. Here, autistic toddlers were captured by a *non-social* audiovisual contingency – the synchrony between the sound of the clapping and the point-light movements of the hands. Klin et al. (2009; see also Klin & Jones, 2008) suggest that these young children show a lack of preferential attention towards biological motion combined with a heightened sensitivity to cross-modal synchrony. The authors suggest that this combination of atypicalities veers children on an altered developmental trajectory from very early on in life, leading them to focus instead on what one might call "socially-irrelevant" information. Although the underlying mechanism, which fails to orient infants towards more relevant, social information, is poorly understood, the possibility that this fundamental (and evolutionarily old) behavior might develop differently in autism offers exciting opportunities for future research.

Despite showing reduced sensitivity to the perception of biological motion, the ability to detect animacy appears to be intact in autism (Celani, 2002; New et al., 2009), while the evidence with respect to perception of causality is somewhat mixed. Studies assessing the latter ability have used Michotte's (1963) launching and reaction events showing the ambiguous movements of two geometric objects (shapes A and B). In launch events, one object (shape A) moves toward a stationary object (shape B). If shape B moves immediately after contact with shape A, typical adults report that "A pushes B" or "A hits B and sets it in motion." In reaction events, shape A approaches shape B, which begins to move *before* contact with shape A; adults attribute intentionality to the animations, including reports of "A chases B" or "B escapes from A." Even 6-month-old infants are sensitive to the causal roles of the agents in habituation paradigms (Schlottman, Surian, & Ray, 2009).

One might expect children with autism, who purportedly show difficulties in theory of mind, to show reduced sensitivity to reaction events specifically, since these appear to automatically trigger psychological attributions. Yet Ray and Schlottman (2007) showed that school-age children with autism had difficulty perceiving launch but (rather paradoxically) not reaction causality. Another study by the same group reported, however, that older children and young people with autism showed no difficulty perceiving either type of causality (Congiu, Schlottmann, & Ray, 2010), despite showing reduced sensitivity to artificial animal movements, strengthening the evidence for atypical biological motion in autism. It is important to note that children with autism in both studies were much older than the age at which perceptual causality typically emerges. These null findings therefore suggest either that initial difficulties might be overcome with age or, alternatively, that older children were using alternative strategies for perceiving such causality.

Difficulty attributing intentional mental states to others upon observing their actions seems, however, to be especially difficult for people with autism. In the classic Heider and Simmel (1944) experiment, participants observed two triangles (one big, one small) and a small circle moving around a larger rectangle, and immediately imbued the triangles' ambiguous movements with social meaning. Typical children and adults find it irresistible to attribute identities ("friend", "bully"), goal-directed actions ("hiding", "trapping"), and mental and emotional states ("angry", "is surprised") to the otherwise ambiguous movements of the triangles. The narratives of individuals with autism, however, are far less mentalistic. Despite being able to pass standard false-belief tasks, they tend not to attribute social meaning to the animated shapes, at least to the same extent as typically developing individuals do (Abell, Happé, & Frith, 2000; Klin, 2000; Klin & Jones, 2006; Zwickel et al., 2010). Furthermore, autistic individuals show different neural activation patterns in the "social brain network" than typical individuals when observing the movement patterns that evoke mental-state attribution (Castelli et al., 2000, 2002).

Atypical patterns of reciprocal eye gaze are also a striking feature of autism. Indeed, this feature forms part of the diagnostic criteria for autism (APA, 2000), and may be one of its earliest (detectable) manifestations (e.g., Baron-Cohen et al., 1996; Zwaigenbaum et al., 2005) (see Nation & Penny, 2008, and Senju & Johnson, 2009, for recent reviews). Children with autism engage less in direct eye-to-eye contact (Sigman, Mundy, Sherman, & Ungerer, 1986) and fixate less on the eyes during spontaneous viewing of faces than typically developing children do (e.g., Pelphrey et al., 2002; but see Fletcher-Watson, Leekam, Benson, Frank, & Findlay, 2009). Furthermore, they tend not to monitor the target of another person's gaze during joint visual attention (e.g., Leekam, Hunnisett, & Moore, 1998). In tasks that ask children to indicate which chocolate a character Charlie wants, or is going to take, from the direction of his eye gaze, children with autism do not use this information as a mentalistic cue (Baron-Cohen et al., 1995), and autistic adults show difficulties inferring another's mental state from viewing expressions in the eyes (Baron-Cohen, Jolliffe, Mortimore, & Robertson, 1997). This "failure" to understand the mentalistic significance of the eyes is thought to be instrumental in causing autistic children's theory of mind difficulties (Baron-Cohen, 1995).

Individuals with autism are not completely insensitive to eye-gaze direction, however. Children with autism show basic knowledge about eyes and seeing (Tan & Harris, 1991), can detect also whether someone is "looking at me" or "looking at not-me" (Baron-Cohen et al., 1995), and are able to follow line of sight (Leekam et al., 1997). Also, children with autism automatically shift their visual attention in response to an eye-gaze cue similar to typical children (e.g., Chawarska, Klin & Volkmar, 2003; Kylliäinen & Hietanen, 2004; Senju, Tojo, Dairoku, & Hasegawa, 2004).

On this basis, some researchers (Baron-Cohen, 1995) have claimed that there is a dissociation between detecting and interpreting eye-gaze direction in autism. Baron-Cohen (1995) argues that eye-gaze discrimination per se is intact in autism: individuals with autism are able to detect the presence of eyes, understand that eyes are for 'seeing,' and can determine direction of eye gaze in non-mentalistic contexts. The real difficulty in autism, instead, is thought to lie in the *interpretation* of directional information from eye gaze during joint (triadic) interactions. In particular, individuals with autism are unable to establish that the self and other are attending to the same object/event, and consequently fail to use gaze direction as an indicator of another's mental state – his/her attention, goals, motives or desires.

SPONTANEOUS THEORY OF MIND IN AUTISM

Together, these and other findings have led some authors (e.g., Frith & Happé, 1999) to suggest that people with autism might lack an "intuitive" or spontaneous theory of mind. These authors argued that success by individuals with autism on traditional false-belief tasks does not provide unequivocal evidence that these individuals have in fact developed a theory of mind. Consistent with this view, individuals with autism who pass standard false-belief tasks tend to perform poorly on more naturalistic tasks like the Heider and Simmel (1944) animated figures (Abell et al., 2000; Castelli et al., 2002; Klin, 2000), and still remain confused by everyday social interactions that require mentalizing (Frith, Happé, & Siddons, 1994). For example, Frith et al. (1991) suggested that cognitively able autistic individuals may have learned or extracted explicit rules about certain social situations, such as "When something in the world changes, people who just happen not to have seen the change occur behave (for some reason) as if they do not know about these changes" (p. 436). These "passers" could therefore be using such alternative (and considerably more effortful) compensatory routes to task success (Eisenmajer & Prior, 1991; Frith et al., 1991; Happé, 1995; Holroyd & Baron-Cohen, 1993; Ozonoff et al., 1991).

Separate sources of evidence favor the possibility that individuals with autism who pass classic false-belief tasks might be "hacking" out the solution using alternative strategies. Neuroimaging studies have provided indirect evidence for this claim, with reports of less activation in "social brain" regions (e.g. medial prefrontal cortex and temporoparietal junction, Mitchell,

Banaji, & Macrae, 2005; Saxe & Kanwisher, 2003; see Frith & Frith, 2003, and Saxe, Carey, & Kanwisher, 2004, for reviews) combined with greater activation in neural regions associated with general problem-solving skills in adults with autism (e.g., Castelli et al., 2002; Happé et al., 1996). More direct evidence comes from a recent eye-tracking study of a paradigm used previously with infants, who are shown a scenario similar to the classic Maxi task. Infants seem to look longer – and therefore show surprise or "violation of expectation" – when Maxi reaches into the location in which the chocolate is currently hiding (the drawer), suggesting that infants show evidence of *implicit* mentalizing ability (Onishi & Baillargeon, 2005; Surian et al., 2007). Frith (2003) suggested that although explicit rule-based mentalizing can be learned in autism, spontaneous mentalizing ability, as shown by infants' eye movements in their second year, might never be accomplished.

To test this possibility, Senju et al. (2009) presented a similar task to adults with Asperger syndrome, who were all able to pass standard theory of mind tasks, and tracked their eye movements as they watched the scenario play out. Typical adults, like typical 25-month-olds (Southgate et al., 2007), immediately looked to the empty box for the ball, where the protagonist falsely believed it to be. Adults with Asperger syndrome, however, reportedly had "mindblind eyes": they looked equally at both boxes, suggesting that they were unable to predict implicitly where the protagonist should look for the ball. Although older and more able individuals with autism may be able to solve standard false-belief tasks, these findings indicate that there is an "absence of *spontaneous* mentalizing in autism" – the sort of processes automatically used by typical infants, toddlers, and children to successfully navigate everyday social interaction, and which might require the integrity of those developmentally early-emerging building blocks of social cognition, including the perception of causality and animacy, sensitivity to biological motion, and the ability to recognize communicative intent using ostensive cues.

Another study from the same group, however, suggests that the story might not be so straightforward. Zwickel, White, Coniston, Senju, and Frith (2010) tracked the eye movements of adults with autism as they watched several Heider and Simmel-type animations. Despite attributing less intentionality to the animate shapes than typical individuals, adults with autism showed *similar* fixation patterns to typical adults; they spent more time watching the triangles rather than other part of the display, and spent an equal amount of time focusing on each triangle, which was especially important for animations involving theory of mind, such as "mocking." They further showed that adults with autism could adopt the visuospatial perspective of another agent – both implicitly and explicitly.

These recent data suggest that the (implicit) abilities to detect social agents and to appreciate how the world looks to another person – spontaneous abilities thought to be potential building blocks for later social cognition – are not lacking in autism. Zwickel et al. (2010) suggest that these particular implicit abilities might be intact in autism because they were "fundamental survival skills" in an evolutionary sense, long before attributing mental states to potential predators became relevant. That said, data from young children with autism suggest that another early-emerging (and evolutionarily "old") skill, spontaneous detection of biological motion, is impoverished (Klin & Jones, 2009). It will be critical to try and assess all of these abilities from the earliest possible ages because it is certainly possible that the reportedly intact spontaneous agency detection and visuospatial perspective-taking skills in adults with autism (Zwickel et al., 2010) may have initially followed a delayed and/or different developmental trajectory.

These investigations are in the early stages, and future work may delineate a clearer picture of precisely which early-emerging sociocognitive building blocks are atypical in autism. This goal of determining how and when infants with autism might begin to follow a different developmental trajectory to that of typically developing infants, however, is difficult to achieve since autism is not usually diagnosed until 2–3 years of age (and in some children, much later). Investigators studying the behaviors of infant siblings of children with autism, who are at a higher risk of developing autism themselves, are optimistic that such studies will provide these important clues (e.g., see Rogers, 2009; Tager-Flusberg, 2010; Yirmiya & Charman, 2010).

Whatever the difficulties in emergent mentalizing skills, atypicalities in these alone, however, will not explain fully the real-life functioning of individuals with autism. There is vast variability both in the extent to which individuals with autism pass traditional theory of mind tests and in their competence during everyday tasks that rely on mentalizing, including making and keeping friends, turn-taking during conservations, and responding to others' needs. Understanding this variability in autism, and further deepening our knowledge of the way that social cognition develops – typically or atypically – requires moving beyond a narrow understanding of theory of mind itself. In the final section of this chapter, I discuss the possibility that the emergence of social cognition may be critically dependent on other non-theory of mind functions.

BEYOND THEORY OF MIND: THE ROLE OF OTHER CONTRIBUTING FACTORS

Contemporary developmental approaches (e.g., Bishop, 1997; Karmiloff-Smith, 1998, 2009; Pennington, 2006) emphasize the dynamic nature of developing systems, where interactions among domains are likely to be the norm. On this view, it is not surprising to suggest that other functions might play a critical role in the development of theory of mind both in typically developing children and in children with autism. In this section, I shall discuss the relationship between children's growing theory of mind and two such functions, language and executive control.

Language and theory of mind

It is well-documented that performance on standard false-belief tasks is correlated with typical children's language ability (for a recent meta-analysis, see Milligan, Astington, & Dack, 2007). False-belief tasks are, of course, highly verbal in nature, and so it is perhaps unremarkable that children who have better language skills tend to pass false-belief tasks from an earlier age. Many researchers, however, have suggested that there is a functional relationship between language and false-belief understanding, although the underlying nature of the relationship is hotly debated. Some theorists have claimed strongly that syntactic development, specifically children's mastery of sentential complements – namely, a tensed proposition embedded under a mental (e.g., *think/believe/know*) or communication (e.g., *said*) verb (e.g., Marc *thinks* [that] his keys are in the kitchen) – might be a necessary prerequisite of a representational theory of mind (e.g., de Villiers & de Villiers, 2000; Hale & Tager-Flusberg, 2003; Lohmann & Tomasello, 2003). Sentences containing complements are unique because the whole sentence can be true (e.g., Marc thinks X) even though the embedded clause may be false (e.g., his key are not in the kitchen). Once the child acquires the ability to understand sentential complements, it allows him/her "to entertain the possible worlds of other minds, by a means that is unavailable without embedded propositions" (de Villiers, 2000, p. 90).

Other researchers, however, have emphasized the important use of language for sociocommunicative purposes. They suggest that language facilitates the development of an explicit theory of mind because conversation with others enables a constant exchange of differing points of view: i.e., it allows children to talk about the mind (Harris, 1996, 2005; Peterson & Siegal, 1995, 1999, 2000). Evidence for these models comes from studies of atypical development, especially children with hearing impairment. Children who are born deaf but grow up in hearing families show impoverished performance on tasks of false-belief attribution purportedly because, unlike children born deaf and raised by deaf parents, they lack the conversational input that is necessary for the typical development of theory of mind (Peterson & Siegal, 1995, 1999, 2000).

Language delay and deviance are one of the defining characteristics of autism. It is not surprising, therefore, that poor verbal ability has been cited as one explanation for autistic children's poor performance on false-belief tasks, and even their delayed development of theory of mind. Indeed, Happé's (1995) review of theory of mind showed that a certain level of verbal ability was necessary for children with autism to succeed on standard false-belief tasks, which was considerably higher than that of typically developing children. An abundance of cross-sectional (e.g., Charman & Baron-Cohen, 1992; Fisher, Happé, & Dunn, 2005; Leekam & Perner, 1991) and some longitudinal (Pellicano, 2010; Steele et al., 2003; Tager-Flusberg & Joseph, 2005) work has since shown that language ability, especially grammatical ability, is significantly related to autistic children's performance on standard false-belief tasks. Whether the mechanism involves mastery of sentential complements or conversation with others (and it will possibly be a combination of both skills), these findings suggest that early language skills might play an important role in facilitating autistic children's understanding of the representational nature of mind.

Executive function in theory of mind

The emergence of another critical function – children's growing self-control or "executive function" – has been offered as an additional explanation of autistic children's (limited) performance on false-belief tasks. Executive function is an umbrella term for a set of higher-order processes, including working memory, inhibitory control, and cognitive flexibility, closely associated with the prefrontal cortex, that are necessary for regulating and controlling behavior, especially in new situations. It shows a protracted developmental trajectory, which begins in early infancy and continues well into adolescence (Diamond, 2002) and shows a boost in development around the

preschool period (Carlson, 2005; Diamond, 2002; Hughes, 1998a; Luciana & Nelson, 1998; Zelazo & Müller, 2002) – precisely when typical preschoolers are beginning to show an explicit awareness of others' minds. They begin, that is, to succeed at tasks that require them to hold information "in mind" and work with it, in addition to inhibiting a salient or prepotent response – two essential features of executive tasks (Pennington et al., 1997).

Typical children's progress in theory of mind has been shown to be intimately tied to improvements in executive function in development. Numerous studies have reported robust correlations between individual differences in tasks tapping theory of mind and tasks tapping several components of executive function, independent of age and general intellectual functioning, in preschoolers (Carlson & Moses, 2001; Carlson, Moses, & Breton, 2002; Carlson, Moses, & Claxton, 2004b; Frye, Zelazo, & Palfai, 1995; Hughes, 1998a, 1998b), and in toddlers (Carlson, Mandell, & Williams, 2004a; Hughes & Ensor, 2007).

The most clear-cut explanation of this relationship is that false-belief prediction tasks used to index theory of mind place considerable demands on children's executive function and, hence, that executive function is thought to contribute to the *expression* of theory of mind rather than to its development (Carlson & Moses, 2001; Leslie, 1994; Leslie & Polizzi, 1998; Moses, 2001; Russell et al., 1991). The executive demands of the classic false-belief task are manifold. Any difficulties keeping track of the protagonist's actions and the whereabouts of the object, and/or inhibiting reference to one's more salient, current (and true) belief could therefore severely limit autistic children's performance on false-belief tasks (see Russell, Saltmarsh, & Hill, 1999, and Russell, Hala, & Hill, 2003, for discussion).

Despite potential difficulties with the false-belief task, however, several theorists have provided good reasons to suppose that there is a more fundamental relationship between these two cognitive domains, where functioning in one domain is critical to the *emergence* of functioning in the other. Such theorists diverge as to the nature of the functional link. Some assert that the abilities to monitor one's actions and to act with volition are critical for reflecting on the mental states of self and other: i.e., that theory of mind emerges from executive function (e.g., Russell, 1996; see also Moses, 2001, and Pacherie, 1997). Conversely, others suggest that the causal arrow is in the opposite direction: children's growing ability to regulate their behavior is dependent on their developing metarepresentational capacity underlying theory of mind (e.g., Perner, 1998; Perner & Lang, 1999).

The very co-occurrence of problems in theory of mind and executive function in autism is suggestive of a link between these domains. Several cross-sectional studies have reported significant correlations between theory of mind (as generally tapped by false-belief understanding) and components of executive function, independent of age, verbal ability, and nonverbal ability (Colvert, Custance, & Swettenham, 2002; Joseph & Tager-Flusberg, 2004; Ozonoff et al., 1991; Pellicano, 2007, 2010). To examine the nature of the association between these skills, Ozonoff et al. (1991) calculated the extent of "impairments" within each cognitive domain by calculating the percentage of individuals with autism who scored below the mean score of the typically developing group. Although difficulties in executive function were near-universal in their sample, theory of mind problems were present in only half of the autism group. On this basis, Ozonoff et al. (1991) suggested both that atypicalities in executive function are primary in autism and that a third factor was required to explain the link between these skills.

Pellicano (2007) re-examined Ozonoff et al.'s (1991) suggestion by investigating the pattern of associations between theory of mind and executive function in 4–7-year-old children with autism, but this time using a more conservative definition of "impairment": the percentage of children with autism who scored more than one standard deviation below the mean of the typically developing group. In her sample, no child with impaired executive function also possessed intact theory of mind – precisely the pattern of results predicted by Russell (1996). Pellicano (2007) therefore concluded that good executive skills are a necessary, but not sufficient, precondition for the development of theory of mind in autism.

Recent longitudinal data have further strengthened this claim. Tager-Flusberg and Joseph (2005) tested children with an autism spectrum condition on numerous theory of mind (including false-belief tests) and executive function tasks at intake and re-evaluated their theory of mind skills 1 year later. Children's early executive skills predicted developmental changes in theory of mind independent of language and initial theory of mind scores, suggesting, akin to Pellicano (2007), that executive function is critical for children's developing theory of mind. Pellicano (2010) extended these findings in a 3-year prospective study of autistic children's cognitive skills to show that, like Tager-Flusberg and Joseph (2005), children's executive abilities at intake were predictive of improvements in theory of mind over the 3-year period. Critically, however, she also showed that predictive relations did not exist in the reverse direction: i.e., early theory of mind did not predict developmental changes in executive function.

These findings show the strongest support yet for the notion that early executive skills might play a critical role in shaping the development of theory of mind in children with autism.

Since Bloom and German's (2000) plea for researchers to abandon the false-belief task as the cornerstone of theory of mind, there has been considerable interest in the way that other functions, especially language and executive function, might influence children's performance on false belief and other tests of theory of mind, but also, and more critically, how these functions might shape the development of an explicit representation of other minds. Certainly, findings from the autism literature suggest that both language and executive function might be important limiting and enabling factors in the (a)typical developmental trajectory of theory of mind. The nature of the relationship, of course, could be mediated by a third factor, such as social interaction (cf. Hughes, 1998b; Luria, 1966). Both good language skills and good executive function capacity might enable children with and without autism to participate in effective social exchanges, especially with peers, which could result in multiple cascading events on children's emerging socio-cognitive skills.

Future research in this area will surely elucidate the precise determinants of explicit belief attribution. The data as they stand, however, already suggest that any theoretical model of sociocognitive development – in autism or in typical children – must delineate how internal (e.g., language, executive function) and external (e.g., social interaction) factors might influence children's developmental trajectories. In so doing, such a model must also identify a means by which key internal factors like executive function shape the development of important early-emerging theory of mind behaviors other than those directly related to false-belief prediction. Some authors have already proposed such a relationship, suggesting that early executive abilities, such as inhibitory control or attentional flexibility, may in fact be critical for the development of joint attention (e.g., Mundy & Newell, 2007; Nichols, Fox, & Mundy, 2005) and pretend play (e.g., Jarrold, 2003).

CONCLUSION

It has been almost three decades since researchers proposed that atypicalities in understanding other minds could explain the core socio-communicative symptoms of autism. During this time, the field has witnessed an explosion of research on the topic, with more recent research dedicated to going both beyond false belief – by identifying the necessary preconditions for the emergence of theory of mind in both typical and atypical development – and beyond theory of mind – to specify the role of other critical functions, which might shape the developmental trajectory of mental-state attribution.

The broadening of the definition of theory of mind to extend beyond false-belief understanding does introduce a degree of circularity in which the first signs of autism (poor gaze monitoring, failure to orient towards social stimuli) are, by definition, components of poor theory of mind (see Hughes & Leekam, 2004, for discussion). Further refinement of the theory will therefore necessitate an understanding and delineation of the underlying *mechanisms* responsible for the development of an implicit theory of mind, and how these might be different in autism, in addition to specifying which of these mechanisms might then be necessary for the emergence of an explicit theory of mind. Are the developmental origins of sociocognitive atypicalities in autism rooted in fundamental difficulties identifying what is relevant versus what is irrelevant in the social world (e.g., detection of another agent) (Klin et al., 2009)? Or are they due to a fundamental lack of interest in the social world (cf. Dawson et al., 2005)? Furthermore, can individuals (with autism) develop an explicit awareness of other minds, created perhaps through compensatory executive function and language skills, despite experiencing atypicalities in early-emerging intuitive mentalizing skills? And if so, is there genuinely a difference at the representational level for those who develop theory of mind via the usual route (implicit → explicit) compared to those who do not?

Researchers will also need to grapple with the pervasiveness of the disadvantage in social cognition in autism. As noted earlier, there are some "islets" of social ability in individuals with autism (e.g., Attwood et al., 1988; Sodian & Frith, 1992). These individuals can attribute judgments of attractiveness and trustworthiness to photographs of faces (White et al., 2006), and acquire culturally transmitted knowledge about stereotypes (Hirschfeld et al., 2007). Other studies have shown, however, that autistic individuals' sociocognitive atypicalities might extend beyond truly "mentalistic" contexts. For example, Pellicano and Macrae (2009) showed that mutual eye gaze does not facilitate basic person-perception judgments (gender categorization) for children with autism, like it does for typically developing children (see also Akechi et al., 2009), rendering it possible that "someone looking at you" does not modulate broader social (in this case, person-construal) processes in autism, rather than failing to do so in mentalistic contexts alone.

Understanding the breadth of weaknesses and strengths in social cognition in autism is critically important for practical efforts aimed at improving the functional outcomes of individuals with autism, and ultimately their well-being. Specifically, it should direct attention towards identifying how we might alleviate the often-profound social difficulties in autism by pinpointing the most promising candidates for intervention. Can we train individuals with autism to attend to (or be motivated by) another agent? Can the spontaneous, implicit theory of mind atypicalities be overcome by compensations in other areas? If so, which other areas should these be? If we can answer these questions experimentally then we might be able to enhance the life experience of people with autism and discover something crucial about social cognition more generally.

There is, however, one final cautionary tale to tell. Several recent studies have attempted to promote social behavior in autism using oxytocin, a hormone that is particularly important in forming parent–child bonds (see Bartz & Hollander, 2008, for review). For example, Andari et al. (2010) asked adults with autism and typical adults to play a computerized ball-tossing game (a game of "catch") with three other virtual players. Typical adults quickly established alliances with some players and not with others, while adults with autism failed to interact selectively with the most socially cooperative player. The experimenters then randomly selected half of the autistic adults to receive a nasal spray of oxytocin. They found that those who had inhaled oxytocin began to cooperate selectively, and subsequently avoid certain players – precisely like typical adults, but quite unlike those adults with autism who were administered a saline placebo. In many respects, this study was extremely successful, with adults with autism exhibiting increased levels of social behavior and affect under oxytocin. Yet one might also suggest that, prior to oxytocin, adults with autism behaved impartially, tossing the ball equally among players, while under oxytocin, this impartiality disappeared, and autistic adults played the game like typical adults, displaying a potentially worrying partiality (Dawson, 2010). These findings highlight the need for caution: making individuals with autism more like us might not be uncomplicatedly a good thing.

ACKNOWLEDGMENTS

I am grateful to Marc Stears and the editors for their thorough comments on a previous version of this chapter. Research at the Centre for Research in Autism and Education (CRAE) is supported by The Clothworkers' Foundation and Pears Foundation.

NOTE

1   False-belief tasks usually consist of only a few experimental trials, where chance performance on each trial is 50% (where the protagonist initially left the object or where it really is now). One should therefore not necessarily expect *all* persons with autism to fail false-belief tasks; some individuals may "pass" due to random responding.

REFERENCES

Abell, F., Happé, F., & Frith, U. (2000). Do triangles play tricks? Attribution of mental states to animated shapes in normal and abnormal development. *Cognitive Development, 15*, 1–16.

Akechi, H., Senju, A., Kikuchi, Y., Tojo, Y., Osanai, H., & Hasegawa, T. (2009). Does gaze direction modulate facial expression processing in children with autism spectrum disorder? *Child Development, 80*, 1134–1146.

American Psychiatric Association (APA) (2000). *Diagnostic and statistical manual of mental disorders* (*DSM-IV-TR*; 4th ed., text revision). Washington, DC: American Psychiatric Association.

Andari, E., Duhamel, J-R., Zalla, T., Herbrecht, E., Leboyer, M., & Sirigu, A. (2010). Promoting social behavior with oxytocin in high-functioning autism spectrum disorders. *Proceedings of the National Academy of Sciences, 107*, 4389–4394.

Attwood, T., Frith, U., & Hermelin, B. (1988). The understanding and use of interpersonal gestures in autistic and Down's syndrome children. *Journal of Autism and Developmental Disorders, 18*, 241–257.

Baldwin, D. A. (1995). Understanding the link between joint attention and language. In C. Moore & P. Dunham (Eds.), *Joint attention: Its origins and role in development* (pp. 131–158). Hillsdale, NJ: Erlbaum

Batki, A., Baron-Cohen, S., Wheelwright, S., Connelan, J., & Ahluwalia, J. (2000). Is there an innate gaze module? Evidence from human neonates. *Infant Behavior and Development, 23*, 223–229.

Baron-Cohen, S. (1987). Autism and symbolic play. *British Journal of Developmental Psychology, 5*, 139–148.

Baron-Cohen, S. (1989). The autistic child's theory of mind: A case of specific developmental delay. *Journal of Child Psychology and Psychiatry, 30*, 285–297.

Baron-Cohen, S. (1992). Debate and argument: On modularity and development in autism: A reply to Burack. *Journal of Child Psychology and Psychiatry, 33*, 623–629.

Baron-Cohen, S. (1993). From attention-goal psychology to belief–desire psychology: The development of a theory of mind, and its dysfunction. In S. Baron-Cohen, H.

Tager-Flusberg & D. J. Cohen (Eds.), *Understanding other minds: Perspectives from autism* (pp. 59–82). Oxford, UK: Oxford University Press.

Baron-Cohen, S. (1994). How to build a baby that can read minds: Cognitive mechanisms in mindreading. *Cahiers de Psychologie Cognitive, 13*, 513–552.

Baron-Cohen, S. (1995). *Mindblindness: An essay on autism and theory of mind*. Cambridge, MA: MIT Press.

Baron-Cohen, S., Campbell, R., Karmiloff-Smith, A., Grant, J., & Walker, J. (1995). Are children with autism blind to the mentalistic significance of the eyes? *British Journal of Developmental Psychology, 13*, 379–398.

Baron-Cohen, S., Cox, A., Baird, G., Swettenham, J., Nightingale, N., Morgan, K., et al. (1996). Psychological markers in the detection of autism in infancy in a large population. *British Journal of Psychiatry, 168*, 158–163.

Baron-Cohen, S., & Goodhart, F. (1994). The "seeing-leads-to-knowing" deficit in autism: The Pratt and Bryant probe. *British Journal of Developmental Psychology, 12*, 397–401.

Baron-Cohen, S., Jolliffe, T., Mortimore, C., & Robertson, M. (1997). Another advanced test of theory of mind: Evidence from very high functioning adults with autism or Asperger syndrome. *Journal of Child Psychology and Psychiatry, 38*, 813–822.

Baron-Cohen, S., Leslie, A. M., & Frith, U. (1985). Does the autistic child have a "theory of mind"? *Cognition, 21*, 37–46.

Baron-Cohen, S., Ring, H., Moriarty, J., Schmitz, B., Costa, D., & Ell, P. (1994). Recognition of mental state terms: Clinical findings in children with autism and a functional neuroimaging study of normal adults. *British Journal of Psychiatry, 165*, 640–649.

Baron-Cohen, S., Spitz, A., & Cross, P. (1993). Can children with autism recognize surprise? *Cognition and Emotion, 7*, 507–516.

Baron-Cohen, S., Tager-Flusberg, H., & Cohen, D.J. (2000). *Understanding other minds: Pperspectives from developmental cognitive neuroscience*. Oxford, UK: Oxford University Press.

Bartz, J. A., & Hollander, E. (2008). Oxytocin and experimental therapeutics in autism spectrum disorders. *Progress in Brain Research, 170*, 451–462.

Bettelheim, B. (1967). *The empty fortress: Infantile autism and the birth of the self*. New York: The Free Press.

Bishop, D. V. M. (1997). Cognitive neuropsychology and developmental disorders: Uncomfortable bedfellows. *Quarterly Journal of Experimental Psychology A, 50A*, 899–923.

Blake, R., Turner, L. M., Smoski, M. J., Pozdol, S. L., & Stone, W. L. (2003). Visual recognition of biological motion is impaired in children with autism. *Psychological Science, 14*, 151–156.

Bloom, P., & German, T. (2000). Two reasons to abandon the false belief task as a test of theory of mind. *Cognition, 77*, B25–B31.

Bowler, D. M. (1992). "Theory of mind" in Asperger's syndrome. *Journal of Child Psychology and Psychiatry, 33*, 877–893.

Bretherton, I. (1991). Intentional communication and the development of mind. In D. Frye & C. Moore (Eds.), *Children's theories of mind: Mental states and social understanding* (pp. 49– 76). Hillsdale, NJ: Erlbaum.

Bushnell, I. W. R., Saï, F., & Mullin, J. T. (1989). Neonatal recognition of the mother's face. *British Journal of Developmental Psychology, 7,* 3–15.

Carlson, S. M. (2005). Developmentally sensitive measures of executive function in preschool children. *Developmental Neuropsychology, 28,* 595–616.

Carlson, S. M., Mandell, D. J., & Williams, K. (2004a). Executive function and theory of mind: Stability and prediction from ages 2 to 3. *Developmental Psychology, 40,* 1105–1122.

Carlson, S. M., & Moses, L. J. (2001). Individual differences in inhibitory control and children's theory of mind. *Child Development, 72,* 1032–1053.

Carlson, S. M., Moses, L. J., & Breton, C. (2002). How specific is the relation between executive function and theory of mind? Contributions of inhibitory control and working memory. *Infant and Child Development, 11,* 73–92.

Carlson, S. M., Moses, L. J., & Claxton, L. J. (2004b). Individual differences in executive functioning and theory of mind: An investigation of inhibitory control and planning ability. *Journal of Experimental Child Psychology, 87,* 299–319.

Carlson, S. M., Moses, L. J., & Hix, H. R. (1998). The role of inhibitory control in young children's difficulties with deception and false belief. *Child Development, 69,* 672–691.

Cassidy, K. W. (1998). Three- and 4-year-old children's ability to use desire- and belief-based reasoning. *Cognition, 66,* B1–B11.

Castelli, F., Frith, C., Happe, F., & Frith, U. (2002). Autism, Asperger syndrome and brain mechanisms for the attribution of mental states to animated shapes. *Brain, 125,* 1839–1849.

Castelli, F., Happé, F., Frith, U., & Frith, C. (2000). Movement and mind: A functional imaging study of perception and interpretation of complex intentional movement patterns. *Neuroimage, 12,* 314–325.

Celani, G. (2002). Human beings, animals and inanimate objects: What do people with autism like? *Autism, 6,* 93–102.

Charman, T., & Baron-Cohen, S. (1992). Understanding drawings and beliefs: A further test of the metarepresentation theory of autism: A research note. *Journal of Child Psychology and Psychiatry, 33,* 1105–1112.

Chawarska, K., Klin, A., & Volkmar, F. (2003). Automatic attention cueing through eye movement in 2-year-old children with autism. *Child Development, 74,* 1108–1122.

Colvert, E., Custance, D., & Swettenham, J. (2002). Rule-based reasoning and theory of mind in autism: A commentary on the work of Zelazo, Jacques, Burack, and Frye. *Infant and Child Development, 11,* 197–200.

Congiu, S., Schlottmann, A., & Ray, E. (2010). Unimpaired perception of causality, but impaired perception of animacy in high-functioning children with autism. *Journal of Autism and Developmental Disorders, 40,* 39–53.

Corkum, V., & Moore, C. (1998). The origins of joint visual attention in infants. *Developmental Psychology, 34,* 28–38.

Csibra, G., & Gergely, G. (1998). The teleological origins of mentalistic action explanations: A developmental hypothesis. *Developmental Science, 1,* 255–259.

Csibra, G., Gergely, G., Biro, S., Koos, O., & Brockbank, M. (1999). Goal attribution without agency cues: The perception of 'pure reason' in infancy. *Cognition, 72,* 237–267.

Dahlgren, S. O., & Trillingsgaard, A. (1996). Theory of mind in non-retarded children with autism and Asperger's syndrome: A research note. *Journal of Child Psychology and Psychiatry, 37,* 759–763.

Dawson, G., & Adams, A. (1984). Imitation and social responsiveness in autistic children. *Journal of Abnormal Child Psychology, 12,* 209–225.

Dawson, G., Webb, S. J., & McPartland, J. (2005). Understanding the nature of face processing impairment in autism: Insights from behavioral and electrophysiological studies. *Developmental Neuropsychology, 27,* 403–424.

Dawson, M. (2010). Oxytocin versus autism: A cure for altruism. URL (Accessed 21st February 2011). http://autismcrisis.blogspot.com/2010/02/oxytocin-versus-autism-cure-for.html

Dennett, D. C. (1978). Beliefs about beliefs. *The Behavioral and Brain Sciences, 4,* 568–570.

Dennett, D. C. (1996). *The intentional stance.* Cambridge, MA: MIT Press

de Villiers, J. (2000). Language and theory of mind: What are the developmental relationships. In S. Baron-Cohen, H. Tager-Flusberg & D. Cohen (Eds.), *Understanding other minds: Perspectives from developmental cognitive neuroscience* (2nd ed., pp. 83–123). Oxford, UK: Oxford University Press.

de Villiers, J., & de Villiers, P. (2000). Linguistic determinism and the understanding of false beliefs. In P. Mitchell & K. J. Riggs (Eds.), *Children's reasoning and the mind* (pp. 191–228). Hove, UK: Psychology Press.

Diamond, A. (2002). Normal development of prefrontal cortex from birth to young adulthood: Cognitive functions, anatomy, and biochemistry. In D. T. Stuss & R. T. Knight (Eds.), *Principles of frontal lobe function* (pp. 466–503). London: Oxford University Press.

Eisenmajer, R., & Prior, M. (1991). Cognitive linguistic correlates of "theory of mind" ability in autistic children. *British Journal of Developmental Psychology, 9,* 351–364.

Farroni, T., Csibra, G., Simion, G., & Johnson, M. H. (2002). Eye contact detection in humans from birth. *Proceedings of the National Academy of Sciences of the United States of America, 99,* 9602–9605.

Farroni, T., Mansfield, E. M., Lai, C., & Johnson, M. H. (2003). Infants perceiving and acting on the eyes: Tests of an evolutionary hypothesis. *Journal of Experimental Child Psychology, 85,* 199–212.

Fisher, N., Happé, F., & Dunn, J. (2005). The relationship between vocabulary, grammar, and false belief task performance in children with autistic spectrum disorders and children with moderate learning difficulties. *Journal of Child Psychology and Psychiatry, 46,* 409–419.

Fletcher-Watson, S., Leekam, S. R., Benson, V., Frank, M. C., & Findlay, J. M. (2009). Eye-movements reveal attention to social information in autism spectrum disorder. *Neuropsychologia, 47,* 248–257.

Frith, U. (2003). *Autism: Explaining the enigma* (2nd ed.). Oxford, England: Blackwell.

Frith, U., & Frith, C. D. (2003). Development and neurophysiology of mentalising. *Philosophical Transactions of the Royal Society of London, Series B, 358,* 459–473.

Frith, U., & Frith, C. (2010). The social brain: Allowing humans to boldly go where no other species has been. *Philos Trans R Soc Lond B Biol Sci, 365,* 165–176.

Frith, U., & Happé, F. (1999). Theory of mind and self-consciousness: What is it like to be autistic? *Mind and Language, 14,* 1–22.

Frith, U., Happé, F., & Siddons, F. (1994). Autism and theory of mind in everyday life. *Social Development, 3,* 108–124.

Frith, U., Morton, J., & Leslie, A. M. (1991). The cognitive basis of a biological disorder: Autism. *Trends in Neurosciences, 14,* 433–438.

Frye, D., Zelazo, P. D., & Palfai, T. (1995). Theory of mind and rule-based reasoning. *Cognitive Development, 10,* 483–527.

Gergely, G., & Csibra, G. (2003). Teleological reasoning in infancy: The naive theory of rational action. *Trends in Cognitive Sciences, 7,* 287–292.

Gergely, G., Nádasdy, Z., Csibra, G., & Bíró, S. (1995). Taking the intentional stance at 12 months of age. *Cognition, 56,* 165–193.

Goren, C. C., Sarty, M., & Wu, P. Y. K. (1975). Visual following and pattern discrimination of face-like stimuli by newborn infants. *Pediatrics, 56,* 544–549.

Hains, S. M., & Muir, D. W. (1996). Infant sensitivity to adult eye direction. *Child Development, 67,* 1940–1951.

Hala, S., & Russell, J. (2001). Executive control within strategic deception: A window on early cognitive development? *Journal of Experimental Child Psychology, 80,* 112–141.

Hale, C. M., & Tager-Flusberg, H. (2003). The influence of language on theory of mind: A training study. *Developmental Science, 61,* 346–359.

Happe, F. (1993). Communicative competence and theory of mind in autism: A test of Relevance Theory. *Cognition, 48,* 101–119.

Happé, F. G. E. (1994). An advanced test of theory of mind: Understanding of story characters' thoughts and feelings by able autistic, mentally handicapped, and normal children and adults. *Journal of Autism and Developmental Disorders, 24,* 129–154.

Happé, F. G. E. (1995). The role of age and verbal ability in the theory of mind task performance of subjects with autism. *Child Development, 66,* 843–855.

Happé, F., Ehlers, S., Fletcher, P., Frith, U., Johansson, M., Gillberg, C., Dolan, R., et al. (1996). "Theory of mind" in the brain. Evidence from a PET scan study of Asperger syndrome. *Neuroreport, 8,* 197–201.

Harris, P. (1996). Desires, beliefs, and language. In P. Carruthers, & P. K. Smith (Eds.), *Theories of theories of mind* (pp. 200–220). Cambridge, UK: Cambridge University Press.

Harris, P. L. (2005). Conversation, pretense, and theory of mind. In J. W. Astington & J. A. Baird (Eds.), *Why language matters for theory of mind* (pp. 70–83). Oxford, UK: Oxford University Press.

Heider, F., & Simmel, M. (1944). An experimental study of apparent behavior. *American Journal of Psychology, 57,* 243–259.

Hirschfeld, L. A., Bartmess, E., White, S., & Frith, U. (2007). Can autistic children predict behaviour by social stereotypes? *Current Biology, 17,*R451–452.

Holroyd, S., & Baron-Cohen, S. (1993). Brief report: How far can people with autism go in developing a theory of mind? *Journal of Autism and Developmental Disorders, 23,* 379–385.

Hughes, C. (1998a). Executive function in preschoolers: Links with theory of mind and verbal ability. *British Journal of Developmental Psychology, 16,* 233–253.

Hughes, C. (1998b). Finding your marbles: Does preschoolers' strategic behavior predict later understanding of mind? *Developmental Psychology, 34,* 1326–1339.

Hughes, C., & Ensor, R. (2007). Executive functions and theory of mind: Predictive relations from 2 to 4. *Developmental Psychology, 43,* 1447–1459.

Hughes, C., & Leekam, S. (2004). What are the links between theory of mind and social relations? Review, reflections and new directions for studies of typical and atypical development. *Social Development, 13,* 590–619.

Hughes, C., Soares-Boucaud, I., Hochmann, J., & Frith, U. (1997). Social behaviour in pervasive developmental disorders: Effects of informant, group and "theory of mind". *European Child and Adolescent Psychiatry, 6,* 191–198.

Jarrold, C. (2003). A review of research into pretend play in autism. *Autism, 7,* 379–390.

Johnson, M. H., Dziurawiec, S., Ellis, H., & Morton, J. (1991). Newborns' preferential tracking of face-like stimuli and its subsequent decline. *Cognition, 40,* 1–19.

Jones, C.R.G., Swettenham, J., Charman, T., Marsden, A.J.S., Tregay, J., Baird, G., Simonoff, E., Happé, F. (2011). No evidence for a fundamental visual motion processing deficit in adolescents with autism spectrum disorders. *Autism Research, 4,* 347–357.

Joseph, R. M., & Tager-Flusberg, H. (2004). The relationship of theory of mind and executive functions to symptom type and severity in children with autism. *Development and Psychopathology, 16,* 137–155.

Kaiser, M., & Shiffrar, M. (2009). The visual perception of motion by observers with ASD: A review and synthesis. *Psychonomic Bulletin & Review, 16,* 761–777.

Kanner, L. (1943). Autistic disturbances of affective contact. *Nervous Child, 2,* 217–250.

Karmiloff-Smith, A. (1998). Development itself is the key to understanding developmental disorders. *Trends in Cognitive Sciences, 2,* 389–398.

Karmiloff-Smith, A. (2009). Nativism versus neuroconstructivism: Rethinking the study of developmental disorders. *Developmental Psychology, 45,* 56–63.

Klin, A. (2000). Attributing social meaning to ambiguous visual stimuli in higher-functioning autism and Asperger syndrome: The social attribution task. *Journal of Child Psychology and Psychiatry, 41,* 831–846.

Klin, A., & Jones, W. (2006). Attributing social and physical meaning to ambiguous visual displays in individuals with higher-functioning autism spectrum disorders. *Brain and Cognition, 61,* 40–53.

Klin, A., & Jones, W. (2008). Altered face scanning and impaired recognition of biological motion in a 15-month-old infant with autism. *Developmental Science, 11,* 40–46.

Klin, A., Jones, W., Schultz, R., & Volkmar, F. (2003). The Enactive Mind – from actions to cognition: Lessons from autism. *Philosophical Transactions of the Royal Society. Biological Sciences, 358,* 345–360.

Klin, A., Jones, W., Schultz, R., Volkmar, F., & Cohen, D. (2002). Visual fixation patterns during viewing of naturalistic social situations as predictors of social competence in individuals with autism. *Arch Gen Psychiatry, 59,* 809–816.

Klin, A., Lin, D., Gorrindo, P., Ramsey, G., & Jones, W. (2009). Two-year-olds with autism orient to non-social contingencies rather than biological motion. *Nature, 459,* 257–261.

Klin, A., Volkmar, F. R., & Sparrow, S. S. (1992). Autistic social dysfunction: Some limitations of the theory of mind hypothesis. *Journal of Child Psychology and Psychiatry, 33,* 861–876.

Koldewyn, K., Whitney, D., & Rivera, S. M. (2010). Coherent motion, coherent form and biological motion perception in autism: A psychophysical study. *Brain, 133,* 599–610.

Kylliäinen, A., & Hietanen, J. K. (2004). Attention orienting by another's gaze direction in children with autism. *Journal of Child Psychology and Psychiatry, 45,* 435–444.

Leekam, S. R., Baron-Cohen, S., Perrett, D., Milders, M., & Brown, S. (1997). Eye-direction detection: A dissociation between geometric and joint attention skills in autism. *British Journal of Developmental Psychology, 15,* 77–95.

Leekam, S. R., & Perner, J. (1991). Does the autistic child have a metarepresentational deficit? *Cognition, 40,* 203–218.

Leslie, A. M. (1987). Pretense and representation: The origins of "theory of mind". *Psychological Review, 94,* 412–426.

Leslie, A. M. (1991). The theory of mind impairment in autism: Evidence for a modular mechanism of development? In A. Whiten (Ed.), *Natural theories of mind: Evolution, development and simulation of everyday mindreading* (pp. 63–78). Oxford, UK: Blackwell.

Leslie, A. M. (1994). ToMM, TOBY, and Agency: Core architecture and domain specificity. In L. A. Hirschfeld & S. A. Gelman (Eds.), *Mapping the mind: Domain specificity in cognition and culture* (pp. 119–148). Cambridge, UK: Cambridge University Press.

Leslie, A. M., & Frith, U. (1988). Autistic children's understanding of seeing, knowing and believing. *British Journal of Developmental Psychology, 6,* 315–324.

Leslie, A. M., & Keeble, S. (1987). Do six-month-old infants perceive causality? *Cognition, 25,* 265–288.

Leslie, A. M., & Polizzi, P. (1998). Inhibitory processing in the false belief task: Two conjectures. *Developmental Science, 1,* 247–253.

Leslie, A. M., & Thaiss, L. (1992). Domain specificity in conceptual development: Neuropsychological evidence from autism. *Cognition, 43,* 225–251.

Levy, S. E., Mandell, D. S., & Schultz, R. T. (2009). Autism. *Lancet, 374,* 1627–1638.

Lohmann, H., & Tomasello, M. (2003). The role of language in the development of false belief understanding: A training study. *Child Development, 74,* 1130–1144.

Luciana, M., & Nelson, C. (1998). The functional emergence of prefrontally-guided working memory systems in four- to eight-year-old children. *Neuropsychologia, 36,* 273–293.

Luria, A. R. (1966). *Higher cortical functions in man.* New York: Basic Books.

Michotte, A. E. (1963). *The perception of causality* (Tr. by T. R. Miles & E. Miles.) New York: Basic Books. (Original work published 1946)

Milligan, K., Astington, J. W., & Dack, L. A. (2007). Language and theory of mind: Meta-analysis of the relation between language ability and false-belief understanding. *Child Development, 78,* 622–646.

Mitchell, J. P., Banaji, M. R., & Macrae, C. N. (2005). General and specific contributions of the medial prefrontal cortex to knowledge about mental states. *Neuroimage, 28,* 757–762.

Moore, C., & Corkum, V. (1994). Social understanding at the end of the first year of life. *Developmental Review, 14,* 349–372.

Moses, L. J. (2001). Executive accounts of theory of mind development. *Child Development, 3,* 688–690.

Mundy, P., & Newell, L. (2007). Attention, joint attention, and social cognition. *Current Directions in Psychological Science, 5,* 269–274.

Mundy, P., & Sigman, M. (1989). Specifying the nature of the social impairment in autism. In G. Dawson (Ed.), *Autism: Nature, diagnosis and treatment* (pp. 3–21). New York: Guilford Press.

Nation, K., & Penny, S. (2008). Sensitivity to eye gaze in autism: Is it normal? Is it automatic? Is it social? *Development and Psychopathology, 20,* 79–97.

New, J. J., Schultz, R. T., Wolf, J., Niehaus, J. L., Klin, A., German, T. C., et al. (2009). The scope of social attention deficits in autism: Prioritized orienting to people and animals in static natural scenes. *Neuropsychologia, 48,* 51–59.

Nichols, K. E., Fox, N., & Mundy, P. (2005). Joint attention, self-regulation, and neurocognitive functions in toddlers. *Infancy, 7,* 35–51.

Oliver, A., Johnson, M. H., Karmiloff-Smith, A., & Pennington, B. (2000) Deviations in the emergence of representations: A neuroconstructivist framework for analysing developmental disorders. *Developmental Science, 3,* 1–23

Onishi, K. H., & Baillargeon, R. (2005). Do 15-month-old infants understand false beliefs? *Science, 308,* 255–258.

Ozonoff, S., Pennington, B. F., & Rogers, S. J. (1991). Executive function deficits in high-functioning autistic individuals: Relationship to theory of mind. *Journal of Child Psychology and Psychiatry, 32,* 1081–1105.

Pacherie, E. (1997). Motor-images, self-consciousness and autism. In J. Russell (Ed.), *Autism as an executive disorder* (pp. 215–255). Oxford, England: Oxford University Press.

Pellicano, E. (2007). Links between theory of mind and executive function in young children with autism: clues to developmental primacy. *Developmental Psychology, 43,* 974–990.

Pellicano, E. (2010). Individual differences in executive function and central coherence predict developmental changes in theory of mind in autism. *Developmental Psychology, 46,* 530–544.

Pellicano, E., & Macrae, C. N. (2009). Mutual eye-gaze enhances gender categorization for typically developing children, but not for children with autism. *Psychonomic Bulletin and Review, 19,* 1094–1099.

Pellicano, E., & Rhodes, G. (2003). The role of eye-gaze in understanding other minds. *British Journal of Developmental Psychology, 21,* 33–43.

Pelphrey, K. A., Sasson, N. J., Reznick, J. S., Paul, G., Goldman, B. D., & Piven, J. (2002). Visual scanning of faces in autism. *Journal of Autism and Developmental Disorders, 32,* 249–261.

Pennington, B. F., Rogers, S. J., Bennetto, L., McMahon, E., Reed, D. T., & Shyu, V. (1997). Validity tests of the executive dysfunction hypothesis of autism. In J. Russell (Ed.), *Autism as an executive disorder* (pp. 143–178). Oxford, England: Oxford University Press.

Pennington, B. F. (2006). From single to multiple deficit models of developmental disorders. *Cognition, 101,* 385–413.

Perner, J. (1998). The meta-intentional nature of executive functions and theory of mind. In P. Carruthers & J. Boucher (Eds.), *Language and thought: Interdisciplinary themes* (pp. 270–283). Cambridge, UK: Cambridge University Press.

Perner, J., & Lang, B. (1999). Development of theory of mind and executive control. *Trends in Cognitive Sciences, 3,* 337–344.

Perner, J., Leekam, S. R., & Wimmer, H. (1987). Three-year-olds' difficulty with false belief: The case for a conceptual deficit. *British Journal of Developmental Psychology, 5,* 125–137.

Perner, J., & Wimmer, H. (1985). "John thinks that Mary thinks that . . .": Attribution of second-order beliefs by 5- to 10-year-old children. *Journal of Experimental Child Psychology, 39,* 437–471.

Peterson, C. C., & Siegal, M. (1995). Deafness, conversation and theory of mind. *Journal of Child Psychology and Psychiatry, 36,* 459–474.

Peterson, C. C., & Siegal, M. (1999). Representing inner worlds: Theory of mind in autistic, deaf, and normal hearing children. *Psychological Science, 10,* 126–129.

Peterson, C. C., & Siegal, M. (2000) Insights into theory of mind from deafness and autism. *Mind & Language, 15,* 123–145.

Phillips, W., Baron-Cohen, S., & Rutter, M. (1998). Understanding intention in normal development and in autism. *British Journal of Developmental Psychology, 16,* 337–348.

Premack, D. (1990). The infant's theory of self-propelled objects. *Cognition, 36,* 1–16.

Premack, D., & Woodruff, G. (1978). Does the chimpanzee have a theory of mind? *Behavioral and Brain Sciences, 4,* 515–526.

Ray, E., & Schlottmann, A. (2007). The perception of social and mechanical causality in young children with autism. *Research in Autism Spectrum Disorders, 1,* 266–280.

Reed, T., & Peterson, C. (1990). A comparative study of autistic subjects' performance at two levels of visual and cognitive perspective taking. *Journal of Autism and Developmental Disorders, 20,* 555–568.

Rogers, S. (2009). What are infant siblings teaching us about autism in infancy? *Autism Research, 2,* 125–137.

Russell, J. (1996). *Agency: Its role in mental development.* Hove, England: Erlbaum.

Russell, J., Hala, S. M., & Hill, E.J. (2003). The automated windows task: Performance of preschool children, children with autism, and children with moderate learning difficulties. *Cognitive Development, 18,* 111–137.

Russell, J., Mauthner, N., Sharpe, S., & Tidswell, T. (1991). The "windows task" as a measure of strategic deception in preschoolers and autistic subjects. *British Journal of Developmental Psychology, 9,* 331–349.

Russell, J., Saltmarsh, R., & Hill, E. L. (1999). What do executive factors contribute to the failure on false belief tasks by children with autism? *Journal of Child Psychology and Psychiatry, 40,* 859–868.

Saxe, R., Carey, S., & Kanwisher, N. (2004). Understanding other minds: linking developmental psychology and functional neuroimaging *Annual Review of Psychology, 55,* 87–124.

Saxe, R., & Kanwisher, N. (2003). People thinking about thinking people. The role of the temporo-parietal junction in "theory of mind." *Neuroimage, 19,* 1835–1842.

Schlottmann, A., & Surian, L. (1999). Do 9-month-olds perceive causation-at-distance? *Perception, 28,* 1105–1113.

Schlottmann, A., Surian, L., & Ray, E. (2009). Eight- and 10-months-old infants' perceive action and reaction. *Journal of Experimental Child Psychology, 103.* 87–107.

Scholl, B. J., & Tremoulet, P. D. (2000). Perceptual animacy and causality. *Trends in Cognitive Sciences, 4,* 299–309.

Senju, A., & Csibra, G. (2008). Gaze following in human infants depends on communicative signals. *Current Biology, 18,* 668–671.

Senju, A., & Csibra, G., & Johnson, M. H. (2008). Understanding the referential nature of looking: Infants' preference for object-directed gaze. *Cognition, 108,* 303–319.

Senju, A., & Johnson, M. H. (2009). Atypical eye contact in autism: Models, mechanisms and development. *Neuroscience and Biobehavioral Reviews, 33,* 1204–1214.

Senju, A., Southgate, V., White, S., & Frith, U. (2009). Mindblind eyes: An absence of spontaneous theory of mind in Asperger syndrome. *Science, 325,* 883–885.

Senju, A., Tojo, Y., Dairoku, H., & Hasegawa, T. (2004). Reflexive orienting in response to eye gaze and an arrow in children with and without autism. *Journal of Child Psychology and Psychiatry, 45,* 445–458.

Sigman, M., Mundy, P., Sherman, T., & Ungerer, J. (1986). Social interactions of autistic, mentally retarded and normal children and their caregivers. *Journal of Child Psychology & Psychiatry, 27,* 647–655.

Simion, F., Regolin, L., & Bulf, H. (2008). A predisposition for biological motion in the newborn baby. *Proceedings of the National Academy of Science, 105,* 809–813.

Sodian, B., & Frith, U. (1992). Deception and sabotage in autistic, retarded and normal children. *Journal of Child Psychology and Psychiatry, 33,* 591–605.

Southgate, V., Senju, A., & Csibra, G. (2007). Action anticipation through attribution of false beliefs by 2-year-olds. *Psychological Science, 18,* 587–592.

Steele, S., Joseph, R. M., & Tager-Flusberg, H. (2003). Brief report: Developmental change in theory of mind abilities in children with autism. *Journal of Autism and Developmental Disorders, 33,* 461–467.

Surian, L., Caldi, S., & Sperber, D. (2007). Attribution of beliefs by 13-month-old infants. *Psychological Science, 18,* 580–586.

Tager-Flusberg, H. (1992). Autistic children's talk about psychological states: Deficits in the early acquisition of a theory of mind. *Child Development, 63,* 161–172.

Tager-Flusberg, H. (2000). Language and understanding minds: Connections in autism. In S. Baron-Cohen, H. Tager-Flusberg & D. J. Cohen (Eds.), *Understanding other minds: Perspectives from developmental cognitive neuroscience* (2nd ed., pp. 124–149). London: Oxford University Press.

Tager-Flusberg, H. (2001). A re-examination of the theory of mind hypothesis of autism. In J. A. Burack, T. Charman, N. Yirmiya, & P. R. Zelazo (Eds.), *The development of autism: Perspectives from theory and research* (pp. 173–193). Mahwah, NJ: Erlbaum.

Tager-Flusberg, H. (2007). Evaluating the theory-of-mind hypothesis of autism. *Current Directions in Psychological Science, 16,* 311–315.

Tager-Flusberg, H. (2010). The origins of social impairments in autism spectrum disorder: Studies of infants at risk. *Neural Networks, 23,* 1072–1076.

Tager-Flusberg, H., & Joseph, R. M. (2005). How language facilitates the acquisition of false-belief understanding in children with autism. In J. W. Astington & J. A. Baird (Eds.), *Why language matters for theory of mind* (pp. 298–318). Oxford, UK: Oxford University Press.

Tager–Flusberg, H., & Sullivan, K. (2000). A componential view of theory of mind: Evidence from Williams syndrome. *Cognition, 76,* 59–89.

Tan, J., & Harris, P. (1991). Autistic children understand seeing and wanting. *Development and Psychopathology, 3,* 163–174.

Tomasello, M. (1995). Joint attention as social cognition. In C. Moore & P. J. Dunham (Eds.), *Joint attention: Its origins and role in development* (pp. 103–130). Hillsdale, NJ: Erlbaum.

Tomasello, M. (2003). *Constructing a language.* Cambridge, MA: Harvard University Press.

Troje, N. F., & Westhoff, C. (2006). Inversion effect in biological motion perception: Evidence for a "life detector"? *Current Biology, 16,* 821–824.

Volkmar, F. R., Sparrow, S. S., Goudreau, D., Cicchetti, D. V., Paul, R., & Cohen, D. J. (1987). Social deficits in autism: An operational approach using the Vineland Adaptive Behavior Scales. *Journal of the American Academy of Child & Adolescent Psychiatry, 26,* 156–161.

White, S., Hill, E., Happé, F., & Frith, U. (2009). Revisiting the strange stories: Revealing mentalizing impairments in autism. *Child Development, 80,* 1097–1117.

White, S., Hill, E., Winston, J., & Frith, U. (2006). An islet of social ability in Asperger syndrome: Judging social attributes from faces. *Brain and Cognition, 61,* 69–77.

Williams, D., & Happé, F. (2010). Representing intentions in self and other: Studies of autism and typical development. *Developmental Science, 13,* 307–319.

Wimmer, H., & Perner, J. (1983). Beliefs about beliefs: Representation and constraining function of wrong beliefs in young children's understanding of deception. *Cognition, 13,* 103–128.

Woodward, A. L. (1998). Infants selectively encode the goal object of an actor's reach. *Cognition, 69,* 1–34.

Yirmiya, N., & Charman, T. (2010). The prodrome of autism: Early behavioral and biological signs, regression, peri- and post-natal development and genetics. *Journal of Child Psychology and Psychiatry, 51,* 432–458.

Zelazo, P. D., & Müller, U. (2002). The balance beam in the balance: Reflections on rules, relational complexity, and developmental processes. *Journal of Experimental Child Psychology, 81,* 458-465.

Ziatas, K., Durkin, K., & Pratt, C. (1998). Belief term development in children with autism, Asperger syndrome, specific language impairment, and normal development: Links to theory of mind development. *Journal of Child Psychology and Psychiatry, 39,* 755–763.

Zwaigenbaum, L., Bryson, S., Rogers, T., Roberts, W., Brian, J., & Szatmari, P. (2005). Behavioral manifestations of autism in the first year of life. *International Journal of Developmental Neuroscience, 23,* 143–152.

Zwickel, J., White, S., Coniston, D., Senju, A., & Frith, U. (2010). Exploring the building blocks of social cognition: Spontaneous agency perception and visual perspective taking in autism. *Social Cognitive and Affective Neuroscience,* http://dx.doi.org/10.1093/scan/nsq088.

22

Social Cognition in Real Worlds: Cultural Psychology and Social Cognition

Beth Morling & Takahiko Masuda

Imagine the following scene: an adult approaches a light fixture resting on a table. He bends at the waist and touches a nearby button with his forehead: the light illuminates, and the adult gives a satisfied nod. The 16-month-old human who witnessed this scene soon approaches the table, and though it would be simpler to push the button with her hand, she, too, illuminates the light by using her forehead (Meltzoff, 1995). Furthermore, if the adult responds to the illuminated light with a frown and an "uh oh!" (indicating that he hit the button by accident), 16-month-olds usually do not engage in any imitation (Carpenter, Akhtar, & Tomasello, 1998).

It may not be obvious how this story relates to a chapter about cultural psychology and social cognition. And yet social cognition – both its very existence and its specific manifestations – is fundamentally shaped by culture. Cultural psychology emphasizes the formative power of culture at two levels: first, as a selection pressure that shaped humans as a species; second, as a diverse set of socially transmitted operating instructions that fundamentally shape human psychological functioning. At the first level, many cultural psychologists argue that the historical selection pressures of culture have shaped *species-wide* social cognitions such as those illustrated in the opening story: a capacity for sharing the intentions of others, and imitating goal-directed actions. At the second level, cultural psychologists argue for

dramatically content-specific, culturally shaped social cognition across human social groups.

Cultural psychologists work within a theoretical framework that emphasizes the ways human beings are significantly shaped by their adaptive participation with accumulated cultural settings, products, and information (Bruner, 1990; Markus & Hamedani, 2007; Shweder, 1989). Human children are born into a real world of "already-there" cultural content. To take advantage of the power of it, human children bring evolved social cognitive abilities to the table – they must be able and willing to imitate, discern others' intent, be open to cooperation, and represent symbolically (Tomasello, 1993, 1999). Because of these species-wide adaptations, humans are able to acquire and use accumulated cultural knowledge and transmit it in a high-fidelity way (Tomasello, 1993). At the same time, these very adaptations suggest that the human species is destined to be variable. Inherited flexibility has made it possible for humans to adapt to a variety of physical settings around the earth. They develop and then socially transmit effective ways of functioning in variable worlds. In turn, the resulting diversity of cultural content shapes its users in culturally variable ways. Therefore, culture has both shaped human social cognition over phylogeny, and also shapes human social cognition during ontogeny.

In this chapter on social cognition and culture, we will be describing psychological manifestations of an evolved human reliance on cultural content. The fact of social cognition is a species-wide adaptation. However, their reliance on culture means that, by virtue of being human, people are psychologically diverse (Geertz, 1973). In the next sections, we define cultural psychology and explain other overlaps between social cognition and cultural psychology. We then outline some methods for cultural psychology and review classic and recent empirical work on culturally shaped social cognition. Finally, we reflect on the current concerns of social-cognitive cultural psychology.

WHAT MAKES A CULTURAL PSYCHOLOGIST?

Although they may not always recognize that social cognition is inherently cultural, most social cognitive psychologists are aware of the advent of the field of cultural psychology. Cultural psychology is the study of culture, mind, and increasingly, brain. Cultural psychologists study how both basic and complex psychological phenomena such as memory, attention, person perception, and self-perception are shaped by people's participation in the concrete content of particular cultural settings. In turn, cultural psychologists also study how such culturally shaped people create, amplify, or reinforce such cultural settings by acting and participating in them. Most definitions of the discipline are influenced by Shweder (1989), who described cultural psychology as the study of "...the ways subject and object, self and other, psyche and culture, person and context, figure and ground, practitioner and practice, live together, require each other, and dynamically, dialectically and jointly make each other up" (p. 73). Cultural psychologists' hypotheses are dynamic ones, about people in cultural settings.

The cultural psychological definition of culture reflects this dynamic. Culture is a dynamic pattern of socially transmitted information about how the world works. It is a set of beliefs, norms, values, procedures, and shortcuts that make effective living possible for human beings (Geertz, 1973). Humans both passively inherit and actively participate in cultural patterns, which are considered *products of action* and *conditioning elements of further action* (paraphrased from Kroeber & Kluckhohn, 1952; see Adams & Markus, 2004). This definition points to cultural psychology's goal, which is not simply to take some psychological phenomenon that has been explored in one culture, and then test to see if it "works" in another. Instead, the discipline dynamically investigates how people's psychologies are affected by

their networks of cultural meaning, and how people actively construct and transmit those networks.

CULTURAL PSYCHOLOGY: ANNOYANCE OR ALLY?

Although having cultural psychologists around could be perceived to be a nuisance, the two fields also share core theoretical perspectives.

Annoying reminders to study the unfamiliar

Cultural psychologists like to remind more mainstream psychologists that they should conduct their research on a larger variety of populations. For example, two recent cultural reviews point out that the overwhelming majority of psychology research is conducted on less than 5% of the world's population – i.e., the American part (Arnett, 2008). This matters, as one set of authors put it, because most of the participants in psychology research have been WEIRD (Henrich, Heine, & Norenzayan, 2010). That is, they are Western, Educated, Industrialized, Rich, and Democratic undergraduate students who, it turns out, act differently from the rest of the world, even in some very basic cognitive and social tasks. For example, WEIRD and non-WEIRD people perceive the length of lines very differently in the Müller–Lyer illusion (McCauley & Henrich, 2006; Segall et al., 1966). And WEIRD people categorize differently; for example, given a triad of concepts such as *carrot, eggplant,* and *rabbit,* people from WEIRD cultures typically categorize taxonomically, grouping the two vegetables together. In contrast, in many other samples studied, people categorize relationally, grouping the carrot and rabbit together. If cultural differences are this profound for seemingly "basic" cognitive processes involving asocial perception and categorization, how much more variable would social cognitive processes be?

Faced with questions like these, non-culturally oriented social cognitive psychologists could feel nagged. Social cognitive research is hard enough to do at home, much less translate, conceptualize, and conduct in other cultural contexts. But if we take cultural psychology seriously, then much of social cognitive theory is culturally specific. After all, social cognitive psychologists believe that other people matter in cognitive processing. If human social life is infused with culture, then all social cognition is cultural, too.

Social cognitive psychologists who do not consider specific cultural content are not responsibly studying human psychology. In the absence of such analysis, they might as well rename their journals, as Arnett (2008) suggests, to *Journal of Social and Personality Psychology of North Americans,* or *Social Cognition of North Americans.*

Another potential source of discomfort is the unusual language that many cultural psychologists use. Cultural psychologists study and talk about "settings," "practices," and "intersubjectivities" just as much as they study and talk about familiar psychological processes like "thoughts," "feelings," and "behaviors." The language and methods reflect the cultural psychologist's refrain: behavior is made meaningful by content outside the head, and cultural settings are made possible by meanings enacted inside the head (Bruner, 1990). Even these two distinctions (inside and outside the head) are not enough – cultural content includes broad ideas, such as theologies or philosophies; socially manufactured ecologies, such as institutions and products; and daily practices and physical settings (Markus & Kitayama, 2010; Miyamoto, Nisbett, & Masuda, 2006; Morling & Lamoreaux, 2008; Oishi & Graham, 2010). These external layers of historically derived systems of information, cooperative social practices, prescriptive norms, and shared values attempt to describe the "already there" worlds into which humans are born, and through which their psychological responses are shaped. Yet these layers may be unfamiliar to social cognitive psychologists who focus on the individual and his or her immediate social setting.

Allied focus on evolutionary processes, content-shaped cognition, and neuroscience

Despite cultural psychology's nagging reminders about non-universality and its unfamiliar discourse about settings and practices, the cultural approach is accessible to social cognitive psychologists. First of all, the fields of cultural psychology and social cognition study many of the same phenomena, such as self-regulation, attribution, stereotyping, and implicit cognition. And the two fields share more theoretical overlap than they might realize. In particular, both fields have been enriched by adopting an evolutionary perspective (e.g., Baumeister, 2005; Schaller, Norenzayan, Heine, Yamagishi, & Kameda, 2010).

In social psychology, evolutionary models have emphasized how humans have adapted to selection pressures such as mating success (Buss, 2010) and group living (Barkow, Cosmides, & Tooby, 1992). But evolutionary analyses should not be limited to passive adaptations to a historically distant African savanna. The trajectory emphasized in cultural psychology, Dual Inheritance Theory, articulates the power of culture as well as genes in shaping human development (Richerson & Boyd, 2005). According to this argument, it is not enough to explain human behavior in terms of genetically inherited responses to past environments: human societies also owe their sophistication and diversity to transmitted culture. The power of socially transmitted information is illustrated in the case of two Illinois communities who settled identical farming environments yet who have dissimilar beliefs about farm management. German-Catholic immigrants value farming as a lifestyle and hope their children will be farmers; immigrants from other American states value farming for its profit and allow their children to pursue other lifestyles (Richerson & Boyd, 2005). The social transmission of cultural values (rather than genes or a learned response to local environments) is the best explanation for these social patterns.

In cultural models of evolution, inheritance is not passive: through social transmission and participation in culture, humans actively create their own environmental niches. It is a highly adaptive process, because such cultural adaptations evolve more quickly than genes in response to challenging environments. Culture enables humans to thrive in a wide range of environments as well as to participate actively in their own evolution.

The dual inheritance perspective also specifies that species-wide social cognitive abilities such as language, theory of mind, imitation, phenotypic flexibility, the desire to share experiences, and cooperation are adaptations that help humans take advantage of a cultural world, as illustrated in this chapter's opening examples (Richerson & Boyd, 2005; Tomasello, 1999, 2009). One such adaptation is an enhanced motivation and ability to exactly *imitate* a model's behavior (e.g., the child pressed the light with her head, not her hand, imitating the model). Another is the ability to *discern the model's intent* – human children identify and imitate intentional, but ignore accidental, behaviors of a model. Other social cognitive abilities that are uniquely adapted for culture include cooperation, the motivation to teach, and the ability to represent the world using linguistic symbols (Tomasello, 1999, 2009). Arguably, these evolved (social cognitive) abilities are especially well-developed in humans. Lab-reared chimpanzees can imitate a human adult who uses a rake to drag in some attractive food. But chimpanzees also improvise: some spontaneously flip the rake so the food will not fall through the tines (Nagell, Olguin, & Tomasello, 1993). In contrast, human 2-year-olds persist in imitating the model, even though the model's technique is not the most efficient. In the short run, such imitative learning may seem maladaptive, but over time, the species who can best imitate successful models is most likely to faithfully transmit successful cultural practices, which makes possible the cumulative transmission of cultural information. People imitate other people, improve on these imitations, and then others imitate the better variations (the "ratchet effect"; Tomasello, 1993, 1999, 2009). In sum, social cognition and cultural psychology can be allies in emphasizing humans' evolved abilities as cultural creatures, and articulating the simultaneous power of genes and culture to understand the human mind.

Another similarity is that both social cognition and cultural psychology fundamentally emphasize that cognition is content-dependent. Social cognition was founded on the assumption that social cognition is not always the same as non-social cognition (Fiske & Taylor, 1991, 2008). People do not think about people in the same way that they think about non-social objects, texts, or scenes. As social cognition matured, researchers focused more on how social cognitive processes are fundamentally and pragmatically shaped by immediate goals (Fiske, 1992), social status (e.g., Barreto, Ellemers, & Fiske, 2010), and biologically prepared orientations to others of our species (Fiske & Taylor, 2008). Cultural psychology's most basic message – that the psyche's activities are shaped by (culturally) specific goals and settings – should sound familiar to social cognitive psychologists.

Finally, cultural psychologists, like social cognitive psychologists, work increasingly in the brain, exploring how cultural differences may be studied in patterns of brain activity (Ames & Fiske, 2010; Chiao & Bebko, in press; Kitayama & Uskul, 2011; Park & Huang, 2010) and in genes (e.g., H. Kim et al., 2010; see also Chapter 26). Neuroscience and genetic techniques are useful tools for both social cognition and cultural psychology. As noted later in this chapter, these techniques can potentially highlight the brain's plasticity (i.e., how cultural experience wires the brain; Park & Huang, 2010), as well as track how the human genome might have adapted as humans migrated to different world regions.

In sum, the overlap in content and theory between social cognition and cultural psychology are fundamental, and we would argue, not normally acknowledged by either side.

RESEARCH METHODS CAN CAPTURE CULTURAL PROCESSES

Cultural psychology pays unique methodological attention to the process of *mutual constitution* – how the culturally-shaped mind shapes cultural content (Shweder, 1989). Social cognitive psychologists, too, have studied how individuals and collectives shape external norms and behaviors (Hogg, 2010; Klein & Snyder, 2003; Sherif, 1935). But cultural psychologists may be more intentional about capturing the full circle of mutual constitution (Cohen, 2007). For example, cultural psychologists often study tangible cultural products and situations. They find, for example, that cultural products such as children's books, magazine ads, and religious texts from East Asia tend to represent more collectivism, and less individualism, than cultural products from North America (Morling & Lamoreaux, 2008). Cultural products studies strive to fit the Shwederian tradition of "mutual constitution."

Cultural psychologists have also measured how people actively produce (or "constitute") cultural settings and products. In choosing which stories or details to model, copy, or share, people participate in shaping the content of culture. For example, one study demonstrated that television and newspaper accounts of Olympic Games athletes were culturally different, focusing on the advice or support of others in Japan and personal characteristics in the United States. Later, the authors asked people in each culture to select appropriate media statements originating in the two countries. Americans preferred to report statements about athletes' personal attributes and unique characteristics, whereas Japanese preferred to report statements about the athletes' coaches, teams, motivation, emotion, and doubts (Markus, Uchida, Omoregie, Townsend, & Kitayama, 2006). Americans and Japanese who are put in the position of (re)creating cultural products produced stories that replicated the cultural settings.

Another method for studying mutual constitution hypotheses is situation sampling (e.g., Kitayama, Markus, Matsumoto, & Norasakkunkit, 1998; Morling, Kitayama, & Miyamoto, 2002). As exemplified in a classic study on self-esteem (Kitayama et al., 1997), the situation sampling method consists of two phases. First, participants (in this case, students from Japan and the United States) described a number of concrete situations in which they experienced success or failure – i.e., self-esteem relevant situations. Second, both American and Japanese participants reported how they would feel in both American and Japanese situations.

By analyzing the situations in the first step, researchers established that Americans listed more self-esteem-increasing situations, whereas Japanese listed more self-esteem-decreasing situations. The second step assessed both cultural people and cultural situations. For example, Americans reported an increase in self-esteem compared to Japanese in both countries' success situations, whereas Japanese reported a decrease in self-esteem compared to Americans in both countries' failure situations. In addition, the cultural origin of each situation mattered. Both American and Japanese participants judged that their self-esteem would decrease relatively more in the "made in Japan" situations and that their self-esteem would increase relatively more in the "made in the US" situations. The findings suggest that American social realities afford self-boosting experiences, whereas Japanese social realities afford self-critical experiences. The method captures the mutual interaction of situations and ontogenetically developed psychological processes (for other examples, see Morling et al., 2002; Savani, Morris, Naidu, Kumar, & Berlia, 2011).

Through developing tools to measure "persons in cultural settings," cultural psychologists have attempted to combine the sophistication of quantitative psychological measurement with the descriptive ideals of ethnography.

SOCIAL COGNITION IN CULTURAL CONTEXT

Research in cultural social cognition is organized by two major interpretive themes:

- cultural self-construals, which are independent or interdependent, organize a variety of research on cognition and emotion (Markus & Kitayama, 1991, 2010).
- the rubric of "analytic vs holistic" world views organizes research on human cognitive and perceptual processes (Nisbett, 2003; Nisbett & Masuda, 2003; Nisbett, Peng, Choi, & Norenzayan, 2001).

These two themes, together, explain a variety of social cognitive phenomena.

Cultural self-construals

Markus and Kitayama (1991) describe two collective understandings of the self that differ across cultures, by now widely recognized as independent and interdependent self-construals.

Independent cultural contexts (emphasized in middle-class European-American settings) foster a view of the self as separate from others, who acts independently and, ideally, consistently from situation to situation. The independent self may be a modern cultural product, historically developed in Western intellectual traditions (Taylor, 2007). When this view of self is intersubjectively shared, people may actively look for attributes they are proud of, establish personal preferences and unique characteristics, and value self-consistency. In contrast, interdependent cultural contexts (emphasized in middle-class Asian and Asian-American contexts, and possibly African and South American settings) foster a view of the self as significantly shaped by others, in which agency is conjoined with and attuned to close others (Markus & Kitayama, 1991, 2010). When this view of self is intersubjectively shared, people emphasize the expectations of significant others, correct imperfect and insufficient aspects of the self, and flexibly adapt themselves to the context.

A pattern of diverse research in social cognition, motivation, and emotion has supported Markus and Kitayama's (1991, 2010) self-construal model. When asked to define themselves in an abstract context, North Americans describe themselves using abstract personal attributes, whereas East Asians describe themselves based on social categories and roles (Bond & Cheung, 1983; Cousins, 1989; Rhee, Uleman, Lee, & Roman, 1995). When asked to define themselves across concrete contexts (e.g., home, school, or work), Japanese flexibly change patterns of reference, whereas North Americans tend to keep consistent references across contexts (Kanagawa, Cross, & Markus, 2001). North Americans are more motivated by self-consistency than East Europeans (Cialdini, Wosinska, Barrett, Butner, & Gornik-Durose, 1999), and compared to Hong Kong Chinese, who incorporate the views of close others into their self-concept, North American self-concepts seem immune to the criticism of others (Kim, Cohen, & Au, 2010). North Americans report undiluted emotions, which are experienced as individual events, whereas East Asians experience more mixed emotions, which are experienced as shared events (Uchida & Kitayama, 2009; Uchida, Townsend, Markus, & Bergsieker, 2009). The emotions of European-Americans become more intense when they are reminded of the self, whereas the emotions of Asian-Americans intensify in situations when the social group is salient (Chentsova-Dutton & Tsai, 2010). North Americans have higher self-esteem than non-Western individuals (Heine, Lehman, Markus, & Kitayama, 1999). North Americans remember their success experiences more than Japanese (Endo & Meijer, 2004) and are motivated to re-engage in a task they are good at, whereas Japanese are motivated to re-engage in a task they are bad at (Heine et al., 2001). North Americans tend to believe that their talent and ability is fixed, whereas Chinese and Japanese tend to believe that their ability is changed by their effort (Azuma, 1994; Stevenson & Stigler, 1992); such beliefs are even encoded in graduation cards (Choi & Ross, 2011). North Americans tend to hold promotion-oriented motivation, whereas Hong Kong Chinese and Japanese tend to hold prevention-oriented motivation (Hamamura, Meijer, Heine, Kamaya, & Hori, 2009; Lee, Aaker, & Gardner, 2000). American political candidates whose photos are judged higher in power (perhaps reflecting independent agency) tend to be elected, whereas Japanese candidates judged higher in warmth (perhaps reflecting interpersonal harmony) tended to be elected (Rule et al., 2010). North Americans report more, and more extreme, instances of influencing the environment (i.e., primary control), whereas Japanese report more, and more extreme, instances of adjustment to the environment (i.e., secondary control; Morling & Evered, 2006; Morling, Kitayama, & Miyamoto, 2002; Weisz, Rothbaum, & Blackburn, 1984). North Americans are more likely than Koreans to express uniqueness (Kim & Markus, 1999). North Americans tend to experience socially disengaged emotions, whereas Japanese tend to experience socially engaged emotions (Kitayama, Markus, & Kurokawa, 2000; Kitayama, Mesquita, & Karasawa, 2006). Self-esteem is strongly associated with North Americans' well-being, whereas the association is weaker outside of North America (Diener & Diener, 1995; Uchida, Kitayama, Mesquita, Reyes, & Morling, 2008). Asian-Americans and Japanese feel a higher life satisfaction when they meet significant others' expectations, compared to when they meet their personal goals (Oishi & Diener, 2003). Focus on others' approval manifests in Asian-American relative preference for name-brand products (Kim & Drolet, 2009). Taken together, most of these cross-cultural research findings can be interpreted as consistent with a culturally held model of self as relatively independent in North America, and relatively interdependent in many other world regions.

Analytic and holistic systems of thought

The dimension of analytic and holistic thought also has explanatory power to interpret and organize a diverse range of cross-cultural differences in social cognition and basic perception (e.g.,

Nisbett, 2003; Nisbett et al., 2001). Psychologists and anthropologists have long questioned the universality of basic human perceptual processes (e.g. Bruner, 1990; Witkin, 1967). The research builds on this tradition, placing emphasis on the role of cultural world views in shaping people's fundamental cognitive and perceptual processes.

According to Nisbett, analytic thinking is characterized by a focus on objects and their attributes. In this view, objects and people are perceived as existing independently from their contexts. Analytic thinkers focus on the attributes that make up the object or person. To categorize things, analytic thinkers focus on the common attributes among objects and persons. To better predict and explain a given phenomenon, analytic thinkers use a set of fixed, abstract rules. In contrast, holistic thinking is characterized by an orientation to the context as a whole. It is a relational way of thinking, where one's attention goes not only to a particular target object and person but also to the relations among the target and the surrounding context. Formal, abstract rules are less important; people rely on case-by-case experiences.

These organized world views have both economic and social origins. Nisbett and his colleagues maintain that these different cultural patterns were distally rooted to available resources in the physical environment and to economic practices that used those resources. Once such patterns of behavior are institutionalized in a given culture, they may become self-sustaining across generations, as the culture's way of understanding the world is socially transmitted (Nisbett, 2003; Nisbett et al., 2001). For example, recent evidence suggests that Turkish fishermen, farmers, and cattlemen differ in their tendency to use holistic and analytic reasoning (Uskul, Kitayama, & Nisbett, 2008). Their reasoning styles, in part, reflect social practices: communal fishing and farming practices seem to foster holistic thinking; solitary herding practices seem to foster analytic thinking. These economic practices were, in turn, fostered by different local resources and geographies. Again, differences in real worlds help explain and maintain differences in social cognition.

Nisbett (2003) maintains that the cultural variations in cognition observable in contemporary members of Western and East Asian cultures are attributable in part to ancient Greek and ancient Chinese civilizations (which, in turn, may have resonated with their own contemporary economic or social practices). Greek, specifically Aristotelian philosophies teach that things fundamentally exist independently and the characteristics of an object are determined by the object's internal attributes. By contrast, Buddhism, Confucianism, and Taoism in China emphasize the holistic nature of things.

Such a holistic understanding of the world became the foundation of a discourse shared by members of East Asian culture such as China, Korea, and Japan, which affords attention to relationships between objects and their contexts.

These historical philosophical influences manifest themselves in an impressive variety of contemporary cross-cultural research on causal attribution, categorization, and judgment about social and physical events. North Americans are more likely to explain an event by referring to internal factors of a target individual; Chinese and Indians pay more attention to the external factors which surround the target (Lee, Hallahan, & Herzog, 1996; Miller, 1984; Morris & Peng, 1994). East Asians are more likely to refer to field information when they explain physical events (Peng & Knowles, 2003). North Americans explain causes of an event by referring to small pieces of information, whereas East Asians refer to peripherally important causes (Choi, Dalal, Kim-Prieto, & Park, 2003), and Canadians equate the size of a cause to the size of the event more so than Chinese (Spina et al., 2010). When categorizing things, North American judgments are based on common attributes, whereas East Asians rely on holistic similarity (Norenzayan, Smith, Kim, & Nisbett, 2002), and relationality (Ji, Peng, & Nisbett, 2000). East Asians are more likely than North Americans to accept contradictions (Choi & Choi, 2002; Koo & Choi, 2005; Peng & Nisbett, 1999; Spencer-Rodgers & Peng, 2004). East Asians are more likely than their North American counterparts to think that even a seemingly stable trend of an event can be reverted (Ji, 2008; Ji, Nisbett, & Su, 2001). Dialectism leads East Asian students to change self-views, rather than self-verify, when feedback is self-discrepant (Spencer-Rodgers, Boucher, Peng, & Wang, 2009).

Such differences in social and non-social cognition are enabled by patterns of attention. For example, Masuda and Nisbett (2001) presented 20-second animated vignettes of underwater scenes to Japanese and American participants. After seeing each video twice, participants were asked to report what they had seen. In their first comments, Americans tended to spotlight the most important scene: "I saw three fish swimming around, one of which had red fins," whereas Japanese tended to refer to the background: "It looks like a deep sea because the water color was much darker than the previous video." Overall, Japanese made more observations about the fields and about relationships between objects and the fields than did Americans. In another experiment, Masuda and Nisbett showed participants images of wildlife, followed by a surprise recall test. In the test, some images showed previously seen wildlife with the original background. Other images showed a previously seen wildlife with a novel background. Although both Japanese and Americans could accurately remember images in their original setting, Japanese were less able to remember the target wildlife with a novel background. The results suggest that Japanese are inclined to memorize the target wildlife by binding it to its scenery. Indeed, eye-tracking data suggest that East Asians alternate their attention to figure and ground more frequently than Americans (Goh, Tan, & Park, 2009).

Analytic and holistic patterns of attention generalize to non-social, abstract images (Ji et al., 2000; Kitayama, Duffy, Kawamura, & Lawson, 2003), as well as to social stimuli. If social experiences are the foundation of the development of attentional patterns, then culturally shaped attention should be intensified when participants observe more social stimuli. Masuda et al. tested this hypothesis by asking Japanese and North Americans to judge the emotions of a target individual who was surrounded by four others (Masuda, Ellsworth, Mesquita, Leu, Tanida, & van de Veerdonk, 2008). In some scenes, the target and the background figures showed congruent facial expressions (e.g., happy target and happy others); other scenes showed incongruent facial expressions (e.g., happy target and sad others). Americans judged the target person's emotion the same in both conditions. However, the Japanese ratings of the emotion were intensified when targets were presented with congruent others than with incongruent others. Eye-tracking data suggested that Japanese allocated their attention to the background figures more often than Americans.

Analytic and holistic cultural patterns are not only carried in individual processes; dominant cultural resources such as artistic conventions also convey analytic or holistic themes to the same and next generation (e.g. Masuda, Gonzalez, Kwan, & Nisbett, 2008). Children may develop analytic or holistic cultural patterns around age 6, perhaps by being exposed to such cultural resources (Duffy, Toriyama, Itakura, & Kitayama, 2009). Therefore, cultural patterns are sustained and carried by cultural products as well as those products' creators (Morling & Lamoreaux, 2008; Richerson & Boyd, 2005; Tomasello, 1999).

Self-construals and systems of thought working together

The independent/interdependent and analytic/holistic dimensions have, to some extent, qualitatively different logic (Spencer-Rodgers & Peng, 2004). However, many researchers find that both forces, used together, can help explain cultural phenomena. Recent evidence suggests that, at the cultural level at least, interdependent social orientation is associated with holistic cognitive styles, and independent social orientation is associated with analytic cognitive styles (Varnum, Grossmann, Kitayama, & Nisbett, 2010). Next we review three concrete examples: the fundamental attribution error, self-awareness, and social influence.

The fundamental attribution error across cultures

The fundamental attribution error, or correspondence bias, describes how people infer that others' observed behavior was produced by some internal disposition, failing to take into account pertinent contextual information (Nisbett & Ross, 1980). Although robust among North Americans (Henrich et al., 2010), this phenomenon does not work the same in cultural contexts that foster holism and interdependence. The correspondence bias is weaker for Koreans and Japanese than for Americans when the social constraint is made salient (Choi & Nisbett, 1998), when the stimulus essays were made less persuasive (Miyamoto & Kitayama, 2002), and when the perceiver is the inducer of the external constraint (Masuda & Kitayama, 2004). Taken together, these results suggest that East Asians show the correspondence bias under Jones and Harris's (1967) original paradigm, but, unlike Americans, when social constraints are made salient, the effect is weakened (Choi, Nisbett, & Norenzayan, 1999).

Why are East Asians less susceptible than North Americans to this bias? Some researchers maintain that the holistic world view shared by East Asians fosters a greater degree of context sensitivity (Norenzayan, Choi, & Nisbett, 2002). For example, East Asians are more likely than North Americans to change their behavior according to a given situation and are also more likely to believe that people's personalities can be changed (presumably in response to changing life settings or contexts). Tolerance for contradiction can mean that East Asians view their in-groups more ambivalently (Ma-Kellams, Spencer-Rodgers, & Peng, 2011). Similarly, Australians are more likely than Asians to expect attitude–behavior consistency in others (Kashima, Siegal, Tanaka, & Kashima, 1992). In addition to dominant thinking styles, social interdependence and harmony concerns can also explain attributional patterns. After reading a fictional dilemma in which a person disagreed with his respected boss, 87% of Americans thought that the protagonist should attempt to change his boss's opinion, whereas 53% of Japanese thought so (Iwao, 1997). By contrast,

23% of Japanese would have shown a smile and not argued, compared to only 6% of Americans. Thus, many East Asian contexts may foster, or even promote, inconsistency between attitudes and behavior, as a way of maintaining interpersonal harmony.

East Asians' weak motivation to maintain attitude–behavior consistency is also expressed in self-consistency. The foot-in-the door phenomenon (Freedman & Fraser, 1966) and cognitive-dissonance theory (Festinger, 1957) are examples of people's motivation to maintain their self-consistency. However, Japanese show weaker cognitive dissonance than North Americans (Heine & Lehman, 1997). Japanese show dissonance effects mainly when the setting evokes the concerns of the public self, such as in front of an incidental poster of schematic drawings of human eyes (Imada & Kitayama, 2010; Kitayama, Snibbe, Markus, & Suzuki, 2004).

These examples of attitude–behavior consistency, manifested in the fundamental attribution error as well as cognitive dissonance, illustrate how self-construals and reasoning styles might interact at the cultural level. Interdependent construals engage people to pay attention to the external factors that surround and influence a target individual. As Markus and Kitayama (1991) write, "If one perceives oneself as embedded within a large context of which one is an interdependent part, it is likely that other objects or events will be perceived in a similar way" (p. 246). Attention to context also resonates with a holistic understanding of the world in which "everything in the world is related to each other" and no single element can be logically viewed as acting independent of anything else. By contrast, independent self-construals encourage people to think that peoples' behavior emerges based on their internal intention, goals, attitudes, or traits – not other people. In addition, this understanding of others resonates with the analytic way of thinking, which maintains that "things exist independent from their context," so single elements may be viewed without acknowledging anything else. Such similarities in understanding are probably not coincidental. Rather, these understandings of the world could be historically interwoven in a given culture (see Varnum et al., 2010).

More immediate cultural tools can supplement self-construals and systems of thought as explanations for the fundamental attribution error. Specifically, different language patterns shape people's attributions and descriptions (Holtgraves & Kashima, 2008). For example, Korean speakers are more likely to use verbs and English speakers more likely to use adjectives when describing themselves and others (Kashima, Kashima, Kim, & Gelfand, 2006). Verbs tend to emphasize situational factors; adjectives emphasize personal factors. In this sense, language use is an example of mutual constitution. Pragmatically, language reflects people's habitual ways of thinking about people, but cultural schemas appear to shape people's language patterns, too (Morris & Mok, 2011; Na & Choi, 2009). Syntactically, dominant language structures (verbs vs adjectives) are able to communicate those ways of thinking to others (Holtgraves & Kashima, 2009). Another example is human-made physical settings (specifically, urban and suburban cityscapes), which are more visually complex in Japan than North America (Miyamoto et al., 2006). Exposure to the more complex cities and towns of Japan make people more holistic in attention than exposure to North American towns. Both language and human-made physical settings are created by culturally shaped humans, but in turn they influence human perception and cognition.

Self-awareness across cultures

Cross-cultural research on subjective self-awareness is a second example of how the two dimensions, analytic vs holistic thought and independent vs interdependent self-construals, can work together. When people recall their own experience subjectively, as if they were the actor in the event, their memory is identical to what they saw at the time. But people can also imagine the same scene, including themselves, objectively, from the third-person point of view. Cohen and Gunz (2002) examined systematic variations in the perspective typically taken by East Asians and North Americans by asking them to report their memories for exciting experiences. The results indicated that Asian-Canadians tended to report the event from the third-person perspective, whereas European-Canadians reported from the first-person perspective (see also Leung & Cohen, 2007; Y. Kim et al., 2010). Perspective taking also shapes ongoing events. Cohen and Hoshino-Browne (2005) asked Asian-Canadian and European-Canadian participants to tap out a tune (such as "Happy Birthday") on the table for another participant. They asked participants to estimate how difficult it was for the listener to identify the target song. European-Canadians were overconfident about their guesses compared to Asian-Canadians, arguably because from their own first-person perspective the task is fairly easy. In contrast, Asian-Canadians, who are likely to apply the third-person perspective, can more accurately guess the constraints on the listener (Cohen & Hoshino-Browne, 2005).

We speculate that both self-construals and styles of thought work together to foster first- or third-person perspectives. The independent self-construal encourages people in the idea that they are the center of their social world. By contrast, the interdependent self-construal encourages people to see themselves as part of a larger social context, and not necessarily at the middle of it. Taking the third-person perspective is a strategy for people to see themselves from others' eyes in a given context. In addition, holistic thinkers attend to the relations within a whole event, so they apply the same context-embedded perspective towards themselves. By contrast, if analytic thinkers attend to focal events while ignoring peripheral influences, they may see themselves as a spectator who holds a single, stable viewpoint. In fact, self-construal and styles of thought may have co-evolved over time, mutually influencing each other. Art historians have argued that the development of individualism and the emergence of single-spectator point of view emerged at around the same time (e.g., Giedion, 1964; for another review, see Varnum et al., 2010).

Social influence across cultures

Recent social influence research provides an example of how self-construal models might cause analytic and holistic reasoning in a goal-focused setting. People in interdependent cultural settings tend to adjust themselves to their surroundings, whereas people in independent cultural settings tend to emphasize influencing their surroundings (e.g. Morling et al., 2002; Savani et al., 2011). Adjustment and influence strategies are well adapted to interdependent and independent contexts, respectively; however, these strategies may require or foster holistic and analytic perceptual skills, at least in some cultures. In a recent experiment (Miyamoto & Wilken, 2010), Americans and Japanese were randomly assigned to be either a leader (influence condition) or a matcher (adjustment condition) in a communication game; the leader described 12 abstract figures to the matcher, so that they could put their cards in the same order. In a later task (a modified rod-and-frame task), Americans assigned to the leader's role had better analytic skills. (Japanese performance was not affected by the manipulations.) Apparently, in the North American cultural setting, social influence goals highlight analytic perceptual skills. In related research, Americans who were asked to recall situations in which they had influenced surrounding others tended to show analytic patterns of cognition during a later task, whereas those who were asked to recall situations in which they had adjusted to surrounding others tended to show holistic patterns of attention (Miyamoto & Ji, 2010).

In sum, a variety of classic and recent research in cultural psychology shows the influence of two dimensions – interdependence and holistic perception and independence and analytic perception. These patterns work together to explain cultural differences in the fundamental attribution error, self-perception, and social influence.

CURRENT THEMES IN CULTURAL PSYCHOLOGY

A reading of the most current literature in cultural psychology suggests three trends in cultural psychology that are likely to shape its intersection with social cognition in future years. The first trend explores the degree to which a "cultural self-concept" can explain differences in cultural behavior. The second trend is the emerging field of cultural neuroscience. The third trend reflects recent research on how cultural meaning systems develop. We devote more space to the first trend here, because the other two have been recently and thoroughly reviewed in other venues.

Is there a "cultural self" stored inside the head?

In this section, we review several recent commentaries that have focused on how cultural differences – especially in the self – should properly be conceived and measured (Chiu et al., 2010; Kashima, 2009; Zou et al., 2009). As outlined earlier, cultures are proposed to differ in their dominant models of the self as either independent or interdependent (Markus & Kitayama, 1991). For the last 20 years, much of cultural psychology research has been conducted in light of that classic paper on culture and the self. The two authors carefully specified that cultural approaches to self-concept are encoded, afforded, constituted in cultural *settings*. But as research tested its hypotheses, much research attempted to locate these cultural differences inside the head – as an internalized self-*concept* that is either "independent" or "interdependent." For example, some researchers used self-report questionnaires to measure cultural differences, asking about private beliefs, values, or attitudes about the self (e.g., "I enjoy being unique and different from others in many respects" or "It is important to me to respect the decisions made by the group," Singelis, 1994; Triandis, 1996; Triandis, Bontempo, Leung, & Hui, 1990). Researchers have used these scales to test hypotheses derived from (but, notably, not stated by) Markus and Kitayama's paper. For instance, many have hypothesized that Asians and European-Americans should differently endorse independent or individualistic self-concept items.

Similarly, some have argued that cultural differences in psychological phenomena (such as conformity, attributional style, or cognitive style) will be mediated by self-concept differences on such measures (e.g., Singelis, Bond, Sharkey, & Lai, 1999). It seems possible that the study of self-construal as self-*concept* was influenced by the schema model in social cognition, which was dominant at that time (e.g., Fiske & Taylor, 1991).

However, data have not provided strong support for this simple prediction. First, sometimes the predicted cultural differences are obtained on these self-concept scales (Oyserman, Coon, & Kemmelmeier, 2002), but sometimes – perhaps more often – not (Chiu et al., 2010; Kitayama, Park, Sevincer, Karasawa, & Uskul, 2009; Matsumoto, 1999; Oyserman et al., 2002; Takano & Osaka, 1999). Second, sometimes cultural psychological phenomena (such as cultural differences in attribution or cultural differences in motivational patterns) are mediated by self-concept measures (Chiao et al. 2009; Lam & Zane, 2004; Na & Kitayama, 2010), other times not. And in some studies, separate aspects of self-concept, such as dispositional attributions, holistic attention, or socially engaged emotions, may not co-occur within a sample of individuals. Correlations among such separate psychological phenomena are sometimes only 0.10 or so within a cultural sample (Kitayama et al., 2009; Na, Grossmann, Varnum, Kitayama, Gonzalez, & Nisbett, 2010).

Some cultural researchers have responded to these findings by addressing methodological problems behind self-report scales – issues such as reference group effects (Heine, Lehman, Peng, & Greenholtz, 2002), response styles (Schimmack, Oishi, & Diener, 2005), and the fact that cultural differences in cultural products are larger than cultural differences in self-reports (Morling & Lamoreaux, 2008). But increasingly, some cultural researchers are disengaging from the search for a cultural self. These cultural psychologists are empirically documenting the idea that cultural differences in independence and interdependence may not be represented by a coherent and internalized "self-concept" stored in the head. There are two aspects of this argument, the "intersubjective culture" model and the "semiotic culture" model.

Intersubjective culture: Culture as common sense

The intersubjective culture or "culture as common sense" argument, outlined by Chiu, Gelfand, Zou, Wan, Morris, Yamagishi, and their colleagues (e.g., Chiu et al., 2010; Wan et al., 2007; Wan, Tam, & Chiu, 2010; Yamagishi, Hashimoto, & Schug, 2008; Zou et al., 2009) has three premises

(Chiu et al., 2010). First, people do not always act according to their internal beliefs and values; instead, they sometimes act according to values and beliefs that they think are common in their culture (Zou et al., 2009). Second, although cultures differ, people do not simply internalize their own culture's norms and influences. People actively negotiate with culture, internalizing some values, ignoring others, attempting to change others (see Sperber, 1996). Third, there can be a mismatch between widespread beliefs and values of a culture and the individual beliefs and values of people living in that culture (Wan et al., 2007).

Chiu and colleagues propose that what may matter in understanding cultural differences in behavior is not what individual members of a culture *personally* believe and value. Instead, what matters is what individuals think *most others* in their culture believe and value. In one study, Zou et al. (2009) empirically demonstrated the first premise of the intersubjective approach. First, they found cultural differences in compliance. Whereas Poles reported being more likely to complete a marketing survey if their peers had (or had not) agreed, North Americans reported being more likely to complete the marketing survey if they had (or had not) usually completed such surveys in the past. The result replicated a past study finding that Poles were more influenced by peers, and North Americans more by consistency concerns (Cialdini et al., 1999). In addition to measuring compliance differences, Zou et al. asked both samples to complete two measures of collectivism: one at a personal level (e.g., how positive participants *personally* thought it was to consult one's family before making an important decision) and one at a collective, or intersubjective level (e.g., how frequent they thought it was *in their country* for people to consult their family before making an important decision). The results for the collectivism measures were twofold. First, there were significant cultural differences in the intersubjective measure (with Poles reporting higher perceived levels of their countrymates' collectivism) but not the measure of personal beliefs (replicating past work by Wan et al., 2007). Second, the intersubjective measure of collectivism (but not the personal measure) mediated the cultural difference in compliance. In three other studies, intersubjective, but not personal, beliefs mediated cultural differences in internal attributions and avoidant regulatory focus. In sum, observed cultural differences in social cognitive behaviors may not be attributable to some coherent *self*-concept stored inside the head. Instead, such behaviors seem to be better explained by the people's concept of what *others* in their culture believe (see Figure 22.1).

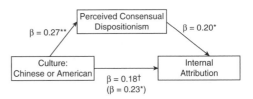

Figure 22.1   Sample result from Zou et al. (2009). People's beliefs about their others' dispositionism, but not their personal beliefs about dispositionism, mediated cultural differences in attributional style. †p<.1; *p<.05; **p .01. (Reproduced with permission from Zou et al., 2009.)

Self as interpretive category

Another version of the argument that cultures are not simply stored in individuals' heads has been articulated by Kashima (2009), who contrasted two possible views of cultural psychology. One he called the "standard model," which proposes that (a) there are culturally different *selves* and (b) these selves *cause* different processes such as attributional reasoning, emotion processing, or compliance. In the standard model, a domain-general psychological construct (such as an interdependent or individualistic "self") exists within people to different degrees depending on the cultural context. In addition, there are cultural differences in several domain-specific constructs (such as attributional styles, holistic or analytic reasoning, compliance, or counterfactual thinking) which are linked to culturally specific demands and tasks. In the standard model, the domain-specific constructs are causally linked to the higher-level construct (such as the independent or interdependent "self").

In contrast, Kashima endorses a semiotic, or interpretive view. In this view, there are still domain-specific psychological constructs which develop as people participate in different cultural tasks such as attending particular schools, using conversational norms, or following particular scripts. And as in the standard model, these domain-specific constructs are distributed differently across cultures (e.g., people in North American cultures are more likely to make dispositional attributions and place blame on individuals rather than groups, whereas people in East Asian contexts are more likely to make situational attributions or place blame on groups rather than individuals). However, participation in cultural tasks does not lead to the development or internalization of a domain-general self. Instead, the domain-general construct emerges simply as an *interpretation* – a meaningful, parsimonious, and accurate interpretation that an observer makes about the distribution of domain-specific constructs in a culture. These *interpretive constructs* help researchers accurately understand and communicate about the particular distribution of domain-specific constructs in a culture. But the domain-general constructs are not internalized inside of people's heads as "selves," and they are not causally linked to domain-specific constructs (see Figure 22.2 for an illustration of the two models).

Kashima's semiotic model is similar to distributed cognitive processing models. It explains why empirical measures of self-concept as independent or interdependent do not always mediate cultural differences in behavior and cognition (when they should, if an independent or interdependent "self" is something that is stored inside people's heads and explains cultural behavior). It also explains why, though there are cultural differences in several domain-specific constructs, these constructs do not always correlate with each other at the individual level of analysis (Kitayama et al., 2009; Na et al., 2010). Culturally specific tasks and settings prompt psychological adaptations that are situational and fragmented. Patterns across individuals make sense when the interpretive frame of independence or interdependence is applied. However, this interpretive frame does not

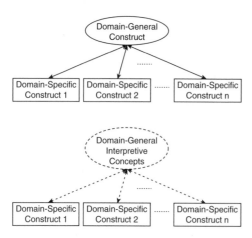

Figure 22.2 Schematic representation of the standard reading (upper panel) and a semiotic reading (lower panel) of the psychological theories of cultural differences. Note: Solid lines indicate *causal links*, with their bibirectional arrows indicating their bidirectional causal relationships. Broken lines indicate *interpretive links*, with their arrowheads indicating an interpretation. (Reproduced with permission from Kashmina, 2009.)

have to be stored inside people's heads in order to be accurate. Individual people may engage to different degrees with different combinations of cultural tasks (Sperber, 1996), so people do not internally replicate the entire cultural pattern of domain-specific constructs. Therefore, within a culture, correlations between domain-specific constructs may be low, even when such correlations across a set of cultures may be high.

In sum, these two important, emerging perspectives are data-driven, complementary responses that question the empirically undersupported view that self-concepts are stored inside the head and have causal explanatory power for cultural differences. (See Kitayama et al., 2009, for a related explanation about why explicit self-concepts do not correlate with domain-specific cultural "tasks.")

Cultural and institutional primes

The intersubjective culture and semiotic models of self provide a lens through which to view recent cultural social cognition studies that have demonstrated "cultural priming" effects. For example, one model of multiculturalism proposed that people with deep experience in two cultures develop two different cultural frames with which to view the world (Hong, Morris, Chiu, & Benet-Martinez, 2000). These frames might be differently active depending on local situation cues and contexts, and they shape how people view the world at that moment. For example, when bicultural Hong Kong Chinese students were exposed to classic American symbols such as the Statue of Liberty, they gave more dispositional answers in an attribution task, but when exposed to classic Chinese symbols such as the Great Wall, they gave more situational answers in the attribution task. Hong et al.'s model (2000) used the language of "frames" or "cultural knowledge structures" to explain how people organize their experiences in two distinct cultures. These knowledge structures may be activated when related concepts, such as flags or symbols, are presented to bicultural people.

Since then, other researchers have demonstrated that cultural primes (e.g., primes for an individual vs a group orientation) can work even among people who are not bicultural, even European-Americans who have never lived abroad. For example, American students who had been primed by circling pronouns that were predominantly self-focused (e.g., "I" or "me") rather than group-focused (e.g., "we" and "us") performed better at an embedded figures task (Kühnen et al., 2001). Dozens of such priming studies have been conducted in the past 10 years. For most tasks, the primes worked similarly in both Western and East Asian samples (Oyserman & Lee, 2008).

Because of these data, Oyserman and colleagues (Oyserman & Lee, 2007, 2008) argue that people in all cultures have access to multifaceted, internalized "mindsets" that may even be contradictory (Oyserman & Sorenson, 2009). According to the model, the commonly observed cultural differences in psychological processes in most studies (such as attributional styles or focus on figure vs ground) can be explained by different relative distributions of cues and primes across cultures. On the one hand, the priming data do provide further evidence in support of Chiu et al.'s (2010) proposition that dominant cultural values are not simply copied into the minds of cultural participants, because people appear to be primable with either individualistic or collectivistic cultural mindsets. On the other hand, the intersubjective culture model proposes that situationally activated mindsets may be less important in explaining cultural behavior than people's beliefs about *others'* mindsets. In addition, Kashima (2009) argues that the primes used in situated cognition studies do not necessarily work because they activate broad, internalized mindsets. Instead, the primes activate isolated domain-specific constructs, which simply prime other domain-specific constructs because the two have been repeatedly activated together in past experience. For example, the pronoun "I" might prime an analytical approach to the embedded figures task in Americans because contexts in which first-person pronouns are used are also contexts in which analytic processing occurs. (For a discussion of how the semiotic model explains cultural priming effects, see Kashima, 2009.)

In addition, the mutual-constitution perspective of cultural psychology raises an additional shortcoming of the situated cognition model. Although priming data indicate that relational or individual elements of knowledge can prime people's behaviors and cognitions, it is silent on the essential, complementary dynamic of how people shape culture. If people's minds house all possible cultural mindsets, then how do culturally different societies, cultural situations, institutions, languages, and other cues come about in the first place? In contrast, cultural psychologists would argue that people socially transmit and recreate local situations and practices as they act in the world – that this is at least half of the explanatory goal. The dynamic argument might also be directed at interpretations of other data. Some work illustrates that cultural differences can be viewed as psychological strategies that respond to different cultural institutions and incentives: for example, the incentive to avoid looking bad in front of others (e.g., Yamagishi et al., 2008) or the tendency of social networks to be stable and cohesive (Schug, Yuki, Horikawa, & Takemura, 2009). Some interpretations of these data argue that cultural differences in social cognitive tendencies are not real (i.e., they do not represent qualitatively divergent psychological processes) because they can be explained away by these culturally different institutions. In contrast, a cultural psychologist would argue that *of course* people's behavior responds to common cultural institutions, incentives, and settings (Oishi & Graham, 2010; Schug et al., 2009), because cultural content definitely matters. However, such critiques commonly neglect to explain the other part of the equation – how the cultural content of institutions, incentives, and practices are actively maintained and created by cultural people.

Summary of the self-concept debate and implications for social cognition

It is clear that a current conceptual issue is the existence, placement, and importance of the self in cultural analyses. It will be essential for future cultural researchers to be clear about the extent to which they wish to endorse internalized, generalized cultural selves (or mindsets) that have causal power. It may well be the case that the existence and explanatory power of cultural self-*construals* (stored in practices, messages, and institutions both outside and between individuals) do not necessarily require that abstract, generalizable cultural self-*concepts* of interdependence and independence be stored inside people's heads. Perhaps independence and independence can be stored as neutral knowledge structures (i.e., Kashima's interpretive concepts) that do not imply some motivational–emotional–evaluative homunculus. And Zou, Chiu, Morris, and others remind us that even if culturally different self-concepts exist, what probably matters more is people's meta-social cognitions about their cultural peers, not what they believe deep down inside.

When the dust settles, how might these internal debates among cultural psychologists impact social cognition researchers? First, it's possible that social cognitive researchers will inherit a new explanatory model about how we cultural creatures act. Perhaps much of human behavior is meta-social cognitive, in that beliefs about the collective mediate social cognition (Chiu et al., 2010; Prentice & Miller, 1994; Zou et al., 2009). (Indeed, this meta-social cognition is a likely capacity of the evolved cultural animal.) Second, Kashima's views of the power of semiotic, negotiated meaning (Holtgraves & Kashima, 2008; Kashima, 2009) might revive social cognitive interest in studying how people work together to create common ground and understanding, and how language shapes this process. Third, if an internalized, general, explicit "self" is found to have reduced explanatory power in cultural psychology, it might translate into a view of self – even in social cognitive research – that is emergent, compartmentalized, and task-specific. And finally, if cultural psychologists ultimately decide that the self is an emergent and interpretive construct, not a causal one, then it might create an elevated view of description (rather than causation) in social science (Kashima, 2009).

Cultural psychology and the brain

A second recent wave in cultural psychology is cultural neuroscience. This literature has been ably and recently reviewed by many of the key players in this growing field (Ames & Fiske, 2010; Chiao & Bebko, in press; Kitayama & Uskul, 2011; Park & Huang, 2010; see also Chapter 26), so we will not recapitulate their reviews and arguments here. However, all of these reviews acknowledge a basic theme: the brain is not a fixed biological entity – it adapts in response to repeated practice at tasks in the world. Years of specific cultural experience can wire the brain in significant ways (Park & Huang, 2010).

A few examples illustrate the theme. One functional magnetic resonance imaging (fMRI) study showed that among Chinese participants, the medial prefrontal cortex (MPFC) region, known to be active for self-relevant information processing, was active even when people were asked to think of their mothers, whereas North Americans activated the same region only when they think of themselves (Zhu, Zhang, Fan, & Han, 2007). Similarly, using the event-related (brain) potential (ERP) technique, researchers found that British men showed larger frontal lobe amplitude when identifying self-portraits than when identifying their friend's portraits, whereas Chinese men showed the opposite pattern (Sui, Liu, & Han, 2009). Neural differences correspond to behavioral patterns in analytic and holistic processing, too: the brain patterns of a sample of Singapore Chinese worked more efficiently at context-relevant tasks than European-Americans (Goh et al., 2007). As might be expected from studies of brain plasticity, accumulated cultural experience shapes the brain.

Research on how the plastic human brain responds to a single lifetime of cultural experience is complemented by research on genetic diversity, which documents how cultural brains presumably evolved over generations. As humans migrated around the world, their physiologies evolved in response to local physical and social environments. These changes are reflected in different allelic distributions across ethnic populations, some of which are related to psychological function (Chiao & Blizinsky, 2010; Gelernter, Kranzler, & Cubells, 1997). Local culture also shapes allelic expression: certain alleles appear to be expressed differently, depending upon cultural background (e.g., H. Kim et al., 2010). In the coming decade, we expect to see more research in cultural neuroscience, and expect it to promote sophisticated theories about the interaction of culture, mind, and brain.

Cultural origin, maintenance, and change

Finally, cultural psychologists are building theories about how cultural patterns emerge and change over time. In this effort, cultural psychologists are adopting theories of sociologists, economists, marketing researchers, evolutionary biologists, and earlier theories of psychology (Brunswik, 1943; Lewin, 1939). These theories attempt to identify the biological, physical, and social demands in past human populations that made particular patterns of values and behavior more adaptive.

One example is parasite prevalence theory, based on the finding that cultural patterns of collectivism and individualism are correlated with regional differences in the prevalence of infectious disease (Schaller & Murray, 2010). According to the argument, sticking with familiar other people can reduce one's risk of exposure to pathogens, an adaptive behavioral defense where infection risks are high (Schaller, 2006; Schaller & Murray, 2010).

Another example is the idea that individualistic and independent cultural patterns emerged as adaptive responses to frontier exploration (Kitayama et al., 2010; Kitayama & Uskul, 2011). That is, cultural practices favoring self-protection, self-promotion, believing in self-efficacy and hard work (a constellation favoring independence of self from others) are proposed as adaptive reactions to the harsh ecological conditions of the frontiers of Western America and Hokkaido, Japan (Kitayama & Bowman, 2010; Kitayama, Ishii, Imada, Takemura, & Ramaswamy, 2006). A related argument is the residential mobility hypothesis (Oishi, 2010) that people who move a lot endorse and develop more individualistic psychological tendencies.

Such models are complemented by socioecological approaches to culture (Oishi & Graham, 2010), which identify the institutions and economies that underlie psychological patterns. One well-known and clear example is the culture of honor, found in the Southern United States, in which men respond vehemently, strongly, and clearly in response to insult (Nisbett & Cohen, 1996). The Southern culture of honor may have emerged as an adaptive response to the economic practice of herding (in which one's reputation for defensive violence can affect whether or not one's herd will be rustled), which in turn, was adapted to hilly areas or arid plains. Although the situational supports for cultures of violence may have dropped out (or, at least, changed) since earlier herding times (Daly & Wilson, 2009), cultural practices of violence appear to be shaped and maintained by both social transmission and economic factors.

Oishi and Graham (2010) explain how a socioecological approach complements cultural explanations of behavior. The origins of certain cultural practices and ideas (such as laws sanctioning insult-based violence or practices for self-reliance) are probably rooted in socioecologies (such as the economic practice of herding, or the physical challenges of a frontier), some of which predated their cultural values.

Research on cultural production and change faces some key challenges. One is that there are limits to the influence of a physical ecology on culture. For any given physical or social setting, there may be different possible cultural solutions (Cohen, 2001). An example comes from two Sudanese cultures, the Dinka and the Nuer, who both practice herding in the same physical environment, and yet have developed very different agricultural and kinship traditions (Edgerton, 1971; Richerson & Boyd, 2005). So, physical ecology may not be the strongest single determinant of culture – social transmission matters, too. Another challenge is to predict and explain which new cultural patterns will be adopted. For new cultural patterns to catch on, they must be adaptive – rational and effective – in some existing context. (For example, the pattern of individualism is relatively more adaptive in the context of high residential mobility; Oishi, 2010.) Effective cultural patterns might need to be adopted by key figures in a social group, such as high-status people or highly visible models (for a comprehensive review of these dynamics, see Cohen, 2001). Recent cultural research has begun to study how people's values are influenced by the nonverbal signals of others (Weisbuch & Ambady, 2009), how people's behaviors are implicitly tuned to the social majority (Shytenberg, 2010), and how conversational grounding helps cultural ideas perpetuate (Fast, Heath, & Wu, 2009). Such mechanisms help explain how cultural patterns, once established, may be socially transmitted.

Research on cultural origins and cultural change expands the science of cultural psychology beyond psychologies and cultural settings to a broader level of mutual constitution: how larger cultural patterns and institutions are created, copied, or sustained by culturally shaped people.

GOING FORWARD TOGETHER: CULTURAL PSYCHOLOGY AND SOCIAL COGNITION

As social cognition and cultural psychology move forward, we hope that the subdisciplines will continue to influence one another. Such mutual influence is already happening on many fronts. Many social cognitive psychologists not only believe their theories are universal but also test that assumption. For example, the stereotype content model, proposed as a universal, has been tested in dozens of world countries (Cuddy et al., 2009). Warmth and competence organize group stereotypes across cultures, although individualists are more likely to place in-groups in the most positive quadrant (high competence, high warmth). In addition, cultures with more economic inequality place more social groups in ambivalent quadrants (i.e., high competence but low warmth, or low competence but high warmth), perhaps to both placate and justify low-status groups (Durante et al., 2011).

Other social cognitive psychologists are incorporating cultural questions by studying social class culture. Whereas middle-class contexts emphasize uniqueness and individual control, working-class contexts emphasize individual integrity and self-control (Snibbe & Markus, 2005). People from lower social classes also perceive less control over personal outcomes, which is associated with a tendency to notice and use contextual explanations for people's behavior (Kraus, Piff, & Keltner, 2009). Social class is a potentially valuable area for expansion in social cognition – most social cognition models were built on data from European-American, middle-class contexts, but these models may not follow the same logic in lower-class settings. Furthermore, social class is an accessible way for social cognitive researchers to get involved in cultural research – it requires no language translation and has a much smaller travel budget (see Norenzayan & Heine, 2005 on universality testing).

A final example is the rapidly expanding set of research on how specific metaphors and bodily experiences shape social cognition. Embodied cognition research documents ways that social cognition is reflected in or shaped by movements of the physical body. And conceptual metaphors, a bit more broadly, investigate how metaphorical representations (such as clean vs dirty, or close vs distant) might affect people's behaviors and interpretations (such as moral vs immoral or liking vs disliking, respectively) (Landau, Meier, & Keefer, 2010). This work represents another potential bridge between social cognition and cultural psychology. The metaphors involved (cleanliness, motion, distance, warmth) may in some cases be universally meaningful; in other cases not. For example, warm objects may symbolize social inclusion universally, because physical closeness is literally warm (Zhong & Leornardelli, 2008), and height may symbolize power in most cultural contexts (Landau et al., 2010). But Landau and colleagues noted that other movements – such as head nodding indicating assent, or time being represented by horizontal movement – are culturally specific. For example, a bowed vs upright head posture invokes cognitions related to dishonor and honor, respectively, among men from honor cultures, but not among men from other cultural contexts (Cohen & Leung, 2009). Thus, in different cultural contexts, physical movements are repeatedly practiced in association with particular meanings, so that later, those physical movements prime social cognitive patterns. Once again, real cultural contents – in the form of physical movements and practices – shape social cognition. If embodied or metaphorical social cognitions are grounded in repeated, concrete actions, it re-emphasizes that human cognition, affect, and motivation are best understood as grounded in real worlds, settings, and activities.

Cultural psychology and non-cultural social cognition share the same dedication to describing human cognition as pragmatically situated in real worlds. They share a similar dedication to evolutionary and neural underpinnings of the phenomena they study. And the two fields share an interest in explaining the ways human social cognition is uniquely suited to absorb, transmit, and develop cultural information. In the past, social cognition has outlined a wide topography of research areas for cultural psychologists to study in cultural context. If, in turn, social cognition researchers imitate cultural psychologists in their intent to explain *people in contexts*, the combination could ratchet forward our ability to create comprehensive models of human thought.

ACKNOWLEDGMENT

We thank Vinai Norasakkunkit, Ken Ito, and Sawa Senzaki for their helpful comments on the chapter.

REFERENCES

Adams, G., & Markus, H. R. (2004). Toward a conception of culture suitable for a social psychology of culture. In M. Schaller & C. S. Crandall (Eds.), The psychological foundations of culture (pp. 335–360). Hillsdale, NJ: Erlbaum.

Ames, D. L., & Fiske, S. T. (2010). Cultural neuroscience. *Asian Journal of Social Psychology, 13*, 72–82.

Arnett, J. J. (2008). The neglected 95%: Why American psychology needs to become less American. *American Psychologist, 63*(7), 602–614.

Azuma, H. (1994). Nihonjin no shitake to kyoiku – hattatsu no nichibeihikaku ni motozuite [Education and socialization in Japan: A comparison between Japan and the United States]. Tokyo: University of Tokyo Press.

Barkow, J. H., Cosmides, L., & Tooby, J. (Eds.) (1992). *The adapted mind: Evolutionary psychology and the generation of culture.* New York: Oxford University Press.

Barreto, M., Ellemers, N., & Fiske, S. T. (2010). "What did you say, and who do you think you are?" How power differences affect emotional reactions to prejudice. *Journal of Social Issues, 66*, 477–492.

Baumeister, R. F. (2005). *The cultural animal: Human nature, meaning, and social life.* New York: Oxford University Press.

Bond, M. H., & Cheung, T. (1983). College students' spontaneous self-concept. *Journal of Cross-Cultural Psychology, 14*, 153–171.

Bruner, J. (1990). *Acts of meaning: Four lectures on mind and culture.* Cambridge, MA: Harvard University Press.

Brunswik, E. (1943). Organismic achievement and environmental probability. *Psychological Review, 50*, 255–272.

Buss, D.M. (2010). Origins of mating behavior. In N. B. Moore, J. K. Davidson, & T. D. Fisher (Eds.), *Speaking of sexuality* (pp. 45–57). New York: Oxford University Press.

Carpenter, M., Akhtar, N., & Tomasello, M. (1998). Fourteen- to 18-month-old infants differentially imitate intentional and accidental actions. *Infant Behavior and Development, 21*, 315–330.

Chentsova-Dutton, Y. E., & Tsai, J. L. (2010). Self-focused attention and emotional reactivity: The role of culture. *Journal of Personality and Social Psychology, 98*, 507–519.

Chiao, J. Y., & Bebko, G. M. (in press). Cultural neuroscience of social cognition. In S. Han & E. Poeppel (Eds.) *Culture and identity: Neural frames of social cognition.* New York: Springer Press.

Chiao J. Y., & Blizinsky, K.D. (2010). Culture–gene coevolution of individualism–collectivism and the serotonin transporter gene. *Proceedings of Biological Sciences, 277*, 529–537.

Chiao, J. Y., Harada, T., Komeda, H., Li, Z., Mano, Y., Saito, D. N., et al. (2009). Neural basis of individualistic and collectivistic views of self. *Human Brain Mapping, 30*(9), 2813–2820.

Chiu, C., Gelfand, M. J., Yamagishi, T., Shteynberg, G., & Wan, C. (2010). Intersubjective culture: The role of intersubjective perceptions in cross-cultural research. *Perspectives on Psychological Science, 5*, 482–493.

Choi, I., & Choi, Y. (2002). Culture and self-concept flexibility. *Personality and Social Psychology Bulletin, 28*, 1508–1517.

Choi, I., Dalal, R., Kim-Prieto, C., & Park, H. (2003). Culture and judgment of causal relevance. *Journal of Personality and Social Psychology, 84*, 46–59.

Choi, I., & Nisbett, R. E. (1998). The situational salience and cultural differences in the correspondence bias and the actor–observer bias. *Personality and Social Psychology Bulletin, 24*, 949–960.

Choi, I., Nisbett, R. E., & Norenzayan, A. (1999). Causal attribution across cultures: Variation and universality. *Psychological Bulletin,125*, 47–63.

Choi, K., & Ross, M. (2011). Cultural differences in process and person focus: Congratulations on your hard work versus celebrating your exceptional brain. *Journal of Experimental Social Psychology, 47*, 343–349.

Cialdini, R. B., Wosinska, W., Barrett, D. W., Butner, J., & Gornik-Durose, M. (1999). Compliance with a request in two cultures: The differential influence of social proof and commitment/consistency on collectivists and individualists. *Personality and Social Psychology Bulletin, 25*, 1242–1253.

Cohen, D. (2001). Cultural variation: Considerations and implications. *Psychological Bulletin, 127*, 451–471.

Cohen, D. (2007). Methods in cultural psychology. In S. Kitayama & D. Cohen (Eds.), *Handbook of cultural psychology*. New York: Guilford Press.

Cohen, D., & Gunz, A. (2002). As seen by the other...: Perspectives on the self in the memories and emotional perceptions of Easterners and Westerners. *Psychological Science, 13*, 55–59.

Cohen, D., & Hoshino-Browne, E. (2005). Insider and outsider perspectives on the self and social world. In R. M. Sorrention, D. Cohen, J. M Olson, & M. P. Zanna (Eds.), *Culture and social behaviour: The Tenth Ontario Symposium* (pp. 49–76). Hillsdale, NJ: Laurence Erlbaum.

Cohen, D., & Leung, A. K. Y. (2009). The hard embodiment of culture. *European Journal of Social Psychology, 29*, 1278–1289.

Cousins, S. D. (1989). Culture and selfhood in Japan and the U.S. *Journal of Personality and Social Psychology, 56*, 124–131.

Cuddy, A. J. C., Fiske, S. T., Kwan, V. S. Y., Glick, P., Demoulin, S., Leyens, J., et al. (2009). Stereotype content model across cultures: Towards universal similarities and some differences. *British Journal of Social Psychology, 48*(1), 1–33.

Daly, M., & Wilson, M. (2010). Cultural inertia, economic incentives, and the persistence of "Southern violence". In M. Schaller, A. Norenzayan, S. J. Heine, T. Yamagishi, & T. Kameda (Eds.), *Evolution, culture, and the human mind* (pp. 229–241). New York: Psychology Press.

Diener, E., & Diener, M. (1995). Cross-cultural correlates of life satisfaction and self-esteem. *Journal of Personality and Social Psychology, 68*, 653–663.

Duffy, S., Toriyama, R., Itakura, S., & Kitayama, S. (2009). Development of cultural strategies of attention in North American and Japanese children. *Journal of Experimental Child Psychology, 102*, 351–359.

Durante, F., Fiske, S. T., Cuddy, A. J., Kervyn, N., et al. (2011). *Income inequality increases ambivalence in the stereotype content model: Cross-national patterns*. Unpublished paper.

Edgerton, R. B. (1971). *The individual in cultural adaptation: A study of four East African peoples*. Berkeley, CA: University of California Press.

Endo, Y., & Meijer, Z. (2004). Autobiographical memory of success and failure experiences. In Y. Kashima, Y. Endo, E. S. Kashima, C. Leung, & J. McClure (Eds.), *Progress in Asian social psychology* (Vol. 4, pp. 67–84). Seoul: Kyoyook-Kwahak-Sa Publishing Company.

Fast, N. J., Heath, C., & Wu, G. (2009). Common ground and cultural prominence: How conversation reinforces culture. *Psychological Science, 20*, 904–911.

Festinger, L. (1957). *A theory of cognitive dissonance*. Stanford, CA: Stanford University Press.

Fiske, S. T. (1992). Thinking is for doing: Portraits of social cognition from daguerreotype to laserphoto. *Journal of Personality and Social Psychology, 63*(6), 877–889.

Fiske, S. T., & Taylor, S. E. (1991). *Social cognition* (2nd ed.). New York: McGraw-Hill.

Fiske, S. T., & Taylor, S. E. (2008). *Social cognition: From brains to culture*. New York: McGraw-Hill.

Freedman, J. L., & Fraser, S. C. (1966). Compliance without pressure: The foot-in-the-door technique. *Journal of Personality and Social Psychology, 4*, 195–202.

Geertz, C. (1973*). The interpretation of cultures*. New York: Basic Books.

Gelernter J., Kranzler, H., & Cubells, J. F. (1997) Serotonin transporter protein (SLC6A4) allele and haplotype frequencies and linkage disequilibria in African- and European-American and Japanese populations and in alcohol-dependent subjects. *Human Genetics, 101*, 243–246.

Giedion, S. (1964). *Space, time and architecture: The growth of a new tradition* (4th ed.). Cambridge, MA: Harvard University Press.

Goh, J. O., Chee, M. W., Tan, J. C., Venkatraman, V., Hebrank, A., Leshikar, E. D., et al. (2007). Age and culture modulate object processing and object–science binding in the ventral visual area. *Cognitive, Affective & Behavioral Neuroscience, 7*, 44–52.

Goh, J. O., Tan, J. C., & Park, D. C. (2009). Culture modulates eye-movements to visual novelty. *PLoS ONE, 4(12)*, e8238.

Hamamura, T., Meijer, Z., Heine, S. J., Kamaya, K., & Hori, I. (2009). Approach–avoidance motivations and information processing: A cross-cultural analysis. *Personality and Social Psychology Bulletin, 35*, 454–462.

Heine, S. J., Kitayama, S., Lehman, D. R., Takata, T., Ide, E., Leung, C., et al. (2001). Divergent consequences of success and failure in Japan and North America: An investigation of self-improving motivations and malleable selves. *Journal of Personality and Social Psychology, 81*, 599–615.

Heine, S. J., & Lehman, D. R. (1997). Culture, dissonance, and self-affirmation. *Personality and Social Psychology Bulletin, 23*, 389–400.

Heine, S. J., Lehman, D. R., Markus, H. R., & Kitayama, S. (1999). Is there a universal need for positive self-regard? *Psychological Review, 106*, 766–794.

Heine, S. J., Lehman, D. R., Peng, K., & Greenholtz, J. (2002). What's wrong with cross-cultural comparisons of subjective Likert scales: The reference-group problem. *Journal of Personality and Social Psychology, 82*, 903–918.

Henrich, J., Heine, S. J., & Norenzayan, A. (2010). The weirdest people in the world? *Behavioral and Brain Sciences, 33*(2–3), 61–83.

Hogg, M. A. (2010). Influence and leadership. In S. T. Fiske, D. T. Gilbert, & G. Lindzey (Eds.), *The handbook of social psychology* (5th ed., Vol. 2, pp. 1166–1206). New York: Wiley.

Holtgraves, T. M., & Kashima, Y. (2008). Language, meaning, and social cognition. *Personality and Social Psychology Review, 12*(1), 73–94.

Hong, Y., Morris, M. W., Chiu, C., & Benet-Martínez, V. (2000). Multicultural minds: A dynamic constructivist approach to culture and cognition. *American Psychologist, 55*(7), 709–720.

Imada, T., & Kitayama, S. (2010). Social eyes and choice justification: Culture and dissonance revisited. *Social Cognition, 28*(5), 589–608.

Iwao, S. (1997). Consistency orientation and models of social behavior: Is it not time for West to meet East? *Japanese Psychological Research, 39*, 323–332.

Ji, L. (2008). The leopard cannot change his spots, or can he? Culture and the development of lay theories of change. *Personality and Social Psychology Bulletin, 34*, 613–622.

Ji, L., Nisbett, R. E., & Su, Y. (2001). Culture, change and prediction. *Psychological Science, 12*, 450–456.

Ji, L., Peng, K., & Nisbett, R. E. (2000). Culture, control, and perception of relationships in the environment. *Journal of Personality and Social Psychology, 78*, 943–955.

Jones, E. E., & Harris, V. A. (1967). The attribution of attitudes. *Journal of Experimental Social Psychology, 3*, 1–24.

Kanagawa, C., Cross, S. E., & Markus, H. R. (2001). "Who am I?": The cultural psychology of the conceptual self. *Personality and Social Psychology Bulletin, 27*, 90–103

Kashima, Y. (2009). Culture comparison and culture priming: A critical analysis. In R. S. Wyer, C. Chiu, & Y. Hong (Eds.), *Understanding culture: Theory, research, and application* (pp. 53–77). New York: Psychology Press.

Kashima, Y., Kashima, E. S., Kim, U., & Gelfand, M. (2006). Describing the social world: Object-centered versus process-centered descriptions. *Journal of Experimental Social Psychology, 42*, 388–396.

Kashima, Y., Siegal, M., Tanaka, K., & Kashima, E. (1992). Do people believe behaviors are consistent with attitudes? Toward a cultural psychology of attribution processes. *British Journal of Social Psychology, 31*, 111–124.

Kim, H. S., & Drolet, A. (2009). Express your social self: Cultural differences in choice of brand-name versus generic products. *Personality and Social Psychology Bulletin, 35*(12), 1555–1566.

Kim, H. S., & Markus, H. R. (1999). Deviance or uniqueness, harmony or conformity? A cultural analysis. *Journal of Personality and Social Psychology, 77*, 785–800.

Kim, H. S., Sherman, D. K., Sasaki, J. Y., Xu, J., Chu, T. Q., Ryu, C., et al. (2010). Culture, distress, and oxytocin receptor polymorphism (OXTR) interact to influence emotional support seeking. *PNAS Proceedings of the National Academy of Sciences of the United States of America, 107*(36), 15717–15721.

Kim, Y.-H., Cohen, D. & Au, W.-T. (2010). The jury and abjury of my peers: The self in face and dignity culture. *Journal of Personality and Social Psychology, 98*, 904–916.

Kitayama, S., & Bowman, N. A. (2010). Cultural consequences of voluntary settlement in the frontier: Evidence and implications. In M. Schaller, A. Norenzayan, S. J. Heine, T. Yamagishi, & T. Kameda (Eds.), *Evolution, culture, and the human mind* (pp. 205–227). New York: Psychology Press.

Kitayama, S., Conway, L. G., III, Pietromonaco, P. R., Park, H., & Plaut, V. C. (2010). Ethos of independence across regions in the United States: The production–adoption model of cultural change. *American Psychologist, 65*(6), 559–574.

Kitayama, S., Duffy, S., Kawamura, T., & Larsen, J. T. (2003). Perceiving an object and its context in different cultures: A cultural look at New Look. *Psychological Science, 14*, 201–206.

Kitayama, S., Ishii, K., Imada, T., Takemura, K., & Ramaswamy, J. (2006). Voluntary settlement and the spirit of independence: Evidence from Japan's "Northern frontier". *Journal of Personality and Social Psychology, 91*(3), 369–384.

Kitayama, S., Markus, H. R., & Kurokawa, M. (2000). Culture, emotion, and well-being: Good feeling in Japan and the United States. *Cognition & Emotion, 14*, 93–124.

Kitayama, S., Markus, H. R., Matsumoto, H., & Norasakkunkit, V. (1997). Individual and collective processes in the construction of the self: Self-enhancement in the United States and self-criticism in Japan. *Journal of Personality and Social Psychology, 72*, 1245–1267.

Kitayama, S., Mesquita, B., & Karasawa, M. (2006). Cultural affordances and emotional experience: Socially engaging and disengaging emotions in Japan and the United States. *Journal of Personality and Social Psychology, 91*, 890–903.

Kitayama, S., Park, H., Sevincer, A. T., Karasawa, M., & Uskul, A. K. (2009). A cultural task analysis of implicit independence: Comparing North America, Western Europe, and East Asia. *Journal of Personality and Social Psychology, 97*(2), 236–255.

Kitayama, S., Snibbe, A. C., Markus, H. R., & Suzuki, T. (2004). Is there any "free" choice? Self and dissonance in two cultures. *Psychological Science, 15*(8), 527–533.

Kitayama, S., & Uskul, A. K. (2011). Culture, mind, and the brain: Current evidence and future directions. *Annual Review of Psychology, 62*, 419–449.

Klein, O., & Snyder, M. (2003). Stereotypes and behavioral confirmation: From interpersonal to intergroup perspectives. In M. P. Zanna (Ed.), *Advances in experimental social psychology* (Vol. 35, pp. 153–234). San Diego, CA: Academic Press.

Koo, M., & Choi, I. (2005). Becoming a holistic thinker: Training effect of Oriental medicine on reasoning. *Personality and Social Psychology Bulletin, 31*, 1264–1272.

Kraus, M. W., Piff, P. K., & Keltner, D. (2009). Social class, sense of control, and social explanation. *Journal of Personality and Social Psychology, 97*(6), 992–1004.

Kroeber, A. L., & Kluckhohn, C. (1952). *Culture: A critical review of concepts and definitions.* New York: Random House.

Kühnen, U., Hannover, B., Roeder, U., Shah, A. A., Schubert, B., Upmeyer, A., et al. (2001). Cross-cultural variations in identifying embedded figures: Comparisons from the United States, Germany, Russia, and Malaysia. *Journal of Cross-Cultural Psychology, 32*(3), 365–371.

Lam, A. G., & Zane, N. W. S. (2004). Ethnic differences in coping with interpersonal stressors: A test of self-construals as cultural mediators. *Journal of Cross-Cultural Psychology, 35*, 446–459.

Landau, M. J., Meier, B. P., & Keefer, L. A. (2010). A metaphor-enriched social cognition. *Psychological Bulletin, 136*, 1045–1067.

Lee, A. Y., Aaker, J. L., & Gardner, W. L. (2000). The pleasures and pains of distinct self-construals: The role of interdependence in regulatory focus. *Journal of Personality and Social Psychology, 78*, 1122–1134.

Lee, F., Hallahan, M., & Herzog, T. (1996). Explaining real-life events: How culture and domain shape attributions. *Personality and Social Psychology Bulletin, 22*, 732–741.

Leung, A. K., & Cohen, D. (2007). The soft embodiment of culture: Camera angles and motion through time and space. *Psychological Science, 18*(9), 824–830.

Lewin, K. (1939). Field theory and experiment in social psychology: Concepts and methods. *American Journal of Sociology, 44*, 868–896.

Ma-Kellams, C., Spencer-Rodgers, J., & Peng, K. (2011). I am against us? Unpacking cultural differences in ingroup favoritism via dialecticism. *Personality and Social Psychology Bulletin, 37*(1), 15–27.

Markus, H. R., & Hamedani, M. G. (2007). Sociocultural psychology: The dynamic interdependence among self systems and social systems. In S. Kitayama & D. Cohen (Eds.), *Handbook of cultural psychology* (pp. 3–39). New York: Guilford Press.

Markus, H. R., & Kitayama, S. (1991). Culture and the self: Implications for cognition, emotion, and motivation. *Psychological Review, 98*(2), 224–253.

Markus, H. R., & Kitayama, S. (2010). Cultures and selves: A cycle of mutual constitution. *Perspectives on Psychological Science, 5*(4), 420–430.

Markus, H. R., Uchida, Y., Omoregie, H., Townsend, S. S. M., & Kitayama, S. (2006). Going for the gold: Models of agency in Japanese and American contexts. *Psychological Science, 17*, 103–112.

Masuda, T., Ellsworth, P., Mesquita, B., Leu, J., Tanida, S., & van de Veerdonk, E. (2008). Placing the face in context: Cultural differences in the perception of facial emotion. *Journal of Personality and Social Psychology, 94*, 365–381.

Masuda, T., Gonzalez, R., Kwan, L., & Nisbett, R. E. (2008). Culture and aesthetic preference: Comparing the attention to context of East Asians and European Americans. *Personality and Social Psychology Bulletin, 34*, 1260–1275.

Masuda, T., & Kitayama, S. (2004). Perceived-induced constraint and attitude attribution in Japan and in the US: A case for cultural dependence of the correspondence bias. *Journal of Experimental Social Psychology, 40*, 409–416.

Masuda, T., & Nisbett, R. E. (2001). Attending holistically vs. analytically: Comparing the context sensitivity of Japanese and Americans. *Journal of Personality and Social Psychology, 81*, 922–934.

Matsumoto, D. (1999). Culture and self: An empirical assessment of Markus and Kitayama's theory of independent and interdependent self-construals. *Asian Journal of Social Psychology, 2*, 289–310.

McCauley, R., & Henrich, J. (2006) Susceptibility to the Müller–Lyer illusion, theory-neutral observation, and the diachronic penetrability of the visual input system. *Philosophical Psychology, 19*, 1–23.

Meltzoff, A. (1995). Understanding the intentions of others: Re-enactment of intended acts by 18 month old children. *Developmental Psychology, 31*, 838–850.

Miller, J. G. (1984). Culture and development of everyday social explanation. *Journal of Personality and Social Psychology, 46*, 961–983.

Miyamoto, Y., & Ji, L.-J. (2010). *Influencing others fosters analytic cognition, whereas adjusting to others fosters holistic cognition.* Unpublished manuscript, University of Wisconsin.

Miyamoto, Y., & Kitayama, S. (2002). Cultural variation in correspondence bias: The critical role of attitude diagnosticity of socially constrained behaviour. *Journal of Personality and Social Psychology, 83*, 1239–1248.

Miyamoto, Y., Nisbett, R. E., & Masuda, T. (2006). Culture and the physical environment: Holistic versus analytic perceptual affordances. *Psychological Science, 17*, 113–119.

Miyamoto, Y., & Wilken, B. (2010). Culturally contingent situated cognition: Influencing othersfosters analytic perception in the U.S. but not in Japan. *Psychological Science, 21*, 1616–1622.Morling, B. cultural "tasks."), & Evered, S. (2006). Secondary control reviewed and defined. *Psychological Bulletin, 132*, 269–296.

Morling, B., & Lamoreaux, M. (2008). Measuring culture outside the head: A meta-analysis of individualism–collectivism in cultural products. *Personality and Social Psychology Review, 12*(3), 199–221.

Morling, B., Kitayama, S., & Miyamoto, Y. (2002). Cultural practices emphasize influence in the United States and adjustment in Japan. *Personality and Social Psychology Bulletin, 28*, 311–323.

Morris, M. W., & Mok, A. (2011). Isolating effects of cultural schemas: Cultural priming shifts Asian-Americans' biases in social description and memory. *Journal of Experimental Social Psychology, 47*(1), 117–126.

Morris, M. W., & Peng, K. (1994). Culture and cause: American and Chinese attributions for social and physical events. *Journal of Personality and Social Psychology, 67,* 949–971.

Na, J., & Choi, I. (2009). Culture and first-person pronouns. *Personality and Social Psychology Bulletin, 35*(11), 1492–1499.

Na, J., Grossmann, I., Varnum, M. E. W., Kitayama, S., Gonzalez, R., & Nisbett, R. E. (2010). Cultural differences are not always reducible to individual differences. *Proceedings of the National Academy of Sciences of the United States of America, 107*(14), 6192–6197.

Na, J., & Kitayama, S. (2010). *Trait-based person perception is culture-specific: Behavioral and neural evidence.* Manuscript submitted for publication.

Nagell, K., Olguin, R. S., & Tomasello, M. (1993). Processes of social learning in the tool use of chimpanzees (*Pan troglodytes*) and human children (*Homo sapiens*). *Journal of Comparative Psychology, 107,* 174–186.

Nisbett, R. E. (2003). *The geography of thought.* New York: Free Press.

Nisbett, R. E., & Cohen, D. (1996). *Culture of honor: The psychology of violence in the South.* Boulder, CO: Westview Press.

Nisbett, R. E., & Masuda, T. (2003). Culture and point of view. *Proceedings of the National Academy of Sciences of the United States of America, 100,* 11163–11175.

Nisbett, R. E., Peng, K., Choi, I., & Norenzayan, A. (2001). Culture and systems of thought: Holistic vs. analytic cognition. *Psychological Review, 108,* 291–310.

Nisbett, R. E., & Ross, L. (1980). *Human inference: Strategies and shortcomings of social judgment.* Englewood Cliffs, NJ: Prentice Hall.

Norenzayan, A., Choi, I., & Nisbett, R. E. (2002). Cultural similarities and differences in social influence: Evidence from behavioural predictions and lay theories of behaviour. *Personality and Social Psychology Bulletin, 28,* 109–120.

Norenzayan, A., & Heine, S. J. (2005). Psychological universals: What are they and how can we know? *Psychological Bulletin, 135,* 763–784.

Norenzayan, A., Smith, E. E., Kim, B. J., & Nisbett, R. E. (2002). Cultural preferences for formal versus intuitive reasoning. *Cognitive Science, 26,* 653–684.

Oishi, S. (2010). The psychology of residential mobility: Implications for the self, social relationships, and well-being. *Perspectives on Psychological Science, 5*(1), 5–21.

Oishi, S., & Diener, E. (2003). Culture and well-being: The cycle of action, evaluation and decision. *Personality and Social Psychology Bulletin, 29,* 939–949.

Oishi, S., & Graham, J. (2010). Social ecology: Lost and found in psychological science. *Perspectives on Psychological Science, 5*(4), 356–377.

Oyserman, D., Coon, H., & Kemmelmeier, M. (2002). Rethinking individualism and collectivism: Evaluation of theoretical assumptions and meta-analyses. *Psychological Bulletin, 128,* 3–73.

Oyserman, D., & Lee, S. W. (2007). Priming "culture": Culture as situated cognition. In S. Kitayama, & D. Cohen (Eds.), *Handbook of cultural psychology* (pp. 255–279). New York: Guilford Press.

Oyserman, D., & Lee, S. W. (2008). Does culture influence what and how we think? Effects of priming individualism and collectivism. *Psychological Bulletin, 134,* 311–342.

Oyserman, D., & Sorensen, N. (2009). Understanding cultural syndrome effects on what and how we think: A situated cognition model. In R. S. Wyer, C. Chiu, & Y. Hong (Eds.), *Understanding culture: Theory, research, and application* (pp. 25–52). New York: Psychology Press.

Park, D. C., & Huang, C. (2010). Culture wires the brain: A cognitive neuroscience perspective. *Perspectives on Psychological Science, 5*(4), 391–400.

Peng, K., & Knowles, E. D. (2003). Culture, education, and the attribution of physical causality. *Personality and Social Psychology Bulletin, 29,* 1272–1284.

Peng, K., & Nisbett, R. E. (1999). Culture, dialecticism, and reasoning about contradiction. *American Psychologist, 54,* 741–754.

Prentice, D. A., & Miller, D. T. (1996). Pluralistic ignorance and the perpetuation of social norms by unwitting actors. In M. P. Zanna (Ed.), *Advances in experimental social psychology* (Vol. 28, pp. 161–209). San Diego, CA: Academic Press.

Rhee, E., Uleman, J. S., Lee, H., & Roman, R. J. (1995). Spontaneous self-descriptions and ethnic identities in individualistic and collectivistic cultures. *Journal of Personality & Social Psychology, 69,* 142–152.

Richerson, P. J., & Boyd, R. (2005). *Not by genes alone: How culture transformed human evolution.* Chicago, IL: University of Chicago Press.

Rule, N. O., Ambady, N., Adams, R. B, Ozono, H., Nakashima, S., Yoshikawa, S., et al. (2010). Polling the face: Prediction and consensus across cultures. *Journal of Personality and Social Psychology, 98,* 1–15.

Savani, K., Morris, M. W., Naidu, N. V. R., Kumar, S., & Berlia, N. V. (2011). Cultural conditioning: Understanding interpersonal accommodation in India and the United States in terms of the modal characteristics of interpersonal influence situations. *Journal of Personality and Social Psychology, 100,* 84–102.

Schaller, M. (2006). Parasites, behavioral defenses, and the social psychological mechanisms through which cultures are evoked. *Psychological Inquiry, 17*(2), 96–137.

Schaller, M., & Murray, D. R. (2010). Infectious diseases and the evolution of cross-cultural differences. In M. Schaller, A. Norenzayan, S. J. Heine, T. Yamagishi & T. Kameda (Eds.), *Evolution, culture, and the human mind* (pp. 243–256). New York: Psychology Press.

Schaller, M., Norenzayan, A., Heine, S. J., Yamagishi, T., & Kameda, T. (Eds.) (2010). *Evolution, culture, and the human mind.* New York: Psychology Press.

Schimmack, U., Oishi, S., & Diener, E. (2005). Individualism: A valid and important dimension of cultural differences between nations. *Personality and Social Psychology Review, 9,* 17–31.

Schug, J., Yuki, M., Horikawa, H., & Takemura, K. (2009). Similarity attraction and actually selecting similar others: How cross-societal differences in relational mobility affect interpersonal similarity in Japan and the USA. *Asian Journal of Social Psychology, 12*(2), 95–103.

Segall, M., Campbell, D., & Herskovits, M. J. (1966) *The influence of culture on visual perception.* New York: The Bobbs-Merrill Company.

Sherif, M. (1935). A study of some social factors in perception. *Archives of Psychology, 27*(187), 17–22.

Shweder, R. (1989). Cultural psychology: What is it? In J. Stigler, R. Shweder, & G. Herdt (Eds.), *Cultural psychology: The Chicago Symposia on Culture and Development* (pp. 1–46). New York: Cambridge University Press.

Shytenberg, G. (2010). A silent emergence of culture: The social tuning effect. *Journal of Personality and Social Psychology, 99,* 683–689.

Singelis, T. M. (1994). The measurement of independent and interdependent self-construals. *Personality and Social Psychology Bulletin, 20*(5), 580–591.

Singelis, T. M., Bond, M. H., Sharkey, W. F., & Lai, C. S. Y. (1999). Unpackaging culture's influence on self-esteem and embarrassability: The role of self-construals. *Journal of Cross-Cultural Psychology, 30,* 315–341.

Snibbe, A. C., & Markus, H. R. (2005). You can't always get what you want: Educational attainment, agency, and choice. *Journal of Personality and Social Psychology, 88,* 703–720.

Spencer-Rodgers, J., Boucher, H. C., Peng, K., & Wang, L. (2009). Cultural differences in self-verification: The role of naïve dialecticism. *Journal of Experimental Social Psychology, 45*(4), 860–866.

Spencer-Rodgers, J., & Peng, K. (2004). The dialectical self: Contradiction, change, and holism in the East Asian self-concept. In R. M. Sorrentino, D. Cohen, J. M. Olsen, & M. P. Zanna (Eds.), *Culture and social behavior: The Ontario Symposium* (Vol. 10, pp. 227–250). Mahwah, NJ: Lawrence Erlbaum.

Sperber, D. (1996). *Explaining culture: A naturalistic approach.* Oxford, UK: Blackwell.

Spina, R. R., Ji, L., Guo, T., Zhang, Z., Li, Y., & Fabrigar, L. (2010). Cultural differences in the representativeness heuristic: Expecting a correspondence in magnitude between cause and effect. *Personality and Social Psychology Bulletin, 36*(5), 583–597.

Stevenson, H. W., & Stigler, J. W. (1992). *The learning gap: Why our schools are failing and what we can learn from Japanese and Chinese education.* New York: Summit Books.

Sui, J., Liu, C. H., & Han, S. (2009). Cultural difference in neural mechanisms of self-recognition. *Social Neuroscience, 4,* 402–411.

Takano, Y., & Osaka, E . (1999). An unsupported common view: Comparing Japan and the U.S. on individualism–collectivism. *Asian Journal of Social Psychology, 2,* 311–341.

Taylor, C. (2007) *A secular age.* Cambridge, MA: Harvard University Press.

Tomasello, M. (1993). Cultural learning. *Behavioral and Brain Sciences, 16,* 495–552.

Tomasello, M. (1999). *The cultural origins of human cognition.* Cambridge, MA: Harvard University Press.

Tomasello, M. (2009). *Why we cooperate.* Cambridge, MA: MIT Press.

Triandis, H. C. (1996). The psychological measurement of cultural syndromes. *American Psychologist, 51,* 407–415.

Triandis, H. C., Bontempo, R., Leung, K., & Hui, C. K. (1990). A method for determining cultural, demographic, and personal constructs. *Journal of Cross-Cultural Psychology, 21,* 302–318.

Uchida, Y., & Kitayama, S. (2009). Happiness and unhappiness in east and west: Themes and variations. *Emotion, 9,* 441–456.

Uchida, Y., Kitayama, S., Mesquita, B., Reyes, J. A. S., & Morling, B. (2008). Is perceived emotional support beneficial? Well-being and health in independent and interdependent cultures. *Personality and Social Psychology Bulletin, 34,* 741–754.

Uchida, Y., Townsend, S. S. M., Markus, H. R., & Bergsieker, H. B. (2009). Emotions as within or between people? Cultural variation in lay theories of emotion expression and inference. *Personality and Social Psychology Bulletin, 35,* 1427–1439.

Uskul, A. K., Kitayama, S., & Nisbett, R. E. (2008). Ecocultural basis of cognition: Farmers and fishermen are more holistic than herders. *Proceedings of National Academy of Sciences of the United States of America, 105,* 8552–8556.

Varnum, M. E. W., Grossmann, I., Kitayama, S., & Nisbett, R. E. (2010). The origin of cultural differences in cognition: The social orientation hypothesis. *Current Directions in Psychological Science, 19*(1), 9–13.

Wan, C., Chiu, C., Peng, S., & Tam, K. (2007). Measuring cultures through intersubjective cultural norms: Implications for predicting relative identification with two or more cultures. *Journal of Cross-Cultural Psychology, 38*(2), 213–226.

Wan C., Tam K.-P., & Chiu C.-Y. (2010). Intersubjective cultural representations predicting behavior: The case of political culture and voting. *Asian Journal of Social Psychology, 13,* 200–273.

Weisbuch, M., & Ambady, N. (2009). Unspoken cultural influence: Exposure to and influence of nonverbal bias. *Journal of Personality and Social Psychology, 96,* 1104–1119.

Weisz, J. R., Rothbaum, F. M., & Blackburn, T. C. (1984). Standing out and standing in: The psychology of control in America and Japan. *American Psychologist, 39,* 955–969.

Witkin, H. A. A. (1967). Cognitive-style approach to cross-cultural research. *International Journal of Psychology, 2,* 233–250.

Yamagishi, T., Hashimoto, H., & Schug, J. (2008). Preferences versus strategies as explanations for culture-specific behavior. *Psychological Science, 19*(6), 579–584.

Zhong, C., & Leonardelli, G. J. (2008). Cold and lonely: Does social exclusion literally feel cold? *Psychological Science, 19*(9), 838–842.

Zhu, Y., Zhang, L., Fan, J., & Han, S. (2007). Neural basis of cultural influence on self-representation. *NeuroImage, 34,* 1310–1316.

Zou, X., Tam, K., Morris, M. W., Lee, S., Lau, I. Y., & Chiu, C. (2009). Culture as common sense: Perceived consensus versus personal beliefs as mechanisms of cultural influence. *Journal of Personality and Social Psychology, 97*(4), 579–597.

23

Evolutionary Perspectives on Social Cognition

Joshua M. Ackerman, Julie Y. Huang, & John A. Bargh

INTRODUCTION

Social cognition evolved. This statement seems simple and uncontroversial enough. After all, social cognition is a product of biological structures (brain and body), and "nothing in biology makes sense except in the light of evolution" (Dobzhansky, 1964, p. 449). It was not until relatively recently, however, that an evolutionary perspective began to gain real traction within the field of social psychology. Over the past few decades, application of evolutionary theory to the understanding of psychological phenomena has taken off, emerging in a wide number of specialty and flagship journals (Webster, 2007). Database searches for terms like "evolution" show that in primary social psychological sources, even the 2000s represent a twofold increase in appearance over the 1990s. This Handbook is a good example – no previous incarnation of the *Handbook of Social Cognition* featured a chapter on evolutionary perspectives. Perhaps Kenrick, Schaller, and Simpson (2006, p. 2) summarized it best:

> Once upon a time, social cognition represented a relatively small and austere little niche in the study of social behavior. Today, it hardly makes sense to treat social cognition as a specialized domain of inquiry or to separate the study of social cognition from the study of psychology more broadly... The same trajectory now characterizes the evolutionary perspective on social psychology.

The growth and acceptance of the evolutionary perspective on human sociality has not followed an easy progression. Early applications of sociobiology (the precursor of evolutionary psychology) to humans were met with strong resistance. Following the publication of his landmark *Sociobiology: The New Synthesis* (1975), of which only the final of 27 chapters was devoted to humans, the eminent biologist E. O. Wilson was harangued by scholars within and outside of his own department (in one example, Wilson had water poured on his head by a protestor during a conference) (Wilson, 1995). Even today, misunderstandings exist (e.g., Buller, 2005; but see Barrett, Frederick, Haselton, & Kurzban, 2006; Cosmides, Tooby, Fiddick, & Bryant, 2005; Kenrick, 1995). (For a review of the "standard" objections to evolutionary psychology, including issues of automaticity, learning, cultural variation, and interpretive errors such as the naturalistic fallacy and concerns about theoretical falsifiability, see Confer et al., 2010; Conway & Schaller, 2002; Kenrick, Ackerman, & Ledlow, 2003; Neuberg, Kenrick, & Schaller, 2010; Symons, 1992.) Thus, it may help to begin this chapter by establishing a general understanding of an evolutionary perspective within psychology. Following this, we highlight how this perspective carves social cognition at different conceptual joints than has traditionally been the case. Finally, we consider how a recent synthesis of evolutionary and developmental perspectives – scaffolding theory – can help to frame the emergence of linkages between specific social cognitive processes over the course of an individual's as well as a species' history.

An evolutionary perspective

At its core, an evolutionary perspective is a collection of specialized principles united by the common theme of adaptive design. How people think, feel, act, and exist is the result of selective forces that, over long periods of time, have shaped the body and mind to promote effective propagation of those same design features. To properly account for the outcomes of this process, an evolutionary perspective must be goal-based, engineering-focused, and interactionist in principle. As a *goal-based perspective*, the many mental adaptations studied by evolutionary researchers are initially considered to provide solutions to fine-grained, specific goals which themselves serve the "end" goal of differential reproduction. This goal framework reinforces the notion that cognition is for action (e.g., Morsella, Bargh, & Gollwitzer, 2008). Viewing the regularities and biases of social cognition as potential adaptations provides insight into why those features might exist as well as how to study them.

Typically, an evolutionary analysis also requires an *engineering focus*. For instance, Tooby and Cosmides (1992) detail five central components of such an analysis: investigators should identify an adaptive target (a proposed biologically successful outcome), background conditions (a description of the relevant ancestral environment in which the mental feature likely emerged), a design (a detailed depiction of the components and boundaries of the feature), a performance examination (how the feature acts in the world and the outcomes it produces), and a performance evaluation (an assessment of how well the design has met the adaptive target). This process can help to determine whether a particular mental feature is likely to be an adaptation. An engineering focus also highlights the historical constraints that restrict existing adaptations from achieving optimal functionality.

Finally, as is apparent from this analysis, an evolutionary perspective necessitates an *interactionist approach*. Selection acts on phenotypes (e.g., bodies, behaviors), which emerge as a result of gene–environment interactions. Although an evolutionary perspective is commonly misunderstood as advancing the idea of inevitable and immutable traits, evolutionary theories recognize the importance of *epigenetic* influences on development which occur after birth in response to the specific contingencies of one's environment (see Table 23.1). Epigenetic alterations are particularly important in the face of rapid environmental

change; in some species they have been known to dramatically alter both the phenotype and the genotype within a single generation (Gottlieb, 1998; Weber & Depew, 2003). For all species, including humans, adaptations arose to solve problems within specific contexts, and therefore they are at least somewhat sensitive to intrapersonal, interpersonal, and cultural contexts. These contexts provide the critical information and affordances to which people respond (Gibson, 1979; McArthur & Baron, 1983). In sum, "nothing about humans could possibly be immune from developmental intervention" (Tooby & Cosmides, 1992, p. 80).

Unlike many psychological approaches, an evolutionary perspective connects humans to the rest of the biological world. Evolution affects all organisms. Indeed, hypotheses about humans are often drawn from observing the behavior of other species, and this comparative research has demonstrated both connections across species and the species-specific nature of human cognition and behavior relative to that of other animals. For instance, work on the social behavior of other primates has improved our understanding of human morality (de Waal, 2006) as well as shown the universality of biases and states such as loss aversion and cognitive dissonance (Chen, Lakshminaryanan, & Santos, 2006; Egan, Santos, & Bloom, 2007). With respect to loss aversion, a large amount of research suggests that people overweight losses relative to equivalent gains (e.g., Tversky & Kahneman, 1991), and thus prefer to avoid situations where losses could be incurred. Monkeys show the same tendencies. Given the choice between one piece of apple and two pieces of apple from which one piece was always removed prior to the transaction (making the expected value of each choice equal), capuchin monkeys strongly prefer the single apple offers (Chen et al., 2006). They dislike incurring the "loss," even though the end result is identical across choices. The presence of such sophisticated biases in "economic" reasoning within distantly related primates has shed new theoretical light on evolved unconscious cognitive and motivational processes in humans (Bargh & Morsella, 2008); as a consequence, these are now being looked for, and detected, in young children for the first time (see, e.g., Dunham, Baron, & Banaji, 2008).

Although an understanding of human as animal is true of certain other research approaches (e.g., using rats and pigeons as models for human behavior), and has historically been important within the broader field of psychology (Darwin, 1872; James, 1890/1950; McDougall, 1926), many researchers had moved away from this position before the advent of sociobiology and evolutionary psychology. For instance, Maslow

Table 23.1   Glossary of terms

Term	Definition	Example
Affordance	Informational relationship between individual and environment, specifically the utility offered by an external cue for a perceiver	A smiling person affords possible friendship; a growling lion affords potential injury
Costly signaling	Demonstrations (behavioral, physical) of fitness quality that occur at a cost and thus are relatively "honest" signals	Wearing expensive items shows the possession of and (likely) ability to acquire resources
Differential parental investment	Cost of producing and rearing offspring dictates mating-related selectivity	Women tend to be romantically choosier than men
Epigenetic factors	Influences on gene expression that occur without altering the DNA sequence	Resource scarcity, toxin exposure, operational sex ratio
Genotype	Genetic makeup (specific alleles) of an individual	
Inclusive fitness	Combination of individual fitness with fitness produced by providing for genetic relatives	People often allocate support to relatives proportional to their relatedness
Loss aversion	Tendency to overweight and thus prefer avoiding losses relative to making equivalent gains	People may show twice as much negativity to a $5 price increase as they do happiness to a $5 price discount
Ontogeny	Developmental trajectory of organisms over the life span	
Phenotype	Observable characteristics of an individual, including (internal and external) morphology and behavior	Height, eye color, posture, language
Phylogeny	Evolutionary history of a species, especially in terms of ancestral relations to other species	
Scaffolding	Referring to connections between mental structures (concepts, goals) that emerge from ontogenetic or phylogenetic processes	Physical warmth (temperature) and social warmth (trust) are mentally associated
Sexual selection	Process focusing on traits that promote success at intrasexual competition and intersexual mate choice, often at a cost to survival-related fitness	Sexual dimorphisms, costly signaling

(1943, p. 392) claimed in his seminal work on motivation, "It is no more necessary to study animals before one can study man than it is to study mathematics before one can study geology or psychology or biology." Instead, an evolutionary perspective provides a meta-theory that helps to integrate research from a diverse range of fields that speak to social cognitive processes, from psychology to anthropology to economics.

ADAPTIVE SOCIAL COGNITION

Research using an evolutionary perspective has demonstrated how a wide span of social cognitive processes are tuned to produce functional solutions to adaptively important goals. Much of this research falls into two structural bins: lower-order perception effects and higher-order, interpersonally relevant processing. Within these bins, many of the standard topics in social cognition – accuracy and bias, attention and memory, categorization, person perception, stereotypes, emotion, theory of mind, and so on – have been reframed in an evolutionary light. Such processes address goals at multiple levels of analysis (e.g., proximal, developmental), but the general focus of most evolutionary research has been on providing answers to the question of the ultimate function, or biological adaptiveness, of cognitive structures (Kenrick, Griskevicius, Neuberg, & Schaller,

2010; Tinbergen, 1963). That is, what is this process good for? Why does it exist? How might it have aided a person over the course of evolutionary time? This latter question is critical, because although cognitive processes are likely to have been adaptive when they emerged in the ancestral past, it is also likely that relatively recent ecological and cultural changes have created environments in which some of these processes no longer maintain the same adaptive value. Thus, evolutionary researchers typically pursue questions of historical function, and of the related issue of historical contingency (i.e., Do features exist as they do simply because their evolution has been constrained by what previously existed?).

A focus on function does not imply that mental adaptations produce perfect outcomes. Changes in environments over time can lead to errors in information processing. People also make errors even in situations that match ancestrally relevant problems. Researchers have traditionally regarded such problems as the result of improperly applied heuristics or as motivated by a desire to enhance proximate feelings of self-esteem (e.g., Greenberg et al., 1993; Kahneman, Slovic, & Tversky, 1982; Miller & Ross, 1975). However, many error-generating cognitive biases are entirely consistent with, and in fact predicted by, an evolutionary approach. Factual accuracy is not necessarily the purpose of natural selection. Instead, biases should arise wherever they promote more functional outcomes for basic adaptive problems. This notion is detailed by *error management theory* (EMT), which suggests that cognitive biases are often not flaws, but design features that improve responses under uncertainty (Haselton & Buss, 2000; Haselton & Nettle, 2006; see also Ackerman, Shapiro, & Maner, 2009; Gigerenzer & Goldstein, 1996; Goldstein & Gigerenzer, 2002; Nesse, 2005). EMT considers information processing as a signal detection problem, and points out that false-negative and false-positive judgments or decisions may actually aid people's fundamental goal pursuit. When judgments are uncertain, people may err on the side of overinclusiveness (a false-positive bias) or underinclusiveness (a false-negative bias). Though it may seem that both errors are substandard outcomes, uncertainty will inevitably produce errors, and thus it pays for people to exhibit the "correct" form of bias. EMT describes the evolutionary pressures that led to particular directions of bias as, on average, a function of minimizing the more adaptively costly errors.

For example, people may overweight public self-relevant information as in the case of the spotlight effect. In this effect, people presume their actions are more salient to others than is true (Gilovich, Medvec, & Savitsky, 2000; Savitsky,

Epley, & Gilovich, 2001). Strictly speaking, such beliefs can be considered to be errors (e.g., involving anchoring and adjustment), but the *direction* of these errors suggests that they may also be adaptive solutions to uncertainty. Public self-relevant information is critically important to one's place in a social group, and thus giving this information more weight than it deserves may encourage people to maintain their social affiliations by adhering to group norms and self-censoring deviant behavior. In another example of error management, people tend to underweight signals of forgiveness after committing transgressions (Friesen, Fletcher, & Overall, 2005). Doing so may encourage stronger, and more effective, reconciliation attempts than would otherwise occur. In sum, oversensitivity to reputational information and undersensitivity to forgiveness information may help prevent consequences that could be deadly in ancestral environments, such as ostracism and aggression (Baumeister & Leary, 1995; Haselton & Nettle, 2006). Thus, social cognitive biases should be viewed in terms of their ultimate, adaptive effects, and not whether they represent logical or "accurate" ways of thinking.

Highlighting adaptive function in this way shifts the conceptual frame typically applied to social cognition. It suggests that classic formulations – those that organize the mind according to process or mental structure – might (unintentionally) present commonalities between processes or structures that evolved for quite distinct purposes. For example, understanding how emotion works in general is a worthwhile pursuit, but different emotions serve (and likely arose to serve) very different functions; thus, we might predict that particular emotions are somewhat different in both what they do *and* how they do it. The same may be true of most classic social cognitive constructions, including stereotypes, social comparisons, and so on (e.g., Todd, Hertwig, & Hoffrage, 2005). The mental gerrymandering in which we typically engage, although useful, may interfere with an understanding of the mind as a toolbox for solving specific types of problems. It is important to point out that answering questions of function has historically been integral to research on human cognition (e.g., James, 1890/1950). The modern advent of sociobiology and evolutionary psychology has given this problem-based approach the theoretical spotlight. To shine in this spotlight, then, we might first want to answer: What problems might cognitive processes have evolved to solve?

Fundamental social domains

There are innumerable goals that humans pursue on a day-to-day basis, yet the vast majority of these are representative of a set of fundamental social goals. In fact, these fundamental goals themselves filter down into one primary purpose – facilitating differential reproduction. Reproduction, and the reproductive fitness of offspring, is the final cause (in the Aristotelian sense) of social cognition. (Readers unfamiliar with this approach should note that this problem of differential reproduction, along with those discussed below, is ultimate in nature and not necessarily what a person would explicitly or even implicitly report.) Considering all aspects of social cognition as (potentially) feeding into this one primary purpose illuminates research questions that would otherwise go unasked, and reshapes our understanding of how and how well cognition works. Of course, there are many steps that people take to address this purpose. A number of researchers have attempted to organize these steps into functional domains of social life (e.g., Ackerman & Kenrick, 2008; Bugental, 2000; Buss, 1999; Fiske, 1992; Kenrick, Li, & Butner, 2003; Kenrick et al., 2010). Such organizations share a great deal of commonality (good for those theorists positing universal mechanisms), allowing us to consider social cognitive processing from the standpoint of relatively few adaptive functions. These domains include interpersonal aggression (enacting and reacting to physical threats), disease avoidance (protecting oneself from contagious agents), mating (selecting, attracting, and keeping romantic partners), status (power and prestige considerations), affiliation (managing social connections), and inclusive fitness (managing relationships with biologically related others). These fundamental domains, which we now review, incorporate most of the common problems a person might encounter in social situations.

Interpersonal aggression

The domain of interpersonal aggression refers to the ways in which people physically threaten and are threatened by others. Much of the social cognitive work in this domain has investigated responses to direct or indirect threat cues. Perhaps the most commonly studied direct threat cue is the angry expression. A large literature suggests that people are especially attuned to the presence of angry individuals, and devote a high degree of cognitive resources to these individuals. This is true from a very early age, as infants rapidly visually discriminate anger and respond with functionally appropriate negative behaviors (e.g., Serrano, Iglesias, & Loeches, 1995). As adults, people also find it difficult to disengage their visual attention from angry faces, and they exhibit enhanced memory for such faces (e.g., Ackerman, Shapiro, Becker, Neuberg, & Kenrick, 2011; Fox et al.,

2000; Jackson, Wu, Linden, & Raymond, 2009; Öhman, Flykt, & Esteves, 2001). These patterns are especially strong in high-anxiety individuals or individuals primed with other cues to threat (e.g., Fox, Russo, Bowles, & Dutton, 2001), suggesting that the goal to avoid harm sensitizes (and perhaps oversensitizes) people to potential dangers. Interestingly, identification of anger is quicker when it appears on male faces than on female faces (Becker, Kenrick, Neuberg, Blackwell, & Smith, 2007). This effect appears to be due to the evolution of the physical structure of male and female faces, and not existing gender stereotypes. Specialized attunement to male anger may be quite functional, as men are more likely to inflict physical damage on others (Vivian & Langhinrichsen-Rohling, 1994), and more likely to engage in extreme aggressive thinking (e.g., homicidal fantasies) (Buss, 2005; Kenrick & Sheets, 1993).

Indirect safety threats can take many forms, but evolutionary accounts have largely focused on group membership as a cue to the presence or absence of potential threat. Humans are naturally group-forming creatures (Baumeister & Leary, 1995; Caporael, 1997), and the group boundaries we create afford other people relevance for our fundamental goals. That is, the interpersonal interactions that mattered most to individuals' evolutionary outcomes (e.g., mate selection, reciprocal exchange, negotiation of status hierarchies) historically occurred within coalitional groups. This is still largely true today (Fiske, 1992). We are also more interdependent and empathetic with these "in-group" members. Indeed, when faced with safety threats, in-group members band together, increasing the likelihood of in-group prosocial behavior (e.g., Griskevicius et al., 2006; Van Vugt, De Cremer, & Janssen, 2007). Because of the diversity of outcomes these close ties allow, in-group interactions necessitate more complex inferences than interactions with out-group members.

Whereas in-group members afford us a variety of potential benefits, over evolutionary time, out-group members have typically not. As a result, out-group membership serves as an easy cue to potential threat (this is true even if the base rate of threats is higher within in-groups). Consistent with this idea, people heuristically associate many out-group members with harm (e.g., Becker et al., 2010; Cottrell & Neuberg, 2005; Eberhardt, Goff, Purdie, & Davies, 2004; Faulkner, Schaller, Park, & Duncan, 2004; Navarrete et al., 2009; Trawalter, Todd, Baird, & Richeson, 2008). People also more readily perceive intentions of threat in out-group members (Maner et al., 2005), especially when primed by cues to danger such as ambient darkness (Schaller, Park, & Mueller, 2003). Out-group members may also frequently be the targets of cognitions that facilitate aggression, such as dehumanization (e.g., Bandura, Underwood, & Fromson, 1975; Harris & Fiske, 2006).

Out-group membership often has been operationalized in terms of racial differences (in fact, race is not itself a "natural" category, but a proxy for group membership; Kurzban, Tooby, & Cosmides, 2001), but can be indicated by religious, cultural, gender, and many other individual differences as well. Combinations of group cues also may produce particular functional relevancies (e.g., Black men are more associated with physical threat than Black women; Navarrete, McDonald, Molina, & Sidanius, 2010). Indirect threat cues become especially powerful in their effects on cognition when accompanied by direct threat cues. For instance, subliminally priming images of guns and knives leads White perceivers to visually attend more to Black men (Eberhardt et al., 2004). Angry expressions can amplify memory for Black men, even countering cognitive processing deficits typically found for out-group members (Ackerman et al., 2006; also see Becker et al., 2010). At an evaluative level, although people's judgments of stimuli typically contrast away from extreme examples (Schwarz & Bless, 1992), White individuals viewing angry Black men assimilate the perceived threat to other, non-angry Black faces (Shapiro, Ackerman, Neuberg, Maner, Becker, & Kenrick, 2009). Such findings highlight the functional tuning of a number of cognitive processes – by devoting more resources to the processing of potential safety threats, people are likely better able to track and respond to (and less likely to miss) these dangers.

Disease avoidance

Interpersonal aggression is not the only safety-related danger associated with social interaction. People are also carriers of contagious diseases. This is not simply due to the advent of large, modern societies. Disease-causing organisms have been a recurrent problem throughout human evolutionary history (Gangestad & Buss, 1993; Low, 1990). People, therefore, likely acquired specific cognitive strategies for managing disease-relevant cues (Gangestad, Haselton, & Buss, 2006; Kurzban & Leary, 2001; Park, Faulkner, & Schaller, 2003; Zebrowitz & Collins, 1997). Although these strategies should produce somewhat similar responses to those in the interpersonal aggression domain, there are important differences. For example, the emotion of disgust functions in the service of disease avoidance (Tybur, Lieberman, & Griskevicius, 2009), and is seen in reaction to targets associated with disease, whereas anger is generally not (Cottrell & Neuberg, 2005). The relatively indirect and invisible nature

of disease transmission suggests that people may be especially likely to over-perceive or over-react to a wide variety of cues (Haselton & Nettle, 2006; Kurzban & Leary, 2001; Li, Ackerman, White, Neuberg, & Kenrick, 2011; Tybur, Bryan, Magnan, & Caldwell Hooper, 2011). That is, although people may have developed some lay theory of contagion (probably mediated by physical contact), the uncertain and constantly changing nature of disease threats would promote heuristic avoidance responses to many cues that are actually not indicative of contagion.

Indeed, people associate a large number of physical and behavioral abnormalities with disease (e.g., Park, Schaller, & Crandall, 2007; Schaller, Park, & Faulkner, 2003; Zebrowitz, Fellous, Mignault, & Andreoletti, 2003). For example, people attend to but show decreased preference for others with unusual facial features such as birthmarks, scars, and other asymmetries (e.g., Ackerman et al., 2009; Grammer & Thornhill, 1994; Kurzban & Leary, 2001). (Such asymmetries may in fact be indicative of early-life exposure to disease agents [Thornhill & Gangestad, 1993].) When primed with other cues to disease, people also become more suspicious of out-group members (who may be carriers of diseases to which perceivers have not developed immunity), infer less extraversion and openness in themselves (which can inhibit interpersonal contact), and behaviorally avoid others (e.g., Heinemann, Pellander, Vogelbusch, & Wojtek, 1981; Houston & Bull, 1994; Mortensen, Becker, Ackerman, Neuberg, & Kenrick, 2010). A number of other yet-untested formulations of classic social cognitive constructs may emerge from a motivation to avoid disease.

Mating

A large portion of research taking an evolutionary approach has focused, to some degree, on the topic of mating. It is clear why – differential reproduction represents the primary end of the evolutionary game. However, mating processes are also linked by Darwin's other major theory, sexual selection. Sexual selection suggests that heritable traits that promote competitive success for mates will be selected, even if they negatively affect survival (Darwin, 1871). Thus, people may take risks, spend themselves into the poorhouse, or even kill each other as a function of (ultimate, unconscious) reproductive pressures (e.g., Daly & Wilson, 1983, 1988; Miller, 1998, 2000).

Within the broad domain of mating, several unique types of problems exist (Miller & Todd, 1998). People must select, attract, and retain romantic partners. Selection, as with all forms of judgment and decision making, involves evaluation of relevant criteria and determination that those criteria pass some threshold of acceptability. There is broad agreement about the criteria that are important for "good" mating decisions (e.g., most people want romantic partners who are kind, trustworthy, intelligent, and likable), but much research has also examined sex differences in the qualities people desire in mates (Buss, 1989; Li, Bailey, Kenrick, & Linsenmeier, 2002; Schmitt, 2005). This work has consistently shown that women tend to prefer status and resource-acquisition potential in potential mates more than men do, whereas men tend to prefer indicators of physical attractiveness and fecundity more than women do (e.g., Buss, 1989; Buss & Barnes, 1986; Buunk, Dijkstra, Fetchenhauer, & Kenrick, 2002; Li et al., 2002). Generally, women are more selective than men in the qualities they judge to be romantically acceptable (Buss & Schmitt, 1993; Kenrick, Sadalla, Groth, & Trost, 1990). This discrepancy is explained by the principle of parental investment, which stresses that in any sexual species marked by differential investment in offspring, the sex that invests more will be choosier in selecting mates (Trivers, 1972). In people, women spend more physiological resources to produce eggs than men do to produce sperm, and women spend more time rearing children; thus, women are romantically choosier. Of course, degree of choosiness also depends on the type of relationship, or mating strategy, people pursue (Gangestad & Simpson, 2000). When looking for long-term, committed partners, men and women often look for similar qualities, though when looking for short-term partners (a situation that exaggerates the costs of choosing poorly) women tend to be somewhat pickier than men (Buss & Schmitt, 1993; Clark & Hatfield, 1989; Kenrick et al., 1990; Li & Kenrick, 2006).

The ways in which people attract and retain romantic partners extend these patterns of evaluation. Because parental investment leads women to be choosier than men, women often play the role of selector and men often play the role of selectee (Miller, 1998). In terms of mate quality (reproductive potential), everyone is not created equal, and thus men typically compete to be selected (Buss, 1988; Geary, Vigil, & Byrd-Craven, 2004). This competition can be direct, through combat or ritualized events, but it commonly takes the form of *costly signaling*. Such signals require significant investment and are designed (at a functional level) to demonstrate the quality of a particular man over and above that of other men. Think peacock tails (although in men we see other forms of conspicuous consumption, such as sports cars and picking up the check at meals). When presented with mating-relevant cues, men exhibit increased attention to attractive women as well as correspondingly

riskier judgments, less conformity, more creativity, and a variety of other cognitive changes that act as costly signals (e.g., Griskevicius, Cialdini, & Kenrick, 2006; Griskevicius et al., 2007; Maner et al., 2003; Miller, 2000; Van den Bergh, Dewitte, & Warlop, 2008). In some instances, men may be motivated to pursue more rapid romantic commitment (Ackerman, Griskevicius, & Li, 2011), and they may even begin to think cooperatively in order to overcome the romantic thresholds that women (utilizing their own forms of cooperation as a method of quality control) set (Ackerman & Kenrick, 2009).

Once a romantic couple forms, people's cognition shifts to a mate-retention mindset. This produces increased attentional focus on desirable members of the same sex (to ward off potential interlopers), paired with a reduction in attraction to the opposite sex (to reduce the potential of straying). A host of additional defensive strategies also come on-line (e.g., Buss & Shackelford, 1997; Campbell & Ellis, 2005; Maner, Gailliot, Rouby, & Miller, 2007; Maner, Rouby, Gonzaga, 2008; Shackelford, Goetz, & Buss, 2005; Simpson, Gangestad, & Lerma, 1990). These kinds of empirical findings highlight the importance of romantic concerns at an ultimate, if not a proximate level, and indicate that many outcomes beyond simple direct mating decisions are influenced by mating-related cognition.

Status

The drive for power and prestige within social groups is a hallmark of all societies (Barkow, 1989; Brown, 1991; Eibl-Eibesfeldt, 1989). The motivation to acquire status likely stems from the natural tendency for human groups to form dominance hierarchies (indeed, this is true of all group-living primates), and for higher-ranking members of those hierarchies to prosper (for a more detailed review of status-based processes, see Fiske, 2010). In fact, attaining status can result in greater interpersonal influence (Miller, Collins, & Brief, 1995), material resources (Cummins, 1998), and self-esteem (Tesser, 1988), as well as decreases in stress-related health problems (Adler, Epel, Castellazzo, & Ickovics, 2000; Cummins, 2008). Objective status is thus certainly valuable, but even perceiving relatively high levels of status can produce many of these benefits independent of actual status (Cummins, 2008).

It is no surprise, then, that people possess a number of cognitive adaptations that facilitate status seeking. For example, many of the positive illusions people exhibit, from unrealistic optimism to a heightened sense of personal control, likely function by encouraging successful actions, promoting the signaling of high-quality traits, and buffering against failures (Campbell, 1986; Haselton & Nettle, 2006; Weinstein, 1980). These illusions act as forms of self- and other-deception that can aid people faced with status challenges (Cummins, 2008; von Hippel & Trivers, 2011). Competing motivations to maintain group membership may help to constrain unrealistic status perceptions within groups, however (Anderson, Srivastava, Beer, Spataro, & Chatman, 2006). Other cognitions motivated by status seeking include legitimizing perceptions of rigid social structures (Sidanius & Pratto, 2001), the desire for leadership (Van Vugt, Hogan, & Kaiser, 2008), and preferences for the use of particular social exchange rules (Ackerman & Kenrick, 2008; Fiske, 1992). Interestingly, the manner in which our minds are shaped by status ambitions may depend on the stability of one's status position. We might expect that status attainment is associated with competitive thoughts, and indeed, people who acquire high status act competitively (or selfishly) when status hierarchies are unstable. However, when one's position is relatively safe, high-status individuals instead behave more cooperatively, focusing on group goals (Maner & Mead, 2010).

Although women gain a number of social and material benefits by elevating their power and prestige, men gain a unique benefit from rising in the status hierarchy – an increase in mating attractiveness. As mentioned earlier, status confers romantic desirability on men to a much stronger degree than it does on women (Baize & Schroeder, 1995; Buss, 1989; Li et al., 2002). Thus, the advertisement of status by men is largely a function of sexual selection pressures. Men therefore are more attuned than women to potential losses of status (Daly & Wilson, 1988; Gutierres, Kenrick, & Partch, 1999). This cross-domain benefit of status suggests that status cognitions overlap with mating cognitions, at least for men. For example, men who perceive a higher proportion of males relative to females in their environment (a cue to mating competition) respond by mentally discounting the future and accepting more risk in their decisions (a status-relevant outcome) (Griskevicius, Tybur, Ackerman, Delton, & Robertson, in press). The same is not true for women. We might expect similar forms of overlap in other situations that cue mating and status.

Affiliation

People everywhere desire to form social groups (Baumeister & Leary, 1995; Caporael, 1997; Leary & Cox, 2007). In-group relationships afford a number of benefits – safety, romance, direction in uncertain situations – and thus people attempt to manage those social connections using a variety of rules, incentives, and cognitive biases. Perhaps the best-known decision rule that helps to maintain effective group functioning is reciprocal altruism (Axelrod & Hamilton, 1981; Trivers, 1971). From an evolutionary perspective, cooperation between unrelated individuals is a puzzle (Why help others if it doesn't help my own genes?), but reciprocal altruism ensures that many interactions will involve relatively equal exchanges (Clark, Mills, & Powell, 1986; Fiske, 1992; see also Cosmides & Tooby, 1992). Indeed, many in-group relationships are reciprocal in nature (Ackerman & Kenrick, 2008; van Lange, 1999; Van Vugt & van Lange, 2006). The notion that people (and many other animals; Trivers, 1971) are inclined towards exchanges that are often time delayed and content varying requires the use of particular social cognitive abilities. People must remember their interaction partners, and they must be able to calculate the abstract value of exchange goods and services. Additionally, people need to be on the lookout for free riders – those trying to cheat the system by drawing physical or social resources without adequate repayment (Price, Cosmides, & Tooby, 2002; Yamagishi, 1986). Although social norms help to reduce cheating behavior, people have evolved specialized mechanisms for detecting cheaters in social exchanges (e.g., Cosmides, 1989) and for responding negatively to exchange violations (e.g., Fehr & Gächter, 2002).

The fundamental nature of the goal for social connection is acutely made by research on threats to one's place in a group – the problem of social exclusion. Forms of exclusion (rejection, ostracism, being ignored) are hugely impactful on individuals, producing an array of negative consequences on judgment, self-control, emotion, and mental health (Baumeister & Leary, 1995; Williams, 2007a, 2007b). For example, after being excluded, people feel pain (Eisenberger, Lieberman, & Williams, 2003), exhibit deficits in intelligent thought and the ability to self-regulate appropriately (Baumeister & DeWall, 2005), and experience aspects of emotional numbness (DeWall, Baumeister, & Masicampo, 2009). When given the opportunity, people also display a compensatory motivation to make connections with new and old interaction partners. For instance, excluded people conform more to others' opinions (Williams, Cheung, & Choi, 2000), form more positive impressions of and desires to interact with new people (Maner, DeWall, Baumeister, & Schaller, 2007), and spend money in the service of identifying with others (Mead, Baumeister, Stillman, Rawn, & Vohs, 2011). These patterns make functional sense. Over evolutionary time, exclusion would have been tantamount to a death sentence, and thus people should possess mechanisms that are especially sensitive to exclusion.

Therefore, people are attuned to cues of potential rejection, like averted gaze (Wirth, Sacco, Hugenberg, & Williams, 2010), and they may also over-respond by anthropomorphizing animals and objects after exclusion (Epley, Waytz, & Cacioppo, 2007). One important cognitive mechanism that helps to regulate social connections is self-esteem. Instead of representing a domain-general evaluative mechanism, as it has traditionally been considered, self-esteem may have evolved as an indicator of one's level of acceptance in social groups (Leary, Tambor, Terdal, & Downs, 1995; also see Kirkpatrick, & Ellis, 2001).

Inclusive fitness

The domain of inclusive fitness refers to the manner in which people manage relationships with biologically related others. Biological kinship involves a different type of interpersonal tie, characterized by unique psychological mechanisms, than the typical affiliative relationship (Park & Ackerman, 2011). Overlapping genetic structure can itself create an incentive to interact prosocially, if genes for altruism are shared between kin. Thus, the typical (cooperative) decision rule active among related individuals is a function of the cost to oneself relative to the benefit to the other, multiplied by the probability that the relevant gene is shared (Hamilton, 1964). Higher degrees of relatedness often lead to higher degrees of help, in terms of social support (Kivett, 1985), physical safety (Daly & Wilson, 1998), economic inheritance (Smith, Kish, & Crawford, 1987), and even willingness to rush into a burning building to save someone (Burnstein, Crandall, & Kitayama, 1994). However, a high degree of relatedness also often leads to lowered sexual attraction in order to minimize genetic problems with incest (Ackerman, Kenrick, & Schaller, 2007; Fessler & Navarrete, 2004).

These forms of processing do not necessitate many of the cognitive requirements of strategies like reciprocal altruism, but they do require a means of distinguishing kin from non-kin, and closer kin from less close kin. In humans, perceived similarity, familiarity (especially co-residence during childhood), and maternal perinatal association (seeing one's mother caring for an infant from birth) all may act as signals of relatedness (DeBruine, 2005; Lieberman, Tooby, & Cosmides, 2007; Park, Schaller, & Van Vugt, 2008). When such cues are present, people may be over-inclusive, mentally representing unrelated others using kin-based psychological mechanisms (Park & Ackerman, 2011; Shepher, 1971; Westermarck, 1921). This can support outcomes such as surrogate parenting by unrelated individuals (stepparents, friends, elders, etc.), a behavior that, interestingly,

has historically been performed more often by women than men. Kinship over-inclusion is also a likely contributor to "implicit egotism" effects in which liking of and identification with others (as well as with occupations and places to live) is often based merely on superficial similarities such as sharing initials or birthdays (Cohen, Garcia, Apfel, & Master, 2006; Jones, Pelham, Carvallo, & Mirenberg, 2004).

An interesting extension of inclusive fitness involves parent–offspring conflict (Godfray, 1995; Trivers, 1974). Functional, gene-level goals sometimes differ for children and parents, producing tensions over issues of resource investment (e.g., how much and for how long children should be supported), prosocial vs egotistic behavior, and even the decisions children make as adults. For instance, parents often attempt to exert direct or indirect influence over the romantic choices their children make, and these attempts typically stress a different set of mate qualities than children prefer (Buunk, Park, & Dubbs, 2008; Dubbs & Buunk, 2010). In sum, inclusive fitness as a domain of inquiry represents an important, but understudied, window into social cognition.

Domain-specific and domain-flexible cognitive processing

An evolutionary perspective suggests specific ways in which information relevant to functional problems, such as those that arise within fundamental domains, is likely to be processed. Solutions to a given problem are thought to entail the use of distinct, or modular, computational mechanisms that are relatively independent of those used to address other functional problems (Barrett & Kurzban, 2006; Kurzban & Aktipis, 2007; Santos, Hauser, & Spelke, 2002; Sherry & Schacter, 1987; Sperber, 2001; Tooby & Cosmides, 1992). For instance, people use different decision rules and memory procedures to manage language learning, food aversion, facial memory, and spatial location. This modularity involves specificity of processing (e.g., which inputs relate to which functions) but it does not necessarily imply fixed at birth or completely encapsulated responses. Organisms typically possess a number of open-ended mental programs that draw on environmental information to shape those mechanisms' development (Mayr, 1976), or "fill the tank" (consider that cars, which are specialized to accept gasoline as input, can also run on vegetable oil). This information is often fitted to species-specific ecological tasks. For example, rats, which have poor vision and rely on taste and smell to find food at night, easily condition aversions to novel tastes but not to novel visual stimuli (Garcia &

Koelling, 1966). Although commonly misunderstood as "less evolved" than closed programs (which are fixed), open programs are clearly adaptive. Creatures would simply not last long if they were unable to respond to the changing requirements of dynamic environments. People may have an even greater degree of flexibility than many animals in the kinds of information that they apply to particular functional problems, but some degree of processing specificity still exists. We rarely see people trying to make friends with shrubbery or compete for status with sandwiches.

Despite the general lack of one-upmanship between person and lunch, a significant amount of flexibility exists in how domain-relevant information is processed and applied. Cognitive systems may be designed to manage novelty (Flinn, 2006; Gangestad et al., 2006; Miller, 2000) or cast a wide net in terms of which stimuli are perceived as relevant (Bargh, Green, & Fitzsimons, 2008; Haselton & Nettle, 2006), and the biases these systems produce can appear to apply beyond the problems for which they evolved. Consider two examples. From an evolutionary perspective, a mating motivation is designed to promote the search for suitable romantic partners, which, for humans, includes only other humans. However, the decision rules that direct evaluation of suitable mating characteristics may affect a broader set of evaluations. One such characteristic is peak life stage (broadly, time of maximal fecundity). Studies show that an active mating goal causes preferential attunement to targets representing a peak stage of development, such as women in early adulthood but not as toddlers or older adults (Huang & Bargh, 2008). Demonstrating the wide net this motivation may cast, mating-primed peak preference also occurs for other living targets, including bananas and flowers, but not for inorganic objects such as cars.

Another example of flexible processing involves the manner in which people think about their friends. Friendship is a functionally different form of relationship than is biological kinship in that we are not genetically related to our friends. Yet, friends experience many kinship-relevant psychological cues such as prosociality, attitudinal similarity, and self–other overlap (e.g., Park & Schaller, 2005; Park et al., 2008). For a number of reasons, women may experience many of these cues more strongly than men, which may increase the probability that women sometimes view friends as akin to family members (Ackerman et al., 2007). Indeed, women's responses to friends on two important kinship indicators (disgust in response to sexual activity and nepotistic benevolence) suggest that they may process friends using the same mechanisms as those used to process kin (Ackerman et al., 2007; Park & Ackerman, 2011).

Consistent with this, in their work on "befriending" in response to stress, Taylor and colleagues suggest that friendship processes "may have piggybacked onto the attachment-caregiving system" employed in kinship interactions (Taylor et al., 2000, p. 412).

These two examples, peak attunement and friendship processing, demonstrate that the inputs considered relevant for a particular cognitive system may extend beyond the domain for which that system evolved. Along similar conceptual lines, emerging work in the fields of social cognition and neuroscience suggests that open-ended systems might allow for cognitive connections to emerge between seemingly different domains of processing. In the next section, we review the ideas underlying this research and suggest that the cross-modular development of the mind can be explained by one particular perspective – scaffolding theory.

A SCAFFOLDED MIND

An understanding of the human social world requires, and historically has required, great cognitive flexibility. How might people manage the novel information to which they are continually exposed? One possibility is by "fitting" this new information to existing knowledge structures. This process of conceptual integration is the hallmark of *scaffolding* (Williams, Huang, & Bargh, 2009). In architecture, scaffolding refers to supporting physical structures used to shape and construct buildings (we might also think of physical foundations as being a form of scaffolding). This imagery can also be applied to mental structures. In the mind, scaffolding refers to the utilization of primitive (foundational, pre-existing) concepts as the basis for the development of derived (later) conceptual knowledge. This process may be one of active construction, as when parents provide contextual support for language learning (Cazden, 1983; Wood, Bruner, & Ross, 1976), but the focus of much recent work, and our review here, is on the passive, unintentional co-opting of primitive mental structures. In particular, existing work suggests that a key source for primitive concepts involves knowledge of the physical world (Shepard, 1984, 2001; Tooby & Cosmides, 1992), whereas a key source for derived concepts involves more abstract knowledge, including our understanding of the social world. It is clear why – people, and other organisms, must interact with the physical world before they are able to make use of social information. This is of course an overgeneralization, but it remains essentially true. Newborns encounter a host of physical, sensory inputs before developing the mental capacities to understand complex social interactions (Mandler, 1992).

Scaffolding is an experiential process, but its roots extend into the natural history of humans and biological organisms more generally. In fact, our use of the terms *primitive* and *derived* is itself co-opted from the literature on anatomical evolution. In this literature, a derived feature is a physical structure (e.g., a wing) that is adapted from a pre-existing structure (e.g., an arm). As Mayr (1960, p. 377) pointed out, "The emergence of new structures is normally due to the acquisition of a new function by an existing structure . . . the resulting 'new' structure is merely a modification of a preceding structure." The evolutionary development of mental structures likely proceeded in a similar fashion (Bargh & Morsella, 2008; Buss, Haselton, Shackelford, Bleske, & Wakefield, 1998; Kenrick et al., 2010; Panksepp, 2004). More recent mental systems – designed to manage new, recurrent and species-specific needs – were not fashioned out of whole cloth, but built in part from existing materials. These pre-existing structures therefore would have established the groundwork (by analogy, a schema) for the processing of information in novel domains, and likewise set constraints on how the derived structure could function (of course, some modification would necessarily occur in order for the new cognitive system to be adaptive; Wakefield, 1999). Psychologically, then, information processing within a derived domain should retain many of the hallmarks of information processing within the relevant primitive domain. This process of recruiting previously evolved mental systems can be referred to as *phylogenetic scaffolding* (Williams et al., 2009).

Phylogenetic scaffolding is likely widespread throughout the human mind. Over evolutionary time, all organisms have faced certain basic, critical goals – for example, finding and processing food, avoiding predation or environmental damage, and reproduction. As species evolved, some developed more complex social (and psychological) systems. These systems required new ways of managing information, but they also relied on many of the same information-processing mechanisms. The social world is largely physical, after all. Thus, when people deal with interpersonal and intrapersonal psychological issues – e.g., How do I know if she is a good person? How do I know if I'm a good person? – how these issues are addressed is in part influenced by mechanisms that existed previously. This influence could occur simply through constraint of how derived mental mechanisms function (e.g., use of only certain inputs), through recruitment of pre-existing neural regions, or some other process (Anderson, 2007a,

2010). Such questions remain to be answered, but we expect that no one answer is universally true.

In comparison to phylogenetic scaffolding, the application of (primitive) concepts that are experienced over the course of human development to later-experienced information (derived concepts) is referred to as *ontogenetic scaffolding* (Williams et al., 2009). Through ontogenetic scaffolding, basic sensorimotor experiences encountered over the course of development serve as a foundation for understanding later, more abstract concepts. Much of the work supporting the idea of ontogenetic scaffolding, and our focus here, again involves the passive process of utilizing early physical knowledge in the service of later abstract knowledge. This form of scaffolding may recruit phylogenetic linkages, and it may also involve relatively domain-general physical concepts (e.g., sensations) that support integration of higher-level concepts (e.g., beliefs, impressions).

How ontogenetic scaffolding might work is a hotly contested question at present (see Anderson, 2010; Barsalou, 1999; Boroditsky & Ramscar, 2002; Hurley, 2008; Niedenthal, Barsalou, Winkielman, Krauth-Gruber, & Ric, 2005). Generally, research has tended to support the idea that abstract mental tasks recruit brain regions associated with sensorimotor functioning (e.g., thinking about verbs/actions activates motor control areas and thinking about nouns/objects activates vision areas; Damasio & Tranel, 1993). The same is likely true for higher-order cognition, as we describe below.

At least two models strongly make the case for sensorimotor processing serving as the primitive feature on which abstract (and social) processing is scaffolded. One of these, the "neural exploitation hypothesis," suggests that because cognition is for action, thinking about things (simulation) requires activation of action-related brain regions (Gallese, 2008; Gallese & Lakoff, 2005). This occurs because, just as the premotor system functions to control and structure perception and action patterns, the premotor system (becomes decoupled from these procedures and then) is used to control and structure later-arising social cognitive procedures (Gallese, 2008). As Anderson (2010) describes it, people develop schemas through experiences with objects and events that guide actions related to those objects and events. The components of these schemas are used to construct concepts that have some (broadly defined) functional relation to elements of the prior experiences. A second model, the "shared circuits model," provides a more complex, hierarchical construction of feedback loops that are predicated on sensorimotor processes and facilitate social cognitive processing (e.g., mindreading) (for details, see Hurley, 2008). Additional possible models exist, however. For instance, certain emerging theories in neuroscience highlight the re-use of previously existing neural structures, and some of these go beyond the re-use of sensorimotor mechanisms (e.g., Anderson, 2007b, 2010; Dehaene & Cohen, 2007).

In the following empirical review, we focus on the contribution of sensorimotor processing to more abstract social processing. This conceptualization of scaffolding suggests the primacy of physical processing over social processing, which we believe characterizes much of the recent work in the related field of embodied cognition and is generally consistent with evolutionary history (others have seen things differently; e.g., Ostrom, 1984). This should not be taken to mean that social cognition is in any way less important than non-social cognition. Humans are fundamentally a social species, perhaps more so than any other. This fact may argue that people necessarily possess a high degree of specialized, un-scaffolded mental structures for processing the social world; however, it could likewise suggest that a means of facilitating social cognition (through scaffolding) might be an especially important adaptation for humans.

Our claim is not that physical processing can account for the sophisticated nature of *all* human social processing; rather, scaffolding advances our understanding of the development and consequences of this conceptual integration when it does occur. A scaffolding approach also may be uniquely powerful in helping to explain the role of incidental influences on both social judgments and decisions, as well as on goal pursuit. Moreover, it can provide a framework with which to predict domains where these connections are likely to occur. Below, we concentrate on research that employs priming methods to demonstrate such physical and social associations. Because links between primitive and derived structures are often retained, priming methods can be especially useful in revealing these underlying structural connections (Bargh & Chartrand, 2000).

Scaffolded concepts

Work in the realm of embodied social cognition is quite varied, but a representative sample has focused on the manner through which tactile sensory experiences make associated concepts more mentally accessible. Consider the tactile dimension of warmth–coldness, a fundamental object property (Lederman & Klatzky, 1987) and also a fundamental component of interpersonal evaluation (Asch, 1946; Fiske, Cuddy, & Glick, 2007). The conceptual understanding of interpersonal warmth (i.e., trust, helpfulness) may be scaffolded on the sensation of physical warmth because early-life experiences with physical warmth were often manifested during times of care and trust, such as infant–mother contact (Bowlby, 1969; Harlow, 1958). If so, later contact with warm objects should conceptually prime trust and helpfulness. Indeed, in one study, people who briefly held a cup of hot coffee were more likely to rate another person as socially warm than were people who held a cup of iced coffee (Williams & Bargh, 2008). In a second study from this paper, briefly touching a heated therapeutic pad (as opposed to a cold therapeutic pad) increased the likelihood that participants would choose to give a gift to their friends rather than take it for themselves. It also appears that similar neural regions are involved in processing physical and social warmth (Meyer-Lindenberg, 2008). For instance, during an economic trust ("dictator") game, touching a warm product increased people's willingness to sacrifice their own immediate gains for potential future shared profits with a partner, and this increase was mediated by activation in the insula (Kang, Williams, Clark, Gray, & Bargh, 2011). Indeed, the same specific region of insula became activated following physical cold temperature sensation as well as after betrayals of trust (i.e., social coldness) in the economics game (Kang et al., 2011, Study 2).

In addition to temperature, there are three other fundamental object-related properties about which people acquire knowledge – weight, texture, and hardness (Lederman & Klatzky, 1987). Evidence suggests that unique abstract concepts are scaffolded onto these properties as well. Physical weight (heaviness) appears to be associated with importance and seriousness, physical texture (roughness) with difficulty and argumentativeness, and physical hardness with evaluative rigidity. In several studies, people holding heavy clipboards judged job candidates as being more seriously interested in the position, viewed currency as having more value, and engaged in more cognitive elaboration during preference formation tasks (Ackerman, Nocera, & Bargh, 2010; Jostmann, Lakens, & Schubert, 2009). In other studies, touching rough puzzles made social interactions seem less coordinated and effortless, whereas touching hard objects (and even sitting in hard chairs) led people to view others as both more stable and strict, and themselves to engage in more rigid negotiations (Ackerman et al., 2010). Such findings demonstrate how tactile sensorimotor experiences may serve as the conceptual foundation for (facilitating understanding of) derived, abstract knowledge. We have suggested a speculative reason why aspects of social warmth would be commonly tied to physical warmth (cueing infant–caretaker closeness), and the same may be true for other tactile forms of scaffolding (e.g., important things generally are physically heavier, the friction caused by physical roughness makes movement more difficult, hard things are inherently rigid). However, important questions remain as to whether these, and other, scaffolded links are themselves adaptive.

Scaffolded goal pursuit

Much of the research into scaffolded cognition has focused on conceptual linkages. Emerging research, though, suggests that scaffolding may also be implicated in goal-related processes (Williams et al., 2009). A goal is a mental representation of a desired end state, including the means through which to attain that end state (Aarts & Dijksterhuis, 2000; Bargh, 1990; Kruglanski et al., 2002). Mental representations of goals are distinguishable from concepts through their abilities to turn on, persist in activation through a delay, and deactivate following achievement of the end state (Fishbach & Ferguson, 2007). Through scaffolding, one goal may act as a primitive and one as a derived goal such that the activation, operation, and completion of one goal may influence pursuit of the other goal (Williams et al., 2009). Thus, pursuit of one goal may inform progress of the other, linked goal.

Some basic evidence supports the association of physical and social goal processing. For instance, Zhong and Leonardelli (2008) show that participants who recall being socially excluded (an experimental manipulation that threatens affiliation goals; Park & Maner, 2009) rate the ambient temperature as colder compared to participants who do not recall being socially excluded. Both neural regions and genes that process social affiliation threats also appear to overlap with those that process physical pain (Eisenberger, Lieberman, & Williams, 2003; Way, Taylor, & Eisenberger, 2009). For example, social rejection can trigger feelings of physical numbness (DeWall & Baumeister, 2006), which has been identified as a defensive mechanism in the human body to minimize distress from physical injury. If we presume that goal processes which serve social rejection concerns are scaffolded on goal systems that respond to physical pain (see also MacDonald & Leary, 2005), management of pain goals also may interfere with management of rejection goals.

Consistent with this possibility, ingesting a physical painkiller (Tylenol [acetaminophen]) can decrease both affective and neural reactions to social rejection (DeWall et al., 2010). In another set of studies, socially excluded individuals were found to have an increased need for affiliation, but

this need disappeared (i.e., was apparently satisfied) if they had briefly held something warm following the exclusion experience (Bargh & Shalev, in press). Furthermore, even simulating physically safe experiences can interrupt people's goal-driven responses to social rejection, specifically by reducing experienced negative affect as well as intentions to behave prosocially (Huang, Ackerman, & Bargh, 2011).

Another example of goal scaffolding involves the processing of physical and moral contagion. Concerns about physical contagion stem from the fundamental desire to avoid disease transmission. The desired end state of contagion goals involves avoiding physical impurities (social indicators of which are discussed above), and the means through which to attain this state include specific avoidance behaviors and emotions such as disgust (Rozin & Fallon, 1987; Rozin, Millman, & Nemeroff, 1986). Interestingly, concerns about *moral* contagion involve similar outcomes (avoiding moral impurities) attained by similar means (avoidant actions, felt disgust) (Haidt, 2007; Rozin et al., 1999). Consider the moral euphemisms of a "dirty player" who cheats at a game or of "washing away one's sins." Again, we should expect that scaffolding will set the stage for goal-related actions at one level to interfere with goal pursuit at another level. Typically, people judge unethical acts quite negatively. Deliberating on such acts can elicit a desire for physical cleanliness, and engaging in physical cleaning actions can make moral offenses appear less wrong and actually interrupt the goal to restore one's own moral purity (Schnall, Benton, & Harvey, 2009; Zhong & Liljenquist, 2006). The nature of this physical and moral scaffolding may even be specific to the motor modality involved. Verbal offenses trigger a desire to clean the mouth but not the hands, and written offenses trigger a desire to clean the hands but not the mouth (Lee & Schwarz, 2010). It is not yet known whether actual interruptions of social goal pursuits by physical means are modality-specific in this way.

FUTURE DIRECTIONS

Scaffolding

A number of open questions remain regarding a scaffolded view of the human mind. For instance, to what extent are metaphoric priming effects dissociable from pure semantic priming effects? Semantic priming can account for many metaphoric priming effects through the hypothesized process of ontogenetic scaffolding, such that the original physical concept (e.g., hardness) acquires additional, analogous meanings over the course of one's experiences. The process would be similar to that of stereotype formation and eventual automatization. As stereotypes form, the original group-differentiating information (e.g., skin color, gender, age) becomes associated over time with additional group-related content (e.g., stereotypic group qualities gleaned passively from the media, parents, peers, other cultural sources). With sufficient use of the stereotype representation, the new meanings eventually become co-activated with the old in an all-or-none fashion (Devine, 1989; Hayes-Roth, 1977). In this way, the (more concrete) features that activated the original concept (e.g., physical hardness) now also activate the accrued (more abstract) features as well (e.g., decreased willingness to compromise).

There is no reason why embodied grounding or metaphoric priming effects must all have the same underlying cause. There may well be multiple causes: semantic priming may be responsible for some types of connections, possibly hard/soft or rough/smooth, but not be as necessary in the production of others, such as warm/cold, which are supported by specific anatomical connections (Kang et al., 2011). It is here that developmental research on infants and toddlers (pre-verbal children), as well as on non-human primates, would be especially useful in distinguishing between possible innate, early-experience, and semantic priming accounts of physical-to-psychological influences (see Dunham et al., 2008). If these physical influences on social judgments and behavior are found in children who have not yet developed complex semantic knowledge, or in other primates, this would favor an innate account over a semantic priming interpretation. We consider such developmental-comparative approaches as critical for future investigations of the scaffolded human mind.

Reconceptualizing social cognition

The domain-oriented approach espoused by evolutionary perspectives represents a shift from traditional phenomenon- or process-oriented approaches to social cognition. Cognitive structures previously examined in terms of process (i.e., how they work) may be fruitfully re-examined in terms of function (i.e., why they work). One prime candidate for functional reappraisal is the self-construct. The self, and various processes related to the self (e.g., self-esteem, self-enhancement, self-control, self-consistency), are standard topics within social cognition (e.g., Bandura, 1989; Brewer, 1991; Kihlstrom & Klein, 1994). Such aspects of the self-construct are typically considered quite

broadly in their function, even when the self is divided into multiple component structures such as good selves, bad selves, ought selves, and ideal selves (Markus & Nurius, 1986).

Yet, from an evolutionary perspective, component selves cannot be generally good or bad, but only good or bad *for some purpose*. The notion of a coherent, singular self makes even less sense (Bargh & Huang, 2009; Kurzban & Aktipis, 2007). Different aspects of the self likely arose for different purposes, and at different times. Indeed, this evolutionarily derived, function-driven perspective has been applied to multiple aspects of mental life that have traditionally been considered under the aegis of the self, including self-representations (Kurzban & Aktipis, 2007), beliefs (von Hippel & Trivers, 2011), motivations (Bargh & Huang, 2009; Tetlock, 2002), and phenomenal states associated with consciousness (Morsella, 2005). Similar conclusions might be drawn about other traditional concepts, such as contrast and assimilation effects (Shapiro et al., 2009). Across various functional domains, these phenomena may exhibit important differences of process and outcome, suggesting that we may wish to view the mind first in terms of function and only then in terms of process.

Reconsidering how the conceptual joints of social cognitive research are carved offers other intriguing implications. The very term *unconscious* has been used in social cognition, and cognitive science more generally, primarily to refer to effects that occur when a person is unaware of the presence of a stimulus, thus operationalizing "unconscious" processes in terms of what the mind can do with subliminally presented stimuli (e.g., Dehaene, Changeux, Naccache, Sackur, & Sergent, 2006; Loftus & Klinger, 1992). That same term, however, has long been used in evolutionary theory to refer to the *unintended* aspects of a process, which were assumed to involve supraliminal, not subliminal stimuli. Darwin (1859) used the term "unconscious" (Freud was only 3 at the time) when describing how farmers and stockbreeders produced larger ears of corn and fatter sheep by implicitly following the laws of natural selection. Moreover, Dawkins (1976) wrote of nature as the "blind watchmaker, the unconscious watchmaker," stressing that there was no intentional guiding hand in producing complex, evolved designs (see also Bargh & Morsella, 2008; Buss et al., 1998; Dennett, 1991, 1995). Limiting (theoretically) the powers of unconscious influence to how the mind can handle subliminally presented stimuli is a conceptual mistake, as it confuses the operational definition of an unconscious process with the actual scope or domain of its operation (Bargh, 1992; Morsella & Bargh, 2011). It also puts a conceptual roadblock in the way of appreciating the role of the unconscious over evolutionary time periods, because it is difficult to understand why such a supposedly sophisticated system would be adapted merely to process rarely-if-ever occurring subliminal-strength stimuli. After all, natural selection shaped the human unconscious over the eons through experience with normal, supraliminal stimuli, not subliminal stimuli.

CONCLUSION

Recent decades have seen a rapid expansion in interest in applying an evolutionary perspective to questions of social cognition. We expect that this trend will continue. Evolutionary approaches are especially interesting to people wishing to connect human cognition with the rest of the biological world, and they help answer the call for "bigger picture" theorizing in the field of psychology (e.g., Bargh, 2006; Conway & Schaller, 2002; Kruglanski, 2001). Any number of novel hypotheses may be spawned by explicitly considering social cognition in terms of adaptive problems rather than traditional constructs. After all, "Is it not reasonable to anticipate that our understanding of the human mind would be aided greatly by knowing the purpose for which it was designed?" (Williams, 1966, p. 16). However, we do not expect evolutionary psychology to become an encapsulated research area within psychology more generally. It is simply a metatheoretical approach to situating psychological effects and to hypothesis generation, and as such, must be integrated with other metatheoretical approaches to explain social cognitive (and other) phenomena at multiple levels of analysis. This process is now well underway (e.g., Gangestad et al., 2006; Kenrick et al., 2010; Low, 1998; Norenzayan, Schaller, & Heine, 2006).

The notion of scaffolding, along with other models of mental derivation, may facilitate the understanding of higher-order cognitive processes across these multiple analytical levels. We hope that these models will help to integrate evolutionary theorizing with the increasingly expanding field of embodied cognition. The accuracy of such models remains to be determined, of course, but it is inescapable that how we think about ourselves and others is in large part a product of our species' evolutionary history. This recognition should bring a sense of satisfaction to all psychologists desirous of connecting their work to the other natural sciences. But it should also excite those who appreciate the new light that an evolutionary perspective can shed on the fundamental questions of social cognition.

REFERENCES

Aarts, H., & Dijksterhuis, A. (2000). Habits as knowledge structures: Automaticity in goal-directed behavior. *Journal of Personality and Social Psychology, 78,* 53–63.

Ackerman, J. M., Becker, D. V., Mortensen, C. R., Sasaki, T., Neuberg, S. L., & Kenrick, D. T. (2009). A pox on the mind: Disjunction of attention and memory in processing physical disfigurement. *Journal of Experimental Social Psychology, 45,* 478–485.

Ackerman, J. M., Griskevicius, V., & Li, N. P. (2011). Let's get serious: Communicating commitment in romantic relationships. *Journal of Personality and Social Psychology, 100,* 1079–1094.

Ackerman, J. M., & Kenrick, D. T. (2008). The costs of benefits: Help–refusals highlight key trade-offs of social life. *Personality and Social Psychology Review, 12,* 118–140.

Ackerman, J. M., & Kenrick, D. T. (2009). Cooperative courtship: Helping friends raise and raze relationship barriers. *Personality and Social Psychology Bulletin, 35,* 1285–1300.

Ackerman, J. M., Kenrick, D. T., & Schaller, M. (2007). Is friendship akin to kinship? *Evolution & Human Behavior, 28,* 365–374.

Ackerman, J. M., Nocera, C. C., & Bargh, J. A. (2010). Incidental haptic sensations influence social judgments and decisions. *Science, 328,* 1712–1715.

Ackerman, J. M., Shapiro, J. R., Becker, D. V., Neuberg, S. L., & Kenrick, D. T. (2011). *The emotional bystander: Effects of emotional expression on memory for the unexpressive.* Manuscript submitted for publication.

Ackerman, J. M., Shapiro, J. R., & Maner, J. K. (2009). When is it good to believe bad things? *Behavioral and Brain Sciences, 32,* 510–511.

Ackerman, J. M., Shapiro, J. R., Neuberg, S. L., Kenrick, D. T., Becker, D. V., Griskevicius, V., et al. (2006). They all look the same to me (unless they're angry): From out-group homogeneity to out-group heterogeneity. *Psychological Science, 17,* 836–840.

Adler, N. E., Epel, E. S., Castellazzo, G., & Ickovics, J. R. (2000). Relationship of subjective and objective social status with psychological and physiological functioning: Preliminary data in healthy white women. *Health Psychology, 19,* 586–92.

Anderson, C., Srivastava, S., Beer, J. S., Spataro, S. E., & Chatman, J. A. (2006). Knowing your place: Self-perceptions of status in face-to-face groups. *Journal of Personality and Social Psychology, 91,* 1094–1110.

Anderson, M. L. (2007a). Evolution of cognitive function via redeployment of brain areas. *The Neuroscientist, 13,* 13–21.

Anderson, M.L. (2007b). The massive redeployment hypothesis and the functional topography of the brain. *Philosophical Psychology, 20,* 143–174.

Anderson, M.L. (2010). Neural reuse: A fundamental organizational principle of the brain. *Behavioral and Brain Sciences, 33,* 245–266.

Asch, S. E. (1946). Forming impressions of personality. *Journal of Abnormal and Social Psychology, 41,* 258–290.

Axelrod, R., & Hamilton, W. D. (1981). The evolution of cooperation. *Science, 211*, 1390–1396.

Baize, H. R., & Schroeder, J. E. (1995). Personality and mate
selection in personal ads: Evolutionary preferences in a
public mate selection process. *Journal of Social Behavior
and Personality, 10*, 517–536.

Bandura, A. (1989). Human agency in social cognitive theory.
American Psychologist, 44, 1175–1184.

Bandura, A., Underwood, B., & Fromson, M. E. (1975).
Disinhibition of aggression through diffusion of responsibil-
ity and dehumanization of victims. *Journal of Research in
Personality, 9*, 253–269.

Bargh, J. A. (1990). Auto-motives: Preconscious determinants
of social interaction. In E. T. Higgins & R. M. Sorrentino
(Eds.), *Handbook of motivation and cognition* (Vol. 2,
pp. 93–130). New York: Guilford Press.

Bargh, J. A. (1992). Why subliminality does not matter to
social psychology: Awareness of the stimulus versus
awareness of its influence. In R. F. Bornstein & T. S. Pittman
(Eds.), *Perception without awareness* (pp. 236–255).
New York: Guilford Press.

Bargh, J. A. (2006). What have we been priming all these
years? On the development, mechanisms, and ecology of
nonconscious social behavior. *European Journal of Social
Psychology, 36*, 147–168.

Bargh, J. A., & Chartrand, T. L. (2000). The mind in the middle:
A practical guide to priming and automaticity research.
In H. T. Reis & C. M. Judd (Eds.), *Handbook of research
methods in social and personality psychology*. New York:
Cambridge University Press.

Bargh, J. A., Green, M. L., & Fitzsimons, G. M. (2008). The
selfish goal: Unintended consequences of intended goal
pursuits. *Social Cognition, 26*, 520–540.

Bargh, J.A., & Huang, J.Y. (2009). The selfish goal. In
G. Moskowitz & H. Grant (Eds.), *The psychology of goals*
(pp. 127–150). New York: Guilford Press.

Bargh, J. A., & Morsella, E. (2008). The unconscious mind.
Perspectives on Psychological Science, 3, 73–79.

Bargh, J. A., & Shalev, I. (in press). The substitutability
of physical warmth and social warmth in daily life.
Emotion.

Barkow, J. H. (1989). *Darwin, sex, and status: Biological
approaches to mind and culture.* Toronto, Canada:
University of Toronto Press.

Barrett, H. C., Frederick, D. A., Haselton, M. G., & Kurzban, R.
(2006). Can manipulations of cognitive load be used to test
evolutionary hypotheses? *Journal of Personality and Social
Psychology, 91*, 513–518.

Barrett, H. C., & Kurzban, R. (2006). Modularity in cognition:
Framing the debate. *Psychological Review, 113*,
628–647.

Barsalou, L. W. (1999). Perceptual symbol systems. *Behavioral
and Brain Sciences, 22*, 577–609.

Baumeister, R. F., & DeWall, C. N. (2005). Inner disruption
following social exclusion: Reduced intelligent thought
and self-regulation failure. In K. D. Williams, J. P. Forgas, &
W. von Hippel (Eds.), *The social outcast: Ostracism, social
exclusion, rejection, and bullying* (pp. 53–73). New York:
Psychology Press.

Baumeister, R. F., & Leary, M. R. (1995). The need to
belong: Desire for interpersonal attachments as a fundamental human motivation. *Psychological Bulletin, 117*,
497–529.

Becker, D. V., Kenrick, D. T., Neuberg, S. L., Blackwell, K. C.,
& Smith, D. M. (2007). The confounded nature of angry
men and happy women. *Journal of Personality and Social
Psychology, 92*, 179–190.

Becker, D. V., Neuberg, S. L., Maner, J. K., Shapiro, J. R.,
Ackerman, J. M., Schaller, M., et al. (2010). More memory
bang for the attentional buck: Self-protection goals
enhance encoding efficiency for potentially threatening
males. *Social Psychological and Personality Science, 1*,
182–189.

Boroditsky, L., & Ramscar, M. (2002). The roles of body
and mind in abstract thought. *Psychological Science, 13*,
185–188.

Bowlby, J. (1969). *Attachment and loss.* London: Hogarth
Press.

Brewer, M. B., (1991). The social self: On being the same and
different at the same time. *Personality and Social Psychology
Bulletin, 17*, 475–482.

Brown, D. E. (1991). *Human universals.* Philadelphia, PA:
Temple University Press.

Bugental, D. (2000). Acquisition of the algorithms of social
life: A domain-based approach. *Psychological Bulletin,
126*, 187–219.

Buller, D. J. (2005). *Adapting minds: Evolutionary psychology
and the persistent quest for human nature.* Cambridge,
MA: MIT Press.

Burnstein, E., Crandall, C., & Kitayama, S. (1994). Some
neo-Darwinian decision rules for altruism: Weighing
cues for inclusive fitness as a function of the biological
importance of the decision. *Journal of Personality and
Social Psychology, 67*, 773–789.

Buss, D. M. (1988). The evolution of human intrasexual
competition: Tactics of mate attraction. *Journal of
Personality and Social Psychology, 54*, 661–628.

Buss, D. M. (1989). Sex differences in human mate preferences: Evolutionary hypotheses tested in 37 cultures.
Behavioral and Brain Sciences, 12, 1–49.

Buss, D. M. (1999). Adaptive individual differences revisited.
Journal of Personality, 67(2), 259–264.

Buss, D. M. (2005). *The murderer next door: Why the mind is
designed to kill.* New York: The Penguin Press.

Buss, D. M., & Barnes, M. L. (1986). Preferences in human
mate selection. *Journal of Personality and Social Psychology,
50*, 559–570.

Buss, D. M., Haselton, M. G., Shackelford, T. K., Bleske, A. L.,
& Wakefield, J. C. (1998). Adaptations, exaptations, and
spandrels. *American Psychologist, 53*, 533–548.

Buss, D. M., & Schmitt, D. P. (1993). Sexual strategies theory:
An evolutionary perspective on human mating. *Psychological
Review, 100*, 204–232.

Buss, D. M., & Shackelford, T. K. (1997). From vigilance to
violence: Mate retention tactics in married couples. *Journal
of Personality and Social Psychology, 72*, 346–361.

Buunk, B. P., Dijkstra, P., Fetchenhauer, D., & Kenrick, D. T.
(2002). Age and gender differences in mate selection

criteria for various involvement levels. *Personal Relationships, 9,* 271–278.

Buunk, A. P., Park, J. H., & Dubbs, S. L. (2008). Parent–offspring conflict in mate preferences. *Review of General Psychology, 12,* 47–62.

Campbell, J. D. (1986). Similarity and uniqueness: The effects of attribute type, relevance and individual differences in self-esteem and depression. *Journal of Personality and Social Psychology, 50,* 281–294.

Campbell, L., & Ellis, B. J. (2005). Commitment, love, and mate retention. In D. M. Buss (Ed.), *The handbook of evolutionary psychology* (pp. 419–442). Hoboken, NJ: Wiley.

Caporael, L. R. (1997). The evolution of truly social cognition: The core configurations model. *Personality and Social Psychology Review, 1,* 276–298.

Cazden, C. B. (1983). Adult assistance to language development: Scaffolds, models, and direct instruction. In R. P. Parker & F. A. Davis (Eds.), *Developing literacy: Young children's use of language* (pp. 3–17). Newark, DE: International Reading Association.

Chen, M. K., Lakshminaryanan, V., & Santos, L. R. (2006). The evolution of our preferences: Evidence from capuchin monkey trading behavior. *Journal of Political Economy, 114,* 517–537.

Clark, M. S., Mills, J., & Powell, M. (1986). Keeping track of needs in exchange and communal relationships. *Journal of Personality and Social Psychology, 37,* 333–338.

Clark, R. D. III, & Hatfield, E. (1989). Gender differences in receptivity to sexual offers. *Journal of Psychology and Human Sexuality, 2,* 39–55.

Cohen, G. L., Garcia, J., Apfel, N., & Master, A. (2006). Reducing the racial achievement gap: A social–psychological intervention. *Science, 313,* 1307–1310.

Confer, J. C., Easton, J. A., Fleischman, D. S., Goetz, C., Lewis, D. L., Perilloux, C., et al. (2010). Evolutionary psychology: Questions, prospects, and limitations. *American Psychologist, 65,* 110–126.

Conway, L. G., III, & Schaller, M. (2002). On the verifiability of evolutionary psychological theories: An analysis of the psychology of scientific persuasion. *Personality and Social Psychology Review, 6,* 152–166.

Cosmides, L. (1989). The logic of social exchange: Has natural selection shaped how humans reason? Studies with the Wason selection task. *Cognition, 31,* 187–276.

Cosmides, L., & Tooby, J. (1992). Cognitive adaptations for social exchange. In J. H. Barkow, L. Cosmides, & J. Tooby (Eds.), *The adapted mind: Evolutionary psychology and the generation of culture* (pp. 163–228). New York: Oxford University Press.

Cosmides, L, Tooby, J., Fiddick, L., & Bryant, G. (2005). Detecting cheaters. *Trends in Cognitive Sciences, 9,* 505–506.

Cottrell, C. A., & Neuberg, S. L. (2005). Different emotional reactions to different groups: A sociofunctional threat-based approach to 'prejudice.' *Journal of Personality and Social Psychology, 88,* 770–789.

Cummins, R. A. (1998). The second approximation to an international standard for life satisfaction. *Social Indicators Research, 43,* 307–334.

Daly, M., & Wilson, M. I. (1983). *Sex, evolution, and behavior: Adaptations for reproduction* (2nd ed.). Boston, MA: Willard Grant Press.

Daly, M., & Wilson, M. (1988). *Homicide.* Hawthorne, NY: Aldine de Gruyter.

Daly, M., & Wilson, M. (1998). *The truth about Cinderella.* London: Weidenfeld & Nicolson Publishers.

Damasio, A., & Tranel, D. (1993). Nouns and verbs are retrieved with differently distributed neural systems. *Proceedings of the National Academy of Sciences, 90,* 4957–4960.

Darwin, C. (1859). *On the origin of species by means of natural selection, or the preservation of favoured races in the struggle for life.* London: John Murray.

Darwin, C. (1871). *The descent of man, and selection in relation to sex.* London: John Murray.

Darwin, C. (1872). *The expression of the emotions in man and animals.* London: John Murray.

Dawkins, R. (1976). *The selfish gene.* New York: Oxford University Press.

DeBruine, L. M. (2005). Trustworthy but not lustworthy: Context-specific effects of facial resemblance. *Proceedings of the Royal Society of London B, 272,* 919–922.

Dehaene, S., Changeux, J.-P., Naccache, L., Sackur, J., & Sergent, C. (2006). Conscious, preconscious, and subliminal processing: A testable taxonomy. *Trends in Cognitive Science, 10,* 204–211.

Dehaene, S., & Cohen L. (2007). Cultural recycling of cortical maps. *Neuron, 56,* 384–398.

Dennett, D. C. (1991). *Consciousness explained.* Boston: Little, Brown.

Dennett, D. C. (1995). *Darwin's dangerous idea: Evolution and the meanings of life.* New York: Simon & Schuster.

Devine, P. (1989). Stereotypes and prejudice: Their automatic and controlled components. *Journal of Personality and Social Psychology, 56,* 5–18.

de Waal, F. B. M. (2006). *Primates & philosophers: How morality evolved.* Princeton, NJ: Princeton University Press.

DeWall, C. N., & Baumeister, R. F. (2006). Alone but feeling no pain: Effects of social exclusion on physical pain tolerance and pain threshold, affective forecasting, and interpersonal empathy. *Journal of Personality and Social Psychology, 91,* 1–15.

DeWall, C. N., Baumeister, R. F., & Masicampo, E. J. (2009). Feeling rejected but not much else: Resolving the paradox of emotional numbness after exclusion. In A. L. Vangelisti (Ed.), *Feeling hurt in close relationships* (pp. 123–142). New York: Cambridge University Press.

DeWall C. N., MacDonald, G., Webster, G. D., Masten, C., Baumeister, R. F., Powell, C., et al. (2010). Acetaminophen reduces social pain: Behavioral and neural evidence. *Psychological Science, 21,* 931–937.

Dobzhansky, T. (1964). Biology: Molecular and organismic. *American Zoologist, 4,* 443–452.

Dubbs, S. L., & Buunk, A. P. (2010). Parents just don't understand: Parent–offspring conflict over mate choice. *Evolutionary Psychology, 8,* 586–598.

Dunham, Y., Baron, A. S., & Banaji, M. R. (2008). The development of implicit intergroup cognition. *Trends in Cognitive Sciences, 12*, 248–253.

Eberhardt, J. L., Goff, P. A., Purdie, V. J., & Davies, P. G. (2004). Seeing black: Race, representation, and visual perception. *Journal of Personality and Social Psychology, 87*, 876–893.

Egan, L. C., Santos, L. R., & Bloom, P. (2007). The origins of cognitive dissonance: Evidence from children and monkeys. *Psychological Science, 11*, 978–983.

Eibl-Eibesfeldt, I. (1989). *Human ethology*. New York: Aldine de Gruyter.

Eisenberger, N. I., Lieberman, M. D., & Williams, K. D. (2003). Does rejection hurt? An fMRI study of social exclusion. *Science, 203*, 290–292.

Epley, N., Waytz, A., & Cacioppo, J. T. (2007). On seeing human: A three-factor theory of anthropomorphism. *Psychological Review, 114* (4), 864–886.

Faulkner, J., Schaller, M., Park, J. H., & Duncan, L. A. (2004). Evolved disease-avoidance processes and contemporary xenophobic attitudes. *Group Processes and Intergroup Behavior, 7*, 333–353.

Fehr, E., & Gächter, S. (2002). Altruistic punishment in humans. *Nature, 415*, 137–140.

Fessler, D. M. T., & Navarrete, C. D. (2004) Third-party attitudes toward sibling incest: Evidence for Westermarck's hypotheses. *Evolution and Human Behavior, 25*, 277–294.

Fishbach, A., & Ferguson, M. J. (2007). The goal construct in social psychology. In A. W. Kruglanski & E. T. Higgins (Eds.), *Social psychology: Handbook of basic principles* (Vol. 2). New York: Guilford Press.

Fiske, A. P. (1992). The four elementary forms of sociality: Framework for a unified theory of social relations. *Psychological Review, 99*, 689–723.

Fiske, S. T. (2010). Interpersonal stratification: Status, power, and subordination. In S. T. Fiske, D. T., Gilbert, & G. Lindzey (Eds.), *Handbook of social psychology* (5th ed., pp. 941–982). New York: Wiley.

Fiske, S. T., Cuddy, A. J. C., & Glick, P. (2007). Universal dimensions of social cognition: Warmth and competence. *Trends in Cognitive Sciences, 11*, 77–83.

Flinn, M. V. (2006). Cross-cultural universals and variations: The evolutionary paradox of informational novelty. *Psychological Inquiry, 17*, 118–123.

Fox, E., Lester, V., Russo, R., Bowles, R. J., Pichler, A., & Dutton, K. (2000). Facial expressions of emotion: Are angry faces detected more efficiently? *Cognition & Emotion, 14*, 61–92.

Fox, E., Russo, R., Bowles, R. J., & Dutton, K. (2001). Do threatening stimuli draw or hold visual attention in subclinical anxiety? *Journal of Experimental Psychology: General, 130*, 681–700.

Friesen, M. D., Fletcher, G. J. O., & Overall, N. C. (2005). A dyadic assessment of forgiveness in intimate relationships. *Personal Relationships, 12*, 61–77.

Gallese, V. (2008). Mirror neurons and the social nature of language: The neural exploitation hypothesis. *Social Neuroscience, 3*, 317–333.

Gallese, V., & Lakoff, G. (2005). The brain's concepts: The role of the sensory-motor system in reason and language. *Cognitive Neuropsychology, 22*, 455–479.

Gangestad, S. G., Haselton, M. G., & Buss, D. M. (2006). Evolutionary foundations of cultural variation: An illustration using human mate preferences. *Psychological Inquiry, 2*, 75–95.

Gangestad, S. W., & Buss, D. M. (1993). Pathogen prevalence and human mate preferences. *Ethology and Sociobiology, 14*, 89–96.

Gangestad, S. W., & Simpson, J. A. (2000). The evolution of human mating: Trade-offs and strategic pluralism. *Behavioral and Brain Sciences, 23*, 573–587.

Garcia, J., & Koelling, R. A. (1966). Relation of cue to consequence in avoidance learning. *Psychonomic Science, 4*, 123–124.

Geary, D. C., Vigil, J., & Byrd-Craven, J. (2004). Evolution of human mate choice. *Journal of Sex Research, 41*, 27–42.

Gibson, J. J. (1979). *The ecological approach to visual perception*. Boston, MA: Houghton Mifflin.

Gigerenzer, G., & Goldstein, D. G. (1996). Reasoning the fast and frugal way: Models of bounded rationality. *Psychological Review, 103*, 650–669.

Gilovich, T., Medvec, V. H., & Savitsky, K. (2000). The spotlight effect in social judgment: An egocentric bias in estimates of the salience of one's own actions and appearance. *Journal of Personality and Social Psychology, 78*, 211–222.

Godfray, H. J. C (1995). Signalling of need between parents and young: Parent–offspring conflict and sibling rivalry. *The American Naturalist, 146*, 1–24.

Goldstein, D. G., & Gigerenzer, G. (2002). Models of ecological rationality: The recognition heuristic. *Psychological Review, 109*, 75–90.

Gottlieb, G. (1998). Normally occurring environmental and behavioral influences on gene activity: From central dogma to probabilistic epigenesit. *Psychological Review, 105*, 792–802.

Grammer, K., & Thornhill, R. (1994). Human (homo sapiens) facial attractiveness and sexual selection: The role of symmetry and averageness. *Journal of Comparative Psychology, 108*, 233–242.

Greenberg, J., Pyszczynski, T., Solomon, S., Pinel, E., Simon, L., & Jordan, K. (1993). Effects of self-esteem on vulnerability-denying defensive distortions: Further evidence of an anxiety-buffering function of self-esteem. *Journal of Experimental Social Psychology, 29*, 229–251.

Griskevicius, V., Cialdini, R. B., & Kenrick, D.T. (2006). Peacocks, Picasso, and parental investment: The effects of romantic motives on creativity. *Journal of Personality and Social Psychology, 91*, 63–76.

Griskevicius, V., Tybur, J. M., Ackerman, J. M., Delton, A. W., & Robertson, T. E. (in press). The financial consequences of too many men: Sex ratio effects on saving, borrowing, and spending. *Journal of Personality and Social Psychology*.

Griskevicius, V., Tybur, J. M., Sundie, J. M., Cialdini, R. B., Miller, G. F., & Kenrick, D. T. (2007). Blatant benevolence and conspicuous consumption: When romantic motives elicit strategic costly signals. *Journal of Personality and Social Psychology, 93*, 85–102.

Gutierres, S. E., Kenrick, D. T., & Partch, J. (1999). Beauty, dominance, and the mating game: Contrast effects in self assessment reflect gender differences in mate selection criteria. *Personality & Social Psychology Bulletin, 25*, 1126–1134.

Haidt, J. (2007). The new synthesis in moral psychology. *Science, 316*, 998–1001.

Hamilton, W. D. (1964). The genetical evolution of social behaviour. I, II. *Journal of Theoretical Biology, 7*, 1–52.

Harlow, H. (1958). The nature of love. *American Psychologist, 13*, 573–685.

Harris, L. T., & Fiske, S. T. (2006). Dehumanizing the lowest of the low: Neuroimaging responses to extreme outgroups. *Psychological Science, 17*, 847–853.

Haselton, M. G., & Buss, D. M. (2000). Error management theory: A new perspective on biases in cross-sex mind reading. *Journal of Personality and Social Psychology, 78*, 81–91.

Haselton, M. G., & Nettle, D. (2006). The paranoid optimist: An integrative evolutionary model of cognitive biases. *Personality and Social Psychology Review, 10*, 47–66.

Hayes-Roth, B. (1977). Evolution of cognitive structures and processes. *Psychological Review, 84*, 260–278.

Heinemann, W., Pellander, F., Vogelbusch, A., & Wojtek, B. (1981). Meeting a deviant person: Subjective norms and affective reactions. *European Journal of Social Psychology, 11*, 1–25.

Houston, V., & Bull, R. (1994). Do people avoid sitting next to someone who is facially disfigured? *European Journal of Social Psychology, 24*, 279–284.

Huang, J. Y., Ackerman, J. M., & Bargh, J. A. (2011). *Goal scaffolding: Physical safety interrupts psychological self-protection goals*. Manuscript submitted for publication.

Huang, J. Y., & Bargh, J. A. (2008). Peak of desire: Activating the mating goal changes life stage preferences across living kinds. *Psychological Science, 19*, 573–578.

Hurley, S. L. (2008). The shared circuits model (SCM): How control, mirroring, and simulation can enable imitation, deliberation, and mindreading. *Behavioral and Brain Sciences, 31*, 1–58.

Jackson, M. C., Wu, C., Linden, D. E. J., & Raymond, J. E. (2009). Enhanced visual short-term memory for angry faces. *Journal of Experimental Psychology: Human Perception and Performance, 35*, 363–374.

James, W. (1890/1950). *The principles of psychology* (2 vols.). New York: Dover.

Jones, J. T., Pelham, B. W., Carvallo, M., & Mirenberg, M. C. (2004). How do I love thee? Let me count the Js: Implicit egotism and interpersonal attraction. *Journal of Personality and Social Psychology, 87*, 665–683.

Jostmann, N. B., Lakens, D., & Schubert, T. W. (2009). Weight as an embodiment of importance. *Psychological Science, 20*, 1169–1174.

Kahneman, D., Slovic, P., & Tversky, A. (1982). *Judgment under uncertainty: Heuristics and biases*. New York: Cambridge University Press.

Kang, Y., Williams, L., Clark, M., Gray, J., & Bargh, J. (2011). Physical temperature effects on trust behavior: The role of insula. *Social Cognitive and Affective Neuroscience, 6*, 507–515.

Kenrick, D. T. (1995). Evolutionary theory versus the confederacy of dunces. *Psychological Inquiry, 6*, 56–61.

Kenrick, D. T., Ackerman, J., & Ledlow, S. (2003). Evolutionary social psychology: Adaptive predispositions and human culture. In J. DeLamater (Ed.), *Handbook of social psychology* (pp. 103–124). New York: Kluwer–Plenum.

Kenrick, D. T., Griskevicius, V., Neuberg, S. L., & Schaller, M. (2010). Renovating the pyramid of needs: Contemporary extensions built upon ancient foundations. *Perspectives on Psychological Science, 5*, 292–314.

Kenrick, D. T., Li, N. P., & Butner, J. (2003). Dynamical evolutionary psychology: Individual decision-rules and emergent social norms. *Psychological Review, 110*, 3–28.

Kenrick, D. T., Sadalla, E. K., Groth, G., & Trost, M. R. (1990). Evolution, traits, and the stages of human courtship: Qualifying the parental investment model. *Journal of Personality, 58*, 97–116.

Kenrick, D. T., Schaller, M., & Simpson, J. (2006). Evolution is the new cognition. In M. Schaller, J. Simpson, & D. T. Kenrick (eds.) *Evolution and social psychology* (pp. 1–16). New York: Psychology Press.

Kenrick, D. T., & Sheets, V. (1993). Homicidal fantasies. *Ethology and Sociobiology, 14*, 231–246.

Kihlstrom, J. F., & Klein, S. B. (1994). The self as a knowledge structure. In R. S. Wyer & T. K. Srull (Eds.), *Handbook of social cognition* (2nd ed., Vol. 1, pp. 153–208). Hillsdale, NJ: Lawrence Erlbaum.

Kirkpatrick, L. A., & Ellis, B. J. (2001). An evolutionary–psychological approach to self-esteem: Multiple domains and multiple functions. In G. Fletcher & M. Clark (Eds.), *The Blackwell handbook of social psychology: Vol. 2. Interpersonal processes* (pp. 411–436). Oxford, UK: Blackwell.

Kivett, V. R. (1985). Consanguinity and kin level: Their relative importance in the helping network of older adults. *Journal of Gerontology, 40*, 228–234.

Kruglanski, A. W. (2001). That "vision thing": theory construction in social and personality psychology at the edge of the new millennium. *Journal of Personality and Social Psychology, 80*, 871–875.

Kruglanski, A. W., Shah, J. Y., Fishbach, A., Friedman, R., Chun, W. Y., & Sleeth-Keppler, D. (2002). A theory of goal systems. In M. P. Zanna (Ed.), *Advances in experimental social psychology* (Vol. 34, pp. 331–378). San Diego, CA: Academic Press.

Kurzban, R., & Aktipis, C. A. (2007). Modularity and the social mind: Are psychologists too self-ish? *Personality and Social Psychology Review, 11*, 131–149.

Kurzban, R., & Leary, M. R. (2001). Evolutionary origins of stigmatization: The functions of social exclusion. *Psychological Bulletin, 127*, 187–208.

Kurzban, R., Tooby, J., & Cosmides, L. (2001). Can race be erased?: Coalitional computation and social categorization. *Proceedings of the National Academy of Sciences, 98*, 15387–15392.

Leary, M. R., & Cox, C. (2007). Belongingness motivation: A mainspring of social action. In J. Shah & W. Gardner (Eds.), *Handbook of motivation science* (pp. 27–40). New York: Guilford Press.

Leary, M. R., Tambor, E. S., Terdal, S. K., & Downs, D. L. (1995). Self-esteem as an interpersonal monitor: The sociometer hypothesis. *Journal of Personality & Social Psychology, 68,* 518–530.

Lederman, S. J., & Klatzky, R. L. (1987). Hand movements: A window into haptic object recognition. *Cognitive Psychology, 19,* 342–368.

Lee, S. W. S., & Schwarz, N. (2010). Dirty hands and dirty mouths: Embodiment of the moral-purity metaphor is specific to the motor modality involved in moral transgression. *Psychological Science, 21,* 1423–1425.

Li, N. P., Bailey, J. M., Kenrick, D. T., & Linsenmeier, J.A. (2002). The necessities and luxuries of mate preferences: Testing the trade-offs. *Journal of Personality and Social Psychology, 82,* 947–955.

Li, N. P., & Kenrick, D. T. (2006). Sex similarities and differences in preferences for short-term mates: What, whether, and why. *Journal of Personality and Social Psychology, 90,* 468–489.

Li, Y. J., Ackerman, J. M., White, A. E., Neuberg, S. L., & Kenrick, D. T. (2011). *What's cooking? Disease concern enhances preferences for familiar versus unfamiliar foods.* Manuscript under review.

Lieberman, D., Tooby, J., & Cosmides, L. (2007), *The architecture of human kin detection. Nature, 44,* 727–731.

Loftus, E. F., & Klinger, M. R. (1992). Is the unconscious smart or dumb? *American Psychologist, 47,* 761–765.

Low, B. S. (1990). Marriage systems and pathogen stress in human societies. *American Zoologist, 30,* 325–339.

Low, B. S. (1998). The evolution of human life histories. In C. B. Crawford & D. L. Krebs (Eds.), *Handbook of evolutionary psychology: Ideas, issues, and applications* (pp. 131–161). Mahwah, NJ: Lawrence Erlbaum.

MacDonald, G., & Leary M. R. (2005). Why does social exclusion hurt? The relationship between social and physical pain. *Psychological Bulletin, 131,* 202–223.

Mandler, J. M. (1992). How to build a baby: II. Conceptual primitives. *Psychological Review, 99,* 587–604.

Maner, J. K., DeWall, C. N., Baumeister, R. F., & Schaller, M. (2007). Does social exclusion motivate interpersonal reconnection? Resolving the "porcupine problem." *Journal of Personality and Social Psychology, 92,* 42–55.

Maner, J. K., Gailliot, M. T., Rouby, D. A., & Miller, S. L. (2007). Can't take my eyes off you: Attentional adhesion to mates and rivals. *Journal of Personality and Social Psychology, 93,* 389–401.

Maner, J. K., Kenrick, D. T., Becker, D. V., Delton, A. W., Hofer, B., Wilbur, C., & et al. (2003). Sexually selective cognition: Beauty captures the mind of the beholder. *Journal of Personality and Social Psychology, 85,* 1107–1120.

Maner, J. K., Kenrick, D. T., Neuberg, S. L., Becker, D. V., Robertson, T., Hofer, B., et al. (2005). Functional projection: How fundamental social motives can bias interpersonal perception. *Journal of Personality and Social Psychology, 88,* 63–78.

Maner, J. K., & Mead, N. (2010). The essential tension between leadership and power: When leaders sacrifice group goals for the sake of self-interest. *Journal of Personality and Social Psychology, 99,* 482–497.

Maner, J. K., Rouby, D. A., & Gonzaga, G. (2008). Automatic inattention to attractive alternatives: The evolved psychology of relationship maintenance. *Evolution & Human Behavior, 29,* 343–349.

Markus, H., & Nurius, P. (1986). Possible selves. *American Psychologist, 41,* 954–969.

Maslow, A. H. (1943). A theory of human motivation. *Psychological Review, 50,* 370–396.

Mayr, E. (1960). The emergence of evolutionary novelties. In S. Tax (Ed.), *Evolution after Darwin: Vol. 1: The evolution of life: Its origin, history, and future* (pp. 349–380). Chicago, IL: University of Chicago Press.

Mayr, E. (1976). *Evolution and the diversity of life.* Cambridge, MA: Harvard University Press.

McArthur, L. Z., & Baron, R. M. (1983). Toward an ecological theory of social perception. *Psychological Review, 90,* 215–238.

McDougall, W. (1926). *An introduction to social psychology* (rev. ed.). Boston, MA: Luce.

Mead, N. L., Baumeister, R. F., Stillman, T. F., Rawn, C. D., & Vohs, K. D. (2011). Social exclusion causes people to spend and consume in the service of affiliation. *Journal of Consumer Research, 37,* 902–919.

Meyer-Lindenberg, A. (2008). Trust me on this. *Science, 321,* 778–780.

Miller, A. G., Collins, B. E., & Brief, D. E. (1995). Perspectives on obedience to authority: The legacy of the Milgram experiments. *Journal of Social Issues, 51,* 1–19.

Miller, D. T., & Ross, M. (1975). Self-serving biases in the attribution of causality: Fact or fiction? *Psychological Bulletin, 82,* 213–225.

Miller, G. (2000). *The mating mind.* New York: Doubleday.

Miller, G. F. (1998). How mate choice shaped human nature: A review of sexual selection and human evolution. In C. Crawford & D. Krebs (Eds.), *Handbook of evolutionary psychology: Ideas, issues, and applications* (pp. 87–129). Mahwah, NJ: Lawrence Erlbaum.

Miller, G. F., & Todd, P. M. (1998). Mate choice turns cognitive. *Trends in Cognitive Sciences, 2,* 190–198.

Morsella, E. (2005). The function of phenomenal states: Supramodular interaction theory. *Psychological Review, 112,* 1000–1021.

Morsella, E., & Bargh, J. A. (2011). Unconscious action tendencies: Sources of 'un-intergrated' action. In J. Decety & J. T. Cacioppo (Eds.), *The Oxford handbook of social neuroscience* (pp. 335–347). New York: Oxford University Press.

Morsella, E., Bargh, J. A., & Gollwitzer, P. M. (2008). *Oxford handbook of human action.* New York: Oxford University Press.

Mortensen, C. R., Becker, D. V., Ackerman, J. M., Neuberg, S. L., & Kenrick, D. T. (2010). Infection breeds reticence: The effects of disease salience on self-perceptions of personality and behavioral avoidance tendencies. *Psychological Science, 21,* 440–447.

Navarrete, C. D., McDonald, M., Molina, L., & Sidanius, J. (2010). Prejudice at the nexus of race and gender: An outgroup male target hypothesis. *Journal of Personality & Social Psychology, 98*(6), 933–945.

Navarrete, C. D., Olsson, A., Ho, A., Mendes, W., Thomsen, L., & Sidanius, J. (2009). Fear extinction to an outgroup face: The role of target gender. *Psychological Science, 20*, 155–158.

Nesse, R. M. (2005). Natural selection and the regulation of defenses: A signal detection analysis of the smoke detector principle. *Evolution and Human Behavior, 26*, 88–105.

Neuberg, S. L, Kenrick, D. T., & Schaller, M. (2010). Evolutionary social psychology. In S. T. Fiske, D. T. Gilbert, & G. Lindzey (Eds.), *Handbook of social psychology* (5th ed., Vol. II, pp. 761–796). New York: John Wiley & Sons.

Niedenthal, P. M., Barsalou, L. W., Winkielman, P., Krauth-Gruber, S., & Ric, F. (2005). Embodiment in attitudes, social perception, and emotion. *Personality and Social Psychology Review, 9*, 184–211.

Norenzayan, A., Schaller, M., & Heine, S. (2006). Evolution and culture. In M. Schaller, J. Simpson, & D. Kenrick (Eds.), *Evolution and social psychology* (pp. 343–366). New York: Psychology Press.

Öhman, A., Flykt, A., & Esteves, F. (2001). Emotion drives attention: Detecting the snake in the grass. *Journal of Experimental Psychology: General, 130*, 466–478.

Ostrom, T. M. (1984). The sovereignty of social cognition. In R. S. Wyer and T. K. Srull (Eds.), *Handbook of social cognition* (Vol. 1, pp. 1–38). Hillsdale, NJ: Lawrence Erlbaum.

Panksepp, J. (2004). *Affective neuroscience: The foundations of human and animal emotions.* New York: Oxford University Press.

Park, J. H., & Ackerman, J. M. (2011). Passion and compassion: Psychology of kin relations within and beyond the family. In C. Salmon and T. Shackelford (Eds.), *Oxford handbook of evolutionary family psychology* (pp. 329–344). New York: Oxford University Press.

Park, J. H., Faulkner, J., & Schaller, M. (2003). Evolved disease-avoidance processes and contemporary anti-social behavior: Prejudicial attitudes and avoidance of people with physical disabilities. *Journal of Nonverbal Behavior, 27*, 65–87.

Park, J. H., & Schaller, M. (2005). Does attitude similarity serve as a heuristic cue for kinship? Evidence of an implicit cognitive association. *Evolution and Human Behavior, 26*, 158–170.

Park, J. H., Schaller, M., & Crandall, C. S. (2007). Pathogen-avoidance mechanisms and the stigmatization of obese people. *Evolution and Human Behavior, 28*, 410–414.

Park, J. H., Schaller, M., & Van Vugt, M. (2008). Psychology of human kin recognition: Heuristic cues, erroneous inferences, and their implications. *Review of General Psychology, 12*, 215–235.

Park, L., & Maner, J. K. (2009). Does self-threat promote social connection? The role of self-esteem and contingencies of self-worth. *Journal of Personality and Social Psychology, 96*, 203–217.

Price, M. E., Cosmides, L., & Tooby, J. (2002). Punitive sentiment as an anti-free rider psychological device. *Evolution and Human Behavior, 23*, 203–231.

Rozin, P., & Fallon, A. E. (1987). A perspective on disgust. *Psychological Review, 94*, 23–41.

Rozin, P., Lowery, L., Imada, S., & Haidt, J. (1999). The CAD triad hypothesis: A mapping between three moral emotions (contempt, anger, disgust) and three moral codes (community, autonomy, divinity). *Journal of Personality and Social Psychology, 76*, 574–586.

Rozin, P., Millman, L., & Nemeroff, C. (1986). Operation of the laws of sympathetic magic in disgust and other domains. *Journal of Personality and Social Psychology, 50*, 703–712.

Santos, L. R., Hauser, M. D., & Spelke, E. S. (2002). Domain-specific knowledge in human children and nonhuman primates: Artifacts and foods. In M. Bekoff, C. Allen, & G. M. Burghardt (Eds.), *The cognitive animal: Empirical and theoretical perspectives on animal cognition* (pp. 205–215). Cambridge, MA: MIT Press.

Savitsky, K., Epley, N., & Gilovich, T. (2001). Is it as bad as we fear? Overestimating the extremity of others' judgments. *Journal of Personality and Social Psychology, 81*, 44–56.

Schaller, M., Park, J. H., & Faulkner, J. (2003). Prehistoric dangers and contemporary prejudices. *European Review of Social Psychology, 14*, 105–137.

Schaller, M., Park, J. H., & Mueller, A. (2003). Fear of the dark: Interactive effects of beliefs about danger and ambient darkness on ethnic stereotypes. *Personality and Social Psychology Bulletin, 29*, 637–649.

Schmitt, D. P. (2005). Fundamentals of human mating strategies. In D. M. Buss (Ed.), *The handbook of evolutionary psychology* (pp. 258–291). New York: Wiley.

Schnall, S., Benton, J., & Harvey, S. (2008). With a clean conscience: Cleanliness reduces the severity of moral judgments. *Psychological Science, 19*, 1219–1222.

Schwarz, N., & Bless, H. (1992). Constructing reality and its alternatives: An inclusion/exclusion model of assimilation and contrast effects in social judgment. In L. Martin & A. Tesser (Eds.), *The construction of social judgments* (pp. 217–245). Hillsdale, NJ: Lawrence Erlbaum.

Serrano, J. M., Iglesias, J., & Loeches, A. (1995). Infants' responses to adult static facial expressions. *Infant Behavior and Development, 18*, 477–482.

Shackelford, T. K., Goetz, A. T., & Buss, D. M. (2005). Mate retention in marriage: Further evidence of the reliability of the Mate Retention Inventory. *Personality and Individual Differences, 39*, 415–425.

Shapiro, J. R., Ackerman, J. M., Neuberg, S. L., Maner, J. K., Becker, D. V., & Kenrick, D. T. (2009). Following in the wake of anger: When not discriminating is discriminating. *Personality & Social Psychology Bulletin, 35*, 1356–1367.

Shepard, R. N. (1984). Ecological constraints on internal representation: Resonant kinematics of perceiving, imagining, thinking and dreaming. *Psychological Review, 91*, 417–447.

Shepard, R. N. (2001). Perceptual-cognitive universals as reflections of the world. *Behavioral and Brain Sciences, 24,* 581–601.

Shepher, J. (1971). Mate selection among second generation kibbutz adolescents and adults: Incest avoidance and negative imprinting. *Archives of Sexual Behavior, 1,* 293–307.

Sherry, D. F., & Schacter, D. L. (1987). The evolution of multiple memory systems. *Psychological Review, 94,* 439–454.

Sidanius, J., & Pratto, F. (2001). *Social dominance: An intergroup theory of social hierarchy and oppression.* New York: Cambridge University Press.

Simpson, J. A., Gangestad, S. W., & Lerma, M. (1990). Perception of physical attractiveness: Mechanisms involved in the maintenance of romantic relationships. *Journal of Personality and Social Psychology, 59,* 1192–1201.

Smith, M. S., Kish, B. L., & Crawford, C. B. (1987). Inheritance of wealth as human kin investment. *Ethology and Sociobiology, 8,* 171–182.

Sperber, D. (2001). In defense of massive modularity. In E. Dupoux (Ed.), Language, brain, and cognitive development: *Essays in honor of Jacques Mehler* (pp. 47–57). Cambridge, MA: MIT Press.

Symons, D. (1992). On the use and misuse of Darwinism in the study of human behavior. In J. Barkow, L. Cosmides, & J. Tooby, J. (Eds.), *The adapted mind: Evolutionary psychology and the generation of culture* (pp. 137–159). New York: Oxford University Press.

Taylor, S. E., Klein, L. C., Lewis, B. P., Gruenewald, T. L., Gurung, R. A. R., & Updegraff, J. A. (2000). Biobehavioral responses to stress in females: Tend-and-befriend, not fight-or-flight. *Psychological Review, 107,* 411–429.

Tesser, A. (1988). Toward a self-evaluation maintenance model of social behavior. In L. Berkowitz (Ed.), *Advances in experimental social psychology* (Vol 21, pp. 181–227). New York: Academic Press.

Tetlock, P. E. (2002). Social-functionalist metaphors for judgment and choice: The intuitive politician, theologian, and prosecutor. *Psychological Review, 109,* 451–472.

Thornhill, R., & Gangestad, S. W. (1993). Human facial beauty: Averageness, symmetry and parasite resistance. *Human Nature, 4,* 237–269.

Tinbergen, N. (1963). On aims and methods of ethology. *Zeitschrift für Tierpsychologie, 20,* 410–433.

Todd, P. M., Hertwig, R., & Hoffrage, U. (2005). The evolutionary psychology of cognition. In D. Buss (Ed.), *The handbook of evolutionary psychology* (pp. 776–802). Hoboken: Wiley.

Tooby, J., & Cosmides, L. (1992). The psychological foundations of culture. In J. H. Barkow, L. Cosmides, & J. Tooby (Eds.), *The adapted mind: Evolutionary psychology and the generation of culture* (pp. 19–136). New York: Oxford University Press.

Trawalter, S., Todd, A., Baird, A. A., & Richeson, J. A. (2008). Attending to threat: Race-based patterns of selective attention. *Journal of Experimental Social Psychology, 44,* 1322–1327.

Trivers, R. L. (1971). The evolution of reciprocal altruism. *Quarterly Review of Biology, 46,* 35–57.

Trivers, R. L. (1972). Parental investment and sexual selection. In B. H. Campbell (Ed.), *Sexual selection and the descent of man, 1871–1971* (pp. 136–179). Chicago, IL: Aldine.

Trivers, R. L. (1974). Parent–offspring conflict. *American Zoologist, 14,* 249–264.

Tversky, A., & Kahneman, D. (1991). Loss aversion in riskless choice: A reference dependent model. *Quarterly Journal of Economics, 106,* 1039–1061.

Tybur, J. M., Bryan, A. D., Magnan, R. E., & Caldwell Hooper, A. E. (2011). Smells like safe sex: Olfactory pathogen primes increase intentions to use condoms. *Psychological Science, 22,* 478–480.

Tyber, J. M., Lieberman, D., & Griskevicius, V. (2009). Microbes, mating, and morality: Individual differences in three functional domains of disgust. *Journal of Personality and Social Psychology, 97,* 103–122.

Van den Bergh, B., Dewitte, S., & Warlop, L. (2008). Bikinis instigate generalized impatience in intertemporal choice. *Journal of Consumer Research, 35,* 85–97.

Van Lange, P. A. M. (1999). The pursuit of joint outcomes and equality in outcomes: An integrative model of social value orientation. *Journal of Personality and Social Psychology, 77,* 337–349.

Van Vugt, M., De Cremer, D., & Janssen, D. (2007). Gender differences in competition and cooperation: The male warrior hypothesis. *Psychological Science, 18,* 19–23.

Van Vugt, M., Hogan, R., & Kaiser, R. (2008). Leadership, followership, and evolution: Some lessons from the past. *American Psychologist, 63,* 182–196.

Van Vugt, M., & Van Lange, P. A. M. (2006). The altruism puzzle: Psychological adaptations for prosocial behavior. In M. Schaller, J. A. Simpson, & D. T. Kenrick (Eds.), *Evolution and social psychology* (pp. 237–261). Madison, CT: Psychosocial Press.

Vivian, D., & Langhinrichsen-Rohling, J. (1994). Are bidirectionally violent couples mutually victimized? A gender sensitive comparison. *Violence and Victims, 9,* 107–124.

Von Hippel, W., & Trivers, R. (2011). The evolution and psychology of self-deception. *Brain and Behavioral Sciences, 34,* 1–16.

Wakefield, J. C. (1999). Evolutionary versus prototype analyses of the concept of disorder. *Journal of Abnormal Psychology, 108,* 374–399.

Way, B. M., Taylor, S. E., & Eisenberger, N. I. (2009). Variation in the mu-opioid receptor gene (OPRM1) is associated with dispositional and neural sensitivity to social rejection. *Proceedings of the National Academy of Sciences, 106,* 15079–15084.

Weber, B. H., & Depew, D. J. (Eds.) (2003). *Evolution and learning: The Baldwin effect reconsidered.* Cambridge, MA: MIT Press.

Webster, G. D. (2007). Evolutionary theory's increasing role in personality and social psychology. *Evolutionary Psychology, 5,* 84–91.

Weinstein, N. D. (1980). Unrealistic optimism about future life events. *Journal of Personality and Social Psychology, 39,* 806–820.

Westermarck, E. A. (1921). *The history of human marriage* (5th ed.). London: Macmillan.

Williams, G. C. (1966). *Adaptation and natural selection.* Princeton, NJ: Princeton University Press.

Williams, K. D. (2007a). Ostracism. *Annual Review of Psychology, 58,* 425–452.

Williams, K. D. (2007b). Ostracism: The kiss of social death. *Social and Personality Compass, 1,* 236–247.

Williams, K. D., Cheung, C. K. T., & Choi, W. (2000). Cyberostracism: Effects of being ignored over the internet. *Journal of Personality and Social Psychology, 79,* 748–762.

Williams, L. E., & Bargh, J. A. (2008). Experiencing physical warmth promotes interpersonal warmth. *Science, 322,* 606–607.

Williams, L. E., Huang, J. Y., & Bargh, J. A. (2009). The scaffolded mind: Higher mental processes are grounded in early experience of the physical world. *European Journal of Social Psychology, 39,* 1257–1267.

Wilson, E. O. (1975). *Sociobiology: The new synthesis.* Cambridge, MA: Harvard University Press.

Wilson, E. O. (1995). *Naturalist.* New York: Warner Books, Inc.

Wirth, J. H., Sacco, D. F., Hugenberg, K., & Williams, K. D. (2010). Eye gaze as relational evaluation: Averted eye gaze leads to feelings of ostracism and relational devaluation. *Personality and Social Psychology Bulletin, 36,* 869–882.

Wood, D. J., Bruner, J. S., & Ross, G. (1976). The role of tutoring in problem solving. *Journal of Child Psychiatry and Psychology, 17,* 89–100.

Yamagishi, T. (1986). The provision of a sanctioning system as a public good. *Journal of Personality and Social Psychology, 51,* 110–116.

Zebrowitz, L. A., & Collins, M. A. (1997). Accurate social perception at zero acquaintance: The affordances of a Gibsonian approach. *Personality and Social Psychology Review, 1,* 203–222.

Zebrowitz, L. A., Fellous, J. M., Mignault, A., & Andreoletti, C. (2003). Trait impressions as overgeneralized responses to adaptively significant facial qualities: Evidence from connectionist modeling. *Personality and Social Psychology Review, 7,* 194–215.

Zhong, C.-B., & Leonardelli, G. J. (2008). Cold and lonely: Does social exclusion literally feel cold? *Psychological Science, 19,* 838–842.

Zhong, C.-B., & Liljenquist, K. (2006). Washing away your sins: Threatened morality and physical cleansing. *Science, 313,* 1451–1452.

24

Thinkers' Personalities: On Individual Differences in the Processes of Sense Making

Arie W. Kruglanski & Anna Sheveland

Psychologically speaking, humans share two defining attributes, one cognitive and the other social. The cognitive attribute refers to the sense-making process in which people continually engage. The social element refers to the collective nature of sense making and its grounding in collective world views and shared realities. Jointly, the cognitive and the social elements define the field of study known as social cognition, which over the last century has made substantial contributions to understanding how people think, judge, and ultimately produce intelligible action (Fiske, 1992).

Like the broader discipline of social psychology of which it is part, the social cognition domain has traditionally emphasized the situation and de-emphasized personality and individual differences as the determinants of people's sense-making activity. The large preponderance of social cognition studies have used experimental designs in which participants are randomly assigned to conditions and the relevant variable is manipulated in the laboratory. In this category fall the various priming studies, where the construct of interest is activated in the participants' minds by the experimenter (for a review, see Förster & Liberman, 2007); the cognitive load studies (e.g., see Gilbert, 1989), in which a person's cognitive capacity is situationally restricted; person perception or persuasion studies, where the information given to participants is manipulated in the experimental setting; or meta-cognitive research (for a review,

see Petty, Brinol, Tormala, & Wegener, 2007), where people's inferences about their cognitive states are systematically varied.

Indeed, occasionally, social psychologists have implied that individual differences are of lesser theoretical importance than are situations, and have treated such differences as noise or "error variance" whose main function resides in serving as a statistical backdrop against which the ubiquitous "power of the situation" may be assessed. The situational emphasis in social psychology can be traced to Kurt Lewin's (1939) ahistorical approach and his theorizing about the mental representation of one's momentary "life space," and the field of forces impinging on the individual's psyche in specific circumstances. The juxtaposition of the person and the situation was echoed by developments in the field of personality, spearheaded by Walter Mischel's (1968) skepticism about the cross-situational predictive ability of personality factors, leading him to conclude that "with the possible exception of intelligence, highly generalized behavioral consistencies have not been demonstrated, and the concept of personality traits as broad response predispositions is thus untenable" (p. 146). Decades later, Ross and Nisbett (1991) voiced a similar indictment of personality research, arguing that "a half-century of research has taught us that in most [...] novel situations, one cannot predict with any accuracy how particular people will respond [...] using information about an individual's personal dispositions" (p. 2).

Subsequent developments, however, mitigated the "wholesale" rejection of the individual differences program. In a well-known paper, Bem and Allen (1974) argued that people differ in their degree of trans-situational consistency, and hence that it should be possible to predict "some of the people some of the time." And Edward Jones (1998) stated that both factions of the situationism–dispositionism debate accept the premise that the person and the situational context interact to determine individuals' behavior. Where social and personality researchers have historically, and continue to, differ concerns which of the two components of the person–situation interaction is emphasized. The notion of individual differences was interpreted in cognitive terms (rather than rejected out of hand) by Mischel and Shoda (1995), who assumed that people may differ in "if–then" action rules to which they subscribe. Such individual differences in relatively stable action schemata account for differences between individuals across situations.

In the domain of personality research, the trait approach has been revived and appears to be thriving. In a recent chapter, Funder and Fast (2010) state that despite the long decades of analysis and criticism, the study of personality these days is alive and well. There is general consensus in the field that the Big Five personality factors (Costa & McCrae, 1992) constitute the major dimensions of personality and, as Funder (1994) summarized it 16 years ago, "...*there is something integral to human psychology that maintains its behavioral effectiveness over long periods of time. We could call that personality*" (p. 125).

PERSONALITY AND SITUATION AS DETERMINANTS OF PSYCHOLOGICAL STATES

In the present chapter we take a yet different approach to the personality–situation issue. We consider both as separate determinants of psychological states that ultimately drive behavior. Individual differences have behavioral consequences if they operationally define stable psychological constructs that are relevant to behavior, and so do situations. This view echoes Higgins' (2008) conception of personality "as simply one source of variability in the functioning of psychological principles that also vary across momentary situations" (p. 612). That is, contrary to the conceptualization of personality and situation factors as qualitatively distinct, we see them as sharing a core similarity in constituting ways of thinking and operationalizing psychological variables. An important upshot of this approach is that the very same psychological constructs could be embodied (or operationalized) via a dimension of a stable individual difference as well as by a transient situation. In the former case, the behavior of interest might be stable across relevant situations, whereas in the latter case, the same behavior would be situationally specific.

THE PRESENT CHAPTER

In this chapter, we review individual differences in variables affecting the socio-cognitive process, presently treated as the process of sense-making and knowledge construction. Consistent with the discussion above, for the most part the individual factors we will consider would have been discussed previously in terms of their situational manifestations, or could have been so considered, as they refer to psychological constructs that can vary both by person and by situation. As a preview of what is to come, we first discuss the knowledge construction process as it has been portrayed in our lay epistemic theory (Kruglanski, 1989, 2004). We use this theory as an organizing framework for discussing individual difference variables in various categories as they relate to theoretically identified factors affecting knowledge formation.

Specifically, we discuss the role of lay theories in knowledge formation – specifically, lay theories concerning the nature of evidence, the essence of human attributes (i.e., entity vs incremental theories), and the deservedness of outcomes (i.e., the *belief in a just world* and the *Protestant work ethic*). We then review motivational factors relevant to knowledge formation, including the need for cognition, the need for cognitive closure, preference for consistency, and regulatory focus (i.e., promotion and prevention) and regulatory mode (i.e., locomotion and assessment) conceptions. Next, our discussion of cognitive ability factors will center on individual differences in working memory capacity, ability to achieve structure, cognitive complexity, and schematicity. We also discuss the interrelations among the foregoing three classes of factors.

THE PROCESS OF KNOWLEDGE FORMATION: HOW DO WE "KNOW" WHAT WE "KNOW"

The process of knowledge formation is ubiquitous, and reflected in all forms of social (and, non-social) reasoning and judgment. Kruglanski's (1989) lay epistemic theory and subsequent work building upon it (e.g., Erb et al., 2003; Kruglanski

& Gigerenzer, 2011) outline a general theoretical framework that explicates this process and that serves as a framework for our subsequent discussion of individual differences in social cognition.

Kruglanski and colleagues (e.g., Kruglanski, 1989, 2004; Kruglanski & Gigerenzer, 2011; Kruglanski & Sleeth-Keppler, 2007) have proposed that, at bottom, all human "knowledge" (treated as subjective beliefs on various topics) is formed in fundamentally the same way: by reasoning syllogistically from evidence to conclusion. More specifically, knowledge is derived from relevant information via the utilization of if–then inference rules. In terminology of syllogistic reasoning, these inference rules constitute the major premises (of the "if X then Y" variety), where X is some manner of evidence and Y is the conclusion to be drawn on the basis of that evidence. For example, one might subscribe to the inference rule that "*if* a person is a doctor, *then* he or she is intelligent." Learning that a new neighbor is a cardiovascular surgeon would, thus, serve to inform and facilitate the judgment that she is bright.

Three important points can be illustrated with this example. First, a key component of the knowledge formation process is not simply the utilization of inference rules (i.e., major premises), but also the recognition that some new information given in the situation affirms the antecedent condition of the rule, and hence constitutes evidence (e.g., "this person is a cardiovascular surgeon"). This latter contribution to the knowledge formation processes constitutes, in syllogistic terms, the minor premise.

Second, as alluded to, not all individuals subscribe to the same inference rules. Consequently, different individuals may draw highly divergent conclusions from the same salient piece of information, or cue. For instance, whereas Person A might believe that all doctors are intelligent, Person B may hold a more context-specific inference rule regarding doctors, believing that this applies only to those who have earned degrees from prestigious universities. Thus, for Person B, knowledge of the new neighbor's occupation would not be sufficient to enable a judgment about her intelligence; instead, judgment would need to be reserved until more information (i.e., what institution the physician earned her degree from) was available. Moreover, Person C might hold no inference rule at all relating the profession of medical doctor to intelligence. For him, learning that the new neighbor is a surgeon would not prompt the formation of a judgment along the attribute dimension of intelligence.

The third point is that stereotypes, a major topic of interest to social cognition researchers, may be thought of as inference rules in which the individual's social category (e.g., gender, age, race or profession) constitute the antecedent term and the properties assumed to be tied to the category – the consequent. For instance, the stereotype of professors as absent minded can be expressed as a major premise whereby "if X is a professor, then X is absent minded." Although not all inference rules are stereotypes, stereotypes represent a class of inference rules of great social import and, thus, a concrete example of the relevance of the present conceptualization of the knowledge formation process to the social realm.

BEYOND SUBJECTIVE LOGIC: FACTORS OF MOTIVATION AND ABILITY IN KNOWLEDGE FORMATION

Although, ultimately, the formation of knowledge is carried out via subjective logic, its application in specific contexts may depend on the individuals' cognitive motivation and abilities. We consider these in turn.

Motivation

The process of knowledge formation involves the retrieval (activation) from memory of the pertinent inference rules (major premises), as well as gleaning from the ambient environment of information relevant to the rules (minor premises). This process may vary in difficulty across circumstances. Inference rules may vary in their strength, or the degree (or likelihood) that the antecedent X is believed to imply the consequent Y. For example, whereas one individual may believe that going more than 10 miles per hour over the speed limit is very likely to get you ticketed, another may believe such an outcome is far less likely to result from speeding of that magnitude. Furthermore, some inference rules may be more readily retrievable (e.g., more accessible) than others, and individuals may vary in their readiness to persist in the rule retrieval process in order to optimize their judgmental outcomes (i.e., to find the most reliable judgmental rule in the situation). Such readiness may depend on individuals' degree of epistemic motivation: i.e., motivations relevant to the formation of knowledge. Some epistemic motivations are non-directional in that they do not bias the judgmental process toward the contents of any particular conclusion. The need for accuracy is non-directional, as is the need for cognitive closure (Kruglanski, 2004), or the need for cognition (Cacioppo & Petty, 1982). Other motivations are directional: the need for self-enhancement (e.g., Dunning, 1999; Kunda, 1990; Kunda & Sinclair, 1999; Murray & Holmes, 1999) is known to bias judgments toward esteem-enhancing judgments; the need for control, toward judgments implying control, etc.

In all cases, the epistemic motivation affects the extent and selectivity of information processing en route to a judgment. For instance, a strong motivation for cognitive closure would arrest information processing on an early judgment, whereas a strong accuracy motivation would prolong the elaboration process and induce an extensive evaluation of numerous possibilities. A strong need for esteem would cut the process short where an esteem-promoting judgment was afforded, and would prolong the process where an esteem-undermining judgment seemed suggested, etc. (for discussions, see Kruglanski, 1980, 2004; Kruglanski, Pierro, Mannetti, & DeGrada, 2006; Kruglanski & Webster, 1986).

Cognitive capacity

The amount of effort individuals are prepared to invest in judgmentally relevant information processing should also depend on their attentional capacity: i.e., on the amount of cognitive resources they can bring to bear on the judgment-forming activity. Situationally, cognitive capacity is determined by concurrent cognitive tasks in which the individual is engaged (defining the amount of load imposed on this individual's cognitive system), and it is also affected by prior capacity-depleting activities (Baumeister et al., 2002; Kruglanski, 1989), or the place in the circadian cycle at which individuals find themselves (Pierro & Kruglanski, 2008). The extent of an individual's cognitive capacity should affect the amount of effort the individual is likely to invest in information processing. The lesser the capacity, the sooner the individual would be inclined to bring the elaboration process to a close and proceed to crystallize a firm judgment. Often, restricted cognitive capacity (stemming from an imposition of cognitive load, for example) may exert its effects through arousal of a motivation for cognitive closure – which, in turn, may curtail information processing as mentioned above. For instance, reduction of cognitive capacity via time pressure, noise, alcoholic intoxication, or a nadir in one's circadian cycle has been found to limit individuals' extent of information processing and increase the tendency to form judgments quickly, and on the basis of limited information (Kruglanski, 2004).

Cognitive ability

Distinct from cognitive capacity, which primarily has to do with the amount of attentional resources at the individual's disposal, is the individual's ability to generate inference rules in a given domain and to detect information pertinent to those rules. In part, such ability may have to do with individuals' degree of expertise or sophistication in the domain, with the experts possessing a richer, more differentiated, and complex "arsenal" of available knowledge than the novices. In turn, the complexity of one's cognitive representations may determine one's facility with respect to informational elaboration and the ease of generating and applying inferential rules on a given topic.

As an interim summary, the lay epistemic theory posits a universal process through which knowledge is derived via the identification of "evidence" (the minor premise) pluggable into specific inference rules (the major premise) and the joint utilization of those premises toward the drawing of conclusions. Although this process is assumed to be fundamentally equivalent across individuals and judgments of different kinds, the content of the inference rules adhered to, and hence the determination of what constitutes evidence, can vary greatly inter-individually as well as situationally. Specifically, different rules can be primed, hence made accessible, in different situational contexts, and different individuals may have different rules chronically accessible to them (Higgins, 1996).

The utilization of inference rules in specific contexts may require considerable effort on the part of individuals. The readiness to expend the effort, in turn, depends on the magnitude of epistemic motivation that individuals bring to the knowledge formation context, and the cognitive capacity that they can apply to the knowledge formation process. Again, the motivational magnitude as well as type may be determined situationally and also vary across individuals, representing dimensions of individual differences.

In what follows, we use the foregoing organizational scheme suggested by the lay epistemic theory to review major individual difference variables in social cognition. We first review factors relevant to the inferential rules and application of the syllogistic logic in judgment formation. Subsequently, we review individual differences in cognitive ability and motivation.

INDIVIDUAL DIFFERENCES IN INFERENTIAL RULES: THE CONCEPT OF LAY THEORIES

People form new knowledge by applying their understandings of how different things hang together, and what the implicational relations are among categories of events. In the preceding pages, we characterized those perceived relations as inferential rules of an "if–then" form. More traditionally in social cognition, such conceptual linkages in people's minds have been characterized as lay theories. The notion of lay theories goes back to Heider's (1958) "common-sense psychology" and his view of the average person as a naïve scientist, who actively works to make sense out of his world. To that end, people were assumed to construct "naïve theories" about how objects in their social world are related.

As discussed earlier, lay theories comprise inference rules; they function by providing individuals with expectations that help them interpret and make judgments about information they encounter in their social worlds. Because lay theories constitute beliefs about (implicational) relations between categories, they may differ considerably among cultures, groups, and individuals. Some lay theories have attracted more theoretical and empirical attention from psychological scientists than others. Below, we review lay theories related, respectively, to the nature of personal attributes, the deservedness of outcomes, and to ascriptions of epistemic authority.

The nature of personal attributes

Dweck and her colleagues (e.g., Dweck, 1999; Dweck, Hong, & Chiu, 1993; Dweck & Leggett, 1988; Hong, Chiu, & Dweck, 1995) have investigated individual differences in lay theories concerning the nature of personal attributes. Specifically, they have explored individual variability in assumptions about the fixedness of human attributes; these were assumed to be rooted in two competing lay theories, *entity theory* and *incremental theory*. Whereas entity theorists view human attributes as stable across times and contexts, incremental theorists view human traits as malleable and capable of changing as a function of learning.

Endorsement of entity versus incremental theories has implications for judgments about the self as well as others. Compared to incremental theorists, entity theorists are more prone to attribute personal academic failures and setbacks to their own intellectual inferiority (Henderson & Dweck, 1990). Relatedly, entity and incremental theorists differ in their responses to failure: incremental theorists are more likely to report that, in the face of failure, they would adopt new strategies or increase their level of effort, compared to entity theorists (Zhao & Dweck, 1994, cited in Dweck, 1999).

Compared to incremental theorists, entity theorists tend to draw stronger trait inferences from others' behavior, anticipate greater consistency in trait-relevant behavior across situations, and are more confident in behavioral predictions based on information about a person's traits (Chiu, Hong, & Dweck, 1997). The tendency of entity theorists to place greater emphasis on the role of stable traits in explaining behavior has been explored also in the context of judgments of guilt and innocence. In this context, Gervey, Chiu, Hong, and Dweck (1999) found that among participants who were asked to render a verdict in a fictitious murder trial, potentially trait-relevant information (e.g., the defendant's attire at the time of the murder, intended to provide information about the defendant's respectability, or lack thereof) had a substantially greater impact on the judgments of entity theorists relative to those of incremental theorists. Finally, entity theorists also appear to endorse ethnic stereotypes (of Blacks, Asians, Caucasians, Hispanics, and Jews) to a significantly greater extent than incremental theorists, despite comparable knowledge about the content of widely-held societal stereotypes associated with those groups (Levy, Stroessner, & Dweck, 1998).

The deservedness of outcomes

Belief in a just world
The just-world hypothesis (Lerner, 1965) states that "individuals have a need to believe that they live in a world where people generally get what they deserve" (Lerner & Miller, 1978, p. 1030), which allows them to see world as stable and orderly and, thus, predictable. One of the earliest tests of this hypothesis was conducted by Lerner and Simmons (1966). In this experiment, female participants watched a young woman participate in a "learning experiment" in which she was given electric shocks for every mistake she made (i.e., a negative reinforcement condition). In the next session, some participants were given the chance to vote to have the "victim" placed in an alternative positive reinforcement condition, in which she would be given money for correct answers rather than shocks for incorrect ones. Other participants were not given this opportunity to restore "justice." When later asked to evaluate the victim's attractiveness, participants in the unresolved injustice condition rated her less favorably (i.e., derogated her more) than participants who were able to place her in the positive reinforcement condition and learned that, in fact, the switch had been made. That is, when participants were confronted with an unresolved situation of injustice (an innocent person suffering), they appeared to

cognitively resolve it by devaluing the victim, thus making her fate more palatable. Participants for whom justice had been restored already, however, exhibited no such tendency.

Although early studies on the just-world hypothesis demonstrated that people generally have a need to view the world as one in which outcomes are just, the extent to which individuals subscribe to this view (i.e., their belief in a just world; Lerner, 1980) varies. Next, we will discuss some of the phenomena associated with individual differences in just-world belief (for a more extensive review, see Dalbert, 2009).

Consistent with Lerner and Simmons' early findings regarding victim derogation, evidence suggests that individuals with stronger just-world beliefs are more likely to blame rape victims (Sakalli-Uğurlu, Sila Yalçin, & Glick, 2007) and report that AIDS sufferers deserve their illness (Glennon & Joseph, 1993) compared to individuals with weaker just-world beliefs. The belief in a just world also appears to increase one's susceptibility to the halo effect. Specifically, in a study exploring the relationship between the belief in a just world and physical attractiveness stereotyping, participants with stronger beliefs in a just world rated an attractive male as possessing more socially desirable personality qualities and as more likely to have better life outcomes than an unattractive male (Dion & Dion, 1987).

In addition to perceiving greater congruence between the personal qualities and outcomes of others, individuals with stronger just-world beliefs also appear to view their own outcomes as more just (Dalbert, 2009). For example, Dalbert and Filke (2007) found that among male inmates at a German prison, those with strong just-world beliefs viewed their personal experiences and circumstances related to their imprisonment (e.g., the legal proceedings that resulted in their incarceration, their treatment by prison officials) as more just than inmates without strong just-world beliefs. Finally, in keeping with the general just-world notion that bad things happen to bad people and good things to good people, the belief in a just world appears to be negatively associated with perceptions of personal risk (Hafer, Bogaert, & McMullen, 2001), and positively associated with a sense of obligation to reciprocate a good deed (Edlund, Sagarin, & Johnson, 2007). (Dalbert, 2009).

Protestant work ethic

The Protestant work ethic (Weber, 1905/1958) centers on the belief that success is the reward for hard work, whereas poor outcomes reflect insufficient effort, and represent, therefore, just deserts.

Accordingly, individuals who strongly endorse the Protestant work ethic tend to view people as more responsible for their own outcomes (Christopher & Schlenker, 2005). For example, participants with a strong Protestant work ethic belief are more prone to make internal attributions for unemployment and are more opposed to welfare payments (Furnham, 1982). The association between the Protestant work ethic and a strong belief in people's personal responsibility for outcomes also explains Katz and Hass' (1988) finding that endorsement of the Protestant work ethic is positively associated with racial prejudice.

Of present interest, the Protestant work ethic does not appear to hold the same meaning for everyone. Whereas for White Americans, endorsement of this ethic generally serves to justify inequality, for Black and Latino Americans it assumes a more egalitarian meaning, suggesting that all members of society can achieve success (Levy, Ramirez, & Vellila, 2005, as cited in Levy, Chiu, & Hong, 2006). Moreover, there also appear to be age differences among White Americans, in that 10 and 15-year-olds are more likely to emphasize the egalitarian meaning, whereas older individuals tend to extract the inequality justifier meaning (Levy, West, Ramirez, & Karafantis, 2006).

Ascriptions of epistemic authority

Contrasted against Dweck's incremental and entitative theories, and Protestant work ethic and just-world beliefs, an altogether different type of lay theory concerns more generally what sources individuals turn to for information. Individuals differ in theories they hold about reliable sources of information: i.e., about whom or what constitutes a trusted epistemic authority (Kruglanski, 1989; Kruglanski et al., 2005). As do other lay theories, epistemic authority beliefs constitute "if–then" assertions about the validity attachable to given sources (i.e., "if Source X made statement Y, then statement Y is valid"). Epistemic authorities can be specific – for example, teachers, parents, religious authorities, government officials, and celebrities can constitute epistemic authorities for some individuals, and so can an individual's own self (referring to a self-ascribed epistemic authority). Epistemic authorities can be general, consisting not of a single person or entity (e.g., the *New York Times*) but a category or class such as an occupation, level of seniority, or level of education. An epistemic authority may be relied upon for guidance in numerous areas of a person's life, or may be influential only in a limited number of domains or even a single domain (e.g., a plumber or a dentist would likely be trusted as authorities in their own areas of specialization) (Kruglanski et al., 2005).

Individuals differ in the degree to which they ascribe epistemic authority to different sources. For some people, religious leaders (e.g., the Pope) may serve as important epistemic authorities, whereas, for others, religious leaders may wield little epistemic authority. Such individual differences in the distribution of ascribed epistemic authority across various sources are assumed to arise from different socialization histories (Kruglanski et al., 2005), and have important implications for differences in people's judgments in similar situations.

Not surprisingly, individuals appear to rely on information from dominant epistemic authorities to a greater extent than on information from less-trusted sources. For example, Bar (1999; cited in Kruglanski et al., 2005) found that participants sought out information from dominant epistemic authorities first, spent more time examining this information than information from other sources, and were more confident in judgments they made based upon recommendations from these dominant epistemic authorities.

The self can also serve as an important epistemic authority. Accordingly, individuals with higher self-ascribed epistemic authority in a particular domain tend to seek out less external information in that domain. Moreover, this tendency is moderated by the need for cognitive closure, such that among individuals with a low self-ascribed epistemic authority in the specific domain of interest, the higher the need for cognitive closure, the stronger their tendency to seek out external information, whereas among individuals with a high self-ascribed epistemic authority, the higher their need for closure, the lower their tendency to seek out external information (Pierro & Mannetti, 2004; cited in Kruglanski et al., 2005). Individuals with higher self-ascribed epistemic authority are also better at discriminating between information that is relevant versus irrelevant to their decision (ibid.), and appear to learn more from personal experience, presumably because they place more trust in their own interpretations of their experiences, treating these as valid sources of evidence.

INDIVIDUAL DIFFERENCES IN COGNITIVE ABILITY AND COMPLEXITY

Having covered individual differences manifested in the content of lay theories, we now turn to a second class of individual difference factors – cognitive ability (i.e., working memory capacity

and ability to achieve structure) and cognitive sophistication (i.e., a person's cognitive complexity, schematicity, and expertise in a domain) – that affect the sense-making process. These dimensions of individual differences affect the most basic levels of information processing and are, therefore, highly consequential for a variety of socio-cognitive processes and outcomes.

Cognitive ability

Working memory capacity
Working memory capacity has been defined as "the capacity for controlled, sustained attention in the face of interference or distraction" (Engle, Kane, & Tuholski, 1999, p. 104). Although working memory can be assessed in a variety of ways (see, e.g., Oberauer, 2005), it is typically measured using "span" tasks that require participants to remember information (e.g., numbers) presented to them during a complex secondary processing task. In these conditions, an individual's working memory capacity is assessed in terms of the number of correctly recalled memory items. For example, the operation span task (Turner & Engle, 1989) has participants perform a string of arithmetic operations – e.g., $(6 \times 2) - 3 = 10$ (yes/no) – each of which is paired with a word (e.g., "Fish") that serves as the memory item the participant must later recall. Individual differences in cognitive capacity have particularly consequential implications where requirements for controlled, elaborative processing are high (see also, Barrett, Tugade, & Engle, 2004).

As can be expected, individuals' working memory capacity may vary across situational circumstances. Individuals preoccupied with various concerns may have a more limited capacity at their disposal than others not similarly encumbered. Alert individuals may have greater working memory capacity than these people when drowsy, mentally fatigued or at the nadir of their circadian cycle. Of greater present interest are stable individual differences in working memory capacity. One phenomenon where this has been demonstrated is the suppression of unwanted thoughts. The "white bear" effect (Wegner, Schneider, Carter, & White, 1987) describes a phenomenon wherein asking participants to suppress thoughts of a particular kind (in this case, a white bear) actually leads to increased accessibility of the construct. Utilizing this classic paradigm, Brewin and Beaton (2002) showed that, compared to participants with low working memory capacity, those with a high stable degree of such capacity were significantly better able to suppress thoughts of a white bear when instructed to do so. The superior ability of individuals with higher working memory capacity to suppress unwanted thoughts has important implications for mental well-being, as higher working memory capacity is apparently related to the suppression of anxious autobiographical memories (Geraerts, Merckelbach, Jelicic, & Habets, 2007) and of other unwanted thoughts of various kinds (Brewin & Smart, 2005).

Apart from keeping unwanted thoughts from entering consciousness, working memory capacity may enable keeping desired thoughts active in consciousness; this conclusion was suggested by McVay and Kane's (2009) finding that working memory capacity is negatively related to goal neglect. Specifically, participants with lower working memory capacity experienced a greater number of goal-neglect failures on a sustained attention to response task, and this relationship was partially mediated by mind-wandering (i.e., a reduced ability to control conscious thought).

Individual differences in working memory capacity are also associated with variation in the recall of memories. Specifically, lower working memory capacity is associated with overgeneralized autobiographical memory – i.e., a greater number of categorical autobiographical memories relative to specific autobiographical memories (Ros, Latorre, & Serrano, 2010) – as well as with false-memory recall (Gerrie & Garry, 2007; Jaschinski & Wentura, 2002). This latter finding holds important implications for real-world situations such as court cases involving eyewitness testimony (Jaschinski & Wentura, 2002).

Individual differences in working memory capacity also appear to affect people's ability to bias their judgments in a motivationally desirable direction, as illustrated by a study by Chen (2009). Participants in their research were University of Maryland (UMD) students who received information about a series of track and field competitions between Duke and UMD. This information, if considered carefully, ultimately favored Duke. However, its sheer processing (i.e., the sheer comprehension of the facts) required considerable capacity, so that little capacity was left for effecting the motivational distortion. As a consequence, individuals with high working memory capacity were able to bend the facts in their desirable direction and concluded that UMD was the winner after all. In contrast, individuals with low working memory capacity did not have a sufficient cognitive ability to distort the information and thus reached the (correct!) conclusion that UMD was inferior to Duke across a greater number of different athletic events.

Individual differences in working memory capacity may also affect moral judgments. Moore, Clark, and Kane (2008) presented participants with variants of the classic moral dilemma of killing one person to save several others. Participants read a series of vignettes in which they were to imagine themselves as the protagonist confronting a tough moral choice and were asked, for each scenario, to judge the appropriateness of sacrificing the life of one person to save the lives of multiple others. The vignettes differed from each other in (a) whether the act of killing was impersonal (e.g., activating a system that eliminates oxygen from a hall in a burning building) or personal (e.g., using the body of an injured man as a battering-ram to break through burning blockage preventing the escape of others), and (b) whether the death of the person to be sacrificed was inevitable or not. Participants with high (vs low) working memory capacity deemed personally killing someone whose death was inevitable to be more acceptable. Thus, working memory capacity appears to be implicated in moral rationalization, such that individuals with high working memory capacity are better able to justify killing one person to save others when the person killed is already "slated" to die.

Finally, individual differences in working memory capacity have been implicated in probability judgments, judgments which involve simultaneously comparing a focal hypothesis with its alternatives, thus requiring one to hold considerable information active in working memory (Sprenger & Dougherty, 2006). Specifically, the accuracy of probability judgments is negatively correlated with working memory capacity. This deficiency in probability judgments associated with lower working memory capacity may have important consequences for individuals' everyday lives. For example, given that goal striving is in part a function of the expectancy of goal attainment (i.e., a probability judgment), individuals low in working memory capacity may inefficiently appropriate their motivational resources based on erroneous assessments of the likelihood of attaining their various goals. That is, inaccurate expectancy estimates might lead individuals with lower working memory to chase goals whose true probability of attainment does not warrant their pursuit, while neglecting goals that are more likely to be attained. Similarly, inaccurate estimates of the relative instrumentality of different means to a goal might lead one to adopt a suboptimal strategy in the pursuit of that goal.

Ability to achieve cognitive structure

There are situations in which the individual may desire certainty, and the comfort of assured knowledge, whereas in other situations certainty and assurance may be less desirable. The need for cognitive closure or structure (Kruglanski &

Freund, 1983; Kruglanski, 1989, 2004),[1] discussed in detail later, represents a psychological construct expressing the magnitude of such desire that may vary across situations. Yet situations may also vary in the difficulty of attaining closure. For instance, closure may be difficult to attain where the individual receives a considerable amount of inconsistent information on a topic, or is cognitively busy, and hence less capable of "connecting the dots" and piecing together a coherent belief from seemingly disparate bits of available information. Both the desire for closure/structure and the ability to attain it have been studied as dimensions of individual differences as well. In this vein, Yoram Bar-Tal et al. (1997) defined the ability to achieve cognitive structure as the "extent to which individuals are able to use information-processing strategies (cognitive structuring or piecemeal) consistent with the level of their need for structure" (p. 1158). Bar-Tal and his colleagues have explored the interactive effects of individual differences in the ability to achieve cognitive structure and the motivation to do so (i.e., the need for cognitive structure or closure) on cognitive structuring outcomes.

Specifically, Bar-Tal has proposed that the need for cognitive structure should affect judgment only insofar as individuals are capable of achieving the level of structure they desire (i.e., their ability to achieve cognitive structure) and that, likewise, the ability to achieve cognitive structure should influence judgmental outcomes only among individuals who desire cognitive structure (i.e., those who are high in need for cognitive closure). In other words, for individuals low in the need for cognitive structure, the ability to achieve cognitive structure should be irrelevant because they are unmotivated to strive for structure in the first place; and for individuals low in the ability to achieve cognitive structure, the need for cognitive structure should be irrelevant because they are unable to achieve cognitive structure regardless of its perceived desirability. Building upon this idea, Bar-Tal (1994; with Kishon-Rabin & Tabak, 1997) has investigated the joint effects of the ability to achieve cognitive structure and the need for cognitive structure on a number of decisional outcomes. Specifically, in a series of five studies, Bar-Tal, Kishon-Rabin, and Tabak (1997) demonstrated that the ability to achieve cognitive structure and the need for cognitive structure jointly determine cognitive structuring behavior, just as these authors hypothesized.

One way in which cognitive structure can be achieved is through the filtering of schema-inconsistent and schema-irrelevant information. In this vein, Bar-Tal et al. (1997) found that the need for cognitive structure was associated with the recruitment of such structuring strategies only

when the ability to achieve cognitive structure was high. For participants low in that ability, the need for cognitive structure, as such, did not affect these individuals' cognitive structuring behavior.

A different strategy for achieving cognitive structure is the use of simplified generalizations and abstract (vs concrete) category labels, as these imply greater stability (and, thus, greater certainty) across both times and situations (for a review, see Kruglanski, 2004). Pertinent to this phenomenon, Bar-Tal and his colleagues (1997) found that high need for cognitive structure participants exhibited greater global (vs situation-specific) self-attributions and evinced lesser variability in their ratings of both an individual and a group (Palestinians) across multiple dimensions (implying non-specific, generalized conceptualizations), but only when their ability to achieve cognitive structure was high. This tendency for high need for cognitive closure individuals to rely on generalized and abstract knowledge structures when able to do so (i.e., when their ability to achieve cognitive structure is high) is consistent with the finding that the need for cognitive structure/closure is positively related to stereotypical thinking (a form of cognitive structuring) only for individuals who are high in the ability to achieve cognitive structure (Bar-Tal, 1991; cited in Bar-Tal, 1994).

Bar-Tal (1994) also explored the joint effect of the ability to achieve cognitive structure and the need for cognitive structure/closure on coping with decision-making in conflicted situations, which he regarded as a specific instantiation of psychological uncertainty. In the face of uncertainty, individuals who were both motivated (those high in the need for cognitive structure who experienced heightened levels of discomfort from the uncertainty) and able to structure the situation so as to reach decisional closure more quickly did so, and also reported the least amount of difficulty in making their decision.

Cognitive complexity

Situationally given information may contain elements that are more or less clearly differentiated; furthermore, those elements may operate together to a lesser or greater extent, and hence be more or less integrated in performing an overall function. The elements of differentiation and integration appear as twin dimensions of an individual-difference variable known as "cognitive complexity." Thus, a cognitively complex individual will differentiate between a large number of cognitive elements and have well-developed representations of the interrelations between them, whereas a cognitively non-complex individual will distinguish between few cognitive elements and lack a clear conceptualization of their interrelatedness.

Although cognitive complexity has been measured in a variety of ways, the two popular methods of its assessment are:

(a) variations of Scott's (1962) Object-Sorting Test, in which participants are either provided with or asked to generate themselves a number of objects (e.g., countries) and group them in as many ways (i.e., along as many dimensions) as possible, and

(b) the Paragraph Completion Test (Schroder, Driver, & Streufert, 1967), in which participants are asked to complete sentence stems about various topics. Tetlock (e.g., 1984, 1985, 1988) has also used the Paragraph Completion Test scale with archival data (e.g., speeches, interviews) in order to assess the complexity of high-profile political actors.

Cognitive complexity is implicated in judgment in a number of different ways. For instance, it is associated with the extremity of judgments rendered about others. Specifically, individuals low in cognitive complexity generate more extreme ratings of target persons than individuals high in complexity (Frauenfelder, 1974), and college males with relatively complex (vs non-complex) representations of older males have been found to evaluate older male targets more extremely in both positive and negative directions (Linville, 1982). In a related vein, cognitive complexity is also associated with individual differences in in-group and out-group perceptions such that, compared to participants low in cognitive complexity, those high in complexity perceive greater variability within both in-groups and out-groups and, consistent with the previously discussed findings, form less extreme evaluations of in-groups and out-groups (Ben-Ari, Kedem, & Levy-Weiner, 1992).

Cognitive complexity has also been implicated in judgments about the self. It is related to greater confidence in self-evaluative judgments (Adams-Webber, 2003), and appears to moderate the relationship between global self-evaluation and self-reported depression, such that the relationship is attenuated for individuals higher in cognitive complexity (Gara, Woolfolk, & Allen, 2002). Linville (1985, 1987) extended the cognitive complexity construct to the domain of self more explicitly with the concept of "self-complexity," defined as "the number of aspects that one uses to cognitively organize knowledge about the self, and the degree of relatedness of these aspects" to one another (Linville, 1985, p. 97). Her research suggests that self-complexity serves to buffer

individuals from the adverse effects of stress such as depression and illness (but see Rafaeli-Mor & Steinberg, 2002, for a challenging viewpoint and review of the literature). It is possible to view these results in terms of substitutability of different means to the goal of positive self-regard. The highly self-complex individuals have multiple such means (corresponding to the large number of self-dimensions that they distinguish), and hence the failure of endeavors regarding one of the aspects can be compensated for by pursuit of one or more of the remaining aspects.

Beginning in the 1980s, implications of cognitive complexity for the political domain – specifically, the notion of a relationship between cognitive complexity and ideological orientation – began to attract the attention of various researchers. Tetlock's (1986) value pluralism model proposes that greater cognitive complexity will be engendered by pluralistic ideologies in which core values are often in conflict with each other, compared to monistic ideologies in which only one value, or a set of values that are highly congruent with each other, are viewed as important. Furthermore, Tetlock (1993) has argued that the center-left position on the ideological spectrum inherently creates the highest levels of value conflict because it places considerable value on both freedom and equality, two values that often are in conflict when it comes to public policy initiatives. In this view, therefore, moderate liberals should exhibit the highest levels of cognitive complexity, while ideological extremists, for whom one value presumably trumps all others, should be the least cognitively complex. Alternatively, Sidanius' (e.g., 1984) context theory proposes that extremists at both ends of the political spectrum will actually be the most politically sophisticated, and thus exhibit greater levels of cognitive complexity than individuals closer to the ideological center.

Evidence supporting both theories has been mixed, with Tetlock (1984, 1986) providing empirical evidence in support of the value pluralism model and Sidanius (1988) providing empirical evidence in support of context theory (Van Hiel & Mervielde, 2003). Van Hiel and Mervielde (2003) have suggested that one explanation for these inconsistent findings might be grounded in methodology. Specifically, they point out that whereas Tetlock's work has been primarily conducted via content analysis of archival data (e.g., speeches) from political elites, Sidanius' has been based on Swedish student samples using Sidanius' (1978) political prediction task, in which participants predict the likelihood of political outcomes (e.g., rioting) from provided information, as a measure of cognitive complexity. In their own investigation into the complexity–ideology relationship, Van Hiel and Mervielde found greater support, across multiple samples and operationalizations of cognitive complexity, for the positive relationship between political extremism and cognitive complexity hypothesized by Sidanius.

Schematicity

Another way that individuals can differ in cognitive sophistication is in the extent to which they engage in the schematic processing of information within a given domain. Bem's (1981) gender schema theory posits that sex-typed individuals are more likely than their non-sex-typed (e.g., androgynous) counterparts to engage in gender-schematic processing, in which gender information (about the self as well as others) is encoded and organized simplistically, along the sole dimension of masculinity/femininity. Gender-schematic individuals (as assessed via Bem's Sex Role Inventory) are more likely to stereotype sports as masculine or feminine (Koivula, 1995) and confuse individuals belonging to the same gender group (Frable & Bem, 1985), and gender-schematic males are more likely to sexually objectify women following exposure to pornographic stimuli (McKenzie-Mohr & Zanna, 1990). In addition to gender schematicity, race schematicity (e.g., Levy, 2000), physical appearance schematicity (e.g., Hargreaves & Tiggemann, 2002), and self-monitoring schematicity (e.g., Mellema & Bassilli, 1995) have also been investigated.

INDIVIDUAL DIFFERENCES IN MOTIVATED COGNITION

The view of the thinker in social cognition research has changed considerably throughout the history of social psychology (Fiske & Taylor, 2007). Among the most notable developments has been the growing recognition of the profound role that motivational forces can play in cognitive processes. Below, as a third and final class of factors discussed in this chapter we will review some prominent examples of such motivational constructs in social cognition research in particular reference to individual variation on the dimensions these constructs represent.

The need for cognition

The need for cognition (Cacioppo & Petty, 1982) is an individual-difference variable defined as a "tendency to engage in and enjoy thinking" (p. 130). Individuals may occupy varying locations along a need for cognition continuum that

spans from cognitive misers to intensive cognizers (Cacioppo, Petty, Feinstein, & Jarvis, 1996). Thus, although situational factors may affect the extent to which individuals are willing to engage in effortful cognition, the need for cognition has been conceptualized and assessed as a dimension of stable individual differences.

The need for cognition is associated with a variety of processes and outcomes relevant to judgment (for a review, see Cacioppo et al., 1996). Because it describes a tendency toward, and the enjoyment of, thinking, the need for cognition is positively associated with the seeking out and processing of information. Indeed, there is evidence that individuals high in the need for cognition engage in more extensive information search when tasked with making a decision (Verplanken, Hazenberg, & Palenéwen, 1992) and appear to process information more thoroughly; the latter has been demonstrated by the finding that, in the realm of persuasion, argument quality has a greater impact on message evaluations, source impressions, and, ultimately, attitudes for individuals high in the need for cognition (Cacioppo, Petty, & Morris, 1983). Furthermore, for individuals high (vs low) in the need for cognition, attitude change effected by a persuasive message persists longer and is more resistant to counter-attitudinal influences (Haugtvedt & Petty, 1992).

The need for cognition also appears to reduce one's susceptibility to a number of judgmental biases, primarily those that stem from insufficient information processing. Specifically, individuals high in the need for cognition are less susceptible to the correspondence bias (i.e., the tendency to overemphasize the role of internal factors when explaining an individual's behavior to the neglect of external factors; D'Agostino & Fincher-Kiefer, 1992), the attractiveness bias (i.e., the tendency to believe attractive people also possess other desirable traits; Perlini & Hansen, 2001), and primacy (Ahlering & Parker, 1989) and framing effects (Smith & Levin, 1996), presumably because their propensity to engage in a greater amount of thinking allows them to correct, at least in part, for the biasing processes involved. Moreover, when forming impressions of others, individuals high in the need for cognition tend to engage more in explanatory thinking (Lassiter, Briggs, & Slaw, 1991) and appear to be less prone to forming expectancy-consistent impressions than their low need for cognition counterparts (Dudley & Harris, 2003). In the same vein, the judgments of individuals low in the need for cognition are more heavily influenced by stereotypes, presumably because they require lesser cognitive effort (Crawford & Skowronski, 1998).

However, although relative to their low need for cognition counterparts, individuals high in the need for cognition seem to enjoy a number of advantages in rendering unbiased judgments, Cacioppo et al. (1996) have emphasized that this need not always be the case. Rather, the need for cognition may in some circumstances actually promote biased judgments, insofar as the process of engaging in more thought leads to more opportunity for that thought to be influenced by biasing factors such as mood (Petty, Schumann, Richman, & Strathman, 1993) and priming effects (Petty & Jarvis, 1996).

In addition to the foregoing implications of the need for cognition for a variety of general cognitive processes, the need for cognition is also associated with a number of content-specific judgments. For one, individuals high (vs low) in the need for cognition are less supportive of punitive measures toward criminals, a relationship apparently mediated by greater attributional complexity of individuals high in the need for cognition (Sargent, 2004). However, this relationship is moderated by authoritarianism, such that, for individuals high in right-wing authoritarianism (RWA) or social dominance orientation (SDO), the need for cognition is associated with increased support for punitive measures and dispositional attributions of crimes, and reduced support for the rehabilitation of criminals (Tam, Leung, & Chiu, 2008). Similarly, although the need for cognition has been shown to be generally negatively associated with racial prejudice (Waller, 1993), it has been shown to predict increased rationalization of a racially discriminatory practice (the failure of a White taxi driver to pick up a Black man) in participants who held strong anti-Black attitudes (Khan & Lambert, 2001). Thus, although the need for cognition is generally associated with reduced levels of punitiveness and racial prejudice, strongly held orientations (i.e., SDO and RWA orientations, and anti-Black attitudes) appear to not merely negate but actually reverse this effect. This shouldn't be too surprising: After all, high need for cognition has implications only for the extent of processing, not for its content. Thus, the content of judgment finally reached should depend heavily on the sequencing of informational contents. Where a given piece of information comes early in the sequence and its opposite later in the sequence, low need for cognition may favor the early information and high need for cognition the later information, whatever the contents of the early and later information might be.

The need for cognitive closure

A motivational variable heavily implicated in sense making and the construction of subjective knowledge is the need for cognitive closure (Kruglanski, 1989), which describes a desire for a definitive answer to a question (i.e., "closure"), as opposed to prolonged uncertainty, confusion, or ambiguity. The need for cognitive closure is conceptualized as containing the dual tendencies of urgency and permanency; these are assumed to work in concert to provide and maintain cognitive closure, and ward off a lack of closure. Whereas the urgency tendency promotes "seizing" upon early information, allowing the individual to render an immediate judgment and thus obtain closure quickly, the permanency tendency promotes "freezing" upon the resulting judgment such that the obtained closure is maintained (Webster, 1993).

The need for cognitive closure may appear to be closely, and negatively, related to the need for cognition. However, these two needs should not be thought of as simply opposite ends of a single bipolar dimension. Empirically, although the need for cognition and the need for cognitive closure are correlated, the magnitude of the correlation is modest – e.g., Webster and Kruglanski (1994) found a correlation of only – 0.24 between the two measures – inconsistent with the notion of a single latent construct underlying these two motivational forces. More importantly, the two constructs differ conceptually: whereas the need for cognition emphasizes the cognitive process (i.e., the act of engaging in cognitive endeavors), the need for closure emphasizes a desired outcome, i.e., a goal of that process (closure). Put differently, the need for cognition defines the cognitive process as an *end in itself*, whereas the need for closure defines it as a *means to an end*.

As has been typically the case with the presently reviewed variables, the need for cognitive closure may vary as function of the situation and the person. Indeed, empirical findings based on situational and dispositional operationalizations of the need for cognitive closure have been found to consistently converge (for reviews, see Kruglanski, 2004; Kruglanski & Fishman, 2009).

Individual differences in the need for cognitive closure are implicated in judgment in a number of ways. Individuals who are high (vs low) in the need for cognitive closure search for less information (Mayseless & Kruglanski, 1987; Webster, Richter, & Kruglanski, 1996) and generate fewer alternative hypotheses before forming a crystallized judgment (Mayseless & Kruglanski, 1987). Ironically, however, they are subjectively more confident in their decisions than their low need for cognitive closure counterparts (e.g., Kruglanski, Webster, & Klem, 1993), perhaps because they are less cognizant of alternative judgmental possibilities (Kruglanski & Fishman, 2009).

Unsurprisingly, given their predisposition toward quick "seizing" upon information that allows them to reach closure, individuals high in the need for cognitive closure demonstrate a heightened susceptibility to primacy effects in impression formation (Webster & Kruglanski, 1994) when the impression formation goal is introduced prior to the presentation of information, but are more prone to succumb to recency effects when the impression formation goal is introduced only after exposure to the pertinent information (Richter & Kruglanski, 1999). The need for cognitive closure is also associated with an increased reliance on stereotypes (Dijksterhuis, van Knippenberg, Kruglanski, & Schaper, 1996; Kruglanski & Freund, 1983), an augmentation of the correspondence bias (Webster, 1993), and a reduced ability to take the perspective of and feel empathy for a dissimilar target (Webster-Nelson, Klein, & Irvin, 2003); presumably all these phenomena arise from the curtailment of cognitive exertion that accompanies a drive toward closure.

Of special social psychological interest, the need for cognitive closure plays a significant role in intergroup evaluative and perceptual phenomena. For one, need for cognitive closure is associated with greater in-group liking. In a study by Shah, Kruglanski, and Thompson (1998), participants were provided with information about fictional individuals, who they expected to be either their partners or their competitors in a future task. Compared to participants low in the need for cognitive closure, those high in the need for cognitive closure reported more liking for their own "teammates" and less liking for presumed members of the other teams. A heightened need for cognitive closure is also associated with greater linguistic intergroup bias (Webster, Kruglanski, & Pattison, 1997), in that it increases the extent to which positive in-group behaviors and negative out-group behaviors are described in abstract terms, thereby implying stable, fundamental traits. Generally speaking, the need for closure may lead to greater "group centrism" (Kruglanski, Pierro, Mannetti, & DeGrada, 2006), a tendency that manifests itself in greater striving for group uniformity, greater intolerance of opinion deviancy and diversity, and a tendency to prefer autocratic, hierarchical, group decision-making structures that increase the likelihood of a quick arrival at consensual closure and a firm shared reality.

Preference for consistency

An assumption underlying much early social psychological theorizing – e.g., Festinger's (1957) cognitive dissonance theory, or Heider's (1958) cognitive balance theory – is that maintaining consistency among one's cognitions constitutes a driving human motivation. In attempting to account for why, despite the richness of these consistency theories, empirical evidence demonstrating such effects could be difficult to produce, Cialdini, Trost, and Newsom (1995) proposed that there might exist individual differences in the extent to which people place a premium on cognitive consistency. In turn, these differences were assumed to have considerable implications for a number of seminal social psychological theories predicated on the notion of a universal human need for consistency.

To test these ideas, Cialdini et al. (1995) developed the preference for consistency scale. Research conducted with this instrument found that individuals did, in fact, differ in their preference for consistency and, more importantly, that these differences significantly moderated two classic consistency-related phenomena – cognitive balance and cognitive dissonance – such that individuals with a low preference for consistency did not exhibit classic cognitive balance and dissonance effects. These findings support the notion that, contrary to the traditional view of cognitive consistency as a universal human need, or drive, consistency is merely a means of knowledge construction (consistent cognitions validating a knowledge structure, and inconsistent ones undermining it) rather than an end in itself. In cases where such knowledge is desirable, consistency would be preferred over inconsistency; however, where the knowledge was aversive, or had negative implications for one's well-being, inconsistency that undermined such negative knowledge would be welcome and much preferred over consistency that supports it (for a discussion, see Kruglanski & Shteynberg, in press).

Regulatory focus

An important example of the motivation–cognition interplay is represented in Higgins' (1997) theory of regulatory focus. According to this theory, a useful distinction can be made between two types of basic human needs – promotion needs, concerned with advancement, growth, and accomplishment, and prevention needs, concerned with protection, safety, and responsibility (Higgins, 1997).

Higgins proposed that these different regulatory foci give rise to divergent modes of goal pursuit: namely, with a promotion regulatory focus, people are attuned to the presence and absence of gains and the pursuit of "ideals," whereas with a prevention regulatory focus, people are attuned to the presence and absence of losses and the pursuit of "oughts." These different mind-sets have a wide array of implications for social cognitive processes and outcomes (Molden, Lee, & Higgins, 2008).

As with the need for cognitive closure, the magnitude of prevention and promotion orientations is assumed to vary both as a function of the person and of the situation. Concerning a situational induction, a promotion motivation is activated by, among other things, gain-focused incentives, growth needs, independence concerns, and ideal self-standards. The prevention motivation, on the other hand, is activated by, among other things, loss-focused incentives, security needs, interdependence concerns, and ought self-standards. These same factors that can lead to variation as a function of situational factors are also thought to foster the development of stable inter-individual differences in regulatory focus, insofar as they lead to the chronic activation of promotion or prevention needs (Molden, Lee, & Higgins, 2008).

Promotion and prevention needs have been implicated in judgment in a number of different ways. Compared to promotion-focused individuals, prevention-focused individuals generate fewer hypotheses (i.e., better to miss being right than risk being wrong; Molden, Lee, & Higgins, 2008) when making a decision and, as a result, make more certain predictions about others' future behavior (Liberman, Molden, Idson, & Higgins, 2001). The regulatory foci also engender differential sensitivities to certain kinds of information. Specifically, prevention-focused individuals are more sensitive to information regarding security and loss, whereas promotion-focused individuals are more sensitive to information regarding advancement and gains. For example, Markman, Baldwin, and Maddox (2005) found that promotion-focused participants performed best on a classification task when payoffs were structured in terms of gains, whereas prevention-focused participants performed more optimally when the payoffs were structured in terms of losses. The different regulatory foci also have implications for goal commitment insofar as they affect the importance placed on the perceived expectancy of attaining the goal, as demonstrated by Shah and Higgins (1997). Whereas promotion-focused individuals exhibited the classic maximized utility (expectancy X value) effect for goal commitment, for prevention-focused individuals, as the value of the goal increased (and, presumably, prevention-focused individuals began to view it as a necessity), its perceived expectancy carried less weight in determining goal commitment.

Finally, prevention and promotion concerns have also been implicated in intergroup phenomena such as intergroup bias. Across a series of studies, Shah, Brazy, and Higgins (2004) found that a promotion focus was positively related to in-group bias (e.g., cheerfulness and approach-related behaviors toward in-group members), whereas a prevention focus was positively related to out-group bias (e.g., agitation and avoidance-related behaviors toward out-group members).

Regulatory mode

Regulatory mode theory (Higgins et al., 2003; Kruglanski et al., 2000) posits the existence of two largely orthogonal core components of self-regulation – locomotion and assessment – that jointly enable goal pursuit. Locomotion refers to the act of moving either toward or away from an end state (i.e., goal) and, more importantly, away from a current state. A locomotion mindset is associated with, among other things, commitment to prompt action, an achievement orientation, the ability to stay focused on a task, psychological vitality or energy, and conscientiousness. Assessment, on the other hand, refers to the act of comparing one object (e.g., a present state) to another (e.g., a desired end state, or goal). An assessment mindset is associated with, among other things, a fear of invalidity, discomfort with ambiguity, public and private self-consciousness, a mastery orientation, and neuroticism. (Kruglanski et al., 2000).

Similar to regulatory focus theory, regulatory mode theory assumes that the magnitude of an individual's orientation toward each mode can vary as a function of situational features, and can also represent relatively stable individual differences that arise from both temperament and socialization factors (Higgins, Kruglanski, & Pierro, 2003). Locomotion and assessment are implicated in judgment in a number of ways. Below we review empirical findings regarding each mode individually, followed by a discussion of outcomes related to their joint operation.

Because individuals higher in an assessment orientation are more heavily influenced by social norms, or by a concern with doing the "right" thing (Pierro, Mannetti, Higgins, & Kruglanski, 2002), it is not surprising that assessment is negatively correlated with self-esteem and optimism, and positively correlated with social anxiety, depression (Kruglanski et al., 2000), counterfactual thinking, and regret (Pierro et al., 2008). Assessment also has direct implications for goal pursuit. For example, Kruglanski and his colleagues (2000) asked college students to list five personal attributes they wanted to attain (i.e., goals), the perceived value and attainability of each goal, and an unspecified number of means for each goal. Participants' assessment scores were positively associated with goal value (but not goal attainability) and the number of means generated per goal (but not the speed with which the means were generated).

In contrast to the assessment orientation's emphasis on comparison and deliberation, a heightened locomotion orientation reflects a concern with simply moving from one state to another, or doing something just to be doing anything. Locomotion is positively correlated with self-esteem and optimism, and negatively correlated with social anxiety, depression (Kruglanski et al., 2000), counterfactual thinking, and regret (Pierro et al., 2008). And, regarding goal pursuit, locomotion is positively related to the expectancy of goal attainment (but not goal evaluation) and the speed with which means to a given goal are generated (but not the overall quantity of means generated) (Kruglanski et al., 2000).

Arguably, the most illuminating empirical findings regarding the locomotion and assessment modes have to do with their concurrent, as compared to their isolated, operation. Specifically, the quality of self-regulatory outcomes appear to be contingent on the joint operation of locomotion and assessment, with individuals relatively high in both outperforming individuals high on one but not the other, or low on both. Kruglanski et al. (2000) found that both undergraduates' academic achievement (as assessed via grade point average) and soldiers' successful completion of elite military training were the greatest among those high in both locomotion and assessment. The benefit of locomotion and assessment operating conjointly appears to extend to group composition, as well, such that groups composed of equal numbers of individuals high on assessment and on locomotion orientations outperform groups composed of high assessors only and high locomotors only (Mauro, Pierro, Kruglanski, & Higgins, 2009).

It may be well at this juncture to differentiate between the assessment and locomotion mode distinction and the delineation between deliberative and implemental mindsets (e.g., Gollwitzer, 1990). At first blush one might presume that the terms are redundant; specifically, that the assessment component of goal pursuit corresponds with the deliberative phase of self-regulation, whereas the locomotion phase corresponds with the implemental phase. However, both locomotion and assessment concerns are implicated in deliberative and implemental mindsets. That is, deliberation is concerned with the comparison and evaluation of multiple goals, whereas implementation is concerned with the comparison and evaluation of multiple means; therefore, both processes necessarily entail assessment. Moreover,

both the deliberation and implementation phases of self-regulation must be set in motion, which necessarily requires locomotion. Thus, the locomotion and assessment modes of goal pursuit are neither redundant with nor extraneous to the implemental and deliberative phases of self-regulation; rather, they are implicated in both, albeit perhaps to differing degrees. (cf. Higgins et al., 2003).

INTERRELATIONS BETWEEN COGNITIVE CAPACITY/SOPHISTICATION, MOTIVATION, AND LAY THEORIES

Though we discussed them separately, the three classes of individual difference factors discussed in this chapter – cognitive capacity and sophistication, motivation, and lay theories – often operate jointly rather than in isolation from one another. We have already discussed a few ways in which these three classes of factors may interrelate. Here we recapitulate those examples and add a few additional ones.

As discussed previously, Bar-Tal (1994; with Kishon-Rabin & Tabak, 1997) has shown that the effect of the need for cognitive closure/structure on cognitive structuring outcomes is dependent upon the individual's ability to achieve the desired structure, such that for an individual low in the ability to achieve cognitive structure, the need for cognitive closure/structure has little effect on information processing. In this case then, motivation and ability interact to determine the outcomes of cognitive structuring.

In some instances, cognitive capacity and motivation might be causally related to each other. In this vein, Kossowska, Orehek, and Kruglanski (2010) investigated the possibility that dispositional need for cognitive closure may at least partially result from aspects of working memory capacity. That is, they hypothesized that for individuals with lower working memory capacity, the reduced ability to handle large amounts of information in their environments may engender a high need for cognitive closure. Although the correlational nature of their research makes it difficult to definitively prove the existence or direction of a causal relationship, Kossowska et al. did find that working memory capacity was inversely associated to the need for cognitive closure, consistent with their hypothesis.

Illustrating the inverse trend, Tetlock's (1986) value pluralism theory proposes that cognitive sophistication may be driven by motivational concerns. Specifically, value pluralism theory posits that cognitive complexity in the sociopolitical realm arises from conflict between important values that an individual holds and a motivation to resolve this conflict.

Finally, the need for cognitive closure appears to play a role in the operation of lay theories. Specifically, a heightened need for cognitive closure increases reliance on implicit cultural theories, i.e., lay theories that are chronically accessible due to the cultural context an individual is immersed in (Chiu, Morris, Hong, & Menon, 2000), and dominant epistemic authorities (Pierro & Mannetti, 2004), presumably because these provide the individual with a way of quickly reaching the desired closure. Also, it seems intuitive that individuals high in the need for cognitive closure should favor the entity theory of personal attributes over the incremental view, as a belief that traits are relatively fixed across time and situations should provide more closure. To our knowledge, thus far this particular hypothesis has not been explicitly tested.

CONCLUSION

In this chapter we reviewed (albeit not exhaustively) extensive bodies of literature about individual differences in cognitive functions pertaining to knowledge formation. Our approach rested on two assumptions: (1) that basic parameters of knowledge formation pertain to the processes of knowledge validation in light of (subjectively pertinent) evidence, as well as cognitive ability/ sophistication and motivation factors affecting such validation; and (2) that individuals may stably differ on those parameters, in the same way that situations (or cultures) may so differ.

We have proposed that the process of knowledge validation is determined by subjective rules to which different individuals subscribe and which are embedded in their lay theories. Accordingly, we have reviewed a number of major such theories and the related conceptions of schematicity and ascribed epistemic authority. Digging for evidence that bears on the validity of one's knowledge often requires the investment of substantial mental effort and "cognitive work." Individuals' ability to expend such effort is determined in various ways by their general cognitive resources (such as their working memory capacity), and their sophistication in a given domain of knowledge. Whereas the general amount of cognitive capacity corresponds to a "hardware" aspect of the human mind, their sophistication and domain expertise pertain to the "software" aspect. Finally, individuals' motivation to expend the effort is determined by their stable epistemic goals having to do with the process of knowledge formation (exemplified,

e.g., by the need for cognition construct) as well as its outcomes, such as possession of (any) firm knowledge on a topic, or firm knowledge of a specific desired content.

For analytic purposes, we have accorded a separate discussion to each of those categories of factors. We also specified, however, how in reality they typically work interactively and in functional dependence on each other. Finally, the existence of individual differences in cognitive and motivational variables relevant to judgment and sense making does not imply that individuals would exhibit fixed patterns of information processing. Often, their stable cognitive and motivational proclivities may be overridden by situational determinants of the relevant epistemic processes, attesting to the dynamic and flexible manner in which people go about their sense-making endeavors across times and circumstances.

NOTE

1 The labels *cognitive closure* and *cognitive structure* have been used interchangeably in lay epistemic research to denote the desire for firm knowledge and the eschewal of ambiguity. The term *structure* was used in early papers on this topic (e.g. Kruglanski & Freund, 1983); it was replaced by the term *closure* in Kruglanski's (1989) volume, which has been used subsequently in discussions of relevant phenomena.

REFERENCES

Adams-Webber, J. (2003). Cognitive complexity and confidence in evaluating self. *Journal of Constructivist Psychology, 16*, 273–279.

Ahlering, R., & Parker, L. (1989). Need for cognition as a moderator of the primacy effect. *Journal of Research in Personality, 23*, 313–317.

Bar, R. (1999). *The impact of epistemic needs and authorities on judgment and decision making.* Unpublished doctoral dissertation, Tel Aviv University.

Bar-Tal, Y. (1991). *When the need for cognitive structure does not cause stereotypical thinking: The moderating effect of the ability to achieve cognitive structure.* Unpublished manuscript, Tel-Aviv University.

Bar-Tal, Y. (1994). The effect on mundane decision-making of the need and ability to achieve cognitive structure. *European Journal of Personality, 8*, 45–58.

Bar-Tal, Y., Kishon-Rabin, L., & Tabak, N. (1997). The effect of need and ability to achieve cognitive structuring on cognitive structuring. *Journal of Personality and Social Psychology, 73*, 1158–1176.

Barrett, L. F., Tugade, M. M., & Engle, R. W. (2004). Individual differences in working memory capacity and dual-process theories of the mind. *Psychological Bulletin, 130*, 553–573.

Baumeister, R. F., Twenge, J. M., & Nuss, C. (2002). Effects of social exclusion on cognitive processes: Anticipated aloneness reduces intelligent thought. *Journal of Personality and Social Psychology, 83*, 817–827.

Bem, D. J., & Allen, A. (1974). On predicting some of the people some of the time: The search for cross-situational consistencies in behavior. *Psychological Review, 81*, 506–520.

Bem, S. L. (1981). Gender schema theory: A cognitive account of sex typing. *Psychological Review, 88*, 354–364.

Ben-Ari, R., Kedem, P., & Levy-Weiner, N. (1992). Cognitive complexity and intergroup perception and evaluation. *Personality and Individual Differences, 13*, 1291–1298.

Brewin, C. R., & Beaton, A. (2002). Thought suppression, intelligence, and working memory capacity. *Behavior Research and Therapy, 40*, 923–930.

Brewin, C. R., & Smart, L. (2005). Working memory capacity and suppression of intrusive thoughts. *Journal of Behavior Therapy and Experimental Psychiatry, 36*, 61–68.

Cacioppo, J. T., & Petty, R. E. (1982). The need for cognition. *Journal of Personality and Social Psychology, 42*, 116–131.

Cacioppo, J. T., Petty, R. E., Feinstein, J. A., & Jarvis, W. B. G. (1996). Dispositional differences in cognitive motivation: The life and times of individuals varying in need for cognition. *Psychological Bulletin, 119*, 197–253.

Cacioppo, J. T., Petty, R., & Morris, K. (1983). Effects of need for cognition on message evaluation, recall, and persuasion. *Journal of Personality and Social Psychology, 45*, 805–818.

Chen, X. (2009). *Cognitive and motivational parameters in motivated biases in human judgment*. Unpublished doctoral dissertation, University of Maryland.

Chiu, C., Hong, Y., & Dweck, C. (1997). Lay dispositionism and implicit theories of personality. *Journal of Personality and Social Psychology, 73*, 19–30.

Chiu, C. Y., Morris, M. W., Hong, Y. Y., & Menon, T. (2000). Motivated cultural cognition: The impact of implicit cultural theories on dispositional attribution varies as a function of need for closure. *Journal of Personality and Social Psychology, 78*, 247–259.

Christopher, A., & Schlenker, B. (2005). The Protestant work ethic and attributions of responsibility: Applications of the triangle model. *Journal of Applied Social Psychology, 35*, 1502–1518.

Cialdini, R. B., Trost, M. R., & Newsom, J. T. (1995). Preference for consistency: Development of a valid measure and the discovery of surprising behavioral implications. *Journal of Personality and Social Psychology, 69*, 318–328.

Costa, P. T., & McCrae, R. R. (1992) The five-factor model of personality and its relevance to personality disorders. *Journal of Personality Disorders, 6*, 343–359.

Crawford, M., & Skowronski, J. (1998). When motivated thought leads to heightened bias: High need for cognition can enhance the impact of stereotypes on memory. *Personality and Social Psychology Bulletin, 24*, 1075–1088.

D'Agostino, P., & Fincher-Kiefer, R. (1992). Need for cognition and the correspondence bias. *Social Cognition, 10*, 151–163.

Dalbert, C. (2009). Belief in a just world. In M. R. Leary, & R. H. Hoyle (Eds.), *Handbook of individual differences in social behavior* (pp. 288–298). New York: Guilford Press.

Dalbert, C., & Filke, E. (2007). Belief in a personal just world, justice judgments, and their functions for prisoners. *Criminal Justice and Behavior, 34*, 1516–1527.

Dijksterhuis, A., van Knippenberg, A., Kruglanski, A. W., & Schaper, C. (1996). Motivated social cognition: Need for closure effects on memory and judgments. *Journal of Experimental Social Psychology, 32*, 254–270.

Dion, K., & Dion, K. (1987). Belief in a just world and physical attractiveness stereotyping. *Journal of Personality and Social Psychology, 52*, 775–780.

Dudley, M., & Harris, M. (2003). To think or not to think: The moderating role of need for cognition in expectancy-consistent impression formation. *Personality and Individual Differences, 35*, 1657–1667.

Dunning, D. (1999). A newer look: Motivated social cognition and the schematic representation of social concepts. *Psychological Inquiry, 10*, 1–11.

Dweck, C. (1999). *Self-theories: Their role in motivation, personality, and development*. New York: Psychology Press.

Dweck, C., Hong, Y., & Chiu, C. (1993). Implicit theories: Individual differences in the likelihood and meaning of dispositional inference. *Personality and Social Psychology Bulletin, 19*, 644–656.

Dweck, C., & Leggett, E. (1988). A social-cognitive approach to motivation and personality. *Psychological Review, 95*, 256–273.

Edlund, J., Sagarin, B., & Johnson, B. (2007). Reciprocity and the belief in a just world. *Personality and Individual Differences, 43*, 589–596.

Engle, R. W., Kane, M. J., & Tuholski, S. W. (1999). Individual differences in working memory capacity and what they tell us about controlled attention, general fluid intelligence, and functions of the prefrontal cortex. In M. Akira & P. Shah (Eds.), *Models of working memory: Mechanisms of active maintenance and executive control* (pp. 102–134). New York: Cambridge University Press.

Erb, H.-P., Kruglanski, A. W., Chun, W. Y., Pierro, A., Mannetti, L., & Spiegel, S. (2003). Searching for commonalities in human judgment: The parametric unimodel and its dual mode alternatives. *European Review of Social Psychology, 14*, 1–47.

Festinger, L. (1957). *A theory of cognitive dissonance*. Evanston, IL: Row, Peterson.

Fiske, S. T. (1992). Thinking is for doing: Portraits of social cognition from daguerreotype to laserphoto. *Journal of Personality and Social Psychology, 63*, 877–889.

Fiske, S. T., & Taylor, S. E. (2007). *Social cognition: From brains to culture*. New York: McGraw-Hill.

Förster, J., & Liberman, N. (2007). Seven principles of goal activation: A systematic approach to distinguishing goal priming from priming of non-goal constructs. *Personality and Social Psychology Review, 11*, 211–233.

Frable, D. E., & Bem, S. L. (1985). If you are gender schematic, all members of the opposite sex look alike. *Journal of Personality and Social Psychology, 49*, 459–468.

Frauenfelder, K. (1974). Integrative complexity and extreme responses. *Psychological Reports, 34*, 770.

Funder, D. C. (1994). Explaining traits. *Psychological Inquiry, 5*, 125–127.

Funder, D. C., & Fast, L. A. (2010). Personality in social psychology. In S. T. Fiske, D. T. Gilbert, & L. Gardner (Eds.), *Handbook of social psychology* (5th ed., pp. 668–697). New York: Wiley.

Furnham, A. (1982). The Protestant work ethic and attitudes toward unemployment. *Journal of Occupational Psychology, 55*, 277–285.

Gara, M., Woolfolk, R., & Allen, L. (2002). Social cognitive complexity and depression: Cognitive complexity moderates the correlation between depression self-ratings and global self-evaluation. *Journal of Nervous and Mental Disease, 190*, 670–676.

Geraerts, E., Merckelbach, H., Jelicic, M., & Habets, P. (2007). Suppression of intrusive thoughts and working memory capacity in repressive coping. *The American Journal of Psychology, 120*, 205–218.

Gerrie, M., & Garry, M. (2007). Individual differences in working memory capacity affect false memories for missing aspects of events. *Memory, 15*, 561–571.

Gervey, B., Chiu, C., Hong, Y., & Dweck, C. (1999). Differential use of person information in decisions about guilt versus innocence: The role of implicit theories. *Personality and Social Psychology Bulletin, 25*, 17–2.

Gilbert, D. T. (1989). Thinking lightly about others: Automatic components of the social inference process. In J. S. Uleman & J. A. Bargh (Eds.), *Unintended thought* (pp. 189–211). New York: Guilford Press.

Glennon, F., & Joseph, S. (1993). Just world beliefs, self-esteem, and attitudes towards homosexuals with AIDS. *Psychological Reports, 72*, 584–586.

Gollwitzer, P. M. (1990). Action phases and mind-sets. In E. T. Higgins & R. M. Sorrentino (Eds.), *Handbook of motivation and cognition: Foundations of social behavior* (Vol. 2, pp. 53–92), New York: Guilford Press.

Hafer, C., Bogaert, A., & McMullen, S. (2001). Belief in a just world and condom use in a sample of gay and bisexual men. *Journal of Applied Social Psychology, 31*, 1892–1910.

Hargreaves, D., & Tiggemann, M. (2002). The role of appearance schematicity in the development of adolescent body dissatisfaction. *Cognitive Therapy and Research, 26*, 691–700.

Haugtvedt, C., & Petty, R. (1992). Personality and persuasion: Need for cognition moderates the persistence and resistance of attitude changes. *Journal of Personality and Social Psychology, 63*, 308–319.

Heider, F. (1958). *The psychology of interpersonal relations.* Hoboken, NJ: John Wiley & Sons.

Henderson, V., & Dweck, C. (1990). Motivation and achievement. In S. S. Feldman & G. R. Elliot (Eds.), *At the threshold: The developing adolescent* (pp. 308–329). Cambridge, MA: Harvard University Press.

Higgins, E. T. (1996). The 'self-digest': Self-knowledge serving self-regulatory functions. *Journal of Personality and Social Psychology, 71*, 1062–1083.

Higgins, E. T. (1997). Beyond pleasure and pain. *American Psychologist, 52*, 1280–1300.

Higgins, E. T. (2008). Culture and personality: Variability across universal motives as the missing link. *Social and Personality Compass, 2*, 608–634.

Higgins, E. T., Kruglanski, A., & Pierro, A. (2003). Regulatory mode: Locomotion and assessment as distinct orientations. In M. P. Zanna (Ed.), *Advances in experimental social psychology* (Vol. 35, pp. 293–344). New York: Academic Press.

Hong, Y., Chiu, C., & Dweck, C. (1995). Implicit theories of intelligence: Reconsidering the role of confidence in achievement motivation. In M. H. Kernis (Ed.), *Efficacy, agency, and self-esteem* (pp. 197–216). New York: Plenum Press.

Jaschinski, U., & Wentura, D. (2002). Misleading postevent information and working memory capacity: An individual differences approach to eyewitness memory. *Applied Cognitive Psychology, 16*, 223–231.

Jones, E. E. (1998). Major developments in five decades of social psychology. In D. T. Gilbert, S. T. Fiske, & L. Gardner (Eds.), *Handbook of social psychology* (4th ed., pp. 3–57). New York: McGraw-Hill.

Katz, I., & Hass, R. (1988). Racial ambivalence and American value conflict: Correlational and priming studies of dual cognitive structures. *Journal of Personality and Social Psychology, 55*, 893–905.

Khan, S., & Lambert, A. (2001). Perceptions of rational discrimination: When do people attempt to justify race-based prejudice?. *Basic and Applied Social Psychology, 23*, 43–53.

Koivula, N. (1995). Ratings of gender appropriateness of sports participation: Effects of gender-based schematic processing. *Sex Roles, 37*, 543–557.

Kossowska, M., Orehek, E., & Kruglanski, A. W. (2010). Motivation towards closure and cognitive resources: An individual differences approach. In A. Gruszka, G. Matthews & B. Szymura (Eds.), *Handbook of individual differences in cognition: Attention, memory and executive control* (pp. 369–382). New York: Springer.

Kruglanski, A. W. (1980). Lay epistemologic process and contents: Another look at attribution theory. *Psychological Review, 87*, 70–87.

Kruglanski, A. W. (1989). *Lay epistemics and human knowledge: Cognitive and motivational bases.* New York: Plenum Press.

Kruglanski, A. W. (2004). *The psychology of closed mindedness.* New York: Psychology Press.

Kruglanski, A. W., & Fishman, S. (2009). The need for cognitive closure. In M. R. Leary, & R. H. Hoyle (Eds.), *Handbook of individual differences in social behavior* (pp. 343–353). New York: Guilford Press.

Kruglanski, A. W., & Freund, T. (1983). The freezing and unfreezing of lay-inferences: Effects on impressional primacy, ethnic stereotyping and numerical anchoring. *Journal of Experimental Social Psychology, 19*, 448–68.

Kruglanski, A. W., & Gigerenzer, G. (2011). Intuitive and deliberate judgments are based on common principles. *Psychological Review,* 97–109.

Kruglanski, A. W., Pierro, A., Mannetti, L., & DeGrada, E. (2006). Groups as epistemic providers: Need for closure and the emergence of group centrism. *Psychological Review, 113*, 84–100.

Kruglanski, A. W., Raviv, A., Bar-Tal, D., Raviv, A., Sharvit, K., Ellis, S., et al. (2005). Says who? Epistemic authority effects in social judgment. *Advances in experimental social psychology* (Vol. 37, pp. 345–392). San Diego, CA: Elsevier Academic Press.

Kruglanski, A. W., & Shteynberg, G. (in press). Cognitive consistency as means to an end: How subjective logic affords knowledge. In B. Gawronski & F. Strack (Eds.), *Cognitive consistency: A unifying concept in social psychology.* New York: Guilford Press.

Kruglanski, A. W., & Sleeth-Keppler, D. (2007). The principles of social judgment. In A. W. Kruglanski & E. T. Higgins (Eds.), *Social psychology: Handbook of basic principles* (pp. 116–137). New York: Guilford Press.

Kruglanski, A. W., Thompson, E. P., Higgins, E. T., Atash, M. N., Pierro, A., Shah, J. Y., et al. (2000). To do the right thing! or to just do it! Locomotion and assessment as distinct self-regulatory imperatives. *Journal of Personality and Social Psychology, 79*, 793–815.

Kruglanski, A. W., & Webster, D. M. (1996). Motivated closing of the mind: "Seizing" and "freezing." *Psychological Review, 103*, 263–83.

Kruglanski, A. W., Webster, D. M., & Klem, A. (1993). Motivated resistance and openness to persuasion in the presence or absence of prior information. *Journal of Personality and Social Psychology, 65*, 861–876.

Kunda, Z. (1990). The case for motivated reasoning. *Psychological Bulletin, 108*, 480–498.

Kunda, Z., & Sinclair, L. (1999). Motivated reasoning with stereotypes: Activation, application, and inhibition. *Psychological Inquiry, 10*, 12–22.

Lassiter, G., Briggs, M., & Slaw, R. (1991). Need for cognition, causal processing, and memory for behavior. *Personality and Social Psychology Bulletin, 17*, 694–700.

Lerner, M. J. (1965). Evaluation of performance as a function of performer's reward and attractiveness. *Journal of Personality and Social Psychology, 1*, 355–360.

Lerner, M. J. (1980). *The belief in a just world: A fundamental delusion.* New York: Plenum.

Lerner, M. J., & Miller, D. T. (1978). Just world research and the attribution process: Looking back and ahead. *Psychological Bulletin, 85*, 1030–1051.

Lerner, M. J., & Simmons, C. (1966). Observer's reaction to the 'innocent victim': Compassion or rejection? *Journal of Personality and Social Psychology, 4*, 203–210.

Lerner, M. J., & Miller, D. T. (1978). Just world research and the attribution process: Looking back and ahead. *Psychological Bulletin, 85*, 1030–1051.

Levy, G. D. (2000). Individual differences in race schematicity as predictors of African American and White children's race-relevant memories and peer preferences. *The Journal of Genetic Psychology: Research and Theory on Human Development, 161*, 400–419.

Levy, S. R., Chiu, C., & Hong Y. (2006). Lay theories and intergroup relations. *Group Processes and Intergroup Relations, 9*, 5–24.

Levy, S. R., Ramirez, L., & Vellila, E. (2005). *The role of culture and context on the intergroup meaning of the Protestant work ethic.* Unpublished manuscript, State University of New York at Stony Brook.

Levy, S. R., Stroessner, S., & Dweck, C. S. (1998). Stereotype formation and endorsement: The role of implicit theories. *Journal of Personality and Social Psychology, 74*, 1421–1436.

Levy, S. R., West, T., Ramirez, L., & Karafantis, D. (2006). The Protestant Work Ethic: A lay theory with dual intergroup implications. *Group Processes and Intergroup Relations, 9*, 95–115.

Lewin, K. (1939). Field theory and experiment in social psychology: Concepts and methods. *American Journal of Sociology, 44*, 868–896.

Liberman, N., Molden, D., Idson, L., & Higgins, E. (2001). Promotion and prevention focus on alternative hypotheses: Implications for attributional functions. *Journal of Personality and Social Psychology, 80*, 5–18.

Linville, P. (1982). The complexity extremity effect and age-based stereotyping. *Journal of Personality and Social Psychology, 42*, 193–211.

Linville, P. (1985). Self-complexity and affective extremity: Don't put all of your eggs in one cognitive basket. *Social Cognition, 3*, 94–120.

Linville, P. (1987). Self-complexity as a cognitive buffer against stress-related illness and depression. *Journal of Personality and Social Psychology, 52*, 663–676.

Markman, A., Baldwin, G., & Maddox, W. (2005). The interaction of payoff structure and regulatory focus in classification. *Psychological Science, 16*, 852–855.

Mauro, R., Pierro, A., Kruglanski, A. W., & Higgins, E. T. (2009). The perfect mix: Regulatory complementarity and the speed–accuracy balance in group performance. *Psychological Science, 20*, 681–685.

Mayseless, O., & Kruglanski, A. W. (1987). What makes you so sure? Effects of epistemic motivations on judgmental confidence. *Organizational Behavior and Human Decision Processes, 39*, 162–183.

McKenzie-Mohr, D., & Zanna, M. P. (1990). Treating women as sexual objects: Look to the (gender schematic) male who has viewed pornography. *Personality and Social Psychology Bulletin, 16*, 296–308.

McVay, J., & Kane, M. (2009). Conducting the train of thought: Working memory capacity, goal neglect, and mind wandering in an executive-control task. *Journal of Experimental Psychology: Learning, Memory, and Cognition, 35*, 196–204.

Mellema, A., & Bassilli, J. N. (1995). On the relationship between attitudes and values: Exploring the moderating effects of self-monitoring and self-monitoring schematicity. *Personality and Social Psychology Bulletin, 21*, 885–892.

Mischel, W. (1968). *Personality and assessment.* New York: John Wiley and Sons.

Mischel, W., & Shoda, Y. (1995) A cognitive-affective system theory of personality: Reconceptualizing situations, dispositions, dynamics, and invariance in personality structure. *Psychological Review, 102,* 246–268.

Molden, D. C., Lee, A. Y., & Higgins, E. T. (2008). In J. Shah & W. Gardner (Eds.), Motivations for promotion and prevention. *Handbook of motivation science* (pp. 169–187). New York: Guilford Press.

Moore, A. B., Clark, B. A., & Kane, M. J. (2008). Who shalt not kill? Individual differences in working memory capacity, executive control, and moral judgment. *Psychological Science, 19,* 549–557.

Murray, S. L., & Holmes, J. G. (1999). The (mental) ties that bind: Cognitive structures that predict relationship resilience. *Journal of Personality and Social Psychology, 77,* 1228–1244.

Oberauer, K. (2005). The measurement of working memory capacity. In O. Wilhelm & R. W. Engle (Eds.), *Handbook of understanding and measuring intelligence* (pp. 393–407). Thousand Oaks, CA: Sage Publications.

Perlini, A. H., & Hansen, S. D. (2001). Moderating effects of need for cognition on attractiveness stereotyping. *Social Behavior and Personality, 29,* 313–321.

Petty, R. E., Brinol, P., Tormala, Z. L., & Wegener, D. T. (2007). The role of metacognition in social judgment. In A. W. Kruglanski & E. T. Higgins (Eds.), *Social psychology: handbook of basic principles* (pp. 254–284). New York: Guilford Press.

Petty, R. E., & Jarvis, W. (1996). An individual differences perspective on assessing cognitive processes. In N. Schwarz & S. Sudman (Eds.), *Answering questions:Methodology for determining cognitive and communicative processes in survey research* (pp. 221–257). San Francisco, CA: Jossey-Bass.

Petty, R. E., Schumann, D., Richman, S., & Strathman, A. (1993). Positive mood and persuasion: Different roles for affect under high- and low-elaboration conditions. *Journal of Personality and Social Psychology, 64,* 5–20.

Perlini, A., & Hansen, S. (2001). Moderating effects of need for cognition on attractiveness stereotyping. *Social Behavior and Personality, 29,* 313–321.

Pierro, A., & Kruglanski, A. W. (2008). 'Seizing and freezing' on a significant-person schema: Need for closure and the transference effect in social judgment. *Personality and Social Psychology Bulletin, 34,* 1492–1503.

Pierro, P., Leder, S., Mannetti, L., Higgins, E. T., Kruglanski, A. W., & Aiello, A. (2008). Regulatory mode effects on counterfactual thinking and regret. *Journal of Experimental Social Psychology, 44,* 321–329.

Pierro, A., & Mannetti, L. (2004). *Motivated consumer search behavior: The effects of epistemic authority.* Unpublished manuscript, University of Rome "La Sapienza."

Pierro, A., Mannetti, L., Higgins, E. T., & Kruglanski, A. W. (2002). *Moderating role of regulatory mode on relationships between theory of planned behavior variables.* Unpublished manuscript, University of Rome "La Sapienza."

Rafaeli-Mor, E., & Steinberg, J. (2002). Self-complexity and well-being: A review and research synthesis. *Personality and Social Psychology Review, 6,* 31–58.

Richter, L., & Kruglanski, A.W. (1999). Motivated search for common ground: Need for closure effects on audience design in interpersonal communication. *Personality and Social Psychology Bulletin, 25,* 1101–1114.

Ros, L., Latorre, J., & Serrano, J. (2010). Working memory capacity and overgeneral autobiographical memory in young and older adults. *Aging, Neuropsychology, and Cognition, 17,* 89–107.

Ross, L., & Nisbett, R. (1991). *The person and the situation: Perspectives of social psychology.* New York: McGraw-Hill.

Sakalli-Uğurlu, N., Sila Yalçin, Z., & Glick, P. (2007). Ambivalent sexism, belief in a just world, and empathy as predictors of Turkish students' attitudes toward rape victims. *Sex Roles, 57,* 889–895.

Sargent, M. (2004). Less thought, more punishment: Need for cognition predicts support for punitive responses to crime. *Personality and Social Psychology Bulletin, 30,* 1485–1493.

Schroder, H., Driver, M., & S. Streufert, S. (1967). *Human information processing.* New York: Holt, Rinehart, & Winston.

Scott, W. A. (1962). Cognitive complexity and cognitive flexibility. *Sociometry, 25,* 405–414.

Shah, J. Y., Brazy, P., & Higgins, E. T. (2004). Promoting us or preventing them: Regulatory focus and manifestations of intergroup bias. *Personality and Social Psychology Bulletin, 30,* 433–446.

Shah, J. Y., & Higgins, E. T. (1997). Expectancy × value effects: Regulatory focus as determinant of magnitude and direction. *Journal of Personality and Social Psychology, 73,* 447–458.

Shah, J. Y., Kruglanski, A. W., & Thompson, E. P. (1998). Membership has its (epistemic) rewards: Need for closure effects on ingroup bias. *Journal of Personality and Social Psychology, 75,* 383–393.

Sidanius, J. (1978). Cognitive functioning and socio-politico ideology: An exploratory study. *Perceptual and Motor Skills, 46,* 515–530.

Sidanius, J. (1984). Political interest, political information search, and ideological homogeneity as a function of sociopolitical ideology: A tale of three theories. *Human Relations, 37,* 811–828.

Sidanius, J. (1988). Political sophistication and political deviance: A structural equation examination of context theory. *Journal of Personality and Social Psychology, 55,* 37–51.

Smith, S., & Levin, I. (1996). Need for cognition and choice framing effects. *Journal of Behavioral Decision Making, 9,* 283–290.

Sprenger, A., & Dougherty, M. (2006). Differences between probability and frequency judgments: The role of individual differences in working memory capacity. *Organizational Behavior and Human Decision Processes, 99,* 202–211.

Tam, K., Leung, A., & Chiu, C. (2008). On being a mindful authoritarian: Is need for cognition always associated with less punitiveness?. *Political Psychology, 29,* 77–91.

Tetlock, P. (1984). Cognitive style and political belief systems in the British House of Commons. *Journal of Personality and Social Psychology, 46*, 365–375.

Tetlock, P. (1985). Integrative complexity of American and Soviet foreign policy rhetoric: A time-series analysis. *Journal of Personality and Social Psychology, 49*, 1565–1585.

Tetlock, P. (1986). A value pluralism model of ideological reasoning. *Journal of Personality and Social Psychology, 50*, 819–827.

Tetlock, P. (1988). Monitoring the integrative complexity of American and Soviet policy rhetoric: What can be learned?. *Journal of Social Issues, 44*, 101–131.

Tetlock, P. (1993). Cognitive structural analysis of political rhetoric: Methodological and theoretical issues. In S. Iyengar & W. J. McGuire (Eds.), *Explorations in political psychology* (pp. 380–405). Durham, NC: Duke University Press.

Turner, M. L., & Engle, R. W. (1989). Is working memory capacity task-dependent? *Journal of Memory and Language, 28*, 127–154.

Van Hiel, A., & Mervielde, I. (2003). The measurement of cognitive complexity and its relationship with political extremism. *Political Psychology, 24*, 781–801.

Verplanken, B., Hazenberg, P., & Palenéwen, G. (1992). Need for cognition and external information search effort. *Journal of Research in Personality, 26*, 128–136.

Waller, J. (1993). Correlation of need for cognition and modern racism. *Psychological Reports, 73*, 542.

Weber, M. (1905/1958). *The protestant work ethic and the spirit of capitalism* (T. Parsons, Trans.). New York: Scribner's.

Webster, D. M. (1993). Motivated augmentation and reduction of the overattribution bias. *Journal of Personality and Social Psychology, 65*, 261–271.

Webster, D. M., & Kruglanski, A. W. (1994). Individual differences in need for cognitive closure. *Journal of Personality and Social Psychology, 67*, 1049–1062.

Webster, D. M., Kruglanski, A. W., & Pattison, D. A. (1997). Motivated language use in intergroup contexts: Need for closure effects on the linguistic intergroup bias. *Journal of Personality and Social Psychology, 72*, 1122–1131.

Webster, D. M., Richter, L., & Kruglanski, A. W. (1996). On leaping to conclusions when feeling tired: Mental fatigue effects on impressional primacy. *Journal of Experimental Social Psychology, 32*, 181–195.

Webster-Nelson, D. M., Klein, C. F., & Irvin, J. E. (2003). Motivational antecedents of empathy:Inhibiting effects of fatigue. *Basic and Applied Social Psychology, 25*, 37–50.

Wegner, D., Schneider, D., Carter, S., & White, T. (1987). Paradoxical effects of thought suppression. *Journal of Personality and Social Psychology, 53*, 5–13.

Zhao, W., & Dweck, C. S. (1994). *Implicit theories and vulnerability to depression-like responses.* Unpublished manuscript, Columbia University.

25

The Ideological Toolbox: Ideologies as Tools of Motivated Social Cognition

Aaron C. Kay & Richard P. Eibach

INTRODUCTION

The popular image of the ideologue is someone who is rigid and impractical. When we say that a person's thinking is influenced by ideology we often mean that they are blind to the dynamics of the immediate situation. This is in sharp contrast to the highly pragmatic portrayal of human thought that has come to characterize the field of social cognition. One of the most influential messages of social cognition has been that mental constructs such as goals (Bargh, Gollwitzer, Lee-Chai, Barndollar, & Trötschel, 2001), attitudes (Ferguson & Bargh, 2004), self-perceptions (Markus & Wurf, 1987), and stereotypes (Kunda & Spencer, 2003) fluctuate adaptively in relation to cues of situational relevance and immediate needs. So, at first, the topic of ideologies may seem to be a poor fit for a handbook of social cognition.

However, we will review research that shows that, much like these other social-cognitive constructs, ideological knowledge can be activated and applied flexibly in response to changing situational dynamics and personal goals. We will apply the classic social-cognitive distinction between chronic and temporary accessibility of cognitive content to ideological knowledge in order to show that individual differences interact with situational demands to influence the expression of ideology in people's thoughts and behavior. We will present a model suggesting that,

through their exposure to competing ideologies in the social environment, people acquire diverse ideological resources that they can use to interpret events in their personal lives and the broader world.

Differences in individuals' psychological needs and their relative exposure to and frequency of activation of specific ideologies produce variability in the chronic accessibility of specific ideological resources. However, while certain ideologies may be more chronically accessible for a given individual, we suggest that most individuals also have diverse ideological resources to draw on, some that are chronically accessible and others that become accessible only when prompted by relevant situational cues. We will suggest that people draw on their ideological resources to construct situated ideologies that help them make sense of events, provide meaning and coherence to their actions, and rationalize their circumstances and personal choices. In short, to borrow a metaphor from the sociology of knowledge (Swidler, 1986), ideologies are like tools that people use to solve specific functional problems and accomplish particular tasks. Individuals may differ in the content and organization of their ideological toolboxes, but most people have diverse ideological tools to draw on. Some of these ideological tools may be more readily at hand than others but people will usually attempt to find the tool that best fits the particular task they are working on at any given moment.

This ideological toolbox metaphor provides an original perspective on a long-standing controversy regarding whether American voters actually have ideologies. Ever since Converse's (1964) devastating depiction of the inconsistencies in American voters' political opinions, political scientists have argued that the average American is too politically unsophisticated to have anything resembling a coherent ideology guiding their judgments. From this point of view, highly educated elites may have ideologies, but average people do not. Others such as Jost (2006) have argued that Converse overstated the case and there actually is sufficient underlying stability and coherence in average voters' political opinions to characterize their judgments as based on ideology. Our model of chronic and temporary accessibility of ideological knowledge provides a resolution to this controversy and explains both the inconsistencies and the underlying stability in average voters' political judgments. Contrary to Converse (1964), we would argue that voters' political judgments are inconsistent not because they have *too little* ideology but because they have *too much* ideology. That is, if exposure to diverse ideological positions in their social environment causes people to acquire diverse forms of ideological knowledge, then people will draw on different ideological resources to construct judgments in different contexts, depending on what ideological resources seem to provide the best fit to a particular problem. Thus, what Converse and others see as ideological incoherence may actually reflect the flexible application of ideological resources to diverse problems.

To illustrate, the case for ideological incoherence has often cited examples where average voters appear to take ideologically inconsistent positions on the same issue, depending on superficial variations in how the issue is framed. For example, Schuman and Presser (1981) showed that while a majority of Americans said that the United States should not "forbid public speeches in favor of communism," a majority of Americans said that the United States should not "allow public speeches in favor of communism." Thus, when the question is worded in terms of forbidding speech most Americans look like civil libertarians, but when the question is worded in terms of allowing speech most Americans look like authoritarians. Converse might say that this means that Americans' ideologies are neither libertarian nor authoritarian but rather that they are so hopelessly inconsistent that they have no underlying ideological structure to speak of. By contrast, we would argue that most Americans have diverse ideological knowledge to draw on and that the particular ideological resources that they apply in any given situation will depend on what the situation

has prompted. So, the oppressive overtones of a word like "forbid" may activate Americans' libertarian proclivities, while the extreme permissiveness of a word like "allow" in the context of a threatening belief system like communism may activate their authoritarian proclivities.

While analyses of average citizens' responses to closed-ended questions in political surveys have often led researchers to conclude that their attitudes lack ideological structuring, analyses of responses to open-ended questions have suggested a more complex picture of the role of ideology in political judgment. For instance, in response to open-ended questions about public welfare and resource distribution, Americans readily draw on ideological concepts to describe and justify their positions (Feldman & Zaller, 1992; Hochschild, 1981). However, their responses also suggest that Americans have a great deal of ideological ambivalence regarding public welfare, because this issue brings up their conflicting values of individualism, humanitarianism, and opposition to big government (Feldman & Zaller, 1992). Moreover, this kind of value pluralism tends to be associated with more sophisticated, integratively complex forms of ideological reasoning as people seek to balance their conflicting values to arrive at a position on a given issue (Tetlock, 1986). This is consistent with our suggestion that far from being empty-headed when it comes to ideology, people may actually have a variety of ideological resources that they draw on flexibly as the situation demands.

Our model can also explain why, amidst the inconsistencies in their political judgments across contexts, people also show a good degree of underlying stability. We would argue that the stability that Jost (2006) and others document reflects people's chronically accessible ideological views. These are the ideological tools that are most readily at hand and that people will use by default unless the context prompts them to draw on a less readily accessible ideological tool.

Defining ideology

In this chapter we define an ideology as a set of general beliefs or abstract values by which people define the social and political arrangements that they believe ought to be preferred. Ideologies thus function like generative grammars for constructing and justifying positions on specific social and political issues (Rohan & Zanna, 2001). The ideologies that we will be discussing in this chapter are primarily concerned with two issues: (1) specifying the legitimate grounds for distributing material, symbolic, and social resources, and (2) defining the nature and scope of moral authority. Debates over how to distribute resources and how to define moral authority animate many of today's major ideological conflicts. For instance, while free-market individualists believe that resources should be distributed based on individual choice in a free market (Nozick, 1974), liberal egalitarians believe that resources should be distributed in ways that ensure that the least well-off members of society are better off than they would be under any alternative arrangement (Rawls, 1971), and moral traditionalists often believe that resource distributions should reward those who display virtuous character traits.

In addition to ideological variation in beliefs about the legitimate bases for distributing resources, ideologies also differ in their definitions of the nature and scope of moral authority. According to Hunter (1991), the modern culture wars are rooted in fundamental disagreements about moral authority that pit morally orthodox ideologies against morally progressive ideologies. The morally orthodox define moral authority as "external, definable, and transcendent" (Hunter, 1991, p. 120). Different orthodox communities base moral authority on different sources, such as sacred scripture, moral tradition, "natural law," or the teaching authority of religious leaders, but in all cases moral authority is seen as being rooted in fundamental moral truths that are not subject to human interpretation or revision. By contrast, moral progressives define moral authority "as a process, as a reality that is ever unfolding" (Hunter, p. 44) and, which, "can only be understood and expressed in human (which is to say, historical and institutional terms)" (Hunter, 1991, p. 123). Attending to these moral dimensions of ideological conflict is particularly important because attitudes that are rooted in moral convictions tend to promote greater political involvement, lead to greater intolerance of (and social distancing from) those who disagree, are more likely to override concerns about procedural justice, promote greater resistance to counter-attitudinal decisions by authorities, are more resistant to counter-attitudinal norms and conformity pressures, and are more opposed to value tradeoffs compared to equally strong but non-moral attitudes (Skitka, 2010).

Jost, Federico, and Napier (2009) suggest that political ideologies can be situated on a left-to-right continuum depending on their implications for equality and their openness to changes in the social order. Ideologies on the left-wing end of the continuum highly value social equality and are relatively open to change in the system, whereas ideologies on the right-wing end of the continuum tend to place less emphasis on social equality and are more supportive of the status quo.

Others suggest that political ideology is multidimensional, involving a more complex mix of potentially conflicting values (Haidt, Graham, & Joseph, 2009; Tetlock, 1986). These authors suggest that liberals and conservatives often disagree on policy issues not because conservatives do not value social equality but because they adhere to other values such as in-group loyalty and moral purity that sometimes come into conflict with equality (Haidt & Graham, 2009).

If ideologies are the generative grammars for constructing and justifying social and political attitudes, then our model would suggest that, when it comes to ideology, people might be considered multilingual. Thus, what appears to be ideological incoherence may be better described as the ideological equivalent of linguistic code-switching. That is, the same person may, depending on what situation they are in, alternate between the codes of libertarian individualism and communitarianism, meritocracy and egalitarianism, or moral relativism and universalism. If people tend to assimilate elements from these and other opposing ideologies without fully committing themselves to any given ideology, then they may draw on different ideologies depending on what best fits their immediate situation. Their outwardly inconsistent attitudes, judgments, and behaviors may appear to suggest that people do not have ideologies at all but the reality may be that they have diverse ideological resources that they draw on selectively, depending on the issue and the broader situation they are facing.

Using this model of chronic and temporary accessibility as our guiding framework, we will discuss and integrate a range of social psychological factors that contribute to the formation of chronic (first half of the chapter) and temporary (second half of the chapter) ideological beliefs and perspectives.

CHRONIC DIFFERENCES IN THE APPLICATION OF IDEOLOGICAL PERSPECTIVES

There is considerable evidence that people, chronically, differ in their ideological predispositions. Although it may be tempting to assume such chronic, "personality" (Adorno et al., 1950) differences are outside the scope of social-cognitive inquiry, this is not necessarily the case (Jost, Glaser, Kruglanski, & Sulloway, 2003a). According to Higgins (1996), consistent differences in preferences, perceptions, judgments, and even behavior may reflect chronic differences in cognitive features: namely, construct accessibility. Put simply, constructs that are more chronically accessible are more likely to be applied in a given situation.

For those for whom a given ideological principle or construct is chronically accessible, therefore, specific types of ideological judgments will be more likely across situations. What might predict these chronic differences in ideological resources? Below, we review several documented sources of chronic variance in ideological predispositions, including genetics, chronic motivational differences, and differing formative experiences.

Influence of biological factors on ideological predispositions

Monozygotic twins are more concordant in liberal-conservative political ideology than dyzygotic twins, and estimates derived from these data indicate that approximately 43% of the variance in political ideology is heritable (Alford, Funk, & Hibbing, 2005). To explain how heritable variation produces ideological differences, Jost (2009) suggested that genetically based differences in personality or cognitive style could create affinities for different political ideologies. The idea is that people are channeled towards political ideologies that form a suitable match to their personality or cognitive style. In the following sections we review research on the neurophysiological, personality, and cognitive correlates of political ideologies that provide insights into the individual differences that may be the sources of people's affinities for specific ideologies.

Neurocognitive and physiological correlates

Neurocognitive research finds that liberals show stronger evoked-reaction potential activity in the anterior cingulate region than conservatives during a go/no-go task, in which participants had to switch their behavioral responses between trials (Amodio, Jost, Master, & Yee, 2007). This pattern of neuroactivity suggests that liberals are more sensitive to response conflict and thus better able to inhibit habitual responses. Consistent with this account, the researchers also found that liberals were more accurate than conservatives on the go/no-go task. Other studies show that conservatives are more physiologically reactive to threatening stimuli than liberals are, as measured through startle eye-blink responses and changes in skin-conductance arousal in response to non-political threatening stimuli (Oxley et al., 2008). It is possible that these differences in liberals' and conservatives' physiological reactions to response conflict and threatening stimuli are some of the heritable factors that contribute to variance in political ideology. Of course, it is also possible

that the direction of causation runs in the other direction, with ideology causing people to experience psychophysiological changes, or these ideological differences in psychophysiology could be due to differences in individuals' social experiences rather than heritable differences.

Intelligence and cognitive style

Another heritable factor that may be the source of ideological differences is general intelligence. In research with nationally representative samples, individuals with higher IQs tend to be more liberal than individuals with lower IQs (Deary, Batty, & Gale, 2008; Kanazawa, 2010). This association of socio-political ideology with IQ remains significant even when age, sex, race, education, income, and religiosity are controlled. One explanation for this association is that liberalism's greater attraction to novelty and difference may involve types of abstract thought associated with higher IQ (Deary et al., 2008). Another explanation stresses that liberal attitudes often require people to override a default conservative response when they make attributions about the causes of events (Skitka, Mullen, Griffin, Hutchinson, & Chamberlin, 2002), evaluate whether a harmless but offensive action is immoral (Haidt, Koller, & Dias, 1993), or decide between the status quo and change (Eidelman & Crandall, 2009). Because people with higher IQs have greater cognitive resources, they may have more ability to override these default conservative responses.

Personality

Researchers have also examined the relationship of political ideology to the Big 5 dimensions of personality, which have a heritable basis and thus could account for some of the genetic variation related to political ideology. Numerous studies with a variety of samples have found that liberals score higher than conservatives on self-report measures of openness and conservatives score higher than liberals on self-report measures of conscientiousness (Carney, Jost, & Gosling, 2008; Hirsh, DeYoung, Xu, & Peterson, 2010; Jost et al., 2003a). Moving beyond self-report measures of personality, researchers have also coded the contents of people's bedrooms and offices for behavioral traces of openness and conscientiousness (Carney et al., 2008). The contents of their bedrooms and offices indicate that liberals tend to seek out more novel and diverse experiences than do conservatives. Research using other behavioral measures also supports the conclusion that liberals are more open to experience than conservatives. For instance, a recent study using a non-political measure of exploratory behavior found that liberals explore novel stimuli more actively than conservatives when forming attitudes (Shook & Fazio, 2009).

In addition to studies establishing associations of political ideology with the openness and conscientiousness dimensions of personality, recent research has documented that different components of the agreeableness dimension are associated with liberal and conservative ideologies (Hirsh et al., 2010). Specifically, this research finds that conservatives are higher than liberals in the politeness component of agreeableness, whereas liberals are higher than conservatives in the compassion component. Conservatives' greater politeness may explain why they tend to be more traditional than liberals, whereas liberals' greater compassion may explain why they tend to be more egalitarian than conservatives.

In addition to these differences in liberals' and conservatives' scores on broad personality dimensions, other research has investigated the relation between ideology and more specific, theoretically relevant traits. For instance, some have speculated that political ideology might be associated with disgust–sensitivity because liberals, in the tradition of John Stuart Mill (1859), tend to oppose legal restrictions on behaviors that are harmless but offensive to many members of the community, while conservatives, like Lord Patrick Devlin (1965), tend to defend legal restrictions on harmless but offensive behaviors (Haidt & Hersh, 2001; Nussbaum, 2010). People with a strong disgust response might be motivated to restrict behaviors that offend them, which would make the conservative position on using the law as a mechanism for enforcing morality more attractive to them. Consistent with this hypothesis, recent studies have found that liberals report weaker disgust reactions than conservatives, even in response to non-political disgusting actions (e.g., accidentally drinking from a stranger's soda can) (Inbar, Pizarro, & Bloom, 2009).

Since personality traits have a heritable basis and show consistent relations to ideology, it makes sense that personality differences might be an important mediating link between genetic differences and ideologies. Suggestive evidence for such a connection comes from a recent study that identified an interesting gene–environment interaction that predicts political liberalism. Specifically, this study found that if a person has the 7R variant of the dopamine receptor gene (*DRD4*), a gene variant that tends to be associated with novelty seeking, they are more likely to report having a liberal ideology, but only if the person also has a relatively large friendship network (Settle, Dawes, Hatemi, Christakis, & Fowler, 2010). Novelty seeking, which is a

component of openness to experience, may be the personality dimension that provides the motivation and a large friendship network may be the structural factor that provides the opportunity to explore diverse perspectives on social issues and events, and it may be this experience of diverse perspectives that then leads people to be more liberal. This work is too preliminary to support any definitive conclusions, but future research on gene–environment interactions may help to illuminate the links between, genes, personality, and the development of political ideologies.

Influence of chronic needs on ideological predispositions

Information processing and judgment can be powerfully impacted by motivational- and need-based states (Kunda, 1990). This includes the recruitment and use of knowledge structures that help the individual interpret their environment in ways most useful for a given need (Kunda & Sanitioso, 1989; Kunda & Spencer, 2003). When a given need is most salient, specific schemas, stereotypes, and perceptual filters become more likely to be applied in that situation. This form of motivated cognition – in which a chronic need renders a certain mode or style of information processing chronically more active – has been shown to powerfully predict ideological judgments across a wide range of contexts.

Lerner (1980) famously argued that people hold a need to believe in a just and fair world. Since Lerner's seminal treatise on this topic, hundreds of studies have demonstrated that individual variation in this need predicts the casual inferences people make when confronted with victims of misfortune (Hafer & Bègue, 2005). Although the specific nature of this finding differs slightly from one study to the next, the general message is that those higher in the need to believe in a just world are more apt to perceive an individual's actions or character as causally related to that individual's fate (Hafer & Bègue, 2005) – i.e., they are more likely to construe people as personally responsible for their outcomes, a noted difference between left- and right-wing social perception. This proclivity can even be predicted via reaction time measures that gauge the cognitive accessibility of fairness-related constructs (Hafer, 2000). This type of effect – in which chronic needs influence the interpretation of social information – has now been demonstrated across a wide range of psychological needs and ideological judgments.

In their review of the literature, Jost et al. (2003a) demonstrate that a host of chronic needs – including uncertainty tolerance, death anxiety, and needs for order, structure, and closure – predict resistance to change and justification of inequality, two variables that, they and others suggest, represent the core of conservative ideology. In their article, Jost and colleagues argue that, "… conservatism as a belief system is a function of many different kinds of variables, but that a matching relationship holds between certain kinds of psychological motives and specific ideological outcomes" (p. 342). In their review, they note, for example, that those higher in intolerance of ambiguity, uncertainty avoidance, and need for cognitive closure tend to be more conservative socially and politically. In other words, Jost and colleagues suggest that specific needs give rise to specific ways of interpreting and processing the social world, which, in turn, gives rise to specific ideological positions – in this case, conservatism. Lerner's view, that the need to believe in a just world will manifest as increased perceptions of personal responsibility also offers a content-specific perspective on how chronic needs can translate into information-processing biases that represent a particular type of ideology. More recently, Kay, Gaucher, Napier, Callan, and Laurin (2008) have offered a similarly content-specific prediction regarding the effects of chronic needs, but in the context of views toward government intervention and religious belief. Specifically, they suggest that those who are higher in needs for order and structure are more apt to construe the government as a necessary means of providing the world with order, rather than as an impediment to personal freedom (Kay, Whitson, Gaucher, & Galinsky, 2009b; see also Adorno et al., 1950).

There is also a class of psychological theories that, while sharing this same emphasis on the effects of chronic needs on ideological beliefs, suggest a more content-free set of consequences (Greenberg & Jonas, 2003). Terror management theory, the meaning maintenance model (Heine, Proulx, & Vohs, 2006), theories of world-view verification (e.g., Major, Kaiser, O'Brien, & McCoy, 2007), and theories of uncertainty management and conviction (e.g., McGregor, 2003) argue that specific existential and epistemic needs will shape ideological beliefs, but not necessarily in one, uniform direction. According to these perspectives, psychological needs can and do manifest in ideological judgments, but whether that need will lead to more left- or right-leaning cognitions in a given individual may depend on several factors, including (but not limited to) dominant cultural views, previously held beliefs, and characteristics of the status quo (also see Kay et al., 2009a). According to terror management theory, for example, needs to avoid acknowledging one's mortality influence ideological judgments, but the manner in which they do so will be a function of what a given individual believes is the commonly accepted world view in his or her environment – concerns about mortality will cause individuals to gravitate toward whatever is the predominant world view (Greenberg & Jonas, 2003; but see Jost, Glaser, Kruglanski, & Sulloway, 2003b).

Importantly, though, it need not be the case that these two classes of theories are mutually exclusive; some needs may be best satisfied by a specific class of beliefs, whereas others may simply require strong beliefs, regardless of their content. For the purposes of the present chapter, all that is relevant is the common feature between all of these approaches: that ideological beliefs can be shaped by chronic needs that lead to an increased use of the cognitive tools (e.g., schemas, frameworks) to understand and interpret the social world. That is, chronic needs render certain tools for interpreting and understanding the world more and less likely to be applied, and these chronic differences can result in consistently different ideological tendencies. In this way, chronic needs can shape the cognitive processes that mediate ideologically relevant judgments. Those high in the need to believe in a just world, for example, may have notions of personal responsibility especially accessible, which should affect the causal inferences they make when they encounter a situation in which a tragedy needs to be explained.

Experiential influences on ideological predispositions

Individual differences in the recruitment and application of specific ideological concepts are not, however, just a function of differences in psychological needs. They also can be determined by powerful social experiences. We now turn our attention to a discussion of experiential influences on ideological predispositions, and how they can shape the ways in which people interpret and understand ideologically relevant issues. Specifically, we discuss how learning, exposure to moral cultures, social status, peer-group influences, and chance experiences can shape the chronic tendency of people to draw on specific ideological concepts when forming political beliefs.

Learning

Sears' theory of symbolic politics (2001) proposes that in early life people form affective associations to political symbols through classical conditioning processes, and that these affective associations remain an important source of people's political predispositions over the course of their lives. For example, a person who grows up in an environment in which poor people are often depicted in negative ways in media imagery and everyday discourse will tend to form an enduring antipathy towards the poor that may reduce their support for redistributive economic policies, such as welfare for people who fall below the poverty line. Support for this theory has been found in studies showing that measures of people's affective evaluations of relevant political symbols are often stronger predictors of their policy positions than measures of their self-interest with respect to those policies (Kinder & Sears, 1981; Sears, Lau, Tyler, & Allen, 1980). Also supporting the theory is research showing that people's political predispositions remain largely stable over the course of their lives (Sears & Funk, 1999).

Learning about the effects of different social arrangements can also play a role in shaping people's ideological leanings. Breer and Locke (1965) found that people adopted more authoritarian attitudes if they received false feedback indicating that they had performed better when they worked in a leader-directed groups than when they worked in a more democratically structured group, but they adopted more egalitarian attitudes if they received false feedback indicating that they had performed better when working in a democratically structured group than when working in a leader-directed group.

Social status

Research generally finds that self-interest has, at best, a weak influence on people's political attitudes (Sears & Funk, 1991). For example, winning the lottery is associated with attitudes that are narrowly relevant to a lottery winner's self-interest, such as opposition to the estate tax, but not with more general conservative views on economic stratification, which would also be consistent with a lottery winner's self-interest (Doherty, Gerber, & Green, 2006). While self-interest does not appear to be a reliable determinant of political ideology, evidence suggests that group interests may play a more important role in shaping people's political ideologies. In particular, research suggests that people who are members of low-status social groups are more likely to adopt egalitarian ideologies, perceive greater need for egalitarian reform, and support hierarchy-attenuating social policies than people who are members of high-status social groups (Adams, O'Brien, & Nelson, 2006; Bobo, 1983; Bobo & Hutchings, 1996; Eagly, Diekman, Johannesen-Smith, & Koenig, 2004; Eibach & Ehrlinger, 2006, 2010; Hunt, 1996; Kahn, Ho, Sidanius, & Pratto, 2009; Kluegel & Smith, 1986; O'Brien, Blodorn, Alsbrooks, Dube, Adams, & Nelson, 2009; Pratto, Stallworth, Sidanius, & Sears, 1997; Robinson,

2008; Sidanius & Pratto, 1999; Siegelman & Welch, 1991). For members of high-status groups, both the motive to advance the in-group's interests and the motive to defend the system should undermine support for egalitarianism. However, for members of low-status groups, these two motives pull in opposite directions. The motive to advance the in-group's interests should make egalitarian ideology more attractive to members of low-status groups than it is to members of high-status groups. However, this should be an ambivalent and fragile attraction, even for members of low-status groups, because the motive to defend the system (Jost & Banaji, 1994), which they tend to share with high-status groups, works against egalitarianism.

There is considerable evidence that members of low-status groups tend to endorse egalitarian ideologies more strongly than members of high-status groups. One particularly compelling line of evidence for this is research on group differences in social dominance orientation (SDO), a measure of individual differences in preferences for group dominance hierarchies over more egalitarian social arrangements (Sidanius & Pratto, 1999; but also see Jost & Thompson, 2000). This research shows that members of high-status social groups tend to have higher SDO scores than members of low-status social groups. For example, within the United States the lowest-status ethnic groups, Black Americans and Latino Americans, have the lowest mean SDO scores, while the highest-status ethnic group, White Americans, has the highest mean SDO score, with the intermediate-status ethnic group, Asian Americans, having a mean SDO score that falls between these higher- and lower-status groups (Sidanius & Pratto, 1999). The domination of women by men also seems to lead to men being lower in egalitarianism and higher in SDO than women in most societies in which these gender differences have been examined, including the United States, Canada, Sweden, Australia, the Soviet Union, China, and Israel (Pratto et al., 2000; Sidanius, Levin, Liu, & Pratto, 2000; Sidanius & Pratto, 1999; Sidanius, Pratto, & Brief, 1995).

Furthermore, evidence indicates that group differences in ideology are due to the groups' perceptions of their differential status in their society's dominance hierarchy. For instance, in Northern Ireland, Irish Catholics have higher SDO scores than Irish Protestants among participants who believe that Irish Catholics are the dominant group, but Irish Protestants have higher SDO scores than Irish Catholics among participants who believe that Irish Protestants are the dominant group (Levin, 2004).

Other research suggests a more complicated relationship between social status and ideology. For instance, a 19-nation study of working-class authoritarianism found evidence that economically advantaged and economically disadvantaged groups are drawn to conservative ideology for different reasons (Napier & Jost, 2008a). Whereas economically advantaged groups endorse conservative ideology to defend their status privileges, economically disadvantaged groups endorse conservative ideology to express ethnic and moral intolerance that helps them cope with their experiences of economic threat.

Role socialization

Social roles often have associated ideologies, and the process of psychologically adapting to social roles may involve adopting role-congruent ideologies. For instance, the criminal justice system often functions to maintain social hierarchies because members of low-status social groups (e.g., African Americans) tend to be disproportionately punished by the criminal justice system, which perpetuates their low status. People who work in hierarchy-enhancing roles within the criminal justice system, such as police, tend to be higher in SDO than people who work in hierarchy-attenuating roles such as public defenders (Sidanius & Pratto, 1999). These data could indicate that people's pre-existing SDO beliefs influence which roles within the criminal justice system they seek out or they could indicate that people adapt their SDO beliefs to their roles. The latter possibility is better supported by longitudinal studies which show that, over time, as people become socialized into their role within a hierarchy-maintaining social institution, such as the police or their country's military, they adopt attitudes that justify group dominance (Guimond, 2000; Teahan, 1975). Evidence also suggests that experience in system-challenging roles can affect a person's ideology. For instance, McAdam (1988) collected longitudinal data to test the long-term effects of civil rights activism on the attitudes of a sample of activists who participated in a high-profile civil rights event and a control sample who, although they applied to participate in the same event, did not ultimately participate in it. The activists reported becoming more critical of dominant social institutions, shifted their attitudes further toward the left, and were more active in subsequent system-challenging protest movements than the control sample, despite the fact that there was little evidence that the activists and the control sample differed in their political attitudes, values, and motivations prior to this civil rights event.

Gender role socialization is another potential source of ideological variation. Specifically, women's socialization into caretaking roles has been used to explain why women tend to be higher in socially compassionate attitudes, such as government intervention to reduce income inequalities, and moral traditionalism, such as disapproval of divorce and legalization of marijuana, compared to men (Eagly et al., 2004). Women's overrepresentation in child-rearing roles may explain their greater social compassion because raising children involves caretaking activities and it may explain women's greater moral traditionalism because child-rearing involves nurturing children's character development.

Peer-group influences

The groups that people belong to and the social networks that they participate in can play a powerful role in shaping their political attitudes and behavior (Huckfeldt & Sprague, 1995; McAdam, 1986; Snow, Zurcher, & Ekland-Olson, 1980). People have fundamental affiliative needs (Baumeister & Leary, 1995) and individuals may adopt a peer-group's ideology in order to better integrate themselves into that group. Describing the process by which social contacts can shape ideologies, Bandura (1982) writes, "[O]nce individuals become attached to a primary group, they are socialized into its ideology and life-style through a vast network of proximal rewards and sanctions that members provide each other in daily transactions" (p. 752).

The classic demonstration of the impact of reference groups on ideology is Newcomb's (1943) Bennington College study. Newcomb studied the development of political ideologies in a sample of undergraduates who, during the 1930s, enrolled at Bennington College, a small liberal arts college for women located in Bennington, Vermont. The students who enrolled at Bennington mostly came from wealthy, conservative Republican families who were largely hostile to the New Deal policies of the Roosevelt administration. Due to its small size and recent establishment, Bennington College was a highly cohesive community where the students had close interactions with the faculty who were mostly young, liberal-minded supporters of the New Deal. Newcomb documented how the Bennington students shifted away from their families' conservative ideology in their freshman year to an increasingly liberal ideology as they advanced towards graduation. This liberal shift appears to initially have served a social adjustment function as the Bennington students adopted liberal beliefs in order to be viewed favorably by the faculty and upper-class students. Indeed, liberal students were more popular and were judged to be better representatives of the College compared to their conservative peers.

Although the initial motivation to adopt liberal beliefs seems to have been social adjustment, many of the Bennington students eventually internalized the liberal beliefs that they outwardly professed. Indeed, the Bennington students' liberalism persisted up to 50 years after they graduated (Alwin, Cohen, & Newcomb, 1991; Newcomb, Koenig, Flacks, & Warwick, 1967). However, reference groups may have played a role even in the long-term persistence of the Bennington graduates' liberal ideology because this liberal ideology was more likely to persist over time if they had married liberal spouses and formed lasting friendships with other liberals (Alwin et al., 1991). Another interpretation of these data is that the Bennington graduates who were more strongly committed to liberalism, and thus more likely to remain liberal over the ensuing decades, were also those who were more likely to have formed social ties to others liberals.

Moral cultures

Liberal and conservative ideologies may also be rooted in people's socialization into different moral cultures. Research by Haidt, Graham, and colleagues suggests that conservatives tend to moralize a broader range of behaviors and interpersonal relationships than do liberals (Graham, Haidt, Nosek, 2009; Haidt & Graham, 2009). Liberals' moral concerns tend to be narrowly confined to issues of fairness, equality, and alleviating suffering. Conservatives, for the most part, share liberals' moral concerns about these issues, but conservatives also have moral concerns about respecting authority, remaining loyal to one's group, and maintaining sexual and bodily purity that liberals typically lack. Thus, issues that liberals would see as matters of taste or preference, conservatives see as matters of moral concern. For instance, research shows that while both liberals and conservatives tend to express moral disapproval of acts that violate values of fairness, equality, and compassion towards others, conservatives tend to morally disapprove of acts that violate values of respect for authority, in-group loyalty, and bodily purity more strongly than do liberals (Graham et al., 2009).

What is the source of these differences in liberals' and conservatives' moral values? Haidt and Graham (2009) suggest that these differences may be rooted in the different cultures that liberals and conservatives experience from living in differently structured communities. Specifically, they suggest that the three distinctively conservative values of respect for authority, in-group loyalty, and concern for moral purity may be more likely to be cultivated in small, close-knit, culturally homogeneous communities. It is in such communities that people will experience the kind of tight interpersonal connections that are conducive to developing strong values for authority, group loyalty, and sacredness.

In addition to differing in their moral cultures, liberals and conservatives may also differ in the mental models that they use to conceptualize the political system. Lakoff (1996) suggests that because the State is an abstract and vastly complex concept that may be very difficult for individuals to comprehend, people may use more concrete relationships from their everyday lives as metaphors for understanding the relationship between the State and its citizens. In particular, Lakoff suggests that many people use the relationship between parents and children as a metaphor for understanding the proper relationship between citizens and the State. If the family is used as a metaphor for understanding the State, then differences in people's conceptions of parent–child relations may be an important source of ideological differences in their conceptions of good government.

In particular, Lakoff suggests that the dominant model of parent–child relations for conservatives is a "strict father" model that emphasizes parental authority and strict rules, with rewards for children's compliance with parental rules, and punishments for children's deviations from parental rules. This is consistent with classic work linking authoritarianism to harsh parental discipline (Adorno et al., 1950). By contrast, the dominant model of parent–child relations for liberals, according to Lakoff, is a "nurturant parent" model that emphasizes parental responsibility for tending to their children's emotional needs and fostering their development into happy and fulfilled adults. Lakoff argues that when conservatives apply their "strict father" model to politics, this leads them to support State actions that reward those who comply with societal norms and punish those who deviate. By contrast, when liberals apply their "nurturant parent" model to politics, this leads them to support State actions that intervene to reduce the suffering that can arise in a market-based economy and to cultivate citizens' skills and opportunities for success. If Lakoff's analysis is correct, then the ideological differences between liberals and conservatives may be rooted in the different family cultures that liberals and conservatives experience in their everyday lives.

There is some evidence to support Lakoff's hypothesis that liberals and conservatives may have different models of the family. For example, Barker and Tinnick (2006) found that conservative political attitudes are associated with harsh disciplinarian attitudes towards child-rearing, while liberal political attitudes are associated with nurturant attitudes towards child-rearing. Also, a recent study found that when they describe significant autobiographical events conservatives tend to emphasize themes such as self-discipline and rule-following, which are associated with the "strict father" model, whereas liberals tend to emphasize themes of empathy, openness, and growth, which are associated with the "nurturant parent" model (McAdams, Albaugh, Farber, Daniels, Logan, & Olson, 2008).

Chance encounters

Although it may be possible to make predictions about a person's ideological leanings based on information about such factors as their personality and cognitive style, cultural background, early socialization experiences, social status, and social network ties, there is likely to be a significant component of variance in ideology that is unpredictable because it is due to chance encounters that people have during the course of their lives (Bandura, 1982). This idea that random experiences might shape a person's ideology is captured in the common saying that "a liberal is someone who has never been mugged." And while this particular effect does not appear to hold – crime victimization is not a reliable predictor of conservative attitudes towards crime (King & Maruna, 2009; Unnever, Cullen, & Fisher, 2007) – the more general idea that chance experiences may influence a person's ideology remains a viable hypothesis.

For instance, in a study of women in racist movements, Blee (2002) found evidence that chance social encounters can influence people to adopt extremist ideologies. Blee reports that many of the women she interviewed developed racist ideologies through chance contacts with individuals who were already involved in the hate movement. It appears that it was often these social contacts rather than unusual background characteristics or preexisting racist beliefs that led many of these women to develop extreme racist ideologies. Blee reports that while some of these women were raised in families with extreme racist beliefs, many others were not, and some were even from liberal or progressive families who they became estranged from after they joined hate groups. Also, while many of these women had racist beliefs before they joined hate groups, their beliefs were not that different from racist views that are quite widespread in American culture. Indeed, it was only after they joined hate groups that many of the women developed more extreme racist beliefs, through their exposure to the movement's ideology.

SITUATIONAL AND CONTEXTUAL DETERMINANTS OF THE APPLICATION OF IDEOLOGICAL KNOWLEDGE

Without disputing the obvious fact that certain beliefs and modes of information processing are more chronic than others for specific individuals, it is clear that the processing of social information is also influenced by one's immediate context, needs, and situational constraints (Kunda, 1990). At a cognitive level of analysis, it has been observed, for instance, that temporary increases in the accessibility of a given construct (achieved via subliminal priming) influence social information processing and perception, regardless of whether people are a priori chronically high (or low) in accessibility for that construct (Bargh, Bond, Lombardi, & Tota, 1986). Consistent with this perspective, it has been shown that although people differ in their chronic tendencies to apply stereotypes when evaluating other groups, this tendency also fluctuates as a function of transient, situational factors, including self and social threat (e.g., Fein & Spencer, 1997; Kay, Jost, & Young, 2005) and environmental triggers of stereotype accessibility (for a review, see Wheeler & Petty, 2001).

The application of ideological knowledge functions no differently. Situational constraints and contextual cues can strongly influence the likelihood that people will bring to mind (i.e., render more cognitively accessible) and apply specific ideological resources in making ideological judgments. In the next sections, we describe four such influences on beliefs and attitudes in ideologically relevant domains: threat, framing, priming, and role salience.

Threat

A long tradition of research has demonstrated that, following specific psychological threats, cognitive resources are mobilized to help the individual most efficiently deal with that threat. Across various domains of research – ranging from self and interpersonal perception to social stereotyping to basic cognitive processing (e.g., Baldwin & Main, 2001; Fein & Spencer, 1997; Mathews & MacLeod, 1985) – it has been observed that immediate threats can activate specific modes of information processing. Similar findings have also been observed in the context of ideological perceptions, judgments, and inferences. That is, ideological judgments and beliefs have also been shown to be influenced by the salience of immediate threats.

Sales, for example, reasoned that contexts of economic threat and turmoil should cause people to temporarily construe authoritarian institutions as more attractive (Sales, 1972, 1973). In support of this, Sales noted that during times of threat (such as the Great Depression and other economic downturns), people exhibited increases in many of the behaviors and beliefs associated with authoritarianism, according to Adorno et al.'s (1950) definition. For example, he observed that, in times of economic threat, conversion rates into religious sects offering high levels of imposed order increased, conversion rates into religious sects offering low levels of imposed order decreased, people became more loyal to authority, people perceived others more cynically, and superstitious belief increased.

Sales' research was influential but the measures were limited to what was available in archival sources, the methodology was strictly correlational, and it lacked a clear mechanistic account. More recently, researchers have developed other models of the influence of threat on ideological processes that more precisely specify and measure underlying mechanisms and provide the experimental data needed to more definitively test patterns of causal influence. All of these more recent models pivot on the notion that when a specific motivational state is starved, people will relatively immediately act in ways that promote the satiation of that specific motivation (or, conversely, when a specific motive is satiated, people will relatively immediately disengage from those processes specific to that motive). This is consistent with social cognitive goal theory, which suggests that, just as meeting a desired end state greatly reduces motivated cognitive processes generally used to achieve that end state (e.g., Förster, Liberman, & Higgins, 2005), blocking a desired end state results in increased efforts to reach it (Atkinson & Birch, 1970; Bargh et al., 2001). In a social psychological context, this process is perhaps most vividly illustrated via the myriad demonstrations that self-threat (affirmation) manipulations increase (decrease) the proclivity to engage in self-defensive processes (e.g., Fein & Spencer, 1997; Sherman & Cohen, 2002; Steele, 1988). Following self-threat (or self-affirmation), this research demonstrates that people engage in (or disengage from) a number of social-cognitive processes, including stereotyping, shifts in self-construal, and shifts in self-identification, that help them protect their views of their self-worth.

Similar types of processes manifest in ideological contexts, too, shaping people's perceptions and judgments regarding a range of political, religious, and institutional issues. Following mortality threats, terror management theorists suggest

people engage in the defense of worldviews (including political and religious ones) that can serve to establish their symbolic immortality and attachment to something larger than their physical selves (Greenberg, Solomon, Pyszczynski, 1997). In the context of ideology, terror management researchers have observed that following specific mortality threats, for example:

- people preferred leaders that emphasized the superiority of the in-group (Cohen, Solomon, Maxfield, Pyszczynski, & Greenberg, 2004)
- people became more supportive of George W. Bush's policies in Iraq (Cohen, Ogilvie, Solomon, Greenberg, & Pyszczynski, 2005; Landau et al., 2004)
- Middle Eastern participants became more positive towards a student who supported martyrdom and American conservative participants became more supportive towards aggressive, likely fatal military policies (Pyszczynski, Abdollahi, Solomon, Greenberg, Cohen, & Weise, 2006)
- liberal students' attitudes towards capital punishment, abortion, and gay people became more conservative (Nail, McGregor, Drinkwater, Steele, & Thompson, 2009).

In each of these cases, terror management researchers suggest, mortality salience led people to filter their social perceptions, apply social schemas, and generally arrive at conclusions that provided evidence for the worth and permanence of the social ideas and groups they identify with.

Compensatory control theory, like terror management theory, also posits a model of threat and compensation. But, unlike terror management, compensatory control theory emphasizes (i) people's motivation to maintain a view of the world as a structured, non-random place and (ii) the substitutability of people's means for doing so (Kay et al., 2008, 2009b, 2010c). To maintain a view of the world as structured and non-random, the theory suggests, people rely on a combination of their own personal control, and the structure and control exerted on them via secular and religious structural forces (e.g., governments, institutions, religions, organizations, etc.). As such, when the integrity of one of these control-maintaining outlets is threatened or challenged, people can augment their faith in the others.

Such a model holds implications for political and religious ideology. It suggests, for example, that when personal control is threatened, people should become more likely to believe in and endorse government control and religious control. Indeed, both of these effects have been observed. Following experimental inductions of personal control threat, people become more likely to believe in a controlling God (Kay et al., 2008; Kay, Moscovitch & Laurin, 2010b; Laurin, Kay, & Moscovitch, 2008), more likely to support government intervention (Kay et al., 2008), and more likely to believe their political leaders are capable of controlling their lives (Banfield & Kay, 2010). This model also suggests that threats to one source of external control should cause increased support for another. This, too, has been observed. Following experimentally generated or naturally occurring threats to one's political system, people become more likely to report believing that a controlling God exists (Kay, Shepherd, Blatz, Chua, & Galinsky, 2010c). Likewise, following information that threatens belief in the existence of a controlling God, people become more likely to support those aspects of the government that provide order and stability (Kay et al., 2010c). Finally, following control threat, people have even been shown to become more likely to believe that catastrophes were caused by conspirators (rather than random forces; Whitson & Galinsky, 2008) and that personal enemies (rather than random chance) are to blame for negative outcomes (Sullivan, Landau, & Rothschild, 2010). Thus, following contextual threats that deprive individuals of one specific means for maintaining their belief in the order and structure of the world, people begin to perceive order in other domains (Kay, Whitson, Gaucher, & Galinsky, 2009b). This perceptual interpretation is buttressed by data demonstrating that, following control threat, people are more likely to see patterns even in random visual stimuli (Whitson & Galinsky, 2008).

Finally, system justification theory suggests that, for various epistemic, existential, and relational reasons, people hold a fundamental need to believe in the integrity, legitimacy, and desirability of the systems (including political ones) within which they function (Jost & Banaji, 1994; Jost, Banaji, & Nosek, 2004). To the extent this is so, events that threaten people's beliefs in the integrity and legitimacy of their system should cause people to engage in social-cognitive processes that reassert that system's legitimacy. This process can manifest itself in ways that have profound effects on ideological judgments. For example, following exposure to fake newspaper articles that suggest their national system is decaying (i.e., system threat manipulations), people become more likely to endorse stereotypes that justify inequality in both liberal (complementary stereotypes that offer an illusion of equality) and conservative (victim derogating stereotypes that reaffirm meritocracy) ways (Jost, Kivetz, Rubini, Guermandi, & Mosso, 2005; Kay & Jost, 2003; Kay, Jost, & Young, 2005; Kay et al., 2007). Following similar system threat manipulations,

people also have been shown to resist changes to the gender imbalance in business contexts (Kay et al., 2009a) and prefer romantic partners who hold benevolent sexist ideologies (Lau, Kay, & Spencer, 2008). A similar system threat analysis has also been used to explain a range of real-world phenomena, from victim blame following Hurricane Katrina (Napier, Mandisodza, Andersen, & Jost, 2006) to increased nationalism following terrorist attacks or the threat thereof (Ullrich & Cohrs, 2007; Willer & Adams, 2008), to the resistance to environmental policy that suggests the system is failing (Feygina, Jost, & Goldsmith, 2010).

Other theories also have implications for the effects of immediate contextual threats on ideological beliefs and judgments, but we do not have the space to review them all here. These include, but are not limited to, McGregor and colleagues' model of reactive approach motivation (McGregor, Nash, & Prentice, 2010), Hogg's uncertainty-identity theory (Hogg, 2005, 2007), and van den Bos and Lind's model of uncertainty management and fairness judgments (van den Bos & Lind, 2002). It is also worth noting that just as psychological threat can increase the recruitment and application of specific ideological judgments and social perceptions, psychological affirmations can decrease them. For example, whereas mortality threats have been shown to make people more likely to gravitate towards a strong, charismatic leader and support the Iraq war (Landau et al., 2004; Pyszczynski et al., 2006), reminders of secure attachment figures cause people to less strongly endorse these worldview buffering beliefs (Gillath & Hart, 2010).

Different types of threat activate distinct versions of conservative ideology

Some motivational models of ideology propose that there is a more specific mapping from particular threats to corresponding ideologies. For instance, Duckitt's (2001) dual-process model of ideology posits that distinct forms of conservatism are responsive to different types of threat. Duckitt proposes that conservative ideology is composed of two distinct underlying ideologies, which he identifies as right-wing authoritarian ideology and social dominance ideology. According to Duckitt's model, these two ideologies are rooted in two different worldviews. Specifically, right-wing authoritarianism (RWA) is rooted in the perception that the world is a dangerous place, whereas SDO is rooted in the perception that the world is a competitive jungle. Supporting the idea that these different conservative ideologies are rooted in different worldviews, research shows that RWA, but not SDO, tends to correlate with beliefs that the world is a dangerous place, whereas SDO, but not RWA, tends to correlate with belief in a competitive, zero-sum world (Duckitt, 2001).

If RWA and SDO are rooted in distinct world-views, as these correlational results suggest, then manipulations that raise the salience of threats related to one or the other of these worldviews should selectively activate that worldview's associated ideology. Specifically, if right-wing authoritarian ideology is rooted in perception that the world is a dangerous place then events that highlight dangers and disorder in the world should tend to selectively activate authoritarian attitudes and behavior. Consistent with this hypothesis, research shows that when researchers experimentally induce participants to perceive dangers, disorder, and decline in the world people tend to report higher RWA scores, but not higher SDO scores (Altemeyer, 1988; Duckitt & Fisher, 2003).

While events that highlight threats and dangers in the world should selectively activate right-wing authoritarian ideology, events that highlight intergroup competition for access to resources and social status should selectively activate social dominance ideology. Researchers have used a variety of methods to test how manipulations that highlight intergroup competition moderate the effects of social dominance ideology on people's political perceptions and attitudes. When threats to the in-group's status are highlighted, people who are high in SDO have a stronger implicit preference for their in-group over out-groups compared to people who are low in SDO (Pratto & Shih, 2000). SDO also has a stronger influence on people's perceptions of social conditions when participants are induced to perceive resources and opportunities as zero-sum than when they are induced to perceive resources as non-zero-sum (Eibach & Keegan, 2006; Eibach & Purdie-Vaughns, 2009). Other research has found that the relationship between SDO and negative attitudes (Esses, Dovidio, Jackson, & Armstrong, 2001) and aggression (Thomsen, Green, & Sidanius, 2008) toward immigrants is amplified when immigrants are perceived to be a competitive threat. Importantly for Duckitt's dual-process model, this research also shows that information that highlights immigrant's competitive threat does not increase the influence of RWA on aggression towards immigrants (Thomsen et al., 2008).

Priming

Just like threat, other contextual factors can also influence which of their diverse ideological resources people draw on when forming an

opinion on a given ideological issue. Priming, or recency of prior activation of an ideological resource, may be one factor that influences which ideological resources influence people's political attitudes, perceptions, and behavior (Zaller, 1992). To support this hypothesis, Zaller (1992) cites research showing carryover effects of prior questions on answers to subsequent questions in opinion surveying. For example, Zaller (1992) cites research by Tourangeau, Rasinski, Bradburn, and D'Andrade (1989) showing that American participants were significantly less likely to criticize defense spending as being too high if they were responding to a version of the survey in which a previous question asked about the Soviet military threat than they were if they were responding to a version of the survey in which the previous question asked not about the Soviet military threat but about the issue of arms control. Although such an effect could be driven by the types of threat reactions described above, it also could be because the relevant ideas that were activated in response to a preceding question remained accessible when a subsequent question was encountered, making this information more accessible and readily applied to the subsequent question.

In a recent study that provided clearer evidence for ideological priming, Bryan, Dweck, Ross, Kay, and Mislavsky (2009) tested the hypothesis that most Americans carry around conflicting ideas about the role of personal merit versus good fortune in determining people's outcomes in life. Bryan et al. hypothesized that which of these ideas people have in mind when they consider a given social policy may determine whether they adopt a conservative or a liberal position toward that policy because conservative policies tend to assume that people are responsible for their circumstances whereas liberal policies assume that a person's social position may be determined by forces beyond his or her control. Consistent with this reasoning, the researchers found that when personal merit was primed people adopted more conservative policy positions than they did when good fortune was primed. (For other examples of priming effects in an ideological context, see Berger, Meredith, & Wheeler, 2008; Wakslak, Jost, Tyler, & Chen, 2007.)

Role salience

Ideologies are sometimes associated with particular social roles, which may mean that people will be more likely to express a given ideology when a relevant role is situationally salient. Just like primes and threats, therefore, the salience of social roles or identities may make specific ideological resources more likely to be recruited and applied when judging specific social issues. A number of studies have investigated the effects of manipulating social role salience on various measures of ideology. For example, Catholic participants expressed attitudes that were more consistent with the ideology of their Church if their role as Catholics was made salient by mentioning it in a prior question (Charters & Newcomb, 1958). Also, Black American voters expressed less approval of conservative Republican President Ronald Reagan when they were interviewed by a Black interviewer who specifically mentioned that he was surveying the attitudes of Black Americans than when they were interviewed by a White interviewer who did not mention race (Zaller, 1992).

Levin (cited in Sidanius & Pratto, 1999) hypothesized that which of a person's social identities is salient in a given situation can influence that person's expression of social dominance ideology. Specifically, she hypothesized that when a person's membership in a low-status group is situationally salient, that person should tend to score lower in SDO than they do when their membership in a high-status group is situationally salient. To test this hypothesis, Levin studied social dominance ideology among three ethnic groups of Israeli Jews: Ashkenazi Jews, who have a higher status than other Jews; Sephardic Jews, who have a lower status than other Jews; and mixed-ethnicity Jews, who have intermediate status. This was a promising context to study the effects of social identity salience on social dominance ideology because all three groups of Jews have higher status relative to Palestinians. Thus, when national identity (Israeli vs Palestinian) is salient, all three groups of Jews should tend to endorse social dominance ideology at comparably high levels. However, when Jews' ethnic identities (Askenazi vs Sephardic vs mixed ethnicity) are situationally salient, endorsement of social dominance ideology should be highest for the highest-status ethnic group (Ashkenazi Jews), intermediate for the intermediate status group (mixed-ethnicity Jews), and lowest for the lowest-status group (Sephardic Jews). Levin experimentally varied whether Israeli nationality or Jewish ethnicity was situationally salient before participants' endorsement of social dominance ideology was measured. In the ethnic prime condition, the ethnic hierarchy within the Jewish in-group was made salient by having participants answer a number of questions about Ashkenazi and Sephardic Jews. In the nationality prime condition, the hierarchical relationship between Israelis and Palestinians was made salient by having participants answer a number of questions about Israelis and Palestinians. As Levin predicted, all three ethnic groups of Jews endorsed social dominance ideology at comparably high levels in the nationality prime condition. However, as Levin hypothesized, in the ethnicity prime condition participants' endorsement of social dominance ideology corresponded to the status of their ethnic group: social dominance scores were highest for Ashkenazi Jews, intermediate for mixed-ethnicity Jews, and lowest for Sephardic Jews.

Other research has examined the effects of situational variance in social role salience on people's political and moral attitudes and ideologies. For example, when their parental role is made salient, parents perceive the world to be a more dangerous place (Eibach & Libby, 2009; Eibach & Mock, 2011) and adopt more paternalistic moral attitudes (Eibach, Libby, & Ehrlinger, 2009). Also, research has examined how variation in people's subjective identification with a social role interacts with their beliefs about the ideological entailments of that role to predict political and moral attitudes. For example, when middle-aged and older adults were induced to feel subjectively older and primed with the stereotype that older people are more rigid, this caused them to adopt more morally traditionalist beliefs and to more strongly oppose extension of marriage rights to same-sex couples, compared to participants who had not been induced to feel older or were not primed with the rigidity stereotype (Eibach, Mock, & Courtney, 2010).

Framing

Threat, priming, and role salience, however, are not the only factors that dictate which of a person's diverse ideological resources he or she will apply to any given political judgment or decision. This is because even once a given ideological concept becomes activated (via, for example, threat), it must then be applied to the specific, concrete issue at hand, and this application process is often far from straightforward. There is rarely a direct one-to-one mapping from an ideology to a position on a particular issue, because ideologies tend to be abstract whereas political issues are often more concrete. Indeed, the same ideology could often be used to support opposite positions on the same issue. Consider, for example, egalitarian ideology. This specific ideology has been used to both support a more open immigration policy – based on the reasoning that immigration restrictions are invariably applied in an unequal manner to people from different ethnic or cultural backgrounds (Ngai, 2010) – and to oppose it – based on the grounds that open immigration creates downward pressure on wages for low-skilled workers, who are often members of low-status ethnic or cultural groups within the host society (Swain, 2010).

How an ideological concept gets translated into specific political beliefs and judgments for a given issue, therefore, can be an ambiguous process. People may thus look for external cues to guide their selection and application of ideological concepts to specific policy questions. In particular, people may rely on *frames,* offered by opinion elites and social movement activists, to determine how to map their own ideological views onto specific policy issues. One of the most powerful ways in which media discourse (Iyengar, 1991) and social movement activists (Snow, 2004) influence public opinion is through the work they do to frame public issues. Most public issues are complex and can often be seen from a variety of ideological perspectives. From the range of potentially relevant ideological perspectives, frames select a particular perspective and interpret the issue from that perspective, highlighting those features of the issue that are relevant to that ideological perspective and relatively downplaying or ignoring features of the issue that are not relevant to the selected perspective. Thus, framing simplifies the construal of an issue by narrowing the range of relevant ideological considerations that people apply to the issue. For example, the issue of global climate change would look very different depending on whether one viewed it from the perspective of a consequentialist's concerns about maximizing human flourishing over the long run, an evangelical Christian's concerns about responsible stewardship over Creation, an egalitarian's concerns about global injustices in the distribution of the benefits and costs of resource consumption, or a libertarian's concerns about protecting human freedom. By selecting which of these perspectives to emphasize, politicians, media figures, and activists can influence what ideological considerations the public draws on to form an opinion on a given issue.

Kinder and Sanders (1996) conducted a series of experiments to test whether the perspective from which a public issue is framed determines which of a person's relevant ideological concepts most influences the opinions they form about that issue. In these studies, Kinder and Sanders measured a number of relevant ideological predispositions by having participants complete a battery of ideological scales. They then manipulated the ideological framing of a particular policy issue to which participants were exposed. After participants considered the issue from the assigned frame, the researchers then assessed the strength of the associations between measures of participants' ideological predispositions and the positions they took on the relevant issue. When an ideological concept was referenced in the framing of a policy issue, measures of participants' endorsement of that ideological concept were stronger predictors of their stance toward the policy than when that ideological concept was not referenced in the frame.

CONCLUSION

Social psychologists (Augoustinos, 1998; Billig, 1995; Essed, 1991), feminist scholars (Bem, 1994), and media critics (van Dijk, 1998) have observed that ideology is a pervasive feature of everyday life. Ideology is not only conveyed overtly – as in the discourse of political leaders, social movement activists, and media pundits – but also more subtly in a variety of everyday practices that convey meta-messages about how society ought to be structured (Bem, 1994; Shweder, Jensen, & Goldstein, 1995). Given people's extensive exposure to ideology in everyday life, it should not be surprising that ideology comes to influence their own thought processes and behavior. Even if people do not fully understand or accept the various ideologies they encounter in everyday life, these ideologies may nevertheless affect how they think about the world and the choices they make (Feagin, 2000).

Whereas in past eras there may have been a single dominant ideology that most people adhered to, the contemporary era seems to be characterized by a fractured mix of diverse ideologies (Augustinos, 1998). Given this extensive ideological pluralism within the culture, it should not be surprising that people show a great deal of ideological heterogeneity in their own thought processes and behavior. Thus, the inconsistencies in expressions of ideology that some observers have taken to suggest a lack of ideology on the part of ordinary people may actually suggest that people flexibly sample from the heterogeneous ideological environment in which they are immersed.

To explain how immersion in this heterogeneous ideological environment may affect people's thinking and behavior, we borrowed a conceptual framework from the field of social cognition that emphasizes the classic distinction between chronic and temporary accessibility of cognitive constructs (Bargh et al., 1986; Higgins, 1996). We reviewed research showing that people vary in their chronically accessible ideologies, owing to their affinities for particular ideologies that fit their own temperament or cognitive style, and their degree of prior exposure to different ideologies. We also reviewed research showing that people vary in the temporary accessibility of ideological concepts, depending on their immediate need states and the recency of prior activation of those ideological concepts. Thus, the dynamic patterns of activation of ideological concepts seem to follow that of other cognitive constructs.

This variation in chronic and temporary accessibility of ideological concepts suggests that, in their use of ideology, people do not fit the stereotype of the rigid ideologue. Instead, people seem to flexibly draw on ideological concepts as tools to solve particular problems, such as understanding events and broader conditions (Skitka, 1999; Skitka et al., 2002), deciding what position to take on a particular social issue (Feldman & Zaller, 1992), rationalizing social arrangements (Jost & Hunyady, 2002; Sidanius & Pratto, 1999), and managing their own emotions about social conditions (Jost & Hunyady, 2002; Napier & Jost, 2008b; Wakslak et al., 2007). While this image of people as flexible ideological tool users may not fit some definitions of ideologies as coherent and consistent systems of thought, it does fit with the pragmatic image of human thought processes that has been more generally advanced within the social cognition literature.

REFERENCES

Adams, G., O'Brien, L. T., & Nelson, J. C. (2006). Perceptions of racism in Hurricane Katrina: A liberation psychology analysis. *Analyses of Social Issues and Public Policy, 6,* 215–235.

Adorno, T. W, Frenkel-Brunswik, E., Levinson, D. J., & Sanford, R. N. (1950). *The authoritarian personality.* New York: W.W. Norton.

Altemeyer, B. (1988). *Enemies of freedom.* San Francisco, CA: Jossey-Bass.

Alford, J. R., Funk, C. L., & Hibbing, J. R. (2005). Are political orientations genetically transmitted? *American Political Science Review, 99,* 153–168.

Alwin, D. F., Cohen, R. L., & Newcomb, T. M. (1991). *Political attitudes over the life span.* Madison, WI: University of Wisconsin Press.

Amodio, D. M., Jost, J. T., Master, S. L., & Yee, C. M. (2007). Neurocognitive correlates of liberalism and conservatism. *Nature Neuroscience, 10,* 1246–1247.

Atkinson, J. W., & Birch, D. (1970). *The dynamics of action.* New York: John Wiley.

Augoustinos, M. (1998). Social representations and ideology: Towards the study of ideological representations. In U. Flick (Ed.), *The psychology of the social* (pp. 156–169). New York: Cambridge University Press.

Baldwin, M. W., & Main, K. J. (2001). Social anxiety and the cued activation of relational knowledge. *Personality and Social Psychology Bulletin, 27,* 1637–1647.

Bandura, A. (1982). The psychology of chance encounter and the life path. *American Psychologist, 37,* 747–755.

Bargh, J. A., Bond, R. N., Lombardi, W. J., & Tota, M. E. (1986). The additive nature of chronic and temporary sources of construct accessibility. *Journal of Personality and Social Psychology, 50,* 869–878.

Bargh, J. A., Gollwitzer, P. M., Lee-Chai, A., Barndollar, K., & Trötschel, R. (2001). The automated will: Nonconscious activation and pursuit of behavioral goals. *Journal of Personality and Social Psychology, 81,* 1014–1027.

Barker, D. C., & Tinnick, J. T. (2006). Competing visions of parental roles and ideological constraint. *American Political Science Review, 100,* 249–263.

Baumeister, R. F., & Leary, M. R. (1995). The need to belong: Desire for interpersonal attachments as a fundamental human motive. *Psychological Bulletin, 117,* 497–529.

Bem, S. L. (1994). *The lenses of gender: Transforming the debate on sexual inequality.* New Haven, CT: Yale University Press.

Berger, J., Meredith, M., & Wheeler, S. C. (2008). Does where you vote affect how you vote? The impact of environmental cues on voting behavior. *Proceedings of the National Academy of Science, 105,* 8846–8849.

Billig, M. (1995). *Banal nationalism.* London, UK: SAGE.

Blee, K. N. (2002). *Inside organized racism: Women in the hate movement.* Berkeley, CA: University of California Press.

Bobo, L. (1983). Whites opposition to busing: Symbolic racism or realistic group conflict? *Journal of Personality and Social Psychology, 45,* 1196–1210.

Bobo, L., & Hutchings, V. L. (1996). Perceptions of racial group competition: Extending Blumer's theory of group position to a multiracial social context. *American Sociological Review, 61,* 951–972.

Breer, P. E., & Locke, E. A. (1965). *Task experience as a source of attitudes.* Homewood, IL: Dosey Press.

Bryan, C. J., Dweck, C. S., Ross, L., Kay, A. C., & Mislavsky, N. O. (2009). Political mindset: Effects of schema priming on liberal-conservative political positions. *Journal of Experimental Social Psychology, 45,* 890–895.

Carney, D. R., Jost, J. T., & Gosling, S. D. (2008). The secret lives of liberals and conservatives: Personality profiles, interaction styles, and the things they leave behind. *Political Psychology, 29,* 807–840.

Charters, W. W., Jr., & Newcomb, T. M. (1958). Some attitudinal effects of experimentally increased salience of group membership. In E. Macoby, T. Newcomb, & E. Hartley (Eds.), *Readings in social psychology* (3rd ed.,). New York: Holt Rinehart.

Cohen, F., Ogilvie, D. M., Solomon, S., Greenberg, J., & Pyszczynski, T. (2005). American roulette: The effect of reminders of death on support for George W. Bush in the 2004 presidential election. *Analyses of Social Issues and Public Policy, 5,* 177–187.

Cohen, F., Solomon, S., Maxfield, M., Pyszczynski, T., & Greenberg, J. (2004). Fatal attraction: The effects of mortality salience on political preferences as a function of leadership style. *Psychological Science, 15,* 846–851.

Converse, P. E. (1964). The nature of belief systems in mass publics. In D. Apter (Ed.), *Ideology and discontent* (pp. 206–261). New York: The Free Press.

Deary I. J., Batty, G. D., & Gale C. R. (2008). Childhood intelligence predicts voter turnout, voting preferences, and political involvement in adulthood: The 1970 British Cohort Study. *Intelligence, 36,* 548–555.

Devlin, P. (1965). *The enforcement of morals.* Oxford, UK: Oxford University Press.

Doherty, D., Gerber, A. S., & Green, D. P. (2006). Personal income and attitudes toward redistribution: A study of lottery winners. *Political Psychology, 27,* 441–458.

Duckitt, J. (2001). A cognitive-motivational theory of ideology and prejudice. In M.P. Zanna (Ed.), *Advances in experimental social psychology* (Vol. 33, pp. 41–113). San Diego, CA: Academic Press.

Duckitt, J., & Fisher, K. (2003). Social threat, worldview, and ideological attitudes. *Political Psychology, 24,* 199–222.

Eagly, A. H., Diekman, A. B., Johannesen-Schmidt, M. C., & Koenig, A. G. (2004). Gender gaps in sociopolitical attitudes: A social psychological analysis. *Journal of Personality and Social Psychology, 87,* 796–816.

Eibach, R. P., & Ehrlinger, J. (2006). "Keep your eyes on the prize": Reference points and group differences in assessing progress towards equality. *Personality and Social Psychology Bulletin, 32,* 66–77.

Eibach, R. P., & Keegan, T. (2006). Free at last? Social dominance, loss aversion, and White and Black Americans' differing assessments of progress towards racial equality. *Journal of Personality and Social Psychology, 90,* 453–467.

Eibach, R. P., & Libby, L. K. (2009). Ideology of the good old days: Exaggerated perceptions of moral decline and conservative politics. In J. T. Jost, A. Kay, & H. Thorisdottir (Eds.), *Social and psychological bases of ideology and system justification* (pp. 402–423). New York: Oxford University Press.

Eibach, R. P., Libby, L. K., & Ehrlinger, J. (2009). Priming family values: How being a parent affects moral evaluations of harmless but offensive acts. *Journal of Experimental Social Psychology, 45,* 1160–1163.

Eibach, R. P., & Mock, S. E. (2011). The vigilant parent: Parental role salience affects parents' risk perceptions, risk-aversion, and trust in strangers. *Journal of Experimental Social Psychology, 47,* 694–697.

Eibach, R. P., Mock, S. E., & Courtney, E. A. (2010). Having a "senior moment": Induced aging phenomenology, subjective age, and susceptibility to ageist stereotypes. *Journal of Experimental Social Psychology, 46,* 643–649.

Eibach, R. P., & Purdie-Vaughns, V. (2009). Change we can believe in? Barack Obama's framing strategies for bridging racial divisions. *Du Bois Review, 6,* 137–152.

Eidelman, S., & Crandall, C. S. (2009). On the psychological advantage of the status quo. In J. T. Jost, A. C. Kay, & H. Thorisdottir (Eds.), *Social and psychological bases of ideology and system justification.* New York: Oxford University Press.

Essed, P. (1991). *Understanding everyday racism: An interdisciplinary theory.* Newbury Park, CA: SAGE.

Esses, V. M., Dovidio, J. F., Jackson, L. M., & Armstrong, T. L. (2001). The immigration dilemma: The role of perceived group competition, ethnic prejudice, and national identity. *Journal of Social Issues, 57,* 389–412.

Feagin, J. A. (2000). *Racist America: Roots, current realities, and future reparations.* New York: Routledge.

Fein, S., & Spencer, S. J. (1997). Prejudice as self-image maintenance: Affirming the self through derogating others. *Journal of Personality and Social Psychology, 73,* 31–44.

Feldman, S., & Zaller, J. (1992). The political culture of ambivalence: Ideological responses to the welfare state. *American Journal of Political Science, 36,* 268–307.

Ferguson, M. J., & Bargh, J. A. (2004). Liking is for doing: The effects of goal pursuit on automatic evaluation. *Journal of Personality and Social Psychology, 87,* 557–572.

Feygina, I., Jost, J. T., & Goldsmith, R. (2010). System justification, the denial of global warming, and the possibility of "system-sanctioned change." *Personality and Social Psychology Bulletin, 36,* 326–338.

Förster, J., Liberman, N., & Higgins, E.T. (2005). Accessibility from active and fulfilled goals. *Journal of Experimental Social Psychology, 41,* 220–239.

Gillath, O., & Hart, J. J. (2010). The effects of psychological security and insecurity on political attitudes and leadership preferences. *European Journal of Social Psychology, 40,* 122–134.

Graham, J., Haidt, J., & Nosek, B. (2009). Liberals and conservatives rely on different sets of moral foundations. *Journal of Personality and Social Psychology, 96,* 1029–1046.

Greenberg, J., & Jonas, E. (2003). Psychological motives and political orientation – the left, the right, and the rigid: Comment on Jost et al. (2003). *Psychological Bulletin, 129,* 376–382.

Greenberg , J., Solomon, S., & Pyszczynski, T. (1997). Terror management theory of self-esteem and cultural worldviews: Empirical assessments and conceptual refinements. *Advances in Experimental Social Psychology, 29,* 61–139.

Guimond, S. (2000). Group socialization and prejudice: The social transmission of intergroup attitudes and beliefs. *European Journal of Social Psychology, 30,* 335–354.

Haidt, J., & Graham, J. (2009). Planet of the Durkheimians: Where community, authority, and sacredness are foundations of morality. In J. T. Jost, A. Kay, & H. Thorisdottir (Eds.), *Social and psychological bases of ideology and system justification* (pp. 371–401). New York: Oxford University Press.

Haidt, J., Graham, J., & Joseph, C. (2009). Above and below left–right: Ideological narratives and moral foundations. *Psychological Inquiry, 20,* 110–119.

Haidt, J., & Hersh, M. (2001). Sexual morality: The cultures and emotions of conservatives and liberals. *Journal of Applied Social Psychology, 31,* 191–221.

Haidt, J., Koller, S., & Dias, M. (1993). Affect, culture, and morality, or is it wrong to eat your dog? *Journal of Personality and Social Psychology, 65,* 613–628.

Hafer, C. L. (2000). Do innocent victims threaten the belief in a just world? Evidence from a modified Stroop task. *Journal of Personality and Social Psychology, 79,* 165–173.

Hafer, C. L., & Bègue, L. (2005). Experimental research on just-world theory: Problems, developments, and future challenges. *Psychological Bulletin, 131,* 128–167.

Heine, S. J., Proulx, T., & Vohs, K. D. (2006). The meaning maintenance model: On the coherence of social motivations. *Personality and Social Psychology Review, 10,* 88–110.

Higgins, E. T. (1996). Knowledge activation: Accessibility, applicability, and salience. In E. T. Higgins & A. W. Kruglanski (Eds.), *Social psychology: Handbook of basic principles* (pp. 133–168). New York: Guilford Press.

Hirsh, J. B., DeYoung, C. G., Xu, X., & Peterson, J. B. (2010). Compassionate liberals and polite conservatives: Associations of agreeableness with political ideology and moral values. *Personality and Social Psychology Bulletin, 36,* 655–664.

Hochschild, J. L. (1981). *What's fair? American beliefs about distributive justice.* Cambridge, MA: Harvard University Press.

Hogg, M. A. (2005). Uncertainty, social identity and ideology. In S. R. Thye & E. J. Lawler (Eds.), *Advances in group processes* (Vol. 22, pp. 203–230). New York: Elsevier.

Hogg, M. A. (2007). Uncertainty-identity theory. In M. P. Zanna (Ed.), *Advances in experimental social psychology* (Vol. 39, pp. 69–126). San Diego, CA: Academic Press.

Hunt, M. O. (1996). The individual, society, or both? Comparison of Black, Latino, and White beliefs about the causes of poverty. *Social Forces, 75,* 293–322.

Hunter, J. D. (1991). *Culture wars.* New York: Basic Books.

Huckfeldt, R., & Sprague, J. (1995). *Citizens, politics, and social communication: Information and influence in an election campaign.* New York: Cambridge University Press.

Inbar, Y., Pizarro, D. A., & Bloom, P. (2009) Conservatives are more easily disgusted than liberals. *Cognition and Emotion, 23,* 714–725.

Iyengar, S. (1991). *Is anyone responsible? How television frames political issues.* Chicago, IL: University of Chicago Press.

Jost, J. T. (2006). The end of the end of ideology. *American Psychologist, 61,* 651–670.

Jost, J. T. (2009). "Elective affinities": On the psychological bases of left–right ideological differences. *Psychological Inquiry, 20,* 129–141.

Jost, J. T., & Banaji, M. R. (1994). The role of stereotyping in system-justification and the production of false consciousness. *British Journal of Social Psychology, 33,* 1–27.

Jost, J. T., Banaji, M. R., & Nosek, B. A. (2004). A decade of system justification theory: Accumulated evidence of conscious and unconscious bolstering of the status quo. *Political Psychology, 25,* 881–920.

Jost, J.T., Federico, C.M., & Napier, J.L. (2009). Political ideology: Its structure, functions, and elective affinities. *Annual Review of Psychology, 60,* 307–333.

Jost, J.T., Glaser, J., Kruglanski, A.W., & Sulloway, F. (2003a). Political conservatism as motivated social cognition. *Psychological Bulletin, 129,* 339–375.

Jost, J.T., Glaser, J., Kruglanski, A.W., & Sulloway, F. (2003b). Exceptions that prove the rule: Using a theory of motivated social cognition to account for ideological incongruities and political anomalies. *Psychological Bulletin, 129,* 383–393.

Jost, J.T., & Hunyady, O. (2002). The psychology of system justification and the palliative function of ideology. *European Review of Social Psychology, 13,* 111–153.

Jost, J. T., Kivetz, Y., Rubini, M., Guermandi, G., & Mosso, C. (2005). System-justifying functions of complementary regional and ethnic stereotypes: Cross-national evidence. *Social Justice Research, 18,* 305–333.

Jost, J. T., & Thompson, E. P. (2000). Group-based dominance and opposition to equality as independent predictors of self-esteem, ethnocentrism, and social policy attitudes among African Americans and European Americans. *Journal of Experimental Social Psychology, 36,* 209–232.

Kahn, K., Ho, A. K., Sidanius, J., & Pratto, F. (2009). The space between us and them: Perceptions of status differences. *Group Processes and Intergroup Relations, 12,* 591–604.

Kanazawa, S. (2010). Why liberals and atheists are more intelligent. *Social Psychology Quarterly, 73,* 33–57.

Kay, A. C., Gaucher, D., Napier, J. L., Callan, M. J., & Laurin, K. (2008). God and the government: Testing a compensatory control mechanism for the support of external systems. *Journal of Personality and Social Psychology, 95,* 18–35.

Kay, A. C. Gaucher, D., Peach, J. M., Friesen, J., Laurin, K., Zanna, M. P., et al. (2009a). Inequality, discrimination, and the power of the status quo: Direct evidence for a motivation to view what is as what should be. *Journal of Personality and Social Psychology, 97,* 421–434.

Kay, A. C., & Jost, J. T. (2003). Complementary justice: Effects of "poor but happy" and "poor but honest" stereotype exemplars on system justification and implicit activation of the justice motive. *Journal of Personality and Social Psychology, 85,* 823–837.

Kay, A. C., Jost, J. T., Mandisodza, A. N., Sherman , S. J., Petrocelli, J. V., & Johnson, A. L. (2007). Panglossian ideology in the service of system justification: How complementary stereotypes help us to rationalize inequality. In M. Zanna (Ed.), *Advances in experimental social psychology* (Vol. 39, pp. 305–358). San Diego, CA: Elsevier.

Kay, A. C., Jost, J. T., & Young, S. (2005). Victim derogation and victim enhancement as alternate routes to system justification. *Psychological Science, 16,* 240–246.

Kay, A. C., Moscovitch, D. M., & Laurin, K. (2010b). Randomness, attributions of arousal, and belief in God. *Psychological Science, 21,* 216–218.

Kay, A. C., Shepherd, S., Blatz, C. W., Chua, S. N., & Galinsky, A. D. (2010c). For God (or) country: The hydraulic relation between government instability and belief in religious sources of control. *Journal of Personality and Social Psychology, 5,* 725–739.

Kay, A. C., Whitson, J. A., Gaucher, D., & Galinksy, A. D. (2009b). Compensatory control: Achieving order through the mind, our institutions, and the heavens. *Current Directions in Psychological Science, 18,* 264–268.

Kinder, D. R., & Sanders, L. M. (1996). *Divided by color: Racial politics and democratic ideals.* Chicago, IL: University of Chicago Press.

Kinder, D. R., & Sears, D. O. (1981). Prejudice and politics: Symbolic racism versus racial threats to the good life. *Journal of Personality and Social Psychology, 40,* 414–431.

King, A., & Maruna, S. (2009). Is a Conservative just a liberal who has been mugged? Exploring the origins of punitive views. *Punishment Society, 11,* 147–169.

Kluegel, J. R., & Smith, E. R. (1986). *Beliefs about inequality: Americans views of what is and what ought to be.* New York: Aldine De Gruyter.

Kunda, Z. (1990). The case for motivated reasoning. *Psychological Bulletin, 108,* 480–498.

Kunda, Z., & Sanitioso, R. (1989). Motivated changes in the self-concept. *Journal of Experimental Social Psychology, 25,* 272–285.

Kunda, Z., & Spencer, S. J. (2003). When do stereotypes come to mind and when do they color judgment? A goal-based theory of stereotype activation and application. *Psychological Bulletin, 129,* 522–544.

Landau, M. J., Solomon, S., Greenberg, J., Cohen, F., Pyszczynski, T., Arndt, J., et al. (2004). Deliver us from evil: The effects of mortality salience and reminders of 9/11 on support for President George W. Bush. *Personality and Social Psychology Bulletin, 30,* 1136–1150.

Lakoff, G. (1996). *Moral politics: What conservatives know that liberals don't.* Chicago, IL: University of Chicago Press.

Lau, G. P., Kay, A. C., & Spencer, S. J. (2008). Loving those who justify inequality: The effects of system threat on attraction to women who embody benevolent sexist ideals. *Psychological Science, 19,* 20–21.

Laurin, K., Kay, A. C., & Moscovitch, D. M. (2008). On the belief in God: Towards an understanding of the emotional substrates of compensatory control. *Journal of Experimental Social Psychology, 44,* 1559–1562.

Lerner, M. J. (1980). *The belief in a just world: A fundamental delusion.* New York: Plenum Press.

Levin, S. (2004). Perceived group status differences and the effects of gender, ethnicity, and religion, on social dominance orientation. *Political Psychology, 25,* 31–48.

Major, B., Kaiser, C. R., O'Brien, L. T., & McCoy, S. K. (2007). Perceived discrimination as worldview threat or worldview confirmation: Implications for self-esteem. *Journal of Personality and Social Psychology, 92,* 1068–1086.

Markus, H., & Wurf, E. (1987). The dynamic self-concept: A social psychological perspective. *Annual Review of Psychology, 38,* 299–337.

Mathews, A., & MacLeod, C. (1985). Selective processing of threat cues in anxiety states. *Behaviour Research & Therapy, 23,* 563–569.

McAdam, D. (1986). Recruitment to high-risk activism: The case of freedom summer. *American Journal of Sociology, 92,* 64–90.

McAdam, D. (1988). *Freedom summer.* New York: Oxford University Press.

McAdams, D. P., Albaugh, M., Farber, E., Daniels, J., Logan, R. L., & Olson, B. (2008). Family metaphors and moral intuitions: How conservatives and liberals narrate their lives. *Journal of Personality and Social Psychology, 95,* 978–990.

McGregor, I. (2003). Defensive zeal: Compensatory conviction about attitudes, values, goals, groups, and self-definition in the face of personal uncertainty. In S. Spencer, S. Fein, & M. Zanna (Eds.), *Motivated social perception: The Ontario Symposium* (Vol. 9, pp. 73–92). Mahwah, NJ: Erlbaum.

McGregor, I., Nash, K., & Prentice, M. (2010). Reactive approach motivation (RAM) for religion. *Journal of Personality and Social Psychology, 99,* 148–161.

Mill, J. S. (1859). *On liberty.* Indianapolis, IN: Library of Liberal Arts.

Nail, P. R., McGregor, I., Drinkwater, A., Steele, G., & Thompson, A. (2009). Threat causes liberals to think like conservatives. *Journal of Experimental Social Psychology, 45,* 901–907.

Napier, J. L., & Jost, J. T. (2008a). The "antidemocratic personality" revisited: A cross-national investigation of working-class authoritarianism. *Journal of Social Issues, 64,* 595–617.

Napier, J. L., & Jost, J. T. (2008b). Why are conservatives happier than liberals? *Psychological Science, 19,* 565–572.

Napier, J. L., Mandisodza, A., Andersen, S. M., & Jost, J. T. (2006). System justification in responding to the poor and displaced in the aftermath of Hurricane Katrina. *Analyses of Social Issues and Public Policy, 6,* 57–73.

Newcomb, T. M. (1943). *Personality and social change: Attitude formation in a student community.* New York: Dryden Press.

Newcomb, T. M., Koenig, K. E., Flacks, R., & Warwick, D. P. (1967). *Persistence and change: Bennington College and its students after twenty-five years.* New York: Wiley.

Ngai, M. M. (2010). Response. In J. H Carens (Ed.), *Immigrants and the right to stay* (pp. 55–4). Cambridge, MA: MIT Press.

Nozick, R. (1974). *Anarchy, state, and utopia.* New York: Basic Books.

Nussbaum, M. (2010). *From disgust to humanity: Sexual orientation and constitutional law.* New York: Oxford University Press.

O'Brien, L. T., Blodorn, A., Alsbrooks, A., Dube, R., Adams, G., & Nelson, J. C. (2009). Understanding White Americans' perceptions of racism in Hurricane Katrina-related events. *Group Processes and Intergroup Relations, 12,* 431–44.

Oxley, D. R., Smith, K. B., Alford, J. R., Hibbing, M. V., Miller, J. L., Scalora, M., et al. (2008). Political attitudes vary with physiological traits. *Science, 321,* 1667–1670.

Pratto, F., Liu, J. H., Levin, S., Sidanius, J., Shih, M., Bacharach, H., et al. (2000). Social dominance orientation and the legitimization of inequality across cultures. *Journal of Cross-Cultural Psychology, 31,* 369–409.

Pratto, F., & Shih, M. (2000). Social dominance orientation and group context in implicit group prejudice. *Psychological Science, 11,* 515–518.

Pratto, F., Stallworth, L. M., Sidanius, J., & Siers, B. (1997). The gender gap in occupational role attainment: A social dominance approach. *Journal of Personality and Social Psychology, 72,* 37–53.

Pyszczynski, T., Abdollahi, A., Solomon, S., Greenberg, J., Cohen, F., & Weise, D. (2006). Mortality salience, martyrdom, and military might: The Great Satan versus the Axis of Evil. *Personality and Social Psychology Bulletin, 32,* 525–537.

Rawls, J. (1971). *A theory of justice.* Cambridge, MA: Harvard University Press.

Robinson, R. K. (2008). Perceptual segregation. *Columbia Law Review, 108,* 1093–1180.

Rohan, M. J., & Zanna, M. P. (2001). Values and ideologies. In A. Tesser & N. Schwarz (Eds.), *Blackwell handbook of social psychology: Intraindividual processes* (pp. 458–478). Oxford, UK: Blackwell.

Sales, S. M. (1972). Economic threat as a determinant of conversion rates in authoritarian and nonauthoritarian churches. *Journal of Personality and Social Psychology, 23,* 420–428.

Sales, S. M. (1973). Threat as a factor in authoritarianism: An analysis of archival data. *Journal of Personality and Social Psychology, 28,* 44–57.

Schuman, H., & Presser, S. (1981) *Questions and answers in attitude surveys.* New York: Academic Press.

Sears, D. O. (2001). The role of affect in symbolic politics. In J. H. Kuklinski (Ed.), *Citizens and politics: Perspectives from political psychology* (pp. 14–40). New York: Cambridge University Press.

Sears, D. O., & Funk, C. L. (1991). The role of self-interest in social and political attitudes. In L. Berkowitz (Ed.), *Advances in experimental social psychology* (Vol. 24, pp. 1–91). New York: Academic Press.

Sears, D. O., & Funk, C. L. (1999). Evidence of the long-term persistence of adults' political predispositions. *Journal of Politics, 61,* 1–28.

Sears, D. O., Lau, R. R., Tyler, T. R., & Allen, H. M. (1980). Self-interest vs. symbolic politics in policy attitudes and presidential voting. *American Journal of Political Science, 74,* 670–684.

Settle, J. E., Dawes, C. T., Hatemi, P. K., Christakis, N. A., & Fowler, J. H. (2010). Friendships moderate an association between a dopamine gene variant and political ideology. *Journal of Politics, 72,* 1189–1198.

Sherman, D. K., & Cohen, G. L. (2002). Accepting threatening information: Self-affirmation and the reduction of defensive biases. *Current Directions in Psychological Science, 11,* 119–123.

Shook, N. J., & Fazio, R. H. (2009). Political ideology, exploration of novel stimuli, and attitude formation. *Journal of Experimental Social Psychology, 45,* 995–998.

Shweder, R. A., Jensen, L. A., & Goldstein, W. M. (1995). Who sleeps by whom revisited: A method for extracting the moral goods implicit in practice. *New Directions for Child Development, 67,* 21–39.

Sidanius, J., Levin, S., Liu, J.H., & Pratto, F. (2000). Social dominance orientation and the political psychology of gender: An extension and cross-cultural replication. *European Journal of Social Psychology, 30,* 41–67.

Sidanius, J., & Pratto, F. (1999). *Social dominance.* New York: Cambridge University Press.

Sidanius, J., Pratto, F., & Brief, D. (1995). Group dominance and the political psychology of gender: A cross-cultural comparison. *Political Psychology, 16,* 381–396.

Siegelman, L., & Welch, S. (1991). *Black Americans' views of racial inequality: The dream deferred.* New York: Cambridge University Press.

Skitka, L. J. (1999). Ideological and attributional boundaries on public compassion: Reactions to individuals and communities affected by natural disasters. *Personality and Social Psychology Bulletin, 25,* 793–808.

Skitka, L. J. (2010). The psychology of moral conviction. *Social and Personality Psychology Compass, 4,* 267–281.

Skitka, L. J., Mullen, E., Griffin, T., Hutchinson, S., & Chamberlin, B. (2002). Dispositions, ideological scripts, or motivated correction? Understanding ideological differences in attributions for social problems. *Journal of Personality and Social Psychology, 83,* 470–487.

Snow, D. A. (2004). Framing processes, ideology, and discursive fields. In D. A. Snow, S. A. Soule, & H. Kreisei (Eds.), *The Blackwell companion to social movements* (pp. 380–412). Malden, MA: Blackwell.

Snow, D. A., Zurcher, L. A., & Ekland-Olson, S. (1980). Social networks and social movements: A microstructural approach to differential recruitment. *American Sociological Review, 45,* 787–801.

Steele, C. M. (1988). The psychology of self-affirmation: Sustaining the integrity of the self. In L. Berkowitz (Ed.), *Advances in experimental social psychology* (Vol. 21, pp. 261–302). New York: Academic Press.

Sullivan, D., Landau, M. J., & Rothschild, Z. (2010). An existential function of enemyship: Evidence that people attribute influence to personal and political enemies to compensate for threats to control. *Journal of Personality and Social Psychology, 98,* 434–449.

Swain, C. M. (2010). Response. In J. H Carens (Ed.), *Immigrants and the right to stay* (pp. 65–72). Cambridge, MA: MIT Press.

Swidler, A. (1986). Culture in action: Symbols and strategies. *American Sociological Review, 51,* 273–286.

Teahan, J. E. (1975). Role playing and group experiences to facilitate attitude and value changes. *Journal of Social Issues, 31,* 35–45.

Tetlock, P. E. (1986). A value pluralism model of ideological reasoning. *Journal of Personality and Social Psychology, 50,* 819–827.

Thomsen, L., Green. E. G. T., & Sidanius, J. (2008). We will hunt them down: How social dominance orientation and right-wing authoritarianism fuel ethnic persecution of immigrants in fundamentally different ways. *Journal of Experimental Social Psychology, 44,* 1455–1464.

Tourangeau, R., Rasinski, K. A., Bradburn, N., & D'Andrade, R. (1989). Belief accessibility and context effects in attitude measurement. *Journal of Experimental Social Psychology, 25,* 401–421.

Ullrich, J., & Cohrs, J. C. (2007). Terrorism salience increases system justification: Experimental evidence. *Social Justice Research, 20,* 117–139.

Unnever, J. D., Cullen, F. T., & Fisher, B. S. (2007). A liberal is someone who has not been mugged: Criminal victimization and political beliefs. *Justice Quarterly, 24,* 309–334.

Van den Bos, K., & Lind, E. A. (2002). Uncertainty management by means of fairness judgments. In M. P. Zanna (Ed.), *Advances in experimental social psychology, 34,* 1–60). San Diego, CA: Academic Press.

Van Dijk, T. A. (1998). Opinions and ideologies in the press. In A. Bell & P. Garrett (Eds.), *Approaches to media discourse* (pp. 21–63). Malden, MA: Blackwell.

Wakslak, C., Jost, J. T., Tyler, T. R., & Chen, E. (2007). Moral outrage mediates the dampening effect of system justification on support for redistributive social policies. *Psychological Science, 18,* 267–274.

Wheeler, S. C., & Petty, R. E. (2001). The effects of stereotype activation on behavior: A review of possible mechanisms. *Psychological Bulletin, 127,* 797–826.

Whitson, J. A., & Galinsky, A. D. (2008). Lacking control increases illusory pattern perception. *Science, 322,* 115–117, 268.

Willer, R., & Adams, N. (2008). The threat of terrorism and support for the 2008 presidential candidates: Results of a national field experiment. *Current Research in Social Psychology, 14,* 1–22.

Zaller, J. R. (1992). *The nature and origin of mass opinion.* New York: Cambridge University Press.

26

Gene × Environment Interaction in Social Cognition

Joan Y. Chiao, Bobby K. Cheon,
Genna M. Bebko, Robert W. Livingston,
& Ying-Yi Hong

INTRODUCTION

> In an ideal world the scientist should find a method to prevent the most severe forms of autism but allow the milder forms to survive. After all, the really social people did not invent the first stone spear. It was probably invented by an Aspie who chipped away at rocks while the other people socialized around the campfire. Without autism traits we might still be living in caves. (Temple Grandin, 1996)

How can we explain the nature and origin of social cognition? One of the most remarkable hallmarks of human and non-human primate living is the ability to successfully coexist over centuries in incredibly complex social groups of varying size, from small-scale hunter-gatherer tribes, ranging from a few to a few hundred people, to large-scale settled horticultural tribes, ranging from a few hundred to a few thousand people. According to the social brain hypothesis, this versatility in social living arrangements is possible due to humans having evolved an unusually large brain with increased cognitive capacities (Brothers, 2001; Dunbar, 1998). Supporting this view, a number of quantitative studies have shown that, among primates, the relative volume of the neocortex is positively correlated with a range of

markers of social group complexity, including the average size of a social group, number of females in the group, grooming group size, frequency of coalitions, prevalence of social play, prevalence of deception, and frequency of social learning (Dunbar & Shultz, 2007). These findings illustrate the evolutionary role of the brain mechanisms involved in facilitating social cognition as well as genes that facilitate their transmission across generations (see Chapter 23).

Whereas the capacity for social cognition is largely ubiquitous across individuals and social groups, the extent to which people are adept at understanding other people varies across individuals and cultures. These differences in understanding can be seen in individuals with autism, who have difficulty reading the minds of others, to individuals with Williams syndrome, who display hypersociality (see Chapter 21). Understanding how and why such a wide range of social-cognitive ability exists in society throughout human history requires an understanding of how genetic and environmental factors, such as cultural values, practices, and beliefs, give rise to social cognition and its underlying neural substrates, as well as the evolutionary basis for such social-cognitive abilities.

Here we adopt the cultural neuroscience framework for understanding how genetic and environmental influences shape social cognition across cultural contexts (Chiao & Ambady, 2007; Chiao, 2009; Chiao, 2011; see Figure 26.1). The idea that complex behavior results from the dynamic interaction of genes and cultural environment is not new (Caspi & Moffitt, 2007; Johnson, 1997; Li, 2003); however, cultural neuroscience represents a novel empirical approach to demonstrating bidirectional interactions between culture and biology by integrating theory and methods from cultural psychology (Kitayama & Cohen, 2007), neuroscience (Gazzaniga, Ivry, & Mangun, 2002), and neurogenetics (Canli & Lesch, 2006; Green et al., 2008, Hariri, Drabant, & Weinberger, 2006). Similar to other interdisciplinary fields, cultural neuroscience aims to explain a given mental phenomenon in terms of a synergistic product of mental, neural, and genetic events. Cultural neuroscience shares overlapping research goals with social neuroscience, in particular, as understanding how neurobiological mechanisms facilitate cultural transmission involves investigating primary social processes that enable humans to learn from one another, such as imitative learning. However, cultural neuroscience is also unique from related disciplines in that it focuses explicitly on ways that mental and neural events vary as a function of culture and genetic traits in some meaningful way (Figure 26.2). Additionally, cultural neuroscience illustrates how cultural and genetic traits may alter neurobiological and psychological processes beyond those that facilitate social experience and behavior, such as perception and cognition.

Over the past decade, social-cognitive neuroscientists have been uncovering with rapid precision how our unusually large human brain has enabled complex social behavior by mapping networks of brain structures to complex social functions (Lieberman, 2010; Ochsner & Lieberman, 2001). Convergent social neuroscience evidence to date indicates that a core network of brain regions underlie the capacity for social cognition or thinking about other people, including the extrastriate cortex, superior temporal gyrus, medial prefrontal cortex, temporoparietal junction, amygdala and lateral prefrontal regions, and anterior insula and secondary somatosensory cortex (Figure 26.3). Regions of extrastriate cortex, such as the fusiform gyrus, and superior temporal gyrus, are involved in the ability to recognize personal identity, from perceptual cues such as the face (Kanwisher, McDermott, & Chun, 1997) and the voice (Belin et al., 2000). Medial prefrontal cortex (MPFC) and temporoparietal junction (TPJ) play important roles in the ability to infer other people's thoughts, feelings, and intentions through either simulated (Mitchell, 2009) or conceptual (Saxe, 2006) processing of

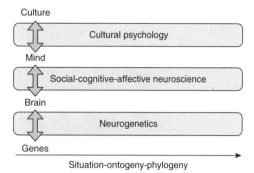

Figure 26.1   Illustration of the cultural neuroscience framework (adapted from Chiao, 2011).

social cues in the environment. Limbic circuitry, such as the amygdala, facilitate an emotional (Pessoa & Adolphs, 2010) and motivational (Cunningham & Zelazo, 2007) response to threatening or ambiguous signals in the environment, whereas prefrontal cortex, including orbital and lateral regions, are associated with the regulation of this emotional response in the context with social and cultural norms (Olsson & Ochsner, 2008; Quirk & Beer, 2006). Finally, anterior

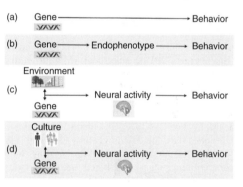

Figure 26.2   Illustration of different models of gene-to-behavior pathways. (a) The direct linear approach to gene and behavior. (b) The endophenotype approach, which assumes that the gene-to-behavior pathway is mediated by proximate or intermediate phenotypes such as neural activity. (c) The gene-by-environment approach, which assumes interaction between genetic and environmental factors influences neural activity and behavior. (d) The culture-by-gene approach, which identifies specific cultural traits and genes that interact and mutually influence neural activity and subsequent behavior (Chiao, 2011).

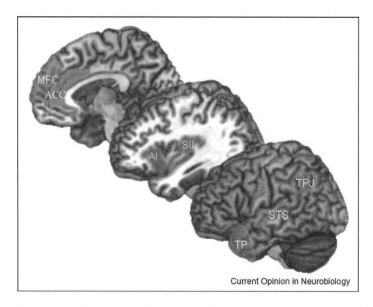

Current Opinion in Neurobiology

Figure 26.3   Illustration of network of brain regions involved in understanding the mental states of self and others (adapted from Hein & Singer, 2008). MFC, medial prefrontal cortex; ACC, anterior cingulate cortex; AI, anterior insula; SII, secondary somatosensory cortex; TP, temporal poles; STS, superior temporal sulcus; TPJ, temporoparietal junction.

insula and secondary somatosensory cortex are brain regions associated with responding to the perception and sharing of the experience of social (Eisenberger, 2010), emotional (Mathur et al., 2010), and physical pain (Apkarian, Baliki, & Geha, 2009; Lamm, Decety, & Singer, 2011).

Some of these brain regions underlie related social-cognitive abilities in non-human primates as well. For instance, dominant male rhesus macaques show increased right amygdala and right superior temporal sulcus response during mate competition, suggesting shared neural circuitry associated with social vigilance across species (Rilling, Winslow, & Kilts, 2004). Additionally, some components of the social-cognitive brain are engaged during childhood, and to a greater extent, compared to adults. For instance, children showed heightened amygdala activation in response to emotional faces relative to adults (Hoehl & Striano, 2010). Even in early infancy, the superior temporal sulcus can distinguish between vocal and non-vocal sounds, setting the stage for neural discrimination of auditory cues facilitating conspecific communication (Belin & Grosbras, 2010). The existence of a core network of brain regions across species and engaged early in development suggests that the human ability to navigate the social world, to distinguish between one's self and others, between a person's intentions from their thoughts and desires, to understand one as

part of a group, and to infer consciousness of others from both perceptual and conceptual information is reliant, at least in part, on innate biological machinery that facilitates transmission of social-cognitive processes across phylogeny and ontogeny.

GENETIC BASIS OF SOCIAL COGNITION

The notion of social cognition as arising from innate machinery is supported by evidence from twin studies showing that several foundational social skills, such as empathy, motivation, and decision making, are between 15 and 50% heritable (Ebstein et al., 2010), or shared to a greater extent between monozygotic (MZ) compared to dizygotic (DZ) twins. MZ twins share nearly 100% of their genome, whereas DZ twins only share 50%. Assuming that both MZ and DZ twins are raised in a similar shared environment, differences in correlation of behavior between MZ and DZ twins can be attributed to a genetic influence (see also Constantino & Todd, 2000).

Furthermore, behavioral and neurogenetic studies of social behavior in human and non-human primates have made significant progress in associating specific functional polymorphisms (SNPs) or genes with specific social-cognitive processes underlying interpersonal processes. For instance, the serotonin transporter gene (*SLC6A4*) is typically associated with emotional (Hariri et al., 2002) and social-cognitive processes (Canli & Lesch, 2007). People who carry the short (S) allele of the serotonin transporter gene are more likely to show greater emotional reactivity and amygdala response to emotional information compared to those who carry the long (L) allele (Munafo, Brown, & Hariri, 2008). Empathy, or the ability to feel what others are feeling, is associated with the oxytocin receptor gene (*OXTR*). Recent evidence shows that the rs2254298A allele of *OXTR* is significantly associated with larger bilateral amygdala, but not hippocampal, volume (Inoue et al., 2010). Monoamine oxidase A (MAOA) genotype has been associated with antisocial behavior across a number of studies (Taylor & Kim-Cohen, 2007). In addition, recent behavioral genetics further suggests evidence of a genetic basis for intergroup processes as well. For example, in a large-sample twin study, Lewis and Bates (2010) revealed that MZ twins displayed significantly more similar levels of intergroup bias relative to DZ twins, and both shared genes and environment contributed to this process. Hence, social cognition underlying both interpersonal and intergroup processes arises, at least in part, due to genes regulating brain regions underlying emotional and social processes.

CULTURAL BASIS OF SOCIAL COGNITION

Whereas emerging behavioral and neurogenetics work shows that social cognition is due at least in part to genetic factors, a plethora of cultural psychology (Chapter 22) and cultural neuroscience evidence (Chiao & Bebko, 2010; Han & Northoff, 2009) indicates that environmental factors, such as cultural values, practices, and beliefs, have a tremendous influence on a range of core skills underlying the human capacity to understand and think about other people.

Self and other knowledge

One of the most robust ways that values, such as individualism and collectivism, influence human behavior is in self-construal, or how people think about themselves in relation to others. Individualists think of themselves as autonomous from others, while collectivists think of themselves as highly interconnected with others (Markus & Kitayama, 1991; Triandis, 1995). Recent cultural neuroscience evidence indicates that the brain basis of the self is modulated by cultural values

of individualism and collectivism (Chiao et al., 2009; Han & Northoff, 2008). For instance, research has shown Caucasians, but not Chinese, showed greater neural activity within the MPFC during evaluation of personality traits of one's self relative to a close other (i.e., mother), suggesting cultural variation in MPFC response during self-evaluation (Zhu et al., 2007; see Figure 26.4). More recent evidence has demonstrated that cultural values (i.e., individualism–collectivism), rather than cultural affiliation (i.e., East Asian–Westerners) per se, modulate neural response during self-evaluation. In another cross-cultural neuroimaging study, people in both Japan and the United States who endorsed individualistic values showed greater MPFC activity for general relative to contextual self-descriptions, whereas people who endorsed collectivistic values demonstrated greater MPFC activation for contextual relative to general self-descriptions (Chiao et al., 2009; see Figure 26.5). Supporting this view, another study using cultural priming (Hong et al., 2000) showed that even temporarily heightening awareness of individualistic and collectivistic values in bicultural individuals (i.e., bicultural Asian-Americans) modulates MPFC and posterior cingulate cortex (PCC) in a similar manner (Chiao et al., 2010; see Figure 26.6). In addition to cultural values modulating neural responses during explicit self-processing, a further neuroimaging study shows that dorsal, but not ventral, regions of MPFC are modulated by cultural priming of individualism and collectivism when thinking about one's self in an implicit manner (Harada, Li, & Chiao, 2010; see Figure 26.7). Such findings suggest that cultural values dynamically shape neural representations during the evaluation, rather than the detection, of self-relevant information. Taken together, these studies provide convergent evidence that environmental factors, such as cultural values of individualism–collectivism, shape the psychological and neural basis of the self.

In addition to cultural values of individualism–collectivism, religious beliefs may also play an important role in modulating neural responses underlying social cognition. One set of neuroimaging studies examining the neural substrates of religiosity found that activity within Theory of Mind (ToM) regions, including left precuneus, left temporoparietal junction, and left middle frontal gyrus, was correlated with the degree of one's religiosity (Kapogiannis et al., 2009). Additionally, religious practices, such as praying, also modulate neural responses within ToM regions. For instance, compared to formalized prayer and secular cognition, improvised praying activated the temporopolar region, medial prefrontal cortex, temporoparietal junction, and precuneus (Schjoedt et al., 2009). Finally, religious

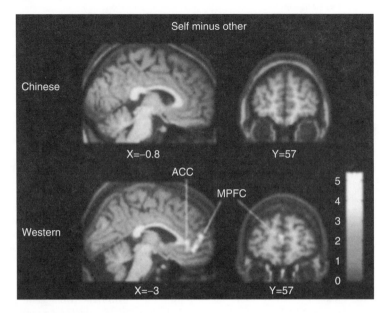

Figure 26.4   Cultural difference in medial prefrontal cortex (MPFC) during explicit self-judgments between Chinese and Westerners living in China (adapted from Zhu et al., 2007). ACC, anterior cingulate cortex.

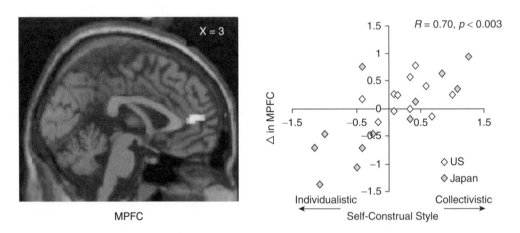

Figure 26.5   In both Japan and the United States, the degree of collectivistic or individualistic cultural values predicts neural response within medial prefrontal cortex (MPFC) to contextual or general self-judgments, respectively (adapted from Chiao et al., 2009).

beliefs affect neural representations of the self. Whereas atheists typically recruit ventral MPFC during self-evaluation, religious individuals show greater response within dorsal MPFC, suggesting that religious beliefs promote greater evaluation, rather than representation, of one's self (Han et al., 2008). Hence, the human ability to possess

religious beliefs and exercise religious practices relies on ToM and mentalizing brain regions that facilitate the representation and evaluation of own and others (e.g., human, God) mental states.

Although the lion's share of cultural neuroscience research on knowledge of self and others has been conducted with human neuroimaging

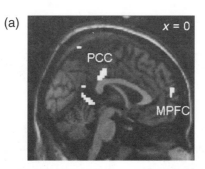

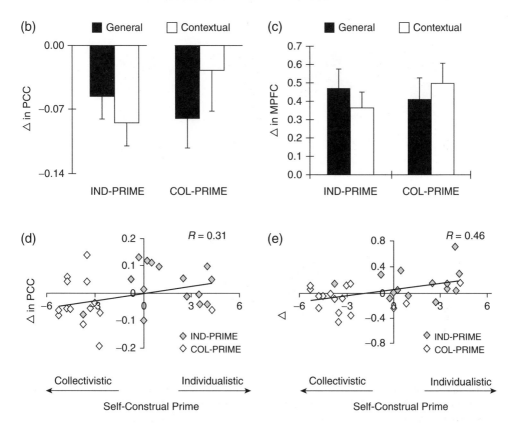

Figure 26.6   Dynamic cultural influences on neural response to self-judgments. (a–c) Bicultural individuals primed with collectivistic cultural values show greater medial prefrontal cortex (MPFC) and posterior cingulate cortex (PCC) response to explicit contextual self-judgments, whereas bicultural individuals primed with individualistic cultural values show greater MPFC and PCC response to explicit general self-judgments (adapted from Chiao et al., 2010). (d–e) Degree of cultural priming predicts neural response to culturally congruent self-judgments within both MPFC and PCC.

methodology, a couple of recent studies have examined the effect of culture on electrophysiological indices of social cognition. In one study, Lewis and colleagues (2008) measured event-related potentials (ERPs) while participants

completed the oddball task, where they are shown visual stimuli in either a frequent or infrequent (i.e., oddball stimulus) manner. Results demonstrated that European-American participants showed greater novelty P3, or late positive

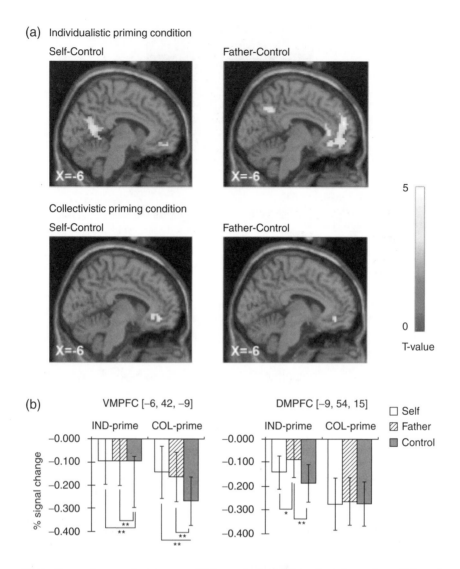

Figure 26.7   Dynamic neural response within ventral and dorsal regions of medial prefrontal cortex (VMPFC and DMPFC) during implicit self-judgments (Harada, Li, & Chiao, 2010). (a) Neural response during self-relevant and father-relevant trials compared to control trials for both individualistic and collectivistic priming conditions. (b) Mean parameter estimates within VMPFC and DMPFC during implicit self-judgments.

potential, amplitude for target events, whereas East Asians showed greater P3 amplitude for oddball events. Another study by Iishi and colleagues (2009) found that amplitude of the N400, a late negative potential, was significantly larger when individuals perceived incongruent relative to congruent information and the degree of late negativity activity was reliably predicted by chronic social orientation (e.g., interdependence) for females. Both electrophysiological studies demonstrate the effect of cultural values of individualism–collectivism on how people respond to information that is either congruent or incongruent to one another. Hence, cultural values of individualism–collectivism not only affect how people represent knowledge about self and others but also respond to congruent or incongruent informational cues in the environment.

Interpersonal perception

Minute perceptual cues from the body, such as the eye region of the face, can convey a wealth of information about what people are thinking and feeling. Recent neuroimaging evidence indicates cultural variation in neural responses when inferring the internal states of others, particularly from the eye region (Adams et al., 2010). Native Japanese and US Caucasian participants performed the "Reading the Mind in the Eyes" Test (RME), a measure of mental state decoding from visual stimuli only depicting an individual's eyes (Baron-Cohen, Wheelwright, Hill, Raste, & Plumb, 2001). In the study participants were more accurate at decoding the mental state of members of one's own culture relative to members of another culture, and activity within the posterior superior temporal sulcus (pSTS) increased during the same-culture mental state decoding relative to other-culture mental state decoding (see Figure 26.8). Additionally, the intracultural advantage was significantly negatively correlated with pSTS activity during other-culture mental state decoding such that as pSTS activity increased, the intracultural advantage decreased. This correlation was not significant for same-culture mental state decoding from the eyes, suggesting that the intracultural advantage may be due to less pSTS recruitment during other-culture mental state decoding. These findings support the universal recruitment of pSTS in ToM, while at the same time revealing culturally modulated pSTS recruitment underlying the intracultural advantage in ToM. Another recent study found that activity within the mesolimbic system responds more for culturally congruent dominant and submissive facial cues (Freeman et al., 2009). Individuals from egalitarian cultures, such as the United States, show greater mesolimbic response to dominant facial cues, whereas individuals from hierarchical cultures, such as Japan, show greater mesolimbic response to submissive facial cues. Taken together, these studies highlight how cultural variation in attribution styles may modulate neural activity underlying processes related to interpersonal perception.

Emotion recognition

Culture affects how people prefer to experience, express, recognize, and regulate their emotions (Mesquita & Leu, 2007). East Asians prefer to experience low-arousal relative to high-arousal positive emotions (Tsai, 2007) and are more likely to suppress their emotions relative to Westerners (Butler, Lee, & Gross, 2007). Additionally, both East Asians and Westerners demonstrate cultural specificity in emotion recognition, whereby they show greater recognition for emotions expressed by their own cultural group members relative to members of other cultural groups (Elfenbein & Ambady, 2002). Recent cultural neuroscience of emotion research has shown cultural specificity effects within a number of brain regions involved in emotion recognition. Moriguchi and colleagues (2005) found greater activation in the posterior cingulate, supplementary motor cortex, and amygdala in Caucasians, relative to Japanese, who showed greater activity within the right inferior frontal, premotor cortex, and left insula when participants were asked to explicit recognize emotions from the face. Chiao and colleagues (2008) examined neural responses in adults living in either the United States or Japan and found that across cultures people exhibit greater bilateral amygdala response to fear faces expressed by own-culture relative to other-culture members (Chiao et al., 2008, Figure 26.9). Another recent neuroimaging study comparing neural responses during emotion recognition in Asians and Europeans found a significant negative correlation between duration of stay and amygdala response, such that amygdala response during emotion recognition was higher in individuals who were recent immigrants to the region, suggesting that experience alters neural responses to emotional expressions (Derntl et al., 2009). Taken together, this research indicates that activity within the human amygdala is modulated by cultural group membership. An important question for future research will be to determine whether neural mechanisms that support other facets of emotion, such as experience and regulation, are affected by culture.

Empathy

Empathy is the capacity to share the emotional states of others (Batson, Duncan, Ackerman, Buckley, & Birch, 1981; Preston & de Waal, 2002). The perception–action model of empathy indicates that empathy is a key motivator (Decety & Grèzes, 2006) and the proximate mechanism (de Waal, 2008) of altruistic behavior, whereby an individual perceives and shares in the distress of another person, and acts to reduce his or her suffering (Preston & de Waal, 2002). Prior social neuroscience research indicates that empathy is a multi-component process that includes affect sharing, cognitive perspective taking, and cognitive appraisal (Decety & Jackson, 2004; Hein & Singer, 2008; Lamm, Batson, & Decety, 2007; Olsson & Ochsner, 2008). Empathy for pain is supported by neuroanatomical circuits underlying both affective and cognitive processes (Decety & Jackson, 2004; Hein & Singer, 2008; Lamm et al., 2007; Olsson & Ochsner, 2008). A distinct neural matrix, including bilateral anterior insula (AI) and anterior cingulate cortex (ACC) (Decety &

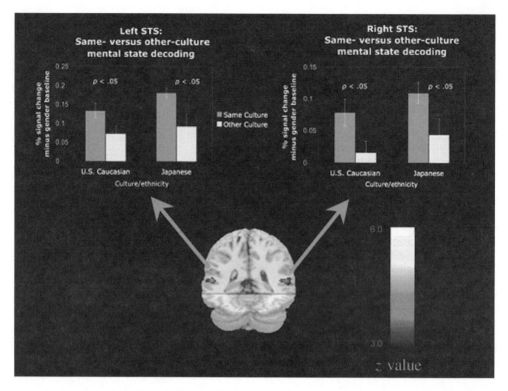

Figure 26.8 Graphs depict regions of left and right posterior superior temporal sulcus (pSTS) activation for same- versus other-culture mental state decoding (Adams et al., 2010). Neural response within STS is heightened for same- versus other-culture mental state decoding across both cultural groups.

Jackson, 2004; Hein & Singer, 2008; Olsson & Ochsner, 2008) is thought to underlie the affective components of empathy. AI and ACC code the autonomic and affective dimension of pain and, in particular, the subjective experience of empathy when perceiving pain or distress in others (Decety & Jackson, 2004; Hein & Singer, 2008; Olsson & Ochsner, 2008).

Recent evidence indicates that empathic neural response is modulated by culture. For instance, a recent neuroimaging study by Xu and colleagues (2009) examined whether or not cultural group membership modulates neural response during the perception of pain in others. Chinese and Caucasian participants were scanned while observing Chinese and Caucasian targets either in physically painful (e.g., needlestick) or neutral (e.g., Q-tip probe) scenes. All participants showed greater ACC and AI response to painful relative to neutral scenes; however, they also showed greater ACC response to in-group relative to out-group members (see Figure 26.10). Furthermore, recent transcranial magnetic stimulation (TMS) findings

by Avenanti and colleagues (2010) show that both Black and White participants showed greater muscle-specific corticospinal inhibition when watching a needle penetrate the hand, but only when the hand was a person of the same race, indicating an in-group bias in the activation of pain representations within the perceiver's sensorimotor system. Importantly, however, both groups of participants showed increased neural response to violet hands, highlights a pivotal role for culture in changing how and when humans share and respond to the suffering of same and other races (see Figure 26.11). Taken together, these findings demonstrate that cultural group membership affects neural responses to perceived physical pain of others and suggest a neural precursor to group selection in altruistic behavior (Wilson, 2006).

Theory of Mind

Another key social cognitive process is theory of mind (ToM), or the ability to understand and represent the psychological state of others (Wellman,

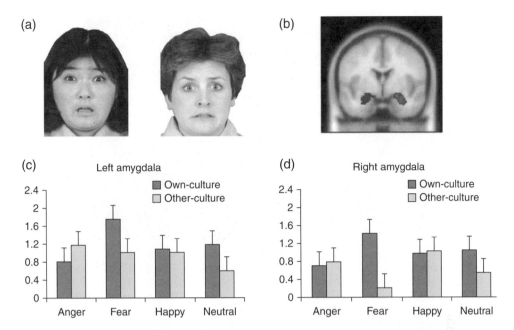

Figure 26.9   Cultural specificity in bilateral amygdala response to fear faces (adapted from Chiao et al., 2008). (a) Examples of Japanese and Caucasian-American fear faces. (b) Bilateral amygdala. (c, d) Participants show greater left (c) and right (d) amygdala response to fear expressed by members of one's own cultural group.

Cross, & Watson, 2001). Normally developing children demonstrate ToM starting at 4 years of age, while younger children and children with autism typically fail to demonstrate ToM (Baron-Cohen, Leslie, & Frith, 1985). Such developmental findings provide evidence for ToM as a universal developmental process (Fodor, 1983; Leslie, Friedman, & German, 2004; Scholl & Leslie, 1999) with an underlying biological basis (Frith & Frith, 2001; Scholl & Leslie, 1999). While some cross-cultural studies support the universality of ToM, other studies suggest ToM may be culturally and linguistically dependent (for review, see Kobayashi, Glover, & Temple, 2006). For example, variation in cultural attribution styles may influence ToM performance in Asian children (Naito, 2003) who are raised in a culture that attributes behavior to external and contextual causes rather than to internal causes, as in American–European cultures (Masuda & Nisbett, 2001; Nisbett, 2003). Similarly, speaking a non-English language with few mental state verbs may negatively influence children's performance on ToM tasks (Vinden, 1996).

Neuroimaging provides further evidence for both the universal (Saxe, 2006; Saxe & Kanwisher, 2003) and culturally specific influences on ToM

processes (Kobayashi, Glover, & Temple, 2006). A number of prior neuroimaging studies of ToM conducted on individuals from Western populations have found greater activity within the right temporoparietal junction (rTPJ), specifically when participants read stories about another person's thoughts (Saxe, 2006; Saxe & Kanwisher, 2003). Recently, Kobayashi and colleagues (2006) used functional magnetic resonance imaging (fMRI) to examine cultural and linguistic influences on neural activity underlying ToM in American English-speaking monolinguals and Japanese-English late bilinguals. Neural activity was recorded using fMRI while participants completed second-order false-belief ToM stories in both English and Japanese languages. Universally recruited brain regions associated with ToM processing included the right MPFC, right anterior cingulate cortex (ACC), right MFG/DLPFC (middle frontal gyrus/dorsal-lateral prefrontal cortex), and TPJ. In the American English-speaking monolinguals, culturally modulated neural activity underlying ToM was observed in the right insula, bilateral temporal poles, and right MPFC relative to the Japanese-English bilinguals, while the Japanese-English late bilinguals showed culturally modulated neural activity in the right

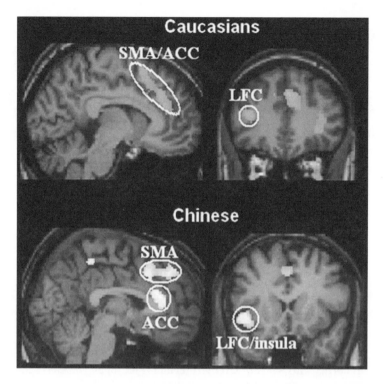

Figure 26.10 Increased activations in the anterior cingulate cortex (ACC) and the frontal/insula cortex when participants perceived racial in-group faces (Xu et al., 2009). LFC, lateral frontal cortex; SMA, supplementary motor area.

orbitofrontal gyrus (OFG) and right inferior frontal gyrus (IFG) associated with ToM processing relative to the American English-speaking monolinguals. Greater insular and TP activity in the American English-speaking monolinguals suggest that ToM in American culture emphasizes integrating sensory modalities with limbic input, whereas greater OFG and IFG activity in the Japanese-English late bilinguals suggest ToM in Japanese culture may rely more on emotional mentalizing. Taken together, these findings demonstrate universality and cultural diversity in neural mechanisms underlying theory of mind.

Intergroup perception

Recent evidence from social cognition and social neuroscience has demonstrated that diverse mechanisms are involved in the perception and processing of group membership, and, in particular, has highlighted the role of social context in modulating neural response to in-group and out-group targets. Early work on the social neuroscience of interracial perception demonstrated greater amygdala reactivity when viewing the faces of

out-group members relative to in-group members (Hart et al., 2000; Phelps et al., 2000), which reflected, in part, unconscious racial bias (Cunningham et al., 2004; Phelps et al., 2000; Richeson et al., 2003; Wheeler & Fiske, 2005).

Biases in intergroup perception and processing may be represented through other patterns of neural reactivity not directly related to evaluation or detection of threat. For instance, an individual with damage to the bilateral amygdala is still capable of exhibiting negative racial biases (Phelps, Cannistraci, & Cunningham, 2003), suggesting that other neural correlates may be involved. Though negative biases, evaluations, or stereotypes may be spontaneously activated, such automatic processes may be followed by controlled inhibitory processes (Devine, 1989; Shelton, 2003). Such regulatory activity may be reflected by responses in the ACC, which may detect inappropriate potential responses, and the dorsal-lateral prefrontal cortex (DLPFC), a region involved in inhibitory processes (Amodio et al., 2004; Cunningham et al., 2004). Supporting this view, Richeson and colleagues (2003) demonstrated that implicit racial bias was associated with increased reactivity within the ACC and

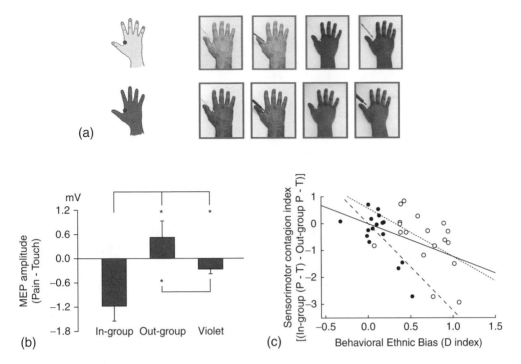

Figure 26.11   Empathic sensorimotor contagion as a function of race (Avenanti, Sirigu, & Aglioti, 2010; Chiao & Mathur, 2010). (a) Black and White participants observe a needle penetrating a specific muscle in a Black, White, or Violet hand. (b) For Black and White participants, motor-evoked potential (MEP) inhibition is greater for in-group relative to out-group hands. (c) Unconscious racial bias predicts degree of in-group bias in empathic sensorimotor contagion.

DLPFC when White participants viewed Black faces during neuroimaging. Moreover, the level of cognitive depletion experienced by White participants following face-to-face interracial interaction with a Black target corresponded to greater reactivity in the DLPFC when viewing Black faces during neuroimaging. These findings suggest that neural responses underlying intergroup bias are modulated by the degree of self-monitoring or regulation exerted by participants when processing in-group and out-group members.

Finally, intergroup processes may be reflected not only in the activation and suppression of potentially negative evaluations but also the withholding of activity in regions that may be involved in prosocial responding. One critical contribution from social neuroscience to social cognition has been the demonstration that cognitive processes recruit qualitatively different neural processes within social and non-social contexts. For example, the MPFC is typically recruited when one thinks about or infers the traits and characteristics of others, but less so when similar cognitions or

inferences are applied to understanding non-social phenomena (Amodio & Frith, 2006; Mitchell, Macrae, & Banaji, 2005). This "social" profile of cognitive activity may be attenuated when perceiving out-group relative to in-group members. For instance, when viewing highly stigmatized out-group members, participants show lower levels of MPFC response, suggesting stigmatized out-group members are processed in a de-individuated fashion more similar to aversive objects rather than people (Harris & Fiske, 2006, 2007).

GENE-BY-ENVIRONMENT INTERACTION IN SOCIAL COGNITION

Understanding how and when environmental factors such as culture shape social-cognitive brain function is a laudable and necessary stepping stone to the larger project of understanding how the interaction of genetic and environmental factors give rise to a range of social-cognitive abilities (Canli & Lesch, 2007; Caspi et al., 2010). Groundbreaking work by Suomi and colleagues, for instance, has revealed a gene-by-environment interaction in aggression levels of non-human primates (Suomi, 1994). Specifically, levels of high-risk aggression in male macaques carrying the S allele of the serotonin transporter gene (*SLC6A4*) were significantly higher if they were also exposed to early adversity in the form of peer rearing (Schwandt et al., 2010). Environmental influence on the expression of the serotonin transporter gene has similarly been found in humans. In an early seminal study, Caspi and colleagues (2003) found that humans carrying at least one S allele were significantly more likely to experience depressive episodes compared to those carrying the L allele, but only when exposed to major life stress, such as threat of loss of a significant other (see also Risch et al., 2009). This model of gene-by-environment interaction associated with the serotonin transporter gene has similarly been found at the neural level in humans. For instance, Canli and colleagues (2005) recently showed that life stress interacts with the effect of serotonin transporter genotype on both amygdala and hippocampal resting activation in humans. Taken together, these studies indicate the importance of understanding how environmental factors interact with genes in the production of socio-emotional behavior, and their underlying neural bases.

Intriguingly, recent research has begun to demonstrate culture–gene interaction in production and maintenance of complex behavior. In one recent study, Kim and colleagues (2010) found an interaction between the 5-HTR1A genotype and culture, such that Koreans were more likely to attend to the field compared to European-Americans, and this cultural difference in locus of attention was moderated by the serotonin 1A receptor polymorphism (5-HTR1A). Specifically, European-Americans carriers of the G allele recently showed increased attention to focal objects, whereas Korean carriers of the G allele showed increased attention to the context. In another recent study, Kim and colleagues (2010) found that distressed American carriers of the GG/AG genotype of the oxytocin receptor polymorphism (*OXTR*) rs53576 reported seeking more emotional social support, compared with those with the AA genotype, whereas Korean participants did not differ significantly by genotype. By contrast, *OXTR* groups did not differ significantly in either cultural group when not in distress. Taken together, these findings illustrate specific functional polymorphisms that are sensitive to input from the social environment – specifically cultural norms – in both basic visual perception and emotional support seeking.

FUTURE DIRECTIONS IN GENE-BY-ENVIRONMENT INTERACTION IN SOCIAL COGNITION

How and why does social cognition emerge from gene-by-environment and culture–gene interaction? One possible theory, alluded to at the beginning of this chapter, is that culture–gene coevolutionary forces have shaped the social-cognitive brain (Boyd & Richerson, 1985). By this view, environmental pressures, such as the presence of infectious diseases (Fincher et al., 2006), made it important throughout human history to have the cultural capacity to infer the mental states of conspecifics and having this trait was adaptive and selected for across successive generations, giving human and non-human primates the ability to coexist with each other and coordinate tasks essential to group survival. Genes would then enable the refinement of cognitive and neural architecture underlying social cognitive capacities across successive generations. Finally, any geographic variation of environmental pressures driving social cognition would then lead to cultural variation in the psychological and biological mechanisms underlying how to understand each other's thoughts, intentions, and feelings (see Chapter 22). An important puzzle for future research is to understand how culture–gene coevolution may have shaped mechanisms in the social mind and brain differently across cultural contexts, due to diversity of selection pressures across geographical regions.

Supporting this view, recent cross-national culture–gene association studies have identified specific cultural and genetic factors associated with social cognition. Chiao and Blizinsky (2010) found that cultural values of individualism and collectivism are associated with the serotonin transporter across nations (see Figure 26.12). Collectivistic cultures were significantly more likely to be composed of individuals carrying the S allele of the 5-HTTLPR across 29 nations. Furthermore, across nations, global pathogen prevalence was positively associated with collectivistic social norms, due, at least in part, to selection of the S allele of the serotonin transporter gene. Way and Lieberman (2010) have similarly found that additional genes important to social cognition and social sensitivity, such as *MAOA -uVNTR* and opioid (*OPRM1 A118G*) receptor genes, vary cross-nationally and appear to confer similar adaptive benefits, such as reduced prevalence of mood disorders.

Importantly, recent cross-cultural behavioral genetics studies have similarly revealed the importance of genetic and cultural factors underlying social cognition. Recent cross-cultural behavioral

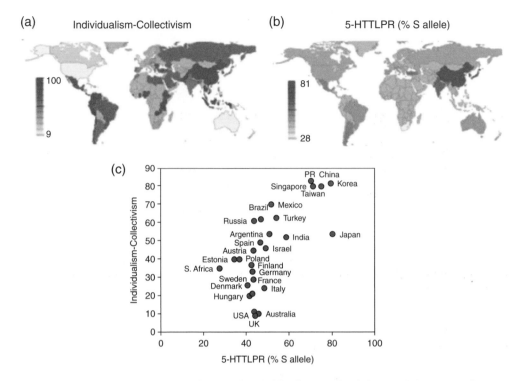

Figure 26.12   Culture–gene coevolution of individualism–collectivism and the serotonin transporter gene (5-HTTLPR) (Chiao & Blizinsky, 2010). (a) Color map of frequency distribution of IND-COL from Hofstede (2001). (b) Color map of frequency distribution of S alleles of 5-HTTLPR. (c) Collectivistic nations showed higher prevalence of S allele carriers.

genetics work further suggests that the G allele is associated with different behavioral phenotypes, depending on culture and environment (Kim et al., 2010, see Figure 26.13). The oxcytocin receptor polymorphism (*OXTR*) contains a polymorphism in the third intron of *OXTR* that has two known allelic variants, the G allele and the A allele. In Western populations, people carrying the G allele of *OXTR*, relative to those with the A allele, show increased maternal sensitivity (Bakermans-Kranenburg & van Ijzendoorg, 2008), empathy (Rodrigues et al., 2009), and positive emotion (Lucht et al., 2009). Distressed Americans who carry the G allele are more likely to seek emotional support relative to those who carry the A allele, whereas equally distressed Koreans who carry the G allele do not (Kim et al., 2010). Given the allelic frequency variation of the *OXTR* polymorphism, it is possible that carrying the A rather than the G allele in East Asian cultures is advantageous and thus is selected for disproportionately within the geographic region and confers differential functional utility across cultures, which is observable in brain and behavior.

Despite some early clues regarding the nature and origin of social cognition, many questions remain. For instance, what kinds of evolutionary selection pressures have led to diversity in cultural and genetic factors underlying social cognition? How might the human brain construct and constrain a diversity of social cognitive styles across cultures? Future work adopting a cultural neuroscience approach to social cognition may be helpful for illuminating these questions (Chiao & Bebko, 2010; Han & Northoff, 2009).

IMPLICATIONS OF GENE-BY-ENVIRONMENT INTERACTION MODELS OF SOCIAL COGNITION

Theory

To date, theories of social cognition have focused primarily on the role of environmental factors, such as the situation and culture, and how they

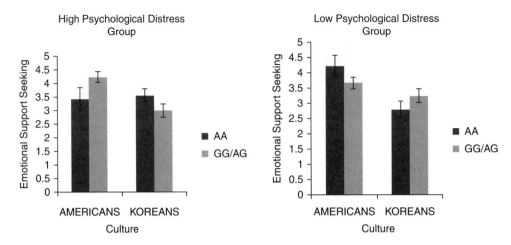

Figure 26.13   Gene-by-culture interaction and emotional support seeking as a function of level of psychological distress (adapted from Kim et al., 2010). Allelic variants, the G and A alleles (see text).

contribute to the extent to which people infer the mental states of others. However, less well understood is how both genetic and environmental factors affect mental-state inference and social behavior across cultures. Given that frequency of allelic variation in genes associated with social cognition, such as the serotonin transporter gene and oxcytocin receptor polymorphism, varies across geographic regions and is known to interact with environmental factors, such culture, an important direction for future research in social cognition is to examine how both genetic and environmental factors contribute to social cognition across cultures.

Application

Disruptions in social cognition, including autism, Williams syndrome, prosopagnosia, social phobia, and schizophrenia, underlie some of the most complex and challenging mental health disorders around the globe. While these mental health disorders may simply reflect naturally occurring individual variation in social cognition that may even confer adaptive benefits to the population as a whole, individuals with autism or Williams syndrome often suffer detriments to the quality of their social life and will seek treatment as a means of reducing the emotional burden of living with the disorder. However, the cost of treating mental health disorders is often exorbitant for individuals and institutions alike. Ganz (2006) estimates that caring for an autistic person alone can cost about $3.2 million over his or her lifetime and that caring for all people with autism over their

lifetimes costs an estimated $35 billion per year within the United States. Similar to other kinds of complex atypical behavior, such as mood disorders, the source and nature of these social-cognitive disorders likely results from complex interactions between genetic and environmental factors. Developing a more precise model of gene-by-environment interaction in social cognition may enable us to discover how to effectively treat such complex health disorders as well as create a richer basic science understanding of how social-cognitive mechanisms in the mind and brain give rise to the fundamental human capacity for social living.

REFERENCES

Adams, R. B., Rule, N. O., Franklin, R. G., Wang, E., Stevenson, M. T., Yoshikawa, S., et al. (2010). Cross-cultural reading the mind in the eyes: An fMRI investigation. *Journal of Cognitive Neuroscience, 22*(1), 97–108.

Adolphs, R., Tranel, D., Damasio, H., & Damasio, A.R. (1995). Fear and the human amygdala. *Journal of Neuroscience, 15*, 5879–5891.

Amodio, D. M., & Frith, C. D. (2006). Meeting of minds: The media frontal cortex and social cognition. *Nature Reviews Neuroscience, 7*, 268–277.

Amodio, D. M., Harmon-Jones, E., Devine, P. G., Curtin, J. J., Hartley, S. L., & Covert, A. E. (2004). Neural signals for the detection of unintentional race bias. *Psychological Science, 15*, 88–93.

Apkarian, V. A., Baliki, M. N., & Geha, P. Y. (2009). Towards a theory of chronic pain. *Progress in Neurobiology.*

Avenanti, A., Sirigu, A., & Aglioti S. M. (2010). Racial bias reduces empathic sensorimotor resonance with other-race pain. *Current Biology, 20*(11), 1018–1022.

Bakermans-Kranenburg, M. J., & van Ijzendoorn, M. H. (2008). Oxytocin receptor (OXTR) and serotonin transporter (5-HTT) genes associated with observed parenting. *Social Cognitive and Affective Neuroscience, 3*(2), 128–134.

Baron-Cohen, S., Leslie, A. M., & Frith, U. (1985). Does the autistic child have a "theory of mind"? *Cognition, 21,* 37–46.

Baron-Cohen, S., Wheelwright, S., Hill, J., Raste, Y., & Plumb, I. (2001). The 'Reading the Mind in the Eyes' Test revised version: A study with normal adults, and adults with Asperger syndrome or high-functioning autism. *Journal of Child Psychiatry and Psychiatry, 42,* 241–252.

Batson, C. D., Duncan, B. D., Ackerman, P., Buckley, T., & Birch, K. (1981). Is empathic emotion a source of altruistic motivation? *Journal of Personality and Social Psychology 40,* 290–302.

Baumgartner, T., Heinrichs, M., Vonlanthen, A., Fishbacher, U., & Fehr, E. (2008). Oxytocin shapes the neural circuitry of trust and trust adaptation in humans. *Neuron, 58*(4), 639–650.

Belin, P., & Grosbras, M-H. (2010). Before speech: Cerebral voice processing in infants. *Neuron, 65*(6), 733–735.

Belin, P., Zatorre, R.J., Lafaille, P., Ahad, P., & Pike, B. (2000). Voice-selective areas in human auditory cortex. *Nature, 403*(6767), 309–312.

Blasi, G., Mattay, V. S., Bertolino, A., Elvevåg, B., Callicott, J. H., Das, S., et al. (2005). Effect of catechol-*O*-methyltransferase *val158met* genotype on attentional control. *Journal of Neuroscience, 25*(20), 5038–5045.

Boyd, R., & Richerson, P. J. (1985). *Culture and the evolutionary process.* Chicago, IL: University of Chicago Press.

Brothers, L. (2001). *Friday's footprint: How society shapes the human mind.* New York: Oxford University Press.

Butler, E. A., Lee, T. L., & Gross, J. J. (2007). Emotion regulation and culture: Are the social consequences of emotion suppression culture-specific? *Emotion, 7,* 30–48.

Canli, T., & Lesch, K. P. (2007). Long story short: The serotonin transporter in emotion regulation and social cognition. *Nature Neuroscience, 10,* 1103–1109.

Canli, T., Omura, K., Haas, B. W., Fallgatter, A., & Constable, R. T. (2005). Beyond affect: A role for genetic variation of the serotonin transporter in neural activation during a cognitive attention task. *Proceedings of the National Academy of Sciences USA* 102(34): 12224–12229.

Caspi, A., Hariri, A. R., Holmes, A., Uher, R., & Moffitt, T. E. (2010). Genetic sensitivity to the environment: The case of the serotonin transporter gene and its implications for studying complex diseases and traits, *American Journal of Psychiatry, 167*(5), 509–527.

Caspi, A., & Moffitt, T. (2006). Gene–environment interactions in psychiatry: Joining forces with neuroscience. *Nature Reviews Neuroscience 7,* 583–590.

Caspi, A., Sugden, K., Moffitt, T. E., Taylor, A., Craig, I. W., Harrington, H., et al. (2003). Influence of life stress on depression: Moderation by a polymorphism in the 5-HTT gene. *Science, 301*(5631), 386–389.

Chiao, J. Y. (2009). Cultural neuroscience: A once and future discipline. *Progress in Brain Research, 178,* 287–304.

Chiao, J. Y. (2011). Cultural neuroscience: Visualizing culture–gene influences on brain function. In J. Decety & J. Cacioppo (Eds.), *Handbook of social neuroscience,* Oxford, UK: Oxford University Press.

Chiao, J. Y., & Ambady, N. (2007). Cultural neuroscience: Parsing universality and diversity across levels of analysis. In S. Kitayama, & D. Cohen (Eds.), *Handbook of cultural psychology* (pp. 237–254). NewYork: Guilford Press.

Chiao, J. Y., & Bebko, G. M. (2011). Cultural neuroscience of social cognition. In S. Han & E. Poeppel (Eds.), *Culture and identity: Neural frames of social cognition.* New York: Springer Press.

Chiao, J. Y., & Blizinsky, K.D. (2010). Culture–gene coevolution of individualism–collectivism and the serotonin transporter gene (5-HTTLPR). *Proceedings of the Royal Society B: Biological Sciences, 277*(1681), 529–537.

Chiao, J. Y., Harada, T., Komeda, H., Li, Z., Mano, Y., Saito, D. N., et al. (2009). Neural basis of individualistic and collectivistic views of self. *Human Brain Mapping, 30*(9), 2813–2820.

Chiao, J. Y., Hariri, A. R., Harada, T., Mano, Y., Sadato, N., Parrish, T. B., et al. (2010). Theory and methods in cultural neuroscience. *Social Cognitive and Affective Neuroscience, 5*(2–3), 356–361.

Chiao, J. Y., Iidaka, T., Gordon, H. L., Nogawa, J., Bar, M., Aminoff, E., et al. (2008). Cultural specificity in amygdala response to fear faces. *Journal of Cognitive Neuroscience, 20*(12), 2167–2174.

Constantino, J. N., & Todd, R. D. (2000). Genetic structure of reciprocal social behavior. *American Journal of Psychiatry, 157,* 2043–2045.

Cunningham, W. A., Johnson, M. K., Ravel, C. L., Gatenby, J. C., Gore, J. C., & Banaji, M. R. (2004). Separable neural components in the processing of Black and White faces. *Psychological Science, 15*(12), 806–813.

Cunningham, W. A., & Zelazo, P. D. (2007). Attitudes and evaluations: A social cognitive neuroscience perspective. *Trends in Cognitive Science, 11*(3), 97–104.

Decety, J., & Grèzes, J. (2006). The power of simulation: Imagining one's own and other's behavior. *Brain Research, 1079,* 4–14.

Decety, J., & Jackson, P.L. (2004). The functional architecture of human empathy. *Behavioral and Cognitive Neuroscience Reviews, 3,* 71–100.

De Dreu, C. K. W., Greer, L. L., Handgraaf, M. J. J., Shalvi, S., Van Kleef, G. A., Baas, M., et al. (2010). The neuropeptide oxytocin regulates parochial altruism in intergroup conflict among humans. *Science, 328,* 1408–1411.

De Dreu, C. K. W., Greer, L. L., Van Kleef, G. A., Shalvi, S., & Handgraaf. M. J. J. (2011). Oxcytocin promotes human ethnocentrism. *Proceedings of the National Academy of Sciences, 108*(4), 1262–1266.

Dertnl, B., Habel, U., Robinson, S., Windischberger, C., Kryspin-Exner, I., Gur, R. C., et al. (2009). Amygdala activation during recognition of emotions in a foreign ethnic group is associated with duration of stay. *Social Neuroscience, 4*(4), 294–307.

Devine, P. G. (1989). Stereotypes and prejudice: Their automatic and controlled components. *Journal of Personality and Social Psychology, 56*(1), 5–18.

de Waal, F. B. M. (2008). Putting the altruism back into altruism: The evolution of empathy. *Annual Review of Psychology, 59*, 279–300.

Dunbar, R. I. M. (1998). The social brain hypothesis. *Evolutionary Anthropology, 6*(5), 178–190.

Dunbar, R. I. M., & Shultz, S. (2007). Evolution in the social brain. *Science 317*, 1344–1347.

Ebstein, R. P., Israel, S., Chew, S. H., Zhong, S., & Knafo, A. (2010). Genetics of human social behavior. *Neuron, 65*(6), 831–844.

Eisenberger, N. I. (2010). The neural basis of social pain: Findings and implications. In G. MacDonald & L. A. Jensen-Campbell (Eds.), *Social pain: Neuropsychological and health implications of loss and exclusion* (pp. 53–78). Washington, DC: American Psychological Association.

Elfenbein, H. A., & Ambady, N. (2002). Is there an in-group advantage in emotion recognition? *Psychological Bulletin, 128*, 243–249.

Fincher, C. L., Thornhill, R., Murray, D. R., & Schaller, M. (2008). Pathogen prevalence predicts human cross-cultural variability in individualism/collectivism. *Proceedings of the Royal Society B, 275*, 1279–1285.

Fodor, J. A. (1983). *The modularity of mind.* Cambridge, MA: MIT Press.

Freeman, J. B., Rule, N. O., Adams, R. B., Jr., & Ambady, N. (2009). Culture shapes mesolimbic response to signals of dominance and subordination that associates with behavior. *NeuroImage, 47*, 353–359.

Frith, U., & Frith, C. (2001). The biological basis of social interaction. *Current Directions in Psychological Science, 10*, 151–155.

Ganz, M. L. (2006). The lifetime distribution of the incremental societal costs of autism. *Archive of Pediatric Adolescent Medicine, 161*(4), 343–349.

Gazzaniga, M. S., Ivry, R., & Mangun, G. R. (2002). *Cognitive neuroscience: The biology of the mind.* New York: W. W. Norton.

Green, A. E., Munafo, M. R., DeYoung, C. G., Fossella, J. A., Fan, J., & Gray, J. R. (2008). Using genetic data in cognitive neuroscience: From growing pains to genuine insights. *Nature Reviews Neuroscience, 9*, 710–720.

Han, S., Mao, L., Gu, X., Zhu, Y., Ge, J., & Ma, Y. (2008). Neural consequences of religious belief on self-referential processing. *Social Neuroscience, 3*, 1–15.

Han, S., & Northoff, G. (2008). Culture-sensitive neural substrates of human cognition: A transcultural neuroimaging approach. *Nature Review Neuroscience, 9*, 646–654.

Harada, T., Li, Z., & Chiao, J. Y. (2010). Differential dorsal and ventral medial prefrontal representations of the implicit self modulated by individualism and collectivism: An fMRI study. *Social Neuroscience, 22*, 1–15.

Hariri, A. R., Drabant, E. M., & Weinberger, D. R. (2006). Imaging genetics: Perspectives from studies of genetically driven variation in serotonin function and corticolimbic affective processing. *Biological Psychiatry, 59*(10), 888–897.

Hariri A. R., Mattay V. S., Tessitore A., Kolachana B. S., Fera F., Goldman D., et al. (2002). Serotonin transporter genetic variation and the response of the human amygdala. *Science, 297*, 400–403.

Harris, L. T., & Fiske, S. T. (2006). Dehumanizing the lowest of the low: Neuroimaging responses to extreme out-groups. *Psychological Science, 17*(10), 847–853.

Hart, A. J., Whalen, P. J., Shin. L. M., McInerney, S. C., Fischer, H., & Rauch S. L. (2000). Differential response in the human amygdala to racial outgroup vs ingroup face stimuli. *Neuroreport, 11*(113), 2351–2355.

Hein, G., & Singer, T. (2008). I feel how you feel but not always: The empathic brain and its modulation. *Current Opinion in Neurobiology, 18*, 153–158.

Hoehl, S., & Striano, T. (2010). The development of emotional face and eye gaze processing. *Developmental Science, 13*(6), 813–825.

Hong, Y., Morris, M. W., Chiu, C., & Benet-Martinez, V. (2000). Multicultural minds: A dynamic constructivist approach to culture and cognition. *American Psychologist, 55*, 709–720.

Iishi, K., Kobayashi, Y., & Kitayama, S., (2010). Interdependence modulates the brain response to word–voice incongruity. *Social Cognitive and Affective Neuroscience, 5*(2–3), 307–317.

Inoue, H., Yamasue, H., Tochigi, M., Abe, O., Liu, X., Kawamura, Y., et al. (2010). Association between the oxytocin receptor gene and amygdalar volume in healthy adults. *Biological Psychiatry, 68*(11), 1066–1072.

Israel, S., Lerer, E., Shalev, I., Uzefovsky, F., Riebold, M., Laiba, E., et al. (2009). The oxytocin receptor (OXTR) contributes to prosocial fund allocations in the dictator game and the social value orientations task. *PLoS ONE, 4*, e5535.

Johnson, M. H. (1997). *Developmental cognitive neuroscience: An introduction.* Oxford, UK: Blackwell.

Kanwisher, N., McDermott, J., & Chun, M. (1997) The fusiform face area: A module in human extrastriate cortex specialized for the perception of faces. *Journal of Neuroscience, 17*, 4302–4311.

Kapogiannis, D., Barbey, A. K., Su, M., Zamboni, G., Krueger, F., & Grafman, J. (2009). Cognitive and neural foundations of religious belief. *Proceedings of the National Academy of Sciences, 106*(12), 4876–4881.

Kim, H. S, Sherman, D. K., Sasaki, J. Y., Xu, J., Chu, T. Q., Ryu, C., et al. (2010). Culture, distress, and oxytocin receptor polymorphism (OXTR) interact to influence emotional support seeking. *Proceedings of the National Academy of Sciences, 107*(36), 15717–15721.

Kitayama, S., & Cohen, D. (2007). *Handbook of cultural psychology.* New York: Guilford Press.

Kobayashi, C., Glover, G., & Temple, E. (2006). Cultural and linguistic influence on neural bases of 'Theory of Mind': An fMRI study with Japanese bilinguals. *Brain and Language, 98*, 210–220.

Kosfeld, M., Heinrichs, M., Zak, P. J., Fischbacher, U., & Fehr, E. (2005). Oxytocin increases trust in humans. *Nature, 435*, 673–676.

Lamm, C., Batson, C.D., & Decety, J. (2007). The neural substrate of human empathy: Effects of perspective-taking and cognitive appraisal. *Journal of Cognitive Neuroscience, 19*, 42–58.

Lamm, C., Decety, J., & Singer, T. (2011). Meta-analytic evidence for common and distinct neural networks associated with directly experienced pain and empathy for pain. *Neuroimage, 54*, 2492–2502.

Leslie, A. M., Friedman, O., & German, T. P. (2004). Core mechanisms in theory of mind. *Trends in Cognitive Sciences, 8*(12), 528–533.

Lewis, G. J., & Bates, T. C. (2010). Genetic evidence for multiple biological mechanisms underlying in-group favoritism. *Psychological Science, 21*(11), 1623–1628.

Lewis, R. S., Goto, S. G., & Kong, L. L. (2008). Culture and context: East Asian American and European American differences in P3 event-related potentials and self-construal. *Personality and Social Psychology Bulletin, 34*(5), 623–634.

Li, S. C. (2003). Biocultural orchestration of developmental plasticity across levels: The interplay of biology and culture in shaping the mind and behavior across the life span. *Psychological Bulletin, 129*(2), 171–194.

Lieberman, M. D. (2010). Social cognitive neuroscience. In S. T. Fiske, D. T. Gilbert, & G. Lindzey (Eds), *Handbook of social psychology* (5th ed., pp. 143–193). New York: McGraw-Hill.

Lucht, M. J., Barnow, S., Sonnenfeld, C., Rosenberger, A., Grabe, H. J., Schroeder, W., et al. (2009). Associations between the oxytocin receptor gene (OXTR) and affect, loneliness and intelligence in normal subjects. *Progress in the Neuropsychopharmacology and Biological Psychiatry, 33*(5), 860–866.

Markus, H. R., & Kitayama, S. (1991). Culture and the self: Implications for cognition, emotion and motivation. *Psychological Review, 98*, 224–253.

Masuda, T., & Nisbett, R. E. (2001). Attending holistically vs. analytically: Comparing the context sensitivity of Japanese and Americans. *Journal of Personality and Social Psychology, 81*, 922–934.

Mathur, V. A., Harda, T., Lipke, T., & Chiao, J. Y. (2010). Neural basis of extraordinary empathy and altruistic motivation. *Neuroimage, 51*(4), 1468–1475.

Mesquita, B., & Leu, J. (2007). The cultural psychology of emotion. In S. Kitayama & D. Cohen (Eds.), *Handbook for cultural psychology*. New York: Guilford Press.

Mitchell, J. P. (2009). Inferences about mental states. *Philosophical Transactions of the Royal Society London B: Biological Sciences, 364*(1521), 1309–1316.

Mitchell, J. P., Banaji, M. R., & Macrae, C. N. (2005). General and specific contributions of the medial prefrontal cortex to knowledge about mental states. *Neuroimage, 28*, 757–762.

Moriguchi, Y., Ohnishi, T., Kawachi, T., Mori, T., Hirakata, M., Yamada, M., et al. (2005). Specific brain activation in Japanese and Caucasian people to fearful faces. *Neuroreport, 16*(2), 133–136.

Munafò, M. R., Brown, S. M., & Hariri, A. R. (2008). Serotonin transporter (5HTTLPR) genotype and amygdala activation: A meta-analysis. *Biological Psychiatry, 63*(9), 852–857.

Naito, M. (2003). The relationship between theory of mind and episodic memory: Evidence for the development of autonoetic consciousness. *Journal of Experimental Child Psychology, 85*, 312–336.

Nisbett, R. E. (2003). *The geography of thought*. New York: The Free Press.

Ochsner, K. N., & Lieberman, M. D. (2001). The emergence of social cognitive neuroscience. *American Psychologist, 56*, 717–734.

Olsson, A., & Ochsner, K. N. (2008). The role of social cognition in emotion. *Trends in Cognitive Sciences, 12*(2), 65–71.

Pessoa, L., & Adolphs, R. (2010). Emotion processing and the amygdala: From a 'low road' to 'many roads' of evaluating biological significance. *Nature Reviews Neuroscience, 11*(11), 773–783.

Phelps, E. A., Cannistraci, C. J., & Cunningham, W. A. (2003). Intact performance on an indirect measure of race bias following amygdala damage. *Neuropsychologia, 41*(2), 203–208.

Phelps, E. A., O'Connor, K. J., Cunningham, W. A., Funayama, E. S., Gatenby, J. C., Gore, J. C., et al. (2000). Performance on indirect measures of race evaluation predicts amygdala activation. *Journal of Cognitive Neuroscience, 12*(5), 729–738.

Preston, S. D., & de Waal, F. B. M. (2002). Empathy: Its ultimate and proximate bases. *Behavioral and Brain Sciences, 25*(1), 1–71.

Quirk, G. J., & Beer, J. S. (2006). Prefrontal involvement in the regulation of emotion: Convergence of rat and human studies. *Current Opinion in Neurobiology, 16*, 723–727.

Richeson, J. A., Baird, A. A., Gordon, H. L., Heatherton, T. F, Wyland, C. L., Trawalter, S., et al. (2003). An fMRI examination of the impact of interracial contact on executive function. *Nature Neuroscience, 6*, 1323–1328.

Rilling, J. K., Winslow, J. T., & Kilts, C. D. (2004). The neural correlates of mate competition in dominant male rhesus macaques. *Biological Psychiatry, 56*(5), 364–375.

Risch, N., Herrell, R., Lehner, T., Liang, K-Y., Eaves, L., Hoh, J., et al. (2009). Interaction between the serotonin transporter gene (5-HTTLPR), stressful life events, and risk of depression. *Journal of the American Medical Association, 301*(23), 2462–2471.

Rodrigues, S. M., Saslow, L. R., Garcia, N., John, O. P., & Keltner, D. (2009). Oxytocin receptor genetic variation relates to empathy and stress reactivity in humans. *Proceedings of the National Academy of Sciences USA, 106*(50), 21437–21441.

Saxe, R. (2006). Why and how to study theory of mind with fMRI. *Brain Research, 1079*(1), 57–65.

Saxe, R., & Kanwisher, N. (2003). People thinking about thinking people – fMRI studies of theory of mind. *Neuroimage, 19*(4), 1835–1842.

Schjoedt, U., Stodkilde-Jorgensen, H., Geertz, A.W., & Roepstorff, A. (2009). Highly religious participants recruit areas of social cognition in personal prayer. *Social Cognitive and Affective Neuroscience, 4*(2), 199–207.

Scholl, B. J., & Leslie, A. M. (1999). Modularity, development and 'theory of mind'. *Mind and Language, 14,* 131–153.

Schwandt, M. L., Lindell, S. G., Sjöberg, R. L., Chisholm, K. L., Higley, J. D., Suomi, S. J., et al. (2010). Gene–environment interactions and response to social intrusion in male and female rhesus macaques. *Biological Psychiatry, 67*(4), 323–330.

Shelton, J. N. (2003). Interpersonal concerns in social encounters between majority and minority group members. *Group Processes & Intergroup Relations, 6*(2), 171–185.

Singer, T., Seymour, B., O'Doherty, J. P., Stephan, K. E., Dolan, R. J., & Frith, C. D. (2006). Empathic neural responses are modulated by the perceived fairness of others. *Nature, 439,* 466–469.

Suomi. S. J. (1994). Risk, resilience and gene × environment interactions in rhesus monkeys. *Annals of the New York Academy of Sciences,* 52–62.

Tan, H., Chen, Q., Goldberg, T. E., Mattay, V. S., Meyer-Lindenberg, A., Weinberger, D. R., et al. (2007). Catechol-*O*-methyltransferase Val158Met modulation of prefrontal–parietal–striatal brain systems during arithmetic and temporal transformations in working memory. *Journal of Neuroscience, 27,* 13393–13401.

Taylor, A., & Kim-Cohen, J. (2007). Meta-analysis of gene–environment interactions in developmental psychopathology. *Development and Psychopathology, 19,* 1029–1037.

Taylor, S. E., Klein, L. C., Lewis, B. P., Gruenewald, T. L., Gurung, R. A., & Updegraff, J. A. (2000). Biobehavioral responses to stress in females: Tend-and-befriend, not fight-or-flight. *Psychological Review, 107,* 411–429.

Triandis, H. C. (1995). *Individualism and collectivism.* Boulder, CO: Westview.

Tsai, J. L. (2007). Ideal affect: Cultural causes and behavioral consequences. *Perspectives on Psychological Science, 2,* 242–259.

Vinden, P. (1996). Junin Quechua children's understanding of mind. *Child Development, 67,* 1707–1716.

Way, B. M., & Lieberman, M. D. (2010). Is there a genetic contribution to cultural differences? Collectivism, individualism and genetic markers of social sensitivity. *Social Cognitive & Affective Neuroscience, 5*(2–3), 203–211.

Wellman, H. M., Cross, D., & Watson, J. (2001). A meta-analysis of theory of mind development: The truth about false belief. *Child Development, 72,* 655–684.

Wheeler, M. E., & Fiske, S. T. (2005). Social-cognitive goals affect amygdala and stereotype activation. *Psychological Science, 16*(1), 56–63.

Wilson, D. S. (2006). Human groups as adaptive units: Toward a permanent consensus. In P. Carruthers, S. Laurence, & S. Stich (Eds.), *The innate mind: Culture and cognition.* Oxford, UK: Oxford University Press.

Xu, X., Zuo, X., Wang, X., & Han, S. (2009). Do you feel my pain? Racial group membership modulates empathic neural responses. *Journal of Neuroscience, 29,* 8525–8529.

Zhu, Y., Zhang, Li., Fan, J., & Han. S. (2007). Neural basis of cultural influence on self representation. *Neuroimage, 34,* 1310–1317.

27

"One Word: Plasticity" – Social Cognition's Futures

Susan T. Fiske

Social cognition is thriving, and not only in this *Sage Handbook*. We are everywhere, popular now for fascinating factoids, thanks to our friends in science journalism (e.g., Brooks, 2005, 2011; Gladwell, 2000, 2005, 2008), as well as our talented peers who write for lay audiences (e.g., Feldman, 2009; Gilbert, 2006; Taylor, 1989). We twitter, we blog, we YouTube, and future media will doubtless go on loving us. We are simply too much fun to ignore. But our nuggets are nowhere without the science. We are not only fun but also too important to ignore, now and in the future. Social cognition research matters because it focuses on how people make sense of themselves and others. Social cognition is an everyday miracle: thinking for doing (Fiske, 1992, paraphrasing James, 1890). Social cognition homes in on that sweet spot, the center of people's lives, because we are about what matters to people. And, like people's sociality, we as a field are adaptive and pragmatic. If nothing else, our functional value guarantees our future as a field. In other words, people survive and thrive through social cognition, so our field has a bright future.

What is that future? In one word: plasticity. This is both a popular and a scientific reference. In the 1967 film *The Graduate*, a just-minted BA, Benjamin Braddock, played by Dustin Hoffman, during the party in his honor, is led outside by a family friend, Mr McGuire, who has noticed him wallowing in indecision and offers the avuncular advice: "Just one word." "Yessir." "Are you listening?" "Yes. I am.": "Plastics." A puzzled Benjamin asks for clarification, to which the response is,

"There's a great future in plastics. Think about it. Will you think about it?" Unlike Mr McGuire, I will not insist "Shh! Enough said"; instead, let's share our field's promising little secret.

We are already plastic, in three respects: people are plastic; our field is plastic; and the context is plastic. This malleability at all levels is our future, as the science appreciates more and more about human plasticity. Social psychologists can get people to do about anything, so in that sense we have always been about human plasticity. Our most influential work as social psychologists has dramatized the mighty-mouse phenomenon: how a small change in an independent variable can have huge effect on an important dependent variable. Social psychologists have classically known this, as in the iconic studies associated with great names in the field (Festinger, Tajfel, Milgram, Zimbardo, Cialdini, Aronson, Ross, Darley, et al.). And social cognition classics share the same magic, priming undergraduates to be elderly walkers or smarter trivial pursuers, recording split-second judgments that predict electing politicians or shooting suspects, or showing failures to predict happiness or suppress white bears (respectively, Bargh, Dijksterhuis, Todorov, Payne, Gilbert, and Wegner). In each paradigm, a small, subtle manipulation (e.g., remember this phone number) creates an interesting demonstration of people's plasticity.

Our field also is already plastic. Operationally, social cognition research often borrows or invents methods to examine fundamental processes of social understanding, focused on mental processes and internal representations. This will not change, but our focus on sociality has made us avoid anything biology-related as too deterministic (evolution, genes, temperament, hormones, brains, bodies). But biology isn't destiny! Biology, too, reflects context (e.g., Taylor & Stanton, 2007). So we are now heading more in that direction.

Finally, the context itself is plastic. Our world is changing, and social cognitionists, like other social psychologists, acutely attune to social issues raised by the current human situation. For example, American social psychologists began, during World War II, by measuring attitudes for propaganda purposes and documenting stereotypes to understand the Holocaust and racial integration of the military. Attitudes and stereotyping research have continued to flourish under the social cognition umbrella, and, given globalization, this trend will doubtless continue. What's more, changing demographics predict changes to our field in the future. This chapter thus examines social cognition's future in plasticity three ways: human behavior's malleability; our field's nimble adaptation; and changing demographic contexts.

SOCIALLY ATTUNED: PEOPLE ARE INCREDIBLY PLASTIC

The term *plasticity* is far more state of the art in cellular neuroscience, where the first demonstrations are Nobel Prize material. Instead of neurons' numbers being fixed at birth, as assumed for decades, neuronal firing increases neuronal wiring and even neurogenesis. According to a now-established perspective, brain plasticity results from experience (for reviews, see Kolb & Whishaw, 1998; McEwen & Gianaros, 2011). Most relevant here, social experience shapes hormones (Carney, Cuddy, & Yap, 2010) and neuro-plasticity itself (Stranahan, Khalil, & Gould, 2006). For example, parenting is intensely affected by hormones such as oxytocin and affects other hormones such as testosterone. Overall, social encounters also deeply involve the influence of hormones in attachment, trust, dominance, sexuality, stress, social support, and more. Social cognition researchers have opportunities here.

Extrapolating upward several levels of analysis, and admittedly linking loosely, social cognition research illustrates other versions of plasticity, finding that people modify their responses with remarkable alacrity. Closer to the neural plasticity metaphor, we are also capable of developing new social-cognitive habits. Human social cognition is plastic in both senses.

Humans are socially agile, even on automatic

Because humans are famously social, our everyday adaptation and our long-term viability both depend on getting along and playing nicely with others. Being warm and trustworthy is a primary dimension of social cognition, for good reason. Much evidence indicates that humans do best when they cooperate (Fiske, 2010). Being responsive to others requires being attuned. Thus, we adjust to each other, to our immediate social context. Social psychologists know this; it is our stock-in-trade. Social cognition research will continue to examine the fine-grained mechanisms of sociality.

Human are socially agile, and in that sense plastic. We are hard-wired to be attuned, but not precisely how to respond, which depends on context. Social cognition appreciated this most eloquently when one of our most cherished "universal" principles yielded to culture context. We learned – and we thought we knew it was fundamental – that people are biased to view behavior as a product of the actor's predispositions, neglecting situational constraints (Gilbert, 1998). We even do this automatically. According to an ad hoc PsychNet search (January 2011), our articles on social attribution accelerated from about zero in the 1960s to nearly 2000 per year in 2010. But articles showing cultural variations, while about a tenth of the total, show that our earlier results may have described WEIRD (Western, educated, individualistic, rich, democratic) people more than the rest of the world (Henrich, Heine, & Norenzayan, 2010a, 2010b). Other people, maybe even most, understand the power of the situation more than we do (A. Fiske et al., 1998). So while all of us are socially agile, responding to the situation, some cultures recognize this more than others do.

Social agility overthrew another thing we thought we knew. Automatic priming of behavior boasts some of our most amazing, "science is stranger than fiction" demonstrations. People easily respond to social demands even without knowing what influenced them. We thought this was an inevitable situational control, but now we find out that even automaticity is – paradoxically – malleable too. In this volume, Keith Payne (Chapter 2) describes how automatically we respond, at the same time that neither our automaticity nor our control is absolute. The future of research on automaticity will be in understanding just how plastic it is. Also in this volume, Ezequiel Morsella and Avi Ben-Zeev (Chapter 14) describe how not only cognitive representations but also action representations impel behavior. The future of social cognition predicting action lies in the flexibility and attunement of these varied knowledge formats.

Even our automatic cognition and behavior depend on goals and motivation, as Henk Aarts shows in Chapter 5. Just as people are swayed by shortcuts, environmental anchors, accessible information, and confirmatory evidence, and biased toward immediate, certain, loss prevention, we also are swayed by emotional states; all this nudges us to some reflexive judgments and decisions over others, as David Dunning notes (Chapter 13). The future of motivated thinking and doing lies in better understanding these intrapersonal dynamics.

Perceiving other people likewise is remarkably automatic but also remarkably plastic. Perceiving faces, as Alexander Todorov shows in Chapter 6, is special: rapid and consequential, with dedicated neural networks, reflecting the peculiar importance of other people as objects of perception. In addition, we readily infer traits, status, and intents from other people, which Daniel Ames and Malia Mason demonstrate in reviewing mind perception (Chapter 7): how, how well, and where we mind-read. Social perception per se enters the first really early moments of perception (e.g., neural systems), and much remains to clarify and specify about how we represent other faces and other minds.

These social cognitive representations are not only mental, as a growing mountain of evidence shows, but also embodied cognition, emotion, and attitudes show how plastic our forms of representation can be. As Gün Semin, Margarida Garrido, and Tomás Palma show (Chapter 8), cognition emerges from sensorimotor interactions with the environment, in dynamic and adaptive ways, challenging received wisdom in social cognition research. As in cognitions, so too in emotions: Autumn Hostetter, Martha Alibali, and Paula Niedenthal (Chapter 11) link social cognition, emotion, and gesture to understand embodied social thought. From such controversial, forward-thinking provocations come the next bandwagons.

Regardless of representational format, social cognition operates at varying levels of abstraction, be they long-term new habits or back-and-forth switching. People regulate their own construal levels, depending on context, as Oren Shapira, Nira Liberman, Yaacov Trope, and SoYon Rim explain in Chapter 12. Also, social cognition operates at varying levels of consciousness, from unconscious to meta-conscious, as Piotr Winkielman and Jonathan Schooler review in Chapter 4.

To illustrate how far we have come: social cognition research used to be viewed as reductionist and determinist, insufficiently social. But as the future fades into the present, the field shows more and more just how socially adaptive we are, for most everyday purposes. Evolutionary perspectives, as Joshua Ackerman, Julie Huang, and John Bargh point out (Chapter 23), link adaptive processes within individuals' and species' social development.

For an example of social adaption from our lab, prior work had shown that social interdependence makes people pay attention to others and think about their predispositions, presumably for adaptive control. An independently identified area of the medial prefrontal cortex differentiates partners one needs for a goal, and especially the most diagnostic information for making sense of them (Ames & Fiske, 2011). People's socially attunement starts at the most fine-grained levels, as we collectively learn to measure them.

OUR NIMBLE FIELD

Our field is incredibly plastic, as befits researchers who study attunement to situations. Our nimble science adapts to new trends and adopts new theories and methods; this is our rapid response to new insights, shifting with exhilarating speed for an academic discipline. Several classic social cognition topics have ebbed and flowed accordingly, suggesting alternative future worlds.

Oldies and goodies

Our field is constantly discovering new functions served by social cognition. At first, social thinkers seemed to be cognitive misers who simply conserve scarce mental resources. Then, the field turned to viewing thinkers as motivated tacticians, who chose among processes. Recently, we have viewed social thinkers as activated actors, who must both think and behave in the course of social interaction (Fiske & Taylor, 2008, Chapter 1).

Constant among these views of the social perceiver are nevertheless some key factors. One key functional representation, the expectancy, dates back to the earliest social cognition research (Bruner & Postman, 1949). Expectancy has gone by various terms such as *schema* and *prototype* in the thick of the cognitive revolution, and for the last few decades, they yielded to frameworks such as the social categories documented in Chapter 16 by Galen Bodenhausen, Sonia Kang, and Destiny Peery. Social categories serve various functions for perceivers, consistent with the theme that perceivers adapt to contextual contingencies. Bodenhausen and colleagues suggest that the future must tackle both the intersection of multiple categories and the possible ambiguity in category membership, for example, in multi-racial individuals, or immigrants balancing old country and new identities. Besides new problems to tackle, as new methods continue to emerge – such as neuroimaging over the last decade – our understanding of expectancies' processes and representation will grow.

More than just a shift in terms or in methods, social psychology as a whole has moved from studying initial *attraction* and *first impressions* to study ongoing *close relationships*. Social cognition research has informed this transition. As reviewed by Susan Andersen, Adil Saribay, and Elizabeth Przybylinski (Chapter 18), people's stored knowledge about significant others is evoked by context, with important consequences for beliefs, feelings, and actions in social responses even beyond the close relationship itself. The future, informed by new methods such as experience sampling and diary studies, as well as the multilevel modeling needed to analyze such data, promises to be productive.

Another topic, *attitudes*, foundational to the field of social psychology, has shifted focus several times over the decades, and doubtless will continue to do so. In the context of cognitive approaches to attitudes, the biggest recent and ongoing impact has been indirect measures of attitudes. As Brian Nosek, Carlee Hawkins, and Rebecca Frazier note (Chapter 3), measures can catalyze theories of mechanisms and applications to new domains. Methods that started in controversy have resolved into a bandwagon, judging not least from PsycNet hits, and doubtless the upward trend in implicit attitudes research will continue.

Even the core topics in attitudes acknowledge the newest indirect measures of attitudes but, as related to social cognition, delve further into representation and process. Melissa Ferguson and Jun Fukukura document in Chapter 9 that likes and dislikes form easily but predict judgment and behavior, varying across time and situation. We probably know more about attitude representation and process than any other social psychological concept, and its futures expand still farther into contending with neural correlates, peripheral physiology, and subtle links to behavior.

Moving to more general feeling states, another established area, *emotions*, has bright social-cognitive futures. Emotions in social contexts reflect motivating social cognitions, as Batja Mesquita, Claudia Marinetti, and Ellen Delvaux remind us in Chapter 15. Feeling, like thinking, is for doing, and in particular social doing, whether in dyads or groups, even though people sometimes fail to respond adaptively.

Much emotion is communicated nonverbally, as Nora Murphy's account of cues, perceivers, targets, and interactions shows (Chapter 10). The social-cognitive angle focuses on accuracy in complex and nuanced decoding. *Nonverbal behavior* will continue to be important, as we measure ever-more subtle expressions, e.g., using EMG (electromyography), and as we measure ever-more subtle perceptions, e.g., using eye-tracking of facial stimuli.

Psychology and physiology marry also in continuing work on the *self-concept*. People evaluate and know themselves, Jennifer Beer notes (Chapter 17), through both internal and external sources of information, and social-cognitive approaches examine neural, cognitive, and bodily representations. We will not stop studying the self anytime soon, as is true of other classics – expectancies, relationships, attitudes, emotions, and nonverbal communication – all seen in new ways.

Taboo topics

How will we know when these social cognitive foundations are shifting as the future temblors shake us? Like earthquakes, tectonic shifts in the field are unpredictable except that we know they will happen. The intellectual shake-ups matter not for their speed but for re-orienting the landscape. Feeling unsettled is a good predictor of magnitude, as in the notion (urban myth?) about animals sensing earthquakes before people do. Discomfort can index an idea whose time may have come to shake things up a bit (Fiske, 2003).

Uncomfortable new ideas often overcome old taboos. In social cognition (as in much of social psychology), personality sometimes is relegated to the error heap. Arie Kruglanski and Anna Sheveland (Chapter 24) argue that personality is not anti-social, or a-social, but that both domains can operationalize the same conceptual variables. Sense-making varies as a function of both perceivers and situations, disciplinary chauvinism aside.

In another resolution, ideology and science need not oppose each other. Social-cognitive scientists can study ideological knowledge not as rigid, fixed ideas, but instead as flexibly activated concepts, depending again on both person and situation, as Aaron Kay and Richard Eibach note (Chapter 25). While the field rethinks its relationship to politics, science can adapt older concepts (e.g., chronic and temporary accessibility) to new domains. Deeply divided political times need all the scientific insight we can get.

Politics aplenty have come into nature–nurture debates of the past, now mostly behind us, fortunately. As gene × environment interactions demonstrate, the twain shall indeed meet. We have not only biological but social brains, as described by Joan Chiao, Bobby Cheon, Genna Bebko, Robert Livingston, and Ying-yi Hong (Chapter 26) examining the gene–culture mix in social cognition.

From controversy to bandwagons

Not every controversy produces a parade, marching bands, and a crowd of followers. But, safe to say, researchers greet noisy new ideas with skepticism, as indeed we should. Why rearrange the traffic patterns unless we must? Our field's flexibility is impressive but not unbridled. It's a fine line between same-old science (Have we learned anything new here?) and far-out anomalies (ESP, Bem, 2011).

The rocky road toward new approaches used to include social cognition research, strange as that may seem now. Social psychologists originally found social cognition research too asocial and reductionist, whereas cognitive psychologists found it insufficiently cognitive and rigorous. Before enough people joined up, social cognition researchers were caught in heavy crossfire. History has repeated itself with social neuroscience, now well accepted. Doubtless, the future will bring more such public disturbances. We can only hope.

SHIFTING DEMOGRAPHICS

People, in general, and in our field, in particular, adapt to change. Our field always responds to social change – war, racism, environment, gender roles – with relevant theory-based research. In that sense, our larger social–political–economic world is plastic, too. Hence, changing demographics predict the topics of the future: globalization, immigration, aging boomers, changing family patterns, earlier diagnosis of mental disorders, and overall economic volatility, especially income inequality. Let's speculate about each in turn.

Globalization, the shrinkage of distance and boundaries, expands opportunities for contact across cultures. As cultures collide, the field will increasingly address the formative power of culture, as Beth Morling and Takahiko Masuda aptly describe it (Chapter 22). Cultures, of course, shape all humans to adapt to their immediate context, in order to survive and thrive. And specific cultures transmit guidelines for psychological functioning, including the lens of social cognition.

We are only beginning to understand the alternative realities that cultures constitute.

Although not appearing in this volume, immigration provides an opportunity for social cognition research, but not just in terms of immigrants as objects of attitudes and stereotypes. Immigration oversees an abrupt change in social cognitions about culture, identity, goals, ideology, and more. If we can address people's transitions to new cultures, and the duality of the immigrant experience, social cognition researchers will access countless natural experiments on change in the content, representation, or even the processes of social thinking.

Our population is aging. Hence, another kind of natural experiment is also occurring within-subject, and that is the natural aging process. Reviewed in Chapter 20 by William von Hippel and Julie Henry, social-cognitive aging demonstrates decline in some mechanics of social cognition, especially certain controlled processes and the speed of automatic ones, but also an increase in experience, resulting in a lifetime's accumulation of knowledge. The interplay among these processes and contents provides a window on distinct processes perhaps otherwise hard to dissociate. The aging demographic bulge provides an opportunity also for focusing on intergeneration tensions that are unique among in-group–out-group dynamics because of the moving window of this boundary (North & Fiske, 2011). Interactions between generations often occur within families, an understudied site for social cognition.

Simultaneously, social cognition research is moving downward in age, as well as upward in age. The growth area of social-cognitive development, reviewed by Talee Ziv and Mahzarin Banaji (Chapter 19), explores the origins of the processes and knowledge that appear throughout this volume. Changing family patterns here present the opportunity for exploring the role of different caretaker patterns (e.g., by gender, by sheer number) in developing early-childhood social cognition.

Younger research participants also enter specifically into the origins of atypical social cognition, described in Chapter 21 by Elizabeth Pellicano. As the larger field learns more about autism, for example, diagnoses increase and start earlier. Autism, deeply implicated in social-cognitive processes, focuses attention on the building blocks of interpersonal perception: for example, intention, biological motion, and communication signals.

Standing back from age and culture, economic issues provide a larger context for social cognition. Social cognition researchers have many opportunities here. Income inequality predicts a nation's lay theories of how society and its groups operate (Durante et al., 2011). Economic volatility creates uncertainty that undermines health and well-being (Wilkinson & Pickett, 2010), and uncertainty exaggerates toxic status divides (Fiske, 2011). Social class is one such status system that influences formal social-cognitive training in school, but also less formal world views that construct everyday social encounters (for a collection of initial endeavors, see Fiske & Markus, 2012).

Besides globalization, immigration, aging baby boomers, changing family patterns, earlier diagnosis of mental disorders, and overall economic volatility, especially income inequality, the larger scientific context provides new opportunities for our field. As illustrated throughout, new methods and theories cross the borders from adjacent fields to social cognition, enriching and growing the endeavor.

REPRISE: PLASTICITY FUTURES

Humans are socially agile, providing constant opportunity for social cognition researchers to document people's functional and dysfunctional adaptations. Doubtless, this dominant trend will continue to value human malleability. Our science has displayed its nimble adoption of new paradigms that move from controversy to bandwagons; so as scientists too, we are agile, and alert to new opportunities that the context offers. One potent predictor of societal and therefore scientific context is demographic shifts. If we pay attention to these larger contexts, we will see even more opportunities on the horizon.

REFERENCES

Ames, D. L., & Fiske, S. T. (2011). Encountering the unexpected under outcome dependency: Power relations alter the neural substrates of impression formation.

Bem, D. J. (2011). Feeling the future: Experimental evidence for anomalous retroactive influences on cognition and affect. *Journal of Personality and Social Psychology, 100*(3), 407–425.

Brooks, D. (2005). *On Paradise Drive: How we live now (and always have) in the future tense.* New York: Simon & Schuster.

Brooks, D. (2011). *The social animal: The hidden sources of love, character, and achievement.* New York: Random House.

Bruner, J. S., & Postman, L. (1949). On the perception of incongruity: A paradigm. *Journal of Personality, 18,* 206–223.

Carney, D. R., Cuddy, A. J. C., & Yap. A. J. (2010). Power posing: Brief nonverbal displays affect neuroendocrine levels and risk tolerance. *Psychological Science, 21*(10), 1363–1368.

Durante, F., Fiske, S. T., Cuddy, A. J. C., Kervyn, N., et al. (2011). Nations' income inequality predicts ambivalence in stereotype content: How societies mind the gap.

Feldman, R. (2009). *The liar in your life: The way to truthful relationships.* New York: Twelve/Hachette Book Group.

Fiske, A. P., Kitayama, S., Markus, H. R., & Nisbett, R. E. (1998). The cultural matrix of social psychology. In D. T. Gilbert, S. T. Fiske, & G. Lindzey (Eds.), *The handbook of social psychology* (4th ed., Vol. 2, pp. 915–981). New York: McGraw-Hill.

Fiske, S. T. (1992). Thinking is for doing: Portraits of social cognition from daguerreotype to laserphoto. *Journal of Personality and Social Psychology, 63,* 877–889.

Fiske, S. T. (2003). The discomfort index: How to spot a really good idea whose time has come. *Psychological Inquiry, 14,* 201–206.

Fiske, S. T. (2010). *Social beings: Core motives in social psychology* (2nd ed.). New York: Wiley.

Fiske, S. T. (2011). *Envy up, scorn down: How status divides us.* New York: Russell Sage Foundation.

Fiske, S. T., & Markus, H. R. (Eds.) (2012). *Facing social class: How societal rank influences interaction.* New York: Russell Sage Foundation.

Fiske, S. T., & Taylor, S. E. (2008). *Social cognition: From brains to culture.* New York: McGraw-Hill.

Gilbert, D. T. (1998). Ordinary personology. In D. T. Gilbert, S. T. Fiske, & G. Lindzey (Eds.), *The handbook of social psychology.* (4th ed., Vol. 1, pp. 89–150). New York: McGraw-Hill.

Gilbert, D. T. (2006). *Stumbling on happiness.* New York: Knopf.

Gladwell, M. (2000). *The tipping point: How little things can make a big difference.* New York: Little, Brown.

Gladwell, M. (2005). *Blink: The power of thinking without thinking.* New York: Little, Brown and Co.

Gladwell, M. (2008). *Outliers: The story of success.* New York: Little, Brown and Co.

Henrich, J., Heine, S. J., & Norenzayan, A. (2010a). Beyond WEIRD: Towards a broad-based behavioral science. *Behavioral and Brain Sciences, 33*(2–3), 111–135.

Henrich, J., Heine, S. J., & Norenzayan, A. (2010b). The weirdest people in the world? *Behavioral and Brain Sciences, 33*(2–3), 61–83.

James, W. (1983). *The principles of psychology.* Cambridge, MA: Harvard University Press. (Originally published 1890)

Kolb, B., & Whishaw, I. Q. (1998). Brain plasticity and behavior. *Annual Review of Psychology, 49,* 43–64.

McEwen, B. S., & Gianaros, P. J. (2011). Stress- and allostasis-induced brain plasticity. *Annual Review of Medicine, 62,* 431–445.

North, M. S., & Fiske, S. T. (2011). The young and the ageist: Intergenerational tensions over succession, identity, and consumption.

Stranahan, A. M., Khalil, D., & Gould, E. (2006). Social isolation delays the positive effects of running on adult neurogenesis. *Nature Neuroscience 9,* 526–533.

Taylor, S. E. (1989). *Positive illusions: Creative self-deception and the healthy mind.* New York: Basic Books.

Taylor, S. E., & Stanton, A. L. (2007). Coping resources, coping processes, and mental health. *Annual Review of Clinical Psychology, 3,* 377–401.

Wilkinson, R. G., & Pickett, K. E. (2010). *The spirit level. Why equality is better for everyone.* London: Penguin.

Name Index

Subject Index